The Handbook of
Contemporary Syntactic Theory

Blackwell Handbooks in Linguistics

This outstanding multi-volume series covers all the major subdisciplines within linguistics today and, when complete, will offer a comprehensive survey of linguistics as a whole.

Published works:

The Handbook of Child Language
Edited by PAUL FLETCHER and BRIAN MACWHINNEY

The Handbook of Phonological Theory
Edited by JOHN GOLDSMITH

The Handbook of Contemporary Semantic Theory
Edited by SHALOM LAPPIN

The Handbook of Sociolinguistics
Edited by FLORIAN COULMAS

The Handbook of Phonetic Sciences
Edited by WILLIAM HARDCASTLE and JOHN LAVER

The Handbook of Morphology
Edited by ANDREW SPENCER and ARNOLD ZWICKY

The Handbook of Japanese Linguistics
Edited by NATSUKO TSUJIMURA

The Handbook of Linguistics
Edited by MARK ARONOFF and JANIE REES-MILLER

The Handbook of Contemporary Syntactic Theory
Edited by MARK BALTIN and CHRIS COLLINS

The Handbook of Contemporary Syntactic Theory

Edited by

Mark Baltin and Chris Collins

Copyright © Blackwell Publishers Ltd 2001

First published 2001

2 4 6 8 10 9 7 5 3 1

Blackwell Publishers Inc.
350 Main Street
Malden, Massachusetts 02148
USA

Blackwell Publishers Ltd
108 Cowley Road
Oxford OX4 1JF
UK

Library of Congress Cataloging-in-Publication Data

The handbook of contemporary syntactic theory / edited by Mark Baltin and Chris Collins.
    p. cm. — (Blackwell handbooks in linguistics)
  Includes bibliographical references and index.
  ISBN 0–631–20507–1 (alk. paper)
  1. Grammar, Comparative and general—Syntax—Handbooks, manuals, etc. I. Baltin, Mark R. (Mark Reuben), 1950– II. Collins, Chris, 1963– III. Series.
P291.H246 2000
415—dc21   99–087402

British Library Cataloguing in Publication Data

A CIP catalogue record for this book is available from the British Library.

Typeset in 10/12pt Palatino
by Graphicraft Limited, Hong Kong
Printed in Great Britain by T.J. International, Padstow, Cornwall

This book is printed on acid-free paper.

This book is dedicated to our families: Roberta and Amy and Atsupe, Betty and Essi who make it all worthwhile.

Contents

Contributors

Mark Baker has taught in the linguistics department at McGill University, and most recently at Rutgers University. His specialty is in the syntax of under-studied non-Indo-European languages, especially native American and African languages. He is the author of two books (*Incorporation* and *The Polysynthesis Parameter*) and numerous articles on syntax and related topics in the morphology and semantics of such languages.

Mark Baltin is Professor of Linguistics at New York University, where he has taught since receiving his PhD from MIT in 1978. He has written numerous articles on movement rules, ellipsis, phrase structure, and predication, which have appeared in *Linguistic Inquiry* and various edited volumes. He coedited, with Anthony S. Kroch, *Alternative Conceptions of Phrase-Structure*, and has served on the National Science Foundation's Advisory Panel for Linguistics.

Andrew Barss is Associate Professor of Linguistics at the University of Arizona, where he has taught since receiving his PhD from MIT in 1986. Dr Barss's research focusses on several closely connected areas of syntactic theory and the syntax–semantics interface, conducted predominantly in the Minimalist framework.

Adriana Belletti is Associate Professor of Linguistics at the University of Siena. She is the author of, among other essays, the monograph "Generalized Verb Movement" and the article "The Case of Unaccusatives" (*Linguistic Inquiry*). She has served as European editor of *Linguistic Inquiry* and is now on the associate editorial board of the journal.

Judy B. Bernstein is Assistant Professor of Linguistics at Syracuse University. Her research interests include syntax, particularly comparative syntax, and language acquisition. Within syntax, she has worked extensively on the internal structure of noun phrases, and within language acquisition, she has recently conducted experiments on various aspects of the acquisition of relative clauses in English-speaking children.

John Bowers is Professor of Linguistics at Cornell University. In addition to his recent work on predication, he has published work on X'-theory, constraints on transformations, and the syntax–semantics interface. He is currently working on a Minimalist approach to argument structure and adverbial modification.

Joan Bresnan is Howard H. and Jesse T. Watkins University Professor of Linguistics at Stanford University. She has also taught at the University of Massachusetts, Amherst, and at MIT. Bresnan's research interests include syntactic theory and the design of universal grammar, computational linguistics, and the structure of Bantu and Australian aboriginal languages. Among her publications are *Theory of Complementation in English Syntax, Linguistic Theory and Psychological Reality* (coedited with Halle and Miller), and *The Mental Representation of Grammatical Relations*. A principal architect of the theory of Lexical Functional Grammar, she has also contributed to Optimality Theoretic morphosyntax, and has been a Fellow at the Center for Advanced Study in the Behavioral Sciences, and a Guggenheim Fellow.

Chris Collins is currently Associate Professor in the Department of Linguistics at Cornell University, where he has been since 1993. He does research on the syntax of African languages, including Ewe (spoken in West Africa) and =Hoan (spoken in Botswana). His other main interest is in economy conditions in syntax. He is the author of *Local Economy*.

Martin Everaert is Associate Professor at the Utrecht Institute of Linguistics OTS. He has published on anaphora and idioms and is currently on the editorial board of *Linguistic Inquiry* and the *Journal of Comparative Germanic Linguistics*.

Janet Dean Fodor is Distinguished Professor of Linguistics at the Graduate School of the City University of New York. Following her PhD at MIT, she worked on semantics for a few years before turning to psycholinguistics. She has published many papers on sentence processing, with emphasis on universal properties of the human sentence parsing routines. More recently she has been working on issues of the learnability of natural language. In 1997 she was President of the Linguistic Society of America.

Naoki Fukui is Professor of Linguistics and Director of Graduate Studies at the University of California, Irvine. He has published numerous books and articles (in both English and Japanese) on phrase structure, movement, philosophy of linguistics, and the theory of comparative syntax. He is also an editorial board member of various international journals such as *Linguistic Inquiry, Linguistic Review, Lingua*, the *Journal of East Asian Linguistics*, etc.

Jeffrey S. Gruber is known for his seminal work on semantic role structure – thematic relations or "theta-theory" – stemming from his influential MIT dissertation of 1965. He has published work on thematic, lexical, and conceptual structure, as well as essays on the adoption of a universal auxiliary language. Following field research in Botswana on the Khoisan language =Hoan in the early 1970s, he held appointments as Professor and Head of Department of

Linguistics at Awolowo University at Ife and at the University of Benin, Benin City, Nigeria, until 1992. He is currently a visiting scholar in the Department of Linguistics and Philosophy at MIT.

Kyle Johnson teaches theoretic syntax at the University of Massachusetts, Amherst, and is perhaps best known for his work on word order and its relation to grammatical functions. In recent years he has been exploring the relationships between ellipses phenomena, word order variation in Germanic, and the mechanisms that assign scope to quantificational arguments.

Anthony S. Kroch is Professor of Linguistics at the University of Pennsylvania and a member of the University's Institute for Research in Cognitive Science. He is a specialist in problems of natural language syntax and the syntax–semantics interface. In addition to his publications in formal syntax and the syntax–semantics interface, he has done several statistical studies of the historical syntax of English, for which he designed and supervised the construction of a one-million-word parsed treebank of Middle English, the Penn–Helsinki Parsed Corpus of Middle English, which is available to scholars world-wide.

Howard Lasnik is Professor of Linguistics at the University of Connecticut, where he has taught since receiving his PhD from MIT in 1972. He has supervised 34 completed PhD dissertations, on morphology, on language acquisition, and, especially, on syntactic theory. His main research areas are syntactic theory and the syntax–semantics interface. His publications include scores of articles and six books, the most recent being *Minimalist Analysis* and, with Marcela Depiante and Arthur Stepanov, *Syntactic Structures Revisited: Contemporary Lectures on Classic Transformational Theory*.

Giuseppe Longobardi is Professor of Linguistics at the University of Trieste, and taught previously at the University of Venice. He is the author, with Allesandra Giorgi, of *The Syntax of Noun Phrases*, as well as numerous articles on various aspects of the syntax and semantics of nominal expressions.

Eric J. Reuland is Professor of Linguistics at Utrecht University, and Academic Director of the Utrecht Institute of Linguistics OTS and the National Graduate School of Linguistics in the Netherlands LOT. He has published on a wide range of topics, including syntactic categories, (in)definiteness, and binding, in journals such as *Linguistic Inquiry* and in various books. He has also edited a number of books on these topics, and is currently serving as the European Editor of *Linguistic Inquiry*.

Luigi Rizzi is Professor of Linguistics at the University of Siena. His main research domains are syntactic theory and comparative syntax, with special reference to the Romance languages; he has also worked on language acquisition. He is the author of *Issues in Italian Syntax* and *Relativized Minimality*.

Ian Roberts teaches linguistics at the University of Stuttgart. He has published numerous articles on diachronic syntax and on various aspects of head movement.

Anna Szabolcsi is Professor of Linguistics at New York University, previously at UCLA. Her interests are in formal semantics, the syntax–semantics interface, and Hungarian syntax. Her recent books are *Ways of Scope Taking* and *Verbal Complexes* (with Hilda Koopman). She is an Associate Editor of *Linguistics and Philosophy*.

Höskuldur Thráinsson is Professor of Icelandic Linguistics at the University of Iceland in Reykjavik. He has mainly worked on Icelandic and Scandinavian syntax, writing on topics like verb movement, word order, reflexives, etc., and in recent years Faroese has become one of his favorite languages. He is the Editor of *Islenskt mal*, the Icelandic linguistic journal, has coedited several linguistic anthologies, and has worked on several editorial boards.

Hiroyuki Ura is Associate Professor of Linguistics at Osaka University. He has published several articles on agreement, case, grammatical functions/relations, and typology of voice in journals and books. He is the author of *Checking Theory and Grammatical Functions in Universal Grammar*.

Akira Watanabe teaches syntax in the Department of English at the University of Tokyo. His research interests include *wh*-movement and scope, case, binding and control, and lexical syntax. Among his publications are *Case Absorption and Wh-Agreement* and articles in the *Journal of East Asian Linguistics*.

Raffaella Zanuttini is Associate Professor of Linguistics at Georgetown University, and has published extensively on Romance negation. She is the author of *Negation and Clausal Structure*.

Introduction

The goal of this *Handbook* is to provide an overview to researchers and students about the current state of research in syntax, a difficult but not impossible task because the field of syntax is not monolithic: there are schools of thought, and areas of disagreement, but there are also shared assumptions among many schools of thought which we shall try to bring out below.

We decided to follow the twin paths of ecumenicalism and comprehensiveness of empirical coverage by focussing on areas of grammar for our coverage, rather than particular frameworks, of which there are several (Government Binding, Minimalism, Categorial Grammar, Lexical Functional Grammar, Head Driven Phrase Grammar). We intended no slight to these approaches and indeed while most of the chapters in this volume are written with a Minimalist/ GB orientation (but not all of them), we would hope that the observations and analyses could serve as a point of departure for investigators in other frameworks.

When we first agreed to edit the *Handbook of Contemporary Syntactic Theory* for Blackwell, we did so in order to convey to others, both in and out of the field of syntax, the fascination that we constantly feel on an almost daily basis about how restricted syntactic systems, the systems of natural language that are responsible for the construction of sentences, are in comparison to what they could be. This emphasis, and its proper characterization, have been at the foreground of syntactic research since the 1960s, when Chomsky, in 1962, noticed the following restriction on the formation of constituent questions (Chomsky 1962). Sentence (1) is ambiguous; under one interpretation, the man is in the room, and on the other, the prepositional phrase *in the room* is an adverbial modifier of the verb *see*:

(1)   John saw the man in the room.

Questioning the prepositional object of *in*, however, removes the ambiguity. Only the latter interpretation of the PP is possible:

(2) Which room did John see the man in?

There is a great deal of evidence that sentences are structured into constituents, or groups, and the representations of such groupings are termed phrase-markers. Hence, (1) would have two distinct phrase-markers, roughly (very roughly), as in (3):

(3) a.

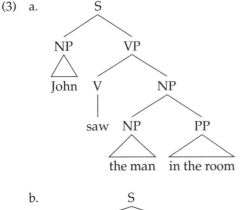

b.

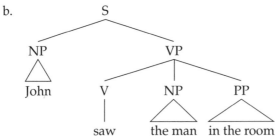

In these structures, NP stands for noun phrase, VP for verb phrase, and PP for prepositional phrase. Chomsky's restriction was that processes such as the one for forming constituent questions cannot move elements out of larger elements of the same type, so that, e.g. an NP could not be moved out of an NP. This constraint was dubbed the A-over-A Constraint. Subsequently, Ross (Ross 1967a) demonstrated that the A-over-A Constraint was both too strong (ruling out movements that are perfectly fine) and too weak (allowing movements that result in unacceptability). Since that time, a large amount of research has unearthed even more such restrictions (for example, Perlmutter 1971, Postal 1971, Chomsky 1973, 1981, and many others).

In fact, on an extremely regular basis, syntacticians notice that an otherwise general process does not occur in a given instance. If one looks at traditional grammars, such as Curme (1931) or Jesperson (1946), one finds no mention of such restrictions. Much of the reason for this lack of emphasis, we suspect, lies with the primary method of gathering the data for syntactic analysis, which was essentially philological in nature, i.e., the examination of texts. If one's method of collecting data is observation rather than experimentation, one's primary focus, although not inexorably, will be on what one actually encounters, and one would have to be somewhat cautious about the absence of certain expressions. The introduction of introspective data into the battery of techniques that linguists use to do syntactic analysis has allowed greater confidence in the judgment that certain expressions are absent because they are unacceptable, rather than fortuitously missing in a certain corpus of data.

However, we suspect that an equally compelling reason for the current emphasis in syntactic analysis on constraints lies in a shift in the view of how to do research. The view of philosophy of science that guided pre-Chomskyan structuralist linguistics was that scientific theories were formulated inductively, and hence, abstract linguistic principles emphasized the formulation of procedures of data analysis, with no pre-judgment of what the results of those procedures would be (Wells 1947, Harris 1951). In short, the theory of grammar, Universal Grammar, was just those procedures. Under such a view, one would not view certain results as being expected or unexpected. It is only when one has certain expectations about the system itself, the end result of analysis, that one views divergences from this system as being noteworthy and requiring explanation.

So, to return to the missing interpretation of the question in (2), it is surprising for the following reason: we assume that grammatical rules operate in the simplest, least-specified manner possible. Some initial evidence for the correctness of this assumption is the acceptability of fronting a *wh*-phrase from a position that is apparently indefinitely far away from the position in which it ends up, as in (4):

(4)   Who did John think that Bill claimed that Mary suspected that everybody liked__?

The fronted *wh*-phrase, interpreted as the object of *liked*, starts out within a clause that is embedded within a clause that is three clauses down from the root of the sentence. If we assume, on the basis of data such as (4), that *wh*-fronting occurs from any position relative to the one in which it ends up, the missing interpretation in (2), which corresponds to the impossibility of *wh*-fronting a noun phrase from within a noun phrase, becomes paradoxical. The point that we would emphasize, however, is that the noteworthiness of this restriction, and indeed all such restrictions, is made in the context of the theoretical assumption that grammatical rules operate in the simplest, least-specified manner possible. Without this assumption about what grammatical processes should be, everything is equally expected.

We could go on and on with such examples. To take just one more case, consider the interpretation of the negative following the modal *could*:

(5)   John could not visit Sally.

Sentence (5) could mean either that (a) it is not the case that John is able to visit Sally; or (b) John could refrain from visiting Sally. Notice that (6) could only mean (b) and could not mean (a):

(6)   What John could do is not visit Sally.

Negatives can contract in English casual speech, and when we contract the negative in (5), the result is (7):

(7)   John couldn't visit Sally.

We note, again, that (7) is more restricted in its interpretation than (5) is (we say "again" to note the parallelism with (2), the case of constituent questions); in this case, (7) can only mean (a), and not (b).

How do we make sense of these facts? Many linguists, following Klima (Klima 1964) and Jackendoff (Jackendoff 1969), distinguish two kinds of nega-tion (see Zanuttini's chapter in this volume), which are termed sentential nega-tion and constituent negation. The scope of sentential negation, as the term implies, is the entire clause, while the scope of constituent negation is the phrase in which the negative occurs. The (a) interpretation of (5) is one in which the negative element is an instance of sentential negation, while the (b) interpreta-tion is one in which the negative is an instance of constituent negation, in this case modifying the verb phrase. The standard analysis of sentential negation, following Pollock (Pollock 1989), has the negative occurring outside the verb phrase. Examples such as (6), in which the negative must be constituent nega-tion, are most naturally analyzed as instances in which the negative is a modi-fier of the verb phrase, occurring within the verb phrase. We would then have to say there is some restriction on contracting a negative that occurs as a modifier within the verb phrase, and Baltin (Baltin in preparation) relates this restriction to a restriction on the occurrence of inflected prepositions in Modern Irish (McCloskey 1984).

These are but two examples of restrictions on grammatical processes, and the introduction to a handbook is not the place to simply catalogue such restric-tions. However, we would note that the examples indicate that grammatical processes such as *wh*-fronting and negative contraction must refer to constitu-ent structure, rather than simply linear order. Given that constituent structure is not directly present in the sentences to which we are exposed, it is difficult if not impossible to see how constituent structure could be learned. There-fore, the structure-dependence of such rules is, as Chomsky (1975) observed, an argument for innate principles of language.

We would observe that innateness has its critics (Elman et al. 1995), but we would argue nevertheless that any theory of, e.g., language acquisition or language processing – indeed, any account that requires an account of what language is – must now take into account the huge amount of research since the mid-1960s or so into the nature of the structure of language, and the picture that emerges is of a system that is quite restricted in its nature. A great deal of research was initially devoted to the simple observation of these restrictions, given their lack of note in previous syntactic research, but since the late 1970s or so there has also been a more theoretical emphasis on the proper characterization and the nature of such restrictions. How are they encoded into Universal Grammar? Ross's dissertation (Ross 1967a) was a monumental achievement in the observation of syntactic islands, such as the Complex Noun Phrase Constraint, the Coordinate Structure Constraint, the Left-Branch Constraint, etc. However, it is extremely implausible to believe that the theory of grammar has, in addition to phrase-structure rules, phonological rules, transformations, etc., which operate in the grammar in its constructive sense, a set of diverse stipulations as to where the "normal rules" cannot operate, and indeed, following the appearance of this work, much research was devoted to attempting to unify these constraints (Chomsky 1973, 1986b, Cattell 1976).

Indeed, Gazdar, Klein, Pullum, and Sag proposed a model of grammar (Gazdar et al. 1985) whose account of unbounded dependencies such as those in (4) would account for the fact that such dependencies cannot occur out of adjuncts, as noted by Cattell (1976) and Huang (Huang 1982), but in a way that does not need to stipulate this fact, and has it follow from the basic mechanisms of their grammar. An example of this restriction is given in (8):

(8) *Who does John visit Sally because he likes__?

While their account is ultimately untenable because it blocks extraction of adjuncts, as in (9), as well as extraction from adjuncts, it is noteworthy as an attempt to eliminate separate stipulations in the form of constraints, and to have the restrictions be theorems of the basic mechanisms of grammar; exactly the right move in our opinion:

(9) Why did John leave?

We have tried to provide an overview, in this introduction, of what syntax looks like today. It is fitting, we feel, to quote from the scholar who, more than anyone else, has made syntax what it is, in the work that revolutionized this field:

> The search for rigorous formulation in linguistics has a much more serious motivation than mere concern for logical niceties or the desire to purify well-established methods of linguistic analysis. By pushing a precise but inadequate formulation to an unacceptable conclusion, we can often expose the exact source of this inadequacy, and, consequently, gain a deeper understanding of the linguistic data. (Preface to Chomsky 1957)

In short, by taking seriously the idea that a grammar is a formal theory, with mentalistic embodiment, we can ask precise, testable questions about the nature of some very interesting things, such as the human mind, in a way that would have been meaningless even in the late 1930s.

Given this background, we will now summarize the chapters contained in this *Handbook*. All syntactic theories recognize that syntax makes infinite use of finite means, but there is a fundamental distinction between theories as to how this is done. Some theories postulate a derivational approach, where structures are built incrementally by various operations (such as Merge and Move in the Minimalist Program). In other theories, structures are taken as given, and they are evaluated with respect to various conditions. The issue of derivation versus representation has proved to be one of the most elusive and difficult to settle in syntactic theory. Even researchers who otherwise adopt very similar sets of assumptions will differ as to whether they consider syntax to be derivational or representational.

In part I, Howard Lasnik shows that even within the assumptions of the Minimalist Program, it is often a subtle matter to determine if some condition should be stated derivationally or representationally. Chris Collins assumes a derivational theory and shows how many syntactic constraints can be viewed as economy conditions which guarantee that operations, derivations, and representations are minimal. Joan Bresnan assumes the representational framework of Optimality Theory syntax, and shows how various morphosyntactic facts can be given a natural treatment. Lastly, Luigi Rizzi's paper largely assumes a representational treatment of Relativized Minimality (as a condition on Logical Form), but makes some comparison to the derivational treatment of similar facts by Chomsky (Chomsky 1995b).

All theories assume that syntactic theory must account for dependencies of the kind in (2), where a constituent seems to be displaced from the position where it is interpreted. In part II, Ian Roberts takes up the issue of head movement of elements such as nouns and verbs. Akira Watanabe's chapter shows that the phenomenon of "*wh*-in-situ" is not a unitary phenomenon, with certain languages showing movement characteristics of question words that superficially remain in place, while other languages do not. This issue raises interesting learnability problems (for which see Janet Dean Fodor's chapter in part VI). Mark Baltin compares a wide variety of theories which differ in their analysis of what, in Government Binding Theory/Minimalism, is treated as movement to argument positions (A-positions). Höskuldur Thráinsson gives an overview of object shift and scrambling, and discusses how these movement types fit into the A/A' distinction.

In recent years, there has been an increased emphasis on reducing the role of a heavily specified primitive phrase-structure component. In part III, Jeffrey S. Gruber's chapter considers the nature of thematic relations, their expression in lexical representations, and the correct account of their linking with syntactic positions. John Bowers examines various theories of the syntactic expression of the predication relation and presents additional evidence for the existence of a Pred Phrase. Hiroyuki Ura's chapter discusses a universal theory of Case and the structural conditions for the realization of Case, arguing, within a principles and parameters approach, that Agr projections are not necessary for Case-checking (but see Adriana Belletti's chapter in part IV for a different point of view). Naoki Fukui's chapter shows what is meant by the idea that phrase structure rules – the rules that generate initial syntactic structures – can be eliminated, and how the work that is done by phrase structure rules can be accommodated with other devices. Mark C. Baker argues that the source of apparent non-configurationality can differ in different languages. In Japanese, movement is the source of non-configurationality, while in Warlpiri, it is claimed that the apparent arguments are really adjuncts. Kyle Johnson's chapter considers the twin problems of VP-ellipsis: the characterization of the licensing environments and the nature of the elided VP. He argues that null VPs are not silent pro-forms.

An important thread in current formal syntactic research is the existence of non-lexical, or functional, categories. In part IV, Raffaella Zanuttini considers the cross-linguistic generalizations that can be made about the categorial status and syntactic position of negation. Adriana Belletti reviews the evidence for AGR projections, and concludes with some comments on the attempts by Chomsky (Chomsky 1995b: ch. 4) to dispense with Agr projections in favor of multiple specifiers of a v ("light verb") node. Two of the chapters in this part, Judy B. Bernstein's and Guiseppe Longobardi's, consider the evidence that nominals are in fact determiner phrases, as proposed by Abney (Abney 1987) and Brame (Brame 1982). Adopting complementary evidence, they argue for additional structure within nominal phrases. Judy Bernstein explores the parallels between nominal structure and clausal structure with respect to head movement. Giuseppe Longobardi argues for the existence of PRO within noun phrases, a position also argued for in Baltin (1995).

The next part deals with the interplay between syntactic structures and semantic phenomena, principally anaphora and the scope of logical operators. Anna Szabolcsi considers the role of syntactic structure in establishing the relative scope of logical operators, comparing various treatments of "inverse scope," in which a superficially less prominent logical operator takes scope over a more prominent one. Martin Everaert and Eric Reuland discuss the role of syntactic structure in the determination of coreference, and the question of whether coreference is fully determined by the grammar. Andrew Barss's chapter deals with the optimal treatment of reconstruction, the phenomenon by which moved elements are interpreted as though they were in their pre-movement positions. He considers various analyses of the well-known asymmetry between moved predicative phrases and non-predicative phrases.

An important piece of the evidence in the evaluation of a grammar is its fit with domains which require the formulation of a grammar. In part VI, Anthony S. Kroch examines the way in which synchronic syntactic theory can inform and be informed by an account of possible syntactic change. Janet Fodor's paper explores the mechanisms by which children would have to be said to set the parameters of grammar variation that are posited by many linguistic theories.

This should give a flavor of this volume. We have undoubtedly offended many who would have chosen a different set of topics, but we would hope that the volume is comprehensive enough to serve a wide community.

I Derivation versus Representation

1 Explaining Morphosyntactic Competition

JOAN BRESNAN

0 Introduction

Morphosyntactic markedness theory classically assumes dynamic competition among the members of a paradigm. They are in opposition within a system of contrasts, and their meaning, or use, is determined by their relation to each other in the paradigm, not by their intrinsic features alone. This idea is embodied in Jakobson's (1984: 1) often-cited formulation of morphosyntactic unmarkedness in his work on the structure of the Russian verb:

> When a linguist investigates two morphological categories in mutual opposition, he often starts from the assumption that both categories should be of equal value, and that each of them should possess a positive meaning of its own: Category I should signify A, while Category II should signify B; or at least I should signify A, and II the absence or negation of A. In reality, the **general meanings** of correlative categories are distributed in a different way: If Category I announces the existence of A, then Category II does not announce the existence of A, i.e. it does not state whether A is present or not. The general meaning of the unmarked Category II, as compared to the marked Category I, is restricted to the lack of "A-signalization."

Jakobson gives (1) as a simple example:

(1) Russian: *oslíca* "she-ass," *osël* "donkey"
     èto oslíca? "Is it a she-ass?" – *nét, osël* "no, a donkey."

Here a Russian feminine gender noun *oslíca* "she-ass" is the marked category used only for a female animal of the species, where the corresponding masculine gender noun *osël* "donkey" is used for animals of both sexes. However, in a specific context of contrast the female meaning may be cancelled, leaving only the male meaning: *èto oslíca?* "Is it a she-ass?" – *nét, osël* "no, a donkey." Thus, depending on context, the unmarked (neutral) form can be used either inclusively, subsuming the marked, or exclusively, in opposition to the marked. This general idea that "the unmarked member acts as a surrogate for the entire category" (Greenberg 1966: 61) is widely instantiated in phonology, in morphology, and in morphosyntactic systems such as case, agreement, and voice, as well as in other syntactic, semantic, and pragmatic domains.

If we represent Jakobson's "marked" as in (2) by a feature specification such as [FEM] for the feminine gender variant, then the "unmarked" is the neutral form, lacking any specification such as [MASC] or ¬[FEM]:

(2)   marked: [FEM]
      unmarked: [   ]

Observe that the specifications in (3a, b) fail to capture the inclusive use of the unmarked form by excluding the feminine gender:

(3)   a.   [MASC]
      b.   ¬[FEM]
      c.   [MASC] ∨ [FEM]

An inclusive meaning *is* represented in (3c) by stipulating a disjunction of features. But *any* disjunction of features could be stipulated in this way. What is not captured is that the meaning of a neutral form derives dynamically from its role within a paradigm: it may subsume or contrast with the meanings of the other elements in relation to it.

The representation of neutral forms as featurally unmarked raises well-known problems for syntactic theory, however. Suppose, for example, that there is gender concord in a language that has a marked feminine gender as in (2). If concord between two elements is represented as checking for compatibility, or unification, of their feature structures, then the unmarked masculine form would wrongly be expected to be compatible with both feminine and masculine genders. To solve this problem, most feature-logic based syntactic theories (including LFG, categorial unification grammar, and HPSG) have resorted to overspecification of the unmarked form by adopting negations and disjunctions of features, as in (3) (Karttunen 1984, Pollard and Sag 1987, Maxwell and Kaplan 1995).[1]

1   Markedness in Blocking Theories

Overspecification of the unmarked form has been criticized by Andrews (1990) and Blevins (1995) as leading to loss of significant linguistic generalizations. The most fundamental generalization to be captured is what Jakobson (1984) recognizes: the meaning of the unmarked form depends not statically on its inherent feature specifications, but dynamically on its relation to other elements in opposition to it. This generalization is what Andrews's (1982: 495) Morphological Blocking Condition in (4) is designed to capture:

(4) **Morphological Blocking Condition** (Andrews 1982: 495)
If the constraint equations of a form A are a subset of those of a form B
from the same paradigm, and if the equations of B are satisfied at a
position X, then A may not be inserted at X.

Andrews's condition is a unification-based version of the Elsewhere Principle
found in phonology (Anderson 1969, Kiparsky 1973): if both a specific and a
general form from the same morphological paradigm are compatible with a
syntactic position, the more specific one must be used. Because the lexical
specifications of a verb or other head may unify with those of the syntactic
context, Andrews's principle allows morphologically inflected forms to compete with and block certain syntactic elements in a construction. In the gender
concord example, this condition would prevent the use of the unmarked masculine form where the marked feminine form is equally compatible because
the empty set of features is a subset of any set, by definition.[2]

The dependence of the meaning of the unmarked form on competing elements from the same paradigm is illustrated by contrasting verbal paradigms
in English and Ulster Irish (Andrews 1990). The English present tense paradigm and Ulster Irish conditional paradigm are shown in (5). The marked
forms are shown in bold type:

(5)   English present tense paradigm: Ulster Irish conditional paradigm:

	Singular	Plural		Singular	Plural
1	hit	hit	1	**chuirfinn**	**chuirfimis**
2	hit	hit	2	**chuirfeá**	chuirfeadh
3	**hits**	hit	3	chuirfeadh	chuirfeadh

In English the unmarked form (*hit*) is used in the complement of morphosyntactic environments of the marked form (the third person singular):

(6)   I/you/*he/*she/we/they hit the ball.

The same is true in Ulster Irish: the unmarked conditional form *chuirfeadh* is
used in the complement of the morphosyntactic environments of the marked
forms (the first person singular, first person plural, and second person
singular):

(7)   Chuirfeadh *mé/*tú/*muid/sibh/sé/sí/siad   isteach ar an phost sin.
      put-Cond   I/you-Sg/we/you-Pl/he/she/they in   on the job   that
      "*I/*you(sg)/*we/you(pl)/he/she/they would put in for that job."

How do we know from these facts alone that the forms *hit* in English and
chuirfeadh in Ulster Irish are indeed unmarked in Jakobson's sense? In the
domain of morphosyntax, unlike the domain of lexical meaning in Jakobson's
donkey example, it is difficult to find contexts in which a putatively unmarked

form can substitute for a marked form and thus demonstrate the presence of the inclusive meaning. The reason is that morphosyntactic constraints are generally too rigid to allow arbitrary substitution in grammatical constructions. This fact indeed has led to criticisms of Jakobson's definition of unmarkedness by Kuryłowicz, Dokulil, and other members of the Prague School (Dokulil 1994). They have argued that in morphosyntax the unmarked forms are better understood in terms of ambiguity, having primary and secondary meanings, than in terms of the general, inclusive meaning described by Jakobson. What evidence is there then that the meaning of these morphologically unmarked forms is in fact general rather than ambiguous?

On the Jakobsonian definition the inherent meaning of the unmarked is general (non-specific or vague) and its specific interpretations in various contexts depend on the marked form(s) to which it is in opposition. Hence there is a *dynamic* relation between the unmarked and marked forms. If the paradigm grows or shrinks in its marked forms, then the use of the unmarked form correspondingly diminishes or extends, augmenting or diminishing its range of specific interpretations. Thus Andrews (1990: 525) surveys the variation in use of verb forms in Irish dialects. The general tendency is that as the number of marked (inflected) forms increases from North to South, the use of the general (uninflected) forms correspondingly decreases. (In some areas there is a situation of free variation, with both marked and unmarked variants of certain categories in use; but Andrews notes (1990: n. 24, 530) that the co-occurring forms are sometimes reported to be differentiated by social register, suggesting the presence of closely related sociolinguistically competing grammars.) This dynamic relation is not captured by ambiguity analyses, for they provide no intrinsic connection between the loss of a marked form and the addition of its meaning to the unmarked form. The loss of inflected forms could simply lead to unfilled gaps in the paradigm, for example; or the gaps could be filled by extensions of other inflected forms.

To capture linguistic generalizations of this kind, syntactic theories must have some mechanism to represent competition among related morphosyntactic expressions. Though blocking was earlier applied in generative grammar to kinship terms and words (Gruber 1973, Aronoff 1976), Andrews's Morphological Blocking Principle (1982, 1984, 1990), couched within the LFG framework, is the first proposal within the generative tradition to capture morphosyntactic blocking. Blevins (1995) extends Andrews's proposal to HPSG by adding structured lexical paradigms to global feature type hierarchies ordered by subsumption and disjointness. In the distributed morphology framework, a rule-based theory of morphosyntax (Lumsden 1992, Halle and Marantz 1993, Bonet 1995), there is competition between more or less specified lexical items for insertion into a fully specified syntactic tree; the competition is implemented by rule ordering. For example, Lumsden (1992: 480) proposes that "A form that is specified for a relevant feature value must be inserted before a form that is unspecified for that feature." (This theory also admits ordering of morphological rules that non-monotonically alter featural composition.)

2 Some Limitations of Blocking Theories

The lexical blocking approaches to morphosyntactic competition all depend on two ideas. The first is that lexical forms compete for insertion into the same syntactic position. The field of competition is thus narrowly localized to a single preterminal (X^0) in the syntactic structure. The second idea is that a more specific or featurally complex form pre-empts a more general, featurally simple form. The possible relations of competing forms are thus restricted in terms of content to featural subsumption.

These restrictions are not intrinsic to the concept of paradigmatic competition, however. A more abstract conception of the paradigm is evident in the classic work of the European structuralists and the Prague School (represented by Jakobson). There the paradigm is viewed as a set of oppositions or dimensions of contrasts in general categories of meaning, a view which informs modern feature based conceptions of inflectional morphology as well (e.g. Matthews 1972, Anderson 1992). In an important development in theoretical morphosyntax, Vincent and Börjars (1996) and Börjars et al. (1997) show that this abstract way of defining the paradigm can be captured in modern feature-logic based theories of syntax such as LFG and HPSG. Instead of restricting the paradigm to sets of words that can be lexically inserted into the same syntactic position in a tree, they expand the paradigm to sets of forms of expression (whether words or phrases) that correspond to the same type of feature structure. They argue that this model of the paradigm can play an explanatory role in the synchronic distribution and historical development of periphrases, suppletion, and pronominal inflections.

This more general conception of paradigm makes the prediction that paradigmatic competition could occur between morphological and syntactic forms of expression of the same general categories of meaning; in particular, blocking could cross the boundaries of X^0 categories into the phrasal domain. And indeed, this phenomenon is widely attested. Blocking is implicit in periphrasis itself. Greenberg (1966: 30) observes that periphrasis is an instance of "defectivation," Hjelmslev's (1953) term for the propensity of marked categories to have defective paradigms. As an example Greenberg gives the perfective verbal system in Latin, where the active verb has a perfect inflection but the (marked) passive verbal form relies on periphrastic expressions for the perfect. (Börjars et al. (1997) provide the same example with an analysis using LFG feature structures.) In such cases a syntactic form is used where the morphological paradigm is defective. If we return to the Ulster Irish examples in (5) and (7), we see that syntactic constructions (namely a verb plus pronominal subject) fill the gaps in the inflectional paradigm (second plural, third singular, and third plural). The synthetic forms block the use of the syntactic construction to convey the specific information that is already expressed morphologically. In this way the blocking relation crosses the boundaries of the word into the syntactic domain.

A case of periphrasis in Basque is cited by Poser (1992: 122) as an example of the blocking of phrasal constructions by lexical items: in Basque a phrasal construction is used for progressive aspect except with verbs that have a progressive inflection. Another example of blocking from morphology into syntax cited by Poser (and already analyzed as morphosyntactic blocking by Andrews 1984) is English comparative and superlative adjectival inflections, which are supplemented with phrasal forms where adjectives are uninflected:

(8)   cheaper/cheapest, *more/*most cheap
       *expensiver/*expensivest, more/most expensive

Poser (1992) hypothesizes that blocking of phrases by words is permitted only where the phrases are "small categories" consisting entirely of X^0 categories and created by morphological rules (see also Sells 1996). But this structurally local characterization of morphosyntactic blocking cannot account for the Ulster Irish cases, where as we saw in (7), the entire periphrastic construction containing a main verb and a subject pronoun is blocked by the synthetic verbs which are inflected for subject pronominal features. The Irish main verb and subject can constitute an entire clause – quite a large category in its constituency. Nor would the small category hypothesis explain the English comparative, for although Poser (1992: 127) assumes that *more intelligent* is a small category consisting entirely of X^0s, syntactic work on English comparatives (e.g. Bresnan 1973) reveals a full X″ phrasal structure for comparative measure phrases: witness [*How much more*] *expensive is it? – It is* [*so much more*] *expensive,* [*exactly three times more*] *expensive.* Nor would the Latin passive example plausibly be restricted to a small category, since there a single verb form competes with a major phrasal configuration [V VP] or [I VP]. Consequently the blocking of a syntactic construction by a morphological word cannot be so narrowly localized in X′-theoretic terms as Poser (1992) proposes.

Compared with other generative blocking theories, feature-logic based theories of morphological blocking (e.g. Andrews 1990, Blevins 1995) greatly extend the explanatory scope of the Elsewhere Principle into syntax. For example, the competition within the Ulster Irish conditional paradigm is easily explained by Andrews (1990) because he captures the periphrastic relation by means of LFG feature structures, not by the operation of morphological rules on X^0 categories. In LFG, crucially, words and phrases, though constructed from different elements and by different principles of composition, may specify feature structures of the same type (Bresnan and Mchombo 1995, Bresnan 1998a, Nordlinger 1998). All feature-logic based theories share this property to a greater or lesser extent (e.g. Blevins 1995, Ackerman and Webelhuth 1998, Goldberg 1996). In Andrews's (1990) analysis of the Irish synthetic inflections (5) the marked verb forms specify several attributes of their clauses: namely, the main predicator, the conditional mood, and the pronominal subject for certain persons and numbers. Andrews represents these by a complex feature structure (f-structure in LFG); a version of this type of analysis is illustrated in (9):

(9)
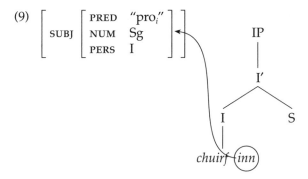

The unmarked verb forms are blocked in syntactic contexts that express the same constellation of information, represented by a similar complex feature structure arising from the unification of the head verb and subject pronoun feature structures with that of the clause (Andrews 1990: 519). Blocking in the English adjectival comparatives is explained by Andrews (1984) in the same framework. Many other cases of the blocking of syntactic phrases by morphologically formed words have been documented and explained in feature-logic based theories of syntax: in Chicheŵa (Bresnan and Mchombo 1987: 768–75; Bresnan in press a), Hungarian and Estonian (Ackerman 1990, Ackerman and Webelhuth to appear), Japanese and Korean (Sells 1997a, 1997b), Russian (King 1995), and Persian (Goldberg 1996). Both Andrews (1990) and Sadler (1997) analyze blocking between clitic-head constructions and phrasal pronominal constructions in French, Spanish, and Welsh, suggesting the quasi-morphological status of verbal clitics in these languages.

Despite the success of the feature-logic based theories of morphosyntactic blocking, these blocking theories nevertheless have other limitations stemming from the basic idea of a more specific or complex form pre-empting the lexical insertion of a more general or simple form into a periphrastic construction. Blocking is predicted only in the special case where one lexical item is more specified than another (that is, where one is properly subsumed by the other informationally). What happens when two forms compete but are not related by proper subsumption? Their features might only intersect, for example, each being unspecified for some feature of the other so that two different dimensions of markedness could be at play (Avery Andrews, personal communication, May 1997). The blocking theories say nothing principled about such cases, but they exist.

Consider the verb *are*, which is the most general form in the suppletive paradigm for present tense *be* in Standard English:

(10)

	Sg	Pl
1	am	are
2	are	are
3	is	are

The hypothesis that *are* is general in its meaning (unmarked in a Jakobsonian sense) rather than ambiguous would be supported by the existence of English dialects in which the historical person–number neutralization has converged on *are*. Such dialects exist. According to the *Survey of English Dialects* (Orton and Dieth 1962–) *are* is generalized to the first person singular *Are I?*, *I are* in some localities of the southern counties (vol. 4, part 3, 1121, 1131–2, 1134–7) and the East Midland counties (vol. 3, part 3, 1287, 1299, 1302). These dialects retain marking only for third singular of present tense *be*:

(11)   Southern and East Midland counties (Orton and Dieth 1962–71)

	Sg	Pl
1	am	are
2	are	are
3	is	are

I are. Are I?

Although I have not found neutralization of all persons in the present, there are dialects which converge on *were* across all persons in the past. For example, in the West and East Midlands non-standard dialects described by Cheshire et al. (1993: 80) there occur *I were singing. So were John. Mary weren't singing:*[3]

(12)   West and East Midlands (Cheshire et al. 1993: 80):

	Sg	Pl
1	were	were
2	were	were
3	were	were

I were singing. So were John. Mary weren't singing.

In addition to the evidence from dialect variation, there is rare but telling evidence within Standard English showing that the general form *are* can replace the specific first person singular form *am* in certain contexts. For most of the verb forms in (10), a negative affix *-n't* can be attached. (The contracted form of the negation *-n't* is often called a clitic, but Zwicky and Pullum (1983) argue convincingly that it has become an affixal negation.) However, the negative paradigm has a gap in the first person:

(13)

	Sg	Pl
1		aren't
2	aren't	aren't
3	isn't	aren't

In declarative sentences the gap is filled by the coexisting syntactic expression *am not*. But this syntactic form is unavailable in presubject position in questions:

(14)   a.   *Am not I going?
       b.   I am not going.

In just this position in Standard English, the general *aren't* may fill the gap:

(15)   a.   Aren't I going?
       b.   *I aren't going.

The fact that *aren't* does not occur in the declarative construction (15b) could be explained by the availability of the less marked syntactic form for this construction (14b). If so, then we have here a syntactic construction competing with an equivalent morphological one, as observed by Dixon (1982: 236–8) and Bresnan (in press a). (Of course, it needs to be explained why another competing construction *Am I not going?* does not suffice to block *Aren't I going?*, as Hudson (1997) rightly observes, and why blocking is not observed in coexisting forms such as *isn't* and *is not*. We return to both these questions below in section 4.)[4]

Interestingly, morphological blocking fails to explain this phenomenon. The negatively inflected form *aren't* in (15b) is neither more general nor more specific than *am* in the syntactic construction *am not* in (14b); *am* specifies person and number, but not negation, while *aren't* specifies negation but not person and number. Even if we enlarge the comparison to *aren't* and *am not*, treating *am not* as a "small construction" in Poser's (1992) sense, we cannot explain the phenomenon. In Poser's as in all the morphosyntactic blocking theories, a word or smaller syntactic construction pre-empts an equivalent larger construction, in a kind of economizing of phrasal structure (cf. Bresnan 1998a, forthcoming a, Sells 1997a, Ackerman and Webelhuth 1998, to appear, Sadler 1997). Here, however, the syntactic construction is blocking the morphological form.

The same kind of competition between syntactic and morphological expressions of negation occurs in other English dialects. In some Scottish dialects, *amn't* may be used (Hughes and Trudgill 1979: 14), but is restricted just as *aren't* is in the dialects which use that form (Dixon 1982: 237, Richard Hudson, personal communication, April 7, 1997):

(16)   Scottish English dialects
       Amn't I your friend?
       *I amn't your friend.

In Hiberno-English, in contrast, *amn't* is used in both positions (Jim Mcloskey, personal communication, October 1996, Siobhán Cottell, personal communication, April 7, 1997):

(17)   Hiberno-English
       Amn't I your friend?
       I amn't your friend.

What would explain these variations? Unlike Hiberno-English, Scottish English has a distinct clitic *nae* for sentence negation, which cannot invert (Brown 1991: 80, 97–8, April McMahon, personal communication, October 29, 1997):

(18)   He couldnae have been working.
       *Couldnae he have been working?

These facts suggest that the native Scottish clitic *nae* is competing with the English *-n't* and blocking it. (Again it needs to be explained why another competing construction of Scots, *Am I no your friend?*, does not also block *Amn't I your friend?* (Hudson 1997). This question is addressed in section 4.) These facts, too, are unexplained by morphological blocking, for the two negative elements are not distinguished by featural subsumption. Nor does the "smaller" (affixal) form of negation block the "larger" (clitic) form: as the contrast between (16) and (17) shows, the morphological form appears only where the clitic form is unavailable.

In sum, competition between morphological and syntactic forms of expression is correctly predicted by the feature-logic based models of the paradigm (Andrews 1990, Blevins 1995, Börjars et al. 1997), given the classic conception of paradigmatic competition. Yet we have no real explanation for the full range of morphosyntactic competition that has been documented. The blocking theories of markedness localize the field of competition too narrowly in syntactic structure or too restrictively in morphosyntactic content. Optimality Theory (Prince and Smolensky 1993) suggests a more general approach.

3   Markedness in Optimality Theory

Optimality Theory (OT) is a general theory of constraint interaction and comparative grammaticality. The basic structure of OT grammar is shown in (19) as a function from inputs to outputs.[5] The inputs in this case are phonological segment strings and the outputs are syllabifications of the strings according to a simplified CV theory (Prince and Smolensky 1993, Smolensky 1996a).

(19)   **Optimality Theory: CV Theory** (Prince and Smolensky 1993)
       (a)   INPUT   CANDIDATES   OUTPUT

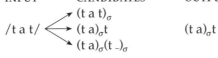

(b)   GEN: INPUT ⇒ CANDIDATES
(c)   EVAL: CANDIDATES ⇒ OUTPUT

A generator GEN produces candidate structural analyses or realizations of the input, and these are evaluated according to a function EVAL, whose basic properties are given in (20):[6]

(20)   EVAL
    (i)   A universal Constraint Set; constraints conflict and are violable.
    (ii) A language-particular strict dominance ranking of the Constraint Set.
    (iii) An algorithm for harmonic ordering: the optimal/most harmonic/ least marked candidate (= the output for a given input) is one that best satisfies the top ranked constraint on which it differs from its competitors.

Two fundamental requirements of the theory must be noted. First, GEN must be universal. That is, the input and the candidate set are the same for all languages. Systematic differences between languages arise from different constraint rankings, which affect how the candidates are evaluated (Prince and Smolensky 1993, Smolensky 1996a). Second, to ensure learnability the input must be recoverable from the output and the output itself must contain the overt perceptible data (Tesar and Smolensky 1996).

Now in the domain of morphosyntax, universality of the input would be ensured by an abstract multidimensional space of dimensions of contrast as formally modelled by complex feature structures. Recoverability of the input from the overt perceptible output would be ensured by a well-defined correspondence between feature structures and the types of overt forms of expression which may realize them. Both of these requirements can be met by taking the morphosyntactic GEN to be one of the feature-logic based models of morphosyntax. This line of research is being actively developed in LFG (Choi 1996, forthcoming, Bresnan 1998b, 1998c, in press a, in press b, forthcoming b, forthcoming c, Sells 1997b, 1998b, Butt et al. 1997, Frank et al. 1998, Morimoto 1998, Vincent 1998a, 1998b, Johnson forthcoming, Lee 1998). In what follows I will therefore assume for morphosyntax that the universal input is modeled by sets of f-structures and the universal candidate set consists of pairs of a c-structure and its corresponding f-structure, which may be matched to the input f-structure by a correspondence theory of input–output relations (cf. McCarthy and Prince 1995, Bresnan in press a, in press b, forthcoming c).[7] The overall scheme is illustrated (with simplifications) in (21).[8] Following Jakobson (1984) and Andrews (1990), we may assume that morphosyntactic candidates may have general (non-specific or vague) meanings; generality is represented by fewer feature specifications. Output indeterminacy of this sort must not be confused with underspecification in the phonological sense (Steriade 1995). The latter involves the omission of features in underlying structures which are required at the overt level:

(21)   **An Optimality Theoretic Framework for Morphosyntax**

INPUT   CANDIDATES   OUTPUT

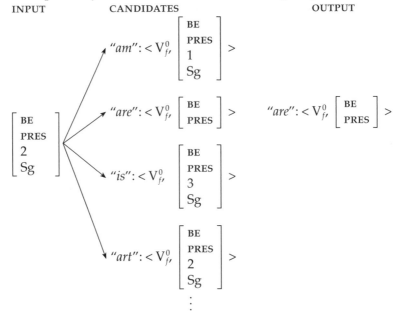

On this conception of GEN the input represents language-independent "content" or points in the multidimensional spaces of possible grammatical and lexical contrasts, to be expressed with varying fidelity by the candidate forms, which carry with them their own interpretations of that content. For each input, GEN enumerates the set of all possible types of formal realizations of that input that are available across languages. In morphosyntax as in phonology, systematic variation is derived by the rerankings of universal constraints rather than by language-particular specifications of differences in input or lexical inventory. Thus it is presumably a systematic fact about English that it has auxiliary verbs. In (21) V_f^0 stands for a finite auxiliary or "functional" verb. There are many other categorial realizations of the input among the candidate set – for example, as main verbs, verbal inflections, copular particles, or no structure at all; by hypothesis these alternatives are all less optimal than the auxiliary verb analysis under the constraint ranking for English. Likewise, it is a systematic fact about English that person and number distinctions are neutralized throughout the verbal paradigm except in third singular present (and in first singular present for *be*). As shown in (21) the candidate set includes a second person singular present tense form. The fact that second person verb forms are lacking in Standard English is a result of this neutralization; it follows from their non-optimality under the current constraint ranking, and their presence in non-standard English dialects (such as those of Somerset where *art* or *be'st* are used (Ihalainen 1991: 107–8)) arises from alternative rankings, as we will see.

What is not systematic is not derived from the general theory but must be specified as a language-particular property. Thus in (21) the names *"am," "is," "are"* in quotation marks stand for the English spellings (pronunciations) of candidates which have the abstract universal characterizations represented in angled brackets. These spellings are a language-particular property of English which distinguishes it from other languages independently of systematic differences in constraint ranking. Given the constraint ranking for English, the English-particular lexicon is a sampling of the output (Smolensky 1996a) that associates pronunciations and other unsystematic properties with the abstract morphosyntactic characterization. (The form pronounced *"art"* is of course no longer used in Standard English; it is included here simply as a convenient label for the candidate form which most faithfully matches the input in (21), but is nevertheless not optimal under the constraint rankings of present-day Standard English, which neutralize second person.)

Now markedness in Optimality Theory results from the relative ranking of the two types of constraints shown in (22) and (23) – constraints on faithfulness to the input ("FAITH") and constraints on the structural markedness or well-formedness of forms ("STRUCT") (Prince and Smolensky 1993, Smolensky 1996a):

(22) **Faithfulness Constraint** (FAITH):
FAITH$^{P \& N}$: preserve input person and number in the output[9]

(23) **Structural Markedness Constraints** (STRUCT):
    (a)   *Pl, *Sg
    (b)   *2, *1, *3

"FAITH$^{P \& N}$" is violated by any candidate which fails to match the input in both person and number. Note that faithfulness in fusional morphology is assumed here to respect *sets* of values, such as person and number combined in FAITH$^{P \& N}$.[10] Different faithfulness constraints may be instantiated for various morphosyntactically defined domains (Urbanczyk 1995, Benua 1995, Smith 1997). In Standard English the three present tense verbal paradigms (*be*, modal verbs, and other verbs) are thus represented by three different FAITH$^{P \& N}$ constraints, of which we will be concerned here only with FAITH$_{be}^{P \& N}$.

In general, faithfulness constraints favor featurally more complex forms, and hence more informative forms. Opposing faithfulness, however, are structural markedness constraints, which penalize the complexity of forms. The STRUCT constraints *2, *1, *3 are respectively violated by candidates specified for second, first, and third person values. Faithfulness constraints serve the major communicative function of preserving contrasts, making it possible for languages to have perceptibly different expressions for different meanings. But markedness constraints work to erode these contrasts by simplifying expressions.

Suppose now that the structural markedness constraints are ranked with respect to the faithfulness constraints as in (24). ("$c_1 \gg c_2$" means that constraint c_1 outranks constraint c_2 in the constraint hierarchy. The ranking relations of constraints separated by commas are not specified here.)

(24)   *Pl, *2 $\gg$ FAITH$_{be}^{\text{P \& N}}$ $\gg$ *Sg, *1, *3

The ranking of the markedness constraints for second person and plural above the faithfulness constraint means that violations of the former are worse than violations of the latter. Thus it is worse to express these features than to be unfaithful to the input by failing to preserve them. Hence a general form unmarked for second person or plural number will be preferred over candidates specifically marked for these features. On the other hand, the ranking of faithfulness above the other markedness constraints means that it is worse to fail to express the input features of singular number and first or third person than to bear the complexity penality against marking them. The end result of these rankings will be that specific forms for first or third person singular will be optimal when they match the input, as we see in (25), and the general unmarked form will be optimal elsewhere, as we see in (26). In OT, this is how one could derive the blocking of the general form *are* of the present tense *be* paradigm by the specific forms *am*, *is*.

In these tableaux the constraints are ordered from left to right according to their relative ranking. Violations of constraints are indicated by a *, and the ! denotes a fatal violation, rendering a candidate non-optimal. The optimal candidate(s) are designated by ☞. Constraint evaluations which have no effect in determining the outcome are shaded gray. Thus the marks incurred in (25) by "am," which violates *1 and *Sg by bearing the features 1 and Sg, are nevertheless overridden by the fatal marks incurred by its unfaithful competitor candidates and have no role here in determining the outcome:

(25)   input: [BE PRES 1 Sg]

	*Pl, *2	FAITH$_{be}^{\text{P \& N}}$	*Sg, *1, *3
☞ "am": [BE PRES 1 Sg]			**
"is": [BE PRES 3 Sg]		*!	**
"are": [BE PRES]		*!	
"art": [BE PRES 2 Sg]	*!	*	*

(26)   input: [BE PRES 2 Sg]

	*Pl, *2	FAITH$_{be}^{P\,\&\,N}$	*Sg, *1, *3
"am": [BE PRES 1 Sg]		*	*!*
"is": [BE PRES 3 Sg]		*	*!*
☞ "are": [BE PRES]		*	
"art": [BE PRES 2 Sg]	*!		*

Observe in (26) that if the markedness constraint against second person were to be demoted below faithfulness, the second person form would now become optimal, as in the Somerset dialects (Ihalainen 1991: 107–8). Conversely, if the markedness constraint against first person were promoted above faithfulness, *are* would be generalized to first singular, as in the southern and East Midland dialects (11).

A number of researchers in OT have proposed that in the initial state of the language learner all structural markedness constraints dominate faithfulness constraints; maximal unmarked forms are thus optimal during the initial stages of language acquisition. Then during the acquisition of marked forms, markedness constraints are subsequently demoted, allowing marked forms to become optimal. (See Smolensky 1996a for discussion and references; cf. Hale and Reiss 1997 for an opposing view; for a symmetric demotion-and-promotion learning strategy, see Boersma 1997.) On this view the absence of a marked form from a language would reflect the persistence of the initial high ranking of the relevant markedness constraints. In this case the learner never encounters the evidence needed to demote the relevant markedness constraints.

4   Analytic and Synthetic Negation in English

We have now seen how the present OT framework for morphosyntax can capture blocking effects. (See Sells 1997a, 1997b, for further examples from Japanese and Korean.) Unlike the blocking theories the present framework can also explain competition effects that are not localized to a single pre-terminal node in a syntactic tree and which do not follow the default logic of feature subsumption hierarchies. The competition between analytic and synthetic negation in English dialects sketched in section 2 will provide our demonstration.

We begin by observing that the overall structure of our framework for morphosyntax (21) applies as well to larger syntactic structures (Bresnan in press a):

(27)   INPUT

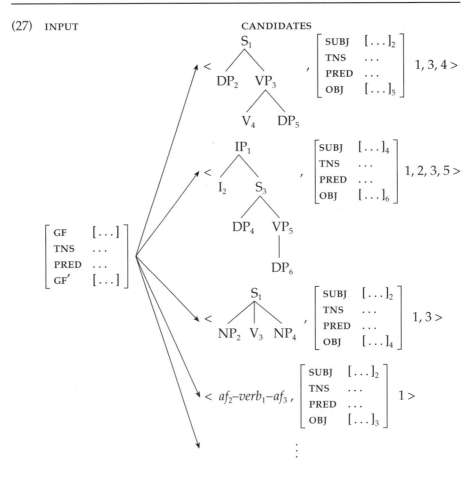

The inputs are again f-structures (with undifferentiated argument function types GF, GF'), and the candidates are again pairs of expressions and their corresponding f-structures, but this time at the level of sentence structure (as in LFG and similar syntactic frameworks). Expressions of syntax are actually composite, consisting of c-structure and their lexical instantiations.[11]

To determine what constraints will apply, we must next set English negation within the morphosyntactic typology of sentence negation. Klima (1964) distinguishes *sentential negation* from *constituent negation* by a number of tests including polarity reversal in confirmatory tag questions. Sentential negation can take scope over the entire sentence and reverse the polarity of tags, as illustrated by the postverbal *not* in (28a). Constituent negation cannot, as illustrated by *un-* and *not* in (28b–c):

(28)   a.   Louise is not happy, is she?   (sentential negation)
       b.   Louise is unhappy, isn't she?   (constituent negation)
       c.   Louise likes not being happy, doesn't she?   (constituent negation)

Sentential negation may also be expressed in English by negated or inherently negative quantifier phrases, as in (28a, b):

(29) a. Not many books survived the fire, did they?
      b. No books survived the fire, did they?

From this it would seem that sentential negation could simply be defined as *any* expression of negation having the sentence as its semantic scope. However, the expressions standardly used to negate sentences do not always have sentential scope semantically. For one thing, the actual semantic scope of sentential negation varies with the focus structure of the sentence (Jackendoff 1972).[12] For another, certain sentence operators like the initial adverb in (30b) and the modal verb *must* in (31b) take scope over sentential negation (cf. Stockwell et al. 1973: 248, Payne 1985: 200):

(30) a. He hasn't often paid taxes, has he?   NOT(OFTEN(S))
      b. ?Often he hasn't paid taxes, has he?   OFTEN(NOT(S))

(31) a. He can't pay taxes, can he?   NOT(POSSIBLE(S))
      b. ?He mustn't pay taxes, must he?   NECESSARY(NOT(S))

Thus "sentential negation" does not take sentential scope under all conditions, only under conditions of neutral focus and the absence of widest-scope sentence operators.

To circumvent these problems of identification, Payne (1985) defines *standard negation* as the expression of (sentential) negation in the basic sentences of a language, which are the minimal sentence constructions that exclude optional dependents such as adverbials and modifiers. Standard negation will coincide with sentential negation (semantically scoping over the sentence) in the simplest cases, and thus identified, it can be extended to cases where the semantic scope of the same expression of negation is reduced by focus or widest-scope sentence operators. Non-standard negation will then encompass constituent negation as in (28b, c) and any types of sentential negation which are expressed only in non-basic sentences (e.g. (29a, b)). We will be concerned here only with standard negation.

Languages vary in their repertoires of negative expressions; many lack negative quantifiers, for example. But according to Payne (1985: 223) all languages possess standard negation and typologically, standard negation is overwhelmingly a verbal category. Crosslinguistically, it appears as a negative lexical verb or auxiliary, a negative verbal inflection, or an analytic negation expression adjoined to a verbal category, in which are included here V, VP, I (the postsubject finite auxiliary position), and C (the inverted verb position in English). Only rarely does standard negation appear as a nominal category, and the single instance cited by Payne (1985: 228) shows signs of a deverbal origin. Following the OT markedness logic presented in the previous section, these assumptions suggest the markedness constraints in (32):

(32)   **Structural Markedness Constraints:**

    (a)   *NEG-C, *NEG-I, *NEG-V, *NEG-VP: mark an analytic negation expression adjoined to C, I, V, VP.

    (b) $*NINFL\text{-}V_f^0$, $*NINFL\text{-}V_{lex}^0$: mark a synthetic negation expression, inflecting functional (auxiliary) or lexical verbs.

    (c)   *NEG-LEX-V: mark a negation expression lexicalized as a verb.

Note that these structural markedness constraints apply to the expression component of the candidates in the present framework (27). Expressions are formally modelled by c-structures, representing the overt, perceptible configuration of syntactic elements. Thus the constraints on analytic negation such as *NEG-C and *NEG-I are violated by c-structures containing the substructures (33a) and (33b), respectively:

(33)   a.   b.

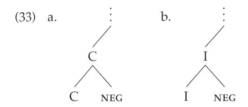

No syntactic movements are assumed in this constraint-based, output-oriented framework, and none need be, because the correspondence mapping between the parallel c- and f-structures[13] functionally replaces the coindexing between different substructures of the same tree invoked in derivational representations of movement (Bresnan in press a). Thus, rather than concern ourselves with a hypothetical base-generated tree position from which expressions of standard negation must be moved to their observable surface positions (as first proposed by Klima 1964 and still assumed in derivational syntactic frameworks), we simply let GEN enumerate the full typological space of possible surface realizations of standard negation, with corresponding f-structures showing the clausal polarity information they provide. From this point of view (33a, b) are two independent structures produced by GEN by simple adjunction of NEG directly to C (occupied by a complementizer or pre-subject verb) or I (occupied by the finite auxiliary in English).[14] In sum, the constraints in (32) simply impose marks against specific surface verbal positions or categories where negation might be overtly realized. (The *NINFL constraints are a special case of Sells's 1997a, 1997b "Avoid Affix.") Intuitively, these constraints penalize the additional structural complexity contributed by various expressions of negation at the lexical, morphological, or syntactic level.

    Opposed to these markedness constraints is the faithfulness constraint of (34):

(34)   **Faithfulness Constraint:**

    FAITH^{NEG}: preserve input scope of negation in the output[15]

Our interpretation of FAITH^{NEG} will be that any of the verbal expressions of negation in (32a–c) can parse the sentential scope of standard negation, but only the structurally appropriate expressions can parse constituent negation. Thus a negation expression attached to a VP can in principle have either sentence scope or constituent scope over VP, while a negation expression attached to I^0 can have sentence (IP) scope but not constituent scope over VP.[16]

By ranking FAITH^{NEG} among the family of markedness constraints for expressions of negation, we can derive the particular inventory of expressions of negation used in a given language following the same logic of markedness as in the preceding section. For example, if all of the structural markedness constraints for negation are ranked above the faithfulness constraint FAITH^{NEG}, the markedness of negative expressions will be worse than the failure to express negation. The resulting grammar would define a hypothetical language severely limited in its expressibility by the absence of specialized expressions for negation. Demotion of the constraint marking verbal lexicalization of negation (32c) below FAITH^{NEG} would yield a language whose inventory of negative expressions for standard negation consists of lexical verbs. An example would be the Nilo-Saharan language Majang, which employs a transitive negating verb *ku-* "which is neither an affix nor an auxiliary, but a full verb root" (Unseth 1994: 12):

(35)   Majang (Unseth 1994)
      $\ldots \gg$ FAITH$^{\text{NEG}} \gg$ *NEG-LEX-V

Swahili expresses standard negation synthetically by means of affixation to lexical verb stems, and this inventory follows from the ranking illustrated in (36), where the sole structural markedness constraint demoted below faithfulness is that against negatively inflected lexical verbs:

(36)   Swahili (Ashton 1982)
      $\ldots \gg$ FAITH$^{\text{NEG}} \gg$ *NINFL-V$^0_{lex}$

Russian, according to King (1995), expresses negation analytically by adjoining *ne* to I:

(37)   Russian (King 1995)
      $\ldots \gg$ FAITH$^{\text{NEG}} \gg$ *NEG-I

This framework can also illuminate the variable forms of standard negation in English dialects.

Standard English has both analytic negation (*not*) and synthetic negation (the negative verbal affix *-n't*). Restricting attention first to analytic negation, we see that the same invariant negation expression *not* is used to negate sentences as in (38a) and non-finite VP constituents as in (38b), leading to ambiguities as in (38c):

(38)　a.　She does not see him.　　　　　　　　　(sentence negation)
　　　b.　She kept not seeing him.　　　　　(VP-constituent negation)
　　　c.　She could not have been working.　　　　　　　　(ambiguous)

One possible analysis within our framework would be to say that *not* in (38) is always adjoined to non-finite VP, where it can (under the right conditions) parse either sentential scope or VP-scope negation. This account would be descriptively attractive from an English-internal standpoint, because it capitalizes on the sameness of form of *not* in its various uses. Yet it offers no explanation for the fact that standard *not* requires the proximity of a finite auxiliary or modal verb on its left:[17]

(39)　a.　*Marianne not left.
　　　b.　*Marianne left not.
　　　c.　Marianne did not leave.

An alternative analysis is proposed (with minor differences ignored here) by Payne (1985) and Bresnan (in press a). According to this analysis, the ambiguity of (38c) represents a choice between NEG-I right-adjoined to the modal/finite auxiliary position I^0 or NEG-VP left-adjoined to the VP:

(40)　a.　He [could not] have been working.　　　　　　　　NEG-I
　　　b.　He could [not have been working].　　　　　　　　NEG-VP

In support of this two-structure analysis of English *not*, Payne (1985: 240–1) points out that it is typologically common for languages to have different forms of negation for main (or fully tensed) and subordinate clauses. Observe that with the modal *can*, English orthography actually distinguishes the two forms. As shown in (41), the NEG-I form is spelled as a single word *cannot*, while the NEG-VP construction is spelled as two separate words *can not*:

(41)　a.　He cannot have been working.　　　　　$\neg(\text{POSS}(\text{work}(\text{he})))$
　　　b.　He can (just/simply) not have been working.　　$\text{POSS}(\neg(\text{work}(\text{he})))$

We will make use of this convenient orthographic representation of the distinction in what follows.

The two-structure analysis can be expressed in the present framework by the constraint ranking in (42):

(42)　English
　　　. . . *NEG-C ≫ FAITH^NEG ≫ *NEG-VP ≫ *NEG-I

This ranking allows two analytic forms of negation into the Standard English inventory: *not* adjoined to VP and *not* adjoined to I^0. By hypothesis both can parse wide scope (sentence) negation, but only the former can parse constituent negation of VP. Now assume that the input specifies sentential scope negation; because *NEG-VP is ranked higher than *NEG-I, it provides a worse violation, and therefore *not* adjoined to VP will be less harmonic than *not* adjoined to I^0 for this reading. But when the input specifies VP-scope negation, *not* adjoined to VP will be optimal by our interpretation of FAITH^{NEG} (34). This ranking therefore derives the contrast seen in (41), assuming that *cannot* has *not* adjoined to I^0, while *can not* has *not* adjoined to VP. See (43):

(43)

	FAITH^{NEG}	*NEG-VP	*NEG-I
input: ¬(poss(work(he)))			
☞ *he cannot have been working*			*
he can not have been working		*!	
input: poss(¬(work(he)))			
he cannot have been working	*!		*
☞ *he can not have been working*		*	

How does this analysis apply to the other modals? The modal verbs *could*, *may* (in the permission sense), and *need* are like *can* in allowing standard negation to have wider (sentential) scope (cf. (31a)). With these modal verbs, therefore, the structural ambiguity between NEG-I and NEG-VP coincides with a clear semantic difference in scope as above. But *may* (in the possibility sense), *might*, and *will* are widest scope sentential operators like *must* in (31b). With widest scope modals the structural ambiguity between NEG-I and NEG-VP obviously does not coincide with the scope difference. Neverthless, both negation structures are syntactically available with these modals, as (44) illustrates:

(44) a. You [must not] simply [not work].
       b. He [may not] just [not have been working].

Thus the essential difference with these modals is that their faithfulness to the widest scope property overrides faithfulness to wide scope negation. A full Optimality Theoretic analysis of the English modal verbs would take us too far afield in the present study, however. In what follows *can* or *could* will continue to be our exemplar, because they conveniently signal the structural ambiguity of negation by a scope ambiguity.

The proposed analysis of Standard English *not* finds support in the Hawick Scots dialect of English, as very usefully described by Brown (1991). Analytic negation in Hawick Scots takes two forms: there is a negative clitic *nae*, which attaches to the finite auxiliary or modal, and a negative isolate *no*:

(45)   Hawick Scots (Brown 1991: 83):
    (a)   ?She couldnae have told him, but she did.
        ("It was impossible for her to have told him, but she did tell him.")
    (b)   She could no have told him, but she did.
        ("It was possible for her not to have told him, but she did tell him.")

The clitic *nae* in Hawick Scots closely corresponds to the Standard English *not* adjoined to I^0. First, as shown in (45a), *nae* unambiguously takes wide scope over the modal, creating a contradiction with the following conjunct. Second, like the Standard English *not*, *nae* cannot invert with the auxiliary:

(46)   a.   *Isnae he coming?   (Hawick Scots – Brown 1991: 80)
     b.   *Is not he coming?   (Standard English)

Assuming that the inverted auxiliary of both dialects is the C^0 position, these shared properties of Standard English and Hawick Scots reflect the ranking of *NEG-C above FAITH^NEG and *NEG-I below it given in (42). (Inversion itself is not treated here; see Grimshaw 1997 and Bresnan in press a.) A structure will incur a mark under *NEG-C when syntactic negation (*not* in Standard English, *nae* in Scots) appears in the inverted position (adjoined to C^0). Only the overt perceptible position of the negative element is considered in assessing STRUCT marks, by the design of our general framework (21).

    The Hawick Scots isolate *no* corresponds to English *not* adjoined to VP; it "normally shows narrow scope negation" (Brown 1991: 83). However, Brown (1991: 83) notes that there is "a small complication:" a sentence like *She could no have told him* is "potentially ambiguous between a narrow scope reading and a negative stressed wide scope reading." This fact would follow if we assume that clitics and other reduced, atonic forms cannot express what Brown calls stressed negation; only forms that can carry primary stress have this property. By ranking a FAITH^STRESS constraint together with FAITH^NEG among the FAITH constraints, we allow the need to express stressed negation to override the greater markedness of the isolate *no* as a competitor to the clitic *nae*:[18]

(47)   Hawick Scots:
    . . . *NEG-C ≫ FAITH ≫ *NEG-VP ≫ *NEG-I

This ranking gives us the basic generalizations for the use of Hawick Scots *no* and *nae* in simple sentence declaratives and interrogatives, as described by Brown (1991). In the following tableaux the set of faithfulness constraints – FAITH^NEG, FAITH^STRESS – has again been abbreviated simply as FAITH:[19]

(48)   Hawick Scots:

	*NEG-C	FAITH	*NEG-VP	*NEG-I
input: ¬(poss(work(he)))				
☞ *he couldnae work*				*
he could no work			*!	
input: STRESS¬(poss(work(he)))				
he couldnae work		*!		*
☞ *he could no work*			*	
input: Q(¬(poss(work(he))))				
couldnae he work?	*!			
☞ *could he no work?*			*	

The results are straightforward. In declaratives, the clitic *nae* is the optimal form for expressing sentence-scope negation; the isolate *no* is possible with stressed negation and required for VP-scope negation. In interrogatives, the isolate *no* is the optimal form for expressing sentence negation, regardless of stress.

Under the analysis proposed here (following Bresnan in press a), Standard English is very similar to Hawick Scots in its inventory of syntactic expressions of (analytic) negation, differing in the spelling (pronunciation) of the two analytic forms:

(49)

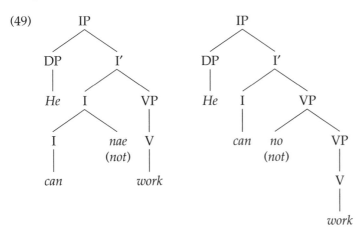

Let us now turn to synthetic negation. The negative affix *-n't* has the same form in the two dialects, but somewhat different properties. Consider first

Standard English. In declaratives the *-n't* form alternates as an expression of wide scope negation with *not* adjoined to I:

(50) a.   He can't have been working. $\neg(\text{POSS}(\text{work}(he)))$
       b.   He cannot have been working. $\neg(\text{POSS}(\text{work}(he)))$
       c.   He can not have been working. $\text{POSS}(\neg\text{work}(he))$

In interrogatives having unstressed wide scope negation, *-n't* widely replaces *not* in the contemporary spoken standard:[20]

(51) a.   Can't he have been working? $\text{Q}(\neg(\text{POSS}(\text{work}(he))))$
       b.   Can he not have been working? $\text{Q}(\text{POSS}(\neg(\text{work}(he))))$
       c.   *Can he not have been working? $\text{Q}(\neg(\text{POSS}(\text{work}(he))))$
            (marked: very formal or stilted)

This pattern results from the constraint ranking shown in (52). The constraint $^*\text{NINFL-V}_f^0$ is the structural markedness constraint for negative inflections on functional verbs (auxiliaries and modals). It is here grouped with the lowest ranked of the markedness constraints on analytic negation, $^*\text{NEG-I}$ from (42).

(52)   Spoken Standard English:
        . . . $^*\text{NEG-C} \gg \text{FAITH} \gg {}^*\text{NEG-VP} \gg {}^*\text{NEG-I}, {}^*\text{NINFL-V}_f^0$

The properties of the negative forms given in (50)–(51) follow:

(53)   Spoken Standard English:

	*NEG-C	FAITH	*NEG-VP	*NEG-I, *NINFL-V$_f^0$
input: $\neg(\text{POSS}(\text{work}(he)))$				
☞ *he can't have been working*				*
☞ *he cannot have been working*				*
he can not have been working			*!	
input: $\text{Q}(\neg(\text{POSS}(\text{work}(he))))$				
☞ *can't he have been working?*				*
cannot he have been working?	*!			
can he not have been working?			*!	
input: $\text{Q}(\text{POSS}(\neg(\text{work}(he))))$				
can't he have been working?		*!		*
cannot he have been working?	*!	*		
☞ *can he not have been working?*			*	

Observe that in (53) two alternate forms – *can't* and *cannot* – are optimal in simple declaratives. This results from treating *NEG-I and *NINFL-v$_f^0$ as tied constraints in (53). In the present context, this device is merely a simplification, abstracting away from the exact conditions (such as stress, emphasis, or style) under which the two forms may be differentially used.[21] Within OT, tying of constraints is one way in which optional alternate forms can arise (Tesar and Smolensky 1996), although in a large grammar consisting of massive numbers of constraints there are certain to be some that distinguish the forms. Another way to model optionality is to adopt partially ordered rankings which define sets of coexisting competing grammars (Anttila 1997, to appear). Yet another way in which optional alternate forms can arise is from allowing variable ranking, such as random variation around ranking values of constraints on a continuous scale, which can produce different frequencies of production of optionally varying forms (Boersma 1997) as well as gradient judgments (Hayes in press).

The main point of this analysis of the English synthetic negation is that its relatively unmarked status effectively eliminates NEG-VP from the competition for expressing sentential negation. (It appears, of course, when narrower scope is required, as in the examples like *They will obviously not have time to change* cited by Kim and Sag 1996.)

Consider now synthetic negation in Scottish English. The same English form *-n't* is also used, but it is considerably more marked. In Hawick Scots, *-n't* is lexically restricted to a subset of the verbs which can be negated with *nae* (Brown 1991: 93). Thus *can, must, will* do not have *-n't* forms, though *could* does:

(54) cannae, mustnae, willnae, couldnae, ...
      *can't, *mustn't, *won't, couldn't, ...

Brown (1991: 80) remarks that *-n't* is "not usually available in main clause negatives" but "seems to occur freely in tags," where ... *isn't he?* contrasts with ... *is he no?* in both intonation and pragmatic implication. The markedness of the English form in Scottish English generally is reinforced by Miller's (1993: 114) sociolinguistic description, where *-n't* is said to be preferred by educated speakers in formal contexts. An asymmetry in the distribution of *-n't* in Scottish English is also pointed to by Dixon (1982: 237), cited in section 2 above (16):

(55) Scottish English dialects (Dixon 1982)
      Amn't I your friend?
      *I amn't your friend.

Exactly this asymmetric distribution of *-n't* would result from the constraint ranking in (56):

(56) Scottish English:
      ... *NEG-C ≫ FAITH ≫ *NEG-VP, *NINFL-v$_f^0$ ≫ *NEG-I

Here $*$NINFL-v_f^0 is ranked higher, and thus makes a worse markedness violation, than is Standard English (52).[22] As a result *-n't* forms in Scottish English compete less well with the $*$NEG-I form than in Standard English. The results are shown in (57):

(57)   Scottish English:

	*NEG-C	FAITH	*NEG-VP, *NINFL-v_f^0	*NEG-I
input: ¬(poss(work(he)))				
he couldn't work			*!	
☞ *he couldnae work*				*
he could no work			*!	
input: STRESS¬(poss(work(he)))				
he couldn't work		*!	*	
he couldnae work		*!		*
☞ *he could no work*			*	
input: Q(¬(poss(work(he))))				
☞ *couldn't he work?*			*	
couldnae he work?	*!			
☞ *could he no work?*			*	

This ranking explains why *-n't* appears only where *nae* cannot appear. It also predicts a contrast in the scope of NEG-VP in Scottish English and spoken Standard English. In spoken Standard English questions, as we saw in (53), the inverted contracted form *-n't* has replaced the sentence-scope use of NEG-VP *not*. In Scottish English, in contrast, *-n't* is more marked and fares less well against the sentence-scope use of NEG-VP *no* in interrogatives.

In areas of Ireland the negative affix shows the same markedness rank as in Standard English, yielding a symmetrical pattern, as noted in section 2 above:

(58)   Hiberno-English
       Amn't I your friend?
       I amn't your friend.

The contrast between (55) and (58) is quite interesting theoretically. The essential difference between the two dialects is that $*$NINFL-v_f^0 is higher ranked (hence more marked) compared to NEG-I in Scots than in Hiberno-English:

(59) a. Hiberno-English:
         ... $\text{*NEG-C} \gg \text{FAITH} \gg \text{*NEG-VP} \gg \text{*NEG-I, *NINFL-V}_f^0$
      b. Scottish English:
         ... $\text{*NEG-C} \gg \text{FAITH} \gg \text{*NEG-VP, *NINFL-V}_f^0 \gg \text{*NEG-I}$

There is no evident structural basis for this difference in markedness. Compared to *amn't*, *amnae* is neither more economical in phrase structure nodes nor more specific in featural content, whether compared in parts or as a whole.[23] Hence the pre-emption of *amn't* by *amnae* (where the latter is available) has no evident structural basis internal to Scots. Also unanswered in purely structural terms is why the NEG-I structure blocks NINFL-v_f^0 in Scots but not in Hiberno-English.

Thus the markedness difference between NINFL-v_f^0 and NEG-I in the two dialects cannot be explained by the blocking theories. Nor should it be. NEG-I in Scots is of course the native Scots form *nae*, while NEG-I in Hiberno-English is the Standard English form *not*. The fact that *NINFL-v_f^0, a Standard English form *-n't* in both dialects, is more marked compared to NEG-I in Scots than in Hiberno-Irish may simply reflect the social competition between the Scots and the Standard English forms of expression. If so, the competition cannot be explained in terms of purely structural properties of the forms themselves, but instead reflects historical and social factors that have shaped the universally available typological possibilities in slightly different ways through constraint ranking. Recall from section 3 that the language-particular lexicon is a sampling of the output that associates spellings, or pronunciations, and other unsystematic properties with the abstract morphosyntactic characterization. Here the unsystematic property is the social value of the standard and nonstandard pronunciations of NEG-I.[24]

Standard English itself, as we noted in section 2, lacks the first person singular negative form of *be* used in (58) and (55). Various reasons have been suggested for the presence of this gap. Dixon (1982) proposes a phonological reduction of *am* to [a:] before *-n't* to avoid the [mn] sequence. Another suggestion[25] is that *ain't* may be an older regular first person present negative form which became socially stigmatized after its use spread to other persons. Whatever its causes, it manifests itself by the absence of a recognized pronunciation for the pair in (60), given our (simplified) framework of section 3:

$$(60) \quad \text{`` ''}: < V_f^0 + \textit{ninfl}, \begin{bmatrix} \text{BE} \\ \text{PRES} \\ 1 \\ \text{Sg} \\ \text{NEG} \end{bmatrix} >$$

To model accidental lexical gaps in OT, assume a highly ranked constraint which requires that candidates normally have pronunciations;[26] the absence of a pronunciation for (60) will filter it out from the candidate set. Because it is the job of the lexicon to pair the inventory of abstractly characterized candidates selected by the constraint ranking with the unsystematic language-particular pronunciations by which they are used, this constraint is called LEX.[27]

The presence of this lexical gap in Standard English eliminates a competitor from the candidate set. To understand the results, consider first the tableaux in (61), which simply add LEX in a position dominating the spoken Standard English constraints of (53). The FAITH[NEG] and FAITH[STRESS] constraints are abbreviated as FAITH in (53):

(61)   Possible effect of a lexical gap (I):

	LEX	*NEG-C	FAITH	*NEG-VP	*NEG-I, *NINFL
(declarative, wide negative, 1 Sg)					
I amn't (60) *working*	*!				*
☞ *I am not working*					*
I am [*not working*]				*!	
(interrogative, wide negative, 1 Sg)					
Amn't (60) *I working?*	*!				*
Am not I working?		*!			
☞ *Am I* [*not working*]?				*	

For declaratives the result is that the syntactic construction *am not* is optimal;[28] for interrogatives, the syntactic construction with *am* inverted and *not* adjoined to VP is optimal. Here syntactic constructions with *am . . . not* replace the missing first person singular negative inflected form of *be*.

Though some speakers may avoid the lexical gap by using a syntactic construction everywhere, it is much more common (certainly in informal spoken Standard American English) to use *Aren't I . . . ?*, the apparent "first person" *aren't* (Langendoen 1970, Hudson 1977, 1997, Dixon 1982, Gazdar et al. 1982, Kim and Sag 1996, Bresnan in press a), as discussed in section 2.[29] What is happening is that faithfulness to person and number is sacrificed in order to avoid the very marked use of VP-negation with wide scope. For these speakers, *NEG-VP dominates $FAITH_{be}^{P\ \&\ N}$ in the constraint hierarchy, as shown in (62):

(62) $*\text{NEG-VP} \gg \text{FAITH}_{be}^{P\ \&\ N}$
       $\text{FAITH}_{be}^{P\ \&\ N} \gg *\text{NEG-I}, *\text{NINFL-V}_f^0$

With all other constraint rankings the same as before, this means that it is a worse violation to use VP negation (for wide scope input) than to violate faithfulness to number and person. The main result is shown in (63), where F^{NEG} and F^{PN} designate faithfulness to negation and to person and number, respectively:

(63) Possible effect of a lexical gap (II):

	LEX	*NEG-C	F^{NEG}	*NEG-VP	F^{PN}	*NEG-I, *NINFL
(declarative, wide negative, 1 Sg)						
I amn't (60) *working*	*!					*
I aren't working					*!	*
☞ *I am not working*						*
I am [*not working*]				*!		
(interrogative, wide negative, 1 Sg)						
Amn't (60) *I working?*	*!					*
☞ *Aren't I working?*					*	*
Am not I working?		*!				
Am I [*not working*]?				*!		

Let us recall from section 3 why the form *aren't* is optimal here. Consider the theory of person–number marking in section 3. As expressions of third and first person singular, the special forms based on *is* and *am* are optimal, as shown in (64) and (65):[30]

(64) INPUT: [NEG 3 Sg] (declarative)

	LEX	*NEG-C	...	F^{PN}	...	*Sg, *1, *3	...
☞ i isn't [NEG 3 Sg]						**	
☞ ii is not [NEG 3 Sg]						**	
iii aren't [NEG]				*!			
iv are not [NEG]				*!			
v am not [NEG 1 Sg]				*!		**	
vi amn't (60)	*!			*		**	

(65)   INPUT: [NEG 1 Sg] (declarative)

	LEX	*NEG-C	. . .	F^PN	. . .	*Sg, *1, *3	. . .
i isn't [NEG 3 Sg]				*!		**	
ii is not [NEG 3 Sg]				*!		**	
iii aren't [NEG]				*!			
iv are not [NEG]				*!			
☞ v am not [NEG 1 Sg]						**	
vi amn't (60)	*!					**	

Observe in (65) how the lexical gap corresponding to *amn't* in other dialects is filled by the analytic form *am not*. (66) shows that when the input conflicts with feature values of the most specified forms, the general forms will be optimal, as we expect:

(66)   INPUT: [NEG 1 Pl] (declarative)

	LEX	*NEG-C	. . .	F^PN	. . .	*Sg, *1, *3	. . .
i isn't [NEG 3 Sg]				*		*!*	
ii is not [NEG 3 Sg]				*		*!*	
☞ iii aren't [NEG]				*			
☞ iv are not [NEG]				*			
v am not [NEG 1 Sg]				*		*!*	
vi amn't (60)	*!			*		**	

Now in all these tableaux the analytic (*not*) forms are equally harmonic with the synthetic negative forms available as long as both are in postsubject position (I⁰). When inverted (in C⁰ position), however, the analytic form will incur a mark by *NEG-C, and the synthetic form becomes more harmonic. This is fine in all cases except for (65) (the first person singular input), where a synthetic first person singular form is lacking. The analytic form still cannot be used in this (inverted) case, which tells us that *NEG-C must outrank the PARSE constraints at least. In just this case, the optimal candidate becomes *aren't*, as shown in (67). (*Am I not . . . ?* is excluded by *NEG-VP which dominates FAITH$_{be}^{\text{P \& N}}$ as in (63).)

(67)   INPUT: [NEG 1 Sg] (interrogative)

	LEX	*NEG-C	...	F^PN	...	*Sg, *1, *3	...
i isn't [NEG 3 Sg]				*		*!*	
ii is not [NEG 3 Sg]		*!		*		**	
☞ iii aren't [NEG]				*			
iv are not [NEG]		*!		*			
v am not [NEG 1 Sg]		*!				**	
vi amn't (60)	*!					**	

We see, then, that the appearance of *aren't* in the inverted position for the first person singular follows from its unmarked status for person and number in the verbal paradigm for *be*, given the strong constraints against using the analytic forms with inversion. Its appearance in *only* the inverted position results from the competition by the more harmonic analytic form in the uninverted position. In the latter situation we have another case where a syntactic construction "blocks" a morphological one.

What is most striking about the use of negation in these English dialects is that the specific properties of the output form depend upon the other surface forms (both morphological and syntactic) that actively compete with it, and not on the details of the derivation of its formal structure, as in the classical generative approach to syntax. The results are attained by letting surface morphological and syntactic forms express the same kinds of abstract information, as in the feature-structure representations of syntax. Optimality Theory, incorporating a feature-logic based theory of the candidate set, shows us that small (and even externally motivated) differences in the evaluation of surface forms of expression can have visible and unexpected repercussions in the syntax and semantics of verbal negation and inversion.

Although we have been concerned here with variations among closely related dialects of English, the same overall framework for morphosyntax can be applied to much broader typological variations (e.g. Bresnan 1998a, in press a, in press b, forthcoming c) – an inviting project for future research.

NOTES

*   I am grateful to Avery Andrews, Mark Baltin, Jim Blevins, Andrew Bredenkamp, Chris Collins, Edward Flemming, Jane Grimshaw, Dick

Hudson, Mark Johnson, Knud Lambrecht, Andrew Carstairs-McCarthy, Scott Myers, Alan Prince, Geoff Pullum, Peter Sells, Petr Sgall, Paul Smolensky, Ida Toivonen, David Wilkins, Mary McGee Wood, and Nigel Vincent for critical suggestions, though I am solely responsible for the use made of their comments.

1   For discussion of further problems of feature-logic based theories, see Ingria (1990) and Johnson and Bayer (1995), who use properties of neutral forms to argue against unification, and Dalrymple and Kaplan (1997) for a rebuttal and unification-based counterproposal, utilizing a set-based theory of indeterminate feature values.

2   See Andrews (1990: 519) for a reformulation in terms of subsumption of feature structures (Shieber 1986), rather than subsets of feature specifications.

3   This dialect can be heard spoken by the unemployed Sheffield steelworkers' families portrayed in the British motion picture *The Full Monty*.

4   Hudson's (1997) own analysis using multiple inheritance involves overspecification of the general form *aren't*.

5   This original conception has recently been generalized to abstract away from the input–output function (Smolensky 1996b). Nevertheless, the schema shown is useful as one illustrative instantiation of the general theory.

6   The general algorithm for determining the optimal, or most harmonic, output is given by Tesar and Smolensky (1996).

7   The candidates could equally well be represented as c-structures with "annotated" feature structures, as in some variants of LFG (Andrews and

Manning 1993) and construction grammar (Goldberg 1996). On the formal architecture of LFG see Dalrymple et al. (1995) and Bresnan (forthcoming a).

8   Among the simplifications are these: the label "BE" stands for an index to the appropriate lexical semantics, "2" and "SG" should specify the person and number of an argument (the subject) of the verb, and "PRES" should specify a clausal property. Some issues involving detailed representations are discussed by Butt et al. (1997). Note also that monovalent (privative) features are used here; these are represented uniquely by their values. The natural contrasts among sets of such features (e.g. SG vs. PL) follow from their inherent meanings, obviating a purely formal representation by equipollent feature values. Such a representation is not necessary to the present theory, however, and the standard feature-logic attribute value system can be substituted.

9   FAITH$^{P \& N}$ comprises two constraints: IDENT-IO (PERS & NUM) and MAX-IO (PERS & NUM) in the correspondence theory of faithfulness (McCarthy and Prince 1995). See Bresnan (forthcoming b) for further discussion.

10 Faithfulness to sets of values cannot be eliminated by the local conjunction (Legendre et al. 1998) of constraints on single feature values. The local conjunction of FAITH (PERS) and FAITH (NUM) is violated only when both conjuncts are violated. Hence in (26) the local conjunction interpretation would favor fully specified forms *is, am* that partly match the input over the general form (*are*) that completely fails to match the input. Logical conjunction could be used instead (Hewitt and Crowhurst to appear).

Nigel Vincent (personal communication, November 11, 1997) suggests that logical conjunction of constraints may be characteristic of fusional and suppletive morphology; see Börjars and Vincent (1997) for discussion of specific properties of fusional morphology.

11 Hence, the candidates are more accurately thought of as *n*-tuples of lexical strings, trees, feature structures, and their correspondence functions.

12 For example, the negation in (i) (adapted from Payne 1985: 199) has a reading in which its semantic scope is restricted to the focussed PP, yet still passes the test for sentential negation in requiring polarity reversal in a confirmatory tag:

   (i)   Celia didn't kiss John IN THE
         RAIN, did she?
         ("It's true of Celia, isn't it, that
         she didn't kiss John in the rain"
         or "It's true, isn't it, that it was
         not in the rain that Celia kissed
         John")

13 And a-structures (Bresnan and Zaenen 1990).

14 Variable positioning of verbs within the clause follows from the correspondence mapping; see Kroeger (1993), King (1995), Bresnan (in press a, forthcoming a), Berman (1996, 1997, 1998), Sadler (1997), Sells (1998a, 1998b), and the references cited in these.

15 Technically, the semantic scope information is not represented in f-structures, which are unspecified with respect to scope relations (Genabith and Crouch 1996, Dalrymple et al. 1995) but in a parallel information structure of the input.

16 This generalization does not rule out the attraction of standard negation scope to focal phrases, as discussed

above, but it does exclude a NEG-I expression from negating only a VP in the absence of special focus or other operators.

17 Grimshaw (1997) offers an account of this fact within OT assuming a NegP; see Bresnan (in press a) for discussion.

18 I use the terms "stressed negation," FAITH^{STRESS}, and STRESS as convenient shorthand for what may well involve constraints on focus structure.

19 I set aside here the constraints which yield inversion for yes/no questions; see Bresnan (in press a) for the specifics assumed here.

20 Palmer and Blandford (1969: 293) observe that negative sentences on the pattern *Does John not drink coffee?* are occasionally used in very formal speech, adding "but most good speakers feel that this style is stilted and unnatural."

21 Thus we can eliminate the tie by having FAITH$^{\text{FEAT}} \gg$ *NEG-I $\gg$ *NINFL-v_f^0, which in declaratives would make *can't* optimal for negative inputs without FEATURE and *cannot* optimal for negation with FEAT. In general, our tied constraints could be eliminated with a more fine-grained theory of the input than there is scope for here.

22 Again the tie between constraints is a simplification to be replaced by a more fine-grained theory of the factors affecting choice of forms (cf. n. 21).

23 Indeed, the opposite is true. *am* in *amnae* is less specific than *amn't* and equally economical in phrase structure nodes, occupying a single I^0. Likewise, the entire verb plus clitic construction *amnae* is more complex in phrase structure nodes than *amn't*, and equally specific in features. Only if we invented a feature [SCOTS] and attached it to the

entire complex of verb plus clitic, leaving the English form *-n't* unspecified for this feature, could we say that *amnae* blocks *amn't* by proper featural subsumption. However, this move would take the native Scots form to be the marked form, despite the clear dialect-internal evidence that the English form *-n't* is more marked; see the discussion surrounding (54) above.

24   By "unsystematic" I mean "not deriving from the abstract system of grammatical contrasts and structural expressions." Social factors may of course also be systematized in language; formal politeness systems are one example.

25   From a usage note, *The American Heritage Dictionary*.

26   "Normally" would refer to cases where the structural form of the candidate, represented by the left member of the pair in (60), is non-empty. Null structure occurs in some candidates, such as zero pronouns (Bresnan in press a, forthcoming c, Grimshaw and Samek-Lodovici 1998).

27   This constraint is used only for truly accidental gaps, which cannot be explained systematically. The discovery of an explanation in terms of systematic constraints would allow the latter to replace LEX in our subsequent analysis. The LEX constraint follows suggestions from Edward Flemming (personal communication, Fall 1996) and Scott Myers (personal communication, April 1997).

28   The choice between the full verb *am* and the reduced *'m* is an orthogonal issue that is not addressed here. See Pullum and Zwicky (1997) for discussion.

29   See also n. 20 above.

30   Only the relevant features, constraints, and candidates are shown.

2 Economy Conditions in Syntax

CHRIS COLLINS

0 Introduction

An important theme in recent generative grammar is that linguistic operations, derivations, and representations are subject to economy conditions which guarantee that they are optimal in some sense (see Chomsky 1998b).

Consider an operation OP applying in a derivation D leading to the representations (PF, LF) (phonetic form and logical form). Economy considerations suggest that OP be as small as possible, and be applied in a way that minimizes search. Given a series of operations that form a derivation D, economy conditions suggest that the length or cost of the derivation must be minimized in some way. Lastly, economy considerations suggest that the representations formed in the course of a derivation should be as simple as possible, consisting of a minimal number of syntactic objects, each of which is interpretable (at either LF or PF).

The main purpose of this chapter is to give an overview of the economy conditions that have been proposed for syntax and to discuss how the various conditions are related. I will also present what I consider to be the outstanding problems and interesting research issues.

This chapter is organized as follows. In section 1, I will discuss Last Resort. In section 2, I will discuss Minimality. In section 3, I will discuss the Shortest Derivation Requirement. In section 4, I will discuss timing principles, such as ASAP (As Soon As Possible) and Procrastinate. In section 5, I will discuss the issue of local versus global economy conditions. In section 6, I will discuss economy of representation. Section 7 is the conclusion.

1 Last Resort

The principle of Last Resort is perhaps the most widely used economy condition. The most intuitive way to state the condition is along the following lines:

(1)   An operation OP may apply only if the derivation would otherwise result in an ungrammatical representation (at PF or LF).

A number of immediate questions arise about this formulation. First, are all operations subject to Last Resort (e.g. Move, Merge), or just some limited subset (e.g. the spelling out of resumptive elements, *do*-support)? Second, what kind of ungrammaticality can sanction an operation to apply (a violation of the Empty Category Principle (ECP), non-convergence, any type of violation)? I will comment on both of these (largely unresolved issues) in the following exposition.

This very general formulation describes a number of different phenomena, investigated by a number of different authors, not all of whom use the term Last Resort. Consider the case of *do*-support. Chomsky (1991) analyses *do*-support as resulting from an interpretation of "least effort" such that language specific operations are more costly than operations that are specified as part of Universal Grammar (UG). In particular, *do*-support is assumed to be a language specific operation, and movement is assumed to be an operation specified as part of UG.

Given these assumptions, consider the following data (I simplify Chomsky's account for matters of exposition):

(2)   a.   John Infl Agr wrote books
     b.   *John [$_{Infl}$ did] Agr write books
     c.   *John Infl not Agr wrote books
     d.   John [$_{Infl}$ did] not Agr write books

Example (2a) involves the following steps: Infl lowers to Agr, and then Agr lowers to V, and then V raises back to Infl at LF (via Agr). (2b) is blocked, since "inserting" *do* in Infl involves a language specific operation that is more costly than the lowering and raising found in (2a). Example (2c) is disallowed by the ECP. Once Infl lowers to Agr and Agr lowers to V, V is blocked from raising back to Infl at LF by negation. Example (2d) is allowed, because even though lowering and raising is less costly than *do*-support, lowering and raising would lead to a violation of the ECP. In other words, it is the ungrammaticality of the derivation leading to (2c) that licenses (2d). In this example, there is a mechanism of *do*-support, which steps in just when the derivation would have been ungrammatical otherwise.

An alternative account of *do*-support that has recently gained some support is based on adjacency (Bobaljik 1995, Lasnik 1995b). The basic intuition of this approach is that in (2) above the inflectional head Infl contains an affix. This affix may combine morphologically with the following bare verb under adjacency, as in (2a). If negation is present (as in (2c)), adjacency is blocked and the dummy *do* is inserted to support the affix (as in (2d)). A natural way to block *do*-support in the sentence (2b) is Last Resort. In other words, *do* can only be inserted when the derivation would otherwise lead to a stranded affix.

Koopman and Sportiche (1986: 362, 366) claim that the distribution of resumptive pronouns, resumptive verbs, and adjunct extraction particles is determined by "minimalist strategies." They note "It is an often made observation that languages seem to adopt 'minimalist strategies' as unmarked strategies when possible; licensing processes are invoked only when necessary." From this point of view consider the following sentences:

(3) a. yEsO n   dIdO-dIdO suO   la
           how you cut-M-cut-M tree-det WH
           "How did you cut the tree?"
     b. n dI suO   fafa
           I cut tree-det quickly
           "I cut the tree quickly."
           (*dIdOdIdO)

(4) a. alO *(O)   nU mI la
           who he-resum did it   WH
           "Who did it?"
     b. yI   Kofi nU la
           what Kofi did WH
           "What did Kofi do?"

(5) nU Kofi ka   mI nU
     do Kofi Fut-Aux it do
     "Kofi will DO it."

According to Koopman and Sportiche, the reduplication of the verb seen in (3a) is needed to govern the trace of the extracted adjunct properly. If the adjunct has not been extracted, no such morphology is possible. Similarly, in (4a), a subject trace does not obey the ECP, therefore the trace must be spelled out. The trace of an object does obey the ECP, and so no resumptive pronoun is possible. Similar reasoning holds for resumptive verbs, seen in the predicate cleft construction in (5). Since the verbal trace would violate the ECP, an overt copy must be spelled out at the tail of the verbal chain.

Other authors that have a similar analysis of resumptive elements include Rizzi (1990), Ura (1996), Shlonsky (1992), and Pesetsky (1997: 168) on resumptive pronouns. For example, Shlonsky (1992: 443) states that "resumptive pronouns only occur as a Last Resort, when wh-movement fails to yield a grammatical structure."

With respect to the questions asked above, the operation of spelling out the trace of movement (in resumptive pronoun constructions, and in predicate cleft constructions) is considered to be an operation that applies only as a last resort. The principle that triggers the operation is the ECP.

Last Resort like principles are also possible to state in non-derivational frameworks. For example, in the Relational Grammar framework, the Motivated Chomeur Law is a kind of Last Resort principle. This principle states that

Cho arcs arise only when there would otherwise be a violation of Stratal Uniqueness (see Perlmutter and Postal 1983: 99). In particular, one of the consequences of this law is that there can be no spontaneous creation of a chomeur. Last Resort like principles are also used in phonology (for example, the analysis of epenthesis in Prince and Smolensky 1993).

The full range of cases falling under the general form of Last Resort in (1) is not known. But it is without a doubt true that natural language obeys something like (1). In section 5, I will return to the issue of whether the general form of Last Resort in (1) is global or local.

1.1   Last resort and inertness

An implicit assumption of much recent work is that once a syntactic relation is formed it cannot be altered. For example, if X dominates Y and Z, then it is impossible to change the dominance relations, so that later in the derivation X dominates only Y, or X dominates Y, Z, and W (see in particular Collins 1997; see also Watanabe 1995). In addition, if X is the head of a constituent Y, then it is impossible to change the head of Y, so that later in the derivation Z becomes the head of Y. If an empty element ec is a PRO at some step in the derivation, then it cannot become a A'-trace at some later step.

I will state this condition as follows:

(6)   Once a syntactic relation (or syntactic object) is formed, it cannot be changed.

I will call this general principle Inertness or Inalterability. Last Resort and Inertness seem to be two sides of the same coin. Last Resort gives the conditions under which an operation can take place. Inertness gives the conditions under which an operation cannot take place.

For example, consider the discussion of Case assignment in Babby (1987: 96): "a NP is assigned case only once and there are no rules that change one case to another." Babby calls this principle "inertness" and uses it to account for the fact that in Russian the object of a verb that assigns lexical Case (e.g. dative) cannot be passivized (since that would involve the NP being assigned nominative).

This principle has the effect of limiting the number of operations that can affect a particular element (say a NP), and so it seems justified to call it an economy condition. Inertness is obviously related to Chomsky's (1995b) analysis of feature checking, where an uninterpretable feature, once deleted and erased, is inaccessible to further operations. As another example, Chomsky (1998a) postulates that the sisterhood and c-command relations that a label enters into cannot be changed.

As another example, Richards (1998: esp. n. 32) postulates Principle of Minimal Compliance, which may also be a form of Inertness. For example, in his discussion of Subjacency, Richards states "it appears to be true quite generally that in cases involving multiple wh-movement to a single [+wh] complementizer, only the first moved wh-word will have to obey Subjacency." It appears that when a structure acquires the status of obeying Subjacency, that status cannot be changed later in the derivation.

C-command does not seem to be subject to (6). Suppose X c-commands Y, then Y moves to a position where it c-commands X. In this case, the relation of c-command has been altered. The force of this counter-example to (6) depends in part on interpretation of the copy theory of movement, and in part on whether c-command is even a real syntactic relation.

The topic of Inertness has never been investigated in a systematic way. The question is what syntactic relations cannot be changed, and which ones can be changed, and what distinguishes the two sets.

1.2   *Last resort and movement*

In the Minimalist Framework (Chomsky 1995b), the discussion of Last Resort has been mostly focussed on Move, which is a generalization of traditional movement operations such as constituent questions, clefting, passive, and raising. The original insight that Move is subject to a Last Resort condition is due to Chomsky (1986a: 143, 160). He claimed that Move-alpha is applied only when a failure to apply it would lead to a structure that violates a grammatical condition such as the Case filter. The main generalization that Chomsky wanted to explain is what is often called the Chain Condition:

(7)   In an A-chain of the form $(\alpha_1, \ldots, \alpha_n)$, α_1 occupies its unique
         Case position and α_n occupies its unique theta-position. (modified from
         Chomsky 1986a: 137)

In particular, Chomsky was concerned about the part of the generalization above that states that only the head of a chain (not the tail) is in a Case position. The basic reasoning is that if a NP has had Case assigned to it, then it would not have to move any more to satisfy the Case Filter.

Chomsky (1993, 1995b: 200, 201) picks up the notion of Last Resort again, defining it as follows: "a step in a derivation is legitimate only if it is necessary for convergence." Chomsky refines Last Resort to make it self-serving. This is the condition of Greed (self-serving Last Resort), stated below:

(8)   Move α applies to an element α only if the morphological properties of α
         itself are not otherwise satisfied.

In this regard, consider the following sentence:

(9)   *John seems that [$_{TP}$ t is nice]
         "John seems to be nice."

The question is why *John* could not raise from the embedded subject position to the matrix subject position. According to Chomsky, this is blocked by Greed, since at the time of the raising, the Case feature of *John* is already checked.

The condition of self-serving Last Resort or Greed has been argued against most extensively by Lasnik (1995a) and Collins (1995, 1997). Lasnik argues that in a large number of cases no independent condition of Greed is needed. For example, Lasnik points out that (9) is ruled out by an independent principle that states that if T has an unchecked Case assigning feature, then the derivation crashes. Since the Case feature of *John* is checked in the embedded clause, it no longer can check the Case assigning feature of the matrix T. So no principle of Greed is needed to block (9).

Collins (1995, 1997) points out that successive cyclic movement, ECM, locative inversion, and quotative inversion all seem to demand a weakening of the condition in (8). First consider successive cyclic movement:

(10)   a.   [$_{IP}$ John to be [$_{SC}$ t nice]]
       b.   [$_{IP}$ John seems [$_{IP}$ t to be [$_{SC}$ t nice]]]

A structure involving successive cyclic movement is illustrated in (10b). In order to form this structure it is necessary, at some point in the derivation, to raise *John* to the intermediate Spec IP position (to satisfy what has traditionally been called the EPP, or extended projection principle). The problem is that this movement is not licensed by the condition in (8), since the morphological properties of *John* would have been satisfied if *John* had raised directly to the matrix Spec IP position (without passing through the embedded Spec IP). This would give rise to the following representation:

(11)   [$_{IP}$ John seems [$_{IP}$ to be [$_{SC}$ t nice]]]

This representation violates the EPP, but that is not relevant to the movement of *John*. In addition to this criticism, Collins (1997) also argues that (8) is inherently global (see section 5 below), because it refers to alternate derivations (this is what the word "otherwise" means).

Lastly, Collins (1997) argues that quotative inversion and locative inversion do not satisfy (8). Consider the following:

(12)   a.   "I am so happy", thought John
       b.   down the hill rolled John

Collins argues that the quotation in (12a) undergoes movement to the specifier of TP, but that this movement does not result in the checking of Case (since the Case feature of the quotation has already been checked). The movement is purely the result of the need to check the EPP feature of the matrix T.

Given these considerations, Collins (1995, 1997), Lasnik (1995a), and Chomsky (1995b, 1998a) all argue that (8) should be weakened to a condition like the following:

(13)   Move raises α to the checking domain of a head H with a feature F only
       if the feature F of H enters into a checking relation with a feature F of α.

(14)   F1 and F2 enter a checking relation iff F2 is in the checking domain of F1 and F1 is deleted (F2 may also be deleted).

The crucial aspect of this condition is that checking relation is defined *asymmetrically*. What this means is that movement of a constituent α does not have to result in the features of α being checked. We can illustrate this with the example in (10a). Assume, with Chomsky (1995b), that the infinitival *to* checks its EPP feature against the D feature of *John*. In that case, the movement in (10a) satisfies (13), since a checking relation has been established. Note that the checking relation is asymmetric, since the D feature of *John* has not been deleted.

This account of Last Resort as it affects movement answers the questions under (1) above in the following way. First, all movement operations are subject to Last Resort. Second, only morphological feature checking can trigger movement, nothing else (such as the ECP, or another syntactic condition).

Is the narrow form of Last Resort in (13) reducible to the general form of Last Resort in (1)? This is far from clear, and the issue has not been addressed systematically.

The version of Last Resort in (13) takes the point of view of the head H that contains a feature F. This feature needs to be checked in order for movement operation to take place. It is in part for this reason that Chomsky (1995b: 297) reinterprets Last Resort as part of the definition of Attract (see section 2 for a similar remark about the Minimal Link Condition). Chomsky (1998a) also assumes that the narrow form of Last Resort in (13) is a part of the definition of applying an operation. In order to apply some operation OP (Agree or Merge), a probe or selector must be found, and then satisfied.

2   Minimality

Minimality states that given a choice between two comparable operations, the smallest is chosen. This way of stating Minimality is more general than the statements usually found in the literature (see Rizzi 1990, Chomsky 1995b). Looked at this way, Minimality bears a strong resemblance to the Shortest Derivation Requirement (see below) that says that the number of operations in a derivation should be minimized. The intuition behind both conditions is that a grammar tends to minimize whatever can be ranked along some scale: length of movements, steps in a derivation, or the number of violations of some condition (at least in OT syntax/phonology).

Consider Chomsky's (1995b: 296) Minimal Link Condition:

(15)   Minimal Link Condition (Chomsky 1995b: 296)
       α can raise to a target K only if there is no operation (satisfying Last Resort) Move β targeting K, where β is closer to K.

To illustrate, consider the following example:

(16)   *John$_i$ seems that it was told t$_i$ that Mary left

In this example, the DP *John* raises from the embedded clause to target the matrix T'. In the embedded clause, it checks the Case and EPP feature of T. The problem is that the DP *it* is closer to the matrix T' than *John*, and so it blocks movement of *John* by the MLC in (15).

Chomsky's MLC (in (15)) takes the point of view of the head H containing the feature F that needs to be satisfied. The feature F' closest to F is the one that can enter into a checking relation with F. This is natural, as Chomsky points out, if the MLC is built into the definition of Attract (just as Last Resort was in section 1). Chomsky (1998a) develops this line of reasoning even further, proposing that the MLC is just one reflection of a general constraint that the search needed to apply an operation is minimized.

There are many other cases of Minimality conditions in syntax, which have just begun to be investigated. For example, Nakamura (1994, 1997) claims that extraction in Tagalog and Bantu applicative constructions is mediated by a type of Minimal Link Condition. Collins (1997) claims that binary branching in syntax is a result of Minimality. Richards (1997) claims that the order of *wh*-phrases in Slavic multiple *wh*-movement is the result of Minimality. Takahashi (1994a) attempts to derive the CED from the Minimal Link Condition. There are also several Minimality like conditions in phonology, including the EDGEMOST condition of Prince and Smolensky (1993).

One of the most exciting areas of syntax is the search for examples where Minimality like conditions play a role, and to unify these conditions. At this point in the search for phenomena, the largest possible net should be cast.

Since Rizzi (in this *Handbook*) takes up the issue of Relativized Minimality, I will not elaborate any further on these notions.

3   Shortest Derivation Requirement

The principle that the number of steps in a derivation be minimized is often called the Shortest Derivation Requirement (SDR), and it is stated below:

(17)   Minimize the number of operations necessary for convergence.

Note that there must be some way in which derivations are comparable in order for (17) to be useful. If any derivation could be compared to any other derivation, the zero derivation (with no operations) would always win. The set of comparable derivations is often called the reference set.

There are a number of different proposals as to how to define the reference set. Under one account, if derivations D1 and D2 are both convergent, and start from the same Numeration, then they are comparable (see Chomsky 1995b). Under another account, if D1 and D2 are both convergent, and they both lead to the same interpretations, then they are comparable (see Fox 1995).

Other researchers that have employed the Shortest Derivation Requirement are Kitahara (1997), Chomsky (1991, 1995b), and Epstein (1992). In particular,

Collins (1994a) uses the Shortest Derivation Requirement to rule out cases of chain interleaving.

Of all the economy conditions, the Shortest Derivation Requirement is the one with the least intuitive appeal. For example, consider a derivation with 18 steps. By the Shortest Derivation Requirement this derivation will be blocked by any comparable derivation (having the same Numeration) with 17 or fewer steps. This appears to be a case of the grammar counting, in a way that has long been held to be impossible. What grammars seem to be able to do well is to verify whether some simple condition holds of a representation or an operation (e.g. does the representation R satisfy condition A? Does Move X result in a feature being checked?).

To illustrate what is at issue, consider the following example that has been employed by Chomsky (1995b: 357) and Kitahara (1997: 19) to illustrate the Shortest Derivation Requirement. The following sentence illustrates object shift in Icelandic:

(18) a. Í gær   las Jón bækurnar ekki.
          yesterday read John the books not
          "Yesterday, John did not read the books."
      b. *Í gær   las bækurnar Jón ekki.
          yesterday read the books John not
          "Yesterday, John did not read the books."

The question is why the inverted structure in (18b) is unacceptable. Given the clause structure in Chomsky (1995b: 352), where there are no Agr projections, sentence (18a) would have the following structure (I leave out V-movement and V/2-effects for convenience of exposition):

(19)

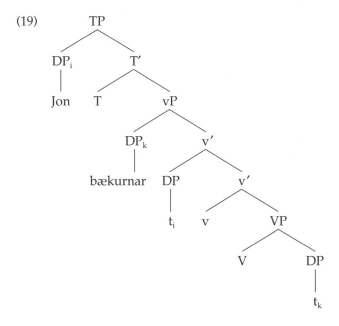

The derivation of this structure is as follows. The DP *bækurnar* "the books" has raised over negation (which is adjoined to v′), to the outer specifier of vP. In this position, *bækurnar* checks the accusative Case of v, and the EPP feature of v (the feature which Chomsky (1995b) assumes drives overt object shift). Second, the subject raises from the inner specifier of vP to the specifier of TP. In this position, the DP *Jón* checks the nominative Case and the EPP feature of T.

But there is a second possible derivation, the one which leads to (18b). Suppose after the object raises to Spec vP (checking the Case and EPP of v), it then raises to Spec TP (satisfying only the EPP feature of T). At this point, the only features left to check are the Case and phi-features of T and the Case feature of the DP *Jón*. Finally, the FF(Jón) (Case, D, phi features) raises covertly and adjoins to T at LF. Therefore, there is a good derivation of (18b).

Chomsky (1995b) proposes that this derivation is ruled out in the following way. Consider again the two relevant derivations:

(20)   Non-inverted derivation: (= 18a)
    a.   the DP *bækurnar* moves to Spec vP
    b.   the DP *Jón* moves to Spec TP

(21)   Inverted derivation: (= 18b)
    a.   the DP *bækurnar* moves to Spec vP
    b.   the DP *bækurnar* moves to Spec TP
    c.   the FF(*Jón*) moves to adjoin to T

Since the inverted derivation has one more step than the non-inverted derivation, and both converge, the inverted derivation is blocked by the Shortest Derivation Requirement.

Although inversion in (18b) is blocked by the Shortest Derivation Requirement, Collins (1997) argues extensively that the Shortest Derivation Requirement makes the wrong empirical predictions about inversion phenomena in English, in particular quotative inversion and locative inversion. Therefore, it is worthwhile asking whether there is not a different explanation of the unacceptability of (18b).

Chomsky (1998a) proposes that if the Case feature of a DP is checked, the DP becomes inactive and cannot undergo any further movement or participate in any further agreement relation. Such a condition would immediately rule out (21) with no further stipulation (a point made by Chomsky 1998a: 45).

In conclusion, we see that even examples that apparently show that the Shortest Derivation Requirement is needed can be explained in different ways.

One question that we have not addressed is the relation of the Shortest Derivation Requirement to Last Resort, stated in (1), and repeated below:

(22)   An operation OP may apply only if the derivation would otherwise result in an ungrammatical representation (at PF or LF).

Clearly the two principles are related. In many cases, both principles prefer a shorter derivation over a longer derivation. However, the two principles have a slightly different emphasis. We could imagine a scenario where the number of steps in derivation D1 is less than or equal to the number of steps in derivation D2, but D2 is chosen over D1 on the basis of the general form of Last Resort (1). This situation arises in the analysis of *do*-support as a last resort operation (see (2)). Also, the principle of Procrastinate below has the effect of making overt operations last resort operations, and choosing a derivation D2 over D1 even if they have exactly the same number of steps.

4 Timing Principles

Timing principles are principles that regulate when an operation can and must apply in a derivation. The two principles that I will discuss are Procrastinate and ASAP (As Soon As Possible).

4.1 *Procrastinate*

Perhaps the most famous timing principle is Chomsky's (1993) Procrastinate, which can be stated as follows:

(23) Covert movement is less costly than overt movement.

According to this principle, overt movement is not allowed, unless the derivation would otherwise crash. A derivation crashes at some interface level (either PF or LF) if there is some feature present that is not interpretable at that level. For example, if a Case feature is present at LF, the derivation crashes. If a strong feature is present at PF, the derivation crashes (Chomsky 1993).

As pointed out above, Procrastinate can be interpreted as an instance of Last Resort condition (see (1)). An overt operation OP can apply only if otherwise the derivation would crash.

The principal motivation for Procrastinate is to describe the differences between languages as to whether movement occurs overtly or not. Consider the following two examples illustrating the difference between French and English:

(24) a. *John kisses often Mary
      b. John often kisses Mary

(25) a. Jean embrasse souvent Marie   (French)
          John kisses   often   Mary
      b. *Jean souvent   embrasse Marie
          John often   kisses   Mary

Assuming that the adverb occupies some position (adjoined or specifier) between T and V, this paradigm can be described in the following way. In English, the verb cannot raise to T. In French, the verb must raise to T.

Chomsky (1993: 30) proposes to account for this paradigm in terms of feature strength. In French, the V feature of T is strong, and in English the V feature of T is weak. Chomsky makes the assumption that strong features are visible at PF, and weak features are not. He further assumes that strong features are not legitimate PF objects (unlike the feature [labial], or some other phonological feature). Therefore, if the strong V feature of T in French is not checked (or deleted), it will cause the derivation to crash. Thus the verb raises in French to ensure convergence.

Since the V feature of T is weak English, the verb does not have to raise. Chomsky proposed in addition that the verb is forced to stay in situ by Procrastinate, given in (23). Therefore, Procrastinate rules out (24a).

Chomsky also assumes that Procrastinate selects among the set of convergent derivations (1994: 428). This is necessary, since otherwise overt movement of the verb in (25a) would be blocked by the unacceptable (25b). Since the derivation leading to (25b) does not converge (since the strong V feature of T has not been checked), it does not compete with the derivation leading to (25a).

Procrastinate postulates a fundamental difference between overt and covert movements: overt movements are more costly than covert movements. Chomsky (1995b: 262) proposes that there is a more principled distinction that can be made between overt and covert movement.

Consider the following example. If a *wh*-movement takes place in order for the *wh*-feature of the *wh*-phrase to enter into a checking relation with the Q feature of Comp, then it is strange that the whole DP (including phonetic and semantic features) raises to Spec CP:

(26) $[_{CP} [_{DP}$ which book$]_i$ $[_{C'}$ did John read $t_i]]$

Chomsky (1995b) suggests that the Q feature of Comp attracts only the *wh*-feature of the DP, but the rest of the DP (the phonetic and semantic features) is pied-piped, or carried along. The reason for this pied-piping is that separating the formal features from a word before Spell-Out would cause the derivation to crash.

To regulate this kind of generalized pied-piping, Chomsky postulates the following economy condition (see also Watanabe 1992a: 57, for similar remarks). I will call this condition the Weight Condition, since it is equivalent to saying that what is moved should be as small or as light as possible:

(27)   F carries along just enough material for convergence.

In the covert component (after Spell-Out), there is nothing to prevent a feature from being separated from its lexical item. Therefore, according to (27) only bare features (and not whole categories) can move in the covert component.

Chomsky (1998a) develops this line of thought even further, and proposes that there is no covert movement at all. Rather, there are agreement relations that are established (e.g. between a Q Comp and a *wh*-feature), some of which are accompanied by the overt movement of some constituent.

4.2   ASAP

As opposed to Procrastinate, there seems to be another condition in grammar which, following Yang (1997), we can call ASAP (see Pesetsky 1989 for a related condition). This is stated below:

(28)   If it is possible for an operation to apply, then it must apply. (See Collins 1999.)

The first question to ask is whether ASAP is actually an economy condition. In fact, ASAP looks like an anti-economy condition, the opposite of Procrastinate. But in one important sense ASAP is an economy condition, since it allows simplification in the computation needed to decide whether a particular operation applies. Suppose that OP can apply at a particular step S in the derivation. If UG permitted a choice between applying or not applying OP at step S, a decision would have to be made. Information that allowed the decision to be made would have to be found. It would be considerably simpler to adopt (28). Condition (28) is very similar to Chomsky's (1999) condition "Maximize matching effects."

Perhaps the most obvious instantiation of this principle has to do with checking. ASAP states that if a checking relation can be established, it must (see especially Chomsky 1995b: 280). Consider the following example:

(29)   [$_{IP}$ John$_i$ seems that [$_{IP}$ t$_i$ is nice]]

Chomsky (1995b: 284) and Lasnik (1995a) claim that this sentence is unacceptable for the following reason. Suppose that the NP John has a Case feature, and that finite Infl has a Case feature. At some point in the derivation, the following representation will be formed:

(30)   [$_{I'}$ seems that [$_{IP}$ John$_i$ is nice]]

At this step, the Case feature of *John* and the Case assigning feature of the embedded finite Infl enter into a checking relation, and they are both deleted. Because of this, *John* does not have a Case feature, and therefore, the Case feature of the matrix Infl can never be checked, even if *John* moves to the matrix Spec IP position as in (29).

This account crucially relies on the assumption that the checking of nominative Case in the embedded clause in (30) must be symmetric (see section 1.2 above for a discussion of asymmetric feature checking). Symmetric feature checking is forced by ASAP.

It is possible that ASAP is related to the "Disjunctive Principle" of Gruber (1973: 440). Gruber discusses the use of kinship terms in =Hoan (a Khoisan language of Botswana) and notes that the use of specific terms for a kinship relation always takes precedence over general terms. As Gruber states: "The disjunctive principle operates in the lexical attachment process to delimit the environment of applicability of a lexical item by that of another which is an inclusive subcategorization of it."

To see what the issues are, consider a similar example closer to home (roughly following Halle and Marantz 1993). We use the suppletive form *went* to the exclusion of the analytic form *go-ed*. Suppose at some point in the derivation we form [V_{go} + Past], where V_{go} is a set of semantic and syntactic features that is spelled out as "go" in infinitival contexts. In order to spell out [V_{go} + Past] we have a choice. The first choice is to spell out V_{go} as "go" and then Past as "-ed." The second choice is to spell out [V_{go} + Past] as "went." The second option is preferred on the basis of Gruber's Disjunction Principle. It is also preferred on the basis of ASAP (or similarly maximize matching effects), since the first option does not spell out Past as quickly as possible. Note that the second option may also be preferred since it uses fewer morphemes (see section 6 below for a related principle).

The above explanation assumes that there is no economy condition that minimizes the number of features spelled out (or features checked) at a particular step in the derivation.

All three principles (ASAP, Disjunction Principle, maximize matching effects) are essentially economy principles. It is unclear for the moment what the empirical scope of each of the principles is, or whether any can be eliminated.

5   Global versus Local Economy

One issue that is becoming increasingly important in linguistic theory is the distinction between global and local theories. This distinction cross-cuts the derivational/representational distinction. Basically, a theory is a local theory if the decision about whether or not an operation OP may apply to a representation R is made only on the basis of information available in R (and not some other representation). Given this definition, Procrastinate is global. Consider again the example in (24). In order to determine whether V-movement must take place in English, it is necessary to see what happens at the PF interface. If not doing V-movement causes the derivation to crash, the V-movement is allowed.

A similar definition can be made for representational theories. We can say that a representational theory of syntax is local if the evaluation of whether a predicate P holds of R is restricted to information in R. For example, OT Syntax/Phonology is definitely global, since the evaluation of the predicate "R is optimal" crucially necessitates comparing R to other representations.

Procrastinate and the Shortest Derivation Requirement are global principles. Is the general form of Last Resort in (1) a global principle? The question is whether the application of some operation needs to make reference to global information.

Consider again the issue of resumptive verbs in a predicate cleft construction (see (5) above). I claimed (following Koopman and Sportiche 1986) that spelling out the tail of the verbal chain is a last resort operation triggered by a potential violation of the ECP. Does the spelling out of the trace of the moved verb make reference to global information? This answer is not entirely clear.

Many researchers are now adopting the point of view that global conditions should be avoided (see Collins 1997, Chomsky 1998a, Poole 1995, Ura 1996, Yang 1997).

6 Economy of Representation

In most of the analyses described above, an operation or derivation is guaranteed to be minimal by an economy condition. We can now ask whether there is a condition on representations that they must be minimal in some way. Chomsky (1986a) proposes the condition of Full Interpretation that requires that each element in a PF or LF representation must be licensed. For example, Chomsky states that "at the PF level each phonetic element must be licensed by some physical interpretation." Chomsky (1995b: 219) articulates Full Interpretation further, stating that a representation meets Full Interpretation if it consists of legitimate objects that can be interpreted (at the interface levels).

Are there further economy conditions on representations over and above Full Interpretation? A good example is the treatment of finite and infinitival clauses in Bošković (1997b). Bošković gives the following condition on representations:

(31) **The Minimal Structure Principle**
Provided that lexical requirements of relevant elements are satisfied, if two representations have the same lexical structure and serve the same function, then the representation that has fewer projections is to be chosen as the syntactic representation serving that function.

Bošković claims that the MSP can be used to rule out certain infinitival relative clauses. Consider the following example:

(32) a. *The man [$_{CP}$ Op$_i$ Comp [$_{IP}$ t$_i$ likes John]]
 b. *The man [$_{IP}$ Op$_i$ [$_{IP}$ t$_i$ likes John]]
 c. The man [$_{CP}$ Op$_i$ that [$_{IP}$ t$_i$ likes John]]

Bošković argues that the MSP chooses representation (32b) over (32a), since (32a) and (32b) have the same lexical items and (32b) has fewer projections. Note that (32c) is not blocked by (32b), since (32c) involves an additional lexical item "that" (which is nominal in nature) and is therefore not comparable with the other structures.

In addition, (32b) is ruled out by an economy condition that prohibits move-ment operations that are too short (at least one category must be crossed; a single segment of an adjunction structure does not count). Bošković calls this the "ban on superfluous steps."

Bošković notes that his MSP has an element of globality (since it compares two representations). To avoid this problem, Bošković gives a derivational account of the MSP. This leads us to the natural hypothesis that there are no economy conditions that compare two different representations.

There still may be economy conditions on representations, other than Full Interpretation? One possibility is the economy condition proposed by Emonds (1994: 162): "The most economic realization of a given deep structure mini-mizes insertions of free morphemes ('Use as few words as possible')." Emonds calls this "Economy of Derivation," but I think it is naturally construed as an economy condition governing the spelling out of representations. As such, it is not part of the syntactic computation (from the Numeration to LF), but rather a part of Spell-Out. Adopting a framework like that of Distributed Morphology and Gruber (1973), we can say that at Spell-Out, the lexical items and syntactic structures are provided with actual phonetic content.

There is a wide array of data that seems to support such a principle. For example, Emonds claims that his economy condition favors French *au* "to the" over *à le*. Emonds also claims that this economy condition chooses *bigger* over *more big*. There is an obvious similarity between Emonds's constraint and the Fewest Morphemes constraint of section 4.2, which I will highlight by calling Emonds's constraint the Fewest Free Morphemes constraint. Emonds's con-straint might explain the fact that in pro-drop languages, expletive pronouns are obligatorily absent. Related conditions include Chomsky's (1981: 65) Avoid Pronoun principle, and Koopman's (1983: 175) Avoid Phonetics.

In addition, Emonds's constraint might be at the root of the generalization that resumptive elements (verbs or pronouns) are normally avoided. More generally, consider the chain (X, Y). Suppose that the head of the chain and not the tail is pronounced (e.g. John$_i$ was seen t$_i$). We can characterize this in one of two ways. We can say that the phonetic content of the tail of the chain was deleted at Spell-Out. Alternatively, we can say that the phonetic content of the tail of the chain was never provided at Spell-Out. Either way, spelling out the tail of the chain (as a resumptive pronoun, or full copy in predicate cleft) involves an extra word, and so is prohibited by Emonds's constraint.

One of the issues in finding economy conditions on representations is decid-ing how much of syntactic theory is derivational and representational (see Lasnik, this volume). The above discussion has assumed for the most part that syntactic structures are formed through a derivation, involving minimally some type of mechanism to build phrase structure (Merge) and some type of mechan-ism to capture syntactic dependencies (Move, Attract, Agree). The economy principles seem to be natural in this kind of framework.

However, the issue is not as simple as it appears at first. As mentioned above, representational theories often have economy like conditions. The reason for this is that extra steps in a derivation usually correspond to extra symbols (or extra violations) in a representation. As a consequence, economy conditions on derivations can sometimes be restated as economy conditions on representations (e.g. minimize the number of symbols, or minimize the number of violations).

However, there are other reasons to adopt a derivational theory. For example, consider the c-command asymmetry involved in chains (the head of the chain c-commands the tail). This seems like a fairly robust empirical generalization and follows without stipulation on the derivational approach (see, for example, Collins 1997 or Chomsky 1998a). In fact, the derivational approach to syntax provides structures with a natural asymmetry (some parts are built before others), which is reflected in the many asymmetrical properties of chains.

7   Conclusion

I have tried to give an overview of economy conditions in syntax in this chapter. I have discussed Last Resort, Inertness, Minimality, the Shortest Derivation Requirement, Procrastinate, the Weight Condition, ASAP, maximize matching effects, Fewest Morphemes, the Minimal Structure Principle, the ban on superfluous steps, and Fewest Free Morphemes.

As representations are simplified to a greater degree, it will become more and more necessary to articulate the theory of economy conditions. For example, Collins (1999) attempts to eliminate labels on phrasal constituents (such as NP and VP). This simplification is only possible when the economy conditions are articulated in a certain way.

One point that has not been made in the preceding discussion is the importance of optionality for research into economy conditions. Suppose that at a particular step in the derivation either OP1 or OP2 can apply. Then it follows that OP1 and OP2 have the same cost associated with them. Therefore, optionality provides a direct probe into measuring the cost of operations (see Chomsky 1991).

The whole range of economy conditions and the interrelations between them have just begun to be charted. What can be said with certainty is that our understanding of economy at this point is minimal.

NOTE

*   I wish to thank Mark Baltin and
    Yoshi Dobashi for helpful comments
    on a draft version of this chapter.

3 Derivation and Representation in Modern Transformational Syntax

HOWARD LASNIK

0 Introduction

The general issue of derivational vs. representational approaches to syntax has received considerable attention throughout the history of generative grammar. Internal to the major derivational approach, transformational grammar, a related issue arises: are well-formedness conditions imposed specifically at the particular levels of representation[1] made available in the theory, or are they imposed "internal" to the derivation leading to those levels? This second question will be the topic of this chapter. Like the first question, it is a subtle one, perhaps even more subtle than the first, but since Chomsky (1973), there has been increasing investigation of it, and important argument and evidence have been brought to bear. I will be examining a range of arguments, some old and some new, concerning (i) locality constraints on movement, and (ii) the property forcing (overt) movement, especially as this issue arises within the "minimalist" program of Chomsky (1995b).

1 Locality of Movement: Subjacency and the ECP

The apparent contradiction between unbounded movement as in (1) and strict locality as in (2) has long played a central role in syntactic investigations in general and studies of the role of derivation in particular:

(1) Who do you think Mary said John likes

(2) ?*Who did you ask whether Mary knows why John likes

Based on the unacceptability of such examples as (2), Chomsky (1973), rejecting earlier views (including the highly influential Ross 1967a) proposed that long distance movement is *never* possible. (1) must then be the result of a series of short movements, short movements that are, for some reason, not available in the derivation of (2). In roughly the terms of Chomsky (1973), movement across more than one bounding node is prohibited by Subjacency and S is a bounding node. Consider (3), a representation of (1), with the successive positions of *Who* indicated by *t* (trace):

(3) [$_{S'}$ Who [$_S$ you think [$_{S'}$ *t* [$_S$ Mary said [$_{S'}$ *t* [$_S$ John likes *t*]]]]]]

Movement is via "Comp," given the phrase structure:

(4) S' → Comp S

In (2), on the other hand, the lower Comps are occupied, as shown in (5):

(5) [$_{S'}$ Who [$_S$ you ask [$_{S'}$ whether [$_S$ Mary knows [$_{S'}$ why [$_S$ John likes *t*]]]]]]

Therefore Subjacency is necessarily violated: the movement of *Who* must have been in one long step, crossing three Ss on the way.

  Immediately, a question arises about long movement out of certain non-"islands":

(6) Who do you think that Mary said that John likes

(6) has the grammaticality status of (1), but does not seem relevantly different from (2) in its structure:

(7) [$_{S'}$ Who [$_S$ you think [$_{S'}$ that [$_S$ Mary said [$_{S'}$ that [$_S$ John likes *t*]]]]]]

Chomsky's solution to this problem was a strictly derivational account of locality effects (though he did not make a big fuss about it at the time). The proposal was that in the course of the syntactic derivation, the structure of (6) is identical to that of (1), namely (3). Movement proceeds via successive Comps in both derivations. The difference is that in (6), at a very late level in the derivation the non-matrix Comps are spelled out as *that*. Thus, at that late level, Subjacency appears to be violated, even though in the course of the derivation every step is legitimate. This is the paradigmatic type of situation Chomsky frequently alludes to in his recent writings when he argues for a derivational approach to syntax.

  In the early 1980s, particularly under the impetus of Huang (1981/2, 1982), attention began to focus on certain locality "asymmetries." For instance, while movement of an argument across two bounding nodes results in substantial degradation, movement of an adjunct yields total unacceptability:

(8) ?Which problem do you wonder whether Mary solved

(9) *How do you wonder whether Mary solved the problem

Huang, extending ideas from Chomsky (1981), appealed to the Empty Category Principle (ECP), a constraint independent of Subjacency, demanding
locality between a (non-argument) trace and its antecedent. (9) is then worse
than (8) because (8) violates only Subjacency while (9) violates both Subjacency
and the ECP. Now notice that by the above reasoning, the ECP too must be
satisfiable "online," or (10) would incorrectly be assigned the status of an ECP
violation:

(10)   How do you think that Mary solved the problem

Lasnik and Saito (1984), developing Huang's ideas further, explored the ECP
requirements of intermediate movement positions. Consider the unacceptable
long movement in (11):

(11)   *How do you wonder whether John said (that) Mary solved the problem

In the derivation of (11), movement can proceed via the lower Comp, as in
(10). This step is clearly licit, and the adjunct trace in the lower clause must be
in satisfaction of the ECP, given the grammaticality of (10). The next step of
movement is in violation of Subjacency, but the descriptive problem is that (11)
is worse than a mere Subjacency violation, as in the structurally parallel (12):

(12)   ??Which problem do you wonder whether John said (that) Mary solved

Following Chomsky's proposal (adopted by Huang) that the ECP is specifically a requirement on traces, Lasnik and Saito concluded that even intermediate
traces must satisfy the requirement (must be "properly governed"). Consider
first the structure of the version of (11) without *that*:

(13)   How [$_S$ do you wonder [$_{S'}$ whether [$_S$ John said [$_{S'}$ t' [$_S$ Mary solved the
       problem t]]]]]

The initial trace t is properly governed by the intermediate trace t'. But the
intermediate trace is too distant from its antecedent *How*, causing a violation
of the ECP.
   The version of (11) with *that* seems trivial. The *that* in (14) presumably keeps
the initial trace from being properly governed:

(14)   How [$_S$ do you wonder [$_{S'}$ whether [$_S$ John said [$_{S'}$ that [$_S$ Mary solved the
       problem t]]]]]

However, this simple account must be rejected. If it were correct, then (10),
repeated as (15), would be incorrectly ruled out.

(15)   How did you think that Mary solved the problem

Recall that earlier, I indicated, based on (15), that the ECP must be satisfiable "online." That is, the initial trace must be established as properly governed at a point in the derivation where the *that* is not present. That point might be before *that* is inserted, as suggested above. Alternatively, as proposed by Lasnik and Saito, the point might be after *that* is inserted and subsequently deleted in the LF component. Under the assumption that operations in the "covert" component mapping S-structure to LF are just those that are potentially available overtly (in the D-structure to S-structure portion of a derivation), Lasnik and Saito argued that the availability of an overt Complementizer deletion process entails the availability of a covert analogue. Under either alternative, the question is how we can resolve the apparent contradiction between the unacceptable (11) and the acceptable (15).

2 Constraints on Adjunct Movement: Representational and/or Derivational

The analysis provided by Lasnik and Saito has clear implications for the derivation vs. representation issue. They argued that the proper government requirement must be satisfied specifically at *levels* (S-structure or LF), and not at arbitrary points of the derivation. The reasoning was as follows. We have already seen that allowing online satisfaction of the ECP (gamma-marking of trace, in the Lasnik–Saito technology and notation) has the incorrect consequence of allowing derivations such as (13), where an adjunct makes a short licit move followed by a long illicit move. Yet we still must allow (15). Earlier, I noted that Lasnik and Saito argued that *that* can be deleted in the LF component. Simplifying slightly, immediately following the deletion, the representation of (15) is (16):

(16)   How do you think [$_{S'}$ [$_S$ Mary solved the problem *t*]]

Then, nothing prevents Move alpha, the basic and general movement operation of the grammar, from "lowering" *How* to the lower Comp, then re-raising it to the matrix Comp, leaving a trace in the intermediate Comp. Both traces are now in the appropriate locality configuration with their nearest antecedents for gamma-marking to operate, and the sentence is correctly allowed.

Chomsky (1986b) offers an alternative "derivational" approach to the locality constraints on adjunct movement. Chomsky rejects the "representational" stipulation that gamma-marking is only at levels. The crucial example to consider is (11), which I argued above is ruled out on the representational approach but incorrectly allowed on the derivational approach. At this point, I slightly alter the structures of the relevant sentences in accord with the extended X-theory introduced by Chomsky (1986b). Chomsky proposes that S' is actually CP, the maximal projection of Comp (and S is actually IP, the maximal projection of the tense-agreement inflectional element of the sentence). *Wh*-movement is then not literally to C, but rather to Spec of C, in accord with a generalized structure preservation constraint. Note in passing that this renders the acceptable (15) straightforwardly unproblematic. On these assumptions, presence or absence of *that* is evidently irrelevant (though Chomsky's Minimality condition on proper government, which I will put aside here, makes it relevant again in certain circumstances). (11) then has (17) as one step in its derivation, and at that point in the derivation, the initial trace can be gamma-marked:

(17)   [$_{CP}$ [$_{C'}$ do [$_{IP}$ you wonder [$_{CP}$ whether [$_{IP}$ John said [$_{CP}$ How [$_{C'}$ (that) [$_{IP}$ Mary solved the problem *t*]]]]]]]]

How then moves to matrix Spec of CP, violating Subjacency. Further, if this movement leaves a trace, that trace will also violate the ECP. But the worry of Lasnik and Saito was that the movement would not obligatorily leave a trace, since no principle demands a trace in this intermediate position. Or, if a trace is left, no principle prevents its deletion. Chomsky (in lectures in the late 1980s) addressed this worry with the following principle:

(18)   Adjuncts must be fully represented.

The intent of (18) is that every step of adjunct movement must leave a trace, and none of these traces can be deleted. Thus, the continuation of (17) will necessarily be (19), and *t′* will necessarily be in violation of the ECP, an "offending trace" in Lasnik and Saito's term:

(19)   [$_{CP}$ How [$_{C'}$ do [$_{IP}$ you wonder [$_{CP}$ whether [$_{IP}$ John said [$_{CP}$ *t′* [$_{C'}$ (that) [$_{IP}$ Mary solved the problem *t*]]]]]]]]

Note that we also have here the beginnings of an explanation of the adjunct–argument asymmetry in long movement. For argument movement, the variable trace must of course be present, but nothing (including (18)) demands that intermediate traces be present. Parallel to (19), we thus can have (20) with the structure (21), where the offending trace *t′* is deleted:

(20)   ??Which problem do you wonder whether John said (that) Mary solved

(21)   [$_{CP}$ Which problem [$_{C'}$ do [$_{IP}$ you wonder [$_{CP}$ whether [$_{IP}$ John said [$_{CP}$ *t′* [$_{C'}$ (that) [$_{IP}$ Mary solved *t*]]]]]]]]

As noted above, the long argument movement in (20) is not perfect, but is not nearly as degraded as long adjunct movement. The fact that it is not perfect follows on Chomsky's completely derivational view of Subjacency. Since one step of movement was too long, the example is marked as degraded. But since the offending trace is gone following deletion, (21) is not an ECP violation. As Chomsky and Lasnik (1993: 547) describe the situation, "An expression . . . is a Subjacency violation if its derivation forms a starred trace. It is an ECP violation if, furthermore, this starred trace remains at LF." This is the residue of the Lasnik and Saito distinction between gamma-marking and the gamma filter (i.e., the ECP). Significantly, even on this "derivational" analysis, the ECP is actually not entirely derivational. It is derivational to the extent that potential violations are marked online anywhere in the course of the derivation. But it is representational in that whether the potential violations are actual violations is determined strictly at the *level* of LF.

Thus, as often turns out to be the case, there is empirically little to choose between the representational approach and the derivational one, and even technically, the difference is not very sharp. In this particular instance, Lasnik and Saito's representational account of adjunct movement locality and Chomsky's derivational (and partially representational) one both capture the facts, and both have a cost. For the former, the cost is the stipulation that gamma-marking is *strictly* representational, operating only at levels. For the latter, it is (18), which is evidently relevant solely for the phenomenon at issue.

3   Intermediate Trace Deletion and Economy

Chomsky (1991) (see also Chomsky and Lasnik 1993) proposes a more general way of capturing the effects of (18). Following Chomsky, for concreteness suppose that a trace in violation of the ECP is marked *. Further, continue to assume that deletion is one of the operations affecting phrase markers, but abandon the assumption that movement only optionally leaves a trace. Rather, if a trace is missing in a position from or through which movement has taken place, it is by virtue of deletion. What is then at issue is a deletability asymmetry between intermediate traces in adjunct chains and those in argument chains. Chomsky's account of this asymmetry is in terms of the theory of "economy" that he began to develop in detail in Chomsky (1991) (and which formed the basis for the "minimalist framework"). I briefly summarize the relevant concepts here.

First, the level of LF must satisfy the principle of Full Interpretation (FI). This principle is parallel to economy of derivation. Just as economy of derivation demands that there be no superfluous steps in derivations, FI requires that there be no superfluous symbols in representations. In particular, every element in an LF representation must be "legitimate." Chomsky (1995a: 153–4) suggests that only:[2]

> the following elements are permitted at LF, each a chain . . . :
> 1. Arguments: each element is in an A-position . . .
> 2. Adjuncts: each element is in an Ā-position.
> 3. Lexical elements: each element is in an X^0 position.
> 4. Predicates, possibly predicate chains if there is predicate raising . . .
> 5. Operator-variable constructions, each a chain (α_1, α_2), where the operator α_1 is in an Ā-position and the variable α_2 is in an A-position.

Then deletion, one instance of "Affect α," "may apply (and must apply) only to yield such an element, given an illegitimate object."

Successive cyclic Ā-movement from an A-position will produce a chain that is not one of the legitimate LF objects. The "tail" of the chain is in an A-position while all of the other links are in Ā-positions, so the chain is neither an argument chain nor an adjunct chain. Nor is it an operator-variable construction, since those are limited to two-membered chains. The only way to make such a chain into a legitimate LF object is to delete the intermediate traces, whereupon it becomes an operator-variable construction. Notice that if one or more of those intermediate traces had been marked * in the course of the derivation, those *s would be eliminated when the traces are deleted.

Now consider the case of successive cyclic adjunct movement. This time, all of the members of the chain are in Ā-positions. Hence, the chain is one of the legitimate objects – an adjunct chain. By economy of derivation, no deletion of intermediate traces can take place. Thus, if any of those intermediate traces were marked * (by virtue of a too-long step of movement having taken place), by economy of derivation those *s could not be eliminated. They would remain at the level of LF. The result is a legitimate object, but one that happens not to be well formed. Thus does Chomsky derive the argument-adjunct asymmetry with respect to long movement. It is principled just to the extent that the categorization of legitimate LF objects is, particularly the illegitimacy of a complete chain of *wh*-movement of an argument, as contrasted with the legitimacy of a corresponding adjunct chain. As before, the approach is derivational, in that the marking of a trace as being in violation of the ECP crucially takes place in the course of the derivation. In fact, it can be immediately upon the creation of the trace. Yet it is representational in the way that a derivational violation can be remedied. If no offending trace remains at the level of LF, the resulting structure is not an ECP violation, even if online it was.

Subjacency remains strictly derivational:[3] a long movement, even of an argument, causes some degradation of the sentence, as we have seen. Thus, it is evidently not the LF representation that is responsible for determining violation of Subjacency. Rather, violation is determined online. This is all rather standard in Chomskyan work of the last several years. Interestingly, if we look back two decades before that, we can find a paradigm intriguingly parallel to the one arguing that the proper treatment of the ECP is partly representational. Ross (1969), in his seminal discussion of Sluicing, argued extensively that ellipsis involves deletion, and, given that, showed that deletion ameliorates island violations. Sluicing is the ellipsis phenomenon often found in embedded questions, given appropriate discourse context:

(22)   Mary hired someone.
       Tell me who ~~Mary hired~~.

In (22), the *wh*-movement has been internal to one clause. Sluicing is also possible when the *wh*-movement has been long distance:

(23) I heard that Mary hired someone.
Tell me who ~~you heard that Mary hired~~.

Now notice that if the long movement is out of an "island" (in this case, an adjunct island), the usual degradation is significantly lessened in the Sluicing construction:

(24) I resigned because Mary hired someone.
?*Tell me who you resigned because Mary hired.
?Tell me who ~~you resigned because Mary hired~~.

If Sluicing is, indeed, a deletion phenomenon, as Ross argued (and as Chomsky has consistently maintained about ellipsis in general), then (24) provides evidence that Subjacency violation is not determined strictly online. This is because the Sluiced and non-Sluiced versions of (24) are identical throughout the syntactic portion of the derivation, and, in particular, at the point in the derivation where the excessively long step of movement takes place. The improvement created by Sluicing suggests that a Subjacency violation, rather like an ECP violation, places a * at some specific place in the structure, perhaps on the constituent constituting the island (rather than on the trace, in order to maintain the distinction between Subjacency violations and ECP violations). Deletion of (a constituent containing) the island then eliminates the *. If deletion is a PF process, then, rather curiously, we are led to the tentative speculation that it is the PF level that ultimately determines Subjacency violations, while, as we saw, it is the LF level that ultimately determines ECP violations.

4   When Derivational Locality is Obscured by Later Operations

For both ECP and Subjacency, we have seen evidence that an online violation can be improved (if not remedied entirely) by a later operation that results in a change in the ultimate representation, LF in the first case, PF in the second. Interestingly, Chomsky argues for the reality of syntactic derivations by appealing to virtually the opposite state of affairs: situations where the ECP is *satisfied* online, but where the ultimate LF representation appears to be in *violation*, yet the resulting sentence is good. I quote one of Chomsky's discussions:

> Viewed derivationally, computation typically involves simple steps expressible in terms of natural relations and properties, with the context that makes them natural "wiped out" by later operations, hence not visible in the representations to which the derivation converges. Thus, in syntax, crucial relations are typically local, but a sequence of operations may yield a representation in which the locality is obscured. Head movement, for example, is narrowly "local," but several such operations may leave a head separated from its trace by an intervening

head. This happens, for example, when N incorporates to V, leaving the trace t_N and the [$_V$ V-N] complex then raises to I, leaving the trace t_V: the chain (N, t_N) at the output level violates the locality property, and further operations (say, XP-fronting) may obscure it even more radically, but locality is observed in each individual step. (Chomsky 1995a: 223–4)

Consider the structure at issue, where, for concreteness, I assume that V right-adjoins to I, and complements are to the right of heads:

(25)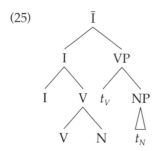

Chomsky's assumption, which I share, is that in this configuration, N is too distant from its trace to satisfy the Head Movement Constraint (a head cannot be separated from its trace by an intervening head), or whatever it derives from (the ECP or some version of relativized minimality,[4] on a fairly standard view). At the immediately prior point of the derivation, however, HMC is evidently satisfied:

(26)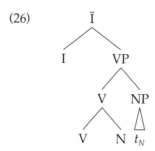

At this stage of the derivation, N is attached to the next head up from its trace, so there is no intervening head. The locality demanded by HMC obtains. But, as Chomsky notes, the next local step of movement has the effect of obscuring the locality of the first step. If we examined the LF output to determine locality satisfaction, we would incorrectly exclude (25), or so it seems.

One can, however, imagine a representational alternative. True, in (25), the V trace intervenes between the moved N and its trace. But what exactly is the V trace? Chomsky, among others, has argued that a trace in a position is a copy of the item that moved from that position. Under that hypothesis, consider the more articulated version of (25), where the 'traces' are in italics:

(27)

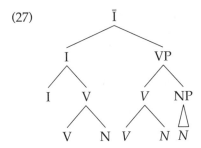

Now if N "antecedent governs" its trace in (26), presumably the intermediate N likewise antecedent governs the initial trace N in (27). Thus, under the copy theory of traces, even at the level of LF the locality requirement on head movement (i.e., on the traces of head movement) is arguably satisfied.

Interestingly, Chomsky himself alludes to this alternative to the strictly derivational analysis, but he rejects it:

> It is generally possible to formulate the desired result in terms of outputs. In the head movement case, for example, one can appeal to the (plausible) assumption that the trace is a copy, so the intermediate V-trace includes within it a record of the local N → V raising. But surely this is the wrong move. The relevant chains at LF are (N, t_N) and (V, t_V), and in these the locality relation satisfied by successive raising has been lost. (1995a: 224)

Chomsky's objection to the representational alternative raises an important question. If, as I assume Chomsky implies here, the relevant chain at LF consists of just the moved item and its *initial* trace, his argument is fairly compelling. The representational alternative makes crucial reference to intermediate traces, but if they have no relevance at LF, such reference is plausibly illicit. (Note that no such conceptual objection applies to the derivational approach: in the whole range of theories I am considering here, intermediate *steps* exist regardless of whether they still leave evidence of their existence in the form of traces (copies) at LF.) However, there is reason to believe that (at least some) chains at LF are not just two-membered, but rather include intermediate traces along with the initial one. Recall the Chomsky (1991) analysis summarized above of the *wh* adjunct-argument asymmetry with respect to degree of unacceptability of island violations. That analysis demanded that every intermediate step of movement leave a trace, and that when a particular step is too long, the trace created is marked *. At LF, a * marked trace indicates ungrammaticality. This much could, of course, be easily restated in strictly derivational terms. But the account of the *asymmetry* had a fundamentally representational aspect. Both adjuncts and arguments make successive short moves leaving traces; and in both instances, when the step of movement is too long, the trace is marked *, whether the step is the first step of movement or a later step. But intermediate traces of adjuncts cannot be eliminated (given that the chain already is a well-formed object, conforming to the second criterion

– Adjuncts: each element is in an Ā-position). Intermediate traces of arguments undergoing Ā-movement can be eliminated (in fact must be, on Chomsky's account). Then at LF, if the former kind of derivation involved a long intermediate step, the chain will contain a * marked intermediate trace. A corresponding derivation involving movement of an argument, on the other hand, will not contain such a trace, all intermediate traces having been eliminated so that the chain will conform to the fifth criterion: Operator-variable constructions, each a chain (α_1, α_2), where the operator α_1 is in an Ā-position and the variable α_2 is in an A-position. As far as I know, there is still no better way to account for the adjunct-argument asymmetry, or even one equally good. To the extent that this is so, we have evidence that (at least some) intermediate traces exist at LF. The strongest possible form of the conceptual argument against intermediate traces as licensors of lower traces can thus be answered.[5]

5   Locality and Reconstruction

There is also evidence that, as Chomsky himself suggests, a trace is indeed a copy of the moved item. This assumption is clearly necessary for the representational treatment of ECP satisfaction in the head movement case under consideration. The evidence comes from so-called reconstruction effects, where for certain purposes, especially those having to do with anaphoric connection, a moved item behaves as if it were in the position of one of its traces. Barss (1986) provides an extensive discussion of such phenomena, and Chomsky (1993) concludes from them that traces are copies and that they exist at LF, the level of representation that Chomsky takes to be relevant to "Binding Theory." (28) is based on one of Chomsky's examples, of a standard type:

(28)   Mary wondered which picture of himself Bill saw *t*

The point is that *Bill* can serve as the antecedent of *himself* in (28) even though *Bill* does not seem to c-command *himself*. Chomsky's analysis of this fact relies on the trace being a copy of the moved item. Abstracting away from details that are irrelevant here, the binding requirement of the anaphor *himself* is satisfied by virtue of the copy of *himself* in the "trace." On this approach, at least initial traces exist at LF, and they are copies. I turn now to the issue of intermediate traces, since intermediate traces were directly relevant to the adjunct-argument asymmetry discussion.

With respect to intermediate traces, there is evidence like that in (28) for the existence of such traces, and for their status as copies. But, as we will see, that evidence will actually run counter to the conclusion based on the adjunct-argument asymmetry. First, the evidence for intermediate traces: Barss (1986) observes that the kind of reconstruction effect with respect to initial position seen in (28) also arises with respect to intermediate position. Consider (29), whose derivation involves successive movement:

(29)   Which picture of himself does Mary think that John said that Susan likes

Obviously, with the *wh*-phrase in its surface position, *himself* is not in an appropriate c-command relation with its antecedent *John*. Further, the initial position of the *wh*-phrase, object of the most deeply embedded verb, has *himself* too distant from *John*, as evidenced by (30):

(30)   *Mary thinks that John said that Susan likes pictures of himself

The appropriate position seems to be Spec of the lowest CP, as seen in the approximately parallel (31):

(31)   Mary thinks that John said that pictures of himself, Susan likes

A trace (copy) in the intermediate position would thus provide the necessary structural relation to license the anaphoric connection.

I have thus far summarized two arguments for the existence of intermediate traces. Unfortunately, they rather neatly contradict each other. The argument based on the adjunct-argument asymmetry presupposes an analysis under which intermediate traces of arguments are eliminated prior to the LF level (while intermediate traces of adjuncts remain). But the reconstruction effects just examined, evidently implicating intermediate traces, involved *wh*-argument movement. The two lines of reasoning cannot both be correct. I do not know of a good counter to the first line of reasoning, so I will assume that it is correct. That leaves the intermediate reconstruction facts to be addressed in another way.

As indicated above, Chomsky's specific approach to reconstruction in general centers on traces (copies) visible at the LF level, a strongly representational approach, interestingly enough. According to Chomsky (1993), developing a suggestion of Chomsky and Lasnik (1993), if the basic aspects of Binding Theory hold only at the LF interface, then we can move toward a simple interpretive version of Binding Theory which directly maps structural properties into semantic ones. There is no syntactic filtering of the sort found in the three binding conditions of Chomsky (1981). In fundamental respects, this represents a return to much earlier generative treatments of anaphora, such as RI (Rule of Interpretation), the Chomsky (1973) ancestor of Condition B, and the Disjoint Reference Rule of Lasnik (1976), the ancestor of Condition C. But, as we saw, this approach seems to demand the presence at LF of intermediate traces (even of arguments), a consequence incompatible with the treatment of the adjunct-argument island asymmetry.

An appealing alternative would rely on a more derivational approach to anaphoric connection. Belletti and Rizzi (1988) present just such a theory, at least for one class of binding phenomena. They argue that Condition A can be satisfied online, at any point in the derivation. Their concern is, of course, reconstruction effects abstractly similar to those discussed above. The crucial property is that at the output of the derivation, Condition A is apparently not satisfied while at some prior point in the derivation, it would have been. In empirical effect, the online proposal is very close to the LF trace account. The technical difference is that it precisely does not rely on LF traces, so it would allow us to preserve the account of the adjunct-argument asymmetry that demands the elimination of intermediate argument traces. Note that if we take the Binding Theory to consist not of conditions on form, but rather of interpretive principles, as suggested in the preceding paragraph, then this amounts to saying that there is no specific *level* of LF. That is, there is no one single representation that uniquely interfaces with semantics.

Within generative grammar, there are numerous antecedents for this possibility. For example, in the classic formulation of generative grammar in the mid-1950s, the closest analogue to LF is the "T-marker," the record of the transformational derivation. Later, in the orthodox form of the "Extended Standard Theory" (EST) of the early 1970s, the input to semantic interpretation consisted of two representations – Deep Structure and Surface Structure. Variant EST formulations existed at the same time, some of them clearly anticipating the Belletti–Rizzi approach. Jackendoff (1972), for example, proposed a theory of anaphora that included interpretive rules operating at the end of each syntactic cycle. Similarly, Lasnik (1972) suggested "cyclic" interpretation of the scope of negation, and Lasnik (1976) extended this to the scope of other operators. There are analogues on the PF side of the grammar as well, as with the Bresnan (1971) arguments that the rule responsible for the assignment of sentence stress in English applies not at Surface Structure, as had been assumed, but at the end of each syntactic cycle. Needless to say, all of these analyses are fundamentally derivational. There is a modern version of these approaches which is even more derivational. Epstein (in press) (see also Uriagereka in press) suggests that *all* interpretive information is provided online, in the course of the syntactic derivation. In a way reminiscent of Chomsky (1955), there is no *level* of LF per se. Under Epstein's approach, after each syntactic operation, any structural information relevant to semantics (and presumably phonetics as well, though Epstein's specific arguments are not concerned with that interface) is available. This approach can easily accommodate the reconstruction phenomena sketched above. However, it seems that it is not consistent with the account of the adjunct-argument asymmetry discussed here, or with any close variants, since such accounts crucially rely on a late representation masking properties present earlier in the derivation (illicitly long steps of movement in this case).[6] For present purposes, then, I will continue to assume one of the hybrid approaches incorporating derivational and representational aspects.

6   The Motivation for Movement

Thus far, I have been examining the "derivation" vs. "representation" question with respect to general locality constraints on movement. At this point, I turn to an arguably more fundamental aspect of the question: what determines whether movement occurs in the first place? Chomsky (1995a) argues on conceptual and, to some extent, empirical grounds that movement is always morphologically driven. That is, there is some formal feature that needs to be checked, and movement provides the configuration in which the checking can take place. Chomsky also provides strong reason to believe that, all else being equal, covert movement (that in the LF component) is preferred to overt movement, a preference that Chomsky calls "Procrastinate." When movement is overt, rather than covert, then, it must have been forced to operate "early" by some special requirement. The major phenomenon that Chomsky considers in these terms is verb raising (which Chomsky takes to be overt in French and covert in English). He also hints at a contrast in object shift, overt in some languages and covert in others. Chomsky (1993, 1994, 1995a)[7] codes the driving force for overt movement into "strong features," and presents three successive distinct theories of precisely how strong features drive overt movement. These three theories, which I will summarize immediately, are of interest to my central question, since the first two of them are explicitly representational in the relevant sense, while the third is derivational:

(32) a. A strong feature that is not checked in overt syntax causes a derivation to crash at PF. (Chomsky 1993)
      b. A strong feature that is not checked (and eliminated) in overt syntax causes a derivation to crash at LF. (Chomsky 1994)
      c. A strong feature must be eliminated (almost) immediately upon its introduction into the phrase marker. (Chomsky 1995a)

All three of these proposals are designed to force overt movement in the relevant instances (e.g. verb raising in French; a strong V feature of Infl will cause a violation in one of the three ways listed in (32)) and all are framed within a "Minimalist" conception of grammar. In addition to what was indicated in the preceding paragraph, the most pertinent aspect of this conception is the reduction of levels from the four that were standard in Government Binding analyses (D-structure, S-structure, LF, and PF) to just the last two, the "interface" levels LF and PF. There is no D-structure level of representation since the work of building a structure is done by generalized transformations, as it was before recursion in the base was introduced in Chomsky (1965). Interestingly, this return to an earlier approach replaces a representational view with a strongly derivational one. As for S-structure, it remains, but merely as the point where the derivation branches off toward LF on one path and toward PF on another. Chomsky calls this point "Spell-Out." The claim is that it has no further properties. In particular, it is not the locus of satisfaction of any conditions or constraints (as it obviously had been in Government Binding work). With this much background, we can proceed to a more careful consideration of the three proposals in (32).

Chomsky (1993) argues that the treatment in (32a) follows from the fact that parametric differences in movement, like other parametric differences, must be based on morphological properties reflected at PF. (32a) makes this explicit. Chomsky suggests two possible implementations of the approach:

> "strong" features are visible at PF and "weak" features invisible at PF. These features are not legitimate objects at PF; they are not proper components of phonetic matrices. Therefore, if a strong feature remains after Spell-Out, the derivation crashes . . . Alternatively, weak features are deleted in the PF component so that PF rules can apply to the phonological matrix that remains; strong features are not deleted so that PF rules do not apply, causing the derivation to crash at PF. (Chomsky 1993: 198)

There is presumably only one other possible type of representational approach, given minimalist assumptions: one that involves LF, rather than PF. Chomsky (1994) proposes such an analysis, (32b), based on an empirical shortcoming of (32a). What is at issue is the unacceptability of sentences like (33):

(33)   *John read what?

Assuming that the strong feature forcing overt *wh*-movement in English resides in interrogative C,[8] the potential concern is that that C might be introduced in the LF component, where, checked or not, it could not possibly cause a PF crash, since, as far as PF knows, the item does not exist at all. Yet (33) is bad, so such a derivation must be blocked. This problem arises in the general context of fitting lexical insertion into the grammar. In most circumstances, there is no need for a specific prohibition against accessing the lexicon in the PF or LF component. (33) represents a rare problem for the assumption that lexical insertion is free to apply anywhere. I quote Chomsky's discussion of this point.

> Spell-Out can apply anywhere, the derivation crashing if a "wrong choice" is made . . . If the phonological component adds a lexical item at the root, it will introduce semantic features, and the derivation will crash at PF. If the covert component does the same, it will introduce phonological features, and the derivation will therefore crash at LF . . . Suppose that root C (complementizer) has a strong feature that requires overt WH-movement. We now want to say that unless this feature is checked before Spell-Out it will cause the derivation to crash at LF to avoid the possibility of accessing C after Spell-Out in the covert component. (Chomsky 1994: 60)

Chomsky proposes to implement this basic idea in the following way: "Slightly adjusting the account in Chomsky (1993), we now say that a checked strong feature will be stripped away by Spell-Out, but is otherwise ineliminable" (Chomsky 1994: 60).

Chomsky (1995a) rejects the representational approach in (32a), and the conceptual argument he gives evidently applies equally to the alternative representational approach in (32b). He discounts such an account as an "evasion," and proposes what he claims is a more straightforward statement of the phenomenon:

formulation of strength in terms of PF convergence is a restatement of the basic property, not a true explanation. In fact, there seems to be no way to improve upon the bare statement of the properties of strength. Suppose, then, that we put an end to evasion and simply define a strong feature as one that a derivation "cannot tolerate": a derivation D→Σ is canceled if Σ contains a strong feature. (Chomsky 1995a: 233)

Chomsky's summary of that approach is given in (34):

(34) "A strong feature ... triggers a rule that eliminates it: [strength] is associated with a pair of operations, one that introduces it into the derivation ... a second that (quickly) eliminates it." (Chomsky 1995a: 233)

This approach is strongly derivational.

In addition to the claim that (32c) avoids the evasion present in (32a) (and presumably in (32b) as well), Chomsky implies that (32c) is superior to the representational theories on another ground as well: that of computational complexity. While under theory (32c), the determination that overt movement is needed is made online, immediately as the head containing the strong feature is introduced into the structure, the two representational theories require considerable "look-ahead."[9] At a given point in the overt portion of a derivation, it is necessary to inspect the PF or LF representation to see whether Procrastinate is to be evaded.

At this point, I want to give a fuller elaboration of (32c), since that fuller elaboration is of interest in its own right, but also because a potential problem emerges. Chomsky suggests the following: "The intuitive idea is that the strong feature merged at the root must be eliminated before it becomes part of a larger structure by further operations" (Chomsky 1995a: 234). After considering how derivations work in general, he goes on to indicate that: "the descriptive property of strength is [(35)]. Suppose that the derivation D has formed Σ containing α with a strong feature F. Then [(35)] D is canceled if α is in a category not headed by α" (1995a: 234).

According to Chomsky, there are two significant consequences of this approach: (i) that cyclicity follows;[10] (ii) that a strong feature is checked by an overt operation: "We ... virtually derive the conclusion that a strong feature triggers an *overt* operation to eliminate it by checking. This conclusion follows with a single exception: covert merger (at the root) of a lexical item that has a strong feature but no phonological features" (1995a: 233). This exception involves a kind of example we have seen before:

(36) *John read what

Recall that it was exactly this type of example that led Chomsky to reject the PF crash theory (32a) in favor of the LF crash theory (32b). But, as Chomsky in effect acknowledges, the problem now re-arises in the derivational theory. To be specific, how can derivation (37) be blocked?[11]

(37) Spell-Out: John read what
        LF: C [strong Q] John read what

The structure in (37) never needs to become part of a larger structure, so the fact that the strong feature of C was not checked overtly should not hinder the derivation. Chomsky proposes to bar such covert insertion of an item bearing a strong feature with the economy principle (38):

(38) α enters the Numeration only if it has an effect on output.

The Numeration is basically the set of items chosen from the lexicon that will form the basis for the derivation. (38) is intended to mean that an item can be chosen from the lexicon only if it will have a phonetic consequence or a semantic consequence. This immediately raises a question concerning the central argument for the derivational approach – that it eliminates the look-ahead inherent in the PF and LF approaches. There is extreme look-ahead here, all the way from the very beginning of the derivation, the Numeration, to the very ends, the phonetic and semantic interfaces.

Apart from this conceptual question, there is an empirical question about whether the correct result is obtained. There is reason to think that it is not. Consider the situation at issue, insertion in the LF component of interrogative C in English, a language in which C has a strong *wh* feature. (38) purports to prevent this. To see whether it does, we first have to ask whether this C has an effect on output. By definition, covert insertion of a C will have no phonetic effect. Will it have an effect at the LF output? Either it will or it will not. If it will, then covert insertion is allowed, and we generate (36) with structure (39):

(39) C [$_{IP}$ John read what]

Since this is not the correct result, suppose instead that C will not have a semantic effect. Then we cannot generate (36) with structure (39), so the problem is apparently solved under the assumption that insertion of interrogative C has no effect on semantic output. As Chomsky states the situation:[12] "the interface representations (π, λ) are virtually identical whether the operation takes place or not. The PF representations are in fact identical, and the LF ones differ only trivially in form, and not at all in interpretation" (1995a: 294). But the goal is actually more general than just ruling out (36) with structure (39). Rather, it is ruling out (36) altogether. Under the assumptions just spelled out, (36) is successfully excluded with C covertly inserted. But what if C is not inserted at all? That is, what if the LF is just the same as the "S-structure"?

(40) [$_{IP}$ John read what]

(40) violates no morphological requirements, and, if C has no effect on output, the assumption that was necessary in order to exclude (36) *with* C inserted, then it should mean exactly *What did John read?* To summarize, if C has a semantic effect, inserting it in LF should be permitted. And if it does not have

a semantic effect, *not* inserting it should be of no consequence. Thus, even given the new economy condition (38), (36) is allowed as a standard interrogative, an incorrect result. In this regard, then, the derivational theory of strong features ultimately fares no better than the PF theory. Either theory demands an additional stipulation, perhaps just that lexical insertion is prohibited in the covert component[13] (a result Chomsky was trying to deduce, but, as we have just seen, not completely successfully).

7   The Nature of Strong Features

There are further phenomena that might bear on the question of representational vs. derivational approach to strong features. The derivational approach outlined above demands that a strong feature triggering overt movement is always a feature of the position that an item is moving to (a feature of an "attracting head"). This is so since a strong feature in an item that will move would virtually never be able to be eliminated before that item is embedded, by a generalized transformation, in a larger structure. The derivation would therefore fatally terminate before the feature ever had a chance to be checked and deleted. Evidence for a strong feature in an item forcing that item to move would therefore be evidence against the derivational approach, at least as formulated in (32c). Certain ellipsis paradigms provide such evidence, at least on the face of it. I turn to one such paradigm now, involving Pseudogapping.[14]

(41) presents a few examples of Pseudogapping from the classic study by Levin (1978):

(41)   a.   If you don't believe me, you will ø the weatherman
    b.   I rolled up a newspaper, and Lynn did ø a magazine
    c.   Kathy likes astronomy, but she doesn't ø meteorology

While in many instances, it might appear that the process is simply elision of the main verb, there is evidence that more is involved. In the examples in (42), the ellipsis site includes the main verb plus (a) the small clause predicate or (b) the second object in a double object construction:

(42)   a.   The DA proved Jones guilty and the Assistant DA will ~~prove~~ Smith
     ~~guilty~~
    b.   ?John gave Bill a lot of money, and Mary will ~~give~~ Susan ~~a lot of~~
     ~~money~~

Rejecting the possibility of an ellipsis rule affecting a discontinuous portion of the structure, Jayaseelan (1990) proposes that Pseudogapping constructions result from VP ellipsis, with the remnant NP having moved out of the VP by Heavy NP Shift. In Lasnik (1995c) I argue that this proposal is correct in its essentials, though wrong in certain details. I modify Jayaseelan's analysis by positing raising to Spec of Agr$_o$, instead of HNPS, as the process removing the remnant from the ellipsis site.

Under "standard" Minimalist assumptions, going back to Chomsky (1991), raising to Spec of Agr_o is covert, taking place in the LF component. Given Jayaseelan's goal, adopted also in Lasnik (1995c), of analyzing Pseudogapping as affecting a constituent, the ellipsis process must then be analyzed as copying in the LF component, rather than deletion in the PF component. However, on the theory of LF movement advocated by Chomsky (1995a), and further defended by Lasnik (1995c, 1995d), the necessary structure would not be created even in *covert* syntax. On that theory, since movement is invariably triggered by the need for formal features to be checked, all else being equal only formal features move. When movement is overt (triggered by a strong feature), PF requirements demand that an entire constituent move, via a sort of pied-piping. However, when movement is covert, PF requirements are irrelevant so economy dictates that movement *not* be of the entire constituent. But it is very difficult to see how covert raising of just the formal features (FF) of NP to Spec of Agr_o could possibly create a suitable ellipsis licensing configuration. The structure of the second conjunct of (43) would be as in (44), with *believe* incorrectly within the ellipsis site rather than outside of it:

(43)   Mary will believe Susan, and you will Bob

(44)

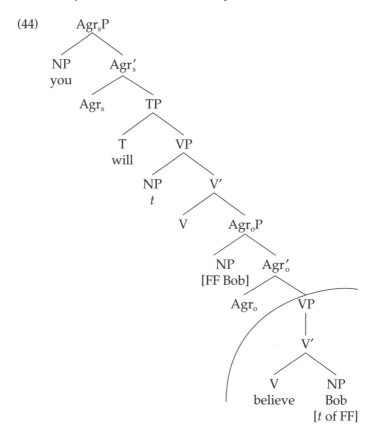

It seems then that if movement newly creates a configuration licensing ellipsis, the movement must be overt rather than covert. Before I indicate how that is possible in the present instance, I note that if the movement is overt, then the conclusion above, that ellipsis must involve LF copying, no longer follows. If the licensing configuration must be created prior to the LF/PF split regardless, then ellipsis could just as easily be a PF deletion phenomenon.

Now early Minimalist literature, such as Chomsky (1991, 1993) and Chomsky and Lasnik (1993), did have accusative NP raising to Spec of Agr$_o$, but covertly rather than overtly. However, Koizumi (1993, 1995), developing ideas from Johnson (1991), argues, instead, that that raising is always overt, driven, as usual, by a strong feature. In Lasnik (1995f) I suggest that the strong feature in this instance is an "EPP feature" residing in Agr, hence the same feature that drives overt subject raising, the modern technological implementation of the Extended Projection Principle of Chomsky (1981). I will have little more to say here about this particular strong feature. I will, however, address another strong feature that must be involved in simple transitive sentences without ellipsis. Given that word order in English is V-O rather than O-V, if object raises out of VP, verb must normally raise still higher. Koizumi's proposal, which he calls the split VP hypothesis, is that V raises, via Agr$_o$, to a higher "shell" V position, as shown in (46) for the sentence in (45):

(45) You will believe Bob

(46)

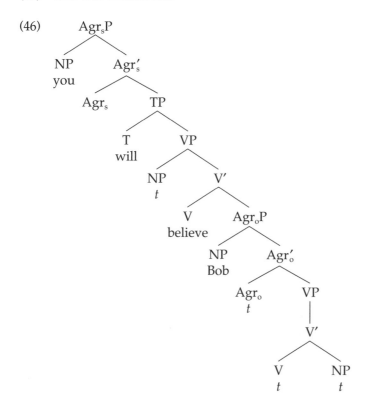

Under this general hypothesis, consider a simple Pseudogapping example such as (47):

(47)   You might not believe me but you will Bob

If *Bob* overtly raises to Spec of Agr$_o$ while *believe* remains in situ, then deletion of the residual VP produces (47). The relevant structure is shown in (48):

(48)

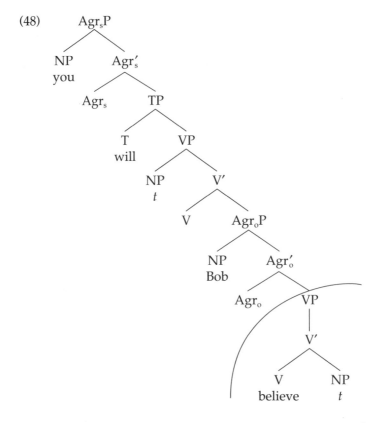

Deletion of the lower VP yields the Pseudogapping example in (47).

The question that now arises is why the V need not raise in Pseudogapping constructions, given that in non-elliptical sentences it must:

(49)   *You will Bob believe

By hypothesis, a strong feature is involved. Yet there seem to be two possibilities for a convergent derivation. The verb can raise as in (46), presumably checking the relevant strong feature. Alternatively, the verb can be deleted along with its containing VP as in (48). This state of affairs receives a straightforward account under theory (32a) of strong features, the PF approach, under the new hypothesis that the strong feature forcing the verb to raise overtly is a feature of the lexical verb itself, rather than of the target position it raises to. The overt raising derivation is essentially unaffected by this change in perspective. The ellipsis structure is more interesting. Consider (48) from this point of view:

(50)

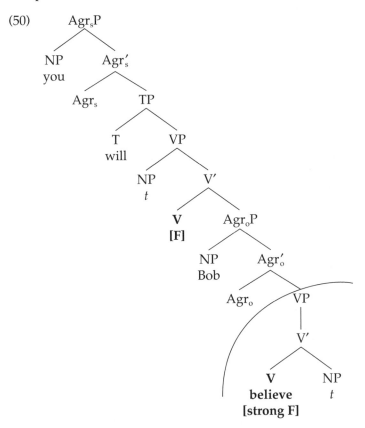

If *believe* fails to raise, and no other relevant process takes place, the strong feature that is not overtly checked causes (50) to crash at PF. But if the lower VP containing *believe* is deleted in the PF component, then, patently, the strong feature cannot cause a PF crash, since the (category containing the) feature will be gone at that level. It is not obvious how to capture this result under theory (32b), the LF crash account of strong features (since even if the strong feature is deleted in PF, it will still be present at LF), or theory (32c), the derivational theory. Thus, we apparently have an argument for theory (32a).

Surprisingly, it turns out that the ellipsis facts can be reconciled with the derivational theory. There is a possible alternative analysis of those ellipsis facts, based on the Chomsky (1995a) theory of "pied-piping," particularly as explicated by Ochi (1997, 1999).[15]

Ochi, following Chomsky, considers the nature of pied-piping, the usual reflex of movement triggered by a strong feature. Chomsky (1995a) gives the following characterization:

> For the most part – perhaps completely – it is properties of the phonological component that require pied-piping. Isolated features and other scattered parts of words may not be subject to its rules, in which case the derivation is canceled; or the derivation might proceed to PF with elements that are "unpronounceable," violating F[ull] I[nterpretation]. (Chomsky 1995a: 262)

Overt movement consists of a complex of operations under this approach:

> Applied to the feature F, the operation Move thus creates at least one and perhaps two "derivative chains" alongside the chain $CH_F = (F, t_F)$ constructed by the operation itself. One is $CH_{FF} = (FF[F], t_{FF[F]})$, consisting of the set of formal features FF[F] and its trace; the other is $CH_{CAT} = (\alpha, t_\alpha)$, α a category carried along by generalized pied-piping and including at least the lexical item containing F. CH_{FF} is always constructed, CH_{CAT} only when required for convergence ... As noted, CH_{CAT} should be completely dispensable, were it not for the need to accommodate to the sensorimotor apparatus. (1995a: 265)

Note that this seems to assume the second of the two possibilities Chomsky mentioned in the prior passage, that is, that failure of pied-piping causes a violation specifically at PF. Chomsky goes on to observe that even overt movement might be possible without pied-piping under certain circumstances, if no phonological requirement is violated: "Just how broadly considerations of PF convergence might extend is unclear, pending better understanding of morphology and the internal structure of phrases. Note that such considerations could permit raising without pied-piping even overtly, depending on morphological structure" (1995a: 264).

Consider now how the ellipsis phenomena examined above might be reanalyzed in terms of this theory. Recall my analysis of Pseudogapping in terms of the PF crash theory of strong features. Assuming the split VP hypothesis, in a non-elliptical transitive sentence, for example, the object raises to Spec of Agr_o and the lexical V raises to the higher shell V position in order that a strong feature of the lexical V will be checked. If the V does not raise, a PF crash will ensue, but only if the offending item exists at that level. Hence, under a deletion account of ellipsis, ellipsis provides another way to salvage the derivation. When the lower VP is deleted without the V having raised, a PF crash is avoided and the result is acceptable Pseudogapping.

The alternative account preserves the idea of deletion averting a PF crash, but the potential crash now has another cause. The feature driving overt V-raising could be a strong feature of the *higher* V. Once the matching feature of the lower lexical V is "attracted" out of the lower V, the lower V becomes defective. A PF crash will be avoided if either pied-piping or deletion of a category containing the lower V (VP Deletion = Pseudogapping in the relevant instances) takes place. This is illustrated in (51):[16]

(51)

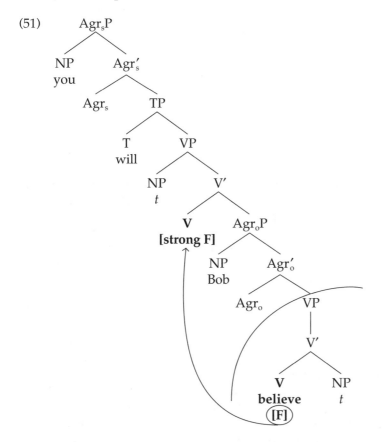

Even under the derivational theory of strong features, then, there is a way to capture the saving effect of ellipsis in the Pseudogapping construction.

Thus, the essence of the PF account of the ellipsis facts based on the PF theory of strong features can be captured under the derivational theory as well, a rather surprising result, and, perhaps, a welcome one if Chomsky's conceptual arguments for the derivational theory are accepted. It must be noted, though, that even the account of the ellipsis facts relying on the derivational approach to strong features does ultimately rely on a property of the PF interface level. Before concluding, I will briefly mention one well-known, and rather powerful, argument that strong features reside in some moving categories (not just in attracting heads), and that the basic premise of the derivational theory (32c) is therefore incorrect. There is a great deal of literature, going back to Toman (1982) and Rudin (1982, 1988), discussing the phenomenon of multiple *wh*-movement in the Slavic languages. Bošković (1998) presents a treatment of Serbo-Croatian multiple *wh*-movement in terms directly relevant to the present discussion. Bošković argues that in Serbo-Croatian, *wh*-phrases have a strong focus feature, and that that is why they all have to move overtly:

(52)   Ko   šta   gdje   kupuje?
       who what where buys   "Who buys what where?"
       *Ko kupuje šta gdje?
       *Ko šta kupuje gdje?
       *Ko gdje kupuje šta?

Whether he is right about the precise identity of the feature will not be of concern here. Regardless, the fact that all of the *wh*-phrases must move overtly strongly suggests Bošković's basic conclusion, that the strong feature driving the movement resides in the *wh*-phrases themselves. If, instead, it resided in the head to which they move (or just in that head), why would not the movement of just one of them suffice (as in English)? But if the *wh*-phrases contain strong features to be checked against higher heads, there is no way that strong features can invariably be eliminated immediately upon their insertion into the structure. Thus, the technology behind the Chomsky (1995b) strictly derivational approach to strong features cannot be accepted in its entirety.

8   Summary

In summary, the issue of derivation vs. representation in transformational grammar turned out to be every bit as subtle as it seemed that it would. But there is some reason for optimism that the topic is not completely intractable. Consideration of certain movement locality asymmetries (adjunct vs. argument; full form vs. elliptical) at least helped bring the issue into sharper focus. Those locality effects seem to demand a hybrid account that is crucially derivational, measuring length of each successive step of movement, but is partly representational as well, inspecting the LF and PF representations for violation markers. The attempt to reconcile the treatment of long adjunct/argument movement asymmetry with intermediate position reconstruction effects led to the tentative conclusion that Binding Conditions (or at least condition A) are satisfied "derivationally." Also derivational is the third of Chomsky's three analyses of the strong features which provide the driving force for overt movement. Interactions between ellipsis and (lack of) overt movement at first appeared to argue against that derivational view and in favor of a PF account, but on closer inspection turned out to be consistent with it, given plausible assumptions about feature movement and pied-piping. How to reconcile this with the facts of multiple *wh*-fronting in Slavic, and, indeed, how to fit all of these pieces together into a coherent whole, remains a task for further investigation.

NOTES

* I am indebted to Željko Bošković for very helpful suggestions at every stage of this research, and to Chris Collins for valuable recommendations for improvement of the presentation.

1 In the technical sense of Chomsky (1955).

2 See Browning (1987) and Déprez (1989) for antecedents of this typology.

3 See Freidin (1978) for an early representational view of Subjacency as well as for important discussion of the whole derivation–representation question.

4 The history of this particular condition is interestingly relevant to the theme of this chapter. The earliest version (though not under this particular name) appears in Rizzi (1986b), in the context of an argument against derivation and for a strictly representational approach. Chomsky (1991) and Chomsky and Lasnik (1993), however, present a derivational formulation, based on Rizzi (1990).

5 Note that this line of reasoning also seems to run directly counter to the Chomsky (1995a: 224) argument cited above. This is so since the logic of the intermediate trace deletion account of argument vs. adjunct movement also should extend to head movement, precluding intermediate trace deletion in that situation as well. In fact, Chomsky (1991), after spelling out the adjunct movement analysis, indicates that head movement should behave in parallel, though he gives no examples. A relevant example would involve licit short head movement followed by illicit long head movement, with the resulting sentence totally unacceptable. A potential instance is shown in (i), where *is* has raised to Infl in the lower clause, then to Comp in the matrix:

(i) *Is Mary has said John clever

6 Chris Collins (personal communication) suggests an interesting reinterpretation of the mechanism of trace deletion outlined above that might render it consistent with the Epstein approach: suppose that immediately upon their creation, intermediate traces of argument *wh*-movement are deleted, while, as before, adjunct traces are not eliminated. Then the presence of a starred trace at any step in the derivation would yield an ECP violation. I hope to explore this possibility in future research.

7 Page references to Chomsky (1994) will be to pages in Campos and Kempchinsky (1995), one of two books where the article was published (the other being Webelhuth 1995a). I use the 1994 citation for ease of exposition, and to keep the historical development of the ideas I am exploring clear. Page references to Chomsky (1993) will be to the reprint in Chomsky (1995b).

8 Notice that in English, the relevant strong feature could not reside in the *wh*-phrase, since in multiple interrogation, all but one of the *wh*s remain in situ, hence unchecked in overt syntax:

(i) Who gave what to who

9 See Collins (1997) for extensive discussion of the issue of

computational complexity and look-ahead.

10   At least for overt movement, though Chomsky does not add this qualification.

11   As Máire Noonan pointed out in the discussion following my presentation of some of this material at the 1997 Open Linguistics Forum in Ottawa, even *overt* insertion of C in the matrix without overt *wh*-movement seems to be incorrectly allowed by Chomsky's formulation: "[A] strong feature merged at the root must be eliminated before it becomes part of a larger structure by further operations" (1995a: 234). Chomsky elaborates this as follows: "Suppose that the derivation D has formed Σ containing α with a strong feature F. Then . . . D is canceled if α is in a category not headed by α" (1995a: 234). When, as in the example now under consideration, the interrogative will not be embedded, hence will never be part of a larger structure, nothing demands that the strong feature be checked overtly.

12   Here I am somewhat reinterpreting what Chomsky actually said, since prior context indicates that Chomsky was referring to the operation of "insertion of strong features." But I do not see how to fit such an operation (insertion of strong features independent of the item of which they are features) into the theory. Possibly I am missing something crucial.

13   Or at least lexical insertion of an item with a strong feature.

14   In Lasnik (1999) I provide a parallel argument based on Sluicing.

15   Ochi's concern is the locality of movement, in particular the fact that only relativized minimality effects follow in any natural way from Attract F. Other island effects seem to make sense only from the point of view of the moving item, rather than the target. Ochi proposes that the feature chain, created by Attract F, is responsible for the relativized minimality effects while the pied-piping chain, created by Move α in order to remedy the defect in α created by the movement of the formal features out of α, is responsible for other island effects.

16   The entire tree is shown in (51) just for expository purposes. In the actual derivation, the strong feature of the higher V would attract the corresponding feature of *believe* immediately upon the introduction of the former into the phrase marker, in accord with the derivational theory.

4 Relativized Minimality Effects

LUIGI RIZZI

0 Introduction

Natural language expressions are potentially unbounded in length and depth of embedding, as a consequence of the recursive nature of natural language syntax. Nevertheless, the core of syntactic processes is inherently local, in that such processes are bound to apply within limited structural domains. The search for the relevant locality principles is one of the central topics of generative grammar. In this chapter I would like to report on a subclass of locality effect which has been the focus of intensive research since the late 1980s or so. Such effects are all amenable to the following abstract form: in the configuration:

(1) $\ldots X \ldots Z \ldots Y \ldots$

Y cannot be related to X if Z intervenes and Z has certain characteristics in common with X. So, in order to be related to X, Y must be in a minimal configuration with X, where Minimality is relativized to the nature of the structural relation to be established. The major cases illustrating such Relativized Minimality (RM) effects involve the theory of chains: in the general case, a chain cannot be built between X and Y in configuration (1). In the first part of this chapter, I will present Relativized Minimality effects on the different types of chain through a representational formulation of the relevant locality principle, as in Rizzi (1990). I will then focus on A'-chains and refine the approach to deal with complex patterns of Minimality effects induced by different kinds of adverbial modifier. This part will also contain a brief comparison with the derivational approach proposed by Chomsky (1995b). I will conclude with a discussion of Minimality effects in head-phrase interactions.

1 Relativized Minimality

It is a central property of natural languages that elements can be pronounced in positions different from those in which they are interpreted as thematic arguments, as theta-assigners, as modifiers of various sorts, etc. By "chain" I mean the connection between a displaced element and its traces, down to the relevant interpretive position. I will not take a position here on the question of whether such a connection is established by movement (an operation distinct from the fundamental structure-building operation, which perhaps simply consists in stringing together two elements into a third element, "Merge" in Chomsky's 1995b sense) or is read off configurations (Rizzi 1986) created by the fundamental structure-building operation uniquely. When I mention movement from now on, I simply use the term metaphorically, to refer to an abstract relation between two structural positions.

On the other hand, following Chomsky's (1995b) approach, I will assume that traces are silent copies of antecedents, and I will express them as fully specified positions within angled brackets (as in Starke 1997; in other environments I will use more standard symbols for traces such as "t" or "____".). So, (2a) will have a representation like (2b):

(2) a. How did you solve the problem?
     b. How did you solve the problem <how>?

Now, it is well known that certain structural environments block chain formation; for instance, a *wh*-chain starting from an adverb position fails across an indirect question:

(3) a. I wonder who could solve the problem in this way.
     b. *How do you wonder who could solve this problem <how>?

It is natural to think of (3b) as illustrating pattern (1): a chain cannot connect *how* and its trace in (3b) because another *wh*-element intervenes in the lower Spec of C.

In order to express the effect precisely, I will adopt the following principle (a simplification and updating of RM in Rizzi 1990):

(4) Y is in a Minimal Configuration (MC) with X iff
     there is no Z such that
     (i)   Z is of the same structural type as X, and
     (ii) Z intervenes between X and Y

So, if we think of Y as the position from which the relevant relation is computed, and X as the target of the computation (i.e., in the case of chain formation, the trace Y seeks for an antecedent X), the two elements are in a minimal configuration when there is no intervening element having certain structural characteristics in common with the target. A proper typology of positions is critical for the system to work; i.e., we must achieve the result that none of the intervening positions blocks the chain in the well-formed (2b), while at least one position does in (3b). The typology must involve at least two irreducible distinctions:

(5) (i)   between heads and phrases and, in the latter class,
     (ii) between positions of arguments (A′-positions) and of non-arguments
           (A′-positions).

Intervention could be defined hierarchically, in terms of c-command (Z c-commands one but not the other), but it could also be relativized to the kind of relation looked at (particularly if we want to extend the system to deal with locality in ellipsis, on which see below).

We can now define a chain through the notion of minimal configuration (4), as follows:

(6) $(A_1, \ldots, A_n)$ is a chain iff, for $1 \leq i < n$
     (i) $A_i = A_{i+1}$
     (ii) A_i c-commands A_{i+1}
     (iii) A_{i+1} is in a MC with A_i

So, each chain link involves identity (under the copy-theory of traces), c-command and Minimality.

Going back to (3b), chain formation between how and <how> fails because the two are not in a minimal configuration due to the intervention of *who*, an element of the same structural kind as *how*, an A′-specifier.

Notice that locality as expressed by (4) does not involve c-command. It seems to be the case that prominence (expressed by c-command) and locality (expressed by (4)) are two fundamental and independent configurational notions that natural languages use. Chains require both prominence and locality to hold, but other complex relations dissociate them. For instance, the possibility of interpreting a pronoun as a variable bound by a quantified expression requires c-command, hence (8) is out, but it is totally insensitive to locality, as in (7):

(7) a. *No candidate* can predict how many people will vote for *him*.
     b. *Every politician* is worried when the press starts attacking *him*.
     c. *Which politician* appointed the journalist who supported *him*?

(8) *The fact that *no candidate* was elected shows that *he* was inadequate.

The converse case may also exist: certain kinds of ellipsis seem to involve locality but not c-command. E.g., the gapped verb in (9) can be interpreted as identical to the local verb *buy*, not to the non-local verb *sell* (see Koster 1978 for relevant discussion):

(9) John sells books, Mary buys records and Bill V newspapers.

We have seen that chains involve both locality and c-command to hold. The fourth case may also exist: simple coreference requires neither:

(10) The question of whether *John* met Mary worries the people who support *him*.

Going back to chains, they divide into three fundamental kinds, depending on the nature of the displaced element and on the nature of the position it occupies. The first crucial distinction is between X chains and XP chains; then within the latter class, we want to distinguish at least between Argument chains (involved in passive, raising, and in fact any movement to subject position under the VP internal subject hypothesis, as well as object movement to various IP internal positions) and operator chains (involved in questions, relatives, exclamatives, focus movement, etc.). By and large, argument chains involve IP internal positions, while operator chains involve the CP system of the clause, the left periphery, even though the distinction is not absolute (see below). Different descriptive locality conditions hold of the three kinds of chain, head chains being by far the most local, and operator chains the most liberal. The system sketched out here is an attempt to subsume such descriptive conditions under a unified principle. We will now consider the different kinds of chain separately.

2   Head Chains

In general, heads cannot move across other heads: heads can be displaced over significant distances in the tree provided that they move through all the intervening head positions; as soon as one position is skipped, ill-formedness results. This is the Head Movement Constraint of Travis (1984). It is illustrated, for instance, by the fact that only the highest functional verb can move to C in English questions:

(11) a.   They have left.
      b.   Have they <have> left?

(12) a.   They could have left.
      b.   *Have they could <have> left?
      c.   Could they <could> have left?

or by the fact that lexical verbs, unable to reach I in Modern English (as in 13c), cannot be moved to C in interrogatives (as in 13d):

(13) a.   He has often   seen Mary.
      b.   He *I*   often sees Mary.
      c.   *He sees often <sees> Mary.
      d.   *Sees he *I*   often <sees> Mary?

In earlier phases of English, when movement of the lexical V to I was possible, the continuation of the movement to C was also allowed (Roberts 1993b).

Modern French allows (in fact, requires) movement of the lexical V to I (Pollock 1989), and the continuation of this movement to C in interrogatives:[1]

(14) a. Il   a   souvent vu   Marie.
           "He has often   seen Marie."
      b. Il   voit souvent <voit> Marie.
           "He sees often   Marie."
      c. Voit-il <voit> souvent <voit> Marie?
           "Sees he   often   Marie?"

Consider also the fact that in Italian gerundival (Rizzi 1982) and participial (Belletti 1981) clauses the non-finite verb moves to C; but the participle cannot move across the gerundival auxiliary:[2]

(15) a. Essendo Mario <essendo> tornato a Milano, . . .
           "Having Mario come back to Milan, . . ."
      b. Tornato Mario <tornato> a Milano, . . .
           "Come back Mario to Milan, . . ."
      c. *Tornato Mario essendo <tornato> a Milano . . .
           "Come back Mario having to Milan, . . ."

The same constraint is also illustrated by the fact that non-finite functional verbs in English can optionally move to the left of *not* (Pollock 1989), but can never cross the infinitive marker *to*:

(16) a. Not to be
      b. To not be
      c. To be not
      d. *Be to not
      e. *Be not to

Assuming that *to* can occupy at least two functional head positions, higher and lower than *not*, and the latter is the specifier of NegP, *be* can optionally move head to head across *not* (16c), but cannot cross *to*.

The impermeability of *to* to movement is only a special instance of the general fact that particle like elements in the inflectional system have the effect of blocking V-movement. For instance, in Creole languages, in which the inflectional field is typically realized by a rich system of particles designating tense, mood, and aspect, we never find V-movement to C in interrogatives and related constructions. For example, Haitian Creole does not involve movement of the verb to C in interrogatives, contrary to French, etc. Evidently, the particles do not enter into head movement to C, but their presence suffices to block head movement to C of some lower verbal element, as expected under RM. Of particular interest here is the case of mixed systems, pointed out by Guglielmo Cinque. Cinque (1999) observes that languages having both affixes and particles to express properties of the inflectional field may give rise to configurations like:

(17)   ... Aff ... Prt ... V ...

where a structurally higher property is expressed by a verbal affix and a lower property by a particle in the inflectional field. In such cases, the language never resolves the situation by having the V move to the affix by jumping across the particle; rather the language reverts to the insertion of an auxiliary in a position higher than the particle, a semantically empty verb capable of supporting the relevant affix. Evidently, a strong structural constraint is operative to block movement here, forcing the language to complicate the representation in order to achieve morphological well-formedness. A case in point discussed by Cinque is Welsh: tense and agreement suffixes are normally attached to a main verb, but if aspectual particles *wedi* (perfective) or *yn* (progressive) are present, the language reverts to an auxiliary verb (be) to carry tense and agreement suffixes:

(18)   a.   Cana   i yfory.
             sing-Fut-1Sg I tomorrow
             "I will sing tomorrow."
       b.   Bydda   i wedi canu erbyn saith o'r gloch.
             be-Fut-1Sg I Perf sing by   seven o'clock
             "I will have sung by seven o'clock."
       c.   Bydda   i 'n   canu yfory.
             be-Fut-1Sg I Prog sing tomorrow
             "I will be singing tomorrow."

All these cases straightforwardly follow from the assumption that chain links must satisfy RM, as formally expressed by our principles (4) and (6).

3   A-Chains

A subject raised to a higher subject position cannot skip an intervening subject position; the banned configuration has been called "Super Raising":

(19)   a.   It seems that it is likely that John will win.
       b.   It seems that John is likely t to win.
       c.   John seems t to be likely t to win.
       d.   *John seems that it is likely t to win.

One could think that the impossibility of (19d) is related to the impossibility of extracting the subject from the tensed clause:

(20)   *John seems (that) t will win.

If A-movement is triggered by Case, one could think that the DP simply moves to the closest case position, so it cannot move further from the embedded subject position in (20) and cannot skip the embedded subject position in (19d).

But in fact, the problem is more general: a pure Case approach is not plausible for cases of languages allowing raising out of tensed clauses, such as the dialect of Turkish discussed in Moore (1998). These languages clearly dissociate (19d) and (20):

(21) Biz   san-a   viski-yi   iç-ti-k   gibi gorun-du-k.
     We-Nom you-Dat whiskey-Acc drink-Past-1Pl like appear-Past-1Pl
     "We appeared to you (we) have drunk the whiskey."

(22) Cok viski   iç-ti   san-d1-n   gibi gorun-du-0
     Much whiskey drink-Past-1Sg believe-Past-2Sg like appear-Past-3Sg
     "It appears you believed I have drunk a lot of whiskey."

(23) *Cok viski   iç-ti   san-d1-n   gibi gorun-du-m
     Much whiskey drink-Past-1Sg believe-Past-2Sg like appear-Past-1Sg
     "I appear you believe (I) have drunk a lot of whiskey."

As raising is possible in this variety from the subject position of a finite clause, where the raised DP could receive Case (as in 21a), the locality effect shown by (21c) seems to be independent from attraction to the closest Case position. What this pattern suggests is that intervening subject positions of the kind involved in the satisfaction of the Extended Projection Principle (EPP) block any kind of A-chains, regardless of case considerations, as Moore points out.

This is also shown by the fact that intervening subjects also block A-chains not aiming at another (cased) subject position, but to a different kind of A-position. Consider for instance past participle agreement, triggered by a displaced object in French (e.g. in a *wh*-construction):

(24) Les voitures qu'il a t' conduites t
     "The cars that he has driven(FP)"

I will assume (following in essence Kayne 1989) that agreement is triggered by the passage of the displaced object through a specifier position of the relevant agreement head (t' in (24)). It has been observed (Kayne 1989a, Déprez 1989) that this agreement is local. For instance, in case of *wh*-extraction of the object, it cannot be triggered on the verb of the higher clause:

(25) Les voitures qu'il a dit(*es) qu'il a conduit(es)
     "The cars that he has said(FP) that he has driven(FP)"

The structure involving the higher agreement could have a representation like the following:

(26)　Les voitures qu'il a t''' dites (t'') qu'il a t' conduites t

(t, t') is a well-formed link of an A-chain, but (t', t''') is not: if t'' is present in the spec of some C-projection, the chain moves from an A-position to an A'-position back to an A-position, a case of improper movement. If t'' is not there, the link (t', t''') crosses a subject position, again a Super Raising violation. All these cases are excluded by RM for X, Z = A specifiers.[3]

4　A'-Chains: The Asymmetries

Huang (1982) observed that the effect shown in (3) is not fully homogeneous. While adverbial elements strongly resist *wh*-extraction from *wh*-islands, *wh*-arguments are at least marginally extractable, as is shown by near-minimal pairs like the following (only the relevant extraction trace is indicated):

(27)　a.　?Which problem do you wonder how to solve <which problem>?
　　　b.　*How do you wonder which problem to solve <how>?

So, while adverbs fully manifest the expected RM effects for A'-chains, arguments somehow manage to escape, at least in part. Since the mid-1980s, much work has been devoted to the exact structural characterization of the asymmetries, and to the identification of the class of "interveners" determining RM effects in A'-chains. Let us consider these two issues in turn.

If much work in the 1980s treated the contrast in (27) as an asymmetry between arguments and adverbs (or adjuncts), later it became clear that a more accurate characterization should set aside arguments from everything else. An instance of this wider generalization is offered by cases in which part of an argument can be moved out of the DP, apparently in free alternation with movement of the whole DP, as with *combien* extraction in French:

(28)　a.　Combien de problèmes sais-tu résoudre ____?
　　　　　"How many of problems can you solve?"
　　　b.　Combien sais-tu résoudre [____ de problèmes]?
　　　　　"How many can you solve of problems?"

Now, extraction of the whole direct object out of a *wh*-island is marginally acceptable, but extraction of *combien* alone is barred:

(29)　a.　?Combien de problèmes sais-tu comment résoudre ____?
　　　　　"How many of problems do you know how to solve?"
　　　b.　*Combien sais-tu comment résoudre [____ de problèmes]?
　　　　　"How many do you know how to solve of problems?"

So, here we have an asymmetry between an argument and a proper part of an argument, the latter resisting extraction. Moreover, if pied-piped arguments are marginally extractable from *wh*-islands, pied-piped predicates are not (Baltin 1992):

(30) a. How many people do you consider ____ intelligent?
　　 b. How intelligent do you consider John ____?

(31) a. ??How many people do you wonder whether I consider ____ intelligent?
　　 b. *How intelligent do you wonder whether I consider John ____?

In conclusion, the asymmetry appears to be between arguments and everything else: predicates, adverbs and proper subparts of arguments resist extraction from *wh*-islands.

An additional restriction, more subtle but clearly detectable in many cases, was then brought to light. It was observed that *wh*-arguments are optimally extractable only with a special interpretation, i.e., when the range of the variable is pre-established in discourse, or presupposed (Comorovski 1989, Cinque 1990b). This disourse-linked (D-linked: Pesetsky 1987) or presupposed interpretation is favored or forced by certain lexical choices for the *wh*-operator (e.g. by *which* in English), while certain types of *wh*-phrase like *what the hell*, *what on earth* are incompatible with it (Pesetsky's "aggressively non-D-linked" *wh*-expressions), whence such contrasts as:

(32) a. ?Which problem do you wonder how to solve ____?
　　 b. *What the hell do you wonder how to say ____?

The necessity of a pre-established range emerges with clarity also in the interpretation of other *wh*-operators. Consider the following contrast in Italian (and see Frampton 1991 for the discussion of similar pairs in English):

(33) a. ?Quanti problemi non sai come risolvere ____?
　　　 "How many problems don't you know how to solve?"
　　 b. *Quanti soldi non sai come guadagnare ____?
　　　 "How much money don't you know how to make?"

While it is natural to assume that there may be a known set of problems of which (33a) can be asked, in general (33b) will not be asked about a known set of objects (say, sums of money pre-established in discourse). On the other hand, even sentences like (33b) can improve if the partitive form of the interrogative DP is used, explicitly stating that the question bears on a specific sum of money:

(34) ?Quanti dei soldi che ti servono non sai come guadagnare ____?
　　 "How much of the money that you need don't you know how to make?"

In conclusion, *wh*-extraction from a *wh*-clause is generally barred, as expected under RM. A systematic exception involves D-linked argumental *wh*-phrases, which are marginally extractable. In order to accommodate the exception, it was proposed in Rizzi (1990) that such *wh*-phrases can be related to their traces through a mechanism different from ordinary chain formation as expressed by (6), and as such are not submitted to locality. As the theory must admit a way to relate positions non-locally in order to accommodate long distance binding of a pronoun by a quantified expression (see (7) and the related discussion), the proposal was made that D-linked argumental *wh*-phrases can exploit such a mechanism to be related long distance to their traces. This idea was implemented in Cinque (1990b) and Rizzi (1990) by assuming that only D-linked and argumental (theta-marked) *wh*-phrases could bear (and share with their traces) a referential index capable of ensuring the antecedent–trace connection non-locally. Much of the discussion on this approach was centered on the legitimacy and appropriateness of using referential indices as a technical device to permit long distance dependencies (see Frampton 1991 for a critical discussion, Chomsky 1995b on the possibility of dispensing with indices, and Manzini 1992 for a different view on the asymmetries).

Here I would like to suggest a different implementation, which does not resort to indices and fully exploits the analogy with (7).[4] Let me first introduce a mechanism to deal with the latter case and, in general, with long distance binding of pronouns from quantified expressions. Following fairly standard assumptions, I will assume that binding holds when the following conditions are met:

(35)   A binds B iff:
    (i)   A and B are non-distinct DPs, and
    (ii)   A c-commands B.

It is natural to restrict binding to DPs (possibly to DPs and CPs), the only categories that can enter into referential dependencies. Featural non-distinctness is needed to ensure feature matching between the binder and the bindee (here we cannot require the stronger condition of full structural identity as in (6i): a bound pronoun is not identical to its binder); and c-command must hold (cf. (8)).

Now, suppose that (35) is the grammatical device that can be used as an alternative to "being in a minimal configuration" in chain formation (condition (6iii)). Given the fact that (35) is restricted to DPs, the non-local mechanism is not available with *wh*-dependencies involving adjuncts (27b), predicates (31b), or parts of DPs (29b). What about non-D-linked *wh*-DPs? Following Frampton (1991) I will assume that in such cases "reconstruction" must apply, leaving the bare *wh*-operator in the left periphery, and reconstructing the rest of the DP in situ. If we adopt the core idea of the theory of reconstruction in Chomsky (1995b), exploiting the copy theory of traces, S-structure (36a) is thus converted into LF (36b) by deleting the non-operator material from the left periphery (an operation which automatically triggers the consequence that the lexical restriction is "exported" from the trace in (36b), if the trace is understood as an identical copy of the antecedent):

(36) a. Quanti soldi non sai come guadagnare <quanti soldi>
     b. Quanti ____ non sai come guadagnare <quanti> soldi

Therefore, at LF the *wh*-dependency in the non-D-linked interpretation is not a DP dependency, but a bare QP dependency, so that mechanism (35) is not available, locality must be met in the strict form of (6iii), and (36b) is correctly ruled out. Following again Frampton (1991) and Chomsky (1995b), we can account for the obligatoriness of reconstruction here by assuming that the principle of Full Interpretation is strong enough to enforce it: the lexical restriction is not licensed by a left-peripheral mechanism in (36), so it must delete in the syntax of LF.

Now, what about D-linked *wh*-phrases, e.g. in (33a)? Following the logic of the argument, the lexical restriction in D-linked *wh*-elements must be allowed to stay in the left periphery at LF, in order to permit a non-local DP dependency to be established through (35). Why is this legitimate? I continue to assume that D-linked means "pre-established in discourse," hence topic like; of course, topic interpretation licenses elements in the left periphery (e.g. through the formal device discussed in Rizzi 1997), so we can think that the lexical restriction can remain in the left periphery as it is licensed *qua* topic at LF.

In conclusion, the selective sensitivity to *wh*-islands can be reduced to the formal distinction between DP and non-DP dependencies at LF. Among the *wh*-dependencies, only D-linked phrases allow DP dependencies at LF, which can exploit the non-local connecting device (35), and survive across a *wh*-island. Adjunct, predicative, and bare *wh*- (extracted from DP) dependencies are not DP dependencies, so they must obey RM; non-D-linked *wh*-dependencies like (36) are DP dependencies at S-structure, but not at LF, the level where RM applies, so that they are expected to obey strict locality under this approach.[5, 6]

5 A'-Chains: The Interveners

It was observed in the early 1990s that the class of possible interveners triggering minimality effects is not coextensive with the class of target positions, but significantly wider. For instance, asymmetries of the kind illustrated by (29) are also determined by an intervening negation:

(37) a. Combien de problèmes ne sais-tu pas résoudre ____?
        "How many of problems can't you solve?"
     b. *Combien ne sais-tu pas résoudre [____ de problèmes]?
        "How many can't you solve of problems?"

This is a particular case of the selective islands induced by negation, which non-arguments are generally sensitive to (Ross 1983 and, for recent critical discussion, Szabolcsi and Zwarts 1997, Kuno and Takami 1997, and the references cited there).

Certain kinds of quantificational adverb expressing the frequency of an action, or the intensity of a state, determine similar asymmetries in French (Obenauer 1983, 1994):

(38) a. Combien de livres a-t-il beaucoup consultés ____?
          "How many of books has he a lot consulted?"
      b. *Combien a-t-il beaucoup consulté ____ de livres?
          "How many has he a lot consulted of books?"
      c. Combien de films a-t-elle peu aimés ____
          "How many films did she little like?"
      d. *Combien a-t-elle peu aimé [____ de films]?
          "How many did she little like of films?"

Given the width of the blocking effects, it seemed natural to define the structural typology relevant for RM in a very broad way. As *wh*, negation, and quantificational adverbs like *beaucoup, peu, souvent*, etc. plausibly have in common the fact of occupying an A'-specifier position, the formulation of the principle in Rizzi (1990) referred to the sole distinction between A- and A'-specifiers to express the typology of elements triggering minimality effects at the XP level.

On the other hand, the plausibility of such a purely geometric approach was immediately threatened by the observation that non-quantificational adverbs do not induce a similar Minimality effect (Obenauer 1983, 1994, Laenzlinger 1996): compare (36) with the following:

(39) a. Combien de livres a-t-il attentivement consultés ____?
          "How many of books did he carefully consult?"
      b. Combien a-t-il attentivement consulté [____ de livres]?
          "How many did he carefully consult of books?"

Now, it appears unlikely that the position of a non-quantificational adverb like *attentivement* differs enough in tree geometry from the position of *beaucoup, peu*, etc. to allow us to maintain a purely geometric approach. This is even more so in view of recent advances on the study of adverbial positions *qua* specifiers of particular functional heads (Cinque 1999, Laenzlinger 1996) and on the opportunity of eliminating the distinction between specifier and adjoined position (Kayne 1994). If these approaches are on the right track, then the theory of phrase structure has no resources to differentiate the position of these adverbs uniquely in terms of configurations.

Clearly, a more selective characterization of the Minimality inducing factor is needed. An extremely selective characterization is in fact provided in the reinterpretation of RM effects in Chomsky (1995b). According to Chomsky, movement is triggered by feature attraction: a head endowed with a certain feature attracts a phrase bearing the same specification to its immediate structural domain (say, in traditional X-bar terminology, to occupy its specifier position). This attract operation is phrased in such a way that only the closest "attractee" can move:

(40)   **Minimal Link Condition:**
        K attracts a only if there is no b, b closer to K than a, such that K attracts b. (Chomsky 1995b: 311)

(40) differs from (4) in two major respects. First, it is a principle that operates on derivations, not a well-formedness condition on representations, so it requires one to take the "movement metaphor" literally, whereas (4) does not. Moreover, it makes the Minimality effect sensitive to identity of features; i.e., in the derivation of (41) the higher C endowed with the *wh*-feature (element K in (40)) fails to attract the *wh*-phrase *how* from the embedded clause due to the intervention of a closer attractee, the *wh*-phrase in the embedded Spec of C:

(41)   C you wonder [which problem C [to solve how]]

Here I will not address the important distinction between derivational and representational approaches to locality (but see n. 6), and will focus on the different selectivity of the two approaches. It is clear that (40) suffers from the opposite problem with respect to (4): it is too selective to account for cases of Minimality such as (37b) and (38b–d), in which the intervener bears a feature different (formally and interpretively) from the one of the attractor. If we want to maintain that a genuine generalization underlies (29b) and these other examples we cannot adopt this approach to RM effects.[7]

What seems to be needed is an intermediate position between the geometric approach and the one based on identity of features. Features determining chain formation seem to cluster into natural classes, such that Minimality effects are determined within classes, but not across them.

6   Classes of Features

In accordance with much current work, I will assume that specifiers must be licensed by the sharing of certain features with the respective heads. One can think of this licensing as a special need that certain features have (they must be "checked" in a local environment, as in Chomsky's 1995b system), or a subcase of head-XP selection, mutual selection with respect to certain formal features. In this family of approaches, it is natural to assume that the typology of specifier positions is determined by the licensing features. So, the typology of positions reduces to the clustering of features into natural classes.

What question and negative elements have in common with adverbs like *beaucoup, peu, souvent* is their quantificational character (Rizzi 1990, Laenzlinger 1996). As in the core case A'-positions are scope positions of quantificational elements, one could think of restricting minimality effects in the A'-system to such scope positions, thus correctly excluding cases like (39b) from the domain of the principle. On the other hand, one cannot simply exclude non-quantificational adverbs from RM effects without further qualifications: intervening adverbs of all kinds generally determine a Minimality effect on certain kinds of adverb movement, a fact often pointed out in the relevant literature (now reviewed in detail in Cinque 1999, a study on which the following discussion is based). For instance, Koster (1978) observed that, given the hierarchy of adverbs in IP internal position in Dutch, shown by the relative order in the embedded clause (42a) (vs. the ill-formedness of (42b)), the lower epistemic adverb "probably" cannot be moved in a V-2 construction across the higher evaluative adverb "unfortunately," as in (43b); if no other adverb intervenes, the epistemic adverb can be moved to the first position in V-2, as in (43c):[8]

(42) a. Het is zo dat hij helaas waarschijnlijk ziek is.
          "It is so that he unfortunately probably sick is."
      b. *Het is zo dat hij waarschijnlijk helaas ziek is.
          "It is so that he probably unfortunately sick is."

(43) a. Helaas is hij ____ waarschijnlijk ziek.
          "Unfortunately is he probably sick."
      b. *Waarschijnlijk is hij helaas ____ ziek.
          "Probably is he unfortunately sick."
      c. Waarschijnlijk is hij ____ ziek.
          "Probably is he sick."

This preservation of the ordering under movement is clearly reminiscent of RM (and in fact it is explained by a very similar principle in Koster's account, as Cinque points out).

We observe the same effect with adverb preposing in Italian, except that, of course, preposing does not trigger V-2 in this language: a lower adverb like *rapidamente* can be fronted to pre-IP position, as in (44a), but not across a higher epistemic adverb, as in (44c):

(44) a. I tecnici hanno (probabilmente) risolto rapidamente il problema.
          "The technicians have probably resolved rapidly the problem."
      b. Rapidamente, i tecnici hanno risolto ____ il problema.
          "Rapidly, the technicians have resolved the problem."
      c. *Rapidamente, i tecnici hanno probabilmente risolto ____ il problema.
          "Rapidly, the technicians have probably resolved the problem."

On the other hand, it is not the case that movement of an adverb across another adverb is barred in general. The Minimality effect is observed when the landing site is another adverbial position. If the landing site is different in nature, the Minimality effect may not arise. This is clearly shown by a contrast observed in French by Schlyter (1974) and mentioned in Cinque (1999): simple fronting of a lower adverb across *probablement* is banned, as in the Italian example (see (45b)), but focalization of the lower adverb in a cleft construction across the higher adverb is fine (see (45c)):

(45) a. Il a probablement travaillé énergiquement.
          "He has probably worked energetically."
      b. *Energiquement, il a probablement travaillé.
          "Energetically, he has probably worked."
      c. C'est énergiquement qu'il a probablement travaillé.
          "It is energetically that he has probably worked."

The same effect is found in Italian: (44c) clearly improves if the adverb is focalized:

(46) RAPIDAMENTE i tecnici hanno probabilmente risolto il problema (non lentamente).
      "RAPIDLY the technicians have probably solved the problem (not slowly)."

Cinque quotes an observation by Moltmann to the effect that a preposed adverb can cross a higher adverb in a V-2 construction if the adverb is focused, as in the following German example:

(47) SEHR OFT hat Karl Marie wahrscheinlich gesehen
      "VERY OFTEN has Karl Marie probably seen"

In conclusion, the descriptive statement capturing RM effects with adverbs is quite complex. *Wh*-movement of elements different from D-linked arguments is sensitive to the intervention of *wh*, negation, and quantificational adverbs, but not of non-quantificational adverbs. Adverb movement on the other hand is sensitive to the intervention of any adverb, quantificational or not; but if the moved adverb targets a position different from an adverbial position, say a focus position, then intervening adverbs determine no blocking effect.

In the spirit of the licensing approach mentioned above, adverb positions typically sit in specifier positions of heads possessing certain licensing features. I will call such features "modifier features," and adopt the hierarchy of the relevant heads arrived at in Cinque (1999): evaluative adverbs like *unfortunately* occupy the specifier position of a higher head than epistemic adverbs like *probably*, which in turn are higher than amount/frequency adverbs, manner adverbs, etc. Moreover, adverbs may be moved from the IP system to the CP system in cases like (43a–c), (44b), etc. Following Haegeman (1998) I will assume that in such cases the initial adverb "sets the scene" for the following proposition (see also Cinque (1999) on this notion); technically, this can be expressed through the assumption that adverb movement targets the specifier of a modifier head in the CP system where the adverb is interpreted as setting the scene for the event expressed by the following IP.[9]

Now, some modifier features such as amount, extent, frequency, etc. are quantificational features, too, so the Spec positions occupied by adverbs of amount, frequency, etc. have the dual status of modifier and quantificational positions. We end up with (at least) the following two classes of specifier-licensing features in the A'-system:

(48)   Quantificational: *wh*, Neg, amount/frequency, . . .

(49)   Modifier: evaluative, epistemic, amount/frequency, manner, . . .

The crucial step now is to assume that RM only holds within classes of feature, but not across them. So, the quantificational amount/frequency adverb *beaucoup* will determine a Minimality effect on the quantificational chain aiming at a *wh*-position in (38b), while the pure modifier manner adverb *attentivement* will have no effect on the *wh*-chain in (39b). On the other hand, the chains involved in adverb movement in (43b) and (44c), aiming at a modifier position (the "scene setting position" in the CP system), will undergo Minimality effects triggered from any modifier position, i.e., any intervening adverbial position, no matter whether quantificational or not.[10]

Concerning the observed improvement under focus movement, the adverb clearly does not aim at a modifier position in (45c), (46), and (47), but at a focus position, identified by a focus feature distinct from modifier features. The minimality effect is then correctly excluded (we will not take a position here on whether focus belongs to the class of quantificational features or uniquely to another subclass of discourse-related or pragmatic A'-features).

7   Local Actions on Phrases by Heads

In this final section, I will try to show that the scope of our locality principle (4) is not limited to chain formation: it also constrains the local actions that heads can perform on neighboring phrases. Consider a simple syntactic action that a head can be responsible for, such as the licensing of a case feature on a DP. Even if we do not consider the possibility of LF checking (Chomsky 1995b) and just look at surface environments, case licensing remains possible in a small class of local configurations. A head is capable of licensing a case feature on its specifier (50), on its complement (51), and on the specifier of its complement (52):

(50) a. [He has left]
 b. [His book] is nice

(51) a. Bill [saw him]
 b. Bill works [with him]

(52) a. John [believes [him to be a nice guy]]
 b. John [considers [him a nice guy]]
 c. [For [him to do that]] would be a mistake
 d. [With [him sick]], the team is in trouble

but not on the specifier of a higher head or on the complement of a complement. Consider first the specifier of a higher head:

(53) a. *[A man to [be t in the garden]] is unlikely
 b. *[A man to [come t]] is unlikely
 c. *[John to [call]] would be unlikely
 d. *[This conclusion to be arrived [at t]] is surprising
 (meaning: That this conclusion will be arrived at is surprising)

In (53a, b, c) the verb is unable to assign whatever case feature it possesses (possibly partitive in a, b: Belletti 1988, Lasnik 1992, as in *There is a man in the garden. There came a man*, and accusative in c, as in *John called Bill*) to the DP moved to the specifier of I to satisfy the EPP. More generally, a verb does not determine the case of its subject in VP-external position, which is determined by the properties of the inflectional system; an apparent exception is the case of quirky subjects, but quirky case is plausibly assigned in VP-internal position and then licensed in the inflectional system in a position of structural case assignment. In (53d) the preposition *at* cannot assign case to a DP moved out of its projection.

The following cases illustrate the fact that a head cannot license the case on the complement of a complement:

(54) a. John discussed [(about) it]
 b. John believes [that he/*him is sick]
 c. *John tries [C him to win]
 d. *John wonders [where C him to go]

In (54a) when the preposition is present the verb cannot determine the case on the prepositional object; the preposition does (as is shown by languages in which verbs and prepositions assign morphologically distinct cases). A higher verb cannot determine the case of a lower IP specifier across an intervening C layer, so that the embedded subject in such configurations can only receive whatever case I assigns (nominative in (54b), none or null case (Chomsky and Lasnik's chapter in Chomsky 1995b) in (54c–d)). In general, a higher verb can never license a case on the embedded subject if an (overt or covert) C intervenes.

The following scheme summarizes the possible surface configurations in which a head can perform case-licensing actions (aP, bP, etc. = arbitrary phrases):

(55)

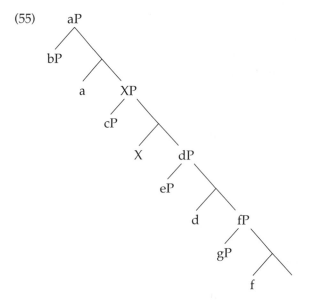

X can license case on its specifier cP, on its complement dP and on the specifier of its complement eP, but not on the specifier of the head selecting its maximal projection bP or on the complement of its complement fP or on the specifier of the complement of its complement gP, etc. This state of affairs suggests a simple formal generalization: a head cannot license a case across an intervening head, either upward or downward. In fact, in (55) a intervenes between X and bP, d intervenes between X and fP, gP, etc., but no other head intervenes between X and cP, dP, eP. Of course, this is the generalization we expect to hold, if case licensing is constrained by RM. In order to achieve this result formally, some ingenuity is needed, as the case licensing head is sometimes lower and sometimes higher than the DP.

We can reason in the following way: case-licensing procedures typically involve minimal c-command, that is to say the conjunction of c-command and Minimality, along the following lines:

(56) Case Feature K is licensed on (X, YP) only if YP is in a MC with X and X
      c-commands/is c-commanded by YP.

(56) states that the minimal configuration, as defined in (4), is always computed from the phrase YP, which is looking for the case-licensing head X, so that any intervening head in the path from the phrase to the head (either upward or downward) will induce a Minimality effect, as desired. On the other hand, the

required direction of c-command between the two elements may be flipped around depending on the specific case feature licensed. Some cases require that the head minimally c-commands the phrase: objective case in many languages, the case assigned by prepositions, case-assigning complementizers, etc. Other cases require that the phrase minimally c-commands the licensing head: nominative case in many languages, accusative under object shift and, in general, OV order, the case assigned by postpositions, genitive in languages like English, etc. Following traditional terminology, we may continue to call "agreement" the configuration in which the phrase minimally c-commands the head, and "government" the configuration in which the head minimally c-commands the phrase, but this terminology should not obscure the fact that these two configurations are not primitive theoretical entities: they are made of the same elementary ingredients, minimality and c-command, and differentiated by the simple flipping around of the direction of the c-command relation. So, the direction of c-command is a simple parameter differentiating, e.g., accusative assignment in English and in OV languages, etc.[11]

This approach naturally extends to the licensing action of heads on traces. Consider a standard subject object asymmetry like the following:

(57) a. Who do you think that Bill likes t?
      b. Who do you think that Bill believes t to be innocent?
      c. *Who do you think that t believes John to be innocent?
      d. *Who would you prefer for t to win the race?

(57a–b) illustrate the fact that a verb provides an adequate licensing environment for a trace (in a head-complement or head/specifier-of-the-complement environment), a fact that various versions of the Empty Category Principle have attempted to capture. (57c–d) show that a complementizer (of this sort) does not license a trace; moreover, the higher verbs *think*, *prefer* evidently are too far away from t to have any beneficial effect on it. Similarly, a raising trace is well formed in Italian in a local environment with the raising verb (58a), but not if the infinitival complementizer *di* intervenes (*di* is possible with *seem* in the control construction (58c): see Kayne 1984: ch. 5, Rizzi 1982: ch. 3):

(58) a. Gianni sembra t essere stanco.
          "John seems t to be tired."
      b. *Gianni sembra di t essere stanco.
          "John seems 'di' t to be tired."
      c. Mi sembra di PRO essere stanco.
          "It seems to me 'di' PRO to be tired."

So there seems to be a licensing requirement on traces such that they must be minimally c-commanded by a head of a certain kind, i.e., a V counts and a C normally does not (but it may in special circumstances, e.g. through the mechanism illustrated in Rizzi 1990). Again, c-command must be minimal in that another head cannot intervene between the licensing head and the licensed trace:[12]

(59)   X licenses t only if X c-commands t in a LC.

It is worth noticing, as a concluding remark, that from the perspective developed here the possibility of a direct relation between a head and the specifier of its complement naturally falls out without the need to stipulate an independent government relation: this possibility is generated by the simple composition of the elementary relations of c-command and Minimality, and there is no conceptual gain in trying to rule it out. So, in a sense, this system meets the desideratum expressed in Chomsky (1995b) of eliminating head government from the inventory of primitive structural relations, while at the same time preserving the option of a direct action of a head on the specifier of its complement, a possibility which receives strong empirical support from considerations of case licensing and trace licensing.

NOTES

1   Mainland Scandinavian Languages disallow the equivalent of (13c) (in non V-2 environments) and still permit (13d): evidently in these languages, contrary to Modern English, there is no absolute ban against moving lexical verbs to I, but only a blocking due to other derivational possibilities, say through Chomsky's (1995b) principle Procrastinate. When no other possibilities exist, e.g. in questions, nothing blocks movement of the lexical verb to C via I. In Modern English, on the other hand, I is specialized for functional verbs (a fact which may in turn be related to the existence of a special class of functional verbs, the modals), hence it disallows movement of the lexical verb, direct movement of the latter to C being banned by the Head Movement Constraint, subsumed under RM.

2   In fairy-tale registers of Italian we have structures with preposed participles across the finite inflectional system:

(i)   Tornato che fu a Milano, . . .
      "Come back that he was to
      Milan, . . ."

But this construction is more akin to remnant VP topicalization in Germanic (den Besten and Webelhuth 1989) than to genuine head movement, as is suggested by the fact that the participle appears in an XP position, to the left of the C *che*, and also by the fact that pied-piping of the verbal complement is only somewhat cumbersome, not categorically excluded:

(ii) ?Tornato a Milano che fu, . . .
      "Come back to Milan that he
      was, . . ."

I suspect that cases of so-called "long head-movement" to the left periphery often reported in the literature could be analyzed as more or less disguised instances of remnant VP topicalization.

3 I will not address here the problems raised by the postulation of Spec Agr positions higher than the basic position of the subject and to which the object moves for case or other reasons. Clearly, a version of RM simply referring to A-positions is insufficient for such cases. See Chomsky (1995b), Bobaljik and Jonas (1996), Collins and Thráinsson (1993), Haegeman (1993b), and the references cited there for different technical solutions which are expressible into the representational approach adopted here.

4 The analogy is only partial. Both D-linked A'-chains and pronominal binding by quantified expressions are insensitive to "weak islands" (intervention of *wh*, negation, quantificational adverbs, etc.); on the other hand, D-linked A'-chains are sensitive to strong islands (extraction out of a relative, and other complex DPs, etc.) while pronominal binding is not. I will continue to assume that all chains (including D-linked A'-chains) are submitted to an independent bounding principle, Subjacency, which is responsible for strong island effects; this principle is not operative on non-chain dependencies such as pronominal binding.

5 Argumental *wh*-PPs generally allow extraction from *wh*-islands; so either we extend (35) to PPs, or we assume that reconstruction can always put the preposition back in situ, thus transforming the PP dependency into a DP dependency at LF.

6 Notice that if this argument is correct, we have evidence for a representational approach to locality with RM applying at LF: a derivational variant of RM applying

on the attract operation would not naturally draw the distinction between (33a) and (33b), and, in general, between D-linked and non D-linked *wh*-DPs, because *wh*-attraction to the higher C involves the whole DP in both cases.

7 Consider also, in this respect, the argument given in connection with (17) and related facts: even if the particle is not attracted by the affix (or by some other functional head, like a *wh*-C) its presence suffices to block movement of V. In general, an approach based on the attraction of a specific feature seems to be too selective to account for the fact that a moving head can almost never skip an intervening head (i.e., the Head Movement Constraint holds very generally, with extremely limited exceptions): this approach predicts free movement of a head across a head not marked for the relevant attracting feature:

(i) $X_{+F} \ldots X_{-F} \ldots X_{+F} \ldots$

a freedom which is not empirically supported.

8 The same effects are found in German, according to Bartsch (1976: 229), as reported in Cinque (1999):

(i) Wahrscheinlich kommt Peter oft
     "Probably comes Peter often"

(ii) *Oft kommt Peter wahrscheinlich
      "Often comes Peter probably"

9 Here I differ from Rizzi (1997) where adverb preposing was analyzed, in essence, as a subcase of topicalization. See Haegeman (1998) for arguments in favor of a structural distinction between argument topicalization and adverb preposing.

10 It has been observed that certain quantified DPs such as *everyone*,

someone, etc. differ from those in (48) in that they do not determine Minimality effects. Without going into the scopal properties of such DPs here, I will simply assume that their LF representations are different enough from those of (48) to allow a structural distinction to be drawn (without necessarily relying on the Specifier/adjunction distinction as in Rizzi 1990).

11   If theta-marking involves spec-head and head-complement relations, and cannot involve head/spec-of-the-complement relations (which is not obvious: Rizzi 1992b), this may be due to the fact that theta-marking involves some kind of binding of theta-slots in the grid associated to the theta-assigner (Stowell 1981), so that c-command from the assignee is demanded. If this view is correct, a head could not theta-mark the specifier of its complement because the latter would be unable to bind the appropriate slot in the theta-marker's grid.

12   In the spec-head relation and in the head/spec-of-the-complement relation asymmetric c-command holds (from the phrase and from the head, respectively), whereas heads and complements symmetrically c-command each other. Does this have adverse consequences? The issue may arise e.g. for the licensing of past participle agreement in French, not possible in situ but possible when the object moves:

(i)   a.   J'ai mis(*e) la voiture dans le garage
           "I have put the car in the garage"
      b.   Je l'ai mise dans le garage
           "I have put it in the garage"

If this instance of Agr requires minimal c-command by the phrase, why is this requirement not satisfied by the object in its in situ position? But notice that under current assumptions this agreement specification is not licensed in the VP, but on a higher autonomous X-bar subtree headed by an Agr node. So, in (ia) the object is not in a position to license Agr, and the problem does not arise (see Belletti, this volume, and references cited there).

Is there any genuine case of Agr licensing under minimal c-command by the complement? Our approach may lead us to expect it. One reasonable candidate may be C-agreement in Germanic (Haegeman 1992), which could then be analyzed as involving direct agreement from C to IP rather than LF (feature) movement of the subject to C. Perhaps also the pervasive agreement phenomena within the Romance DP (*I suoi molti bei libri* = The+MP his+MP many+MP beautiful+MP books+MP), not easily amenable to spec-head configurations, may be analyzed in this way.

II Movement

5 Head Movement

IAN ROBERTS

0 Introduction

Head movement is the case of Move-α where the value of α is X°. As a case of Move-α, standard conditions on movement apply to it. These include locality, structure preservation, and the requirement that movement leave a well-formed trace. The principal locality condition on head movement is the Head Movement Constraint (HMC), originally proposed by Travis (1984) and given informally in (1):

(1) Head movement of X to Y cannot "skip" an intervening head Z.

In section 4 I discuss the theoretical status of (1) in detail. Its empirical consequences will be illustrated in sections 1, 2, and 3. The structure preservation requirement on head movement has the consequence that the landing site of head movement must always be another head.[1] Typically (notably in Baker 1988), head movement is taken to be adjunction of the moved head X° to the target head Y°; Kayne (1991, 1994) proposes that this must always be left-adjunction. Finally, head movement must leave a well-formed trace. Since a major well-formedness condition on traces is that they must be c-commanded by their antecedents, this forces head movement always to take place in an upward direction, where "upward" is understood as defined by c-command (some possible exceptions to this idea will be briefly discussed in section 2).

Taking these conditions together, we arrive at the following general schema for head movement of X° to Y°:

(2)

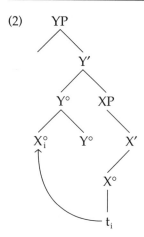

Applied to this configuration, the HMC bans movement of $X°$ directly to a head $Z°$ which asymmetrically c-commands $Y°$ (i.e., in the simplest case, which takes YP as its complement). However, since, like other kinds of movement, head movement can be iterated, $X°$ can move to $Z°$ if $Y°$ containing $X°$ moves to $Z°$. We will see a number of concrete examples of such iterated head movement below.

The principal cases of head movement which have been discussed in the literature are instances of verb movement, i.e., cases where the moved $X°$ is a verb, and the target of movement is a position in the clausal functional structure. Such movement is frequently iterated through the functional structure, a canonical example being verb movement in verb-second clauses in the Germanic languages. Such cases were first discussed in the context of a theory of head movement in Travis (1984) (although they are discussed under rather different theoretical assumptions in Williams 1974, Emonds 1976, and den Besten 1975, 1983). Assuming that the functional structure of the clause comprises CP and IP, the structure of a simple V2 clause like (3a) in Danish, for example, would be (3b) in Travis's system (see Koopman 1984, Vikner 1994a):

(3)   a.   Kaffe   drikker Peter aldrig.
         Coffee drinks   Peter never
         "Peter never drinks coffee."

b.

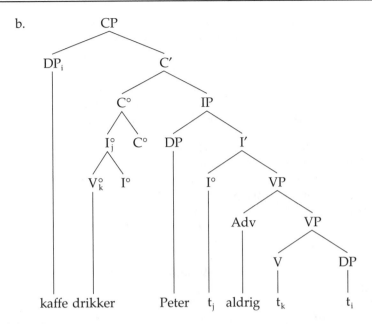

We look at Verb Second in section 2.2. Travis's theory of head movement was developed and applied to a wide range of cases, in conjunction with Case theory deriving many instances of grammatical function changing phenomena, in Baker (1988). In section 1 I summarize the main points of Baker's theory. A further area where assuming head movement has yielded interesting results is within DP; section 3 is devoted to this. Finally, as mentioned above, section 4 discusses the place of head movement in the general theory of locality.

1   Baker's (1988) Theory of Incorporation

Arguably the most influential work on head movement was Baker (1988). Baker uses head movement to derive morphologically complex words from more basic elements (roots, stems, or affixes). Baker analyses noun-incorporation (N-to-V movement), applicative constructions (P-to-V movement), causatives (V-to-V movement), and passives (V-to-PASS movement) in terms of head movement. Examples and schemata of the relevant parts of the structure are given in (4)–(7):

(4)   **Noun incorporation** (Mohawk: Baker 1988: 81–3):
　　a.　Yao-wir-aʔa ye-　　　nuhweʔ-s ne ka-**nuhs**-aʔ.
　　　　Pre-baby-Suf 3SgF/3N-like-Asp   the Pre-house-Suf
　　　　"The baby likes the house."
　　b.　Yao-wir-aʔa ye-　　　**nuhs**-nuhweʔ-s ʔ.
　　　　Pre-baby-Suf 3SgF/3N-house-like-Asp
　　　　"The baby likes the house."

(5) **Applicatives** (Chichewa: Baker 1988: 229ff):
   a. Ndi-na-tumiz-a   chipanda cha mowa kwa mfumu.
       1SgSubj-Past-send-Asp calabash of beer   to   chief
       "I sent a calabash of beer to the chief."
   b. Ndi-na-tumiz-ir-a   [$_{PP}$ t$_{ir}$ mfumu] chipanda cha mowa.
       1SgSubj-Past-send-to-Asp chief   calabash of   beer
       "I sent a calabash of beer to the chief."

(6) **Causatives** (Chichewa: Baker 1988: 148–9):
   a. Mtsikana ana-chit-its-a   kuti mtsuko   u-gw-e.
       girl   Agr-do-make-Asp that waterpot Agr-fall-Asp
       "The girl made the waterpot fall."
   b. Mtsikana anau-gw-ets-a [$_{VP}$ t$_{gw-}$ mtsuko].
       girl   Agr-fall-make-Asp   waterpot
       "The girl made the waterpot fall."

(7) **Passives** (English: Baker 1988: 307–9; see also Baker et al. 1989):
   a. Someone stole my car.
   b. My car was stolen.
   c.

A central aspect of Baker's theory is that the complex head retains or inherits certain properties of the incorporated head in derived structures like those in (4b)–(7b). The relevant principle is the Government Transparency Corollary (GTC):

(8) An Y° which has an X° incorporated into it governs everything which X° governed in its original structural position.

The GTC has the effect that incorporation may "extend" government domains. From it, Baker is able to derive many of the effects of what in other theories are seen as grammatical function changing processes. Take, for example, applicative constructions. It is well known that in examples like (5b) the "applied object" (the DP which is the complement of the Preposition in the non-applied (5a) and which, on Baker's analysis, is the object of the incorporated Preposition) has all the canonical properties of a direct object: in Chichewa, it may be "pro-dropped," be passivized, and trigger object agreement. Baker argues that these properties result from the fact that, after P-to-V incorporation, this DP is governed by V. Direct object properties can be derived from government by V, and hence the applied object takes on direct object properties. In this way, Baker's theory of incorporation, and notably the GTC, go a very long way toward providing a fully configurational theory of grammatical function changing operations.

Another important aspect of Baker's theory is that he takes head movement to leave a trace subject, like all other traces in Government Binding theory, to the Empty Category Principle (ECP). The ECP states that all traces must be both head governed and antecedent governed. The head government require-ment means that the trace of head movement must be inside the immediate X′ complement of the head targeted by movement; in other words, where X° moves to Y° in (2) XP must be the structural complement of Y. Antecedent government amounts to Relativized Minimality (see Rizzi, this volume), and, in the case of head movement, effectively derives the Head Movement Con-straint – see section 4.

In addition to deriving the Head Movement Constraint, subjecting the trace of head movement to the ECP has three consequences: (i) it explains why head movement is impossible from subjects and adjuncts; (ii) it accounts for the impossibility of downgrading heads; (iii) "excorporation" is banned. We now consider these consequences one by one.

The head government part of the ECP rules out the possibility of head movement from a non-complement category. Thus the heads of subjects and adjuncts cannot be moved to other heads without the ensuing trace violating the ECP. Schematically, then, cases like the following are ruled out by the ECP in Baker's system:

(9) a. **Incorporation from a subject:**

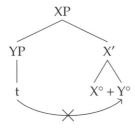

b. **Incorporation from an adjunct:**

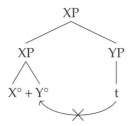

Baker shows in detail that there are indeed no cases of noun incorporation, causative formation, or applicative formation which move the head of a subject or adjunct to another head position. This is a significant result, and one which follows naturally from the theory of head movement combined with a well-formedness condition on traces such as the ECP.

Second, as mentioned in the introduction, downgrading to a non-c-commanding head is ruled out. The ECP prevents this since c-command is a necessary condition for both antecedent government and head government. Downgrading is schematized in (10):

(10)

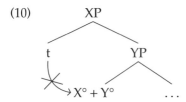

One case of head movement which may actually be an instance of this schema is an updated version of Chomsky's (1957) Affix Hopping rule. This rule arguably places Infl-material (tense and agreement features) on V in simple clauses lacking an auxiliary verb in English, as illustrated in (11):

(11) a. John left.
      b.

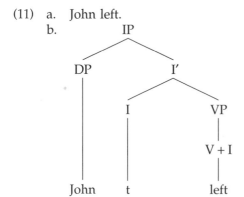

As Pollock (1989) points out, there are two ways of dealing with this case. On the one hand, one can postulate LF-raising of the inflected verb to I, "covering" the offending trace in I; this is proposed in Chomsky (1991), for example. Alternatively, one can propose that I-lowering is a morphological rule applying the PF-component and as such not required to leave a trace; this possibility is argued for in Bobaljik (1995).

Finally, the antecedent government requirement arguably rules out "excorporation." Excorporation is successive-cyclic head movement where one head simply moves through another, first incorporating and then moving on – hence the term excorporation. Schematically, excorporation is shown in (12):

(12)

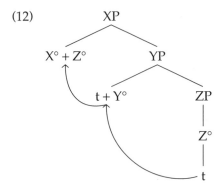

A possible case of this type involves the interaction of Verb Raising and Verb Second in Dutch. The relevant kind of example is (13):

(13) Gisteren   had ik [mijn vriendin op t] willen bellen.
      Yesterday had I   my   girlfriend up want call
      "Yesterday I wanted to call my girlfriend up."

A commonly held analysis of Verb Raising (see Evers 1975, den Besten and Edmonson 1983, Rutten 1991) is that the verbal cluster *willen bellen* (itself formed by head adjunction of *bellen* to *willen*) right-adjoins to I, or at any rate the clause-final position of the finite verb before the application of Verb Second. In clauses where Verb Second does not apply, the finite verb combined with the infinitives forms an uninterruptible cluster: *[[had] willen bellen]*. Where Verb Second applies, however, it appears that the finite verb excorporates from this cluster and moves to C, as shown in (13).

Baker (1988: 73) rules out excorporation by the claim that words cannot contain traces. However, it is possible that Y° blocks antecedent government of the intermediate trace in (12) (see Roberts 1991). If so, all cases of excorporation effectively reduce to the Head Movement Constraint, i.e., to Relativized Minimality (see n. 7 on this point).

To summarize, Baker's theory utilizes head movement in order to derive the properties of many grammatical function changing operations. This is achieved through the interaction of the nature of head movement itself with the Government Transparency Corollary and the ECP. In Baker's approach the advantages of assuming that head movement is exactly like all other types of movement emerge rather clearly against the background of fairly standard assumptions of Government Binding theory.

2 Verb Movement

In this section, I concentrate on verb movement to functional positions higher in the clause than VP, V-to-V movement having been briefly discussed in the previous section (see (6)).

Assuming a clause structure of the general type shown in (3b), there are two main types of verb movement to functional positions: movement into the I-system and movement into the C-system. Here I discuss each of these in turn, followed by a brief discussion of the question of whether VSO orders are derived by movement to C or by movement to I.

2.1   *Verb movement to I*

It was originally argued by Emonds (1978) that French has a rule moving finite verbs out of VP, while English does not. The basic form of the observation is as follows: there is a class of elements X that can be regarded as positioned approximately on the left edge of VP. These elements include VP-adverbs, clausal negation, and floated quantifiers. In French, finite main verbs must precede X, while English main verbs always follow X. The relevant paradigms are as follows:

(14)   **Adverb:**
   a.   Jean **embrasse souvent** Marie.
        *Jean **souvent embrasse** Marie.
   b.   *John **kisses often** Mary.
        John **often kisses** Mary.

(15)   **Negation:**
   a.   Jean (ne) **mange pas** du chocolat.
        *Jean (ne) **pas mange** du chocolat.
   b.   *John **eats not** chocolate.
        John does **not eat** chocolate.

(16)   **Floated quantifiers:**
   a.   Les enfants **mangent tous** le chocolat.
        *Les enfants **tous mangent** le chocolat.
   b.   *The children **eat all** chocolate.
        The children **all eat** chocolate.

The evidence clearly shows that finite verbs are in different positions in the two languages. The alternative is to suggest that the X-elements differ between the two languages (this approach was developed by Williams 1994). Emonds also pointed out that English auxiliaries, particularly *have* and *be* (when they are auxiliaries, usage varies across dialect and register with possessive *have*), appear to move like French main verbs in that they systematically precede X. (17) illustrates for perfect *have*:

(17)   a.   John **has often** kissed Mary.
   b.   John **has not** kissed Mary.

  c. The kids **have all** eaten the chocolate.
  d. **Has John** seen Mary?

These facts led Emonds to propose a special rule of *have/be* raising for English.

 Pollock (1989) observed that the same auxiliary vs. main verb split shows up in infinitival clauses in French:

(18) a. N'**avoir/*posséder pas** de voiture en banlieue crée des problèmes.
   To have/possess not a car in the suburbs creates problems.
  b. N'**être/*sembler pas** heureux est une condition pour écrire des romans.
   To be/seem not happy is a condition for writing novels.

A second very important empirical observation was that the class X is not unitary in this respect: main verb infinitives cannot raise over negation, as (18) shows, but may optionally precede VP-adverbs and floated quantifiers (I illustrate with adverbs):

(19) a. Souvent paraître triste pendant son voyage de noce, c'est rare.
   Often to-appear sad during one's honeymoon is rare.
  b. Paraître souvent triste pendant son voyage de noce, c'est rare.
   To-appear often sad during one's honeymoon is rare.

The contrasts between (18) and (19) led Pollock to propose the "split-Infl" clause structure, illustrated in (20) (NegP is motivated primarily by facts connected to English *do*-support, which I will leave aside here):

(20)

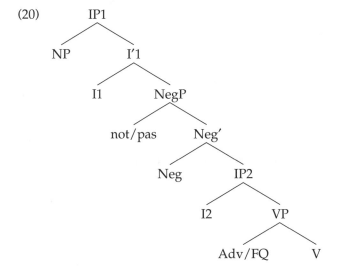

French main verb infinitives optionally move to I2, French finite main verbs obligatorily move to I1, and both French and English auxiliaries move optionally to either position. English main verbs are immobile.

Chomsky (1993, 1995b) proposes that the parameter distinguishing English and French concerns the value of an abstract morphological feature that licenses verbs, and is associated with I. This feature is called I's V-feature. In Chomsky's system, such features are generated both on V and on I, and must be cancelled out by a checking operation prior to LF since they have no semantic content and will thus violate the Principle of Full Interpretation unless eliminated. The feature varies parametrically as either strong or weak. If it is strong, it is visible to the PF component, and hence must be eliminated prior to the mapping to that level of representation, Spell-Out. Since feature checking takes place in a highly local domain (essentially Specifier-head or head-to-head adjunction, the latter being relevant in this case), V must move to I in order for feature checking to take place. Thus where the V-feature is strong, V raises overtly to I. Where the feature is weak, the Procrastinate principle, which delays movement to the covert, post-Spell-Out part of the grammar wherever possible, prevents this movement from taking place overtly. In these terms, then, French I has a strong V-feature and English I has a weak V-feature.[2]

Pollock originally identified I1 in (21) as T and I2 as Agr. Belletti (1990) proposed instead that I1 should be identified with Agr and I2 with T. There are three main reasons for this. First, the order Agr-T is consistent with Baker's (1985) Mirror principle, which requires the order of affixation in morphologically complex words to reflect the order of syntactic operations associated with those affixes; typically in many languages, including the Romance ones, tense affixes are closer to the verb stem than agreement affixes (e.g. Italian *canta-v$_{Tense}$-ano$_{Agr}$* "they were singing"), suggesting that tense features are associated with, or checked by, the verb before Agreement features are. Second, it seems more natural for the canonical subject position to be Spec, AgrP rather than Spec, TP, since the subject agrees with the verb in a Spec–head relation. Third, Belletti shows that Italian infinitives raise to the highest I-position, like finite main verbs in French. She relates this difference between Italian and French to the fact that Italian is a null-subject language with "rich" Agr, while French is not.

Chomsky (1991) adopts a combination of Pollock's proposal and Belletti's proposal, positing two AgrPs in the clause, one above and one below T. The upper one is associated with subject agreement and Nominative Case, and the lower one with object agreement and Accusative Case:

(21)

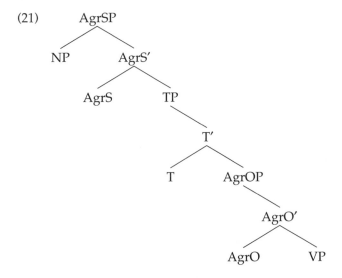

In terms of this structure, finite main verbs in French move to AgrS. As the foregoing shows, the role of the study of verb movement in postulating this elaborated clause structure has been central.

2.2   *Verb-movement to C*

Standard assumptions about inversion (subject-aux inversion in English, subject-clitic inversion in French, and V2 inversion in Germanic languages) deriving from the seminal work of den Besten (1983) treat this operation as involving movement of I to C. Given the Head Movement Constraint in (1), V cannot move directly to C, and so inversion of main verbs depends on the prior operation of V-movement into the I-system, in fact to the highest position in the I-system, to feed it. Thus we find that French main verbs are able to undergo inversion (subject to the independent restriction that the subject be a clitic – cf. Rizzi and Roberts 1989), while English main verbs are unable to do so:

(22)   a.   **Voit-il** le cheval?
       b.   *****Sees he** the horse?

The contrast in (22) is a consequence of the fact that French main verbs move into the I-system while their English counterparts do not.[3]

There are two views on the nature of V2. The first, originally argued for by den Besten (1983), is that it always involves movement of the inflected verb into C. The second, originally argued for by Travis (1984) and more recently by Zwart (1993a, 1997), is that this is the case only where the initial XP is not the subject; in subject initial V2 clauses the verb only moves as far as the I-system.

According to the first view, then, in all the following German examples (taken from Tomaselli 1989), the initial XP is in CP and the finite verb in C:

(23)   a.   [$_{CP}$ Ich [$_{C}$ las] [$_{IP}$ schon letztes Jahr diesen Roman]].
            I read already last year this book.
       b.   [$_{CP}$ Ich [$_{C}$ habe] [$_{IP}$ schon letztes Jahr diesen Roman gelesen]].
            I have already last year this book read.

(24)   a.   [$_{CP}$ Diesen Roman [$_{C}$ las] [$_{IP}$ ich schon letztes Jahr]].
            This book read I already last year.
       b.   [$_{CP}$ Diesen Roman [$_{C}$ habe] [$_{IP}$ ich schon letztes Jahr gelesen]].
            This book have I already last year read.

(25)   a.   [$_{CP}$ Schon letztes Jahr [$_{C}$ las] [$_{IP}$ ich diesen Roman]].
            Already last year read I this book.
       b.   [$_{CP}$ Schon letztes Jahr [$_{C}$ habe] [$_{IP}$ ich diesen Roman gelesen]].
            Already last year have I this book read.

There are two principal pieces of evidence that the finite verb is in C in V2 clauses. First, the finite verb is in complementary distribution with complementizers, themselves undoubtedly in C: this can be seen most clearly in German, where in certain embedded clauses the complementizer *daß* is obligatorily associated with verb final order and alternates with complementizerless clauses (prescriptively at least, in the subjunctive) showing V2 order:

(26)   a.   Er sagte, gestern sei er schon angekommen.   (embedded V2)
            He said, yesterday have he already arrived.
       b.   Er sagte daß er gestern schon angekommen ist.
                                              (C filled, no embedded V2)
            He said that he yesterday already arrived has.
            "He said he'd already arrived yesterday."

Second, den Besten (1983) observed that weak pronouns in Dutch are obligatorily adjacent either to a complementizer in a non-V2 clause or to the inflected verb in a V2 clause. This is illustrated in (27), where *je* and *ze* are weak pronouns:

(27)   a.   . . . dat je gisteren/*gisteren je ziek was.
            . . . that you yesterday/yesterday you sick were.
       b.   Was ze gisteren/*gisteren ze ziek?
            Were you yesterday/yesterday you sick?

If the verb is in C in V2 clauses, the generalization regarding these weak pronouns is simply that they are dependent on C ((27b) is a yes/no question with the verb apparently first; it is standardly assumed, however, that SpecCP is occupied by a null operator in this kind of clause).

The unified approach to V2 clearly makes it possible to treat V2 as triggered by a property of C. In Minimalist terms, it is easy to state that C in a V2 language has a strong V- (or perhaps I- or T-feature); in fact, starting with den Besten's original work, it has frequently been proposed that C has some I-like property in V2 languages – cf. Platzack (1987), Holmberg and Platzack (1991, 1995), Tomaselli (1989), and Roberts and Roussou (1998) for varying proposals. This leaves open the question of what causes XP-movement to SpecCP. One idea, first proposed in Roberts (1993b: 56), is that this is the Extended Projection Principle (EPP) applying at the C-level. Applying at the I (or AgrS) level, the EPP requires that SpecIP be filled by a DP owing to the fact that I is inherently associated with agreement features; applying at the C-level, on the other hand, it arguably simply requires that the Specifier be filled by an XP of any category, since there is no inherent requirement for agreement with features of C – see Roberts and Roussou (1998) for a defence and elaboration of this idea.

Turning now to the second approach, Zwart (1993b, 1997) gives evidence that subject–verb orders in V2 languages are structurally distinct from other V2 orders (from now on I refer to the former as SV orders and the latter as VS orders). The principal evidence comes from differences in the form of agreement morphemes in Standard Dutch and various dialects which correlate with SV and VS order, and facts about the placement of subject clitics. In Standard Dutch the 2-Sg agreement form ends in -*t* in SV clauses (and in embedded clauses) while in VS clauses it is a bare stem:

(28) a. . . . dat jij naar huis **gaat**/***ga**.
      . . . that you to home go.
     b. Jij **gaat**/***ga** naar huis.
      You go to home.
     c. Vandaag **ga**/***gaat** jij naar huis.
      Today go you to home.
     d. Wanneer **ga**/***gaat** jij naar huis?
      When go you home?

In some Dutch dialects, the forms for complementizer agreement and verbal agreement differ. Strikingly, Zwart shows that in these dialects the complementizer agreement shows up on the verb in VS clauses, while the verb has the other form in SV clauses. I illustrate from East Netherlandic (although Zwart shows that the same facts hold in Brabantish and West Flemish):

(29) a. dat-**e** wij speul-**t**.
      that-1Pl we play-1Pl
     b. Wij speul-**t**/*-**e**.
      We play-1Pl.
     c. Wat speul-**e**/*-**t** wij?
      What play-1Pl we?
     d. Vandaag speul-**e**/*-**t** wij.
      Today play-1Pl we.

Also, subject clitics in Standard Dutch precede the verb only in SV main clauses but follow V in VS clauses, while they follow C in embedded clauses:

(30) a. **'k** eet vandaag appels.
    I(Cl) eat today apples.
  b. Natuurlijk eet **'k** vandaag appels.
    Of course eat I(Cl) today apples.
  c. . . . dat **'k** vandaag appels eet.
    . . . that I today apples eat.

(A similar argument was made by Travis 1984 based on weak forms of certain German pronouns, but cf. Tomaselli 1989 for an alternative.)

Zwart interprets this evidence as showing that the subject is in SpecAgrSP and the verb in AgrS° in SV clauses, while XP is in SpecCP and the verb in C in VS clauses. He proposes that AgrS has a strong V-feature, attracting V, and a strong N-feature, attracting N. In VS clauses, C has a strong V-feature and a further strong feature (*wh*, Topic, etc.) lacking in SV clauses; in this way V is attracted to C and an XP to SpecCP.

A further issue, touched on by Zwart (1997), concerns the nature of the C-system. Rizzi (1997) argues that at the left periphery of the clause, above IP, there are the separate projections ForceP, FocusP, and FiniteP, interspersed with possibly recursive TopPs. The categories I am most interested in here are Fin and Force: Fin marks the clause as finite or not and Force is the position associated with clausal typing.

Typical complementizers like English *that* mark two things: that the clause they introduce is declarative and that it is finite. In this respect, they are associated with features of two heads, Force and Fin, just as a finite verb is associated with properties of V and I. So we might expect that crosslinguistically, some complementizers are overtly realized in Force and others in Fin. Straightforward evidence from this comes from McCloskey's (1993) evidence that C apparently lowers to I in Irish. The argument is based on the observation that in general across languages sentential adverbs do not adjoin to CP:

(31) a. In general, he understands what's going on.
  b. It's probable that in general he understands what's going on.
  c. *It's probable [$_{CP}$ in general [$_{CP}$ that he understands what's going on]].
  d. *[In general [that he understands what's going on]] is surprising.

In (31c, d) the bracketing is meant to indicate that the adverb should be interpreted as modifying the *that*-clause. These readings are impossible in English. McCloskey calls this general ban on the adjunction of adverbs to CP the Adjunction Prohibition.

Irish shows the opposite distribution of adverbs in relation to CPs:

(32) Is doíche [faoi cheann   cúpla lá [go bhféadfaí imeacht]]
    is probable at-the-end-of couple day that could   leave
             Adv   C   I

McCloskey also shows that we cannot maintain that Irish simply lacks the Adjunction Prohibition (however exactly this idea might be formulated). The evidence against this idea is that the order *adverb–wh-phrase* is bad:

(33)   *Ní bhfuair siad amach ariamh an bhliain sin cé   a   bhí
        Neg found they out   ever   the year   that who Prt was
        ag goid a gcuid móna
        stealing their turf
        "They never found out who was stealing their turf that year."

McCloskey proposes (i) that sentential adverbs adjoin to IP in Irish just as in English (and other languages), and (ii) that Irish has a rule which lowers C to I. The C-to-I lowering rule derives orders like that in (32). Schematically, the relevant parts of (32) have the following structure:

(34)   t [$_{IP}$ Adv [$_{IP}$ C+I . . .

The split-C system provides a way of handling McCloskey's data without having recourse to a C-to-I lowering operation. The basic idea is to capitalize on the overall similarity between the structure of McCloskey's argument and the structure of Emonds's (1978) arguments for V-to-I raising in French and I-to-V lowering in English. As we saw in section 2.1, Emonds observed, *inter alia*, the following contrast between French and English:

(35)   a.   *French:* V+Infl Adv   direct object
       b.   *English:*   Adv V+Infl direct object

Pollock (1989) concluded that V raises to Infl in French, but that Infl lowers to V in English. The Irish–English contrast that we saw in (31) vs. (32) can be handled in an analogous way, given the split-C system. Here what we have is the following:

(36)   a.   *Irish:*   [$_{ForceP}$ [$_{TopP}$Adv [$_{FinP}$ Comp IP . . .
       b.   *English:* [$_{ForceP}$ Comp [$_{TopP}$Adv [$_{FinP}$ IP . . .

So the possibility emerges of saying that Irish complementizers occupy a different position from their English counterparts. Does Comp raise to Force in English or is it merged there? In fact, the answer may be different for different languages. "CP-recursion" examples like (37) provide a relevant indication:

(37)   I said that never in my life had I seen a place like Bangor.

If V is in Foc and the negative constituent in SpecFocP here, *that* cannot have raised to Force. To account for this, we may assume that *that* is base-generated in Force and the relevant Fin-features raise to combine with Force (see Chomsky 1995b on feature movement). Since *daß* is incompatible with CP-recursion in standard German (Vikner 1994a), we conclude that it is base-generated in Fin and moves to Force. We thus see three different parametric properties of Force: in Irish, it is inert, and complementizers occupy Fin; in English, *that* is inserted in it and it attracts Fin-features; in German, it attracts *daß*. A fourth possibility is illustrated by Welsh. In Welsh there are two par-ticles – *fe* and *mi* – which introduce affirmative main clauses (under certain conditions). Adverbs can occur before these particles, but not in between them and the verb:

(38) a. Bore   'ma, mi glywes i 'r newyddion ar y radio.
          Morning this, Prt heard I the news   on the radio
      b. *Mi bore   'ma glywes i 'r newyddion ar y radio.
          Prt morning this heard   I the news   on the radio
          "This morning, I heard the news on the radio."

Again we can apply our analysis of McCloskey's Irish data and take it that *fe/ mi* are in Fin. In addition, Welsh has a focussing strategy which allows exactly one XP to be fronted over the verb, followed by *a* or *y* and the rest of the clause:

(39) a. Y   dynion a   werthodd y   ci.
          The men   Prt sold   the dog
          "It's the men who have sold the dog."
      b. Ym Mangor y   siaradais i llynedd.
          In Bangor Prt spoke   I last-year
          "It was in Bangor I spoke last year."

When embedded, clauses with a fronted focussed XP like those in (39) are preceded by one of a special class of complementizers, as in (40) (examples from Tallerman 1996):

(40) Dywedais i **mai** ['r dynion a   werthith y   ci].
      Said   I MAI the men   Prt will-sell the dog
      "I said that it's the men who will sell the dog."

Rouveret (1994) and Tallermann (1996) treat these structures as involving "CP-recursion." Tallerman observes that adverbs can appear between *mai* and the focussed constituent, but not – with embedded scope – before *mai*:

(41) a. ??Dywedais i **mai** fel arfer y   dynion a   werthith y   ci.
          Said   I MAI as usual the men   Prt will-sell the dog
      b. Dywedais i **mai** 'r dynion fel arfer a   werthith y   ci.
          Said   I MAI the men   as usual Prt will-sell the dog

c. *Dywedais i fel arfer **mai** ['r dynion **a** werthith y ci].
Said I as usual MAI the men Prt will-sell the dog
"I said that it's the men as usual who will sell the dog."

The preferred order is (41b), where the adverb intervenes between the focussed XP and *a*. Thus the natural position for *a* is in Fin. It seems reasonable to situate the focussed XP in SpecFoc; this implies that the adverb in (41b) occupies a position in between Foc and Fin (possibly SpecFinP). We consider *mai* and other elements that introduce "CP-recursion" of the kind illustrated in (40) to be in Force. In Welsh, then, both Force and Fin can be simultaneously filled by different complementizers.

These proposals point the way to an account of root-embedded asymmetries in verb movement, a typical feature of many Germanic languages. Let us make one specific hypothesis about the structural difference between root and embedded clauses:

(42) ForceP is either absent or inert in root declaratives.

(42) is linked to the idea that root declaratives are the unmarked clause type. In embedded clauses, typical complementizers like English *that* (and German *daß*) raise from Fin to Force due to the nature of the Force head in these languages. Let us suppose further, following den Besten (1983) and the other references given above, that both full and residual V2 are the reflex of a dependency between T and Fin which holds in finite clauses: essentially, in a V2 language Fin attracts T. In embedded declarative clauses, Force attracts a complementizer from Fin. Following den Besten (1983), the presence of the complementizer in Fin blocks T-movement to Fin (although features may move, giving rise to agreeing complementizers in a number of varieties – see Zwart 1997 for an elaboration of this idea). Significantly, all the Germanic V2 languages differ from English in requiring the presence of a complementizer in finite embedded declaratives, with the notable exception of German, which requires embedded V2 exactly where the complementizer is missing; see (26) above. Since embedded V2 typically requires the presence of the equivalent of *that* in other Germanic languages (see Vikner 1994a for discussion and illustration), these elements also presumably occupy Force.

In *wh*-complements where no overt complementizer is present something more must be said. Here we can capitalize on an observation by Stowell (1981: 422) to the effect that selection for +*wh* neutralizes selection for Fin. This can be illustrated by paradigms such as the following:

(43) a. I explained how to fix the sink.   [+*wh*, −Fin]
b. I explained how we should fix the sink.   [+*wh*, +Fin]
c. I explained that we should fix the sink.   [−*wh*, +Fin]
d. *I explained to fix the sink.   [−*wh*, −Fin]

In Rizzi's system, this is straightforwardly accounted for by the fact that both Force and Foc are structurally higher than Fin. Suppose, concretely, that if Force is selected as +Q then this activates Foc as +*wh*, but no feature of Fin is selected. More generally, we can think the presence of Foc blocks the selectional relation between Force and Fin – this follows from standard assumptions about the locality of selection which go back to Chomsky (1965). Whether Foc requires/allows Fin to be morphologically realized varies from language to language: where it does (e.g. in Dutch), *wh–that* sequences are found; where it does not, they are not.

The above sketch of the root embedded asymmetry, which is in some ways an adaptation of den Besten's (1983) analysis to the split-C system of Rizzi, links the root embedded asymmetry in verb movement to the fact that matrix clauses cannot have complementizers (in the languages in question), since by hypothesis root ForceP is either absent or inert. It also implies that in languages in which complementizers are generated in Force but in which Force does not determine movement of Fin, T should be able to freely raise to Fin, giving rise to the absence of root embedded asymmetries. This may well be the situation in the "symmetric" V2 languages Yiddish and Icelandic. In Irish and Welsh Force also does not attract Fin, as the evidence given above shows. Given this, we can understand why there are no root embedded asymmetries in verb movement in the Celtic languages; V could be analyzed as moving to Fin, as in Yiddish and Icelandic (although then it left-adjoins to the particles, *contra* Kayne 1994). I return to the issue of the position of V in VSO languages in section 2.3.

So we see that Force may be overtly realized by Merge (insertion of a complementizer) or Move (attraction of Fin), both (although in this case only features of Fin are moved) or neither. Welsh realizes the first option, German the second, English the third, and Irish the fourth. Combining this with (42) gives rise to an account of root embedded asymmetries.

2.3   VSO orders

Emonds (1980) was the first to propose that VSO orders are derived by verb movement. In general terms, Emonds's idea was that the existence of VSO orders is not incompatible with the postulation of an underlying VP constituent. As long as verb movement rules exist (and this is not in doubt), such a rule can move the verb out of the VP and to the left over the subject. This gives a derived VSO order from an underlying SVO or SOV order.

I take Welsh as an example of a canonical VSO language, mentioning other Celtic languages and Semitic VSO languages (notably Classical Arabic) where relevant. In Welsh, we can very clearly see that something like what Emonds described is going on in VSO clauses. There is a general possibility of what we can think of as free "*do*-insertion." Free "*do*-insertion" is available in the future and preterite tenses, as illustrated in (44):

(44) a.   Mi **welais** i Megan.
           Prt saw   I Megan
           "I saw Megan."
      b.   Mi **wnes** i weld Megan.
           Prt did   I see   Megan
           "I saw Megan."

It seems clear that the lexical verb *welais* in (44a) is in the same position as the auxiliary verb *wnes* in (44b). Both elements appear in between the clause initial particle *mi* and the subject *i*. Moreover, the *only* thing which can appear in between the particle and the subject is a finite verb or auxiliary. It seems natural to think that this position is the one for the finite element of the clause. If the verb is chosen as the finite element, it moves to that position; if an auxiliary is chosen, the main verb remains in VP. (44b) shows that the order of elements in the clause following the position for the finite element is SVO.

Sproat (1985) gives a number of other arguments for the same conclusion; in particular, he argues that non-finite verbs typically appear in SVO orders, and that non-finite VPs could be fronted along with their complement, stranding the subject. The relevant facts are illustrated in (45a) and (45b), respectively:

(45) a.   [Cyn i Siôn laddu draig], y mae rhaid   iddo   brynu
           Before to John kill   dragon, Prt is   necessary to-him buy
           llaeth i'r   gath.
           milk for-the cat
           "Before John kills a dragon, he has to buy milk for the cat." (Sproat
           1985: 205)
      b.   [Gadael y   glwyd ar agor] a wnaeth y   ffermwyr.
           Leave   the gate on open Prt did   the farmer
           "Leave the gate open, the farmer did." (Rouveret 1994: 77)

We conclude with Sproat, and following the general consensus of work on Welsh (and the Celtic languages in general; see, for example, the introduction to Borsley and Roberts 1996) that VSO clauses involve an operation which moves the verb out of VP to the left over the subject.

The above considerations are straightforward and easy to motivate. However, it is much harder to say (i) what the position that V moves to is, or (ii) what the position of the subject is. In a theory which posits the existence of one or more functional categories above VP (see section 2.1), a range of different options is available in this connection. The one thing we have to ensure is that the finite verb occupies a position higher than that of the subject at Spell-Out.

On the basis of the above considerations, it should be clear what the simplest analysis of VSO would be. We could posit a derived structure like the following for (44a):

(46)

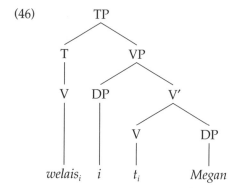

In addition to this being adopted in Chomsky (1993, 1995b), Koopmann and Sportiche (1991) also consider it as a possibility. There are, however, a number of arguments against an analysis of the type in (46).

The first argument has to do with adjacency effects. McCloskey (1991) shows that V must be adjacent to the subject in VSO clauses in Irish:

(47) *Dúirt sí go dtabharfadh amárach a   mac turas orm.
      said   she that would-give tomorrow her son visit on-me.
                      V   X   S
      "She said that tomorrow her son would visit me."

The same observation holds for Welsh:

(48) *Mi welith yfory   Emrys ddraig.
      Prt will-see tomorrow Emrys dragon
         V   X   S
      "Tomorrow Emrys will see a dragon."

It is widely assumed that the space between T and VP contains positions in which adverbs of various kinds can appear (whether adjoined to VP, to other functional categories, or to X'-level projections or in Specifier positions is a matter of debate). If so, then we expect such adverbs to intervene between the raised verb and the subject if the structure of a VSO clause is (46). The fact that these orders are impossible indicates that (46) is not the correct analysis of VSO clauses.

The second argument was noticed by Koopman and Sportiche (1991). In spoken Modern Welsh, the form of negation seems to be similar to French *ne ... pas*, in that there are two elements, one a preverbal, clitic like element and the other a postverbal, adverb like element. The relevant observation in the present context is that the second element of negation follows the subject:

(49) (Ni)   ddarllenodd Emrys ddim o'r   llyfr.
      (Neg) read   Emrys Neg of-the book.
      "Emrys didn't read the book."

If we assimilate *(d)dim* to French *pas*, then we take it to occupy a VP-external position lower than T and higher than the position in which the subject is merged. In that case, the order *subject–ddim–object* in (49) shows us that the subject is not in its merged (VP-internal) position. Concretely, let us follow Pollock (1989) in assuming that the *pas*-type negative is in SpecNegP and that NegP intervenes between TP and VP. In that case, the situation is illustrated both for Welsh and for the comparable French sentence in (50):

(50) *(Ni)ddarllenodd Emrys . . .*
       Jean   ne   lut   . . .

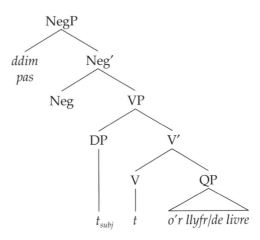

We must conclude that the subject raises from VP.

   Not all the Celtic languages are like Welsh as regards the relative order of the subject and the second part of negation. The Goidelic languages just have preverbal negation (Irish *ní* (present), *níor* (past); Scots Gaelic *cha*). However, McCloskey (1993: 39) shows that certain adverbs which it is plausible to think of as attached to VP intervene between the subject and the object in Irish VSO clauses (and, given the argument made above, cannot intervene between the verb and the subject):

(51) Níor shaotaigh **Eoghan ariamh** pingin.
       Neg earned   Owen   ever   penny
       "Owen has never earned a penny."

This example indicates that the subject leaves VP in Irish.

   The third argument is due to McCloskey (1996), who makes the argument for Irish, although it carries over to Welsh. McCloskey points out that the standard A-dependencies raising, passive, and unaccusative are all found in Irish; such constructions are also found in Welsh. On Minimalist assumptions, such movement must be driven exclusively by the need to check features. Features are assumed to be checked in the checking domain of functional heads. It follows from these assumptions that movement to Spec, VP – a position in the checking domain of a lexical head – is impossible; lexical heads do not offer the possibility of feature checking. Now, if the subject position were VP-internal, A-dependencies would precisely involve movement to Spec, VP. Hence the derived subjects of raising, passive, and unaccusative verbs cannot be in Spec, VP. Since these subjects are no different in their position in their clauses from other subjects, then we have an argument that subjects in general are not VP-internal.

Finally, let us briefly consider an argument that subjects leave VP that has been made on the basis of data from Northern dialects of Irish (the construction is also found in Scots Gaelic – see Adger 1996). The argument, first made by Bobaljik and Carnie (1996) (see also Carnie 1995), is based on the existence of SOV order in infinitives in these varieties, as in:[4]

(52)   Ba mhaith liom   [(é)   an teach   a   thógáil].
       is good   with-me (him) a   house-Acc Prt build
       "I would like him to build the house."

In Southern dialects, the direct object is Genitive and the order is SVO:

(53)   Ba mhaith liom   [(é)   a thógáil an tí]
       is good   with-me (him) to build   Prt house-Gen
       "I would like him to build the house."

Bobaljik and Carnie propose that the Accusative form of the object is found when the object moves to SpecAgrOP. Therefore the subject must have raised out of VP, because it precedes the object. The lowest available position for the subject is SpecTP. Therefore V is higher than T. They conclude that V is in AgrS.[5]

In conclusion, we have seen several reasons to reject an analysis of the kind given in (46). All our arguments point in the same direction: the subject is raised from its base position. We now know that the subject is in the specifier of a functional category, and we can be sure that the verb is in a functional head position higher than the subject. Moreover, the adjacency evidence of McCloskey (1991), illustrated in (47) and (48) above, suggests that the subject is in the specifier position of the functional category which is the complement of the one whose head V moves to (and that further adjunction to this category is impossible). Schematically, the situation must be as follows:

(54)

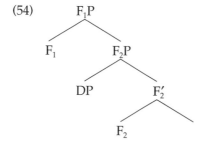

A natural hypothesis is that F_1 is C and F_2 is I. We saw in the previous section that we can think of V as moving to Fin in Celtic, except for the fact that this requires to assume it right-adjoins to the particle in Fin, *contra* Kayne (1994).

Of course, this argumentation is restricted to Welsh. It may be that V does raise into the C-system in other VSO languages (although Fassi Fehri 1993 concludes that V does not raise out of the I-system in Arabic, on the basis of arguments similar to those just given for Welsh). Carnie et al. (1996) argue that V raised to C in Old Irish.

3   Head Movement in Nominals

The general tendencies seen in the development of theories of clause structure that I reviewed in the previous section are also apparent in recent work on nominals. Above all, functional categories and head movement have been shown to play a central role in this domain, too. The most important functional category in nominals is the Determiner Phrase, or DP. This was originally proposed by Abney (1987) and by Fukui and Speas (1986).

A further parallel with work on clause structure concerns the idea that N may raise to D (or to another functional head inside DP). This idea can account for two kinds of phenomenon. First, it has been used (by Taraldsen 1990, Delsing 1990) to account for postnominal articles of the type found in the Scandinavian languages. Thus, a form like *hus-et* ("house-the") is derived by N-movement adjoining *hus* to *-et* in D in a structure like the following:

(55)

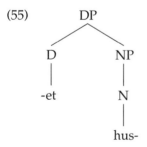

The phenomenon of postnominal articles can then be reduced to the operation of a movement rule. Longobardi (1994) argues that this movement rule applies at LF in those languages where it does not apply overtly, in order to give referential value to the N.

Second, the Semitic construct state construction may feature N-to-D raising. This has been argued for by Mohammad (1988), Ritter (1988), Fassi Fehri (1993), and Siloni (1991, 1994, 1997) for Semitic, and the analysis carries over naturally to Celtic possessives (see below). The parallel with the way in which verb movement in clauses gives rise to VSO order is striking, especially given that overt, productive constructs are found just in languages that are either fully or residually VSO: Celtic and Semitic (see section 2.2).

The Semitic construct state construction displays the following properties (this presentation is based on that in Longobardi 1996, which in turn relies on Siloni 1994):

(56) a. The noun heading the construction occurs first in the whole nominal phrase.
      b. A phrase semantically understood as a genitive argument always follows the head noun.
      c. The article of the head noun disappears.
      d. The preposition usually introducing genitive arguments disappears.
      e. Strict adjacency (i.e., no intervening adjective) is required between the head noun and the argument.
      f. The head noun occurs deaccented and often with vowels phonologically reduced.
      g. The definiteness value of the head noun depends on (is harmonic with) the ±definite status of the complement.

We illustrate these with Hebrew examples, unless otherwise indicated. Properties (56a, b) are illustrated by (57):

(57) beyt ha-iʃ
      home the-man
      "the man's home"

Following (56c), the article is impossible on the head noun here:

(58) *ha-beyt ha-iʃ
      the-home the-man

There is clearly no possessive preposition in (57) (see (56d)), and (59) shows that no adjective can intervene between the head noun and the possessor:

(59) *beyt ha-gadol ha-iʃ
      home the-big the-man

The word for *home* here is phonologically reduced; its usual form is *bayit* – see (56f). Definiteness harmony – (56g) – is illustrated by the fact that an adjective modifying the head noun must agree in definiteness with the possessor noun; in other words, definiteness is shared between the possessor and the head noun:

(60) a. beyt ha-iʃ   ha-gadol
          house the-man the big
          "the big man's house/the man's big house"

    b.   beyt iʃ   gadol
        house man big
        "a big man's house/a man's big house"
    c.   *beyt ha-iʃ   gadol
        house the-man big
        "the big man's house/the man's big house"

Properties (56a, c, e) are immediately accounted for if the head noun raises to D, nothing can appear in SpecDP, the possessor appears in the Specifier position immediately subjacent to D (given as NP in 61)), and APs are unable to adjoin to the complement of D:

(61)

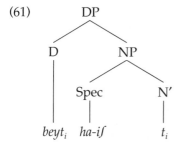

Properties (56b, d) are connected to the fact that N-to-D movement licenses Genitive Case assignment – see Longobardi (1996) for specific proposals as to how this works. Definiteness harmony is accounted for by the interaction of Spec–head agreement for definiteness in a lower projection (say, NP in (61)) and movement of the head of that projection to D; thus D and the possessor DP in the lower Specifier position must have the same value for ±definite. Finally, (56f) may be connected to the presence of a strong feature in D which triggers N-raising.

    In Celtic, possessive constructions have properties very similar to those of the Semitic construct state (see in particular Guilfoyle 1988 and Duffield 1996 on Irish, and Rouveret 1994 on Welsh). Properties (56a–d) are illustrated in the following examples, and thus provide clear evidence for N-to-D movement:

(62) a.   llyfr John   (Welsh)
         book John
         "John's book"
      b.   teach an fhir   (Irish)
         house the man
         "the man's house"

On the other hand, property (62e) does *not* hold in Celtic (see Duffield 1996). If the possessed noun is modified by an AP, that AP intervenes between the noun and the possessor:

(63) a. llyfr newydd John   (Welsh)
           book new   John
           "John's new book"
      b. guth láidir an tsagairt   (Irish)
           voice strong the priest-Gen
           "the priest's powerful voice"

The order *N–Poss–A* is obligatorily interpreted such that the adjective modifies
the possessor. In this respect, Celtic differs from Semitic, as pointed out by
Duffield (1996) on the basis of the following contrasts:

(64) a. teach an tsagairt   chiúin   (Irish)
           house the priest-Gen quiet-Gen
           "the quiet priest's house" (*"the priest's quiet house")
      b. ħu   ir-raġel   il-kbir   (Maltese)
           brother(MSg) the-man(MSg) the-big
           "the man's big brother/the big man's brother"

Duffield analyzes this difference in terms of differential movement of the possessors; in Semitic languages, possessors appear in the immediately subjacent
specifier to D, while in the Celtic languages the possessor remains in SpecNP.
Following essentially Duffield's proposal, then, the structures of (64a, b) are:

(65)

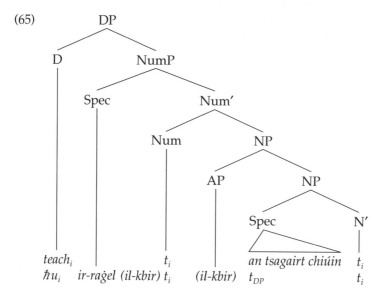

Here we see a difference between the Celtic and the Semitic languages.

   Property (56f) does not appear to hold in Celtic. Regarding property (56g),
what is at issue here is the interpretation of the head noun as definite or
indefinite in the absence of the possibility of marking this by the presence or

absence of the definite article. In Celtic, there is no overt definiteness marking on adjectives, and so purely interpretive evidence must be used:

(66)   mab brenin   (Welsh)
       son king
       "the son of a king/a son of a king" (Rouveret (1994: 184))

Definiteness harmony only holds in one direction in Welsh, in that, as (66) shows, the head noun can either be definite or "inherit" indefiniteness from the possessor. What is impossible, however, is an indefinite interpretation for the head noun where the possessor is definite. By N-to-D movement indefiniteness can be "inherited" from the possessor, but D can otherwise have a default definite value (Duffield 1996: 329–30) shows that the situation is the same in Irish.

We see then that N-to-D movement can explain the striking properties of possessive constructions in the Celtic and Semitic languages. Longobardi (1996) shows that the same mechanism is at work, although less obviously, in possessive constructions in both Romance and Germanic.

In Romance, overt N-to-D raising in possessive constructions is restricted to proper names and "a few singular common nouns, essentially a proper subset of the class of kinship nouns and the word for 'home'" (Longobardi 1996: 2). Thus we find DPs like the following in Italian:

(67)   a.   Il mio Gianni ha finalmente telefonato.
            The my Gianni has finally called.
       b.   Gianni mio ha finalmente telefonato.
            Gianni my has finally called.
       c.   *Mio Gianni ha finalmente telefonato.
            My Gianni has finally called.

(68)   a.   La mia case è più bella della tua.
            The my house is more beautiful than the yours.
       b.   Casa mia è più bella della tua.
            House my is more beautiful than the yours.
       c.   *Mia casa è più bella della tua.
            My house is more beautiful than the yours.

Longobardi shows in detail that all the properties of Semitic constructs given in (56) can be detected in these Romance constructions, and concludes that N-to-D raising is available in a restricted fashion in possessives in these languages.

Finally, there is some evidence that a similar process occurs covertly with certain nouns in Germanic. In English, the noun *home* may occur without an article and with an understood possessor, just like its Romance counterparts which overtly raise to D:

(69) a.   Home is always the best place to relax.
      b.   John was heading home.

Since *home* always follows adjectives, there is no question of overt N-to-D movement. Longobardi thus proposes that it may move to D in LF.

  More generally, Longobardi suggests that the Germanic "Saxon Genitive" may be a case of LF N-to-D movement. One argument for this is that this construction is incompatible with demonstratives, which occupy either the head or Specifier of D (Giusti 1993):

(70)   *diese Ottos wunderbaren Bücher
        these Otto's wonderful books

If this is correct, then N-to-D movement is found universally, in possessive constructions and with certain types of head noun (proper names and others). Whether the movement is overt depends on the strength of the relevant features of D.

4   The Local Nature of Head Movement

In this section, I want to consider in more detail the theoretical status of the Head Movement Constraint, repeated here:

(1)   Head movement of X to Y cannot "skip" an intervening head Z.

As pointed out by Rizzi (1990, this volume), (1) can be derived from Relativized Minimality. In Rizzi (this volume), Relativized Minimality is stated in terms of the notion of Minimal Configuration (MC) and the definition of chains, as follows:

(71)   Y is in a MC with X iff there is no Z such that
        (i)   Z is of the same structural type as X, and
       (ii)   Z intervenes between X and Y.

Intervention can be defined in terms of asymmetric c-command: Z intervenes between X and Y iff Z asymmetrically c-commands Y and does not asymmetrically c-command Z.[6]

(72) $(\alpha_1 \ldots \alpha_n)$ is a chain iff, for $1 \leq i < n$
        (i) $\alpha_i = \alpha_{i+1}$
       (ii) α_i c-commands α_{i+1}
      (iii) α_{i+1} is in an MC with α_i

Assuming the copy theory of traces, then, each chain link involves identity, c-command, and Minimality.

As Rizzi points out, the notion of "same structural type" in (71i) is crucial. Whatever the precise details here (see in particular section 6 of Rizzi's chapter, this volume, on this), it is clear that heads can naturally be viewed as being of the same structural type as other heads. In that case, applied to head chains, (71) and (72) block the formation of a head chain across an intervening head; this is of course exactly what (1) rules out. The configuration that violates (1) is thus:

(73)

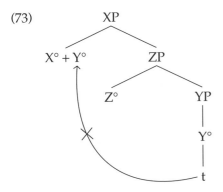

This is violated in standard cases of the type discussed by Rizzi (this volume), e.g.:

(74) a. *[$_C$ Have] they [$_I$ could] [$_V$ t] left?
       b. *[$_C$ Tornato]   Mario [$_I$ essendo] [$_V$ t] a Milano.
           Come-back Mario   being   to Milan

It seems clear that XP-movement is constrained in a more fine-grained way, at least along the lines of the distinction between A- and A′-positions, probably with a further distinction among types of A′-positions (see again Rizzi this volume); the distinctions seem to relate to the feature content of the XPs. Since heads bear features, a natural question to ask is whether head movement is sensitive to the feature content of intervening heads. Evidence for this conclusion would come in the form of structure where a head moves from Y to X across a structural intervener Z, but where the structural intervener is not a *featural* intervener between X and Y (MC can be trivially defined in terms of featural interveners by substituting "featural" for "structural" in (72); in fact, though, I continue to assume that both notions are needed together – see n. 11). In such cases, we would need to show both (i) that Y-movement is genuine head movement and not disguised YP-movement, and (ii) that there are featural interveners Z which block formation of the X–Y chain. A construction which seems to have exactly these properties is long V-movement in Breton, as discussed by Borsley et al. (1996). Long V-movement is illustrated in (75):

(75)   Lennet en   deus Yann al levr.
       Read   3SgM has   Yann the book
       "Yann has read the book."

Superficially, the order here resembles that seen in remnant topicalization constructions in Dutch and German (see Koster 1987, den Besten and Webelhuth 1989, and Rizzi this volume: n. 2):

(76)   Gelesen hat er das Buch nicht.
       Read   has he the book not
       "He hasn't read the book."

Examples like (76) are standardly analyzed as involving scrambling of the object *das Buch* to some VP-external position, followed by topicalization to SpecCP of the remnant VP, whose sole overt exponent is the participle *gelesen* (although it also contains the trace of the scrambled object; for a detailed discussion of remnant movement in German and its possible theoretical implications see Müller 1997). However, there are two important differences between topicalization, including VP-topicalization, and long V-movement: long V-movement is clause bound, while topicalization is not (see 77)); and long V-movement is blocked by negation, while topicalization is not (see 78)):

(77)   a.   *Desket am eus klevet he deus Anna he c'hlentelioù.

                                                        long V-movement

            learnt 1Sg have heard 3SgF have Anna 3SgF lesson
            "I have heard that Anna has learnt her lessons."
       b.   O lenn al levr a ouian emañ Yann.   VP-topicalization
            Prog read the book Prt know-1Sg is Yann
            "I know Yann is reading the book."

(78)   a.   *Lennet n'en deus ket Tom al levr.   long V-movement
            Read Neg 3SgM have Neg Tom the book
            "Tom hasn't read the book."
       b.   O lenn al levr n'emañ ket Yann.   VP-topicalization
            Prog read the book Neg is Neg Yann
            "Yann isn't reading the book."

It seems then that Breton long V-movement cannot be reduced to remnant fronting. See Borsley et al. (1996) for further argumentation on this point.

   Borsley et al. (1996) go on to identify long V-movement with various processes found in a range of Slavic and Romance languages moving verbs or clitics by what appear to be long head movement (LHM) into the C-system (see Rivero 1991, 1994, Lema and Rivero 1990, 1991, 1992, Roberts 1994). These processes all share four important properties, also shared by long V-movement in Breton:

(79) a. LHM is a root phenomenon:
    *Lavaret he deus Anna lennet en deus Tom al levr.
    Said 3SgF have Anna read 3SgM have Tom the book
    "Anna said Tom had read the book."
  b. LHM is blocked by negation – see (78a).
  c. LHM is incompatible with movement to SpecCP (e.g. topicalization):
    Al levr lennet en deus Tom.
    the book read 3SgM have Tom
  d. LHM is licensed only by certain auxiliaries, e.g. perfect (see (75)),
    but not progressive:
    *O lenn emañ Yann al levr.
    Prog read is Yann the book

Borsley et al. (1996) conclude that the derived structure of examples like (75)
is (80):[7]

(80)

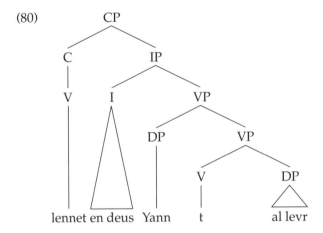

Here we can see that the participle *lennet* has undergone head movement over
I. So we have a *prima facie* case of the kind of head movement which would
motivate a featural, in addition to a structural, characterization of interveners
for head movement. Borsley et al.'s arguments that long V-movement is distinct from remnant VP-topicalization show that this operation is genuine head
movement. Moreover, the fact that this operation is blocked by negation (78a)
and by certain auxiliaries (79d) shows that it is sensitive to certain kinds of
intervening head.

If we grant that Breton long V-movement provides a case for a featural
definition of interveners for head movement, we then have to provide a characterization of the relevant features. On the basis of the work on other possible
LHM structures referred to above, combined with what is known about the
triggers for head movement generally, we could suggest as a first pass distinction between C-heads and I-heads. Suppose then that I-heads block movement
of other I-heads and C-heads block movement of other C-heads. This alone

will guarantee that most cases of head-movement in the clausal domain are highly local, as is standardly observed. Moreover, since many cases of head movement into the C-system, e.g. all full and residual V2, plausibly involve the attraction of T, rather than V (see section 2.2), we can see why these cases of head movement are also strictly local. Also, canonical cases of V-movement into the I-system involve checking of Tense and Agreement features, and so V will not be able to skip the relevant positions. The residue of all of this consists essentially of movement of non-finite V into the C-system, where an auxiliary or particle realizes whatever features of the I-system require checking, and where C has some feature which requires checking which cannot be checked by I-elements. (This feature seems to be related to the EPP property which causes SpecCP to be filled in full V2 systems; see Roberts and Roussou 1998.) This is exactly what seems to be going on in Breton and in comparable cases discussed in the references given above. Note that, in these terms, the clause boundedness of long V-movement is automatically accounted for; an intervening C will block movement to a higher C (cyclic movement is ruled out since it is an instance of excorporation; C itself never overtly incorporates into a higher clause for reasons that are unclear).[8]

However, two considerations lead us to modify this first pass slightly, and to take the featural characterization of the interveners for head movement a step in the direction of the characterization given by Rizzi (this volume) for XPs. We saw above that two kinds of head appear to block long V-movement: negation and certain auxiliaries. Neither of these is in any obvious way a C-head. To take account of this, I propose the following typology of heads in place of the C-head vs. I-head distinction just adumbrated:

(81) a. Lexical vs. functional heads (cf. Baker and Hale 1990).
      b. Among functional heads, operator vs. non-operator heads.

Rivero (1991, 1994) distinguishes lexical from functional auxiliaries according to a range of criteria: in these terms the Breton progressive would be a lexical auxiliary, while the perfect is a functional auxiliary. The obvious way to construe this distinction is by saying that functional auxiliaries are Is while lexical auxiliaries are Vs (cf. the standard way of distinguishing English modals from aspectual *have* and *be*). Then lexical auxiliaries will always block V-movement; whatever attracts the lexical V will preferentially attract the lexical auxiliary.

The blocking effect of negation justifies (81b). Essentially, then, we treat T and Agr (and presumably Asp, etc.) as non-operator heads, while C-heads and Neg are operator heads. It may at first sight seem arbitrary to say that T is not an operator but Fin is, but it is plausible to think of T as a predicate giving an ordering relation on times (see Stowell 1998) while Fin is associated with quantification over times (or worlds, to the extent that its content is modal). If long V-movement in Breton is movement to Fin (see Roberts and Roussou

1998), then this movement will not be blocked by intervening non-operator heads in the I-system, but will be blocked by negation.[9]

We thus group temporal/modal quantification, *wh* (as a canonical C-feature), and negation together, in opposition to agreement positions; this bifurcation is very close to that proposed by Rizzi (1990, this volume) for XP-movement. To the extent that the relevant features can be associated both with heads and with XPs this is a natural and welcome result.[10] This kind of approach is probably consistent with Chomsky's recent formulation of the Minimal Link Condition (MLC):

(82)   L attracts α only if there is no β, β closer to K than α, such that K attracts β.

Of course, attraction has to be relativized to classes of features, not individual features, and much remains to be done in determining what these classes are.[11]

5   Conclusion

The above sections have attempted to illustrate the workings of head movement from an empirical and a theoretical point of view. The empirical evidence for head movement in underlying grammatical function changing operations, and accounting for word order differences crosslinguistically at the clausal and nominal level, is impressive. Theoretically, most, if not all, the properties of head movement can be deduced from the simple statement that we began with: head-movement is Move-α for α a head. In fact, we can now reformulate this as Move-F(eature) where the feature is morphologized on a word. This formulation forces us to a view of locality like that sketched in n. 11. This is particularly clear if heads can be shown to obey the fundamental locality constraints – of which Relativized Minimality may well be the most important – exactly as XPs do; in the last section I suggested that this was the case.

Recently, however, Chomsky has proposed (in class lectures) that head movement may not truly be part of the syntax at all, but rather part of the phonology. This proposal is certainly consistent with representational approaches to the movement phenomenon of the type espoused by Brody (1995) and Rizzi (1990, this volume). The properties of head movement reduce to those of head chains, formed subject to (71) and (72) as modified in section 4. Where a given head is spelt out in a head chain is a matter partly determined by morphology; see Brody (1995) and Roberts and Roussou (1997) for slightly different suggestions (the latter doing away at the same time with notion of checking). To the extent that the claim that head movement is "a PF-phenomenon" means anything substantive, it can be interpreted – crucially in the context of a representational theory – to mean this.

NOTES

*   I would like to thank Anna Roussou for valuable comments on an earlier draft of this paper. All the errors are mine.

1   The Uniformity Condition on Chains of Chomsky (1995b: 253) has the same effect, as long as we assume that head movement forms a chain (again, a standard assumption regarding movement):

(i)   A chain is uniform with regard to phrase structure status.

"Phrase structure status" here refers to the X^n status of the positions which make up the chain.

2   Chomsky accounts for *have/be* raising with the suggestion that these elements cannot obey Procrastinate since they lack an LF interpretation, and so must be eliminated prior to that level. For criticism of this idea, and different alternative approaches to *have/be* raising in a minimalist framework, see Lasnik (1995a) and Roberts (1998).

3   The straightforward implication that a language allows inversion only if it has the French-style orders in (14)–(16) does not hold. The mainland Scandinavian languages – Swedish, Danish, and Norwegian – are Verb Second in root clauses and pattern like English with respect to the Pollock/Emonds tests in embedded clauses (Platzack 1987, Holmberg and Platzack 1995, Vikner 1994a). If at least some V2 clauses involve V-to-I movement, as proposed by Travis (1984) and Zwart (1993a) (see below), then the generalization can be maintained.

4   The subject can always be optionally realized as an Accusative DP in non-finite clauses in Irish. See Chung and McCloskey (1987).

5   For further discussion of this issue, and a summary of a number of recent analyses of SOV order in non-finite clauses in Irish, see Carnie (1995: 81–118). For my purposes here, it is enough to show how these orders argue for the idea that the subject leaves VP in Irish.

6   Note that this formulation makes Z an intervener even if it symmetrically c-commands X. If c-command is defined in terms of branching nodes, so that segments determine c-command domains (*contra* Kayne 1994), then this can rule out excorporation – cf. Roberts (1991) and the discussion in section 1.

7   Note that Borsley et al. (1996) place the Breton subject in SpecVP and the inflected verb in I. As examples like (78b) show, Breton subjects differ from those of Welsh in following the second element of negation *ket*, hence there is no obvious bar to placing the subject here. See the discussion of VSO orders in section 2.3.

8   Chomsky (1998a) suggests that selection is a kind of attraction. Complement C is always lexically selected, and so is attracted by V. Perhaps for this reason it cannot be attracted in any other way (i.e. so as to trigger movement). Incorporation from non-selected CPs is ruled out by (the relevant updating of) Baker's account summarized in section 1.

9   Long V-movement must be adjunction to Fin as the presence of the particle *a* shows (which appears to be exactly like its Welsh counterpart discussed in section 2.3 – see Hendrick 1988) in (i):

(i)   Lenn a ra Anna al levr.
       "Anna reads the book."

10   Rizzi (this volume) proposes that
       modifier XPs act as interveners
       for other modifier XPs. Whether
       this class of features affects head
       movement could be determined
       by a close examination of head
       movement relations inside APs,
       an issue that has been largely
       neglected, but see Donati (1996).

11   As Anna Roussou (personal
       communication) points out,
       we could in fact, following the
       proposals in Chomsky (1995b),
       eliminate the notion of structural
       intervener entirely. All movement
is triggered by features of heads,
and we might think XPs are
attracted to the extent that they
realize features that can be checked
with attracting heads. For example,
Agr attracts DPs (although it may
be able to attract Ds, giving rise
to cliticization), C attracts *wh*-XPs,
but any head with a V-feature will
attract a verb rather than a VP. This
would be the natural extension of
locality in terms of the current
theory, although many details
remain to be worked out. In any
case, proposing a featural
characterization of the intervener
for head movement seems more
than justified in this context.

6 Object Shift and Scrambling

HÖSKULDUR THRÁINSSON

0 Introduction

The purpose of this chapter is to give an overview of the most important descriptive issues involved in the so-called Object Shift (henceforth OS) and Scrambling constructions, and to discuss some of the theoretical implications of the facts. There is an extensive literature on these constructions, written in a number of different frameworks and arguing for quite different analyses.[1] For reasons of space I will concentrate on facts from Germanic languages in the descriptive part of the chapter, mainly the Scandinavian languages for OS, and German and Dutch for Scrambling.[2]

Since most of the literature on these constructions assumes derivational accounts and movement rules (see e.g. the papers in Grewendorf and Sternefeld 1990b, Corver and Riemsdijk 1994b), I will basically assume that kind of analysis in the presentation of the data.[3] I will, however, try to save most of the theoretical issues for the second half of the chapter and make an attempt to keep the first half relatively descriptive and theory-neutral in order to give the reader a reasonable overview.

The relevant constructions are exemplified in (1b) and (2b) (where t_i indicates trace in the position where the "moved" object is generally assumed to have been base generated):

(1) a. Nemandinn las   ekki bókina.   (Ic)
       student-the read   not book-the
   b. Nemandinn las   **bókina**$_i$ ekki t_i
       "The student didn't read the book."

(2) a. Der Student hat   nicht das Buch gelesen.   (Ge)
       the student has   not the book read
   b. Der Student hat **das Buch**$_i$ nicht t_i gelesen.
       "The student hasn't read the book."

Under the standard assumption that Icelandic (1b) and German (2b) involve OS and Scrambling, respectively, it is immediately obvious that there are certain similarities between the two constructions, or the two movement rules: both can move objects to the left and across a clause-medial adverb like the negation. In addition, it is frequently possible to find subtle semantic differences between sentences of the b-type and those of the a-type, and these tend to be similar in Icelandic and German, for instance (see section 2.4.1 below). Hence the two constructions/movements are sometimes grouped together under the label of Object Movement (see e.g. Déprez 1989, 1994, Diesing 1997).

Despite this, there are considerable differences between OS in Icelandic and Scrambling in German, for instance. First, the structural conditions appear to be different. As Holmberg was the first to point out (1986), OS in Icelandic only applies when the main verb is finite and has arguably "moved" out of the VP, whereas German Scrambling also takes place in clauses with non-finite main verbs and auxiliaries (like (2b), for instance). Second, Icelandic OS only applies to objects of verbs whereas German Scrambling can also apply to other maximal projections, e.g. prepositional phrases. Third, it has been argued that OS in Icelandic moves the object to a relatively low position (one suggestion is SpecAgrOP, cf. sections 2.1.1 and 2.2.3) whereas German Scrambling appears to move constituents to a higher position, at least in some instances (a common suggestion is adjunction to IP). But if differences of this sort exist, then one would like to know why they exist, what they are related to, whether comparable constructions in other languages have similar properties, and, if so, why that might be. As we will see, the study of OS and Scrambling phenomena in various languages has raised a number of intriguing questions of this sort and shed light on many issues having to do with crosslinguistic similarities and differences, the nature of syntactic structure, and the relationship between syntax, semantics, and phonology.

The organization of this chapter is as follows: in section 1 I outline some of the basic properties of the constructions, summarizing the apparent similarities and differences between OS and Scrambling in section 1.3. Section 2 then discusses some of the theoretical issues that have arisen in recent discussions of OS and Scrambling. These issues concern the nature of syntactic structure and the interaction between syntax, semantics, morphology, and phonology. Finally, section 3 concludes the chapter.

1 Basic Properties of Object Shift and Scrambling

1.1 *Object shift in Scandinavian*

1.1.1 *The movable constituents*
OS in Icelandic was first discussed within the generative framework by Holmberg (cf. Holmberg 1986). As he pointed out, sentences similar to (1b)

can also be found in Mainland Scandinavian (Danish, Norwegian, Swedish, henceforth MSc), provided that the object is a simple, unstressed definite pronoun. This is also true for Icelandic and Faroese, but as illustrated below, pronominal OS tends to be obligatory in Scandinavian,[4] contrary to the OS of full NPs (or DPs) in Icelandic (the sign % indicates that the sentence may be possible in certain dialects):

(3) a. *Nemandinn las   ekki hana.   (Ic)
         *Studenten   læste   ikke den.   (Da)
         *Næmingurin las   ikki hana.   (Fa)
         %Studenten   läste   inte den.   (Sw)
         student-the read   not it
     b. Nemandinn   las   **hana**$_i$ ekki t$_i$ (Ic)
         Studenten   læste **den**$_i$ ikke t$_i$ (Da)
         Næmingurin   las   **hana**$_i$ ikki t$_i$ (Fa)
         Studenten   läste **den**$_i$ inte t$_i$ (Sw)
         student-the read it   not
         "The student didn't read it."

It is generally assumed in the literature that Icelandic is the only modern Scandinavian language that has OS of full NPs (DPs) since sentences corresponding to (1b) are bad in the others:[5]

(4) a. *Studenten   læste **bogen**$_i$ ikke t$_i$ (Da)
     b. *Næmingurin las   **bókina**$_i$ ikki t$_i$ (Fa)
     c. *Studenten   leste **boken**$_i$ ikke t$_i$ (No)
     d. *Studenten   läste **boken**$_i$ inte t$_i$ (Sw)
         student-the   read   book-the not

Similarly, stressed, modified and conjoined pronouns cannot be shifted in MSc or in Faroese, whereas they can in Icelandic. Thus we find contrasts like those in (5) (the other MSc languages would work like Norwegian, cf. Holmberg and Platzack 1995: 162n):

(5) a. Hún sá **mig**$_i$/**MIG**$_i$/**[mig og þig]**$_i$/**[þennan á hjólinu]**$_i$ ekki t$_i$ (Ic)
     b. Hun så **meg**$_i$/*MEG$_i$/*[meg og deg]$_i$/*[ham på sykkelen]$_i$ ikke t$_i$
                                                                              (No)
         she saw me   ME   me and you   him on the bike   not
         "She didn't see me/me and you/him on the bike."

As illustrated, all the objects in question can be fronted in Icelandic, but in Norwegian only the unstressed pronominal object can.

Icelandic OS only applies to objects of verbs, not to objects of prepositions, PPs, or APs (either predicates or secondary predicates), for instance. This is illustrated in (6)–(7):[6]

(6) a. Jón talaði   ekki [$_{PP}$ við Maríu].   (Ic)
         Jon spoke   not   to   Mary(A)
         "John didn't speak to Mary."
    b. *Jón talaði **Maríu**$_i$ ekki [$_{PP}$ við t$_i$]
    c. *Jón talaði [$_{PP}$ **við Maríu**]$_i$ ekki t$_i$

(7) a. Fyrirlestrar hans eru   alltaf   skemmtilegastir.
         talks   his   are   always most-interesting
         "His talks are always the most interesting ones."
    b. *Fyrirlestrar hans eru **skemmtilegastir**$_i$ alltaf   t$_i$
    c. Jón málaði   ekki hurðina dökkgræna.
         Jón painted   not door-the dark green
         "John didn't paint the door dark green."
    d. *Jón málaði **dökkgræna**$_i$ ekki hurðina t$_i$

Pronominal objects of prepositions, or PPs containing (weak) pronouns, cannot be shifted either (see e.g. Vikner 1989: 147, 1991: 287, Holmberg 1986: 199).

All the examples of shifted objects given so far involve definite NPs (DPs) or definite pronouns (personal pronouns). The reason is that indefinite objects can only be shifted when they receive a special interpretation, as will be discussed in section 2.4.1. Thus (8b) is impossible in Icelandic:

(8) a. Hún keypti   ekki kaffi.   (Ic)
         she   bought   not   coffee
    b. *Hún keypti **kaffi**$_i$ ekki t$_i$
         "She didn't buy coffee."

Similarly, it appears that indefinite pronouns do not readily shift, either in MSc or in Icelandic (see also Diesing 1996: 76):

(9)   Nei, jeg har   ingen paraply,   (No)
         no   I   have no   umbrella
    a.   men jeg køper   muligens en   i morgen.
            but I   buy   possibly one tomorrow
    b. *. . . men jeg køper **en**$_i$ muligens t$_i$ i morgen.
         "I don't have an umbrella, but I may buy one tomorrow."

(10)   Ég á   ekkert   eftir Chomsky.   (Ic)
         I   have nothing by   Chomsky
    a. Átt þú   ekki eitthvað?
         have you   not   something
    b. *Átt þú **eitthvað**$_i$ ekki t$_i$?
         "I don't have anything by Chomsky. Don't you have something?"

Having looked at the types of constituent that can be moved in Scandinavian OS, we can now consider the structural conditions involved in more detail.[7]

1.1.2   *The structural conditions on Scandinavian Object Shift*

In this section we will first look at the relationship between Scandinavian OS and verb movement (position of the finite verb) and then the applicability of OS in particle verb constructions and in double object constructions.

As pointed out by Holmberg (1986), OS in Scandinavian is restricted by the position of the main verb. Thus when the main verb is finite and appears to move out of the VP, as it does in all types of clause in Icelandic and in main clauses in MSc, OS is applicable, but it does not apply in auxiliary constructions, when the main verb apparently stays inside the VP, or in MSc embedded clauses where a finite main verb cannot move out of the VP. Thus we get contrasts like the following (cf. Holmberg 1986: 165, Vikner 1989, Josefsson 1992, 1993; *v* indicates the verb's base position):

(11)   a.   Af hverju lásu nemendurnir **bækurnar**$_i$ ekki [$_{VP}$ v   t$_i$]?   (Ic)
            for what   read students-the books-the not
            "Why didn't the students read the books?"

      b.   *Af hverju hafa nemendurnir **bækurnar**$_i$ ekki [$_{VP}$ lesið t$_i$]?
            for what   have students-the books-the not   read

      c.   Hún spurði [$_{CP}$ af hverju stúdentarnir læsu **bækurnar**$_i$ ekki [$_{VP}$ v t$_i$]]
            she asked   for what   students-the   read books-the not
            "She asked why the students didn't read the books."

(12)   a.   Varför läste studenterna   **den**$_i$ inte [$_{VP}$ v   t$_i$]?   (Sw)
            why   read students-the   it   not
            "Why didn't the students read it?"

      b.   *Varför har   studenterna   **den**$_i$ inte [$_{VP}$ läst t$_i$]?
            why   have students-the   it   not   read

      c.   *Hon frågade [$_{CP}$ varför studenterna **den**$_i$ inte [$_{VP}$ läste t$_i$]]
            he   asked   why   students-the it   not   read

Since Holmberg's dissertation (1986), the observation that there is a relationship between the position of the main verb and the shiftability of the object in Scandinavian has come to be known as Holmberg's Generalization. We will return to it in section 2.2.5 below.[8]

OS can apply in particle constructions in Scandinavian, for instance in Icelandic (see e.g. Collins and Thráinsson 1996: 429ff):[9]

(13)   a.   Hún hefur   ekki [$_{VP}$ skrifað upp kvæðið]   (Ic)
            she has   not   written up poem-the
            "She has not written up the poem."

      b.   Hún skrifaði **kvæðið**$_i$ ekki [$_{VP}$ v   upp t$_i$]
            she wrote   poem-the not   up
            "She didn't write up the poem."

Finally, consider the applicability of OS in double object constructions in Scandinavian, beginning with the shift of full NP (or DP) objects in Icelandic. As Collins and Thráinsson (1996) observe, it is not simple to test the "shiftability" of the objects in double object constructions. The acceptability of the sentences involved is influenced by various independent phenomena, including stress, person, and animacy of the objects, and the so-called Inversion phenomenon (i.e. the ability of certain verbs to allow both the (normal) IO DO order (the Indirect Object preceding the Direct Object, that is) and the (exceptional) DO IO order, cf. Rögnvaldsson 1982, Zaenen et al. 1985, Falk 1990, Holmberg 1991b, Holmberg and Platzack 1995, Ottósson 1991, 1993).[10] These factors are controlled for in the following examples:[11]

(14)　a.　Mannræninginn skilaði　aldrei foreldrunum　börnunum.
　　　　　kidnapper-the　returned never parents-the(D) kids-the(D)
　　　　　"The kidnapper never returned the kids to the parents."
　　　b.　Mannræninginn skilaði **foreldrunum**$_i$ aldrei t_i börnunum.
　　　c.　*Mannræninginn skilaði **börnunum**$_j$　aldrei foreldrunum t_j
　　　　　(ungrammatical in the sense: ". . . never returned the kids to the parents.")
　　　d.　Mannræninginn skilaði **foreldrunum**$_i$ **börnunum**$_j$ aldrei t_i t_j

As these examples indicate, it is possible to shift the IO (cf. (14b)) or both the IO and the DO but the DO does not seem to be able to shift across the IO (cf. (14c)).

Some puzzling restrictions on the shiftability of objects in double object constructions will be discussed in section 2 below (especially section 2.1.4).

1.1.3　Apparent landing sites involved in Scandinavian Object Shift

In all the examples of Scandinavian OS given above, the "moved" objects have "landed" immediately to the left of a sentential adverb or the negation. The standard assumption is that these adverbs are left-adjoined to VP in Scandinavian (see e.g. Vikner 1995, Holmberg and Platzack 1995, Jonas 1996a, 1996b, Bobaljik 1995, Jonas and Bobaljik 1993, Collins and Thráinsson 1996, Bobaljik and Thráinsson 1998, and references cited by these authors). If we accept that assumption, we only have evidence so far for the objects shifting "just out of" the VP and not to some higher position. As a matter of fact, it seems very difficult to find evidence for any "long OS" in Scandinavian, e.g. one where the shifted object has landed to the left of a postverbal subject, say in a Topicalization structure. Observe (15):

(15)　a.　Þá　máluðu allir strákarnir　　　　stundum　bílana　rauða.
　　　　　　　　　　　　　　　　　　　　　　　　　　　　　　(Ic)
　　　　　then painted all boys-the(N)　　stundum cars-the(A) red(A)
　　　b.　Þá　máluðu allir strákarnir **bílana**$_i$ stundum　t_i　　　rauða.
　　　　　"Then all the boys sometimes painted the cars red."
　　　c.　*Þá　máluðu **bílana**$_i$ allir strákarnir stundum　t_i　　　rauða.

As can be seen here, the shifted object *bílana* "the cars" can only shift as far as immediately across the sentential adverb *stundum* "sometimes," not across the subject *allir strákarnir* "all the boys."[12]

All the examples of pronominal OS given so far are also instances of "short OS." Although this is the general rule, there are some examples of "long pronominal OS" in Modern Swedish dialects and in some older Scandinavian texts. Representative examples are given in (16) (see Holmberg 1986: 230ff, Hellan and Platzack 1995: 58–60, Josefsson 1992):

(16)   a.   Varför gömde **sig**$_i$ barnen   t$_i$?   (Sw)
              why   hid   self children-the
              "Why did the children hide?"

        b.   Gav **dej**$_i$ snuten t$_i$ körkortet   tillbaka?   (Sw)
              gave you cop-the   driver's-license-the back
              "Did the cop give you your driver's license back?"

        c.   Nu befallde **oss**$_i$ rånaren   t$_i$ att vara tysta.   (Sw)
              now ordered us   robber-the   to be   silent
              "Now the robber ordered us to be silent."

        d.   Ekki hryggja **mig**$_i$ hót   þín t$_i$ (OIc)
              not grieve me threats your
              "Your threats don't disturb me."

        e.   Snart indfandt **sig**$_i$ dette t$_i$ (No 1833)
              soon presented itself this
              "Soon this presented itself."

        f.   Derfor   forekommer **mig**$_i$ maaske det hele   t$_i$ mere   (Da 1860)
              therefore seems   me perhaps the whole more
              betydningsfuldt.
              important
              "Therefore the whole thing perhaps appears more important to me."

As can be seen here, the pronominal objects are either reflexive, 1st or 2nd person pronouns and according to Holmberg (1986: 230) and Hellan and Platzack (1995), one could not substitute a 3rd person pronominal object in (16a) or (16c), for instance. The reason for this restriction is unclear.

After this descriptive overview of Scandinavian OS we will now give a parallel overview of German and Dutch Scrambling.

1.2   Scrambling in German and Dutch

1.2.1   The movable constituents

The term Scrambling for a rule describing word order variation originates with Ross (1967a), although the phenomenon was already discussed in a generative framework by Bierwisch (1963). Ross originally proposed this rule to account for so-called "free word order" in languages like Latin and suggested that it be considered a part of the "stylistic component" rather than the transformational component proper. In recent literature the term is normally used in a more restricted sense, namely to refer to "fronting" (or "raising") of constituents like objects, indirect objects, and even PPs in various languages (cf. e.g. the discussion in Grewendorf and Sternefeld 1990a, the papers in Grewendorf and Sternefeld 1990b, and in Corver and van Riemsdijk 1994b).

In the so-called Principles and Parameters approach, usually traced to Chomsky (1981), the emphasis has shifted from the description of language-particular rules (cf. e.g. the discussion in Epstein et al. 1996) and a standard claim is that there is only "one transformational rule," namely "Move α," where α is some syntactic constituent. In that sense the "rule" of Scrambling is just "Move α" and thus not different from, say, the "rule" of OS discussed above. Nevertheless it has been argued that the structures created by (German and Dutch, henceforth GD) Scrambling are different from those created by (Scandinavian) OS. The purpose of this section is to outline some of these properties and compare them to those of the OS just discussed.

What will qualify as Scrambling data in GD depends on one's assumptions about the underlying order of the main verb and the object in GD. Under the traditional assumption that Dutch and German are OV languages, examples like those in (17) provide no evidence for Scrambling whereas the ones in (18) do (or may). But if we assume with Kayne (1994) that all languages are underlyingly VO, as Zwart (1993a, 1997) and Roberts (1997) do, for instance, then even the sentences in (17) would provide evidence for Scrambling (namely movement of the object to the left across the verb, cf. e.g. Zwart 1997: 30ff; see also Haider et al. 1995: 14ff):

(17) a. . . . dat Jan gisteren Marie gekust heeft.   (Du)
      b. . . . dass Jens gestern   Maria geküsst hat.   (Ge)
               that John yesterday Mary kissed   has
          ". . . that John kissed Mary yesterday."

(18) a. . . . dat Jan **Marie** gisteren   gekust heeft.   (Du)
      b. . . . dass Jens **Maria** gestern   geküsst hat.   (Ge)
               that John Mary   yesterday kissed   has
          ". . . that John kissed Mary yesterday."

In the following I will for the most part adopt the traditional assumption and only consider GD evidence where the relevant constituents appear to have shifted to the left across (at least) an adverbial phrase of some sort. This means that the trace of the moved objects in (18) would be between "yesterday" and "kissed" whereas the objects in (17) would presumably be in situ.[13]

Assuming this, we can now try to establish what kinds of constituent GD Scrambling may apply to. As shown in (19)–(21), it applies to NPs and PPs but not to (secondary predicate) APs (cf. e.g. Grewendorf and Sternefeld 1990a, de Hoop 1992, Corver and van Riemsdijk 1994a, Neeleman 1994, Vikner 1994b, Haider et al. 1995: 14ff, Costa 1996, Zwart 1997, and references cited by these authors):

(19) a.   . . . dass Jens   nicht die Bücher kauft.   (Ge)
      b.   . . . dat Jan   niet de boeken koopt.   (Du)
            that John   not   the books buys
      c.   . . . dass Jens **die Bücher**$_i$ nicht t$_i$ kauft.
      d.   . . . dat Jan **de boeken**$_i$ niet t$_i$ koopt.

(20) a.   . . . dass Jens   kaum   auf meine Bemerkung reagierte.   (Ge)
      b.   . . . dat Jan   nauwelijks op mijn opmerking   reageerde. (Du)
            that John   hardly   on my remark   reacted
      c.   . . . dass Jens **auf meine Bemerkung**$_i$ kaum   t$_i$ reagierte.
      d.   . . . dat Jan **op mijn opmerking**$_i$ nauwelijks t$_i$ reageerde.

(21) a.   . . . dass Jens   morgen   die Tür dunkelgrün   streicht.   (Ge)
      b.   . . . dat Jan   morgen   de deur donkergroen verft.   (Du)
            that John   tomorrow the door dark green   paints
      c.   *. . . dass Jens **dunkelgrün**$_i$ morgen die Tür t$_i$ streicht.
      d.   *. . . dat Jan **donkergroen**$_i$ morgen de deur t$_i$ verft.

Thus we see that GD Scrambling is similar to Icelandic OS in that neither applies to APs, but GD Scrambling is different from Scandinavian OS in applying to PPs. The question is how this difference might be explained. I will consider some proposed explanations in section 2 (e.g. 2.2.4 and 2.3.1).

Having compared the movable constituents in GD Scrambling and Scandinavian OS, I will now compare these "rules" in more detail with respect to structural conditions on their application.

1.2.2.   The structural conditions on German and Dutch Scrambling

As illustrated in section 1.1.2 above, Scandinavian OS appears to be restricted by the position of the main verb. Thus if there is an auxiliary verb in the clause and the main verb is hence non-finite and follows sentential adverbs and the negation, OS cannot apply. As already mentioned, GD Scrambling is not restricted in this fashion. This is illustrated in (22) with a German example (see e.g. Vikner 1994b: 498ff, Zwart 1997: 90ff):

(22) a.   . . . dass Jens   gestern   das Buch gekauft hat.   (Ge)
            that John   yesterday the book bought has
      b.   . . . dass Jens **das Buch**$_i$ gestern   t$_i$ gekauft hat.
            ". . . that John bought the book yesterday."

This is an intriguing difference which has given rise to a number of theoretical proposals, as we shall see in section 2 below (see e.g. 2.2.5).

Since the constituents that can be moved by Scrambling seem to be partially different from those undergoing OS, and also because the structural conditions on the two constructions appear to be different, one might wonder whether the landing sites (the positions that the constituents move to) could be the same. There appear to be some differences, as we shall now see.

1.2.3　Apparent landing sites

As demonstrated by Vikner (1994b: 487–8), for instance, examples of, say, German Scrambling and Danish (pronominal) OS can look very similar:

(23)　a.　I går　　læste han **dem**$_i$ ikke　t$_i$　　　　　　　　　(Da)
　　　b.　Gestern　las　er　**sie**$_i$　nicht t$_i$　　　　　　　　(Ge)
　　　　　yesterday read　he　them not

As readers familiar with work on Germanic languages will notice, the sentences in (23) involve preposing of a non-subject (*i går, gestern* "yesterday"), so the finite main verb shows up in second position in both Danish and German since both are Verb-Second (V2) languages. Since the objects *dem, sie* "them" precede the negation, the standard assumption is that they have moved to the left and out of the VP. If the negation is left-adjoined to the VP, then the moved objects could be left-adjoined to the VP also (i.e., "on top of" the negation).

There is some evidence, however, that GD Scrambling may move elements "higher" than Scandinavian OS normally does. This is especially true for German (cf. e.g. Grewendorf and Sternefeld 1990a: 9, Czepluch 1990: 174):

(24)　a.　. . . dass　　der Schüler　　**den Lehrer**$_i$　　nicht t$_i$ überzeugt. (Ge)
　　　　　　　　that　　the student-Nom　the teacher-Acc　not　　convinces
　　　b.　(?) . . . dass **den Lehrer**$_i$　　der Schüler　　nicht t$_i$ überzeugt.
　　　　　" . . . that the student does not convince the teacher."
　　　c.　(?) . . . dass die Antwort　　**den Lehrer**$_i$　　nicht t$_i$ überzeugt.
　　　　　　　　that the answer-Nom　the teacher-Acc　not　　convinces
　　　d.　. . . dass　　**den Lehrer**$_i$　　die Antwort　　nicht t$_i$ überzeugt.
　　　　　" . . . that the answer does not convince the teacher."
　　　e.　. . . dass　　**den Max**$_i$　　jeder　　　　　t$_i$ kennt.
　　　　　　　　that　　Max　　　everybody　　　　knows
　　　　　" . . . that everybody knows Max."

As shown in (24b, d, e), it is possible in German to scramble an object across a subject, with some variation in acceptability, depending on the nature of the subject and object (cf. Czepluch 1990: 174).[14] As mentioned in section 1.1.3 above, such movement of object across a subject appears to be impossible in Icelandic full NP OS. Thus it seems that German Scrambling can move constituents further to the left than Icelandic OS, perhaps adjoining them to IP (in addition to VP) (cf. e.g. Müller and Sternefeld 1994: 342).

The situation is slightly different in Dutch. There Scrambling of an object across a subject is apparently only possible when a special "focus" reading is involved, as indicated by contrasts like the following (based on Neeleman 1994: 395–6):

(25) a. . . . dat   Jan   **die boeken$_i$**   niet t$_i$ koopt. (Du)
          that   John   the books   not   buys
      b. *. . . dat **die boeken$_i$** Jan   niet t$_i$ koopt.
      c. . . . dat   zelfs Jan **zulke boeken$_i$** niet t$_i$ koopt.
          that   even John such books   not   buys
      d. . . . dat **zulke boeken$_i$** zelfs Jan   niet t$_i$ koopt.

In (25b) we see that a regular object like *die boeken* "the books" cannot be scrambled across the subject, whereas the object *zulke boeken* "such books" can be scrambled across the subject *zelfs Jan* "even John" in (25d). Thus although Dutch Scrambling normally moves elements to a lower position, one could argue that it can exceptionally adjoin them to a higher position (like IP, for instance).[15] Zwart (1997) refers to this special kind of (long) Scrambling in Dutch as "focus Scrambling" and treats it as a different process.[16]

As in Scandinavian, movement of unstressed pronominal objects tends to be obligatory in German and Dutch.

1.3   Summary of similarities and differences observed so far

Concentrating on Scandinavian OS and GD Scrambling, we can summarize as follows the similarities and differences between the two constructions found so far (with some simplification, as is always involved in tables of this sort – see also the systematic comparison in Vikner 1994):

(26)

	Scandinavian OS		GD Scrambling	
	Icelandic	*Other Scand. lgs*	*German*	*Dutch*
Moves full NPs	yes	no	yes	yes
Moves pronominal NPs	yes	yes	yes	yes
Moves PPs	no	no	yes	yes
Moves (secondary) predic. APs	no	no	no	no
Dependent main verb pos.	yes	yes	no	no
Moves to a low (VP-adj.?) pos.	yes	yes	yes	yes

The similarities and differences summarized here call for explanations, and these are bound to differ depending on the theoretical framework assumed. But the particular theoretical approaches will typically also uncover other similarities and differences between the constructions in question, and increase our understanding of and knowledge about syntactic structure in general and the nature of the relationship between syntax, semantics, morphology, and phonology. Some examples are discussed in section 2.

2 Some Theoretical Issues Concerning Object Shift and Scrambling

Studies of OS and Scrambling, including comparison of these two types of construction, have shed light on various theoretical questions, including the following:

(27) a. What is the nature of constituent structure and how does it vary crosslinguistically?

b. How can syntactic movement rules be classified, how are they restricted, and what are the possible "landing sites" for movement?

c. What is the relationship between morphology and syntactic structure in general and syntactic movement rules in particular?

d. To what extent are syntactic movement rules optional and to what extent do they interact with semantics and/or phonology?

The organization of this section reflects the issues listed in (27) and in some instances they have been broken down into more specific questions.

2.1 The nature of constituent structure

2.1.1 Hierarchical clause structure, functional projections, and directionality

Within a syntactic theory that assumes movement of constituents, there are two ways to account for free word order, or variation in word order. One is to assume extensive movement, the other to assume variation in underlying structure. Both approaches, however, raise a similar question: why do languages differ with respect to the ordering of constituents they allow? But within a reasonably rich theory which assumes movement but also allows for some variability in underlying structure, it should be possible in principle to distinguish between word order alternations that derive from different underlying structures and those that are derived by movement. Thus Webelhuth (1992) argues that Scrambling structures obey the so-called island constraints first discussed by Ross (1967a) and that this suggests that movement is involved (cf. also Corver and van Riemsdijk 1994a: 3–4).

A radical approach to crosslinguistic differences with respect to freedom of word order is the non-configurationality hypothesis (see e.g. Hale 1983, 1994; see also Baker's contribution to this volume). Some linguists have attributed the relatively free word order of languages like German and Old Norse to non-configurationality (see Haider 1988, Faarlund 1990; for different positions see Webelhuth 1984–5, Rögnvaldsson 1995). This approach will not be discussed further here.

Another approach to the crosslinguistic variability observed in OS and Scrambling phenomena is to attribute them to some extent to different underlying structure of the languages in question. Thus it has been claimed that the reason Modern Icelandic (and Old Norse and the MSc languages in previous centuries) have OS of full NPs may have something to do with a richer functional structure, e.g. because of different (or "stronger") agreement features associated with IP in Icelandic (and Old Norse etc.), allowing for different licensing of nominal arguments (see e.g. Holmberg and Platzack 1990, 1995), or because of different licensing properties of the argumental positions (see e.g. Jonas and Bobaljik 1993, Jonas 1994, 1996a, 1996b, Bobaljik and Jonas 1996), or else because Modern Icelandic (and Old Norse, etc.) has a more complex functional structure than MSc, allowing for more surface positions of the arguments (see Thráinsson 1996, Bobaljik 1995, Bobaljik and Thráinsson 1998). We will return to issues of this kind in section 2.2 (especially sections 2.2.2 and 2.2.3).

While some of the studies just referred to argue that the crosslinguistic variation in word order frequently attributed to object movement of some sort can be traced to differences in underlying structure and the different movement possibilities resulting from these, a different tack is taken by those linguists who claim that there are only minimal differences (if any) in underlying structure between languages. In particular, these linguists claim that languages generally have VO-order within the VP underlyingly and the observed differences in surface word order result from different movement rules. The basic idea goes back to Kayne's influential book (1994) and has been applied to "Scrambling" languages by linguists like Zwart (1997; Dutch) and Roberts (1997; older stages of English). If languages like Dutch and German, for instance, are VO-languages, then that obviously means more extensive application of Scrambling (or something like it) to derive the surface word orders, as already mentioned in section 1.2.1 above. Space does not permit further discussion of the theoretical issues involved (but see Thráinsson 1997 for some relevant points).

2.1.2   Adverb positions

Studies of OS and Scrambling have forced linguists to look more closely at individual aspects of syntactic structure. One such aspect is the positioning of adverbs, since (sentential) adverbs figure prominently in the study of OS and Scrambling as landmarks of syntactic structure, as seen above.

The basic problem with using adverbs as evidence for the syntactic position of other constituents is the fact that adverbs can typically occur in a number of different positions within the clause (see e.g. Jackendoff 1972, McConnell-Ginet 1982, Higginbotham 1985, Travis 1988, McCawley 1988, Alexiadou 1997, Cinque 1997). But despite attempts to account explicitly for the interaction between the syntax and semantics of adverbs, it seems that most studies of OS and Scrambling assume a relatively unsophisticated theory of adverbs. The crucial assumption in most of these studies is that adverbs that precede the position of the main verb (in a VO-language) must be adjoined no lower than to VP. Consequently, if an object appears to the left of such an adverb in such a language, it must have moved out of the VP. A classic paradigm is repeated in (28) for ease of reference:

(28)   a.   Jón hefur   **aldrei** lesið bókina.   (Ic)
            John has   never read book-the
            "John has never read the book."
       b.   *Jón hefur   lesið **aldrei**   bókina.
            John has   read never   book-the
       c.   *Jón hefur   lesið bókina   **aldrei**.
            John has   read book-the never
       d.   Jón las   **aldrei** v   bókina.
            John read   never   book-the
       e.   Jón las   bókinaᵢ **aldrei** v   tᵢ
            "John never read the book."

In (28a) the finite verb is the auxiliary *hefur* "has." It is standardly assumed that the main verb stays in the VP in such clauses and we see that it follows the sentential adverb *aldrei*. As (28b) shows, the adverb *aldrei* cannot intervene between the non-finite main verb and the object in such clauses, and (28c) shows that it cannot follow the object. But when there is no auxiliary verb and the main verb is finite, it can precede sentential adverbs like *aldrei*, as illustrated in (28d). Consequently it is assumed that it has moved out of the VP. Finally, (28e) shows that in such contexts the object can also precede this adverb and this is, of course, the classic instance of OS under discussion here.

   While a paradigm of this kind indicates that the object may shift out of the VP in languages like Icelandic when the verb also leaves the VP, as in (28e), it does not really show that the verb and the object could not also have moved out of the VP in sentences like (28a). This is so because the adverb *aldrei* could in principle be adjoined higher than to the VP (e.g. to TP in a complex functional structure). More specifically, the question is why the structure of (28a) could not be like (29):

(29)   [$_{AgrSP}$ Jón hefur [$_{TP}$ aldrei [$_{TP}$ lesið [$_{AgrOP}$ bókina [$_{VP}$ v tᵢ]]]]]

Here the subject *Jón* would be in SpecAgrSP, the finite auxiliary *hefur* in AgrS, the adverb *aldrei* adjoined to TP, the non-finite main verb in T, and the object could then have shifted to SpecAgrOP. To rule this out, we need an explicit theory of movement which specifies *why* the elements in question move where they supposedly move. One such is the checking theory proposed by Chomsky (1993, 1995b) and related work. Under such a theory, it could be argued that the non-finite main verb *lesið* would not have any feature to check in T. Note also that if we assume that the non-finite verb could move out of the VP and to T, we would expect that it could cross an adverb adjoined to VP. If the object remained in situ, we should then get a structure like (28b), but if the object shifted out of the VP and across the adverb, we should get a structure like (28c). As indicated above, however, both structures are ungrammatical in Icelandic.

We see then that while a sophisticated theory of adverb placement would certainly be welcomed by those who try to account for the apparent variability in surface positions of verbs and objects, the standard arguments reviewed above are not implausible. But if one assumes, like Zwart (1997), for instance, that Dutch is a VO-language, then one is forced to conclude that the object has not only moved (undergone Scrambling) in (30b) but also in (30a), as indicated by the traces (see e.g. Zwart 1997: 91):

(30) a.   . . . dat Jan **gisteren** Marie$_i$ gekust t$_i$ heeft.   (Du)
          that John yesterday Mary   kissed   has
      b.   . . . dat Jan   Marie$_i$ **gisteren** gekust t$_i$ heeft.
          ". . . that John has kissed Mary yesterday."

Zwart thus has to assume that the object is in the same position in (30a) and (30b) and that it is the adverb *gisteren* which shows up in different places. As Zwart himself points out, this claim bears on theories about the semantic interpretation of shifted and unshifted objects, a topic which we shall return to in section 2.4.1 below. But it also makes clear that it would be nice to have some way of distinguishing between different positions of adverbs. It does not seem implausible, for instance, that a given type of adverb may have a default position within the clause although it can also under certain circumstances appear elsewhere (see e.g. Bobaljik and Thráinsson 1998 for discussion).

One way in which research on OS and Scrambling can tell us something about adverb placement is the following: suppose we have two adverbs which can adjoin to different positions. If one can adjoin to VP and the other to some higher functional projection, we might expect to be able to get the order Adv1–Object–Adv2 if the object shifts to, say, SpecAgrOP. Interestingly, some pairs of adverbs allow this kind of ordering in Icelandic while others do not. This is illustrated in (31)–(32):

(31) a.   Jón   las   bókina   **náttúrulega aldrei**.
          John read   book-the naturally   never
      b.   (?)Jón las   **náttúrulega** bókina   **aldrei**.
          "John naturally never read the book."

(32) a.   Jón   las   bókina   **eflaust**   **aldrei**.
          John read   book-the doubtlessly never
          "John doubtlessly never read the book."
      b.   *Jón las   **eflaust** bókina   **aldrei**.

As shown here, the object can intervene between *náttúrulega* and *aldrei* but not between *eflaust* and *aldrei*. This may suggest that *náttúrulega* can more easily adjoin to a higher position than *aldrei* can. This is not surprising, since *náttúrulega* is one of the adverbs that can also intervene between the subject and the finite verb in the so-called V3 construction in Icelandic (see e.g. Thráinsson 1986, Sigurðsson 1986):

(33) Jón **náttúrulega** las aldrei bókina.
      John naturally   read never book-the
      "John naturally never read the book."

Interestingly, the class of adverbial expressions that can "straddle" a moved object does not seem to be the same in the Scandinavian languages and German, for instance, as Vikner (1994b: 493ff) has shown:

(34) a. ...dass er das Buch   **ohne Zweifel nicht** gelesen hat.   (Ge)
              that he the book   without doubt not   read   has
      b. ...dass er **ohne Zweifel** das Buch   **nicht** gelesen hat.
          "...that he has undoubtedly not read the book."

(35) a. Peter læste den **uden tvivl**   **ikke**.   (Da)
          Peter read it   without doubt not
          "Peter undoubtedly didn't read it."
      b. *Peter læste **uden tvivl**   den   **ikke**.

One possible explanation is that GD Scrambling is adjunction to VP and hence scrambled elements can intervene between adverbs that also adjoin to the VP, whereas Scandinavian OS moves elements out of the VP. Another possibility is that the possible adjunction sites of the adverbial expressions in question are not the same in these languages. Examples like the following show that adverbials seem to have considerable freedom of occurrence in Dutch, for instance (cf. Zwart 1997: 64):

(36) a. ...dat **gisteren** Jan Marie gekust heeft.   (Du)
              that yesterday John Mary kissed has
          "...that John has kissed Mary yesterday."
      b. ...dat Jan **gisteren** Marie **waarschijnlijk** gekust heeft.
              that John yesterday Mary probably   kissed has
          "...that John has probably kissed Mary yesterday."

All this indicates that the research on OS and Scrambling has shed light on adverb placement possibilities, although a restrictive and enlightening theory of adverb placement is still needed.[17]

2.1.3 The structure of particle constructions

As Johnson (1991) points out, there is a striking parallelism between Scandinavian OS and the word order alternations found in the so-called particle constructions in English. Some examples are given in (37)–(38) (the English examples are mostly from Johnson 1991 and references he cites):

(37) a. Mickey looked   up the reference.
     b. Mickey looked   the reference   up.
     c. *Mickey looked   up it.
     d. Mickey looked   it   up.
     e. Mickey looked   up THEM.
     f. Mickey looked   up him and her.
     g. Mickey teamed   up with the women.
     h. *Mickey teamed   with the women   up.
     i. Mickey pointed   out [that Gary had left].
     j. *Mickey pointed [that Gary had left]   out.
     k. Mickey slips   up all the time.
     l. *Mickey slips   all the time   up.

(38) a. Jón   las   ekki bókina.   (Ic)
         John read   not book-the
     b. Jón   las   **bókina$_i$**   ekki t$_i$
     c. *Jón las   ekki hana.
         John read   not it.
     d. Jón   las   **hana$_i$**   ekki.
     e. Jón   las   ekki HANA.
     f. Jón   hitti   ekki hana og hann.
         John met   not him and her.
     g. Jón   talaði   ekki við konurnar.
         John talked   not to women-the
     h. *Jón talaði **við konurnar$_i$** ekki t$_i$
     i. Jón   sagði   ekki [að   María hefði farið].
         John said   not that Mary had   left
     j. *Jón sagði **[að María hefði farið]$_i$** ekki t$_i$
     k. Jón   talaði   ekki allan daginn.
         John spoke   not all   day-the
         "John didn't speak for the whole day."
     l. *Jón talaði **allan daginn$_i$** ekki t$_i$

In the (a) and (b) examples we see that a full NP-object can occur on either side of the particle in English and on either side of the sentential adverb (here the negation) in Icelandic constructions where OS is possible. The (c), (d), (e), and (f) examples show that pronouns have to appear to the left of the particle in English, and to the left of the sentential adverb in Icelandic, unless they are stressed (the (e) examples) or conjoined (the (f) examples). The (g) and (h) examples show that prepositional complements cannot occur to the left of the particle in English or to the left of the adverb in Icelandic, and the (i), (j), (k), and (l) examples show that the same is true of clausal complements and of adverbial NPs (adjuncts).

The parallelism just reviewed is truly striking and calls for an explanation. Johnson's (1991) account is that English has OS and verb movement, just like

Scandinavian, although it is not always visible to the same extent. He suggests (1991: 628) that the (main) verb in English may move to T and the object to SpecAgrOP in a complex functional structure.

Despite the parallelism between (English) particle constructions and Scandinavian OS constructions just reviewed, there are interesting crosslinguistic twists to the story. First, restrictions on particle constructions in Icelandic mirror those of Icelandic OS to a great extent, as already pointed out by Rögnvaldsson (1982). Thus compare (39) to (37)–(38):

(39) a. Jón   tók   upp   bókina.   (Ic)
          John picked   up   book-the
      b. Jón   tók   bókina   upp.
          "John picked up the book."
      c. *Jón tók   upp   hana.
          John picked   up   it.
      d. Jón   tók   hana   upp.
      e. Jón   tók   upp   HANA.
      f. Jón   rak   út   hana og hann.
          John kicked   out   him and her.
      g. Jón   hélt   til   hjá systrunum.
          John held   to   with sisters-the
          "John stayed with the sisters." [e.g. had room and board there]
      h. *Jón hélt   hjá systrunum   til.
      i. Jón   tók   fram [að María hefði farið].
          John took   forth that Mary had   left.
          "John explicitly mentioned that Mary had left."
      j. *Jón tók   [að María hefði farið] fram.
      k. Jón   kastaði   upp   allan daginn.
          John threw   up   all   day-the
      l. ?*Jón kastaði allan daginn   upp.

As shown by Collins and Thráinsson (1996: 430), however, the "shift" of the object in particle constructions is not dependent on movement of the main verb the way "normal" OS is. Thus the "shifted" versions of (39) are just as good with a finite auxiliary and a non-finite main verb in situ, as illustrated in (40):

(40) a. Jón hefur tekið bókina upp.   (cf. (39b))
          John has   picked book-the up
          "John has picked up the book."
      b. Jón hefur tekið hana   upp.   (cf. (39d))

This suggests that if some sort of OS is involved in particle constructions, it shifts the object to a lower position than the one involved in "regular" OS. Hence the structure of particle constructions may be more complex than it would seem at first, and this is the tack taken by a number of linguists. Thus

Collins and Thráinsson (1996) tie this in with their analysis of double object constructions (see also section 2.1.4 below). Others have suggested some sort of a biclausal analysis of particle constructions (see e.g. Bolinger 1971, Kayne 1985, den Dikken 1995, Svenonius 1996).

Space does not permit a further discussion of the different proposals about particle constructions and their relationship to OS constructions. But there is an interesting crosslinguistic twist here, potentially relevant for the topic at hand: while all the MSc languages allow pronominal OS but typically not OS of full NPs, Danish and Norwegian allow the "OS" in particle constructions to apply to full NPs (optionally) as well as to pronouns (obligatorily), but neither version applies in Swedish (see e.g. Åfarli 1985, Holmberg 1986: 166, 200, Svenonius 1996, Holmberg and Platzack 1995: 203):

(41) a. Jeg   skrev   op nummeret/*det.   (Da)
          I   wrote   up number-the/it
      b. Jeg   skrev   brevet/det op.
          "I wrote the number/it down."
      c. Han   spiste   opp tørrfisken/*den.   (No)
          he   ate   upp dryfish-the/it
      d. Hann   spiste   tørrfisken/den opp.
          "He ate the dried fish/it up."
      e. Hon   kastade   ut Johan/honum.   (Sw)
          she   threw   out John/him
          "She threw John/him out."
      f. *Hon   kastade Johan/honom ut.

This again suggests that the "OS" found in particle constructions may not be exactly the same kind of OS as the one found elsewhere in Scandinavian, despite striking similarities.[18]

2.1.4   The structure of double object constructions

Studies of OS and Scrambling have also played an important role in the analysis of double object constructions. Here the most important question has been whether and under what circumstances the direct object (DO) can move (shift or scramble) across the indirect object (IO) and what this can tell us about the nature of the relevant structures.

First, Dutch seems to differ from both German and Yiddish in not allowing the DO to scramble freely across the IO.[19] This is illustrated in (42)–(44) (see e.g. Haider et al. 1995: 17–18, Weerman 1997: 431–3, Diesing 1997: 402, etc.):

(42)

a. ...dat de vrouw   waarschijnlijk de mannen de film   toont.   (Du)
    that the woman probably   the men   the picture shows
b. ...dat de vrouw   **de mannen**$_i$ waarschijnlijk t$_i$ de film toont.
    "...that the woman probably shows the picture to the men."
c. *...dat de vrouw   **de film**$_j$ waarschijnlijk de mannen t$_j$ toont.

(43) a. . . . dass die Firma   nicht meinem Onkel die Möbel   (Ge)
              that the company not   my uncle-Dat   the furniture-Acc
           zugestellt hat.
           delivered has
       b. . . . dass dies Firma **meinem Onkel**$_i$ nicht t$_i$ die Möbel zugestellt
           hat.
       c. . . . dass die Firma **die Möbel**$_j$ nicht meinem Onkel t$_j$
           zugestellt hat.
           ". . . that the company has not delivered the furniture to my uncle."

(44) a. Max hot   nit gegebn Rifken dos bukh.   (Yi)
           Max has   not given   Rifken the book
       b. Max hot **Rifken**$_i$ nit gegebn t$_i$ dos bukh.
       c. Max hot **dos bukh**$_j$ nit gegebn Rifken t$_j$
           "Max has not given Rifken the book."

A couple of comments are in order here. First, it is reported that "marked
stress patterns" improve examples like (42c) in Dutch (cf. Zwart 1997: 32,
Weerman 1997: 431). Second, not all DOs scramble equally easily across the
IOs in German. Thus it seems difficult to scramble an accusative object across
another accusative in German, and also to scramble a genitive object across an
accusative (cf. Czepluch 1990: 176, de Hoop 1992):

(45) a. . . . dass der Lehrer nicht die Schüler   diese Sprache   (Ge)
              that the teacher not   the students-Acc this language-Acc
           lehrt.
           teaches
           ". . . that the teacher doesn't teach the students this language."
       b. ?*. . . dass der Lehrer **diese Sprache**$_i$ nicht die Schüler t$_i$ lehrt.
       c. Sie hat wahrscheinlich einen Angestellten des Diebstahls
           she has probably   a staff-member-Acc the theft-Gen
           bezichtigt.
           accused-of
           "She has probably accused a staff member of the theft."
       d. ??Sie hat **des Diebstahls**$_i$ wahrscheinlich einen Angestellten t$_i$
           bezichtigt.

These details aside, it seems clear that there is some difference here between
Dutch (and Modern Frisian) on the one hand and German and Yiddish on the
other. Weerman (1997) wants to relate it to the loss of morphological case in
Dutch. While the Yiddish facts do not refute this hypothesis, it is clear that
case considerations cannot be the whole story about possible orderings of IOs
and DOs. This is so because (clearly overtly case marked) DOs cannot shift
across IOs in Icelandic, as shown by Collins and Thráinsson (1996). Here we
get the following possibilities:[20]

(46) a. Ég skilaði   ekki manninum bókinni. (Ic)
      I   returned   not   man-the-Dat book-the-Acc
     b. Ég skilaði **manninum**$_i$ ekki t$_i$ bókinni.
     c. Ég skilaði **manninum**$_i$ **bókinni**$_j$ ekki t$_i$ t$_j$
       "I didn't return the book to the man."
     d. *Ég skilaði **bókinni**$_j$ ekki manninum t$_j$

Similar facts are found in Swedish pronominal OS (cf. Collins and Thráinsson 1996: 421, Holmberg 1991b: 145):

(47) a. ?Jag gav   slutligen Sara den.   (Sw)
      I   gave   finally   Sara it
       "I finally gave it to Sara."
     b. *Jag gav **den**$_j$ slutligen Sara t$_j$
     c. Jag gav **henne**$_i$ **den**$_j$ slutligen t$_i$ t$_j$
      I   gave her   it   finally
       "I finally gave it to her."

Here the crucial example is (47b), which shows that a pronominal DO cannot shift over an in situ IO, although both objects can move if both are pronouns, as shown in (47c).

Within a theory which assumes movement, it seems natural to search for an explanation of the crosslinguistic differences observed so far by studying the alleged movements more closely, both their type and the possible landing sites of the movements. The next section gives an overview of that kind of research.

2.2 Landing sites and movement types

2.2.1 Clause-boundedness and landing sites

Studies of OS and Scrambling have made interesting contributions to the general theory of movement types and landing sites. Thus one of the standard claims about Scandinavian OS and GD Scrambling is that they are "clause bounded." In movement theory terms, this means that the rules in question cannot move constituents out of clauses, in contrast with Topicalization, for instance:

(48) a. María   telur   ekki [að Harald   vanti peninga]
       Mary(N) believes   not that Harold-Acc needs money-Acc
       "Mary doesn't believe that Harold needs money."
     b. *María   telur   **Harald**$_i$ ekki [að t$_i$ vanti peninga]
     c. **Harald**$_i$ telur María   ekki [að t$_i$ vanti peninga]
       "Harold, Mary doesn't believe needs money."

Here we see that the embedded (accusative) subject *Harald*[21] cannot be shifted out of the embedded clause and across the matrix negation *ekki* "not," although it can be topicalized out of such a clause and moved to matrix-initial position, as shown in (48c). Since (48c) is good, the ungrammaticality of (48b) cannot be attributed to anything like an Icelandic equivalent of the *"that-*trace filter" of Chomsky and Lasnik (1977), as Icelandic does not in general show *that*-trace effects (cf. e.g. Maling and Zaenen 1978).

Ross (1967a) had already maintained that German Scrambling is clause bounded, as opposed to Topicalization. The phenomenon can be illustrated by examples like the following (see e.g. Grewendorf and Sternefeld 1990a: 9; cf. also Grewendorf and Sabel 1994: 264, Müller and Sternefeld 1994: 338–9, Corver and Riemsdijk 1994a: 4–5, and references cited there):

(49) a. Ich glaube   nicht [dass jeder   den Max kennt]
         I   believe   not   that everybody the Max knows
         "I don't believe that everybody-Nom knows Max-Acc."
     b. *Ich glaube **den Max**$_i$ nicht [dass jeder   t$_i$ kennt]
     c. **Den Max**$_i$ glaube ich nicht dass jeder   t$_i$ kennt
         "Max, I don't believe that everybody knows."

The object cannot be scrambled out of the finite complement clause in (49), as (49b) shows, although it can be topicalized out of it, as illustrated by (49c). The ungrammaticality of (49b) cannot be due to some kind of a restriction on the Scrambling of objects across subjects since such a restriction does not hold in German in general, as we have seen.

Clause-boundedness does not seem to be a general property of Scrambling (or Scrambling-like processes), however. Thus it has been reported that non-clause-bounded Scrambling is found in languages like Hindi, Japanese, Persian, and Russian, for instance (see e.g. Corver and Riemsdijk 1994a: 4–5, Kitahara 1997: 80ff, with references). In addition, it seems that arguments can be shifted or scrambled out of certain types of non-finite complements in Scandinavian, German, Dutch, and Yiddish. First, the so-called Accusative-with-Infinitive (or Subject-to-Object Raising or Exceptional Case Marking (ECM)) constructions in Scandinavian share some properties with Scandinavian OS (see Holmberg 1986: 220ff), which suggests that they involve movement of the accusative subject out of the infinitival clause (see also Thráinsson 1979). Second, arguments can be scrambled out of some non-finite complements in German, for instance (cf. e.g. Fanselow 1990: 199ff, Grewendorf and Sabel 1994: 264). These constructions will not be discussed further here, but the degree of clause-boundedness of movement rules is clearly among the properties that should be explained in terms of the nature of the rule, such as the possible "landing sites." We now turn to issues of that kind.[22]

2.2.2 Adjunctions and adjunction sites

Some of the movement analyses of Scandinavian OS and probably most movement analyses of Scrambling argue (or at least assume) that the movement rules involved adjoin the moved constituents to some maximal projection, such as VP or IP, for instance. Now we have seen that there appear to be some crosslinguistic differences with respect to the "locality" of the movement rules (cf. sections 1.1.3 and 1.2.3 above). Hence it has been suggested that there is an adjunction site parameter for Scrambling positions such that some languages could allow adjunction to VP only while others could also allow adjunction to IP and even CP (cf. Müller and Sternefeld 1994: 342, also Vikner 1994b: 487ff). But unless the value of this adjunction site parameter is related to something else in the grammar, suggesting this parameter only amounts to stating a descriptive generalization in specific terms.

Without going into the argumentation, we can summarize some recent proposals for the adjunction sites involved in Scandinavian OS and DG Scrambling as in (50):

(50)   a.   Scandinavian OS may be adjunction to VP (or possibly some "low" functional projection like ActP), cf. e.g. Vikner (1994b), Holmberg and Platzack (1995: 142ff).

b.   German Scrambling may be adjunction to VP or IP (see e.g. Grewendorf and Sternefeld 1990a: 10ff, see also Müller and Sternefeld 1994: 342) or possibly just to IP (see e.g. Fanselow 1990: 116ff, cf. also Czepluch 1990: 172ff).

c.   Dutch Scrambling may be adjunction to VP (cf. the "traditional" analysis outlined in Zwart 1997: 50 and the references he cites).

This could give partial (and simplified) structures like (51a, b) for Icelandic and German, for instance, when an object has been scrambled (assuming the VP-Internal Subject Hypothesis and the kind of constituent structure adopted by most of the studies under consideration):

(51)   a.   b.

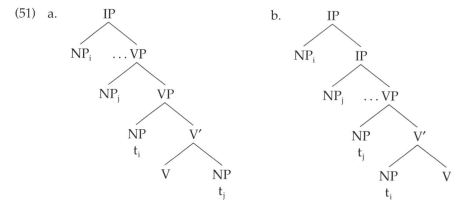

Here the displaced object-NP has been adjoined to the VP in Icelandic but to the IP in German.

Now if movement involving adjunction has special properties, then these adjunction theories are making claims not only about the possible landing sites involved but also about the nature of the movement. Similarly, the alternative proposals that Scandinavian OS and GD Scrambling may involve substitution into the specifier position of some functional projection rather than adjunction should make different predictions about the nature of the rules. We will now consider such proposals.

2.2.3 *Substitutions and specifier positions*

Before Pollock's influential paper on the structure of the IP (1989), linguists standardly assumed two functional projections above the VP, namely CP and IP. The specifier position of the former was (and is) typically thought to be the landing site for Topicalization and *wh*-movement, whereas Spec-IP was considered the canonical subject position. Since GD Scrambling and Scandinavian OS seemed to move elements to positions different from both Spec-CP and Spec-IP (cf. sections 1.1.3 and 1.2.3 above), linguists who wanted to argue for movement analyses of these constructions were forced to some sort of adjunction analysis, as just outlined. But with the "explosion" of the IP after Pollock's (1989) and especially Chomsky's (1991) papers, new possibilities for substitution analyses opened up.

The earliest attempts to analyze Scrambling and OS as substitution into the specifier position of some functional projection include Mahajan (1990), Wyngærd (1989), Déprez (1989, see also Déprez 1994) and Moltmann (1990). Mahajan was mainly concerned with Scrambling in Hindi, but also wanted to account for crosslinguistic differences with reference to the properties of object movement (cf. section 2.2.4 below). Wyngaerd mainly discusses Dutch Scrambling, despite the name of his paper. Déprez discusses both GD Scrambling and Scandinavian OS, while Moltmann concentrated on German Scrambling. More recently Zwart (1997) has argued for a substitution analysis of Dutch Scrambling, but it is probably fair to say that adjunction analyses of GD Scrambling have been more common. But a number of linguists have argued for substitution analyses of Icelandic OS, such as Jonas and Bobaljik (1993), Jonas (1994, 1996b), Bobaljik (1995), Thráinsson (1996), Ferguson (1996), Collins and Thráinsson (1996), and Bobaljik and Thráinsson (1998). Details aside, the diagram in (52) gives an idea of the "substitution" operation typically assumed in studies of this kind:

(52)

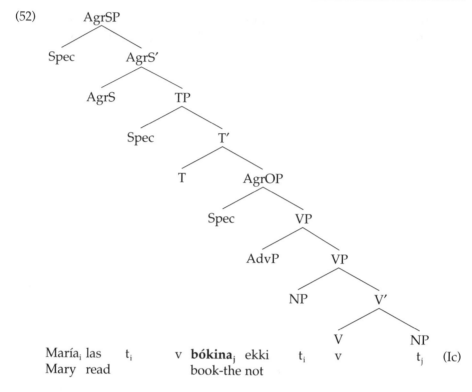

María$_i$ las   t$_i$ v **bókina**$_j$ ekki   t$_i$ v   t$_j$ (Ic)
Mary read   book-the not

The analyses of Icelandic OS as movement to the specifier position of a functional projection usually argue that the movement is to Spec-AgrOP, as indicated in (52). Since there is some evidence that the landing site for GD Scrambling can be higher than that for Scandinavian OS (cf. sections 1.1.3 and 1.2.3 above), Déprez originally assumed (1989: 283) that German Scrambling can move constituents to different specifier positions above the VP. But how could one distinguish between adjunction and substitution? One potentially relevant theoretical notion is discussed in 2.2.4.

2.2.4   A- or A-bar-movement?

In studies written in the Government Binding (GB) framework, one of the most heavily debated theoretical issues concerning OS and (especially) Scrambling is whether the movement involved is "A-movement" (like e.g. Passive) or "A-bar-movement" (like e.g. Topicalization). Here the basic question is whether the landing site of the movement has the properties of an argument position (A-position) or a non-argument position (A-bar, $\bar{\text{A}}$, A') in the sense of Chomsky (1981). Chomsky's original definition of an argument position was as follows (cf. Chomsky 1981: 47):

(53)   An A-position is a potential theta-role position.

This means that an A-position is one that *can* be assigned a thematic role, although it need not have one in all instances. Thus the canonical subject and object positions will be A-positions.[23] For Chomsky (1981), then, the main A-positions and A'-positions would be the ones shown in (54):

(54)

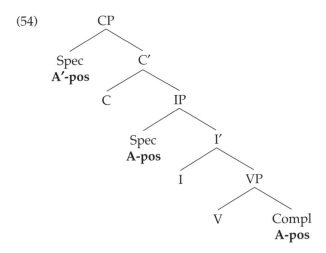

The basic idea behind this is that different structural positions have different properties. Some have the properties of an A-position, others do not. Obviously, the question of whether the landing site of OS and Scrambling is an A- or A'-position ties in with the question discussed in the preceding section: is the landing site some specifier position (like SpecAgrOP) or is it an adjoined position? Thus it has sometimes been assumed that no adjoined positions are A-positions (cf. below) whereas some specifier positions are, as we have seen. This is one of the reasons why linguists have tried to find out whether the landing site of OS and Scrambling has A- or A'-position properties. A huge body of literature deals with questions of this sort, especially with reference to Scrambling in German, Dutch, Hindi, Japanese, and other languages (see e.g. the overviews in Grewendorf and Sternefeld 1990a: 6ff, Corver and van Riemsdijk 1994a: 5ff, Haider et al. 1995: 15–16, Webelhuth 1995a: 64–9, with references), but also in connection with pronominal and non-pronominal OS in Scandinavian (see e.g. Vikner 1994b: 488–91, Holmberg and Platzack 1995: 145ff). This research has shed light not only on the nature of OS and Scrambling constructions but also more generally on the nature of movement processes and properties of different structural positions.

The standard strategy is to compare OS and Scrambling to typical A- and A'-movements (e.g. Passive vs. Topicalization) and ask to what extent they are similar to or different from these. Some of the tests or questions asked have been formulated in terms of properties of the moved constituent, others in terms of properties of the resulting construction or even the movement process itself:

(55) a. Is the movement **clause bounded**?
    b. Does the moved constituent license a **parasitic gap**?
    c. Does the movement influence **binding relations**?
    d. Does the movement induce **weak crossover** violations?
    e. Does the movement have something to do with **case** (or Case)?

We have already discussed the clause-boundedness issue in section 2.2.1. It is mentioned here because it is standardly believed that A-movement rules (such as Passive) are typically clause bounded whereas A'-movement rules are not. As we have seen, OS is basically clause bounded whereas the clause-boundedness of Scrambling seems to vary somewhat from language to language. The argument would be, however, that to the extent OS or Scrambling is clause bounded, it is not a typical A'-movement rule.

Licensing of "parasitic gaps" is probably the most hotly debated issue in connection with OS and (especially) Scrambling. As originally shown by Engdahl (cf. Engdahl 1983), a parasitic gap is a gap which is dependent on the presence of another gap. A classic illustration is given in (56) (where the relevant gap is indicated by *e*):

(56) a. Did Harold sell the book$_i$ without reading it$_i$/*e_i?
    b. Which book$_i$ did Harold sell t$_i$ without reading it$_i$/e_i?

The gap in the object position of *reading* is impossible in (56a) but possible in (56b). As indicated, there is another "gap" (or non-overt element) in (56b), namely the trace of the *wh*-moved NP *which book*. Thus it seems that the gap in the object position of *reading* is dependent on the preceding one and we can say that they are both licensed by (and coindexed with) the *wh*-moved NP. This indicates, then, that *wh*-moved constituents license parasitic gaps. Examples like (57) suggest that passivized elements do not:

(57) The book$_i$ was sold t$_i$ without reading it/*e.

More generally, it is standardly believed that A-moved constituents do not license parasitic gaps whereas A'-moved constituents do. Hence licensing of parasitic gaps is taken to be an important diagnostic to distinguish between A- and A'-movement.

Turning now to OS and (GD) Scrambling, it has frequently been argued that the former does not license parasitic gaps whereas the latter does (cf. Vikner 1994: 490–1, Holmberg and Platzack 1995: 146, Webelhuth 1989: 356, Zwart 1997: 50, with references):

(58) a. Pétur bauð **Maríu$_i$** aldrei t$_i$ án   þess að sækja hana$_i$/*e_i (Ic)
    Peter invited Mary not   without it to fetch her
    "Peter never invited Mary without picking her up."

b. Peter inviterede **dem**$_i$ ikke t$_i$ uden   at kende dem$_i$/*e$_i$ på   (Da)
   Peter invited   them not   without to know them   in
   forhånd.
   advance
   "Peter didn't invite them without knowing them beforehand."

c. ... weil er **den Patienten**$_i$ ohne   vorher ihn$_i$/?e$_i$ (Ge)
      because he the patient without first   him
   zu untersuchen t$_i$ operierte.
   to examine   operated
   "... because he operated on the patient without first examining him."

d. ... dat Jan **Marie**$_i$ zonder ze$_i$/e$_i$ aan te kijken t$_i$ gekust   (Du)
      that John Mary without her   on to look   kissed
   heeft.
   has
   "... that John kissed Mary without looking at her."

Some linguists have interpreted this difference as suggesting that OS may be A-movement but (GD) Scrambling A'-movement. But this is not uncontroversial. One problem is that the parasitic gap examples involving Scrambling tend to be less than perfect (cf. the ? on the German example above). It has also been argued that it is sometimes possible for elements in A-positions to license parasitic gaps, e.g. the passive subject in the following Dutch example (cf. de Hoop 1992: 140):

(59) Ik weet dat **deze boeken**$_i$ gisteren   door Peter zonder   e$_i$ te lezen
      I know that these books   yesterday by Peter   without   to read
      t$_i$ werden teruggebracht
         were   taken-back
      "I know that these books were taken back by Peter without (his) reading (them)."

The arguments based on binding relations are even more problematic than those having to do with parasitic gaps. The relevant question about "influencing" binding relations is sometimes phrased as in (60):

(60) Do OS and Scrambling create new binding relations or destroy old ones?

This is a somewhat misleading formulation (under standard assumptions all movements of NPs, for instance, "create new binding relations," namely those between the moved NP and its trace) but it is helpful in explaining what is involved. As is well known, standard Binding Theory maintains that anaphors have to be bound and binding obtains between a c-commanding antecedent and a coindexed anaphor. Thus an antecedent in subject position may bind an anaphor (like the reflexive pronoun in English) in object position but not vice versa:

(61) a.   Mary$_i$ has always liked herself$_i$.
      b.   *Herself$_i$ has always liked Mary$_i$.

The binding relations in (61a) are not destroyed by topicalizing *herself* and thus changing the precede and c-command relations, nor are examples like (61b) improved by topicalizing *Mary* and thus make it precede and c-command *herself*:

(62) a.   Herself$_i$ Mary has always liked t$_i$
      b.   *Mary$_i$, herself$_i$ has always liked t$_i$

Thus it is standardly believed that A'-movements like Topicalization can neither "create new binding relationships" in the intended sense nor destroy old ones. Arguably, examples like the following show that A-movements like Raising are different in this respect:

(63) a.   [e] seem to each other$_i$ [they$_i$ to be nice]
      b.   They$_i$ seem to each other$_i$ [t$_i$ to be nice]

Here (63a) is the standardly assumed underlying structure for a raising construction like (63b). In (63a) the c-command relations are obviously not appropriate for the binding of *each other* by *they*, which is the subject of the embedded infinitival complement of *seem*. But raising *they* to the matrix subject position of *seem* apparently creates a new binding relationship, since (63b) is good.

With this in mind, it should in principle be possible to test whether OS and Scrambling have A-movement properties or A'-movement properties with respect to binding. Unfortunately, this is not as simple as it might seem. First, we have seen (in sections 1.1.3 and 1.2.3 above) that Scandinavian OS and Dutch Scrambling do not shift objects across indirect objects or across subjects. This makes it difficult to test whether the relevant movement would create new binding relations or destroy old ones in these languages. Second, there are some semantic restrictions on the binders of reflexives and reciprocals. Consider the following examples from Icelandic:

(64) a.   Ég taldi   **Harald$_i$** vera latan, honum$_i$/*sér$_i$ til mikillar undrunar.
           I   believed Harold   be   lazy, him/self   to great   surprise
           "I believed Harold to be lazy, to his great surprise."
      b.   **Haraldur$_i$** var talinn   t$_i$ vera latur, ?honum$_i$/sér$_i$ til mikillar
           Harold   was believed be   lazy,   him/self   to great
           undrunar.
           surprise
           "Harold was believed to be lazy, to his great surprise."

As shown here, the object *Harald* in (64a) cannot bind a reflexive in the adverbial (or parenthetical) phrase that follows, whereas the (passive) subject in (64b) can.[24] For this reason, it is not surprising that arguments about the nature of OS and Scrambling based on binding relations tend to be inconclusive. The following are based on examples in Holmberg and Platzack (1995: 148–9):

(65) a. Ég taldi,   þeim$_i$/*sér$_i$ til undrunar, [Ólaf og Martein]$_i$ (Ic)
          I   believed them-Dat/self-Dat to surprise   Olaf and Martin
          vera jafngóða.
          be   equally-good
          "I believed, to their surprise, Olaf and Martin to be equally good."
     b. Ég taldi   [Ólaf og Martein]$_i$, þeim$_i$/*sér$_i$ til undrunar, t$_i$
          I   believed Olaf and Martin   them-Dat/self-Dat to surprise
          vera jafngóða.
          be   equally-good
          "I believed Olaf and Martin, to their suprise, to be equally good."

(66) a. Jag ansåg   till deras$_i$/*sin$_i$ besvikelse [Per och Martin]$_i$ (Sw)
          I   believed to their/self's disappointment Per and Martin
          vara lika   bra.
          be   equally good
          "I believed, to their disappointment, Per and Martin to be equally good."
     b. Jag ansåg   dem$_i$ till deras$_i$/*sin$_i$ besvikelse   t$_i$, vara   (Sw)
          I   believed them to their/self's disappointment   be
          lika   bra.
          equally good
          "I believed them, to their disappointment, to be equally good."

Holmberg and Platzack claim that if OS (which they take to be involved in ECM (Exceptional Case Marking) constructions like these, cf. the discussion in 2.2.1 and n. 22) were A-movement, it should make the shifted object a possible binder for the reflexives in the adverbial (or parenthetical) phrase in the (b) examples above (Holmberg and Platzack also give examples with a reciprocal anaphor). So whereas the parasitic gap test above suggested that Scandinavian OS is A-movement, Holmberg and Platzack (1995) argue that binding facts of the type just shown suggest that it is *not* A-movement, which would seem paradoxical. But this is not a very convincing argument. First, Holmberg and Platzack do in fact show that OS in ECM constructions can influence binding relations. This can be seen from contrasts like the following (cf. Holmberg and Platzack 1995: 148, n. 5):

(67) a. Han ansåg   till Marias$_i$ besvikelse   henne$_i$ vara för ung.
          he   believed   to Mary's disappointment her   be   too young
          "To Mary's disappointment, he believed her to be too young."
     b. *Han ansåg henne$_i$ till Marias$_i$ besvikelse   t   vara för ung.

Second, it is well known that the binding of reflexives and reciprocals can be semantically restricted, as pointed out above. Hence one needs to test that the relevant object (or subject of an infinitive in this case) in situ would bind a reflexive or a reciprocal contained in a following parenthetical of this kind, but Holmberg and Platzack do not give such examples.[25] Thus it is not clear that any kind of paradox is involved or that the status of OS as an A-movement has been refuted. We will return to this issue in section 2.4.2 below.

The above-mentioned restrictions on Dutch Scrambling (no scrambling of DOs across IOs or subjects) make it difficult to test its interaction with binding principles.[26] Relevant examples should be easier to construct in German, since German Scrambling is not subject to the same restrictions. The following are based on examples in Müller and Sternefeld (1994: 351ff):

(68)   a.   *... dass ich sich$_i$ den Patienten$_i$ im   Spiegel zeigte.
                  that I   self-Dat the patient-Acc in-the mirror showed
         b.   ... dass ich **den Patienten**$_i$ *ihm$_i$/(?)sich$_i$ t$_i$ im   Spiegel
                  that I   the patient-Acc him-Dat/self-Dat   in-the mirror
              zeigte.
              showed
              "... that I showed the patient to himself in the mirror."

Here the basic idea would be that the DO in situ in (68a) cannot bind the preceding IO reflexive *sich*, whereas scrambling the DO across the IO makes such binding possible (and also rules out the personal pronoun *ihm* in the IO position), as shown in (68b). This would be unexpected if German Scrambling were an A'-movement. But Müller and Sternefeld argue (based on facts from Grewendorf 1988: 58) that the argument is suspect because the IO in sentences of this type does not seem to be able to bind a following DO anaphor but requires a personal pronoun instead:

(69)   ... dass ich dem Patienten$_i$ *sich$_i$/(?)ihn$_i$ im   Spiegel zeigte.
              that I   the patient-Dat self-Acc/him-Acc in-the mirror showed

A possible interpretation of facts of this sort would be that a DO–IO order is base generated here (which in turn could explain why German appears to be different from Dutch in allowing Scrambling of DO across IO, cf. section 1.2.3 above).

We can conclude, then, that binding facts do not provide very clear arguments about the nature of OS and GD Scrambling.

Another frequently used argument about the nature of OS and Scrambling, also crucially involving coreference (or coindexation), has to do with so-called weak crossover effects. The basis for this argument is the ungrammaticality of sentences like (70b):

(70)   a.   [His$_i$ mother] loves John$_i$.
         b.   *Who$_i$ does [his$_i$ mother] love t$_i$?

The claim here is that moving an R-expression across a non-c-commanding coindexed pronoun (*his* in (70b)) leads to the observed ungrammaticality (see, e.g., the overview in Huang 1995: 138ff). Now if all and only A'-movement rules give rise to this kind of ungrammaticality, one could use it as a diagnostic for the nature of OS and Scrambling.

Once again, however, the facts are not very straightforward. Since Scandinavian OS and Dutch Scrambling do not shift a DO across an IO or across a subject, it is quite difficult to construct relevant examples. Holmberg and Platzack (1995: 147) give the following examples and judgments, attempting to contrast *wh*-movement and pronominal OS in Swedish:

(71) a. ?Vem$_i$ tilldelade dom   i [hans$_i$ frånvaro] t$_i$ priset?
         who   awarded they   in his absence   prize-the
      b. Dom   tilldelade **honom$_i$** i [hans$_i$ frånvaro] t$_i$ priset.
         they awarded him   in his absence   prize-the
         "They awarded him the prize in his absence."

According to Holmberg and Platzack, (71a) is "marginal" but (71b) "perfectly grammatical." The problem is, however, that the base position of the (parenthetical) PP *i hans frånvaro* is perhaps not crystal clear. Hence it is not obvious that any OS has taken place in (71b).[27]

Examples like the following (based on examples in Zwart 1997: 65) show a somewhat similar contrast between *wh*-movement and Scrambling in Dutch, assuming that it is clear that the object (*iederen*) has been scrambled in (72b):

(72) a. ?Wie$_i$ hebben [zijn$_i$ ouders] t$_i$ onterfd?   (Du)
         who   have   his parents   disinherited
      b. Jan heeft **iedereen$_i$** op [hun$_i$ voorhoofd] t$_i$ gekust.
         Jan has   everybody on their forehead   kissed
         "Jan kissed everybody on their forehead."

Again, it should be easier to construct the relevant examples in German, due to the more relaxed restrictions on German Scrambling. Thus examples like (73), where a DO has been scrambled across a subject, seem to indicate that German Scrambling does not give rise to weak crossover effects (cf. Müller and Sternefeld 1994: 368):

(73) ... dass **jeden$_i$**   [seine$_i$ Mutter]   t$_i$ mag.   (Ge)
         that everybody-Acc his mother-Nom   likes

Now this would seem surprising if German Scrambling were an A'-movement. Consequently, weak crossover facts have been used to argue that German Scrambling may be A-movement (see e.g. the discussion in Lee and Santorini 1994: 260ff and references cited there). Müller and Sternefeld (1994: 368ff) argue, however, that weak crossover facts cannot tell us much about the nature of German Scrambling since *wh*-movement does not induce weak crossover effects either (see also Lasnik and Stowell 1991 on non-quantificational A'-movement not inducing weak crossover effects):

(74) Wen$_i$ hat [seine$_i$ Mutter]   nicht t$_i$ gemocht?   (Ge)
       whom-Acc has his mother-Nom not   liked

Once again, therefore, the picture is not crystal clear.

The issue of the relationship between OS and Scrambling with case (or abstract Case) is of a different nature and simpler to deal with. A standard GB analysis of A-movement phenomena like Passive and Raising maintains that they are triggered by the need of the relevant NPs to be assigned Case (or to have their Case checked, if one assumes a checking account of the Minimalist type, cf. e.g. Chomsky 1993, 1995b). A'-movements like Topicalization or *wh*-movement, on the other hand, do not seem to have anything to do with Case (or case). This could be the reason why Passive and Raising only apply to NPs whereas Topicalization also applies to PPs, for instance. Now if OS and Scrambling only applied to NPs (or DPs), it would make them similar to the A-movement rules in this respect and different from A'-movement. As shown in sections 1.1.2 and 1.2.2 above, Scandinavian OS only applies to NPs whereas GD Scrambling also applies to PPs. Hence it is clear that GD Scrambling cannot have anything to do with Case, although Scandinavian OS could. We will return to this issue in section 2.3 (cf. especially sections 2.3.1 and 2.3.3).

The picture that has emerged in this section is not very clear. OS and Scrambling do not seem to fall unambiguously into the category of A-movement rules or that of A'-movement rules. Arguably, Scandinavian OS has more in common with typical A-movement rules than GD Scrambling does, but Dutch Scrambling appears to be more like A-movement rules than German Scrambling is. Yet there are linguists who have argued that German Scrambling is an A-movement rule (cf. Corver and van Riemsdijk 1994b: 5ff). How can this be explained?

First, it is possible that the so-called OS and Scrambling rules vary from one language to another and hence it is useless to try to classify them uniformly as A-movement or A'-movement rules. We have already seen that there seems to be some crosslinguistic difference with reference to the possible landing sites of OS and Scrambling (cf. the summary in 1.3) and it has in fact been argued that the alleged A-/A'-difference depends on the landing sites rather than the elements moved (operators or non-operators, for instance, cf. Déprez 1994). A variant of this kind of account is to say, as Lee and Santorini (1994) do, for instance, that the different properties of Scrambling depend on how local the Scrambling operation is, long distance Scrambling (across subject) being more A'-like than local Scrambling. Related accounts have been proposed by Mahajan (1994b) and Merchant (1996), and Fanselow (1990) has also argued that the A-/A'-status of Scrambling varies crosslinguistically.

But we are not only dealing with crosslinguistic variation here. Webelhuth (1989) was one of the first to discover that Scrambling may exhibit paradoxical

A-/A'-properties within a given language (in his case German – Lee and Santorini (1994) try to account for his so-called paradox). Seemingly paradoxical properties of Scrambling phenomena have also been reported for other languages, e.g. Hindi (Mahajan 1990), Korean (see e.g. the overview in Kim 1996), etc. This has made several linguists suspicious of the A-/A'-dichotomy itself. Interestingly enough, recent development in syntactic theory has made it difficult to maintain in its original version, although most linguists would agree that there is something intuitively correct about the distinction. Since we cannot go into any details about the nature and validity of this distinction here, a few comments will have to suffice.

First, consider the original definition of A-position given in Chomsky 1981, repeated from above:

(53)   An A-position is a potential theta-role position.

The qualification "potential" is already somewhat suspicious here. More importantly, recall that the "canonical subject position" SpecIP was assumed to be an A-position (see the diagram in (54) above). But if one assumes the widely accepted "VP-internal subject hypothesis" (see e.g. McCloskey 1997, with references), then the subject is generated in the specifier position of VP and (presumably) assigned a thematic role there. This means that SpecIP (or its descendants SpecTP and SpecAgrSP) will not be "assigned a thematic role" any more and thus not be A-positions according to the original definition. This makes it even harder than before to come up with a coherent definition of the concept of an A- vs. A'-position (see also Epstein et al. 1996: 37n). Chomsky (1993: 27–9) has suggested that the notion of L-relatedness (relation to morphological features of lexical items, such as tense, agreement) can be used to define the relevant distinction between structural positions. This would mean, for instance, that the specifier positions of TP (tense phrase) and AgrP (agreement phrase) would be L-related positions but the specifier position of CP would not be (assuming that C does not check morphological features of lexical categories). The question then arises what the status would be of a position adjoined to the projection of a head checking a lexical feature. Chomsky refers to such positions as "broadly L-related" and says that their status has been "debated, particularly in the theory of scrambling" (1993: 29). But if OS is movement to SpecAgrOP, then that should be an L-related position (or "narrowly L-related," to be exact). The question still remains whether this distinction is relevant in explaining some of the observed differences between OS and Scrambling. We will have reason to return to it in the following section, where we discuss an issue where the A-/A'- or L-related/non-L-related distinction becomes relevant again.

2.2.5   Minimality violations?

A major task in syntactic movement theory has always been to try to determine how movement is restricted: which elements can (or cannot) move where and why? One observation that has frequently been made can be informally stated as follows:

(75) Movement to a specific kind of landing site does not skip landing sites of the same type.

The notion "same type" here is standardly taken to include head positions for heads, A-positions for A-movement, and A'-positions for A'-movement, so this issue is related to the distinction discussed in the preceding section. Travis's Head Movement Constraint (1984), Rizzi's Relativized Minimality (1990), and recent attempts to define "Shortest Move" (see e.g. Chomsky 1993, Jonas and Bobaljik 1993, Ferguson 1996, Zwart 1996, with references) are all ways of accounting for this phenomenon.

As shown above, verbs that only allow one order of IO and DO in Icelandic (non-inversion verbs, cf. Collins and Thráinsson 1996, cf. also n. 20 above) only allow the first object to passivize:

(76) a. Sjórinn   svipti   konuna   eiginmanninum.   (Ic)
          ocean-the deprived woman-the-Acc husband-the-Dat
          "The ocean deprived the woman of her husband."
      b. **Konan**$_i$ var svipt t_i eiginmanninum.
          woman-the-Nom   was deprived   husband-the-Dat
          "The woman was deprived of her husband."
      c. ***Eiginmanninum**$_j$ var svipt   konan t_j
          husband-the-Dat   was deprived woman-the-Nom

Thus we see that the second object of *svipta* cannot be passivized "over" the first object, and it cannot be moved across it by OS either, as we have already seen:

(77) a. Sjórinn   svipti   ekki konuna   eiginmanninum.
          ocean-the deprived   not woman-the-Acc husband-the-Dat
          "The ocean did not deprive the woman of her husband."
      b. Sjórinn   svipti **konuna**$_i$ ekki t_i eiginmanninum.
      c. *Sjórinn   svipti **eiginmanninum**$_j$ ekki konuna t_j

It seems reasonable to assume that these restrictions on Passive and OS are related and it has been argued that they are "Minimality" phenomena in some sense: the object which is seeking an appropriate landing site cannot cross another object position. A similar account could be given of the fact that Dutch DOs do not seem to scramble over IOs (see the discussion in section 2.1.4 above). Now note, however, that DOs can freely topicalize over IOs, e.g. in Icelandic:

(78) **Eiginmanninum**$_i$ svipti   sjórinn   konuna t_i
      husband-the   deprived ocean-the-Nom woman-the-Acc
      "The husband, the ocean deprived the woman (of)."

Thus the intervening object position apparently does not count as a position of "the same type" as the landing site of Topicalization whereas it seems to count as a position of the same type as the landing site of Passive and OS. But here the difference between Dutch Scrambling on the one hand and German and Yiddish Scrambling on the other becomes interesting, since DOs freely scramble over IOs and subjects in German and Yiddish but not in Dutch (cf. e.g. Diesing 1997: 404–7, with references). Should that be taken as evidence that OS and Dutch Scrambling are A-movements whereas German and Yiddish Scrambling have A'-movement properties? And what about the fact that objects must always shift and scramble over a subject position if subjects are base generated in SpecVP, as the VP-internal subject hypothesis maintains?

This last point has been an issue of considerable debate in the recent literature, e.g. in connection with OS in Icelandic. Assume that Icelandic OS is movement to SpecAgrOP, as suggested by Déprez (1989), Jonas and Bobaljik (1993), and later studies. That would give a partial derivation like this:

(79)

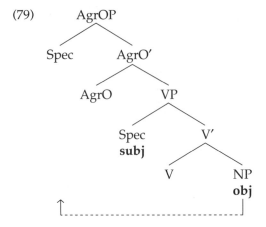

As (79) indicates, OS to SpecAgrOP would move the object across the subject position in SpecVP. In the light of the preceding discussion, this might seem surprising, and it has in fact been used as argument against the claim that Scandinavian OS could be A-movement (cf. Holmberg and Platzack 1995: 147). Others have tried to find a special explanation for this, while still assuming that OS is A-movement. Thus Vikner (1994b: 498) suggests that the base generated subject position does not count as an "intervener" because it is a theta-marked position. Unless some additional evidence is given for such an account, it looks like an ad-hoc stipulation.

An interesting account derives from Chomsky's (1993: 17–18) notion of shortest move and equidistance. Chomsky defined equidistance like this:

(80)   If α, β are in the same minimal domain, they are equidistant from γ.

The minimal domain of a head X includes its complement, its specifier, and also whatever is adjoined to the head, to its specifier, or to its maximal projection (cf. Chomsky 1993: 11–12), namely everything that is in bold type in (81):

(81)

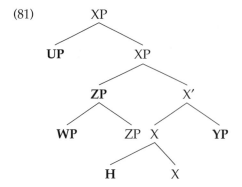

The "Shortest Move" version of the Minimality constraint basically maintains that the shortest move possible will be selected (for reasons of economy).

Now if OS moves an element across SpecVP to SpecAgrOP, as illustrated in (79) above, then the question is why that does not count as a violation of Shortest Move, since moving the object to SpecVP would seem to be a shorter move. Here Chomsky argues that if the V-head raises to Agr, the minimal domain of V is extended to include AgrOP (see Chomsky 1993: 18). This will mean that SpecVP and SpecAgrOP will be equidistant from the object position inVP. Thus moving the object across the subject in SpecVP to SpecAgrOP will no longer be a violation of Shortest Move, since this movement is technically not "longer" than the movement to SpecVP would be. Chomsky argues that this is exactly what is found in Scandinavian OS because here OS is dependent on movement of the verb out of the VP (cf. section 1.1.2 above). This approach to Icelandic OS – and the account it implies of Holmberg's Generalization – was then further developed by Jonas and Bobaljik (1993) and has figured prominently in much recent work on OS in Icelandic (e.g. Bobaljik 1995, Bobaljik and Jonas 1996, Jonas 1996a, 1996b, Thráinsson 1996, Ferguson 1996, Collins and Thráinsson 1996, Kitahara 1997: 43, Bobaljik and Thráinsson 1998; see Déprez 1994: 133ff for a somewhat different account).

As seen above, GD Scrambling is not dependent on verb movement the way Scandinavian OS seems to be. This could be explained if Scrambling were of a different nature, e.g. A'-movement (as Jonas and Bobaljik 1993: 68 assume, for instance) or triggered by the need to check (or attract) a different kind of feature (some sort of an "operator" feature as opposed to an "argument" feature, cf. Kitahara 1997: 78).[28] As shown above, there is some evidence for this, especially as far as German Scrambling is concerned. The evidence regarding Dutch Scrambling is weaker (except for the "focus" Scrambling in Dutch which can shift objects around subjects, cf. Zwart 1997: 31). Another possibility would be to say that Holmberg's Generalization is indeed also valid for Dutch and German, although we do not see the movement involved since it moves formal features only. This has recently been suggested by Zwart (1997: 242–3), but it is rather difficult to test that kind of analysis empirically.

The equidistance account of Holmberg's Generalization does not solve all theoretical and empirical problems concerning OS, Scrambling, and verb movement, however. First, it has nothing interesting to say about the apparent optionality of full NP OS in Icelandic (see section 2.4.1 below). Second, it does not explain why OS in Icelandic applies to both full NP objects and pronominal objects, whereas MSc OS only applies to pronominal objects but yet seems to be just as dependent on verb movement as OS in Icelandic. We will leave these issues aside for the moment and next consider the possible involvement of morphology in OS and Scrambling.

2.3 *Morphological aspects*

2.3.1 *Abstract Case and overt morphological case*
Scandinavian OS only applies to nominal objects of verbs whereas GD Scrambling also applies to PPs, as we have seen. This makes it tempting to try to relate OS in some way to the property that characterizes verbal objects: they are in some sense assigned case (and/or Case) by the verb. Relating GD Scrambling to Case does not seem very promising *a priori* (see, however, section 2.3.3). But trying to relate OS to case (or Case) raises questions of empirical and theoretical interest.

In his ground-breaking dissertation, Holmberg (1986) did in fact attempt to relate it to abstract Case and morphological case. An important aspect of this is his attempt to explain the fact that OS applies only to pronominal objects in MSc but also to full NPs in Icelandic. To explain this, he argues that the shifted object would not be assigned Case by any Case assigner. Hence it should violate the Case Filter (which states that all NPs must have Case). The reason no Icelandic NPs violate the Case Filter when they are moved to a non-Case position by OS is supposedly that they do have morphological case. MSc pronominal objects also have morphological case and hence can undergo OS and move to a non-Case position. But since MSc nouns do not have morphological case they cannot undergo OS (cf. Holmberg 1986: 208).

In this connection Holmberg also refers to the "well-known generalization that languages with rich case morphology have 'free word order'" (1986: 214)." Similarly, Neeleman (1994: 416ff) wants to relate the fact that German DOs have a greater freedom of occurrence than their Dutch counterparts (they scramble over IOs and subjects, cf. above) to the differences in case distinctions (Dutch nouns do not show morphological case distinctions, German nouns do). But despite the common belief that there is some relationship between rich morphology and freedom of word order, it has proven to be difficult to capture in any formal way.[29] We return to this issue in section 2.3.3 below.

There are certain empirical problems with this approach to OS. Holmberg's original idea is that shifted objects will not be assigned any Case (such as Nom by I°) and that will not cause any problem as long as they are marked by a morphological object case (in Icelandic Acc, Dat, or Gen, cf. Holmberg 1986:

215–16). A similar idea has been expressed by Holmberg and Platzack (1995: 168, passim), who add that "nominative Case on a shifted object cannot be licensed (or structurally checked)" but if "the shifted object has a non-nominative m[orphological]-case, it will not be assigned nominative, and can be licensed structurally." One problem with this is that Icelandic has nominative objects (cf. e.g. Zaenen et al. 1985, Yip et al. 1987, Sigurðsson 1989) and these can undergo OS just as easily as any other objects (see also Thráinsson 1997: 507):

(82) a. Mér   líka   ekki þessar bækur.
          me-Dat like   not these books
      b. Mér   líka þessar bækur$_i$ ekki t$_i$
          me   like these books   not
          "I don't like these books."

Second, as Vikner (1994b: 502) and others have pointed out, morphological case marking on nouns (or full NPs) does not seem to be a sufficient condition for full NP OS, since Faroese has rich case inflection of nouns (and adjectives) but only pronominal OS. Holmberg and Platzack (1995: 173ff) attempt to account for this by claiming that morphological case in Faroese is of a weaker type than morphological case in Icelandic and thus "does not suffice to provide a DP with inherent Case." While there are some differences in the behavior of morphological case in Icelandic and Faroese (cf. e.g. Petersen et al. 1998, Thráinsson 1999, Smith 1994), it is not clear that morphological case in Faroese is "weak" in the sense Holmberg and Platzack (1995) need it to be.[30]

While Holmberg and Platzack (1995) attempt to account for crosslinguistic variation in OS by referring to varying strength of case systems, others have attributed restrictions on object movement within a given language to "weakness" of certain cases. Thus de Hoop (1992: 136ff) maintains that objects that have "weak Case" cannot scramble in Dutch. But since she is basically referring to semantic distinctions (which correlate to some extent with morphological case in other languages, e.g. Turkish, Finnish), we will return to some of the facts she discusses in section 2.4.1.

Finally, several linguists have noted that OS and Scrambling seem to have been lost or become more restricted in the history of various languages, e.g. English and Dutch (cf. Roberts 1997, Weerman 1997, with references). Since the case system has also been simplified in these languages (case distinctions have been lost), it is tempting to try to relate these changes. Thus Weerman (1997: 432–3) points out that DOs could precede IOs in Middle Dutch and in Old English:

(83) a. so began si oc **getugnesse** hem   te geheue.   (MidDu)
          so began she also testimony-Acc him-Dat to give
          "so she also began to give him testimony."
      b. Ac gif we þa **mirran** gode   gastlice geoffriað   (OE)
          but if we then myrrh-Acc God-Dat spiritually offer
          "but if we offer myrrh to God spiritually"

As we have seen, DOs cannot be scrambled across IOs in Modern Dutch whereas they can in Modern German. Middle Dutch had morphological case distinctions on nouns, as Modern German has, but Modern Dutch does not. Hence Weerman suggests the following generalization (1997: 433):

(84)   The order of indirect object and direct object has to remain constant unless there is a morphological case system.

He then sets out to give a theoretical account of this phenomenon. But this cannot be the whole story since DOs do not shift across IOs in Modern Icelandic, as we have seen, although Modern Icelandic has a rich case system (see also Thráinsson 1997). Old Icelandic, on the other hand, seems to have had a considerably freer word order, allowing word orders reminiscent of Modern German Scrambling (see Rögnvaldsson 1992, 1995, Thráinsson 1997: 506). Yet the case morphology of Icelandic does not seem to have undergone any changes to speak of.

2.3.2   Relation to verbal morphology

Linguists have also attempted to relate crosslinguistic differences in word order to verbal morphology. A common line of argumentation goes like this: if the functional projections AgrSP (subject-agreement phrase), AgrOP (object-agreement phrase), and TP (tense phrase) have something to do with morphological agreement with subject/object or morphological tense distinctions, as their names would suggest, then one might expect them to figure prominently in the syntactic structure of languages that do have rich verbal morphology but not in languages with poor verbal morphology. This would then imply that we would not expect to find object movement to SpecAgrOP in languages that do not have "rich verbal morphology." This kind of argumentation can be found in Bobaljik (1995) and Thráinsson (1996) and it is further developed in Bobaljik and Thráinsson (1998). They argue that there is a correlation between rich verbal morphology and "split IP," namely the presence of the functional projections AgrSP, AgrOP, and TP. In particular, they maintain that Icelandic has "split IP" whereas MSc does not (i.e., it only has IP where Icelandic has AgrSP+TP+AgrOP). If full NP OS in Icelandic is movement of SpecAgrOP, this structural difference between Icelandic and MSc could explain why MSc does not have full NP OS (it has no SpecAgrOP to move full NPs to). This means, however, that Bobaljik and Thráinsson (1998) have to assume that the pronominal OS found in MSc must be of a different nature, presumably some sort of head movement (as suggested, e.g., by Josefsson 1992, 1993, and assumed by Jonas and Bobaljik 1993, Bobaljik and Jonas 1996, Jonas 1996a, 1996b, etc.).[31]

Vikner (1994b: 502ff) also wants to argue that the crucial syntactic difference between Icelandic on the one hand and Faroese and MSc on the other is somehow related to agreement morphology (although he admits that the distribution of full NP OS is still a puzzle (1994: 506)). And while the accounts of OS and Scrambling suggested by many linguists, including Déprez (1989, 1994) and Mahajan (1990), rely on "a multitude of functional categories related to the agreement system," Lee and Santorini (1994: 291) argue against such approaches and claim that "the properties of scrambling . . . are strikingly similar regardless of whether a language exhibits both subject and direct object agreement (Hindi), only subject agreement (German), or minimal or no agreement whatsoever (Korean, Japanese)." But if OS and Scrambling are in fact different kinds of movement, in the sense that only the former is movement to SpecAgrOP, then this statement would not be incompatible with the approach advocated by Bobaljik and Thráinsson (1998), for instance.

2.4   Semantic interpretation, focus, and stress

2.4.1   The semantic effects of Object Shift and Scrambling

As seen above, OS of full NPs in Icelandic and GD Scrambling is "optional" in a sense in which pronominal OS is not: full NP-objects in Icelandic can be left in situ and the same is true of objects in Scrambling languages like German and Dutch. In most cases the movement (OS or Scrambling) does not seem to have any semantic effect, i.e., the objects are interpreted the same way in situ and when they have been shifted. But as observed in Diesing and Jelinek (1993, 1995; see also Diesing 1992, 1996, 1997), this is not so when we pick NPs of a certain kind, such as indefinite or quantificational NPs. This is illustrated in (85)–(86) (most of these examples are based on examples in Diesing's work):

(85)   a.   Nemandinn las   ekki þrjár bækur.   (Ic)
            student-the read not   three books
            "It is not the case that the student read three books."[32]

       b.   Nemandinn las   **þrjár bækur** ekki t_i
            student-the read three books   not
            "There are three books that the student didn't read."

       c.   Ég les   sjaldan lengstu bókina.   (Ic)
            I   read rarely   longest book-the
            "I rarely read the longest book (whichever it is)."

       d.   Ég les   **lengstu bókina**$_i$ sjaldan t_i
            I   read longest book-the rarely
            "There is a book that is the longest and I rarely read it."

(86)   a.   . . . weil ich selten   jedes Cello spiele.   (Ge)
                  since I   seldom every cello play
            ". . . since I seldom play every cello."
            (i.e., "It is rarely the case that I play every cello.")

       b.   . . . weil ich **jedes Cello**$_i$ selten t_i spiele.
                  since I   every cello seldom   play
            ". . . since I play every cello (only) seldom."
            (i.e., "It holds for every cello that I rarely play it.")

    c. ... weil ich selten die kleinste Katze streichle.   (Ge)
           since I   seldom the smallest cat   pet
           "... since I seldom pet the smallest cat (whichever cat is the smallest)."
    d. ... weil ich **die kleinste Katze**$_i$ selten   t$_i$ streichle.
           since I   the smallest cat   seldom   pet
           "... since I pet the smallest cat (only) seldom."
           (i.e., "There is a cat which is the smallest and I rarely pet it.")

As can be seen from these examples, the differences in interpretation are similar in Icelandic non-OS/OS sentences and German non-Scrambling/Scrambling sentences.

    Diesing (1992, and also Diesing and Jelinek 1993, 1995, and Diesing in her later work) wants to try to relate these differences to a particular theory of semantic interpretation developed by Heim (1982) and others. The basic idea is that syntactic structures "map" into semantic structures in a particular fashion, as stated in the Mapping Hypothesis (this formulation is based on Diesing 1997: 373):

(87) **The Mapping Hypothesis**
    1. VP maps into the Nuclear Scope (the domain of existential closure).
    2. IP [functional projections above VP] maps into the Restriction (of an operator).

Thus in sentences like (85a) the object is inside the VP and hence receives a predicational reading and there is no presupposition of existence. In (85b), on the other hand, the object has moved out of the VP and "into the IP" in some sense and hence receives a specific (or quantificational) interpretation. The interpretational differences in the other pairs in (85)–(86) would be accounted for in the same fashion.

    Diesing and Jelinek (1993, 1995) also use this semantic approach to account for other facts about Scandinavian OS and GD Scrambling. First, as shown by examples like (3) above, pronominal OS is obligatory in Scandinavian (except for (dialects of) Swedish). The semantic account for this is supposed to be that the interpretation of unstressed pronouns is incompatible with VP-type interpretation (the "existential closure" interpretation) and hence unstressed pronouns have to shift out of the VP. Focussing or (contrastively) stressing the pronoun, on the other hand, introduces a "novelty" aspect, which is compatible with the VP-interpretation. Hence stressed pronominal objects stay in situ in Scandinavian (cf. the discussion around (5) in section 1.1.1 above). Diesing (1996: 72, 1997: 417) also maintains that definite objects in German tend to get a contrastive reading (aided by stress on the noun) when left in situ in examples like the following, whereas this reading is not present for the scrambled object:

(88) a. ?... weil ich selten   die Katze streichle.   (Ge)
             since I   seldom the cat   pet
             "... since I seldom pet the cat (and not the dog)."

b. ... weil ich **die Katze**ᵢ selten   tᵢ streichle.
    since I   the cat   seldom   pet
    "... since I seldom pet the cat."

Finally, Diesing and Jelinek (1993: 23–4) point out interpretational differences like the following:

(89) a. Ég las   ekki bók.
          I read not book
          "I didn't read (a single) book."
      b. *Ég las **bók**ᵢ ekki tᵢ
          I read book not
      c. Ég les   ekki bækur.
          I read not books
          "I don't read books."
      d. Ég les   **bækur**ᵢ ekki tᵢ
          I read books not
          "I don't read books (I only buy them)."

In (89a) the indefinite singular object *bók* "(a) book" can receive the regular VP-internal existential interpretation but when it is shifted out of the VP, as in (89b), no interpretation is available for it.[33] Similarly, in (89c) the plural indefinite object *bækur* "books" receives an existential interpretation in situ, but when it is shifted out of the VP, as in (89d), it can be interpreted generically: "As for books, I don't read them (but possibly just buy them)."[34]

In their later work, Diesing and Jelinek (cf. Diesing and Jelinek 1995, Diesing 1997) are more specific about the theoretical implementation of this approach to the syntax of OS and Scrambling. Here the so-called Scoping Condition plays an important role (see Diesing 1997: 375):

(90) **Scoping:** The scope of operators must be syntactically fixed.

The basic idea is then that the OS and Scrambling are ways of satisfying the Scoping Condition.

The work by Diesing and Jelinek has clearly added an important dimension to the study of OS and Scrambling. But the facts are actually somewhat more complicated than we have made them out to be. A few observations must suffice here for reasons of space.

As Diesing recognizes (see especially Diesing 1997: 419ff), the Diesing and Jelinek approach to Scandinavian OS faces a disturbing complication: although OS is supposed to be driven by the semantics, as it were, it only applies when the syntax allows it to. As the reader will recall, Scandinavian OS is dependent on verb movement: if the lexical verb does not leave the VP, the object cannot shift. Now the Diesing and Jelinek approach maintains that objects move out of the VP for interpretational reasons. But if pronominal objects have to move out of the VP for interpretational reasons in sentences like (91a) (only the version in (91b) is grammatical), how can they be interpreted inside the VP in sentences like (91c), where they do not (cf. (91d)) undergo OS?

(91) a. *Nemendurnir lásu   ekki   hana.
          students-the   read   not   it
      b. Nemendurnir lásu **hana**$_i$ ekki   t$_i$
          students-the   read it   not
          "The students didn't read it."
      c. Nemendurnir hafa   ekki lesið hana.
          students-the   have   not read it
          "The students haven't read it."
      d. *Nemendurnir hafa **hana**$_i$ ekki lesið t$_i$
          students-the   have it   not read

Similarly, the object *þrjár bækur* "three books" in (92b) can clearly have the specific (or quantificational) reading that it has in (92a), although it has not raised out of the VP in (92b) (and cannot because the lexical verb has not moved):[35]

(92) a. Nemandinn las   **þrjár bækur**$_i$ ekki t$_i$
          student-the read three books   not
          "There are three books that the student didn't read (namely . . .)."
      b. Nemandinn hefur ekki lesið þrjár bækur.
          student-the has   not   read three books
          "It is not the case that the student has read three books." or:
          "There are three books that the student hasn't read (namely . . .)."

Complications of this sort force Diesing to assume that some objects move out of the VP at LF when they cannot do so overtly. As she points out herself (1997: 420), this would appear to be a violation of the Procrastinate principle of Chomsky (1993: 30 and later work), which can be stated as follows:

(93) **Procrastinate:** Delay movement to LF whenever possible.

Obviously, LF-movement of objects cannot be allowed to obliterate relevant scope relations established by overt OS and Scrambling. Without going into the technical details, we can note that although Scoping is stated as a syntactic constraint, it is not a hard constraint which leads to ungrammaticality if it is violated, at least not when it cannot be obeyed for syntactic reasons.

The "softness" of this constraint is reminiscent of the nature of constraints in Optimality Theory (OT). The basic tenet of OT is that constraints are violable and the "best" derivation (of a sentence or a phonological form) is the one that violates the lowest ranked constraints. Thus OT maintains that sentences can be grammatical although they violate certain syntactic constraints. Hence Vikner

(1997b) argues that the violability of the Scoping Condition in Scandinavian OS indicates that an OT approach to Scandinavian OS is superior to a Minimalist approach of the kind proposed by Diesing (1997), for instance. Vikner bases his argumentation on examples of the following type (the examples are somewhat simplified here but the account of the readings is based on Vikner's):

(94)   a.   Þau sýna alltaf   [viðtöl við Clinton]   klukkan ellefu.   (Ic)
            they show always interviews with Clinton clock   eleven
            "They always show interviews with Clinton at 11 o'clock."
                                                                  (existential)
            (i.e., "It is always the case that they show interviews with Clinton at
            11 o'clock.")

       b.   Þau sýna **[viðtöl við Clinton]**ᵢ   alltaf   tᵢ klukkan ellefu.
            they show interviews with Clinton always   clock   eleven
            "They show interviews with Clinton always at 11 o'clock."
                                                                  (generic)
            (i.e., "Whenever there are interviews with Clinton, they are always
            shown at 11 o'clock.")

       c.   Þau hafa alltaf   sýnt   [viðtöl við Clinton]   klukkan ellefu.
            they have always shown interviews with Clinton clock   eleven
            "They have always shown interviews with Clinton at 11 o'clock."
                                                                  (ambiguous)

       d.   *Þau hafa **[viðtöl við Clinton]**ᵢ   alltaf   sýnt   tᵢ klukkan ellefu.
            they have interviews with Clinton always shown   clock   eleven

Vikner's basic point is that the non-shifted and the shifted indefinite objects in (94a, b) have different readings, but the indefinite object in (94c) is ambiguous because it cannot shift. Basing his semantic account (partially) on Diesing's, he argues that when OS does not apply in sentences like (94a), the adverb (here *alltaf* "always") has scope over the object, but when OS does apply, as in (94b), the object has scope over the adverb. But when an indefinite object cannot move out of the VP, as in (94c) (here the main verb cannot move because there is an auxiliary present and hence OS is impossible), it will have an ambiguous interpretation. Vikner then gives an OT account of this, assuming among other things an OT constraint which is based on Diesing's Scoping Condition:

(95)   **Scoping:** An element has the position in the clause that corresponds to
       its relative scope.

It should be clear, however, that Vikner's account crucially depends on the claim that a non-moved object which can move will have a narrower scope than an adverb that c-commands it. Diesing (1997) also assumed that if objects with the definite/specific/strong ... reading could move out of the VP, they would do so. That implies that sentences like the following should not be ambiguous:

(96) a. . . . dat de politie gisteren   veel taalkundigen opgepakt heeft. (Du)
             that the police yesterday many linguists   arrested has
             ". . . that the police arrested many linguists yesterday."
      b. Þau sýna alltaf [viðtöl við Clinton]   klukkan ellefu. (cf. (94a))
             they show always interviews with Clinton clock   eleven
             "They always show interviews with Clinton at 11 o'clock."

Example (96a) is taken from de Hoop (1992: 139) and she states explicitly that
it "can have either a weak (existential) or a strong (partitive) reading." In other
words, an object with a strong reading does not have to scramble, according to
her. Example (96b) is modeled on the examples in Vikner (1997b), and speakers of Icelandic seem to agree that it *can* have the "strong" reading, although
the "weak" reading is more natural. When these objects scramble or shift, on
the other hand, the weak reading seems to be eliminated (see also de Hoop
1992: 139):

(97) a. . . . dat de politie **[veel taalkundigen]**$_i$ gisteren   t$_i$ (Du)
             that the police many linguists   yesterday
          opgepakt heeft.
          arrested   has
             ". . . that the police arrested many linguists yesterday."
      b. Þau sýna **[viðtöl við Clinton]**$_i$ alltaf   t$_i$ klukkan   (cf. (94b))
             they show interviews with Clinton always   clock
          ellefu.
          eleven
             "They show interviews with Clinton always at 11 o'clock."

Thus the correct generalization seems to be that the weak/existential reading
is incompatible with OS and Scrambling but objects having the strong/
quantificational/specific reading do not necessarily have to shift or scramble.
Facts of this sort are obviously relevant for the general issue of optionality: to
what extent can syntactic movement rules be truly optional? The Minimalist
Program predicts that such rules should not exist, since if constituents do not
have to move, they should not move, due to the principle of Procrastinate
(cf. (93) above).

    As seen above, various terms have been used about the relevant semantic
distinctions involved in OS and Scrambling. This reflects the fact that the nature
of these is not entirely clear. Thus Jonas (1996b) talks about the checking of a
D-feature (cf. Chomsky 1995b: 232, passim), a feature supposed to have something to do with Determiners and hence possibly definiteness or specificity.
Diesing (1996: 72) and others have emphasized the "novelty effect," something
which could also be related to ideas about new vs. old information and focussing (see also Bobaljik 1995: 127–8). De Hoop (1992) calls the basic distinction
"strong" and "weak," attempting to relate this distinction to that between strong
and weak quantifiers usually attributed to Milsark (1974, 1977).[36] Furthermore,

she wants to relate this distinction to proposals about strong and weak Case.[37] Now it seems a rather questionable move in itself to call something a Case distinction in one language just because it is reminiscent of a distinction correlating with morphological case in another language. But the contrasts clearly need to be explained.[38]

2.4.2   The role of focus and stress

In the preceding sections we have frequently seen the part that stress may play in influencing the acceptability of sentences involving OS and Scrambling. Details aside, it thus seems clear that Scrambling is incompatible with focus stress, as argued by Grewendorf and Sternefeld (1990a: 15), for instance:

(98) a.   . . . weil   der Professor   dem Studenten das Buch   (Ge)
               because the professor-Nom the Student-Dat the book-Acc
            ausgeliehen hat.
            lent   has

      b.   *. . . weil   **dem Studenten$_i$ DAS BUCH$_j$** der Professor   t$_i$ t$_j$
               because the student-Dat the book-Acc the professor-Nom
            ausgeliehen hat.
            lent   has

      c.   . . . weil   **dem Studenten$_i$ das Buch$_j$**   DER PROFESSOR t$_i$ t$_j$
               because the student-Dat the book-Acc the professor-Nom
            ausgeliehen hat.
            lent   has

The examples in (98) illustrate that both IO and DO can be scrambled over the subject in German, as we have already seen, but if, say, the scrambled DO is stressed, as in (98b), the result is ungrammatical, whereas the in situ subject can be stressed, as shown in (98c).

Some linguists have also suggested that OS could be a PF-rule. Holmberg originally argued (1986: 167ff) that OS could not be a PF rule since it had to apply before a syntactic rule, namely Topicalization (see also Holmberg and Platzack 1995: 150–1). But recently Holmberg (1997) has argued that Scandinavian OS is in fact a PF-rule. He argues that since OS has neither the properties expected of an A-movement rule nor those of an A'-movement rule it must be a PF-rule. His major argument against the A-movement status of OS involves binding relations, i.e., he argues that OS does not "create new binding possibilities," as it should if it were an A-movement rule. But as discussed in section 2.2.4 above, his arguments against the A-movement status of OS are rather unconvincing.

Holmberg (1997) also maintains that OS is dependent on verb movement because phonological material may block OS and hence the verb has to "get out of the way," as it were. He argues, for instance, that particles may block OS in Swedish, because Swedish differs from, say, Icelandic in not shifting pronominal objects obligatorily around particles. As Bobaljik (1998) has pointed out, however, the facts seem to be a bit more complicated and call for a different explanation, cf. (99):

(99) a. *Dom kastade **den**$_i$ inte ut t$_i$ (Sw)
         they threw   it   not out
      b. Dom stängde **den**$_i$ inte av t$_i$
         they closed it   not off
         "They didn't switch it off."

This does not mean that there could not be a phonological component to OS and Holmberg's Generalization. But no convincing arguments have been presented for the claim that OS is a PF rule.

3 Concluding Remarks

As shown by the overview in this chapter, the study of Scandinavian OS and GD Scrambling has led to the discovery of many theoretically interesting facts about the languages in question and language in general. The theoretical relevance of OS and Scrambling studies would have become even clearer if we had been able to include more references to "similar phenomena" in other languages, e.g. the non-Germanic languages discussed in Corver and van Riemsdijk (1994b).

In conclusion, let us consider briefly the phrase "similar phenomena" used above. Before the introduction of the Principles and Parameters (P&P) approach by Chomsky (1981), syntacticians tended to concentrate on language-specific and construction-specific phenomena, whereas typical GB studies in the P&P approach emphasized that all movement rules were in fact "the same rule," i.e., "Move α," applying freely but constrained by general principles. Hence it might seem rather out of place to ask whether a given phenomenon in Language X shows that it has a rule of OS or Scrambling, or just some "different rule." Yet a typical argumentation in the literature goes like this:

(100) Rule Y in Language X has properties a, b, c. Scrambling (e.g. in German) is known to have properties a, b, c. Hence Rule Y must be an instance of Scrambling.

Thus Alexiadou and Anagnastopoulou (1997: 143) point out, for instance, that because so-called Clitic Doubling in Greek is "sensitive to Specificity," like (Germanic) Scrambling, it has been suggested that the two should be "unified." Now Alexiadou and Anagnastopoulou (1997) assume the Minimalist approach, and one could argue that within the checking theory inherent in the Minimalist Program it makes more sense than before to ask questions like "same rule?" or "different rule?". If checking of the same features is involved, then it is at least obvious that the rules in question have more in common than some of the processes that have been unified under the general label "Move α."

NOTES

1   See e.g. the overview in Corver and van Riemsdijk 1994a, especially their table on p. 13.

2   Among discussions of OS and Scrambling in other languages one could mention the following: First, the closest relatives of German and Dutch, namely Swiss German, Frisian, (West) Flemish, Afrikaans, and Yiddish, have all been claimed to "have" Scrambling or Object Movement of some sort (see e.g. Vikner 1994b, Neeleman 1994, den Dikken 1996, Diesing 1997).

Second, although it is usually assumed that Modern English does not have OS or Scrambling, some linguists claim that it does, as evidenced, for instance, by particle constructions (see e.g. Johnson 1991, Diesing and Jelinek 1993, Koizumi 1993, 1995, Runner 1995). A more common position is that Old English, Middle English, and even Early Modern English had Scrambling (or OS) but that the relevant word orders were later "lost" (see e.g. Kemenade 1987, Roberts 1995, 1997, with references).

Third, a number of other European languages have been reported to have OS or Scrambling of some sort, including Italian (PP-scrambling, cf. Belletti and Shlonsky 1995), Portuguese (Costa 1996), Spanish (clitic doubling with some OS properties, cf. Suñer 1998), Hungarian (Fanselow 1990, É. Kiss 1994), Russian (Müller and Sternefeld 1994), Greek (clitic doubling with some Scrambling properties, cf. Alexiadou 1997, Alexiadou and Anagnostopoulou 1997), and Turkish (Fanselow 1990,

Bayer and Kornfilt 1994, Haider 1997).

Fourth, a number of Asian languages appear to have OS or Scrambling, such as Hindi (cf. Mahajan 1990, 1994b), Persian (Browning and Karimi 1994), Bangla (Senegupta 1990), Japanese (cf. e.g. Kuno 1973, Saito 1989, 1992, Ueyama 1994, Kim 1996, Kitahara 1997), and Korean (cf. Lee and Santorini 1994, Kim 1996).

Fifth, one could mention a couple of "exotic" languages where such phenomena reportedly exist, such as Selayarese (Finer 1994), Warlpiri (Hale 1994), and West Greenlandic (Fanselow 1990).

3   Non-movement analyses include non-configurational analyses along the lines of Hale (1983), "base-generation" accounts in GB-type frameworks (like Weerman 1989, Neeleman 1994), and accounts in frameworks that do not assume "transformations" or "movement rules" at all (cf. e.g. Pollard and Sag 1993). There are also "mixed approaches," which assume that some of the variation in the order of constituents should be accounted for by movement rules while other instances of such variation go back to underlying differences (cf. Czepluch 1990, Bayer and Kornfilt 1994, Hale 1994, Collins and Thráinsson 1996).

4   As Holmberg (1986: 228–9) points out, citing Faarlund (1977), some Swedish and Norwegian dialects appear to allow unstressed pronominal objects to stay in situ, whereas Danish and Icelandic do not (see also Vikner 1989, 1991). "True clitics" (i.e., reduced

pronominal forms) can also follow the negation in Swedish and Norwegian dialects (cf. Hellan and Platzack 1995: 55–6, Josefsson 1993: 23):

(i) a. Jag såg inte'na.
　　　　(Sw) ['na from OSw *hana,*
　　　　not Modern Sw. *henne* "her"]
　　b. Æ såg itj'a
　　　　I　　saw not-her
　　　　(Trøndersk – a dialect of
　　　　Norway around Trondheim)

Faroese seems to follow Icelandic and Danish here (see e.g. Petersen et al. 1998). The reason for this variation is unclear. It is indicated by the % sign in (3a) but it will be ignored for the most part in this chapter.

5　As Nielsen (1997) observes, the Norwegian facts are somewhat more complicated than usually assumed. He gives complex but passable sentences which appear to involve OS in Norwegian. See also n. 17.

6　Here, and for the rest of the chapter, traces (t) are used for convenience to indicate the "base position" of the moved elements without any strong theoretical claims about their nature or even their existence in some cases.

7　Although Scandinavian OS by and large only applies to arguments, it has been noted (e.g. by Haider et al. 1995: 20–1) that unstressed (presumably) non-argumental *der* "there" has similar distribution with respect to adverbs to that of shiftable pronominal objects. In particular, its position is influenced by verb movement. Unstressed *þar* "there" in Icelandic behaves in a similar fashion, except that it does not seem to have to "shift" (Danish based on Haider et al. 1995: 20–1):

(i)
a. *Peter sov　　ikke der.　(Da)
　　Peter slept　　not there
b. Peter sov　**der**$_i$ ikke t$_i$
c. Peter har　　ikke sovet der.
d. Peter has　　not slept there
e. *Peter har　**der**$_i$ ikke sovet t$_i$
f. Pétur svaf　ekki þar.　(Ic)
g. Peter slept　not there
h. Pétur svaf　**þar**$_i$ ekki t$_i$
i. Pétur hefur　ekki sofið þar.
　　Peter has　　not slept there
j. *Pétur hefur **þar**$_i$ ekki sofið t$_i$

The parallelism is interesting and indicates that there is still a lot that we do not understand about the nature of OS.

8　Sentences containing "negative objects" seem to constitute an interesting exception to Holmberg's Generalization in Scandinavian, however (cf. Christensen 1986 Rögnvaldsson 1987, Jónsson 1996: sec. 3.4):

(i) a. Jeg har　**ingen**$_i$/　　(No)
　　　　I　have no one/
　　　　***henne**$_i$ set　t$_i$.
　　　　*her　　seen
　　　　"I haven't seen anyone."
　　b. Ég hef　**enga bók**$_i$/　(Ic)
　　　　I　have no book/
　　　　***þessa bók**$_i$ lesið t$_i$.
　　　　*this book　read
　　　　"I haven't read any book."

As shown here, negative objects like Norwegian *ingen* "no one" and Icelandic *enga bók* "no book" can shift to the left of the non-finite main verb although the Norwegian pronoun *henne* "her" and the Icelandic "positive NP" *þessa bók* "this book" cannot. Something special needs to be said about this kind of OS and it will be ignored for the most part in this chapter.

It should be mentioned here that Zwart (1997: 241) argues against the validity of Holmberg's Generalization. We return to his arguments in section 2 below (especially section 2.2.5).

9 Pronominal OS in Danish and Norwegian works the same way, but the Swedish facts are different, as shown by Holmberg (1986), due to special properties of the particle construction in Swedish (see also Svenonius 1996):

(i) a. Hún skrifaði það upp/*upp
     það.   (Ic)
   b. Hon skrev *det upp/upp
     det.   (Sw)
   c. Hun skrev det op/*op det.
                (Da)
     she wrote it up/up it

10 Czepluch (1990: 176) refers to studies that argue for "alternative projections from one lexical structure," i.e., different underlying orders of objects for different verbs in German – and also verbs where two orders are equally unmarked, a phenomenon somewhat similar to Icelandic Inversion as analyzed by Collins and Thráinsson 1996, for instance. Czepluch argues that this may be the proper account for some variations in object order in German.

11 Except for the special behavior of unstressed (and sometimes also the reduced) pronouns, stress, and intonation factors will not be discussed in any detail in this chapter because they are too complex to deal with in a comparative chapter of this sort. Some effects of stress on the acceptability of various word order configurations in Icelandic are discussed by Collins and Thráinsson 1996, and Zwart 1997 contains numerous observations on the interaction of object positions and intonation (e.g. 92ff).

12 There is some evidence, however, that a full NP object can shift across an indefinite quantified subject (possibly in SpecVP) or across a quantifier "floated" off a subject, as shown in (ia, b), respectively:

(i) a. Þá máluðu **bílana**$_i$ (Ic)
     then painted cars-the(A)
     stundum einhverjir strákar
     sometimes some boys(N)
     t_i rauða.
      red
     "Then some boys sometimes
     painted the cars red."
   b. Þá máluðu strákarnir
     then painted boys-the(N)
     bílana$_i$ stundum allir
     cars-the(A) sometimes all(N)
     t_i rauða.
      red
     "Then all the boys sometimes
     painted the cars red."

This is clearly something which needs to be accounted for, e.g. with respect to Minimality (see e.g. section 2.2.5).

13 This issue has been discussed from a more general point of view by various researchers, see e.g. Czepluch (1990) for German (with references) and Diesing (1997) for Yiddish (with references). Diesing (1997) argues that Yiddish is underlyingly VO and thus that OV-orders in Yiddish are derived by Scrambling. This makes Yiddish special among the Germanic VO-languages, she maintains, since Scrambling (as opposed to OS) is otherwise only found in the Germanic OV-languages. I will return to this issue below when I try to compare Scrambling and OS.

14 The fact that the finite verb does not immediately follow the fronted element in clauses of this type, as it does when something is topicalized (the V2 phenomenon), is generally

taken to indicate that Topicalization is not involved here.

15 Neeleman (1994: 395) refers to *zelfs* "even" and *zulke* "such" as "focus markers" and argues that they make this Scrambling possible. He argues for a base generated analysis of the orders in (25a, c) and maintains that the scrambled objects in (25b, d) are adjoined to VP.

16 This seems likely in fact, since Zwart argues (1997: 31–2) that this process is unbounded and applies to elements that otherwise do not undergo Scrambling in Dutch, such as resultative predicates.

17 One of the things that such a theory needs to account for is the apparent contrast between sentences like the following in Norwegian, as already mentioned in n. 5 (cf. Nielsen 1997: 19, passim):

(i) a. *Etter dette slo   Guri Per
           after this   beat Guri Per
           altid i sjakk.
           always in chess
     b. Etter dette slo   Guri Per
           after this   beat Guri Per
           ærlig talt   heldigvis
           honestly spoken fortunately
           ikke lenger   alltid
           not   any-longer always
           i sjakk.
           in chess.
           "After this, Guri honestly spoken fortunately didn't any longer always beat Per in chess."

Although OS of full NPs across a single sentential adverb is standardly bad in Norwegian, as in (ia), sentences like (ib), where the object precedes a long string of adverbs, are markedly better.

18 Interestingly, Swedish also differs somewhat, at least dialectally, from the other Scandinavian languages in that it allows unstressed objects to remain in situ in contexts where pronominal OS is obligatory in the other Scandinavian languages; cf. the examples in (3) and n. 4. Maybe there is some sort of a link here.

19 According to Weerman (1997: 431), Modern Frisian has similar restrictions to Dutch on the ordering of objects.

20 As Collins and Thráinsson show (1996: 415ff), the Icelandic facts are complicated by the existence of the so-called Inversion structures first discussed by Rögnvaldsson (1982; see also Holmberg 1991b), i.e. base generated DO–IO order allowed by a subclass of ditransitive verbs. When we abstract away from this and select a non-inversion verb like *skila* "return," it becomes clear that a DO cannot shift over an in situ IO.

21 The embedded verb *vanta* "need, lack" is one of the verbs that take accusative subjects in Icelandic. For a discussion of these see, e.g., Zaenen et al. 1985 and references cited there.

22 The relevant Scandinavian facts include sentences of the following sort:

(i) a. *Hann telur   (Ic)
           he-Nom believes
           sjálfur [hana   vera fífl]
           self-Nom her-AccF be   fool
     b. Hann telur **hana**ᵢ
           sjálfur [tᵢ   vera fífl]
           "He himself believes her to be a fool."
     c. Hann   hefur
           He-NomF has
           sjálfur   talið
           self-NomF believed
           [hana   vera fífl]
           her-AccF be   fool
           "He himself has believed her to be a fool."
     d. *Hann   hefur **hana**ᵢ
           sjálfur   talið
           [tᵢ   vera fífl]

As (ia, b) show, when the matrix main verb is finite a pronominal accusative subject has to be shifted out of an infinitival complement of this sort and hence it precedes the (quantifier-like) emphatic *sjálfur* "self," which agrees in case, gender, and number with the matrix subject. (If this accusative subject is a full NP, this movement is optional.) When the matrix verb is non-finite, on the other hand, this raising of the accusative subject cannot take place, as indicated by (ic, d). This is obviously very reminiscent of Icelandic OS.

Relevant German examples include these (based on examples in Fanselow 1990, Grewendorf and Sabel 1994):

(ii) a. weil   niemand
          because   nobody
          [mich die Bücher lesen]
          me   the books read
          liess/sah.
          made/saw
      b. weil   **mich**ᵢ niemand
          [tᵢ   die Bücher lesen
          liess/sah.
          "because nobody made/
          saw me read the books."
      c. dass   keiner
          that   nobody
          [PRO den Hund zu füttern]
             the dog   to feed
          versuchte
          tried
      d. dass **den Hund**ᵢ keiner
          [PRO tᵢ   zu füttern]
          versuchte
          "that nobody tried to feed
          the dog."

23 The reason for the hedging ("a *potential* theta-role position") was that although object positions were believed to be assigned a theta-role in all instances, the subject position in, say, passives and raising

constructions (with verbs of the *seem*-type, for instance) do not appear to have a thematic role of their own.

24 As we will see below (example 67b)), there is reason to believe that a raised ("object shifted") accusative subject of infinitival complements of this sort does c-command an adjoined parenthetical like *X til mikillar undrunar* "to X's great surprise." Hence the ungrammaticality of the reflexive in (64a) suggests that *Harald* is not a semantically appropriate antecedent for a reflexive, whereas the passive subject *Haraldur* in (64b) is.

25 Relevant examples would include sentences of the following type, and here the reflexive seems bad:

      (i) Jag ansåg   [Per och Martin]ᵢ (Sw)
           I   believed Per and Martin
           vara lika bra,   till
           be   equally good, to
           derasᵢ/?*sinᵢ besvikelse
           their/self's disappointment
           "I believed Per and Martin to
           be equally good, to their
           disappointment."

26 Note, for instance, that the example Neeleman (1994: 394) gives to argue for the influence of Dutch Scrambling on binding relations arguably does not involve Scrambling of an object across an indirect object but rather the base generated order DO–prepositional IO, as he himself points out in n. 3.

27 Holmberg (1986: 174) argues that PPs like *i Xs frånvaro* are "left-adjoined to I'" and hence sentences similar to (71b) must involve OS (otherwise the object would not precede the PP). That means then that sentences like (ia) should be bad (since full NP-objects cannot shift in Swedish) and (ib) should be fine, but neither he nor Holmberg

and Platzack (1995) gives such examples:

(i) a. Dom tilldelade Peter
         they awarded Peter
         i min frånvaro priset.
         in my absence prize-the
     b. Dom tilldelade
         they awarded
         i min frånvaro Peter
         in my absence Peter
         priset.
         prize-the

28 It should be noted, however, that Kitahara (1997) assumes that short Scrambling in German is triggered by an "argument feature" rather than an "operator feature," making it on a par with A-movement rather than A′-movement.

29 Note, for instance, that English pronouns show similar case marking distinctions to their MSc counterparts but do not appear to undergo the same kind of OS. Conversely, although Dutch nouns do not show case distinctions any more than MSc ones, Dutch NP objects are more movable than MSc NP objects, as we have seen (cf. also Déprez 1994: 119–21).

30 In addition, it seems counterintuitive to say that the morphological case on Faroese nouns (which show Nom/Acc/Dat distinctions in sg. and pl.) is in some sense "weaker" than that of, say, Swedish personal pronouns (where the Acc/Dat distinction has disappeared altogether).

31 Under this approach, the lack of full NO OS in Faroese could be related to the fact that Faroese has a much poorer agreement system than Icelandic, although richer than MSc. The problem is that Faroese has some word order traits in common with Icelandic, at least dialectally (cf. Jonas 1996a, 1996b, Petersen et al. 1998).

32 Below we will claim that sentences like this one are not unambiguous, although the "predicational" (or existential closure) reading given here is the most natural one.

33 There is no indefinite article in Icelandic so all indefinites are "bare indefinites." Maybe the interpretational possibilities of bare indefinites are more restricted than those of indefinites with the indefinite article. Thus Zwart (1997: 91) reports an interpretational difference for examples of the following sort in Dutch, involving a singular indefinite NP:

(i) a. ... dat Jan gisteren
             that Jan yesterday
         en meisje gekust heeft.
         a girl   kissed has
         "... that Jan kissed a girl yesterday."
     b. ... dat Jan **en meisje**$_i$
             that Jan a girl
         gisteren   t$_i$ gekust heeft.
         yesterday   kissed has
         "... that Jan kissed a (particular) girl yesterday."

34 This latter interpretation can be aided by stressing the verb. See also the discussion of the influence of stress on the shiftability of (indefinite) objects in Collins and Thráinsson 1996.

35 Needless to say, a similar situation obtains when unstressed pronominal objects cannot shift in MSc embedded clauses where no verb movement occurs (cf. Diesing 1997: 411, Vikner 1997b: 11ff).

36 As Vangsnes (1995) has shown, the distinction between strong and weak quantifiers appears to play a role in the licensing of different argument positions in Scandinavian expletive constructions.

37 The reason is that in some languages, e.g. Turkish and Finnish,

it seems that morphological case distinctions correlate with semantic distinctions of the type under discussion. In addition, NPs marked with the "weak" morphological case are not as movable as the ones marked with the strong case. According to de Hoop (1992: 137), this can be illustrated by Turkish examples (the following are based on de Hoop's examples, borrowed from Kornfilt 1990):

(i)   a.   Ben dün akşam   (Tu)
           I   yesterday evening
           [çok güzel bir biftek]
           very nice a steak-Part
           yedim.
           ate
           "I ate a very nice steak
           yesterday evening."
      b.   *Ben **[çok güzel bir biftek]**$_i$
           dün akşam t$_i$ yedim.

(ii) a.   Ben dün akşam
           I   yesterday evening
           bifteg-i   yedim.
           steak-Acc ate
      b.   Ben **bifteg-i**$_i$
           I   steak-Acc
           dün akşam   t$_i$ yedim.
           yesterday evening   ate
           "I ate the steak yesterday
           evening."

This is meant to illustrate that the object in (i) cannot shift, because it is in the "weak" partitive case, whereas the object in (ii) can, since it is in the "strong" accusative case. De Hoop then wants to extend the same kind of analysis to Dutch to account for contrasts like the following:

(iii) a.   . . . dat de politie   (Du)
           that the police
           de taalkundigen$_i$ gisteren
           the linguists   yesterday
           t$_i$ opgepakt heeft.
           arrested   has

"... that the police arrested the linguists yesterday."

      b.   *. . . dat de politie
           that the police
           taalkundigen$_i$ gisteren
           linguists   yesterday
           t$_i$ opgepakt heeft.
           arrested   has

We cannot go further into this account here for reasons of space.

38   As de Hoop (1992: 141–2) points out, Scrambling of PPs does not seem to have any effects on the reading:

(i)   a.   . . . omdat Petra   (Du)
           because   Petra
                          altijd
                          always
           [op haar conditie] vertrouwt.
           on her contition   relies
      b.   . . . omdat Petra
           because   Petra
           [op haar conditie]$_i$ altijd
           on her condition   always
           t$_i$ vertrouwt.
                               relies
           "... because Petra always
           relies on her condition."

This would be expected if the semantic effects of Scrambling had something to do with Case, since PPs do not have Case. In this connection one could also mention that it has been argued that Scrambling in Japanese is a "semantically vacuous A'-movement" (cf. Saito 1989), and Browning and Karimi (1994) argue that only the A-movement like variant of Scrambling in Persian is semantically restricted (in terms of specificity), whereas the A'-movement like variants are not so restricted and have nothing to do with Case (or case). This is intriguing and warrants further research.

7 *Wh*-in-situ Languages

AKIRA WATANABE

1 A Movement Approach to *Wh*-in-situ

Research on *wh*-movement has occupied a central place in generative grammar since Chomsky (1964) and Ross (1967a), leading to important insights into the nature of transformational operations (see Chomsky 1977, 1986b, Rizzi 1990, in particular: cf. Baltin and Ura, both in this volume). In languages like Chinese and Japanese, however, *wh*-phrases do not have to be displaced in overt syntax, as can be seen from comparison between an English sentence (1) and a Chinese example (2):

(1)   John wonders [what$_i$ Mary bought t_i].

(2)   Zhangsan xiang-zhidao [Lisi mai-le shenme]
      Zhangsan wonder   Lisi bought what
      "Zhangsan wonders what Lisi bought."

Huang (1982a, 1982b) has extended the domain of inquiry by treating *wh*-in-situ in terms of LF *wh*-movement. According to Huang's proposal, the *wh*-phrase in (2) undergoes LF movement after mapping to PF to produce the following LF representation:

(3)   Zhangsan xiang-zhidao [$_{CP}$ shenme$_i$ [$_{IP}$ Lisi mai-le t_i]].[1]
      Zhangsan wonder   what   Lisi bought

Note that the LF representation (3) is parallel to the structure in (1).

Huang's LF movement approach to *wh*-in-situ in languages like Chinese makes it possible to directly compare *wh*-in-situ languages with English-type languages where *wh*-phrases are overtly displaced. One immediate consequence, Huang argues, is that we can capture the parallelism in scope and selection between English-type languages and *wh*-in-situ languages by looking at the LF representations.

Consider the following Chinese examples:

(4) a. Zhangsan yiwei Lisi mai-le shenme?
         Zhangsan think Lisi bought what
         "What does Zhangsan think Lisi bought?"
     b. Zhangsan xiang-zhidao Lisi mai-le shenme.
         Zhangsan wonder   Lisi bought what
         "Zhangsan wonders what Lisi bought."

(4a) must be interpreted as a direct question, whereas (4b) has only the reading of an indirect question where the *wh*-phrase takes the embedded scope.
The situation is analogous to what we find in English-type languages, as shown
in (5):

(5) a. What does John think Mary bought *t*?
     b. *John thinks what Mary bought *t*.
     c. John wonders what Mary bought *t*.
     d. *What does John wonder Mary bought *t*?

(5b) is ungrammatical because *think* selects a declarative clause and is incompatible with a *wh*-phrase in Spec of its complement CP. (5d) is ruled out
because *wonder* takes an interrogative clause and requires a *wh*-phrase in Spec
of its complement CP. Now, if *wh*-phrases in (4) undergo LF movement, we
have the following possibilities to consider:

(6) a. [$_{CP}$ shenme$_i$ [$_{IP}$ Zhangsan yiwei [$_{CP}$ [$_{IP}$ Lisi mai-le t_i]]]]
             what   Zhangsan think   Lisi bought
     b. Zhangsan yiwei [$_{CP}$ shenme$_i$ [$_{IP}$ Lisi mai-le t_i]]
         Zhangsan think   what   Lisi bought
     c. Zhangsan xiang-zhidao [$_{CP}$ shenme$_i$ [$_{IP}$ Lisi mai-le t_i]]
         Zhangsan wonder   what   Lisi bought
     d. [$_{CP}$ shenme$_i$ [$_{IP}$ Zhangsan xiang-zhidao [$_{CP}$ [$_{IP}$ Lisi mai-le t_i]]]]
             what   Zhangsan wonder   Lisi bought

Of these, (6b) and (6d) are ruled out for the same reason as (5b) and (5d)
are ungrammatical: violation of selectional requirements. Notice that the LF
representations in (6) display the same structural pattern as the visible effects
of *wh*-movement in (5). The advantage of the LF movement approach to *wh*-in-
situ is that we can state the selectional restrictions as straightforward formal
conditions on LF representations, applicable to English-type languages as well
as to Chinese-type languages. The two types of language simply differ in
whether *wh*-movement takes place in overt syntax or at LF.
   The significance of Huang's proposal is, of course, not limited to the statement
of selectional properties. His discussion of restrictions on LF movement generated a series of important works dealing with locality of movement (see Aoun

and Li 1993c, Lasnik and Saito 1984, 1992, for example). This chapter looks at various issues concerning the treatment of *wh*-in-situ in the Chinese–Japanese type of languages. Section 2 considers the possibility that the *wh*-movement posited for *wh*-in-situ languages takes place in overt syntax, contrary to appearances. Section 3 turns to the morphological basis that separates *wh*-in-situ languages from English-type languages, and then takes up the parametric split among *wh*-in-situ languages.

2   LF Movement or Overt Movement?

Huang's proposal has turned *wh*-in-situ into an important tool with which to investigate the locality of movement. At the same time, to the extent that the behavior of *wh*-in-situ mimics the nature of overt movement, the LF movement hypothesis receives further support. Thus, the empirical question is to what extent overt syntactic movement and the postulated LF *wh*-movement behave in the same way. This section explores this question by concentrating on Japanese data.[2]

2.1   Locality of **wh-*movement***

It is well known that overt *wh*-movement cannot extract a *wh*-phrase from an island, as illustrated by English examples in (7):

(7)   a.   ??Who is he reading a book that criticizes *t*?
       b.   ??What do you remember where we bought *t*?

(7a) is an instance of a complex NP island; (7b) a *wh*-island. (See Fukui in this volume for a general discussion of islands.) Both (7a) and (7b) violate Subjacency. When we turn to Japanese, we get a mixed result: the counterpart of (7a) is OK but that of (7b) is not. Consider examples in (8):

(8)   a.   kare-wa [dare-ga   kaita] hon-o   yonde-iru no?
           he-Top   who-Nom wrote book-Acc read-Prog Q
           "Is he reading a book that who wrote?"
       b.   ??[nani-o   doko-de   katta   ka] oboete-iru   no?
           what-Acc where-At bought Q   remember-Prog Q
           "What do you remember where we bought?"

(8a), which corresponds to (7a), is acceptable. In (8b), on the other hand, the reading in which *nani-o* "what-Acc" takes the matrix scope is very difficult to get.[3] What sense can we make of this situation?

Nishigauchi (1990), Choe (1987), and Pesetsky (1987) claim that LF movement is also subject to Subjacency, taking (8b) as manifesting a Subjacency violation in a transparent way. The LF representation for (8b) under the relevant reading is shown below:

(8′) b.   [$_{CP}$ nani$_i$-o [$_{IP}$ pro$_{you}$ [$_{CP}$ doko-de$_j$ [$_{IP}$ pro$_{we}$ t_i t_j katta]   ka]
           what-Acc   where-at   bought Q
       oboete-iru]   no]
       remember-Prog Q

In (8′b), the embedded object *nani-o* "what-Acc" is extracted out of a *wh*-island, just as in (7b). It is (8a) which needs a special treatment. According to Nishigauchi, Choe, and Pesetsky, LF movement is entirely parallel to overt movement, obeying the same constraint. This conclusion thus strengthens Huang's LF movement analysis of *wh*-in-situ. To handle (8a), Nishigauchi, Choe, and Pesetsky propose not that what undergoes LF movement in (8a) is the *wh*-phrase *dare*, but that the entire complex NP *[dare-ga kaita] hon* is pied-piped. According to this proposal, (9) is the LF representation of (8a):

(9)   [$_{CP}$ [dare-ga   kaita] hon$_i$-o [$_{IP}$ kare-wa t_i yonde-iru] no]
        who-Nom wrote book-Acc he-Top   read-Prog Q

Since movement of the complex NP itself does not cross an island in (9), (8a) is grammatical. There are languages such as Sinhala (Kishimoto 1992) which have the device of obligatorily indicating the size of *wh*-phrases so that large-scale pied-piping is overtly marked. Cf. Pesetsky's (1987) discussion of a similar (but not obligatory) device in Japanese. See the references cited for further arguments for large-scale pied-piping and von Stechow (1996) for a critical discussion.[4]

   The pied-piping hypothesis has to deal with the fact that certain adjuncts do not allow large-scale pied-piping. This fact is indicated by the ill-formedness of (10):

(10)   *kare-wa [John-ga   naze kaita] hon-o   yonde-iru no?
        he-Top   John-Nom why wrote book-Acc read-Prog Q
        "Is he reading a book that John wrote why?"

If large-scale pied-piping were possible, (10) should be grammatical, since there would be no extraction from an island. We are thus led to assume that large-scale pied-piping is not possible with adjuncts like *naze* "why." The strong unacceptability of (10) is attributed to some kind of Subjacency effect. In the framework of Chomsky (1986b) and Lasnik and Saito (1984, 1992), the ill-formedness of (10) has been analyzed as an ECP effect, which is stronger than an ordinary Subjacency violation. The same strong ungrammaticality is incurred by overt adjunct extraction in English illustrated in (11) with the indicated structure:

(11)   *Why is he reading [a book [that John wrote *t*]]?

See Lasnik and Saito (1984, 1992), Nishigauchi (1990), and Saito (1994a) for further discussion of the behavior of adjuncts within islands.

Returning to the locality of LF movement, an interesting question arises when we compare Japanese-type languages and English-type languages. *Wh*-in-situ is not limited to languages like Chinese and Japanese. Multiple questions in English-type languages also involve *wh*-in-situ, as in (12):

(12)   Who bought what?

It is also well known[5] that *wh*-in-situ in languages like English does not display island effects. Consider the sentences in (13):

(13)   a.   Who is reading a book that criticizes who?
       b.   Who remembers where we bought what?

In (13a) and (13b), the *wh*-direct object in the embedded clause can take the matrix clause as its scope, so that (13a) is a direct question asking for a pair of people, and (13b) a pair of a person who remembers and a thing bought.[6] Suppose the LF movement analysis is also applicable to *wh*-in-situ in languages like English. The LF representations for (the relevant readings of) the sentences in (13) are:

(14)   a.   [$_{CP}$ who$_j$ who$_i$ [$_{IP}$ t_i is reading a book that criticizes t_j]]
       b.   [$_{CP}$ what$_j$ who$_i$ [$_{IP}$ t_i remembers where we bought t_j]]

We are then faced with a dilemma. When we consider LF movement in languages like English, we have to conclude that it is not subject to Subjacency, behaving differently from overt movement. But if we look at LF movement in Japanese, it obeys the same restriction as overt movement: Subjacency. How can we reconcile these two apparently contradictory conclusions?

One possibility explored by Watanabe (1992a, 1992b) is to assume that *wh*-questions in Japanese in fact involve movement in overt syntax, not LF movement. According to this hypothesis, part of the *wh*-phrase, which is a phonologically invisible operator, undergoes overt movement, so that (15a) is associated with the representation (15b) in overt syntax:

(15)   a.   Boku-wa [$_{CP}$ [$_{IP}$ John-ga   nani-o   katta]   ka] shiritai.
            I-Top   John-Nom what-Acc bought Q want-to-know
            "I want to know what John bought."
       b.   Boku-wa [$_{CP}$ Op$_i$ [$_{IP}$ John-ga [t_i nani]-o katta] Q] shiritai.

Under this analysis, the absence of an island effect in (8a) is due to generation of the *wh*-operator on the complex NP itself, in which case movement does not cross an island. We will return to the identity of this invisible operator in the next section.

If Watanabe's hypothesis is adopted, it becomes possible to reconcile the facts about English and those about Japanese. The island effects shown by Japanese *wh*-questions no longer are due to LF movement, but should be attributed to overt movement. It is therefore not surprising that Japanese *wh*-questions behave in the same way as overt movement in languages like English, obeying Subjacency, in contrast to LF movement involved in *wh*-in-situ in languages like English. LF *wh*-movement is simply immune to Subjacency, if we continue to assume that LF movement applies to *wh*-in-situ in multiple questions.[7] Watanabe further observes that the parallelism between Japanese and English is strengthened if we look at multiple *wh*-questions in Japanese. The data which are used to show the island-sensitivity of Japanese *wh*-questions are limited to interrogatives which involve single *wh*-phrases. It is therefore interesting to see what happens in multiple questions. Surprisingly, the *wh*-island effect disappears in this context. Consider the contrast in (16):

(16) a.   ??John-wa [Mary-ga   nani-o   katta   kadooka] Tom-ni
          John-Top   Mary-Nom what-Acc bought whether   Tom-Dat
          tazuneta no?
          asked   Q
          "What did John ask Tom whether Mary bought?"
     b.   John-wa [Mary-ga   nani-o   katta   kadooka] dare-ni
          John-Top Mary-Nom what-Acc bought whether   who-Dat
          tazuneta no?
          asked   Q
          "Who did John ask whether Mary bought what?"

In (16), the *wh*-phrase *nani-o* "what-Acc" inside the embedded *wh*-clause necessarily takes matrix scope, since it is incompatible with *kadooka* "whether." This ends up as a familiar case of the *wh*-island effect in (16a). (16b) shows that when a second *wh*-phrase is added outside of the island, the sentence improves. The contrast in (16) is essentially the same as what we find in English examples in (17), where *what* in (17b) can take matrix scope:

(17) a.   ??What do you remember where we bought?
     b.   Who remembers where we bought what?

The contrast in (16) can be accounted for on the assumption that only one *wh*-element must undergo overt movement in Japanese, an assumption needed for languages like English anyway in view of the ungrammaticality of the examples in (18):

(18) a.   *I wonder [$_{CP}$ who what [$_{IP}$ *t* bought *t*]]
     b.   *I wonder [$_{CP}$ what who [$_{IP}$ *t* bought *t*]]

Returning to the Japanese example (16b), the *wh*-phrase *dare-ni* "who-Dat" launches an operator in overt syntax. Since this movement does not cross an island, it is legitimate. The *wh*-phrase inside the *wh*-island, *nani-o* "what-Acc," does not have to launch overt movement.

To sum up so far, on the basis of Japanese data, Huang's movement approach to *wh*-in-situ can be strengthened to the idea that *wh*-in-situ involves overt movement, not LF movement, in Japanese-type languages, contrary to appearances. Japanese-type languages and English type-languages are maximally similar, requiring movement of exactly one *wh*-element to Spec of an interrogative CP in overt syntax. Furthermore, overt movement, but not LF movement, is subject to Subjacency.

2.2   *Category movement or feature movement?*

The overt movement analysis of *wh*-in-situ raises questions about the nature of the invisible operator that undergoes overt movement in Japanese interrogative sentences. The intuitive idea is that the essence of a *wh*-phrase is extracted, leaving behind the rest of the phrase. What then is the essence of a *wh*-phrase?

It is interesting to consider this question in light of a recent proposal about the nature of movement put forth by Chomsky (1995a). He claims that the movement operation should raise only the morphosyntactic formal features, if movement in general is driven by morphological considerations. *Wh*-elements such as *who* and *what* consist of a *wh*-feature, an indefinite part, and the [±human] feature.[8] In case of *wh*-movement, only the *wh*-feature needs to be raised, according to Chomsky's (1995a) view. This is not the case in English, however, where the entire *wh*-phrase must be raised. Chomsky calls this effect generalized pied-piping and attributes it to morphophonological requirements. His proposal is that the derivation crashes at PF when parts of a word are scattered. Since LF movement should be free from such requirements, it follows that only features undergo movement in the LF component in general. In Japanese, on the other hand, we can hypothesize that morphophonological considerations allow movement of the *wh*-feature alone even in overt syntax, leaving the rest of the *wh*-feature in situ.[9] The question of morphology is taken up in section 3.

Watanabe (1992a), also based on morphological considerations, proposes a somewhat more conservative approach, according to which the invisible operator originates in Spec of the DP which is a *wh*-phrase such as *nani* "what." Movement of this operator proceeds as in (19):

(19) $[_{CP} Op [_{IP} \dots DP \dots] Q]$

Under this proposal, what undergoes movement is a maximal projection.

Choice between these two approaches at our current level of understanding is difficult, especially in view of uncertainties in the treatment of island effects in the general framework of Chomsky (1995a).[10] The two approaches may eventually converge, the movement in (19) carrying only the *wh*-feature (but not the entire category), if we adopt Takahashi's (1997) suggestion that a null operator undergoes pure feature movement even in overt syntax because it is free from PF considerations. Cf. Bošković (to appear). Here, I put aside this question and consider one important aspect in the treatment of *wh*-in-situ which is significant in evaluating theories of invisible operator movement in overt syntax, in order to spell out a theoretical problem behind the treatment of island effects.

The conclusion of section 2.1 rests on the assumption that *wh*-in-situ in English-type languages undergoes LF movement. It is not obvious, however, that we can justify this assumption. Remember that this hypothesized LF movement is different from overt movement in not obeying Subjacency. Suppose *wh*-in-situ in English-type languages does not undergo LF movement, licensed by some kind of unselective binding instead.[11] The absence of island effects follows as a natural consequence. See Chomsky (1995a) for considerations that lead to this hypothesis, and Reinhart (1997b, 1998) in particular for interpretive problems raised by *wh*-in-situ in English. At the same time, the island sensitivity of *wh*-in-situ in Japanese can be explained if we continue to assume the LF movement analysis of Japanese *wh*-in-situ. To accommodate the range of facts discussed in section 2.1, we only need the assumption that movement obeys Subjacency whether it applies in overt syntax or at LF, and that only one *wh*-feature is required to be raised to Spec of an interrogative CP in Japanese as well as in English. We have to look for further evidence.

The crucial argument that Watanabe (1992a, 1992b) presents for the overt movement treatment of Japanese *wh*-in-situ has to do with the blocking effect that *wh*-clauses have for another type of overt A'-movement, Comparative Deletion. Kikuchi (1987) (see also Ishii 1991) shows that Comparative Deletion is derived by movement in overt syntax. This means that Comparative Deletion displays island effects. Significantly for us, an indirect question constitutes an island for Comparative Deletion. This is illustrated in (20).

(20)   *[Minna-ga   [naze Paul-ga *t* yonda ka] siritagatteiru yori]
         everyone-Nom why Paul-Nom read   Q   want-to-know than
         John-ga   takusan-no hon-o   yonda.
         John-Nom many-Gen book-Acc read
         "John read more books than everyone wants to know why Paul read."

(20) shows that Comparative Deletion in Japanese is sensitive to a *wh*-island in the same way as in English (Chomsky 1977). If *wh*-in-situ in Japanese is assumed to undergo only LF movement, the embedded question in (20) has the same structure as a declarative clause in overt syntax, so that it cannot

function as a *wh*-island at that stage of the derivation. (20) would be indistinguishable from (21), which is acceptable:

(21) [Minna-ga   [Paul-ga *t* yonda to] uwasasiteiru yori] John-ga
      everyone-Nom Paul-Nom read   C° rumor   than John-Nom
      takusan-no hon-o   yonda.
      many-Gen book-Acc read
      "John read more books than everyone rumors that Paul read."

If *wh*-in-situ launches an invisible operator in overt syntax, on the other hand, we can expect the *wh*-island effect created by the embedded question. Thus, we are led to conclude that *wh*-questions in Japanese involve overt movement.

At this point, let us return to the choice between the *wh*-feature movement analysis and Watanabe's (1992a) original proposal. To solve this question, it is important to consider exactly what induces the *wh*-island effect. In the traditional account, the *wh*-island effect arises from the configuration in (22), where YP tries to move across XP, which occupies Spec of CP:[12]

(22) ... [$_{CP}$ XP C° [$_{IP}$ ... YP

This movement is ruled out by the Relativized Minimality of Rizzi (1990) or by the Minimal Link Condition (MLC) of Chomsky and Lasnik (1993). Cf. Ura in this volume.

In the framework of Chomsky (1995a), MLC is incorporated into the definition of the movement operation, and furthermore, movement is characterized in terms of attraction. A somewhat simplified definition of Attract is given in (23):[13]

(23) K attracts F if F is the closest feature that can enter into a checking
      relation with K.

The movement of YP in (22) is blocked by this definition only if XP has the closest feature that can enter into a checking relation with the head that is supposed to check the relevant feature of YP. In the interaction of Comparative Deletion with a *wh*-question in (20), it is doubtful whether the *wh*-feature can enter into a checking relation with the complementizer that triggers Comparative Deletion. The problem is not limited to *wh*-in-situ, however, because Comparative Deletion is blocked by a *wh*-island even in languages like English.

Let us now consider the *wh*-feature movement analysis. Chomsky (1995a) argues that feature movement necessarily results in adjunction to a head. The configuration for the *wh*-island should be something like (24):

(24) ... [$_{CP}$ C°+wh [$_{IP}$ ... YP

First of all, the Relativized Minimality of Rizzi (1990) or the MLC of Chomsky and Lasnik (1993) cannot handle the island effect in (24) because Spec of CP is not filled. In this sense, the blocking effect in (20) is an argument for Watanabe's (1992a) proposal of invisible operator movement under the framework which assumes the Relativized Minimality of Rizzi (1990) or the MLC of Chomsky and Lasnik (1993), as long as Comparative Deletion involves movement of a maximal projection. On the other hand, it does not matter for Attract in (23) whether the *wh*-feature is located in Spec or the head. The *wh*-feature in (24) is certainly closer to K than the feature in YP. Still, the same problem remains: the *wh*-feature cannot enter into a checking relation with the trigger of Comparative Deletion. Thus, to the extent that the Attract approach can be modified to handle the interaction between *wh*-question movement and Comparative Deletion (or more generally, two types of A′-movement), we do not have grounds on which to choose between the *wh*-feature movement analysis or the invisible operator movement analysis. Future research has to address this issue.

   To summarize the discussion, an independent argument is presented for the idea that *wh*-in-situ in Japanese-type languages involves movement in overt syntax. The identity of the entity that undergoes this overt movement is also discussed. Two possibilities are considered, namely that it is a *wh*-feature and that it is an operator that originates in Spec of DP.

3   Morphology and the Typological Perspective

It is mentioned in section 2.2 that morphological considerations are significant in determining whether *wh*-in-situ is allowed. This section pursues this question in some detail. This discussion is also related to fine-grained differences among *wh*-in-situ languages.

3.1   Factors that allow wh-in-situ

There is an interesting property that characterizes *wh*-in-situ languages like Chinese and Japanese. The quantificational system in these languages builds on expressions that are used in *wh*-phrases. Thus, it is well known (Huang 1995) that in Chinese, *shenme* can be interpreted as a *wh*-phrase, a universal quantifier, a negative polarity item, or an existential quantifier, depending on the context in which it appears:

(25)   a.   ni   xiang mai shenme (ne)?
             you want buy what   Q
             "What do you want to buy?"
       b.   wo shenme   dou mai.
             I   everything all   buy
             "I want to buy everything."

c. wo bu xiang mai shenme.
    I   not want buy anything
    "I don't want to buy anything."
d. ta dagai   mai-le   shenme   le.
    he probably buy-Perf something-Part
    "He probably bought something."

See Cheng (1991, 1995), Cheng and Huang (1996), and Li (1992) for detailed discussions of the licensing conditions on non-*wh* readings in Chinese. In Japanese, too, *wh*-expressions can be used as quantificational expressions, but only when a particle is attached, as illustrated in (26):[14]

(26) a. dare-ga   ringo-o   tabeta no?
          who-Nom apple-Acc ate   Q
          "Who ate an apple?"
      b. daremo-ga   ringo-o   tabeta.
          everyone-Nom apple-Acc ate
          "Everyone ate an apple."
      c. daremo ringo-o   tabe-nak-atta.
          anyone apple-Acc eat-Neg-Past
          "No one ate an apple."
      d. dareka-ga   ringo-o   tabeta.
          someone-Nom apple-Acc ate
          "Someone ate an apple."

The syntactic and semantic roles of these particles have received a lot of attention in generative studies of Japanese since Kuroda (1965). See Aoyagi and Ishii (1994), Brockett (1994), Hasegawa (1991), Kawashima (1994), and Nishigauchi (1990), among many others, for discussion. See also Haspelmath (1997) for typological patterns in the use of these particles.

Watanabe (1992a) claims that this morphosyntactic property, namely, the existence of indeterminate elements which receive various quantificational interpretations governed by morphosyntactic environments, allows *wh*-in-situ in these languages. Cheng (1991), on the other hand, observes that *wh*-in-situ languages tend to have overt question particles as complementizers (*ne* in Chinese *wh*-questions and *no/ka* in Japanese questions in general), and argues that the presence of an overt particle in CP obviates the need of moving an overt *wh*-element, allowing *wh*-in-situ and forcing *wh*-in-situ because of Economy (see Baltin in this volume), since a particle is sufficient to indicate that the clause is a question. Kayne (1994) pursues yet another possibility that links word order with *wh*-in-situ. Kayne claims that when the complementizer is clause final, IP is raised into Spec of CP, using up the potential landing site for a *wh*-phrase. It follows that *wh*-in-situ is the only option for languages with clause final complementizers.

Each of these positions has its own empirical problems because they are not based on exception-free generalizations. One point worth mentioning here is that Takahashi (1993, 1994a) argues that Japanese allows overt *wh*-movement of an entire DP in addition to *wh*-in-situ. If his analysis is on the right track, we also need to explain why both options coexist in a single language.[15] Further research may show that all the three positions above point to a deeper, single property that is common to all *wh*-in-situ languages,[16] or it may turn out that *wh*-in-situ languages are not uniform after all and that each of these proposals deals with different types of *wh*-in-situ languages. In the next section, it will be shown that Chinese and Japanese (and perhaps Korean) contrast in some crucial respects, suggesting that *wh*-in-situ languages are indeed not uniform. At the same time, I do not want to deny the need to search for a deeper account of the factors that contribute to *wh*-in-situ.

3.2   Types of **wh-*in-situ* language**

So far, we have proceeded on the pretense that Chinese and Japanese *wh*-questions behave in the same way. It is now time to compare these two languages more closely.

3.2.1   *Chinese vs. Japanese*

Aoun and Li (1993a, 1993b) and Tsai (1994a) have recently proposed that Chinese *wh*-in-situ does not undergo movement, contrary to Huang's original proposal. Among the empirical considerations that lead to this conclusion are a number of differences between Chinese and Japanese in the behavior of *wh*-in-situ and quantificational expressions. Here, I will discuss some of these.

We have seen in section 2.1 that *wh*-in-situ in Japanese is sensitive to *wh*-islands. The relevant example (8b) is repeated here:

(8)   b.   ??[nani-o doko-de katta   ka] oboete-iru   no?
           what-Acc where-At bought Q   remember-Prog Q
           "What do you remember where we bought?"

Interestingly, the *wh*-island effect is absent in Chinese, as originally noted by Huang (1981/2). Compare (8b) with (27):

(27)   ni   xiang-zhidao [wo weishenme mai shenme]?
       you wonder   I   why   buy what
       "What do you wonder why I bought?"

Wh-movement in Japanese is subject to another type of blocking created by a c-commanding quantifier, an observation originally due to Hoji (1985), whereas there is no such effect in Chinese:

(28) a.   *?daremo-ga   nani-o   katta   no?   (Japanese)
           everyone-Nom what-Acc bought Q
      b.   nani-o daremo-ga *t* katta no?
      c.   meigeren dou mai-le   shenme?   (Chinese)
           everyone all   buy-Perf what
           "What did everyone buy?"

The contrast in the *wh*-island effect is explained by the hypothesis that *wh*-movement takes place in Japanese, but not in Chinese. Recall from section 2.2 that the *wh*-island effect arises from the nature of movement. If movement is not responsible for the *wh*-dependency in the Chinese example (27), the absence of the *wh*-island effect is not surprising. How, then, does the *wh*-phrase get interpreted in Chinese? Aoun and Li (1993a, 1993b) and Tsai (1994a) both claim that Chinese makes use of unselective binding in the sense of Heim (1982). In particular, Tsai (1994a) develops a comprehensive theory of operator-variable binding according to which Chinese generates unselective binders at the clausal level while Japanese does so at the DP level. Thus, Chinese *wh*-questions have the following schematic representation base generated directly:

(29) $[_{CP} Op_X [_{IP} \ldots wh(x) \ldots]]$

The operator-variable pair in (29) is immune to the *wh*-island effect because it is not created by movement.

The contrast with respect to blocking by QP in (28) should receive a similar account if the blocking effect is due to movement.[17] That is, a c-commanding QP *daremo-ga* blocks *wh*-movement in (28a), yielding ill-formedness. If the *wh*-phrase is scrambled over the QP, the sentence becomes grammatical, as in (28b). Since *wh*-movement does not take place in the first place in the Chinese counterpart (28c), no such blocking takes place, on the assumption that unselective binding is not blocked by an intervening quantified expression.[18] We return to interaction with QP in section 3.2.3.

The next question is why *wh*-in-situ gets interpreted via unselective binding in Chinese and involves movement in Japanese. At this point, the morphological difference in the quantificational system, noted in section 3.1, becomes relevant. Recall that Japanese uses special particles to build various quantificational expressions out of indeterminate elements, while Chinese does not employ particles. Aoun and Li (1993b) claim that this morphological difference reflects a syntactic difference in the quantificational system. The use of particles indicates that the language allows an operator to be base generated with the DP which it is associated with and be subsequently moved away from that DP. Chinese places unselective binders elsewhere, namely, at the clausal level.[19]

This morphosyntactic characterization of the difference between Chinese and Japanese meshes well with the possibility of large-scale pied-piping in Japanese, which we have reviewed in section 2.1 above. Remember that the pied-piped phrase is a DP, the type of category which can be associated with the operator that undergoes movement. At the same time, as in the case of large-scale pied-piping, the non-movement characterization of Chinese must be modified somewhat, again, in order to accommodate the behavior of adjuncts. (27) above shows that Chinese lacks *wh*-island effects, but this holds only for arguments. A certain class of adjuncts systematically exhibits *wh*-island effects, as shown in (30):

(30)   ni   xiang-zhidao [wo weishenme mai shenme]?
          you wonder   I   why   buy what
     a.   What is the thing x such that you wonder why I bought x?
     b.   *What is the reason x such that you wonder what I bought for x?

(30) allows the reading (a) in which the argument *shenme* can take the matrix scope, but not the reading (b) where the adjunct *weishenme* is extracted over a *wh*-island. Reinhart (1998) claims that the same class of English adjuncts lacks a nominal head which provides a variable. Extending this idea to Chinese, we can say that these Chinese adjuncts resist unselective binding due to lack of a variable to be bound and therefore must undergo movement, subject to Subjacency. The (b) reading of (30) is hence blocked. See Lin (1992) and Tsai (1994a, 1994b) for discussion.

The idea that certain adjuncts resist unselective binding also explains their inability to undergo large-scale pied-piping in Japanese (see (10) above). In our discussion of semantics of large-scale pied-piping in n. 4, we have seen that pied-piping of a complex NP yields a kind of multiple question interpretation. This is another instance of unselective binding, as Nishigauchi (1990) originally claims. But then, these adjuncts will be excluded from large-scale pied-piping, correctly.

3.2.2   Scope marking strategy

Let us turn to another type of *wh*-in-situ language, represented by Hindi and Iraqi Arabic.[20] A very remarkable characteristic of *wh*-in-situ in these languages is stricter locality. Compare the Chinese and Japanese examples in (31) with those of Hindi and Iraqi Arabic in (32):

(31) a.   Zhangsan yiwei [Lisi mai-le shenme]?   (Chinese)
           Zhangsan think Lisi bought what
           "What does Zhangsan think Lisi bought?"
      b.   John-wa [dare-ga   kita to] omotteiru no?   (Japanese)
           John-Top who-Nom came that think   Q
           "Who does John think came?"

(32) a.   *raam-ne socaa   [ki   kOn aayaa hE]?   (Hindi)
           Ram-Erg thought that who come has
           "Who did Ram think had come?"[21]

b. *Mona tsawwarit [Ali ishtara sheno]?   (Iraqi Arabic)
    Mona thought   Ali bought what
    "What did Mona think Ali bought?"

The *wh*-phrase in the embedded clause can take the matrix scope in Chinese and Japanese without any trouble, but not in Hindi nor in Iraqi Arabic. The *wh*-in-situ strategy itself is legitimate as long as the *wh*-phrase appears in the clause where it takes scope, as shown in (33):

(33) a. raam-ne puuchaa [ki   mohan-ne kis-ko dekhaa]   (Hindi)
          Ram-Erg asked   that Mohan-Erg who   saw
          "Ram asked who Mohan saw."
      b. Mona se?lat Ali [Ro?a ishtarat sheno]   (Iraqi Arabic)
          Mona asked Ali Ro?a bought what
          "Mona asked Ali what Ro?a bought."

In other words, *wh*-in-situ in Hindi and Iraqi Arabic only allows a clause bound *wh*-dependency.[22]

One way of expressing the intended readings of (32) is to raise the *wh*-phrase into the matrix clause, as in (34):

(34) a. kOn raam-ne socaa [ki *t* aayaa hE]?   (Hindi)
          "Who did Ram think had come?"
      b. sheno tsawwarit Mona [Ali ishtara *t*]?   (Iraqi Arabic)
          "What did Mona think Ali bought?"

Mahajan (1990) and Dayal (1996) argue that the movement in question is scrambling in Hindi, whereas Wahba (1991) assumes that the preposed *wh*-phrase is placed in Spec of CP in Iraqi Arabic.

Another way of expressing the intended readings is to place a special scope marker, glossed as SM, in the matrix clause, as in (35):

(35) a. raam-ne kyaa socaa   [ki   kOn aayaa hE]?   (Hindi)
          Ram-Erg SM   thought that who come has
      b. sh-tsawwarit Mona [Ali ishtara sheno]?   (Iraqi Arabic)
          SM-thought Mona Ali bought what

The scope marking strategy finds its counterpart in overt *wh*-movement languages such as German, where the *wh*-phrase moves at least to Spec of an intermediate CP and takes the matrix scope indicated by the marker *was*, as in (36):

(36) Was glaubt Hans [$_{CP}$ mit   wem [$_{IP}$ Jakob jetzt spricht]]?
      SM   believe Hans   with whom   Jakob now speak
      "With whom does Hans think that Jakob is now talking?"

The scope marker tends to use the *wh*-form corresponding to "what" cross-linguistically.[23] The scope marking strategy of the German kind is also employed by children learning English at some point during the acquisition process. See Thornton (1990) and McDaniel et al. (1995).

The scope marking strategy displays the clause bounded nature, too, as illustrated by the Hindi example in (37):

(37)   raam-ne *(kyaa) socaa   [ki   ravii-ne *(kyaa) kahaa
       Ram-Erg SM   thought that Ravi-Erg SM   said
       [ki   kOn sa aadmii aayaa thaa]]]?
       that which man   came
       "Which man did Ram think that Ravi said came?"

Notice that when there is an additional clause between the matrix and the *wh*-phrase, every such intervening clause must contain a scope marker.[24] This very strict locality requirement holds even with multiple questions, as in Hindi example (38):

(38)   kis-ne *(kyaa) socaa   [ki   siitaa-ne kis-ko dekhaa]?
       who-Erg SM   thought that Sita-Erg who   saw
       "Who thought that Sita saw whom?"

The presence of a *wh*-phrase in the matrix clause is not sufficient to license the *wh*-phrase in the embedded clause. The scope marker has to be added to satisfy locality. This contrasts with the movement strategy, which affects only one of the *wh*-phrases that take the same scope, so that the locality holds only for the one that is affected by movement. The relevant examples in English and Japanese are repeated here:

(13)   a.   Who is reading a book that criticizes who?
       b.   Who remembers where we bought what?

(16)   a.   ??John-wa [Mary-ga   nani-o   katta   kadooka] Tom-ni
            John-Top   Mary-Nom what-Acc bought whether   Tom-Dat
            tazuneta no?
            asked   Q
            "What did John ask Tom whether Mary bought?"
       b.   John-wa [Mary-ga   nani-o   katta   kadooka] dare-ni
            John-Top Mary-Nom what-Acc bought whether   who-Dat
            tazuneta no?
            asked   Q
            "Who did John ask whether Mary bought what?"

The *wh*-in-situ in English can occur within an island, as in (13). The *wh*-island effect disappears in the Japanese example (16b), once another *wh*-phrase is added outside the island to take the same scope. The Hindi multiple question in (38) behaves rather differently in this respect.[25]

This contrast between the movement strategy and the strictly local scope marking strategy can be found within a single language. According to McDaniel (1989), the *wh*-in-situ in German multiple questions does not require a local scope marker, as shown in (39a):

(39) a. Wer glaubt [dass ich meinte [dass Jakob mit wem gesprochen
          who believe that I   thought that Jacob with whom spoken
          hat]]?
          has
    b. *Wer glaubt [dass ich meinte [mit wem Jakob gesprochen hat]]?
          who believe that I   thought with whom Jacob spoken   has
    c. Wer glaubt [was ich meinte [mit wem Jakob gesprochen hat]]?
          who believe SM I   thought with whom Jacob spoken   has

Once the embedded *wh*-phrase moves to Spec of the lowest CP as in (39b, c), however, the intermediate clause must host a scope marker.

One of the major issues in the literature on the scope marking strategy is how the *wh*-dependency is formed at LF. One possibility (Bayer 1996, Beck 1996, McDaniel 1989, Müller and Sternefeld 1996) is to assume that the *wh*-phrase undergoes LF movement to replace the scope marker. Challenging to this approach are syntactic and semantic differences between the direct movement strategy and the scope marking strategy. Rizzi (1992), for example, observes that the scope marking strategy is blocked by negation whereas full movement is not:

(40) a. Mit wem glaubst du nicht [dass Hans gesprochen hat]?
          with whom believe you not   that Hans spoken   has
    b. *Was glaubst du nicht [mit wem Hans gesprochen hat]?
          SM   believe you not   with whom Hans spoken   has
      "Who don't you think that Hans has talked to?"

The same blocking is found in Hindi, too, according to Dayal (1994, 1996). The putative LF movement must be blocked by negation. Bošković (1997, to appear) argues that the similar clause-boundedness of *wh*-in-situ in French should be captured in terms of LF feature movement. See also Beck (1996) as well as Rizzi (1992).

It is worth mentioning that expletive replacement in the *there*-construction displays a similar blocking. Chomsky (1991) observes that *many* takes narrow scope in (41a), in contrast to the ordinary transitive clause (41b), which allows scope ambiguity:

(41) a. There aren't many linguistics students here.
    b. I haven't met many linguistics students.

One might say that movement of the quantificational feature is blocked by negation in (41a), in a way analogous to (40b). This blocking leads to direct ungrammaticality in (40b) because the interrogative reading requires the existential quantificational feature. Movement of the Case and phi-features alone will do in (41a), on the other hand, so that the quantificational feature can be left behind. To the extent that the *there*-construction involves LF movement of the postcopular NP, the contrast in (40) in fact supports the LF movement approach to the scope marking strategy.

Another approach (Dayal 1994, 1996) is to interpret structures with a scope marker like (36) directly, without moving the *wh*-phrase to the scope position. This means that *wh*-in-situ moves only to the local CP in Hindi. The scope marker binds a propositional variable, whose content is supplied by the clause headed by a *wh*-expression. The contrast in (40) is not surprising from this perspective, since (40a) and (40b) involve different processes, but the contrast itself remains to be accounted for. Dayal (1996) claims that the clause-boundedness in Hindi *wh*-questions comes from the islandhood of the complement clause, arguing that finite complement clauses are extraposed in Hindi. Mahajan (1994a) and Ouhalla (1996a) observe, however, that a rather strong unacceptability induced by the absence of a scope marker in (32) and (38) is qualitatively different from ordinary island violations found in these languages, which are much milder. If so, the source of the strict locality must be sought somewhere else.

Yet another possibility (Mahajan 1990) is to adjoin to the scope marker the clause that contains the *wh*-phrase which also undergoes clause internal raising, thereby bringing the *wh*-phrase close enough to the scope position. Mahajan (1990, 1994a) proposes that *wh*-phrases in Hindi are essentially quantifier phrases, lacking the movement ability of familiar *wh*-phrases. As a result, they can only undergo QR, which is clause bound. The scope marker is therefore needed to extend the scope of *wh*-phrases.

Ouhalla (1996a) points out, however, that *wh*-phrases in Hindi and Iraqi Arabic do not allow any quantificational readings other than as *wh*-interrogatives, unlike their Chinese counterparts. It is unclear why *wh*-phrases in Hindi and Iraqi Arabic do not have uses as non-*wh* quantifiers, if their movement is analogous to QR, movement of quantifiers.[26] Ouhalla (1996a) instead proposes that unselective binding is parametrized so that a certain kind of *wh*-phrase, exemplified by those in Hindi and Iraqi Arabic, must be bound within the smallest finite clause.

The discussion in the literature is inconclusive, leaving many questions open. Horvath (1997) claims that the scope marking strategy is not uniform across languages after all. Much further work is needed for proper understanding of the scope marking strategy.

3.2.3   Interaction with QP

Lastly, let us take up interaction between *wh*-in-situ and QP again. Recall from section 3.2.1 above that Japanese and Chinese contrast in whether a *wh*-phrase can be c-commanded by a QP. The relevant examples are repeated here:

(28)   a.   *?daremo-ga   nani-o   katta   no?   (Japanese)
             everyone-Nom what-Acc bought Q
       b.   nani-o daremo-ga *t* katta no?
       c.   meigeren dou mai-le   shenme?   (Chinese)
             everyone all   buy-Perf what
             "What did everyone buy?"

There is a further parametric difference worth noting in this connection. As discussed in detail by Aoun and Li (1993c), the Chinese question (28c) allows a pair-list answer like (42), which is rendered in English:

(42)   John bought beer, Mary a bottle of wine, . . .

In this respect, Chinese is parallel to English, which also allows a pair-list answer for a question like (43), a phenomenon first discussed in depth by May (1985). See also Lasnik and Saito (1992), Chierchia (1993), Dayal (1996), Beghelli (1997), and Szabolcsi (1997a):

(43)   What does every student buy?

In Japanese, on the other hand, not only is (28a) unacceptable (at least for some speakers) but also the acceptable (28b) lacks a pair-list reading, as originally observed by Hoji (1985, 1986). Even those who find (28a) acceptable do not get the pair-list reading. Dayal (1996: 114) briefly mentions that Hindi also allows a pair-list answer for questions with the scope marking strategy, as in (44):

(44)   a.   jaun kyaa soctaa hai [har   bacca kaun   kitaab khariidegaa]
             John SM   think-Pres every child which book   buy-Future
             "Which book does John think that every child will buy?"
       b.   jaun soctaa hai [ki   ravi laal phuul khariidegaa aur raam godaan
             John think-Pres that Ravi laal phuul buy-Future and Ram godaan
             khariidegaa]
             buy-Future
             "John thinks that Ravi will buy laal phuul and Ram will buy godaan."

The possibility of pair-list answers in case of *wh*-QP interaction seems to suggest that among *wh*-in-situ languages, Hindi and Chinese should be treated in a similar way, in contrast to Japanese. It is interesting to observe that the scope marking strategy in German as in (45) allows a pair-list answer in *wh*-QP interaction, according to Beck (1996):[27]

(45)   Was glaubt   jeder   wen   Karl gesehen hat?
        SM   believes   everyone   whom   Karl   seen   has
        "Who does everyone believe that Karl saw?"

It should be noted, at the same time, that English and Japanese, both of which are assumed to involve movement, contrast in the availability of the pair-list reading.

Recent attempts (Saito 1994b, 1997, Watanabe 1997) to explain the absence of the pair-list reading in the Japanese questions in (28) appeal to a parametric difference in the quantificational system of a particular language. Saito (1997) points to the use of the domain-widening particle *mo* (Kadmon and Landman 1993, Kawashima 1994) in the universal quantifier as causing a pragmatic problem in case of the pair-list answer, while Watanabe (1997) suggests that the type of absorption found in languages like English, which is crucial in obtaining the pair-list reading (cf. Chierchia 1993), is absent in Japanese. It is an important question for future inquiry whether an approach based on systematic analysis of particular languages' quantification system produces fruitful results in wider crosslinguistic contexts.

NOTES

*   I would like to thank the editors Mark Baltin and Chris Collins for comments and Veneeta Dayal, Kazuki Kuwabara, and Yasuo Ishii for discussion. The work reported here is supported by the Japanese Ministry of Education Grant-in-Aid for Center of Excellence (# 08CE1001).

1   Throughout this chapter, it is assumed that *wh*-movement fills Spec of CP unless indicated otherwise, though Huang's proposal antedates widespread use of the CP system.

2   Chinese and other in situ languages are taken up in section 3.

3   (8b) has another reading where the indirect question asks for the thing bought and the place of purchase. This reading does not involve *wh*-movement out of a *wh*-island, and therefore is irrelevant.

4   von Stechow (1996) claims that large-scale pied-piping is problematic from the viewpoint of semantic interpretation. Assuming with Hamblin (1973) and Karttunen (1977) that the meaning of a question is a set of propositions which determines answerhood, von Stechow claims that the LF representation (9) should be interpreted as (i):

(i) $\lambda p \exists x \exists y [\text{person}(x) \wedge \text{book}(y) \wedge \text{wrote}(x, y) \wedge p = {}^{\wedge}\text{reading }(he, y)]$

Since the form of the propositions which can be used as answers is "he is reading y" according to (i), it is wrongly predicted that answers like "he is reading *War and Peace*" would be appropriate, contrary to fact.

Von Stechow's claim is based on Nishigauchi's (1990: 111) remark that the pied-piped part is interpreted as "which x, y, x a person, y a book that x wrote." At another place (1990: 52), however, Nishigauchi observes that a question like (8a) is after the identity of books in terms of the person who wrote them. I would like to claim that there is a better way of cashing in on Nishigauchi's latter observation. Let us suppose that questions involving large-scale pied-piping call for functional answers, as in Engdahl's (1986) analysis of the question–answer pair in (ii). Cf. also Chierchia (1993):

(ii) a. Who does every boy love?
      b. His mother.

Informally, then, (8a) is interpreted as something like "which f, x, x a person and $f(x)$ a book that x wrote, he is reading $f(x)$." More precisely, this interpretation is expressed by (iii):

(iii) $\lambda p \exists f \exists x [person(x) \land book(f(x)) \land wrote(x, f(x)) \land p = {}^\wedge reading (he, f(x))]$

Note that answers like "he is reading *War and Peace*" are not appropriate for the question in (iii) because *War and Peace* does not count as an appropriate function that the question is after. (iii) also captures native speakers' intuition, discussed by Nishigauchi (1990) in detail, that an appropriate short answer to (8a) includes the description of the book as well as its author, as in (iv):

(iv) Austen-ga   kaita hon desu.
      Austen-Nom wrote book be
      "It's a book Austen wrote."

This intuition is missed if we simply assume that the effect of pied-piping is not reflected in the interpretation, as von Stechow does.

Veneeta Dayal has independently come up with the same proposal about the semantics of large-scale pied-piping. See Dayal (in preparation) for details.

5   The observation goes back to Baker (1970) and Chomsky (1973).

6   (13b) has another reading where the embedded clause is a multiple indirect question asking for a pair of a place and a thing bought. This reading is irrelevant for the present purposes.

7   See Richards (1997) for a theory that tries to explain why overt movement and LF movement contrast in this way with respect to Subjacency.

8   This idea goes back to Chomsky (1964).

9   See Maki (1995) for an attempt to account for various properties of *wh*-questions in Japanese in terms of LF *wh*-feature movement. Below, we will turn to evidence that seems to favor overt movement over LF movement, whether it is *wh*-feature movement or not.

10 But see Fukui (1997) and Takahashi (1994a) for important discussions.

11 Below, I discuss the proposal that Chinese *wh*-in-situ employs unselective binding.

12 We represent the head-initial structure in which IP follows the C° head, but nothing in our account hinges on this point.

13 Modified from Chomsky (1995a: 297). I abstract away from further elaborations.

14 Korean is closer to Japanese than to Chinese in making use of particles, but there are also some differences. See Choe (1995) and Kim (1991).

15 Coexistence of movement and *wh*-in-situ options may be found in other languages. According to Cole and Hermon (1994), Ancash Quechua is such a language.

16 See Fukui and Takano (1998) for an attempt to unify the latter two approaches. Haspelmath (1997) considers the typological correlation between word order and indeterminate elements, though the relation with *wh*-in-situ is not explored.

17 See Watanabe (1997) for a Minimalist account of this phenomenon. It should also be mentioned that there are speakers who find (28a) acceptable.

18 This assumption may be too simplistic. See Li (1992) for a detailed discussion of interaction between *wh*-construals and licensers of other readings of indeterminate elements.

19 Cole and Hermon (1994) analyze *wh*-in-situ in Ancash Quechua as involving unselective binding. Ancash Quechua, nevertheless, uses a particle to build quantificational expressions out of indeterminate elements, as in Japanese. It should be pointed out, though, that Cole and Hermon do not discuss *wh*-islands.

20 The Hindi examples in this chapter are mostly taken from Mahajan (1990). The Iraqi Arabic examples come from Wahba (1991) and Ouhalla (1996a).

   Bengali (Bayer 1996) and Hungarian (Horvath 1997, Marácz 1988) also display essentially the same grammatical properties.

21 The Hindi verb *socaa* is ambiguous between "think" and "wonder." I ignore the latter reading.

22 Bošković (1997a, to appear) observes that *wh*-in-situ in French, which is allowed only for root questions, is clause bound and is also blocked by negation. See the text discussion below for blocking of the scope marking strategy by negation.

23 The Iraqi Arabic *sh-* is a contracted form of *sheno* "what." Dayal (1994, 1996) claims, on the basis of the evidence from Warlpiri, that a more precise characterization is that the scope marker is a *wh*-form quantifying over propositions.

24 German behaves in the same way according to McDaniel (1989). Dayal (1996) and Müller and Sternefeld (1996) report, however, that there are dialects which do not require a scope marker in the intermediate clause. Thus, (ib) is unacceptable for some speakers, but sounds good for others:

(i) a. Was glaubst du [was Peter
         SM believe you SM Peter
         meint [mit wem Maria
         think with whom Maria
         gesprochen hat]]?
         spoken   has
     b. (*)Was glaubst du [dass
         SM   believe you that
         Peter meint [mit wem
         Peter think with whom
         Maria gesprochen hat]]?
         Maria spoken   has
         "Who do you believe that
         Peter thinks that Maria has
         talked to?"

This could be just a matter of morphological realization. But see also Bayer (1996), Dayal (1996), and the papers in Lutz and Müller (1995) for further differences between Hindi and German.

25 Iraqi Arabic patterns with Hindi. Wahba (1991) notes that a clause boundary in a multiple question leads to ungrammaticality, as in (i):

(i) *sh-i'tiqdit   Mona [meno
     SM-believed Mona who
     tsawwar [Ali sa'ad meno]]?
     thought   Ali helped who
     "Who did Mona believe thought
     Ali helped who?"

26 It should also be noted that the existence of QR itself is called into question in the recent literature. See Hornstein (1995), Kitahara (1996), Pica and Snyder (1995), and Watanabe (1997) for some discussion.

27 Beck (1996), however, claims that a single answer reading is disallowed for (47). This restriction is not found in Chinese or in Hindi.

8 A-Movements

MARK R. BALTIN

0 Introduction

This chapter will concentrate on a range of phenomena that have crucially been held to involve (within Government Binding theory and now Minimalism) movement of an element to what is known as an argument position – roughly, a position in which an element can be base generated and bear a crucial semantic role with respect to the main predicate of a clause. It is to be distinguished from movement to an A' (read A-bar, or non-argument) position. The two types of movement have very different properties, most notably with respect to binding and *wanna*-contraction. (1) contains examples of A-movements, and (2) contains examples of A'-movements:

(1) a. John^i seems t^i to be polite.
     b. John^i was murdered t^i.
     c. John^i died t^i.

(2) a. Who^i did he think t^i would win?
     b. John^i he thought t^i would win.

The trace of an element in an A-position is thought to behave, for the purposes of the binding theory, as an anaphor, while the trace of an element in an A'-position is thought to behave as an R-expression (although Postal 1994 has argued that certain A'-traces behave as pronouns). Hence, the trace in (3), a case of strong crossover (Postal 1971) has been thought to be an R-expression, causing the structure for (3) to violate Condition C of the binding theory, while (4) is acceptable because the trace is an anaphor:

(3) *John^i, who he^i thought t^i would win, . . .

(4) They^i seem to each other^i t^i to be polite.

Another difference that has been less cited (first noted in Jaeggli 1980, to my knowledge), is that traces of A-movements do not block *wanna*-contraction, while traces of A'-movements, as has been well known since at least 1970 (due to Larry Horn's original unpublished observation), do block *wanna*-contraction. For example, the verb *need* induces A-movements by the diagnostics that I will be discussing shortly, and, in my casual speech, induces a flap which I take to be diagnostic of *wanna*-contraction:

(5)   Does there really niyDa be a separate constraint?

The flap pronounciation cannot occur when *need* and *to* are separated by a *wh*-trace, as in (6b), corresponding to (6a):

(6)   a.   I need Sally to be there.
     b.   *Whoi do you niyDa be there?

Of course, the invisibility of raising traces with respect to *wanna*-contraction and binding might in face indicate that they are just not there, and in fact, given the structure preserving nature of these movements, that raising and, more generally, A-movements do not exist. This line has been taken since at least the 1970s by Bresnan (1978, 1982b), Pollard and Sag (1987, 1994), Foley and Van Valin (1984), Van Valin (1993), and many others. These theories, while disagreeing with each other on many issues, have in common the view that passives and unaccusatives are to be related by a lexical redundancy rule, which states roughly that if a given subcategorization A exists, with a linking L (mapping of semantic roles onto argument positions), then another sub-categorization A' exists, with a distinct linking L', so that the arguments in L, while expressing the same semantic roles as the arguments in L', will map them onto distinct argument positions. For the passive construction, the lexical rule will map all of the semantic roles in the active onto a different array of arguments in the passive. With respect to the unaccusative construction, as in (1c), while there may be transitive–unaccusative doublets, as in *freeze, melt*, or *break*, such doublets need not exist, and there would in fact be no semantic role corresponding to a transitive subject for an unaccusative. Manzini makes this point with respect to the pair in (7) (Manzini 1983):

(7)   a.   *The boat sank to collect the insurance.
     b.   The boat was sunk to collect the insurance.

(7a)'s main verb is considered to induce unaccusativity, and its unacceptability is thought to be due to the fact that there is no implicit agent in unaccusative *sink*'s lexical entry that would control the unexpressed subject of the purpose clause. In (7b), on the other hand, the passive of *sink* would have an implicit agent, optionally expressed as an adjunct *by*-phrase.

With respect to the raising construction exemplified in (1a), the proponents of the lexical approach have typically analyzed the infinitival complement as a VP, as they have for control constructions, as in (8):

(8)   John wants to win.

One desideratum for distinguishing, and giving a special treatment to, the constructions in which A-movement is implicated lies in the statement of linking regularities, the idea behind which is that grammatical relations can be predicted on the basis of the semantic roles of the arguments that bear those grammatical relations (Fillmore 1968, Carter 1976). More specifically, the idea is that a given thematic role can be assigned to a unique syntactic position, so that, e.g., agents are subjects, themes are direct objects, and so on. Passives, unaccusatives, and raised subjects on the face of it complicate the statement of linking regularities, but linking regularities can be preserved, it is thought, if these three constructions are derived, either lexically (so that linking regularities are stated over "unmarked" lexical entries) or syntactically (so that linking regularities are stated over initial syntactic representations).

To be sure, however, linking has never, to my knowledge, been used as an argument for either the lexical or syntactic derivation of passives, unaccusatives, or sentences with subject-to-subject raising predicates. Rather, such derivations have been justified on other grounds, to be discussed below, and the end result has tended to allow a simplification of the theory of linking.

In this chapter, I will focus on these three constructions – unaccusatives, passives, and subject-to-subject raisings – as evidence for A-movements, in order to examine their commonalities, and I will try to focus on the comparison between the lexical approach and the movement approach. The reason for this sort of focus is a desire to hold some significant grammatical phenomenon constant as a way of comparing distinct grammatical theories. I will be opting for the movement approach and arguing against the lexical approach, to be sure, and one problem with my argumentation will be that I will be relying on analyses of other grammatical phenomena, necessarily holding constant, because of space limitations, the analysis of these other phenomena in the theories that I will be contrasting. In this sense, my arguments cannot be taken as definitive, of course, but one has to start somewhere. I will attempt, however, to provide the justification for the claims on which my analyses will rest, rather than relying on parochial, theory-internal assumptions.

Passives, unaccusatives, and subject-to subject raising constructions are considered to be the most widely-held examples of A-movements, and it is for this reason that I will be focussing on these constructions. More recently, Collins and Thráinsson have analyzed object shift in the Germanic languages, specifically Icelandic, as an example of A-movement (Collins and Thráinsson 1996), but because object shift is treated by Thráinsson in this volume, I will largely ignore its treatment here.

Also, within Government Binding theory, two other constructions have been analyzed as relying on A-movement: the double object construction (Larson 1988) and, principally because of backwards binding facts, experiencer verbs with theme subjects and accusative experiencer objects (Belletti and Rizzi 1988). The motivation for implicating A-movements in the analysis of these latter two constructions is quite dubious, however, as I will show at the end of this chapter.

By A-movement, then, I mean movement to a c-commanding position, typically a specifier position, of a projection whose head is lexical in nature.

1 Passives

What is usually referred to as a passive does not always involve A-movement. It does always seem, however, to involve a characteristic morphology on the verb, and some sort of variant realization of the corresponding active verb's arguments (see Perlmutter and Postal 1977 for a useful survey of passive constructions, as well as Jaeggli 1986 and Baker et al. 1989). English passives always seem to correspond to active transitive verbs, but this is not universal, as can be seen by looking at what are called the impersonal passives, found in languages such as Dutch and German (examples below). In these languages, the passive can correspond to an intransitive active verb, so long as the subject of the corresponding active intransitive is agentive:[1]

(9)   Es wurde bis spat in die Nacht getrunken.   (German)
      It was till late in the night drunk.
      "Drinking went on till late in the night." (Jaeggli 1986: ex. (22b))

(10) In de zomer wordt er hier vaak gezwommen.   (Dutch)
      In the summer it is swum here frequently. (Perlmutter 1978: ex. (68))

Indeed, even in languages in which the corresponding active must be transitive, such as Spanish (Jaeggli 1986), French, and Italian (Belletti 1988) the object can apparently remain in situ:

(11) Le fué entregado un libro a Maria por Pedro.   (Spanish)
      To-her was handed a book to Maria by Pedro. (Jaeggli 1986: ex. (13))

(12) Il a étè tué un homme.   (French)
      There has been killed a man. (Belletti 1988: ex. (10))

(13) É stato messo un libro sul tavolo.   (Italian)
      Has been put a book on the table. (Belletti 1988: ex. (18a))

Spanish and Italian allow subjects to be postposed, and French allows stylistic inversion (Kayne and Pollock 1978). Therefore, one might ask whether the objects are actually in situ, or are in the postposed construction. Belletti (1988) shows, on the basis of ordering restrictions *vis-à-vis* subcategorized PPs and extraction facts, that both possibilities exist in Italian. For example, some original objects may precede subcategorized PPs, and some may follow:

(14)   All'improvviso é entrato un uomo dalla finestra.
       Suddenly entered a man from the window. (Belletti 1988: ex. (17a))

(15)   All'improvviso é entrato dalla finestra l'uomo.
       Suddenly entered from the window the man.

Moreover, there is an interesting restriction on the nominal that may intervene between the verb and the subcategorized PP: it must be indefinite, so that (13) contrasts with (16):

(16)   *É stato messo il libro sul tavolo. (Belletti 1988: ex. (18b))

Belletti takes these distinctions to diagnose two distinct positions for postverbal subjects. The position of postverbal indefinite nominals which precede subcategorized PPs, when the latter occur, is taken to be the complement position to the head, while the position of postverbal definite nominals, which follow subcategorized PPs when they occur, is taken to be a VP-adjoined position. Belletti is assuming the framework of Government and Binding theory presented in *Barriers*, in which the complement position to a head is taken to be L-marked, and hence not an inherent barrier (Chomsky 1986b), while the VP-adjoined position would not be L-marked, and hence would be a barrier. She then assumes Huang's Condition on Extraction Domains (Huang 1982), which claims that extraction can only occur out of properly governed phrases, i.e., non-barriers.

To return to the focus of this chapter, A-movement, the significance of Belletti's distinctions is that the first postverbal position that she diagnoses, the complement position, would correspond to the position of an unmoved nominal in its original position. In other words, she is claiming that A-movement, while normally obligatory, can sometimes be suspended. We will return to the significance of this distinction below, but it is noteworthy to ask how other frameworks capture the distinction, or whether they can.

Government Binding (GB) theory and its direct descendant, Minimalism, assume that all nominals must receive Case (or, in the current parlance, have Case-features that are checked; see Ura in this volume). The affixation of a passive morpheme is thought to destroy an active verb's ability to license Case on its object, and movement to subject position, when subject position is a position in which Case may be assigned or checked, is forced by this need for the nominal's Case feature to be checked. However, Belletti's claim is that indefinite objects may receive a second Case, which she dubs partitive, as opposed to the normal accusative Case that the active transitive verb would participate in checking. When the indefinite object gets this second Case, there is no reason for it to move, and hence it may remain in situ. Definites, however, may not receive partitive Case.

Other frameworks do not assume movement in the formation of passives. For example, Relational Grammar assumes that there is a class of relation changing rules, and that grammatical relations are primitive. The relation changing rules are dubbed "advancement rules," with the numeral 1 representing subjects, 2 representing objects, and 3 representing indirect objects. Passive would then be represented, in the framework of Relational Grammar, as (17):

(17)   2→1

The original 1, when there is one, would become what is known as a chomeur (literally, "unemployed"). In GB, what would correspond to the active subject would be an adjunct. The impersonal passives of Dutch and German are considered to really be personal passives, formed by rule (17), with what is known as a "dummy," or empty nominal, being inserted as a 2, and then advancing to 1.

Lexical-Functional Grammar (Bresnan 1982c), like Relational Grammar, assumes that grammatical relations are primitive, and analyzes passive as a lexical rule that maps the thematic role linked to the object in the active onto the subject in the passive.

Head-Driven Phrase-Structure Grammar (Pollard and Sag 1987) also employs a lexical redundancy rule that expresses a correspondence, or alternative realization of the semantic roles of the arguments of the predicate, between active and passive structures, as does Role and Reference Grammar (Foley and Van Valin 1984, Van Valin 1990, 1993).

It is difficult to see how the theories that do not generate the nominal in complement position, and which tie it to a conversion of the object into a subject, cope with the inertness of these indefinite objects. One can say that they are subjects in complement position, and it is true that at least Relational Grammar and Lexical-Functional Grammar view grammatical relations as primitive, and independent of constituent structure configurations, but one would expect at least some evidence that these nominals in complement position behave as subjects.

Of course, Belletti's analysis is plausible only to the extent that it fits into a general account of the interaction of A-movement and inherent Case. For example, the account allows nominals with inherent Case to remain in situ when the normal structural Case environment is no longer an available environment for Case-licensing. In Icelandic, however, as shown by Andrews (1990), nominals that receive inherent Case (so-called "quirky Case") must still be fronted in Passives.

It is always instructive to contrast verbal passives with a passive construction which is less controversially viewed as a totally lexical passive, namely the adjectival passive, a construction that has been discussed by Siegel (1973),

Wasow (1977, 1980), Bresnan (1982d), and Levin and Rappaport (1986a). As is well known, English verbal passives have somewhat looser restrictions on the correspondence between their subjects and the nominal following the corresponding active verbs than do English adjectival passives, as shown by the following examples (the *un-* prefix before the adjectival examples brings out their adjectival quality, when the *un-* is not interpreted as reversative: Siegel 1973):

(18)   a.   The bed was unmade.
     b.   *Headway was unmade.
     c.   John was unknown.
     d.   *John was unknown to be the murderer.

Wasow (1977), in discussing these restrictions, observes that the subject of an adjectival passive must bear a much closer relationship to the corresponding active verb than the subject of a verbal passive must bear, and claims that the subject of an adjectival passive must correspond to the theme of the corresponding active. He takes the difference in the range of the two constructions, adjectival versus verbal passives, to be symptomatic of two different methods of derivation of them; verbal passives would be derived via movement from postverbal position of the nominal into subject position, while the formation of adjectival passives would involve a process dubbed externalization (Levin and Rappaport 1986a's term), in which the thematic role of theme, normally linked to an internal argument position, would instead be linked to the position of the external argument of the adjective.

In short, the lexical process that forms adjectival passives was viewed by Wasow, Bresnan, and others to crucially mention the theme role of the internal argument of the corresponding active verb. Because the subject of the adjectival passive is stipulated to necessarily correspond to the theme of the active verb, the inability of idiom chunks (21b) or nominals that bear no relation to the passivized verb (dubbed Exceptional Case-Marked nominals (Chomsky 1981) or subjects raised to object position (Postal 1974)) is accounted for (18d).

Wasow (1977) argued that the wider domain of application of the process forming verbal passives resulted from its transformational nature, given that transformations are purely structure dependent operations, insensitive to thematic role or grammatical relation of any term involved. Hence, a transformation that actually moved the nominal in the formation of verbal passives would just move any postverbal nominal to preverbal position.[2]

In a later paper (Wasow 1980), Wasow draws rather different conclusions about the distinction between verbal and adjectival passives in English. He proposes a distinction between major and minor lexical rules, so that minor lexical rules make reference to thematic relations, while major lexical rules refer to grammatical relations. It is assumed that the postverbal nominal in (19) is an object that has been raised from the subject position of the following infinitive, either syntactically (Postal 1974) or lexically (Bresnan 1978, 1982d):

(19)   We knew John to be the murderer.

Therefore, the major lexical rule of verbal passivization will refer to grammatical relations. Wasow's distinction between major and minor lexical rules seems to correspond, as far as I can see, to Pinker's distinction (Pinker 1989), in his acquisitional study, of broad range and narrow range lexical rules.

Levin and Rappaport (1986a), however, demonstrated that adjectival passives are not in fact subject to a thematic restriction at all. They give numerous examples of adjectival passives with non-themes that are externalized. For example, the verbs *teach* and *feed* can take goals as their sole complements:

(20)   He taught the children.

(21)   He fed the children.

And adjectival passive formation is possible for these verbs:

(22)   The children were untaught.

(23)   The children were unfed.

Levin and Rappaport (1986a) propose that there is no specific thematic restriction on adjectival passives, but rather that the formation makes crucial reference to an argument structure, roughly, a representation of the adicity of the predicate together with a distinction between the external argument and internal arguments. Hence, one might represent the argument structures of *feed* and *teach* as in (24):

(24)   x <y (z)>

with the argument outside of the angled brackets as the external argument, and the arguments inside as the internal ones. Parentheses, as usual, would indicate optionality. We would then say that major lexical rules refer to grammatical relations, while minor ones would refer to argument structure. As far as I can see, Wasow's distinction could be maintained by replacing a thematic restriction on adjectival passive formation with an argument structure one.

In any event, viewing the distinction between adjectival passives and verbal passives as a distinction between minor lexical rules and major lexical rules commits one to the view that the set of environments for adjectival passive formation is a proper subset of the set of environments for verbal passive formation.

With this in mind, let us turn our attention to a Case-marking phenomenon in Russian that has been discussed in detail by Babby (1980) and later by Pesetsky (1982), known as the genitive of negation.

Basically, negated objects of transitive verbs in Russian, in addition to taking accusative Case, may optionally appear in the genitive. As discussed by Babby (1980), when certain subjects of negated intransitive verbs are being asserted not to exist, they may also appear in the genitive. Examples are given in (25) and (26):

(25) V-nasem-lesu-ne-ratet-gribov.
In –our-forest-Neg-grow-3Sg-mushrooms-GenPl
There are no mushrooms growing in our forest. (Babby 1980: ex. (4b))

(26) Ne-ostalos'-somnenij.
Neg-remained-3NSg-doubts-GenPl
"Nothing remained." (Babby 1980: ex. (6b))

Subjects of negated transitive verbs that are nominative in the affirmative cannot take the genitive:

(27) ni odna gazeta ne pecataet takuji erundu.
Not one newspaper-Neg prints such nonsense.
FNomSg 3Sg FAccSg (Pesetsky 1982: ex. (15))

Also, agentive subjects of negated intransitive verbs cannot appear in the genitive.

Babby's generalization is that those subjects that can appear in the genitive of negation are in the scope of negation at D-Structure, in fact are D-Structure direct objects. Hence, the class of verbs whose subjects may appear in the genitive of negation is that of the subjects of verbal passives, and the subjects of unaccusative verbs, to be discussed in the next section. Examples are given in (28) and (29):

(28) Razdalsja-lay, no-ni-odnoj-sobaki-ne-pokazalos'.
Resounded-bark, but-not-single-dog-Gen-Neg-appeared-NSg (Babby 1980: ex. (12a))

(29) Ne-naslos'-mesta.
Neg-be-found-NSg-seat/place-Gen-NSg
There was not a seat to be found. (Babby 1980: ex. (24a))

As discussed in Pesetsky (1982), however, Russian has adjectival passives, and when an adjectival passive is negated, its subject cannot appear in the genitive of negation. Hence, Pesetsky gives the following contrast:

(30) *takix maner nikogda ne prinjato v xorosix klubax.
Such manners-FGenPl are never acceptable in good clubs. (Pesetsky 1982: ex. (50b))

(31) takix studentov nikogda ne prinjato v universitet.
Such students-MGenPl are never accepted in the university. (Pesetsky 1982: ex. (49b))

It would seem that the distinction between major and minor lexical rules would be of no utility in allowing us to capture the differential behavior of adjectival and verbal passive subjects in Russian with respect to the genitive of negation. Because adjectival passive formation is a minor lexical rule in this approach, and verbal passive formation is a major lexical rule, the inputs to the process of adjectival passive formation will be almost, but not quite, a proper subset of the inputs to the process of verbal passive formation.[3] On the other hand, a grammar which claims a different source, and a different derivation for adjectival and verbal passives, will be able to account for the differential behavior of the subjects of these two passives with respect to the genitive of negation.

Another argument against a representation of English verbal passives in which the passive subject is not generated postverbally comes from a consideration of the placement of floated quantifiers in infinitives. As noted by Sportiche (1988), and developed in Baltin (1995), floated quantifiers are restricted in their appearance before the infinitive marker *to*. They may appear immediately before *to* when the infinitive takes a lexical subject[4] but not when the subject is unexpressed (to be neutral about the status of this unexpressed subject). Floated quantifiers can always appear immediately after *to*:

(32)   *They tried all to like John.

(33)   I believed these students all to like John.

(34)   They tried to all like John.

(35)   I believed these students to all like John.

This behavior is mirrored by the behavior of certain adverbs, such as *ever*:

(36)   ?*Did he try ever to talk to the student?

(37)   Did you believe him ever to have made an effort to talk to the student?

(38)   Did he try to ever be attentive to the needs of students?

(39)   Did you believe him to ever have made an effort to talk to the student?

The account of these restrictions in Baltin (1995) runs as follows. Assume that there is a notion of a syntactic predicate (see Reinhart and Reuland 1993, for example, who distinguish syntactic and semantic predicates), and let us define a syntactic predicate as an X' projection that has a D'' in its specifier position. Floating quantifiers and adverbs such as *ever* are dubbed predicate specifiers, meaning that they are restricted to introducing predicates[5] (with *ever*, of course, also being a polarity item).

Now, if we assume that the unexpressed subject of an infinitive is syntactically represented as PRO, and that it is generated as a specifier to the VP following *to*, the appearance of the floating quantifier and *ever* immediately after *to* is accounted for; because they are predicate specifiers, and predicates are defined as X' projections that take DP specifiers, the V' of the V" complement of *to* is a predicate, and hence introducible by a predicate specifier. Assuming that all subjects are either generated by (if underlying subjects) or moving through (if derived) this VP-internal position, (34), (35), (38), and (39) are predicted to be acceptable.

We assume, then, that the lexical subject of an infinitive always occurs as the specifier of the VP complement of *to*, and must move to the specifier position of *to*, presumably for Case reasons. It will be noted that movement to the specifier position of *to* will cause the X' projection headed by *to* to become a predicate, by this definition of predicate. The *to* immediate projection will hence be introducible by a predicate specifier, and hence (37) and (33) are acceptable.

On the other hand, the PRO subject of an infinitive is analyzed as not getting Case, at least not in the specifier position of *to*, and therefore there would be no reason for it to move to *to*'s specifier position. Assuming what is known as "Last Resort" (Chomsky 1991), in which movement only occurs if it is necessitated, the fact that PRO does not have to move makes it ineligible for movement to *to*'s specifier position.

Because *to*'s immediate projection does not have a DP in its specifier position (PRO remaining in the specifier position of *to*'s V" complement) in this instance, it would not meet the syntactic definition of a predicate, and would therefore not be introducible by predicate specifiers. In this way, the unacceptability of (35) and (39) is accounted for.

As noted in Baltin (1995), many other theories of grammar do not represent the understood subject of infinitives syntactically at all, such as variants of Categorial Grammar (Bach 1979), Lexical-Functional Grammar (Bresnan 1982a), Head-Driven Phrase-Structure Grammar (Pollard and Sag 1994), and Generalized Phrase-Structure Grammar (Gazdar et al. 1985). Ladusaw and Dowty (1988) work out an analysis that is typical of this view of understood subjects. The subject is not represented syntactically, but is rather inferred. Control is considered to be a two-place relation between an individual and a property (Chierchia 1984 takes properties to be primitive types), and the understood subject is inferred to simply be the possessor of the relevant property.

I cannot see how this view of understood subjects deals with the facts about predicate specifiers that I have just discussed. To be sure, these analyses take floating quantifiers to be adverbs (Brodie 1985), an analysis with which I agree, given the similar behavior of *ever*,[6] but I cannot see how they provide an insightful analysis of the positioning of these adverbs.

Let us return to the analysis of A-movement phenomena. We are contrasting theories in which there is either an empty category in a "pre-movement" position, or the moved element actually occurred in that position, on the one hand, with theories which capture A-movement dependencies via lexical redundancy rules, on the other. It is instructive to consider the distribution of predicate specifiers in infinitival complements of passivized verbs:

(40) They were believed all to be quite diligent.

(41) Was he believed ever to fail students?

Assuming the presence of a predicate specifier as a probe for the presence of a nominal in the higher specifier position at some relevant point in a syntactic derivation, the acceptability of these preverbs before *to* in (40) and (41) indicates that a nominal must have occurred after the matrix passivized verb in these sentences. This seems to be additional evidence against the lexical redundancy rule account, in the absence of a competing story about the placement of preverbs within frameworks that posit lexical redundancy rules to handle A-movement phenomena.

2   Unaccusatives

Unaccusatives differ from passives, as far as I can see, chiefly in two respects: (i) the absence of distinctive verbal morphology as an implicating factor in A-movement, and (ii) the absence of any thematic role other than the one that is assigned to the verbal complement. This point was discussed above in connection with the contrast in (7).[7]

Perlmutter (1978) originally distinguished, principally from evidence in Italian, two types of intransitive verb: those with underlying subjects but no objects (dubbed unergative verbs in Government Binding theory), on the one hand, and those with underlying objects but no subjects (dubbed unaccusative verbs in Government Binding theory). The verb *telefonnare* ("to telephone") is an example of a verb in the former class, and the verb *arrivare* ("to arrive") is said to be an example of a verb in the latter class.

The evidence for this distinction will be discussed below, but before proceeding to that discussion, it is important to note that the distinction between these two types of intransitive verb has important implications for theories of grammatical relations and the statement of linking regularities between thematic roles and grammatical relations. For example, categorial grammar defines grammatical relations in terms of the order of combination of arguments with predicates to form sentences. Dowty (1982) defines indirect objects as the third from the last argument to combine with the predicate, the direct object being the penultimate argument to combine with the predicate, and the subject being the last argument to combine. Such a system, of course, would have no way of distinguishing two classes of monadic predicate,[8] and would predict that all monadic predicates would involve combination of a predicate with a subject.

Similarly, Larson (1988), for example, advocates a theory of linking in which there exists a hierarchy of thematic relations, with elements higher on the thematic hierarchy being projected onto syntactic positions in accordance with the principle that more prominent thematic relations are projected onto syntactically more prominent (i.e., higher in the phrase marker) positions. The theory is a relational, rather than an absolute, theory of linking, in that a given thematic role is not forced to occur in a unique position; its position is always fixed relative to the other thematic relations that are specified by the predicate. Themes, for instance, are more prominent than goals, so that themes will appear in positions superordinate to goals in the phrase markers in which the main predicates select both themes and goals, whereas they will appear in the positions in which goals appear when the relevant predicates do not select goals. For example, *give*'s theme would appear in the specifier position of *give*, while *read*'s theme would appear in *read*'s complement position in the simplified underlying structures[9] below:

(42)   [V″ [D″ John][V′ [V e][V″ [D″ a book][V′ [V give] [P″ to Sally]]]]]]

(43)   [V″[D″ John] [V′[V read][D″ a book]]]

Again, a relational theory of linking would have no way to capture the distinction between unaccusatives and unergatives, a distinction which claims that the single argument of a monadic predicate will be realized in one position for one type of predicate and another for another type of predicate.[10]

With respect to the evidence for the distinction, Perlmutter's original support for the distinction between the two types of monadic predicate in Italian came from auxiliary selection and the distribution of the clitic *ne*. Specifically, Italian takes two types of perfect auxiliary: *avere* (have) and *essere* (be). *Avere* is the auxiliary that is used with transitive verbs and agentive intransitives, while *essere* is used with all other verbs, specifically non-agentive intransitives, passives, and subject-to-subject raising verbs. It is also used, as noted by Burzio (1986), with reflexive transitives when the reflexive clitic *si* is used (Italian also has a strong reflexive *se stesso*). Hence, we have the following pattern, where (A) = *avere* and (E) = *essere*:

(44)   L'artigliera ha affondato due navi memiche.
       The artillery has (A) sunk two enemy ships. (Burzio 1986: ex. (80a))

(45)   Giovanni ha telefonato.
       John has (A) telephoned. (Burzio 1986: ex. (79b))

(46)   Giovanni é arrivato.
       John has (E) arrived. (Burzio 1986: ex. (79a))

(47)   Maria é stata accusata.
       Mary has (E) been accused. (Burzio 1986: ex. (81a))

(48) Molti studenti erano sembrati superare l'esame.
Many students had (E) seemed to pass the exam. (Burzio 1986: ch. l, n. i, ex. (ia))

(49) Ci si era accusati.
Themselves were accused.
"We had accused ourselves/each other." (Burzio 1986: ex. (85b))

The clitic *ne* modifies direct objects and postverbal non-agentive subjects of intransitives. It cannot modify preverbal subjects, postposed subjects of agentive intransitives, or postposed subjects of transitives.

Let us first turn our attention to perfect auxiliary selection in Italian, and ask how to determine the commonalities of the two classes of verb that take the two auxiliaries. With respect to agentive intransitives, we note that agents are practically without exception subjects of transitive verbs in non-ergative languages. We might therefore link the agent role to the subject position. We can also assume that subjects of transitive verbs are generated in subject position. Hence, we might say that *avere* is the perfect auxiliary for those verbs whose superficial subjects are also their underlying subjects.

With respect to *essere*, it is the perfect auxiliary for passive verbs, whose superficial subjects are not their underlying subjects, and subject-to-subject raising verbs (see next section), whose subjects are also not their underlying subjects (assuming movement), in addition to the subjects of (roughly) non-agentive intransitives, and subjects of transitive verbs which take the reflexive clitic *si*. Examples of each of these are given in (50)–(53):

(50) **Passive:**
Maria é stata accusata.
Mary is been accused-F (Burzio 1986: ex. (1.81a))

(51) **Subject-to-subject raising:**
Molti studenti erano sembrati superare l'esame.
Many students were ("had") seemed to pass the exam. (Burzio 1986: ch. 1, n. i, ex. (i))

(52) **Non-agentive intransitives:**
Maria é arrivata.
Mary is arrived-F (Burzio 1986: ex. (1.81c))

(53) a. **Transitive verbs with clitic *si*:**
Maria si é tagliata.
Mary-Refl is cut.
"Mary cut herself."
b. **Transitive verbs without clitic *si*:**
Maria ha tagliato se stessa.
Mary has cut [her]self.
"Mary cut herself." (Van Valin 1990)

Burzio claims that *essere* is the auxiliary that is selected when a particular binding relation holds between the subject position and the postverbal nominal. This binding relation would include the antecedent–trace relation and the antecedent–*si* relationship. Crucially, it would not include the binding relationship between the subject and the strong reflexive *se stesso*.

The binding relationship would also have to take into account the relationship between a null subject and a postverbal that is unmoved, as in (54):

(54)   Sono affondate due navi nemiche.
       Are sunk two enemy ships.
       "Two enemy ships sank."

Burzio and Belletti (1988) analyze the postverbal nominal as remaining in place, with a null expletive in subject position. The above characterization of the distribution of *essere* would necessitate the postulation of binding between the null expletive and the postverbal nominal, analogous to the relationship between the English expletive *there* and the nominal that Chomsky (1991) calls its associate:

(55)   There hangs in the Louvre one of the greatest masterpieces known.

Given the agreement between the verb and the postverbal nominal, Chomsky (1995) distinguishes two types of expletive–associate pair. One type is exemplified by the relationship between English *there* and its associate, and the other type is exemplified by the relationship between English *it* and a clausal argument. Restricting attention to the first type, which subsumes the Italian cases here, the expletive is analyzed as being inserted to satisfy the Extended Projection Principle (called a strong D-feature), while the associate's person, number, and gender features are analyzed as moving up covertly to be checked by Infl.

Crucially, for our purposes, Chomsky's (1995b) analysis does not take *there* to be an actual relationship established in the grammar between the *there*-type expletive and its associate directly. If this is right, the naturalness of the class of conditions which trigger *essere* selection is called into question.

Turning our attention to the distribution of the clitic *ne*, it seems that *ne* can basically modify objects of transitive verbs and indefinite postverbal subjects of non-agentive intransitives, and only these:

(56)   a.   Giovanni ne invitera molti.
            John of-them will invite many. (Burzio 1986: ex. (1.7a))
       b.   Ne arriveranno molti.
            Of them will arrive many.
            "Many of them will arrive." (Burzio 1986: ex. (1.5i))
       c.   *Ne telefoneranno molti.
            Of-them will telephone many. (Burzio 1986: ex. (1.5ii))

  d.   *Ne esamineranno il caso molti.
       Of-them will examine the case many. (Burzio 1986: ex. (1.5iii))
  e.   *Molti ne arriveranno.
       Many of-them arrive. (Burzio 1986: ex. (1.7c))
  f.   *Molti ne telefoneranno.
       Many of-them will telephone. (Burzio 1986: ex. (1.7d))

The argument for *ne*-cliticization is that the host of *ne* must be, within GB/ Minimalism terms, the c-command domain of *ne*. The postverbal indefinites are analyzed as simply being the D-structure objects of the verb that remain in their D-structure positions, claimed by Belletti (1988) to receive an inherent partitive Case. The other postverbal subjects are analyzed as being adjoined to VP, a position from which they are not c-commanded by *ne*. The requirement that *ne* c-command the nominal which it modifies is simply Fiengo's (1974, 1977) proper binding requirement on traces, assuming that *ne* has moved out of the nominal.

By and large, then, one would expect postverbal indefinites of non-agentive intransitives to be able to host *ne*-cliticization, and this ability to correlate directly with *essere* selection by the predicate, a prediction made by Levin and Rappaport Hovav (1995: #104).

Schwartz (1993, cited in Van Valin 1990) notes, however, that this correlation does not hold. Predicate adjectives take *essere* in Italian, and allow final indefinite subjects; but these indefinite subjects do not host *ne*-cliticization. An example that is discussed in Van Valin (1990) is the following:

(57) a.   *Ne sono buon-i molti/sono molti buoni.
           Of them are good-Pl many/are many good.
           "Many of them are good."
      b.   Molti esperti sono stat-i buon-i.
           Many experts are be-Past Part-Pl good-Pl. (Van Valin 1990: ex. (19b))

If we adopt Belletti's account, in which the postverbal subjects that can host *ne*-cliticization are really those which were never in fact subjects at all, but simply those nominals which were allowed to remain in their original positions because they received partitive Case there, Schwartz's observation is immediately accounted for. Presumably, adjectives do not assign partitive Case – only verbs do, and the class of verbs that assign partitive Case does not include *essere*.

With respect to the fact that these predicate adjectives take *essere*, as pointed out to me by Tony Kroch (personal communication), one might claim that *essere* is a raising predicate, and hence, would itself take *essere* as its auxiliary, as with (57b).

It seems to me that one can, in a sense, distinguish two types of argument for the unaccusative hypothesis. One type is a class argument, and basically groups a number of different types of predicate together and tries to find a common characteristic. The other is an argument of a somewhat more direct type, for the nominal actually being in the complement position to V at the relevant stage for the application of some grammatical process. So, for example, the *avere/essere* argument claims that passives, subject-to-subject raising, non-agentive transitives, and agentive transitives with *si* have some property in common. The fact that this property correlates with auxiliary selection is obviously language particular. For instance, English does not trigger selection for the cognates of *avere* and *essere*, *have* and *be*, on the basis of the same factors as Italian.

On the other hand, if we adopt the partitive Case mechanism for allowing the relevant nominals to remain in situ, all of the facts about *ne*-cliticization are accounted for rather simply, by appealing to a universal mechanism, the Proper Binding condition on traces. This mechanism also accounts for Baker (1988)'s observation that, in languages that allow noun incorporation, objects incorporate but transitive subjects do not, and nor do agentive intransitive subjects, while non-agentive intransitive subjects do. Again, assuming that incorporated nouns leave traces, the traces are subject to the Proper Binding Requirement, i.e., that traces must be c-commanded by their antecedents.

In short, it seems to me that the *avere/essere* distinction has a much less firm foundation as an argument for unaccusativity than do the *ne*-cliticization circumstances.

In this vein, it is instructive to examine Van Valin's discussion of *avere/essere* selection and *ne*-cliticization.

Van Valin's framework, Role and Reference Grammar (RRG), has only a single level of syntactic representation. Predicates are divided into Vendler (1967)'s classification of states, activities, accomplishments, and achievements. This quadripartite distinction is represented, along the lines of Dowty (1979), in terms of lexical decomposition into a meta-language which contains a small number of operators such as DO (Ross 1972) for agentive activity verbs, CAUSE for accomplishments, and BECOME for achievements. As in Jackendoff (1990b) and Levin and Rappaport (1986b), thematic roles are not primitive, but rather are simply labels for particular argument slots in representations in the meta-language. In addition to these thematic roles, which are read off from the meta-language representations, RRG postulates a notion of, in effect, a "super-thematic role" which certain distinguished arguments may bear, known as a macro-role. There are two macro-roles, *actor* and *undergoer*. These are assigned to arguments bearing particular thematic roles in accordance with (58) (Van Valin 1990: fig. 1):

(58)   **Actor**   **Undergoer**

　　Agent　　Effector　　Experiencer　　Locative　　Theme Patient

There are never more than two macro-roles being assigned in a simple sentence, even though there can be more than two arguments bearing thematic roles in a simple sentence (for details, see Van Valin 1990, 1993).

With this all-too-brief introduction to RRG, Van Valin posits the following principles governing *essere* selection and *ne*-cliticization within that framework:

(59) **Auxiliary selection with intransitive verbs:** Select *essere* if the LS of the verb contains a state predicate. (Van Valin 1990: ex. (17))

(60) ***Ne*-cliticization:** *Ne* realizes the lowest-ranking argument on the Actor–Undergoer hierarchy in the state predicate in the LF of the predicate in the clause. (Van Valin 1990: ex. (18))

With respect to (59), the claim that *essere* is the auxiliary for those predicates which realize or contain state predicates, we would note that it is the auxiliary for those predicates which are, in GB/Minimalism terms, subject-to-subject raising predicates. Interestingly, English *seem* passes at least one test for statehood, in that it does not progressivize. However, there is at least one English subject-to-subject raising predicate that does progressivize, and therefore seems to be activity-like: the verb *tend*:

(61) There is tending to be more and more discussion of these issues.

The question is: does Italian have verbs such as *tend*, which progressivize, and, if so, what is the auxiliary? I leave this question open.

My objection to the RRG analysis of the *ne*-cliticization facts is that it is essentially unrelated to any other grammatical phenomena in which unaccusativity has been claimed to be implicated. For example, the Proper Binding Condition accounts for Baker's observations about the extent of noun incorporation as well as the *ne*-cliticization facts in Italian. The RRG formulation essentially treats *ne*-cliticization as a process that is disconnected from the noun incorporation facts.

Moreover, the RRG framework must deal with the fact that preverbal elements cannot host *ne*-cliticization but postverbal ones can. Van Valin acknowledges this in a footnote, and gives a different formulation of the conditions for *ne*-cliticization in Van Valin (1993):

(62) ***Ne*-cliticization:** *Ne* realizes the topical head of an NP with a focal quantifier, and this NP must be the lowest ranking argument (in terms of the Actor–Undergoer hierarchy) of the state predicate in the LS of the predicate in the clause. (Van Valin 1990: 85)

A focal quantifier is one that follows the main predicate of the clause. With this in mind, we are now in a position to compare the RRG formulation of *ne*-cliticization with the GB formulation, since Belletti (1988)'s analysis of postverbal ("focal" in the RRG terms) distinguishes two such positions: one in which a postverbal nominal is simply remaining in place, in complement position, and the other adjoined to the VP. (63a), in which the nominal precedes a subcategorized PP, exemplifies the first postverbal position, and (63b), in which the nominal follows the PP, exemplifies the second (the examples are based on Belletti's 17b):

(63)   a.   Ne all'improvisso sono entrati molti dalla finestra.
       b.   *?Ne all'improvisso sono entrati dalla finestra molti.

Belletti's analysis would predict unacceptability for (63b), which should be parallel to (56c), while Van Valin (1990)'s analysis would predict acceptability for both, since his representations would simply assign postfocal status to the *ne* hosts in both sentences.

In fact, the native speakers of Italian whom I have consulted uniformly find a contrast – a fact which would be difficult, as far as I can see, for a theory that has no VP, and which would attempt to capture the positions in terms of focus. The position following the predicate is too general a characterization; the semantic role of the quantifier is also not a relevant factor, since the semantic role is the same for *molti* in (63) both before and after the subcategorized PP. One would have to characterize the postverbal position preceding subcategorized PPs as a sort of "neutral" or "unmarked" position, but this would just be another way of saying that it is the basic position from which movement does not occur, and I do not then see what claims would be made by a theory that claimed to be monostratal.

3   Subject-to-Subject Raising

Subject-to-subject raising is the term given to the process by which the subject of an infinitival complement is raised to become the subject of the main predicate which selects the infinitival complement. It is distinguished from control, known in some frameworks as Equi. Examples of sentences which exhibit subject-to-subject raising are given in (64), and sentences which exhibit control are given in (65):

(64)   a.   John seemed to be a great linguist.
       b.   John proved to be a great linguist.
       c.   There tended to be a lot of discussion.
       d.   There promises to be a storm tonight.

(65)   a.   John tried to be a good boy.
       b.   John strived to be successful.
       c.   John wanted to improve his lot in life.
       d.   John expected to win.

The basic distinction between subject-to-subject raising and control is that the matrix predicate in subject-to-subject-raising constructions does not bear any relation, other than person, number, and gender features (for finite verbs) to its subject, while the matrix predicate in control constructions does impose restrictions on its subject. Hence, the matrix subjects in (65) must all be animate, while any nominal can be the subject of one of the infinitive-taking predicates in (64), as long as it is a possible subject of the infinitive predicate. For some reason that has always been mysterious to me, the controlling nominal of a control predicate must bear a particular restriction: it must be animate. While this is true of predicates which take infinitival complements that must be controlled, there are other constructions in which control is said to be implicated where this restriction does not hold. In particular, the degree complements of the English degree words *too* and *enough* are infinitival, and can be controlled, but there is no animacy restriction on the subject. An example is given in (66):

(66)   This book is too dense to be read in one sitting.

One might then ask whether the antecedent for the understood subject of infinitive relationship in degree complements should be distinguished from raising at all. The answer is clearly in the affirmative, given that expletives cannot be the antecedents for understood subjects in this construction, while they can in the raising construction, a point made by Safir (1985). Hence, we have the contrast between (67a) and (67b):

(67)   a.   *There is too likely to be a riot to be a serious discussion of the issues.
       b.   There is too likely to be a riot for there to be a serious discussion of the issues.

Many theories of grammar have nevertheless assumed that one might simply view raising as that species of control in which the controller gets no restrictions from its superficial position, but rather from the controlled position. Jacobson (1990) points out a number of distinctions between raising and control, albeit in the framework of categorial grammar. One restriction, for example, shows up in the omissibility of the infinitive.[11] The subjectless infinitive can be omitted in the control construction, but not in the raising construction. To be sure, the omissibility of the subjectless infinitive is a matter of lexical variation, depending on the matrix predicate, but there are no raising predicates at all that allow for an optional infinitive complement. Examples of the former are given in (68) (Jacobson's ex. (27)):

(68)   a.   John {tried.}
                 {forgot.}
                 {remembered.}
                 {refused.}
       b.   John is {eager.}
                 {willing.}

However, there are no raising predicates that allow the infinitive complement to be omitted, so that the following are unacceptable, a point made by Jacobson (1990: ex. (30), reproduced as (69) here):

(69)   *Bill seems to be obnoxious, but I don't think that Sam {seems.}
                                                              {happens.}
                                                              {turns out.}
                                                              {appears.}
                                                              {tends.}

Most theories of grammar have a counterpart to Government Binding's theta-criterion, which requires, *inter alia*, that every semantically contentful argument receive a theta-role from the predicate. For instance, Lexical-Functional Grammar posits a condition known as the coherence condition, which has this effect (Bresnan 1982a: 71). Noting the pattern in (63), Bresnan (1982a: 71) proposes that "if the verbal complement of an equi verb is omitted, the result will be functionally incomplete but coherent; while if the verbal complement of a raising verb is omitted, the result will be incoherent as well as incomplete." Given the existence of null complement anaphora, however, or implicit arguments, one might well ask why a predicate which is null cannot be inferred by the mechanism that interprets implicit arguments, in turn licensing the argument of which it is predicated.

Another difference between raising and control that is quite striking is one noted originally by Kayne (1981b), concerning the inability of raising infinitives to be introduced by an overt complementizer, while control infinitives are not subject to this restriction. French and Italian, for example, show this contrast. Kayne gives the following examples:

(70)   Jean a essayé/oublié/decidé de partir.
       John tried/forgot/decided to leave. (Kayne 1981b: ex. (24))

(71)   *Jean semble/parait/se trouve/s'avere d'etre parti.
       "John seems/appears/is found/has just left." (Kayne 1981b: ex. (26))

Andrews (1982) reports the same contrast in Icelandic infinitives, and indeed, Higgins (1989), in discussing the history of raising and control in English, shows that raising did not enter the language until the Middle Ages, and was the result of essentially two changes for the relevant predicates, which were analyzed as control predicates until a certain point: (i) the loosening of selectional restrictions on the controller, and (ii) the ability of infinitives to drop their complementizers.

The restriction on raising out of clauses with overt complementizers is quite striking, and leads us to ask whether it follows from any of the theories that we have considered. It certainly does not seem to follow from any theory that views raising as simply a species of control in which the controller gets all of its characteristics from the controlled position. Does it follow from anything within Government Binding theory or Minimalism?

Kayne (1981b) characterized the restriction on raising out of clauses introduced by overt complementizers in terms of the Empty Category Principle (ECP: Chomsky 1981), which required that traces be properly governed, with the idea that Infl and Comp are not proper governors. Hence, raising out of a clause introduced by an overt complementizer would be parallel to a that-trace violation. However, it is well known that it is possible to superficially violate the *that*-trace filter (Chomsky 1981, Perlmutter 1971, Maling and Zaenen 1978, Rizzi 1982, 1990), but it does not seem to be possible to violate the restriction on raising out of clauses introduced by complementizers. Furthermore, the ECP is not viewed to be a primitive in the theory of grammar in the Minimalist view.

It might be worthwhile to consider the disparity between *that*-trace violations and complementizer raising violations. Rizzi (1990) argues that at least one strategy that a language might employ for allowing *that*-trace violations is to permit the complementizer to become a proper head governor if it takes on agreement features with an element in its specifier position. Hence, if a *wh*-phrase in such a language were to pass through the Spec of a CP, it could "activate" the Comp as a head governor, which would then legitimate a trace in subject position.

This option would be unavailable for raising out a clause introduced by an overt complementizer, however. Such movement would necessitate the raised subject first moving into the specifier position of CP, and then ultimately into the matrix subject position – in other words, first moving into an A'-position, with subsequent movement into an A-position – and such movement is ruled out in a variety of approaches within Government Binding theory/Minimalism (see May 1981 for one early example).

Jacobson (1990) has an interesting approach to raising within the framework of categorial grammar. She adduces a number of arguments to show that the lexical entailment approach to control cannot be extended to raising cases, noting that such an approach to raising would be difficult to prevent within a framework that maintained that control was simply inferred. Her approach to raising employs crucially the notion of function composition, in which two functions combine to form a composite function. For example, adverbs are usually assigned the grammatical category IV/IV, and transitive verbs are assigned the category IV/t, and so functional application for both categories yields a "composed function," as in *John [[ate [the steak]]quickly]*. Raising verbs are specifically stated so as to have to compose, and so *seem*, for example, is designated as $S/^0S$, and when it composes with S/NP, the new composed function is just S/NP.

Hence, the subject of the composed function has all of the characteristics of the subject of the clause with which the raising predicate composes. However, as noted in Baltin (1995), there is a contrast between (32), repeated here as (72), and (73):

(72)   *They tried all to like John.

(73)   They seemed all to like John.

Specifically, the floated quantifier can appear before *to* when *to* heads the complement of a raising predicate, but not a control predicate. This is explicable, assuming Baltin (1995), if *to* had a DP in its specifier in the raising construction, but not in the control construction. However, Jacobson's function composition mechanism does not posit an actual stage at which the subject of the raising predicate is actually in the specifier position of the infinitive, and so I do not see how this contrast is realized within that analysis.[12]

To sum up this section, then, subject-to-subject raising exhibits significant differences from control, suggesting rather different treatments in grammar, and there is some evidence that the raised subject must occupy the specifier position of the infinitive at some point.

A rather interesting raising construction exists in Irish, as shown by McCloskey (1984), and in Modern Greek, as shown by Joseph (1976). In this construction, the subject of the complement clauses raises into the matrix clause to become the object of a preposition. An example is given in (74):

(74)   B' eigean do-n-a ainm a bheith I mbeal na ndaoine.
        Cop-Past to-his name be-Fin in mouth the people-Gen
        "His name must have been in the mouth of the people." (McCloskey
        1984: ex. (16a))

As noted by McCloskey (1984), if the raised subject remains in the matrix V' in Irish, this poses a number of problems for some central tenets of Government Binding theory (Chomsky (1981), including the Proper Binding condition, discussed above, which holds that a moved element must c-command its trace, and the Projection principle, which holds that selectional properties of lexical items must be observed at D-Structure, S-Structure, and LF. The raised subject, were it to reside within the matrix V' as a complement to V, would be in a position that is reserved for items theta-marked by the matrix V, and yet it obviously would not be theta-marked. Subject-to-object raising, as argued for most notably by Postal (1974), would be incompatible with the Projection principle and the claim that the complement to V must be theta-marked by V (but see Postal and Pullum 1988 for arguments against the latter claim). We will consider Subject-to-object raising in more detail below.

Stowell (1989a) has reanalyzed the phenomenon of raising to the object position of a preposition by arguing: (i) the preposition is not a true preposition, but rather a Case-marker, so that the projection is really a nominal projection which would c-command a nominal trace; and (ii) the prepositional object is really in subject position.

4 Subject-to-Object Raising

The existence of an A-movement in which the subject of an infinitival complement is raised to become the object of the verb that selects the infinitival complement is somewhat more controversial. The most detailed justification for such an operation is Postal (1974). For example, (75) would have essentially the structure bracketed (abstracting away from particular theories in which traces or empty categories do not occur in the infinitive subject position):

(75) John [VP believes [Sally] [t to be polite]]

Chomsky (1973) has proposed various theoretical tenets that would ban subject-to-object raising, but, as Lasnik and Saito (1991) have noted, many of Postal's original arguments remain. Two arguments in particular that seem quite strong are based on the interaction of the proposed structure with binding principles and the placement of matrix adverbials. For example, the contrast between (76) and (77) remains unexplained if the underlined nominal is in the complement clause in both sentences, but a structure for (76) in which the nominal is in the main clause, and hence c-commands material inside of the matrix adverbial, would be correctly ruled out by principle C of the binding theory (Chomsky 1981):

(76) *Joan believes <u>him</u>[i] to be a genius even more fervently than Bob[i] does.

(77) Joan believes he[i] is a genius even more fervently than Bob[i] does.

Similarly, adverbs which intervene between the nominal and the infinitival complement can modify the matrix sentence, while adverbs that intervene between a nominal and a finite predicate cannot. Hence, (78) is acceptable, while (79) is not:

(78) I believe John with all my heart to be a fine person.

(79) *I believe John with all my heart is a fine person.

There is another class of verbs which occurs with nominal plus infinitive sequences, exemplified by the verbs *want*, *like*, *hate*, and *prefer*. These verbs, interestingly enough, do not allow the immediately following nominals to be passivized:

(80) a. *John is wanted to win.
      b. We want John to win.

(81) a. *John would be liked to win.
      b. We would like John to win.

(82) a. *John would be hated to win.
       b. We would hate John to win.

(83) a. *John would be preferred to be the candidate.
       b. We would prefer John to be the candidate.

These verbs have yet another interesting characteristic: they can all allow the infinitive to be introduced by the complementizer *for*, in contrast to the verbs that allow the following nominal to be passivized:

(84) I would want for John to win.

(85) I would like for John to win.

(86) I would hate for John to win.

(87) I would prefer for John to be the candidate.

We might account for the behavior of the two classes of verbs by allowing subject-to-object raising for the verbs that do not take infinitives with overt complementizers (such as *believe* and *prove*), and disallowing it for verbs that do take overt complementizers, such as *want* and *prefer*. The failure of the subjects of the infinitival complements of the verbs of the latter class to be A-moved in the passive construction would then be a consequence of the restriction noted in the last section on subject-to-subject raising occurring across an overt complementizer. The non-occurrence of the complementizers, as in the (b) examples of (80)–(83), would be due to PF deletion.

The problem with this bifurcation into two classes of verbs that take infinitival complements is that when we return to the original evidence, given above, for subject-to-object raising, we predict a disparity in behavior between the two classes that is non-existent. For example, it seems that a nominal intervening between a matrix verb and following infinitive binds into a final matrix adverbial with verbs of the *want*-class, but only when the complementizer *for* is absent:

(88) *Sally would prefer him^i to be the candidate even more fervently than Bob^i would.

(89) Sally would prefer for him^i to be the candidate even more fervently than Bob^i would.

Similarly, an adverb that intervenes between the matrix postverbal nominal and the infinitive can modify the matrix clause just as easily when the verb is of the *want*-class as it can if the verb is of the *believe*-class. Again, significantly, the presence of the complementizer *for* seems to affect acceptability:

(90)   I would love (*for) Sally with all my heart to be the one to get the job.

It is striking that the complementizer's presence, forcing an analysis in which the pre-infinitival nominal is in the complement sentence, prevents a pre-infinitival adverb from taking matrix scope, and correlates with the nominal's failure to bind material in the matrix sentence. Interestingly enough, Zidani-Eroglu (1997) also presents evidence from Turkish, from adverbial modification and negative polarity items, for subject-to-object raising as well.

Of course, the failure of the postverbal nominal to passivize when the verb is of the *want*-class requires an account.

5   Conclusion

In this chapter, I have attempted to analyze the data that have motivated movement to an A-position within a transformational framework from a variety of perspectives, comparing the adequacy of the transformational account with alternatives that have appeared. It is my view that there is a real distinction between A-movement phenomena, and their treatment, and lexical phenomena, and that it is impossible to reduce all of the phenomena to a single treatment.

NOTES

* I would like to thank many people who were kind enough to help me as I was writing this; Leonard Babby, Polly Jacobson, Tony Kroch, David Pesetsky, Paul Postal, Chris Collins, Mark Steedman, and Robert Van Valin. The usual disclaimers apply.

1   The existence of such impersonal passives would seem to be problematic for a "phrasal" theory of passives, found within categorial grammar as advocated by Keenan (1980), in which passives are considered to be derived by a rule which converts transitive verb phrases into intransitive verb phrases. In languages such as German and Dutch, the verb phrases are intransitive to begin with.

Nevertheless, Keenan's (1980) observation that passives are identified solely by characteristics of the passive verb phrase will be useful in our discussion of Van Valin (1990) below.

2   As Paul Postal (personal communication) has pointed out, there is a wide range of examples of postverbal nominals that cannot appear as the subjects of verbal passives, and the inability of these nominals to undergo A-movement must be explained, such as the nominals following the verbs *resemble* and *write*:

(i)   *His brother is resembled by John.

(ii)   *John was written by Fred.

corresponding to (iii):

(iii)   Fred wrote John.

Interestingly, as Postal notes, the postverbal nominal in this subcategorization of *write* is also frozen by *wh*-movement:

(iv)   *Who did Fred write?

Postal suggests that the frozen nature of the nominal following *write* makes reference to grammatical relations, such that the nominal is actually an indirect object. As has been noted since at least Fillmore (1965), nominals corresponding to the first objects of double-object verbs cannot be passivized when the double-object construction is interpreted as a variant of the for-dative, and first objects generally cannot be *wh*-moved:

(v)   John bought Sally a cake.

(vi)   John bought a cake for Sally.

(vii)   *Sally was bought a cake by John.

(viii)   *Who did John buy a cake?

(ix)   *Who did John give a book?

The idea would be that English passives would crucially turn English direct objects into subjects, as in the text. The situation seems somewhat more complicated, however, in view of the fact that such verbs as *teach* and *feed*, to be discussed below, have the same privileges of occurrence as *write*, and yet the postverbal nominals passivize and *wh*-move:

(x)   John taught Sally (French).

(xi)   Sally was taught by John.

(xii)   Who did John teach?

(xiii)   John fed Sally (steak).

(xiv)   Sally was fed by John.

(xv)   Who did John feed?

Hence, the situation seems somewhat unclear. As for the verb *resemble* (discussed by Chomsky 1965) I would note that the object is intensional, so that one could be said to resemble a unicorn, and Pustejovsky (1987) has noted that subjects must be extensional. Hence, we have the following contrast:

(xvi)   John fears unicorns.

(xvii)   *Unicorns are feared by John.

(xviii)   *Unicorns frighten John.

Apart from these remarks, to quote Chomsky (1995b), "I leave such examples without useful comment."

3   The subset relation will be destroyed by the assumption of a grammatical relation other than direct object to an internal argument. For example, Lexical-Functional Grammar countenances the grammatical function OBJ2, for second objects in double-object constructions, or INDOBJ, for indirect objects.

4   Or when the subject is raised, as discussed in the next section.

5   It will be noted that I am analyzing these preverbs as predicate specifiers, and subjects are also predicate specifiers. I am therefore committed to the existence of multiple specifiers, as argued for in Baltin (1995) and independently by (Koizumi 1995) and (Chomsky 1995b).

6   Indeed, this is one of the arguments against (Sportiche 1988), which analyzes floated quantifiers as involving movement of the quantified nominal with the quantifier remaining in place. Sportiche's analysis cannot extend to the distribution of *ever*.

7 It is important to note that the distinction between the three types of A-movement discussed here (passives, unaccusatives, and subject-to-subject raising) is actually made by only some of the theories that we are discussing here. For example, in Government Binding theory or Minimalism, the distinction is not actually captured by the theory itself. Chomsky (1995b), for instance, takes movement in general simply to be feature-attraction, with entire categories being moved for phonological reasons when the movement is overt. The distinction between A-movements and A'-movements depends on the characteristics of the "attracting" category. In this connection, the two distinctions between passives and unaccusatives that I have made in the text do not always go together. For example, as noted by Keenan (1980), some languages have morphologically distinguished passives that do not allow the equivalent of oblique active subjects. Indeed, English has at least one passive that has no corresponding active, and certainly no *by*-phrase is permitted here: the passive *be rumored*:

(i) *The American Spectator rumored Clinton to be having an affair.

(ii) Clinton is rumored (*by the American Spectator) to be having an affair.

It is meaningless to ask whether *be rumored* is passive or unaccusative.

8 A theory that defined grammatical relations in terms of order of combination with the predicate would also be forced to claim that an indirect object could only exist in a sentence that also contained a direct object and a subject. In this connection, one might note that English, for example, has datives with no syntactically expressed direct object, as in (i):

(i) He gave__to charity.

For these reasons, I am skeptical of the order-of-composition view of grammatical relations.

9 Larson argues that empty Vs are generated in sentences and the phonologically contentful V raises to the position of the empty V. For details and arguments, see Larson (1988).

10 It is occasionally claimed that unergatives take a "cognate object" (Hale and Keyser 1993), which can typically be realized under the right conditions. Examples are given in (i) and (ii):

(i) He dreamed a long and satisfying dream.

(ii) He slept a long and satisfying sleep.

Therefore, the argument runs, unergatives are not truly monadic. There are two responses to this argument. First, with respect to the relational theory of linking, unless this cognate object bears a thematic role, it would appear to be irrelevant to the relational theory of linking. Second, the factual basis of Hale and Keyser's observation seems questionable, as noted by Baker (1997b).

11 Bresnan (1982a) also makes this observation about missing infinitives, citing Williams (1980), in an unpublished paper that I have not seen.

12 Interestingly, Tony Kroch has pointed out to me that, within the framework of Tree-Adjoining Grammars, raising predicates are,

in effect, inserted between subjects and the predicates out of which they raise, and hence the possibility of placing the floating quantifier between the raising predicate and the infinitive marker simply reduces to the possibility of placing the floating quantifier between a lexical subject of an infinitive and the infinitive marker, as in the ECM case (36) in the text.

III Argument Structure and Phrase Structure

9 Thematic Relations in Syntax

JEFFREY S. GRUBER

1 Thematic Roles and Grammatical Arguments

The grammatical arguments in a sentence are commonly described in terms of their relations in the eventuality expressed (Gruber 1965, Fillmore 1968). For example, in (1a), the subject "John" is described as an Agent of the action, and the object "the house" is described as a Patient or Theme. Similarly, in (1b), the subject "the electrode" is a Source, while the object "ions" is a Theme and "the medium" a Goal. In (1c), "ions" is again a Theme, but subject, while the Goal, "the electrode," is object. In (d), "ions" is a Theme and object while the subject "the medium" is a Location. These all consist in relations to a Theme. They have therefore been called thematic relations (Jackendoff 1972) or theta-roles (Chomsky 1981). In (1d) there is a Location–Theme relation, while in (1b) and (1c) Source and Goal are initial and final Locations of the Theme. The Agent in (1a) is a Source[1] whose Theme is the action as a whole:

(1) a. John destroyed the house.
     b. The electrode emitted ions into the medium.
     c. Ions struck the electrode.
     d. The medium contains ions.

Thematic relations are basically conceptual. The claim, however, is that they are necessary for determining grammatical arguments. In this way thematic theory, or theta-theory, seeks to characterize possible predicates in overt syntax. The central question is how thematic relations and grammatical arguments correspond – the linking problem of argument projection. Linking regularities have been propounded and described in terms of the Universal Alignment Hypothesis (Perlmutter and Postal 1984), the Uniformity of Theta Assignment Hypothesis (Baker 1988, 1996), linking rules and hierarchies (Carter 1988, Jackendoff 1990b), and projection asymmetries (Gruber 1994, 1997).

(1a) is a prime example of an asymmetry in linking: the Agent is expressed as subject and the Patient/Theme as object, and not the reverse. Thus there can be no verb like *bestroy* as in (2a), with the meaning of *destroy* but with Patient/Theme as subject and Agent as direct object. If Agent is a kind of Source, (1b) illustrates, in part, the same asymmetry: Source can be subject but not object. Note that the apparent Source object of *leave* in (2b) cannot become the subject of a passive (2c):[2] it is perhaps rather an implicit prepositional (*from*) phrase. In contrast, (1c) does passivize (2d), showing that a Goal can be a direct object (see section 1.4):

(2) a. *The house destroyed John.
     b. Ions left the electrode.
     c. *The electrode was left by ions.
     d. The electrode was struck by ions.

In the remainder of this section we discuss the information content of simple thematic structures and some projection asymmetries involving them. Complex thematic structures and the significance of aspect are discussed in section 2. The locus of thematic information and the "grain" of theta-role projection are considered in section 3, and the derivation of linking asymmetries in section 4.

1.1   *Elemental thematic functions*

Asymmetries of argument projection show the need to represent conceptual distinctions in a relational system that will appropriately map to syntactic form. Theta-roles are not feature like, constituting arbitrary, lexically specific sets or theta-grids (Stowell 1981, Marantz 1984). Rather they are defined in fixed elemental functions (Gruber 1965, 1994, 1997, Jackendoff 1976, 1987, 1990b).

(1) and (3) illustrate two simple types of thematic function. In a Locational function, (1d) and (3a), there are two thematic roles, Theme Θ and Location Λ. These are defined in relation to each other: viz., the denotation of the Theme is found in that of the Location. In a Motional function, (1a–c) and (3b), there are three roles, Theme, Source Σ, and Goal Γ. The Source has the sense of a preceding Location and the Goal a subsequent one. These are then "Locational" roles, defined by their relation to a Theme and a sequential relation to each other:

(3) a. The ball lies in the box. $<\Theta, \Lambda>$
     b. The ball rolled from the bush to the tree. $<\Theta, \Sigma, \Gamma>$

Thus thematic theory is a theory not only of possible overt syntactic predicates, but of conceptual predicates: these must be based on the elemental Theme–Location relation. Conceptual predicates of arbitrary argument structure cannot be hypothesized. For example, the "subject" of the predicate CAUSE must be analyzed as a Source whose Theme is the Causee clause.

Various ways that theta-roles can correspond to grammatical arguments are shown in (4). In the notation, theta-roles of a function are arrayed on a horizontal line under the grammatical arguments that express them.[3] A vertical stroke marks the lexical predicate head. A Locational function may be expressed intransitively (4a) with Theme subject, or transitively (4b) with Location subject and Theme object. A Motional function may be intransitive with Theme subject (4c), or transitive with Source subject and Theme object (4d), or Theme subject and Goal object (4d):

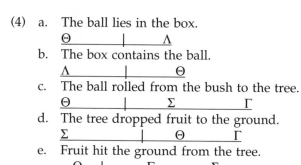

(4) a.   The ball lies in the box.
         Θ | Λ
     b.   The box contains the ball.
         Λ | Θ
     c.   The ball rolled from the bush to the tree.
         Θ | Σ   Γ
     d.   The tree dropped fruit to the ground.
         Σ | Θ   Γ
     e.   Fruit hit the ground from the tree.
         Θ | Γ   Σ

Elemental thematic functions may be combined into complex structures. Non-agentive resultatives provide clear examples. As shown in (5), resultatives consist of Motional functions combined in a relation of consequence (CSQ). The functions are shown stepwise with the precedent one below the consequent one. (Implicit Source is omitted.) In both sentences the precedent function means "the stone hit the pole," where "the stone" is Theme and "the pole" Goal. In (5a) the consequent function means "the stone entered the road," with "the stone" Theme and "the road" Goal. In (5b) the consequent function signifies "the pole entered the road," with "the pole" Theme and "the road" Goal. Note that in each resultative, a theta-role of each function is linked, or "colinked," to the same grammatical argument:

(5) a.   The stone knocked against the pole into the road.

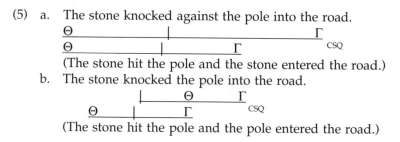

         Θ | Γ
         Θ | Γ   CSQ
         (The stone hit the pole and the stone entered the road.)
     b.   The stone knocked the pole into the road.
                      | Θ   Γ
         Θ | Γ   CSQ
         (The stone hit the pole and the pole entered the road.)

1.2   *Thematic functional integrity*

Since theta-roles are defined relationally within thematic functions, each theta-role of a function is always present conceptually. A Theme entails a Location and vice versa. A Goal entails a preceding Location, hence a Source; a Source entails a following one, hence a Goal. Thematic functions thus maintain their integrity as specific theta-role sets. This is akin to the theta-criterion (Chomsky 1981), which requires lexically specified sets of theta-roles to correspond to grammatical arguments. It is, however, more substantial by characterizing these sets, and therefore has greater predictive power for syntactic form. For example, a Motional predicate (6b, c), but not a Locational predicate (6a), can include a Goal or Source in its complement of theta-roles. In (6), Motional predicates are distinguished by their acceptance of adverbs *gradually* or *at once*. This correlates with Goal or Source arguments identified by their "semantic" Case marking (*to* or *from*).[4] Since the subject of (6b) is a Source, a Goal but not another Source can occur with it. Since in (6c) the Goal is the object, a Source but not another Goal can appear.[5] Similarly, more than one Source or Goal is impossible when both are oblique (6d):[6]

(6) a. The box (*gradually/*at once) contained the ball (*to the ground/ *from the tree).
   b. The tree (gradually) dropped its fruit (to the ground/*from the clouds).
   c. Fruit (at once) hit the roof (from the tree/*against the ground).
   d. Fruit dropped from the tree (*from the clouds)/fell against the house (*against the ground).

An implication of thematic functional integrity is that lexical specification should be in terms of thematic functions rather than theta-roles per se. Each theta-role of an expressed thematic function must be at least implicit and, if so, generally optionally expressed.[7] This is true of the Goal and Source arguments in (6b, c). In (7a) Theme and Goal are explicit, while Source is implicit or optional. (7b) is problematic since an oblique Source is not expressible. However, the content of the subject in (7b) is not that of a Theme but a Source. The Theme may be a generic category like "tree" in (7a), but not a category in taxonomic opposition to Source or Goal, like "cedar" in (7b). Rather the subject Theme in (7b) is identified in content with the absent Source, $\Theta[:\Sigma]$ in (7c). The same occurs between Theme and Goal, $\Theta[:\Gamma]$ in (7d):

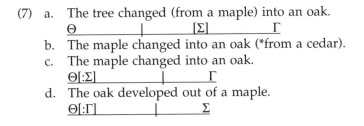

(7) a. The tree changed (from a maple) into an oak.
       Θ | [Σ] Γ
   b. The maple changed into an oak (*from a cedar).
   c. The maple changed into an oak.
       $\Theta[:\Sigma]$ | Γ
   d. The oak developed out of a maple.
       $\Theta[:\Gamma]$ | Σ

1.3   Cross-field generalization

Thematic functions express relations in various conceptual fields or dimensions. This phenomenon of "cross-field generalization" (Jackendoff 1976) is the categorial aspect of thematic structure. Thus *lie*, *roll*, and *contain* express relations of physical position, while *hit* and *drop* involve contact. These are of the Positional and Contact dimensions, respectively. *Change* concerns category identification and is termed Identificational. In the following examples of various dimensions, the subject appears to be Theme and the object or complement Goal, while Source is implicit:

(8) a. The train reached the station.   Positional (PST)
         Θ   PST| Γ
     b. The branches knocked against the wall.   Contact (CTT)
     c. The child became a man.   Identificational (IDT)
     d. The party lasted till midnight.   Temporal (TMP)
     e. The dog went crazy.   State (STE)
     f. It struck John that it was so.   Propositional (PRP)
     g. It came to John that it was so.   Informational (INF)
     h. The snake saw into the nest.   Sensory (SNS)
     i. Hard work resulted in high grades.   Causational (CST)
     j. The farm passed to John.   Possessional (PSS)

The integrity of thematic functions applies in abstract dimensions. *Strike* (8f), *impress on*, and *believe* are Propositional, involving the holding or transferring of propositional attitudes. (9a, b) accept *gradually/at once*, and so are Motional functions. An oblique Source occurs in (9a), so that the direct arguments are Theme and Goal. An oblique Source cannot occur in (9b) because the subject is Source. Neither the adverbs nor an oblique Source can occur with a Locational function (9c):

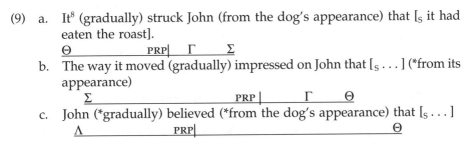

(9) a. It[8] (gradually) struck John (from the dog's appearance) that [s it had
         eaten the roast].
         Θ   PRP| Γ   Σ
     b. The way it moved (gradually) impressed on John that [s ...] (*from its
         appearance)
              Σ   PRP | Γ   Θ
     c. John (*gradually) believed (*from the dog's appearance) that [s ...]
              Λ   PRP| Θ

Essential for a falsifiable theory is the identification of thematic roles by meaning alone. This entails a universal characterization of the set of conceptual dimensions together with a definition of thematic relation independent of any particular dimension. Suppose each dimension determines a space of variable values in which the image of a category is defined. Let us call this its denotation in the conceptual space. The elemental Theme–Location relation then signifies that the denotation of the Theme in some space is found in that of the Location: that is, it asserts a mapping from Theme, as independent variable, to Location. This is a concretization of the Theme–Location relation as figure–ground (Talmy 1978). Thus the Positional dimension would determine (ordinary) physical space. In the Locational function (4a, b), "the ball," a Physical Object, denotes the set of variable values (positions) defining the space occupied by the ball, and "(in) the box" denotes the space occupied by (the inside) of the box. The function means that the space of the Theme maps into that of the Location. Similarly, the Propositional dimension in (9) could determine a space of (truth) conditions, such that the denotation of a clause is the set of conditions under which it is true, while the denotation of an Animate being is the set of conditions it holds true. (9c) asserts that the conditions under which "it had eaten the meat" is true maps into those that John holds true. The clausal argument is thereby identified as Theme and the Animate subject as Location.

Possessional conceptual dimensions contrast with Spatial ones in that they have no independently defined conceptual space. The denotation of the Theme in the thematic relation is the Theme itself. While the change of the Positional space of an entity, i.e., its position, is Spatial, as in (8a), the transfer of the entity itself, such as landed property in (8j), is Possessional. Propositional predicates (8f) are Spatial, while Informational predicates (8g) are Possessional. The latter express the holding or transfer of information denoted directly by the clausal Theme, not as denoted in an independent conceptual space (such as truth conditions).

1.4 Projection asymmetries of simple thematic functions

Locational and Motional functions exhibit projection asymmetries in which their theta-roles correspond differently to grammatical arguments. For Locational functions, the Location is either subject or an oblique complement, but never a direct object. In contrast the Theme is either subject or object, but not normally an oblique complement. The two possible predicate forms are as illustrated in (4a–b). We may state the asymmetry as in (10):

(10) **The Location–Theme Subject–Object Asymmetry**
      For a predicate expressing a simple Locational eventuality:
      a. if the predicate is transitive, the Location is subject and the Theme is direct object;
      b. if the predicate is intransitive the Theme is subject and the Location is oblique.

This asymmetry, as well as those that follow, is valid only for predicates that express truly simple thematic functions, and are truly transitive or intransitive as indicated. Therefore apparent counter-examples must be carefully considered. These are illustrated in (11) for the half of the asymmetry concerned with transitive predicates (10a). First of all, an apparent Location object may be an implicit oblique, as in (2b) and (11a), where the verb cannot be passivized. Second, the predicate may express more than a simple thematic function. For example, it may be agentive (11b), in which a theta-role is colinked with Agent in the subject (section 2.2); or the object may express colinked theta-roles (11c) (section 2.1). Other apparent exceptions occur when the theta-role of the object is misidentified: for example, it may be a Goal (11d) or Path (11e):[9]

(11) a. The chair abuts the wall/*the wall is abutted by the chair.
      b. John is touching the wall/the wall is being touched by John.
      c. A bear occupies/inhabits the cave (cf. water fills the tub).
      d. The electric main joins the house circuit in the basement/the house circuit is joined by the electric main in the basement.
      e. The fence straddles the sidewalk/the sidewalk is straddled by the fence.

An exception to the intransitive half of the Location–Theme asymmetry (10b) is an oblique attributive Theme (12a). The form is marginally used predicatively (12b):[10]

(12) a. The man with a book.
      b. ?The man is with a book.

Source and Goal of simple Motional functions also enter into a projection asymmetry. When projected directly, Source becomes subject and Goal object. We may state this as (13):

(13) **The Source–Goal Subject–Object Asymmetry**
      For a predicate expressing a simple Motional eventuality, either:
      a. the subject is Theme and the Source and Goal are oblique, or
      b. the direct object is Theme, with Source as subject, or
      c. the direct object is Goal, with Theme as subject.

(4c–d) show the three predicate forms of a simple Motional function allowed by (13). Source subject transitives (13b) include causatives and production verbs like *cause, produce, derive,* and verbs of the Substance/Source alternation (14a, Levin 1993). Goal object forms (13c) are *reach, join, see, regard, conclude, realize, notice,* and verbs of contact with intransitive alternates (14b):

(14) a. *drop, drip, leak, gush, ooze, sprout, shine, . . .*
          The tree dropped fruit onto the rooftop/fruit dropped from the tree onto the rooftop.
      b. *hit, strike, slap, kick, rub, touch, . . .*
          Fruit hit the rooftop from the tree/fruit hit against the rooftop from the tree.

Apparent counter-examples to the asymmetry with respect to Source (13b) are shown in (15). A Source appearing to be object but without a passive is an implicit oblique (15a). The Source may be object if the predicate is agentive (15b). A Path role can be projected as a direct object (15c):

(15) a. Gas escaped the tube/*the tube was escaped by gas.
  b. The terrorist escaped the prison cell/the prison cell was escaped by the terrorist.
  c. The rolling stone avoided the river/the river was avoided by the rolling stone.

Apparent counter-examples to the asymmetry with respect to Goal (13c) are shown in (16). A Goal subject is possible if the predicate is agentive (16a), or complex (16b). The asymmetry implies that the Theme in a simple Motional cannot be oblique. An apparent exception is *fill* (16c), in which Goal also appears as subject. But this is again a complex structure with another Theme colinked in the subject (section 2.1). The verbs in (16d) have Goal subjects but are of the type characterized as "Possessional," which naturally projects Goal as subject:

(16) a. The agents caught the terrorist.
  b. The sponge soaked up the water.
  c. The tub filled with water.
  d. John received a book/learned a lesson.

In Possessional Motional predicates, as opposed to Spatial ones, Goal as a direct argument behaves like Source, projecting as subject rather than object. We may state this asymmetry as in (17):

(17) **The Possessional–Spatial Subject–Object Asymmetry**
  For a predicate expressing a simple Motional eventuality:
  a. if the verb is Spatial a Goal may be object but not subject;
  b. if the verb is Possessional a Goal may be subject but not object.

For example (cf. Jackendoff 1990b, Carter 1988), there is neither a verb like *bereach* with the Spatial (Positional PST) meaning of *reach*[11] but with Goal subject (18a, b), nor a verb like *acceive* with the Possessional (PSS) meaning of *receive* but with Goal object (18c, d). (See section 4.5, Gruber 1996.) *Get to* (19) has meaning similar to *reach*, but only *get to* with oblique Goal, not *reach* with Goal object, can be Possessional in sense:

(18) a. The parcel reached John.
    $$\underline{\Theta \qquad\qquad \text{PST}|\quad \Gamma}$$
  b. *John bereached the parcel.
    $$\underline{\Gamma \qquad \text{PST}|\qquad \Theta}$$
  c. John received the parcel.
    $$\underline{\Gamma \qquad \text{PSS}|\qquad \Theta}$$
  d. *The parcel acceived John.
    $$\underline{\Theta \qquad\qquad \text{PSS}|\quad \Gamma}$$

(19) The farm finally got to/*reached John after much litigation.

2 Complex Thematic Structures

2.1 *Resultative structures and asymmetries*

The resultatives in (5) express complex structures combining elemental thematic functions in a sense of consequence. Colinking between such functions appears to be obligatory. In (5a) the Theme of the precedent Contact function is colinked with the Theme of the consequent Positional function in the subject: Theme;Theme colinking (Θ;Θ). In (5b) the precedent Goal is colinked with the consequent Theme in the object: Goal;Theme colinking (Γ;Θ).

The particular function to which a theta-role belongs is significant for argument projection. Of the numerous logical possibilities for obligatory colinking amongst resultative structures, only five occur, three in addition to (5). One constraint is that the obligatorily colinked role of the consequent function or subevent must be Theme. Various asymmetries also have an effect. A Source–Goal asymmetry like (13) applies to roles of the precedent subevent (precedent roles) in a resultative (20). (20a) allows (5b), similar to (21a). (20b) allows (21b). (21c) and (d) are disallowed:

(20) **The Source–Goal Subject–Object Asymmetry in Resultatives**
When theta-roles are colinked in the object of a simple (non-agentive) resultative, then:
  a. the precedent role expressed in the object can be Goal, but not Source;
  b. the precedent role expressed in the subject can be Source, but not Goal.

(21) a. Water filled the cup (high).
$$\text{STE|} \qquad \Theta \qquad \Gamma$$
$$\overline{\Theta \text{ PST|} \qquad \Gamma}$$
  (Water entered the cup and the cup became filled up high.)
  b. The cup leaked water free.
$$\text{STE|} \qquad \Theta \quad \Gamma$$
$$\overline{\Sigma \text{ PST|} \qquad \Theta}$$
  (Water left the cup and became free.)
  c. *Water emptied the cup.
$$\text{STE|} \qquad \Theta$$
$$\overline{\Theta \text{ PST|} \qquad \Sigma}$$
  (Water left the cup and the cup became empty.)
  d. *The cup filled the water high.
$$\text{STE|} \qquad \Theta \qquad \Gamma$$
$$\overline{\Gamma \text{ PST|} \qquad \Theta}$$
  (Water entered the cup and the cup became filled up high.)

The above exhausts the possibilities amongst the roles Θ, Σ, and Γ for obligatory colinking in the object of simple resultatives. In the subject, besides Θ;Θ colinking (5a), there are Γ;Θ and Σ;Θ colinking (22). This exhibits another Source–Goal asymmetry (23), noted by Talmy (1985). Note that while there are contrasted transitive/intransitive predicates for Goal colinked with Theme (21a, 22a), there is only the intransitive predicate for Source (21c, 22b).

(22)   a.   The cup filled with/*of water.

   Θ   STE|
   Γ   PST| Θ

(Water entered the cup and the cup became full.)

   b.   The cup emptied of/*with water.

   Θ   STE|
   Σ   PST| Θ

(Water left the cup and the cup became empty.)

(23)   **The Source–Goal Oblique Theme Asymmetry**
   In simple (non-agentive) resultative structures, if a precedent role colinked in the subject is:
   a.   Goal, the precedent Theme has instrumental/comitative-like Case (*with*); if
   b.   Source, the precedent Theme has genitive-like Case (*of*).

   This completes possible linkages in non-agentive resultatives. An aspectual asymmetry among these (24) distinguishes colinking in subject or object, illustrated in (25) and (26) respectively. In (25a) with Γ;Θ colinking in the subject, a continuous subevent "logs piling onto the barge" precedes the consequent one, "the barge becoming 'high' with logs." This is impossible with colinking in the object (26a). In contrast, in (26b) with Γ;Θ colinking in the object, a punctual subevent "a stone entering the road" precedes the consequent one "the road becoming blocked," impossible with subject colinking (25b). For Σ;Θ subject colinking, the precedent subevent is relatively continuous (25c), not punctual (25d). For Θ;Θ object colinking, the precedent subevent is relatively punctual (26d), not continuous (26c):

(24)   **The Aspectual Colinking Subject–Object Asymmetry**
   In simple (non-agentive) resultative structures:
   a.   the precedent subevent is multi-staged (an iterated or continuous process) relative to the consequent subevent if colinking is in the subject;
   b.   the precedent subevent is single-staged (punctual) relative to the consequent subevent if colinking is in the object.

(25)   a.   the barge piled high with logs (≈ 22a)
   b.   *the road blocked with a stone
   c.   the bottle drained empty of liquid (≈ 22b)
   d.   *the branch dropped bare of its apple

(26) a. *the logs piled the barge high
 b. a stone blocked the road (≈ 21a)
 c. *the bottle drained the liquid free
 d. the branch dropped its apple free (≈ 21b)

If projected as a direct argument, a role from a precedent subevent becomes subject while a role of the consequent subevent becomes object. The relevant asymmetries may be stated as (27). The precedent role subject condition (27a) is illustrated in the above examples.[12] The subject may express a precedent role that is colinked (5a, 22a, b) or not (5a, 21a, b). But it cannot express an uncolinked consequent role. The thematic structure acceptably expressed in (28a) cannot be expressed with the consequent Source as subject (28b). This is so even though the Source can be expressed this way if the thematic structure is simple (28c). Thus a verb may have alternate projection patterns, such as the Contact predicate CTT in (28d, e); but adding a precedent subpredicate, e.g. <PST>, is acceptable only for the alternate for which this results in obligatory colinking in the subject (28d):

(27) **Precedent–Consequent Theta-role Asymmetries**
 a. **Precedent Role Subject Condition:** The subject must project a theta-role of the most precedent subevent.
 b. **Consequent Role Object Condition:** A direct object must project a theta-role of the most consequent subevent.
 c. **Consequent Role Complement Condition:** A complement argument is projected with respect to its most consequent role.

(28) a. Some branches broke off of the tree.

$$\frac{\Theta \quad \text{CTT}|}{\Theta \quad \text{STE}|} \quad \Sigma$$

 (Some branches broke and fell off the tree.)
 b. *The tree broke off some branches.

$$\frac{\Sigma \quad \text{CTT}|}{\text{STE}|} \quad \Theta$$

 c. The tree dropped/lost some branches.

$$\Sigma \qquad \frac{\text{CTT}|}{} \quad \Theta$$

 d. Water bubbled (up) out of the kettle.

$$\frac{\Theta \quad \text{CTT}|}{(\Theta \quad \text{PST}| \qquad \Gamma)} \quad \Sigma$$

 e. The kettle bubbled water (*up) (* = d).

$$\frac{\Sigma \qquad \text{CTT}| \quad \Theta}{(\text{PST}| \qquad \Theta \qquad \Gamma)}$$

The consequent role object condition (27b) means that in a linking pattern like (22a), the complement role, even though Theme, cannot be expressed as direct object (29a). This is because it is of the precedent subevent. Similarly in an event structure like (5a) the precedent Goal cannot be expressed as object (29b). A consequent subpredicate may be added to an event structure in such a way that an erstwhile object role is no longer most consequent. In that case it ceases to be projectable as object (29c), and is projected obliquely (d). This is the essence of the locative alternation in lexical causatives:

(29)   a.   *The cup filled water.

$$\Theta \quad \text{STE}|$$
$$\overline{\Gamma \ \text{PST}| \qquad \Theta}$$

(* = Water entered the cup and the cup became full.)

   b.   *The stone knocked the pole into the road.[13]

$$\Theta \qquad\qquad \text{PST}| \qquad\qquad\qquad\qquad \Gamma$$
$$\overline{\Theta \qquad\qquad \text{CTT}| \qquad\qquad \Gamma}$$

(* = The stone hit the pole and went into the road.)

   c.   The tub leaked water (*empty).

$$(\Theta \qquad\quad \text{STE}| \qquad\qquad \Gamma)$$
$$\overline{\Sigma \qquad\quad \text{CTT}| \qquad \Theta}$$

   d.   The tub leaked empty of water.

$$\Theta \qquad\quad \text{STE}| \quad \Gamma$$
$$\overline{\Sigma \qquad\quad \text{CTT}| \qquad\qquad\qquad \Theta}$$

The consequent role complement condition (27c) states that oblique complements as well as objects will be projected with respect to their most consequent role. This has been observed by Jackendoff (1990), referring to the least embedded or "dominant" theta-role. It covers such facts as why a colinked precedent Goal in a thematic structure like (5b) cannot be projected semantically (30). That is, in the precedent subevent of (30), "the pole" is a Goal, which in itself can be realized as the complement of "against," as in (5a). In the consequent subevent of (30), however, "the pole" is a Theme, which cannot be so realized. The theta-role of the consequent subevent prevails:

(30)   *The stone knocked against the pole into the road.

$$\text{PST}| \qquad\qquad\quad \Theta \qquad\qquad\qquad \Gamma$$
$$\overline{\Theta \qquad\quad \text{CTT}| \qquad\qquad \Gamma}$$

(* = The stone hit the pole and the pole entered the road.)

2.2   Causative structures and asymmetries

The thematic structure of a lexical causative (31b) differs from that of a resultative (31a). The subject of a causative, not a resultative, is expressible obliquely as a *from*-phrase (31c, d). It is Source in a matrix Causational function (CST), i.e., a Cause, whose Theme is the Causee function or predicate as a whole. The Goal of the Causational function, the Patient, appears in a *do to* paraphrase (31f). It is colinked with the theta-role of the Causee function that is projected as object, Theme in (31b). This follows if the matrix function CAUSE, like the verb *cause*, content-identifies Theme with Goal [:Γ], hence Goal with the Causee function and with the theta-role that raises out of it to object. This role is usually Theme but may be any role (see examples 34b, d). In this way also lexical causatives differ from resultatives, since in the latter the consequent obligatorily colinked role is always Theme:

(31) a. Hail stones broke the window.

STE| Θ

Θ   CTT| Γ   CSQ

(Hail stones struck the window and it broke.)

    b. The force of the wind broke the window.

STE| Θ

Σ   CST|Θ   [:Γ]

(The force of the wind caused the window to break.)

    c. *The window broke from hail stones.

    d. The window broke from the force of the wind.

    e. ?What hail stones did to the window was break it.

    f. What the force of the wind did to the window was break it.

The overall structure of a Causational predicate is that of a simple Motional. The subject–object asymmetry between Agent and Patient (1a/2a, 32) then falls under the generalization (13b) about simple Motional predicates. If projected directly, the Cause/Agent (Source) projects to subject while a theta-role of the Causee (Theme) predicate, identified as Patient, projects to object. Otherwise, falling under the generalization (13a), if the Cause is projected obliquely, a theta-role of the Causee predicate, now the main clause, projects to subject, as in (31d):

(32) **The Agent–Patient Subject–Object Asymmetry**

In an agentive (causative) transitive predicate the Agent (Cause) is projected as subject while the Patient is projected as object.

Common agentive verbs have Cause or Agent colinked in the subject with some theta-role of the Causee predicate. This "incidental" colinking seems to be free with lexical specification, and obviates all projection asymmetries except the Agent–Patient asymmetry itself. Thus, that Spatial Goal cannot be projected to subject can be violated if the subject is also Agent (33a). Violations affecting the object are also rendered acceptable if the verb is agentive, e.g. the object of a simple Motional transitive can be a Source (33b, cf. 15a):

(33) a. The agents caught the terrorist.

Γ   PST| Θ

Σ   CST|Θ   [:Γ]

   b. The terrorist escaped the prison cell

$$\frac{\Theta \quad \text{PST}| \qquad\qquad \Sigma}{\Sigma \quad \text{CST}|\Theta \qquad\qquad [:\Gamma]}$$

/the prison cell was escaped by the terrorist.

The lexical causative of a simple Motional predicate exhibits an oblique Theme alternation. Either the Theme is object with oblique Goal or Source (34a, c), or Goal or Source is object with oblique Theme (34b, d). These correspond to semantic or direct Goal/Source in the lexically related non-causative. The Case of the oblique Theme depends on whether Goal or Source is direct, as in the resultative oblique Theme asymmetry (23). In contrast, the lexical causative of a Locational predicate shows no alternation. The Location is semantic in the causative, regardless of whether semantic (34e) or direct (34f) in the related non-causative. The asymmetries are summarized in (35) and (36):

(34) a. John hit the stone against the wall.

$$\frac{\text{CTT}| \quad \Theta \qquad\qquad \Gamma}{\Sigma \quad \text{CST}|\Theta \quad [:\Gamma]}$$

(cf. The stone hit against the wall.)

   b. John hit the wall with the stone.

$$\frac{\text{CTT}| \quad \Gamma \qquad\qquad \Theta}{\Sigma \quad \text{CST}|\Theta \, [:\Gamma]}$$

(cf. The stone hit the wall.)

   c. John tapped some wine from a barrel.

$$\frac{\text{CTT}\,| \qquad \Theta \qquad\qquad \Sigma}{\Sigma \qquad \text{CST}|\Theta \qquad [:\Gamma]}$$

(cf. Water dripped from the bottle.)

   d. John tapped a barrel of some wine.

$$\frac{\text{CTT}\,| \qquad \Sigma \qquad\qquad \Theta}{\Sigma \qquad \text{CST}|\Theta \qquad [:\Gamma]}$$

(cf. The bottle dripped some water.)

   e. John laid the book on the table.

$$\frac{\text{PST}| \qquad \Theta \qquad\qquad \Lambda}{\Sigma \quad \text{CST}|\Theta \qquad [:\Gamma]}$$

(cf. The book lay on the table.)

   e' *John laid the table with the book.

   f. John included his name in the list.

$$\frac{| \qquad\quad \Theta \qquad\qquad \Lambda}{\Sigma \qquad \text{CST}|\Theta \qquad [:\Gamma]}$$

(cf. The list included his name.)

   f' *John included the list with his name.

(35) **The Locational–Motional Lexical Causative Asymmetry**
     For the lexical causative of a transitive verb expressing a simple thematic function:

a. if Locational, the Location is oblique (semantic), while the Theme is object;

b. if Motional, the Goal or Source is object, while the Theme is oblique.

(36) **The Source–Goal Oblique Theme Asymmetry in Lexical Causatives**
For the lexical causative of a simple transitive Motional, if the role projected directly is:
a. Goal (erstwhile object), the Theme has instrumental/comitative-like Case (*with*); if
b. Source (erstwhile subject), the Theme has genitive-like Case (*of*).

The causative Motional alternates (34a, b) and (34c, d) mean the same except for the object role colinked with Patient. The so-called locative alternation (37) exhibits the further difference that the object role is colinked with an "affected Theme." This is the Theme in a consequent function expressing a change of state, often completeness. The structure is that of the lexical causative of a resultative:

(37) a. John loaded the bricks onto the truck.

$$\begin{array}{llll} \text{STE}| & \Theta & & \\ \text{PST}| & \Theta & \Gamma & \\ \Sigma \quad \text{CST}|\Theta & [:\Gamma] & & \end{array}$$

b. John loaded the truck with bricks.

$$\begin{array}{llll} \text{STE}| \;[\Gamma] & \Theta & & \\ \text{PST}| & \Gamma & \Theta & \\ \Sigma \quad \text{CST}|\Theta & [:\Gamma] & & \end{array}$$

The need for a precedent Theme to appear obliquely in (37b) reflects the operation of the consequent role object condition (27b) applied to causatives. In this respect the "dative alternation" (38a, b) is similar to the causative Motional alternation (34a, b) rather than the locative alternation (37). In the former two, (38b) the "double object construction" and (34b), the Goal of the Causee function is projected directly as object. The double object construction, restricted to Possessionals in English, differs only in that the Theme of this function is also projected directly. (38c, d) also demonstrate the consequent role object condition: an erstwhile second object Theme $\Theta(\text{PSS})$ must be projected obliquely if a consequent function is added, creating a resultative causative structure:

(38) a. John fed rice to the baby.

$$\begin{array}{ll} \text{PSS}| \;\; \Theta & \Gamma \\ \Sigma \;\; \text{CST}|\Theta \;\; [:\Gamma] & \end{array}$$

b. John fed the baby rice.

$$\begin{array}{ll} \text{PSS}| \;\; \Gamma & \Theta \\ \Sigma \;\; \text{CST}|\Theta \;\; [:\Gamma] & \end{array}$$

   c.   John fed the baby up with rice.

       STE| Θ   Γ

       PSS| Γ   Θ

     Σ CST|Θ   [:Γ]

   d. *John fed the baby rice up.

       STE| Θ   Γ

       PSS| Γ   Θ

     Σ CST|Θ   [:Γ]

2.3   Aspect and affectedness

Tenny (1989, 1994) proposes the relevance of aspect in argument projection, associating "affectedness" with direct objects. But aspect and thematic relations are inseparable facets of event structure. In particular, affectedness, or the measuring out of an event, is a property of the Theme of the most consequent function. This reflects the significance of the Theme as the independent variable in a thematic relation, as discussed in 1.3. The extent of its involvement in a mapping is a measure of the completeness of the event itself. The extent of the involvement of the Locational role, however, as the dependent variable is irrelevant in measuring out the event.

Theme and Locational role are distinguished as independent and dependent variables by event-measuring adverbs like *completely, fully, half(way)*. These measure the extent the eventuality is effected or the Theme is involved, but not how much the Locational role is. In (39a, b) *completely* applied to the eventuality means "all the way into the box," making reference to the Locational role. Applied to Theme it means "the whole [Theme]," i.e., "the whole ball." But it does not apply specifically to the denotation of the Locational role, meaning "the whole (inside of the) box:"

(39) a. The ball lies completely in the box.   } (= the whole ball/

        (≈ 4a, b)   *box/all the way into

    b. The box completely contains the ball. the box)

    c. The train got to the station fully.   } (= the whole train/

        (≈ 4c, e)   *station/all the way

    d. The train reached the station fully.   to the station)

These observations are consistent with Tenny's association of a Theme object with an aspectual role that measures out the event, while a Goal, a Locational role, expresses its terminus. They hold, however, with reference to thematic roles independent of grammatical form. In (39a, b), *completely* applied to Theme "the ball" means "the whole ball," whether subject or object; with reference to Location "the box" it means "all the way into the box," whether subject or oblique. Similarly, in a simple Motional predicate (39c, d), *fully* applied to

Theme means "the whole train," while with reference to Goal it means "all the way to the station," whether object or oblique.[14] In the lexical causative of a simple Motional (40a, b), the interpretations of *completely* are also the same whether with reference to a direct or oblique argument: for Theme it is "the whole stamp;" for Goal it is "all the way against the pad," not "the whole pad." Interpretations of measure adverbs do appear to vary with grammatical form for the causative of a resultative (40c, d), however. This is the locative alternation. Here it is consistently the object to which the adverb applies, since this represents the colinked Theme of the most consequent subevent in a complex thematic structure. Similarly the adverb does not apply to any of the oblique arguments. In particular it does not apply to the oblique Theme in (40d) because this role is of a precedent subevent:

(40) a. Press the stamp against the pad completely.   (= the whole stamp/
          (≈ 34a, b)   *pad/all the way
      b. Press the pad with the stamp completely.   against the pad)
      c. Spray the paint onto the wall completely.   (= all the paint/*the
          (≈ 37a, b)   whole wall)
      d. Spray the wall (red) with the paint   (= the whole wall/
          completely.   *all the paint)

It is thus principally resultative structures with consequent Theme objects to which the association of affectedness and direct objects pertains. In the causative of a simple Motional an object may not be affected in the sense that it measures out the event, while an oblique may be affected in this sense. Therefore there is no separate module that assigns aspectual properties to an object. Rather the most consequent Theme has these properties.

Patient colinking is associated with affectedness because it is obligatory for the object of a causative or agentive verb. However, it is a distinct phenomenon, independent of the affectedness of a Theme object. Thus, while the object in the locative alternation will be both affected and a Patient (41a), a Goal object of a Motional causative will be a Patient, but not affected (41b). Finally, non-causative Motionals and resultatives provide examples of direct objects that are affected, being the most consequent Theme, but are not Patients (41c), or are neither Patients nor affected (41d):

(41) a. What John did to the wall (completely) was   (= the whole wall)
          spray it. (≈ 37b)
      b. What John did to the wall (completely) was   (* = the whole wall)
          hit it. (≈ 34b)
      c. *What the water did to the bottle   (= the whole bottle)
          (completely) was fill it. (≈ 21a)
      d. *What the stone did to the wall (completely) (* = the whole wall)
          was hit it. (≈ 4e)

3   Grain and the Locus of Thematic Representation

The projection asymmetries are couched in an elaborate system of thematic structure. Does this structure map into a correspondingly elaborate initial representation in grammatical syntax, or is the correspondence relatively coarse grained with a comparatively impoverished initial syntax? There are two ways for the latter to be possible. One way is that the mapping is of prototypical theta-roles or "proto-roles": theta-roles are grouped in "fuzzy" sets of similar roles (Dowty 1991) that map to particular syntactic positions. The other way is that linking is relative: theta-roles are prioritized, perhaps in a hierarchy, to be expressed in more prominent syntactic positions relative to others. The two parameters of correspondence – discrete or prototypical theta-roles, relative (including hierarchical) or absolute mapping – provide for at least three types of linking theory:

	Relative/Discrete	*Absolute/Prototypical*	*Absolute/Discrete*
Initial syntactic form	Arguments	Impoverished	Elaborated
Computation	Semantic projection	Syntactic projection	Syntactic projection

A third parameter is the degree of computation between initial syntactic level, at which theta-roles directly correspond, and a surface (or interface) level where grammatical arguments appear. However, this follows from relative or absolute correspondence. The former (Foley and Van Valin 1984, Bresnan and Kanerva 1989, Grimshaw 1990, Jackendoff 1972, 1990b) allows semantic projection, i.e., less syntactic computation. There is therefore comparatively direct correspondence between theta-roles and grammatical arguments. The latter (Baker 1988, 1997b, Hale and Keyser 1993) allows an impoverished initial structure. But this requires syntactic argument projection, i.e., more syntactic computation, because theta-roles simply do not have unique surface argument positions. For example, by the Unaccusative Hypothesis (Perlmutter 1978), the absolute position of Theme must be an initial one, since its surface position differs in intransitives and transitives. Both absolute and discrete correspondence (Gruber 1994, 1997, Gruber and Collins 1997), requires fine-grained linking and elaborated initial structure. Here syntactic computation is needed to derive the less elaborate grammatical argument structure.

The questions then are whether linking can be relative, or can be prototypical. If not, an impoverished initial syntactic structure, such as a "VP-shell" (42), is not representationally adequate: a multiplicity of discrete roles all need unique positions. Suppose prototypically distinctive theta-roles α, β, γ (say, Agent,

Patient/Theme, Goal/Location) correspond to positions in the shell. This would be inadequate, i.e., structural elaboration would be necessary, if it is shown that (i) three such sets are not sufficient to describe linking regularities; and (ii) any such sets may not correspond relativistically (i.e., as a hierarchy):

(42)

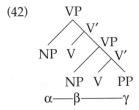

3.1   Discrete roles

The projection asymmetries show that thematic relations must be represented in syntax discretely rather than prototypically. They place theta-roles in the VP-shell positions α, β, γ of (42) as in (43). Each position contains a variety of theta-roles that is inconsistent as a prototype. For example, both α and β contain both Themes and Locational roles. Thus contrary to what is often supposed, Locational roles cannot be said to occupy the same initial position γ as part of the same protorole, since Themes also appear there. On the other hand asymmetries referring to these roles, particularly Source and Goal (13, 20, 23), show that their discreteness is significant for syntax:

(43)   a.   α——β———γ   b.   α———β——γ   c.   α———β——γ
            Θ———°Λ   Λ———Θ   Agt——Θ
            Θ———°Γ   Θ———Γ   Agt——Γ———°Θ
            Θ———°Σ   Σ———Θ   Agt——Σ———°Θ
            Θ———°Θ̲   Γ(pss)–Θ̲   Agt——Γ(pss)—Θ̲
                                Θ̲———Θ

   ° = oblique   Θ̲ = precedent Theme   Γ(pss) = Possessional Goal

While proto-role groupings are not consistent with the projection asymmetries, discrete theta-roles can nearly be accommodated in a VP-shell under a relativized mapping. This is possible for the inner subject and object positions in terms of generalized relative precedence in event structure, defined abstractly. That is, the role in α is precedent to that in β: precedent Theme relative to consequent Theme, Source to Theme, Theme to Goal, Location as ground to Theme (43b), and Agent as Source to Patient colinked with any role (43c). Precedence fails for Possessional (pss) Goal[15] at α in non-agentives (43b), and at β in double object constructions (43c).

Relative precedence does not qualify as a way to define a prototype. Sometimes, members of proto-roles are ranked as "better examples" to prioritize them as arguments. This in essence acknowledges the necessity for discrete roles. For example, Instrument might be part of the same proto-role as Agent, a proto-agent, and so prioritized for subject before (consequent) Theme. But Agent, which becomes subject before Instrument, must be regarded as a better proto-agent. This is the same as saying Agent and Instrument are discrete roles in a hierarchy of agentivity.[16]

3.2　Absolute correspondence and properties of initial positions

Absolute correspondence between theta-roles and syntactic positions, as opposed to relative correspondence, is not directly motivated by projection asymmetries. Traditionally, distinctions in syntactic behavior between un-accusative and unergative intransitives (see Levin and Rappaport 1995) argue against relative correspondence. A single initial syntactic position for prioritized theta-roles cannot explain these differences. They may, however, be attribut-able to conceptual structures apart from grammatical syntax (as in Jackendoff 1990b). A classic example is *ne*-cliticization out of quantified nominals in Ital-ian. It is allowed only for objects and postverbal unaccusative subjects (Belletti 1988, Belletti and Rizzi 1981). This suggests these arguments are initially in the same position and lower than subjects of transitives or unergatives. Their theta-roles, Patient/Theme and Agent respectively, then correspond to unique positions before movement. But the differences could also be attributed to configurations of conceptual structure related to syntax by correspondence rules.[17] Moreover, the unaccusative/unergative distinction motivates absolute correspondence only for prototypical Agent and Patient/Theme.

Direct and unequivocal evidence for multiple discrete theta-roles comes from properties attributable to constant initial positions. In particular, Themes exhibit properties reflecting an initial innermost complement position, while Locational roles show they are determined in an innermost specifier.[18] Clausal arguments of verbs which allow raising to subject or exceptional Case-marking (raising to object) seem to be Themes, while verbs with clausal argu-ments that are Locational roles do not (44). This reflects an initial complement position for Theme, from which raising is possible, and an initial specifier position for Locational roles, out of which raising is not:

(44)　a.　John took Bill [t to be a fool].

　　　$\underline{Γ/Λ \quad | \quad Θ}$

　　　/ . . . *accept, understand, perceive; hold, believe*

　　b.　*John concluded Bill [t to be a fool].

　　　$\underline{Θ \quad | \quad Γ}$

　　　/ . . . *see, realize, notice*

Depictive predicates consistently refer to the most consequent Theme rather than, say, a direct object. This is so, for example, in both forms of the dative alternation (45a, b) (Bowers 1993a, Hale and Keyser 1997), as well as for the alternate forms of the Motional causative (45c, d). However, in the resultat-ive causative (e) only the consequent Theme object can be referred to by the depictive. These facts indicate a constant initial position for the Theme. Indeed, given that the initial position of the Theme is a complement, its first move will be to the immediately higher functional specifier position accessible only to Theme. Such a position must in fact be involved in colinking, hence plausibly a position identified with the subject of the depictive predicate (see Section 4.2):

(45)   a.   Give the bottle to the baby (full/*awake).
      b.   Give the baby the bottle (full/*awake).
      c.   Rub the cloth on the baby (torn/*asleep).
      d.   Rub the baby with the cloth (torn/*asleep).
      e.   Dry the baby with the cloth (asleep/*torn).

The order of nouns in noun–verb compounds must similarly depend only on initial syntactic position. Noun-to-verb incorporation is an alternative to argument projection by XP-movement (Baker 1988).[19] Nouns therefore incorporate from positions from which they have not moved, following the order of initial thematic composition (Pesetsky 1995). Consider N-N-V gerund compounds of causatives. For Locational causatives Theme becomes object and the compound order is Λ-Θ-V (46a, c), not Θ-Λ-V (46b, d). This is so whether corresponding to non-causatives with semantically (46a, b) or structurally (46c, d) projected (Case-marked) Location. Compound order here thus correlates with both projected and initial position. In respect of the latter, Location, appearing farther from the verb, is incorporated after the Theme, implying initial specifier and complement positions respectively:

(46)   a.   [garden [radish growing]]   growing radishes in the garden
      b.   *[radish [garden growing]]   (<radishes grew in the garden)
      c.   [salad [radish including]]   including radishes in the salad
      d.   *[radish [salad including]]   (<the salad included radishes)

For Motional causatives, if Goal or Source is projected semantically (47a, b), the compound order has the Locational role first, as for Locational causatives, i.e., Γ-Θ-V or Σ-Θ-V. This again reflects Locational role and Theme in initial specifier–complement relation. However, if Goal is projected structurally as object (47c), either order is possible in the compound Γ-Θ-V or Θ-Γ-V, while if Source is projected as object (47d, e), we have only the order Σ-Θ-V. Strikingly, even for a verb that has only Source object and oblique Theme (47e), it is Theme that first incorporates in the compound. The implication is that in initial syntactic structure a Motional predicate has two colinked Themes, one in construction with Goal and one with Source. Goal is relative specifier to one and complement to the other, hence either order appears, while Source is relative specifier to both, hence always farthest from the verb:[20]

(47)   a.   [fountain [penny throwing]]   (throwing pennies into fountains)
         *[penny [fountain throwing]]   (*throwing fountains with pennies)
      b.   [airplane [missile dropping]]   (dropping missiles from airplanes)
         *[missile [airplane dropping]]   (*dropping airplanes of missiles)

   c. [fence [stick hitting]]   (hitting sticks against fences)
       [stick [fence hitting]]   (hitting fences with sticks)
   d. [tub [water leaking]]   (leaking some water from tubs)
       *[water [tub leaking]]   (leaking tubs of some water)
   e. [visitor [car robbing]]   (*robbing cars from visitors)
       *[car [visitor robbing]]   (robbing visitors of cars)

The variation in (47) implies a specifier–complement relation between Source and Goal as well. Thus Source appears before Goal in a compound, regardless of how projected. With oblique Source and Goal the pattern is only Σ–Γ–Θ–V (48a–c). With Goal object (48d–f) we also obtain Σ–Θ–Γ–V. But even if Source is object (48g–i) it cannot be nearer the verb than Goal:

(48) a. roof ground ladder lowering   (lowering the ladder from
      b. *roof ladder ground lowering   the roof to the ground)
      c. *ground roof ladder lowering
      d. bottle wall paint squirting   (squirt the wall with paint
      e. bottle paint wall squirting   from a bottle)
      f. *wall bottle paint squirting
      g. tub floor water leaking   (leaking tubs of water onto
      h. *floor water tub leaking   the floor)
      i. *water floor tub leaking

The variable behavior of Goal in Spatial Motional causatives (47c) contrasts with its behavior in Possessional Motional causatives, with dative shift or double object construction alternants. Here it again behaves like Source (cf. 49) always incorporating after Theme. It is therefore configurationally distinct, always in relative specifier to the Theme that projects (Gruber 1996):

(49) a. [student [book lending]]   (lending books to students)
          *[book [student lending]]   (lending students books)
      b. traveler accommodation denying   (*denying accommodation to
                                             a traveler)
          *accommodation traveler denying   (denying a traveler
                                             accommodation)

Motional causatives with Goal or Source object (47c, d) also contrast with resultative causatives where these roles are colinked with a consequent Theme object (50a, b). This Theme incorporates first yielding Θ–Θ–V, hence initially relative complement to the precedent Theme:

(50) a. *[tub [water filling]]   (*filling water into the tub)
          [water [tub filling]]   (filling the tub with water)
      b. *[balloon [helium deflating]]   (*deflating helium from the balloon)
          [helium [balloon deflating]]   (deflating the balloon of (*some)
                                             helium)

Finally, in a causative/agentive, since Cause/Agent is a Source, it is initially in a specifier relative to the Causee subpredicate (Theme) and the role that projects to object out of it. Hence the compound order would be Agent–(oblique)–object–V:

(51) a. [hunter [deer shooting]]   (shooting deer by hunters)
          *[deer [hunter shooting]]
      b. nurse oxygen respirator filling   (filling respirators with oxygen
          *respirator nurse oxygen filling   by nurses)

The specifier–complement relations implied in the above patterns support distinct positions for particular theta-roles at an initial syntactic level. Location, or Locational role, is the specifier of a thematic phrase V, while Theme is its complement (52a). Source and Goal are Locational roles in Locational subpredicates: these are combined as specifier and complement, respectively, of an asymmetric sequential conjunction Cj (52b), forming a Motional predicate. Iteration of this combinatorial process between precedent and consequent Motional subpredicates produces a resultative (52c). A causative/agentive verb (52d) consists of a matrix Motional predicate whose Source is Cause/Agent (projected as subject), whose Goal is Patient (colinked with object), and whose Theme is the Causee predicate | V | (out of which an element raises to object):

(52) a.   b.

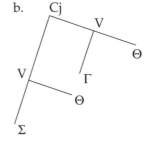

c.

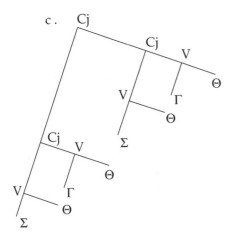

d.

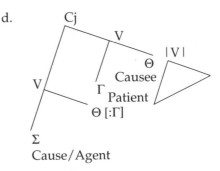

3.3   *Syntactic projection and the epiphenomenality of hierarchies*

If theta-roles are discretely determined in absolute initial syntactic configurations, the latter constitutes thematic signification itself. In fact it shows an iconicity of generalized relative precedence. Argument projection would then be entirely by syntactic computation. In fact it shows characteristics of movement. Theta-roles not always expressed by the same arguments mean dislocated positions for the latter. In particular, subject–object asymmetries distinguish movement from initial specifier and complement positions. The primary case of Agent and Patient/Theme is repeated between Location and Theme, Source and Theme, Theme and Goal, and precedent and consequent Theme. The same distinction is shown in N-N-V compound order.

To illustrate, the Agent α and the role β colinked with Patient, e.g. Theme of the Causee subpredicate (53), are initially in relative specifier–complement positions (54). This accords with the Internal Subject (Kuroda 1988) and Unaccusative Hypothesis (Perlmutter 1978). Optimal movements to functional positions result in Agent projected as subject at F_1, and Patient/Theme as object at F_2. A similar account can be given for projection asymmetries involving the other pairs of roles. (52) provides the required relative specifier–complement positions for them:

(53) **Theta-role subject–object**
     asymmetries

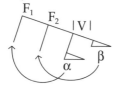

	α	β
	Agent	Patient/Theme
	Location	Theme
	Source	Theme
	Theme	Goal
	Precedent Theme	Consequent Theme

(54) α is *relative specifier/complement* to β, iff in the minimal maximal projection XP containing both α and β, the specifier/complement of XP is or contains α but not β.

Obligatory colinking also shows movement behavior. In a causative/agentive, the role colinked with Patient is whatever raises to object from the Causee. This follows if colinking entails movement into functional positions locally above each combined subpredicate. Moreover, the higher the combinatorial level, the further these positions from basic ones, hence the more diverse the theta-roles reaching them. At the lowest level, combining Locational subpredicates into a Motional, the colinked roles are both Theme. Higher, combining Motionals into a resultative, the precedent role is free.

As seen, theta-role hierarchies are inadequate merely as a sequence of names. Also theta-roles are defined in a complex structure, with many tokens of the same type. Therefore a relative basis to hierarchic principles is preferable,

such as the relative embedding of conceptual arguments in event structure
(Jackendoff 1990b). Indeed, relative specifier–complement positions form a kind
of relative embeddedness, and projection asymmetries constitute hierarchical
correspondences under a generalized notion of precedence. Therefore syntactic
argument projection by movement from these positions renders hierarchies
epiphenomenal.

Syntactic projection also accounts for what hierarchies cannot. The Source–
Goal subject–object asymmetry in resultatives (20), the oblique Theme (23), and
aspectual colinking asymmetry (24) all involve precedent colinked roles. However, hierarchies can refer only to the single role of each grammatical argument
by which it is projected, namely its most consequent (or "dominant") role.

In a relative hierarchy the least embedded role in event structure is preferentially projected. But this works differently for subject and object. It also
depends on whether a precedent subevent in a resultative is represented as a
conceptual argument, e.g. a *by*-phrase, or as the specifier of a sequential conjunction. If the former (as in Jackendoff 1990b) the precedent Theme is more
embedded and is projected as object, while the consequent Theme is projected
as subject, as in (55a). The opposite, however, occurs (55b). Saying that the
precedent Theme is Actor and therefore subject, since Actor is least embedded,
begs the question: why *must* the precedent Theme be Actor?

(55) a.   *The cup knocked the stone apart.

$$\Theta \quad \text{STE}| \qquad \qquad \Gamma$$
$$\Gamma \quad \text{CTT}| \qquad \qquad \Theta$$

   b.   The stone knocked the cup apart.

$$\text{STE}| \qquad \Theta \quad \Gamma$$
$$\Theta \quad \text{CTT}| \qquad \Gamma$$

(56) a.   . . . knock the cup apart with the stone

$$\text{STE}| \qquad \Theta \quad \Gamma$$
$$\text{CTT}| \qquad \Gamma \qquad \qquad \Theta$$

   b.   *. . . knock the stone apart with the cup

$$\text{STE}| \qquad \qquad \Gamma \qquad \Theta$$
$$\text{CTT}| \qquad \Theta \qquad \qquad \Gamma$$

In contrast, this conception of representation and hierarchy works for object
projection in resultative causatives. Here the least embedded Theme becomes
object and the more embedded Theme is oblique (56a), but not the opposite
(56b). Stipulating that the consequent Theme is Patient, and therefore object,
or that the precedent Theme is an adjunct to which Patient colinking cannot
apply, again begs the question: why should the consequent Theme be Patient
and the precedent Theme adjunct? Finally, on the hypothesis that the precedent event is specifier of sequential conjunction, its Theme is least embedded,
and the opposite predictions pertain; we correctly predict the paradigm for the
resultative subject (55), but incorrectly for the causative object (56).

The problem is linking via a single hierarchy for subject and object. The asymmetry is indicative of movement. The subject is projected from the less embedded position and the object from the more embedded. On the hypothesis that the representation of resultatives is by sequential conjunction rather than conceptual arguments or adjuncts, the precedent event is less embedded as specifier. Its Theme is therefore projected as subject, not as object (55a, b). The consequent event is more embedded as complement, and its Theme is projected as object, not as subject (56a, b).

4   Derivations by Syntactic Projection

We outline here feasible means of syntactic computation to derive projection asymmetries (Gruber 1994, 1996, 1997, Gruber and Collins 1997). Configurational determination of Case in positions dislocated from thematic positions is essential.

4.1   *Locational predicates*

The two structural Case positions in (53) explain the Location–Theme asymmetry for transitive predicates (10a). For intransitives (10b), however, ad-hoc stipulation of semantic Case in thematic position for Location but not Theme would be required. A solution is to generalize semantic Case to structural Case, assigning it in a distinct dislocated position accessible only to a specific role, hence theta-related. For Location this is a specifier position A (57a), representing the grammatical-argument/Case-licensing property (cf. Agr) of the thematic head. If Location and Theme are initial specifier and complement respectively, A is above a specifier position T,[21] representing a property (topicality, dislocation) of the thematic head, to which Theme must first move:[22]

(57)   a.   b.   **Locational predicate**

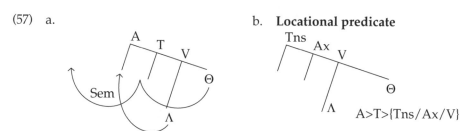

$$A > T > \{Tns / Ax / V\}$$

Properties A and T produce functional extensions of each of three distinct substantives (57b), hence three potential Case/argument positions in Locational predicates. The highest, Tense (Tns), assigns nominative, projecting subject. The lowest, the thematic head (V), assigns semantic Case. An intermediate auxiliary (Ax), perhaps aspectual, assigns accusative, projecting object.[23] V, unlike Tns and Ax, is "thematic," with a lexical initial specifier (long branch), the Location Λ.

Syntactic derivations demonstrating the Location–Theme subject–object asymmetry (10) are shown in (58). Elements in theta-role positions are attracted by functional positions T or A to achieve Case/argumenthood. They move, keeping to minimal links, in a "leap-frogging" fashion (Chomsky 1993, 1995b). The transitive form (58a) is distinguished from the intransitive (58b) by whether Location is projected "structurally," optimally to the highest A position, or "semantically" to the lowest. The A position is facultatively present to Case license a nominal that cannot be attracted higher. Thus Theme cannot be projected as accusative in the extension of Ax in (58b):

(58)   a.   The box contains the ball.

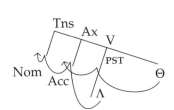

b.   The ball lies in the box.

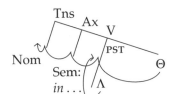

Movements to derive intransitive (59a) and transitive (59b) predicates ruled out by the Location–Theme asymmetry violate the minimal like condition. Theme cannot achieve Case in the semantic position (59a) since to do so either it must cross two specifier positions or the Location must. Similarly for Location to achieve accusative Case (59b) either it or Theme must cross two positions:

(59)   a.   *Λ | °Θ

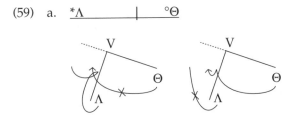

b.   *Θ | Λ

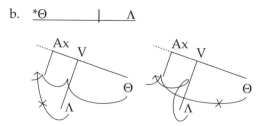

4.2   Motional predicates

We assume substantive and functional categories uniformly extend thematic ones (Cj, V) in a Motional predicate (52b), except for Tns extending the predicate as a whole. The intransitive form with semantically projected Source and Goal is derived in (60). Suppose, consistent with the discussion in section 3.3, elements that move into T extensions of thematic categories under Cj are colinked. Only Theme moves into T extending V, so only Themes may be colinked in a Motional predicate. The two tokens form a single argument (Chain), here moving across the board uniformly through Ax to subject:

(60)   The ball rolled from the bush to the tree.

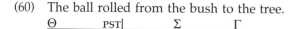

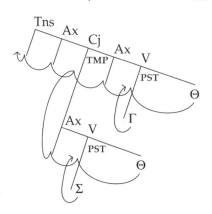

(61) demonstrates the Source–Goal subject–object asymmetry for transitives (13b, c). Either Source or Goal is projected structurally. Only one colinked Theme token can, or needs to, move to a Case position. If Source moves to subject, Theme moves from the complement of Cj to object (61a). If Goal moves to object, Theme moves from the specifier of Cj to subject (61b). The opposite possibilities are impossible. The movement of Source in (61a) into the A extension of matrix Ax as object violates the minimal link condition. Two specifier positions are crossed: the T extensions of matrix Ax and Cj occupied by Theme moving to subject. Similarly Theme in (61b) cannot move to object while Goal moves to subject without violating minimality:

(61)   a.   The tree dropped fruit to the ground.
             Σ   CTT| Θ   Γ

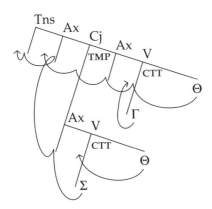

       b.   Fruit hit the ground from the tree.
            Θ CTT| Γ   Σ

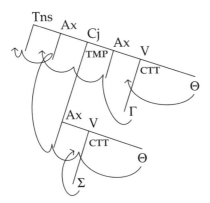

4.3   *Resultative predicates*

The resultative structure (52c) is uniformly extended as in (62), deriving an
intransitive with Sources and Goals projected semantically. Themes are colinked
at each combinatory level and projected across the board to subject. Colinking
under Cj-csq is in the T extensions of Cj-TMP:

(62)   The cup smashed apart against the stone.

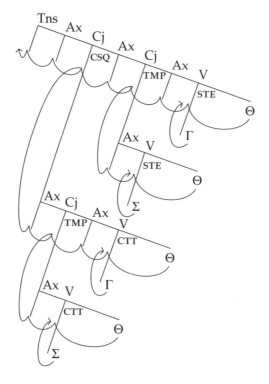

A variety of roles can move into the precedent T-Cj-TMP colinking position, permitting the four remaining resultative derivations. The Source–Goal subject–object asymmetry in resultatives (20) is exhibited by (63a, b), omitting details of consequent Motional subpredicates. These derivations again differ in whether Goal or Source, here of the precedent Motional subpredicate, is projected structurally. While Goal then moves into the position of colinking with consequent Theme object (63a), Source moves uncolinked to subject with precedent Theme colinked with object (63b). Demonstrating the asymmetry, the precedent Goal in (63a) cannot move to subject with Themes colinked in object, since it would cross both specifier of Cj and its T extension bearing the colinked Theme. In (63b) precedent Theme cannot move to subject with precedent Source colinked:

(63)   a.   The stone smashed the cup apart.
            Water filled the cup (up).

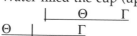

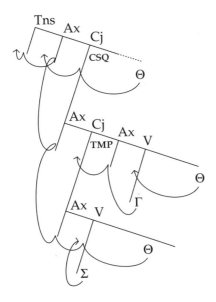

b. The tank leaked the fluid free.

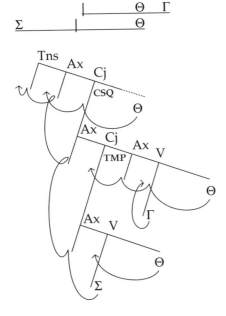

The remaining two possible resultative forms exhibit the Source–Goal oblique Theme asymmetry (23). As shown in (64), Goal and Source are again projected structurally. Unlike (63), however, they move both into the position of colinking with the consequent Theme and through Ax to subject. This strands the precedent Themes in lower positions specific for oblique projection as a *with* or *of* phrase respectively, deriving the asymmetry.[24] The aspectual colinking asymmetry (24) also follows if Ax has an aspectual property satisfied by movement of the colinked element into it:

(64)   a.   The tank filled with petrol out of the pump.

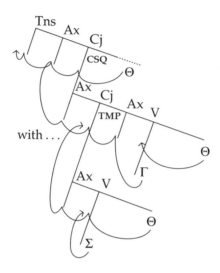

   b.   The cup emptied of water onto the ground.

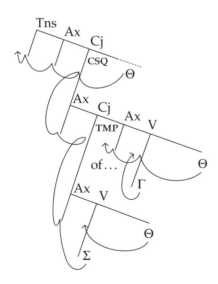

The precedent role subject condition (27a) requiring the subject to project a theta-role of the most precedent subpredicate is demonstrated by the imposs-ibility of (65a) (= 28b). An element out of a consequent subpredicate, here Source, cannot be projected to subject above an element out of a precedent subpredicate, here Theme, without violating the minimal link condition. The consequent role object condition (27b), that an object must project a theta-role of the most consequent subpredicate, is violated in the same way (65b) (= 29a):

(65) a.   *The tree broke off some branches.
            Σ   CTT| Θ
                 STE| Θ

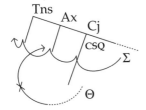

      b.   *The cup filled water.
            Θ STE|
            Γ PST| Θ

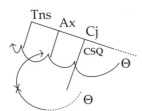

The consequent role complement condition (27c) that a complement projects with respect to its most consequent theta-role is shown by (66) (= 30), impos-sible with the indicated meaning. Given Goal;Theme colinking, projection with respect to Goal means Case in the semantic position (Sem). But once Case-marked nothing drives it to the higher colinking position T-Cj-TMP:

(66)   *The stone knocked against the pole into the road.

$$\underline{\quad\text{PST}|\qquad\qquad\qquad\Theta\qquad\qquad\qquad\Gamma\qquad}$$
$$\Theta\qquad\text{CTT}|\qquad\qquad\qquad\Gamma$$

(* = The stone hit the pole and the pole entered the road.)

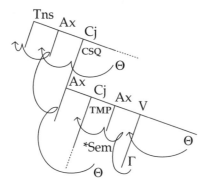

4.4   *Causative predicates*

(67) shows the derivation of a lexical causative, involving uniform extension of (52d). The Agent–Patient asymmetry (32) is demonstrated, the overall scheme of the derivation conforming to the Source–Goal subject–object asymmetry (13b, 61a). The matrix causative is a Motional predicate in which the Source, i.e., Cause or Agent, is projected to subject, while a role ρ raising out of its Theme, the Causee subpredicate | V |, is projected to object. ρ passes through the colinking position T-V where it is colinked with the other Theme of the Motional Causational predicate. But Theme is content identified with Goal, i.e., Patient. Thus the Patient role is colinked with the object:

(67)

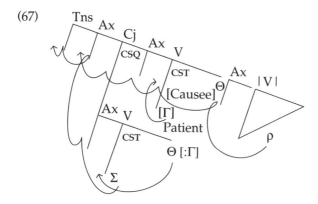

The derivation of agentive verbs with incidental colinking in the subject is similar. The obviation of non-causative asymmetries follows. (See the discussion of (33).) Assuming that the element colinked with Agent does not actually move to subject position, it can be any role. So also the element that moves to object (colinked with Patient) can be any role, since it does not compete in movement with the element colinked with Agent.

In lexical causatives of Locationals the meager structure |V|=V means the oblique position in which erstwhile subject or object is projected is that of semantic Case. Even if Location is specified for structural projection, it is blocked by movement of the Theme and forced for Case in the extension of V, a semantic Case position. The difference between transitive and intransitive is thereby neutralized. Transitive *include* (68b) has the same oblique-Location causative form as intransitive *lay* (68a), hence part (a) of the Locational–Motional lexical causative asymmetry (35):

(68) a. John lay the ball in the box.

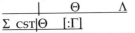

(John caused [the ball lay in the box].)

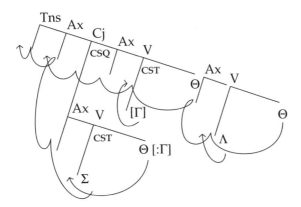

b. John included her name in the list.

$$\overline{\phantom{\Sigma\ \ \text{CST}|\Theta}\underset{\Sigma\ \ \text{CST}|\Theta}{}\overset{\mid\ \ \ \ \ \ \Theta\ \ \ \ \ \ \ \Lambda}{}[:\Gamma]}$$

(John caused [the list include her name].)

In causatives of Motional intransitives the Theme becomes object (69a). For transitives Theme is projected obliquely, whether erstwhile subject with Goal object (69b), or object with Source subject (69c), again a kind of neutralization. (69) thus shows part (b) of the Locational–Motional lexical causative asymmetry (35) and the oblique Theme asymmetry in lexical causatives (36):

(69) a. John rolled the ball from the tree to the bush.

$$\overline{\phantom{\Sigma\ \ \ \text{CST}|\Theta}\overset{\mid\ \ \ \ \ \ \Theta\ \ \ \ \ \ \Sigma\ \ \ \ \ \ \ \ \ \Gamma}{}}_{\Sigma\ \ \ \ \text{CST}|\Theta\ \ \ \ \Theta[:\Gamma]}$$

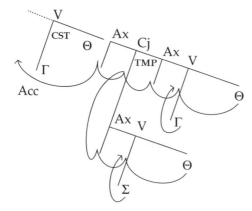

b.   John hit the wall with the stone.

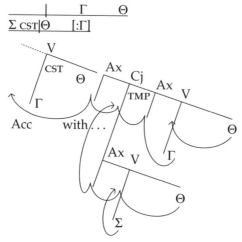

c.   John tapped the bottle of some water.

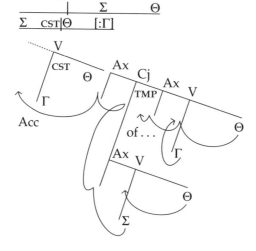

4.5   *Possessional predicates*

Both the Possessional–Spatial asymmetry (17) and Possessional double object constructions (38b) result from a deficiency of Possessional predicates: they lack the conceptual dimension of a head distinct from the Theme. Identificational predicates are also deficient, lacking a head distinct from the Location (Gruber 1996).[25] A complete Possessional predicate is formed by a matrix Identificational subpredicate containing a Possessional one as Location (70a). Thus "John owns the book" or "the book belongs to John" has a basic structure similar to "the book is John's (book)." Identification of Theme or Location with predicate heads (straight arrows) must occur because of the phrasal deficiencies: either one or the other must project as a predicate phrase.[26] Possessional Theme is colinked with Identificational Theme which moves for Case. The derivation of a transitive Locational Possessional predicate is thus analogous to that of a Spatial one (58a), without asymmetry. If a Motional Possessional subpredicate is, like a Locational one, completed by a matrix Identificational subpredicate, the derivation of a predicate with structural Goal (70b) projects Goal as subject, like Source. Thus the Possessional configuration results in the Possessional–Spatial asymmetry. The order Θ-Γ(pss)-V in compounds (49) is also explained:

(70)   a.   John owns the book.

b. John got the book from Bill.

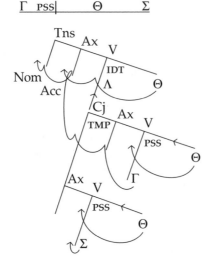

Aside from Possessionals, double object constructions occur in morphological as opposed to lexical causatives (69) in many languages. This suggests the Causee subpredicate in the former is headed by C. Assuming a lexicalization cycle stops at C (Chomsky 1998a) and is associated with agreement (cf. Poletto 1991), Case achieved locally below C would be direct Case. The Possessional double object construction would then be explained if it had the configuration of a morphological causative (71a):

(71) a. John gave Bill the book.

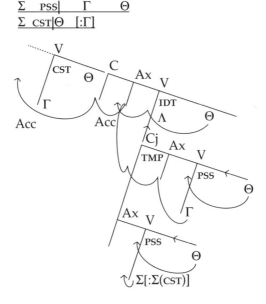

b. *John gave Bill of the book.

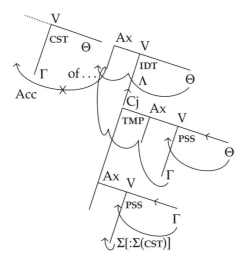

Case in Ax immediately below C would be Accusative. Given the Possessional configuration, a structural Goal is projected above Theme: it is in fact
the raised Goal subject of an erstwhile Possessional transitive. The same configuration makes the projection of a Possessional lexical causative without C
impossible (71b). Projection in Ax heading the Causee blocks the movement of
Theme. Thus Possessional causatives adopt the form of a morphological causative double object construction, in order to have the causative of a structural
Goal predicate at all.

NOTES

* This work was supported in part by the Social Sciences and Humanities Research Council of Canada grant no. 411-92-0012 ("La Modularité de la Grammaire: Arguments, Projections, et Variations") and Fonds Institutionnels de Recherche (University of Quebec at Montreal) to Anna-Maria Di Sciullo.

1 That Agent or Cause is a Source can be seen from the meaning of *for* as in the following:

(i) John sold the car for $100.

(ii) John bought the car for $100.

(iii) John destroyed the house for $100.

The object of *for* is a Theme whose Goal and Source are identified with the complementary role of the main Theme. "John" is Source of "the car" and Goal of the "$100" in (i), but Goal of "the car" and Source of the "$100" in (ii). In (iii) "John" is Goal of the "$100" because he is Agent, i.e. Source of the "destroying."

2 A "true" object is one licensed in a functional projection (AgrOP) specifically blocked in the passive and distinct from that in which semantic Case is licensed.

3 This "thematic functional notation," stemming from work with Ogwueleka (1987), is primarily a descriptive form of conceptual analysis. The term "function" applies to these forms, while, somewhat loosely and interchangeably, the term "event(uality)" will refer to their denotation as part of event structure, and "predicate" to the forms in grammatical syntax that express them.

4 Oblique Case often marked by a preposition contrasts with direct Case, e.g. subject or object, sometimes marked by agreement. Thematically specific semantic Case contrasts with structural Case.

5 The possibility of an explicit Source related to the Goal shows that *hit* cannot be inchoative "come to be at/against" (predicate INCH STATE in Jackendoff 1990b), but must itself be Motional (GO).

6 More precisely, functional integrity is maintained for primary roles. More than one primary Source or Goal per Motional function, whose contents are in taxonomic opposition, produces a contradiction. But a secondary Source or Goal bearing a part–whole relation to the primary Source or Goal (i, ii) does not:

(i) The tree dropped fruit from its upper branches.

(ii) Fruit hit the house against its roof.

Using thematic integrity as a theta-role diagnostic must distinguish primary and secondary roles.

7 The implicitness or explicitness of a theta-role follows independent conditions. Direct arguments must be explicit, unless a lexically specified object (e.g. *eat* FOOD). An implicit oblique Source in relation to a Goal, meaning "from elsewhere," is possible (i), but not an implicit Goal in relation to a Source (ii):

(i) The ball rolled to the tree.

(ii) The ball rolled (*away) from the tree.

In general, oblique arguments of certain (precedent) thematic (sub)functions, like Source, may be implicit.

8 Expletive *it* in the grammatical argument position is labeled, rather than its associate *that*-clause.

9 Path roles, describing Locus of movement (*over*), Direction (*up*), or Accompaniment (*along with*), optionally occur with Motional predicates and are distinguished from simple Source and Goal.

10 This is the normal form of a predicate expressing possession in Setswana:

(i) monna (Λ) o-na   le lokwalo (Θ)
     man   Agr-Cop with book
     "the man has a book"

11 Their example is *enter*, which seems not to be a true transitive (i), while *reach* is (ii):

(i) *The ocean was entered by the river.

(ii) The ocean was reached by the river.

12 The subject theta-role need not be only a precedent Theme (Gruber and Collins 1997), but may be a precedent Source (cf. 21b). The generalization does not apply to

obliquely projected roles of implicit matrix predicates, e.g. oblique Cause in (i), as well as subject Cause of an explicit causative verb (ii):

(i) The food blew off the tray from the force of the wind.

(ii) The force of the wind blew the food off the tray.

13 *Hit* is an apparent transitive in (i), but unpassivizable with this sense (ii), hence an implicit oblique:

(i) The stone hit the pole into the road.
(? = The stone . . . went into the road.)

(ii) The pole was hit by the stone into the road.
(* = The stone . . . went into the road.)

14 The test frame works with Goal but not with atelic Path roles. The object of *go around/surround* actually measures the event, suggesting that Path roles are structurally similar to Theme:

(i) The fence goes fully around/ surrounds the house.
(= the whole house/*the whole fence)

15 For Jackendoff, identified with Patient/Benefactee of the "Action" tier, arguably "precedent."

16 Assuming (consequent) Theme is of a different proto-role, this would explain why Instrument cannot be a direct object over Theme, effectively implying separate subject/object hierarchies.

17 For example, if Agent is above Theme in conceptual structure and Italian allows objects without subjects in syntax, then prohibiting downward correspondences would rule out Agent linking to object.

18 This view contrasts with that commonly assumed (e.g. Williams 1980, Hale and Keyser 1993).

19 N-incorporation does not alter projection asymmetries and occurs only for non-specific NPs. Case would still then be attained by movement, effected by an element (expletive/article) raising out of the NP.

20 Relative specifier/complement is formally defined in (54).

21 This order is explicit in Bantu auxiliary systems (Demuth and Gruber 1995).

22 Chomsky (1998a) attributes a dislocation property to functional categories, essentially the property of T reflected in the Extended Projection Principle to merge an element to topical prominence.

23 Ax is like Chomsky's (1998a) light verb v in that it attracts the direct object. However, the thematic property of v to have a specifier containing Cause is a property of the causative predicate (52a). The two functions are therefore distinct, although their positions form similar VP-shell configurations.

24 The *with* position, in the extension of Cj, is like the position for comitative *with* involving conjunction of Theme. The *of* position, in the extension of Ax and hence analogous to the position of a direct object, is like the position of oblique Case-marking of the object of a nominal (cf. Gruber 1997).

25 In "John has a book," the entity "book" maps directly into (entities possessed by) John; in "the animal is a dog," "the animal" maps into entities directly denoted by "dog." The (in)definiteness effect on the Possessional Theme and Identificational Location of these

deficient verbs reflects their identification with the predicate head.

26   Theme and Location would be distinguished derivationally by the order in which they are selected from the lexicon and merged in syntax: α (Location/Ground) is selected, then β (Theme/Figure) is selected and merged with α. This conception has benefited by discussion with D. Jaspers.

10 Predication

JOHN BOWERS

0 Introduction

Pre-theoretically, I will take for granted the traditional view that a proposition in natural language consists minimally of a distinguished nominal expression referred to as the "subject" and another expression referred to as the "predicate." Predication is the relation between these two constituents. Though this survey is primarily concerned with the syntactic representation of predication, I shall adopt for purposes of discussion the standard Fregean view that a predicate is an unsaturated expression that must combine with an entity expression to form a proposition.

Very early in the literature of transformational-generative grammar the point was made that the notions subject and object are essentially relational in character and it was argued that given an appropriate set of syntactic rules, the relations "subject-of" and "predicate-of" a sentence could be defined in terms of the more basic formal notions of phrase structure such as category, precedence, and dominance. (See Chomsky 1965 for the classic statement of this view.) Though other approaches are possible, notably the assumption of relational grammar that relations themselves are the primitives of grammar, I shall restrict discussion here to the mainstream view that syntactic relations such as predication can be defined in terms of more basic structural notions.

The most obvious instance of predication is main clause predication, which seems universally to involve combining a nominal expression (NP) with a verbal expression (VP):

(1) a. [$_{NP}$ John][$_{VP}$ ate a sandwich]
     b. [$_{NP}$ Bill][$_{VP}$ is very angry]
     c. [$_{NP}$ Fred][$_{VP}$ may be a good fellow]
     d. [$_{NP}$ someone][$_{VP}$ is in the living room]

and it was Chomsky's suggestion that the relation of predication could be defined in terms of the then-standard expansion rule for sentences:

(2) S → NP VP

It was soon noted, however, that in most languages there are at least some instances of so-called "small clause" predication:

(3) a. Mary saw [NP John][VP eat a sandwich]
     b. That made [NP Bill][AP very angry]
     c. I consider [NP Fred][NP a good fellow]
     d. We have [NP someone][PP in the living room]

In these examples, the second bracketed expression is in each case clearly predicated of the first, yet it is far from obvious that there is syntactic motivation for positing a structure in which the two constituents are immediately dominated by an S-node. (See Williams 1975, 1980, 1983a, for classic arguments both pro and con.) The difficulties with the small clause approach were further exacerbated when the "IP" analysis of sentences became widely adopted. According to this view, the subject of main clauses is located in the specifier of a "functional" category "I," apparently requiring that the same structure be assumed in small clauses as well.

Putting aside for the moment the difficulties with the small clause approach, it might appear from the examples in (1) and (3) that simple adjacency of phrases of the appropriate category could provide an adequate basis for a syntactic definition of the predication relation. It is easy to show, however, that adjacency is neither a necessary nor a sufficient condition for predication. Consider the following examples:

(4) a. I consider John a good fellow → John is a good fellow
     b. I gave John an interesting book ↛ John is an interesting book

(5) I found John a good psychotherapist = (a) "I found John to be a good
                                               psychotherapist."
                                           (b) "I found a good
                                               psychotherapist for John."

(6) a. John made Mary a good wife → Mary is a good wife
     b. John made Mary a good husband → John is a good husband

(7) Fred painted the model nude → (a) the model is nude
                                    or (b) Fred is nude

Examples (4a, b) apparently consist of an identical sequence of constituents NP_1-V-NP_2-NP_3, yet in (4a) NP_3 is predicated of NP_2, while the same is not true at all of (4b). Example (5) also contains a sequence of two NPs in postverbal position, yet it is structurally ambiguous: under the (a) interpretation the second NP is predicated of the first, while the same is not true of the (b) interpretation. The examples in (6) have, once again, the same surface sequence of constituents NP_1-V-NP_2-NP_3, yet in (6a) NP_3 is understood to be predicated of NP_2, while in (6b) NP_3 is understood to be predicated of NP_1. Finally, example (7) is ambiguous, depending on whether the AP *nude* is predicated of the object or the subject. Thus the contrasts in (4) and (5) show that simple adjacency of two NPs is not a sufficient condition for predication, while the contrasts in (6) and (7) show that it is not a necessary one.

From these basic observations, we may draw two tentative conclusions: (i) there must be a structural relation between constituents that defines the subject–predicate relation and distinguishes it from other relations that adjacent phrases may bear to one another; (ii) there must be some way of representing "long distance" predication.[1] I shall take it as a methodological given that, all other things being equal, it would be highly desirable if the same structural relation entered into both main clause (MC) and small clause (SC) predication. Certainly the weaker view that predication is realized by entirely different structural relations in different positions should only be adopted as a last resort.

Now let us consider what possibilities there are for the syntactic representation of predication. Given the strong constraints on structural relations imposed by current X'-theory, there are basically only two alternatives: (i) the subject of a predicative expression XP of category X is in [Spec, X]; (ii) there is a functional category F such that the predicative expression XP is the complement of F and its subject is in [Spec, F]. These two possibilities are diagrammed below:

(8) a.   XP   b.   FP

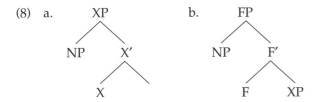

The first view, which I shall refer to henceforth as the Specifier Hypothesis (SH), was originally proposed by Stowell (1981), though only for SC predication. Stowell's view seemed to receive considerable support from the Internal Subject Hypothesis (ISH), proposed originally by Kuroda (1988) and developed in slightly different forms by Fukui (1986), Kitagawa (1986), and Koopman and Sportiche (1985, 1991), among others. According to the ISH, the surface subject in MC predication originates universally in [Spec, V] and is raised, in languages such as English, into [Spec, I] for case theoretic reasons. The ISH thus filled in the missing gap in Stowell's version of the SH, making it possible to claim that all subjects originate uniformly in [Spec, X], X a lexical category.

Until the advent of the ISH, the second view, which I shall refer to henceforth as the Functional Category Hypothesis (FCH), was universally maintained for MC predication, the functional category F being identified as I (or its successor T). The difficulties alluded to above in extending the FCH to SC predication were for the most part simply ignored. The FCH, modified and combined with a slightly different version of the internal subject hypothesis, was extended to SC predication by Bowers (1993a).[2] Under this proposal, the functional category F is no longer identified as I. Instead, I is split up into two separate categories "T" and "Pr" and F is identified as the latter. The category T represents the deictic function of I, while Pr represents its predicational function. (The category label Pr is simply a mnemonic for either "predicate" or "predication," depending on whether the focus is on its categorical or its relational function.) Syntactically, Pr is a functional category that selects the maximal projection XP of any lexical category X and whose maximal projection PrP can either be generated independently (yielding SC predication) or selected by T (yielding MC predication). Note that the position of the internal subject in MCs is simply [Spec, Pr]. I assume in addition that objects originate in [Spec, V] and that Verbs obligatorily adjoin to Pr, thus accounting for their surface position preceding the object (see section 3 for further discussion). It seems likely that Pr is actually a feature complex [+Pr, +/−N, +/−V]. The obligatory raising of the head of the complement VP is then explained by the fact that the lexical category features [+V, −N] are strong in English (perhaps universally). (In contrast, Bowers 1993a assumed that head raising of V to Pr was driven by theta-role assignment. Here I remain neutral as to where theta-roles are assigned.) A feature analysis also explains why the parallel category "Nm" in nominals, proposed in Bowers (1991), shares so many properties with Pr, since the two categories differ only in their lexical categorical features: [+Pr, +V, −N] in the case of the latter, [+Pr, −V, +N] in the case of the former. A feature analysis would also partially, though not completely, resolve the apparent difference between Pr and v (see n. 2). Finally, I will assume, following Bowers (1993a), that the semantic function of Pr is to turn a property expression of type π, assigned to the consitutent XP, into a propositional function (an unsaturated expression) of type <e, p>, whose argument position is then saturated by the entity expression assigned to the NP in [Spec, Pr] (Chierchia 1985, 1989, Chierchia and Turner 1988).[3]

According to this view, then, the basic structures for MC and SC predication would be as shown in (9a, b), respectively:

(9) a.

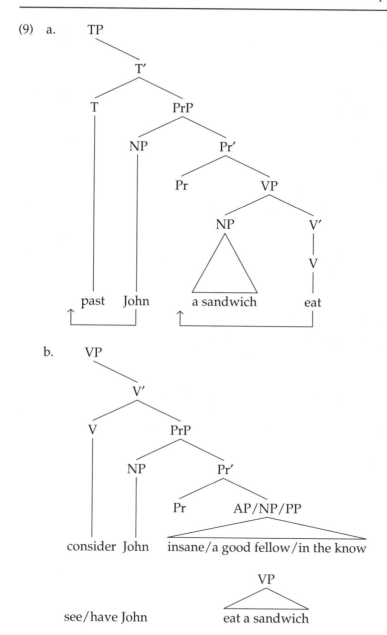

b.

Though there are apparently languages such as Sinhala (Sumangala 1992) in which AP, NP, and PP can be directly selected by Pr in MCs, English obligator-ily requires the copula in such cases. How is this fact to be accounted for? There are two possibilities, both of which have been proposed in the literature: (i) copular *be* is a phonetic spell-out of T; (ii) *be* is a main verb in its own right that selects a SC complement:

(10)   a.   [_TP is [_PrP John [_Pr' Pr [_AP/NP/PP insane/a good fellow/in the know]]]]
       b.   [_TP T [_PrP Pr [_VP be [_PrP John Pr [_AP/NP/PP insane/a good fellow/in the
            know]]]]]

For English at least, it appears that (10b) is correct, because the copula can co-
occur with modals: *John may/might/can/should/must/etc. be insane/a good fellow/in
the know.*[4]

Notice that not only does hypothesizing the category Pr unify MC and SC
predication, providing a purely structural characterization of the predication
relation, but it also solves the related problem of what category to assign SCs
to: a SC is simply the maximal projection of Pr. Moreover, it does so within
the limitations imposed by a uniform two-level version of X'-theory, unlike
proposals such as Fukui (1986), and without resorting to the use of base-
generated adjuncts, as in Koopman and Sportiche (1985, 1991). In addition,
only binary branching is required (Kayne 1984), further narrowing the range
of possible structures permitted.

1   Comparison of the Specifier Hypothesis and the Functional Category Hypothesis

In this section, I discuss a number of very basic problems with applying the
SH to SC predication, all of which can be overcome by adopting the PrP
version of the FCH. The structures that would be assigned to SC constructions
such as those in (3) by the FCH and the SH, respectively, are as follows:

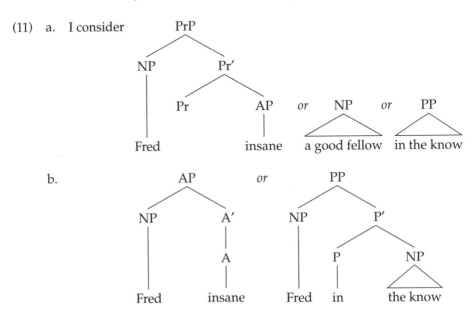

(11)   a.   I consider

       b.

1.1   The subject of predicate nominals

The first problem for the SH is where to put the subject of the SC in predicate nominal constructions. It obviously cannot go in [Spec, N], since it would incorrectly follow any determiner elements, yielding absurd sentences such as *I consider a/my Fred friend*. Equally obviously, it cannot go in [Spec, D] because this position is needed for possessive NPs. The basic problem is that a predicate nominal can in general be an entire DP, not just the maximal projection of N:

(12)   I consider Fred a mensch/the best person for the job/Mary's worst enemy/etc.

Therefore, no matter what Spec position we choose to put the subject of a predicate nominal in, there will always be some class of nominals containing another constituent in that same position. The only alternative would be to posit a Spec position reserved exclusively for subjects of predicate nominals, a move for which there is no independent motivation at all. Under the PrP hypothesis, on the other hand, the complement of Pr could perfectly well be DP. Indeed, given the DP Hypothesis, we would expect the complement of Pr to be a full DP rather than a bare NP.

1.2   The subject of predicate adjectives

As a matter of fact, a similar problem arises for predicate adjectives as well, since APs universally occur with an extensive set of degree modifiers:

(13)   I consider Mary $\left\{\begin{array}{l} \text{so} \\ \text{too} \\ \text{more} \\ \text{as} \\ \text{extremely} \end{array}\right\}$ brilliant at math $\left\{\begin{array}{l} \text{that}\ldots \\ \text{to}\ldots \\ \text{than}\ldots \\ \text{as}\ldots \end{array}\right\}$

Where would these modifiers be located under the SH? Simple adverbial modifiers such as *extremely* might not pose a problem, since they could plausibly be analyzed as A'-adjuncts:

(14)   I consider [_{AP} John [_{A'} extremely [_{A'} brilliant at math]]]

but such an analysis is difficult to maintain for degree modifiers such as *so, too, -er, as*, etc. which may (and sometimes must) select an associated phrasal or sentential complement. Suppose, following Abney (1987), Bowers (1987), and Corver (1990, 1991, 1997), there is a functional category Deg that selects AP or PP (and perhaps DP as well) as its complement and permits various nominal modifiers in [Spec, Deg]:

(15)

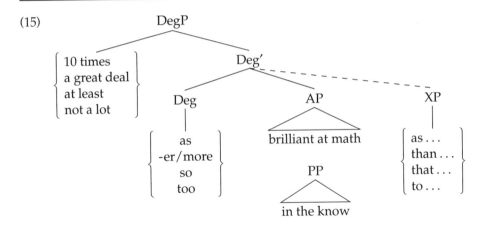

Under the PrP analysis, these extended predicate APs and PPs are easily accommodated by stipulating that Pr select DegP rather than AP or PP. Under the SH, on the other hand, as in the case of predicate nominals, there is no specifier position on the left edge of the DegP that will always be available for the subject of a SC.

1.3   APs with expletive subjects

Consider next predicate AP constructions with an expletive subject such as the following:

(16)   I consider it $\begin{Bmatrix} \text{nice} \\ \text{kind} \\ \text{pleasant} \\ \text{stupid} \end{Bmatrix}$ of Mary to do that.

Since the expletive *it* occupies the subject position in the SC complement of *consider*, the only possible structure under the SH is something like the following:

(17)   [$_{AP}$ it [$_{A'}$ [$_{A'}$ nice [$_{PP}$ of Mary]][$_{TP}$ PRO to do that]]]

But this poses a serious problem, since *Mary* does not c-command PRO and therefore cannot, under the usual assumptions of control theory, be its controller. Under the PrP hypothesis, in contrast, there is nothing to prevent *(of) Mary* from originating in [Spec, A].[5] In order to account for the word order, we may assume, following a recent proposal by Corver (1997), that in addition to the category Deg there is an intermediate category "Q" between Deg and A, parallel to the intermediate category between D and N (named variously "Q" (Abney 1987, Giusti 1991), "Nm" (Bowers 1991), and "Num" (or "#") (Ritter

1991, Valois 1991, Carstens 1991, 1998), and that Q has a strong A-feature that forces Adjectives to adjoin to it:

(18)

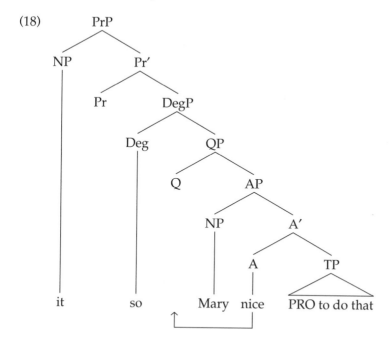

That such an analysis is correct is suggested by the fact that when AP is realized as a pro-form *so*, Q must emerge lexically as *much*:

(19)   John is very fond of Mary. – Yes, too much so.
                              but not more/less so than Bill.

However, further discussion of the intricacies of the English degree system would go beyond the scope of this survey.

1.4   *Unlike category conjunction*

A serious problem for any version of the SH is that it has no way of explaining apparent cases of unlike category conjunction of the predicative elements in SCs:

(20)   I consider Fred [AP crazy] and [DP a fool]
                      both [AP shrewd] and [PP in the know]

as the following diagram shows:

(21)   I consider

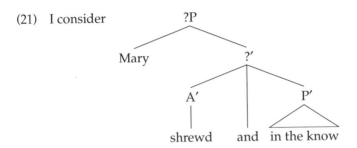

Under the PrP analysis, on the other hand, such examples are easily explained as instances of like category conjunction of the category Pr′:

(22)

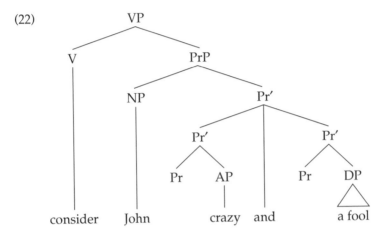

The problem still remains even if (as will be argued later, cf. section 3.1) the subject of the SC must be raised by ATB conjunction:

(23)   I consider Mary

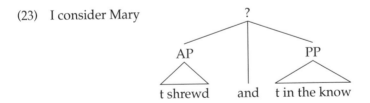

whereas under the PrP analysis, such examples are again easily analyzed as instances of like category conjunction, the category in this case being PrP:

(24)

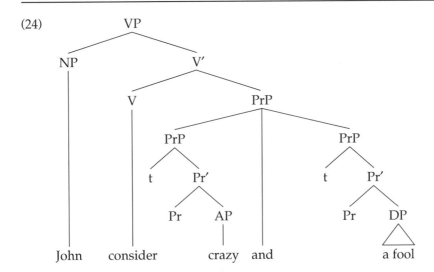

1.5   *Unaccusatives vs. unergatives*

The PrP analysis provides straightforwardly for a structural distinction between unaccusatives and unergatives, the former having a single argument in [Spec, V], the latter a single argument in [Spec, Pr]:

(25)   a.   b.

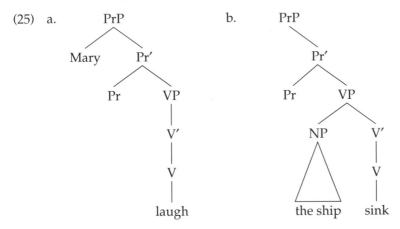

Without Pr, unaccusatives and unergatives could, in principle, be distinguished structurally from one other in the case where each has only a single argument by generating the subject as a complement of V in the former case and in [Spec, V] in the latter case. However, as soon as another PP argument is added, as in the following examples:

(26)   a.   Mary laughed at John.
       b.   The ship sank beneath the waves.

there is only one possible position for both subjects, namely, [Spec, V].[6]

1.6 Lexical realizations of Pr

If there is a functional category Pr, then we might expect to find it lexically realized in at least some instances. In fact, there is growing body of data in support of this conclusion. It was suggested in Bowers (1993a) that the particle *as* that occurs in English in SC constructions such as the following is a (lexically idiosyncratic) realization of Pr:[7]

(27) I regard Fred as ⎧ insane
               ⎨ in the know
               ⎪ my best friend
               ⎩ having a good reputation ⎭

Further support for this view is presented in Bailyn and Rubin (1991) (see also Bailyn 1995a), who show that Russian *kak* and *za* are realizations of Pr and, furthermore, that Pr systematically assigns Instrumental case in SCs. Likewise, Eide and Åfarli (1997) argue that Norwegian *som* and German *als* are realizations of Pr.[8] In addition, Wayne Harbert (personal communication) has suggested that the particle *yn* which occurs systematically in Welsh in predicate nominal constructions such as the following is a lexical realization of Pr:

(28) Mae Rhys yn athro.
     is   Rhys prt a teacher
     "Rhys is a teacher."

An even more systematic lexical realization of Pr occurs in Korean, where the particle *-kye* marks predication in SC constructions such as the following with complete regularity (Jang 1997, Kang 1997, Kim and Maling 1997):

(29) Mary-nun emeni-lul   alumtap-kye sangkakha-n-ta.
     Mary-Nom mother-Acc beautiful-Pr consider-Pres-Dec
     "Mary considers her mother beautiful."

Crucially, as Kang (1997) notes, predicates in SCs cannot occur with the honorific marker *-si* or the tense markers which normally occur in T or AGR, ruling out the possibility that *-kye* is a realization of either of the latter.

Finally, Nishiyama (1998) presents extensive evidence in support of the view that Pr is realized lexically in Japanese in various different phonetic forms. In the class of Adjectives he calls "Nominal Adjectives," Pr is realized as the morpheme *-de*, the full form of which occurs in (30a) and in contracted form in (30b):

(30) a. yoru-ga   sizuka-de ar-u.
         night-Nom quiet-Pr   cop-Pres
         "The night is quiet."

b. yoru-ga   sizuka-da.
   night-Nom quiet-Pr/cop/Pres
   "The night is quiet."

Furthermore, Nishiyama shows that Pr is realized as underlying *-k* in a different morphological class of adjectives he refers to as "Canonical Adjectives," though *-k* is elided in present tense forms such as (31b):

(31) a. yama-ga   taka-k-at-ta.
          mountain-Nom high-Pr-cop-Past
          "The mountain was high."
      b. yama-ga   taka-(k)-i.
          mountain-Nom high-Pr-Pres
          "The mountain is high."

Nishiyama demonstrates convincingly that though Pr has a variety of phonological realizations as the result of the complex interaction of morphological and phonological processes, the underlying syntactic structures are perfectly regular.

In conclusion, it appears that Pr, like other functional categories that have been posited in recent years, may be realized phonologically but need not be. Furthermore, as the Japanese evidence shows, the lexical realization of Pr is subject to morphological syncretism as the result of historical change, as is commonly the case with functional categories.

2   Further Syntactic Arguments in Support of Pr

Having established in a preliminary fashion the plausibility of the PrP version of the FCH, I now turn to some rather more intricate syntactic considerations that provide further syntactic evidence in support of this approach to predication.

2.1   VP conjunction

One such argument can be derived from the fact that English apparently permits ill-formed constituents containing only a direct object and a complement of some kind to conjoin quite freely (Larson 1988, Bowers 1993a):

(32) a. Mary considers John a fool and Bill a wimp.
      b. John regards professors as strange and politicians as creepy.
      c. Sue put the books on the table and the records on the chair.
      d. Harriet gave a mug to John and a scarf to Vivien.
      e. I expect John to win and Harry to lose.
      f. We persuaded Mary to leave and Sue to stay.

g. You eat the fish raw and the beef cooked.
h. I convinced John that it was late and Bill that it was early.
i. They told Sue who to talk to and Virginia when to leave.

Clearly, traditional analyses of the VP fail to shed much light on this phenomenon. A ternary analysis of VP, in particular, makes it impossible to generate such sentences.[9] Under the PrP hypothesis, on the other hand, they are simply instances of ATB extraction of V from a conjoined VP:

(33)

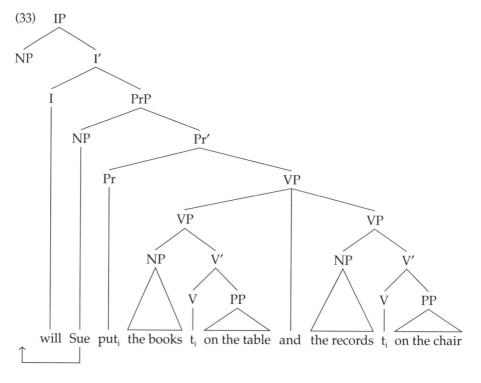

It is known on the basis of comparative evidence that non-auxiliary verbs do not raise to I in English (Emonds 1978, Pollock 1989). Hence, the ATB extraction of V required in these structures is only possible if there is an X^0 position between I and V which the extracted verb can be adjoined to. The needed head position is provided by Pr. Independent evidence for this conclusion can be derived from the existence of RNR sentences (Larson 1990) in which the raised constituent must be a VP containing a V-trace:

(34) a. Smith loaned, and his widow later donated, a valuable collection of manuscripts to the library.
   b. Sue moved, and Mary also transferred, her business to a different location.

c. I succeeded in convincing, even though John had failed to persuade, Mary not to leave.

d. We didn't particularly like, but nevertheless ate, the fish raw.

e. Most people probably consider, even though the courts didn't actually find, Klaus von Bulow guilty of murder.

f. Flo desperately wants, though she doesn't really expect, the Miami Dolphins to be in the Superbowl.

2.2 Adverb positions

Another indirect way demonstrating the need for a category Pr is the following. Modifying Travis (1988) along the lines suggested in Tang (1990), let us make the following fairly restrictive assumptions concerning the structure and licensing of adverb phrases: (i) AdvPs are X'-adjuncts licensed by an X^0 head; (ii) each head licenses one and only one type of AdvP.[10] If it could be shown that there was an adverb type in the appropriate position for which there was no licensing head, and if it could be shown that Pr was a plausible licenser for adverbs of this type, then it could reasonably be concluded that Pr exists. Consider in this light the fact that certain manner adverbs in English can only occur in postverbal position:

(35) a. John learned French perfectly.
b. Bill recited his lines poorly.
c. Mary plays the violin beautifully.

(36) a. *John perfectly learned French.
b. *Bill poorly recited his lines.
c. *Mary beautifully plays the violin.

while other manner adverbs occur in both positions:

(37) a. John learned French immediately.
b. Bill recited his lines slowly.
c. Mary will play the violin soon.

(38) a. John immediately learned French.
b. Bill slowly recited his lines.
c. Mary will soon play the violin.

These two types can co-occur with one another, but cannot be interchanged:

(39) a. John immediately learned French perfectly.
b. John learned French perfectly (almost) immediately.

(40) a. *John perfectly learned French immediately.
      b. *John learned French immediately perfectly. (modulo Heavy Con-
          stituent Shift)

This strongly suggests that they are licensed by different categories. The
problem is that there are at least two further distinct adverb types in English
(making a total of four), none of which can be interchanged with any of the
others:

(41) a. Clearly, John probably will immediately learn French perfectly.
      b. *Clearly, John immediately will probably learn French perfectly.
      c. *Immediately, John probably will clearly learn French perfectly.
      d. *Clearly, John perfectly will immediately learn French probably.
                                      etc.

Since the only three categories available as licensers are V, I, and C, either
another licenser is needed or we must assume that the two types of manner
adverb discussed above are both licensed by V.[11] But if adverbs such as *perfectly* are licensed by V and adverbs such as *immediately* by Pr, then their
distribution follows immediately, as can be seen by examining the following
structures:

(42)

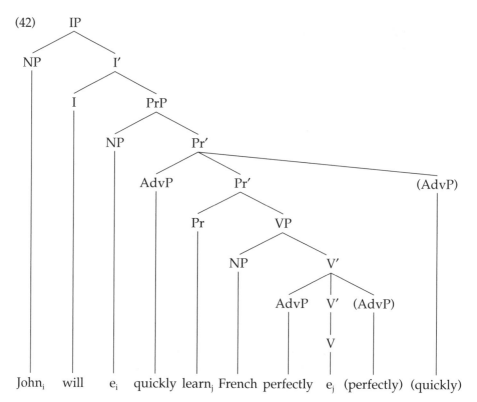

John$_i$ will   e$_i$ quickly learn$_j$ French perfectly   e$_j$ (perfectly) (quickly)

The fact that *perfectly* can only appear in postverbal position is now explained automatically by virtue of obligatory V-raising into Pr, which ensures that the verb is always to the left of the adverb, regardless of whether it is generated as a left or right V'-adjunct. Adverbs such as *quickly*, in contrast, can appear either as left Pr' adjuncts or as right Pr' adjuncts, hence either to the left or to the right of VP. The fact that the two adverb types cannot exchange positions follows from the fact that they are licensed by different heads.[12]

It was noted earlier that Pr, in contrast to a VP shell or the "light" verb v, is always present in both MCs and SCs, regardless of how many arguments a given predicate has. Further evidence in support of this claim is provided by the fact that V-licensed adverbs are uniformly restricted to postverbal position, regardless of how many arguments the verb has and regardless of where they originate:

(43) a. John (*perfectly) rolled the ball (perfectly) down the hill (perfectly).
      b. John (*perfectly) shot the ball (perfectly).
      c. The ball (*perfectly) rolled (perfectly) down the hill (perfectly).
      d. The ball (*perfectly) rolled (perfectly).
      e. John (*intimately) spoke (intimately) to Mary (intimately).
      f. It (*torrentially) rained (torrentially).

It is difficult to explain this distribution of V-licensed adverbs unless there is a fixed Pr position to which the verb must adjoin obligatorily. Strikingly, this generalization holds even in the case of 0-place predicates such as *rain*, as (43f) shows.[13]

This analysis also makes a further correct prediction concerning the distribution of V-licensed adverbs, namely, that they can appear either to the left or to the right of a complement:

(44) a. John spoke French intimately to Mary.
      b. John spoke French to Mary intimately.

(45) a. Mary jumped the horse perfectly over the last fence.
      b. Mary jumped the horse over the last fence perfectly.

This fact also rules out the possibility of analyzing V-licensed adverbs as complements (Larson 1988), since they would then be unable to co-occur with PP complements.

Consider, finally, the well-known fact that adverbs in English strongly resist being placed between a verb and a direct object, though not, as just noted, between a verb and a PP-complement:

(46) a. John spoke French intimately to Mary.
      b. *John spoke intimately French to Mary.

Following Stowell (1981), this restriction on the placement of adverbs in English is usually accounted for in the literature by means of a so-called "adjacency requirement" on case assignment, which stipulates that accusative case can only be assigned by the verb to a NP that it is adjacent to. Apart from the inherent implausibility of restricting case assignment in this way, there are at least two empirical arguments against such an approach. First, adjacency is not a general requirement for case assignment, even in English, since adverbs can occur quite freely between the subject and the I^0 head that assigns it nominative case: *John certainly will win the race.* Second, the adjacency requirement simply does not hold in many languages, even in typologically quite similar languages such as French (Bowers 1993a: section 3.2.1):

(47)   Jean parle souvent le français.

Hence all that remains of the adjacency requirement is a language-specific condition on assignment of accusative case; hardly an explanatory theory, one would think.

Under the analysis proposed here, in contrast, this restriction on the occurrence of adverbs can be explained in purely structural terms. First of all, the fact that V-licensed adverbs such as *perfectly* cannot occur between the verb and its direct object follows immediately from the assumption that these adverbs are V'-adjuncts, together with the linked hypotheses that the canonical position for direct objects is [Spec, V] and that the verb raises obligatorily into Pr^0. These assumptions jointly ensure that there is simply no way of generating an adverb of this type between the verb and its object in English. (Note that for this explanation to work it is crucial that adverbs *not* be treated as XP-adjuncts, contrary to what is frequently assumed in the literature.) Second, these same assumptions ensure that it is impossible to generate adverbs licensed by any other head between the verb and its object. Thus a Pr-licensed adverb, for example, will be generatable either to the left of the raised verb or to the right of the whole VP complement of Pr^0, but not in any other position. The possible positions for adverbs permitted by this theory are indicated in the following structure for (41a):

(48)

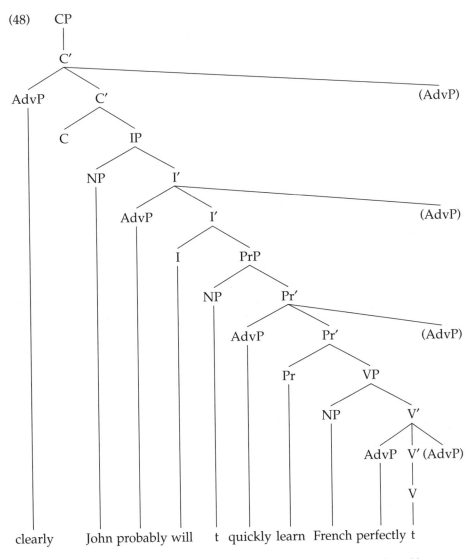

clearly   John probably will   t quickly learn French perfectly t

Finally, the fact that other complements of the verb cannot be ordered between the verb and the direct object:

(49) a. *John spoke to Mary French.
      b. *Mary persuaded to leave John.
      c. *The lions ate raw the meat.
      d. *Sue gave to Bill a book.
      e. *Mary persuaded that he should rest Bill.

can also be explained in purely structural terms. In short, given the theory of predication proposed here, all the ordering properties attributed to the adjacency condition on case assignment can be derived from more basic principles, together with the (perhaps universal) fact that Spec positions are always leftward.[14]

3   The Internal Structure of PrP

In this section I explore briefly some of the syntactic evidence bearing on the internal structure of PrP, particularly the argument structure of VP and the position of small clause adjuncts.

3.1   *Raising to object and the structure of VP*

One particularly significant consequence follows from the claim that objects, as well as subjects, are located in a Spec position. Since Spec positions can in general be theta'-positions, it should be the case that object position, as well as subject position, is a possible theta'-position. In fact, Postal and Pullum (1988) have argued that one of the crucial tests for a theta'-position, namely, occurrence of expletives, holds for object position as well as subject position. This in turn would make it possible, contrary to the standard view, for there to be Raising-to-Object (RO), as well as Raising-to-Subject (RS), without violating the Theta-Criterion.[15]

3.1.1   *Quantifier floating*

An important empirical argument in support of RO can be derived from the facts of so-called "quantifier floating" in English and other languages. The basic observation, due originally to Maling (1976), is that certain quantifiers can "float" to the right of the NP they modify under two conditions: (i) if the NP is a subject; (ii) if it is an object that has a predicative complement following it. Crucially, quantifier floating is not possible from objects that lack a predicative complement:

(50)   a.   The men will all leave.
      b.   We consider the men all fools/totally crazy.
      c.   *I saw the men all.
      d.   *The men were arrested all.
      e.   *The men arrived all.

These facts can be elegantly explained under the following assumptions:

(51)   i.   Floated quantifiers are produced by leftward movement of NP (Sportiche 1988).
      ii.   Raising to object (RO) exists.
      iii. Q is adjoined only to the "propositional" categories PrP and IP.[16]

As shown in (52a), a stranded quantifier is always possible in subject position, since subjects always move from [Spec, Pr] to [Spec, I]; more importantly, the possibility of a stranded quantifier in object position also follows if RO exists, as shown in (52b):

(52) a. [$_{IP}$ the men$_1$ [$_{I'}$ will [$_{PrP}$ all [$_{PrP}$ t$_1$ [$_{Pr'}$ leave$_2$ [$_{VP}$ t$_2$]]]]]]
      b. [$_{IP}$ ... [$_{PrP}$ we [$_{Pr'}$ consider$_1$ [$_{VP}$ the men$_2$ [$_{V'}$ t$_1$ [$_{PrP}$ all [$_{PrP}$ t$_2$ [$_{Pr'}$ e fools]]]]]]]]]

Floating from an object which lacks a complement, as in example (50c), is ruled out, because the object has not been moved. The fact that floated quantifiers are prohibited in postverbal position in passives and unaccusatives, as shown by examples (50d, e), follows from assumption (51iii), which prohibits Q from being adjoined to VP.

   Finally, if this analysis is correct, then we would expect floating quantifiers to occur with PRO as well as trace, as is indeed the case:

(53) a. I persuaded$_1$ [$_{VP}$ the men$_2$ [$_{V'}$ t$_1$ [$_{IP}$ all [$_{IP}$ PRO$_2$ to resign]]]]
      b. The teacher ordered the two boys both to pay close attention.
      c. We put$_1$ [$_{VP}$ the students$_2$ [$_{V'}$ t$_1$ [$_{PrP}$ each [$_{Pr}$ PRO$_2$ [$_{Pr'}$ e in separate desks]]]]]
      d. They returned the books all to their owners.
      e. We painted the chairs all red.
      f. The trainer fed the steaks all to the lions.

These observations lead to the conclusion that goal phrases and dative expressions such as those in (53c, d, f) must in general be SC complements with a PRO subject.[17]

3.1.2   VP fronting
Another important argument in support of RO can be derived from the facts of VP Fronting discussed in Huang (1993). Huang notes that though the anaphor in a fronted complex *wh*-NP has a wider range of coreference possibilities than it does if it remains in situ:

(54) a. Which pictures of himself$_{i/j}$ did John$_i$ think Bill$_j$ liked?
      b. John$_i$ thought Bill$_j$ liked pictures of himself$_{*i/j}$.

the same is not true of fronted VPs:

(55) a. Criticize himself$_{*i/j}$ John$_i$ thinks Bill$_j$ never will.
      b. John$_i$ thinks Bill$_j$ will never criticize himself$_{*i/j}$.

Here the anaphor in the fronted VP can only be coreferential with the NP that would necessarily bind it if it remained in situ. Huang argues that this contrast can be explained if some version of the internal subject hypothesis is correct, for in that case the fronted constituent in (56) will contain a trace of the moved internal subject:

(56) [[$_\alpha$ t$_j$ criticize himself$_j$] John$_i$ thinks Bill$_j$ never will t]

By Condition A of the Binding Theory, *himself* must be bound by the trace left by the moved internal subject, hence must be coreferential with it.

It is now easy to show that the category of α in structures such as (56) must be PrP. Consider first the following example:

(57) Proud of himself$_{*i/j}$ John$_i$ doesn't think Bill$_j$ will ever be.

A fronted AP behaves exactly like a fronted VP with regard to the coreference possibilities of the anaphor contained in it, suggesting that the fronted constituent, whatever it is, must also contain the trace of a raised internal subject:

(58) [[$_\alpha$ t$_j$ proud of himself$_j$] John$_i$ thinks Bill$_j$ will never be t]

Clearly the same process is involved in VP-fronting and AP-fronting. But if the analysis of MC and SC predication proposed here is correct, then the two processes immediately reduce to a single one, since α must be PrP in both cases. Furthermore, it is now possible to construct an independent argument in support of RO. Consider the following example:

(59) Proud of himself$_{*i/j}$ John$_i$ doesn't consider Bill$_j$.

Once again, the coreference facts show that the fronted constituent must contain the trace left by a raised internal subject. In this instance, however, the subject of the SC is not raised to [Spec, I] but rather to [Spec, V], that is, to the object position. If RO were not involved in the derivation of these SC constructions, then we would expect to find fronted PrP constituents of the following sort:

(60) *Bill proud of himself John doesn't consider.

But such sentences are not even marginally acceptable, showing unequivocally that RO exists.[18]

3.1.3 Dative arguments and RO

It has often been noted in the literature that there is a small class of verbs in English which, though apparently transitive in form, cannot be passivized:

(61) a. John went home/*Home was gone by John.
      b. Mary left the room angry/*The room was left angry (by Mary).
      c. John resembles Bill/*Bill is resembled by John.
      d. The package weighed 10 lb/*10 lb was weighed by the package.
      e. This book cost $10/*$10 was cost by this book.
      f. The book cost John $10/*John was cost $10 by the book.

A related phenomenon (commonly referred to in the literature as "Visser's generalization," though the standard account is Bach 1979) is the fact that transitive subject-control verbs lack passives:

(62) a. *John is impressed (by Bill) as pompous.
    b. *The boys were made a good mother (by Aunt Mary).
    c. *The kids were failed (by Max) as a father.
    d. *The men were struck by the idea as nonsense.
    e. *The men were promised (by Frank) to leave.

Interestingly, it has been observed by Maling (1976) that the very same verbs that do not passivize also do not permit floated quantifiers associated with their objects:

(63) a. *He impresses his friends all as pompous.
    b. *Aunt Mary made the boys all a good mother.
    c. *Max failed the kids all as a father.
    d. *The idea struck the men all as nonsense.
    e. *Frank promised the men all to leave.

Clearly, this cannot be an accident, suggesting that there is a structural difference between direct objects and indirect objects. Let us assume the following structures for sentences with *persuade* and *promise*, respectively (see also Larson 1991, for a somewhat different analysis along the same general lines):

(64) a.

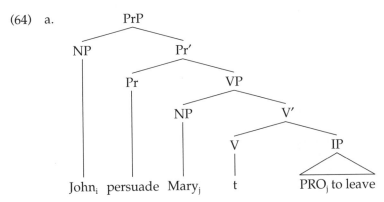

    b.

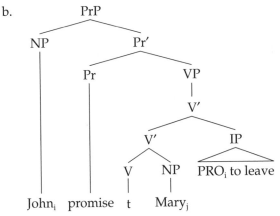

Assuming that *Mary* in (64b) receives inherent Dative case, Visser's generalization follows immediately, since only Accusative case (assigned in [Spec, V]) can be "absorbed" by the passive morphology. This analysis also explains the well-known control properties of these verbs:

(65) a. John$_i$ persuaded Mary$_j$ [PRO$_{*i/j}$ to leave]
     b. John$_i$ promised Mary$_j$ [PRO$_{i/*j}$ to leave]

Assuming the standard view that PRO must be controlled by the nearest c-commanding NP, the control properties indicated in (65) follow at once. Maling's observation concerning quantifier floating is simply a corollary of this solution to the control problem, since only in (64a) does the apparent object c-command the floating quantifier in the complement clause. The remaining examples in (62) are exactly like (64b) in structure except that they contain a SC complement with a PRO subject. An example such as (63d) would therefore be represented as follows:

(66)

Notice that the considerations discussed so far indicate that the argument structure of the PrP must have a fixed structure of the following form:[19]

(67)

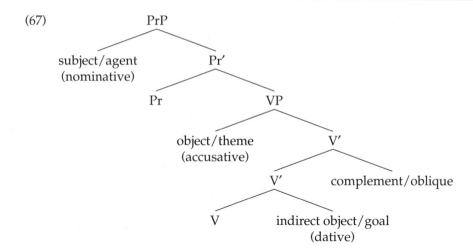

Some further support for the correctness of (67) can be derived from the fact that there are sentences containing all three arguments, a direct object, indirect object, and SC or sentential complement:

(68) a. They feed the meat$_i$ to the lions PRO$_i$ raw.
      b. John put the patient$_i$ in bed PRO$_i$ drunk. (Roberts 1988: 708, n. 3)
      c. I sent John$_i$ to the store PRO$_i$ to get the paper.

As predicted, the direct object, rather than the indirect object, controls the PRO subject of the complement.

Returning now to RO, let us consider its predicted interaction with dative arguments and V-licensed adverbs. As just shown, the latter both occur in positions subordinate to, and to the right of, the direct object. Therefore, if RO exists, the order of these elements must be as follows:

(69) V-Object-(Adverb)-(Dative)-Complement

Remarkably, this prediction is borne out by the facts, as the following data shows:

(70) a. *We proclaimed to the public John to be a hero.
      b. We proclaimed John to the public to be a hero.
      c. *We proclaimed sincerely John to be a hero.
      d. We proclaimed John sincerely to be a hero.
      e. *We proclaimed sincerely to the public John to be a hero.
      f. We proclaimed John sincerely to the public to be a hero.

(71) a. *They represented to the dean Mary as a genuine linguist.
      b. They represented Mary to the dean as a genuine linguist.
      c. *They represented seriously Mary as a genuine linguist.

    d. They represented Mary seriously as a genuine linguist.
    e. *They represented seriously to the dean Mary as a genuine linguist.
    f. They represented Mary seriously to the dean as a genuine linguist.

(72) a. *We proved to the authorities Smith to be the thief.
      b. We proved Smith to the authorities to be the thief.
      c. *We proved conclusively Smith to be the thief.
      d. We proved Smith conclusively to be the thief.
      e. *We proved conclusively to the authorities Smith to be the thief.
      f. We proved Smith conclusively to the authorities to be the thief.

Historically, one of the main objections to admitting RO as a possible operation in the theory of grammar was the fact that it appeared to be string vacuous. As the following derivation shows, this particular objection to RO no longer carries any force:

(73)

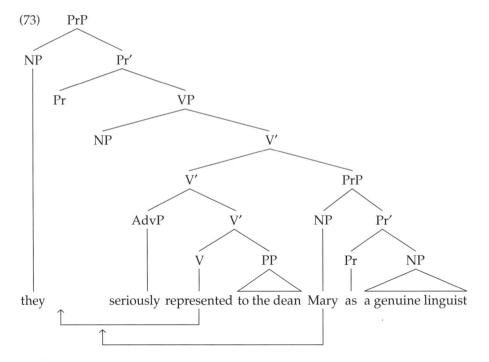

Returning finally to the impassivizible verbs in (61), note that in each case there is at least some independent evidence in support of the view that the apparent direct object is really an underlying dative argument. The apparent object in examples (61a, b) is clearly a directional complement that idiosyncratically lacks a preposition, as revealed by related examples such as *John went to his/the home* (n.b. *John went his/the home), *Mary went out of/away from the room*, etc. The dative character of the apparent object in (61c) shows up in related nominal forms such as *John's resemblance to Bill/the resemblance of John to Bill*. In the case of examples (61d, e) it seems more plausible to suppose that the measure expressions *10 lb* and *$10* are predicates of a SC complement. (61f) further supports this hypothesis, since the (impassivizible) dative object optionally occurs to the left of the measure expression.

3.2   Resultatives

Having demonstrated that RO applies to the subjects of SCs as well as to the subjects of non-finite complement clauses, we might expect to find pairs of SCs that differ only in whether they contain trace or PRO in subject position. In fact, the difference between transitive and intransitive resultative constructions (Carrier and Randall 1992) can be explained in just this fashion. Consider, for example, the following sentences:

(74)   a.   The gardener watered the tulips flat.
       b.   The grocer ground the coffee beans (in)to a fine powder.
       c.   They painted their house a hideous shade of green.

(75)   a.   The joggers ran their Nikes threadbare.
       b.   The kids laughed themselves into a frenzy.
       c.   He sneezed his handkerchief completely soggy.

Bowers (1997b) shows that the syntactic properties of these constructions follow immediately if the former are treated as control constructions and the latter as raising constructions. Otherwise, their structures are identical:

(76)   a.

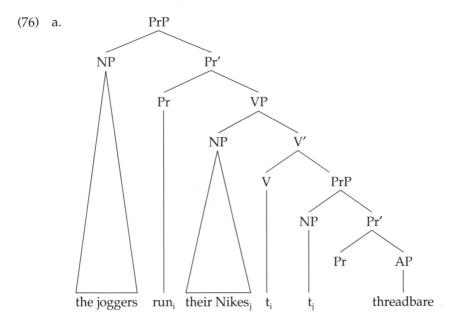

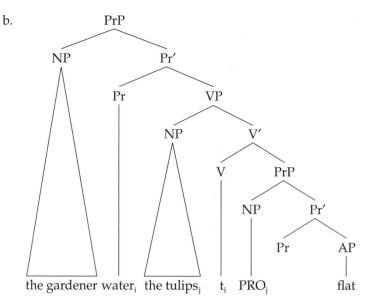

b.

the gardener water$_i$ the tulips$_j$ t$_i$ PRO$_j$ flat

Transitive and intransitive resultatives thus turn out to be exactly analogous to infinitival complements of verbs such as *persuade* and *believe*, respectively.[20]

3.3   SC adjuncts

It was observed at the beginning of this chapter that there must be a way of representing "long distance" predication, since SC complements in postverbal position can, under certain conditions, be construed as predicated of the subject. Consider, for example, the following data from Carrier and Randall (1992) containing "depictive" SCs:

(77)   a.   John$_i$ sketched the model$_j$ [nude]$_j$ [drunk as a skunk]$_j$.
      b.   John$_i$ sketched the model$_j$ [nude]$_j$ [drunk as a skunk]$_i$.
      c.   John$_i$ sketched the model$_j$ [nude]$_i$ [drunk as a skunk]$_i$.
      d.   *John$_i$ sketched the model$_j$ [nude]$_i$ [drunk as a skunk]$_j$.

What this shows is that given two depictives, both may be subject oriented; both may be object oriented; the inner one may be object oriented and the outer one subject oriented; but the inner one may not be subject oriented and the outer one object oriented. The theory proposed here provides a straightforward account of these facts in terms of the usual assumption that PRO is controlled by the nearest c-commanding antecedent. Let us hypothesize that object oriented depictives are simply V'-adjoined PrPs with a PRO subject and that subject oriented depictives are Pr'-adjoined PrPs with a PRO subject. The facts can then be handled as follows. In (77a), shown in (78), the nearest c-commanding antecedent of both *PRO nude* and *PRO drunk* is the object *the model*. In (77b), also shown in (78), the nearest c-commanding antecedent of

PRO nude is the object *the model*, while the nearest c-commanding antecedent of *PRO drunk* is the subject *John*:

(78)

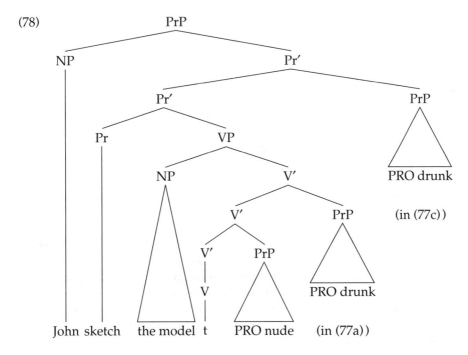

(in (77c))

(in (77a))

In (77c), shown in (79), the nearest c-commanding antecedent of both *PRO nude* and *PRO drunk* is the subject *John*. To get (77d), *PRO drunk* would have to be both c-commanded by *the model* and to the right of *PRO nude*, an impossible configuration:

(79)

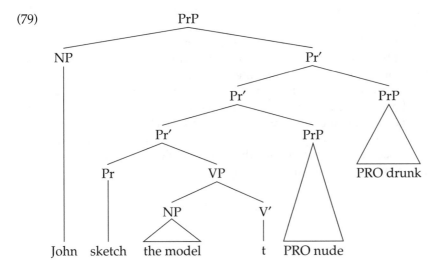

Hence all the facts can be accounted for under standard assumptions about control.

Finally, note that the assumption that object oriented depictives are V'-adjuncts explains why they cannot in general be construed as predicated of PP-complements (Bowers 1993a: 97), given the usual c-command condition on control:

(80) a. They fed the meat$_i$ to the lions$_j$ [$_{PrP}$ PRO$_{i,*j}$ raw]
      b. *The lions ate at the meat$_i$ [$_{PrP}$ PRO$_i$ raw]

Thus it appears that long distance predication can in general be reduced to control theory, given the PrP account of SCs.

4 Conclusion

There could hardly be a relation more fundamental to grammar than predication. Indeed, it could be argued that predication is, in a certain sense, *the* most fundamental relation in both syntax and semantics. Though there are many features of natural language systems that one could imagine eliminating without seriously impairing communication, predication is surely not one of them. Despite the obvious centrality of predication, syntacticians have seldom tried to approach it in a systematic and unified fashion. Instead, the feeling seems to have been that the right characterization of predication would simply fall out, once an adequate description of other more fundamental features of grammar had been attained. While agreeing with the fundamental mainstream assumption that the predication *relation* can be expected to be definable in terms of the more basic structures and categories of grammar, I believe that the work surveyed here shows that a descriptively and explanatorily adequate theory of predication requires positing a grammatical and morphological category Pr, whose function it is to relate subject to predicate. As is the case with other functional categories that have been proposed in recent years, discrete, easily identifiable phonetic reflexes of the category Pr are not always to be found. Instead, the presence of Pr must be inferred indirectly from the effects that it exerts on other categories and the syntactic patterns it induces. Once the category has been recognized, however, and its properties understood, a great many observations, some of them very well known yet never adequately explained, begin to fall into place. The result is, I believe, the beginning of a unified approach to predication, one that gives explicit recognition to the central role it plays in both syntax and semantics.

NOTES

1 An alternative proposed by Williams (1983a) is that adjacent phrases that stand in the predication relation differ only in terms of indexing: I found [John]ᵢ [a good psychotherapist]ᵢ (for the (a) interpretation of (5)) vs. I found [John] [a good psychotherapist] (for the (b) interpretation of (5)). I do not deal with Williams's approach directly here other than to note that many of the phenomena described in this chapter, e.g. unlike category conjunction (section 1.4), VP conjunction (section 2.1), quantifier floating (section 3.1.1), VP fronting (section 3.1.2), and others, simply cannot be described adequately without assuming a SC constituent.

2 Categories partially similar to Pr that have been proposed recently in the literature include the "VP shell" (Larson 1988), Voice (Kratzer 1993), v (Chomsky 1995b), and Tr (Collins 1997). Unlike VP shell and v, Pr is required for predication and is therefore present regardless of how many arguments the verb requires. (See section 2.2 for discussion.) Note also that of these categories Pr is the only one that takes as its complement maximal projections of any lexical category. Hence it is the only one capable of unifying predication in both MCs and SCs.

3 This would then make it possible, as suggested by Chomsky (1981), Rothstein (1983), Chierchia (1989), and Bowers (1993a), to derive the Extended Projection Principle (EPP), which requires that clauses have subjects, from the more basic principle that functions must be saturated. Note, however, that the EPP, as refined in more recent syntactic work, refers to an entirely different parameter, namely, whether or not a language requires that [Spec, T] be filled.

To account for the semantics of true expletives (e.g. the *it*-subject of the verb *seem*), I assume, following Chierchia (1989), that there is a type-shifting operation of "expletivization" E whose logical type is: $p \rightarrow \pi$, i.e., it turns propositions into properties. Applied to the proposition **seem**(p), E yields a property E(**seem**(p)) that predicated of an arbitrarily chosen funny object (indicated by "⊥") yields the proposition **seem**(p); applied to anything other than ⊥, E is undefined. Chierchia shows that such a type-shifting operation is independently motivated in a number of different ways. This makes it possible to retain the assumption that clausal structure universally involves semantic predication, while at the same time avoiding an analysis such as that proposed in Williams (1983b), in which verbs such as *seem* are treated as adverbs semantically.

4 Another possibility, proposed independently by Baker (1997a) and Eide and Åfarli (1997), is to treat the copula *be* as a lexical realization of Pr itself. Lack of space precludes a thorough discussion of the problems with this proposal, but note, for example, that it would make it difficult to account for the difference in meaning between pairs such as *I made John a good teacher/I made John be a good teacher*. See also Rothstein (1997) for arguments that the copula makes an identifiable semantic contribution to the meaning of

sentences, hence cannot be merely a semantically empty phonetic realization of a category such as T or Pr.

5   Notice, incidentally, that this analysis would also make it possible to distinguish structurally between unaccusative and unergative Adjectives, the former having an argument in [Spec, A], the latter an argument in [Spec, Pr]. It has been argued that such a distinction exists in both Italian (Cinque 1990a) and German (Moltmann 1989).

6   In theories that assume a VP shell or "light" verb v, it is usually assumed that unergatives derive uniformly from underlying transitives with an incorporated "cognate object" and an underlying light verb in upper VP (Hale and Keyser 1993). However, the evidence for such derivations is weak at best, in my view. See Rubin (1990), for an interesting use of these structures to explain the properties of Italian experiencer predicates such as *preoccupare* and *piacere*. See also Bowers (1998) for a radically derivational approach to the problem of unergative versus unaccusative predicates, as well as to experiencer predicates in Italian and English.

7   An apparent problem for the claim that *as* is a phonetic realization of Pr is the following example, pointed out to me by Mark Baltin: *I see him as quickly taking advantage of whatever opportunities come his way.* If *quickly* is, as I have argued, a Pr-licensed adverb and if the phrase *taking advantage of . . .* is a VP, then the order should apparently be: **I see him quickly as taking advantage . . .* Note, however, that the gerundive or participial complement in this example must evidently be a full TP (or perhaps DP), as shown by the presence of the perfect

auxiliary in an example such as the following: *I see him as having quickly taken advantage of the situation.* Since T selects PrP, the adverb *quickly* can simply be analyzed as a Pr'-adjunct within the TP (or DP) complement of Pr. Alternatively, it might be the case that *as* in these examples is a complementizer rather than a realization of Pr. Further investigation of the multifarious uses of *as* is clearly needed.

8   Furthermore, they show that the former occurs systematically with predicate nominals, suggesting that its function is to case mark predicate nominals.

9   The only way to do so would be by means of Gapping. For arguments in favor of such an approach, see Jackendoff (1990a); for arguments against, see Larson (1990) and Bowers (1993a).

10 I use the term "license" here in a loose fashion merely to indicate that there is a relationship of some sort between heads and the adverb classes associated with them. The traditional term "modifier" might well be more appropriate, in which case we could refer to "V-modifers," "Pr-modifiers," etc.

11 It is argued in Bowers (1993a) that the latter assumption is untenable.

12 As noted in Bowers (1993a), an adverb may also belong to more than one class, in which case we expect to find subtle meaning differences depending on which position it occurs in.

13 Adverbial modifiers of adjectives and prepositions, in contrast, never seem to be able to occur to the right of the head:

(i) a. John is (so) extremely angry (*(so) extremely) at Mary.
     b. Mary shot the ball right through (*right) the net.

Assuming a structure for (ia) of the sort discussed in section 1.3:

(ii) John is [$_{PrP}$ t [$_{Pr}$ Pr [$_{DegP}$ so [$_{QP}$ extremely [$_{AP}$ angry at Mary]]]]]

it is immediately apparent that adjunction of A to Pr would produce the ungrammatical examples indicated above. A similar argument can be constructed for PP, assuming that *right* is a degree modifier of prepositions (Emonds 1976). It would thus appear that A and P, in contrast to V and N, never raise to Pr. Hence the A-features and P-features of Pr must be weak in English.

14 Apparent violations of these ordering restrictions will arise if there are processes that move objects rightward, as in the case of so-called Heavy-NP Shift (Bowers 1997a): *John spoke perfectly to Mary all the languages that he had learned at his mother's knee*, etc.

15 Under standard Minimalist assumptions, movement is only possible for the purpose of checking morphological features such as Case and Agreement (Last Resort), which can in turn only be checked in [Spec, Agr]. It follows that if RO exists, then either Agr$_O$P must be located between PrP and VP (the "Split VP Hypothesis") or else Case Theory must be revised in such a way as to force raising of the complement subject directly into [Spec, V]. The first possibility has been explored by Koizumi (1993, 1995), Bowers (1993b), and Lasnik (1995a, 1995b, 1995c), while the second is proposed in Bowers (1997a, 1998). The Split VP Hypothesis is apparently inconsistent with the literature on Object Shift in Icelandic, which has been taken to show that object agreement features must be checked in a position *above* whatever category it is that contains the internal subject (in our case, PrP). RO, on the other hand, for which we have amassed a considerable amount of evidence, must clearly raise subjects to a position *below* the Verb in its raised position adjoined to Pr. Hence it would appear that RO and Object Shift cannot both involve movement to Agr$_O$P, or its equivalent.

16 For arguments against Sportiche (1988)'s assumption that the floated quantifier originates inside the moved DP, see Bowers (1993a), section 3.4.1, and Baltin (1995). Note that if the floated quantifier were treated as a Pr'/I'-adjunct, like the adverbs discussed earlier, it would not c-command the trace of the moved NP, making it difficult to assign the scope of the quantifier correctly without further movement. Not only is there no evidence for the required (obligatory) movement but it would also violate standard movement constraints.

17 A potential problem with treating directional and dative PP-complements as control constructions is that the direct object can be omitted with certain verbs that take dative complements, e.g. *he gave to the United Way*, thus apparently violating Bach's generalization that controllers do not delete. It is perfectly possible, however, that the object in such constructions is not deleted, but rather that there is an empty category such as *pro* in object position. In the case of agentless passives such as *the boat was sunk*, there is considerable support for the view that there is an "understood" agent in the syntax.

18 A number of potential problems with Huang's analysis have been

pointed out by Heycock (1995). One problem that is immediately obviated by the analysis proposed here is the fact that fronted predicate DPs behave exactly like other predicative complements with respect to reconstruction possibilities. Heycock assumes that such complements have a structure of the following sort:

(i)   His parents consider [$_{DP}$ Sally [$_{DP}$ Bill's best friend]]

from which it follows, contrary to fact, that a fronted predicate DP should have exactly the same reconstruction possibilities as a fronted argument. Under the analysis proposed here, however, the structure of (i) is exactly parallel to the structure of other predicative complements:

(ii)   His parents consider Sally [$_{PrP}$ t Pr [$_{DP}$ Bill's best friend]]

Since it is PrP, by hypothesis, that is fronted, it is correctly predicted that fronted predicate DPs should have exactly the same coreference possibilities as other predicative complements.

As for the other examples that Heycock cites, there are additional data that blunt considerably her criticisms of Huang's analysis. For example, she notes that there are grammatical cases of coreference that apparently should be ruled out by Huang's analysis:

(iii) a.   How pleased with the pictures Pollock$_i$ painted in his youth do you think he$_i$ really was?
       b.   How afraid of the people Gore$_i$ insulted years ago do you think he$_i$ is now?

Note, however, that the predictions made by Huang's analysis do hold

for topicalized predicate APs (as opposed to *wh*-APs), as the following contrasts show:

(iv)   a.   *Very pleased with pictures Clemente$_i$ has painted recently I don't consider him$_i$.
       b.   Very pleased with pictures he$_i$ has painted recently I don't consider Clemente$_i$.
       c.   How pleased with pictures Clemente$_i$ has painted recently do you consider him$_i$?

(v)   a.   *Afraid of people Gore$_i$ insults I don't consider him$_i$.
       b.   Afraid of people he$_i$ insults I don't consider Gore$_i$.
       c.   How afraid of people Gore$_i$ insults do you consider him$_i$?

Though more work is clearly needed, these data suggest that topicalization of SC complements involves movement of the whole PrP, including the trace of a raised subject, whereas the corresponding *wh*-questions, in contrast, only involve movement of the predicate AP. Assuming Lebeaux (1988, 1990, 1991)'s analysis of adjuncts, the grammaticality of the (c) sentences in (iv)–(v) is then explained by the fact that there is a derivation in which the relative clause adjunct is only added after the phrase in question has been moved out of the c-command domain of the pronoun. There is, however, no comparable way of rescuing the (a) sentences, because the topicalized PrP contains a trace of raised pronominal subject of the predicate AP.

Another potential problem (noted also by Barss 1986), is that an R-expression inside a moved predicate is apparently incorrectly predicted to be free to corefer with the subject of any higher clause. This, however, seems to be true of *both* topicalized PrPs and *wh*-APs:

(vi) a. *How afraid of Margaret$_i$ do you think she$_i$ expects John to be?

      b. *Afraid of Margaret$_i$ I don't think she$_i$ considers John.

suggesting that reconstruction of both topicalized PrPs and *wh*-APs is necessary, contrary to what was assumed in the previous paragraph. How to resolve this apparent contradiction is a question I leave to future research.

19 See Bailyn (1995a, 1995b, 1995c) and Bailyn and Rubin (1991) for work showing that structures identical to these are needed in so-called "free word order" languages such as Russian.

20 For another case in which SC complements may differ only in whether they involve Raising or Control, see the analysis of individual-level and stage-level predicates, respectively, in Bowers (1993b).

11 Case

HIROYUKI URA

0 Introduction

Case has a long history in the grammatical study of human languages. Although it stems from the Classical Greek word that means declension or modification and it was originally used to refer to the variants of a given noun, it came to mean "interrelation between nouns (or words)" in the course of the Middle Ages. In modern linguistics, case is used to refer to something like "grammatical forms expressing some relations that such nominal categories (henceforth, nominals) as nouns, pronouns, or adjectives may bear in a clause," though it is often the case that one framework varies widely from another in its exact denotation. In this chapter I describe case, concentrating on its treatments within the framework of Generative Grammar.

Whatever framework may be assumed, however, it is not easy to tell exactly what kind of role case plays in the grammatical system of natural language: it does not refer merely to the declined forms (morphological shape) of nominals, or the relationships they bear in a clause. Rather, it is the generic term given to what expresses abstract relationships between morphological forms of nominals and the interpretational relations they bear in a clause. In other words it refers to the grammatical category that mediates between form (morphophonology) and meaning (semantics). In this respect it is very interesting to ask what kind of role case plays in syntax, for syntax is often assumed to be the intermediate between semantics and morphophonology, especially within the framework of Generative Grammar. In what follows in this chapter I address myself to some issues that case poses to the theory of syntax.[1]

1 Morphological Case, Abstract Case, and Universal Grammar

In the history of linguistics, case was studied for a long time as one of the main topics of morphology: the study was made primarily by considering such questions as "how does the variance of the forms of case yield the difference in meaning?" or "what kind of case should be employed when such and such a meaning is expressed?" Even in the Generative Grammatical tradition, case was regarded as a merely morphological feature that is assigned by a (kind of transformational) rule to a particular lexical item with such a grammatical relation as SUBJECT or OBJECT (cf. Chomsky 1965, Siegel 1974). Since grammatical relations are structurally determined in the framework of Chomsky (1965), the morphological shape of a given nominal is also determined according to its structural position in this framework.

It is a well-known fact that languages differ in terms of their way of expressing morphological case on nominals. In Latin, for example, every noun has six forms of case, each of which is expressed by declining its stem. While, like Latin, many languages in the world (Russian, Finnish, Georgian, Basque, etc.) have morphologically distinct forms of case for all nominals, it is only for pronouns that English makes the distinction in terms of their morphological shapes, and the distinction is only binary: nominative vs. non-nominative. Still more curiously, in languages like Chinese or Thai, there is simply no morphological distinction of case. It should be noted, however, that the fundamental assumption of Generative Grammar concerning the uniformity of the human language ability (i.e., the assumption about Universal Grammar) demands that the aforementioned differences among languages in terms of the morphologically overt/covert marking of case should be taken to be superficial and attributed to some parametric variations in morphology. The important point is that, whether it is overtly displayed or not, case should be present in all nominals at a more deeply abstract level in the theory of grammar. This abstract notion of case as a theoretical construct is called "abstract Case" to contrast it with the morphological forms of case. Hereafter I will call the former "Case" (capital C) and the latter "case" (small letter c). Under this view of Case and case, the morphological shape of a given DP is regarded as the morphophonological realization of Case, an abstract feature assigned to that DP by some rule.

2 Syntax of Case Marking

Under the aforementioned theory of abstract Case assumed in the Aspects model, Case was connected remotely with syntax, for Case is just marked by the Case marking rule upon a nominal with such and such a grammatical relation. In the late 1970s and the early 1980s, however, Case came to play a significant role in syntactic theory.

2.1 *Theory of abstract Case*

Chomsky (1980), following an idea suggested by Jean-Roger Vergnaud (cf. Rouveret and Vergnaud 1980, Vergnaud 1985), proposed that Case should be regarded as the prerequisite for DP to be active in syntax. That is to say, a sentence containing any (phonologically overt) DP without Case appropriate for its structural positioning is excluded as an ungrammatical one. This idea about the licensing of DP with Case enabled us to give an answer not only to the question concerning the distribution of DP in syntactic structures but also to the question of why certain DPs must undergo the transformation called DP-movement.

Elaborating this idea under a more integrated theory of grammar, Chomsky (1981) made the following proposals (later called Case Theory, which was supposed to be a module of Universal Grammar):[2]

(1) **Case Filter** (applied at S-structure)
    *NP if NP has phonetic content and has no Case. (Chomsky 1981: 49)

(2) **Case Assignment Rules** (Chomsky 1981: 170)
    a.   NP is nominative if governed by AGR.
    b.   NP is objective if governed by V with the subcategorization feature: ____NP (i.e., transitive).
    c.   NP is oblique if governed by P.
    d.   NP is genitive in [$_{NP}$____X'].
    e.   NP is inherently Case-marked as determined by properties of its [−N] governor.

Furthermore, Chomsky (1981) proposed to distinguish Case assigned under (2e) from the others assigned under (2a, b, c, d): the former was named "inherent Case" and the rest "structural Case." He assumed that, while structural Case is dissociated from theta-role and assigned in a purely structural way, inherent Case is linked closely with theta-role. Hence, various theta-roles may be assigned to an element with a given structural Case in principle. This captures a well-known fact concerning a difference between structural Case and inherent Case: in accusative languages like English, Latin, and Japanese, DP as the subject in a clause which is assigned nominative Case under (2a), and DP as the object in a clause which is assigned accusative Case under (2b),[3] may usually have various kinds of theta-role; on the other hand, DP with such inherent Case marking as ablative or instrumental can only have a fixed theta-role such as that associated with Source or Instrumental (cf. Fillmore 1968).[4]

2.2   *Government based Case theory*

Since its original formulation in Chomsky (1980), Case Theory had been continuously elaborated in subsequent work through the GB era (e.g., among many others, Chomsky 1981, 1986a, Stowell 1981, Baker 1988). Most remarkable is the elaboration concerning the unification of structural conditions on

Case marking. Except genitive Case, all other structural Cases are assigned under government. It is theoretically preferable if we can say all Cases are assigned under government. Let us assume, following the lead of Abney (1987), that noun phrases are headed not by N (noun itself) but by D (determiner), the abstract functional category responsible for the inflection within noun phrases. According to this DP-hypothesis, noun phrases such as *John's belief that Mary kissed him* are analyzed as in (3):[5]

(3)

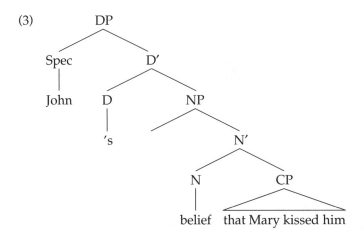

Now suppose that the possessive marker *'s* as a D has the ability to assign genitive Case under government. Then, it is possible to say that it is under government that the assignment of genitive Case to *John* (3) is executed. With this modification of (2d),[6] the assignment of all structural Cases is unified under government; thence, this elaborated Case theory can be called "Government Based Case Theory" (hereafter, G-CT).

Moreover, in formulating (2a), Chomsky (1981) assumed the phrase structure illustrated in (4), where the surface position of Subject counts as a daughter of the S-node, which also dominates Infl (containing AGR-features):

(4)　　　　　S　　　　　(linear order irrelevant)

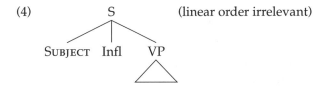

In fact, the position of Subject is indeed governed by Infl in (4), but it is odd from the X′-theoretical point of view since S does not have a head (see Stowell 1981) in (4).[7] Under Chomsky's (1986b) X′-theory, reinforced with the binary branching hypothesis of Kayne (1984), it is assumed that Subject in an indicative affirmative clause usually occupies the Spec of Infl at S-structure, as illustrated in (5):

(5)   IP   (linear order irrelevant)

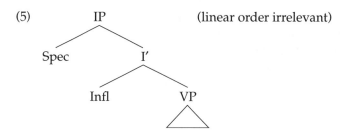

In the structure illustrated in (5), which satisfies the X'-theory, the Spec of Infl is also governed by Infl as required.

With this (elaborated) G-CT, we can appropriately predict which case form of DPs can appear in which positions. Take (6), for example:

(6)   a.   We/*Us/*Our love *they/them/*their.
       b.   *he/*him/his belief that Mary kissed Bill

The first person plural pronoun at the sentence initial position in (6a), which is assumed to occupy the Spec of Infl (a functional head including AGR), is governed by AGR; therefore it is assigned nominative Case and morphophonologically realized as *we* in English. Likewise, the third person plural pronoun, which counts as the object of the transitive verb *love*, must stand in the accusative, for it is governed by the verb and, hence, assigned accusative Case by it.[8] In (6b), on the other hand, the third person masculine singular pronoun is governed by D (just like *John* in (3) above), resulting in its morphological realization of genitive Case.

The above examples in (6) show how the G-CT works to exclude DPs whose assigned Case feature is incorrectly realized in their surface positions. In addition, the G-CT enables us to explain the ungrammaticality of sentences in which DP fails to be assigned a proper Case:

(7)   a.   Mary loves him.
       b.   Mary is fond *(of) him.
       c.   Mary criticized him.
       d.   Mary's criticism *(of) him.

Note that the preposition *of* in these examples has no particular meaning. Then, the ungrammaticality of the sentences without it must be attributed to something other than meaning; namely, form. Given the G-CT, the reason why they are ill formed is that there is no proper Case assignor available. Although the adjective *fond* in (7b) and the noun *criticism* in (7d), respectively, can properly assign a theta-role to *him*, they are not a structural Case assignor. Hence, *him* fails to satisfy the Case Filter, resulting in ungrammaticality, unless some proper preposition like *of* is provided to realize the inherent Case assigned to it together with its theta-role (see Chomsky 1986a, Chomsky and

Lasnik 1993). In (7a, c), on the other hand, the verbs *love* and *criticize*, both of which assign an external theta-role to their subject, can properly assign accusative Case to *him* as required.

Next let us consider (8):

(8)   a.   [That John loves Mary] is doubtful.
    b.   [*(For) John to love Mary] would be doubtful.

In (8a), *John* is properly assigned nominative Case by the Infl in the embedded clause because the Infl in the embedded clause in (8a) is a tensed one and has AGR in English. On the other hand, the Infl in the embedded infinitival clause in (8b) lacks AGR because of its [–AGR] nature in Modern English; therefore *John* in (8b) has no proper Case assignor available unless the prepositional complementizer *for* is provided to assign oblique Case to it (see Chomsky 1981, Stowell 1981, for the prepositional complementizer).[9] It is interesting to notice that the Case Filter (1) requires that Case must be assigned to DP if DP has phonetic content. Then, this allows us to predict that if DP lacks phonetic content, it can occur at a position to which Case is not assigned. This prediction is, indeed, borne out:

(9)   a.   [{ PRO / *(For) him } to go abroad] would be nice.
    b.   John's plan [{ PRO / *(For) him } to go abroad].
    c.   It is nice [{ PRO / *(For) him } to go abroad].

As can be deduced from the discussion thus far, the positions where PRO occurs in the examples in (9) are all Case-less: since the English infinitival Infl has no ability to assign Case to its Spec because of its [–AGR] nature, there is no Case assignor inside the embedded infinitival clauses in (9). Even outside of the clause, there is no Case assignor available, for nouns and adjectives lack any ability to assign Case; therefore, PRO can occur there without any proposition.[10]

2.3   Exceptional Case marking

Here it is important to note that it is because Case is not available from inside or outside of the infinitival clause that phonologically overt DPs (without any prepositional complementizer) are disallowed to occur at the subject position of the infinitival clause lexically selected by a category lacking Case assigning ability such as nouns or adjectives, just as *him* in (9b, c) is disallowed. Given that transitive verbs can assign Case, it is interesting to consider what happens about Case if an infinitival clause is selected by such a verb.

To examine this, take the following examples:

(10)   a.   Mary believed/considered/reported [John/*PRO to have loved her].
     b.   Mary tried/intended/managed/desired [*John/PRO to go abroad].

Since all the verbs in (10) assign an external theta-role, they may count as an accusative Case assignor (see n. 8). This enables us to predict that phonologically overt DPs are allowed to occur at the subject position of the embedded infinitival clauses in (10) because (accusative) Case is available from V from the outside of the clauses. Then, why are they excluded only in (10b)?

Although each verb in (10b) as a transitive one may have the ability to assign accusative Case, it is possible to say that it cannot assign its Case to the subject position of the embedded infinitival clause because it does not govern the position. This is confirmed by the fact that PRO, which can appear only in a non-governed position (see n. 10), can appear there. Then, what prevents the verbs from governing that position in (10b)? It is commonly assumed that such verbs as listed in (10b) select CP as their infinitival complement, so that V cannot govern the Spec of Infl where the subject of the embedded clause occurs. This is due to the so-called Relativized Minimality effect on government (see Rizzi 1990) (that is, C m-commands that position more closely than V m-commands it: cf. the definition of government given in n. 2), as illustrated in (11):

(11)   . . . tried/intended/managed/desired [$_{CP}$ C [$_{IP}$ John to [$_{VP}$ go abroad]]]

Therefore, phonologically overt DPs are excluded in (10b) because Case cannot be assigned to them under government. The verbs that select an infinitival CP-clause as its complement, disallowing phonologically overt DPs in the subject position of the infinitival clause, are called "control verbs."[11]

Returning to the examples in (10a), we can conclude from the prohibition of PRO at the subject position of the embedded infinitival clause that that position is indeed governed. Besides, we have already noted that Case is not available to the subject position of an infinitival clause in English from the inside of the clause. Thus, it must be that the Case of the phonologically overt DP at the subject position of the infinitival clause in (10a) is assigned under government from the outside of the clause; namely, from the matrix V. The fact that the matrix verbs in (10a) are all accusative Case assignors leads us to predict that the Case of the phonologically overt DP must be accusative. This prediction is borne out by the following example:

(12)   Mary believed/considered/reported [him/*he/*his to have loved her].

Next let us consider how the matrix verbs in (12) can assign accusative Case under government to the subject position of the infinitival clause that they select as their complement. If they select a CP-complement just like control verbs, they can never govern that position, as argued above. Hence, the infinitival complement clause they select must be IP, as illustrated in (13):

(13) . . . believed/considered/reported [$_{IP}$ him to [$_{VP}$ love her]]

Since in (13), the verbs m-command *him*, and there is no head such that the verbs c-command it and it c-commands *John* (notice that the Infl *to* m-commands but does not c-command *him*), the verbs govern *him*, resulting in proper assignment of accusative Case to *him*, as required. The verbs that select an infinitival IP-clause as their complement, allowing phonologically overt DP in the subject position of the infinitival clause, are called "ECM (Exceptional Case Marking) verbs." ECM verbs, too, and their constructions have raised a lot of interesting issues concerning Case in the history of Generative Grammar (cf. Postal 1974), some of which are still attracting much interest in the framework under the Minimalist program (cf. Koizumi 1993, Ura 1993, Bošković 1997b).

2.4   *Case and DP-movements*

In the previous subsection we observed that phonologically overt DPs cannot occur at a Case-less position, and that they are excluded as a violation of the Case Filter unless some means to supply them with Case (like inserting a preposition such as *for* or *of* in front of them) is provided. Therefore it is natural to deduce that a phonologically overt DP at a Case-less position can move from there to a position where Case is available in order to get assigned Case. This is the rationale of DP-movements in the GB theory with the G-CT as a module of Universal Grammar (see Baltin in this volume for more details on DP-movements). Vast numbers of studies in the GB era were devoted to confirming that DPs are moved on Case-theoretic grounds in a variety of constructions in a variety of languages (see, among many others, Marantz 1984, Baker 1988, Bittner and Hale 1996a). In this subsection I will sketch out some of the rudimentary applications of the G-CT to DP-movements.[12]

Looking back at the Case assignment rules stated in (2), we realize that (structural) Case assignors are all [–N]. When considering the examples in (7) above, we have already observed that adjectives and nouns, both of which are analyzed as [+N] under the categorial feature classification (cf. Jackendoff 1977), do not have the ability to assign Case to elements they govern. Now it is a traditional claim that past participles behave like adjectives in many respects. In accordance with this tradition, let us assume that past participles lack the specification concerning [±N]. Then, we expect that past participles like adjectives lack the ability to assign Case. Now consider what happens when a structure like the following is constructed at D-structure:

(14) [$_{IP}$ *e* Infl [$_{VP}$ is loved Mary]]. (D-structure)

In (14) the subject position (i.e., the Spec of Infl) is empty (which is represented by *e*). The object *Mary* in (14) cannot get any Case if it stays there at S-structure because the past participle *loved* cannot assign Case. But the subject position, which is now empty, can be provided with nominative Case by the tensed finite Infl. Suppose that in order for *Mary* to get assigned Case by Infl under government to fulfill the Case Filter at S-structure, it is moved from the object position, where it is base generated, to the subject position. This derivation is illustrated in (15):

(15)   [$_{IP}$ Mary$_k$ Infl [$_{VP}$ is loved t$_k$]]. (S-structure)

This is the explanation of the derivation for passive clauses under the G-CT.[13]

Some kinds of adjective that subcategorize a clausal complement assign no theta-role to their subject position. In the theory for the architecture of phrase structures assumed in the GB era (called Projection Principle), the lack of theta-role at a position means that that position is empty at D-structure, and can serve as a landing site of DP-movements and host pleonastic elements like English *it* or *there* (see Roberts 1987, Shlonsky 1987, as well as Fukui in this volume):

(16)   a.   It is certain/likely [that John has loved Mary].
       b.   *e* is certain/likely [John to have loved Mary]. (D-structure)
       c.   John$_k$ is certain/likely [t$_k$ to have loved Mary]. (S-structure)

Given that adjectives cannot assign Case, *John* in (16b) gets no Case if it lingers in the subject position of the infinitival complement at S-structure. The same mechanism as in the passive formation applies here: the Case-less DP is moved from its Case-less base position to the Spec of finite Infl, where nominative case is provided by Infl under government. This DP-movement derives the S-structure illustrated in (16c) from the D-structure in (16b). This is the G-CT analysis of the kinds of DP-movement called "raising."[14]

The analysis of raising with the G-CT gives an account of the reason why raising is prohibited from the subject position of a finite clause:

(17)   a.   *e* is certain/likely [that John has loved Mary]. (D-structure)
       b.   *John$_k$ is certain/likely [that t$_k$ has loved Mary]. (S-structure)

In (17a) *John* is already located at a position where it can get (nominative) Case; therefore, it need not move any more to seek for Case. If the system of the grammar for human language has a Last Resort constraint which forces it to avoid any redundant operation (see Collins in this volume), the movement of *John* illustrated in (17b) violates this constraint, resulting in its degradation in grammaticality.

In this subsection I have sketched out a few instances of DP-movements that are claimed to be caused by Case under the G-CT.[15] As is evident from the discussion presented so far, the G-CT, which consists of the Case Filter and the Case assignment rules stated in (1) and (2), depends crucially on notions such as government, the Projection Principle, the distinction between D- and S-structure, etc. Chomsky (1992), however, casts a strong doubt on these notions as a conceptual construct necessary for the system of the grammar for human language. Hence, in the Minimalist framework initiated by Chomsky (1992) and continuously elaborated in subsequent work (cf. Chomsky 1995b), an approach without resort to those conceptually unnecessary notions has been taken. In section 4 below, I will outline the Case theory assumed in the earlier Minimalist program, which is called "AGR-based Case theory."

Before entering into the discussion on Minimalist Case theory, I will, first, take a look at the issue concerning the significant relationship between abstract Case and grammatical relations, an issue which is very traditional but still central to the study of case/Case in general linguistics.

3 Case and Grammatical Functions/Relations

3.1 Structural determination of Case and grammatical functions/relations

It is commonly held in the literature that every element (mostly, argument) in a clause has its own grammatical functions (hereafter, GFs). Each of the abilities to launch a quantifier floating, to control the missing subject in a subordinate adjunct clause, to bind a (subject oriented) reflexive, to induce subject agreement on the finite verb of the clause, to stand in nominative, etc. is regarded as a GF.[16] Grammatical relations (GRs) such as SUBJECT and OBJECT have been used as a cover term to refer to a set of some of those GFs that a single argument in a clause is supposed to have in general.

A widely held view is that, if some argument A in a clause counts as having the GR SUBJECT (i.e., A assumes SUBJECTHOOD), then A is supposed to have the set of the GFs that are linked with the GR SUBJECT. And it is also widely assumed that, if A has one of the GFs linked to SUBJECTHOOD, then A counts as the SUBJECT of the clause. In English, for example, if a DP counts as having the GR SUBJECT, the DP is expected to have the GFs linked to SUBJECT, such as the ability to induce agreement on the finite verb in the clause and the ability to control the missing subject of a subordinate adjunct clause like the *without*-clause (cf. Postal 1990: 373–4):

(18) a. They$_k$ *has/have hired John$_i$ [without PRO$_{*i/k}$ having to commit themselves$_k$/*himself$_i$ to that salary].

     b. John$_i$ has/*have been hired (by them$_k$) [without PRO$_{i/*k}$ having to commit *themselves$_k$/himself$_i$ to that salary].

Inversely, by differentiating which argument has one of the GFs linked to SUBJECT, we can tell which argument should be the SUBJECT of the clause.

In section 1, we observed that the Case theory assumed in the *Aspect* model associates Case very closely with GRs. We also observed, in section 2, that under the G-CT assumed in the GB theory, the Case of a given DP is determined according to the structural position the DP occupies at S-structure. Independently of the G-CT, Chomsky (1981) proposed the idea that the GR of a given DP which is assumed to be a bundle of certain GFs is also determined according to the structural position of the DP at S-structure. According to this idea, the DP located at the Spec of Infl, for example, is regarded as having GFs linked with the GR SUBJECT. This idea about GFs/GRs has been commonly accepted under the GB theory.[17] The important point is that Case is correlated with GRs through the mediation of structural relations under the GB theory.

3.2   *Problems for structural determination of Case*

Empirical studies on the relationship between Case and GRs/GFs, however, have demonstrated that there are lots of problems for any approach that correlates Case with GRs. Under the GB theory, structural relations are guaranteed to be invariant and universal thanks to the "conventional" X'-theory and the Projection Principle (see Fukui in this volume). Many researchers (e.g., among others, Keenan 1987, Comrie 1989, Palmer 1994, Givón 1997) have revealed that some GFs that an argument with a particular GR is believed to bear are neither absolute nor invariant ones, but they vary from language to language or even from construction to construction in a single language. These kinds of phenomenon (what I call GF-splitting phenomena) in which GFs are split up can hardly be given any consistent account under the theory that considers GRs to be uniformly defined through invariant structural relations. Now that Case is correlated with GRs through structural relations under the GB theory, such GF-splitting phenomena are problematic to the G-CT.[18]

A typical example of GF-splitting phenomena can be found in languages like Icelandic, where, in addition to an ordinary clause where the nominative marked DP has the functions to be associated with the GR SUBJECT (functions such as the ability to induce the agreement inflection, the ability to control, the ability to bind a subject oriented reflexive, etc.), we can find a clause in which a non-nominative marked DP, instead of the nominative marked one, seems to function as the subject of the clause. (This construction is called "Quirky-Subject Construction" (QSC).)

Among QSCs, constructions with a dative subject (Dative Subject Constructions (DSCs)) have been studied most intensively in the literature (see Harley 1995, Ura 1996, forthcoming, for the list of studies on DSCs in a variety of languages). Japanese is one of the languages that allow DSCs. Let us take a look at Japanese DSCs and see how this raises problems to the G-CT. DSCs in Japanese may occur when the predicate in the clause is a kind of so-called psych-predicate:

(19) a. Taroo-ni hebi-ga kowa-i. (Japanese)
Taroo-Dat snake-Nom fearful-Pres
"Taroo is fearful of snakes."

b. Taroo-ni eigo-ga dekir-u.
Taroo-Dat English-Nom understand-Pres
"Taroo understands English."

Many studies on Japanese DSCs have concluded that the dative marked DP in this construction must count as SUBJECT syntactically; that is, it has GFs associated with the GR SUBJECT (see, among many others, Perlmutter 1984 and references there). First, it can bind a subject oriented anaphor:

(20) John-ni$_k$ zibun-ga$_k$/zibun-zishin-ga$_k$ simpai-da. (Japanese)
John-Dat self-Nom/self-self-Nom worry-Cop
"John$_k$ worries about himself$_k$."

The subject oriented anaphora *zibun* and *zibun-zishin* cannot be coreferential with any non-subject even if it is c-commanded, as the ill-formedness of (21) shows:

(21) John-ga$_k$ Mary-o$_i$ [zibun$_{k/*i}$/zibun-zishin-no$_{k/*i}$ sensei]-ni (Japanese)
John-Nom Mary-Acc self/self-self-Gen teacher-to
hikiawaser-(ar)er-u.
introduce-Pot-Pres
"[Lit.] John$_k$ can introduce Mary$_i$ to self's$_{k/*i}$ teacher."

The well-formedness of (22) below, where the non-subject oriented reflexive *kanojo-zishin* is properly bound by *Mary*, shows that *Mary* in (21) indeed c-commands, but not binds, *zibun/zibun-zishin*:

(22) John-ga Mary-o$_i$ [kanojo-zishin-no$_i$ sensei]-ni (Japanese)
John-Nom Mary-Acc herself-Gen teacher-to
hikiawaser-(ar)er-u.
introduce-Pot-Pres
"[Lit.] John can introduce Mary$_i$ to herself's$_i$ teacher."

The conclusion is that the dative marked DP in DSCs can bind a subject oriented anaphor in Japanese.

Second, the dative marked DP in DSCs can control the missing subject of a subordinate adjunct clause:

(23) [PRO$_k$ sutoraiki-o yat-tei-nagara], (Japanese: Perlmutter 1984: 321)
strike-Acc do-Prog-while
roodoosya-ni(-wa)$_k$ sono mokuteki-ga wakara-nakat-ta.
workers-Dat(-Top) its purpose-Nom understand-Neg-Past
"[Lit.] While PRO$_k$ being on strike, the workers$_k$ did not understand its purpose."

As the ill-formedness of (24) shows, PRO in the Japanese *-nagara* construction cannot be controlled by any non-subject (Perlmutter 1984):

(24)   [PRO$_{k/*i}$ ongaku-o   kiki-nagara],   John-ga$_k$ Mary-o$_i$ (Japanese)
                music-Acc listen to-while John-Nom Mary-Acc
       damasi-ta.
       cheat-Past
       "While PRO$_{k/*i}$ listening to music, John$_k$ cheated Mary$_i$."

It is interesting to notice that, as shown in (21) and (24), it is the nominative marked DP that has the ability to bind a subject oriented reflexive, and the ability to control the missing subject of a subordinate adjunct clause when the clause is an ordinary transitive clause with the nominative–accusative pattern. From these observations, it can be justly said that it is not always the case, contrary to Chomsky's (1981) theory of GFs/GRs, that nominative Case is assigned to the DP with the GR Subject.

Far more interesting to our concern is the fact that there is evidence which indicates that the dative marked DP in Japanese DSCs is located at the Spec of Infl at S-structure. Consider (25), in which subject honorification is involved:

(25)   a.   Yamada-sensei-ga   seito-o   o-tasuke-ni   nar-ta.   (Japanese)
            Prof. Yamada-Nom student-Acc Hon-help-to become-Past
            "Prof. Yamada helped a student."
       b.   *Seito-ga   Yamada-sensei-o   o-tasuke-ni   nar-ta.
            student-Nom Prof. Yamada-Acc Hon-help-to become-Past
            "A student helped Prof. Yamada."

Harada (1976) claims that the so-called subject honorification in Japanese is induced solely by the element with the GR Subject. Toribio (1990), recasting this claim under the GB theory, proposes that subject honorification is induced by Spec–head agreement between Infl and the Spec of Infl. According to this hypothesis, the ill-formedness of (25b) results from the fact that *seito-ga* "students-Nom," the DP which is not regarded as honorable, is situated at the Spec of Infl at S-structure with the honorable DP *Yamada-sensei-o* "Prof. Yamada-Acc" being located at the object position of V.

Given Toribio's (1990) proposal, the well-formedness of the following example, therefore, shows that the dative marked DP in Japanese DSCs is indeed located at the Spec of Infl at S-structure, as expected:

(26)   Yamada-sensei-ni [sono mondai]-ga   (Japanese: Perlmutter 1984: 323)
       Prof. Yamada-Dat that   problem-Nom
       o-wakari-ni   nar-u.
       Hon-understand-to become-Pres
       "Prof. Yamada understands that problem."

This conclusion, if correct, counts as a lethal problem for the G-CT commonly assumed in the GB theory. This is because the DP which is located at the Spec of Infl at S-structure is usually assigned nominative Case but can sometimes be assigned dative Case. Moreover, it is not possible to hold that the dative Case assigned to the DP found in a DSC is a mere exception to the G-CT, for the dative marked DP in DSCs assumes the GR SUBJECT, and it is the widely accepted assumption of the GB theory that the GR SUBJECT is linked tightly with nominative Case (in accusative languages; cf. Marantz 1984, Bittner and Hale 1996a). Since QSCs including DSCs can be found in a lot of languages in the world (Korean, Tamil, Quechua, Icelandic, Russian, Spanish, Georgian, Hindi, etc.; see Ura 1996), the problems raised by the GF-splitting found in those constructions cannot be neglected in the theory of the grammar for human languages.

3.3 Ergative languages and split ergativity

One of the best-known GF-splitting phenomena is split ergativity. Studies on ergativity (cf., among many others, Dixon 1979, 1994, Marantz 1984, Bittner and Hale 1996b) have revealed that ergative languages can be divided largely into two types: morphologically ergative languages and syntactically ergative ones. Those of the former type have the so-called ergative Case system for the morphological marking on nominals, but some of them have syntactic properties common to those of the canonical accusative languages like English or Japanese. According to Dixon (1994) no syntactically ergative language with the morphologically accusative Case system has ever been attested so far. Thus, all syntactically ergative languages are morphologically ergative, but some morphologically ergative languages are not syntactically ergative.

To be brief, the ergative Case marking pattern is summarized as follows: the logical, underlying subject in an active transitive clause (most typically, Agent) has a Case marker morphologically different from the logical, underlying subject in an (active) intransitive clause, which has the same Case marker as the logical, underlying object (typically, Patient or Theme) in an active transitive clause. The morphological Case marking for Agent (or Actor) in an active transitive clause is called ERGATIVE, and the one for the subject in an intransitive clause and Patient in an active transitive clause ABSOLUTIVE.

In syntactically pure ergative languages like Dyirbal, DPs have in common a certain set of GFs, most of which are believed to be possessed by a DP with the GR SUBJECT in ordinary accusative languages, if they are marked as absolutive (Dixon 1979, 1994). In languages with only morphological ergativity like Walmatjari (Dixon 1994), Chukchee (Comrie 1979), and Enga (Van Valin 1981), on the other hand, the ergative marked DP in an active transitive clause and the absolutive marked DP in an intransitive clause have in common the GFs that are supposed to be associated with the GR SUBJECT (such as the ability to control, to be a victim of omission, to be relativized, etc.), despite the evident fact that they are differently encoded from a morphological point of view.[19]

Under the hypothesis of GFs/GRs assumed in the GB theory, it must be the case that two elements are located in the same structural position at S-structure if they have those GFs in common, for their sharing of those GFs means that both of them bear the GR SUBJECT, and they must be located at the Spec of Infl at S-structure in order for them to bear the GR SUBJECT. Now that they are located at the Spec of Infl at S-structure, the G-CT demands that they must be marked as the same type of Case whatever the morphological shape of the Case type may be. Put differently, no matter which Case, ergative or absolutive, in ergative languages may correspond with nominative in accusative languages, the G-CT demands that they must be uniformly marked as either ergative or absolutive regardless of whether the clause in which they function as SUBJECT is transitive or intransitive. Therefore, the fact that the ergative marked DP in an active transitive clause and the absolutive marked DP in an intransitive clause have the GFs in common seriously challenges the G-CT on empirical grounds.

In this subsection as well as the previous one I have pointed out some of the empirical problems for the G-CT under the GB theory. After sketching out the conceptual and technical fundamentals of the Minimalist program initiated by Chomsky (1992) and elaborated by subsequent work, I will, in the next section, demonstrate the conceptual and theoretical problems for the G-CT, and propose an alternative theory of Case under the assumptions of the Minimalist program, which is expected to be free from the empirical and conceptual problems involved in the G-CT under the GB theory.

4   Minimalist Case Theory

4.1   The Minimalist program and the theory of formal features

Putting aside many technical details of other modules in addition to the general issue of the entire validation of the Minimalist framework as the theory of the grammar for human language (see Chomsky 1992, 1995a, 1998b), I will, in this subsection, briefly sketch out the fundamental conceptions of the Minimalist program and the theory concerning formal features.

According to Chomsky (1992, 1995a), the Minimalist program (hereafter MP) for linguistic theory aims at establishing the theory of the grammar for human language by postulating only minimal assumptions that are necessary and essential on conceptual grounds alone. As a consequence, there exist a few (hopefully, only one) set(s) of universal principles and a finite array of options as to how they apply (namely, parameters). This is the way to approach the so-called Plato's problem or the "perfectness" of language (or the language faculty of human being) under the MP. Now the task of the MP is to show, by utilizing these highly restricted options in Universal Grammar, that the apparent richness and diversity of linguistic phenomena is illusory and epiphenomenal and that it results from the interactions of the principle(s) and limited sets of fixed parameters.

In the Minimalist framework advocated by Chomsky (1992, 1994, 1995a), two linguistic levels are postulated and only those levels are assumed: they are necessary and essential for linguistic theory as interfaces with the performance systems (namely, articulatory–perceptual (A–P) and conceptual–intentional (C–I) systems). It is also assumed that there is a single computational system C_{HL} for human language and only limited lexical variety, where variations of language are essentially morphological (Chomsky 1994: 3). C_{HL} should be interpreted as mapping some array A of lexical choices to a pair (π, λ), a linguistic expression of a particular language L, where π is a PF representation and λ is an LF representation, each consisting of legitimate objects that can receive an interpretation. Chomsky (1995a: 223) maintains that C_{HL} is strictly derivational, but not representational, in that it involves successive operations leading to (π, λ).[20] Thus, C_{HL} (namely, computation) typically involves simple steps expressible in terms of natural relations and properties, with the context that makes them natural "wiped out" by later operation, hence not visible in the representation to which the derivation converges. Thus in syntax, crucial relations are typically local, but a sequence of operations may yield a representation in which the locality is obscured (cf. Collins 1997, Chomsky 1998b).

A particular language L is an instantiation of the initial state of the cognitive system of the language faculty with options specified, and L determines a set of derivations (= computations). A derivation converges at one of the interface levels if it yields a representation satisfying Full Interpretation, a condition which requires that every entity at an interface level be interpreted. A derivation converges if it converges at both interface levels; otherwise, it crashes.

The array A of lexical choices, which is mapped to (π, λ) by C_{HL}, is the thing that indicates what the lexical choices are and how many times each is selected by C_{HL} in forming (π, λ). Let Numeration be a set of pairs (LI, i), where LI is an item of the lexicon and i is its index, which should be understood to be the number of times that LI is selected. Then, A is a numeration N; C_{HL} maps N to (π, λ). C_{HL} proceeds by selecting an item from N, reducing its index by 1. C_{HL} crashes if all indices are not reduced to zero.

At some point in the computation to LF (i.e., the computation from N to l), there is an operation Spell-Out, which applies to the structure S already formed. Spell-Out strips away from S those elements relevant only to π, leaving the residue S_L, which is mapped to λ by syntactic operations. The subsystem of C_{HL} that maps S to π is called the "phonological component," and the subsystem of C_{HL} that maps S to λ is called the "covert component." The pre-Spell-Out component is called the "overt component." In this system, therefore, there is no direct relation between λ and π (cf. Chomsky 1995a).

Given the numeration N, the operations of C_{HL} recursively construct syntactic objects from items in N and syntactic objects already formed. One of the operations of C_{HL}, which we will call Select, is a procedure that selects a lexical item LI from N, reducing its index by 1, and introduces it into the derivation.

Another operation, which we will call Merge, takes a pair of already formed syntactic objects and replaces them by a new combined syntactic object. The operation Move forms a new syntactic object Λ from two already formed syntactic objects κ and α, where κ is a target and α is the affected, by replacing κ with {Γ, {α, κ}} (= Λ). Since (syntactic) structures are formed only by these three operations, they are built derivationally in a bottom-to-top fashion.

The leading idea about formal features is proposed in Chomsky (1992, 1994) and, especially, Chomsky (1995a), which may be summarized as follows:

I   Formal features (Fs) are the features that have the following properties: (i) they are the only syntactic objects accessible in the course of C_{HL}, and (ii) they are encoded in (or assigned to) a lexical item. Among them, phi-features like gender, person, or number, Case features like nominative or accusative, and categorial features like D-feature play important roles in Minimalist syntax.

II   Fs undergo the operation Feature checking, which motivates syntactic movements under the Last Resort condition (see Collins in this volume). By feature checking, a relation (called Checking Relation) is produced.

III   Feature checking always takes place between two features of the same sort (cf. Ura 1994, Chomsky 1995a).

IV   Feature checking is possible only when the element (= checkee) that possesses the feature to be checked is in the Checking Domain of the element (= checker) that possesses the checking feature.[21]

V   Checked Fs are deleted when possible. Deleted Fs are erased when possible. Deleted Fs are invisible at LF, but accessible to syntactic operations. Erased Fs are not accessible at all in C_{HL}.

VI   There are [+interpretable] and [−interpretable] Fs. [−interpretable] Fs must be checked and deleted at LF, while [+interpretable] ones may not be checked or deleted because they are interpreted at LF; hence, the existence of them at LF does not yield a violation of Full Interpretation at LF. [−interpretable] Fs that remain undeleted at LF cause the derivation to crash. Presumably the interpretability of Fs is universal and invariant among languages: it is universally true that Case features like nominative Case feature are [−interpretable] and categorial features like D-feature are [+interpretable], for example (Chomsky 1995a). As for phi-features, their interpretability depends both on their individual nature and on the morphological characteristics in a given language (see Ura forthcoming for more discussion).

VII   There are strong Fs and weak Fs. Strong Fs must be checked and deleted before Spell-Out, while weak ones can be checked at LF. Strong Fs that remain unchecked at PF cause the derivation to crash.

VIII   Chomsky (1995a) proposes the stipulation that elements introduced (base generated) by Merge in its theta-position cannot undergo feature checking unless they move somewhere other than their base-generated position.[22]

4.2 Agr-based Case theory

Now let us return to the theory of Case. First, recall that the G-CT under the GB theory depends crucially on the structural notion government, the distinction of the abstract syntactic levels D- and S-structure, and the principles that constrain the way of forming syntactic structures (i.e., the "conventional" X'-theory and the Projection Principle). Arguing that they lack any virtual conceptual necessity, Chomsky (1992) makes the claim that government, D- and S-structures, and the Projection Principle should be discarded under the assumptions of the MP, which aims at establishing the theory of the grammar for human language by postulating only minimal assumptions that are necessary and essential on conceptual grounds alone.[23] Besides, Chomsky (1994) shows that it is possible to dispense with the "conventional" X'-theory, which should also be discarded due to its lack of virtual conceptual necessity. Thus the MP is seeking for a new theory of Case without recourse to those conceptually unnecessary notions.

Chomsky (1992) has first incorporated both the Split Infl Hypothesis, initially developed by Pollock (1989) and extended by Chomsky (1989), and the VP-Internal Subject Hypothesis (e.g. Kuroda 1988, Koopman and Sportiche 1991, among others)[24] into the checking theory of formal features, the rudiments of which were outlined in the previous subsection. And then he has proposed the first guiding model of a Minimalist theory of Case. Under this theory, Case is given a syntactically more concrete status than under the G-CT: it counts as a kind of formal feature that has an individual property concerning strength. Moreover, by the LF interface condition (i.e., Full Interpretation), Case is required to be properly licensed (i.e., checked, deleted, and erased) in accordance with the mechanism of feature checking under a certain structural condition (cf. the previous subsection); for Case-feature is universally [−interpretable], and no [−interpretable] features can enter into the interpretation at the conceptual–intentional (C–I) system (i.e., LF level).

To make the discussion more concrete, let us see how Case checking takes place in an ordinary active transitive clause. First, the structure illustrated in (27), where DP_1 is assigned the external theta-role and DP_2 the internal one by V, is built up by Merge according to the VP-Internal Subject Hypothesis:

(27)

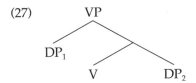

Now V in (27), being a transitive verb with an external theta-role, has an accusative Case feature to be checked with the same type of Case feature in the course of derivation. Although V and the two DPs in (27) seem to be very close to one another, Case checking can never happen in this configuration because (i) DP_2 is not in the checking domain of V, and (ii) DP_1, though in the checking domain of V, cannot enter into any checking relation for the reason that it is located at the position where it is assigned a theta-role (cf. the property (VIII) of formal features stated in the previous subsection). Then, the functional head AgrO, which is assumed to be the locus of object agreement under the extended version of the Split Infl Hypothesis (see Belletti in this volume), is added to (27) by Merge, deriving (28):

(28)   AgrOP

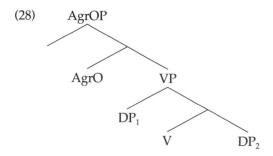

Now suppose that the accusative Case feature of V is strong and, hence, must be erased before Spell-Out. Then, V must move out of VP before Spell-Out in order to have its Case checked off (recall that the checking of V's accusative Case feature is never fulfilled if V stays in VP). Hence, V moves onto AgrO by head movement:

(29)   AgrOP

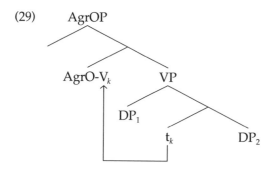

In (29), the Spec of AgrO is empty and, more importantly, it now counts as the checking domain of V, for V is merged with AgrO by head adjunction. At this stage in the derivation illustrated by (29), both DP_1 and DP_2 are eligible to check off the strong accusative Case feature of V if they have the equivalent Case feature.

First, suppose that DP_2 has an accusative Case and DP_1 has a nominative Case. Then, DP_2 can check off the strong accusative Case feature of V by moving to the Spec of AgrO, which is illustrated in (30):

(30)

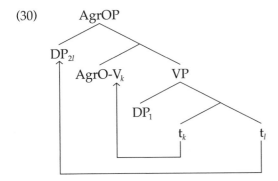

Note that in general, α, an element situated at a position Π_1, cannot move beyond β, another element situated at Π_2, to another position Π_3 if (i) α and β belong to the same type of category and (ii) Π_1 is more remote from Π_3 than Π_2 is (Rizzi's 1990 Relativized Minimality; see Rizzi in this volume). However, by hypothesizing that any two elements α and β are equidistant from a third position γ if α and β are in the same minimal domain, Chomsky (1992) claims that the movement of DP_2 from the complement position of V to the Spec of AgrO beyond DP_1 at the Spec of V is legitimate in (30). Since the Spec of AgrO in (30) falls in the checking domain of V as the result of V's head movement onto AgrO, DP_2 successfully checks off the strong accusative Case feature of V.

As the next step of the derivation, finite Infl with a nominative Case feature is introduced by Merge, as illustrated in (31):

(31)

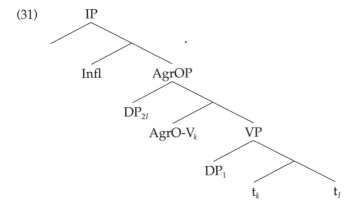

If the commonly assumed hypothesis that every clausal projection has a subject at the surface level is universally true, the Spec of IP must be filled with an argument by LF regardless of the strength of Infl's nominative Case feature, let alone the strength of the other formal features of Infl.[25] In (31), DP_1 and DP_2 are eligible to move to the Spec of Infl to fill it because they are equidistant from the Spec of Infl (they are situated in the minimal domain of V). But even if DP_2 moves there, the nominative Case feature of Infl cannot be checked off by it: DP_2 has already entered into the accusative Case checking relation with V and lost its Case feature. Therefore, DP_1 moves to the Spec of Infl to fill it, deriving (32) from (31):

(32)

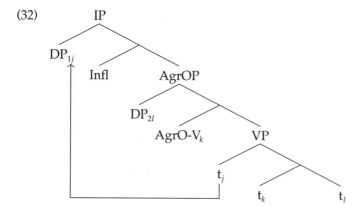

Now that DP_1 has a nominative Case feature, it successfully checks off the nominative Case feature of Infl.[26]

Suppose, instead, that DP_1 has an accusative Case and DP_2 has a nominative Case in (29), which is repeated here:

(29)

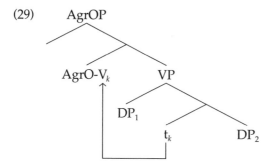

Then, DP_1 moves to the Spec of AgrO to check off the strong accusative Case feature of V, deriving (33) from (29):[27]

(33)

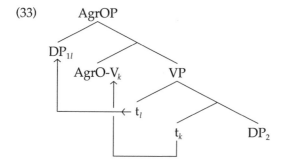

The derivation up to this stage is legitimate. As the next step of the derivation, finite Infl with a nominative Case-feature is introduced by Merge, as illustrated in (34):

(34)

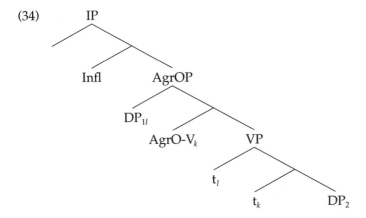

For the purpose of checking the nominative Case of Infl in (34), DP_1 is no longer available because its Case feature is not nominative and, moreover, it has lost its Case feature by entering into a Case checking relation with V. In (34), DP_2 is the only element available for checking off the nominative Case feature of Infl. But DP_2 cannot move to the Spec of Infl beyond DP_1 at the Spec of AgrO, because DP_1 is closer to the Spec of Infl than DP_2 is. Note that in (34), DP_1 is in the minimal domain of V but DP_2 is not located in the minimal domain of V. Therefore, in (34), there is no way to check off the nominative Case feature of Infl (independently of its strength) at LF. Since all Case features are [−interpretable] and must be checked off at LF, this derivation inevitably crashes at LF. This is the reason why the logical, underlying subject is always marked as nominative and the logical, underlying object is always marked as accusative, and not vice versa, in an active transitive clause (in accusative languages). This is the rudiment of the theory of Case under the MP introduced by Chomsky (1992), which is called the Agr-based Case Theory (henceforth, A-CT). This is so named because it depends crucially on the Agr-projections.[28]

One of the most remarkable empirical profits the A-CT brings is its neat treatment of the phenomenon called "Object Shift."[29] It was first noticed by Holmberg (1986) that overt V-movement is prerequisite for the object in the clause to move overtly out of VP in Scandinavian languages (Holmberg's generalization). If Object Shift is caused by some Case reason, this generalization follows immediately from the A-CT: under the A-CT, the accusative Case checking always takes place outside of VP, as we observed thus far. That is to say, in order to fulfill the accusative Case checking between V and the object DP before Spell-Out, both V and the object DP must move out of VP before Spell-Out; therefore, Holmberg's generalization follows.[30]

4.3   *Agr-less checking theory*

Indeed, the A-CT has overcome several conceptual problems involved in the G-CT, as argued above, and it has also brought a fair amount of empirical advantage.[31] Nevertheless, Chomsky (1995a) points out that the A-CT has a serious technical problem for the implementation of the theory.

Chomsky (1995a) claims that the Agr-projections, which play a significant role in the A-CT, should be discarded on conceptual grounds, for they do not receive any interpretation at the interface levels (i.e., PF and LF): they have no meaning and no phonological realization. They function only in syntax and their function is to mediate checking operations. In this subsection, I will outline the core ideas of the Agr-less Checking Theory (henceforce, A-less CT), which is so named because it is a checking theory without recourse to Agr-projections.

In the previous subsection, it was argued that AgrO serves to mediate the accusative Case checking between V and the object DP outside of VP. Then, how is it possible for the strong accusative Case feature of an active transitive verb to be checked off by the object DP in a configuration without AgrO? The A-less CT, first, adopts Hale and Keyser's (1991, 1993) two-layered VP-shell for a simple active transitive verb (Chomsky 1995a), which is illustrated in (35):

(35)

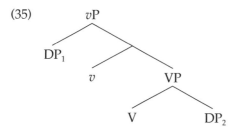

Chomsky (1995a), basically following Hale and Keyser (1991, 1993), assumes that v in (35), which is meant to stand for the higher head of the two-layered VP-shell, has an external theta-role (usually Agent) to be assigned to its Spec and selects as its complement the maximal projection of a simple intransitive verb with only an internal theta-role (usually Theme), which is represented by VP in (35). Thus, the so-called Burzio's generalization (cf. n. 8) can be recaptured by saying that v is the locus of an accusative Case feature. Now that v in (35) has an accusative Case feature, then how and where can its accusative Case feature, if strong, be checked off by the logical, underlying object (DP$_2$ in (35))?

The Minimalist theory of phrase structure (the idea of Bare Phrase Structure presented by Chomsky 1994) allows multiple Specs to be projected by a single head (see Ura 1994, 1996, as well as Chomsky 1994 for extensive discussion). Given this, it is allowed for DP$_2$ in (35) to move to an outer Spec of v in order to check off the strong accusative Case feature of v before Spell-Out. This step of derivation is illustrated in (36):

(36)

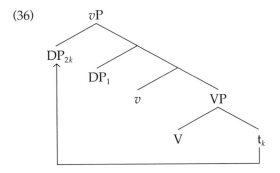

Note that DP_1 at the innermost Spec of v does not prevent the movement of DP_2 out of VP to the outer Spec of v in (36). This is because the target of the movement of DP_2 in this case is in the same minimal domain as the position of DP_1. In fact, Chomsky (1995a) defines this as follows: if β c-commands α and τ is the target of raising, then β is closer to τ than α unless β is in the same minimal domain as (i) τ or (ii) α. Given this, DP_1 does not induce a Relativized Minimality effect on the movement of DP_2 in (36). In (36) DP_2 is now in the checking domain of v and, hence, can check off the accusative Case feature of v.

As the next step of the derivation, finite Infl with a nominative Case feature is introduced by Merge, as illustrated in (37):

(37)

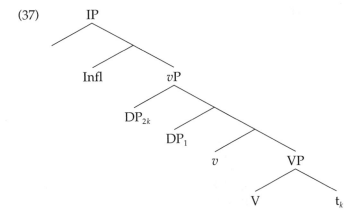

Although DP_1 and DP_2 are both eligible to move to the Spec of Infl to fill it because they are equidistant from the Spec of Infl, it is no use raising DP_2 to that position, for DP_2 has already entered into the accusative Case checking relation with v and lost its Case feature. Instead, DP_1 moves to the Spec of Infl to check off the nominative Case feature of Infl, deriving (38) from (37):

(38)

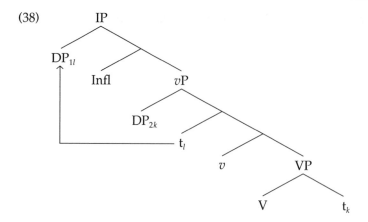

Now that DP$_1$ is in the checking domain of Infl, it successfully checks off the nominative Case feature of Infl. This is the core idea of the A-less CT and its rudimentary application to a simple active transitive clause.

4.4 Agr-less checking theory vs. Agr-based Case theory

Although it might seem that the A-less CT differs drastically from the A-CT in its technical implementation, it is indeed easy to reanalyze the A-CT into the A-less CT, as noted by Watanabe (1996), Collins (1997), and Ura (forthcoming). Nonetheless, it is worth noting that it is not only that the A-less CT surpasses the conceptual problem concerning the *raison d'être* of Agr-projections, but also that there are several empirical advantages of the A-less CT over the A-CT, a few of which I will briefly sketch out in this subsection. The important point is that what the A-CT captures can be also captured by the A-less CT, but not vice versa.

The most remarkable technical difference between those two Case theories under the MP is the (non-)use of multiple Specs. The most explicit advantage of the utilization of multiple Specs is its application to multiple subject constructions (MSCs), in which more than one DP in a single clause stand in the same Case (usually, nominative in accusative languages) and all of them equally function as SUBJECT in the clause (i.e., have the GFs that are typically associated with the GR SUBJECT).[32] Those constructions are found in lots of languages in the world (Arabic, Persian, Uzbek, Alutor, Chukchee, Japanese, Korean, Lahu, Quechua, etc.; see Ura 1994 for a list of languages with MSCs). Under the A-CT, it is imperative to assume multiple Infls (or, more precisely, AgrSs; cf. n. 28) to provide a nominative Case to each of the multiple subjects in a given clause. But there is a serious problem in this account: in languages like Alutor, where subject agreement is morphophonologically represented on the finite verb in a clause, it is usually the case that only a single subject agreement (which is always induced by the innermost subject) appears on the finite verb even when multiple subjects appear in the clause. If multiple Infls in accordance with the number of multiple subjects exist in the clause with multiple subjects, it must be the case that multiple subject agreements appear on the finite verb, just as multiple nominative cases are morphophonologically realized by multiple subjects; however, this is not the case. On the other hand, this fact is given a consistent account under the A-less CT: in a clause with multiple subjects, there is only a single Infl with the ability to enter into multiple nominative Case checking relations,[33] and multiple subjects, located in Specs which are projected by the single Infl, have their nominative Case features checked off by the Infl, which, in turn, enters into a phi-feature checking relation with the innermost subject.[34, 35]

Another empirical advantage of the A-less CT in terms of the utilization of multiple Specs comes from super-raising. Super-raising is the name of the operation by which DP is moved up beyond the subject of a clause to an A-position in a higher clause. (39) exemplifies the operation:

(39)   *John$_i$ seems [$_{CP}$ that [$_{IP}$ it was told t$_i$ [that Mary is a genius]]]

The ill-formedness of (39) is believed to be attributed to a Relativized Minimality effect. But, in Ura (1994), I reported that the following generalization holds true:

(40)   If a language allows MSCs, then it also allows super-raising.

If the aforementioned claim under the A-less CT is true, the generalization stated in (40) follows naturally: under the analysis of MSCs under the A-less CT, it is argued that languages that allow MSCs also have a parametric property to allow multiple Specs to be projected by a single Infl. Thus, an outer Spec of Infl is available for a host of DP in addition to the canonical (i.e., innermost) Spec of Infl in those languages. Furthermore, it is also possible to say that this outer Spec can serve as a landing site of a DP-movement. Then, the super-raising can be schematically illustrated as in (41):

(41)   DP$_{1k}$ ... [$_{IP}$ t$'_k$ [$_{IP}$ DP$_2$ Infl [$_{vP}$ v [$_{VP}$ V t$_k$]]]]

Notice that neither the movement of DP$_1$ from the complement position of V to the outer Spec of Infl, nor its subsequent movement from the outer Spec of Infl to the sentence initial position, is illegitimate in terms of Relativized Minimality; that is, DP$_2$ does not induce any Relativized Minimality effect on those movements. This is because the outer Spec of Infl, which is the target of the first movement and the origin of the second one, is in the same minimal domain as the position where DP$_2$ is located (i.e., the innermost Spec of Infl). Recall that α never induces a Relativized Minimality effect on the movement of β targeting the position γ if α is in the same minimal domain of (i) β or (ii) γ (Chomsky 1995a). If some reason is provided why DP_1 is first attracted to the Spec of Infl in (41), the mechanism of super-raising is explained this way under the A-less CT with special recourse to multiple Specs.[36]

5   A Minimalist Approach to GFs/GRs and Ergativity

In section 3 we observed that in applying the theory of Case to the issues concerning GFs/GRs and the ones concerning ergativity and ergative languages, we find several problems immanent in the Case theory under which Case is correlated with GFs/GRs through the mediation of structural relations. Let us see, in this section, how the Case theory developed under the MP, which was sketched in the previous section, can cope with those problems.

5.1   *Case-feature, feature checking, and grammatical functions*

The problems of the G-CT concerning GFs/GRs lie in its way of defining GRs uniformly in terms of structural relations. Under the theory of phrase structure in the MP (Bare Phrase Structure), however, the structural relation of a given element is defined in terms of the relation the element holds in connection with other elements in the structure (cf. Chomsky 1994, Ura 1994). To put it differently, structural positions are defined not in an absolutely deterministic manner, but relationally. Thus, we can no longer relate GRs and GFs to structural relations in a uniform and deterministic fashion under the assumptions of the MP.

Nevertheless, there is a relationship that can be unambiguously determined in an absolutely deterministic way under this framework; namely, relationship that is created by formal feature checking. In the checking theory of Chomsky (1995a), it is assumed that formal features such as Case features or categorial features are syntactic primitives and that they play the role of entering into checking relations. Therefore, it is quite natural to hypothesize a theory of GFs (and GRs) under this framework, a theory under which GFs (and GRs) are unambiguously defined or determined by checking relations. Here it is important to note that, as long as the feature checking theory is free from conceptually unnecessary assumptions, the theory of GFs (and GRs) just sketched above is also free from them.[37]

Since this idea, together with the theory of multiple feature checking, enables us to expect that two distinct DPs α and β appearing in different constructions may differ from each other in terms of their GFs even if α is located at the same structural position as β, or even if α is marked as the same Case as β, it opens up the possibility of giving a natural account to GF-splitting phenomena as found in QSCs, which seriously challenge the G-CT under the GB theory.[38]

5.2 *A Minimalist approach to ergativity*

In this subsection I will succinctly outline an A-less CT account of the Case marking patterns found in ergative languages, which have been attracting much interest in studying the theory of Case (cf. Marantz 1991, Murasugi 1992, Bobaljik 1993, Bittner and Hale 1996a, 1996b, among many others).

The mystery concerning the Case marking pattern in ergative languages comes from the fact that the logical, underlying subject in an active transitive clause differs from the logical, underlying subject in an (active) intransitive clause in terms of its Case in spite of the fact that they show the same syntactic behaviors (i.e., they have the same GFs) and they occupy the same structural position (i.e., the Spec of Infl). As repeatedly pointed out thus far, this is very difficult to resolve under the G-CT theory. In fact, several proposals have been made under the assumptions of the MP to this mystery, but I will outline, here, an approach by utilizing the A-less CT which is reinforced by the hypothesis of GFs introduced in the previous subsection.

The A-less CT that is reinforced with the theory of multiple feature checking enables us to expect that α and β may differ from each other in their Case shapes even if α in one construction is located at the same structural position as β in another construction. This is because under this theory, DP may have its Case feature checked off at a position which is different from that where it has its phi-features and/or EPP-feature checked off. Aside from the technical details, this theoretically opens up the possibility of giving an account to the ergative Case marking pattern.

Now the question is: how is it possible to implement the technical mechanics to derive the Case marking pattern in ergative languages? Here I would like to propose to hypothesize, contrary to Chomsky's (1995a) stipulation about the ban on the checking of an element at its theta-position, that elements can undergo feature checking in their theta-positions in some languages, while they cannot in other languages. To put it differently, I propose that Chomsky's (1995a) stipulation – viz., that elements introduced (base generated) by Merge in theta-position cannot undergo feature checking – should be parametrized. And I am claiming that elements can undergo feature checking at their theta-positions in ergative languages, while they cannot in accusative languages.

To make the story more concrete, let us see how this hypothesis works by looking at the derivation of a simple active transitive clause and that of a simple active intransitive clause in ergative languages. As argued in section 4.3, the A-less CT adopts Hale and Keyser's (1991, 1993) two-layered VP-shell (illustrated in (42)) as the core structure of a simple transitive verb:

(42)

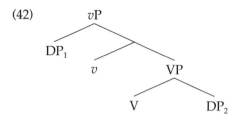

Given the parameter in ergative languages which allows an element to enter into a checking relation at its theta-position, the logical, underlying subject of a transitive verb (DP_1 at the Spec of v in (42)) can enter into a Case checking relation with v at the Spec of v without moving anywhere. Suppose that ergative is the name of the Case that is provided by v in ergative languages and, hence, corresponds to accusative in accusative languages. Then, DP_1 in (42) has entered into an ergative Case feature checking relation with v without moving anywhere.

As the next step of the derivation, finite Infl is introduced by Merge, deriving (43):

(43)

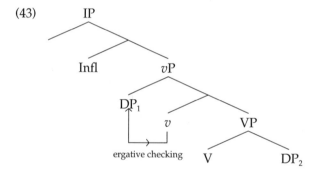

For the reason discussed in section 3, some argument must fill the Spec of Infl before Spell-Out (cf. n. 25). DP_1 is closer to that position than DP_2 is; therefore, DP_1 is moved there to fulfill the above requirement on the clausal subject position. This derives (44) from (43):

(44)

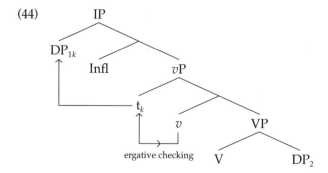

It is important to note that DP₁ can never check the Case feature of Infl in (44), though it may check other formal features of Infl, because it is deprived of its Case feature by having entered into an ergative Case feature checking relation with *v*. DP₂ is the only element that can check off the Case feature of Infl in (44). Thus, DP₂ is moved to the outer Spec of Infl to check off the Case feature of Infl. But notice that the movement of DP₂ to the outer Spec of Infl depends on the strength of the Case feature of Infl: if it is strong, DP₂ moves to the outer Spec of Infl before Spell-Out, which is illustrated in (45):

(45)

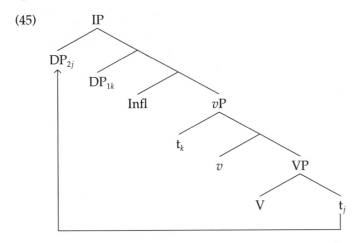

If the Case feature of Infl is weak, then the Case feature of DP₂ is attracted by Infl at LF under Chomsky's (1995a) feature checking theory. So there is no morphophonological output visible at the surface structure in this case. The important point here is that it is the logical, underlying object that enters into a Case checking relation with Infl in a simple active transitive clause in ergative languages, regardless of the strength of the Case feature of Infl.

Now suppose that absolutive is the name of the Case that is provided by finite Infl in ergative languages and, hence, corresponds to nominative in accusative languages. Then, from the above discussion, the fact naturally follows that the logical, underlying subject is marked as ergative and the logical, underlying object is marked as absolutive in a simple active transitive clause in ergative languages.

Next let us consider how a simple intransitive clause is derived in ergative languages. According to Hale and Keyser (1991, 1993), the structure of an unergative verb looks like this:

(46)

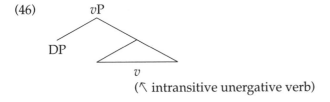

(↖ intransitive unergative verb)

That is, the sole argument of an intransitive unergative verb (i.e., the logical, underlying subject of such a verb) is introduced at the Spec of v, the locus of an ergative/accusative Case feature. Then, just as in the case of the logical, underlying subject of a simple active transitive clause, the sole argument of an intransitive unergative verb, too, can enter into an ergative Case feature checking relation with v without moving anywhere. But, when finite Infl is introduced later in the derivation, a problem arises: Infl has its own Case feature (absolutive), and it must be checked off by LF because it is [−interpretable]. In some ergative languages, the logical, underlying subject of an intransitive unergative verb enters into an absolutive Case feature checking relation with Infl by moving to the Spec of Infl without entering into an ergative Case feature checking relation with v at the Spec of v.[39] But it is possible to predict that, if some ergative languages have the parameter setting that allows their finite Infl not to have its Case feature checked off,[40] they also allow the logical, underlying subject of an intransitive unergative verb to enter into an ergative Case feature checking relation with v, leaving the absolutive Case feature of Infl unchecked. This consistently explains why the logical, underlying subject of an intransitive unergative verb is always marked as absolutive in ergative languages that disallow null subjects, while it can be marked as ergative in ergative languages with null subjects. See Ura (forthcoming) for more discussion.

On the other hand, there is no v in the structure of an intransitive unaccusative clause, according to Hale and Keyser (1991, 1993). The core of the structure of an intransitive unaccusative structure looks like this:

(47)

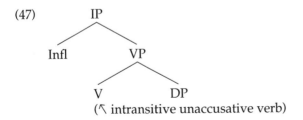

($\nwarrow$ intransitive unaccusative verb)

Thus, there is no way for the sole argument of an intransitive unaccusative verb to enter into an ergative Case checking relation with v. (Recall that V has no Case feature.) Rather, it always enters into an absolutive Case feature checking relation with Infl; otherwise, the derivation crashes at LF because the Case feature of the sole argument in an unaccusative clause, being [−interpretable], remains unchecked at LF. This is the reason why the logical, underlying subject of an intransitive unaccusative verb is always marked as absolutive in every ergative language, regardless of whether it allows null subjects or not.[41]

6   Further Issues and Concluding Remarks

Thus far the following have been observed:

I   The G-CT assumed under the framework of the GB theory involves conceptual and empirical problems, though by explicating the role of abstract Case in the theory of syntax, it gives us an insight to an approach to a variety of syntactic phenomena, especially the distribution of nominals and the properties of DP-movements. The conceptual problems lie in its crucial dependence on the notions whose conceptual necessity seems to be highly dubious in the theory of the grammar for human language, and the empirical problems come from its failure to cope with GF-splitting phenomena such as those found in DSCs and ergative languages.

II The A-CT under the framework of the MP, though it surpasses the G-CT thanks to its abandonment of most conceptually unnecessary notions, is still to blame for utilizing Agr-projections, which are regarded as conceptually unnecessary because of their absence of meaning and form at the interface levels.[42]

III The A-less CT, a modified version of the A-CT, is conceptually superior and brings a wide range of empirical advantages.

I will conclude this chapter by touching upon some residual problems that are expected to be given an explanation by the Case theory.

6.1   *Case and expletive*

Since the beginning of the development of the G-CT into the current theory of Case under the assumptions of the MP, the issues concerning the expletive *there* and its associate have been one of the most controversial topics (cf. Chomsky 1981, 1986a, 1992, 1995a, Shlonsky 1987, Belletti 1988, Lasnik 1992, 1995b, Frampton 1997, to list only a few).

Aside from the problem the expletive *there* itself raises in terms of the general economy condition (see Collins in this volume and references there), there remain several questions about the Case of the associate of *there*:

(48)   a.   There *is/are strangers in that garden.
       b.   There *is/are arriving three men at that station.

As is evident from (48), the associate enters into a phi-feature checking relation with Infl at LF. Then, what about the Case feature of the associate? The seemingly easiest answer to this question is that it also enters into a nominative Case feature checking relation with Infl at LF. But, as Lasnik (1992) points out, it fails to capture the following contrast:

(49)   a.   I consider [there to be a man in that garden].
       b.   *I consider [there a man in that garden].

This fact strongly shows that the associate of the expletive has some connection with the existential *be* in terms of Case, as Belletti (1988) first noted. It is, however, less clear how to implement Belletti's idea about partitive Case under the A-CT or the A-less CT.

Another question concerning the relation between the expletive *there* and Case can be found in the following examples, where the expletive can occur at the position where Case seems to be unavailable (cf. Postal 1974, Ura 1993):

(50)   a.   They alleged [there to have been many strangers in that garden].
      b.   *They alleged [many strangers$_k$ to have been t_k in that garden].
      c.   John wagered [there to have been a stranger in that haunted house].
      d.   *John wagered [a stranger$_k$ to have been t_k in that haunted house].

This puzzle, too, is worth pursuing for the purpose of elaborating the Case theory.[43]

6.2   *Null case and PRO*

As was hinted in section 2 above, it was assumed under the GB theory that PRO must not be governed (i.e., PRO Theorem). Many researchers pointed out, however, that PRO Theorem involves conceptual and empirical problems, and Chomsky and Lasnik (1993) has proposed under the A-CT that PRO has a Case feature of its own (called null Case) and, hence, is required to have its null Case feature checked off by an appropriate checker.

Chomsky and Lasnik (1993) has only hinted that PRO's null Case feature can be checked off by the infinitival Infl, leaving to future research the issue as to exactly what kind of Infl can check it (see Martin 1996 for more discussion on PRO and null Case in the MP). It is obvious that it is not always the case that any kind of infinitival Infl can check the null Case feature of PRO:

(51)   a.   *It is believed/considered [PRO to be intelligent].
      b.   *It seems/appears (to John) [PRO to be intelligent].

(52)   a.   John tried/managed [PRO to kiss Mary].
      b.   John persuaded/told Mary [PRO to kiss him].

(53)   a.   It is illegal/possible [PRO to park here].
      b.   *It is certain/likely [PRO to park here].

Some researchers attempt to relate the null Case feature with the existence of the functional head that introduces a complementizer (= C) (e.g. Watanabe 1993, 1996), while others attempt to relate it with the aspectual/temporal meaning of the infinitival clause (e.g. Martin 1992). In addition, it is interesting, in this respect, to consider other languages in which PRO can appear in a finite clause (cf. Martin 1996, Terzi 1997).

Another interesting question comes from the gerundive construction.[44] There are three types of gerund in English: POSS-ing, PRO-ing, and Acc-ing:

(54) a. **POSS-ing:**
They will discuss [John's protesting against the nuclear test by France].
b. **PRO-ing:**
I will never forget [PRO kissing Mary].
c. **Acc-ing:**
I remember [him hitting Mary].

With respect to the Case theory in connection with null Case, it is interesting to note that some predicates can take both PRO-ing and Acc-ing, though some others can take either of them:

(55) a. I remembered/reported [PRO/him having kissed Mary].
b. I enjoy/detest [PRO/*him taking a bath].
c. I saw/noticed [*PRO/him kissing Mary].

Currently, there seems to be no decisive explanation of the situation where both null Case and accusative Case are equally available.[45]

6.3 Conclusion

Needless to say, many questions and puzzles about Case and its relevance to syntax, which are too numerous to mention here, remain unsolved yet. Nonetheless, Case continues to be one of the hottest topics in the theory of syntax, and the importance of Case theory in studying human languages will be increasing in the future inquiries of linguistic theory, especially when a variety of languages in the world is examined and investigated in a uniform fashion under the assumptions in the MP.

NOTES

* I wish to thank Mark Baltin and Chris Collins for their generous help, which enabled me to write up this chapter. Thanks also go to Noam Chomsky, Ken Hale, Howard Lasnik, Maki Ura, and Akira Watanabe for their comments on an earlier version. Usual disclaimers apply.

1 There are, of course, important issues concerning case with respect to morphology, which I omit discussing here, however. For these morphological issues around case, see Spencer and Zwicky (1998) and Blake (1994).

2 Note that "NP" referred to in Chomsky (1981) corresponds to what I call "DP" in this chapter (see Bernstein in this volume). The definition of government and those of related notions can be stated as in the following manner:

(i) **Government:** A head α governs β iff α m-commands β

and there is no γ, γ another head, such that α c-commands γ and γ c-commands β.

(ii) **M-command:** α m-commands β iff every maximal projection that dominates α also dominates β.

(iii) **C-command:** α c-commands β iff every branching node that dominates α also dominates β.

Note that the definitions of those notions given above are somewhat different from the standard ones commonly assumed in the literature. They are so defined here as to avoid other complications irrelevant to the discussion in this chapter. For the standard definitions of those structural notions and their applications to syntactic analyses, see Fukui (this volume) and references cited there.

3   Instead of "objective," I will use, in this chapter, the more traditional and widely accepted term "accusative" to refer to the same type of Case referred to in (2b).

4   For theta-roles, see Gruber (this volume) and references cited there. For discussion about relationships between theta-roles and Case, see Fillmore (1968), Jackendoff (1972), and Stowell (1981), among others.

5   For details of the DP-hypothesis, see Bernstein and Longobardi (both this volume).

6   There are many interesting issues peculiar to genitive Case assignment and its morphophonological realization, which I will omit discussing in this chapter. For discussion on those issues, see Bernstein (this volume) as well as Chomsky (1986a), Abney (1987), and Siloni (1997).

7   See Fukui (this volume) for detailed discussion on the nature of phrase structures and X'-theory.

8   Precisely speaking, as Burzio (1986) reveals, transitivity is not relevant to V's ability to assign accusative Case; rather, V with an external argument has the ability to assign accusative Case. See Burzio (1986) for more discussion.

9   Thus, we correctly predict that in languages like European Portuguese, whose infinitival Infl may agree (i.e., Infl may have [+AGR]-feature), phonologically overt DP can appear at the subject position of an infinitival clause in which Infl agrees (see Raposo 1987).

10 Notice that the lack of Case assignment is a necessary but not a sufficient condition for the occurrence of PRO. For instance, the examples in (i) below where PRO occurs at a Case-less position are to be excluded as ungrammatical:

(i) a.   *John is fond PRO. (meaning "John is fond of someone.")
    b.   *There was known PRO to everyone. (meaning "Someone was known to everyone.")

Chomsky (1981), assuming that PRO is a pronominal anaphor obeying both A and B of the Binding Theory, maintains that PRO must not be governed, independently of any Case theoretic reason. In (i) PRO occurs at a Case-less but structurally governed position, resulting in their ungrammaticality. For the distribution and referentiality of PRO, see Chomsky (1981, 1986b) and references there. Later in this chapter I will return to the issue concerning the Case of PRO.

11 It is curious that the phonologically overt DP at the subject position of the infinitival complement clause selected by some control verbs cannot be saved in the same way as the phonologically overt DP at the

infinitival complement clause in the examples in (9) is saved, viz., by inserting the prepositional complementizer *for* in front of the phonologically overt DP. Why are examples like (i) ungrammatical?

(i) *Mary tried/managed [for John to go abroad].

Still more mysterious is the fact that the phonologically overt DP at the infinitival complement clause selected by other control verbs can be saved by inserting the prepositional complementizer *for*, as shown in (ii):

(ii) Mary intended/desired [for John to go abroad].

It seems that there has been no satisfactory answer ever provided in the GB era. See Chomsky and Lasnik (1993) and, especially, Martin (1992, 1996) for a Minimalist approach to this question.

12 See, again, Baltin (this volume) for much detailed discussion on DP-movements.

13 There are, of course, not a few technical problems that need resolving. For example, we have to ensure that the subject demotion (i.e., to evacuate the Spec of Infl by making the subject disappear from syntax) can coincide only with past participles; otherwise, we cannot prevent DP-movements from taking place from the object position of adjectives to the subject position (cf. Baker et al. 1989):

(i) a. *Mary is fond. (meaning "Someone is fond of Mary.")
    b. [$_{IP}$ e Infl [$_{VP}$ is fond Mary]]. (D-structure)
    c. [$_{IP}$ Mary$_k$ Infl [$_{VP}$ is fond t$_k$]].

(s-structure)

In addition, we also have to ensure that the Case-less object of past participles cannot be saved just in the same way as the Case-less object of adjectives or nouns can be saved, viz., by inserting the preposition *of* in front of it (cf. (7) above in the text):

(ii) *There/*It was loved of Mary. (meaning "Mary is loved (by someone).")

See Chomsky and Lasnik (1993) for relevant discussion.

The analysis of the passive formation I presented in the text is based on the one suggested by Rouveret and Vergnaud (1980) and Chomsky (1981). As the G-CT developed in the course of the GB era, the analysis of passive also became sophisticated (see Jaeggli 1986, Baker 1988, Baker et al. 1989 for discussion). For a more recent study on passive under the Minimalist framework, see Watanabe's (1996) comprehensive work, in which the question as to why some auxiliaries like English *be* must be accompanied with the passive formation in most languages – a question which has been almost ignored in the previous studies – is extensively discussed in addition to other interesting questions concerning passive in general.

14 Below are some other kinds of raising construction:

(i) a. John$_k$ seems/tends/appears [t$_k$ to have loved Mary].
    b. John$_k$ is believed/ considered/reported [t$_k$ to have loved Mary].

It is evident from the following examples that verbs like *seem/tend/ appear* allow a dethematized subject:

(ii) It seems/appears [that John has loved Mary].

This means that these verbs (called raising verbs) have no external argument as their lexical property. As stated in n. 9 above, verbs that lacks external theta-roles have no ability to assign accusative Case (see Burzio 1986). Thus, *John* in (ia) moves from the subject position of the embedded infinitival clause, where Case is not available, to the matrix subject position, where (nominative) Case is provided by finite Infl under government, just the same way as in the case in (16c). The same reasoning applies to the case illustrated in (ib), where ECM verbs are deprived of (accusative) Case assigning ability under passivization. See Baltin (this volume) for details of raising constructions.

15 Unaccusative constructions are often claimed to be another instance that shows a close relation between Case and DP-movements. Assuming that unaccusative verbs assign a theta-role to their internal argument but do not have the ability to assign Case due to their lack of external theta-role, Burzio (1986) shows that the so-called Unaccusative Hypothesis, which says that the subject of a clause whose main predicate is unaccusative is derivative in the sense that it is derived from the underlying object by a syntactic operation (cf. Perlmutter 1978), is subsumed under the G-CT. See, in addition to Burzio (1986), Shlonsky (1987) and Levin and Rappaport (1995) for further discussion.

16 Thus, GFs should be distinguished clearly from grammatical roles, semantic functions, or semantic roles, all of which are called theta-roles under the GB theory. There are vast numbers of studies concerning GFs in a variety of linguistic theories (see, among many others, Partee 1965 for the Standard Theory, Anderson 1976 for the Extended Standard Theory, Perlmutter 1982 for Relational Grammar, Bresnan 1982a for LFG, Gazder et al. 1985 for GPSG, Baker 1988 in the GB theory, and Ura forthcoming in the Minimalist program). See Palmer (1994), Givón (1997), and Van Valin and LaPolla (1997) for more general discussion on GFs and GRs.

17 See Baker (1988) for more discussion on the standard approach to GFs/ GRs under the GB theory (cf., also, Marantz 1984, Williams 1984, Harley 1995, Bittner and Hale 1996a).

18 See Ura (1996, forthcoming) for extensive discussion on GF-splitting phenomena and their implications in the theory of Universal Grammar.

19 Interestingly enough, in some of these languages only the absolutive marked DP, but not the ergative marked DP, can induce the subject agreement on the finite verb in the clause regardless of the transitivity of the clause (see Comrie 1979, DeLancey 1981, Dixon 1994, Palmer 1994, and references there for more details). In other words, the GFs that the absolutive marked DP assumes in an intransitive clause are split up in an active transitive clause. Some of them (the ability to induce the subject agreement on the finite verb, the ability to stand in absolutive, etc.) are inherited by the absolutive-marked DP (i.e., Theme or Patient in an active transitive clause), and the rest (the ability to control, to be relativized, etc.) by the ergative marked DP (i.e., Agent or Actor). This is clearly a kind of GF-splitting. See Ura (forthcoming) for extensive discussion on split ergativity and its relevance to Case and GFs/GRs.

20 For the issues concerning the representational vs. derivational approaches and their relevance to the general economy condition, see Ura (1995) and Collins (1997) in addition to Lasnik and Collins (both this volume).

21 Relevant definitions are as follows: MAX(α) is the least full-category maximal projection dominating α. The category α dominates β if every segment of α dominates β. The category α contains β if some segment of α dominates β. The domain of α is the set of the nodes contained in Max(α) that are distinct from and do not contain α. The complement domain of α is the subset of the domain reflexively dominated by the complement of α. The residue of α is the domain of α minus the complement domain of α. X is in the minimal domain of α iff X is contained in MAX(α), and X is dominated by no elements in the domain of α other than itself and the elements not distinct from α. Thus, the minimal complement domain of α is the intersection of the minimal domain of α and the complement domain of α. Finally, the checking domain of α is the minimal residue of α. See Chomsky (1992: 15–16) for more.

22 See Ura (forthcoming) for the proposal that this should be parametrized; that is to say, in some languages, elements can undergo feature checking in their theta-positions, while they cannot in the other languages. See section 5.2 in this chapter for more discussion.

23 Due to the space limitation, I omit repeating Chomsky's (1992) argument against those notions. See Lasnik (1993) and Marantz (1995) in addition to Chomsky (1992).

24 For more discussion on the Split Infl Hypothesis and the VP-Internal Subject Hypothesis, see Belletti and Bowers (both this volume) and references cited there.

25 Under the GB theory, this hypothesis was believed to be derived from the Extended Projection Principle (which merely states that every clause has a subject), which has now lost its rationale under the Minimalist assumptions. For recent discussion on the issue as to how this hypothesis is to be technically implemented, see Chomsky (1992, 1995a) and Rothstein (1995).

26 The story presented in the text is fairly idealized and simplified, because we concentrate our attention on Case feature checking. Checking operations involved in a simple transitive clause are far more complicated, for checking operations concerning phi-features and categorial features are involved. See Ura (1996, forthcoming) for details.

27 Even though DP_1 is in the checking domain of V before V head-moves onto AgrO, it cannot enter into an accusative Case feature checking with V. This is just because it is assigned a theta-role at that very position. Recall that we are tentatively assuming that no element can enter into any checking relation if it is located in its theta-position.

28 For extensive discussion on the A-CT and its applications to a variety of phenomena, see Watanabe (1993, 1996). It is commonly assumed under the A-CT, incidentally, that the nominative Case checking between Infl and the DP with a nominative Case feature takes place at the Spec of AgrS, the functional head responsible for subject agreement, as illustrated in (i):

(i)

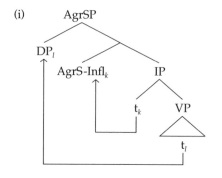

For the sake of brevity of discussion, I omit mentioning this in the text. For discussion, see Belletti (this volume) and Lasnik (1993), Marantz (1995), and Watanabe (1993, 1996) in addition to Chomsky (1989, 1992).

29   See Thráinsson (this volume) and references there for details of Object Shift.

30   A vast number of studies address their attention to Object Shift in various languages. See Watanabe (1993), Bobaljik (1995), Holmberg and Platzack (1995), and references there, in addition to Thráinsson (this volume), for more discussion.

31   For empirical advantages of the A-CT, see, among others, Watanabe's (1993, 1996) extensive studies on a variety of phenomena relevant to Case.

32   For extensive discussion on MSCs and their syntactic properties, see Ura (1994).

33   See Chomsky (1995a) and, especially, Collins (1994b) and Ura (1996, forthcoming) for the technical implementation for the idea that a single head can enter into multiple checking relations.

34   Under the theory of multiple feature checking (cf. Collins 1994b, Ura 1996, forthcoming), it is assumed that formal features that belong to a single head may differ from one another in terms of their properties. Thus, it is possible under this theory

that the phi-features of a head α are strong and can enter into multiple feature checking relations but the Case feature of α is weak and cannot enter into more than one feature checking relation. See Ura (1996, forthcoming) for more discussion.

35   Another argument in favor of the A-less CT in terms of MSCs is provided by Chomsky (1995a), who proposes to analyze the so-called "transitive expletive construction" into a variant of MSCs. According to him, this construction can be explained more explicitly under the A-less CT than under the A-CT. For more discussion, see Chomsky (1995a). For discussion on transitive expletive constructions, see Bobaljik and Jonas (1996) and references there.

36   It is probable that some (strong) formal feature of Infl other than Case feature (possibly, phi-feature) attracts DP_1 to the Spec of Infl to enter into a checking relation before Spell-Out. See Ura (1994) for more discussion.

37   The next question to ask is: in which way is each of the GFs defined in terms of checking relations? Ura (forthcoming) has proposed that the ability to control the missing subject of a subordinate adjunct clause and the ability to bind a subject oriented reflexive, for instance, result, respectively, from a phi-feature checking relation with Infl and from an EPP feature checking relation with Infl. See Ura (forthcoming) for more discussion.

38   Due to the limitations of space, I refer the reader to Ura (1996, forthcoming, in press) for extensive discussion on GF-splitting phenomena under the A-less CT.

39   Note that it is permitted for the Case feature of an intransitive

unergative verb not to be checked off. It is a well-known fact that an intransitive unergative verb sometimes assigns Case but sometimes not (see Burzio 1986 for more discussion).

40 Ura (forthcoming) maintains that this parameter corresponds to the so-called "null subject parameter;" that is, the Case feature of finite Infl need not be checked off in languages with null subjects. See Ura (forthcoming) for details.

41 See Ura (forthcoming), where it is argued that the application of the A-less CT to ergative languages enables us to explain some other issues concerning ergative languages, such as anti-passivization, split-ergativity, GF-splitting, etc.

42 In fact, it is certain that Agr-projections are conceptually problematic, as Chomsky (1998b) points out, but it is also certain that they can provide us with a lot of empirical advantages (see Belletti (this volume) and references there). Nevertheless, tensions of this kind between conceptual merits and empirical ones, which have often emerged in the history of Generative Grammar, are expected to be resolved by giving priority to conceptual merits over empirical ones.

43 In this respect, it might be interesting to touch on the somewhat surprising fact about *wh*-movements and their relevance to Case checking. As shown in (i) and (ii) below, some ungrammatical examples, which are supposed to be degraded for a Case theoretic reason, can be salvaged by the *wh*-extraction of the offending DP (cf. Postal 1974, Kayne 1984):

(i) a. *They alleged [John to have kissed Mary].
     b. Who$_k$ did they allege [t$_k$ to have kissed Mary]?

(ii) a. *They assured Mary [John to be a nice man].
     b. Who$_k$ did they assure Mary [t$_k$ to be a nice man]?

See Ura (1993) and Bošković (1997b) for further discussion.

44 Thanks to Maki Ura for bringing my attention to this construction.

45 It is also interesting, in passing, to note that the accusative marked subject of the embedded gerundive clause cannot be promoted to the matrix subject by passivization:

(i) a. *John$_k$ was reported [t$_k$ having kissed Mary].
     b. John$_k$ was reported [t$_k$ to have kissed Mary].

This indicates that the accusative Case feature of the subject in the embedded gerundive clause has no connection with the matrix verb. Then, how does it have its accusative Case feature checked off? It seems not so easy to give an explicit answer to this question and related puzzles.

12 Phrase Structure

NAOKI FUKUI

0 Introduction

That sentences and phrases in human language have abstract hierarchical structure, not merely sequences of words and formatives, is one of the fundamental discoveries of modern linguistics. Accordingly, any theory of human language must have a component/device that deals with its "phrase structure," regardless of the analyses it offers for other properties of language (such as transformations). In this sense, the theory of phrase structure is a kind of backbone for contemporary linguistic theory.

In earlier generative traditions, the properties of phrase structure were coded in terms of the formal mechanism called "phrase structure rules" of the following form, where α is a single symbol and φ, ψ, and χ are strings of symbols (χ non-null; φ and ψ possibly null):

(1) $\varphi\alpha\psi \rightarrow \varphi\chi\psi$

Phrase structure rules express the basic structural facts of the language in the form of "phrase markers" they generate,[1] with terminal strings drawn from the lexicon. In particular, phrase markers generated by phrase structure rules express three kinds of information about syntactic representations:

(2) i.   the hierarchical grouping of the "constituents" of the structure (Dominance);
     ii. the "type" of each constituent (Labeling);
     iii. the left-to-right order (linear order) of the constituents (Precedence).

For example, the phrase marker (3), generated by the phrase structure rules in (4), indicates that the largest constituent, whose label is S (the designated initial symbol), is made up of a constituent NP (Noun Phrase) preceding the other constituent VP (Verb Phrase); that the NP consists of two constituents,

D(eterminer) and a N(oun), in this order; and that the VP is composed of V(erb) and NP (in this order), and so on:

(3)

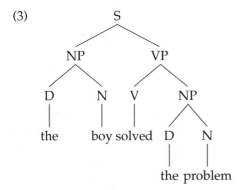

(4)   i.   S → NP VP
       ii. VP → V NP
       iii. NP → D N
       iv. D → the
       v.   N → boy
       vi. N → problem
       vii. V → solved

Phrase structure rules of the kind represented by (4iv)–(4vii), which directly insert lexical items into appropriate places in the structure, were later abolished in favor of the lexicon with subcategorization features (Chomsky 1965). This separation of lexicon from the "computational system" (phrase structure rules) makes it possible to simplify the form of phrase structure rules for human language from the "context-sensitive" (1) to the "context-free" (5) (with φ, ψ necessarily null; other qualifications are the same):

(5) $\alpha \to \chi$

In (5), α is a single "non-terminal" symbol, and χ is either a non-null string of non-terminal symbols or the designated symbol "Δ," into which a lexical item is to be inserted in accordance with its subcategorization features (see Chomsky 1965 for details).

   Thus, context-free phrase structure rules, coupled with the lexicon containing the information about idiosyncratic properties of each lexical item, were assumed in the "Standard Theory" of generative grammar (Chomsky 1965) to be responsible for expressing the properties of phrase structure. However, toward the end of the 1960s, it became apparent that certain important generalizations about the phrase structure of human language cannot be stated in terms of phrase structure rules alone. Recognition of the inadequacies of phrase structure rules, as we will see in the following section, led to the emergence and development of the general theory of phrase structure, "X'-theory," which is a main topic of this chapter.

The organization of this chapter is as follows. Section 1 discusses the basic insights of X'-theory. The section provides a brief explanation as to how this has emerged as an attempt to overcome the deficiencies of phrase structure rules in capturing the basic properties of phrase structure of human language, and summarizes the development of X'-theory from its inception to the Barriers version (Chomsky 1986). Section 2 is concerned with the "post-Barriers" development of the theory of phrase structure, which can be characterized as minimizing the role of X'-theory as an independent principle of Universal Grammar (UG), while maintaining its basic insights, which led to the eventual elimination of X'-theory in the "Minimalist program" (Chomsky 1994). It should be mentioned that the historical overview of these sections is by no means meant to be comprehensive, and the remarks to be made in the presentation are rather selective and schematic. It also goes without saying that the overview benefits from hindsight. Section 3 deals with one of the current issues in the theory of phrase structure, namely, the role of "linear order," in general, and that of the "head parameter," in particular. This section takes up some of the most recent works on the issue of linear order, and examines their basic claims. Section 4 is a summary and conclusion.

As the discussion proceeds, I will occasionally touch on some of the issues of movement (transformations) as well. This is because the theory of phrase structure and the theory of movement have been progressing side by side in the history of generative grammar. Transformations are formal operations applying to linguistic representations constructed in accordance with the general principles of phrase structure. Thus, a substantive change in the theory of phrase structure necessarily has important implications for the theory of transformations.

Throughout the chapter, I will basically confine myself to the discussion of the development of X'-theory, with only scattered references to other approaches to phrase structure, such as categorical grammars (Lambek 1958; see also Wood 1993 and references there), generalized phrase structure grammar (Gazdar et al. 1985) and its various ramifications (head driven phrase structure grammar (Pollard and Sag 1994, for example)), lexical-functional grammar (Bresnan 1982b), etc. This is of course not to dismiss the other approaches, but mainly to keep the discussion coherent and to manageable proportions. In addition, there are also more substantive reasons. First of all, the empirical insights offered by X'-theory are to be captured by any theory of phrase structure, regardless of the difference in formalism. Second, at least given the current version of "X'-theory" (this name may no longer be appropriate, as we will see later), there do not seem to be, as far as the treatment of phrase structure is concerned, so many fundamental differences between "X'-theory" and the other approaches mentioned above. The differences, if any, seem to be only concerned with the way other properties of language (the property of "displacement," for instance) are handled in a given framework.

1 From "Remarks" to *Barriers*: Formulating and Enriching X′-Theory

The basic motivations for X′-theory come from the following two considerations:

(6)   i.   the notion of "possible phrase structure rules";
      ii. cross-categorical generalizations.

The first consideration has to do with what counts as "a possible phrase structure rule" in natural languages. It is observed that while phrase structure rules of the kind in (7) (cf. also the phrase structure rules in (4) above) are widely attested in natural languages, those represented in (8) are systematically excluded in any grammar of human language:

(7)   VP → V (NP) (PP)
     NP → (Det) N (PP)
     PP → P (NP)

(8)   VP → N (PP)
     NP → V (NP) (PP)
     PP → N (VP)

In other words, structures such as those in (9), which are generated by the phrase structure rules in (7), are permitted in human language, whereas structures like those in (10), generated by the phrase structure rules in (8), are systematically excluded in human language:

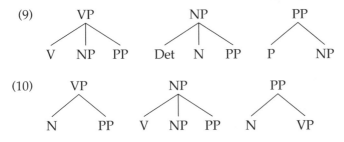

The reason for the impossibility of the phrase structure rules in (8) (and the corresponding structures in (10)) is intuitively clear. VP, for example, is a "Verb Phrase," rather than, say, a "Noun Phrase," and since it is a phrase of a verb, it must have a verb in it. However, the right-hand side of the phrase structure rule VP → N (PP) does not contain any verb. Hence the structure generated by such a phrase structure rule (i.e., the first structure in (10)) is ill formed. The same is true for the other phrase structure rules in (8) (and the corresponding structures in (10)).

In general, an "XP" cannot be a "phrase of X" if there is no X. Put another way, phrase structure in human language is "endocentric," in the sense that it is constructed based on a certain central element (called the "head" of a phrase), which determines the essential properties of the phrase, accompanied by other non-central elements, thus forming a larger structure. This is the right intuition, but, as pointed out by Lyons (1968), the theory of phrase structure grammar simply cannot capture this. Recall that in the general scheme of context-free phrase structure rules in (5), reproduced here as (11), the only formal requirements are that α is a single non-terminal symbol and χ is a non-null string of non-terminal symbols (or the designated symbol Δ):

(11) $\alpha \to \chi$

The phrase structure rules in (7) (which are attested in human language) and those in (8) (which are excluded in human language) are no different as far as the formal "definitions" of phrase structure rules are concerned. Thus, in each of the phrase structure rules in (8), the left-hand side is a single non-terminal symbol ("VP," "NP," and "PP"), and the right-hand side of the rule is a non-null string of nonterminal symbols ("N (PP)," "V (NP) (PP)," and "N (VP)"). These are all legitimate phrase structure rules, satisfying the formal definitions of (context-free) phrase structure rules, just like the phrase structure rules in (7), despite the fact that only the latter type of phrase structure rule is permitted and the former type is never allowed (at least, has never been attested) in human language. Phrase structure rules are too "permissive" as a theory of phrase structure in human language in that they generate phrase structures that are indeed never permitted in human language. We thus need some other mechanism which correctly captures the endocentricity of phrase structure that appears to be a fundamental property of human language.

   The second major motivation for X'-theory is concerned with some observed parallelisms that exist across different categories. Historically, the discussion started out with the treatment of two types of nominal in English, as represented by the following examples:

(12)   a.   John's refusing the offer
       b.   the enemy's destroying the city

(13)   a.   John's refusal of the offer
       b.   the enemy's destruction of the city

Nominals of the type represented in (12) are called "gerundive nominals," whereas those shown in (13) are called "derived nominals." These two types of nominal were treated uniformly in terms of a "nominalization transformation," which derives nominals like, say, (12b) and (13b) from the same source, namely, (the underlying form of) the sentence "the enemy destroyed the city" (see Lees 1960 for details).

Chomsky (1970), however, refutes this "Transformationalist Hypothesis," and argues that the theory of grammar should not allow a nominalization transformation (or any other transformation with similar expressive power) because it performs various operations that are never observed in any other well-argued cases of transformations. Thus, the alleged nominalization transformation (i) changes category types (it changes S to NP and V to N), (ii) introduces the preposition *of*, (iii) changes the morphological shape of the element (*destroy* is changed to *destruction; refuse* is changed to *refusal*, etc.), (iv) deletes all auxiliaries, and so on. These are the operations that other well-attested transformations never perform, and hence should not be allowed, Chomsky argues, if we are to aim at restricting the class of possible grammars.

In particular, Chomsky points out (i) that derived nominals are really "noun-like," not sharing various essential properties with sentences, and (ii) that the relationship between derived nominals and their sentential counterparts is rather unsystematic and sometimes unpredictable (see Chomsky 1970 for more arguments establishing these points). He then concludes that derived nominals should be handled in the lexicon, rather than in terms of transformations which deal with formal and systematic relationships between phrase structure trees. This proposal defines the "Lexicalist Hypothesis," which has become standard for the analysis of derived nominals in particular, and for the characterization of transformations in general.

Once we adopt the Lexicalist Hypothesis, however, an important problem immediately arises as to how to capture certain similarities and parallelisms holding between verb/noun and sentence/nominal pairs. More specifically, the strict subcategorization properties of a verb generally carry over to the corresponding noun, and the identical grammatical relations are observed in both sentences and the corresponding nominals (see Lees 1960 and Chomsky 1970 for detailed illustrations of these points; see also van Riemsdijk and Williams 1986 for a lucid summary). Under the Transformationalist Hypothesis, these parallelisms are captured by the nominalization transformation. With the elimination of such a transformation under the Lexicalist Hypothesis, we now have to seek an alternative way to express the parallelisms in the grammar.

Chomsky (1970) proposes that these parallelisms can be successfully captured if the internal structure of noun phrases is made to be sufficiently similar to that of sentences so that the strict subcategorization properties and grammatical relations can be stated in such a general form as to apply to both verbs/sentences and nouns/nominals. As a concrete means to express these cross-categorical generalizations, Chomsky introduces a preliminary version of X′-theory of the following kind (adapted from Chomsky 1970):

(14) a. $X' \rightarrow X \ldots$
      b. $X'' \rightarrow [\text{Spec}, X'] \, X'$

The "X" in (14) is a variable ranging over the class of lexical categories N(ouns), V(erbs), A(djectives), and (perhaps) P(repositions). The symbol X' (called "X bar," although, for typographical reasons, it is common to use primes rather than bars) stands for a constituent (phrase) containing X as its "head" (the central and essential element of the phrase), as well as those elements appearing in the place indicated by "..." in (14a), the elements called the "complement" of X. The schema (14b) introduces a still larger phrase X" (called "X double bar") containing X' and pre-head elements associated with X', called the "specifier" (Spec) of X' (notated as [Spec, X']).[2] Examples of specifiers include, according to Chomsky, determiners as [Spec, N'], auxiliary elements as [Spec, V'], comparative structures and elements like *very* as [Spec, A'], etc. X' and X", which share the basic properties of the head X, are called "projections" of X, with the latter (X") referred to as the "maximal projection" of X (since it does not project any further).

The X'-schemata in (14) are proposed as a principle of UG on phrase structure, and express the manner in which phrases are constructed in human language. Note that given the X'-schemata, the problem concerning the "possible phrase structure rules" in human language discussed above is immediately resolved. That is, the "endocentricity" of phrases in human language is directly encoded in X'-theory as the generalization that phrases are all projections of their heads. Thus, the non-existing phrase structure rules in (8) are excluded on principled grounds as rules generating the illegitimate structures in (10), which contain phrases lacking the proper heads, in violation of X'-theory.

With respect to the problem of expressing cross-categorical parallelisms, X'-theory provides a generalized structure by which we can uniformly express basic grammatical relations. Thus, the notion of "object-of" X can be stated as an NP that is immediately dominated by X', and the notion of "subject-of" X can be expressed as an NP that is immediately dominated by X", where X in both cases ranges over V, N, etc. Likewise, the strict subcategorization properties of, say, verbs and nouns are stated uniformly in terms of the general X'-scheme. For example, if an X (a verb or a noun) has a subcategorization frame +[_PP], then the PP is realized as the complement of X (the verb or noun).

However, the X'-theoretic generalizations were not complete at this stage of the development of the theory. This is because sentences did not quite fit into the general X'-scheme and were introduced by the following phrase structure rule, which does not really conform to X'-theory (see Chomsky 1970):

(15)   S → N" V"

Given the X'-schemata in (14) and the "S-introducing" phrase structure rule (15), the internal structures of noun phrases such as *the enemy's destruction of the city* and sentences like *the enemy destroyed the city* should be as follows (omitting much detail):

(16) a. **Noun phrases**

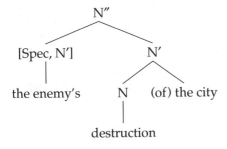

b. **Sentences**

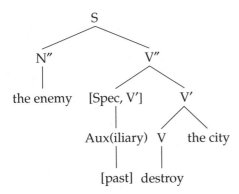

While these internal structures of noun phrases and sentences are sufficiently similar to permit a generalized cross-categorial formulation of grammatical relations and strict subcategorization properties for noun/verb pairs, it is also apparent that further (and rather complete) parallelism could be obtained if sentences are to be analyzed as V″. This issue, however, turns out to be complex and controversial, and in fact motivates much of the subsequent development of X′-theory after Chomsky (1970), as we will see below.

A final tenet of Chomsky's X′-theory concerns the feature analysis of syntactic categories, according to which categories are defined in terms of the two primitive features [±N] (substantive) and [±V] (predicative). The major "lexical categories" are thus defined as follows, using these two primitive features:

(17) N = [+N, −V]
   A = [+N, +V]
   P = [−N, −V]
   V = [−N, +V]

This feature analysis claims that categories in syntax are not really "atoms," but rather, they are decomposable feature complexes characterized by the primitive features, pretty much as "phonemes" are decomposed in terms of distinctive features in phonology. And, as in phonology, this approach makes it possible to define certain "natural classes" of syntactic category with respect to various syntactic operations and principles. Thus, we can capture the generalization that NPs and PPs behave in the same way (as opposed to VPs and APs) with respect to certain transformations, by attributing it to the feature specification [–V]; we can define the class of possible (structural) Case assigners, V and P (as opposed to N and A), by referring to the [–N] feature; we (correctly) predict that N and V never form a natural class because of their completely conflicting feature specifications, and so on (see, among many others, Bresnan 1977, Chomsky 1981).

Summing up the discussion so far, the basic claims of X'-theory of Chomsky (1970) can be stated as follows:

(18)   **The basic claims of X'-theory**
   a.   Every phrase is "headed," i.e., has an endocentric structure, with the head X projecting to larger phrases.[3]
   b.   Heads (categories) are not atomic elements; rather, they are feature complexes, consisting of the primitive features [±N] and [±V].
   c.   UG provides the general X'-schemata of the following sort (cf. (14)), which govern the mode of projection of a head:
         X' → X . . .
         X" → [Spec, X'] X'

The version of X'-theory presented in Chomsky (1970) was in a preliminary form, and there certainly remained details to be worked out more fully. However, it is also true that all the crucial and fundamental insights of X'-theory were already presented in this study and have been subject to little substantive change in the following years. More specifically, the claims (18a) and (18b) above have survived almost in their original forms throughout the following development of grammatical theory and are still assumed in the current framework, while the claim (18c), the existence of the universal X'-schemata, has been subjected to critical scrutiny in recent years, as we will see in the next section.

The proposal of X'-theory was followed by a flux of research on phrase structure in the 1970s, trying to fix some technical problems associated with the initial version of the theory and to expand the scope of X'-theory to extensive descriptive material. The relevant literature in this era is too copious to mention in detail, but to name just a few: Siegel (1974), Bowers (1975), Bresnan (1976, 1977), Emonds (1976), Hornstein (1977), Selkirk (1977), and perhaps most importantly, Jackendoff (1977). From our current perspectives, two important and interrelated problems emerged during this period. They are (i) the analysis of sentences (or clauses) *vis-à-vis* X'-theory, and (ii) the proper characterization of "Spec." Let us look at these issues in some detail.

As we saw above, the sentential structure was handled in Chomsky (1970) by the phrase structure rule (15), which does not conform to the general X'-schemata in (14), thereby making the structure of a sentence a kind of an exception to X'-theory. And this is the main reason for the rather incomplete parallelism between sentences and noun phrases as depicted by (16). Naturally, a proposal has been made, most notably by Jackendoff (1977) (cf. also Kayne 1981c), that a sentence be analyzed as the (maximal) projection of V, with its subject being treated as [Spec, V'] (or [Spec, V"] in Jackendoff's system, since he assumes that X''' is the maximal level for every category). While this proposal has the obvious advantage of making the internal structures of sentences and noun phrases (almost) completely parallel, there exists some evidence against this claim (see Hornstein 1977, among others). The most crucial evidence that counters the $S = V^{max}$ (the maximal projection of V) analysis comes from the close relationship holding between the subject of a sentence and I(nflectional elements, including the traditional notion of AUX) of that sentence. For example, it is the I of a sentence that assigns nominative Case to the subject, and it is also I that the subject agrees with (in terms of number, person, etc.). And this kind of formal relation cannot be straightforwardly stated if the subject is generated inside the projection of V, with I outside of that projection. Thus, even in Chomsky (1981), S is still generated by the following phrase structure rule (adapted from Chomsky 1981), where the subject N" is placed outside the maximal projection of V:

(19) $S \rightarrow N''$ I V"

Huang (1982) proposes (cf. also Stowell 1981, Pesetsky 1982) that S should in fact be analyzed as the maximal projection of I, a natural extension of the spirit of X'-theory. His arguments for this claim mainly come from considerations of the behavior of the subject and I with respect to general principles such as the Empty Category Principle (ECP). In particular, Huang argues that I really behaves like a head in that it governs (but does not properly govern, at least in English) the subject (see Huang 1982 for much detailed discussion). The internal structure of a sentence now looks like the following, which conforms to X'-theory:

(20)

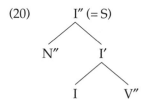

In (20), the subject is the [Spec, I'] and the sentential structure now looks quite "normal" in the sense that there is nothing special with it in light of X'-theory, now extended to a "non-lexical" category I. Note, however, that the incompleteness of parallelism between sentences and noun phrases still remains even under this modified analysis: the subject of a noun phrase is inside its own projection, whereas the subject of a sentence is generated outside of the projection of a verb. This problem was resolved when the new analysis of subjects (called the "Predicate-Internal Subject Hypothesis") was introduced, as we will discuss in the following section.

Returning to the historical discussion of the analysis of sentences, Bresnan (1972), based on extensive study of *wh*-movement phenomena, introduced a larger clausal unit that includes the core part of the sentence (S) and the "sentence-introducer," called C(omplementizer) (e.g., *that, for, whether*, etc.) Thus, the structure of a full clause (notated as S' (S-bar)) should be introduced by the following phrase structure rule (see Bresnan 1972 for details):

(21)   S' → C S

Given the structure of S in (20), the structure of a full clause is:

(22)

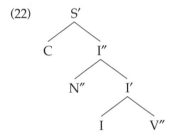

In (22), the top portion of the structure is still an exception to X'-theory. S' is not headed by anything, but rather, branches to two coordinated elements, C and I" (= S). Evidence has been accumulated, however, to show that C functions as a head, in terms of, particularly, the ECP (Fassi Fehri 1980, Stowell 1981, Lasnik and Saito 1984, among others). This led to the proposal of analyzing C as the head of S', thus reanalyzing the latter as C':

(23)

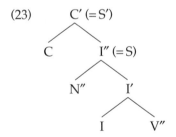

Now the clausal structure is made to fall under X'-theory almost completely, the only problem being the "defectiveness" of the complementizer phrase, i.e., it projects only to C', not to C". To see how this final gap was filled, we should turn to the other major problem that motivated the development of X'-theory, namely, the characterization of Spec.

In Chomsky's (1970) version of X'-theory, "Spec" constituted a rather heterogeneous set, including a variety of "pre-head" elements. Thus, Chomsky suggested that [Spec, V'] includes auxiliary elements of various sorts (with

time adverbials associated), [Spec, N'] is instantiated as determiners, [Spec, A']
contains the system of qualifying elements such as comparative structures,
very, etc. As the research progressed, however, it became increasingly apparent that those pre-head elements can be classified into different types, and that
the notion of Spec should be more narrowly defined to capture the true generalization. Accordingly, some elements that were initially identified as Spec
were later reanalyzed as heads (e.g. auxiliary elements, now analyzed as instances of the head I), or "adjuncts" (modifiers) that are optionally generated
to modify heads (e.g. *very*), although many descriptive questions remain (even
now) with the analysis of the latter.

   The notion of Spec that resulted from these efforts has the following properties: (i) it is typically an NP, and (ii) it bears a certain relationship with the
head. Of the pre-head elements in English, the fronted *wh*-phrase, the subject
of a sentence, and the subject of a noun phrase exhibit these properties. Thus,
the subject of a sentence is identified as [Spec, I'], and the subject of a noun
phrase (as in *the enemy's* destruction) is characterized as [Spec, N'].[4] The fronted
wh-phrase apparently shows the two properties just discussed: it is typically
an NP (or at least a maximal projection), and it bears a certain relationship
with the head C (it is a [+wh] C that triggers *wh*-movement; see Bresnan 1972).
Thus, it is well qualified to be [Spec, C'], patterning with the other Specs. However, to characterize a fronted *wh*-phrase as [Spec, C'] requires a reanalysis of
wh-movement. Namely, *wh*-movement should now be analyzed as "movement
to [Spec, C']," rather than "movement to C," as has been long assumed ever
since Bresnan's pioneering work (Bresnan 1972). This is in fact what Chomsky
(1986b) proposes, with some additional arguments to support this conclusion
(see Chomsky 1986b for details). If a fronted *wh*-phrase occupies [Spec, C'], then
the structure of a full clause now looks like the following, with the projection of
C completely on a par with other projections (i.e., no "defectiveness" of C^{max}):

(24) C" (= S')

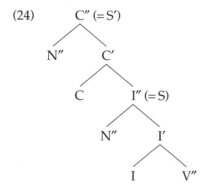

   X'-theory is now in full force, regulating the clausal structure, which has
always been an exception to the theory in one way or another, as well as the
structure of other phrases. The basic ideas of the version of X'-theory presented in Chomsky (1986b) can be stated as follows:[5]

(25)   **X-bar schemata** (cf. Chomsky 1986b)
   a. $X' = X / X' \; Y''$
   b. $X'' = Z'' \; X' / X''$

In (25), X means X^0, a zero-level category (i.e., a head), the "/" sign between symbols indicates that there is a choice between them (e.g. either X or X′ can be chosen in (25a)), and X, Y, Z are variables ranging over possible categories (now including non-lexical categories). Notice that by allowing the same symbol (viz., X′ in (25a) and X″ in (25b)) to occur on both sides of the same equation, we permit "recursion" of the same bar-level structures in a phrase. For example, (25) licenses the following structure, where X′ and X″ each appear twice:

(26)

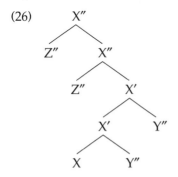

We call the lower Y″ in (26) the "complement" of X, the lower Z″ the "Spec" of X′ (or the Spec of X″ ([Spec, X″]); see n. 2), and the upper Z″ an "adjunct" of X″. The status of the upper Y″ in (26) is ambiguous (it could be a "quasi-complement" or an adjunct, for instance), depending on further articulation of the theory of phrase structure (see Chomsky and Lasnik 1993). Note incidentally that these notions (complement, Spec, and adjunct) are "relational" notions defined in terms of their structural positions, not inherent and categorical ones (unlike notions such as "Noun Phrase," which are categorical). This is an assumption that has been pretty much constant throughout the history of X′-theory.
   A few more general remarks are in order with respect to the X′-scheme in (25). First, one might notice the use of equations in (25), rather than X′-"rules" that have been exploited in previous works on X′-theory. In most earlier works, X′-theory was taken to be a principle of UG that provides the general "rule schemata" that regulate the general form of phrase structure rules of human language. This traditional conception of X′-theory collapsed when the very notion of phrase structure rules was subjected to critical scrutiny, and was eventually eliminated around 1980, when the "principles-and-parameters" approach was first set forth in a systematic way (see Chomsky 1981). Specifically, it was pointed out that phrase structure rules are redundant and dubious devices, recapitulating the information that must be presented in the lexicon. For example, the fact that the verb *persuade* takes an NP and S′ (= C″) complement has to be stated as the verb's lexical property, quite independently

from the phrase structure rule that generates the sequence V-NP-S'/C". And since descriptions of lexical properties in the lexicon are ineliminable, it is the phrase structure rules that ought to be eliminated. Subsequent work such as Stowell (1981) showed that the other information expressed by phrase structure rules (most of which have to do with linear ordering) can in large part be determined by other general principles of UG (such as Case theory; see Stowell 1981). Thus, it was generally believed in the principles-and-parameters approach that phrase structure rules could be entirely eliminated, apart from certain parameters of X'-theory. With the notion of phrase structure rules eliminated from the grammar, X'-theory has become a principle of UG that directly regulates phrase structure of human language.

Second, the X'-scheme in (25) is formulated only in terms of the structural relation "dominance," and does not encode the information regarding linear order. Thus, of the three types of information listed in (2) before, i.e., (2i) Dominance, (2ii) Labeling, and (2iii) linear order (Precedence), only the first two ((2i) and (2ii)) are regulated by X'-theory itself. The linear order of elements (2iii) is to be specified by the "parameter" (called the "head parameter") associated with X'-theory. This is in accordance with the general guidelines of the principles-and-parameters approach, under which UG is conceived of as a finite set of invariant principles each of which is associated with a parameter whose value is to be fixed by experience. There are two values of the head parameter, "head initial" and "head last." If the parameter is set for the value "head initial," the English-type languages follow, in which complements generally follow their heads, whereas if the value is set as "head last," the Japanese-type languages obtain, where complements typically precede their heads.[6] With this move to parametrized X'-theory, the phrase structure system for a particular language is largely restricted to the specification of the parameter(s) that determine(s) the linear ordering of elements.

Finally, given the narrower characterization of Spec as a place for a maximal projection (typically a noun phrase), we now have a much simplified theory of movement. Chomsky (1986b) proposes that there are two types of movement: (i) X^0-movement (movement of a head), and (ii) X" (or X^{max})-movement (movement of a maximal projection). We put aside the discussion of X^0-movement (see Chomsky 1986b, 1995a; see also Roberts in this volume for much detailed discussion of this type of movement). Movement of a maximal projection is divided into two subtypes: (i) substitution, and (ii) adjunction. Chomsky then argues that, apart from X^0-movement to a head position (which we put aside), various principles of UG ensure that substitution (NP-movement and *wh*-movement) always moves a maximal projection to a specifier position (see Chomsky 1986b for details).[7] Thus, the notion of "Spec" now receives a uniform characterization as a landing site for X^{max}-movement: [Spec, C'/C"] is the landing site for *wh*-movement, [Spec, I'/I"] is the landing site for NP-movement (passive and raising), and [Spec, N'/N"] is the landing site for "passive" in a noun phrase. We will return to adjunction later on.

To sum up, Chomsky's (1986b) version of X'-theory has the following characteristics. First, it includes two "non-lexical" categories, I and C, as members of

"X" relevant for X'-theory, so that a full clausal structure is now in full conformity with the principles of X'-theory and "sentences" are no longer exceptions to the theory, a great improvement over earlier versions of X'-theory for which "sentences" have always been treated as exceptions. Second, X'-theory is now parametrized in accordance with the general guidelines of the principles-and-parameters approach, and the theory no longer specifies the linear ordering of elements in the scheme. The ordering restrictions are determined by the value for the parameter (the head parameter) associated with X'-theory, not by X'-theory itself. And finally, the notion of Spec is further sharpened as a landing site for movement of a maximal projection (substitution), with a remarkable simplification of the theory of movement. Some important problems, however, remained open in this version of X'-theory, which motivated further development of the theory in the decade that followed.

2   Minimizing and Deriving X'-Theory

An obvious point in Chomsky's (1986b) version of X'-theory that calls for further improvement is the incomplete parallelism it expresses between noun phrases and clauses/sentences. Compare the following structures which are assigned to noun phrases and clauses in this theory:

(27) a. **Noun phrases**

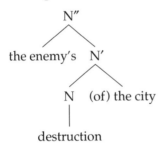

b. **Clauses**

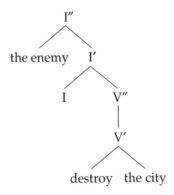

There are various problems with the structures in (27). The source of the problems is the fact that in (27a), all the "arguments" (subject and object) are located within the maximal projection of a single head (N = *destruction*), while in (27b), subject and object are split in two different projections. In other words, in a sentential structure (27b), there is an "additional" structure, due to the existence of the head I; in (27a), on the other hand, there is no such additional structure and all the arguments are located within the projection of N. From this discrepancy, a variety of problems arise. Why is the subject of a sentence located in [Spec, I'], a non-lexical category (I will henceforth follow a more recent practice to notate the Spec), whereas the subject of a noun phrase is located in [Spec, N''], a lexical category? A related question is: why does the "passive" in a sentence (e.g. *the city was destroyed (by the enemy)*) move a maximal projection to the specifier position of a non-lexical category ([Spec, I']), but the corresponding passive in a noun phrase (e.g. *the city's destruction (by the enemy)*) moves a maximal projection to the specifier position of a lexical category ([Spec, N''])? Also, why does V project from V' to V'', without having Spec? And so on. The structures in (27) are clearly not parallel enough to capture the similarities between noun phrases and sentences.

Two proposals were made in the mid- to late 1980s which played important roles in resolving these problems. They are (i) the "DP-analysis" (Fukui and Speas 1986, Abney 1987; see also Brame 1981, 1982), and (ii) the "Predicate-Internal Subject" Hypothesis (see Hale 1978, Kitagawa 1986, Koopman and Sportiche 1991, Kuroda 1988, among others, for various versions of the "VP-Internal Subject" Hypothesis; see Fukui and Speas 1986 for a generalized form of the hypothesis as it is applied to all predicative categories).

The DP-analysis claims that "noun phrases" are in fact "determiner phrases" (DP) headed by the head D which takes a noun phrase as its complement. (See Longobardi in this volume for much relevant discussion, including detailed (crosslinguistic) analyses of the internal structure of noun phrases under this hypothesis.) According to this analysis, then, the internal structure of a noun phrase should be as follows:

(28)

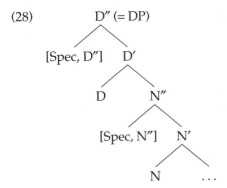

It was argued in the above-mentioned works that the DP-analysis is in fact supported by various syntactic considerations (see also Bernstein and Longobardi in this volume). Furthermore, the DP-analysis of noun phrases received much justification from the semantics of nominal expressions (a similar analysis had in fact been assumed in Montague semantics before the syntactic DP-analysis was proposed). Thus, this analysis has become more or less a standard analysis of noun phrases and is assumed in much current literature.

Notice that the DP-analysis provides a "two-story" structure for noun phrases that looks quite similar to the structure of sentences: in both structures, a non-lexical category (I in a sentence, D in a noun phrase) heads the whole phrase, taking a complement headed by a lexical category (V in a sentence, N in a noun phrase). Given the DP-analysis, then, the parallelism between sentences and noun phrases becomes much more visible and easy to capture than in the traditional analysis of noun phrases.

Where, then, is the subject located in these structures? Quite independently of the DP-analysis, it was proposed that the subject of a sentence should be generated in the projection of a verb (see the references cited above). In fact, the analysis that the subject of a sentence should be generated within a verb's projection is a rather traditional one (see, for example, Jackendoff 1977), which has been challenged by various evidence that the subject of a sentence is in a close relationship with I (see the discussion above). In other words, there seem to be two apparently conflicting sets of evidence regarding the status of the subject in a sentence: one type of evidence (most of which has to do with theta-theoretic considerations) indicates that the subject should be inside the verb's projection, while the other type of evidence (having to do with Case, agreement, government, etc.) suggests that the subject must occupy [Spec, I"]. The "VP-Internal Subject" Hypothesis was proposed mainly to reconcile these two types of evidence. The crucial and novel part of this hypothesis is the movement process that raises the subject (which is generated inside the verb's projection) to [Spec, I"]. This movement is driven by the need for Case assignment. Thus, the subject of a sentence is generated in [Spec, V"] (in some versions of the VP-Internal Subject Hypothesis, not in others), and then, is moved to [Spec, I"] in order to receive Case in that position. The D-structure position of the subject accounts for the subject's theta-theoretic status with respect to the verb, whereas its S-structure position (after the movement) accommodates the evidence indicating its close relationship with the inflectional head (I) (note that Case and agreement are S-structure (or at least non-D-structure) phenomena).

Combining the DP-analysis and the VP-Internal Subject Hypothesis (thus making the latter the "Predicate-Internal Subject" Hypothesis), we have the following completely parallel structures for noun phrases and clauses/sentences (Fukui and Speas 1986):

(29) a. **Noun phrases**

D-structure:

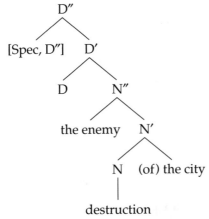

S-structure:

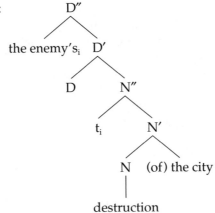

b. **Clauses**

D-structure:

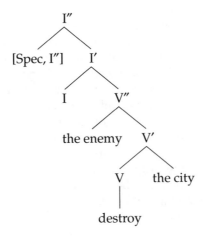

S-structure:

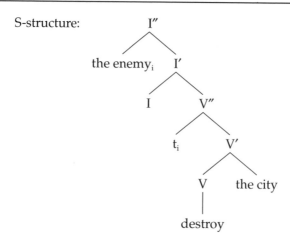

The subjects in both noun phrases and sentences are generated within the projection of the lexical category (N in a noun phrase and V in a sentence), receiving a theta-role in their original positions, and then are raised to the Spec positions of associated non-lexical categories (D in the case of noun phrases, I in sentences) to receive Case (genitive in noun phrases, nominative in sentences).[8] Passives in noun phrases (e.g. *the city's destruction (by the enemy)*) and those in sentences (e.g. *the city was destroyed (by the enemy)*) can be analyzed uniformly as a process involving movement of an object from its base position (the complement position of a predicate N/V) to the Spec of an associated non-lexical category ([Spec, D"] in noun phrases and [Spec, I"] in sentences).

The integration of the DP-analysis and the Predicate-Internal Subject Hypothesis was based on the following ideas about the lexicon as it relates to syntactic computation. (See Fukui and Speas 1986, Abney 1987, for some preliminary discussions; see also Fukui 1986 for further discussion on this and related issues.) Items of the lexicon are divided into two major subtypes: lexical categories and "functional" categories. The latter types of category roughly correspond to the traditional non-lexical categories, renamed in consideration of their nature. Lexical categories have substantive content, and include nouns, verbs, adjectives, etc. They typically enter into theta-marking. Functional categories do not have substantive content, and do not enter into theta-marking (although they do have other feature structures, including categorial features, agreement features, etc.). Lexical categories play an important role in interpretation of linguistic expressions, and indeed, most of the items in the lexicon belong to this type. Functional categories, on the other hand, do not play a comparable role in interpretation of linguistic expressions; their role is largely restricted to "grammatical" (or "computational") aspects of linguistic structure (although some of the proposed functional categories, e.g. I and D, may sometimes function as operators, bearing some "semantic" import). These categories constitute a small (and often closed) set, which include C, I, D (assuming the DP-analysis), and a few others.

Thus, the general view on the nature of these categories is the following division of labor for constructing linguistic expressions:

(30) (i) Lexical categories: the "conceptual" aspects of linguistic structure.
      (ii) Functional categories: the "computational" aspects of linguistic structure.

Lexical categories bear semantic features, including, in particular, features having to do with theta-roles ("theta-grids" in the sense of Stowell 1981). They assign (or "discharge") theta-roles/features associated with them to other phrases, thereby forming larger structures that embed them. Functional categories do not bear theta-roles. Their role is largely restricted to purely formal and computational aspects of linguistic structure such as marking grammatical structures (nominals and clauses) or triggering movement operations. More specifically, some functional categories (functional heads) bear "agreement features," and these agreement features attract a maximal projection to their neighborhoods (their specifier positions), in order for the latter to agree with the former. Thus, functional categories are indeed the "drive" for syntactic movement operations; lexical categories lack agreement features of this kind, and hence do not induce movement.

The idea of functional categories as the major driving force for movement opened up a new way of looking at crosslinguistic variation, and facilitated much subsequent work on comparative syntax in terms of properties of functional elements in languages. Given the nature and role of functional categories, it was proposed that language variation be restricted (apart from ordering restrictions) to the functional domain of the lexicon (Fukui 1986, 1988; see also Borer 1984), and this proposal contributed to constructing a more restrictive theory of comparative syntax. At the same time, numerous "new" functional categories were proposed in the late 1980s, achieving tremendous descriptive success, although from an explanatory point of view, it was clear that the class of possible functional categories has to be severely restricted in a principled way (Fukui 1988, 1995; see also Chomsky 1995a for a "Minimalist" critique of functional elements). See Belletti and Zanuttini (both this volume) and references there for much relevant discussion.

Explicit recognition of the division of labor between lexical and functional categories, as well as increasing emphasis on the importance of features in phrase structure composition, naturally led to a theory of phrase structure called "Relativized X'-theory," which is an attempt to minimize the role of X'-theory, while maintaining its basic insights.[9] The fundamental idea of Relativized X'-theory, inspired by categorial grammars, can be summarized as follows:

(31) Phrase structure composition is driven by feature discharge.

Recall that lexical items have always been assumed, at least since Chomsky (1970), to be feature complexes (see the discussion in section 1). Given the fundamental difference between lexical and functional categories noted above, we can roughly assume the following feature specifications of these categories (see Chomsky 1995a for recent and much more elaborated discussion on features):

(32)   (i)   Lexical categories = {categorial features, theta-features (theta-roles/ theta-grids), subcategorization features, phonological features, etc.}.
       (ii) Functional categories = {categorial features, agreement features, subcategorization features, phonological features, etc.}.

The crucial difference, then, is that lexical categories bear theta-features but not agreement features, whereas functional categories lack theta-features but are associated with agreement features. And this crucial difference is directly reflected in their modes of projection in Relativized X'-theory. Thus, lexical categories project as they discharge their theta-features in the following manner:[10]

(33)   L′ (= L[+projected])

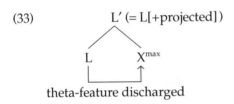

          L   X^{max}

       theta-feature discharged

Lexical categories continue to project, forming larger structures, as they discharge their theta-features, until all the features have been discharged. In other words, the structure created in this process is recursive, and in this sense, the projection of a lexical category is never "closed." Note that in this system, the notion of "maximal projection" can no longer be defined in terms of "bar-levels," as in the standard X'-theory. Thus, maximal projection is defined as follows, in a way that is "relativized" to each head and configuration (see Muysken 1982 for an original proposal of this kind; see also Baltin 1989 for a similar approach):

(34)   The "maximal projection" of X is a category X that does not project further in a given configuration.

The mode of projection of functional categories, although also governed by feature discharge, is different from that of lexical categories, since functional categories do not bear theta-features but instead have agreement features to discharge, and it is claimed that agreement is typically a one-to-one relation (Fukui 1986, Kuroda 1988). Thus, if a functional head F takes a maximal projection, discharging its subcategorization feature to the latter, and then takes another maximal projection for the purpose of agreement, its projection is "closed" at that point, due to the one-to-one nature of agreement:

(35)

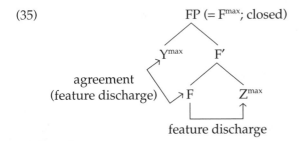

$$\text{FP} \; (= \text{F}^{\text{max}}; \text{closed})$$

Y^max   F'

agreement
(feature discharge)   F   Z^max

feature discharge

Once agreement occurs, therefore, the projection is closed (the closed projection of X is notated as "XP" in this theory, as in (35)), and no further projection is possible. As a closed category cannot project further, it is also a maximal projection. Notice that the reverse is not true. While a closed projection is always a maximal projection, being a maximal projection does not imply it is closed (by agreement). In fact, projections of lexical categories do have maximal projections, but they never have closed projections, simply because lexical heads do not have agreement features (therefore, there is no independent "LP," a closed lexical projection).

Recall that agreement features are the driving force for movement in syntax. Since only functional categories bear these features, it follows that only functional categories induce movement; lexical categories never trigger movement. And this is well in accord with the facts: NP-movement (passive and raising) moves a noun phrase to [Spec, I^{max}]; passive in a noun phrase is the process of moving a noun phrase to [Spec, D^{max}]; and *wh*-movement moves a *wh*-phrase to [Spec, C^{max}] (note that in Relativized X'-theory, maximal projections are not inherently related to bar-levels, even if the latter notion exists at all). It looks as though all typical movements (at least in English) are to the specifier position of a functional category. To sharpen the notion of "Spec" still further, Relativized X'-theory proposes that Spec be defined in terms of agreement:

(36)   The specifier of X is a maximal projection that agrees with X.

Thus, a moved *wh*-phrase, the subject that agrees with I, etc. are all Specs, but lexical categories do not have Specs, since they do not have agreement features to license Specs. The definition of Spec in (36) clarifies the nature of Spec more than ever: Spec is the landing site for movement.

Relativized X'-theory has an important implication for the theory of movement. The issue, again, has to do with the notion of Spec. In the standard theory of movement, an empty category Δ is generated in the position of a specifier at D-structure (or in the course of a derivation; see Chomsky 1993) as a target for substitution. However, it is impossible to justify this empty category in Relativized X'-theory. It is not licensed by theta-assignment, since a functional head never assigns a theta-role, and it is not licensed by agreement because it is the moved maximal projection, not an empty category, that agrees with the functional head. Also, the empty category never appears on the surface;

it is there only to be replaced by a moved category, and it always has to be "erased" before the derivation ends. Therefore, such a superfluous empty category is eliminated in Relativized X'-theory, and hence, substitution operations no longer exist as operations that "substitute for" some existing element. Formally, then, the operation that is involved in "substitution" is no different from Adjunction, in the sense that it does not substitute for anything.[11] Thus, the traditional notion of "substitution" transformation, with the dubious empty category Δ, is eliminated from the theory of grammar (but see n. 11). And if phrase structure composition is also carried out by a formal operation Adjunction (whose application is driven by feature discharge), as we saw above, then it seems that there is one uniform operation which is responsible for both phrase structure building and movement, namely, Adjunction.[12]

Relativized X'-theory minimized, in fact virtually eliminated, the need for an X'-schema, which had been assumed throughout the previous development of X'-theory. It takes seriously the notions (i) projection and (ii) feature discharge, and claims that every position in phrase structure must be licensed in terms of these notions. Since lexical and functional categories have different feature specifications – in particular, only the latter bears agreement features – the modes of projection of these two types of category must reflect the difference. Thus, only functional categories have Specs as a landing site for movement, triggered by agreement features associated with the functional heads, whereas lexical categories never have Specs and their projections are thus never closed. From this, it immediately follows that if a language lacks functional categories (or if its functional system is inert), then the phrase structure of the language is essentially based on the lexical system, phrasal projections in the language are never closed, and no syntactic movement is triggered. Fukui (1986, 1988) argues that this is indeed the case in languages like Japanese, and demonstrates that a variety of typological properties of Japanese, e.g. the lack of *wh*-movement, the existence of multiple-nominative/genitive constructions, scrambling, and many others, are derived from this fundamental parametric property of the language.

The total elimination of X'-theory was proposed and carried out by Chomsky's (1994) "bare phrase structure" theory (see also Kayne 1994 for a different approach). The bare theory is couched within the "Minimalist program" (Chomsky 1993), according to which all the principles and entities of grammar must be motivated and justified either by the properties of two "interface representations," LF and PF, or by considerations of economy (see Chomsky 1993 for details; see also Collins in this volume, and other relevant chapters). Most of the basic claims of Relativized X'-theory carry over to the bare theory, except for a particular characterization of Spec in the former as an X^{max} agreeing with a head (see (36); see also the next section for some relevant discussion).

Chomsky argues that (the standard) X'-theory specifies much redundant information, while the only structural information needed is that a "head" and a "non-head" combine to create a unit. He then proposes that a phrase structure is constructed in a bottom-up fashion by a uniform operation called "Merge," which combines two elements, say α and β, and projects one of them as the head. This is illustrated in (37), where the prime simply means the category is projected (see n. 10):

(37) α β $\xrightarrow{\text{Merge}}$ if α projects $\quad \alpha' (= \alpha[+\text{projected}])$

$$\alpha \quad \beta$$

if β projects $\quad \beta' (= \beta[+\text{projected}])$

$$\alpha \quad \beta$$

Since Merge does not specify the linear order of α and β, the tree structures in (37) can be more formally, and more accurately, represented as in (38):

(38) $K = \{\gamma, \{\alpha, \beta\}\}$, where $\gamma \in \{\alpha, \beta\}$

(38) states that Merge forms a new object K by combining two objects α and β, and specifies one of them as the projecting element (hence the head of K). Merge applies recursively to form a new structure.

Chomsky further argues that Merge is involved in both phrase structure composition and movement processes. Suppose that Merge is to apply to α and K, to form a new unit L, with K projecting:

(39) α K $\xrightarrow{\text{Merge}}$ L $(= K')$

$$\alpha \quad K$$

The only difference between simple phrase structure building and movement is whether α in (39) comes from the lexicon (or from the Numeration, in current terms), as in the case of phrase structure building, or from within K (leaving its copy in the original place), as in the case of movement. Thus, the bare theory unifies phrase structure composition and movement in terms of the single operation Merge (which is somewhat reminiscent of Adjunction in Relativized X'-theory).

A "maximal projection" is also defined relationally in the bare theory: a category that does not project any further in a given configuration is a maximal projection. The terms "complement" and "specifier' are defined in the usual way. Note that the definition of the latter concept (Spec) in the bare theory is different from that of Spec in Relativized X'-theory. In Relativized X'-theory, Spec is defined in terms of agreement (cf. (36)), with the consequence that only functional categories have Specs. In the bare theory, on the other hand, agreement does not play any significant role in defining Spec, and hence Spec is defined in the traditional way as a phrase that is immediately dominated by a maximal projection. This (and the associated distinction between X^{max} (a simple maximal projection) and XP (a closed maximal projection)) seems to be the only substantive difference, apart from details, between Relativized X'-theory and the bare theory. See Fukui (1991), Fukui and Saito (1992), and Saito and Fukui (1998) for some arguments for the necessity of X^{max}/XP distinction. See also the next section for some relevant discussion.

With Chomsky's bare theory, X'-theory is now completely eliminated as an independent module of grammar. The basic insights of X'-theory, in particular, the insight that every phrase is headed in human language (cf. (18a)), is straightforwardly expressed as a fundamental property of the operation Merge, without postulating an additional "principle."

However, of the three kinds of information about syntactic representations listed in (2), i.e., (2i) Dominance, (2ii) Labeling, and (2iii) linear order (Precedence), the last kind of information is not encoded at all in Chomsky's formulation of Merge given above. In fact, whether or not the theory of phrase structure should specify the linear order of elements still remains open in current research, to which we now turn.

3   Linear Order in Phrase Structure

The concept of linear order in a phrase marker was never questioned in an earlier framework of generative grammar. In fact, it was, as stated in (2), one of the few crucial primitive concepts in the theory of phrase structure, and a variety of grammatical rules was formulated with a crucial reference to linear order (see, for example, "pronominalization" transformation in the 1960s). However, it has been increasingly less obvious that linear order plays a role at all in language computation, apart from phonology. Thus, virtually all the principles and conditions assumed in the principles-and-parameters theory in the 1980s are formulated purely in hierarchical terms (in terms of domination and c-command), without referring to linear order. The "head parameter" (and its variants) seems to be the only notion in linguistic theory which crucially refers to linear order.

Kayne (1994) challenges this notion of head parameter. He proposes a universal principle, the Linear Correspondence Axiom (LCA), which states essentially that asymmetric c-command imposes a linear ordering of terminal elements. More specifically, the LCA dictates that if a non-terminal X asymmetrically c-commands a non-terminal Y in a given phrase marker P, then all terminals dominated by X must precede or follow all terminals dominated by Y in P. Kayne takes the relevant ordering to be precedence, rather than subsequence (following), based on his assumptions about the relation between terminals and "time slots" (see Kayne 1994 for more details). Thus, within Kayne's theory, asymmetric c-command relations uniquely map into precedence relations: all terminals dominated by X precede all terminals dominated by Y, in the configuration stated above. It then follows, given Kayne's formulation, that there is a universal S(pecifier)–H(ead)–C(omplement) order (in particular, S(ubject)–V(erb)–O(bject)), with other orders (S-C-H/S-O-V, for example) being derived via movement. With the universal S-H-C order, the head parameter is entirely eliminated.

Note that in Kayne's theory, linear order still plays a role in the core computation of language, though redundantly, because it is entirely determined by asymmetric c-command relations. In other words, Kayne proposes that linear order is not parametrized and that it is uniquely determined by asymmetric c-command relations, given his LCA, which he claims to apply at every syntactic level. But linear order is still defined and remains visible throughout the derivation and could conceivably play a role in the core computation of language.

Chomsky (1994, 1995a), adopting and incorporating the basic insights of Kayne's LCA into his bare theory, makes a step further toward complete elimination of linear order from the core of language computation. As we saw in the preceding section, Chomsky's bare theory, the recursive procedure Merge in particular, does not encode any information regarding linear order of syntactic elements. This is based on his understanding that there is no clear evidence that linear order plays a role at LF or in the core computation of human language.[13] Thus, he assumes that linear order is not defined and hence does not play a role in the core computation of language, and suggests that ordering is a property of the phonological component, a proposal that has been occasionally made in various forms in the literature. Specifically, he claims that a modified version of the LCA applies as a principle of the phonological component to the output of Morphology, a subcomponent of the phonological component (see Chomsky 1995a for detailed discussion). Thus, under Chomsky's proposal, phrase structure is defined without reference to linear order in the core computational part of human language, and will later be assigned linear order by (a modified version of) the LCA in the phonological component.

By contrast, Saito and Fukui (1998) (see also Fukui 1993, Fukui and Saito 1992) claims that linear order indeed plays an important role in the core computational part of human language, and argues that the head parameter, or more precisely a modified version of it, should be maintained. One way, proposed in Saito and Fukui (1998), to incorporate the head parameter into the bare theory is to replace the set notation $\{\alpha, \beta\}$ in (38), reproduced here as (40), by an ordered pair $<\alpha, \beta>$, thereby specifying which of the two elements projects in a given language. Thus, we have (41) instead of (40):

(40)   **Chomsky's Merge:** $K = \{\gamma, \{\alpha, \beta\}\}$, where $\gamma \in \{\alpha, \beta\}$

(41)   **Fukui and Saito's parametrized Merge:** $K = \{\gamma, <\alpha, \beta>\}$, where $\gamma \in \{\alpha, \beta\}$

If γ takes the value "α," we have a "head-initial/left-headed" language such as English, whereas if $\gamma = \beta$, a "head-last/right-headed" language like Japanese is defined. Thus, in left-headed English, elements can be merged only on the *right* side of a head, whereas in right-headed Japanese, Merge occurs only on the *left* side of a head. If something is to be introduced on the opposite side of the structure (i.e., on the left side of a head in English, and on the right side of a head in Japanese), it must be "adjoined" to the target, creating a multi-segment structure (see Chomsky 1986b, 1995a, for relevant discussion on substitution vs. adjunction). A case in point is the status of subjects in these languages. The subject in English is in an adjoined position because it appears on the left side of the head, where projection of the target is prohibited by (41) as it is parametrized for English. The subject in Japanese, on the other hand, is introduced into phrase structure by Merge (i.e., substitution; see below), since it shows up on the left side of the head, where merger is possible (Japanese is a right-headed language). See Saito and Fukui (1998) for more detailed discussion, as well as illustrations of this point.

Saito and Fukui argue that given the parametrized version of Merge (41), it becomes possible to characterize the traditional "adjunction" operations, viz., scrambling in Japanese and heavy NP shift in English, as paradigm cases of Merge (i.e., as substitution, in the sense that they always accompany projection of the target),[14] and hence, given the costless nature of Merge (Chomsky 1995), the optionality of these operations, a matter that has been quite disturbing for the general economy approach to movement (Chomsky 1991), is also straightforwardly accounted for. On the other hand, traditional "substitution" operations (*wh*-movement and NP-movement) are analyzed in this system as genuine adjunction since they never induce projection of the target, creating a multi-segment structure of the target (see Saito and Fukui 1998 for much detail). Further, they point out that the "directionality" of these optional movements correlates with the "directionality" of projection in the language. Thus, head-initial/left-headed English has rightward heavy NP shift, whereas head-last/right-headed Japanese exhibits leftward scrambling, but no other combination is allowed. It is clear that such a correlation can only be captured by a parametrized Merge embodying linear order, as in (41). Saito and Fukui show that a number of other differences between English and Japanese also follow from their theory of phrase structure.

The parametrized Merge has an important implication for the theory of locality on movement. It has been known since Cattell (1976), Kayne (1981c), and Huang (1982) that a non-complement maximal projection forms an island for movement (see also Rizzi, this volume, for some relevant discussion). Thus, extraction out of subjects and adverbial adjuncts results in ungrammaticality, as shown in (42):

(42) a. ?*Who$_i$ did [a picture of t_i] please John
      b. ?*Who$_i$ did John go home [because he saw t_i]

The effects illustrated by (42a) and (42b) are called the Subject Condition effects and the Adjunct Condition effects, respectively. There are two important problems with respect to these effects. One is how to unify them in a natural way. The other problem has to do with the crosslinguistic considerations of these effects. The Adjunct Condition effects are generally assumed to be universal, whereas the Subject Condition effects are known to show crosslinguistic variation. Specifically, it appears that while SVO languages generally exhibit the Subject Condition effects, SOV languages systematically lack the effects (Kayne 1984; see also Aissen 1996 for related discussion). Huang (1982) proposes the Condition on Extraction Domain (CED), which unifies the Subject and Adjunct Condition effects in terms of the notion of "proper government," and suggests a possible way of accounting for the observed crosslinguistic difference with respect to the Subject Condition effects (see Huang 1982 for details). Huang's CED was later incorporated into Chomsky's (1986b) barriers theory as a central ingredient of the latter system.

Takahashi (1994), working under the general "economy" guidelines (see Collins in this volume) and extending Chomsky (1986b) and Chomsky and Lasnik (1993), proposes to derive these effects from the Minimal Link Condition (MLC) and constraints on adjunction sites. The former condition, when interpreted derivationally, requires that movement go through every possible landing site. If any XP dominating the moved element is a potential adjunction site in the case of A'-movement, this implies that the *wh*-phrases in (42) must adjoin to every maximal position that intervenes between their initial positions and the matrix [Spec, CP]. In particular, *who* must adjoin to the subject DP in (42a), and the adverbial CP in (42b). But if adjunction to subjects and adjuncts/modifiers is prohibited, as argued in Chomsky (1986b), then the moved *wh*-phrase must skip a possible landing site in these examples. Hence, (42a–b) both violate the MLC.

The remaining problem is to derive the constraints on adjunction sites. There have been some proposals that treat the subject case and the adjunct (modifier) case separately. (See, for example, Chomsky 1986b, Takahashi 1994a.) However, Saito and Fukui argue that their parametrized Merge approach opens up a refreshingly new way to unify these two cases. Suppose, following a standard assumption, that an adjunct (modifier) appears in a position adjoined to a maximal projection.[15] Then, descriptively, what is prohibited in the adjunct (modifier) case is adjunction to an adjoined phrase. And this extends automatically to the subject case, since a subject in English (or SVO languages generally) is in an adjoined position, as we discussed above. The explanation for the lack of the Subject Condition effects in Japanese (or SOV languages generally) is straightforward: subjects in this language are not in an adjoined position, but rather are introduced into structure by Merge (substitution). The question, thus, reduces to why adjunction to an adjoined position is disallowed.

Saito and Fukui propose that this is due to the indeterminacy of the adjunction site that arises in the relevant case. Consider the following configuration:

(43)

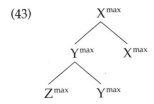

Both X^{max} and Y^{max} neither dominate nor exclude Z^{max} (see Chomsky 1986b for the definitions of these structural notions). Hence, if "adjunction" is defined as in (44), then Z^{max} in (43) is adjoined simultaneously to X^{max} and Y^{max}:

(44)   α *is adjoined to* β $=_{def}$ neither α nor β dominates the other and β does not exclude α.

Adjunction to adjoined phrases, then, is excluded by the following plausible condition:

(45)   An adjunction site must be unique.

   Saito and Fukui argue that the condition (45) need not be stipulated as an independent condition on adjunction site, but rather is an instance of the general uniqueness condition on the licensing of (non-root) elements in a phrase marker. (See Saito and Fukui 1998 for a precise formulation of the principle as well as much detailed discussion on relevant points.) Thus, their parametrized Merge, which incorporates the notion of linear order (the head parameter, in particular), unifies, without having recourse to such notions as "proper government" (Huang 1982) and "L-marking" (Chomsky 1986b), the classical cases of CED (the Subject and the Adjunct Condition effects), offering a natural explanation for the parametric variation associated with the Subject Condition effects.
   The issue of linear order in phrase structure (and movement) is a complex matter and remains open for future research. It is probably conceptually desirable if we can eliminate the concept of linear order from the core part of human language computation, and locate it in the phonological component, where the importance of linear order is firmly established. On the other hand, if the evidence presented in Saito and Fukui's work is real, then it constitutes a rather strong reason for postulating linear order in the portion of grammar where the theory of economy (cf. their arguments with respect to optionality) and that of locality (recall their reunification of CED) are relevant. See also Fukui and Takano (1998) for related discussion on this issue.

4   Summary and Conclusion

This chapter has discussed the development of the theory of phrase structure in generative grammar. Phrase structure of human language was described in terms of phrase structure rules; context-sensitive phrase structure rules in an earlier theory of generative grammar, and then context-free phrase structure rules with an enriched lexicon in the Standard Theory. X'-theory was proposed in the late 1960s based on the recognition of the observed deficiencies of phrase structure rules as a means for explaining the nature of phrase structure of human language: (i) phrase structure rules are "too permissive," in that they allow rules generating various structures that are actually never attested, and (ii) phrase structure rules cannot capture certain systematically observed "cross-categorial" generalizations. X'-theory, as an invariant principle of UG, overcomes these problems by claiming (i) that every phrase is "headed" (i.e., has an endocentric structure), with the head X projecting to larger phrases, (ii) that heads (categories) are not atoms, but rather complexes of universal features, and (iii) that projection of heads conforms to the general "X'-schemata" provided by UG. (See (18a–c) in section 1.)

The development of X'-theory from its inception up until the mid-1980s can be characterized as a process of sharpening and elaborating the format of X'-schemata, in such a way as to expand the scope of X'-theory to extensive descriptive material. As we saw in section 1, during this period, the structure of clauses was reanalyzed so as to fall under the scope of X'-theory, and the notion of "Spec" was gradually narrowed down to directly express its nature in phrase markers.

The subsequent development of X'-theory from the mid-1980s to the present can be described, as we discussed in section 2, as an accumulated attempt to minimize the role of X'-schemata, while maintaining the basic insight of X'-theory. Along the way, some novel analyses of particular constructions in phrase structure were proposed (the DP-analysis and the Predicate-Internal Subject Hypothesis), yielding numerous important empirical (crosslinguistic) studies concerning the structure of clauses and noun phrases. Relativized X'-theory makes a fundamental distinction between lexical categories and functional categories, and claims that phrase structure building is essentially feature driven. A "relativized" notion of maximal projection and the further sharpening of the concept of "Spec" in terms of agreement are also major claims of this theory. Motivated by the Minimalist program, the "bare phrase structure" theory completely eliminates the X'-schemata, in terms of the recursive procedure Merge, keeping the major insight of X'-theory almost intact.

Thus, at the current stage of the theory, of the three basic claims of the classical X'-theory (i)–(iii) stated above, (i) and (ii) are preserved in the bare theory, while the claim (iii), i.e., the existence of the X'-schemata, is explicitly denied. In this sense, there seem to be few fundamental differences between the bare theory and other approaches to phrase structure. Various approaches to phrase structure appear to have started converging and fruitfully influencing each other. For instance, given the foremost importance of features in the theory of phrase structure (and in the Minimalist program generally), the explicit mechanisms of feature systems developed in other approaches (e.g. in the GPSG/HPSG traditions) may well have an important impact on further development of the bare theory.

There are of course numerous remaining problems in the theory of phrase structure, many of which, including the influential "shell" structure proposed by Larson (1988), I could not discuss in this chapter. Section 3 briefly discussed one theoretical problem that remains open, i.e., the status of linear order. Various other theoretical questions remain, and as always, vast numbers of descriptive problems keep challenging the current theory of phrase structure. The theory of phrase structure, in my view, will continue to be one of the central topics of linguistic theory for years to come.

NOTES

*   Portions of the material contained in this article were presented in my lectures ("Phrase Structure and Movement") at the 1997 Linguistic Society of America's Summer Linguistic Institute (Cornell University). I would like to thank the audience there for many valuable questions and suggestions. I am also grateful to the editors of this volume, an anonymous reviewer for the volume, Takao Gunji, and Heizo Nakajima for useful comments and suggestions. The research reported in this article was supported in part by the University of California's Pacific Rim Research Grant (PI: Naoki Fukui).

1   It is not implied here that phrase structure rules directly generate phrase markers. In fact, the standard assumption is that phrase structure rules generate "derivations," from which there is an algorithm to construct phrase markers. See Chomsky (1955, 1959) and especially McCawley (1968) for much relevant discussion on the nature of phrase structure rules and their relation to phrase markers.

2   It is now standard to call these elements the specifier of X″, rather than the specifier of X′, and, accordingly, notate them as [Spec, X″].

3   Ideas of this sort were explored and developed in structural linguistics in terms of discovery procedures of constituent analysis (Harris 1946, 1951).

4   The determiners (such as *the*, *a*, etc.) are also analyzed as [Spec, N′]. As it is hard to analyze determiners as maximal projections (noun phrases, in particular), the identification of determiners as Spec elements poses a problem for the uniform characterization of Spec discussed in the text. This problem was later resolved by the "DP-analysis," as we will see in the next section.

5   The X′-scheme in (25) is my interpretation of what is intended in the proposal of Chomsky (1986b). Chomsky's original formulation is as follows (Chomsky 1986b: 3):

X′-schemata:
a. $X' = X \, X''^*$
b. $X'' = X''^* \, X'$ (where X^* stands for zero or more occurrences of some maximal projection and $X = X^0$)

The crucial difference between (25) and Chomsky's original formulation is that the latter allows "flat" and multiple branching structures at both the single-bar and the double-bar levels, whereas the former (i.e., (25)), while permitting "recursion," never allows flat and multiple branching structures, in accordance with Kayne's (1984) binary branching hypothesis. It seems to me that the schemata in (25) express more properly what was intended by the proposal of Chomsky (1986b).

6   There are of course more complex cases. Whether or not the other linear ordering in the X'-scheme (viz., the Spec–head and head–adjunct order) is subject to parametrization is a complex issue that remains open. See among others Chomsky and Lasnik (1993) and references there for further discussion. We will return to the issue of the head parameter in section 3.

7   The converse is not implied in Chomsky's theory. That is, while X^{max}-movement (substitution) is always to a Spec position, it is not claimed that Spec is always a landing site for X^{max}-movement. Such a claim, which implies further sharpening of the notion of Spec, is in fact put forth in Relativized X'-theory, to be discussed in section 2 below.

8   Details differ in various analyses. For example, we put aside the issue of whether all the subjects of noun phrases are generated within a noun's projection, or some subjects are base generated in [Spec, D"]. There are other problems that remain open. See Longobardi in this volume.

9   Relativized X'-theory was first presented in a preliminary form in Fukui and Speas (1986), and was later developed, in slightly different ways and directions, in Fukui (1986) and Speas (1986, 1990). The following exposition is largely based on Fukui (1986).

10   The formal operation building the structure is assumed to be "Adjunction." Note that Adjunction here is somewhat different from the standard notion of adjunction, which, when applied, creates a multi-segment structure of the target. Adjunction, unlike adjunction, induces a projection of the target element (see the discussion in section 4 of this chapter). Note also that the notion of "bar-level" does not play any significant role in this theory. Thus, X' merely means that X is projected. See also Muysken (1982).

11   To the extent that "substitution" transformations and "adjunction" transformations must be distinguished with respect to their empirical properties, we have to make a distinction somehow, but differently from the traditional definitions. Fukui (1986) attempts to offer appropriate definitions of "substitution" and "adjunction" without having recourse to the empty category Δ, based on the idea that "substitution" is an operation that creates a legitimate structure licensed by (Relativized) X'-theory, whereas "adjunction" creates a structure that is never licensed at the base (in terms of X'-theory). See Fukui (1986: ch. 4). Note incidentally that under these definitions, some instances of Adjunction (see the preceding note), including, for example, scrambling in Japanese, which had been assumed to be adjunction (Saito 1985), should indeed be analyzed as substitution.

12   Notice that this operation includes the traditional "substitution" and the operation that is in charge of building structures, but does not include, perhaps, the traditional "adjunction," which creates a "non-standard" multi-segment structure.

See nn. 10 and 11. See also the discussion in the next section.

13   There are some potentially problematic cases for this claim. The "leftness condition" of Chomsky (1976), carried over into the principles-and-parameters approach in the form of "weak crossover," is one such.

14   Recall the term "substitution" loses its traditional meaning in the bare theory (as well as in Relativized X'-theory), since the dubious empty category Δ is eliminated from the theory of movement. See n. 11.

15   See Ishii (1997) for relevant discussion on this assumption. He proposes that it should be considered a consequence of a general principle on derivation, which he calls the immediate satisfaction principle. It is left open in Saito and Fukui (1998) whether an adjunct (modifier) is directly generated in an adjoined position, or moved there. Under either hypothesis, it follows that an adjunct (modifier) is checked for a feature (the "adverb feature") at the adjoined position, as proposed by Oka (1993) and Lee (1994). (See also Travis 1988 for relevant discussion.) Note finally that since adjunction cannot be a subcase of Merge, it is subject to the Last Resort Principle, as Saito and Fukui argue. See Saito and Fukui (1998) for other details.

13 The Natures of Nonconfigurationality

MARK C. BAKER

0 Introduction

English and French are *configurational* languages, in the sense that the grammatical functions of subject and object consistently appear in particular phrase structure configurations. Thus, virtually every English clause must have some kind of syntactically expressed subject, and clauses with transitive verbs must have syntactically expressed objects as well. The nearly obligatory subject comes before the verb and any auxiliaries, whereas the direct object comes immediately after the verb:

(1)   Pine martens (should) climb trees at night near human habitations.

Furthermore, the object and the verb make up a phrasal unit to the exclusion of the subject, as shown by traditional phrase structure tests like VP-deletion, VP-pronominalization, and VP-fronting:

(2)   a.   Susan [$_{VP}$ hit the table] and Bill did [$_{VP}$ (so)] too.
             Susan said she would hit the table, and [$_{VP}$ hit the table] I guess she did –.
       b.   *[$_{XP}$ John hit] the table and [$_{XP}$ (so)] did the chair too.
             *John said he would hit the table, and [$_{XP}$ John hit] I guess – did it.

Thus, objects are the only NPs that are immediately contained in the surface verb phrase in English, whereas subjects are the only NPs that appear outside the verb phrase in simple English sentences:[1]

(3)

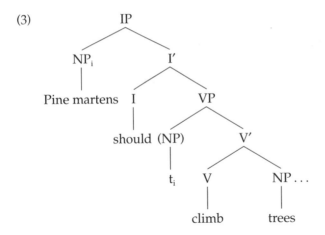

This strict correspondence between grammatical function and phrase structure position opens up the possibility of taking a reductive approach to grammatical functions, eliminating terms like "subject" and "object" from grammatical theory in favor of terms like "NP outside the VP" and "NP that is immediately contained in VP." Historically, this is the approach that has been taken in most narrowly Chomskyan work since the late 1960s (see McCloskey 1997 for a recent overview, focussing on subject positions). Syntactic conditions can then be written in such a way that they are sensitive to these unique phrase structure relationships, in order to capture the various other distinctive properties of subjects and objects. For example, in most Indo-European languages the verb agrees (overtly) with its subject and not its object (unless the subject bears some non-standard case, like dative or ergative). This can be related to the fact that the subject alone has left (overtly) the verb phrase – assuming that being outside the verb phrase and hence inside the local domain of a functional head like I(nfl) is a condition on agreement, as in much current "Minimalist" work (Chomsky 1995b). Similarly, the subject "has prominence" over the object in a variety of ways involving anaphora, coreference, and quantification. Thus, pronouns and anaphors contained in the object can be referentially dependent on the subject, but not vice versa, as sketched in (4):

(4) a. John$_i$ washed himself$_i$.
         John$_i$ washed pictures of himself$_i$.
         Every man$_i$ washed his$_i$ car.
         *He$_i$ washed John's$_i$ car.   (out by Condition C)
     b. *Heself$_i$ washed John$_i$.   (out by Conditions A and C)
         *Friends of himself$_i$ washed John$_i$.   (out by Condition A)
         *His$_i$ friends washed every man$_i$.   (out by weak crossover)
         John's$_i$ friends washed him$_i$.

These patterns are captured by making c-command a condition on referential dependencies, so that X can be referentially dependent on Y if Y c-commands

X (Condition A, weak crossover), but not if X c-commands Y (Condition C) (Reinhart 1983). C-command is defined in (5), with the effect that the subject of a clause c-commands the object of that clause, but not vice versa:

(5) X c-commands Y iff the first phrase that properly contains X also contains Y.

Three of the most important principles governing referential dependency can then be stated as follows:

(6) a. If Y is an anaphor, it can be coreferential with X only if X c-commands Y.
   b. If Y is a pronoun and X is a quantified expression or its trace, Y can be a variable bound by X only if X c-commands Y (weak crossover).
   c. If Y is a lexical NP, it can be coreferential with X only if X does not c-command Y (Condition C).

When this approach is followed to its logical conclusion, phrase structure relationships become absolutely crucial to syntax, whereas traditional grammatical function labels like subject and object survive only as convenient labels for particular phrase structure configurations.

However, it has become increasingly clear since the late 1970s or earlier that not all languages are comfortably configurational in this English sense. In many (perhaps even most) languages, subjects and objects cannot be identified by word order and simple constituency tests in any straightforward way. Classic illustration of this comes from the Australian language Warlpiri – a language which is important both because historically it was used by Kenneth Hale to call these problems to the attention of generative linguists at large, and because by now it is one of the best-studied languages of this type, thanks to the long-term attention of Hale, and his students and colleagues (including David Nash, Jane Simpson, Mary Laughren, and others). Hale (1983) shows that in Warlpiri any word order of the subject, verb, and object is possible, as long as the auxiliary that bears tense and agreement is in the second position in the clause:

(7) a. Kurdu-ngku ka-ju   nya-nyi   ngaju. (Simpson 1983: 140)
      child-Erg   Pres-1SgO see-NonPast I(Abs)
      "The child sees me."
   b. Kurdu-ngku ka-ju ngaju nya-nyi.
   c. Nya-nyi ka-ju kurdu-ngku ngaju.
   d. Ngaju ka-ju nya-nyi kurdu-ngku, etc.

Sometimes more than one word can appear before the auxiliary, as long as those words form a noun phrase or other constituent. However, the verb and its object do not form a constituent in this sense; this is true regardless of whether the object or the verb comes first:

(8)   *Ngaju nya-nyi   ka-ju   kurdu-ngku. (Simpson 1983: 141)
      I(Abs) see-NonPast Pres-1SgO child-Erg
      "The child sees me."

(Neither could the verb plus the subject be topicalized in this way, as one might imagine if they formed a constituent.) Hale (1983: 7) also shows that either the subject or the object or both can be omitted, in which case the "missing" elements are interpreted as pronominals:

(9)   a.   Ngarrka-ngku ka   panti-rni.
           man-Erg   Aux spear-NonPast
           "The man is spearing it."
      b.   Wawirri   ka   panti-rni.
           kangaroo Aux spear-NonPast
           "He/she is spearing the kangaroo."
      c.   Panti-rni   ka.
           spear-NonPast Aux
           "He/she is spearing it."

However, there is no kind of pronominalization that uniquely affects the verb and its object/theme as a unit in Warlpiri. In these and various other respects, the subject and the object appear to behave identically in this language.

   Given facts like these, it is quite natural to suggest that the phrase structure of a Warlpiri clause is symmetrical, as in the following representation of (7a), based on Bresnan (1982a) and Simpson (1991: 99):[2]

(10)

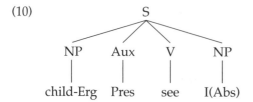

In this structure, I leave open the relationship between S and V: if V is the head of S, then both the subject and object are inside the VP; if it is not, then both are outside (both views have been held). Either way, subjects and objects are not distinguished by phrase structure configurations. Such a language is called *nonconfigurational*.

   More generally, the term "nonconfigurationality" can be used in either a relatively narrow sense, or in a broader sense. In the narrow sense, a nonconfigurational language is one that has the characteristic cluster of features that Hale (1983) identifies for Warlpiri: free word order, possible omission of all grammatical functions, and the possibility of having discontinuous NP constituents (see below for discussion). In a broader sense, languages with a reasonable number of similar properties, or indeed any language in which it seems difficult and/or inappropriate to use phrase structure to distinguish grammatical functions, could be called nonconfigurational.[3] The class of languages that have been called nonconfigurational includes most Australian languages (see, for example, Dyirbal (Dixon 1972), Nunggubuyu (Heath 1986), Jiwarli (Austin in press), Jingulu (Pensalfini 1997)); various American Indian languages, including Salish (Jelinek and Demers 1994) and Uto-Aztecan (Jelinek 1984), Muskogean (Jelinek 1988), Iroquoian (Baker 1996), Algonquian (Reinholtz and Russell 1994), and Klamath/Sahaptin/Nez Perce (Barker 1964; Rude personal communication); certain South American languages, notably Quechua (Lefebvre and Muysken 1988), various New Guinean languages (see, e.g., Yimas (Foley 1991)), South Asian languages such as Malayalam (Mohanan 1982), Hungarian (É. Kiss 1987), Japanese (Farmer 1984), and perhaps even German (see Webelhuth 1992 for a review of the controversy on this). Of course, this is far from a homogeneous group of languages in other respects – an issue that I return to extensively below.

1 Syntactic Similarities Between English and Nonconfigurational Languages

Interestingly, even in highly nonconfigurational languages like Warlpiri some familiar English-like asymmetries between the subject and the object can usually be found. Typically these are seen not in superficial phrase structure phenomena, but in "deeper" patterns of reflexivization, anaphora, and control. For example, Hale (1983) shows that the patient/object in Warlpiri can be an anaphor referentially dependent on the agent/subject, but the subject cannot be an anaphor referentially dependent on the object. This is shown in (11a), where the reflexive element shows up as a clitic on the auxiliary in the slot occupied by object clitics, while the subject is an overt NP in ergative Case. (11b) shows that the reflexive element cannot be a subject clitic next to the auxiliary, while the NP it is dependent on is in the unmarked absolutive Case characteristic of transitive objects:

(11) a. Kurdu-jarra-rlu ka-pala-nyanu paka-rni.
          child-D-Erg   Pres-3DS-ReflO strike-NonPast
          "The two children are striking themselves/each other."
      b. *Ngarrka ka-nyanu-(∅)   nya-nyi. (Hale 1983: 43)
          man-Abs Aux-Refl(-3SgO) see-NonPast
          "*Heself$_i$ sees the man$_i$." (OK as: "He sees himself as a man.")

This is exactly parallel to the English reflexivization facts in (4). Hale (1983: 20–1) also discusses control structures, in which the agent/subject (and only the subject) of a non-finite clause must be phonologically null and is interpreted as the same as a designated argument of the matrix clause (see also Simpson and Bresnan 1983):

(12) Ngarrka-ngku ka   purlapa   yunpa-rni [PRO karli
      man-Erg   Pres corroboree sing-NonPast   boomerang
      jarnti-rninja-karra-rlu].
      trim-Inf-Comp-Erg
      "The man is singing a corroboree song while trimming the boomerang."

Again, these properties are like control of infinitival and participial clauses in English. Therefore, in Warlpiri and many other nonconfigurational languages we find a partial dissociation between direct phrase structure evidence and the kinds of syntactic principle that are held to be defined over phrase structure.

There are in principle two ways to react to this kind of conflict, both of which involve positing additional levels of representation. The standard principles-and-parameters style approach is to say that Warlpiri does have a syntactic representation (such as S-structure, or LF) in which the subject asymmetrically c-commands the object, just as in English. The principles regulating things like anaphora then apply at that level in the usual way. However, for some extrinsic reason this structure is disrupted, so that the verb and the object do not form a constituent on the surface, at least at the level of PF.

The alternative is to say that these facts show that grammatical dependencies such as anaphora and control are not sensitive to phrase structure after all, but rather to grammatical functions or thematic roles that are characterized apart from phrase structure. On this view, the c-command based system in (5) and (6) seems to work as well as it does in English only because subject (and agent) happen to be correlated with a particular structural position in English. However, this need not be so across languages. This is the standard view of most generative theories other than principles-and-parameters (P&P), including Relational Grammar (RG), Lexical Functional Grammar (LFG), and Head-Driven Phrase Structure Grammar (HPSG). For example, Bresnan (1982a) and Simpson (1991) claim that a Warlpiri clause like (7a) has, in addition to its phrase structure representation, a "functional representation" (f-structure) which can be expressed like this:

(13)

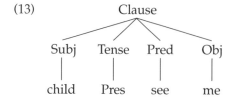

Given this, one can stipulate that only the subject of a non-finite clause can be controlled (see (12)). Similarly, one can state that the Warlpiri reflexive/reciprocal anaphor requires an antecedent that is a subject within the same local clause (Simpson 1983: 187–9). This accounts for the contrast in (11).

Pollard and Sag (1994) develop a similar idea in their "nonconfigurational binding theory," although they generalize it somewhat. They claim that an anaphor must be coindexed with an antecedent that locally o(bliqueness)-commands it, where the local o-command relationship is defined as follows:

(14)   Let Y and Z be [distinct phrases in the same clause], Y referential.
       Then Y locally o-commands Z just in case Y is less oblique than Z.
       (Pollard and Sag 1994: 253)

They define relative obliqueness in terms of a standard hierarchy of grammatical functions: the subject is less oblique than the primary object, which is in turn less oblique than the secondary object, PPs and verbal and/or predicative complements (Pollard and Sag 1994: 24). A similar idea approach to binding and anaphora has been developed in LFG (Bresnan personal communication).[4]

Which of these directions is the correct one has generated substantial debate in the literature, making the topic of nonconfigurational languages much more than a curiosity relevant only to specialists of (say) Australian languages. On the contrary, the question of how to fit nonconfigurational languages into linguistic theory is relevant to some of the deepest issues of linguistics, including the questions of how much variation Universal Grammar allows and what are its proper primitives (phrase structure, grammatical functions, or something else). Bresnan in particular has identified it as a major issue bearing on fundamental design features of linguistic frameworks (Bresnan 1982a, Austin and Bresnan 1996).

Before discussing these questions substantively, it is worth realizing that the difference between these two approaches can in practice be less significant that it seems at first. Both theories involve attributing two distinct representations to Warlpiri, one which is more universal (and hence more English-like) and one which represents more accurately the surface facts of the language. In this respect, the PF representation of P&P is comparable to c-structures such as (10) in LFG, while the S-structure/LF representation of P&P is comparable to f-structures such as (13) in LFG. It is true that the representation scheme of S-structure/LF is formally a phrase marker in P&P, whereas this is not true of f-structure in LFG. However, this phrase marker is not intended to represent linear order or surface constituency in the sense of phonological phrasing; for many P&P practitioners these are left undefined until PF. Indeed, it is in effect often little more than a functional structure that uses the representation schema Subject = [NP, IP] and Object = [NP, VP].[5] Of course, the P&P approach needs to present a satisfying theory of how this abstract phrase marker can be related to word order and phonological phrasing at PF. However, the LFG approach has a parallel need to explain substantively how f-structures may be related to c-structures, and what restrictions hold on how this can happen. In practice, this is not a well-developed aspect of either kind of theory; therefore, it is not currently a useful point of comparison.

2   Three Types of Nonconfigurationality

Before attempting to engage these basic issues of representation, however, it is important to explore the limits of the view that seems to emerge out of the last section, and is taken for granted in some of the literature: that nonconfigurational languages are approximately the same as configurational languages at an abstract, functional level of representation, and differ only at the most concrete level of representation (c-structure or PF). Crudely speaking, the assumption has been that the radical differences appear only in the domain of word order and phrasal groupings, not in other areas. However, this idealization turns out not to be entirely true. Thus, whereas the syntax of reflexives and reciprocals and some features of control seem relatively consistent over all these languages (but see below), other "deep" properties seem to be more variable – at least as far as one can tell from the relatively few languages that have been studied carefully from this perspective.

Consider, for example, Mohawk as described and analyzed by Baker (1991, 1996). Like Warlpiri, Mohawk allows the elements of a simple sentence to appear in any imaginable word order, allows NPs to be omitted freely, and shows no evidence of a verb + object phrasal constituent on the surface. Indeed, Mohawk goes farther still: subjects and objects do not behave differently even for certain anaphora related phenomena.

Thus, a name contained inside the understood direct object can be coreferential with a pronominal subject, just as well as the other way around:

(15)   a.   Wa'-t-há-ya'k-e' [$_{NP}$ ne   thíkʌ Sak raó-[a]'share'].
            Fact-Dup-1SgS-break-Punc PRT that   Sak MSgP-knife
            "He$_i$ broke that knife of Sak's$_i$." (coreference OK)
       b.   Ro-ya'takéhnh-ʌ [$_{NP}$ thíkʌ ne   Sak raó-[a]'share'].
            MSgO-help-Stat   that   PRT Sak MSgP-knife
            "That knife of Sak's$_i$ is helping him$_i$." (coreference OK)

This is rather a puzzle if nonconfigurationality is simply a PF/c-structure phenomenon. In that case, the functional representation of (15a) and (15b) should be essentially the same as the English counterparts, and Condition C should rule out the coreferential interpretation of (15a) (compare the last sentence in (4a)). The easy way out would be to say that Condition C does not hold in Mohawk, but that is a rather undesirable option for at least two reasons. First, Mohawk does have what look like real Condition C effects in other syntactic situations, as shown by Baker (1991, 1996: sec. 2.1.1). Second, Condition C is not the only principle that seems to apply in a peculiar way in Mohawk: weak crossover, for example, shows a similar effect. Thus, a questioned object cannot bind a pronominal inside the understood subject; neither can a questioned subject bind a variable inside the understood object:[6]

(16)   a.   Úhka wa'-akó-[a]ti-'   ne   akaúha ako-núhkwa?
            who Fact-FSgO-lose-Punc PRT her   FSgP-medicine
            *"Who$_i$ lost her$_i$ medicine?" (pronoun deictic only)
       b.   Úhka yako-ya'takéhnha-s   ne   akaúha ako-núhkwa?
            who NSgS/FSgO-help-Hab PRT her   FSgP-medicine
            *"Who$_i$ did her$_i$ medicine help?" (pronoun deictic only)

Crucially, there is an important point of consistency underlying the two "failures" here: in both cases, it seems that there is no c-command relationship between the subject and the object. This suggests that Mohawk structures are different from English ones at the functional level as well as the phrasal one.

Interestingly, facts from Warlpiri make the same point in the opposite way. Farmer et al. (1986: 33) show that English-like subject/object asymmetries are not found with respect to weak crossover in Warlpiri either. However, the observed grammaticality patterns are the opposite of those in Mohawk: the trace of an object is able to bind a pronoun inside the subject:

(17)   Ngana ka   nyanungu-nyangu maliki-rli wajili-pi-nyi.
       who   Pres he-Poss   dog-Erg   chase-NonPast
       "Who$_i$ is his$_i$ dog chasing?" (pronoun can be bound variable)

(The authors do not give an example of an interrogative subject binding a pronoun inside the understood object, but this should be possible as well). Similarly, Simpson (1991: 179–80) reports findings of Mary Laughren that Warlpiri does not have subject/object asymmetries with respect to Condition C either; pronoun arguments of the verb are never coreferential with names embedded in their coarguments:

(18)   a.   Jakamarra-kurlangu maliki   ka   nyanungu-rlu wajili-pi-nyi.
            Jakamarra-Poss   dog-Abs Pres he-Erg   chase-NonPast
            *"He$_i$ chases Jakamarra's$_i$ (own) dog." (coreference is impossible)
       b.   Jakamarra-kurlangu maliki-rli ka   nyanungu wajili-pi-nyi.
            Jakamarra-Poss   dog-Erg   Pres he-Abs   chase-NonPast
            *"Jakamarra's$_i$ (own) dog chases him$_i$." (coreference is impossible)

Again, this grammaticality pattern is the opposite of Mohawk. Thus, in Mohawk it seems that neither the subject nor the object c-commands the other, whereas in Warlpiri it seems that the subject c-commands the object and vice versa. Simpson (1991) concludes that these anaphora conditions should be defined over a flat c-structure like (10) in Warlpiri, but this does not fit comfortably with the early LFG assumption that f-structure is the sole input to the semantic component (Kaplan and Bresnan 1982: 175). Thus, Warlpiri reinforces the impression that the differences between configurational and nonconfigurational languages exist at the "functional" level as well.

A third non-English-like pattern of facts characterizes languages like Japanese and Hindi. In these languages, anaphoric conditions like Condition C and weak crossover seem to be crucially interrelated with word order. If the subject precedes the object, then the subject acts as though it c-commands the object, making coreference between lexical noun phrases impossible and bound variable interpretations possible (Hoji 1985):[7]

(19) a. *Soitu-ga Taroo-no hon-o   mituke-ta
        guy-Nom Taro-Gen book-Acc found-Past
        "The guy$_i$ found Taro's$_i$ book."
    b. Dare$_i$-ga [pro$_i$ e$_k$ hitome   mi-ta]   hito$_k$-o
       Who-Nom   first-glance look-at-Past person-Acc
       sukini natta-no?
       fell-in-love-Q
       "Who$_i$ fell in love with a person s/he$_i$ saw at first glance?"

In this word order, the object does not act as though it c-commands the subject, making coreference between names possible, and bound variable interpretations impossible:

(20) a. Soitu-no hahaoya-ga   Taroo-o sikat-ta
        guy-Gen mother-Nom Taro-Acc scold-Past
        "The guy's$_i$ mother scolded Taro$_i$."
    b. ??[e$_k$ pro$_i$ hitome   mi-ta]   hito$_k$-ga   dare$_i$-o
              first-glance look-at-Past person-Nom who-Acc
       sukini natta-no?
       fell-in-love-Q
       "Who$_i$ did a person that saw him/her$_i$ at first glance fall in love with?"

However, when the object comes before the verb in an OSV word order, the subject no longer acts as though it c-commands it, causing coreference between names to improve (21a). Moreover, the object gains the ability to c-command the subject, making bound variable anaphora possible in (21b):[8]

(21) a. Taroo-no hon-o   soitu-ga mituke-ta
        Taro-Gen book-Acc guy-Nom found-Past
        ?"Taro's$_i$ book, the guy$_i$ found."
    b. Dare$_i$-o [e$_k$ pro$_i$ hitome   mi-ta]   hito$_k$-ga
       who-Acc   first-glance look-at-Past person-Nom
       sukini natta-no?
       fell-in-love-Q
       "Who$_i$ did a person that saw him/her$_i$ at first glance fall in love with?"

These then are languages where anaphoric conditions do not seem sensitive to grammatical functions (or not grammatical functions only), but rather to word order – in contrast not only to English but also to Warlpiri and Mohawk, where word order does not seem to be a crucial factor.

Put together, this range of facts does not pose any inherent problem to the P&P research program of making conditions sensitive to syntactic structure. If anything, it can be construed as supporting that position, since languages where the superficial phrase structure is significantly different from that of English also show significant differences in these other areas. If anything, what is needed is adjustments to P&P's tenets about what phrase structures can be like, rather than the addition of a distinct functional structure.

The other moral of this mini-survey is that it is clearly not the case that all nonconfigurational languages have essentially the same basic syntax. Rather, there seem to be at least three distinct types (and possibly more). This should not be a surprise, since these languages are typologically quite different in other respects as well. In particular, Mohawk is a pure head marking language in the sense of Nichols (1986, 1992): it has very rich agreement morphology and no overt Case marking. Warlpiri, on the other hand, is a dependent mark-ing language, with a well-developed and syntactically significant system of Case morphology. Indeed, fairly closely related languages like Jiwarli are pure dependent marking languages (Austin and Bresnan 1996, Austin in press). Japanese is also a low agreement, dependent marking language, but it has a rather typical head final syntax and a discernible unmarked word order (SOV) – unlike Warlpiri and Mohawk (Mithun 1987, Hale 1992). Furthermore, while available data are fragmentary at best, one can begin to discern what look like non-accidental correlations between the anaphora patterns above and these broad typological classifications. For example, German and Hindi seem to work rather like Japanese in these respects (see Webelhuth 1992: sec. 5.6, Mahajan 1990, Srivastav-Dayal 1993, among others, as well as Mohanan's 1980, 1982, 1983 description of Malayalam, and the discussion in Speas 1990). On the other hand, at least some other Case-poor head marking languages have been found to show the same kind of neutralization of Condition C asymmetries as Mohawk (Baker 1996 cites facts from Southern Tiwa; also Williamson 1984 for Lakhota, Reinholtz and Russell 1994 for Swampy Cree, and Jeff MacSwan personal communication for Nahuatl). Thus, there is not one nonconfigura-tionality challenge, but several.

In the subsequent sections, I discuss these three languages types each in turn. In each case, the same analytic and expositional strategy will be used: I take the facts above at face value as evidence of c-command relationships, and see what this implies about the syntactic structure. Then I consider how that structure might be integrated into what is otherwise known about possible linguistic relationships. The discussions will not be equal in detail, however. My treatment of the Japanese type will be shortest, because this case has been thoroughly studied by communities of native speaker linguists, and a rather well-known standard treatment has emerged. My goal, then, is only to show

how this work fits into the broader topic, and to contrast Japanese with the other kinds of nonconfigurational language. The treatment of the Mohawk type is only slightly fuller; it is a brief summary of the view discussed at length in Baker (1996). Finally, the Warlpiri-type gets the fullest discussion, because here the controversies are sharpest. Indeed, Austin and Bresnan (1996) recently argued that here is where the need for an LFG style architecture is seen most sharply, and there is no standard view of how to approach these languages in a P&P framework. However, I will show that a variant of a suggestion by Speas (1990) (which in turn is a development of Jelinek 1984) can meet many of the challenges of these languages in an interesting way, and I will work out the specific similarities and differences this predicts between Warlpiri and the other types of language. I conclude with some tentative remarks about what Universal Grammar is and is not, based on this discussion.

3   Japanese-Type Nonconfigurationality as Movement

Take Japanese first, then. Recall that when the word order is SOV, the subject acts as though it asymmetrically c-commands the object for purposes of anaphora (and quantifier scope). Thus, there is no barrier to saying that such sentences have a perfectly configurational structure, essentially like English apart from the basic difference in head–complement order. Then OSV orders arise as a result of moving the object to some position higher than the subject, as a normal instance of Move-α. So the phrase structures are:

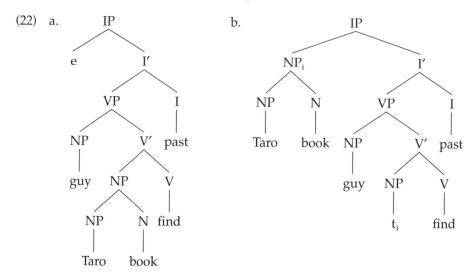

Now in the derived structure (21b) (assuming no reconstruction and a favorable definition of "A-positions"), the object c-commands the subject, and principles like weak crossover and Condition C can apply in a reasonably straightforward way. Note that this is a reasonably unproblematic instance of movement: in particular, it is clause bounded, obeys the Proper Binding Condition that a moved element must c-command its trace, and originates in a properly governed position. (In contrast, one cannot scramble the object of a P, or a genitive NP, for example; see Webelhuth 1992: ch. 5.) Indeed, for purposes of concreteness I have presented the movement as essentially a variant of passive, in which the subject is generated in Spec, VP (as is widely assumed), and the underlying object targets the Spec, IP position, following the version of Kuroda (1988). Notice that passive reverses Condition C and weak crossover patterns in English as well:

(23) a. John's$_i$ car was washed t by him$_i$.   (Compare (4))
       b. Every man$_i$ was criticized by his$_i$ friends.

The major outstanding problems with this approach are how exactly to characterize the landing sites of this kind of scrambling in general (including their status with respect to the A-/A'-distinction) (Mahajan 1990, Webelhuth 1992, Saito 1992, among others), and the question of why this kind of movement that places objects in A-like positions outside of subjects seems to be allowed only in head final languages (Fukui 1993). No doubt much can be said about this analysis, both pro and con, and there are important second-order differences among the languages that I am grouping together as "Japanese-type." But this general approach has been a widely adopted and productive one. I will consider languages like this no further, except by way of contrast with the other, potentially more radical kinds of nonconfigurationality.

4   Mohawk-Type Nonconfigurationality as Dislocation

Consider next the Mohawk type of nonconfigurationality. In this language, examples like (15a) and (16a) show that the NP interpreted as the direct object is outside the c-command domain of the subject, in contrast to English and Japanese in the SOV order. However, other kinds of evidence seem to contradict this result. For example, objects but not subjects can be incorporated into the verb in Mohawk:

(24) a. O-nʌ'y-a'   wa'-t-ka-tsiser-á-hri-ht-e'.
           NSgO-stone-NSF Fact-Dup-NSgS-pane-∅-shatter-Caus-Punc
           "The stone broke the window-pane."
       b. *O-tsíser-a'   wa'-t-ka-nʌy-á-hri-ht-e'.
           NSgO-pane-NSF Fact-Dup-NSgS-stone-∅-shatter-Caus-Punc
           "The stone broke the window."

This shows that the object but not the subject is a governed internal argument of the verb in Mohawk, assuming either the head movement analysis of incorporation in Baker (1988) or something like Selkirk's (1982) First Order Projection Condition on productive synthetic compounding. And there is other data to confirm this as well (Baker 1996).

These conflicting results can be reconciled if we say that there is in fact an object position internal to the smallest VP, but the overt NPs in sentences like (15a) and (16a) cannot be in that position for some reason. What then occupies the true object position in such examples? The most likely answer is a null pronoun (*pro*). Such pronouns are independently known to be possible in Mohawk; indeed, Mohawk has the typical nonconfigurational property of allowing free pro-drop in all syntactic positions (*wa'tháya'ke'* "He broke it" and *wa'akoti'* "She lost it" count as complete clauses by themselves). The possibility of *pro* is also expected theoretically, given that Mohawk is a head-marking language, and there is typically plenty of agreement on the heads to license *pros*. The independent overt NPs, then, are adjoined to the clause as a whole and enter into a dislocation relationship with the null pronouns in the argument position, as in (25):

(25)

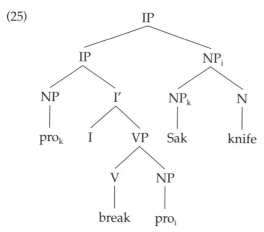

Notice that the overt NP is linked to the direct object position, but it is nevertheless outside the c-command domain of the subject position; therefore a pronominal subject can be coreferential with a name inside the understood object (as in (15a)), whereas an interrogative subject cannot bind a pronoun inside that understood object (as in (16a)). This "dislocation" relation between an overt NP and a weak or null pronoun is not unique to nonconfigurational languages; on the contrary, a similar dislocation construction exists in Romance languages, studied by Cinque (1990b: ch. 2):

(26)   Gianni, lo conosciamo.   (Italian; Cinque 1990b: 61)
       "Gianni, we know him."

This analysis of Mohawk is similar in spirit to the analysis of OSV orders in Japanese given above; in both cases, the object escapes the c-command domain of the subject by entering into some familiar, chainlike relationship. However, the exact relationship entered into is somewhat different in the two cases:[9] the empty object in Mohawk is a *pro* whereas in Japanese it is a *trace*; the NP is base generated in the clause-peripheral position in Mohawk rather than moving there; and the peripheral position is an A'-position rather than an A(-like) position in Mohawk. This last fact implies that the "shifted" object does not gain the ability to bind the subject in Mohawk the way it does in Japanese (compare the grammatical (21b) with the ungrammatical (16b)).

Putting these factors to one side, the most striking difference between Mohawk and Japanese is that in Japanese the movement of the object is optional, whereas in Mohawk the dislocation of the object is apparently obligatory. Thus, the Japanese object has the option of staying in the argument position, in which case the clause has configurational properties quite similar to English, as in (19) and (20). However, the ungrammaticality of (16a) (in any word order) shows that this is not possible in Mohawk: if the NP had the option of appearing in the direct object position, then a bound variable reading of the possessor should be allowed, contrary to fact. Thus, we must say that the argument positions can *only* be null pronouns (or the traces of incorporated nouns) in Mohawk. This is a version of the so-called "Pronominal Argument Hypothesis," a traditional approach to head marking languages introduced into P&P by Jelinek (1984) as a way of handling certain nonconfigurational languages and developed by her in many subsequent papers (see also Van Valin 1985, Mithun 1987, for developments of the same idea in other theoretical frameworks). This fits well with the intuition that Mohawk is a more deeply nonconfigurational language than Japanese, and that unlike Japanese it has no basic word order.

Indeed, the fact that only null pronouns can appear in argument positions in Mohawk does not need to be stipulated as something special about it as a nonconfigurational language. On the contrary, something very similar is found in Romance languages, where the object NP generally *must* be dislocated (or omitted) whenever the object clitic is present on the verb:[10]

(27)   *Lo conosciamo (a) Gianni. (Cinque 1990b: 60)
       "We know Gianni."

The classical Government Binding era account of the ungrammaticality of (27) is to say that the clitic absorbs the accusative Case features of the verb, leaving the object un-Case marked (Borer 1984). The same idea can be applied to Mohawk. The only difference is that whereas object clitics are optionally generated on the verb in Italian, they are obligatory in Mohawk as a basic typological property of the language: Mohawk is by all accounts a pure and obligatory head marking language (the Polysynthesis Parameter of Baker 1996).

Therefore, overt NPs in the object position will *always* be un-Case marked in Mohawk, in violation of the Case Filter.

Certain other differences between the kind of nonconfigurationality manifested by Mohawk and the kind manifested by Japanese also follow from this idea. Perhaps the most obvious is that we predict a much tighter connection between ubiquitous pro-drop and free word for Mohawk-type languages than for Japanese-type languages. The diversity of word orders in Mohawk comes from different choices of where to adjoin a dislocated NP, and this presupposes that the argument position can always be filled by a *pro*. In contrast, new word orders in Japanese come from movement, and this is logically independent of whether *pro* is licensed or not. These predictions seem correct: pronouns are freely omittable in head marking languages like Cree, Nahuatl, Southern Tiwa, and Lakhota; they are also freely omittable in Japanese and Malayalam (Mohanan 1982: 544) but not in other SOV-plus-scrambling languages such as German.

A more subtle difference is that languages like Mohawk do not permit NPs that are referentially defective in some way or another. Since these NPs are not referential, they are in principle unable to be coreferential with the *pro* in argument position, and hence they cannot be unlicensed. Thus, simple NP anaphors and negatively and universally quantified NPs are all impossible in Mohawk, while *wh*-expressions must appear fronted to the Comp position and cannot show the same free word order of other elements (Baker 1996: ch. 2):

(28)   a.   #Sak ro-núhwe'-s   ra-úha.
            Sak   MSgS/MSgO-like-Hab MSgO-self
            "Sak likes himself." (OK as "Sak$_i$ likes him$_k$.")
       b.   *Akwéku wa'-t-ha-[a]hsʌ"tho-'.
            all   Fact-Dup-MSgS-cry-Punc
            "Everybody cried."
       c.   (Oh nahótʌ) Sak wa-ha-hnínu-'   (*oh nahótʌ)?
            what   Sak Fact-MSgS-buy-Punc what
            "What did Sak buy?"

Other head marking nonconfigurational languages are similar in these respects. On the other hand, nonreferential elements can perfectly well be moved; hence simple NP anaphors, nonreferential quantifiers, and interrogatives can be found in languages like Japanese and Hindi, and they can be in both SOV and OSV orders:

(29)   a.   Zibunzisin-o Hanako-ga   t hihansita (koto)   (Japanese)
            self-Acc   Hanako-Nom   criticized fact
            "Herself, Hanako criticized." (Saito 1992)
       b.   Sab-ko   uskii bahin t pyaar kartii   thi.   (Hindi)
            everyone-Acc his   sister   love   do-Fem be-Fem
            "His sister loved everyone." (Chamorro 1992)

c. John-ga   dare-o   nagut-ta no?/ Dare-o   John-ga   nagutta no?
John-Nom who-Acc hit-Past Q/   who-Acc John-Nom hit-Past Q
"Who did John hit?"   (Japanese)

This illustrates nicely the claim that nonconfigurationality has somewhat different causes in typologically different languages; hence it is associated with a predictably different cluster of properties in those languages.

5   Warlpiri-Type Nonconfigurationality as Secondary Predication

Finally, we come back to the case of Warlpiri. This is the most controversial of the three, and there is no standard approach to it within a P&P-style framework. Austin and Bresnan (1996) argue at some length that Jelinek's (1984) Pronominal Argument approach is not appropriate for Warlpiri, in some cases developing arguments that are implicit in Simpson (1991). Their argument is strengthened by comparison with Jiwarli, a related language which is essentially identical to Warlpiri in its nonconfigurational properties, but which has none of the pronominal clitics that Jelinek's analysis seems to depend on (see also Austin in press). These languages thus pose the problem of nonconfigurationality in perhaps its sharpest form. Nevertheless, in the remainder of this chapter I elaborate on a suggestion by Speas (1990) about how to treat languages like these that seems to have promise for incorporating them into the view of Universal Grammar that has been supported in the other cases.

5.1   Basic clause structure in Warlpiri

Again, suppose we begin by taking the Condition C and weak crossover evidence in (17) and (18) at face value, as giving evidence of syntactic c-command relationships.[11] These examples then show that the subject is c-commanded by the object, and that the object is also c-commanded by the subject. Simpson (1991) interprets this as further evidence that there is no VP in Warlpiri, which implies that the difference between subject and object cannot be reduced to phrase structure, and a distinct functional representation is needed. However, the study of Mohawk makes it clear that there is another possibility: what we call informally the "subject" and the "object" could in fact be more complex, chain-like entities with elements in more than one syntactic position. So then the question is: is there ever some kind of expression that is associated with the subject but falls within the c-command domain of the object in well-studied configurational languages? If so, this could be the independently motivated linguistic relationship that plays the same role in the analysis of Warlpiri as Clitic Left Dislocation plays in the analysis of Mohawk and passive-like NP movement plays in the analysis of Japanese.

The answer is maybe yes. Speas (1990) suggests that the actual arguments in Warlpiri are the clitic pronouns on the auxiliary (following Jelinek 1984 and unpublished work by Mary Laughren), and that the lexical nominal expressions have the status of secondary predicates, licensed in essentially the same way as secondary predicates are in English. Now Speas does not explore the syntax of secondary predication in English in any great detail to show exactly where such secondary predicates appear in a structure; she simply notes that it is not easy to construct the crucial examples because it is somewhat rare for secondary predicates to have complements (Speas 1990: 93–4). However, standard constituency tests show rather clearly that subject oriented depictive predicates are inside the VP somewhere (Andrews 1982, Roberts 1988, Legendre 1997):

(30)   John wanted to leave the room happy . . .
    a. —and [$_{VP}$ leave the room happy] he did.
    b. —*and [$_{VP}$ leave the room] he did happy.

Moreover, it has become quite standard in the P&P theory to say that some or all direct objects raise out of the (minimal) VP at some level to a Case-checking position (Chomsky 1995b). This hypothesis is particularly well supported for pronominal objects, which often appear overtly cliticized to Infl (Romance) or shifted leftward (Scandinavian) or rightward (Irish), even in languages where other direct objects seem to remain inside the VP. If we put these two facts together, then we clearly expect (pronominal) objects to c-command secondary predicate material associated with the subject, and subjects to c-command secondary predicate material associated with the object. Arguably this is supported by the following Condition C data, although relevant examples are hard to construct and judgments are delicate:

(31)   a. *He$_i$ always sent soldiers$_k$ to the front [loyal$_k$ to Hitler's$_i$ ideals].
    b. ?*John$_k$ tried to read it$_i$ [sympathetic$_k$ to *Mein Kampf's*$_i$ basic thesis].

The pronominal subject in (31a) clearly cannot be interpreted as coreferential with a name inside the object oriented depictive; however, it is (almost?) as bad to have a pronominal object interpreted as coreferential with a name inside the subject oriented depictive, as shown in (31b).[12] There seems to be no clear contrast here. Similar data involving weak crossover are given in (32):

(32)   a. As much as possible, every dictator$_i$ sends soldiers$_k$ to the front loyal$_k$ to his$_i$ ideals.
    b. As much as possible, John$_i$ reads every book$_k$ sympathetic$_i$ to its$_k$ basic thesis.

Again, there is no clear contrast between a subject's ability to bind into an object oriented depictive (32a) and an object's ability to bind into a subject oriented depictive (32b). (I find both slightly awkward, but basically acceptable.)[13]

If these judgments are correct, then we have supported Speas's claim that the depictive secondary predicate construction has the right properties to serve as a basis for explaining the anaphora facts in Warlpiri. Concretely, we can assume that a simple Warlpiri clause like (7a) has roughly the structure in (33):[14]

(33)

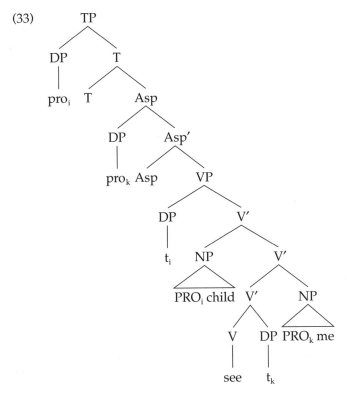

Here there is no reason not to take the basic VP as being as configurational as the English VP on one's favorite version of the VP-internal subject hypothesis. This makes possible a structural account of the basic reflexive and control facts mentioned in section 1, in which Warlpiri works much like English. The secondary predicates are licensed by being in a local configuration with the theta-positions of the corresponding primary arguments; therefore, they are VP-internal as well. (Exactly what the locality condition is is not particularly important. I return below to the question of whether the NPs are predicated directly of the arguments or are predicated of a PRO that is controlled by those arguments.) The pronominal arguments raise to the relevant VP-external specifier positions in the standard way, where they are licensed. Once this happens, the raised positions of the pronouns c-command both secondary predicate positions. In this way, the symmetry of the binding facts is captured without compromising the basic configurationality at the core of the Warlpiri clause.[15]

As Speas points out, part of the attraction of this proposal is that it is clear on anyone's account that nominals in Warlpiri *can* be used as secondary predicates. (34) is a good example of this:

(34)   Nya-nyi   ka-rna-ngku   ngarrka-lku. (Hale 1983)
       see-NonPast Pres-1SgS-2SgO man-after
       "I see you as a man now."

Here since the object pronominal is second person, there is no temptation to analyze the absolutive case nominal *ngarrka* "man" as a true argument; rather it is a depictive predicate of the object. More generally, nominals can freely be used as main predicates in Warlpiri, and anything that can be used as a main predicate can also be a secondary predicate (Simpson 1991). Thus, the general architecture of the grammar is set up so that one expects this case to exist, and Simpson (1991) discusses at length the mechanisms that are needed to account for these NP secondary predicates within LFG. Thus, Speas's proposal does not require that one add any new syntactic resources to the analysis of Warlpiri; it is only a reassessment of which relationships are involved in which particular examples.

One crucial feature of this account is that it takes the true arguments of the verb in a simple clause to be pronominal elements, distinct from the overt nominals. In this, it counts as a variant of Jelinek's Pronominal Argument Hypothesis. We therefore predict that there should be certain syntactic similarities between Warlpiri-type languages and Mohawk-type languages that follow from this shared syntactic feature. This seems to be correct. The first and most obvious prediction is that Warlpiri-type languages should allow *pro*-drop in all positions – like the Mohawk-type languages, but unlike some of the Japanese-type nonconfigurational languages (e.g. German). This is clearly correct for Warlpiri, as illustrated back in (9). It is also true for Jiwarli, even though this language does not have an auxiliary with clitic-like elements (Austin and Bresnan 1996). On a theoretical level, the reason for this is because there is never a syntactic requirement that a secondary predicate be included in a structure, just as there is never a requirement that a sentence have a dislocated element.

More subtle predictions also hold. Recall from above that because of the inherent referentiality of its pronominal arguments, Mohawk cannot have nonreferential NPs like true quantifiers or simple NP anaphors, and interrogative phrases must be fronted by true *wh*-movement. These same effects are found in Warlpiri as well. Bittner and Hale (1995) discuss at length the fact that the way of expressing universal-like quantification in Warlpiri has very different syntax and semantics from phrases with *every* in English. Their idea is that *panu* is not a quantifier at all; it is basically just a noun that means "large group." What look like different quantificational forces are really the interactions of this lexical N meaning with the definiteness ambiguities that are rampant in Warlpiri. (Note also that this element is plural, like English *all*, not singular like *every*.)

(35) Panu ka-rna-jana   nya-nyi.
      many Pres-1SgS-3PlO see-NonPast
      "I see many of them." "I see all of them." "I see them, who are many."
      "I see a large group (of them)." "I see the large group (of them)."
      "I see them, who are a large group."

Second, it is true that Warlpiri has no simple NP anaphor. Reflexive predications
are expressed using a reflexive clitic, which replaces the normal object clitics
in the Aux, as shown in (11a). If this clitic is absent in a matrix clause, no
coreference between the subject and the object is possible (Simpson 1991: 168,
who credits Hale):[16]

(36) Jupurrurla-rlu ka (nyanungu) nya-nyi.
      Jupurrurla-Erg Pres him   seek-NonPast
      "Jupurrurla is looking at him/*himself."

Third, it is the case that nonreferential interrogative phrases must move overtly
to a clause initial, Comp-like position in Warlpiri as in Mohawk. Indeed, Hale
(personal communication) reports that virtually the only ordering constraint
on NPs in Warlpiri is that interrogative phrases are clause initial (see (17) for
an example); this is also true for Jiwarli (Austin classnotes). Thus, there is
good support for the claim that the argument positions in the Australian languages are inherently pronominal. In this respect, the nonconfigurationality of
those languages is more like that of Mohawk than like that of Japanese-type
nonconfigurational languages, which have a discernible unmarked word order,
allow reflexive NPs, have nonreferential quantifiers, permit *wh*-in-situ, and do
not necessarily have free *pro*-drop.[17]

   Austin and Bresnan (1996) argue explicitly against the idea that the Pronominal Argument Hypothesis holds in these Australian languages. Their
simplest argument is that the clitic pronouns that Jelinek (1984) takes to be the
arguments of the verb in Warlpiri are not present in non-finite clauses in
Warlpiri or in any clauses in Jiwarli; nevertheless, these cliticless clauses show
all the same nonconfigurational properties. Strictly speaking, however, this
only argues against the most literal interpretation of Jelinek's hypothesis. Baker
(1991, 1996) takes a slightly different view, more in line with standard P&P
assumptions. He claims that the arguments are not the clitic pronouns, but
rather phonologically null pronouns (*pro*), the clitic/affixes being morphological elements that bear a licensing/agreement relationship to these *pro*s. On
this view, we do not necessarily expect to see an overt manifestation of the
pronominal arguments in Jiwarli. The only thing that might be considered odd
about this language is that *pro*s appear without any agreement morphology
to license them. But it is now well known that the relationship between rich
agreement and the appearance of *pro* is not as tight as was once thought. On
the contrary, languages with no agreement, like Chinese and Japanese, often
allow *pro* as freely as languages like Mohawk with very rich agreement (Jaeggli

and Safir 1989b). Indeed, the fact that null pronouns occur freely in these languages is a feature of the LFG analysis too.[18]

5.2   *Nonconfigurationality and the noun–adjective distinction*

Overall then, there is nothing particularly radical about the proposal that *pro*-drop is possible in the Australian languages, or that nominals can function as secondary predicates. The only radical element of the Speasian approach is the claim that *pro*s are *always* present, and overt nominals are *always* secondary predicates. This strong claim is necessary in order to explain the Condition C facts in (18); if the ergative case nominal had the option of being in the true subject position, then it would be outside the domain of the object pronoun, and the indicated coreference should be possible in (18b). Similarly, if it were possible for overt phrases to be in argument positions, then quantified and anaphoric elements should in principle be possible (although perhaps restricted to a particular clausal position). Therefore, we need to explain why NPs cannot appear in true argument positions in Warlpiri, which makes their status as secondary predicates a necessity, not merely an option. Nor can we use the Baker (1991, 1996) solution to this problem for Mohawk, in which the obligatory agreement morphemes absorb the Case properties of the heads. This analysis would not plausibly extend to Jiwarli, because it does not have such elements.

Speas (1990) offers the beginnings of a proposal for this too: her basic idea is that whatever property of Warlpiri nominals makes them such good secondary predicates also makes them bad arguments. This is conceptually attractive: arguments and predicates are very different logical entities, so one does not necessarily expect the same element to serve as both. Indeed, it should not be taken for granted that NPs can be depictive secondary predicates in Warlpiri and Jiwarli, given that NPs cannot be used as depictive secondary predicates in English (Rapoport 1991: 168–9). This is shown by the contrast in (37):

(37)   a.   I never saw Reagan angry.
       b.   *I never saw Reagan (the) president.
            (Intended meaning: I never saw Reagan when he was president.)

Thus, it is plausible to think that whatever makes NPs usable as secondary predicates in Warlpiri also makes them unusable as arguments.

We can consider taking a step beyond Speas at this point. NPs in English contrast with APs in that APs can serve as depictive secondary predicates (37a). Now it is independently known that in Warlpiri and many other Australian languages there is no syntactic distinction between the class of nouns and adjectives. Bittner and Hale (1995: 81–3) discuss this for Warlpiri, showing that the single morphosyntactic category "nominal" includes names and common nouns (woman, man, food), but also expressions of quality or cardinality (big, sick, many) (see also Simpson 1991: 41). The same general system seems to be present in Jiwarli (Austin classnotes). Now the standard (informal) way of describing this situation is to say that "adjectives" are really nouns in these languages (as Bittner and Hale do). Suppose, however, that we think of this the other way around: that what English speakers naturally think of as nouns are really adjectives in Warlpiri and Jiwarli. At first, this seems almost inconceivable: the intuition is almost universal that noun is a more basic and more universal category than adjective (see, for example, Dixon 1982b, Hopper and Thompson 1984, Bhat 1994). However, strong intuitions often reflect habit more than truth. Based on work by Geach (1962) and Gupta (1980), Larson and Segal (1995: 128–32) suggest that the difference between common nouns and other predicates (including adjectives) is that common nouns are "sortal," meaning that in addition to the condition on applicability that all lexical items have, they also have a condition on identity. If that is correct, then common nouns in English are actually more elaborate in their lexical entries than adjectives are. If neutralization is the loss of additional distinguishing features, then it makes sense that the neutralized category of "nominal" in Warlpiri might be formally more similar to English adjectives than to English nouns. Indeed, this is consistent with what we know about Warlpiri (and Jiwarli) syntax. In English, As differ from Ns in that they can head secondary predicates; in Warlpiri, nominals are like As in this respect, as we have seen. In English, As differ from Ns in that they cannot be the complement of an article (*an intelligent vs. a genius);[19] in Warlpiri, nominals are like As in this respect (and, as a result, the language has no true articles). In English, As differ from Ns in that they can be attributive modifiers of other nominals (an intelligent woman vs. *a genius woman); in Warlpiri, nominals are like As in this respect too. Thus, Hale and Simpson both claim that a valid gloss for (38) is "The childish small thing is chasing it," where the "noun" "child" is a modifier of the "adjective" "small," rather than vice versa:

(38)   Kurdu-ngku wita-ngku ka   wajili-pi-nyi. (Simpson 1991: 265)
       child-Erg   small-Erg Pres chase-NonPast
       "The childish small thing is chasing it." OR "The small child is chasing it."

Last but not least, in English, As differ from Ns in that their projections never appear in argument positions (*Intelligent will solve your problems vs. Brains will solve your problems). And, as we have seen, in Warlpiri nominals cannot appear in argument positions either. Since Warlpiri nominals act like adjectives in all these ways, it makes sense to claim that they really are adjectives – and the fact that Warlpiri is a strongly nonconfigurational pronominal argument language follows immediately from this.[20]

We have already discussed certain similarities between Warlpiri-style nonconfigurationality and Mohawk-style nonconfigurationality that follow from *pros* being present in basic clauses in both languages. We are now in a position to predict certain differences as well, differences that follow from the fact that overt nominals are licensed by forming dislocation chains in Mohawk but by secondary predication in Warlpiri. We have seen one difference already: the fact that overt NP material is inside the c-command domain of the pronominal arguments in Warlpiri, but outside their c-command domain in Mohawk. This leads to the differences in anaphora that got the discussion started. By the same token, we predict that the "scrambling" of constituents should be much more local in Warlpiri than in Mohawk. This seems to be correct. Baker (1996: ch. 3) shows that an NP can be separated from the clause it is interpreted with in Mohawk; this is expected, given that CLLD has the same property in Italian (Cinque 1990b):

(39)   Thíkʌ á'share' wa'-ke-rihwáruk-e'   tsi   Sak wa-ha-[a]táte-ni-'.
        that   knife   Fact-1SgS-hear-Punc that Sak Fact-MSgS-Refl-lend-Punc
        "That knife, I heard that Sak helped himself to it."

On the other hand, a nominal in Warlpiri cannot generally be separated from the clause it is interpreted with. Thus, (40a) is possible, where the embedded verb "dance" and its understood object "corroboree" form a clausal constituent before the second position auxiliary; however, (40b) shows that it is bad for the object to be separated from its verb by the auxiliary, which is an element of the matrix clause (Simpson 1991: 132):

(40)   a.   Purlapa   pi-nja-karra-rlu   kala-lu   pirlirrpa yilya-ja.
               corroboree dance-Inf-Comp-Erg Hab-3PlS spirit   send-Past
               "By dancing a corroboree they would send away the spirit."
        b.   *Purlapa   kala-lu   pi-nja-karra-rlu   pirlirrpa yilya-ja.
               corroboree Hab-3PlS dance-Inf-Comp-Erg spirit   send-Past
               "By dancing a corroboree they would send away the spirit."

Similarly, Austin (classnotes) shows that NPs do not appear separated from the associated verb by material belonging to another clause in Jiwarli, except in one very particular situation where the matrix verb is auxiliary-like and probably undergoes restructuring with the embedded verb. This is what we expect if nominals are licensed as secondary predicates in these languages: such predicates cannot appear outside the verb phrase (cf. English: *Raw, John ate the meat (Rizzi 1990: 48–50)), and thus *a fortiori* they cannot appear adjoined to a higher clause (*Raw, I think John ate the meat).[21]

The other clear difference between Warlpiri-type nonconfigurationality and Mohawk-type nonconfigurationality is that so-called discontinuous expressions are a much freer and more salient characteristic of Warlpiri than they are of Mohawk. Basically, any multiple word NP in Warlpiri can be a discontinuous NP as well, whereas this is certainly not true in Mohawk. (41) shows a typical example of an "adjective" separated from the associated "noun" (Simpson 1991: 257; compare (38)):

(41)   *Kurdu-jarra-ngku* ka-pala   maliki wajili-pi-nyi   *wita-jarra-rlu*.
       child-Dual-Erg   Pres-3DS dog   chase-NonPast small-Dual-Erg
       "Two small children are chasing the dog."

(42) gives a minimal pair of a kind of multiple discontinuous NP that is common in Warlpiri but impossible in Mohawk:

(42)   a.   *Kuyu*   Ø-rna   luwa-rnu   *wawirri*.   (Warlpiri; Hale
            animal Perf-1SgS shoot-Past kangaroo   personal communication)
            "I shot a kangaroo."
       b.   ?*KΛ'tsu ne   auhá'a te-wak-éka'-s   *rababhót*.   (Mohawk;
            fish   PRT most   Cis-1SgO-like-Hab bullhead   Baker 1996)
            "I like bullhead fish the best."

Similarly, demonstratives can be freely split from more contentful nominals in Warlpiri, whereas in Mohawk this is rare and subject to tight syntactic constraints:

(43)   a.   *Wawirri*   kapi-rna   panti-rni   *yalumpu*.   (Warlpiri;
            kangaroo Aux-1SgS spear-NonPast that   Hale 1983: 6)
            "I will spear that kangaroo."
       b.   ?*Kwéskwes* wa-hi-yéna-'   *kíkΛ*.   (Mohawk;
            pig   Fact-1SgS/MSgO-catch-Punc this   Baker 1996)
            "I caught this pig."

This important difference also follows from the difference in how nominals are licensed in the two languages. In Romance languages, only a single NP can be in a dislocation relationship with a given *pro*, presumably because chain formation must take place. Hence, the Mohawk examples are out for essentially the same reason as (44) is in Spanish:

(44)   *Este, lo ví en la fiesta, (el) hombre.*
       "That, I saw him at the party, (the) man."

On the other hand, more than one depictive secondary predicate can be associated with a single argument position in English:

(45)   a.   I only eat fish raw fresh.
       b.   I often send Mary home drunk, and she gets there just fine. The
            problem is that on Tuesday *I sent her home drunk exhausted.*

(Admittedly these examples are unusual; they are accepted only if the first depictive is presupposed, old information and the second bears contrastive focus; hence the context in (45b). Why these pragmatic restrictions hold is unclear.) The Warlpiri examples with multiple realizations of the argument are possible for the same reason as (45).

Finally, it is worth pointing out some typological support for the idea that the neutralization of the noun/adjective contrast can be a factor in causing (a particular type of) nonconfigurationality. Bhat (1994: ch. 9, esp. pp. 168–9) observes that languages with little or no noun/adjective distinction also tend to allow discontinuous constituents, which is a key feature of Hale's notion of nonconfigurationality. Absence of a noun/adjective distinction and nonconfigurationality both seem to be wide spread in Australian languages ranging from Jiwarli to Dyirbal (Dixon 1972). Outside of Australia, other languages that have the typical Australian cluster of nonconfigurational properties (*pro-drop*, free word order, and widespread discontinuous constituents) include Quechua (Lefebvre and Muysken 1988: 162–5), Yimas (Foley 1991: 180–91, 369–76), and languages of the Klamath/Sahaptian family (Barker 1964: 338–9; Noel Rude personal communication). Strikingly, in all these families adjectives and nouns belong to the same lexical class, there being either no distinction at all or at most a very minor one. In particular, the putative adjectives are inflected for the same features as nouns (Quechua: Lefebvre and Muysken 1988: 25–7, Weber 1989; Yimas: Foley 1991: 93–4; Klamath/Sahaptian: Barker 1964: 260–1, 315–18, Noel Rude personal communication). This correlation gives credence to the idea that these two properties are related theoretically.

5.3   A note on syntax and pragmatics

It goes without saying that there are some remaining problems that need to be faced and details of implementation to be worked out before this Jelinek/Speas approach can claim to be a complete theory of Warlpiri-style nonconfigurationality. Unfortunately, limitations of space and insight do not permit me to explore all the relevant issues here.[22] One type of objection is obvious and important enough to demand attention, however. This is a pragmatic problem: sentences with secondary predication in Warlpiri/Jiwarli are not *used* in the same kinds of situation as sentences with secondary predication in English, and they do not have the same communicative effect.

This problem has more than one aspect. For example, depictive APs are used to characterize the way an object is at the time of an event in English only if the object had or could have had a different quality at some other time. As a result, only "stage-level" APs that refer to temporary properties are usable in English (Rapoport 1991). This is clearly not true in Warlpiri, where a nominal characterizes the argument at the time of the event, but there is no implicit contrast with what it was at other times or in other possible worlds. In particular, the secondary predicate nominal can be at individual level in Warlpiri.

Some of the Simpson/Bresnan/Austin criticisms of Jelinek (1984) also fit under this rubric. These authors find it implausible that there is a pronoun for every argument of every clause in Warlpiri, because personal pronouns are always definite, and they typically need some antecedent in the prior context to be felicitous. However, Warlpiri and Jiwarli nominals can be understood as indefinite, and can be used out of the blue at the beginning of a discourse with no discernible change in their syntax. In English, one would not say *John ate it raw* unless the raw thing was already known to the hearer, whereas the Jelinek/Speas approach implies that such an utterance is felicitous in Warlpiri.

Baker (1996: ch. 3) actually faces very much the same issue in Mohawk. There I argue that all nominals in Mohawk are clitic-dislocated, and that NPs have the formal syntactic properties of dislocated elements. However, Mohawk clauses clearly do not have the pragmatics of clitic left dislocation in Romance. For example, only definite NPs can be dislocated in Romance, and the dislocated element functions as a topic in discourse (Cinque 1990b, Rizzi 1997). Baker discusses how to resolve these tensions in some detail.

But, to make a long story short, the lesson of all this might simply be that pragmatics is patently *not* universal. More specifically, if these analyses of nonconfigurational languages are on the right track, Universal Grammar must consist primarily of substantive conditions on syntactic structure, and secondarily of a set of constructions that are consistent with those conditions. However, Universal Grammar must *not* associate a unique pragmatic value to the licit constructions. Rather, the pragmatic values of the particular constructions probably emerge from a variety of considerations. Natural form/function correspondences are presumably one, but another that is likely to be important is some notion of contrast. Since dislocation is a marked option in Romance languages, it comes to be associated with a particular pragmatic value, in contrast to the simpler structure that is also possible and is used in more neutral contexts. This choice between two structures does not exist in Mohawk, since dislocation is forced by Case theory plus the head marking requirement; hence dislocation structures are forced to do a wider range of duties in Mohawk. Similarly, English has a choice between saying "I ate a raw one" and "I ate one raw," so these assume different pragmatic values with regard to definiteness, contrast, and old versus new information structure. Warlpiri, however, has no true nouns, so there is nothing to contrast with the secondary predication structure, and it is used in a wider range of situations. There is much to spell out about how this works out in detail – especially in regard to how definiteness and indefiniteness play out in these articleless languages. But the general picture seems plausible. Indeed, it is just what one would expect on a broadly Chomskyan approach, in which language structure is distinguished from language use.

6 Conclusions

In closing, let me summarize the major lessons that have been learned from investigation into nonconfigurational languages so far.

The first and least controversial lesson is that nonconfigurationality is not a unified phenomenon. Rather, there seem to be several somewhat different kinds of nonconfigurational language. They have non-accidental similarities, but they also have important differences that can be cross-classified in various ways. The kind of nonconfigurationality a language has seems to be related to its other typological properties, such as whether it is head marking or dependent marking, its word order, and its basic category system.

Second, we have seen that the same Universal Grammar holds for this full range of languages, where Universal Grammar is viewed as (primarily) a set of formal constraints and (derivatively) a library of structures that obey those constraints. For example, the whole inquiry has been based on the assumption that things like Condition C and the weak crossover condition are essentially the same across languages. Similarly, the principles that regulate dislocation are basically the same in Mohawk and Italian, while the principles of secondary predication are the same in English and Warlpiri. Even at the points where languages are most different in terms of structure, similar causal factors can be discerned. Thus, the Case filter applies in Mohawk as it does in Romance, forcing dislocation in the presence of object clitics, and whatever bars APs from appearing in argument positions in English also blocks nominals in argument positions in Warlpiri. Indeed, it is the rigidity of Universal Grammar that makes languages look so different on the surface, because a small difference in basic structure caused by the obligatoriness of clitics or the absence of a distinct class of nouns has repercussions for how all the other principles apply. If instead Universal Grammar were a loose-knit collection of functional strategies, one might expect a difference in one area to be compensated for by a counterbalancing difference in another area. In contrast, the pragmatic values of particular constructions do not seem to be defined by Universal Grammar, but emerge out of the system of a particular language taken as a whole.

Finally, we can ask if we have learned anything about what system of grammatical representation is most adequate in general. Here I think the right answer is no. We have seen that languages in which phrase structure is significantly different from English also typically have significant differences in areas like anaphora. Thus, there is no refutation of the P&P idea that "functions" are defined over structure. But there is no direct refutation of an LFG-style architecture either. If it is correct that all Mohawk clauses involve dislocation and all Warlpiri clauses involve secondary predication, this could be expressed in one framework as well as another. Thus, I have parried an attack that LFG has made on P&P, but have not attempted a serious riposte. The choice of overall system of representation probably will have to be made on other grounds. It is worth nothing, however, that these results are compatible with Chomsky's "Minimalist" idea of reducing the number of meaningful grammatical levels to the logical limit (i.e., one: LF), since the same structure seems relevant to both things like word order and anaphora.

NOTES

* The original research reported in this chapter was supported by the Social Sciences and Humanities Research Council of Canada, grant 410-95-0979, and FCAR of Quebec, grant 94ER0578. This chapter never would have come to be if I had not had the opportunity to attend Joan Bresnan's and Peter Austin's seminars on Nonconfigurationality and Australian languages at Stanford University when I was a fellow at the Center for Advanced Studies in the Behavioral Sciences in the fall of 1993. The rich and vigorous discussions in these classes (which also led to Austin and Bresnan 1996) shook me out of my complacency to be content with my views about nonconfigurationality in Mohawk without trying to figure out how those views fit into a more comprehensive picture of nonconfigurationality. I thank them for providing such stimulating forums and a wealth of data. I have also benefited from the chance to present aspects of this material in talks at MIT and McGill University, and thank the audiences there for their input. Special thanks go to Kenneth Hale, Rob Pensalfini, Hidekazu Tanaka, Lisa Travis, Claire Lefebvre, Noel Rude, and Mark Donahue for their comments and information on their languages of expertise. Responsibility for mistakes remains my own.

   Glosses for agreement morphemes in Mohawk include the following elements: indication of person or gender (1, 2, 3, M, F, Z(oic), or N(euter)), indication of number (Sg, Pl, or D(ual)), and indication of "series" (S (roughly subject), O (roughly object), or P (possessor)).

1 These statements are true at the surface level in English. Many linguists believe that the subject originates inside the VP and is raised to the specifier of IP (see McCloskey 1997 for a review), and that the object moves out of the VP abstractly. These points will become relevant below. Presumably the VP is itself configurational in the sense that the subject is generated in a distinctive position within the VP, higher than the object.

2 In more recent LFG work, this structure has been revised somewhat to give a better account of the second position auxiliary. This is taken to be the head of an IP projection, the specifier of which is filled by some constituent taken from the otherwise nonconfigurational clause (Kroeger 1993, Austin and Bresnan 1996). I accept this development, but abstract way from it in this discussion.

3 Thus, at one point even rigid VSO languages like Irish were classed as nonconfigurational, because this word order made it difficult to claim that there was a VP that contained the verb and the object but not the subject. However, there is now a standard configurational analysis of most of these languages, in which their basic clause structure is much like English, except that the verb raises to I and the subject does not raise to Spec, IP (see Speas 1990, McCloskey 1997, for reviews).

4 In contrast, earlier published work in LFG depends on the notion

5   Admittedly this is a somewhat odd-looking representational schema that has evolved historically from the study of English. However, it may in turn be grounded in a principled way in the universal compositional semantics of the clause; see Marantz (1984), Hale and Keyser (1993), and Baker (1997b: sec. 5) for some discussion.

f-command, which does not distinguish subjects from objects within a single clause (Bresnan 1982).

6   These sentences use an overt pronoun rather than a null one in order to avoid the possibility that the possessor is a parasitic gap, an option that some Mohawk speakers – but apparently not all – seem to allow (Baker 1996: sec. 2.1.6).

7   Japanese pronouns are rather different from English ones in certain ways that lie behind how these examples are constructed. The null pronoun *pro* is not convenient for (19a), (20a), and (21a) because its invisibility means that one cannot tell if the object comes before or after the subject. On the other hand, it is not clear that overt anaphoric elements such as the colloquial *soitu* are really pronominal in the sense of being subject to Chomsky's Condition B (hence the use of an epithet-like gloss "the guy" in these examples). Fortunately the exact nature of this element (which is always unbound in these examples) is not directly relevant: the focus of inquiry here is on Condition C with respect to the name *Taro*. I thank H. Tanaka for help with these examples.

8   Technically, the *pro* in (21b) could also be analyzed as a parasitic gap; however, on this interpretation too the category it is contained in must be c-commanded by *dare-o*.

9   In this I disagree with Webelhuth (1992), who conjectures that free word order is always a result of clause internal movement triggered by focus features.

10   Some dialects of Spanish and Romanian are a well-studied exception to this generalization.

11   Note that Simpson (1991: 178) gives data showing that at least some version of Condition C is operative in Warlpiri in cases of clausal embedding.

12   Compare Roberts (1988: 708, n. 5), who admits that his sentence (ia), which is structurally parallel to (31b), is worse than his theory predicts it should be. I have found that some speakers do find (31b) better than (31a), however.

13   Roberts (1988: 709) gives a sentence like (32b) as bad, but he does not contrast it with one like (32a) and his sentence is not very meaningful to begin with.

14   Here I abstract away from the Aux-second affect in Warlpiri (see n. 2). Also, I assume for concreteness that the Case checking position for the pronominal object is the specifier of an Aspect Phrase, but any other functional category position outside the VP would do. In fact, it is possible that the Case of the object pronoun is checked in highest functional category (here TP), given Warlpiri's morphological ergativity (Bittner and Hale 1996b); if so, then it is even clearer that the pronominal object ends up c-commanding the secondary predicate associated with the subject.

15   Chris Collins (personal communication) points out that if one extends this view of Warlpiri clause structure to NP-internal structure in Warlpiri, then this explanation of the Condition C effects in (18) will be lost. In

particular, suppose that the possessor phrase is analyzed as an NP (or AP), predicated of a genitive *pro* that is inside the NP (or AP) that is predicated of the object. Then (i) would be a schematic representation of the structure of (18a):

(i) (He$_i$) [$_{VP}$ chase (it$_k$) [$_{NPk}$ (his$_i$) dog [$_{NPi}$ Jakamarra]]]

The binding theory is satisfied by this indexing. In particular, the *pro* possessor should be able to corefer with the subject by condition B, and the depictive predicate should be outside the domain of Binding Theory and therefore should not affect this possibility.

Fortunately, there is good reason *not* to extend this view of clause structure to NPs in Warlpiri. Simpson (1983, 1991) argues that the possessor suffix in Warlpiri is a kind of derivational Case, which forms adjuncts to NP, not a structural Case that marks an argument of the noun (or a secondary predicate of such an argument). Moreover, according to her rules *pro* is not licensed in possessive positions in this language in the first place. Therefore, the problematic representation in (i) is not available in Warlpiri.

Simpson's treatment of the possessive affix in Warlpiri makes it tempting to compare it to suffixes like *-ian* that derive "referential adjectives" in English (e.g. *the Italian invasion of Albania*, which is a near paraphrase of *Italy's invasion of Albania*, with an ordinary possessive NP). Now, it is known that these "referential adjectives" are not possible antecedents for anaphors or pronouns, even apart from questions of c-command ((iia) is discussed by Kayne 1984: 63, Giorgi and Longobardi 1991: 125–6):

(ii) a. *The Albanian destruction of itself/themselves (was tragic.) (cf. Albania's destruction of itself . . .)

b. The Italian$_i$ invasion of Albania haunted it$_{*i}$ for years. (cf. Italy$_i$'s invasion of Albania haunted it$_i$ for years.)

This raises the intriguing possibility that coreferential interpretations in examples in (18) are ruled out for the same reason as they are in (ii). If so, then these particular sentences turn out not to tell us much about clause structure in Warlpiri after all, *contra* Simpson (1991). More work is needed on these issues.

16 However, there is a complication in embedded clauses. Such clauses have no auxiliary to host clitics, and an empty object in such a clause can apparently be understood as a reflexive (Simpson 1991: 169). This may require some revision of the standard P&P typology of empty categories, but it does not bear directly on the matters at hand.

17 Another property that Warlpiri-type languages and Mohawk-type languages seem to share is that they resist taking clauses as arguments (see Simpson 1991: 20–1 for Warlpiri, Austin personal communication for Jiwarli, and Baker 1996: ch. 10 for Mohawk-type languages). This is another difference between them and Japanese-type languages. This property might also be derivable from the Pronominal Argument Hypothesis, given that the pronominal arguments are inherently nominal and therefore cannot form chain-like relationships with (unnominalized) clauses, due

to the mismatch in syntactic category.

18 Most of the other Simpson and Bresnan/Austin arguments against the Pronominal Argument hypothesis involve the pragmatics associated with having a pronoun in the structure in some way or another. I return briefly to this issue in section 5.3.

19 Bare adjectives in English can sometimes appear following the definite determiner "the," with the nominal as a whole referring generically to the class of people that have this property. However, even in these cases it can be shown that the adjective is the modifier of a null nominal head meaning roughly "people." Hence, the adjective is not technically the complement of the determiner; rather the null N is.

20 Of course it would be desirable to deepen this proposal by showing how these syntactic differences between adjectives and nouns follow in a principled way from a single defining difference – perhaps the fact that Ns are sortal and As are not. I hope to attempt this in future work.

21 The reader should take note, however, that (40) and (39) are not really a minimal pair, since the embedded clause in the Mohawk example is a complement, whereas in the Warlpiri example it is an adjunct. This difference may not be an innocent one, but it is probably unavoidable, if Warlpiri does not have true complement clauses (see n. 17).

22 Perhaps the most important syntactic problem is that it is not clear that the very free word order found in Jiwarli and Warlpiri follows immediately from the analysis of nominals as depictive predicates. These depictive predicates are presumably adjoined to some projection of the verb, and Speas is content to assume that free word order is a theoretical possibility, since no fundamental principle of grammar determines whether they should adjoin to the left or the right of the verbal projection. However, depictive secondary predicates in English are *not* particularly free in their word order: unlike adverbs, they can only be adjoined to the right of VP, and object oriented depictives must adjoin inside of subject oriented ones:

(i) a. I only eat fish raw drunk. (compare "I eat fish slowly drunk.")
     b. *I raw eat fish drunk. (compare "I slowly eat fish drunk.")
     c. *I only eat fish drunk raw. (compare "I eat fish drunk slowly.")

Thus, there is a difference between secondary predication in English and nominals in Warlpiri that still needs to be understood. One promising place to start would be to better understand the special role that Warlpiri's Case morphology plays in the licensing of secondary predication and in control more generally (see Simpson 1991: chs 4, 5, for extensive discussion of the relevant facts), since English does not have Case in this sense.

14 What VP Ellipsis Can Do, and What it Can't, but not Why

KYLE JOHNSON

0 Introduction

VP ellipsis is the name given to instances of anaphora in which a missing predicate, like that marked by "▲" in (2), is able to find an antecedent in the surrounding discourse, as (2) does in the bracketed material of (1):

(1) Holly Golightly won't [eat rutabagas].

(2) I don't think Fred will ▲, either.

We can identify three subproblems which a complete account of this phenomenon must solve:

(3) a. In which syntactic environments is VP ellipsis licensed?
     b. What structural relation may an elided VP and its antecedent have?
     c. How is the meaning of the ellipsis recovered from its antecedent?

These tasks tend to run together, as we shall see; but there is no immediate harm in treating them separately.

1 Licensing the Ellipsis

The first of the problems presents itself with pairs such as (4):

(4) I can't believe Holly Golightly won't eat rutabagas.
     a. I can't believe Fred won't ▲, either.
     b. *I can't believe Fred ▲, either.

These contrasts are typically thought to involve licensing conditions that the environment to the left of the ellipsis invoke. The contrast between (4a) and

(4b), for instance, indicates that the ellipsis site must be in construction with, or perhaps governed by, a member of "Aux," where these can be understood to be just those terms that are able to occupy the highest of the functional projections which clauses are made up of. The modal, *won't*, is an Aux, as are the infinitival *to* and the auxiliaries *have, be*, and *do* in (5):

(5) a. José Ybarra-Jaegger likes rutabagas, and Holly does ▲ too.
     b. José Ybarra-Jaegger ate rutabagas, and Holly has ▲ too.
         José Ybarra-Jaegger should have eaten rutabagas, and Holly should have ▲ too.
     c. José Ybarra-Jaegger is eating rutabagas, and Holly is ▲ too.
         José Ybarra-Jaegger has been eating rutabagas, and Holly has been ▲ too.
     d. Mag Wildwood wants to read Fred's story, and I also want to ▲.

Lobeck (1995: 155ff) and Potsdam (1996b) argue that the sentential negator, *not*, also licenses an ellipsis, as indicated by (6), and so might be considered a member of Aux too:[1]

(6) a. John is leaving but Mary's not ▲.
     b. I consider Bill intelligent and I consider Sally not ▲. (Lobeck 1995: (38c), 156, Potsdam 1996b: (123a), 51)[2]

Note that these examples also demonstrate that the licensing Aux need not actually be in the highest functional projection; that is, they need not be the term that bears finite morphology in finite clauses. (And (6b) also shows that "VP ellipsis" can affect a wider class of predicates than just VPs; see Baltin 1995.) That Auxs differ from other verbal elements in being able to license VP ellipsis is indicated by the contrast these examples have with (7):[3]

(7) a. *Sally Tomato started running down the street, but only after José started ▲.
     b. *Sally Tomato made Mag laugh, and then José made ▲.

   The first step in formulating an account of the licensing conditions on VP ellipsis, then, is to distinguish Auxs from everything else. The second step is to determine why *to* does not always license an ellipsis: (8), for instance, differs from the seemingly similar (5d):

(8) *Mag Wildwood came to read Fred's story, and I also came to ▲.

Lobeck (1987b, 1992, 1995) suggests that the contrast in (8) shows that *to* is by itself unable to license an ellipsis. Being an Aux is therefore not enough to license VP ellipsis. Instead Lobeck argues that it is also necessary that the ellipsis site be head governed by a term related to tense. If we assume that *to* is not a head governor of this sort, then the ungrammaticality of (8) is accounted for. The grammaticality of (5d) would then have to be captured by finding another head governor for the ellipsis. Lobeck suggests *to* is in circumstances like these able to form a government chain with the tense in the higher clause, thereby becoming a licit head governor. She exploits the Government Transparency Corollary, an innovation of Baker's (1988), which allows one head to govern from the position of another when they have Incorporated. She suggests the Government Transparency Corollary should be extended to terms that do not overtly Incorporate, but undergo a kind of covert version of this process. This is what she suggests happens with *to* and the higher tense. Thus, the ellipsis in (5d) satisfies the head government requirement if *to* is able to form a government chain, through *want*, with the tense of the root clause. In (8), however, because the infinitive is an adjunct, the government chain with *to* out of the infinitive will be blocked, in the same way as overt Incorporation would be, and, as a consequence, the elided VP will not become head governed by a term associated with tense.[4]

Zagona (1988a, 1988b) argues, by contrast, that the difference between (5d) and (8) is not due to licensing conditions on VP ellipsis, but instead follows from licensing conditions on *to*. She suggests that *to* must be phonologically bracketed with preceding material when the VP following it is elided – following in this respect Zwicky (1981). Like Lobeck, she assumes that this rebracketing is allowed only when *to* is able to gain proximity to its host; she explicitly resorts to head movement to bring *to* into this proximate position. Hence, the contrast between (5d) and (8) comes about in a parallel way for Zagona: rebracketing is possible in (8) because *to* can undergo head movement to *want*, and impossible in (5d) because head movement to *came* is blocked.

One empirical difference between the two proposals hinges on whether proximity to a term capable of head government is required or not. For Zagona, all that is necessary is that *to* find a method of moving close to some phrase or another; for Lobeck, however, *to* must be able to gain proximity to tense. Zagona cites the grammaticality of examples such as (9) in support of her proposal; Lobeck points to the marginality of (10) in support of hers:[5]

(9) John wants to go on vacation, but he doesn't know when to ▲. (Zagona 1988a: (21), 101)

(10) a. *We wanted to invite someone, but we couldn't decide who to ▲.
     b. *Mary was told to bring something to the party, so she asked Sue what to ▲.
     c. *We might go on vacation if we can ever figure out when to ▲.
     d. *Ron wanted to wear a tuxedo to the party, but Caspar couldn't decide whether to ▲. (Lobeck 1995: (26), 175)

In these cases, *to* is embedded within an indirect question, which is an environment thought to be an island. Exploiting this feature of the examples, Zagona suggests that *to* in (9) remains within the infinitive, moves into C°, and thereby gets close enough to *when*, which sits in Specifier of CP, to rebracket with it. Lobeck also exploits the island-hood of indirect questions and suggests that the ungrammaticality of (10) shows that *to* must form a government chain (a process that is interrupted by islands) out of the infinitive to license the ellipsis.[6] Alas, the difference between (9) and (10) remains puzzling, hampering a decision between the two approaches. But it should be noted that the judgments in (10) are somewhat variable; to my ears, (10d) is considerably better than (10b), for instance.

A much stronger contrast is the one in (11), from Zwicky (1981) and discussed in Lobeck (1995):[7]

(11)   a.   You shouldn't play with rifles because it's dangerous to ▲.
       b.   *You shouldn't play with rifles because to ▲ is dangerous. (Lobeck 1995: (2), 165)

An elided VP cannot be licensed by *to* when the infinitive that *to* heads is in subject position. For both Zagona and Lobeck this will follow from *to*'s need to have the proper relationship to the head on its left. For Zagona, the Generalized Left Branch Condition will prevent *to* from moving out of the subject to get close enough to *because*; and for Lobeck, a similar constraint will block forming a government chain between *to* and the tense in the higher clause.

So, summarizing, in finite clauses, an elided VP is licensed when governed by an Aux. When the ellipsis is governed by an infinitival *to*, there is an additional requirement which, apparently, forces *to* to be "close" to certain other terms. If Zagona and Lobeck are right, "close" is measured in terms similar to those holding of head movement.[8]

There are other known constraints on VP ellipsis which, nonetheless, resist being incorporated into this description of its licensing condition. For example, Sag (1976: ch. 1) argued that VPs elide quite badly when the Aux governing them has *ing* suffixed to it:[9]

(12)   a.   *Doc Golightly is being discussed and Sally is being ▲ too.
       b.   *I remember Doc being discussed, but you recall Sally being ▲.

And for many speakers, VPs headed by *have* resist ellipsis, perhaps because these VPs always fail the licensing condition. The example in (13), for example, does not easily have an interpretation in which the elided VP is understood to be *have eaten rutabagas* (instead, the somewhat strained *eat rutabagas* seems to be the only possibility):[10]

(13)   Sally might have eaten rutabagas, but Holly shouldn't ▲.

What we search for, then, is an account of VP ellipsis that explains why it can be expressed in just those environments governed by an Aux, with the caveats just reviewed.

Before we go any further, however, it is probably relevant to note that linguistic theory banned notions such as VP ellipsis in the late 1970s or so. Gone are all such constructions, and with them their parochial constraints and conditions. Instead, the phenomena which labels like "VP ellipsis" were constructed around are thought to emerge from the interaction of more general processes and constraints. The process VP ellipsis makes use of is, well, ellipsis, whose products almost certainly also include "N'-deletion" and "sluicing," constructions in which an NP or IP are elided, as in (14):

(14) a. Mag will read Fred's [story], and Joe Bell will read Holly's ▲.
      b. José asks that [we go to the meeting], and Sally will tell us when ▲.

The licensing condition on "VP Ellipsis" should therefore be tailored not only to the VP instances of ellipsis, but should also govern where NPs and IPs are elidible. Moreover, this condition should explain why VPs, NPs, IPs, and the AP in (6b) are subject to elision but, in general, phrases of other categories are not. Clearly, then, a licensing condition that is based on proximity to an Aux is too narrow; we must find a way of seeing this as the VP-specific version of a more general licensing condition on ellipsis. Anne Lobeck is, to my knowledge, the only one who has made an extended attack on this project, and there is still much work to be done.[11]

The approaches to the licensing condition which Zagona and Lobeck advocate can be seen as related to the sorts of licensing condition that are used to describe the distribution of other empty categories. One might imagine, for instance, that the conditions which license the null pronominal arguments in Romance, or the conditions that determine where traces may be, are part of the same family that the licensing conditions on ellipsis are in. In both the licensing conditions on null pronouns and those on empty categories, there is a part of the condition that refers to a privileged class of head governors, much as the conditions on ellipsis we have been reviewing do. Luigi Rizzi (1993) has suggested that this head governor requirement is the same in the pronoun and trace situations. He proposes that there is a general head government requirement on these kinds of empty category, and it is natural to imagine that this head government requirement could be extended to ellipsis sites as well. Let me call this part of the licensing condition on null pronouns and traces the Empty Category Principle (ECP), after the version of that condition which is thought to govern the distribution of traces. If we imagine that ellipsis is governed by this condition, then there should be a parallel between the positions in which traces of movement are licensed and the positions in which ellipsis is licensed. This is not obviously correct for the general case of ellipsis. It wrongly leads to the expectation that NP and IP movement should be possible, as in (15), parallel to (14):

(15) a. *It's *story* that Joe Bell will read Holly's *t*.
      b. *It's *we go to the meeting*, that Sally will tell us when *t*.

And it leaves unexplained why prepositional phrases, say, can move and leave a trace, but not elide:

(16) a. It's *to Mag Wildwood* that Joe said Holly can talk *t*.
      b. *Joe can talk [to Mag Wildwood] and Holly can talk ▲ too.
          (where: ▲ = *to Mag Wildwood*)

Perhaps there are particularities of the movement process, and the conditions which it invokes (beyond those shared by ellipsis), that can be used to explain these differences. (Saito and Murasugi 1998 suggest such a strategy for the first of these problems.)

In the specific case of VP ellipsis, however, the match is pretty good. A topicalized VP cannot succeed unless the trace it leaves is governed by an Aux, as the contrast between (17) and (18) shows:

(17) Madame Spanella claimed that . . .
      a. *eat rutabagas*, Holly wouldn't *t*.
      b. *eaten rutabagas*, Holly hasn't *t*.
      c. *eating rutabagas*, Holly should be *t*.
      d. *eating rutabagas*, Holly's not *t*.
      e. *eat rutabagas*, Holly wants to *t*.

(18) Madame Spanella claimed that . . .
      a. **would eat rutabagas*, Holly *t*.
      b. **hasn't eaten rutabagas*, Holly *t*.
      c. ?**eating rutabagas*, Holly started *t*.
      d. ?**eat rutabagas*, Holly made me *t*.

This pattern matches the one we have just witnessed for VP ellipsis. It also extends to the otherwise mysterious block on eliding VPs headed by *have*, since these VPs resist topicalization as well:

(19) *Madame Spanella claimed that *have eaten rutabagas*, Holly should.

What is left unmatched is the prohibition on ellipsis following an *ing* form, a prohibition that is not recapitulated in VP topicalization (see (20)), and the ability of a small clause to elide following *not*, an ability not shared by VP topicalization (see (21)):

(20) Madame Spanella claimed that . . .
      a. *?discussed widely*, Holly is being *t*.
      b. *?discussed widely*, I remember Holly being *t*.

(21) *Madame Spanella claimed that *intelligent*, I consider Holly not *t*.

Still, this is a pretty close fit, and it encourages thinking of the licensing condition on (VP) ellipsis in terms of the licensing condition on traces.

A very sensible question, if this should turn out to be accurate, is why ellipsis sites and traces should be subject to the same licensing condition. In what respect do ellipsis and movement create similar things? One possibility would be explore the thesis that traces and ellipsis sites simply are the same thing. On some conceptions of ellipsis and movement this is very nearly the case. Wasow (1972), for instance, argues that VP ellipsis consists of a full-fledged VP with no lexical items inserted into it; and this is very much like the Copy and Delete view of movement in Chomsky (1995b), according to which traces are full-fledged exemplars of the moved phrase, but with their lexical items removed. On this view, then, traces would turn out to be essentially ellipsis sites, and the Empty Category Principle could be seen as a condition on ellipsis.

Another approach would reduce VP ellipsis to the syntax of movement, and thereby cause the ellipsis site to contain a trace. Recall that when an ellipsis site is governed by infinitival *to* it is sometimes grammatical and sometimes not. It is ungrammatical when in an adjunct or subject infinitival, and variously so when in an indirect question. When the infinitival clause is in complement position, however, the ellipsis is grammatical. This paradigm is reproduced in (22) and (23):

(22) a. *Mag Wildwood came to read Fred's story, and I also came to ▲.
      b. *You shouldn't play with rifles because to ▲ is dangerous.
      c. ??Ron wanted to wear a tuxedo to the party, but Caspar couldn't decide whether to ▲.

(23) a. Mag Wildwood wants to read Fred's story, and I also want to ▲.
      b. You shouldn't play with rifles because it's dangerous to ▲.
      c. It's possible for you to play with rifles, and it's possible for me to ▲ too.

We can add to this that VP ellipsis in an infinitival clause buried within an NP is not good either, as in (24):[12]

(24) a. *Lulamae Barnes recounted a story to remember because Holly had also recounted a story to ▲.
      b. *?I reviewed Joe's attempt to find Holly while you reviewed José's attempt to ▲.
      c. *?Madame Spanella questioned Mag's desire to eat rutabagas, but only after I had questioned Sally's desire to ▲.
      d. *?Sally explained the attempt to arrest Holly, but only after I had denied the decision to ▲.

So, roughly: VP ellipsis cannot strand infinitival *to* when the infinitive that *to* heads is an island (the possible exception to this being the case of indirect questions, as we have seen). This sensitivity to islands, incidentally, is not found for VP ellipses in finite clauses (as Sag 1976 observes):

(25)   a.   John didn't hit a home run, but I know a woman who did ▲.
       b.   That Betsy won the batting crown is not surprising, but that Peter didn't know she did ▲ is indeed surprising.
       c.   Lulamae left although Mag didn't ▲. ((a) and (b) from Sag 1976: (1.1.8–9), 13)

Now on Zagona's approach to these facts, recall, the reason for this paradigm has to do with the defective nature of *to*. It must move to something it can cliticize to when it embeds an elided VP. It is this movement which is responsible for the island effects. I am skeptical, however, that the cause of the finite/non-finite contrast has to do with the defective nature of *to*, because the same paradigm emerges when the ellipses in infinitival clauses are governed by auxiliary verbs. I do not find a contrast in grammaticality between (22) and (26):[13]

(26)   a.   *Mag Wildwood came to be introduced by the barkeep and I also came to be ▲.
       b.   *You shouldn't have played with rifles because to have ▲ is dangerous.
       c.   ??Ron wanted to be wearing a tuxedo to the party, but Caspar didn't know whether to be ▲.
       d.   *Lulamae recounted a story to be remembered because Holly had recounted a story to be ▲.

I think what we search for, then, is something that distinguishes ellipses in infinitival clauses from ellipses in finite clauses, irrespective of the Aux which governs them. That is, we should not blame *to* on the island effects.

Imagine, instead, that VP ellipsis is licensed by VP topicalization. That is, suppose that for a VP to elide it must first topicalize. This, of course, would directly account for why the conditions on VP topicalization and VP ellipsis are so close. But it will also account for the finite/non-finite differences we have just reviewed, because topicalized VPs cannot land inside an infinitival clause in the way that they can in finite clauses:

(27)   a.   ?Lulamae decided that *eating rutabagas*, she should be *t*.
       b.   *Lulamae decided *eating rutabagas*, to be *t*.

Consequently, when a VP in an infinitival clause topicalizes, it must leave that infinitive to find a finite clause to land in. The ellipsis in (23a), for example, would then have the pre-ellipsis representation in (28):

(28)   *read Fred's story*, I also want to *t*.

And the ungrammatical examples of ellipsis in (22) and (24) will have the equally ungrammatical pre-ellipsis representations in (29):

(29) a. *You shouldn't play with rifles because *play with rifles* [to *t*] is dangerous.
      b. ??Ron wanted to wear a tuxedo to the party, but *wear a tuxedo to the party* Caspar couldn't decide whether to *t*.
      c. *Lulamae Barnes recounted a story to remember because *remember* Holly had recounted a story to *t*.

So the island effects we have seen for VPs elided in infinitival clauses can now be traced back to the fact that VPs in infinitival clauses are forced to move out of that infinitival clause, and this movement is subject to island constraints. Moreover, the somewhat variable effects that we have seen in indirect questions – the difference between (9) and (10), for instance – might be traced back to the fact that the *wh*-island constraint is itself quite variable.[14]

If this approach is correct, it suggests a reworking of the licensing conditions on VP ellipsis. The elided VPs in this account are no longer in the positions earlier thought – these positions are instead occupied by the elided VP's trace. Rather, elided VPs stand in a topic position, and therefore the licensing conditions on VP ellipsis should be sought here. This proposal, then, gives VP ellipsis an analysis parallel to the topic drop phenomenon that Huang (1984), among others, discusses.

Alas, this alternative proposal has the shortcoming that it does not explain why the island effects in infinitival clauses are lifted when those infinitival clauses house sentential *not*; (30) is an improvement on (26):[15]

(30) a. Mag Wildwood came to introduce the barkeep but I came (precisely) not to ▲.
      b. You should unload rifles because not to ▲ is dangerous.
      c. If Ron knows whether to wear a tuxedo, and Caspar knows whether not to ▲, do they know different things?
      d. Lulamae recounted a story to remember because Holly had recounted a story not to ▲.

Nor will this proposal gain ground on understanding why elided VPs cannot be governed by *ing* forms. In neither case is there a match with parallel constraints on VP topicalization.

VP ellipsis seems, then, to be subject to a licensing condition which recalls conditions on traces. However, this is not obviously an idea one would have after looking at the licensing condition on the ellipsis of other categories, and so there still remains the challenge of folding the conditions that license elided VPs in with the conditions that license ellipses in general. But if this can be done satisfactorily, it suggests that we should treat ellipses as the same kind of thing a trace is, or, alternatively, that we derive VP ellipsis by way of movement, perhaps in one of the ways just described.

2   Finding the Antecedent

Our second subproblem is to find the conditions which govern where a VP may be for it to serve as antecedent. This is not a well-studied topic, perhaps because there are very few such conditions. Like other forms of anaphora, VP ellipsis (and ellipsis in general) holds over discourses (as (1)/(2) demonstrate), and therefore the placement of antecedents does not seem to be subject to many syntactic conditions.

Nonetheless, there do seem to be some constraints on how the antecedent and elided VP may be structurally related. The question of interest is: are these conditions peculiar to ellipsis phenomena, or are they found in other expressions of anaphora as well? If the latter, then a theory of ellipsis should not be held responsible for explaining them.

For example, while Ross (1967a) finds that elided VPs cannot find antecedents if they command the ellipsis; he suggests that this follows from his more general condition on Backwards Pronominalization.[16] He illustrates the constraint with the contrast in (31),[17] which matches the similar contrast in (32). (I bracket the intended antecedent VPs.)

(31)   a.   If I can ▲, I will [work on it].
       b.   *I will ▲, if I can [work on it]. (Ross 1967a: (5.173), 369)

(32)   a.   If she$_1$ can work, Mag$_1$ will work.
       b.   *She$_1$ will work, if Mag$_1$ can work.

But Sag (1976: 346ff) suggests that these are different phenomena. The condition operative in (32) is not a condition on antecedence, but rather one on expressing "coreferent" relations, as Lasnik (1976) establishes. Thus, even if *she* is provided with an antecedent that is not commanded by it, (32b) does not have the interpretation indicated:

(33)   Mag$_1$ is a workaholic. *She$_1$ will work, if Mag$_1$ can work.

The condition responsible for (31), on the other hand, is a condition on antecedence. The ungrammaticality of (31b) is alleviated if a non-commanded antecedent is provided. Sag demonstrates this with the paradigm in (34):

(34)   a.   *He did ▲ when they asked him to [leave].
       b.   Did Harry [leave]?
            He did ▲ when they asked him to leave. (Sag 1976: (50) and (52), 346)

Therefore, it does not seem that the ungrammatical instances of backwards ellipsis can be reduced to the backwards pronominalization phenomenon.

Still, the condition responsible seems likely to be grounded in general requirements on anaphora, and not ellipsis specific ones; witness the similar patterns in (35):[18]

(35)   a.   ?*He did so when they asked him to [sing].
            ?*He did it when they asked him to [sing].
       b.   Does Joe [sing]?
            He did so when they asked him to sing.
            He did it when they asked him to sing.

In these cases it is an overt anaphoric VP that seems to be subject to the non-command requirement, and, like the VP ellipsis cases, this is a condition on antecedence, not coreference, as (35b) indicates.

Another context in which conditions on antecedents specific to VP ellipsis might be found arise in cases, like (36), first broached by Wasow (1972):

(36)   a.   *A proof that God [exist]s does ▲.
       b.   *A proof that God does ▲ [exist]s. (Wasow 1972: (16), 93)

In an unpublished paper, Christopher Kennedy has suggested that the ungrammaticality of these examples has the same source as the ungrammaticality of (37):[19]

(37)   a.   *Every man who said George would [buy some salmon] did ▲.
       b.   *I [visited every town in every country I had to ▲].

These cases, he notes, contrast with the similar (38):

(38)   a.   Every man who said he would [buy some salmon] did ▲.
       b.   I [visited every town I had to ▲].

Kennedy offers the generalization in (39) as a description of what distinguishes the examples:

(39)   Ellipsis between VP_α and VP_β, VP_β contained in an argument A_α of VP_α, is licensed only if A_α is identical to the parallel argument A_β of VP_β. (Kennedy 1994: (5), 2)

Note that in (37b) and (38b) the antecedent VPs contain the elided ones. These are instances of so-called "Antecedent Contained Deletions." Antecedent Contained Deletions present a, perhaps independent, problem: the bracketed VPs do not have the right form to serve as antecedents for the ellipses. What is called for is an antecedent VP that, in the case of (38b) and (37b) for instance, has the form: *visited t*. That is, what is needed is a VP which, when placed inside the ellipsis site, creates a representation like (40) from (38b) (where the trace in this sentence is bound to the null relative pronoun, represented here with "Op"):

(40)   I visited every town Op_1 I had to [visit t_1].

As we shall see in the following section, a popular method of achieving this is to fashion the required VP out of the ones bracketed in (37b) and (38b) by moving the object which contains the ellipsis out of them. Thus, for example, the antecedent VP for (40) is made from the bracketed phrase in (38b) by moving the object to produce (something like) (41):

(41)   [every town I had to ▲]₁ I [visited t_1.]

   May (1985: 12–13) suggests that this method of producing the antecedent VP for Antecedent Contained Deletions might itself explain the contrast between (37b) and (38b).[20] Note that one feature of this method of resolving Antecedent Contained Deletions (like that, say, in (38b)) is that the index borne by the trace produced when the object moves out of the antecedent VP (as shown for (38b) in (41)) matches the index borne by the null relative pronoun in the vicinity of the elided VP (the "Op" in (40), for example). This is fortunate because the null relative pronoun needs a trace to bind (in general, relative pronouns must bind a trace), and it can only bind the traces it is coindexed with.

   Now, this happenstance of (38b) does not materialize in the ungrammatical (37b). Here, the method of forming an antecedent VP that we have just reviewed will produce something like (42a), which, when plugged into the ellipsis site, yields (42b):

(42)   a.   [every town in every country I had to ▲]₁ I [visited t_1].
       b.   *[every town in every country Op_2 I had to [visit t_1]]₁ I [visited t_1].

As can be seen, the index borne by the trace created in the antecedent is not the same as that borne by the null relative pronoun into whose scope it falls when placed in the ellipsis site.[21] As a consequence, this null relative pronoun will fail to bind a trace, and this causes the sentence to go bad.

   Thus, May's suggestion would capture part of Kennedy's generalization. It does so by, first, adopting the procedure outlined above for forming the antecedent VP in situations of Antecedent Contained Deletions and, second, taking the elided VP to have *exactly* the traces, complete with indices, that their antecedents do. I have illustrated this technique by considering cases where the ellipsis falls inside a direct object, but precisely the same method can be used for all situations where the ellipsis falls within an internal argument of the verb whose VP acts as antecedent. In all of these cases, there will be an Antecedent Contained Deletion, whose resolution will invoke configurations identical to those considered for direct objects.

   In fact, May's procedure might be extended to cases where the ellipsis falls within the subject too, thereby capturing the rest of Kennedy's generalization.

If we exploit the Internal Subjects Hypothesis, which gives subjects an underlying position within VP, then (38a) might get a representation like (43):[22]

(43)   [Every man who$_1$ said he$_1$ would [t_1 buy some salmon]]$_1$ did ▲.

Now if the VP in (43) is placed in the ellipsis site, we achieve the grammatical
(44):

(44)   [Every man who$_1$ said he$_1$ would [t_1 buy some salmon]]$_1$ did [t_1 buy
       some salmon].

By contrast, the Internal Subjects Hypothesis would give to (37a) the representation in (45a), which leads to the ungrammatical representation in (45b) when
the antecedent VP is put in the ellipsis site:

(45)   a.   [Every man who$_1$ said George$_2$ would [t_2 buy some salmon]]$_1$ did ▲.
       b.   [Every man who$_1$ said George$_2$ would [t_2 buy some salmon]]$_1$ did [t_2
            buy some salmon].

What goes wrong in (45b) is very much like what goes wrong in (42b):
the index borne by the trace in the VP does not match the index borne by the
subject which should bind that trace. Wasow's examples fail for exactly the
same reason, as (46) shows. (I distinguish antecedent from elided VPs here
with strikeouts.)

(46)   a.   *[A proof that God$_2$ [t_2 exist]s]$_1$ does [t_2 ~~exist~~].
       b.   *[A proof that God$_2$ does [t_1 ~~exist~~]]$_1$ [t_1 exist]s.

   If correct, this account of Kennedy's generalization would reduce it to the
identity conditions that hold of an elided VP and its antecedent. What originally appears to be a condition on where the antecedents to elided VPs can be
found would be explained away as an effect imposed by the requirement that
antecedent and elided VPs are identical up to the indices they contain.
   Unfortunately, this account is either incomplete or wrong. It is wrong if it
holds that the identity conditions on antecedent and elided VPs require that
the indices in the antecedent are *always* preserved in the ellipsis site. This
would wrongly give to examples such as (47a) the ungrammatical representation in (47b):

(47)   a.   Lulumae should buy salmon and Mag should ▲ too.
       b.   Lulumae$_1$ should [t_1 buy salmon] and Mag$_2$ should [t_1 buy salmon]
            too.

As we shall see in the next section, a requirement that preserves the indices in
antecedent and elided VPs is routinely lifted. So, if May's technique is to be

successful, it needs to be wedded to an account which explains why, in environments that Kennedy's generalization picks out, the indices in elided VPs must match those in the antecedent.

Kennedy proposes to use a part of Fiengo and May (1994)'s conditions on VP ellipsis to provide this additional account. Fiengo and May argue that an elided VP is subject to a condition relative to its antecedent VP that goes beyond matching the elided and antecedent VPs. They suggest that the clauses which contain an elided VP must be "parallel" to clauses containing the antecedent VP. Moreover, they argue that this additional parallelism constraint controls when a variable bound in the antecedent VP may pick up a new binder in the ellipsis site. For example, in (48) his_1 in the antecedent VP may be understood as his_2 in the elided VP:

(48)   a. Joe_1 likes his_1 bar, and $Sally_2$ does ▲ too.
         ▲ = *his₂ bar*
     b. $Joe's_1$ idiosyncrasies bother his_1 patrons, and $Sally's_2$ idiosyncrasies do ▲ too.
         ▲ = *his₂ patrons*

John Ross labeled this fickle relationship pronouns have with their antecedents "sloppiness." Fiengo and May suggest that the kind of interpretation a pronoun must have to invoke a sloppy reading in the ellipsis site triggers the parallelism constraint. Thus, *his* in (48) can accept *Sally* as its binder in the ellipsis site because *Sally* is in a position parallel to that of the binder of *his* (i.e., *Joe*) in the antecedent VP. When this kind of parallelism breaks down, as it does in (49), for example, the sloppy reading for the pronoun is lost:

(49)   a. Joe_1 likes his_1 bar, and $Sally's_2$ patrons do ▲ too.
         ▲ ≠ *his₂ bar*
     b. $Joe's_1$ idiosyncrasies bother his_1 patrons, and $Sally_2$ does ▲ too.
         ▲ ≠ *his₂ patrons*

It is just this kind of sloppy anaphora that is needed to license the different indices on the subject traces in (47). What we seek, then, is a way to prevent recourse to sloppy anaphora in the examples which fall within Kennedy's generalization. The cases in Kennedy's generalization all have a form like that sketched in (50), where one of VP^1 or VP^2 is the antecedent VP, and the other is the elided VP:

(50) $[\ldots X_1 \ldots [_{VP}^{\ 1} \ldots t_1 \ldots] \ldots]_1 \ldots [_{VP}^{\ 2} \ldots t_1 \ldots].$

Kennedy suggests that the special relationship that a pronoun/trace must have to get a sloppy reading precludes this kind of structure. In particular, he blames the fact that these structures place within an argument binding one of these traces a trace with a similar dependency. That is, he suggests that these configurations invoke a kind of circular dependency, much as (51) does, which is fatal:

(51)   [Every picture of itself$_1$]$_1$ arrived.

Heim (1997) also proposes exploiting the Fiengo and May parallelism constraint in an explanation of Kennedy's generalization. But she adopts an interpretation of this constraint that Rooth (1992a) introduces. Rooth argues that there are two completely independent conditions on VP ellipsis. One is responsible for matching the elided VP with its antecedent. This constraint is sensitive to the lexical content of the VPs involved, as well as their syntactic form, but does not care about the indices they hold. Let us call this the "syntactic identity condition." The second constraint is Fiengo and May's parallelism constraint, which Rooth suggests is actually better expressed as a requirement that the elided VP be contained within a constituent which contrasts with a constituent containing the antecedent VP. Let us therefore call this the "contrast condition."[23]

The conditions that determine when two constituents contrast will then influence the form that antecedent and elided VPs may have. On Rooth's proposals, it is also this constraint that determines when the indices in elided and antecedent VPs must match. The contrast condition, which is built upon Rooth's theory of focus,[24] can be abbreviated as (52):

(52)   a.   An elided VP must be contained in a constituent which contrasts with a constituent that contains its antecedent VP.
       b.   α *contrasts* with β iff
            (i)   Neither α nor β contain the other, and
            (ii)   For all assignments g, the semantic value of β with reference to g is an element of the focus value of α with reference to g.
            (iii) The focus value of $[_\xi \ldots \gamma \ldots]$, where γ is focused, is $\{[\![\phi]\!]:$ $[_\phi \ldots x \ldots]\}$, where x ranges over things of the same type as γ and the ordinary semantic value of ξ is identical to $[\![\phi]\!]$ except that x replaces γ.

This condition requires that there be a constituent containing an elided VP which also includes a focussed item.[25] The focussed item will cause that constituent to contrast with another; and (52) requires that the constituent it contrasts with hold the antecedent VP. Further, because (52bii) fixes the values of the indices in the constituents being contrasted, it will have the effect of preventing the indices in antecedent and elided VPs from having different values, unless – by way of (52biii) – they are borne by focussed items.

Consider (53), which illustrates:[26]

(53)   a.   Mag$_1$ ate more than she$_{2F}$ had ▲.
       b.   *Mag$_1$ ate more than she$_2$ could$_F$ ▲.
            (compare: *Mag$_1$ ate more than she$_1$ could$_F$ ▲.*)

In (53a), *she* bears focus, and in (53b), *could* does. Only in (53a) can *she* be understood as bearing a different index than *Mag*. This follows from the contrast condition because only when the subject of the elided VP is focussed will (52b) allow it to bear a different index than the subject of the antecedent VP. Imagine, for concreteness, that the elided VP has the form in (54a) and the antecedent VP has the form in (54b):[27]

(54)   a.   . . . [$_{XP}$ she$_2$ [$_{VP}$ t_2 ~~ate~~]].
       b.   . . . [$_{YP}$ Mag$_1$ [$_{VP}$ t_1 ate]].

For the elided VP in (54a) to satisfy (52), XP must contrast with YP. The definition of contrast requires that XP and YP have the same denotation, except for those terms that are focussed. Because the index on *she* and *Mag* are different, the clauses in (54) will fail this requirement unless *she* is focussed. Thus, the difference in (53).

Because Kennedy's examples involve situations in which the ellipsis is contained within an argument whose index binds a trace within the antecedent VP, they will have to avail themselves of focus in the same way as (53a) does. But it turns out that in a significant range of these situations, this will not be achievable precisely because (52bi) prohibits satisfying the contrast condition when the clause containing the ellipsis is within the contrastive clause containing the antecedent VP.[28]

We have, then, two possible strategies for capturing Kennedy's generalization. Kennedy's own strategy seeks to block these examples from a more general condition on circular reference. Heim's strategy seeks to block them from the necessary contrastiveness that VP ellipsis invokes. Rooth (1992b) and Tancredi (1992), who offers a theory of focus in contexts of ellipsis very like Rooth's, both emphasize that the contrast condition is not peculiar to ellipsis. It is found in cases of anaphoric deaccenting as well, for example. Thus, neither of these strategies demands that there be constraints on the relationship between antecedent and elided VPs that are ellipsis specific.

3   How the Ellipsis Gets its Meaning

Our third subproblem is to determine by which principles the ellipsis site gains its meaning. It is useful to link this question up with the issue of what the ellipsis site is. If the kind of thing that an ellipsis is can be determined, then we might be aided in figuring out what sort of meaning the ellipsis has (and the methods by which it gets that meaning) by examining other things of the same kind.

This approach to the problem hooks up easily with the first subproblem: the question of what conditions an ellipsis is licensed by. It would be natural, for example, to think of the ellipsis site as holding a null pro-form if the licensing condition turns out to be like that for null arguments. And it is natural to think of the ellipsis site as holding a trace, in the event that its licensing condition more nearly matches that of traces. Under the first scenario, we might also try to see the anaphoric properties that ellipsis invokes as making use of the same mechanisms that pronouns in general do. That is, we might speculate that the reason the syntactic conditions on ellipsis are the same (if they are) as those on null arguments is that there is a kind of null pro-form in such cases. But if the licensing conditions on ellipsis seem to be grounded in the principles that govern where traces can be, then it might be advantageous for traces to be thought of as ellipsis sites, along the lines discussed above. The view of what an ellipsis is that best meets this scenario is what I will call the derivational approach. On this conception, an ellipsis site is derivationally related to a full syntactic version of the phrase whose meaning is recovered. So, for example, the surface representation of (2) could be seen as related to the fuller . . . *Fred will eat rutabagas either* through either a deletion process (that removes the VP by way of its anaphoric connection to a previously occurring VP) or a reconstruction process (that forms from the surface representation an LF into which the understood VP is copied).

A glitch to this equation arises if the method I sketched for deriving the licensing conditions on VP ellipsis in section 1 are correct. On this account the elided VP is not actually in the position we might have expected it to be, but instead has moved. This account will manufacture a trace in the position we expect to find the elided VP, thereby invoking the licensing conditions on traces. If this is correct, then the content of the ellipsis and the conditions on its trace no longer connect. It could as easily be a pro-form that topicalizes as it could a full-bodied (elided) VP. Let us therefore keep this caveat in mind.

The pro-form position has as its fullest champion Dan Hardt (see Hardt 1992, 1993); but a similar hypothesis can be found in Schachter (1977a), Partee and Bach (1984), Chao (1987), and Lobeck (1995). Sag (1976), Williams (1977), and Wasow (1972) sponsor the derivational approach.[29]

The difference between these positions engaged much of the early literature on anaphora and ellipsis. (Hankamer and Sag 1976 have an enlightening review.) Grinder and Postal (1971), for example, argue that VP ellipsis is a form of "Identity of Sense" anaphora, a dependency which obtains when the anaphor recovers the semantic content of its antecedent, rather than its antecedent's referent. Thus an antecedent and an Identity of Sense anaphor do not independently express ways of referring to the same entity, but instead constitute expressions with the same denotation. One of their interesting arguments comes from what they dub the "Missing Antecedent" phenomenon, illustrated by (55):

(55)   My uncle doesn't have a spouse but your aunt does ▲ and *he* is lying on the floor. (Grinder and Postal 1971: (17a), 278)

In (55), the VP ellipsis in the *but* clause introduces the indefinite antecedent to *he* (= *a spouse*). That is, the ellipsis site in (55) recycles the semantic material of its antecedent and thereby introduces a referent that the antecedent did not.

This property of ellipsis has a straightforward expression under the derivational approach. Suppose that there is a level of representation where an ellipsis site is made up of a syntactic representation, and it is this representation that is matched against the antecedent. Thus, the ellipsis recycles the linguistic content of its antecedent – in the case of (55) this is *have a spouse*, the very words that make up its antecedent – thereby reinvoking its denotation. The pro-form approach, on the other hand, will have to overcome the fact that the Missing Antecedent phenomenon is not present in the transparent pronominal anaphora of (56), as Bresnan (1971) observes:[30]

(56)   *My uncle didn't buy anything for Christmas, but my aunt did it for him, and *it* was bright red.
(compare: *My uncle didn't buy anything for Christmas, but my aunt did, and it was bright red.*) (Bresnan 1971a: (9), 591)

Hence, the Missing Antecedent phenomenon makes the pro-form approach look doubtful, but fits well the derivational interpretation of ellipsis.

There is a slightly different case which, like the Missing Antecedent phenomenon, suggests that an ellipsis site is made up of linguistic material recovered in the antecedent. This case is found in contexts of extraction, where the ellipsis contains a variable bound to the extracted item, as for example in (57), drawn from Fiengo and May (1994):

(57)   a.   I know which book Max read, and which book Oscar didn't ▲.
       b.   This is the book of which Bill approves, and this is the one of which he doesn't ▲. (Fiengo and May 1994: (99a, c), 229)

In these cases too the ellipsis site seems to have internal parts: in (57a), a variable bound by *which book*, and in (57b), a variable bound to *which*. And, as with the Missing Antecedent phenomenon, obvious pronouns do not seem to tolerate the same kinds of internal part; compare (57) with (58):

(58)   a.   *I know which book José didn't read for class, and which book Lulumae did it for him.
(compare: *I know that José didn't read this book for class, but that Lulumae did it for him.*)
       b.   *This is the book which O. J. Berman reviewed, and this is the one which Fred won't do it.
(compare: *O. J. Berman reviewed this book but Fred won't do it.*)

Just as in (55), then, the ellipses in (57) recover their syntactic form (= [$_{VP}$ *read t*] and [$_{VP}$ *reviewed t*]) from their antecedents. By contrast, pronouns have no syntactic form beyond the lexical item they constitute, and (58) therefore results in a violation of the ban against vacuous quantification. Thus, as in the Missing Antecedent cases, we are led to the conclusion that an ellipsis site should not be seen as consisting of a hidden pronoun.[31]

That the elided material in cases such as (57) does contain syntactic material, and more particularly a trace bound to the A'-moved item, is strengthened by Haïk's (1987) discovery that various island effects hold into the ellipsis site:

(59) a. I know which book Mag read, and which book Mr Yunioshi said that you hadn't ▲.
      b. ?*I know which book Mag read, and which book Mr Yunioshi asked why you hadn't ▲.
      c. ?*I know which book Mag read, and which book Mr Yunioshi read my report that you hadn't ▲.
      d. ?*I know which book Mag read, and which book Mr Yunioshi discussed after I had ▲.

The difference between (59a) and the others is the familiar bounding constraints, whatever they may be, which govern how far a *wh*-phrase may move: descriptively speaking, (59b) is an instance of Chomsky's *Wh*-Island Constraint, (59c) exemplifies Ross's Complex NP Constraint, and (59d) is a result of the Adjunct Condition. Insofar as these conditions are ones that hold of an A'-moved term and its trace, we have reason to believe that there is a trace in the ellipses of these examples.[32]

The cases of Antecedent Contained Deletion discussed in the previous section[33] probably illustrate a similar point. In such cases, the antecedent VP appears to contain the ellipsis, as in (60):

(60) Dulles [suspected everyone who Angleton did ▲].

This is a situation that VP ellipsis permits, but that overt forms of VP anaphora do not:

(61) a. *Dulles suspected everyone who Angleton did it.
      b. *Dulles suspected everyone who Angleton did so.

Of course, this suggests again that VP ellipsis should not be seen as the silent version of a pro-form.

The ungrammaticality of the pro-form anaphora in (61) is no doubt related to the similar difficulties in (62):

(62) a. *Dulles bought [a portrait of it$_1$]$_1$.
      b. *Dulles praised [the picture of a portrait of it$_1$]$_1$.

There is something that prevents the pronouns in (62) from being referentially dependent on the argument containing them; and presumably this same force is at play in (61). It is not immediately clear, however, how (60) can arise even if it is not an instance of pro-form anaphora. On the derivational approach to VP ellipsis, for instance, there is no antecedent with the proper form for the ellipsis in (60), as can be seen in (63):

(63)   Dulles [suspected everyone who Angleton did [~~suspected everyone who Angleton did . . .~~]].

Even if we could figure out how to fill in ". . . ," the elided VP in (63) is not the one that is understood to be elided in (60).

As foreshadowed in the previous section, a popular approach to this problem on derivational theories of VP ellipsis is to view Antecedent Contained Deletions as being licensed by movement of the argument which contains the ellipsis.[34] May (1985), for instance, argues that the argument containing the elision scopes out of the antecedent VP. He argues that there is a level of syntactic representation projected from the surface in which arguments occupy the position at which their scopes are computed. In this level of Logical Form (LF), the object in (60) can be scoped out of the VP which is to serve as antecedent, yielding (64):

(64)   [everyone who Angleton did ▲]$_1$ [Dulles [suspected t_1]].

And in (64), the VP is now of nearly the right form to serve as antecedent, as (65) illustrates:

(65)   [everyone who Angleton did [~~suspected t_1~~]]$_1$ [Dulles [suspected t_1]].

The only difficulty with (65) is that the form of the verb is not appropriate for the ellipsis site. Let us set this aside for the moment.

Hornstein (1994, 1995) offers a variant of this account which credits movement of the object out of the antecedent VP not to QR, but to "Object Shift," the name given to a kind of short Scrambling – an instance of argument movement – found in the Scandinavian languages.[35] On Hornstein's interpretation, Object Shift brings direct and indirect objects into the specifiers of functional projections (which license them, perhaps through Case marking) at LF. These functional projections are thought to lie between the surface position of the subject and the VP. Hence, the LF Hornstein would give to (60) might be as in (66):

(66)   [Dulles [$_{FP}$ [everyone who Angleton did [~~suspected t_1~~]]$_1$ [F° [$_{VP}$ suspected t_1]]]]. (understand "F°" to be the functional head that licenses objects)

How these two variants should be compared will depend on whether "Object Shift" is identified with QR or not.

An interesting consequence of these approaches is that they manufacture in the elided VP a trace, which in turn forces the environment in which the elision arises to have a binder for that trace. In (60), the relative pronoun binds the trace. In fact, a general feature of Antecedent Contained Deletions is that they involve relative clauses. An Antecedent Contained Deletion cannot survive in other kinds of complex NP:

(67) *I [told a rumor that Mag did [~~told a rumor that Mag told a rumor that . . .~~]].

The *that*-clause in (67) cannot be a complement to *rumor*. That is, the content of the rumor I told cannot be *that Mag told a rumor*; instead, the *that*-clause says that Mag and I told the same rumor. So, this fact about Antecedent Contained Deletion, like that in (57), suggests that an elided VP can have enough of the form of a VP to hold a trace.[36] It is this feature of Antecedent Contained Deletions, recall, which May's approach to Kennedy's Generalization exploits.

An unfortunate feature of this last argument for the derivational approach to VP ellipsis is that it rests on locating a phonetically empty term – the trace – within an ellipsis. But as we have all no doubt had occasion to discover, finding the location of invisible things is not trivial. Could we have mislocated it? Might the traces in (60) and (57) in fact be outside the ellipsis, as indicated in (68)?

(68) a. I know which book Max read, and which book$_1$ Oscar didn't ▲ t_1.
      b. Dulles [suspected everyone who$_1$ Angleton did ▲ t_1].

This would be possible if VP ellipsis, or some other ellipsis phenomenon, could elide portions of VPs, leaving remnants in the positions that the traces in (68) occupy. Interestingly, that does seem possible:

(69) a. While O. J. Berman read Fred, he didn't ▲ Dickens.
      b. Sally suspected Joe, but he didn't ▲ Holly.

Levin (1986) dubs these "pseudogaps," and argues that they involve a process different from VP ellipsis. Her reason for distinguishing the two turns on the observation that there are certain environments where VP ellipsis is permitted, but pseudogapping is not. In fronted adverbials, for instance, VP ellipsis but not pseudogapping is licensed (an observation that goes back to Sag's dissertation):

(70) a. Although Holly doesn't ▲, Doc eats rutabagas.
      b. *Although Mag doesn't ▲ eggplants, Sally eats rutabagas.

It is possible, then, that we have mistaken VP ellipsis for pseudogapping in (57) and (60). This is what Jacobson (1992) and Hardt (1993: sec. 2.5), who credits Lappin and McCord (1990), propose. Hardt leans on the fact that cases like (57) and (60) are prohibited in fronted adverbials, and so appear more like pseudogapping than VP ellipsis:

(71) a. ?*Although I don't know which book Sam did ▲, I do know which book Sally read.
      b. ?*Near everyone Angleton did ▲, Dulles stood.
          (compare: *Dulles stood near everyone Angleton did.*)

While it may well be possible to give some of the cases we have examined a pseudogapping source, Haïk (1987), Kennedy (1997), and Tomioka (1997) give compelling reasons for not reducing all such cases to pseudogapping. Pseudogapping is subject to restrictions on the remnants which are not always reflected in those cases of ellipsis involving traces. Pseudogapping, for instance, cannot elide part of a prepositional phrase, as Haïk (1987) and Kennedy (1997) observe, nor may it remove part of a noun phrase, as Tomioka (1997) points out. Illustrative examples are in (72):

(72) a. *Sally will stand near Mag, but he won't ▲ Holly.
      b. *While Holly didn't discuss a report about every boy, she did ▲ every girl.

But traces may be related to these positions, as (73) demonstrates:[37]

(73) a. ?I know which woman FRED will stand near, but I don't know which woman YOU will ▲.
      b. Sally will stand near every woman that you will ▲.
      c. I know which woman HOLLY will discuss a report about, but I don't know which woman YOU will ▲.
      d. Holly discussed a report about every boy that Berman had ▲.

(The badness of (73a) reflects the difficulty in moving *wh*-phrases out of adjuncts, and contrasts with (72a).) These examples at least, then, must not be pseudogaps; and unless some other alternative can be found, it is reasonable to conclude that VP ellipsis has the ability to host a trace.

Moreover, despite the mismatches in licensing environments that Levin catalogues, there is, I think, considerable reason to believe that pseudogapping is a special instance of VP ellipsis. The reason is that the terms which can serve as remnants in pseudogaps are limited in a way that suggests they have moved from the elided VP. That pseudogapping is VP ellipsis from which a remnant has moved is a thesis that Kuno (1981), Jayaseelan (1990), and Lasnik (1995f) have advanced in recent years. Kuno and Jayaseelan argue that pseudogapping is the product of eliding a VP after Heavy NP Shift has occurred. This would explain, for instance, why pseudogapping cannot strand a preposition, since Heavy NP Shift cannot do so either:

(74) *Sam stood near yesterday every one of the women we'd been discussing.

Lasnik, by contrast, argues that Object Shift is responsible for bringing the remnant out of the elided VP. Object Shift, at least as it is found in the Scandinavian languages, shares with Heavy NP Shift an inability to strand prepositions, as noted above. But Object Shift differs from Heavy NP Shift in being able to move pronouns and the first object of a double object construction, things Heavy NP Shift cannot do, as (75) indicates:

(75) a.   *Truman visited yesterday you.
     b.   *Truman told the story Rusty.

Because pronouns and the first object of a double object construction can be the remnants in pseudogapping (as in (76)), Lasnik concludes that Object Shift makes a better candidate than does Heavy NP Shift for the mechanism evacuating remnants from a pseudogapped VP:

(76) a.   While Truman didn't visit me, he did ▲ you.
     b.   While Truman didn't tell me a story, he did ▲ Rusty.

Actually, however, even Object Shift does not have quite the right properties to be the source of the constraints on pseudogapping remnants. Object Shift is unable to move prepositional phrases, for instance; whereas prepositional phrases, though somewhat strained, may be the remnants of pseudogapping:[38]

(77) a.   While José won't talk about Mag, he might ▲ about Holly.
     b.   Although Doc might tell it to you, he won't ▲ to me.

Moreover, Levin notes that pseudogapping seems able to strand remnants which are buried quite deeply in the elided VP. A couple of her examples are in (78):

(78) a.   I'm sure I would like him to eat fruit more than I would ▲ cookies.
     b.   I think you need to show yourself more than you do ▲ anyone else.
        (Levin 1986: (7) and (13), 15–16)

While Levin suggests that cases like these are possible only in comparatives, raising the spectre that they may result from whatever it is that creates (the often peculiar) elisions in these constructions, I think they are not impossible in other contexts. Consider, for example, (79):

(79) a.   ?While I wouldn't like him to eat cookies, I would ▲ fruit.
     b.   ?While I think you need to examine yourself, you don't ▲ anyone else.
     c.   While Truman doesn't want to visit every city, he does ▲ Barcelona.

In (78) and (79), the remnants are the objects of a clause embedded within the elided VP. If Object Shift is the process that brings remnants out of the elision, it would have had to move them clear out of the clause they start in. But Object Shift, at least as it is represented in the Scandinavian languages, cannot move an object that far. For these reasons, then, Object Shift is not quite the right mechanism to blame for bringing remnants out of a pseudogapped VP.

    Still, reducing pseudogapping to VP ellipsis is, I believe, sound. It requires, however, an analogy to the kind of Scrambling that Dutch hosts in its middle field, rather than to Heavy NP or Object Shift. In Dutch, it is possible to Scramble objects, whether they be pronouns or larger, and prepositional phrase complements leftward past adverbs and the like. This Scrambling, like Heavy NP Shift and Object Shift, is also unable to strand prepositions.[39] Thus, Scrambling has the constraints on pseudogapped remnants that Jayaseelan and Lasnik singled out as indicative of movement. Further, Scrambling is able to span long distances, bringing objects out of an embedded clause and beyond the VP which that clause is embedded in, as in (80):

(80)   . . . dat Jan *Marie* heeft geprobeerd [*t* te kussen].
    . . . that Jan Mary has   tried   to kiss
    (. . . that John has tried to kiss Mary)

It therefore has the power to generate the large pseudogaps in (78) and (79); simply let VP ellipsis be fed by long distance Scrambling, as shown in (81):

(81)

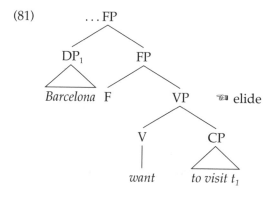

Scrambling, then, shows the features we have encountered so far in pseudo-gapping: it can relocate PPs and DPs, though not if it entails stranding a preposition, and it can do so over long distances.

   Moreover, long distance Scrambling in Dutch and the span that large pseudogaps may have are subject to hauntingly similar constraints. Long distance Scrambling is restricted to certain kinds of non-finite complement clause; it is blocked from adjunct clauses, as in (82a), and from finite complement clauses, as in (82b):

(82)   a. *. . . dat Jan   het boek *zijn vader* gelezen heeft [om *t* te pliezeren]
           . . . that John the book his father read   has   C°   to please
           (. . . that John has read the book to please his father)
    b. *. . . dat Jan *de Krant* beweert [dat Sam *t* leest]
           . . . that John the paper claimed that Sam   read
           (. . . that John claimed that Sam read the paper)

And similarly the remnants of a pseudogap cannot be embedded within an adjunct clause, as in (83a), nor may they be found within a finite complement clause, as in (83b):[40]

(83) a. *While Rusty might leave in order to please Mag, he won't ▲ his father.

   b. *While Doc might claim that O. J. Berman had read his book, he wouldn't ▲ the paper.

And finally, the class of terms that Scrambling may affect probably matches the range of terms that may remain after pseudogapping.[41] Verbal particles, for instance, typically make bad remnants for pseudogaps, as in (84); and they also resist Scrambling, as in (85):

(84) a. *While Perry might switch the TV OFF, he won't [e] ON.
   b. *I'll turn the radio DOWN, but I won't [e] UP.

(85) *... dat Jan de TV uit steeds   zet.
    ... that Jan the TV out all the time puts
    ... dat Jan de TV steeds   uit zet.
    ... that Jan the TV all the time out puts (Zwart 1993: 321)

There are other relevant cases to look at, but in outline it looks as though the pattern of remnants left by pseudogaps matches those that are able to Scramble out of VPs in Dutch. If pseudogapping is VP ellipsis, this finds an explanation: remnants are just those phrases able to move out of the elided VP.

Of course, this leaves the large problem of understanding how English avails itself of Scrambling in these contexts when it is otherwise unable to.[42] And there are other problems for reducing the phenomena of pseudogapping entirely to VP ellipsis. We have already seen (in (70)) that pseudogaps degrade considerably in fronted adverbials, relative to VP ellipsis. But perhaps this difference is related to the fact that in pseudogaps, but not elided VPs, there is an object that must be in a contrastive relationship with a parallel term in the antecedent clause. It is not unreasonable to expect the contrast condition we discussed in the previous section, for example, to be affected by this extra element. Note how much more awkward it is to contrast *rutabagas* in (86b) than it is in (86a):

(86) a. Fred likes eggplants, although he likes RUTABAGAS too.
   b. Although he likes RUTABAGAS too, Fred likes eggplants.

Perhaps, then, there is some fact about focus that makes the contrast condition more difficult to achieve for pseudogaps in fronted adverbials than it does for elided VPs.

Another puzzling way in which pseudogaps and VP ellipsis differ concerns the availability of "sloppy" readings for pronouns. Chris Kennedy points out (and credits the observation to Sag 1976) that the reading indicated for the elided VP in (87a) does not arise for the pseudogap in (87b):[43]

(87)   a.   Fred$_1$ gave flowers to his$_1$ sweetie because Frank$_2$ had ▲.
             ▲ = *given flowers to his$_2$ sweetie*
       b.   Fred$_1$ gave flowers to his$_1$ sweetie because Frank$_2$ had ▲ chocolates.
             ▲ ≠ *given to his$_2$ sweetie*

Pseudogaps do not seem to permit a sloppy reading for their pronouns: The only reading (87b) has is one in which Frank gave chocolates to Fred's sweetie. Perhaps here too, we can seek an account in the fact that pseudogaps invoke the contrast condition in a different way than elided VPs do. The contrast condition in both Rooth (1992a) and Fiengo and May (1994) plays a central role in determining when sloppy readings are available for pronouns, and so this seems a natural place to look for an explanation. At present, however, I cannot see how to give this speculation content.

Finally, it should be noted that, in general, pseudogapping is a much more marginal construction than VP ellipsis. Levin (1986) very carefully explores factors that appear to weaken the acceptability of pseudogaps but have no discernible effect on VP ellipsis. And, perhaps related, pseudogaps resist finding antecedents in other sentences, whereas VP ellipsis has no trouble doing this.[44] The discourse in (88) is decidedly worse than the discourse in (1)–(2):

(88)   a.   Holly won't eat rutabagas.
       b.   ??I don't think Fred will ▲ bananas either.

If a complete reduction of pseudogaps to VP ellipsis is to be successful, the extreme fragility of pseudogapping should be explained.

But if these differences in pseudogapping and VP ellipsis do turn out to be superficial, we have two reasons for doubting that pseudogapping can rescue us from the conclusion that examples like (57) and cases of Antecedent Contained Deletion reveal traces in elided VPs. First, there are some examples of these kinds for which a pseudogapping source is very dubious (namely: (73)). And second, it is not clear that pseudogaps are anything more than elided VPs with traces in them to begin with; the evidence reviewed above raises the suspicion that the remnants in pseudogaps have Scrambled from an elided VP. We might also remember that Kennedy's Generalization (in (39)) is amenable to the kind of account that May, Kennedy, and Heim explore only if instances of Antecedent Contained Deletions invoke traces in the ellipsis site. That is, this Generalization finds an account only if no instances of Antecedent Contained Deletions come by way of a process like that which Levin, Hardt, and others allege pseudogapping to be.

So far as I know, employing an account of pseudogapping which makes it independent of VP ellipsis is the only hope for avoiding the conclusion that elided VPs can contain a trace. To the extent that it fails, then, confidence in the derivational account of VP ellipsis strengthens.

Up to now, all the evidence we have reviewed appears to favor the derivational view of VP ellipsis. There are also facts, however, which have been taken to weigh against this view. Interestingly, though, the derivational approach must be wedded to an additional assumption for these facts to be seen as problematic. The additional assumption is that the "syntactic identity" condition introduced in the previous section requires the form of the elided VP to match perfectly the form of its antecedent VP. This is because these problematic facts are all cases where the antecedent VP could not be copied without change into the ellipsis site. These will then be problems for any theory that holds both (89i) and (89ii):

(89)   i.   An ellipsis site consists of a silent version of the phrase understood to be there.
        ii. The silent phrase in an ellipsis site is lexically and syntactically identical to its antecedent.

Recall that by "lexically and syntactically" we mean that the two VPs can differ with respect to the indices they host, but in no other way. (89i) and (89ii) are not so badly wedded, as most derivational approaches do embrace some sort of syntactic identity condition on antecedent and elided VPs. As might be expected, however, a rabid derivationalist will point to (89ii) as the source of trouble before pointing to (89i).

Let us look at some of these cases, and examine how far into (89) they cut. Some involve the presence of variables within an ellipsis site. Hardt (1993: sec. 2.4), for instance, points out that cases such as (90) should be expected to be ungrammatical under a derivational view:

(90)   a.   China is a country *that* Joe wants to visit *t*, and he will ▲ too, if he gets enough money. (from Webber 1978)
        b.   This is just the kind of thing *that* Harris could have suggested *t*. And in fact, he did ▲.
        c.   Harry is someone they would like to send *t* to the Olympics. And they will ▲ too, if they can finance it. (Hardt 1993: (21)–(22), 15–16)

If the antecedent VPs recycle their trace into the ellipsis site, the results should be on a par with (91):

(91)   a.   . . . he will [visit *t*] too, if he gets the money.
        b.   And in fact, he (did) [suggested *t*].
        c.   And they will [send *t* to the Olympics].

The examples in (91) are ungrammatical, of course, at least in part because they carry an unbound trace. (The form of the main verb in (91b) is also a source of ungrammaticality; we return to this.) But the examples in (90) are just fine. So if VP ellipsis is simply a way of disguising an otherwise normal VP, and antecedent VPs show us what the elided VPs look like, why is there a contrast between (90) and (91)?

A variety of answers appears possible. One, of course, would be to abandon the derivational approach altogether and adopt the analogy to pronominal anaphora which Hardt advises. But then the differences between pronominal anaphora and ellipsis reviewed above will have to be explained. This might be done, perhaps, by imagining that we simply chose the wrong pronouns to compare ellipsis to in the discussion above. Perhaps, for example, we should have analogized to the VP anaphor *do so*, which not only appears to be licensed in contexts like (90) – witness (92a) – but also invokes the Missing Antecedent effect, as can be seen from (92b):

(92) a.   China is a country that Joe wants to visit, and he will do so too, if he gets enough money.
    b.   Jerry wouldn't read a book by Babel, but Meryl has done so and *it* was pretty good.

Moreover, as Hardt points out, the ability of *do so* to license the Missing Antecedent effect suggests that our earlier account of this effect by way of a derivational interpretation of ellipsis is in danger.[45] So perhaps the case for the derivational account is unraveling.

Unfortunately, however, *do so* anaphora does not seem able to host a variable in the same way as VP ellipsis can; (93) contrasts with (57):

(93) a.   *I know which book Max read, and which book Oscar hasn't done so.
    b.   *This is the book of which Bill approves, and this is the one of which he can't do so.

So however it is that *do so* has the abilities that it does, it still fails to have the ones needed to subsume VP ellipsis. Unless some other pro-form can be found whose properties match those of ellipsis, this answer to the problem does not seem promising.

Another possibility would be to maintain that VP ellipsis hides a normal VP, and imagine that in (90) the moved phrase in the antecedent clause binds, somehow, the variable both in the antecedent VP and in the elided VP. That is, we might try to see in (90) the syntax of an across-the-board movement, maybe along the lines sketched in (94):

(94) a.   . . . a country [*that* [[Joe wants to visit *t*], and [he will ~~visit *t*~~ too]], if he gets enough money.
    b.   . . . the kind of thing [*that* [[Harris could have suggested *t*]. And [in fact, he did ~~suggest *t*~~]].
    c.   . . . someone *Op* they would like to send *t* to the Olympics. And they will [~~send *t* to the Olympics~~ too].

(The parses in (94b) and (94c) would require that the second apparently independent sentence be subordinated into the first.) This strategy would give to the rogue trace in the ellipsis site the very same binder as binds the trace in the antecedent VP. But while such an analysis may be possible for (90), it cannot be imported to the similar examples in (95):

(95)   a.   Joe might wish he had ~~visited a country~~, but this isn't a country he
            has visited *t*.
       b.   While I might want to ~~suggest this kind of thing~~, this is the kind of
            thing that Harris has already suggested *t*.

So this solution is not general enough.

A final possibility is the one foreshadowed above: abandon (89ii), the requirement that antecedent VPs are a reliable guide to the form that elided ones have. We have already seen in the previous section that the indices borne by parallel arguments in antecedent and elided VPs need not be identical. But that an additional weakening of (89ii) is needed is shown by examples as simple as (96):

(96)   We like our friends and they do ▲ too.

Here, if the elided VP were required to be absolutely identical to its antecedent, we would expect (96) to have only the meaning found in (97):

(97)   We like our friends and they like our friends too.

But (96) may also have the "sloppy" reading for the genitive pronoun, paraphrased by (98):

(98)   We like our friends and they$_1$ like their$_1$ friends, too.

That is, the genitive understood in the ellipsis can be third person, not the first person pronoun it is in the antecedent VP. Fiengo and May (1994) call the process which allows lexical mismatches of this sort "vehicle change." On their view, the phrases which serve as arguments are merely "vehicles" for the referential indices that come appended to them. These indices, they suggest, are what actually do the work of referring. The phrases they are attached to are not without their own semantic contribution, of course, but can be thought of nonetheless as extricable from the business of referring. As long as their own semantic contribution is minimal enough, they might be seen as interchangeable. Imagine, then, that one VP can act as antecedent for another's ellipsis if they are identical up to the vehicles which their arguments' indices come appended to. If so, perhaps the indices borne by the traces in (90) and (95) can trade those traces in for another vehicle, and thereby avoid violating the condition which guarantees that traces have binders. Fiengo and May suggest, concretely, that it is a resumptive pronoun which trades in for the trace in these examples.[46]

There is a variety of ways in which antecedent and elided VPs may differ, many of which might be amenable to a vehicle change treatment. For example, that (99a) fails to invoke the Binding Theoretic violation illustrated in (99b) when it gets the reading that (99c) paraphrases could be explained if reflexives can trade for pronouns under vehicle change:[47]

(99) a. Rusty$_1$ talked about himself$_1$ only after Holly$_2$ did ▲.
      b. *Rusty$_1$ talked about himself$_1$ only after Holly$_2$ did [talk about himself$_1$].
      c. Rusty$_1$ talked about himself$_1$ only after Holly$_2$ did [talk about him$_1$].

Fiengo and May offer this suggestion, and also explore the possibility that reflexive pronouns can come apart, allowing only the pronoun part to recon-struct into the ellipsis. Hestvik (1992b) offers still another account of these phenomena, which, however, has counter-examples in Hardt (1993: 20).

In these two cases, and others like them, vehicle change exchanges one DP for another of the same type. So in (90), for example, one variable (a trace) is traded for another (a resumptive pronoun). And in (99a), one pronoun (a reflexive) is traded for another (a non-reflexive). Fiengo and May suggest that vehicle change be constrained to changing the values of the Binding Theoretic features [pronoun] and [anaphor], which Chomsky (1981) suggests carve up the space of DP types. This would allow the exchanges we have reviewed, and applies to a variety of other like cases.[48]

There are, however, several situations where an elided VP differs from its antecedent, which cannot be accounted for by so constrained a vehicle change. In one of these, discussed by Sag (1976), a negative polarity item stands in an antecedent VP, but would not be permitted in the elided VP. An example from Hardt (1993) is (100):

(100) We haven't decided to blacklist any firms. But there's a chance we might ▲. (Hardt 1993: (68), 22)

If the antecedent VP in this example is faithfully copied into the ellipsis site, we would expect something as ungrammatical as (101):

(101) *But there's a chance we might [blacklist any firms].

What is required is for something on the order of (102) to be created:

(102) But there's a chance we might blacklist some firms.

A similar effect is found in (103):

(103) I could find no solution, but Holly might ▲.

In this case the elided VP is understood as (104):

(104)   ... but Holly might find a solution.

If vehicle change were to be extended to these sorts of case, it would have to be allowed to make changes to the quantifiers involved, but prevented from making arbitrary switches. We would not want to allow (105), for example, to be synonymous with (106):

(105)   Fred talked about everything before Rusty did ▲.

(106)   Fred talked about everything before Rusty did [talk about something].

It is probably no accident that in the cases where the quantificational force has changed (i.e., (100) and (103)), the fancier indefinites *"any* NP" and *"no* NP" are transformed into the plainer *"a* NP" or *"some* NP." It is perhaps not unimaginable that *"some* NP" or *"a* NP" might be seen as a component of *"any* NP" and *"no* NP." If so, it could be that the changes in quantifiers witnessed above involve a process that strips indefinites of their fancy part, leaving the vanilla *"a* NP" or *"some* NP" as residue. This direction to the problem is strengthened by the observation that (103) gets the reading indicated in (104) only when the antecedent clause has a meaning paraphrased by *I couldn't find a solution*, in which, note, negation has indeed been separated from the vanilla indefinite.

If it is unclear whether vehicle change can be extended to (100) and (103), it is clear that it cannot be so extended to a variety of other mismatches which ellipsis tolerates. Some of these mismatches are dramatic enough, in fact, to weaken (89ii) beyond its usefulness to the derivational approach. But others are amenable to, even supportive of, a derivational treatment.[49]

One of the unthreatening ones is the difference in inflectional class that various of our previous examples have illustrated. As in (107), these examples let a verb of one inflectional type act as antecedent for a verb bearing a different inflectional ending:

(107)   Joe will [go to the store], even though Fred already has [~~gone to the store~~].

These are understandable from a derivational standpoint, if we see verbs and their inflections as coming together during the course of the syntactic derivation. Granting this assumption, VP ellipsis can be seen acting at the stage in the derivation when antecedent and elided verb are in their stem form, and before their inflection causes them to differ. In (107), for example, ellipsis could act on *gone to the store* before *go* gets inflected.[50]

A similar strategy could arguably be employed in (those rare) cases where the antecedent does not match the elided VP in category. It is, for example, possible for an elided VP to take an NP as its antecedent, as in (108), from Hardt:

(108) a. David Begelman is a great [laugher], and when he does ▲, his eyes
crinkle at you the way Lady Brett's did in *The Sun Also Rises*. (from
You'll Never Eat Lunch in This Town Again)

b. Today there is little or no *OFFICIAL* [harassment of lesbians and
gays] by the national government, although autonomous govern-
ments might ▲.

c. The candidate was dogged by charges of infidelity and [avoiding
the draft], or at least trying to ▲. (Hardt 1993: (111), (117), and
(120), 34–5)

In these cases, note, the NP which acts as antecedent (bracketed in each case)
is deverbal. If, as seems increasingly likely, deverbal nouns of this sort are
constructed in the course of the syntactic derivation, then there is a representation in which the verbal portion of this noun exists without its nominalizer.
Imagine, for instance, that underlying (108b) is a representation like (109):

(109)

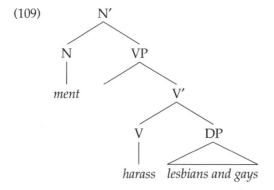

In (109) the required antecedent VP is embedded within the nominal; as in
(90), it exists before movement has applied, in this case to form the deverbal
noun. Perhaps, then, it is this VP which serves as antecedent to the ellipses in
(108).

This is the solution that Fu et al. (1996) explore, and it has the apparently
correct outcome that only deverbal nouns can act as antecedents to elided VPs.
The examples in (108) contrast sharply with those in (110):

(110) a. *David Begelman is a great [artist], and when he does ▲, his eyes
crinkle at you.

b. *The candidate was dogged by charges of [infidelity], or at least
trying to ▲.

This follows because the NPs in (110) have no verbal part, hence lack the
crucial VP.

Perhaps something along these lines could also be put to use in explaining
the fact that passive VPs can antecede active ones:

(111) a. This information could have been released by Gorbachev, but he chose not to ▲.

  b. A lot of this material can be presented in a fairly informal and accessible fashion, and often I do ▲. (Hardt 1993: (131), (134), 37)

And to a slightly less extent, it is also possible for active VPs to serve as antecedents to passive ones:

(112) ?John fired Max, although it was Bill who should have been ▲. (Fiengo and May 1994: 203, n. 10)

If we adopt the commonplace view of the passive/active alternation that it involves a syntactic derivation relating one to the other, we can find a point in this derivation at which antecedent and elided VPs are identical. For example, the first clause in (111a) has an underlying representation whose VP looks something like (113):

(113)

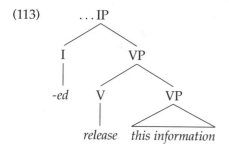

And this VP matches the one elided in (111a).

Nothing quite as simple is possible in (112), where an active VP serves as antecedent for a passive one. This is because even the underlying form of the passive VP (shown in (114)) does not match its active antecedent:

(114)

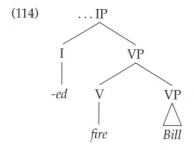

Instead, this case emerges as a special instance of the pseudogapping construction, at least if this construction is a form of VP ellipsis as outlined above. Recall that pseudogaps arise by virtue of emptying a VP-to-be-elided of the phrase which surfaces as remnant. Though we did not touch upon this at the time, this account of pseudogaps requires that the antecedent clause also be able to have that very same form. So, for instance, the antecedent clause in (69a), repeated below, must also be able to be parsed so that the object (*Fred*) has Scrambled out of the VP:

(115)   While O. J. Berman read Fred, he didn't ▲ Dickens.

This is because the elided VP in (115) has the form [$_{VP}$ *read t*] (created by Scrambling *Dickens* out of the VP), which must be matched by a VP in the antecedent clause. Hence, *Fred* must also Scramble in (115). If true, this is not apparent in the overt form of these examples. But, in keeping with the derivational approach, it is conceivable that the LF representation for the antecedent clause has the object Scrambled out of the VP, producing the requisite antecedent. If that is possible in examples like (69a) (= (115)), then in cases like (112) too, it is conceivable that the antecedent clause hosts an invisible Object Scrambling. If the object in the antecedent clause of (112) were Scrambled, a VP of the form "[$_{VP}$ *fire t*]" would be produced, and this is just what is required to match the passivized VP in the ellipsis site.

So in these few cases, there are derivational solutions to the mismatch in antecedent and elided VPs. The accounts of these cases sketched here, then, would rescue the derivational approach to ellipsis by weakening the syntactic identity condition just to the extent that vehicle change allows. So far as I can see, then, these facts do not provide grounds for entirely abandoning either (89i) or (89ii). (In fact, it may be possible to see an argument for (89i) and (89ii) in the restriction to deverbal nouns that the mismatches in (108) illustrate.)

But there are other mismatches which are difficult to reconcile with a strict syntactic identity condition, and which do not fall under even a weakened version of this constraint. A very simply case of this sort, and one that is widely discussed, occurs when there is no apparent linguistic antecedent to the ellipsis at all, as in (116):[51]

(116)   [Mabel Minerva, a Central Park rental horse, begins galloping at full speed with the terrified Fred atop.]
        Fred: "No, no! Don't ▲!"

Where is the identical VP that is recovered in the ellipsis site of such examples? Does it not seem more reasonable to imagine that the ellipsis in such a case is a silent demonstrative, similar, perhaps, to *do that*? A typical response from the derivational camp is to deny the cavalier assumption that linguistic objects always result in speech. Perhaps there is a VP of the right form in (116) to antecede the ellipsis, but one that has simply gone unspoken. Or maybe discourses of this sort are sufficient to license an ellipsis of *do that*.

A more difficult kind of counter-example, however, involves cases where the elided VP has split antecedents, as in (117) from Bonnie Webber (1978):

(117) Wendy is eager to sail around the world and Bruce is eager to climb Kilimanjaro, but neither of them can ▲ because money is too tight.

In these cases the elided VP has the content of none of the VPs occurring previously but seems instead to have cobbled together a meaning from the material in all those VPs. In (117), this material is brought together to form something close in meaning to *sail around the world or climb Kilimanjaro*. Obviously, then, there is no VP here which matches that of the elided one.[52]

So it is not unequivocal, but I think the evidence slouches towards the derivational interpretation of VP ellipsis. At the outset, I linked this interpretation of ellipsis with the ECP based account of where phrases can elide. This might be achieved, I suggested, if we saw the traces left by movement operations – whose distribution the ECP was designed to account for – as made of the same stuff as ellipses are. That is, if we conclude that ellipsis sites are made up of silent syntactic phrases, and not pro-forms, then we could see the similar distribution of traces and ellipsis sites as evidence that traces too are silent syntactic phrases. We could see in this evidence for the Copy and Delete interpretation of movement that Chomsky (1995b) champions.

But it is now clear that this linkage itself has been put at risk by the evidence reviewed above. While the mismatches between antecedent and elided VPs may not close the door on a derivational approach to ellipsis, they do make the strict syntactic identity condition on ellipsis look impossible. Traces, on the other hand, are thought to normally obey a very strict syntactic identity condition with their antecedent: a moved phrase is understood to be exactly the phrase that the trace constitutes. So if we hope to find the theory that determines where ellipses can be in the theory that determines where traces are, we would not be encouraged to do so by letting ellipsis sites and traces be the same thing.[53]

Instead, it seems to me that the most promising way to bring together the questions we have considered here is to, first, adopt an account of VP ellipsis that involves moving the elided VP, as outlined in the first section. This will derive the apparent match between movement and VP ellipsis, without committing us to an outright equation of ellipsis sites with traces. Second, we should abandon an account that sees elided VPs as kinds of null pro-form, for the reasons outlined in this final section. Instead we should seek answers to the (connected) questions: "What is an elided VP?" and "How is it licensed?" by turning to the other members of the ellipsis family: sluicing and N'-deletion. Here we will not be misled into thinking of the ellipsis sites as traces, because – apparently – these are ellipses whose licensing conditions are satisfied in situ. Recall that elided NPs and IPs do not arise in places where moved NPs and IPs do; maybe, then, this is because the conditions on ellipsis are nothing like those on movement. VP ellipsis misled us into thinking so because VP ellipsis involves moving the elided VP.

An elided VP is neither a pro-form nor a trace. It is a creature apart. And if we want to know why it is the way it is, we should look at the other members of its species.

NOTES

* The level of this chapter has been considerably raised by the flood of comments I have received from Mark Baltin, Sigrid Beck, Chris Collins, Dan Hardt, Roger Higgins, Chris Kennedy, Anne Lobeck, Jason Merchant, Orin Percus, Eric Potsdam, and Satoshi Tomioka.

1 That *not* is the licensor in this configuration is shown by the contrasting ungrammaticality of **John is leaving, and Mary's ▲ too.*

2 And see Williams (1994a) and Potsdam (1997).

3 See Bresnan (1976) for an early discussion of this contrast. Lobeck accounts for this by restricting the licensing head government to terms that can have access to tense, something that main verbs are prevented from doing.

4 Lobeck and Zagona adopt the conditions on head movement that Chomsky (1986b) advocates. Lobeck's proposal has empirical consequences very close to that of Napoli (1985), who treats the stranded tensed auxiliaries as the anaphoric items in VP ellipsis.

5 Jason Merchant points out (personal communication) that there are examples parallel to these which are significantly better:

(i) Don't start the motor unless you're sure you know how to.

(ii) Decorating for the holidays is easy if you know how to!

He suggests that we should review this paradigm with constraints on "sprouting" in mind. "Sprouting" is the name Chung et al. (1995) give to the process in sluicing by which a trace can be generated in an elided IP that is not matched by a parallel term in the antecedent IP. (iii) illustrates:

(iii) I know we should solve this problem, but I don't know how.

If VP ellipsis does not allow Sprouting, then we might see the variation in the *Wh*-Island Constraint under examination as actually reflecting whether the *wh*-phrase in these examples must bind a sprouted trace in the elided VP. See Lobeck (1995: 175ff) for a brief exploration of this idea.

6 She makes use of innovations to the Empty Category Principle that Rizzi (1990) offers; see Lobeck (1995: 177). She also suggests that (10b, c) are blocked by the inability of elided VPs to host the variable that the *wh*-phrases in these examples require. The second clause in the title of my chapter shows that this cannot be generally true, however.

7 Mark Baltin points out that (i) is rather good, and a counter-example to this generalization:

(i) For Mary to leave wouldn't bother me, but [for Sally to ▲] would.

This is more in line with Zagona's description of the phenomenon, as in this situation *to* could get into licensing proximity to *for* without being brought out of the clausal subject.

8 Potsdam (1996b) proposes a similar scheme, but measures "closeness' in terms of Grimshaw's (1997) extended projections.

9 See Akmajian and Wasow (1975), Iwakura (1977), Akmajian et al. (1979), Huddleston (1978), Sag (1976), and Warner (1993), among others.

10 An observation of Sag's (1976: 29). And see Zagona (1988b), Lobeck (1987a), and Johnson (1988) for some discussion.

11 And this project should be informed by the sorts of crosslinguistic variation ellipsis tolerates. With respect to VP ellipsis, some of this variation is discussed in the cited works by Zagona and Lobeck, as well as McCloskey (1991) and López (1994).

12 There is some variability in the judgments, the source of which I cannot determine. Lobeck (1995), for instance, suggests that VP ellipsis within infinitival complements to nouns is grammatical, and offers (i) as evidence:

(i) John's decision to run was unexpected, but Bill's decision to ▲ was completely predictable.

(ii) Mary wanted to cheat on the exam, but she failed in her attempt to ▲. (Lobeck 1995: (62)–(63), 185)

The second of these examples does, indeed, sound rather good. The first, note, would also be a counter-example to VP ellipsis's susceptibility to the Subject Condition. Chris Kennedy provides other examples which seem to be an improvement:

(iii) Sally explained why we were going to arrest Holly only after the decision to ▲ had already been made.

(iv) My attempts to solve this puzzle are outmatched only by my desire to ▲.

Kennedy suggests that the comparative improvement these examples get should be related to the fact that these nouns are very verb-like.

13 It is necessary to understand the infinitive in (26a) as a rationale clause, i.e., as an adjunct; otherwise the sentence is grammatical, as expected. On Lobeck's approach, this paradigm would be captured by letting the government chain extend from *to* to the auxiliary verb(s) that follow(s).

14 As Ross (1967a) observes.

15 I owe this observation to Roger Higgins. Perhaps the exceptional licensing ability of *not* is connected to its ability to license the ellipsis in (i) (compare (ii)):

(i) Mag left, and not Sally ▲.

(ii) ?*Mag left, and Sally ▲.

Anne Lobeck suggests, in fact, that Baltin's "predicate ellipsis," which affects a wider class of phrases than just VPs (as in (6), for example) is in fact a different process than VP ellipsis – it does not meet the diagnostic properties of VP ellipsis that she catalogues (see Lobeck 1995: sec. 1.2). Because predicate ellipsis is licensed by *not*, there is the additional possibility that (30) is an instance of it.

16 See Ross (1967b).

17 And see Wasow (1972: 88ff).

18 See Hardt (1997) for additional discussion.

19 See Kennedy (1994). The (b)-example comes from Heim (1997), but represents cases Kennedy discusses.

20 The example he discusses is *Dulles suspected everyone who knew Philby, who Angleton did* ▲, which differs somewhat from the Kennedy/Sag examples, but falls under the generalization in (39).

21 This strategy requires that the index borne by the silent relative pronoun is not "accidentally" the same as that borne by the trace reconstructed into its scope.

22 The pronoun *he* is taken to be coreferent with the trace bound by the relative pronoun. On any other interpretation, this example falls into the case illustrated by (37a), and is ungrammatical.

23 See Tancredi (1992) and Fox (forthcoming) for attempts to collapse these two conditions.

24 See, for instance, Rooth (1992b).

25 At least it will if it is strengthened to prevent x and γ from getting exactly the same assignments from g (i.e., force x and γ to contrast).

26 Understand *she* in (53) to be non-coreferent with *Mag*. The subscript "F" indicates that the item it is attached to receives focus; in the cases at hand, this means that these items will have prominent accent.

27 Neither the contrast condition in (52), nor the particular way it is put to use in these examples, is faithful in details to Heim. I hope, however, that it is close enough to convey her proposal accurately.

28 See Heim's paper for details. As she notes, her technique will not extend to cases like Wasow's (i). Cases like Wasow's (i):

(i) [A proof that God$_2$ does ▲]$_1$ [t_1 exists].

29 Fiengo and May (1994) have a view similar to Wasow's.

30 Though note, as Bresnan does, that it is possible to find an antecedent for *it* in (56) through simple deduction. This, perhaps, explains the improvement (56) enjoys with thought; see Postal (1972) where this effect is elevated to a challenge to Bresnan's interpretation of the (55)/(56) contrast.

31 This argument for the derivational approach can be found in Tancredi (1992), and goes back at least to Chao (1987), who nonetheless holds the pro-form view of VP ellipsis.

32 Haïk (1987) and Kennedy and Merchant (1997) suggest that when the ellipsis would contain the island, the normal degradation associated with island violations is lost. Consider, by way of illustration, the examples in (i), which I owe to Dan Hardt:

(i) I know John explained why he wrote a letter to Susan, and I know Bill explained why he wrote a letter to Mary,
  a. ?but I don't know who Harry did ▲.
     ▲ = *explain why he wrote a letter to t*
  b. *but I don't know who Harry explained why he wrote a letter to.

Indeed, (ia) does sound better than the parallel (ib) and (59). Merchant and Kennedy suggest that this contrast can be accounted for by letting the island constraints hold before the ellipsis is resolved, and to let the ellipsis site itself be bound to the relevant operator. After the ellipsis is resolved, the operator will then pick up its "real" variable. In this way the island effects will be preserved between operator and ellipsis site, but not between the operator and (reconstructed) trace.

Still, in some cases I do find a contrast of the sort denied in (i):

(ii) a. ?I know that Rusty Trawler had met with SOMEone, but exactly WHO only FRED does.
  b. *I know whether Rusty Trawler had met with SOMEone, but exactly WHO only FRED does.
  c. *I read the report that Rusty had met with SOMEone, but exactly WHO only FRED did.

d. *I left after Rusty met with SOMEone, but exactly WHO only FRED did.

33 These cases were introduced by Bouton (1970), who suggested an account not too different from the one relied on by Dan Hardt, and reviewed below.

34 But see Baltin (1987) and Wyngærd and Zwart (1991) for interesting alternatives.

35 See Holmberg (1986), Déprez (1989), and Vikner (1995).

36 Indeed, it is in the context of Antecedent Contained Deletion that Haïk demonstrated island effects:

(i) *John met everyone that Peter wondered when he could ▲. (Haïk 1987: (18), 511)

37 (73b) and (73d) also speak against Hornstein's account of Antecedent Contained Deletion, which, recall, assimilates it to Object Shift. Object Shift is unable to strand a preposition, and this is what would be required of it in (73b); nor is it able to move noun phrases out of other noun phrases, as is necessary in (73d). (Examples illustrating the facts I report here about Object Shift can be found in Holmberg 1986.) This is Kennedy's 1997 point – that Object Shift is not the source of Antecedent Contained Deletion – but his arguments cut against a pseudogapping source for them as well.

38 Kuno (1981), for instance, marks cases like these ungrammatical.

39 The exception to this is the Scrambling of "R-pronouns," discussed in van Riemsdijk (1982); but modern English does not have this phenomenon (except in sluicing contexts).

40 The contrasts in the text would seem to be at odds with the Haïk/

Kennedy and Merchant interpretation – described in n. 32 – of the island effects which arise in ellipsis examples. If pseudogapping is indeed VP ellipsis from which the remnant has extracted, then the ungrammaticality of these examples suggests that there is an island-effect holding of the remnant and the island in the ellipsis. The situation described in n. 32 involved redirecting the island effects so that they held on the relationship between the moved term and the ellipsis. This would not correctly hold for these examples if the judgments I have reported in the text are correct, though this technique could be employed to explain examples like Lobeck's.

41 Though there is plenty of fussing needed for this to come out accurately. So, for instance, Chris Collins notes that finite clauses make fine remnants from pseudogapping, but cannot Scramble in the Germanic languages. Perhaps this discrepancy could be shored up by considering the surface conditions that influence Scrambling – perhaps there is a ban against placing finite clauses in the middle field of German clauses (see, for instance, Stowell 1981). Jason Merchant notes (personal communication) that secondary predicates are incapable of undergoing long distance Scrambling in German and Dutch, but that they too make fine remnants for pseudogapping. It is more difficult to see how this discrepancy can be overcome. One possibility would be to see the constraints on Scrambling making a distinction between long distance and clause bound cases; it may be possible, especially under Zwart (1993a), to see secondary predicates

as undergoing local Scrambling. All that would be needed for the current proposal is for the phrases that can be remnants for pseudogapping to be susceptible to local Scrambling. I do not see presently, however, how this maneuver can preserve the ban against stranding a particle in pseudogapping.

42   Lasnik (1995f) offers a suggestion on this point, but not one that easily accommodates to the long distance cases in (78) and (79).

43   A similar example, but one that involves the relationship between a pronoun and the object, is:

(i)   Mag introduced Sally$_2$ to his$_2$ attorney after Joe did ▲ José$_3$.
      ▲ ≠ *introduced to his$_3$ attorney.*

44   Thanks to Sally McConnell-Ginet and Anne Lobeck for this observation.

45   Hankamer and Sag (1976) make the same point: the Missing Antecedent phenomenon does not appear to be diagnostic of non-pro-forms.

46   This would mean, as they note, that the locality conditions we have witnessed in (59) must hold of resumptive pronouns as well as traces, assuming that vehicle change is available in this scenario as well. See Kennedy (to appear) for an extension of this idea to apparent examples of parasitic gaps within elided VPs (on which also see Kim and Lyle 1996).

47   See Sag (1976), Dalrymple et al. (1991), and Hardt (1993) for a discussion of cases like these.

48   See Fiengo and May (1994: 218ff), and Wyngærd and Zwart (1991) for an application to Antecedent Contained Deletion.

49   One class of interesting cases, which bear on the strictness of the syntactic identity condition between antecedent and elided VPs, involves the scope of quantifiers. As Sag (1976) discussed, there are certain situations where the scope of a quantifier in the *antecedent* VP is influenced by the ellipsis it supports. For example, the wide-scope reading for *everyone* in (i) is lost when it supports the ellipsis in (ii):

(i)   Someone loves everyone.

(ii) Mary doesn't ▲.

Sag thought this was always true, and built his version of the syntactic identity condition around facts of this sort. But Hirschbühler (1982) introduces examples which show that this is not the case; in (iii), for example, *many buildings* may have widest scope in the left conjunct:

(iii) A Canadian flag is in front of many buildings and an American flag is ▲ too.

Fox (1995) develops an approach to Quantifier Raising that will allow this effect to be derived from the syntactic identity condition, whereas Tomioka (1997) develops an approach which derives it from the contrast condition.

50   See Lasnik (1995a) for this idea, and for evidence that auxiliary verbs differ on this score; and see Potsdam (1996a) for problems with Lasnik's characterization of the main verb/ auxiliary verb distinction, and an alternative account based on processing considerations.

51   First famously observed in Schachter (1977b).

52   In general, these instances of split antecedence seem best in contexts where the antecedent VPs are in conjoined clauses. This has led Fiengo and May (1994: 194–200)

to propose that the operation responsible for coordination is itself equipped with the power of fashioning the elided VP in these cases. See Hardt (1997) for a different approach.

53 On the other hand, Hardt (1993) points out that in cases where movement relates a VP to a trace, there are mismatches which look somewhat like those we have just reviewed. For instance, in (ia), there appears to be an invocation of vehicle change; and in (ib) we appear to have a case of split antecedence:

(i) a. We wanted to phone our parents, which Harry also did.

(= We wanted to phone our parents, and Harry wanted to phone his parents.)

b. John wanted to go to India and Harry wanted to go to China, which it turned out they couldn't.

I do not find these fully grammatical, however. Instead, they sound to me as if they are of the same register that allows:

(ii) I've been considering going to Denver, which I don't know whether it is such a good idea.

in which *which* has the syntax of a coordinator. If so, then (i) could involve VP ellipsis, rather than true VP relatives.

IV   Functional Projections

15 Agreement Projections

ADRIANA BELLETTI

1 A Brief History of the Node Agr: Infl, Agr, and T

That clause structure cannot simply be reduced to a configuration involving one major ramification formalizing the subject–predicate relation is not a new idea in the field of generative grammar. It has been present since its beginnings in Chomsky's (1957) *Syntactic Structures*, where a position is generated between the NP subject and the VP predicate to host modals, auxiliaries, and the (few) affixes constituting the paradigm of English verbal morphology. Although the independence (at some level of representation) of verbal morphology and the particular lexical choice of the verb of the clause soon became apparent, its formal and empirical role was obscured, in the 1960s and 1970s, by the common practice of representing clause structure as essentially consisting of the subject–predicate relation, as in the standard rewriting rule S → NP VP. The more or less implicit assumption at the time was that languages displaying a special category of "modals" and "auxiliaries" should involve more formal structure mediating the relation. English[1] was considered a case in point, and nothing in particular was assumed in more general terms. It was only with the "Principles and Parameters" (P&P) approach that the assumption was generalized and taken to be a property of Universal Grammar (UG). The "modal" category of English makes something visible that is always present and may be left less visible (or even invisible) in other languages. With this more or less implicit assumption in mind, a more articulated clause structure was introduced in Chomsky's (1981) *Lectures on Government and Binding*, where the subject–predicate relation is systematically mediated by a functional node labeled Infl(ection), assumed to contain the grammatical information normally associated with the verb such as, typically, tense, mood, and agreement features/affixes.[2] The more articulated clause structure which emerges, and which has been assumed in much work done in P&P terms, is schematized by the rewriting rule: S → NP Infl VP.

One aspect of the format of UG which has been particularly developed within P&P is the X′-module. The leading idea is that phrase structure should not allow for any freedom in the general X′-schema, which thus serves as a rigid constraint. In particular, there should be no room for exocentric projections. Optimally, the clause should not constitute an exception to this general claim. The rule generating clause structure referred to above does not conform to the X′-schema. The idea naturally suggested itself, then, that the clause could also be taken to be an endocentric projection if the node Infl could be considered its head.[3] S can consequently be viewed as a regular maximal projection of I(nflection), the IP (Chomsky 1986b).

It was only in the late 1980s and early 1990s that the more precise nature of Infl became a much debated field of research on its own from at least two main points of view: a conceptual one and an empirical one. On the conceptual side, it appeared that a single head should not be allowed to contain several different sets of features, as was assumed for the Infl head. A head should rather correspond to one single morpheme; if it contains more, this should be the result of the head movement operation, yielding an incorporation configuration. On the empirical side, it appeared that some proposals in Emonds (1978) concerning the respective location of verb and negation could be developed in terms of the assumption of a verb movement operation, as in Emonds's original analysis, such that the differences between English and French in this respect could be interpreted in novel terms and given a straightforward account. These novel terms should imply a more articulated conception of clause structure, ultimately of the nature of the node Infl. Pollock's fundamental contribution in his influential 1989 article played a crucial role in this regard. Pollock's proposal, which has come to be known as the "Split-Infl hypothesis," had the interesting property of simultaneously meeting the conceptual desideratum and empirical adequacy.

The basic lines of Pollock's argument can be summarized as follows. Following Emonds's original proposal, the difference between English and French with respect to the position of the negation (*not* and *pas* respectively) and the lexical verb could be due to the fact that the verb moves out of the VP in French but not in English. Rather, in English an auxiliary (*do*) appears, filling the same position occupied by the lexical verb in French. The basic paradigm concerning the distribution of negation in finite clauses, reviewed in (1)–(4), is thus accounted for through the assumption described for verb movement:

(1)   Jean n'aime pas Marie.

(2)   *John likes not Mary.

(3)   John does not like Mary.

(4)   *Jean ne pas aime Marie.

It is well known, however, that the situation is far more complex since, internally to French, the lexical verb appears to have a non-uniform behavior once non-finite clauses are taken into account. While it appears not to undergo movement when the negative adverb *pas* is considered, it does appear to move if other adverbs are considered. The adverb typically used to illustrate the point in this respect is the adverb *souvent*, which is allowed to follow the lexical verb in both finite and non-finite clauses. However, if compared to English, the situation appears to be contradictory, since in the latter language the lexical verb follows both the negation, as we have just seen, and an adverb like *often*. (5)–(15) illustrate the relevant paradigms:

(5)   Jean rencontre souvent Marie.

(6)   Jean essaye de souvent rencontrer Marie.

(7)   Jean essaye de rencontrer souvent Marie.

(8)   Jean essaye de ne pas rencontrer Marie.

(9)   *Jean essaye de ne rencontrer pas Marie.

(10)   John often meets Mary.

(11)   *John meets often Mary.

(12)   John tries to often meet Mary.

(13)   *John tries to meet often Mary.

(14)   John tries not to meet Mary.

(15)   *John tries to meet not Mary.

Putting aside in this context the question of the apparent optionality of movement of the verb in French infinitives which (6) and (7) illustrate, the crucial conflicting data in French concern the contrast between (7) and (9). While the infinitival lexical verb should be taken not to move if its position with respect to the negation *pas* is considered, it must be taken to move if its position is looked at with respect to the adverb *souvent*. The situation internal to English looks more coherent, since the lexical verb appears not to move with respect to both adverbial classes.[4] These contradictory data found a coherent explanation with Pollock's idea that there is more than one head inflectional position where the verb moves or does not move. If the assumption is made that there are (at least) two inflectional positions which can host the verb, a rational account becomes available. Assume that the position filled by the negation is higher in the clause structure than that filled by an adverb like *souvent*. Assume further that the verb either can or must reach one of the two inflectional positions. The possibility of a complex paradigm becomes available and the English/French contrast receives the following interpretation:

(16) a. **English:** Lexical verbs never move either to the higher or to the lower inflectional position. (Only modals and auxiliaries fill the higher inflectional head.)

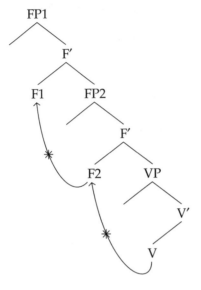

b. **French:** Lexical verbs obligatorily move to the higher inflectional position in finite clauses and optionally move to the lower inflectional position in non-finite clauses.[5]

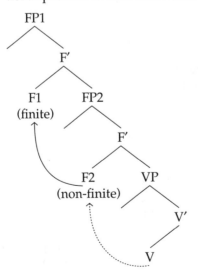

Assuming that the position filled by negation is immediately below the high-est inflectional head available for the verb, and that the one filled by an adverb like *souvent* is immediately below the lowest one, the hypotheses in (16a, b) generate the articulated paradigm above, as can be computed, modulo obligatoriness vs. optionality of the movement.

The following questions arise: what is the nature of the two assumed inflec-tional heads? How can Infl be split? In Pollock's article the proposal was put forward that the crucial role should be played by the features which typically compose finite verbal morphology. In Romance these are typically features of Tense and Agreement, as the French and Italian example of the imperfect indicative clearly illustrates:[6]

(17) Ils parl-ai-ent;   parla-va-no
       They-spoke-Imperf (they)-spoke-Imperf

The single node Infl should best be split into two separate nodes each corres-ponding to the set of Tense and Agreement features, respectively. Now, since the clause is considered an endocentric IP projection of I, it should now rather be seen as the projection of both Agreement and Tense, both interpreted as heads in X'-terms. The hypothesis as to which one of the two heads should be taken to be the highest in the structure, so that the clause should be the max-imal projection of either one, has not been initially uniform.[7] It is now generally assumed that the clause should be interpreted as an AgrP maximal projection of Agr, the TP projection of T being the complement of Agr. In terms of the X'-schema, the basic structure which results is that in (18):

(18)

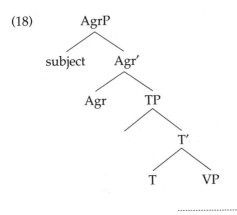

with the subject noun phrase filling the position of Spec/AgrP and the first lexical projection being the VP, complement of T.[8]

Movement of the verb to the highest functional head is then movement to Agr. What the relevant property of an Agr attracting the verb should be is not an easy question to answer. Various attempts have been made in the literature to formulate a notion of "strength" of Agr to be associated with an "attracting" Agr, the most integrated one being that proposed in Chomsky (1995). Although the correlation between "overtness" of inflectional features and attracting property of Agr cannot be established in trivial terms, some crucial role must ultimately be played by it. See the discussion in Belletti (1990); see also Vikner (1997) for a more precise attempt to express the correlation.[9]

Thus, the first Agr projection proposed in the literature is the clause.

2   Agreement Heads in Finite Clauses: AgrS, AgrO . . .

The grammatical features that are contained within Agr are those appearing on the verb entering the subject–verb agreement relation manifested in finite clauses.[10] According to the structure in (18), such an agreement relation does not hold between the subject and the verb directly but is rather mediated through the node Agr. Thus, properly speaking, the phenomenon of subject–verb agreement comes out as the result of two operations: the agreement relation between the subject in Spec/AgrP and the Agr head, plus the realization of the features of Agr on the verb.[11] The Spec–head relation is generally interpreted, both in P&P and within current minimalist assumptions, as a relation of "agreement" in the particular sense of a relation such that the element in Spec and the head share the same features.[12] Probably the most typical manifestation of this relation is the one holding between the subject and Agr, where the features involved are those of person and number, as far as finite verbal morphology is concerned.[13]

Another feature which is currently assumed to be involved in the subject–Agr relation is Case. Agr (or rather Agr+T) carries nominative in finite clauses.[14] Hence, the "agreement" relation directly established through the configuration with its Spec assigns/checks nominative with the subject noun phrase.

In Chomsky (1995b: chs 2, 3) the idea is generalized that the phi-feature Case is systematically checked within an "agreement" configuration involving the mediation of an Agr head. The fact that Case and "agreement" involving other phi-features (e.g. "gender") often "go together" in languages with overt Case morphology provides plausibility to this general hypothesis.[15] However, its generality implies some major change in the conception of clause structure assumed thus far. The most important one is related to the checking procedure of accusative Case, the Case for the direct object in nominative–accusative languages. If an Agr head mediates Case checking under the "agreement" relation, another AgrP projection must be present in the clause to host Case checking for objects. To the extent that accusative is a property of the verb associated to its transitivity, the relevant Agr projection should be found around the VP area. This leads to the introduction of another Agr projection surrounding the VP. This "low" Agr projection is generally referred to as AgrOP, O = object, to distinguish it from the already known higher one, symmetrically referred to as AgrSP, S = subject. Notice that these abbreviations are just given for convenience, since any Agr head is taken to be a collection of phi-features. A clause structure such as the one in (19) thus emerges (details aside):

(19)

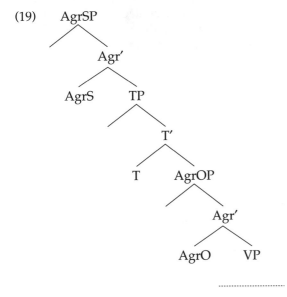

Much as nominative Case is checked in Spec/AgrS of finite tensed clauses under the "agreement" relation, so accusative is checked in Spec/AgrO of clauses containing a transitive verb.[16]

As is easy to see, this geometry implies several consequences. Let us mention two important ones: (i) to the extent that the Case feature of a transitive verb is checked through head movement of the verb into AgrO, V must be assumed to move out of the VP in all languages, at least as far as AgrO; (ii) if accusative Case on the object is checked in Spec/AgrOP, this implies that objects should also move out of VP.[17] Both conclusions require important departures from current assumptions in P&P and also in early formulations of the "Split-Infl" hypothesis. As for the first implication, the hypothesis must combine with the supplementary assumption that Verb movement is either "covert" LF movement or does not go further than AgrO in those English-type languages where it has been assumed to remain in VP, following the by now traditional account of the French/English contrasts reviewed in section 1. As for the second implication, object movement to Spec/AgrO is necessarily "covert" LF movement in those English-type languages displaying (at most) "short" verb movement (to AgrO), while it can be overt in those French-Italian-type languages displaying "long" verb movement. This is so since the final (unmarked) word order of these VO languages is always VO and never OV: *Yesterday I met John/*Yesterday I John met.*[18]

With these considerations in mind, the proposal can be elaborated that (structural) Case checking is part of an "agreement" relation between a noun phrase filling the Spec position and the relevant Agr head. This is the outline of some basic ideas which have lead to the first Minimalist approach to Case theory.

Among the Romance languages, some display overt agreement in phi-features on the verb past participle in particular syntactic configurations. French and Italian are the best studied and most discussed cases.[19] Some representative occurrences of the phenomenon are illustrated in (20)–(27):

(20) Voici les chaises que j'ai repeintes.
      Here are the chairs that I have repainted.

(21) Je les ai repeintes.
      I them-Cl have repainted.

(22) Combien de chaises as-tu repeintes?
      How many chairs have-you repainted?

(23) Les chaises ont été repeintes par moi tout seul.
      The chairs have been repainted by me alone.

(24) Dans cet incident, les femmes sont mortes avant les hommes.
      In this accident the women died before the men.

(25) Le ragazze sono arrivate alle 5.
      The girls arrived at 5.

(26) Le sedie, le ho ridipinte io.
      The chairs, I them-Cl have repainted myself.

(27) (Una volta) ridipinte le sedie, me ne andrò.
      (Once) repainted the chairs, I will go.

In Kayne (1989a) the proposal was put forward for the first time that the phi-features of gender and number appearing on the past participle should be considered the reflex of an established "agreement" relation between the past participle and the moved noun phrase or clitic. The natural assumption to make is that an Agr projection is among the functional projections which surround the past participle and that the moved constituent triggers agreement in its passing through its Spec.

According to this hypothesis a further Agr projection is present in the clause structure, which can be labelled AgrPstPrtP, for convenience. Although there was initially a certain amount of incertitude over the question of whether the same Agr head should be considered responsible for both accusative Case checking and past participle agreement, the idea has become fairly wide spread that the two Agr heads should be distinguished and left separate, as they serve independent requirements.[20] Central in this connection are the observations, on the one side, that assignment/checking of accusative Case is completely independent of presence/absence of a past participial morphology, either overt or covert and, on the other, that past participle agreement is activated independently of presence of accusative Case assignment/checking (cf. presence of past participle agreement with unaccusative past participles; lack of past participle agreement with transitive past participles whose object does not undergo cliticization).

Clause structure is thus enriched with at least three Agr-type projections: AgrS, AgrO, and AgrPstPrt. What all three Agr-heads have in common is the fact of carrying phi-features which undergo (morphological) checking with a noun phrase filling the Spec of the relevant Agr projection, in syntax or LF.[21]

Putting aside the questions related to the presence and the location of other functional categories and their projections in the clause structure, such as NegP, AspP, and ModP, the above conclusion leads to a structure like the following, where the presence of an AuxP is assumed to combine with that of the AgrPstPrt projection:[22]

(28)

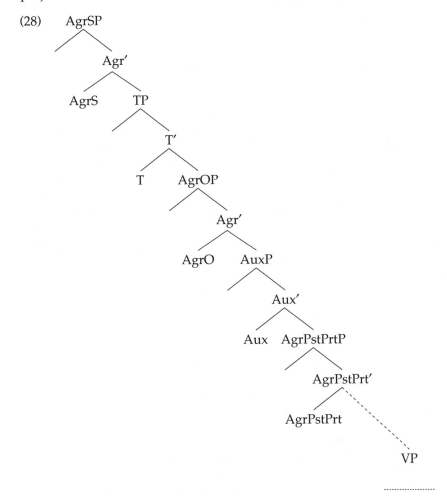

3   On the Uniformity of Clausal Representation: Agreement Projections in Non-Finite Contexts

Characteristically, infinitival clauses do not manifest overt subject–verb agreement morphology. There are well-known "exceptions" to this claim, as the already mentioned case of the Portuguese inflected infinitive construction shows, but this is generally the case. Infinitival clauses do not typically manifest the same richness in phi-features on the verbal morphology as finite clauses do. To take a very simple and clear illustration, consider Italian, which has very rich verbal inflectional morphology in the finite paradigm, especially in the indicative paradigm illustrated in (29), and no overt expression of any phi-feature in the case of the infinitive, as (30) illustrates:

(29)   parl-o, parl-i, parl-a, parl-iamo, parl-ate, parl-ano
       (I, you-Sg, he/she, we, you-Pl, they) speak – first/second/third pers, Sg/Pl

(30)   Ho/hai/ha/abbiamo/avete/hanno deciso di [PRO parlare]
       (I, you-Sg, he/she, we, you-Pl, they) have – first/second/third pers, Sg/Pl

In (30) the PRO subject of the infinitival picks up the referential value of either first, or second, or third person singular/plural according to the choice for the controller in the matrix clause. There is, however, no sign of these differences in the infinitival morphology, which remains invariant. In general, non-finite verbal morphology is much poorer than finite verbal morphology. Considering Italian again, a correct generalization seems to be that non-finite verbal morphology either does not overtly express any phi-feature (infinitive (30), gerund (31)) or expresses "gender" and/or "number" (past participle (20)–(27), including the same situation in French, present participle (32)–(33)), but does not express the feature "person":

(31)   Gianni/Maria stava mangiando.
       Gianni/Maria was eating.

(32)   In quella occasione Gianni/Maria era sorridente.
       On that occasion Gianni/Maria was smiling.

(33)   In quella occasione Gianni e Maria erano sorridenti.
       On that occasion Gianni and Maria were smiling.

What should be concluded from these factual observations? Should one conclude that the functional structure of non-finite clauses is radically different from that of finite clauses? Or should one rather conclude that overt morphological realization is "overt" indication of the existence of a given position but that lack of overtly realized features does not necessarily imply lack of the corresponding syntactic position? The first alternative remains at a purely descriptive level. Now, most of the work in syntactic theory makes a fundamental use of abstract entities whose existence can only be indirectly motivated. A particularly revealing example in this connection is that of "trace" theory and more generally of the (phonetically) empty categories currently admitted in syntactic theorizing. Hence, there is of course nothing in principle wrong in assuming the existence of an entity even if it is not directly visible in a given particular structure. It can rather be assumed, as in the second alternative, that morphological "overtness" is only one criterion which justifies the assumption of a given functional projection, but far from the only one. This allows one to take the most economical track and assume that clause structure is uniform in both finite and non-finite contexts, in particular in both finite and infinitival clauses. Note that this assumption should be taken to hold both language internally and also across languages. We would otherwise be forced to reach the conclusion that languages which differ in the richness of overt verbal morphology should have radically different clause structures attributed to them; an assumption which is implicitly denied in most current work, as the currently assumed analysis of the differences between English and French with respect to the location of negation and other various adverb classes also clearly illustrates. It is an assumption which would furthermore be very costly from the point of view of language acquisition. It can rather be hypothesized that the child learning English and the child learning French start the acquisition process from the same structural skeleton:[23] on the basis of overt evidence they fill in structural positions which are available from UG and attribute the relevant properties to them (e.g. the capacity of attracting the verb). The alternative view would require that children "create" or "invent" positions on the basis of what they hear: it is hard to see what the constraining role of UG would be. Moreover, one should expect significant variation in terms of the functional positions identified, which does not seem to hold.[24] The issue is carefully discussed in Cinque (1999), where, despite the great richness in the kinds of overtly realized affix which different language types display, a substantial uniformity is identified.

To the extent that finite and infinitival clauses have the same structural skeleton attributed to them, the same kinds of process can be taken to occur in both syntactic domains. Briefly consider Case in this respect. As far as accusative Case is concerned, the same checking procedure assumed for finite clauses involving a low AgrO projection can naturally be extended. No difference in the role of AgrO is to be expected. The uniformity hypothesis allows us to also extend the checking procedure for the Case of the subject, assuming a high AgrS projection. The Case will not be nominative, only available in clauses where AgrS combines with a finite T, but rather what Chomsky and Lasnik (1993) have called "null Case," the Case only available in clauses where AgrS combines with non-finite T, i.e., infinitival clauses, and which is only compatible with the null element PRO.

4   Agr in Different Projections: Agr in DP, Agr in CP, Agr in "Small Clauses"

4.1   *Agr in DP*

Abney (1987) has developed the influential proposal that noun phrases should resemble clauses not only in their semantics, as is clearly visible in various instances of nominalization, but also in their structure. Much like clauses, noun phrases should be built around a functional support. In Abney's original proposal, noun phrases are analyzed as DP-projections of the functional category D, the determiner, whose complement is the noun phrase proper, i.e., the projection of the lexical category N.[25] Much work has been done since Abney's dissertation on trying to determine whether the functional structure of the noun phrase should not resemble clause structure even more in displaying a much richer functional architecture. It is not within the scope of the present discussion to review in detail the rich literature on the functional structure of the noun phrase.[26] Nevertheless, it seems appropriate to reconsider the issue from the particular perspective of the role of Agr projections.

The resemblance between clause structure and the structure of the noun phrase has been claimed to be stricter than in Abney's original approach ever since the work by Szabolcsi (1994) in particular. On the basis of evidence from the Hungarian noun phrase, Szabolcsi has proposed that the functional structure of the noun phrase should be built upon an Agr projection of the same nature as the one found in clauses. More specifically, the original DP is assumed to rather correspond to the clausal CP level, external to the clause proper: much like C in the clause, the external D selects an AgrP type projection; more functional structure is then probably involved and the representation ultimately terminates in the NP. The structure which emerges is a representation along the lines in (34):

(34)

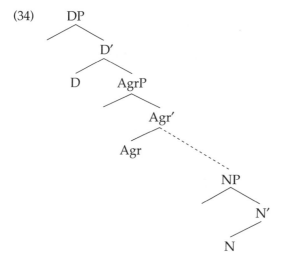

The two basic sets of facts motivating Szabolcsi's proposal find a natural account within the architecture in (34): first, extraction out of DP-phenomena which indicate the A'-status of the Spec/DP position are directly interpreted through the assimilation of the DP-layer to an "external" level of the same type as the CP-layer with respect to the clause; second, the agreement relation overtly established in the Hungarian noun phrase between the possessor and the noun, illustrated in (35), can be directly assimilated to the subject–verb agreement relation overtly established in many languages in finite clauses:[27]

(35) a.   ate ir-od
           you-Nom write-2Sg
      b.   a te titk-od
           the you-Nom secret-2Sg
           your secret

   As these brief remarks suggest, an AgrP can then correspond to either a clause or a noun phrase. What should make the difference between the two is whether other features are ultimately carried by Agr (through head incorporation). "Tense" is likely to be the relevant feature making the difference. An Agr combined with "tense" necessarily corresponds to a clause and is only compatible with selection by C. Lack of "tense" opens the possibility for Agr to be selected by D. In the first case a CP argument is obtained, in the second a DP.[28]

4.2   Agr in CP

There are languages where agreement phi-features are overtly realized in the complementizer. Various Germanic languages have this property to different extent and depending on the syntactic configuration involved.[29] A representative and well-studied case is West Flemish (Haegeman 1992). In West Flemish the finite declarative complementizer overtly agrees with the subject noun phrase, which in turn agrees with the inflected verb. To illustrate, consider the examples in (36) (Haegeman 1992: (6), (9), (49)), where the inflected verb form is given for the first and third person singular with a "strong" (pre-verbal) pronominal subject (36a, c, e, f) and with a "weak" (postverbal)[30] pronominal subject (34b, d, e, f) as well as with the declarative agreeing complementizer (36e, f):

(36) a.   ik goan
      b.   goan-k (ik)
           I go
      c.   zie goat
      d.   goa-se (zie)
           she goes
      e.   Kpeinzen *dan-k* (ik) morgen goan
           I think   that-I (I) tomorrow go
      f.   Kpeinzen *da-se*   (zie) morgen goat
           I think   that-she (she) tomorrow goes

The correspondence in inflectional ending between the complementizer and
the inflected verb (cf. (36b, e) and (36d, f)) is currently interpreted as an indication that a head–head (of the complement) agreement process is operative
between C and the Agr of the complement clause (Rizzi 1990, Haegeman 1992),
as is informally schematized in (37) with a coindexing relation:

(37) $\ldots C_i \ldots Agr_i \ldots$

Since Agr carries the phi-features of the subject noun phrase in Spec/AgrP,
the fact that the same features are also present in C is directly derived.

A slight alternative to this style of account is provided by the proposal in
Shlonsky (1994a) whereby an autonomous AgrP projection (named Agr_cP for
convenience) is assumed to be present within the CP projection. This gives a
CP structure along the lines in (38):

(38)

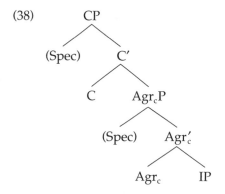

(The symbol IP is an abbreviation for the AgrP corresponding to the clause
utilized, to avoid confusion.) This proposal has several implications concerning in particular the exact location of the subject (lexical, pronominal, doubled
by a clitic or not). A close examination of the issues involved would take the
discussion too far afield and will not be made here. It is worthwhile to just
point out the conceptual advantage of an analysis of this sort, since it tries to
reduce also this instance of agreement in phi-features to the presence of an
Agr-type projection.[31]

Since an "agreement" relation is always automatically provided by the Spec–
head configuration, the idea that a relation of this type is at work at the level
of the CP-layer (possibly mediated by the presence of an AgrP projection, but
see the discussion in n. 31) is very natural. This idea has been developed in
detail in Rizzi (1990) through the proposal that an "agreement" relation in CP
should be held responsible for typical rescuing strategies of long subject extraction cases across a complementizer which would otherwise yield an ECP
violation. Representative cases are the strategies adopted by French, West
Flemish, and English: in the first two languages the "agreement" relation is
overtly signaled by a phonological change in the shape of the complementizer

(*que – qui; da – die*), and in the latter by the absence of an overt realization of the complementizer[32] itself. The relevant examples are given in (39)–(41) (from Rizzi 1990):

(39)   L'homme que je crois [t *qui*/*que[t viendra]]
       The man who I think that will come

(40)   Den vent da Pol peinst [t *die*/*da[t gekommen ist]]
       The man that Pol thinks that come is

(41)   Who do you think [t – /*that [t left]]

In conclusion, languages seem to indicate that agreement is a relevant notion also at the level of CP. This holds both in the sense of overtly displaying phi-features on C, thus possibly indicating the presence of an Agr projection within the CP layer, and in the sense of giving rise to "agreement" relations playing a crucial role in the licensing of various complex syntactic processes such as the case of long *wh*-extraction.

4.3   Agr in "Small Clauses"

Take a language like Italian, which has a fairly rich inflectional morphology. Consider then adjectival and past participial small clauses in this language in examples such as (43) and (44):

(42)   Ritenevo [Maria adatt*a*/*o a questo incarico]
       I considered Maria adequate for this task

(43)   Le ragazze [entrat*e*/*o per ultime] si presentino in portineria
       The girls entered-FemPl/*MascSg = Unmarked form the last must present
       to the reception

(44)   [Arrivat*a*/*o Maria], Gianni uscì dalla stanza
       Arrived-FemSg/*MascSg = Unmarked form Maria, Gianni went out of
       the room

The brackets in (42)–(44) are left without a label on purpose, since the much debated question of the precise determination of the internal structure of small clauses will not be addressed in detail here.[33] Yet, the simple observation of the examples in (42)–(44), combined with the assumption that overt manifestation of phi-features implies the presence of an Agr projection, clearly suggests that these small clauses should imply enough functional structure to include one (or more) Agr projection(s). This is precisely the conclusion reached in various works dealing with the analysis of the structures in (43)–(44) (Belletti 1990, 1994, Siloni 1997, Sportiche 1995, Kayne 1989a, and Starke 1995, among others). What all these analyses have in common is the idea that "small clauses" cannot be so "small" as to only contain the projection of the lexical category which categorially defines them (A, V, in these cases), as originally proposed in Stowell (1983). Generalizing this observation to all kinds of small clause, various authors have reached the conclusion that small clauses actually contain the same structure as full clauses up to the CP level. The difference with full clauses would consist in a somewhat impoverished character/realization of the various functional heads involved.[34] As for Agr projections then, the null assumption in this perspective is that all those assumed for clauses are also present in small clauses (AgrS, AgrO, AgrPstPrt . . .). Furthermore, all those Agr projections assumed within the internal structure of other lexical categories (N, A . . .) should be present in small clauses as well.

5   Agr and Clitics

To the extent that Agr is a container of phi-features of "gender," "number," "person," and "Case," an implicit strong parallelism between Agr and personal pronouns is drawn. Personal pronouns can be analyzed as a collection of grammatical features typically corresponding to "gender," "number," "person," "Case," etc. Even in languages with a relatively poor inflectional morphology, these features are often overtly manifested precisely in the pronominal paradigm. The English case is especially revealing in this respect. The features "number," "person," "Case," and, for the third person singular, also "gender" are overtly expressed in the paradigm of personal pronouns only: *I/me/we/us, he/him/she/her/it/they/them*. The (quasi-)correspondence between Agr and personal pronouns is even more explicit in the Romance languages, which, next to the stressed so-called "strong" forms of pronouns, also have an unstressed paradigm of clitic pronouns. Much like Agr, clitic pronouns are properly analyzed as "heads" in X'-theoretic terms (X°), since they combine with a word (the verb), which is in turn a head (or a derived combination of heads, including functional ones). Note that this holds even if the proper analysis of clitics should be such that they are considered "phonological" clitics which head a maximal projection (XP) at the "syntactic" level and, at this level, behave as maximal projections. Indeed, this seems to be the appropriate analysis of French subject clitics (Kayne 1991, Rizzi and Roberts 1989), to mention a well-known example. Also remaining at the syntactic level, the behavior of clitics can turn out to be non-uniform. To the extent that they undergo syntactic movement, they can do so partly as a maximal projection and partly as a head (Belletti forthcoming). The relation between clitics and Agr is then "substantial" as for the kinds of feature that both express, and goes further, as Agr and clitics are both heads in the sense of X'-theory.

This kind of correspondence between Agr and clitics has inspired much recent work on clitics and the proper analysis of cliticization.[35] Take the case of subject clitics present in most of the dialects of northern Italy. A fairly current analysis interprets them as a direct manifestation of the AgrS node. The lexical subject, possibly present in the same clause together with the subject clitic, is located in the Specifier of the projection of AgrS containing the clitic. Thus, the relevant part of the representation of a sentence like (45), which constitutes a typical instance of a clause containing a lexical subject and a "doubling" subject clitic in northern Italian dialects (e.g. the dialects spoken in Florence, Trento (Brandi and Cordin 1989), Padova, and other northern areas (Poletto 1993a); see also the case of Franco-Provençal (Roberts 1993a)), will correspond to (46):

(45)　La Maria la parla
　　　(the) Mary she-Cl talks

(46)

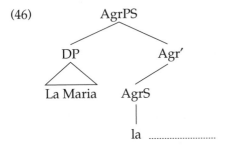

An analysis along the lines of (46) almost inevitably combines with the idea that more than one AgrS projection should be present in the clause. Two AgrS projections should at least be hypothesized to make room for the subject clitic and the (moved) inflected verb. An idea of this sort, explicitly spelled out in Cardinaletti and Roberts (1991) and Belletti (1994), assumes that the upper part of the clause contains more structure at the AgrS level, as illustrated in (47):

(47)

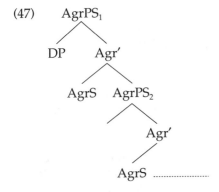

where the upper AgrS hosts the subject clitic and the lower the inflected verb.[36]

Third person object clitics are usually analyzed as belonging to the category D (see the references cited in this section). This assumption is based on the homophony between definite articles and third person clitic pronouns, historically due to the development of both clitics and definite articles from the same

Latin source.[37] Yet a relation with an Agr head is supposed to be established in this case as well. For many analyses the need for the clitic to be related to an Agr head/projection in order to undergo checking of various phi- and Case features is the essence of cliticization. The need for the relation with Agr is given as the fundamental explanation for the question as to why object clitics appear in a displaced position, different from the one where they would belong in the clause. Different solutions have then been proposed as to the exact landing site of the clitic.[38] To the extent that pronominal clitics are generally clitics on the inflected verb, AgrS should ultimately be involved, as the verb systematically ends up in this position in finite clauses (but seen nn. 35, 38): *la conosco*; *l'ho conosciuta* . . . AgrPstPrt is also involved, as the phenomenon of past participle agreement briefly reviewed in (20)–(27) above reveals (thus suggesting movement of the clitic as a maximal projection through the Spec of the AgrPstPrt projection). AgrOP is involved as well, as the clitic must pass through this position on its way to the final landing site. It could also be actively involved if Case checking is one, or even the, factor triggering the displacement of the clitic.[39]

The relation between Agr projections and clitics is thus very strict. Given the identity of the kinds of feature that both Agr and clitic pronouns express, as well as their status as heads, it can go as far as to allow for an assimilation of the two, as in the case of subject clitics of the kind found in the northern Italian dialects. Alternatively, the relation holds in subtler terms in that an Agr head/projection constitutes the designated landing site for the clitic, as in the case of object clitics.

6   The Acquisition of Agr

During the last decade or so, much work has been devoted to the issue of the acquisition of the clausal functional structure.[40] A detailed review of the rich debate which has developed would go well beyond the aims of this work. Nevertheless, some considerations more directly related to the acquisition of Agr seem appropriate.

The empirical area most directly related to this issue and which has received much attention in the field is probably the one which identifies a stage common to the acquisition of several languages, known as the *Optional Infinitive (OI)* (Wexler 1994) or *Root Infinitive (RI)* (Rizzi 1994) stage. The stage is characterized by the fact that children make extensive use of the infinitival form of the verb in root clauses, which typically only allow for finite verbal forms in the adult language. Other properties coexist with the use of root infinitives in this same stage, such as the possibility of null subjects in cases where the target adult language is not a null subject language, or the use of (non-nominative) "default" Case marked subjects of root clauses where the verb is in the infinitival form.[41] (48) illustrates the phenomenon of root infinitives and the co-occurring properties just mentioned:

(48)   a.   Voiture partir (Friedeman 1992)
      b.   Pas laisser tout nu (Friedeman 1992)
      c.   – Want more (Hyams 1986)
      d.   – Boit café (Pierce 1989)
      e.   Him cry/His cry (Schutze 1997)[42]

One interpretation of the attested possibility of using the infinitival form of the verb in root clauses in this particular stage of child language, known as the "truncation hypothesis" (Rizzi 1994), relates it to the possibility assumed to be available for children of utilizing only portions of the clause structure in root clauses. In particular, the CP-level projection is not necessarily reached, as is always the case for adults.[43] Maturation would consist in eliminating this possibility, thus consequently requiring the obligatory projection of the whole CP. To the extent that root clauses can be truncated at different levels of projection at this stage, the highest AgrS node is the most likely one to be involved in the truncation process. Truncation below AgrS has consequences for all processes which are assumed to involve the AgrS projection in one way or other. The most visible consequence should precisely be lack of appearance of phi-agreement features on the verb of the clause, with use of the infinitive becoming possible in root clauses. The other coexisting phenomena could be related to lack of the AgrS projection in various ways and more or less directly. In a nutshell: a "null constant" rather than a *pro* could be responsible for the "apparent" possibility of null subjects, which are then expected to display behaviors different from those of ("adult") null subject languages necessarily involving *pro* (see the discussion in Rizzi 1994, *contra* Hyams 1986); to the extent that nominative is associated with agreement, the expectation is that lack of agreement should induce lack of nominative Case on a lexical (pronominal) subject.[44]

The leading idea of an account of this sort is that the functional structure of the clause is available to the child from the very outset of the acquisition period. Unlike the adult, the child can make use of a reduced portion of it ("truncation" below Agr in Rizzi's 1994 terms) or leave features corresponding to some of the functional heads involved partly unspecified ("tense" in Wexler's 1994 terms; see n. 44).[45] This differs from Radford's (1990) original proposal that no functional structure be available at all for the child at the outset, and significantly limits the enrichment brought about by maturation. This also allows for a natural account of the crucial observed fact that features clearly associated with functional categories are known to the child from the outset, such as the finite/non-finite distinction (Pierce 1989, Guasti 1992). Also important in this respect is the observation that the verbal inflectional agreement endings appear to be known from the outset by children acquiring Italian, as the very low percentage of agreement mistakes during early stages of acquisition reveals (Guasti 1992). The latter observation also directly indicates that both Agr and the morphosyntactic agreement process are known from the early stages.[46]

In conclusion, the acquisition of Agr (and the shapes it takes) appears to play quite a central role in language acquisition, and it reveals potentially rich consequences for the implementation of clause structure in early stages.

Appendix: Some Observations on Agr and Interpretability

Throughout this chapter I have been assuming a conception of clause structure which has become "standard" since Pollock's (1989) article and the numerous works produced since in the same line. As the above discussion has made clear, the rich literature which has grown around the so-called "Split Infl" hypothesis assumes that a central role is played by Agr nodes and projections in clause structure. Agr and Agr projections have also been taken to play a role internal to the projection of categories like CP and DP, as well as various "small clause" types. I have also stressed the relation between Agr and cliticization, specially in Romance, as well as the potentially crucial role played by Agr and its projection in defining particular stages of language acquisition. The central role played by Agr and Agr projections has been recently put into question by Chomsky (1995b). Before concluding the present discussion I would like to make some observations in this connection, although Chomsky's proposal is hard to evaluate since it is still at a fairly sketchy level of elaboration.

In the last part of his "Minimalist Program" Chomsky (1995b) has put forward the innovating hypothesis that nodes of the Agr type should not be present in the clause structure to mark individual syntactic positions; a proposal with pervasive consequences. The hypothesis is based on the distinction made in that system between [+interpretable] and [−interpretable] features, which is supposed to play a central role in the syntactic computation to drive the transition into the interpretive LF component. The phi-features contained in Agr are considered [−interpretable] since they simply express a morphosyntactic relation (an "agreement" relation). They are thus erased once the checking operation with the phi-features of a DP in Spec/Agr is completed. They do not play any role in LF, unlike the nominal phi-features, which are treated as [+interpretable] as they directly determine crucial aspects of the interpretation of DPs.[47] According to Chomsky's proposal [−interpretable] phi-features of the Agr type should not justify a particular syntactic position, as they are not present in LF. They are consequently assumed to be directly part of the composition of other categories (T for AgrS and V for AgrO). A proposal along these lines necessarily requires a corollary hypothesis: the possibility of allowing multiple Spec positions for single projections. This is so since, in the absence of Agr projections, all Spec/Agr positions are also eliminated from clause structure. Consequently, in order for checking of Agr phi-features to be performed, a further Spec position must be created for the category whose head contains those features, beside the one that comes directly from the X'-schema.

The possibility of multiple Spec positions, which amounts to allowing multiple adjunction structures as in previous versions of syntactic theory, may very well be going in the right direction. However, it is clear that its innovating potential will really be such if the hypothesis turns out to be able to make the right predictions in different empirical areas[48] and to derive the results obtained within the traditional, more constrained X'-format, which only allows for one Spec position per head (although necessarily in different terms).[49] Among these results are those reviewed in this chapter where different Agr projections have been taken to play a central role in expressing (overt) morphosyntactic relations, which condition the syntactic computation, and in revealing the presence of individual syntactic positions.

NOTES

1   More generally the Germanic languages, although the comparative approach was less developed at the time than it became in the 1980s and 1990s.

2   The important work by Baker (1988) in the late 1980s on agglutinative languages showed that much more grammatical information can actually be associated with the verb, as these languages overtly manifest. Hence, the assumption must be that the Infl node should have room for even more features/affixes than those mentioned above, characteristically found in more familiar languages. I will abstract away from these considerations. See also n. 6.

3   Arguments showing the head-like behavior of I(nfl) and its autonomy can be provided to empirically support the theory internal conceptual argument. The arguments are based on the observation that I is selected by particular complementizers (C being a head as well), selection being a typical head–head relation.

4   Of course these considerations assume that adverbs have a fixed position in the clause and do not undergo special ad-hoc reordering movements. The only movement operations that adverbs can undergo are the general ones possibly involving any major constituent: *wh*-movement, focus movement, etc. This assumption appears to be the most restrictive one and it has allowed important progresses in such a recalcitrant area. Since the position of adverbs appears to vary significantly across languages, according to this view the site of the variation should rather be recognized in verb syntax, ultimately a morphological property, than in adverb syntax proper. See Cinque (1999) for a most articulated development of this idea, combined with the proposal that the fixed position of adverbs is the Spec of the different functional heads which build up clause structure.

5   Auxiliaries are allowed to move higher in French non-finite clauses, thus reproducing the situation of English, modulo the optionality of movement.

6   In many subsequent works (Pollock 1997, Cinque 1999, to quote some

representative cases) it is argued that the nature of Infl is certainly more articulated than that and other kinds of feature intervene to compose it. "Mode", "Aspect," and "Voice" features are the cases most frequently quoted, also on the basis of crosslinguistic evidence.

7   With Pollock (1989) assuming T to be the highest head, hence the clause a TP on the one side, and with Belletti (1990) and Chomsky (1995b: ch. 3) assuming Agr to be the highest head, hence the clause an AgrP.

8   The French/English paradigms are then accounted for through the assumption that the verb (lexical or auxiliary) obligatorily moves to Agr and optionally moves to T in French finite and non-finite clauses respectively; in English, the lexical verb remains in VP. Auxiliaries, on the other hand, move to Agr obligatorily in English finite clauses and optionally in both English and French non-finite clauses (cfr. *John has not come/does not come // John claims not to have come/to have not come // Jean dit ne pas avoir parlé/ n'avoir pas parlé*).

9   According to which an attracting Agr should express the feature "person" in all tenses.

10   And some non-finite clauses as in the Portuguese inflected infinitive construction, where the inflected infinitive carries the person and number features of the subject (a possibility arising under particular structural conditions and for particular lexical choices; see Raposo 1987).

11   Either through actual incorporation *à la* Baker (1988) of V into Agr in syntax, or directly in the lexicon, with the features to be subjected to morphological checking, in syntax or LF (Chomsky 1995b). Morphological

checking is an operation where the particular features choice made in the lexicon is checked against the actual structure. Matching features are supposed to "erase" after successful checking, which is undertaken through head movement. The Spec–head relation within an X'-maximal projection is the other checking configuration.

12   I will use the notation "agreement" to refer to this type of relation, which is provided by the structural Spec–head configuration and does not necessarily involve the mediation of an Agr node. It does when phi-features are involved. The set of phi-features contains (at least) features such as number, person, gender, and Case.

13   It is not unconceivable that Agr itself be considered as an abbreviation for different contentive heads, such as "number" and "person" (and possibly "gender," a feature typically showing up in non-finite, participial verbal morphology in Romance and which, characteristically, is in complementary distribution with the feature "person"). See Shlonsky (1989) for the sketching of a "Split Agr" hypothesis.

14   Simplifying somewhat, since it is not only T of finite clauses which implies a nominative feature on Agr. Other occurrences of nominative Case in different contexts, such as the Hungarian noun phrase and the inflected infinitive of Portuguese already mentioned, suggest that T is not the only trigger of nominative. Possibly, the feature necessary for nominative to be available is the feature "person," which typically goes with "finiteness," but not necessarily, as in the case of the Portuguese inflected infinitive and the Hungarian possessor in noun

phrases. See below. Also relevant in this respect is the case of Icelandic, where nominative Case appears in non-finite clauses marking what appears to be an object noun phrase (Taraldsen 1995, and the overview in Schutze 1997). For the sake of clarity I continue to assume the simplified hypothesis if not otherwise specified.

15   Which is assumed for so-called Structural Cases: nominative, accusative, possibly some instances of genitive (see below), the "null" Case of infinitivals.

The role played by Case in agreement relations is visible in various situations in different languages. To quote one typical example, take German, where the article, typical carrier of agreeing phi-features in the noun phrase, is also the carrier of Case.

16   It is sometimes said that AgrO is "activated" by the Case feature contained in the lexical information of a transitive verb. This sort of "activation" can be interpreted as the result of the checking operation involving head movement of the verb into AgrO.

17   Not just subjects as in the so-called "VP-internal subject hypothesis" (Kuroda 1988, Koopman and Sportiche 1991, among others).

18   Note that it is no trivial task to compute what the different implications would be in the case of French/Italian type languages, where long Verb movement would anyway obscure the effects of "overt" syntactic movement of the object to Spec/AgrO.

For the first proposal that a certain "amount" of Verb movement should be available also in English, see Johnson (1991). For more recent discussion of these and related issues touching on the phenomenon of "Object Shift" arising in Scandinavian languages, see Vikner (1995) and Collins and Thráinsson (1996), among others.

19   See in particular Kayne (1989a), Belletti and Rizzi (1996), Belletti (1990), and Friedeman and Siloni (1997).

20   See Friedeman and Siloni (1997) for a useful clarification of the issue and the development of empirical and conceptual arguments showing the necessity of the distinction. Possibly, the initial incertitude arose from a "historical" accident: almost simultaneous appearance of Kayne's arguments showing the "existence" of an Agr head/projection in the low VP area, made visible by past participle agreement, and of Chomsky's Minimalist approach to Case checking requiring an Agr head/projection again in the low VP area, and which made direct use of Kayne's arguments.

21   We might notice that whereas nominative Case and other phi-features are checked within the same AgrS projection, two different Agr projections are involved for checking of accusative Case and other phi-features (such as gender and number, which may be overtly realized in the Romance past participle). Possibly, this often assumed asymmetry reveals that some generalization is missed. A promising idea would consist in claiming that no such asymmetry actually holds and that Case and other phi-features are also checked independently in the "upper" part of the clause. This would imply that more than just one AgrS type projection is present there as well. The proposal that more than one "high" AgrS type projection devoted to host a noun phrase subject in its Spec (either as the final landing site

or as a position where the noun phrase passes through on its way to the final landing site) should be assumed to be present is more or less explicitly adopted by several authors. See Belletti (1994) for the adoption of the proposal at least in structures containing an aspectual auxiliary in Romance, also supported by data from north-eastern Italian dialects studied in Poletto (1993a); see too Cardinaletti and Roberts (1991) and Rizzi (1987) for a first hint of a similar idea. Most recently, see Cinque's (1999) typology of clause structure, which includes several so-called DP-related positions, also in the higher part of the clause, which we might assimilate to the Specs of Agr projections. For the proposal that Spec/TP too is a possible subject position, at least in those Germanic languages displaying overt Object Shift and the so-called "Transitive Expletive Construction" (TEC), see Bobaljik and Jonas (1996).

22 The null assumption seems to be that all the positions overtly present in some structures are actually always present in all structures. This naturally leads to the proposal that the structure below AgrO is present independently of the actual realization of a compound tense, overtly involving an Aux and a past participle.

Some further functional head is certainly present in the low part of the clause, between the AgrPstPrt projection and the VP, as the vertical dots in (28) are meant to indicate. In Belletti (1990, 1994) I proposed that an Aspectual phrase is located in this position. On the basis of the rich typological survey undertaken, Cinque (1999) assumes that several aspectual projections are present in this low area, together with the

projection of a functional "Voice" head, which also belongs to the low zone. I disregard here, as I did for the upper part of the clause, the numerous issues related to an exhaustive structural representation of this area, which might include at least other NegP projections (Cinque 1999, Zanuttini 1997), a FocP projection (Belletti and Shlonsky 1995) and others.

23 Or else the skeleton "matures" in different stages. See in this connection the literature on the so-called root/optional infinitives stage (Rizzi 1994, Wexler 1994, and references there). See also section 6 below.

24 Of course this argument is not limited to Agr type functional categories, but extends to all categories constituting the functional structure of the clause.

25 See Grimshaw (1991) for the proposal that DP be viewed as an "extended projection" of N much as IP, and that the projections in which it can be split can be viewed as "extended projections" of V.

26 See, among others, Giusti (1993a, 1997) Cinque (1995), Longobardi (1994), Ritter (1991), Szabolcsi (1994), and Siloni (1997).

27 (35) also illustrates the well-known fact that the possessor not only agrees with the noun in the same form as in the subject–verb agreement relation, but carries nominative Case as well. This kind of fact, hinted at in n. 14, makes it tempting to suggest that the feature relevant in the availability of nominative Case be the feature "person," typically present in the finite verbal morphology, in the Portuguese inflected infinitive, and, it seems plausible to argue, also in the possessor pronoun. This feature should be considered a necessary

but not a sufficient condition for nominative to be available. Concomitant presence of a "verbal" type agreement morphology containing the feature "person" possibly plays a role. If, as is more often the case, a morphology of this kind is not compatible with a nominal base, the Case most typically checked in the noun phrase is not nominative (typically, it is genitive). See Siloni (1997) for an analysis of Hebrew construct and "free state" in this connection.

28   Where only CPs and DPs are possible arguments (Stowell 1989b, Longobardi 1994, Szabolcsi 1994).

The claim that D is the necessary selector of an Agr without "tense" is probably too strong a conclusion, incompatible with the plausible and empirically supported idea that "small clauses" are/can be introduced by C (Starke 1995, Sportiche 1995). On the other hand, the idea that D is the possible selector of an Agr without "tense" makes available a treatment of nominalization such as the one developed in Siloni (1997), named "syntactic nominalization," whereby VP can terminate a DP-extended projection without any violation being created. This is the analysis attributed to reduced relatives and (some) gerunds by Siloni (1997).

Note that the correlation between C and T is an often observed one. See Stowell (1982) and Rizzi (1997), among others.

29   See Bayer (1984) on German, Zwart (1993b) on Dutch, and Bennis and Haegeman (1994) and Haegeman (1992), in particular, on West Flemish.

30   Notice that the weak pronominal subject can be doubled by the strong form, as the parentheses are meant to indicate.

31   The phi-features in Agrc, corresponding to those of the subject, must end up on C, through some version of a head movement operation. Note that this operation is somewhat special since it adjoins the features on Agr to the right of the landing site head C. Usually, head incorporation yields the opposite order, with the incorporating head adjoining to the left of the landing site head. This might indicate that the hypothesis in (36) is a first approximation, but probably more needs to be assumed to derive the correct result. An articulated structure for the CP layer involving more than one C position, such as the one proposed in Rizzi (1997), enriched with an AgrP projection could indicate a possible innovative approach.

32   According to Rizzi's analysis, the so called "agreeing" complementizer of English is phonologically null. "That" and other overt complementizers do not have the relevant "agreeing" property.

Note that the phonological change in the shape of the complementizer in French and West Flemish does not involve realization of typical agreeing phi-features (see Zwart 1993b). This might suggest that even if an AgrP projection is present within the CP layer, it is not involved in the establishment of the relevant relation. Within an articulated conception of the CP internal structure this might be taken as an indication that the "agreement" relation responsible for satisfaction of the head government requirement of the subject trace is established at a level lower than the AgrcP projection, and hence does not involve phi-features.

In Rizzi (1990) it is assumed that languages which (differently from

French and, overtly, West Flemish;
see (35)) do not require that C
agrees with the Agr head of the
clausal AgrP are expected to exist,
and to show variation in the shape
of the complementizer also in cases
of extraction of constituents different
from the subject. The languages
which are brought as possible
illustrations of this case are Irish
(from Chung and McCloskey 1987)
and Kinande (from Schneider-Zioga
1987).

33 See the papers collected in
Cardinaletti and Guasti (1995) for an
overview of the several issues raised
by small clauses in this respect.

34 See in particular the analyses in
Starke (1995), Sportiche (1995), and
Belletti (1994). See also Cinque
(1990a) for the first suggestion that
absolute participial small clauses
should contain a CP level. If one
assumes Rizzi's (1994) idea that
clause structure can be truncated
(as in some stages of acquisition)
in the upper part but cannot be
internally reduced, detection of
a CP level implies that a whole
clause structure is present (as is
specifically discussed in Belletti
1994). See also Belletti (in
preparation) for the detection of
a CP level in some reduced
comparative expressions.

35 The most studied cases involve
the analysis of Romance clitics
(Kayne 1991, Belletti forthcoming,
Uriagereka 1995), but also Semitic
clitics and Germanic so-called "weak
pronouns" have been analyzed from
the perspective discussed in the
text (Shlonsky 1994b, Siloni 1997,
Holmberg 1991a, Haegeman 1993a;
see also Sportiche 1996).

36 Given the argument spelled out in
section 3 above, the richer structure
should be assumed to be present
independently of the presence/

existence of subject clitics in the
language. This immediately gives
a more articulated conception of
the notion of (pre-verbal) "subject
position". See Rizzi (1987) for the
first proposal that the unanalyzed
Infl node should be split into two
nodes, at least in the dialects overtly
revealing it, and Poletto (1993b) for
the idea that Agr projections should
also be assumed at the level of CP
to host the special paradigm of
interrogative subject clitics overtly
present in some dialects.

37 The natural assumption in this
perspective is that the DP
corresponding to first and second
person clitic pronouns, which are
not homophonous with any article,
also contain an Agr projection
hosting the relevant first and second
person, singular/plural features.
Accordingly, the third person
should be taken to correspond to the
default value for Agr.

38 Which can also vary across Romance;
see Bianchi and Figuereido Silva
(1994) on the possibility of Brazilian
clitics cliticizing on the past
participle of finite clauses, and
Rouveret (1989) for the analysis of
cliticization in continental
Portuguese, where clitics can appear
higher in the structure than in the
other Romance languages. However,
the property of being verbal clitics
is shared by Romance pronominal
clitics in general.

39 I am using the movement metaphor
although, possibly, the analysis
could also be phrased in non-
movement terms (as in the original
non-movement approach of Borer
1984, even though it is not obvious
how a non-movement approach
could deal with the past participle
agreement facts). See Belletti
(forthcoming) for the idea that the
AgrO projection is necessarily

involved, as Case checking is the primary factor triggering clitic movement.

40 At least since Radford (1990).

41 (Free) subject inversion is another possibly co-occurring property, at least in French child language, as suggested by the following productions:

(i) a. Ranger tout seul Grégoire.
    b. Fumer Philippe. (Friedeman 1992)

42 Although attested, the RI stage seems to be reduced in a language like Italian compared to the situation in other languages like French, English, Swedish (Platzack 1992), Dutch (Haegeman 1994, etc.), as Guasti (1992) points out. See Rizzi (1994) for a possible interpretation of this asymmetry trying to relate it to the long verb movement process that Italian infinitives appear to undergo (Belletti 1990), contrary to the situation in the other languages quoted.

43 The supplementary assumption being that (related to the obligatory selection that functional categories undergo) it is not possible to eliminate functional projections internally to the part of the clause that has been truncated. This strongly constrains the possible omissions of functional categories from clause structure at any stage of acquisition. The structure, although reduced, is preserved. The expectation is then that the "morphological mistakes" which are found do not occur at random, but are structurally determined. See Rizzi (1994) for discussion. See also White and Prevost (1997) for an analysis introducing a comparison with the situation in ("early" and "adult") L2 acquisition.

44 Possibility of (free) subject inversion could be due to the fact that, in the lack of Spec/AgrS, no problem should arise in a non-null subject (target) language for the licensing of a *pro* in this position; the reader is referred to the relevant quoted literature for detailed discussion.

Schutze (1997) also quotes cases of nominative subjects in root infinitives (*he cry*). He suggests an interpretation whereby Agr ("accord" in his terms) can be present but T is left unspecified. To the extent that third person singular present indicative ending *-s* is the realization of a "tense" feature and not of agreement/Agr, this would explain the availability of nominative in these structures. If this interpretation is on the right track, it suggests that tense underspecification can also be responsible for the emergence of the root infinitives stage, as in the original proposal by Wexler (1994). Note that, as Schutze (1997: 42), 232) clarifies, the various Case possibilities for the subject available in root infinitives also show up in other non-finite root clauses which are possible during the same acquisition period, cf. *me crying*, *her tired*, *my crying*, *I crying*, *she tired*. See n. 14 above for the dissociation of nominative Case from tense.

45 See also Hyams (1996). Functional categories appear to also be present in SLI children (Eyer and Leonard 1995).

46 Recall that root infinitives are relatively few in Italian child language. The very low rate of agreement mistakes indicates that morphological endings are not picked up at random even in early stages but are chosen on the basis of the relevant morphosyntactic Spec/head agreement process. Note that

agreement mistakes can in principle be due to different factors: (i) lack of the node Agr and consequent lack of the related morphosyntactic agreement process; (ii) presence of Agr, but lack of the morphosyntactic agreement process; and (iii) presence of Agr and of the morphosyntactic agreement process, but lack of knowledge of the right morphological ending. The last case seems to better characterize the kind of mistakes found in adult L2 acquisition, according to the discussion in White and Prevost (1997). (i) and (ii) could characterize some attested language pathologies where verbal endings are omitted or substituted for (see for instance Miceli and Caramazza 1988), beside (i) characterizing the child language root infinitives stage discussed in the text.

47 Case is considered a purely formal feature and as such not part of the [+interpretable] features of DP. Note that if the hypotheses discussed in section 4 are on the right track and the phi-features within DP are expressed through an Agr projection, this would mean that not all Agr and Agr projections should have the same status from the point of view of the "interpretability" of the features expressed.

48 But see the "ordering problem" which arises in the so-called "Transitive Expletive Construction" (TEC; Chomsky 1995b), where the expletive pronoun and the associated overt lexical subject of a transitive sentence (also containing an expressed direct object) are predicted to be immediately adjacent to each other, contrary to fact. Note that the inflected verb necessarily intervenes between the expletive and the subject. This would seem to reveal the presence of a further head between the two which could be identified with the AgrS just eliminated.

49 See also Kayne (1994) for crucial use of the most rigid X'-schema.

16 Sentential Negation

RAFFAELLA ZANUTTINI

1 On the Centrality of Sentential Negation

There is a variety of reasons why a proper understanding of the expression of sentential negation is central to our understanding of grammar. Among them are the following:

- Since sentential negation is expressed by all languages, it is interesting to examine the range of possible variation attested crosslinguistically. It is clear even from a superficial investigation of the world's languages that sentential negation is not expressed in as many ways as there are languages. An examination of crosslinguistic differences can tell us what possibilities Universal Grammar (UG) makes available in this domain, and inform us of the kinds of constraint it imposes.
- Negative markers tend to occur in the same part of the structure as realizes other types of grammatical information, standardly considered to be the nucleus of the clause (for example, tense and aspect). Understanding the properties of the negative markers is likely to also shed light on the properties of these elements, through the study of their interaction.
- Negative markers interact with several parts of the grammar of a language. In some cases, they interfere with extraction of maximal projections, in others with movement of heads; they may also determine certain restrictions on the distribution of inherently negative constituents. Interestingly, though, different negative markers have different effects. It is essential that we understand the properties which distinguish negative markers from one another, if we hope to reach a clear understanding of these other phenomena.
- Negative markers can be sensitive to mood, aspectual, or temporal distinctions, as well as to the type of clause in which they occur (e.g. declarative versus imperative). Understanding such sensitivity can shed light on certain (often non-apparent) differences that a language draws among clausal types.

In this chapter, I will discuss only a few of these aspects. My goal will not be to provide a comprehensive overview of recent studies on the syntax of sentential negation; this could not be done in a few pages, given the vastness of this domain of inquiry. Rather, I will outline some of the questions that have been asked on this topic, and some of the approaches taken in the attempt to answer them. The questions I discuss center on the most basic syntactic properties of negative markers, since they are a good starting point for the investigation of many of the complex phenomena relating to sentential negation. Because of the general nature of the discussion, not much attention will be devoted to negation in English, which would require digressions on properties which are language specific. At the same time, because my own research on negation has focussed on Romance languages, many of the arguments discussed in this chapter will be drawn from this language family. However, the reader should not be discouraged by the lack of discussion of a given language or the abundance of arguments from another, since the focus of the chapter is on the *kinds* of question we can ask and on the *kinds* of answer we can give in trying to understand the syntax of sentential negation.

The chapter is structured as follows. In section 2, I first provide a very brief overview of the strategies employed crosslinguistically for the expression of sentential negation; then I outline two basic questions which will guide our voyage through some of the main issues underlying the syntactic study of sentential negation. In section 3, I raise the question of how we can determine the syntactic category to which negative markers belong; then I discuss some proposals on how best to capture their distribution and distinguish them from other elements which have similar, though not identical, distributional properties. In section 4, I address the issue of the phrasal status of negative markers; I discuss some tests which can help us determine whether they behave like heads or like maximal projections. Finally, in section 5, I outline the kinds of question which arise from the proposals discussed throughout the chapter in trying to characterize the options made available by UG for the syntactic expression of sentential negation.

2   The Syntactic Expression of Sentential Negation: A Crosslinguistic View

While space limitations prevent me from doing justice to typological work on negation, let me simply point out the main patterns found across a sample of languages described in one such work, Payne (1985).[1] Even this cursory overview should suffice to justify the assertion of the previous section that the grammatical strategies used to express sentential negation tend to interact with those used to express grammatical meaning typically associated with inflection, e.g. tense, aspect, and mood specifications. Payne (1985) outlines four strategies for the expression of sentential negation; according to his survey, all languages use at least one of these strategies, and some use more than one.

One strategy, found in Polynesian languages, is that of negating a clause by means of a negative marker which has the characteristics of a verb taking a sentential complement. This is exemplified in (1) from Tongan, a Polynesian language analyzed in Chung (1970) and Churchward (1953) (the brackets indicate clausal boundary):[2]

(1) Na'e 'ikai [ke 'alu 'a Siale] (Tongan)
    AspNegAsp-go AbsoluteCharlie
    "Charlie didn't go."

Negative markers of this type share some properties with main verbs, while differing from them in being sensitive to the aspect marking of the clause; in fact, in some cases, such "negative verbs" appear to be a combination of a negative marker and an aspect marker.

Another strategy consists in negating a clause via a negative marker which has the properties of a finite auxiliary (carrying person, number, tense, aspect, or mood affixes) followed by the lexical verb in a non-finite participial form. This type is exemplified in (2) with the Siberian language Evenki, of the Tungus family:

(2) Bi ə-ə-w   dukuwɯn-ma duku-ra. (Evenki)
    I-NegPast1Sg letter-Obj   write-Part
    "I didn't write a letter."

A third, more common strategy uses a negative marker which appears in the form of a "particle," an element which can be invariant (e.g. Russian *ne*) or can exhibit sensitivity to mood (e.g. Hungarian *ne/nem*), tense, or aspect (e.g. Arabic *lam/la*). Negative particles are usually associated with the verb, i.e., in many languages they occur in a position immediately preceding the verb. Pre-verbal negative particles are often "reinforced," in Payne's terminology, by a postverbal negative particle; the position of the latter element is not necessarily adjacent to the verb. A widely known example of such co-occurrence is that of French *ne* and *pas*; an example from Welsh is given in (3):

(3) *Nid* yw'r bachgen (*ddim*) yn hoffi coffi. (Welsh)
    Neg is-the boy   Neg in like coffee
    "The boy does not like coffee."

Finally, negative markers can be part of the derivational morphology of the verb, as a prefix, a suffix, or an infix. For example, Turkish *-me-* precedes the affixes expressing tense, mood, person, and number and follows those indicating reciprocals, reflexives, causatives, and passives.

In this chapter, I will focus on the syntactic characterization of sentential negation in languages which adopt the third of these strategies, namely the use of what Payne calls a negative particle. The term *particle* is a useful descriptive tool in this context, referring to elements which have a unique semantic function, that of contributing an instance of negation, and which do not appear to be easily classified within the traditional syntactic categories. However, it is merely a descriptive term, which leaves their syntactic characterization unstated. My goal will be to guide the reader through some of the recent work on the syntax of sentential negation which has addressed precisely the question of how to characterize so-called negative particles. I will start by asking two basic questions, which will help us classify negative particles (henceforth, "negative markers") in terms of syntactic category and phrasal status:

1   Do negative markers exhibit the same distribution as any other known class of elements (for example, adverbs, markers of tense, aspect, or mood, subject or object pronominal clitics), or are they characterized by a unique distributional pattern?
2   Do negative markers exhibit the syntactic behavior of heads or of maximal projections?

The answers to these two basic questions are essential to set the stage for any further syntactic investigation.

3   The Syntactic Category of Negative Markers

In this section I will address the first of the two questions just outlined, namely whether the distribution of negative markers is the same as that of any known syntactic category or whether it is unique. In particular, I will examine the possibility that negative markers should be assimilated to adverbs or pronominal elements. I present some of the empirical and conceptual arguments given in the recent literature against such an assimilation within the Romance family, demonstrating that negative markers have unique distributional properties. Though the precise kind of evidence discussed here might not be available in all languages, the types of argument presented in support of this conclusion can be seen as paradigmatic.

3.1   *A comparison with VP-adverbs*

A very influential proposal on the syntactic category of negative markers is the one given in Pollock (1989), in the context of a more general discussion of the structure of the clause, based on comparative data from English and French. Pollock observed that the well-known asymmetry in the position of lexical verbs and auxiliary verbs which can be observed in English finite clauses is also found in French, though only in non-finite clauses.

Since Emonds's (1976) and Jackendoff's (1972) work, it has been assumed that, in English finite clauses, auxiliary verbs occur in a higher structural position than lexical verbs. Postulating such an asymmetry provides a straightforward account of the different positions these elements exhibit in questions (cf. 4a vs. 4b), in the presence of VP-adverbs like *often* (cf. 5a vs. 5b), and in the presence of the negative marker *not* (cf. 6a vs. 6b):

(4) a. *Is* <u>Mary</u> running the marathon?
     b. **Runs* <u>Mary</u> the marathon? (Does Mary run the marathon?)

(5) a. Mary *is* <u>often</u> running the marathon.
     b. *Mary *runs* <u>often</u> the marathon. (Mary <u>often</u> *runs* the marathon.)

(6) a. Mary *is* <u>not</u> running the marathon.
     b. *Mary *runs* <u>not</u> the marathon. (Mary does <u>not</u> *run* the marathon.)

Let us suppose that the auxiliary verb *is* moves to the head of the clause, IP, whereas the lexical verb *run* occurs in a lower position, the head of VP. The contrast in (4) can be seen as stemming from the fact that the auxiliary *is* can invert with the subject, moving from I to C; in contrast, the main verb *runs*, unable to move from V to I, will also be unable to move from I to C. In (5), because the auxiliary *is* occurs in I, it precedes the adverb *often*, taken to occur in a lower position; in contrast, the lexical verb *runs* follows the adverb *often* because it is in VP. By similar reasoning, in (6), because *is* occurs in I, it precedes the negative marker *not*, taken to occur in a position intermediate between I and V; in contrast *runs*, which occurs in V, cannot do so, because it occupies a position which is structurally lower than the negative marker.

The asymmetry between auxiliary and lexical verbs found in English finite clauses contrasts with the lack of such an asymmetry in French finite clauses, where lexical verbs and auxiliaries share the same distribution, at least in their relative order with respect to the negative marker and the class of so-called VP-adverbs. Against this background, Pollock (1989) makes the interesting and novel observation that the asymmetry which English exhibits in finite clauses is indeed present in French as well, but only in infinitival clauses. The following examples show that, whereas the auxiliary *être* "to be" can precede the negative marker *pas* (cf. 7b), a lexical verb like *sembler* "to seem" cannot (cf. 8b):[3]

(7) a. Ne <u>pas</u> *être* heureux est une condition   pour écrire   des
         ne pas to-be happy   is a   prerequisite for   to-write of-the
         romans.
         novels
         "Not to be happy is a prerequisite to write novels."
     b. N'*être* <u>pas</u> heureux est une condition pour écrire des romans.

(8) a. Ne <u>pas</u> *sembler* heureux est une condition   pour écrire   des
         ne pas to-seem happy is a   prerequisite for   to-write of-the
         romans.
         novels
         "Not to seem happy is a prerequisite to write novels."
    b. *Ne *sembler* <u>pas</u> heureux est une condition pour écrire des romans.

The same pattern holds for the contrast between *avoir* and other lexical verbs (see Pollock 1989: sec. 2.1). This pattern could be captured by saying that infinitival auxiliaries in French have the option of staying in situ or moving to I, whereas infinitival lexical verbs do not leave the VP. From this it would follow that infinitival auxiliaries can precede the negative marker *pas*, as in (7b), whereas infinitival lexical verbs cannot, as shown in (8b). However, if the relevant contrast were movement to I or lack of such movement, Pollock points out, we would expect that infinitival lexical verbs, which do not move to I, should follow not only the negative marker *pas* but also the class of VP-adverbs, such as the French counterpart of *often*. But this is not what the data show; as illustrated in the following examples, an infinitival lexical verb in French can precede a VP-adverb (cf. 9a), even though it cannot precede *pas* (cf. 9b, parallel to 8b):

(9) a. *Paraître* <u>souvent</u> triste pendant son   voyage de noce, c'est rare.
         to-look often   sad   during one's honeymoon   that-is rare
         "To often look sad during one's honeymoon is rare."
    b. *Ne *paraître* <u>pas</u> triste pendant son   voyage de noce, c'est normal.
         ne to-look *pas* sad   during one's honeymoon,   that-is normal
         "Not to look sad during one's honeymoon is normal."

This contrast leads Pollock to the following conclusion, which has proven extremely influential for the study of negative markers: VP-adverbs like English *often* and French *souvent*, and negative markers like English *not* and French *pas*, do not occupy the same structural position, despite the fact that they both occur between I and V.

To account for the crosslinguistic pattern just described, Pollock proposes that all infinitival verbs in French can raise to a head position which is higher than VP but lower than the position where the negative marker *pas* occurs. Furthermore, infinitival auxiliaries, in contrast with infinitival lexical verbs, can raise even further, to a position from which they precede the negative marker. To account for these positions and for the status of the negative markers, treated separately from adverbs, Pollock suggests that independent syntactic status should be given to three elements traditionally associated with Inflection, namely tense, agreement, and negation. Thus, instead of representing the inflectional part of the clause with the single node IP, Pollock argues that it should be represented as consisting of three distinct syntactic projections, as follows:

(10)

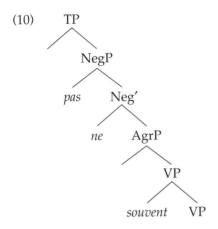

In this representation, an (overt or abstract) tense morpheme heads the TP projection and an (overt or abstract) agreement morpheme the AgrP projection; in French, *ne* heads NegP whereas *pas* occurs in its specifier. The adverbs of the class of *souvent* "often" are assumed to occur in a projection adjoined to VP. Such an articulated view of the clause, combined with the assumption that verbs move to a different extent depending on the language and on whether they are auxiliaries or main verbs, allows an account of the word orders described above, as follows. In English, auxiliaries move to the head of TP, whereas main verbs occur in the heads of VP. This accounts for the pattern in (4)–(6), along the same lines as previous work on the topic. In French, in contrast, both auxiliaries and main verbs move to the head of TP in finite clauses, as already argued in Emonds (1976). In non-finite clauses, Pollock argues, auxiliaries can move to the head of TP, whereas main verbs can only undergo so-called "short verb movement" to the head of a projection intermediate between TP and VP, labelled AgrP. This accounts for the contrast between (7) and (8), as follows. In (7b), the infinitival auxiliary *être* raises to the head of TP, and as a result precedes the negative marker *pas* in linear order (*ne* is assumed to cliticize onto the verb and thus move along with it). In contrast, the infinitival lexical verb *sembler* in (8) only undergoes short verb movement to the head of AgrP; consequently, it follows *pas* in linear order (cf. 8a) and cannot precede it (cf. the ungrammaticality of 8b).[4] Similarly, this proposal accounts for the minimal pair in (9): the infinitival lexical verb *paraître* can undergo short verb movement, and thus land in a position on the left of the adverb *souvent* (assumed to occur in a position adjoined to VP), as shown in (9a); but it cannot raise all the way to the head of TP, and cannot land in a position to the left of *pas*, as shown in (9b).[5]

Pollock's proposal on how to account for the linear order of the verb with respect to VP-adverbs and postverbal negative markers like *pas* constitutes a first important step towards providing an answer for the question of whether or not negative markers have the same distribution as elements belonging to any of the syntactic categories that we know. Pollock's study can be taken to answer a subpart of that question, namely whether postverbal negative markers like French *pas* have the same distribution as VP-adverbs of the class of *souvent* "often." The answer given in this study is negative: this work clearly shows that we need to distinguish *pas* from VP-adverbs, if we want to be able to express the generalization that French exhibits the same restrictions on verb movement as English, though in infinitival rather than in finite clauses. As stated above, this is because infinitival lexical verbs in French can raise past the VP-adverbs, though not past the negative marker *pas*.

3.2   A comparison with pre-verbal clitics

The discussion in the previous section has focussed on the comparison of French *pas* with the class of VP-adverbs; the conclusion that these items must be viewed as belonging to two distinct syntactic classes, on the basis of their distribution, can be extended to other negative markers which occupy the same structural position as French *pas*, for example negative markers found in certain Northern Italian dialects (cf. Zanuttini 1997). It may also extend to the negative markers of many Germanic languages (e.g. German *nicht*, Dutch *niet*, Swedish *inte*), which occur higher than VP but lower than I. But that same conclusion does not straightforwardly extend to negative markers like French *ne*, or Italian *non*, or Spanish *no*, which occur in pre-verbal position. Pollock's arguments, based on the relative word order of auxiliaries and main verbs in relation to VP-adverbs and negative markers, simply do not extend to these elements, which consistently precede the verb, whether finite or non-finite, auxiliary or lexical. At first glance, these elements appear to share the distribution of pronominal clitics, given that they occur immediately adjacent to the verb and, if any element intervenes between them and the verb, it can only be a pronominal clitic. The question then arises whether these negative markers could be viewed as being of the same syntactic category as pronominal clitics.

The idea might seem implausible in light of the fact that they have completely different semantic functions, pronominal clitics being nominal elements which can bear a thematic role, negative markers conveying sentential negation to the interpretation of the clause. In principle, though, it is possible to conceive of a class of elements which have the same distribution without sharing any semantic component. It turns out, however, that this solution would be problematic not only because of their semantic differences, but also because a closer look reveals the existence of a number of discrepancies between the distribution of pronominal clitics and that of this class of negative markers. For example, whereas French *ne* shares the distribution of pronominal clitics in finite and infinitival clauses, where they both precede the verb (cf. 11), Italian *non* exhibits the same distribution as pronominal clitics in finite clauses only (cf. 12a), but not in infinitival clauses. In these contexts, *non* precedes the infinitival verb, whereas pronominal clitics follow it (cf. 12b):

(11)   a.   Jean *ne   les   mange* pas.   (French)
            John Neg Clitic eats   Neg
            "John doesn't eat them."

       b.   Jean voudrait   *ne*   pas *les   manger.*
            John would-want Neg Neg them to-eat
            "John would want not to eat them."

(12)   a.   Gianni *non le   mangia.*   (Italian)
            John   Neg them eats
            "John doesn't eat them."

       b.   Gianni preferisce *non* mangiar*le.*
            John   prefers   Neg to-eat-them
            "John prefers not to eat them."

Moreover, as pointed out in Zanuttini (1991: sec. 2.2.3), Italian *non* can be separated from the verb in certain marginal cases in which the verb can raise past the negative marker, an option which is not given to pronominal clitics. Given the appropriate context, it can also bear contrastive stress (cf. 13, where capitalization indicates phonetic prominence), whereas pronominal clitics can only do so in case of a meta-linguistic repair, i.e., within the template "not x but y":

(13)   a.   Preferisco NON farlo.   (Italian)
            prefer   Neg to-do-it
            "I'd prefer NOT to do it."

       b.   *Preferisco non farLO!

       c.   Preferisco non farLO,   ma farLA!
            prefer   Neg to-do-it (Masc) but to-do-it (Fem)

Differences of this kind warrant the conclusion that the pre-verbal negative markers under discussion are not to be viewed as part of the same syntactic class as pronominal clitics, even on purely distributional grounds. Once again, then, we are examining a class of negative markers whose properties are not the same as those of any other known syntactic category.

The proposal made in Pollock (1989) could be extended to cover these cases in several ways. Recall that, in Pollock's work, French *ne* is viewed as the head of the same projection NegP whose specifier is *pas*, which is generated lower than TP but above VP (see (10)). The reason why *ne* always precedes the verb, which is taken to occur in the head of TP in French, is that it is clitic in nature, and thus adjoins to the verb and raises with it. This proposal expresses the intuition that the negative marker *ne* belongs to a distinct syntactic category from pronominal clitics; at the same time, though, it captures the similarity in the distribution of negative markers and pronominal clitics, by arguing that both cliticize onto the verb. This proposal could be extended to other pre-verbal negative markers in Romance; for example, Belletti (1990, 1994) has extended it to Italian *non*.[6]

A different way of extending Pollock's (1989) proposal to these pre-verbal negative markers consists of exploiting the idea of an independent syntactic projection headed by negative markers, but having the pre-verbal negative marker be the head of a projection distinct from the one of which the postverbal negative marker is a specifier. This has been done, on the basis of different arguments, in Laka (1990) and Zanuttini (1991), among others. Laka (1990) argues for the existence of a functional projection whose possible instantiations are negation and emphatic affirmation. This proposal is based on the complementary distribution of negation and emphatic affirmation found in English and Basque. In English, as already pointed out in Chomsky (1957), sentential negation and emphatic affirmation are in complementary distribution, as shown in (14):

(14)   a.   I didn't, as Bill had thought, go to the store.
       b.   I DID, as Bill had thought, go to the store.
       c.   *I DID not, as Bill had thought, go to the store.

Moreover, the presence of an auxiliary or a modal, or else an instance of *do*-support, is required by both emphatic affirmation and by sentential negation expressed by means of the negative marker. This same requirement is also imposed by the overt element marking emphatic affirmation, *so* (cf. Klima 1964: 257), as illustrated in (15):

(15)   a.   The writers could *so* believe the boy.
       b.   *The writers *so* believed the boy.
       c.   The writers did *so* believe the boy.

Finally, as Laka points out, both negation and emphatic affirmation are in complementary distribution with *so*, as shown in (16):[7]

(16)   a.   *The writers didn't *so* believe the boy.
       b.   *The writers DID *so* believe the boy.

Hence, Laka's work concludes, the sentential negative marker *n't*, the abstract marking of emphatic affirmation, and the overt particle of emphatic affirmation *so* are all possible instantiations of the same functional projection in English, which is given the label P. Similarly, in Basque the negative particle *ez*, the abstract affirmative morpheme, and the emphatic particle *ba* are in complementary distribution and all trigger auxiliary fronting. This is taken to be supportive evidence for the existence of a functional projection with these particular elements. Laka's work extends the proposal concerning the existence of a single functional category housing negation and emphatic affirmation to Romance, arguing that in this language family such a projection occurs in a structural position lower than C but higher than TP. This projection can be headed by the pre-verbal negative markers of Romance, but cannot host the postverbal ones (such as French *pas*), since they occur too high in the structure. Laka's proposal therefore maintains Pollock's (1989) idea that the negative markers project an independent syntactic category, while suggesting that the structural position of such a category is higher than the one proposed in Pollock's work on the basis of the distribution of French *pas*.

Zanuttini (1991) extends Pollock's proposal in a direction similar to Laka's, but on the basis of different considerations. One consideration is that, in contrast with French *ne*, an account of the distribution of Italian *non* which assimilates it to pronominal clitics is problematic. We have already mentioned the differences between *non* and pronominal clitics in their ability to carry phonological prominence; moreover, as we will see in section 4, *non* does not form a cluster with pronononminal clitics, but rather counts as an intervening element which blocks their movement. A second consideration which supports treating Italian *non* as heading a projection other than the one of French *pas* stems from the comparison of pre-verbal negative markers with postverbal negative markers in co-occurrence with imperative verbs. While the former cannot negate a verbal form which is morphologically unique to the imperative (a suppletive verbal form must be used, from the paradigm of the subjunctive, the indicative, or the infinitive), the latter do not show any incompatibility with true imperative forms. Some examples are given below, in which the pre-verbal negative marker of Italian is contrasted with the postverbal negative marker of Piedmontese, a Romance variety spoken in northwestern Italy:

(17) a. Parla! (true imperative form)   (Italian)
          "Talk!" (2Sg)
      b. *Non* parla!
      c. *Non* parlare! (suppletive form)
          Neg to-talk
          "Don't talk!" (2Sg)

(18) a. Parla! (true imperative form)   (Piedmontese)
          "Talk!" (2Sg)
      b. Parla *nen*! (true imperative form)
          talk   Neg
          "Don't talk!"

The incompatibility of the pre-verbal negative marker with true imperative forms is systematically found within Romance whenever a language employs a negative marker which occurs in pre-verbal position and which negates the clause by itself. That is, it is found, among others, in languages like Spanish, Catalan, Italian, and the central and southern Italian dialects, all of which can negate a clause by means of a pre-verbal negative marker alone; but it is not necessarily found in languages where the pre-verbal negative marker must co-occur with another negative element to negate a clause. Zanuttini (1991) suggests that the contrast between pre-verbal and postverbal negative markers in co-occurrence with true imperative forms can best be accounted for by assuming that they each project a functional category (call them NegP-1 and NegP-2) in a different structural position, and with different sensitivities to their complement. In particular, pre-verbal negative markers, which head a projection NegP-1 higher than TP (NegP-1 TP . . . VP), require the presence of some feature in their complement which true imperatives lack, namely tense. In contrast, postverbal negative markers, which occur in a NegP-2 projection lower than at least some components of inflection (TP . . . NEGP-2 . . . VP), are not sensitive to the same properties of their complement.[8] Finally, a third consideration given in this work for extending Pollock's proposal but distinguishing the projection hosting postverbal negative markers like French *pas* from pre-verbal negative markers like Italian *non* is the following. The Romance languages which negate a clause by means of a negative marker like French *pas* or Piedmontese *nen* exhibit sentences where a negative indefinite occurs in postverbal position and is the only overt negative element in the clause. This is illustrated in (19) with an example from Piedmontese. In contrast, the Romance languages which negate a clause by means of a pre-verbal negative marker alone do not license negative indefinites in postverbal position unless they co-occur with a c-commanding negative element. This is illustrated with examples from Italian in the contrast between (20) and (21):

(19) a.   I   sento *gnente.*   (Piedmontese)
           SCl hear   nothing
           "I don't hear anything."
      b.   A   l'è   rivaye   *gnun.*
           SCl SCl'is arrived-there no one
           "Nobody arrived."

(20) a.   *Sento *niente.*   (Italian)
           hear   nothing
           "I don't hear anything."
      b.   *E' arrivato *nessuno.*
           is   arrived no one
           "Nobody arrived."

(21) a.   *Non* sento *niente.*
           "I don't hear anything."
      b.   *Non* è arrivato *nessuno.*
           "Nobody arrived."

Zanuttini (1991) takes this pattern to provide another reason for distinguishing the pre-verbal from the postverbal negative markers in Romance: assuming that they occur in different structural positions allows one to build an account of these contrasts where the strategy employed by a given language for the expression of sentential negation plays a crucial role in determining the licensing conditions for negative indefinites.[9]

3.3 *Negative markers and the projection NegP*

In this section we have seen that the proposals in Pollock (1989) have been extremely influential on recent studies on the syntactic expression of sentential negation. To summarize, one major empirical contribution of that work is the observation that the distribution of negative markers which follow the verb in I and precede the VP is not identical to that of the class of VP-adverbs. This observation, combined with the assumption present in Chomsky (1986) that functional elements have the same phrasal properties as lexical elements, led to a major theoretical innovation, namely the proposal that negative markers be viewed as elements heading an independent syntactic category, whose semantic properties can be characterized as contributing an instance of negation to the clause. This proposal captures the intuition that these negative markers have properties in common with functional elements (e.g. they express grammatical meaning and form a closed class), an intuition shared by researchers working on languages which employ negative markers and verbal affixes to express sentential negation.

This proposal has proven extremely fruitful in analyzing negative markers in many languages, including but also going beyond Germanic and Romance. As was briefly described in section 3.2, Pollock's original proposal has been extended in its empirical domain by proposing that not all negative markers belong to the same projection, but that more than one must be postulated. (In section 5 we will return to the issue of exactly how many distinct functional projections need to be postulated to account for the distribution of negative markers observed crosslinguistically.) Though such projections have been given different labels in different analyses, in this chapter I refer to them with the label NegP for simplicity.

4 The Phrase Structure Status of Negative Markers

We have introduced the hypothesis that negative markers are best viewed as elements which belong to a syntactic category of their own. Assuming that each category abides by X'-theory, we now need to ask, for any given negative marker, whether it is the head of such a category, hence an X°, or whether it is a maximal projection in its specifier, hence an XP. In this section we are going to discuss what kinds of test can tell us whether a negative marker is a head or a maximal projection. Studies on movement phenomena concur that heads interfere with the movement of heads, whereas maximal projections interfere with that of maximal projections. Thus one way to test the phrase structural status of negative markers consists in examining their behavior in the presence of the movement of other heads and maximal projections.

4.1 Negative markers as heads

One approach to the analysis of pronominal clitics in Romance, which follows the seminal work of Kayne on the topic, views them as heads. Given that heads interfere with the movement of heads, we can test the phrasal status of negative markers by observing their interaction with pronominal clitics. In particular, we need a context in which the pronominal clitics can normally undergo head-to-head movement on their way to a certain position; if the presence of a negative marker in that path makes movement of the pronominal clitics impossible, that can be taken as evidence for the head status of the negative marker. Such a situation indeed exists in Romance, and in fact it was the empirical basis for Kayne's (1989b) proposal that pre-verbal negative markers like French *ne* and Italian *non* are heads. In French, pronominal clitics which correspond to arguments of the embedded clause cliticize onto the matrix verb in causative constructions (cf. 22a); such a position is taken to be the result of head-to-head movement of the clitic. As pointed out in Kayne's work, if the negative marker *ne* is present in the embedded clause, movement of the clitic to the matrix clause gives rise to ungrammaticality (cf. 22b):

(22) a. Jean *la* fait   manger par/à Paul.   (French)
          John it makes to-eat   by/to Paul
          "John makes Paul eat it."
      b. *Jean *l'a*   fait   *ne* pas manger à l'enfant.
          John it-has made Neg Neg to-eat   to the-child
          "John made the child not eat it."

To account for this pattern Kayne (1989b) suggests that *ne* be viewed as a head, and that the presence of a head between the clitic on the matrix verb and its trace in the infinitival VP blocks the relation of antecedent government between the clitic and its trace. Kayne then extends this account to the cases of so-called "long clitic climbing" in Italian. These are contexts where a matrix predicate which belongs to the class of so-called "restructuring verbs" (cf. Rizzi 1982, Burzio 1986, among others) takes an infinitival clause as its complement. The pronominal clitics which are arguments of the embedded predicate can appear either in the embedded clause or in the matrix clause (cf. 23a, b). However, if the negative marker *non* is present in the complement clause, long clitic climbing yields results that are less than perfect, ranging from marginal to ungrammatical. This is shown in (24), where the perfectly grammatical example where the clitic is in the complement clause (24a) contrasts with the one where the clitic occurs in the matrix clause as a result of long clitic climbing (24b):[10]

(23) a. Gianni vuole veder*li*.   (Italian)
          John   wants to-see-them
          "John wants to see them."
      b. Gianni *li* vuole vedere.

(24) a. Gianni vuole *non* veder*li.*
          John   wants not to-see-them
          "John wants not to see them."
      b. *Gianni *li* vuole *non* vedere.

The blocking effect of Italian *non* can be given the same explanation as the blocking effect of French *ne*. More generally, the blocking effect of pre-verbal negative markers on pronominal clitics, in striking contrast with the lack of any such effect triggered by postverbal negative markers, can be seen as a good diagnostic test for their status as heads. The main problem with this test is that it is only viable if a language allows long clitic climbing, i.e., movement of pronominal clitics from the embedded to the matrix clause.

A different test which can help us determine whether a negative marker is a head, and which is possible in a different set of languages, consists in examining whether the pre-verbal negative marker interferes with verb movement to C. If the functional projection NegP occurs in a position structurally higher than the one occupied by the finite verb but lower than C, then a negative marker which is a head in terms of phrase structure should block movement of the verb to C. The most straightforward way to test this prediction is to examine a language which exhibits overt verb movement to C. Within Romance, French questions exhibit a different linear order between the finite verb and a pronominal subject than do declarative clauses. Similarly, certain northern Italian dialects exhibit a word order in questions in which the verb precedes the pronominal clitics (also referred to as "subject clitic inversion"). This contrasts with the word order they exhibit in declarative clauses, where the subject clitic precedes the finite verb. Because of the role attributed to the CP projection in the syntax and semantics of questions, this word order has often been analyzed as the result of verb movement to C.[11] Whereas subject clitic inversion is not affected by the presence of the pre-verbal negative marker *ne* in French, it does exhibit sensitivity to the presence of the pre-verbal negative marker in the northern Italian dialects. This can be exemplified with some examples from Paduan, a Romance variety spoken in the northern Italian city of Padua, and studied extensively in works such as Benincà and Vanelli (1982) and Poletto (1993a, 1993b):

(25) a. *El* vien.   (Paduan)
          SCl comes
          "He's coming."
      b. Vien-*lo*?
          comes-SCl
          "Is he coming?"

(26) a. *El no* vien.
          SCl Neg comes
          "He isn't coming."

b.   **No* vien-*lo?*
     Neg comes-SCl
c.   *Nol*   vien?
     Neg-SCl comes
     "Isn't he coming?"

(25) exemplifies the difference in linear order of the subject clitic with respect to the verb in declaratives and yes/no questions: only the latter exhibit
subject clitic inversion. (26) shows that, in the presence of the negative marker
no, subject clitic inversion gives rise to ungrammaticality. One way of analyzing
these data consists in arguing that verb movement to C, obligatory in affirmative yes/no questions (cf. 25b), is blocked by the presence of the negative
marker, which intervenes between the landing site of the verb and its trace.
The reasoning goes as follows: a blocking effect is expected to occur only
between elements of the same phrasal type; given that the verb is a head, the
blocking effect triggered by a negative marker leads to the conclusion that the
negative marker is also a head. I believe that this kind of evidence supports
the head status of certain negative markers, though I do not agree with the
claim often made concerning these cases, namely that they simply lack any
movement to C. The conceptual problem I see with arguing that nothing has
moved to C is the following: CP is generally assumed to play a central role in
the syntax and semantics of questions. Syntactically, in some languages at
least, verb movement to C is a crucial property differentiating a declarative
from an interrogative clause; thus verb movement to C has often been related
to the existence of certain features in CP (in the generativist tradition, from the
Q morpheme of Baker 1970 to the interrogative features of Chomsky 1995b). If
such movement must take place to form a question, whether to satisfy the
needs of an abstract morpheme or to check strong interrogative features, how
can it fail to take place in the presence of a negative marker without giving rise
to ungrammaticality? In other words, how is a clause with a negative marker
marked as a question, if the relevant syntactic operation (namely, verb movement to C) does not take place?
   One could of course conclude that movement to C is not an essential component in forming a question, thus circumventing this conceptual problem;
but the crosslinguistic generalizations which point in the direction of verb
movement to C as central to this clausal type in certain languages are quite
robust, and one is therefore reluctant to set them aside. Alternatively, one
could conclude that, at least in the case of yes/no questions, movement to C is
essential to mark the clause as interrogative, but that such movement does not
necessarily involve the verb. In Zanuttini (1997: sec. 2.4), I have argued that it
is the negative marker itself, a head, which moves to C in such negative questions; this movement suffices to mark the clause as a question. Thus, instead
of viewing the intervening negative marker as blocking verb movement, we
can view it as making verb movement to C unnecessary, by virtue of itself
being able to check the features that need to be checked in yes/no questions.[12]

Independently of this analysis and on the basis of data from several dialects of Chinese, Cheng et al. (1997) have reached the same conclusion. They observe that the question particle *ma* that marks yes/no questions is in complementary distribution with a negative marker in sentence final position, and conclude that the negative marker in Mandarin can fulfill the same function otherwise carried out by the question particle, namely that of syntactically marking a yes/no question.

4.2 Negative markers as maximal projections

Having examined the kind of evidence adduced in support of analyzing certain negative markers as heads, we can now turn our attention to the kind of evidence used to support their status as maximal projections. This comes in two forms: lack of the effects normally induced by heads (i.e., interference with head movement processes, as discussed above) and evidence of interference with movement of maximal projections.[13]

The former type of evidence is clear: in the languages where the verb is assumed to have raised out of the VP in the syntax and the negative markers follow the verb in linear order, they clearly must not block movement of the verb from its base position to its landing site. This is clearly seen in the case of French, already discussed in section 3, where finite verbs and infinitival auxiliaries can raise past the negative marker *pas* without it showing any blocking effect. Identical patterns are found in the other Romance varieties which exhibit postverbal negative markers, such as Catalan *pas* (cf. Espinal 1992), or the Romance varieties spoken in north-western Italy (cf. Parry 1996, 1997, and references there, Zanuttini 1997). The same is true of the Germanic languages, as can be seen in clear cases of verb movement. The following examples, from Holmberg and Platzack (1988), clearly illustrate that the Swedish negative marker *inte*, which precedes the verb in linear order in embedded clauses (cf. 27a), does not block verb movement in matrix clauses (cf. 27b), where the verb moves to second position:

(27) a.   ... om Jan *inte* köpte boken.   (Swedish)
             that John Neg bought books
             "... if John didn't buy books."
      b.   Jan köpte *inte* boken.
             John bought Neg books
             "John didn't buy books."

The second type of evidence mentioned above, namely interference of negative markers with movement of maximal projections, calls for a distinction between maximal projections which occupy an A-position and those which occupy an A'-position. Given the widely held assumption that minimality effects are only triggered by elements of the same type (cf. Rizzi 1990), only the movement of maximal projections in A'-positions is predicted to be affected by the presence of a negative marker, since negative markers occur in non-argument positions. This is the background for the discussion of the interference of negative markers with the extraction of adjuncts, the so-called "inner island" effects of Ross (1983). A purely syntactic account of these patterns is offered in Rizzi (1990), in terms of the blocking effect of the negative marker. Consider the contrast in (28), focussing on the interaction between the negative marker *pas* and the quantifier *beaucoup*:

(28) a. Il n'a   [*pas* [résolu *beaucoup* de problèmes]].   (French)
          he Neg'has Neg solved many   of problems
          "Many problems are such that he didn't solve them." OR
          "Not many problems are such that he solved them."
      b. Il n'a   [*pas* [*beaucoup* résolu [e de problèmes]]].
          he Neg'has Neg many   solved   of problems
          "Not many problems are such that he solved them."

(29) *beaucoup*$_i$ il n'a [*pas* [t$_i$ résolu [e de problèmes]]]

In (28a) the object *beaucoup de problèmes* does not move in the syntax, and the sentence has both the interpretation in which it has wider scope than the negative marker and the one where it has narrower scope than the negative marker. In contrast, in (28b) the quantifier *beaucoup* has moved to an A'-position in the syntax and the sentence can only have the interpretation in which the quantified object has narrower scope than the negative marker. In Rizzi's view the second interpretation is unavailable to (28b) because, if the quantifier raised at LF, it could not establish the proper relation of antecedent government with its trace due to the intervention of *pas*, a maximal projection in an A'-position (cf. the representation in 29). However, a wide scope interpretation is available when the quantifier remains in situ in the syntax, as in (28a), because the trace left in object position by LF-movement is theta-governed by the verb. Leaving aside the issue of whether a purely syntactic account is sufficient to account for negative island effects, this approach does not grant any conclusion concerning the phrasal status of negative markers. This is because negative island phenomena appear in the presence not only of negative markers which are maximal projections, but also of those which are heads by other syntactic tests, for example the pre-verbal negative marker of Italian, *non*. Rizzi (1990) notes this fact and suggests that it should be accounted for by assuming either that all negative markers must be in a specifier position at some level of representation, or that negative markers which are heads co-occur with a phonetically empty operator in their specifier. In effect, this rules out the possibility of using negative island phenomena as a diagnostic test for the phrasal status of negative markers. Suppose in fact that every negative marker which is a head co-occurred with an operator in its specifier; then its behavior with respect to inner island effects would be indistinguishable from that of a negative marker which is itself a maximal projection in a specifier position.

In sum, in this section we have examined some tests which can help one determine whether a negative marker is a head or a maximal projection. Though most of them require a particular constellation of properties in order to be applicable in a given language, I hope they convey a sense of the kinds of question that can be asked in order to determine the phrasal status of negative markers.

5 From Particular Languages to Universal Grammar

In the preceding sections we have discussed some basic tools for the syntactic characterization of negative markers offered to us by recent proposals. In this section, I would like to provide an overview of certain conclusions that have been reached in the literature concerning the syntactic expression of sentential negation in a variety of languages, with the goal of moving a step forward toward being able to define the range of variation permitted by UG in this domain. We will therefore address, albeit in some cases very briefly, the following issues:

- Does every language have a category NegP projected by its sentential negative markers?
- Is the structural position of NegP fixed or can it vary across languages?
- Can there be more than one NegP within a single clause?

The first issue, concerning whether the grammar of every language has a functional projection which expresses sentential negation, is an empirical matter. As we briefly saw in section 2, many languages negate a clause by means of elements descriptively labeled as particles, which we have been calling negative markers. In the case of each individual language, it needs to be established through the relevant syntactic tests whether these elements have the same distributional properties as some other lexical or functional element in that language (for example, adverbs, or pronominal clitics), or whether it is necessary to argue that they belong to an independent distributional class. As we saw in the course of our discussion, in some languages negative markers share the distribution of elements which mark emphatic affirmation, suggesting the existence of a class of functional elements marking a clause's polarity. In other languages, as discussed in Payne (1985), sentential negation is expressed not by negative markers, but by verbal forms. The issue arises concerning such languages, as in languages with negative markers, whether it is advantageous, theoretically and/or empirically, to postulate that negative clauses contain an abstract functional projection with formal features relevant for the expression of sentential negation. Such languages will need to be evaluated on a case by case basis.

The second issue, concerning whether the structural position of NegP is fixed or can vary across languages, has already been addressed indirectly in section 3, while presenting some of the arguments adduced in the literature for the postulation of a projection NegP. If we accept Pollock's arguments distinguishing French *pas* from adverbs, and if we find convincing the reasons for postulating a structural distinction between French *pas* on the one hand and Italian *non* and Spanish *no* on the other, then we reach the conclusion that NegP is not in a fixed position crosslinguistically. In agreement with this conclusion, Ouhalla (1990) proposes that the position of the projection NegP constitutes one of the two ways in which languages can differ with respect to the syntactic expression of sentential negation (the other being whether the negative marker is a head or a maximal projection). His idea is cast in terms of a parameter, which expresses the different structural positions in terms of the selectional properties of the head of the projection NegP:

(30)   **The NEG Parameter** (Ouhalla 1990):
   a.   NEG selects VP.
   b.   NEG selects TNS(P).

This work assumes the following sequence of functional projections: AgrP TP NegP VP. It captures the difference between French *ne* and English *not*, as well as between Berber *ur-* and Turkish *-me-* (cf. 31 below) by assuming that, in each pair, the former takes the tense projection as its complement, whereas the latter takes the VP. This proposal is supported by the relative linear order of the negative marker and the tense morpheme. In Berber, a head initial language, the negative marker immediately precedes the tense morpheme (cf. 31a), the linear order expected to result from the head–complement relation. In Turkish, where the head follows its complement (since it is a head final language), the tense morpheme follows the negative morpheme which in turn follows the verb, a linear order which is seen to result from tense selecting negation, and in turn negation selecting VP (cf. 31b):

(31)   a.   *Ur-ad*-y-xdel   Mohand dudsha.   (Berber)
            Neg-will TNS-3MascSg(AGR)-arrive Mohand tomorrow
            "Mohand will not arrive tomorrow."
       b.   John elmalar-i   *ser-me*-di-().   (Turkish)
            John apples-Acc like-Neg-pastTNS-3Sg(AGR)
            "John does not like apples."

Though more recent studies have suggested that the range of variation in the position of NegP is wider than that suggested by the NEG Parameter, this proposal was the first to explicitly state that the structural position of NegP can vary across languages.

The third issue, whether there can be more than one NegP in a single clause, is addressed at length in Zanuttini (1997: ch. 3). This work examines Romance varieties spoken in northern Italy which negate the clause by means of a postverbal negative marker.[14] Some of these languages have two morphologically distinct postverbal negative markers, which differ both in distribution and in the contribution they make to the interpretation of the clause. The difference in distribution can be detected by analyzing their relative position with respect to different classes of adverbs, following Cinque's (1994b, 1999) classification. When a language has two postverbal negative markers, one of them obligatorily precedes adverbs of the class of "already," as shown in (32) for Piedmontese *pa* and Milanese *minga*:[15]

(32) a. A l'è *pa gia* parti.   (Piedmontese)
          SCl SCl-is Neg already left
          "He hasn't already left."
      b. L'è *minga gemò* partì.   (Milanese)
          SCl-is Neg already left
          "He hasn't already left."

The second negative marker, in contrast, follows "already"; depending on the language, it either precedes the next class of adverbs (i.e., "no more") in the hierarchical structure, as is the case with Piedmontese *nen* and Valdotain *pa*, or else it follows "already" and two other adverb classes, namely "no more" and "always." In the case of Milanese *no*, this can be seen in clauses containing an auxiliary and a past participle. The past participle can occur to the right of *semper* "always," but it can also raise to the head position immediately above it, whose specifier is an adverb of the class of "no more," or to the next head, whose specifier hosts adverbs like "already." This is illustrated schematically below (from Zanuttini 1997: 88):

(33) *minga* - (participle) - *gemò* - (participle) - *pü* - (participle) -
      Neg   already   no more
      semper - (participle)
      always

Crucially, though, the past participle cannot occur to the right of the negative marker *no*, thus suggesting that *no* occurs in a position lower than the one where *semper* occurs:

(34) *minga* - (participle) - *gemò* - (participle) - *pü* - (participle) - *semper* -
      Neg   already   no more   always
      (participle) - *no*
                     Neg

Besides differing in distribution, the negative markers which occur higher than "already" differ from the lower ones in their contribution to the interpretation of the clause: these negative markers are used when the proposition which is being negated is assumed in the discourse, or presupposed (Zanuttini 1997 uses the label "presuppositional negative markers" for this class of elements). The ones which are structurally lower than "already," in contrast, negate a proposition which does not have a special discourse status. Based on these observations, it seems that, within Romance, these is support for the postulation of four distinct projections hosting negative markers, which cannot be collapsed with those hosting adverbs. Distinguishing them by assigning the lowest number to the one which is structurally highest, they can be described as follows: NegP-1 is the projection of negative markers like Italian *non* and Spanish *no*, which precede the finite verb; NegP-2 corresponds to the presuppositional negative markers, exemplified by Piedmontese *pa* and Milanese *minga*, which precede adverbs like "already"; NegP-3 is the projection of Piedmontese *nen*, lower than the one hosting "already" but higher than the one hosting "any more"; NegP-4 is the projection of Milanese *no*, lower than the projection whose specifier is "always." Following Cinque's proposal on both the structure of the clause and the content of the functional projections hosting the adverbs relevant for the distribution of negative markers, Zanuttini (1997: 101) summarizes these positions with the following diagram:

(35)   NegP-1

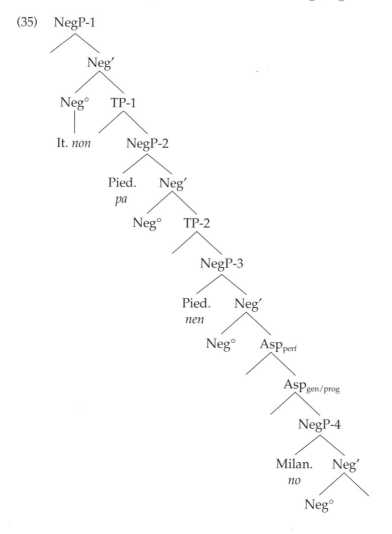

This conclusion, drawn from the study of several varieties of Romance, can be rephrased in more general terms in light of Cinque's work. On the assumption that the sequence of functional projections is made available by UG to all languages, individual languages will differ depending on which ones they instantiate. Thus, rather than thinking of a binary choice between a projection NegP taking TP as a complement and a projection NegP taking VP as a complement, we can think of crosslinguistic variation in this domain as resulting from differences concerning which of the available NegP projections a given language instantiates, and why.

6 Conclusion

In this chapter I have focussed on a set of issues concerning the syntax of sentential negation which center on the proper characterization of negative markers. Although this is only one piece in the mosaic of issues that relate to the grammatical representation of sentential negation, it is an important one both in itself and for the analysis of other grammatical phenomena. The kinds of question raised in this chapter, and the kind of reasoning adopted in searching for answers to them, can hopefully provide a sense of our current understanding of these issues, a useful background for reading current literature on the topic, and the basis for further progress.

NOTES

1 Cf. also Dahl (1979), Dryer (1989), Bernini and Ramat (1992), and Kahrel and van den Berg (1994).

2 All the examples in this section are from Payne (1985).

3 Pollock (1989) points out that modal-like verbs such as *vouloir* "want," *devoir* "must," and *pouvoir* "can" also contrast with lexical verbs in being able to precede *pas* in infinitival clauses.

4 One problem left open by this account concerns the relative order of *ne* and *pas* in cases of short verb movement. If *ne* is the head of the projection of which *pas* is the specifier, and it precedes *pas* in linear order because it raises along with the verb, it should fail to precede *pas* when the verb does not

raise past NegP because it only undergoes short verb movement. However, *ne* always precedes *pas* in linear order, even in cases of short verb movement (cf. 8a).

5 Pollock's (1989) paper makes a very precise proposal concerning what the difference in verb movement should be derived from. Because it is not strictly relevant for the study of sentential negation, I will not discuss it here but simply refer the reader to Pollock's work.

6 Belletti (1990) directly extends Pollock's (1989) proposal for French *ne* to Italian *non*. Belletti (1994) refines the earlier proposal concerning the movement of Italian *non* to pre-verbal position and suggests that this movement is

similar to, though distinct from, that of pronominal clitics.

7   See also Kayne (1989b) for an analysis of the complementary distribution of the negative marker *n't* and the particle of emphatic affirmation *so* in English.

8   The dots in the diagrams are intended to suggest that other functional projections may intervene which do not affect the distribution of NegP. See Zanuttini (1997) for a more comprehensive discussion of the data and of the strengths and weaknesses of two possible approaches to negative imperatives.

9   Due to space limitations, I cannot discuss the proposed account here. I refer the interested reader to Zanuttini (1991) and Ladusaw (1992).

10   The grammaticality of long clitic climbing in the presence of a pre-verbal negative marker is sensitive to a complex set of factors, which include the lexical choice in the matrix predicate, as well as its aspectual properties. For example, Treviño (1991) points out that long clitic climbing across the negative marker *no* is not completely ruled out in Spanish when the matrix predicate is a modal verb.

11   For French, cf. Kayne and Pollock (1978) and Rizzi and Roberts (1989), among others, for the view that such movement takes place in the syntax, and Sportiche (to appear) for the view that it takes place covertly, i.e., at LF.

12   The case of *wh*-questions is slightly different, at least in Paduan: in the presence of a pre-verbal negative marker blocking verb movement, a cleft construction is used. See Zanuttini (1997) for a description and an analysis of this syntactic strategy.

13   As pointed out by the editors of this volume, a third test that can be used to determine the phrasal status of an element is extraction: if a constituent can be moved to a position usually occupied by a maximal projection, then it is a maximal projection. For example, the fact that the adverb *never* in English can be moved to a position generally assumed to be a specifier, as in (i), argues for its status as a maximal projection. In contrast, the impossibility of preposing the negative marker *not*, as in (ii), in conjunction with the differences between *never* and *not* related to the use of do-support, argues for the head status of *not*:

(i)   *Never* had I read such a book.

(ii) *Not had I read such a book.

Though in principle this is a good test, in practice it does not help us distinguish negative markers which are heads from those which are maximal projections, since to my knowledge no negative marker can be fronted in this way. This suggests that factors other than their phrasal status must be at play to block such movement.

14   Although an answer to the question concerning multiple NegPs might also come from languages where a pre-verbal and a postverbal negative marker co-occur, the case of languages which employ only postverbal negative markers is clearer. As we saw in the discussion of French, pre-verbal *ne* and postverbal *pas* might have originated in the same functional projection and have been separated by movement. In this work, I will leave open the issue of where *ne* originates.

15   For the sake of brevity, I will not give the second half of the paradigm, namely the examples where the negative marker follows the adverb corresponding to

"already," which are ungrammatical. Similarly, I will not provide the examples which show that the relative order of adverbs in these languages is the same as the order found by Cinque (1994b) to hold in Italian and French; I refer the reader to Zanuttini (1997: ch. 3). Cinque (1994b, 1999) argues that the relative order of certain classes of adverbs is fixed and holds crosslinguistically, since it reflects the fixed ordering of the functional projections in which they occur. Simplifying his results, for the relevant part of the clause, between the lowest tense projection and the VP, the elements which occur in the specifier of a functional projection are the following, in their relative order: neg – already – no more – always – completely.

17 The DP Hypothesis: Identifying Clausal Properties in the Nominal Domain

JUDY B. BERNSTEIN

0 Introduction

Significant advances in X'-theory came about with Chomsky's (1986b) *Barriers*. In this work, Chomsky proposed that not only lexical elements like nouns and verbs, but also functional elements like complementizers and auxiliaries, project to the phrasal level. So, in addition to VP, *Barriers* advocated the functional categories Complementizer Phrase (CP) and Inflection Phrase (IP), which now constituted the "extended projection" (Grimshaw 1991) of the lexical head, the verb. In *Barriers*, Chomsky never applied this revised notion of X'-theory to the nominal domain, which continued to be represented as NP. In particular, determiner elements, such as definite articles, continued to be generated in SpecNP, although this sort of configuration was inconsistent with at least two aspects of X'-theory: (i) the idea that lexical as well as functional elements project to the phrasal level, and (ii) the notion that specifier positions host phrasal categories (e.g. *wh*-phrases in SpecCP, sentential subjects in SpecIP). These issues were addressed by Abney (1987), whose important work on noun phrases benefited from earlier work by, for example, Szabolcsi (1983) on Hungarian, and Brame (1982).[1] Abney, building on the work of his predecessors, provided theoretical and empirical arguments for the idea that a functional category, Determiner Phrase (DP), is the maximal category projected by the class of determiner elements and heads the noun phrase. Put another way, the DP represents the extended, and maximal, projection of the lexical head, the noun. This pioneering proposal had the immediate advantage of resolving the problems posed for X'-theory by the traditional characterization of NPs, and of unifying the treatment of noun phrases and clauses. The structure Abney proposed for DPs is given in (1):

(1)

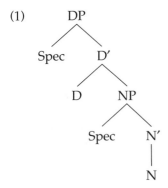

This basic representation has been adopted in much of the subsequent work on nominal structure.

This chapter and the following one by Giuseppe Longobardi are intended as an overview of some of the major issues in and contributions to the study of the syntax of DPs. The advent of what has been labeled "the DP Hypothesis" facilitated the (re-)examination of various aspects of noun phrases. In preparing this chapter, I have focussed on those aspects of DPs that I feel to be most relevant to the issue of parallels between noun phrases and clauses, as well as on those aspects that I am most knowledgeable about. The reader who is intent on pursuing things further is therefore encouraged to track down the relevant sources.

In section 1, I begin by reviewing several proposals that led the way towards assimilating noun phrases to their counterparts in the clausal domain. Of central importance are crosslinguistic morphological, syntactic, and semantic arguments for assuming a nominal counterpart to CP, namely DP. A productive area of inquiry concerns language internal and crosslinguistic word order variations, which are taken up in section 2. A natural question to consider here is whether word order variations reflect fundamental crosslinguistic differences or more superficial differences in syntactic operations. Section 3 addresses the issue of functional categories in DPs. Work on the clause has revealed evidence for functional projections corresponding to, for example, agreement, tense, and negation. This then raises the issue of whether parallel evidence exists for functional projections internal to DP. Indeed, proposals have been made for DP-internal functional projections corresponding to, for example, number (i.e., singular, plural), gender, and case, as well as for a functional category projected by quantifier elements. Several of these proposals will be reviewed and evaluated. Section 4 offers some concluding remarks and observations.

1   From "NP" to "DP"

The DP hypothesis resolves what was a theoretical inconsistency between the treatment of noun phrases and clauses. That is, according to this approach nouns, like verbs, project to a functional category. But is there empirical evidence to support such a proposal?

As it turns out, the theory internal advantages of adopting a DP hypothesis are matched by the compelling empirical arguments for doing so. I will demonstrate that there are morphological, syntactic, and semantic arguments for adopting a DP structure, recalling the sorts of argument made for IP/CP in the clausal domain. In the following subsections, I briefly review some of the most striking empirical support for the DP hypothesis. It is important to keep in mind that these data, in addition to lending support to the DP hypothesis, could not easily be accommodated in a pre-DP framework.

1.1   *Morphological evidence for DP*

Abney (1987: 37–53) discusses languages in which the agreement morphology in the clause and the noun phrase match in terms of both the type of agreement expressed and the manner of expression. In other words, what is observed in these languages is that a possessed noun agrees with its subject in the same way, and with the same agreement morphology, as a verb agrees with its clausal subject. A language falling into this category is Yup'ik, a Central Alaskan Eskimo language. Consider the examples in (2) (from Abney 1987: (24), 39). In Yup'ik, both the verb and its subject are marked with matching ergative case, expressed via an identical agreement suffix (-*t* in this instance), as illustrated in (2a).[2] Similarly, a noun and its possessor are marked for agreement and the morpheme involved (i.e., -*t*), as illustrated in (2b), matches that found in the clause:

(2)   a.   angute-t kiputa-a-t   (Yup'ik)
            man-Erg (Pl) buy-OM-SM
            "the men bought it"
       b.   angute-t kuiga-t
            the man-Erg (Pl) river-SM
            "the men's river"

Matching nominal and clausal agreement morphology also characterizes Mayan languages. Abney illustrates the patterns with data from the Mayan language of Tzutujil (data drawn from Dayley 1985).

Hungarian, a nominative/accusative language, also exhibits identical agreement affixes on nouns and verbs. The data in (3) (Abney 1987: (36), 44, data drawn from Szabolcsi 1983) illustrate the Hungarian nominal agreement pattern, where case is expressed on the possessor and the head noun agrees with the possessor in person and number. In (4) (Szabolcsi 1983: (4), 90), I have illustrated the parallel subject agreement pattern in the clause, where the sentential subject is marked for case and the verb displays number and person agreement with the subject:

(3)   a.   az én-ø vendég-e-m   (Hungarian)
the I-Nom guest-Poss-1Sg
"my guest"

b.   a te-ø vendég-e-d
the you-Nom guest-Poss-2Sg
"your guest"

c.   (a) Mari-ø vendég-e-ø
(the) Mary-Nom guest-Poss-3Sg
"Mary's guest"

(4)   Mari-ø alud-t-ø   (Hungarian)
Mary-Nom sleep-Past-3Sg
"Mary slept"

As Abney discusses and illustrates, Turkish also displays DP-internal agreement (patterns and data Abney examines are from Underhill 1976, Kornfilt 1984). In this language, the possessor displays genitive case and the head noun agrees in number and gender with the possessor. Although Turkish nominal agreement morphology is not identical in form to the corresponding verbal agreement morphology, Kornfilt has shown that both nominal and verbal agreement morphology licenses pro-drop, a property which is apparently also found in the other languages discussed above.

On the basis of patterns and properties of the type reviewed here, both Szabolcsi and Kornfilt have advocated approaches whereby these "sentential NPs" are represented clausally, that is, as (nominal) IPs. An approach along these lines, if strictly adopted, would involve a switch of syntactic category from NP, the category relevant for non-possessive noun phrases, to IP, the category relevant for possessive noun phrases. Abney, building on these basic insights, proposed and developed the idea that the nominal equivalent of the clause is DP. This DP-hypothesis established parallel structural representations for sentences and noun phrases, as suggested by Szabolcsi and Kornfilt and as supported by the Hungarian and Turkish data they examined. At the same time, Abney's distinguishing the sentential functional projections (IP, CP) from the nominal functional projection (DP) obviated a situation where a single clausal projection simultaneously served as the functional category relevant for nouns and verbs.[3]

1.2   Syntactic evidence for DP

Within syntax, there are a number of areas that provide evidence of parallelisms between the nominal and clausal domains. Among these are argument structure, word order, and ellipsis. In this section, I briefly discuss only the first two of these areas of correspondence, namely, argument structure and word order.[4] A more in-depth examination of DP word order phenomena follows in sections 2 and 3.

The basic similarity in argument structure between nouns and verbs may be represented by the well-known examples in (5), adapted from Chomsky (1970). These examples show that nouns, like verbs, may take both internal and external arguments:

(5)   a.   Rome destroyed Carthage
       b.   Rome's destruction of Carthage

Moreover, there is compelling evidence from binding and control phenomena that the arguments in the nominal domain are hierarchically arranged in a manner parallel to that in the clausal domain. Important work by Cinque (1980), for example, demonstrated that only the highest argument in the noun phrase could be extracted (that is, possessivized), lending support to the idea of a hierarchical organization of nominal arguments. The topic of argument structure in the nominal domain has been addressed in recent work by various linguists, including Grimshaw (1990), Picallo (1991), Valois (1991), Siloni (1991, 1994), Taraldsen (1990), and Giorgi and Longobardi (1991). Longobardi (this volume) addresses the topic of the hierarchy of DP arguments (possessor, subject, object), including empty arguments.

An influential proposal concerning the organization of clausal arguments was developed in Sportiche (1988) and Koopman and Sportiche (1991). Their idea was that the internal and external arguments of the verb are generated VP-internally, within the lexical structure of the verbal head, and it is within this VP-projection that thematic roles are assigned. In particular, their analysis incorporated the idea that the subject of the verb is generated in Spec VP rather than directly in SpecIP, as previously assumed. Under this sort of approach, referred to as "the VP-Internal Subject Hypothesis," the specifiers of functional heads are positions moved into, either for case assignment, as in the case of A-movement to SpecIP, or for checking of *wh*-features, as in the case of A'- (e.g. *wh*-)movement to SpecCP.[5] Support for this proposal comes from so-called quantifier float in French, illustrated in the examples in (6) (examples adapted from Sportiche 1988):

(6)   a.   Toutes les filles ont reçu les notes.   (French)
            all the girls have received the grades
            "All the girls received the grades."
       b.   Les filles ont toutes reçu les notes.
            the girls have all received the grades
            "The girls all received the grades."

In the example in (6a), the subject of the sentence *toutes les filles* is assumed to occupy the sentential subject position, SpecIP. Notice that in (6b), the sentential subject *les filles* is separated from the quantifier *toutes*, which nevertheless exhibits morphological (gender and number) agreement with *les filles*. These and other facts argue that *toutes les filles* is generated as a constituent in SpecVP and raises as a unit to SpecIP in (6a). In (6b), on the other hand, only *les filles* raises, stranding the quantifier *toutes* in its base generated position internal to SpecVP.

The internal structure of the DP may be treated along parallel lines. That is, the subject argument of the DP (for example, a possessive) would be generated in SpecNP and the object argument(s) as complement(s) of the noun head.[6] This approach has been taken in work by, for example, Ritter (1988) on Hebrew, whose proposals are examined in section 3.1 in a discussion about DP functional projections. Similarly, Picallo (1991) and Valois (1991) extended proposals about clausal arguments and thematic hierarchy in Romance languages to the domain of the DP, although not all DP-arguments are generated NP-internally in their work. An issue that has not yet been extensively addressed is whether these DP-arguments raise, and if so, to which specifier positions (see, however, Picallo 1994 for an analysis on possessive pronouns in Catalan).

Within the general area of thematic structure, another topic that has been pursued concerns the distinction between A-positions (that is, argument positions) and A'-positions (that is, non-argument positions). Within the domain of the clause, SpecIP is an A-position that hosts the sentential subject and SpecCP is an A'-position that may host *wh*-phrases. Valois (1991), extending proposals made by Szabolcsi (1987), Tellier (1988), and others, developed the idea that SpecDP is an A'-position, on a par with proposals about SpecCP in the clause. Szabolcsi has argued that DP-arguments in Hungarian move to this position, where they receive dative case, and that SpecDP is the landing site for DP-internal *wh*-movement. Tellier proposed that empty operators may occupy SpecDP in French, licensing traces that would not be accessible for *wh*-extraction. Similarly, Valois appeals to the idea of the A'-status of SpecDP to account for the impossibility of extraction from embedded DPs and PPs in French.

The second important area of correspondence between the syntax of noun phrases and clauses concerns word order phenomena. Probably the most compelling type of evidence for assuming syntactic movement in the clause comes from word order variation found across languages, particularly among closely related languages. In early and pioneering work on the clause, Emonds (1978), and later Pollock (1989), argued that word order differences between French and English can be accounted for by assuming the relative presence of verb movement in French and its relative absence in English. This by now famous work appealed to several syntactic properties distinguishing French and English. Of particular significance are facts about the position of adverbs with respect to the verb in French versus English. Simplifying somewhat, the basic pattern in French is that adverbs follow finite verbs (and precede complements), and in English that they precede. The analysis that Pollock developed is that the underlying order of these elements crosslinguistically is adverb followed by verb, and that the surface order found in French is a result of the verb crossing over the adverb. Specifically, it was proposed that the verb in French raises to the relevant functional head in the clause (either T of TensePhrase or Agr of AgrPhrase, corresponding to Pollock's more articulated structure for IP). Pollock claimed that the robustness of verb movement in French, compared with its relative absence in English, correlates with the "rich morphological agreement" characterizing French (see Pollock's article for a formalization of the notion "rich morphological agreement").

Within the nominal domain, the obvious candidate for the correlate of the adverb is the adjective. A natural question to pursue is whether there are similarities between adverbs and adjectives with respect to their position in the clause. In fact, across Romance languages, not only do adverbs tend to be postverbal, but adjectives tend to be postnominal (and they precede noun complements). Recent work on DPs by Cinque (1994a), Crisma (1990, 1996), Bernstein (1991a, 1991b, 1992, 1993a, 1993b), Valois (1991), Picallo (1991), Zamparelli (1993), and others has advanced the idea that, crosslinguistically, the underlying word order in the DP is adjective–noun, which happens to correspond to the surface order found across Germanic languages. According to this approach, the surface order noun–adjective found across Romance languages is the result of the noun raising across the adjective(s) to a functional head situated on the path from N to D.

What about the D-position itself? Is there evidence that the N may raise all the way up to D? In fact, several proposals for N-to-D-raising have been advanced, and for a diverse set of languages. The topic of N-to-D-raising will be taken up in some detail in sections 2.1 and 2.2. The important point to make here is that evidence of N-to-D-movement provides yet another correspondence to what has been discovered about the clause. In particular, it is natural to take N-raising to the highest functional head in the nominal domain (i.e., D) to be equivalent to V-raising to the highest functional head in the clausal domain (i.e., C).[7]

1.3   Semantic evidence for DP

The more highly articulated representation of the clause encoded in Chomsky's (1986b) revision to X'-theory provides a structural correlate for a traditionally semantic partition, namely, the distinction between sentential arguments and non-arguments (propositions).[8] I follow the traditional idea that an argument is a syntactic constituent that bears a thematic role. In Higginbotham's (1987: 45–6) terms, an argument is "saturated" and can be assigned a thematic role. In a CP system, matrix sentences (propositions) would correspond to IP and sentential arguments to CP. Consider the examples in (7)–(9):[9]

(7)   a.   [Isabel llegó].   (Spanish)
      b.   *[Que Isabel llegó].
           "(That) Isabel arrived."

(8)   a.   [Que Isabel llegó] sorprendió a su padre.   (Spanish)
      b.   *[Isabel llegó] sorprendió a su padre.
           "(That) Isabel arrived surprised her father."

(9) a. Creo [que Isabel llegó].   (Spanish)
     b. *Creo [Isabel llegó].
         "I-believe (that) Isabel arrived."

In (7), the Spanish equivalent of the bracketed sentence *Isabel arrived* can only function as a matrix sentence, not an argument, and so the complementizer does not appear. In contrast, the complementizer must introduce the same sentence when it functions as an argument of a verbal predicate (corresponding to the sentential subject in (8) and the verbal complement in (9)). The complementizer may be thought of as a lexicalized marker of the argumenthood of a sentence or, following Szabolcsi (1992: 130), as a "subordinator" that allows a clause to function as an argument.[10]

The CP-system apparently manages the semantic argument/non-argument distinction straightforwardly, treating a proposition as an IP and assigning to the head of CP the complementizer that introduces a sentential argument. Does the DP-system afford the same advantages in the nominal domain? In other words, is there parallel semantic justification for distinguishing NP and DP?

Indeed, semantic properties of noun phrases indicate that the argument/ non-argument distinction is relevant there as well, and furthermore, that non-arguments (i.e., nominal predicates) correspond to NP and arguments to DP (Szabolcsi 1987, Abney 1987, Longobardi 1994, among others) or, alternatively, that NPs are non-referential and DPs are referential (Stowell 1989b). Let us briefly examine some of the applications of these ideas.

Higginbotham's proposal about saturation and its role in the semantics of arguments predicts noun phrase arguments to be saturated and bear thematic roles and noun phrase predicates to be unsaturated and lack theta-roles. Generally speaking, an article may serve to "convert" a predicate NP into an argument DP. Consider the examples in (10) (discussed in Longobardi 1994: 618–19), which display a contrast absent in a language like English:

(10) a. Gianni é medico (*che . . .).   (Italian)
          "John is (a) doctor (that . . .)."
      b. Gianni é un medico (che . . .).
          "John is a doctor (that . . .)."

The articleless nominal expression *medico* in (10a) functions as a predicate of the copula and may be taken to correspond to NP. That (10a) involves an NP-predicate and not a DP-argument is supported by the fact that the nominal expression may not serve as the "head" of a relative clause. Indeed, as Mandelbaum (1994: 14) observes, predicate NPs seem to be adjectival in nature. Predicative NPs also typically appear in vocative contexts. In contrast, the same nominal expression is introduced by an indefinite article in (10b), suggesting that the entire nominal expression is a DP. That this nominal expression is a DP, and therefore an argument, is supported by the fact that *un medico* may serve as the head of a relative clause.

Szabolcsi's proposals about subordinators and their role in establishing argument-hood apply in the nominal domain as well. According to this approach, an NP cannot, on its own, serve as an argument because it is not introduced by a subordinator, which may take the form of, among other things, the definite article.[11] Szabolcsi's analysis is consistent with the accounts put forth by Longobardi, Mandelbaum, and others.

Longobardi (1994, this volume) observes that certain articleless nominal expressions may nevertheless function as arguments. In many European languages, for example, plural and mass nouns may function as arguments, subject to parametric variation in distribution and interpretation. It is natural to assume, as Longobardi does, that these nominal expressions are (DP) arguments introduced by a determiner devoid of lexical content. Also extensively developed is the idea, somewhat simplified here, that another argument-forming strategy is available (subject to parametric variation), namely, raising the N-head to D. This strategy may form DP-arguments from articleless nominal expressions involving proper names (see section 2.1 for further discussion on N-to-D-raising and proper names).

This brief discussion has highlighted some of the ideas developed about structural correlates to semantic functions in the clausal and nominal domains. In particular, there is support for the claim that propositions and clausal arguments correspond to IP and CP, respectively. Analogously, under a DP analysis, nominal predicates correspond to NP and nominal arguments to DP. Another advantage of the DP-analysis is that it provides a functional head (that is, D) that encodes semantic features of determiner elements. Some of the features claimed to be encoded in D are (in)definiteness, specificity, referentiality, and deixis. On these and related topics see, among others, Longobardi (1994), Mandelbaum (1994), Crisma (1997), Zamparelli (1995), Schmitt (1996), and Vangsnes (1996a).

2   Word Order and Movement

Syntactic work on the clause has provided evidence that certain word order patterns (e.g. verb second in Germanic languages) involve verb movement to C, higher than the verb movement proposed by Pollock to account for verb–adverb order in French. Subsequent investigation on Romance languages (see, for example, Belletti 1990) has in fact revealed evidence for a more fine-grained characterization of movement. In other words, verb movement is not necessarily an all-or-nothing phenomenon, but rather, may be characterized in more relative terms. The positing of additional functional categories facilitated proposals for so-called partial verb movement, a situation in which the verb raises somewhat, but not to the highest available (functional) head. What exactly determines how high a verb can raise has not yet been made precise, although some hypotheses have been posited. A distinction must also be made between head movement of a verb to functional heads within CP, and phrasal movement to specifier positions, such as raising of a clausal subject from SpecVP to SpecIP.

A closer look at word order variation within DPs should take into account these clausal patterns and the analyses developed to account for them. In particular, it is important to ask the following three questions: (i) is there evidence for noun movement to D, the highest functional head in the DP?; (ii) is there evidence for movement to positions intervening between N and D, and if so, what is the nature of these positions?; and (iii) is there evidence for phrasal movement internal to DP? As I will demonstrate in the following subsections and have previewed in earlier sections, the answer to all three questions is, remarkably, yes. In other works, there is evidence for N-raising to D, for partial noun movement to functional heads intervening between N and D, and even for phrasal movement internal to DP, further supporting in a strong way the idea that clausal CP and nominal DP are parallel maximal projections.

Arguments for N-to-D-raising have been proposed for Romance languages in Longobardi (1994, 1995) and Bernstein (1991b), for Hebrew in Ritter (1988, 1991) and Siloni (1991), and for Scandinavian languages in Taraldsen (1990), Delsing (1988), Santelmann (1993), and Kester (1993). Some of this work will be discussed in sections 2.1 and 2.2.

Evidence for partial noun movement comes from the variation in the position of the noun relative to the adjective(s) in various Romance varieties. As I will discuss in section 2.2, both the position of a particular type of adjective relative to the noun, and crosslinguistic differences in the basic position for adjectives, support a more fine-grained approach to noun movement.

There have also been proposals for DP-internal phrasal movement. To my knowledge, Szabolcsi (1983) was the first to propose movement of this kind. In particular, she proposed that SpecDP, on a par with SpecCP, is an "escape hatch" for extraction from DP, an idea adopted by Valois (1991) for a language like French. Picallo (1994), in a study of possessive pronouns in Catalan, develops the idea that these elements, which bear thematic roles and which she argues are generated in SpecNP, raise through the specifiers of nominal functional projections (below DP), the highest of which, NumberPhrase (see section 3.1), is a raising category. Another line of proposals (see Bernstein 1993a, Sánchez 1995a, and Martin 1995) argues that the position of (certain) postnominal adjectives in Romance languages is derived by phrasal movement of the extended NP. In addition to these analyses there have been proposals for several other types of phrasal movement internal to DP, two of which I will review in sections 2.3 and 2.4.

In section 2.3, I discuss Kayne's (1994) analysis of relative clauses, which resurrects the idea that the position of the "head" of a relative clause is actually a derived one. In other words, the head noun (and its modifiers) raises leftward from its underlying argument position to its final position to the left of the complementizer. In section 2.4, I review Bernstein's (1997) proposal that the DP-final demonstrative reinforcers found in several Romance languages are the result of a leftward movement of the extended projection of the noun. I show how this analysis generalizes to crosslinguistic (Romance vs. Germanic) differences in the expression of DP-internal focus.

2.1 Proper names and common nouns

To the best of my knowledge, the earliest proposals for movement of the noun to D were based on constructions found in Semitic and Scandinavian languages (see, for example, Ritter 1988, Siloni 1991, for Semitic languages, and Taraldsen 1990, Delsing 1988, for Scandinavian languages; see also Longobardi in this volume for more extensive discussion and references). For both Semitic and Scandinavian languages, arguments of the noun appear postnominally. For both groups of languages, it has been argued that the noun may raise to D, deriving the postnominal position of the arguments. Further support for N-to-D-raising in Hebrew comes from the fact that the definite article does not co-occur with the noun in the genitive "construct state" construction (see section 3.1), arguing that the DP-initial noun substitutes into the D-position. The Scandinavian languages differ from the Semitic in that in Scandinavian the so-called definite article is postnominal and suffixed on the noun, which so far appears consistent with an analysis where N left-adjoins to the definite article in D (but see section 2.2 for a reinterpretation of the Scandinavian facts). Similarly, the postnominal enclitic definite article in Romanian is arguably derived via N-raising and leftward adjunction to D, as essentially suggested in Dobrovie-Sorin (1987) and Grosu (1988) in a pre-DP-framework.

Longobardi (1994) has provided independent evidence for N-to-D-movement in Romance languages. In particular, he argued that proper names raise to the D-position, the locus of referentiality. Longobardi proposed that this noun movement is parameterized, taking place overtly in Romance languages generally, and covertly in Germanic languages. The examples in (11) (from Longobardi 1994) support the idea that proper names not introduced with a definite article must raise to D in the overt syntax in a language like Italian:

(11) a. [$_{DP}$ Il mio Gianni] ha finalmente telefonato. (Italian)
  b. *[$_{DP}$ Mio Gianni] ha finalmente telefonato.
  c. [$_{DP}$ Gianni mio] ha finalmente telefonato.
    (the) my John has finally called
    "My John has finally called."

Example (11a) illustrates how the definite article co-occurs with proper names, and (11b) shows that the entire DP is ungrammatical without an overt D-element. In (11c), the proper name *Gianni* heading NP has crossed over the possessor *mio* and substituted into the D-position, obliterating the definite article. This derivation is detailed in (12):

(12) [$_{DP}$ [$_{D'}$ Gianni$_i$] [$_{AgrP}$ mio [$_{Agr'}$ t$'_i$] [$_{NP}$ t$_i$]]]

Longobardi (1995) has more recently extended the N-to-D-raising analysis to what is arguably a residual case of construct state in Romance languages.

2.2 Representing adjectives

Various proposals have been developed about the internal structure of the noun phrase based on the position of the adjective(s) relative to the noun. This phenomenon has been examined both crosslinguistically and language internally. Crosslinguistically, one of the most salient observations is that across Romance languages, adjectives tend to follow nouns, whereas across Germanic languages, they tend to precede. Even for those languages exhibiting post-nominal adjectives, it has been observed that certain classes of adjective must precede nouns, in a sense disobeying the otherwise unmarked position for adjectives. These sorts of fine-grained distinction might be missed in a study focussing exclusively on Germanic languages due to the relative absence of exceptions to the fairly rigid adjective–noun order obeyed in these languages.

I will adopt the idea that adjectives are organized according to a universal hierarchy that relates to their semantic properties, as developed by Cinque (1994a), whose work relies on crosslinguistic generalizations uncovered by Sproat and Shih (1991; see also Longobardi in this volume for further discussion and references). If so, the variation in the position of the noun relative to the adjective(s) cannot be due to variation in the position of the adjective, but rather, it must be a result of variation in the position of the noun.[12] A rough and informal comparison of Germanic and Romance languages easily confirms the tendency toward adjective–noun order in Germanic languages and noun–adjective order in Romance languages. However, careful consideration of a wide range of Romance varieties suggests that there is parametric variation with respect to how high a noun raises. An observation that can be made is that adjectives have a relatively greater tendency to precede the noun in a language like French than in languages like Spanish and Italian. Under the assumption that noun movement is the mechanism that derives the postnominal surface position of the adjective, the crosslinguistic data suggest that nouns in French do not raise as high as nouns in Spanish and Italian do. Consideration of several less-studied Romance varieties further supports the idea of a continuum between relatively robust and relatively weak noun movement. In Walloon, a moribund Romance language spoken in Belgium, adjectives are overwhelmingly prenominal, contrasting with what I consider to be only a tendency in French (relative to other Romance varieties). The Walloon pattern and how it contrasts with French is illustrated in (13)–(15) (data from Remacle 1952):

(13) a. on neûr tchapê   (Walloon)
          "a black hat"
      b. un chapeau noir   (French)
          a hat black
          "a black hat"

(14) a. lès cûts pans   (Walloon)
          "the baked bread"
      b. les pains (bien) cuits   (French)
          the bread (well) baked
          "the well-baked bread"

(15) a. one bèle bleûve cote   (Walloon)
          "a nice blue dress"
      b. une belle robe bleue   (French)
          a nice dress blue
          "a nice blue dress"

These examples highlight several striking differences between French and Walloon word order. (13) illustrates that color adjectives precede nouns in Walloon, unlike French and the other major Romance languages; (14) illustrates that participial adjectives precede the noun in Walloon, unlike French and other Romance languages; (15) illustrates that the adjectives *nice* and *blue* precede the noun in Walloon, while only *nice* precedes in French.[13] These same two adjectives would both follow the noun in a Romance language like Spanish.

At the other end of the spectrum are Sardinian dialects, spoken on the Italian island of Sardinia. In these dialects, the position of the adjectives is even more rigidly postnominal than that found in Italian, as shown in (16) and (17) (examples from Blasco Ferrer 1986):[14]

(16) a. una dí trista   (Sardinian)
          a day sad
          "a sad day"
      b. una triste giornata   (Italian)
          "a sad day"

(17) a. tempus malu est faendi   (Sardinian)
          weather bad is making
          "the weather is bad"
      b. sta facendo mal tempo   (Italian)
          is making bad weather
          "the weather is bad"

Interestingly, the pattern of variation observed across Romance languages with respect to the relative position of the adjectives follows a geographical continuum: the north-western Romance varieties tend progressively toward prenominal adjectives, and the south-eastern Romance varieties toward postnominal adjectives. From a syntactic perspective, this translates into relatively robust noun movement in the south-eastern Romance varieties and relatively weak noun movement in the north-western varieties.

This discussion of noun raising to derive the postnominal position of adjectives raises an important question about landing sites. Specifically, what position does the noun raise to? So far in this chapter only D has been identified as
a potential landing site for a raised noun. As I have mentioned, compelling
evidence supports the idea that proper names across Romance languages and
common nouns in Romanian overtly raise to D (via substitution in the former
cases and adjunction in the latter). Conspicuously absent, however, are equally
compelling arguments for assuming noun movement to D to derive noun–
adjective order across Romance languages generally. Indeed, there are strong
arguments against such an analysis. For one thing, all of the examples discussed in this section have overt prenominal determiner elements, unlike the
suffixed definite articles found in Romanian. Presumably these prenominal
determiners occupy D. It is unlikely that the nouns also occupy D (for example,
via rightward cliticization to D) because of the possibility for intervening lexical
material. The French example in (15b) nicely illustrates this point. In this case
one adjective precedes and another follows the noun, arguing that the noun
has raised to a position between N and D. The generalization that emerges
from the crosslinguistic data examined may be stated as follows: the higher
the landing site of the noun, the greater the tendency for adjectives to appear
postnominally. At this point, I will simply adopt the idea that the landing sites
between N and D correspond to functional projections that are included in the
"extended projection" of the noun within DP. In section 3, I take up the question of what the precise nature of these landing sites might be.

I return briefly to the Scandinavian word order facts, since the patterns
found in these languages are relevant both to the discussion of N-to-D-
movement and to that of the position of the adjective within DP. Languages
like Norwegian and Swedish exhibit postnominal enclitic definite articles, as
illustrated in (18). This suggests that the N raises to D, as proposed by Taraldsen
and others, and apparently parallel to the pattern found in Romanian:

(18) mannen   (Swedish)
      man-the
      "the man"

Recall next that Germanic languages, including Scandinavian ones, are characterized by prenominal adjectives. Consider the construction in (19), which is
found in several Scandinavian varieties:

(19) det store huset   (Swedish)
      the big house-the
      "the big house"

In this example, the prenominal adjective co-occurs with both a prenominal
adjectival determiner and the postnominal enclitic definite article. The label
"double definiteness" has been applied to these types of example. Examples

like (19) are incompatible with an N-to-D-raising analysis for two basic reasons: (i) the adjectival article, rather than the noun plus enclitic article, occupies the DP-initial position, and (ii) the adjectives appear prenominally. Delsing (1988, 1993), Santelmann (1993), and others have suggested that there is a second lower determiner projection hosting the enclitic article and that the noun raises and left-adjoins to the article in this lower functional head. In order to "block" N-raising to D in examples with prenominal adjectives (cf. (18)), these authors have claimed that the adjectives occupy head positions between N and D.

This sort of analysis has been challenged by several authors (see Giusti 1993b, Bernstein 1997, Kester 1996, Longobardi this volume), who advocate a uniform approach to adjectives, on the one hand, and N-to-D-raising, on the other. The idea adopted is that adjectives uniformly and crosslinguistically occupy specifier positions and that true instances of N-to-D-movement should result in postnominal adjectives and absence of a prenominal (definite) article. These patterns in fact characterize the distribution of proper names across Romance languages as well as common nouns in Romanian, whose definite article is postnominal and phonologically enclitic. Under such a uniform approach to adjectives and N-to-D-raising, the so-called postnominal definite article in Scandinavian languages may be reanalyzed either as a (base generated) nominal agreement marker or the spell-out of an agreement relation between a noun and its specifier in, say, AgrP, a projection lower than what has been proposed for Romance languages. Longobardi (personal communication) has suggested that such a projection could be the landing site of a noun that has raised over argument structure (but not functional structure). This approach is consistent with the fact that nominal arguments appear postnominally across (the relevant) Scandinavian languages.

2.3   *Relative clauses*

Recent work by Kayne (1994) has renewed the idea (going back to Vergnaud 1974) that the relationship between the "head" of the relative clause and the non-adjacent verb that it serves as an argument for involves a disassociation through syntactic movement. Rather than assuming the head to be generated in situ and the relative clause phrase to lower, Kayne maintained that the functional XP containing the noun and its modifiers raises leftward to SpecCP. Kayne's relative clause analysis, which assumes both the CP structure for clauses and the DP structure for noun phrases, involves that underlying structure in (20), where the relative clause CP is a complement of D:[15]

(20) $[_{DP} \; D^{\circ} \; CP]$

So in an example like (21), the extended NP *picture of John*, which corresponds to the head of the relative clause, raises from the complement position of the verb *saw* to SpecCP (Kayne 1994: 87). Notice that according to this approach, the definite article is not directly associated with the (raised) noun, but external to the relative clause CP:

(21)   [$_{DP}$ the [$_{CP}$ [$_{NP}$ picture of John]$_i$ [$_{C'}$ that [Bill saw [e]$_i$]]]]

Support for this approach comes from facts about reflexive binding and the relativization of idiom chunks. In the example in (22) (Kayne 1994: (8)), the antecedent of the reflexive may be either *John* or *Bill*. The only way for *Bill* to be the antecedent for the reflexive is for *Bill* to c-command it at some level of representation, supporting Kayne's proposal that *picture of himself* raises to its surface position:

(22)   John bought the picture of himself that Bill saw.

Another argument in favor of this approach concerns facts about relative clause formation with idiom chunks. A natural approach to idiom chunks is to assume that they involve a relationship rather distinct from, and more fundamental than, that between an ordinary verb and its object. In the example in (23), therefore, the verb *take* and its object *advantage* must be associated with each other at some very basic level, presumably the lexicon:

(23)   a.   to take advantage of
       b.   to make headway

In order to explain the facts in (24), where a piece of the idiom chunk has become the head of the relative clause, Vergnaud argued that the object must have been separated from the verb via movement:[16]

(24)   a.   the advantage that he took . . .
       b.   the headway that we made . . .

Kayne's relative clause analysis is interesting for at least two reasons. If on the right track, it provides evidence that noun phrases, like clauses, admit DP-internal movement, further supporting the assimilation of noun phrases and clauses. A second interesting aspect of the analysis is that it involves a derivation already familiar from work on the clause, namely, phrasal movement (e.g. *wh*-movement) to Spec,CP. It will be interesting to see what other properties these two parallel constructions share.

I turn next to another sort of construction that arguably involves DP-internal movement of an XP.

2.4   Demonstratives, reinforcers, and focus

In Bernstein (1997), I observed that demonstratives and their associated reinforcers must precede the noun in Germanic varieties like non-standard English and the Scandinavian languages, as illustrated in (25):[17]

(25) a. this here guy   (non-standard English)
     b. den här mannen   (Swedish)
         the there man-the
         "this man"

The parallel construction in several Romance languages is formed with a prenominal demonstrative and a postnominal reinforcer, as illustrated for French and Italian in (26):

(26) a. ce livre-ci   (French)
         this book here
         "this book"
     b. questo libro qui   (Italian)
         this book here
         "this book"

I argued that the Germanic-type construction and the Romance-type construction are alike underlyingly. In other words, in the relevant Germanic and Romance languages, both the demonstrative and its reinforcer are generated to the left of the noun as the specifier and head, respectively, of a functional projection FP. I adopted Giusti's (1993a) proposal that demonstratives are generated in the specifier position of a functional projection below DP (see also Carstens 1991, Schmitt 1996).[18] Unlike Giusti, however, who argued that the demonstrative raises to SpecDP universally, I followed the idea in Bernstein (1993a) that the demonstrative head in the Germanic and Romance languages raises and substitutes into D. This is consistent with the fact that the demonstrative may not co-occur with the definite article in these languages. My modification to Giusti's approach does not preclude the possibility that the demonstrative raises to SpecDP in some languages, particularly those with co-occurring prenominal demonstrative and definite article.[19]

What then accounts for the pre- vs. postnominal position of the reinforcer element crosslinguistically? An obvious possibility is that movement derives the postnominal position of the reinforcer in the Romance languages. Indeed, Brugè (1996) would derive the postnominal position of the reinforcer, as well as postnominal demonstratives, via noun movement.[20] That is, an underlyingly prenominal reinforcer is crossed over by the noun in a manner consistent with the derivation of postnominal adjectives in Romance. Brugè's proposal requires a revision to Giusti's basic analysis, namely, that the demonstrative starts out in the specifier of a low (i.e., close to NP) functional projection. This revision yields the DP-final position of the demonstrative after N-raising. It would also derive the postnominal position of the reinforcer in the examples in (26).

I challenged this approach in light of examples like those in (27):

(27) a. ce livre jaune ci   (French)
         this book yellow here
         "this yellow book"

b. ce délégué du ministère ci
this delegate of-the minister here
"this delegate of the minister"

In (27a) the noun is modified by a postnominal adjective and in (27b) by a postnominal complement. Based on these types of example, I argued that the extended NP (including modifiers) crosses over the reinforcer and adjoins to the left of it. The account incorporated the idea that the postnominal position of the adjective(s) is derived by noun movement. Under the assumption that the demonstrative and reinforcer are generated in a functional projection just below DP, it is difficult to see how noun movement alone would derive the phrase final position of the reinforcer. If *livre jaune* raises as a phrasal unit, however, the surface order may be straightforwardly derived. Note that under Brugè's account, which assumes that elements like *cette-ci* are generated below the adjective(s) and above the head noun, the order demonstrative, noun, adjective, reinforcer may be derived by crossing the noun over the reinforcer and the adjective. So (27a), on its own, does not provide convincing evidence for the XP-movement hypothesis, although it is perfectly consistent with such an approach.

The example in (27b), however, provides evidence for the phrasal movement analysis and against the head movement analysis. In order for the head movement analysis to be tenable here, the noun (*délégué*) and its complement (*du ministère*) would somehow have to be reanalyzed as a syntactic head. It is not obvious how to execute such a procedure. Under the XP-movement approach, the noun and its complement would raise as a phrasal unit, thereby unifying the analysis for this example and the one in (27a). The derivation for an example like (27a) under my analysis is given in (28):

(28) $[_{DP}$ ce$_i$ $[_{FP}$ $[_{XP}$ livre$_k$ jaune . . . t$_k]_j$ $[_{FP}$ t$_i$ $[_{F'}$ -ci]]] $[_{XP}$ t]$_j$]

In current work (Bernstein 1999), I observe that the demonstrative reinforcement construction found in languages like French and Italian is only one case of what is actually a more general strategy found in Romance languages, and regularly absent in Germanic languages. Across Romance languages, the right periphery of the DP hosts a series of contrastively focussed elements: reinforcers (e.g. in French and Italian), possessive adjectives (e.g. in Spanish and Italian), quantifiers (e.g. in Spanish and Catalan), and demonstratives (e.g. in Spanish, Catalan, and Romanian; see Roca 1996). All of these elements appear prenominally in the unmarked (i.e., neutral) case in Romance languages and must appear prenominally in most Germanic languages, where focus is typically expressed via contrastive stress. Building on Bernstein (1997), I extend the XP-raising analysis to these DP-final elements and link this movement to general properties of focus constructions.[21] I further observe that properties of the DP-internal focus construction are analogous to properties of "Scrambling," a clause internal focus construction that has been identified in several languages. For example, in both the nominal and clausal focus constructions, the focussed material appears at the right periphery of the constituent and the defocussed material appears in a position that is to the left of its neutral position and to the focussed material.

In this section I have illustrated and discussed examples of what I take to involve DP-internal movement. The patterns uncovered and the analyses developed to account for them contribute to our understanding of the syntactic nature of DPs and further the justification for assimilating noun phrase and clauses. Nevertheless, several important and interesting questions remain. Among them are the following: (i) is there a DP-internal focus position involved in the relevant constructions and if so what is its nature?; (ii) how exactly are DP-internal head and phrasal movement related – for example, is it possible that phrasal movement involves N-raising with pied-piping?;[22] and (iii) what are the parameters determining the availability and robustness of these movement operations crosslinguistically?

3   The Identification of Functional Categories

Throughout this chapter, I have provided arguments for several types of syntactic movement internal to the DP. That is, there is evidence that the noun, in cases of head movement, or the (extended) NP, in cases of phrasal movement, raises to functional projections within DP. This raises the issue of what the nature of these intermediate landing sites might be. Various DP-functional projections have been introduced, recalling proposals developed for clausal functional categories (e.g. TenseP, AgrP). In many cases, these functional projections, although assumed, have not been specifically identified. For example, Cinque's (1994a) universal hierarchy of adjectives entails a highly articulated functional structure, although details about what the functional projections might correspond to have not yet been sufficiently elaborated. In some other cases, however, specific characterizations have been proposed. Among them, DP-functional projections corresponding to number (i.e., singular/plural), gender, and case have been proposed. Shlonsky (1991b) and Giusti (1991) argued that quantifiers are syntactic heads projecting their own functional projection, QP. Due to space limitations, I focus here on proposals for only two DP-functional projections, the first corresponding to number (NumP) and the second to gender (GenP).

3.1   Representing number

As far as I know, Ritter (1991) was the first to propose a functional projection corresponding to a noun's singular/plural marking. In particular, she proposed that Num(ber)P, not NP, is the complement of D in modern Hebrew.

Her arguments appealed to facts distinguishing the construct state noun phrase from the free state noun phrase, both of which Hebrew employs to express genitive.

The construct state construction consists of a head noun followed by its possessor, as in (29). Based on binding facts, Ritter shows that the subject (S) must asymmetrically c-command the object (O), arguing that the NSO-surface order is derived by movement. Ritter proposed that the noun raises from N to D, crossing over the possessor (which occupies a specifier position). This is supported by the fact that the head noun may not be modified by a prenominal definite article (although the postnominal possessor may be). The structure Ritter assigned to an example like (29) is given in (30). In this type of construction, the N must move to D in order for D to be identified and able to assign genitive case to the subject:

(29) parat ikar   (Hebrew)
      cow farmer
      "a farmer's cow"

(30)

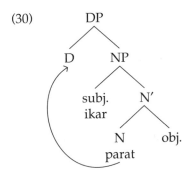

In the free state construction, illustrated in (31), the binding facts and NSO-order are parallel to those of the construct state, arguing that the noun also raises in this construction. However, the head noun in the free state construction cannot raise all the way to D, since free state noun phrases admit the definite article. Ritter argues that the N must raise to a functional head intervening between N and D. Ritter provides evidence from plural formation and word formation processes in Hebrew that the relevant functional head is Num(ber)P, where the singular/plural features of the noun are encoded. Ritter's idea is that, in a language like Hebrew, the noun will raise to NumP to amalgamate with (or check) its number specification.[23] Ritter's derivation for the free state genitive example in (31) is provided in (32):

(31) ha-axila shel Dan et ha-tapuax   (Hebrew)
      the-eating of Dan of the-apple
      "Dan's eating of the apple"

(32)

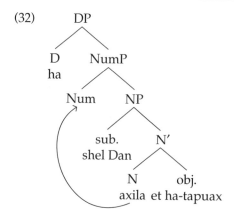

Ritter's basic proposal has been widely adopted and generalized to other languages. For example, Valois (1991) and Picallo (1991) have adopted Ritter's number projection for French and Catalan, respectively. Data from Walloon, discussed in Bernstein (1991a, 1993a), provide some independent support for the adoption of NumP in Romance languages. In particular, Walloon (unlike French) exhibits a special prenominal plural marker that appears (in writing) attached to prenominal adjectives. The masculine plural form appears orthographically as -*s* and the feminine form as -*ès*, as illustrated in the examples in (33) (Walloon examples drawn from Remacle 1952, Morin 1986).[24] Note that word final orthographic -*s* (appearing with both masculine and feminine forms) is not pronounced unless followed by a vowel, a sandhi phenomenon known as *liaison* and indicated in the examples in (33) by the hyphen. Further note that Walloon word final *è* is unstressed (and equivalent in pronunciation to *e* in French *et* "and"):

(33) a. dès vètès-ouh (FPl)   (Walloon)
          "some green doors"
      b. dès nêurs-ouy (MPl)   (Walloon)
          "some black eyes"

Building on work by Morin (1986), I argued that these apparent (orthographic) suffixes should not be analyzed as adjectival suffixes, but rather as the spell-out of the contents of the functional head Num. What evidence is there to support such an analysis? There is, in fact, substantial evidence, which I briefly summarize here.

As I noted earlier, one striking property of Walloon is that adjectives are prenominal, arguing that noun movement is relatively absent in this language. Another remarkable fact about Walloon is that nouns are never marked (except in the orthography) for plural. This contrasts with French, which exhibits plurality on nouns, although not in a particularly robust fashion. The third crucial property about the plural markers, as discussed in Morin (1986), is that they are not phonologically part of the adjective. Instead, Morin provides several arguments supporting the idea that they are phonologically part of the following word, usually a noun. I developed the idea that the syntactic, morphological, and phonological characteristics of the plural marker and its associated noun support the idea and that the prenominal plural marker corresponds to the head of the NumP projection. If on the right track, this work provides evidence for a specific, intermediate, functional projection on the path from N to D, and also for the identification of its role in the functional structure of the noun.

3.2 Is gender a syntactic phenomenon?

My impression is that the idea of a NumP projection has been relatively uncontroversial and therefore rather generally accepted. This is probably owing in part to the morphological and syntactic evidence supporting such an assumption, and also to the fact that number (and its expression) in DPs, like tense in the clause, plays an integral role in the interpretation and legitimacy of a noun phrase. Proposals for a projection corresponding to gender have not been accepted with such unanimous enthusiasm. Nevertheless, it is instructive to examine the arguments and evidence for such a projection.

Unlike the case in English, where the expression of gender is restricted to singular pronominal forms, in many languages gender may be expressed on nouns, determiner elements, adjectives, and/or other modifiers. A relatively simple, yet often robust, gender system is exhibited in European languages, where the inventory of genders expressed is masculine, feminine, and neuter. A familiar pattern from Romance is the distribution of gender in Spanish, where masculine nouns typically end in -*o* and feminine nouns in -*a*, as illustrated in (34). Note that an accompanying determiner and adjective(s) will agree in gender (and number) with the noun. Also note that the gender system applies to all nouns in the language, whether or not they happen to be animate and whether or not they exhibit the typical -*o*/-*a* alternation:

(34) a. el niño pequeño   (Spanish)
        the-MascSg child-MascSg small-MascSg
        "the small child"
     b. la niña pequeña   (Spanish)
        the-FemSg child-FemSg small-FemSg
        "the small child"

Picallo (1991) claimed that gender projects to a functional phrase within the DP, which she labelled Gen(der)P. This functional projection was situated between NP and NumP, reflecting the fact that gender is expressed directly on the noun stem and that number is expressed outside gender, as shown in (35):

(35) mes-a-s   (Spanish)
     table-FemPl
     "tables"

The proposal Picallo made was that the affixes for gender and then number were "picked up" (or checked; Chomsky 1995b) by the noun stem on the path from N to Num, the highest functional head below D (in her system).

Bernstein (1993a, 1993b) suggested a modification to Picallo's GenP. I argued that gender, a morphological property, is expressed in the form of "word markers" (in the sense of Harris 1991), the terminal vowels appearing in a robust way in Spanish- and Italian-type languages. I claimed that it is the word markers, and not gender *per se*, that are responsible for syntactic licensing in certain constructions. Put another way, the word markers in Romance languages represent another instantiation of what has been labeled "rich morphological agreement," a notion which has played an important role in analyses of clausal phenomena such as verb movement (recall Pollock's work discussed in section 1.2) and "pro-drop."

The idea of syntactic licensing by word markers contributed to an analysis for the construction illustrated in (36), where an indefinite determiner element and an adjective appear without an overt noun in Romance languages like Spanish and Italian. The example in (37) shows that the basic form of the masculine singular indefinite article is *un*:

(36)   <u>Uno</u> rojo está encima de la mesa.   (Spanish)
       a red is on the table
       "A red one is on the table."

(37)   <u>Un</u> libro rojo está encima de la mesa.   (Spanish)
       a book red is on the table
       "A red book is on the table."

Based on the distribution of this elliptical nominal construction across Romance languages, I claimed that the word marker appearing on *uno* in (36) corresponds to the head of a functional projection that I labeled WordMarkerP.[25] I further claimed that word markers in these languages are able to license an NP lacking lexical content. The licensing mechanism appealed to was head government, but this licensing can be reformulated in other ways. The basic analysis applied straightforwardly to Italian, and was adapted for and extended to French and Catalan (see Martin 1995 for discussion and revision of the account to accommodate the Catalan data).

Ritter (1993) challenged the idea that gender (or presumably word markers) corresponds to a functional category. Instead, she maintained that gender is a feature and that there is parametric variation in the location of this gender feature crosslinguistically. In a language like Hebrew, she argued, the gender feature is located on the noun stem "at all levels of syntactic representation" (Ritter 1993: 802). In contrast, in Romance languages gender would be located together with the noun's number specification on the functional head Num. In support of her hypothesis about the gender feature in Hebrew, Ritter illustrates derivational (i.e., lexicon internal) word formation processes in Hebrew, where gender manipulation forms new and unpredictable words with non-compositional meanings. Such manipulation does not generally form new words in Romance, except when the words have animate or human reference and in a few other predictable cases, all resulting in compositional interpretations. Ritter appealed to Walloon data of the sort illustrated in (33a), where gender and number are both expressed on the prenominal plural marker, to support her hypothesis about the location of gender (on Num) in Romance languages. The argument rests on the idea (from Bernstein 1991a) that the plural marker may not be decomposed into gender (i.e., Fem -è) and number (i.e., Pl -s). I suggested (in Bernstein 1993a) that perhaps they may. The matter is far from settled.

4   Conclusions

In this chapter, I have surveyed only a sample of the issues addressed and analyses developed on the syntax of DPs. Nevertheless, I believe that even these brief remarks convey the overwhelming theoretical and empirical advantages afforded by the DP-analysis. What is particularly extraordinary is how much progress has been made in the little more than a decade since the pioneering work of Szabolcsi, Abney, and others. As with all progress, however, each step forward raises new questions, fueling further research. Indeed, progress and developments in the investigation of DP syntax have led to a widening of the domains of inquiry, providing fertile testing ground for existing hypotheses, as well as fresh raw data on which to develop new hypotheses. I conclude this chapter by mentioning just two of the expanded domains of study, both of which are contributing in important ways to the growing body of knowledge on the syntax of DPs.

One area of expansion is in the inventory of languages examined. In this chapter, I have mainly focussed on the relatively well-studied western European languages. However, a wide group of languages is now represented in the literature. Among the languages and language families that have been examined are Maori, Japanese, Greek, Kiswahili, Slavic languages, Semitic languages, creole languages, and American Sign Language. The field of language acquisition is another growing and promising domain of investigation. Various aspects of the acquisition of DPs provide insights into the representation of DPs in child vs. adult grammars as well as in L1 vs. L2 grammars. Of particular interest and importance is evidence of correlations between acquisition of functional structure of the clause and functional structure of the noun phrase. The DP properties that have been investigated in the acquisition literature include case marking, plural marking, word order, and the absence vs. appearance of articles and clitics.

Needless to say, much more work remains to be done.

NOTES

* Thanks to Mark Baltin and Chris Collins for comments on an earlier draft of this chapter. Thanks also to Giuseppe Longobardi for his unfailing optimism (despite evidence to the contrary). The usual disclaimers apply.

1 "Noun phrase" is used only as a descriptive term and hence implies no direct correspondence to a particular syntactic projection (e.g. NP or DP).

2 Following Abney (1987), I employ the following abbreviations: OM for object marker and SM for subject marker.

3 On the issue of why DP corresponds to CP rather than IP, see Szabolcsi (1989).

4 Recent work on ellipsis within DPs may be found in Torrego (1987), Lobeck (1995), Kester (1996), Martí (1995), Bernstein (1993a, 1993b), and Sleeman (1996), among others.

5 In this chapter, I abstract away from whether case assignment or checking (Chomsky 1995b) is the relevant notion.

6 It is important to keep in mind that nominal arguments, unlike verbal ones, are often optional.

7 Although beyond the scope of this chapter, so-called verb second effects provide evidence for verb movement to C in Germanic languages (see work by den Besten 1983, Haider and Prinzhorn 1986, Vikner 1995, among others).

8 I am essentially ignoring a vast semantics literature on the subject. In light of the focus (on syntax) of this volume and the necessary brevity of this chapter, I am able to discuss only a small subset of the literature that addresses this subject

and that simultaneously advances the claim that DP is the nominal analog of clausal CP.

9 The inclusion of Spanish examples in (7)–(9) obviates the issue of optional complementizers in English.

10 Szabolcsi (1992: 134–5), following Bhatt and Yoon (1992), shows that the subordinator and clause type indicator (e.g. for declarative) in English are both instantiated as an identical element, the complementizer. This is apparently not the case in all languages. In Hungarian, for example, the element introducing clause type is different from that introducing an argument. Only the latter would correspond to C and function as a subordinator, introducing a sentential argument. Conflation of subordinator and clause type indicator would also apply in the nominal domain in English, but not Hungarian.

11 Mandelbaum (1994) argues that the mere presence of a definite article does not guarantee that a noun phrase is a (DP) argument. The details of this proposal are beyond the scope of this chapter.

12 See Lamarche (1991) and Bouchard (1998) for discussion of problems with and alternatives to an N-raising approach to adjectival position.

13 In fact, there is parametric variation across Walloon dialects with respect to the position of participial adjectives relative to the noun. The position of the participial adjective correlates with other properties of DPs across Walloon varieties (see Bernstein 1993a for discussion).

14 The examples are in the Campidanese dialect of Sardinian.

15 This recalls Szabolcsi's (1983) early work on DPs and re-establishes a blurring of the distinction between nominal projections and verbal ones (see discussion in section 1.1).

16 Mark Baltin points out that an example like (i) (due to Jim McCawley) compromises Kayne's promotion approach to idiom chunks, since *headway* would have to be promoted from within the relative clause:

(i) John made the headway that got us out of here.

He also observes that the grammaticality (for him) of (ii), involving logophoric reflexives in picture NPs, would weaken Kayne's argument based on (22):

(ii) The picture of myself that John took is on the table.

17 I do not consider standard English *this guy here* to be equivalent to non-standard *this here guy*. In this latter type of example, the reinforcer is dependent on the presence of the demonstrative, its absence resulting in ungrammaticality (e.g. **a here guy*). In standard English *this guy here*, substitution of the definite or indefinite article for the demonstrative yields a grammatical result (e.g. *a guy here*).

18 The "phrasal" nature of demonstratives, as implied by the structure assigned to them, can be based on an analogy with adjectives (see Dryer 1992: 120–2). See also Brugè's (1996) discussion of what arguably involves modification of demonstratives in Spanish.

19 See also proposals by Roca (1996) and Vangsnes (1996a) that the demonstrative corresponds to the head of a functional projection, and by Cornilescu (1992) that the

demonstrative may correspond to a specifier or a head.

20 Brugè focussed on postnominal demonstratives, but extended her analysis to reinforcers. I suggest that my proposal for the reinforcers generalizes to the postnominal demonstratives.

21 Androutsopoulou (1997) develops an analysis of DP-focus constructions in Greek that also involves XP-movement. However, the movement operation involved in the Greek construction, unlike what I have described for Romance languages, involves phrasal movement to a focus position outside the DP.

22 This possibility was suggested to me by Giuseppe Longobardi.

23 In a language with noun raising it is not obvious whether amalgamation or checking is the relevant notion. In a language like English, however, the fact that nouns are marked for number and that there is no evidence of overt noun raising suggests that (covert) checking is the correct characterization.

24 The masculine/feminine distinction of the plural marker is not present in all dialects, a fact I am ignoring here (see Bernstein 1993a for discussion of this dialectal variation and its possible significance). The important point for the present discussion is that all dialects will show a prenominal plural marker orthographically attached to a prenominal adjective, regardless of whether there is an accompanying gender distinction in the forms.

25 Delfitto and Schroten (1991) also argued that word markers have syntactic relevance. However, for them word markers correspond to the head of the functional projection NumP.

18 The Structure of DPs: Some Principles, Parameters, and Problems

GIUSEPPE LONGOBARDI

0 Introduction

The investigation of the internal structure of nominal constructions has recently provided important evidence for at least three aspects of syntactic theory:

   i. the syntactic representation of empty categories,
  ii. the deductive depth of parameter theory,
 iii. the form of the syntax–semantics mapping.

The results so achieved begin to provide a preliminary reference framework for parametric descriptions of Determiner Phrases (DPs) across the world's languages: they concern both the lexical structure and the functional structure surrounding head nouns and will be examined in turn.

I Lexical Structure

1 Arguments

1.1 Hierarchies of arguments

The first thing to be observed is that within DPs the principal arguments of the head noun are hierarchically ordered in a way roughly similar to that found in clauses: thematic subjects (e.g. agents) are higher than direct objects (e.g. themes) and other complements. Evidence for this conclusion is found in both English and other Germanic and Romance languages.

   DPs also involve the possibility for another argument or quasi-argument to appear, the so-called possessor or R-related phrase in Higginbotham's (1983) sense, which does not exist in clausal structures. Hierarchically, possessors are higher than subjects. Evidence for this conclusion cannot be found in English, for reasons which will become clear in section 1.4.2 below, and was mainly provided by the Romance languages.

The conjunction of the two generalizations leads one to assume the following hierarchy: P > S > O. The first two arguments will be called external, the third one internal. Converging evidence for such hierarchy comes from two quite distinct domains.

1.1.1   Possessivization evidence

The first and older type of evidence for the hierarchy above comes from the following considerations: most European varieties admit, under variable conditions, two ways of formally realizing the P, S, and O arguments of the noun: (i) through a prepositional form (English *of*, German *von*, Romance *de* or *di*), steadily postnominal; (ii) by means of either a postpositional affix (like Germanic *s*, with crosslinguistically different properties) or a special possessive form, often agreeing with the noun like an adjective or a determiner (cf. section 1.3.1). Now, it is very generally the case that type (ii) realization (henceforth called possessivization) is subject to these limitations:

i.   if only one among P, S, and O is present, then (with one major exception; cf. section 1.2.1) it will always be able to assume type (ii) form;

ii.   if P is overtly present, only it will be able to assume type (ii) form;

iii.   if P is not overtly present and S is, only the latter (i.e., no O) will be able to assume type (ii) form.

These facts, first identified in their entirety by Milner (1978) for French, automatically lead to the assumed hierarchy: P > S > O. In Romance at least the very same hierarchy of arguments so defined by their accessibility to possessivization is reproduced by another class of phenomenon, namely their accessibility to extraction from the DP through *wh*-movement or cliticization. The empirical generalization can be formulated as follows:

> Of the phrases in the frame of a head N, only one representing an argument expressible through possessivization can be extracted from Nmax.

The results of extraction tests, thus, confirm those of possessivization tests (cf. Cinque 1980, Giorgi and Longobardi 1991).

1.1.2   Binding evidence

There is some evidence that this hierarchy in the formal realization of arguments of N is tied to and reflects properties of the NP-internal phrase structure. This evidence comes from a classical constituency testing ground such as c-command relations, as manifested in a number of binding asymmetries between pairs of arguments. For instance, given any pair of arguments among P, S, and O, one containing an anaphorically or quantificationally bound expression and the other representing the antecedent of such a binding relation, it is invariably the case that (essentially irrespectively of the surface linear order) P always represents the binder, O always contains the bindee, and S may bind inside O but never inside P.[1] Given standard assumptions about c-command, these facts suggest an asymmetric c-command hierarchy among the three types of argument precisely of the form P > S > O.

Thus, the hierarchy appears to be structurally represented as follows (order irrelevant):

(1)   [P [S [O ... N ...]]]

The same conclusions are reached from disjointness considerations: an R-expression embedded within O or S is necessarily disjoint from P and one embedded within O is disjoint also from S. No restriction holds vice versa. It is clear that these facts as well are derivable from the structural assumption in (1) and, thus, support it.

Further tests confirm that the only direct argument of some nominalizations corresponding to unaccusative verbs is internal, in the sense of structurally behaving like an O.

It is worth remarking that the suggested structural hierarchy applies, with the same results, to *all* nouns, whether they denote physical objects (*book*, *portrait*) or complex events (singular action nominals like *destruction, assignment*), in Grimshaw's (1990) sense.

1.2   *"Passivization" properties*

1.2.1   *"Affectedness"*
A well-established restriction in English is that some Os cannot appear in the possessivized form even if no overt S or P is present. Most head nouns displaying this restriction are characterized by their assigning a semantically "unaffecting" theta-role to their objects (cf. Anderson 1979):

(2)   a.   The perception/knowledge of the problem
       b.   *The problem's perception/knowledge

A plausible approach to this class of nouns was suggested by Jaeggli (1986): these heads would be unable to give up the syntactic projection of their external argument (S), which would then be obligatorily realized, at least in the form of an empty pronominal category. Such a category, then, and an overt possessivized O phrase can be assumed to compete for one and the same structural position, so that the necessary presence of one (say, the empty subject pronominal) will exclude the other, e.g. an O with the usual 's suffix. The latter item will then be only expressible in the postnominal *of* form. The same constraint is not at work in other languages, like German and Romance (cf. section 1.4.2 below).

The condition on the ineliminability of the syntactic realization of the subject with the lexical heads in question seems independently supported by the analogous impossibility of the lexically corresponding verbs occurring in middle constructions:

(3) *The problem perceives/knows easily

This is another environment where the promotion of the object to a subject-like form appears to necessarily destroy the possibility of syntactic realization of the underlying subject role, as suggested by the known disappearance of control and binding activity on the part of this latter argument:

(4) *The ship sank to collect the insurance.

1.2.2 Passive or middle?

The phenomenon of possessivization of O mentioned above bears some superficial resemblance to passivization in clauses: thus it has often been referred to as "passivization" of NPs. This is likely to be a mislabeling: in fact, at a closer look, the analogy breaks down in at least four respects:

i.   One has already been mentioned in the previous section: in English unaffected objects cannot be possessivized, while they can passivize in clauses.
ii. In English it has been discovered that possessivization of the object destroys any trace of syntactic activity of the understood subject role as a controller (Roeper 1987):

    (5) a. The sinking of the ship (to collect the insurance)
           b. The ship's sinking (*to collect the insurance)

    The same is true for binding relations (Giorgi and Longobardi 1991), which provides a powerful argument against the proposal of treating Roeper's examples as cases of event control rather than argument (subject) control:

    (6) a. The testing of such drugs on oneself
           b. *This drug's testing on oneself

    As noticed, this is paralleled in verbal constructions by middle formation, but not by passives, whose underlying subject role continues to be active in binding and control:

(7)   a.   The ship was sunk to collect the insurance
      b.   This drug must first be tested on oneself

iii.   In some languages other than English or French, where *by* and *par* are used in both constructions, the preposition introducing the expression of the agent in nominals with a possessivized object is not the same as the one expressing the agent in verbal passives (cf. Italian *da* vs. *da parte di*, German *von* vs. *durch*). The difference might perhaps be related to the different intrinsic semantics of the prepositions: *by* and *par* display some independent instrumental meaning, not shared by *da* and *von*.

iv.   Languages normally have quite distinct morphological forms for passive verbs, but not for "passive" nouns; again this recalls middle formation for verbs. Perhaps this fourth is the most basic difference between the processes of object promotion in NPs and clauses, indirectly responsible for the others.

On the whole, then, possessivization of the object of a noun looks rather like the nominal counterpart of middle formation rather than clausal passivization.

Notice that the first two restrictions reduce to the proposed hypothesis that object possessivization precisely obliterates the position for empty realizations of the subject argument (cf. section 1.5.3). This approach implies the important conclusion that both control and binding require a syntactically realized empty category, not just a theta-role in the grid of a lexical head, as an antecedent. The difference with verbal passive could then reside in the fact that the special morphology of passive (as opposed to middle) verbs might take up the task of realizing this argument (cf. Baker et al. 1989).

Finally, it must also be recalled that the properties in (1) and (2) apply to English and Mainland Scandinavian, but do not appear in German and in the Romance languages. For an explanation of this important parametric difference cf. section 1.4.2 below.

1.3   Case

1.3.1   Case positions

The most salient Case theoretic property of nominal constructions is the crosslinguistically frequent contrast between Case realization of both S and O with nouns and in clauses. In other words, many languages tend to use a special Case, Genitive, normally the same employed to express P, for the arguments of nouns whose verbal thematic correspondents bear Nominative and Accusative. The shape assumed by these "genitive" arguments is at first sight quite heterogeneous, both crosslinguistically and often language internally. A major divide, which has already been mentioned, separates instances of Genitive Case realized by means of a *preposition* from the others, which have been collectively gathered under the label "*possessive* or possessivized forms." The apparent maximum of heterogeneity is found among these latter. There are at least five different ways of formal realization:

(8) a. a phrase final affix   (e.g. English *'s*)
    b. a word final affix   (German *s*, Arabic *i*)
    c. an inflectional (really fusional) ending   (Latin or Slavic Genitive)
    d. phi-feature agreement with the noun (Romance/German possessives)
    e. zero-realization   (Hebrew construct state Genitive)

In most of the better-known European languages, at least (8a, b, d, e) sharply contrast with prepositional Genitive because they may surface relatively high in the DP structure, i.e., they can precede attributive adjectives under a normal intonation, a possibility excluded for prepositional genitives. Furthermore, the types in (8a, b, d) may surface prenominally, again as opposed to (stylistically normal) prepositional genitives. (8e) (also accompanied by corresponding agreement on the head in some languages, such as Hungarian) happens to occur just postnominally as well, though normally clearly higher than prepositional genitives, most typically immediately after a noun fronted to the D-position in so-called construct state constructions (cf. section 3.2.5 below for references). Therefore, its postnominal occurrence seems to have nothing in common with that of prepositional Genitive, which appears to be structurally quite lower. (8a, b, d, e) may also occur in postnominal and postadjectival position, though apparently still always preceding prepositional genitives in case of co-occurrence.

Notice, further, that it seems possible, in at least one case, exemplified by German, for two possessive genitives to co-occur, one prenominally and preadjectivally, the other postnominally and postadjectivally:

(9) Marias sorgfältige Beschreibung Ottos
    Mary's accurate description of Otto

As a result and a summary of these observations, the previous scheme (1) could be embedded in the more complex structure (10), made available in principle by Universal Grammar (UG) and slightly parametrized in a way discussed below:

(10) (**1** GenS **2** AP **3** GenO [$_\alpha$ P [S [O ... N ...]] $_\alpha$]]

In (10) the numbered positions **1** through **3** set out some crosslinguistically possible surface positions for the noun (cf. sections 2.1 and 4.2 below), GenS and GenO the high and low position for possessivized Genitive, respectively, and AP a potentially iterated position for attributive APs (cf. section 2.1). As the null hypothesis, one may suppose that the necessarily lower position(s) for prepositional genitives will correspond to the base ones of P, S, and O contained within the phrase α. As above, linear order is essentially undetermined within such a phrase, while it is crucially encoded in the rest of (10).[2]

Finally, we know too little of the syntax of the type in (8c) to establish with certainty whether it patterns like prepositional or possessive genitives, and I will leave the topic for further investigation.[3]

1.3.2   *Equidistance and ergativity*

Crosslinguistically, there are thus two positions for non-prepositional Genitive, one higher than adjectival modifiers, the other lower. Languages make the parametric choice of activating just one or the other or both. As a first approximation, Semitic languages, modern Romance, and Hungarian are likely to activate only the higher one, Celtic languages only the lower, while several continental Germanic varieties might be argued to activate both.

A natural question is whether these positions bear some correspondence to the analogous clausal ones which are used for Nominative and Accusative (or Ergative/Absolutive, respectively, according to Chomsky's 1995b equidistance theory). The clearest evidence of some correspondence is provided by languages like German, activating both positions, though with no formal contrast in the realization of Case. Here, the usual hierarchy P > S > O reappears for the choice among the arguments competing for the higher possessive position. So *Marias* may only be a Subject or a Possessor in (9) above, and *Ottos* must be an Object or a Subject.[4]

This configuration of facts obviously reminds one of the distribution of the higher Case (say, Nominative) and lower Case (say, Accusative) to thematic subjects and objects of transitive verbs, respectively. If only one argument is present, however, it may occur in either position, therefore including the lower one, with any interpretation:

(11)   a.   Marias Beschreibung
            Mary's description
       b.   Die Beschreibung Marias
            The description of/by Mary

In Chomsky's (1995b) terms, this behavior neutralizes for nominals the supposed distinction between Nominative and Absolutive and the relative language types manifested in verbal systems.

1.4   Syntactic realization of arguments

1.4.1   *Order*

We have already briefly sketched some generalizations concerning the order of arguments of nouns relative to the head noun itself and to attributive adjectives. Such generalizations are likely to follow from:

   i.   Case theory (cf. section 1.3 above),
  ii.   the theory of the distribution of adjective phrases (cf. section 2.1 below),
 iii.   the theory of the structural positions within DP attracting the head noun
        (N-raising: cf. sections 2.1 and 4.2.1 below).

The question of the relative ordering of prepositional arguments of nouns with respect to each other is more obscure. As mentioned, they all follow the head noun and adjectives in the best-known languages, but seem to be relatively free in this postnominal position. The Romance languages, which admit an abundant recursion of prepositional arguments in their nominals, should constitute one of the most appropriate testing grounds; but just a few tendencies and empirically subtle preferences can be recorded.

The structural P > S > O hierarchy is only vaguely encoded in the linear order, precisely in the thin and controversial preference often given to P, under a normal flat intonation, as occurring as the outermost prepositional genitive in a cluster of two or three.

Slightly clearer is perhaps the preference for P and S, at least, to precede non-genitive prepositional arguments (PPs not introduced by *de, di*) and for genitive bare nouns to occur adjacent to the head noun:

(12) a. La conversazione di Gianni con Maria
        The conversation of John with Mary
     b. ?La conversazione con Maria di Gianni

(13) a. L'avidità di denaro di Gianni
        John's greed for money
     b. ??L'avidità di Gianni di denaro

In either case, anyway, a lightly marked intonation or heaviness considerations make reverse orders quite acceptable. On the whole, it appears that no clear and theoretically derivable generalization has yet emerged in this domain.

1.4.2 Number of arguments

The most important parametric property of the argument structure of nouns perhaps concerns the number of external positions for arguments which are syntactically realizable. A first observational difference between English and Romance or German is that only one of P and S is overtly expressible in English, while in the other varieties both may occur simultaneously. In other words, it seems that only one external position is syntactically available for a genitive phrase in English nominals, but (at least) two in German and Romance:

(14) *Mary's book of my favorite novelist

(15) Il libro di Maria del mio romanziere preferito

If possessivization of O, discussed earlier, is actually movement to or rather *through* a syntactic external argument position, on the reported analogy with middle formation in clauses, then a whole typological cluster of other, less superficially detectable (and hardly learnable by themselves), differential properties can be parametrically tied to the previous observation about the number of external positions (cf. Giorgi and Longobardi 1991).

The properties in question fall under at least three categories:

i.   control phenomena,
ii.   binding phenomena,
iii.   affectedness constraint (cf. section 1.2.1 above).

It was noticed above (cf. section 1.2.2) how in English binding and control by an understood subject of a noun are possible, but only provided that no possessivization of the O takes place. Now, both processes remain available in Romance and German, irrespectively of whether the O is possessivized or not:

(16)   a.   L'affondamento della nave per riscuotere l'assicurazione
           The sinking of the ship to collect the insurance
       b.   Il suo affondamento per riscuotere l'assicurazione
           Its sinking to collect the insurance

(17)   a.   La sperimentazione di tale droga su se stessi
           The testing of such a drug on oneself
       b.   La sua sperimentazione su se stessi[5]
           Its testing on oneself

Similar examples arise with respect to affectedness restrictions (also Zubizarreta personal communication):

(18)   a.   La percezione/conoscenza del problema
           The perception/knowledge of the problem
       b.   (A proposito del problema) la sua percezione/conoscenza
           (Speaking of the problem) its perception/knowledge

The facts seem to be interpretable as follows: recall the previous hypothesis (cf. section 1.2.2) that binding and control are always syntactic, not just lexical phenomena, requiring an antecedent in the form of a syntactically realized, though possibly empty, phrase. Now, in English (cf. the glosses and section 1.2.2) an empty S competes with a possessivized O for the same syntactic slot, but in German and Romance this is not the case, owing to the independently attested availability of more than one external argument position in nominals. These parametric facts strongly reinforce the argument for syntactically realized empty positions and their role in coreference phenomena.

The treatment of the already mentioned contrast between English/Scandinavian and Romance/German with respect to the affectedness constraint is the same, and follows from the assumptions already made, given the approach to unaffecting head nouns advocated above in section 1.2.1.

On the whole, this crosslinguistic pattern of phenomena reinforces the argument against the proposal of treating Roeper's examples in section 1.2.2 as cases of event control, rather than argument (subject) control.[6]

1.5 *Empty pronominals*

1.5.1 *Null subjects*

The data discussed in the previous section already suggest that the argument structure of nouns *may* and in some cases *must* include empty pronominal categories, at least for S-thematic roles. The latter assumption is widely supported by other evidence, pointing to the existence of a PRO-like category as subject of nouns. It falls into two categories:

  i. evidence that some sort of PRO *may* occur,
  ii. evidence that some sort of PRO *must* occur, with certain nouns.

Type (i), in turn, comes in three subtypes:

  a. evidence from binding,
  b. evidence from arbitrary interpretation,
  c. evidence from construct state.

  (a) First, in many different languages there are cases of binding of an anaphor embedded within an NP by a DP-external apparent antecedent which does not satisfy one of the conditions normally imposed on antecedents of anaphors: *prominence* (c-command), *uniqueness* (non-split nature), *locality*, or *subject-hood* (where the last applies). In all such cases it turns out that the phonetically unrealized subject argument role of the noun is understood as coreferential with the anaphor/antecedent:

(19) La descrizione di se stessa inviata a quella ditta è stata di grande giovamento alla carriera di Anna.
      The description of herself submitted to that firm was very helpful for Anna's career.

Furthermore, the environments in which this type of situation arises are exactly those in which infinitives with controlled PRO-subjects could grammatically replace the head noun in question:

(20) Descrivere se stessa in quel modo è stato di grande giovamento alla carriera di Anna.
      Describing herself that way was very helpful for Anna's career.

The logic of the argument resumes and strengthens that proposed by Higginbotham (1980) with respect to the "gate" function of PRO for weak crossover in examples like (21):

(21) Loving his mother is typical of every Englishman.

(b) Second, some DP-internal anaphors have arbitrary reference without depending on any overt arbitrary binder: again, this only arises when they occur in complement position and are read as bound by the understood subject role of the noun. Thus, some equivalent of PRO could be the primitive source for arbitrariness and occur as subject of N:

(22)   Una buona conoscenza di se stessi è cosa rara.
       A good knowledge of oneself is something rare.

All of this led Giorgi and Longobardi (1991) to the hypothesis that some counterpart of PRO is the invisible subject of such nominals and bridges the otherwise impossible (because notoriously subject to stricter requirements) antecedent–anaphor relation. Of course the syntactic, and not just lexical, nature of this bridging argument is strongly suggested by its parametric interaction with visibly morphosyntactic properties, i.e., the linear positioning and formal realization (possessivization) of an overt O-argument, as evidenced before (cf. section 1.4.2). In this sense, such DP facts, combined with those of section 1.4.2, represent some of the strongest evidence ever for the existence of empty categories in general.

(c) The third subtype of evidence is of a slightly different nature: in so-called Romance construct state nominals (cf. Longobardi 1996) a genitive argument is obligatorily realized *non-prepositionally* and *adjacent* to the head noun, giving rise to surface N + DP + (AP) order:

(23)   a.   Casa Rossi nuova
            Rossi's new home
       b.   *Casa nuova Rossi

However, in some cases a N + (AP) + P(= *di*) + DP sequence appears:

(24)   Case nuova di Rossi

Both apparent irregularities are regularized if the latter sequence is analyzed as actually constituted of N + PRO + (AP) + P + DP, with PRO linked in a chain to the lower genitive PP (= P + DP) and satisfying the condition on adjacency and non-prepositional realization:

(25)   Casa PRO nuova di Rossi

The analysis is independently supported by typological comparison with partially parallel Semitic structures, in which the pronominal category corresponding to Romance PRO is phonetically spelt out.

(c) Here the empty pronominal argument seems necessarily realized in a syntactically high position close to D, where the head noun has been apparently raised. The previous arguments (a, b) provide no evidence as to where exactly a subject empty category may be licensed in the DP structure.

Type (ii) evidence is of the same sort as already seen in (20) above, though it is obtained by replacing the anaphor by a pronoun or name. If with a certain nominal an empty subject *must* occur, it will be disjoint from the pronoun/name by virtue of binding principles B or C. This is exactly the case, for example, in the interpretation of (26):

(26)   La conoscenza di lui/Gianni esibita in quell' occasione (ha molto giovato alla sua carriera).
       The knowledge of him/John exhibited on that occasion (was very helpful for his career).

Again, the facts parallel those holding with control infinitives/gerunds:

(27)   Conoscere *lui/Gianni* (ha molto giovato alla *sua* carriera).
       Knowing him/John (was very helpful for his career).

In either (26) or (27) the understood subject argument can never be coreferential with the object pronoun/name, as made clearer by the impossible coreference of *lui/Gianni* with an external controller of the subject position, such as *sua*, if the latter is added. This suggests that some PRO must syntactically represent it.
       Not all nouns behave this way, however:

(28)   a.   Il ritratto di *lui/Gianni* esibito al museo (ha molto giovato alla *sua* carriera).
            The portrait of him/John exhibited at the museum (was very helpful for his career).
       b.   Ritrarre *lui/Gianni* (ha molto giovato alla *sua* carriera).
            Portraying him/John (was very helpful for his career).

Here no parallelism holds with the corresponding infinitive. Thus, with *ritratto* "portrait," coreference between *lui/Gianni* and the understood agent (author of the (self-)portrait) is not excluded. This suggests that such an understood role is not obligatorily realized as an empty category, which would induce a binding violation, as is actually the case in (28b).
       The *knowledge/portrait* contrast in obligatoriness of a syntactic subject is not surprising, of course, given that *knowledge* was seen to fall anyway into the class of "unaffecting" nouns, requiring an obligatory realization of the external role (cf. section 1.2.1).

1.5.2   *Event vs. object nominals*
Between the two classes is a third one, which in both English and Romance shares with the *knowledge*-class the obligatoriness of a syntactic subject and with the *portrait*-class the option of not assigning the external theta-role. This class is well exemplified by action nominalizations with "affected" objects, such as *destruction*:

(29)   a.   His/The president's moral destruction
      b.   The moral destruction of him/the president was certainly not help-
         ful for his career.

In (29b), the understood agent of *destruction* is necessarily disjoint from *him/the president*. Thus, (29a) suggests that the subject position can be dethematized and obliterated by the raised object, while (29b) suggests that, unless the object raises, the understood subject *must* be syntactically represented.

    The contrast between (29b) and (28) leads to the statement of the following tentative generalization:

(30)   Event nominals (perhaps in the sense of Grimshaw's 1990 *complex event nominals*) require a syntactic external position (occupied by either S or raised O), but object nominals do not.

If correct, (30) draws the most salient syntactic boundary between the two much-debated types of nominal in question.[7]

    In general, thus, one may agree with Grimshaw (1990) that event nominals project their argument structure as obligatorily as verbs. It remains true that O may possessivize in nominals (except for unaffecting nouns), while it cannot always enter a middle construction in the corresponding verbal structure:

(31)   a.   The president's moral destruction
      b.   *The president morally destroyed

Such a difference could perhaps be imputed to Case theory, i.e., to a general optionality of Genitive marking for nominal O as opposed to a lexically conditioned optionality of Accusative marking by verbs (middle formation).

1.5.3   Null objects

In addition to null pronominal subjects, nominals also exhibit null pronominal objects. Some languages, like Italian, display an arbitrary null object of verbs, which is able, among other things, to bind anaphoric expressions (Rizzi 1986a). The same is true with nominals (Giorgi and Longobardi 1991):

(32)   La particolare tecnica delle sue riconciliazioni con se stessi è ciò che ha reso famoso quello psicoanalista.
      The peculiar technique of his reconciliations with oneself is what made that psychoanalyst famous.

Two properties oppose this null object to null subjects. Its licensing is parametrically constrained: as in VPs, it is available in Italian, but forbidden in other languages, such as English. Second, unlike null pronominal subjects and, again, like its verbal counterpart, this empty category can only be arbitrary and never syntactically controlled.

1.5.4 A-positions and the evidence for empty categories

At least thematic subjects and objects of nouns seem to be basically associated with A-positions, from which in fact they are able to regularly bind and control. It was argued before that Romance nominals provide more than one external position, allowing, among other things, co-occurrence of a raised (possessivized) O with a PRO-subject. One may wonder whether all such positions qualify as A- or just the one of thematic subjects. Three types of consideration prove the latter answer to be correct.

Suppose, first, that O is in a configuration where it cannot act as a controller from its base position, say for lack of structural prominence (c-command), but could from a higher (subject) A-position. This is exactly the case in active/passive clausal structures with control into an adverbial infinitival sentence:

(33)   a.   Gianni$_i$ fu condannato dopo PRO$_i$ aver subito un regolare processo.
          John was convicted after facing a regular trial.
      b.   *Hanno condannato Gianni$_i$ dopo PRO$_i$ aver subito un regolare processo.
          They convicted John after facing a regular trial.

A roughly analogous contrast (although sometimes lightly less sharp) can be found within nominals:

(34)   a.   La sua$_i$ condanna dopo PRO$_i$ aver subito un processo irregolare rimarrà un'infamia.
          His conviction after facing an irregular trial will remain a shame.
      b.   ?*La condanna di Gianni$_i$ dopo PRO$_i$ aver subito un processo irregolare rimarrà un'infamia.
          The conviction of John after facing an irregular trial will remain a shame.

In (34b), in order to acquire proper controller status, O must be in (or rather have passed through) a higher A-position, presumably that of S, if and only if no other high position qualifies as A-. Therefore, in these situations a subject empty category should be forbidden in Romance as well and, consequently, no binding ability on the part of an understood S should remain available. Patterns like the following (in particular the ungrammaticality of (36c)) confirm this point (cf. Giorgi and Longobardi 1991 for discussion):

(35)   a.   ?*Disapprovo l'attribuzione del premio a Maria dopo PRO essere stato a lungo in ballottaggio tra i due concorrenti.
          I disapprove of the attribution of the prize to Mary after being long at stake between the two candidates.
      b.   A proposito del premio, disapprovo la sua attribuzione a Maria dopo PRO essere stato a lungo in ballottaggio tra i due concorrenti.
          Speaking of the prize, I disapprove of its attribution to Mary after being long at stake between the two candidates.

(36) a. L'attribuzione del premio a se stessa ha fatto di Maria un tipico
          rappresentante della corruzione odierna.
          The attribution of the prize to herself made Mary into a typical
          representative of today's corruption.
     b. A proposito del premio, la sua attribuzione a se stessa ha fatto di
         Maria un tipico rappresentante della corruzione odierna.
         Speaking of the prize, its attribution to herself made Mary into a
         typical representative of today's corruption.
     c. *A proposito del premio, la sua attribuzione a se stessa dopo PRO
         essere stato a lungo in ballottaggio fra i due concorrenti ha fatto di
         Maria un tipico rappresentante della corruzione odierna.
         Speaking of the prize, its attribution to herself after being long at
         stake between the two candidates made Mary into a typical repres-
         entative of today's corruption.

In fact (35) shows that O must raise to a higher (A-)position in order to control
PRO, (36) that this process interferes with the otherwise possible binding of an
anaphor by the understood subject.

Second, if O, in certain configurations like (37a), is able to control from its
base position, when possessivized it will not need to raise through an A-
position and a null syntactic subject will be available. Indeed the latter may
show its presence by itself performing as a controller:

(37) a. La condanna di Gianni a PRO scontare tre anni di carcere senza PRO
          avergli dato la possibilità di difendersi mi ha scandalizzato.
          The conviction of John to serve three years in prison without giving
          him a chance to defend himself scandalized me.
     b. La sua condanna a PRO scontare tre anni di carcere senza PRO
         avergli dato la possibilità di difendersi mi ha scandalizzato.
         His conviction to serve three years in prison without giving him a
         chance to defend himself scandalized me.

Here O controls the PRO subject of *scontare* "serve," and the understood arbitrary S of *condanna* "conviction" may control the other PRO-subject of the
adverbial *without*-clause. Hence both S and O are syntactically active.

Finally, if the only high A-position is the one of subjects, with "unaffecting"
head nouns, which it was argued cannot dispense with a syntactically realized
S role (cf. section 1.2.1), hence at least an empty category, the object should
never improve its control capabilities through possessivization. This prediction is also borne out:

(38) a. *Non è possibile la conoscenza dell'algebra senza essere studiata bene.
          Knowledge of algebra without being studied well is not possible.
     b. *Non è possibile la sua conoscenza senza essere studiata bene.
         Its knowledge without being studied well is not possible.

Thus, the data suggest that even in languages admitting more than one external position, like Romance language and German as parametrically opposed to English and Scandinavian (cf. section 1.4.2), only one of them counts as an A-position.[8] At the same time these patterns strongly reinforce the evidence for the role played by empty categories within nominal structures.

1.6   Some conclusions

To sum up, the argument structure of nominal phrases is governed by a number of probably universal *principles*, largely shared with clausal structures. Among these are principles concerning:

(39)   a.   the structural hierarchy and obligatoriness/optionality of thematic arguments,
       b.   the existence of two distinct Case positions for non-prepositional arguments,
       c.   the access to such positions,
       d.   the licensing of empty categories.

The main domains of *parametric* variation in this area concern instead.

(40)   a.   the number of external argument positions,
       b.   the number of active Case checking positions,
       c.   the actual forms of non-prepositional Case realization.

The setting of such parameters appears at first sight rather unrelated to the settings and even the structure of parameters in the clausal domain.

2   Modifiers

2.1   Adjectives

Attributive adjectives are traditionally an extensively covered but poorly understood domain of inquiry. Some generalizations began to emerge, however, in recent years, beyond the occurrence of much stylistically conditioned surface variation.

2.1.1   Types and order
The most salient property of adjectives re-evaluated by recent work (Sproat and Shih 1988, Crisma 1990, 1996, Valois 1991) is that they receive different interpretations according to their syntactic position (also cf. Fassi Fehri 1997, Gil 1987). The lexical meaning of some adjectives is compatible with more semantic roles, accordingly allowing them to appear in different positions. That of some others is only compatible with one semantic interpretation, thus freezing their occurrence in certain positions.

The existence of different positions is manifested, rather universally, in the relative linear order of adjectives with respect to each other, and, with some parametric variation, with respect to the head noun.

Sproat and Shih (1988) suggest that a preference hierarchy tends to order adjectives expressing more absolute properties, like shape and color, linearly closer to the head than those expressing relative properties, like quality and size. The hierarchy seems observationally well motivated in languages with steadily prenominal modifiers (e.g. English, Chinese), but yields contrasting results in different languages with superficially postnominal adjectives (within European languages, Celtic retains the same order of adjectives as English, but some non-European languages display its mirror image), and finally has unclear status in languages like the Romance ones, where nouns often surface medially between pairs or sets of adjectives.

Sharper and theoretically more revealing results were provided by including in focus the richer system of adjectival modification found with event nominals. The relevant facts suggest the existence of a fixed crosslinguistic left-to-right sequence of adjectives, paralleling that of adverbs discussed in Jackendoff (1972):

(41)   S-(subject or speaker)oriented > Manner > Argument adjective. (Crisma 1991, 1993)

Some restricted classes of special adjectives (numeral ones and very few others) seem to even precede the sequence of (41) (Bernstein 1991a, Crisma 1991, Zamparelli 1995).

Now, it has been stressed originally by Crisma (1991, 1993, 1996) and Valois (1991) that the head noun surfaces in different positions in different languages, without affecting the relative order of adjectives; cf. the following paradigms representative in turn of event- and object-denoting nominals (with the noun in bold):

(42)   a.   The probable hostile German **reaction**   (English (Germanic))
         b.   La probabile **reazione** ostile tedesca   (Italian (most of Romance))

(43)   a.   A nice blue German **dress**
         b.   One bèle bleuve **cote** alemande   (Walloon)[9]
         c.   Un bel **vestito** azzurro tedesco

The crucial observation is that, as mentioned before, each position corresponds to a distinct semantic role, and many adjectives are lexically able to bear different roles (as the same DP may positionally bear different theta-roles), giving rise to non-synonymous pairs like those in (44) and (45):

(44)   a.   L'astuta risposta ingenua di Gianni
         b.   L'ingenua risposta astuta di Gianni

(45) a. John's clever naive answer
      b. John's naive clever answer[10]

2.1.2   Adjectives and N-raising

Bringing to light these patterns naturally supported the hypothesis that the parametric variation in question does not concern the position of adjectives but rather that of the noun (Bernstein 1991a, 1992, 1993a, Crisma 1991, 1993, 1996, Valois 1991, Cinque 1994a), taken to leftward raise to different positions in different languages and constructions.

This N-raising approach to the noun–adjective order is a generalization of the narrower but parallel analysis proposed in Longobardi (1994) for the N-A-order obligatorily found in Romance with determinerless proper names. Adjectives normally only possible in the D-A-N-order but ungrammatical (or severely constrained in their meaning options) in the D-N-A-order become grammatical (or retain their ordinary prenominal meaning) with proper names in the N-A-sequence (and the A-N-sequence is ungrammatical):

(46) a. La sola Napoli è stata prescelta tra le città italiane.
          The only-SgFemAdj Naples was selected among Italian cities.
      b. *La Napoli sola è stata prescelta tra le città italiane.
          The Naples only was selected among Italian cities.
      c. Napoli sola è stata prescelta tra le città italiane.
          Naples only was selected among Italian cities.
      d. *Sola Napoli è stata prescelta tra le città italiane.
          Only Naples was selected among Italian cities.

The paradigm suggests that N substitutes for D with the adjective remaining basically prenominal. It is perhaps significant that the Romance languages display both N-to-D-raising of proper names and more general leftward N-raising over adjectives, while the Germanic ones lack both, though the question deserves wider typological investigation.

Another type of contrast concerning at least the so-called Manner adjectives, and distinguishing Germanic and Romance in a way parallel to the patterns seen above, is that between *restrictive* and *appositive* modification. With few exceptions, Romance adjectives are only appositive when prenominal; the Germanic ones can be restrictive or appositive:

(47) a. Il **vestito** azzurro
      b. L'azzurro **vestito**

(48) The blue **dress**

This contrast as well has been occasionally suggested to be ultimately reducible to the wider scope (i.e., higher target) of N-raising in Romance (Bernstein 1992, Zamparelli 1994, Crisma 1996). Crosslinguistically, so-called Manner adjectives would be split: the restrictive type might occur lower than the appositive one, with the noun obligatorily raising above the latter adjectives in Romance but not in Germanic. Given (41), this analysis suggests the (perhaps correct) prediction that S-oriented adjectives on one side and argument adjectives on the other should escape the classical appositive/restrictive contrast. (41) could then become (49), with w the potentially universal domain of restrictiveness and N the position normally targeted by raising of common nouns in most Romance varieties:

(49) [S-(subject or speaker-)oriented [Manner$_1$(appositive) N [$_w$Manner$_2$ (restrictive) [Argument adjective . . .]]]]

On the whole, two main conclusions appear to have emerged from recent approaches to adjectival modification:

i. It is possible to profitably pursue a research program based on the idea that adjectives occupy universally fixed positions in the nominal structure with N parametrically taking different orders with respect to such positions.
ii. Attributive adjectives as a whole (i.e., the entire structure of (41) or rather (49)) crosslinguistically occur lower than a genitive position or higher than another genitive position. In other words (41) seems to always occur between the two slots (probably specifier positions) labeled GenS and GenO in (10), a typological conjecture strongly confirmed by a language where both genitives can be realized, such as German (cf. (9) above).[11]

Therefore, properly inserting (49) into (10), the more complete picture turns out to be like the following:

(50) [**1** GenS **2** [S-oriented [Manner$_1$ N [Manner$_2$ [Argument **3** [GenO [$_\alpha$ P [S [O . . . N . . .]] $_\alpha$]]]]]]]

The interaction of N-raising with the lexical structures examined so far will be analyzed in section 4 below.

II   Functional Structure

3   Determiners

3.1   *Types of determiner*

Certain languages are known to introduce the vast majority of their nominal structures by means of one (and often *at most* one) item taken from the (closed) classes of demonstratives, articles, possessives, quantifiers, or cardinal numerals. These five classes, each with peculiarities of its own, are all roughly identified already in traditional grammar and can rather well be defined in relatively obvious semantic terms. As a first approximation, such classes, which, as noticed, normally seem to be mutually exclusive, are collected, precisely on these distributional grounds, under the hyperonymic grammatical category of *determiners* and, as far as their surface location is concerned, in recent works have been variously assigned to the head or specifier position of a D-projection.

Among other things, determiners seem to typically establish the definite/indefinite interpretation of the nominal and to often select between a mass or count reading of morphologically singular head nouns.

The underlying syntactic source of such elements has also been discussed, occasionally giving rise to important conclusions, as in the case of Bernstein's (1997) results about demonstratives and of the considerations discussed in section 3.3 below. I will be primarily concerned with the D-category and principles affecting its surface appearance and will touch on the various determiners only if relevant.

The role of the D-head has been judged so characteristic, in particular since the influential work of Szabolcsi (1981, 1983, 1987, 1989, 1994) and Abney (1987), that it has come more and more generally to be viewed as the head of the whole nominal structure (hence a DP) and as taking NP as its complement (cf. Bernstein this volume for discussion). The following subsections will be devoted to reviewing some crosslinguistic generalizations and some parametrizations concerning the conditions of occurrence or omission of determiners.

3.2   Determinerless NPs

3.2.1   Arguments and non-arguments

Languages superficially appear to differ heavily in the possibility of omitting an overt determiner. However, various constraints on omission have been identified in the recent past. A first principle and a very characteristic feature of the crosslinguistic pattern is that languages seem to distribute in a "subset" or inclusiveness hierarchy with respect to omission environments. In other words we can review the best-known language types in a sequence progressively enlarging the class of environments allowing superficially determinerless NPs.

The most restrictive type seems so far to be best instantiated by French, at least among Indo-European languages. The pattern of determiner omission in French appears close to justifying an influential proposal originally made by Szabolcsi (1987), later adopted in Stowell (1989b, 1991) and Longobardi (1994), namely that a D-position (and its projection) is only necessary for *argument* nominals and may often be dispensable for *non-arguments*. Such a principle has been formulated in forms such as the following:[12]

(51)   DPs can be arguments, NPs cannot.

Thus, French exhibits determinerless NPs as predicates, idioms, exclamations, and vocatives, in addition to certain prepositional complements, but not in classical argument functions. Some non-Indo-European languages might perhaps, at a very first look, be classed with French in the most restrictive type, namely Basque and Maori, and would deserve attentive study in this perspective.[13]

The next macro-type of languages is exemplified by the rest of the Romance varieties and by most of Germanic. Such languages display exactly the same asymmetry between arguments and non-arguments as that exhibited by French, but only with respect to singular count nouns. In other words, in argument position some superficially determinerless NPs do occur but only if headed by a plural or mass noun. Such expressions, whose study was initiated in English by Carlson (1977), still a useful source of information, have come to be known as *bare nouns* (for updated discussion cf. Delfitto to appear).

3.2.2   *Bare nouns*

Argument bare nouns are thus present in all the Romance and Germanic languages (with the noted exception of modern French), but, pending discovery of further languages possibly falling into the same class, we may safely divide the type into two subtypes, well distinct and, again, related to each other by a subset relation.

The two subtypes are instantiated at best by Romance bare nouns on the more restrictive side and by English bare nouns on the other, with the rest of Germanic probably patterning with English, in essentials, although further study of such languages may be required.

Romance and English bare nouns differ with respect to both (52a) and (52b):

(52)   a.   syntactic distribution,
      b.   semantic interpretation.

The first difference essentially amounts to the fact that Romance bare nouns are confined to complement positions and excluded from pre-verbal subject positions, roughly displaying the lexically governed distribution of syntactic variables (*wh*-traces) (cf. Contreras 1986, Lois 1986, Longobardi 1994, among others), while the English ones occur rather freely in all argument positions. Especially since Contreras (1986) it has been speculated that such a distribution in Romance could precisely be due to the presence of an actual empty category as the invisible determiner.

The second difference has to do with the fact that Romance bare nouns can only receive an *indefinite* interpretation (often existential, sometimes generic but only in independently *generic* or *characterizing* sentences), analogous, in the same environments, to that assigned to NPs introduced by overt indefinite determiners (indefinite article, partitive articles) (cf. Casalegno 1987, Dobrovie-Sorin and Laca 1996, Longobardi 1998). English bare nouns, in addition to exhibiting the same interpretive possibilities as the Romance ones, can also apparently occur as kind-referring names, i.e., as referential or definite generics, in argument positions of kind-level (in Carlson's 1977 sense) and of *particular* or *episodic* sentences:

(53) Tomatoes were introduced in Europe after 1492.

In such environments Romance can only resort to DPs headed by overt definite articles:

(54) a. *Pomodori furono introdotti in Europa dopo il 1492.
          Tomatoes were introduced in Europe after 1492.
      b. I pomodori furono introdotti in Europa dopo il 1492.
          The tomatoes were introduced in Europe after 1492.

The two contrasting properties (52a, b) have been suggested to be parametrically tied to each other and to others discussed below (Longobardi 1994, 1996, 1998).

Anyhow, descriptively, what seems clear is that there is a rough hierarchy of inclusiveness ranking languages with respect to such phenomena:

(55) a. languages with no bare nouns,
      b. languages with *stricter* bare nouns,
      c. languages with *freer* bare nouns.

In all these languages, singular count common nouns appear superficially determinerless only in non-argument function. In such non-argument functions the distribution of determiners is more idiosyncratic, and detailed monoglottic and crosslinguistic study of even these well-known languages is still to be pursued.

3.2.3 Bare singulars

In several languages, probably the majority, however, even *singular count* nouns may occur determinerless in argument function. Let me descriptively call such entities *bare singulars*, crucially distinguishing them in this sense from bare nouns as defined above.

A first group of such languages assigns bare singular arguments exactly the same range of interpretations as are assigned to NPs introduced by an overt indefinite article in languages like English, German, or Romance. In essence, in these varieties, such nouns are interpreted as (existential or generic) indefinites, as if they contained a corresponding understood article. Among the most notable such languages, one may apparently cite Icelandic, Welsh and Irish, Hungarian, Hebrew and Arabic, and probably Classical Greek in the varieties of Attic and Koiné prose. Now, it seems to be the case that all these languages, while they have independent overt morphemes with the interpretation of a definite article, lack any overt morpheme which could be identified with the indefinite article of Romance and most of Germanic. That this is not due to chance has been proposed by Crisma (1997) as part of a wider tentative generalization which may be rephrased as follows:

(56)   No language exhibits any free variation between presence and absence of a determiner for nominal arguments.

In other words, if a language has a lexical determiner with a certain meaning (say, the indefinite article), it must obligatorily use it to express that meaning (a synonymous determinerless construction is excluded). If shown to be correct, this will be an important crosslinguistic property of determiner systems, possibly related to some version of the Full Interpretation Principle.

Another type of language allows all types of determinerless argument nominal, including bare singulars, corresponding to either a definite or an indefinite interpretation of western European languages. Typical instantiations of this type are most Slavic languages or Latin. If (56) is correct, it follows that such languages will not have any definite or indefinite lexical article, but just some of the semantically more complex instantiations of the category of determiners mentioned in section 3.1.1 above. The expectation seems to be fulfilled. Also, it seems to remain descriptively true that if a language allows bare singulars it allows bare nouns as well.

Thus we have another pair of language types in a subset relation to one another and to those of (55), so that a fuller picture may now be completed and rephrased as follows:

(57)   a.   languages with no bare nouns (French),
       b.   languages with *stricter* bare nouns (apparently the rest of Romance: Spanish, Italian . . .),
       c.   languages with *freer* bare nouns (English and perhaps most of Germanic),
       d.   languages with indefinite bare singulars (and only a definite lexical article: Icelandic, Celtic, Hebrew . . .),
       e.   languages with ambiguous bare singulars (i.e., articleless languages: Russian, Czech, Latin . . .).

Notice that if crosslinguistic variation were indeed limited to the types of (57), then all such possible languages would be ordered in a full subset hierarchy, trivializing most acquisition issues.

3.2.4   Parametric approaches

Let us now examine this supposedly correct pattern from the viewpoint of a parametric theory. The difference between (57a) and the other types was tentatively but plausibly reduced by Delfitto and Schroten (1992) and Delfitto (1993) to the impoverished number morphology of French nouns as opposed to the rest of Romance, and therefore to an independent morphological parameter. The semantic–syntactic differences between (57b) and (57c) were related by

Longobardi (1994) to a salient Romance/Germanic contrast in the syntax of proper names, for which cf. sections 3.2.6 and 4.1.1 below.

The contrast of the first three types (57a–c) vs. the other two (57d–e) has not been successfully related so far to independently visible differential properties, except for the noted consequences of (55), i.e., the lexical absence of the indefinite or of both articles in (57d) and (57e) respectively. The same is true of the contrast between (57a–d) and (57e).

The relevant distinctions are centered on the notions of *definiteness* interpretation and of *count/mass* selection for morphologically singular nouns. Recall that with overt determiners these are both typical properties of the D-system. The terms *interpretation* and *selection* will be used throughout in this technical sense.

The fact that there seem to exist languages with just bare nouns, but no languages with only bare singulars, may suggest that there is a universally *unmarked* (mass/plural) vs. *marked* (singular count) selectional value.

According to Crisma (1997), in certain languages determinerless arguments would be parametrically limited to the unmarked or *default* selection, while in others they would have *extragrammatical*, i.e., just pragmatic, selection, including the possibility of the marked value, as if they were introduced by actual null articles (*extragrammaticality of count/mass* parameter).

Analogously, while in many languages there are just indefinite determinerless arguments, it is highly dubious that there exist languages with just definite determinerless arguments (e.g. the case of a language complementary to (57d) in the sense of having a lexical indefinite article and missing determiners exclusively understood as a definite one).[14] If this generalization is correct, here too we have to do with an unmarked (*indefinite*) vs. marked (*definite*) interpretive value. Therefore, Crisma (1997) has proposed, again, that in many languages determinerless argument nominals would be limited to the *default* (i.e., indefinite) interpretive value, in others (the languages of (57e), of course, as opposed to those of (57d) and to all those lexically distinguishing two articles of the modern western European type) their interpretation would be extragrammatical, i.e., the assignment of an interpretation with reference to definiteness would be an essentially pragmatic process (*extragrammaticality of definiteness* parameter).

Thus, two main parameters seem to account for most variation affecting null determiners: ±extragrammatical selection, ±extragrammatical interpretation.

This hypothesis provides, among other things, a maximally restrictive theory of the *grammatical* strategies to non-contextually recover the interpretation of an understood determiner. According to this, UG would allow just one such strategy, namely the assignment of a default *indefinite* value. The strategy would be one and the same for two types of phenomenon, which are thus theoretically unified: bare singulars of languages of type (57d) and bare plural/mass nouns of languages of type (57b), like the Romance ones (for (57c) cf. below). Similar considerations might extend to selection recovery: see n. 14 above.

3.2.5   *Contextual identification*

In the previous sections we have examined cases of determinerless NPs whose licensing and interpretation are relatively independent of the grammatical environment surrounding the "missing" D-position. Several languages, however, exhibit interactions between the local (NP-internal) grammatical context and a full range of "missing determiners," thus including nominals with bare singular heads.

There are at least three main cases of this type to be considered:

(58)   a.   Semitic Construct State,
     b.   Saxon Genitive in Germanic,
     c.   Scandinavian definiteness suffixes.

The first construction has been very extensively covered in the recent generative literature, e.g. by Borer (1984, 1994, 1996), Ritter (1986, 1988, 1991), Fassi Fehri (1989, 1993), Siloni (1990, 1994), Hazout (1991), Ouhalla (1988, 1991, 1996b: also on Berber), and Shlonsky (1991a), among many others (also cf. Carstens 1991 on Bantu languages), and has significant parallels in a genitival construction of the Celtic languages (cf. Duffield 1991, Guilfoyle 1993, Rouveret 1995).

In these constructions a determinerless noun is obligatorily followed by a genitival DP and interpreted for definiteness in a way harmonic with the definiteness value of such a DP: in other words the +/−definite reading of the matrix nominal is contextually *inherited* from that of its subordinate. Such constructions all display some evidence of leftward movement of the (matrix) head noun, which in several cases has been plausibly interpreted as raising to an empty D-position, and by some scholars (especially cf. Borer 1994, Siloni 1994) as a necessary component of the semantic process of definiteness inheritance referred to above.

The second construction formally falls into either of the two first types of Genitive realization mentioned in section 1.3.3, depending on the language (English and Scandinavian in the first type, German in the other). From the viewpoint of interpretation, however, it appears to be unitary. As in construct state, no overt determiner may appear introducing such phrases, yet the definiteness value of the matrix nominal is not undetermined, but is likely to depend on the genitival DP. It is arguable (cf. Longobardi 1996 and references there; also Dobrovie-Sorin to appear) that these constructions are variants of the same abstract pattern responsible for the previous subcase, namely construct state. The only difference would be the obvious fact that N-raising does not overtly take place, or at least does not overtly cross past the genitival argument in Saxon Genitive, so as to derive the characteristic Gen-N surface order, as opposed to the N-Gen one of construct state. If so, the interpretive mechanism might be the same, i.e., inheritance of definiteness, with a parametric difference lying just in two distinct types of null Ds, one overtly attracting the head noun (Semitic), the other not (Germanic).

Finally, in the Scandinavian languages, as is known, the unmarked expression of definiteness with common nouns consists of a morpheme suffixed to the head noun (and, in some varieties, homophonous, though without an obvious etymological relation, with the free morpheme presumably occurring in D and functioning as an *indefinite* article), as in the following Norwegian examples:[15]

(59) a. Boken/Huset
          The book/The house
      b. En bok/Et hus
          A book/A house

Such a definiteness suffix cannot, however, be structurally assimilated to a real article, because it does not seem to occupy the D-position. When an adjective is inserted, the difference between this suffix and a real article surfaces: (i) the suffix may (e.g. in Icelandic or archaic forms of Mainland Scandinavian) or must (in most other varieties and styles, except for Danish) co-occur with overt morphemes having a definite or demonstrative interpretation and apparently occupying the D-position (the so-called *double definiteness* phenomenon); (ii) the complex N + suffix obligatorily occurs lower than adjectives in all the languages:

(60) a. Den vidunderlige boken   (Norwegian)
          The wonderful book-the
      b. Frábæra bókinn (/Hin frábæra bók)   (Icelandic)
          Wonderful book-the (/The wonderful book)

These arguments suffice for us to suppose that, while the indefinite morpheme does indeed occupy the D-position, this is not the case for the definiteness suffix, which is then not to be confused with a real enclitic article of the type occurring, for example, in Rumanian (cf. Dobrovie-Sorin 1987, Grosu 1988):

(61) a. Lupul
          Wolf-the
      b. Lup
          Wolf

The difference is that the complex formed by N + suffix occurs first in the Rumanian DP, to the left of adjectives, hence in the normal position of determiners, and cannot be preceded by, say, a demonstrative or any other analogous determination:

(62) a. Lupul frumoas
          Wolf-the beautiful
      b. *Acest lupul frumoas
          This wolf-the beautiful

Thus, while the Rumanian definiteness morpheme may be rather safely taken to occur in D, the Scandinavian one must occur in a lower position. This position is perhaps that labeled **3** in (10) above, since it must be lower than all adjectives and immediately to the left of a position for Genitive Case, as shown by the following phrases:

(63) a.   Den vidunderlige boken hans   (Norwegian)
           The wonderful book-the his
      b.   Frábæra bókinn hans   (Icelandic)
           Wonderful book-the his
           "His wonderful book"

In any event, Scandinavian suffixes positionally are not determiners, hence in one more case something crucially contributes to the definite interpretation of the nominal without lying in D. The same analysis has been persuasively applied to a rather analogous definiteness suffix occurring in Bulgarian (Gambarotto 1995).

In languages where definiteness is grammatically relevant (57a–d), determinerless argument nominals, whenever possible, are thus subject to either of two basic mechanisms of interpretation, i.e., recovery of a definiteness value (cf. Crisma 1997):

(64) a.   *default* interpretation (indefinite),
      b.   definiteness *inheritance*, exemplified in the three subcases of this section.

Now recall that identification of empty determiners seems to be necessary with respect to two properties: recovery of definiteness (except for languages in (57e), of course), and recovery of the mass/count reading selection for singular nouns.

Recovery of the count/mass selection is likely to take place along perfectly analogous lines. Apart from languages where it is extragrammatical, i.e., pragmatic (57d–e), it obtains only by either a *default* strategy (mass/plural) or an *inheritance* process. This has been argued for Saxon Genitive in particular (cf. Crisma 1997, Bernstein et al. in press) since in construct state languages the question is irrelevant, for they seem to independently fall into (57d), i.e., have free selection.

Also, the main difference between Icelandic and the rest of modern Scandinavian (and Germanic in general) would precisely be that in Icelandic selection can be pragmatic, while in the other cognate languages it is at least recovered by inheritance.

Structurally speaking the inheritance processes, though sometimes originating from an embedded argument, presumably in a Spec position, might probably always involve two heads, namely D and a lower one. In construct state, overt movement of the definiteness feature via N-raising to D has been postulated

(Borer 1994, 1996, Siloni 1994). Saxon Genitive has been argued to involve the covert analogue of the same process (Longobardi 1996); it is less clear whether the same could be argued for the Scandinavian process. Only notice that, if such inheritance process were somehow blocked by an intervening adjective, this would explain the obligatory recourse to the overt determiner *den* in Norwegian (63a) and, modulo the pragmatic nature of selection in Icelandic, the minimally contrasting possibility of (63b) in the latter language.

3.2.6 Proper names

In the previous section we have reviewed some generalizations and current hypotheses about the phenomenon of determiner omission with common nouns, i.e., semantically, nouns referring to kinds. Unlike common nouns, proper names, i.e., nouns intrinsically referring to single individual objects, may occur determinerless to a much wider typological extent. Except for Greek (and perhaps Albanian, to judge from Kallulli 1996), at least a subset of proper names, especially place names and names of months and days, seem to be allowed to make arguments without any determiner in all the best-analyzed modern languages, including the ones ranked highest in the hierarchy (57).

A crucial discovery in this respect was that such determinerless arguments are by no means simplex structures and that, furthermore, they are not structurally homogeneous in all languages. Testing the position of determinerless argument proper names with respect to various sorts of adjectives in Romance, Longobardi (1994, 1996) has shown that such names never occupy the same position as determinerless common nouns (e.g. bare nouns), but presumably surface in the D-position, as an effect of N-raising to D (also cf. section 2.1.2 above for examples).

Actually, it was argued that several traditional semantic properties associated with object reference (e.g. transparency in intensional contexts, rigidity of designation) are indeed a necessary correlate of precisely this syntactic raising. The generalization in Romance can thus be formulated as follows:

(65) If N overtly moves to a phonetically empty D then it will be object-referring.

Of course whether an individual noun may bear this interpretation (is "proper") or not (is "common") is a property of its lexical semantics.

Thus, in at least one well-studied language group, the lack of determiners with argument proper names cannot be imputed to the lack or emptiness of the corresponding syntactic position, i.e., D. Further typological support for such N-raising analysis of proper names has been recently proposed, on the grounds of subtler phonological evidence, from the study of Igbo (Niger–Congo) as well (Déchaine and Manfredi 1998).

As anticipated, however, these constructions are not crosslinguistically homogeneous. In English, and presumably in other Germanic languages, argument determinerless proper names seem to have the same structure as bare nouns, i.e., the head noun does not raise to D. Thus, in Germanic Adj + N appears as the surface order of either common or proper determinerless nouns, while in Romance, with the subset of obligatory prenominal adjectives, Adj + N is the surface appearance of bare nouns, N + Adj + t is that of proper names, in argument position.

This necessarily led to the assumption of a parameter of D-strength: descriptively speaking, a lexically empty D is strong in Romance (overtly attracts object-referring nouns) but not, say, in Germanic.

Longobardi (1994, 1996) embedded this parametric hypothesis in what might be defined a "topological" theory of the syntax–semantics mapping in DPs. There would be designated positions within DPs for the interpretation of the various elements, in particular the denotation of the whole DP, hence the referential properties of proper names are read off D (also cf. Zamparelli 1995, Vangsnes 1996b, and references there for the development of theories of further interpretive properties of nominals in a framework of the same spirit). Therefore, object-referring expressions must end up in D, and must do so overtly if the latter is "strong."

The systematic association so discovered between certain referential properties and (movement to) the D-position parallels the more visible and traditionally known holding between scope assignment to *wh*-operators and (*wh*-movement to) Comp.

N-to-D-raising, however, is not the only way for a proper name to satisfy the "strength" requirement of D. In Romance N-to-D often alternates, under dialectal and stylistic conditioning, with proper names introduced by an overt (definite) article. Furthermore, with many names, whose peculiarity is sometimes predictable on complex cognitive grounds, the article strategy is the only available one, and this seems to be the case for *all* proper names in those languages mentioned above like Greek.

Such articles of proper names seem to have an obviously impoverished semantic function and in a few languages also a special morphological form (Catalan, perhaps Frisian to judge from Ebert 1970), Borrowing a useful term from Vergnaud and Zubizarreta (1992), they may be termed *expletive*, since their role, like that of certain subject pronouns, appears to be essentially that of relating a substantive lexical item (the name) to the functional position (D) where it could have been, but was not, moved.

What is relevant here is that, though expletive articles with proper names are attested even in the Germanic languages, i.e., without strong Ds, Art (+ Adj) + N is an available, indeed the only available, alternative to N (+ Adj) + t in languages which must satisfy a strong D.

Therefore, languages where articles are obligatory with *all* proper names can be tentatively viewed as languages with a "strong" setting of the D-parameter, but with an independent blocking of N-to-D-raising, a hypothesis with far-reaching consequences (cf. section 4.1.2 below).

Another category of obvious object-referring expressions is represented by personal pronouns. Thus one could expect them to behave like proper names, i.e., to overtly raise to D in Romance and to stay lower in Germanic. The first expectation, in agreement with the sketched topological theory of DP-interpretation, is fulfilled; the second is not, since, surprisingly, pronouns are likely to surface in D in English as well, essentially in agreement with Postal (1969). So, while (66a, b) minimally contrast, (67a, b) are perfectly parallel:

(66) a. Roma antica/*Antica Roma (fu distrutta dai barbari).
     b. Ancient Rome/*Rome ancient (was destroyed by the barbarians).

(67) a. Noi ricchi/*Ricchi noi ...
     b. We rich/*Rich we ...

Taken together with the crosslinguistic lack of alternations with structures with expletive articles ("*The rich we/*I ricchi noi"), this fact might suggest that pronouns are universally available for base generation in D, thus escaping the effects of the movement parameter affecting proper names.

3.2.7   Empty determiners: arguments and non-arguments

So far, we have tacitly assumed the wide crosslinguistic validity of a principle like (51). We may now wonder whether it can be positively argued that this is correct. The evidence in this direction is at best subtle and the question constitutes an important domain for further inquiry.

Of course, (51) would be naively falsified by a huge number of superficially determinerless arguments were we not to assume the existence of empty determiners. Hence, part of the problem has to do with whether there is positive evidence for empty categories in D in some of the subcases discussed above.

A kind of argument of plausibility can be formulated as follows: the supposed empty determiners display some properties often attributed to empty categories in general. Thus, we have seen that the possibility of determinerless nominals in argument position seems to be subject to two conditions: the *licensing* of the structure (available in, say, Italian, but not in French) and the *identification* or recovery of some features of selection and interpretation usually expressed by determiners. Now, as noticed in Crisma (1997), this is reminiscent of the two analogous requirements proposed by Rizzi (1986a) for empty categories. Furthermore, there is even some analogy between the three types of identification typologically available to missing determiners and those holding for empty pronominals: the *default* strategy could correspond to the assignment of an impersonal (e.g. arbitrary) interpretation; the *contextual* strategy reminds one of the identification of empty subjects by verbal agreement in, for example, Romance *pro*-drop varieties; and the *extragrammatical* (pragmatic) strategy is analogous to that of empty subjects in languages without verbal agreement, like Chinese or Japanese (cf. Jaeggli and Safir 1989a).

Another type of longer-known analogy between missing determiners and empty categories is provided by Contreras's (1986) cited observation that

Romance bare nouns display a "lexically governed" distribution, like certain empty categories, those deprived of intrinsic feature content, according to Chomsky (1981). It is now suggestive that this happens precisely with the cases where the alleged empty determiner would have to be most deprived of intrinsic feature content (default selection + default interpretation).

Of course what is most relevant for (51) is asymmetries between arguments and non-arguments: as noticed, in languages like French, with not even bare nouns, the asymmetry is particularly clear. But also the other Romance languages provide highly suggestive evidence for (51): for two completely independent phenomena, lexical government for bare nouns (which might point to an empty D, cf. above) and N-to-D-raising over adjectives of proper names, are mandatory precisely in argument function, but not necessarily for non-arguments (cf. Longobardi 1994), as exemplified by the following Italian predicates:

(68)   a.   Testimoni saremo noi
            Witnesses will-be1Pl we
       b.   Cinecittà è stata camuffata da antica Roma per il film
            Cinecittà was disguised as ancient Rome for the movie

The coincidence of two unrelated sources of evidence is a strong argument for (51) in Romance, hence for language types (57a–b).

The question is more open for the other types of (57). Though the problem still deserves further attention, argument/non-argument asymmetries pointing to some validity of (51) have been discovered even in some of the most liberal types (i.e., +null article languages). For example, certain lexical items, exactly like Romance proper names, seem to always occur in D (or crucially require an article) in argument position, but can appear determinerless in lower DP-internal positions as non-arguments. Thus they reproduce the $N + Adj + t$ (or $Art + Adj + N$) vs. $Adj + N$ pattern seen to support (51) in Romance. Among such items are some proper names, in particular the word for "God," in varieties of Old English, apparently of type (57d).[16] In addition, personal pronouns have been argued to occur in D in Russian (clearly type (57e)).[17] Albeit still fragmentary, this sort of evidence might suggest the possible universality of (51), and any sound research program should carefully look for it in other languages as well.

3.3   Two sources of determiners

A few tentative speculations are now in order about possibly different sources of determiners. Scattered across languages, in fact, we find slight clues of some distributional non-uniformity of this so far unified category.

That the definite article may basically occur higher than other determiners, probably in what is the D-position proper, is suggested by at least three types of consideration:

i. In Hungarian, where the definite article may overtly co-occur with a prenominal genitive, it always precedes the latter while all other, numeral, demonstrative, or quantificational, determiners necessarily follow it (Szabolcsi 1994):

   (69) a. A Péter könyve
              The Péter's book-3Sg
          b. Péter minden könyve
              Péter's every book-3Sg

ii. In Italian, alternations concerning definite articles and numeral determiners can be interpreted as suggesting that the latter have a lower base position than the former and raise to D if and only if no other determiner is present (e.g. cf. Crisma 1991):

   (70) a. Tre suoi libri
              Three his books
          b. I suoi tre libri
              The his three books
          c. *Suoi tre libri
              His three books

iii. Along such lines, it becomes possible to account for the difference between the Italian and English paradigms in terms of (obligatory) raising/non-raising of numerals to D:

   (71) a. *Three his books
          b. His three books

To this the parallel contrast involving the universal quantifier may be added, where English again essentially behaves like Hungarian:

   (72) a. Ogni suo libro
              Every his book
          b. *Suo ogni libro
              His every book
          c. *Every his book
          d. His every book

In other words, the lack of overt determiner would necessarily overtly attract numerals and "every" to D in Italian, but not in English or Hungarian. It remains to be seen whether this Italian/English contrast in raising to D is parametrically related to the more substantial one involving proper names discussed directly below. In any event, it seems that one can hypothesize the possibility of a head (or phrase?) crosslinguistically occurring lower than D and the GenS position but higher than the whole adjectival structure. Such a position (perhaps identifiable with Szabolcsi's 1994 Det□ and Ritter's 1991 Num□ head of Hebrew) might crosslinguistically be the base position of numerals and at least certain quantificational determiners, which would thus be distributionally distinguishable from definite articles.

4 N-Movement

4.1 N-to-D-raising

4.1.1 *The referentiality parameter: proper names, expletives, generics*
Alternations apparently concerning the surface position of the head noun seem to be quite a widespread phenomenon in several languages. In many a case, for example, the head noun ends up as necessarily initial in the whole nominal phrase, presumably a DP, and is separated from at least some of its thematic arguments, if any, by other material. Since the leftmost position of the nominal phrase is often that of determiner-like elements, such N-first constructions have been typically analyzed as instances of N-raising to D. According to the conditions triggering these movements, at least (and perhaps, hopefully, at most) three types of N-to-D have been identified and are best exemplified by, in turn:

(73)   a.   Rumanian nouns with the enclitic article,
      b.   Semitic construct state,
      c.   Romance proper names.

Descriptively speaking, here D appears to "attract" N, i.e., to be "strong" in Chomsky's (1995b) terms. The question is what the roots of strength are, i.e., what triggers the movement, in the three cases.

As for (73a) (especially studied in Dobrovie-Sorin 1987, Grosu 1988; cf. examples (61)–(62) above; a partly analogous case might be provided by Somali, cf. Lecarme 1989, 1994), the trigger is likely to be plainly morphophonological, i.e., to lie in the consistently enclitic nature of the definite article, with no specifically syntactic strength.

Case (73b), to which an impressive amount of insightful literature has been devoted (cf. the references in section 3.2.5 above), is not characterized by any corresponding segmental morpheme appearing to attract the head noun to D, i.e., the raised noun does not occur suffixed in any way. The most obvious correlate to this case of N-to-D is an interpretive one, i.e., the phenomenon of definiteness inheritance pointed out in section 3.2.5 above. A very plausible proposal, since at least Borer (1994) and Siloni (1994), has been that N-to-D applies in Semitic construct state precisely to check the otherwise unspecified definiteness feature of the lexically empty D-position.[18] Therefore, the strong feature of D seems here to be that of definiteness interpretation.

(73c) is more complicated. As was seen above, it concerns proper names (and a few semantically assimilated nouns: cf. Longobardi 1996) and is descriptively governed by generalization (65), repeated below:

(65)   If N overtly moves to a phonetically empty D then it will be object-referring.

Again, an interpretive property, object reference, seems to be ultimately responsible for this instance of N-to-D in Romance. In this latter case strength would reside in a referentiality feature of D. No relevant phonological consequence seems to arise (though phonological effects are precisely what makes the phenomenon detectable in other languages, according to Déchaine and Manfredi 1998).[19] In addition to proposing generalization (65), Longobardi (1994, 1998) has argued that a D being "strong" precisely in this sense (i.e., overtly attracting object-referring head nouns) typologically correlates with particular distributional and semantic properties of bare *common* nouns, namely those discussed for Romance (as opposed to English) bare nouns in section 3.2.2 above. In particular the following generalization has been proposed to hold:

(74)   A language has kind-referring (i.e., referential generic) bare nouns iff D is not strong.

This latter generalization and the related parametric approach, executed in Longobardi (1994, 1998), thus, are able to unify the two classes of differences between English and Romance noticed in sections 3.2.2 (syntax of proper names) and 3.2.6 (syntax and semantics of bare nouns) above.[20]

4.1.2   N over adjectives

Another source of parametrization noted above and discussed in Bernstein (this volume) concerns the noun's ability to move to the left of some or all its adjectival modifiers. While this is possible (or even necessary), though to variable extents, in certain language types (say, Romance, Celtic, Semitic), it is impossible, at least under normal stylistic conditions, in others, like Germanic, Slavic, and Greek (cf. Androutsopoulou 1995a). Thus, typologically, the portion of DP-internal structure which may host adjectives can be *transparent* or *opaque* to N-raising. For concreteness and just descriptively, suppose that an intermediate head, call it H, occurs to the right of the position of any possible adjective (it is essentially the position labeled **3** in structures (10) and (50) above) and is the maximal target of N-raising in certain languages (i.e., Hmax is an absolute barrier to N-raising).

Recall (cf. section 3.2.6) at this point that a strong D in the sense of (65) forces proper names either to raise or to be introduced by an expletive article (often morphologically neutralized with the definite form). Now, it is plausible to expect N-to-D to be blocked in languages where Hmax is otherwise a barrier to N-raising (i.e., common nouns do not cross over adjectives). Therefore the following conditional should follow as a theorem:

(75)   Strong D + barrierhood of Hmax ⇒ obligatory expletive articles with all
        proper names.

Also recall, then, that a strong D, according to (74), is manifested, among other properties, by the impossibility of expressing referential generics by means of bare nouns. Among the languages cited above with rather steadily prenominal adjectives, there is only one where bare nouns seem never to be kind-referring, i.e., Greek. Greek might thus have the conjunction of strong D and barrierhood of Hmax. It is then highly significant that Greek also displays the noted peculiarity (cf. section 3.2.6) of requiring the article with all proper names. This empirical result confirms the correctness of (75) in a straightforward way, explaining an apparently curious property of Greek proper names as a consequence of deep principles and parameters of UG.

4.2   Raising to intermediate positions

4.2.1   Other functional heads

In the previous section, at least one intermediate functional head between D and N has been tentatively hypothesized as a target for N-raising. Whatever the correctness of that particular hypothesis, a number of proposals in the same spirit have been made in the literature (cf. Bernstein 1991a, 1993a, Picallo 1991, Ritter 1991, Zamparelli 1995, among many others). Three main types of evidence allegedly manifesting such heads were brought to support these claims:

(76)   a.   landing sites for N-raising,[21]
        b.   occurrence of overt (usually clitic[22]) morphemes,
        c.   realization of specific semantic features (e.g. number, gender,
              deixis . . .).

Of course, the most convincing evidence can only be provided by the combination and convergence of these types of argument, e.g. by showing that N-raising to a certain position systematically alternates with an independent realization of a specific morpheme, hopefully identifiable with the expression of a particular semantic feature. A sound research program of this type has been systematically pursued only in Bernstein's groundbreaking work (cf. Bernstein 1991a, 1993a, this volume) on Walloon in comparison to other Romance languages, with some encouraging results.

Owing to reasons of space and competence, I will limit myself here to consider the evidence supposedly provided by N-raising, which is summarized in

(77) below, essentially a generalization of the structures arrived at in (10) and (50) above:

(77) [D [GenS [Num [**H1** [S-or [M$_1$ **H2** [M$_2$ **H3** [Arg **H4** [GenO [$_\alpha$ P [S [O . . . N . . .]]$_\alpha$]]]]]]]]]]]

(77) must be understood according to the parametric specifications (78) and the lexicon (79):

(78) a. In languages like English N is likely not to reach H4.
      b. In the rest of Germanic, Greek, probably Slavic, N reaches H4 and nothing further.[23]
      c. In Romance, Celtic, and Semitic N reaches the various higher heads (from D to H3) according to languages and constructions.

(79) **A lexicon for (77):**
      D = determiner position, target for Romance proper names, Rumanian common Ns with the enclitic article, Semitic construct state Ns
      GenS = position of construct state Genitive, perhaps unmarked Romance possessive As
      Num (unless to be collapsed with H1) = base position for numerals and in many languages for other determiners different from the definite article
      H1 = perhaps target for Sardinian (cf. Bernstein this volume) and Celtic nouns, and Semitic non-construct nouns
      S-or = Subject- or Speaker-oriented adjective
      M$_1$ = Manner1 adjective
      H2 = target for common Ns in most Romance varieties
      M$_2$ = Manner2 adjective
      H3 = target for Walloon Ns
      Arg = argument adjective
      H4 = position of Scandinavian (and Bulgarian?) definite suffixes and target for N-raising in German, Greek, Slavic, Scandinavian suffixed nouns . . .
      GenO = position of postnominal Genitive
      P, S, O = base position for Possessors, External and Internal arguments, respectively
      N = base position for Ns
      α = phrase (perhaps Nmax) including N and its arguments

In (77) four intermediate heads are indicated as potential targets for N-raising. However, no individual language provides evidence for more than one such head, at least on the grounds of N-movement, so their number actually results only from a comparative perspective.[24] It would thus be possible to describe nominal structures in terms of an autosegmental system, with the head sequence made available by UG only consisting of D-H-N, and the realization of the intermediate head H parametrically linked to crosslinguistically different positions in the universally fixed sequence of adjectives and genitival positions assessed above (in (50) and (77)).

In other words, the relation between H and the sequence of adjectives might be that between the following two (possibly universally ordered) levels, with a four-valued linking parameter (or two binary ones):

(80)   a.   [D [GenS [H [GenO [N]]]]
      b.   [S-oriented A [Manner$_1$ A [Manner$_2$ A [Argument A]]]]

The linking module would consist of the crosslinguistic condition (81) and the parametric statements (82):

(81)   Only H may be linked *inside* the sequence (80b).

(82)   a.   The default value is for H to be linked to the extreme right of (80b).[25]
      b.   The typologically attested linking positions for H are immediately before Argument A, Manner$_2$ A, or S-oriented A.

4.2.2   Definiteness suffixes and strength

Let us now consider other crosslinguistic properties of the intermediate head H. To my knowledge, in the best-known languages it is never realized as an independent free (non-clitic) morpheme, and there is no evidence for it as an empty category not targeted by N-movement (like, for example, the empty D hypothesized for certain bare nouns). In other words its visibility is always a function of its being "strong" with respect to N-raising. Except for this fact, H bears some analogy to D. For in some varieties it appears as an overt clitic morpheme, such as the Scandinavian definiteness suffix, to which N adjoins. In other languages it is only signaled as the landing site of N. These recall the two main subtypes of N-to-D (cf. (73)), to an enclitic article or to a segmentally null head.[26]

As with (73a), the strength of H in the first subcase can be easily taken to be of a morphophonological nature, attracting N to satisfy its enclitic properties. A more interesting question arises for the second subtype: is there an independent manifestation of the strength properties of H here? Notice that in the Romance–Germanic domain the languages displaying this subtype of movement are likely to be all the Romance varieties (N crosses over at least some adjectives) and German (N crosses over genitives), as opposed to Scandinavian, essentially displaying the first subtype (enclitic suffixes), and English, providing no evidence for N-movement. This distribution reminds one of that noted in section 1.4.2 for the possibility of licensing more than one external argument position, allowing Possessors or raised Objects to co-occur with Subjects. It is plausible, then, that the two phenomena are parametrically related. The possibility of projecting an extra position for arguments would be contingent on the presence of a *syntactically* strong (not just phonologically clitic, given the patterning of Scandinavian) H.[27] If this tentative line of reasoning is correct, then one of the parameters left open at the end of section 1.6 can be eliminated and reduced to the independent existence in the language of such a strong H.

4.3   Conclusions

It is now possible to sum up a few principles and parameters of DP structure discussed along this review.

To the potentially universal principles pointed out in (39) above, after examining the argument structure (repeated below as (83a–d)), at least (83e) must be added:

(83)   **UG principles:**
   a.   the structural hierarchy and obligatoriness/optionality of thematic arguments,
   b.   the existence of two distinct Case positions for non-prepositional arguments,
   c.   the access to such positions,
   d.   the licensing of empty categories,
   e.   the hierarchy of adjectival and Case checking position (cf. (77)).

As could be expected, most of the overall parametric variation concentrates in the functional structure rather than in the lexical one. In addition, one of the parameters identified in (40) has been tentatively reduced to a parameter of functional structure in section 4.2.1. The main parametric dimensions identified can thus be summarized as follows, with a rough estimation of the number of binary parameters minimally necessary for each dimension in parentheses:

(84)   **Parameters:**
   a.   about the number of active Case checking positions (cf. section 1.3.2),
                                                                    (2)
   b.   about the actual forms of non-prepositional Case realization (cf. section 1.3.1),   (2)
   c.   about overt realization of D (cf. section 3.2.4),   (3)
   d.   about the position of H (section 4.2.1),   (2)
   e.   about syntactic strength of D and H (cf. sections 3.2.6 and 4.2.2), (2)
   f.   about enclitic status of D and H.   (2)

On the whole, it is not too hazardous a guess to expect that the order of magnitude of core grammatical variation in the DP-domain may ultimately turn out to be roughly equivalent to something between 15 and 20 binary parameters, perhaps even including intrinsically morphophonological parameters like (84b) and (84f).

Finally, it must be recalled that a substantial number of problems are still to be addressed theoretically and typologically. Among them at least a few seem to be worth mentioning here. For example, are there really languages with phrase-final D and other mirror-image phenomena (e.g. cf. Williamson 1987, among others)? And, if so, how are they to be treated? Why do most languages seem to display only one type of Case (Genitive) for arguments of nouns as opposed to normally dual Case systems (Nominative/Accusative, Absolutive/Ergative . . .) for clauses (also cf. n. 22)? Last, but of the highest importance, is the question of the universal or language particular validity of a condition like (51), a problem to which detailed and promising attention has recently begun to be given even outside the domain of the best-studied European languages.[28]

NOTES

1 Cf. Giorgi and Longobardi (1991), with results confirmed by Siloni (1990) and Taraldsen (1990) among others.

2 Data such as those studied by Pearce (to appear) suggest the possibility of a parametrization according to which in some languages it would just be the structural position of the genitive that determines its form, while in others, like Maori, it would rather be the thematic interpretation that plays such a role.

3 A conceivable generalization concerning languages with type (8c) genitives might be that they do not display (alternations with) prepositional genitives, as is the case with the other four listed cases.

4 Classical coordination tests suggest that the linear sequence in (10) corresponds to a regularly right-branching hierarchical structure:

   i. Marias [sorgfältige Beschreibung Ottos und wunderbare Photographie Zeldas]
       Mary's accurate description of Otto and beautiful photograph of Zelda

   ii. Marias wunderbare [Beschreibungen Ottos and Photographien Zeldas]
       Mary's accurate descriptions of Otto and beautiful photographs of Zelda

   Marias in (i) and *Marias wunderbare* in (ii) are both understood as having semantic import over the whole bracketed sequences, which appear thus to represent coordinated constituents, hence constituents.

5 It seems thus possible in Romance for an O to raise over S provided that the latter is a null pronominal, apparently violating the possessivization hierarchy of section 1.1.1. This may suggest that Chomsky's (1995b) equidistance principle must be relativized, perhaps in the sense of limiting it to overtly Case marked categories, thus excluding PRO from its scope.

6 Under this proposal, the crosslinguistic lack of any effect comparable to the Romance ones of the text with middle verbal constructions might be elegantly attributed to the universal

uniqueness of the external argument in clauses.

7 If PROs cannot be meteorological subjects, unless controlled, nouns like *snow(storm)*, *rain(storm)*, etc. are unlikely to ever count as event nominals.

8 Though, however, overtly realized Possessors seem to count as A-positions in some binding phenomena.

9 The Walloon example has been adapted from Bernstein (1991a).

10 The possibility of coordinations like the following, in the intended reading, is on a par with those of n. 4 above and suggests, again, that the linear ordering of such sequences corresponds to a regular right-branching structure:

    i. the probable hostile [German reactions and Italian comments]
    ii. the probable [hostile German reactions and favorable Italian comments]

11 The question arose whether prenominal adjectives are heads (i.e., complements to D or to each other) in the extended projection from N to D, or rather full XPs occurring as specifiers of invisible functional heads (or even stacked specifiers of the noun itself). This problem turns out to be hardly decidable on empirical grounds. A reasonable and balanced suggestion was made by Bernstein (1993a), attempting to treat the higher adjectives as heads and the lower ones as specifiers.

12 On the "closing" function of D for arguments also cf. Higginbotham (1983).

13 For Maori an important source is Pearce's (1997, to appear) work.

14 This possibility has been tentatively and erroneously suggested in the literature only for a restricted group of areally contiguous languages, essentially varieties of Turkish,

Persian, and Indo-Aryan (Kravmskyv 1972, Porterfield and Srivastav 1988, Singh 1992). Since in such languages bare mass/plural nouns are not necessarily definite but grammatically ambiguous, Crisma (1997) noticed that the supposed lexical indefinite article is likely not to mark indefiniteness, which would be extragrammatical as in (57e), but rather non-default selection, with mass/plural as the universal default selection for bare indefinites.

15 Cf. Taraldsen (1990), Delsing (1993), and the various papers collected or cited in Holmberg (1992), among many others.

16 Cf. Mustanoja (1973), Crisma (1997). Furthermore, argument/non-argument asymmetries in Hungarian, another language presumably of type (57d), were used by Szabolcsi (1987) to originally propose and motivate (51).

17 Cf. Gambarotto (1995).

18 Even in this case, however, in many languages with most lexical choices the syntactic fronting of the noun in construct state correlates with some detectable effects on the morphophonological structure of the noun itself, which could be attributed to the combination of the lexical entry of the noun with an exclusively prosodic (non-segmental) morpheme lying in D (cf. Ritter 1988). This might suggest that some abstract (occasionally neutralized in some languages or constructions) phonological trigger is in principle at work in all instances of overt N-to-D.

19 Prosodic alternations on head nouns dependent on their use as object referring expressions have been reconstructed for some stage of Proto-Indoeuropean by Lazzeroni (1997); at an historical date, variation in the position of the

accent on the same word according to whether it is used as a common noun/adjective or as a proper name (and in other environments according to slightly different manifestations of an abstract scale of referentiality) are still sporadically documented for Greek and Aryan. These alternating forms are probably lexicalized as different entries at that stage, but might go back to a productive system in the prehistoric language. If this proposal is correct it may be the case that even this version of "strength" of D correlates in principle with morphophonological effects/triggers, detectable in some languages, perhaps neutralized in others.

20   As anticipated in section 3.2.4, this parametric approach, extending to the distributional properties of bare nouns (cf. section 3.2.2), allows one to treat the two classes of languages (57b, c) as just one and the same with respect to parameters licensing determinerless NPs, their contrast independently following from the strong/weak nature of D. Other consequences of the proposed single parametric difference arise in interaction with specific assumptions about Case theory (Longobardi 1996). In particular it has been proposed that only languages where D is weak allow for genitives to superficially precede the head noun, as e.g. in Germanic Saxon Genitive. In languages where D is strong it must actually attract the noun in order for Genitive to be checked in the high (GenS) position (essentially construct state), except for possessives agreeing in features with the noun itself. On the complex question of Genitive checking also cf. Dobrovie-Sorin (to appear) and Pearce (to appear).

21   It has been assumed throughout that rules fronting N within the DP are instances of head movement, necessarily landing into head positions. Fronting of N as part of instances of phrasal movement has also been postulated, e.g. in Androutsopoulou (1995b), Kayne (1994), Sanchéz (1995b, 1996), Bernstein (1997), and Bhattacharya (to appear). These hypotheses will not be reviewed here, owing to space limits.

22   To my knowledge, in European languages, the supposed intermediate functional heads, unlike those found in the clausal domain, do not appear as free stressed morphemes. The fact deserves an explanation as well as the observation that only one nominal Case, Genitive, normally corresponds to both Nominative and Accusative (Benveniste 1966) (the latter fact does not seem to necessarily hold in all languages: cf. Chung 1973, Pearce to appear on Polynesian). Taken together, they could suggest that an intermediate head of nominals is more an extension of some features of N than an independent category like the semantically more complex ones selecting verbs in clauses. This "nominal" character might perhaps be also warranted by the ability to license an extra argument of the noun, if the hypothesis put forward in section 4.2.2 below were correct.

23   The main motivation to distinguish English from these other languages lies in the fact that English, unlike, say, German, does not show evidence that the noun ever raises to the left of an argument checking Genitive in the GenO position.

24   In other words, language internal alternations concerning the surface appearance of N among the various

positions labeled H in (77) are likely not to exist.

25 If (and only if) H happens to be linked to the default position, it may be assumed to universally project a barrier to N-to-D in the sense relevant for section 4.1.2.

26 Other less parallel properties of H with respect to D can derive from the different semantic features constituting the two categories (also cf. the remarks of n. 22).

27 Under this hypothesis the scheme (77) has to be further slightly revised to better accommodate the external argument positions: a plausible attempt is the following, with the extra P position (in parentheses), here conventionally marked next to each potential location for H, only available if the latter is strong:

i. [D [GenS [Num [(P) **H1** [S-or [M_1 [(P) **H2** [M_2 [(P) **H3** [Arg [(P) **H4** [GenO [$_\alpha$ P/S [O . . . **N** . . .]]]$_\alpha$]]]]]]]]]]]

Of course, if this extra Possessor argument surfaces as a postnominal prepositional genitive phrase, the thematic position so projected may be actually occupied by a pronominal empty category, linked in a chain to the lower PP, rather in the way discussed for (25) above.

28 Especially see Carstens (1991) on Bantu, Cheng and Sybesma (to appear), Li (1997), Del Gobbo (1999) about Mandarin and Cantonese, among several others. Also cf. Pearce's (1997, to appear) series of works on Maori DPs.

V Interface with Interpretation

19 The Syntax of Scope

ANNA SZABOLCSI

0 Introduction

This chapter reviews some representative examples of scopal dependency and focusses on the issue of how the scope of quantifiers is determined. In particular, we will ask to what extent independently motivated syntactic considerations decide, delimit, or interact with scope interpretation. Many of the theories to be reviewed postulate a level of representation called Logical Form (LF). Originally, this level was invented for the purpose of determining quantifier scope. In current Minimalist theory, all output conditions (the theta-criterion, the case filter, Subjacency, binding theory, etc.) are checked at LF. Thus, the study of LF is enormously broader than the study of the syntax of scope. The present chapter will not attempt to cover this broader topic.

1 Scope Relations and Determining Scope

1.1 Scope relations

We are going to take the following definition as a point of departure:

(1) The scope of an operator is the domain within which it has the ability to affect the interpretation of other expressions.

Some uncontroversial examples of an operator having scope over an expression and affecting some aspect of its interpretation are as follows:

- quantifier–quantifier,
- quantifier–pronoun,
- quantifier–negative polarity item (NPI).

Examples (2a, b) each have a reading on which *every boy* affects the interpretation of *a planet* by inducing referential variation: the planets can vary with the boys. In (2c), the teachers cannot vary with the boys:

(2) a. Every boy named a planet.
     "for every boy, there is a possibly different planet that he named"
  b. I showed every boy a planet.
     "for every boy, there is a possibly different planet that I showed him"
  c. That every boy left upset a teacher.
     *"for every boy, there is a possibly different teacher who was upset by the fact that the boy left"

Note the following convention: when an example is annotated with one interpretation as in (2), we are only claiming that this interpretation is available (or, if it is starred, unavailable), and we are not making any claim as to whether other interpretations are possible.

Similar variation is induced in (3a, b), with the mediation of *his* being interpreted as a variable bound by *every boy*. No bound variable interpretation is available in (3c), and *his* must refer to a contextually specified person:

(3) a. Every boy$_i$ read his$_i$ book.
  b. I showed every boy$_i$ his$_i$ book.
  c. *That every boy$_i$ left upset his$_i$ teacher.

Notice that the quantifier–bound pronoun relation is syntactically more constrained than the name–coreferential pronoun relation: *That John$_i$ left upset his$_i$ teacher* is fine.

In (4a, b), the negative polarity item *any [of the books]* is licensed (becomes interpretable) in view of being in the scope of the downward entailing operator *few boys*; in (4c) it is not licensed:

(4) a. Few boys read any of the books.
  b. I showed few boys any of the books.
  c. *That few boys came upset any of the teachers.

The notion of scope in (1) is quite similar to its counterpart in logical syntax. The scope of a logical operator is that segment of the formula, demarcated by parentheses (possibly suppressed when notational conventions make them recoverable), over which the operator can have a semantic effect. In (5a), only the x in fx is bound by the universal quantifier; in (5b), only the conjunction $fa \wedge ga$ is affected by negation:

(5) a. $\forall x[fx \wedge ga] \wedge hx$
  b. $\neg(fa \wedge ga) \vee \exists x[hx]$

Definition (1) is syntactic in that it identifies the scope of an operator as the domain within which it has the potential to affect another expression's interpretation. Just as in logic, it does not require that the expressions within this domain be actually affected in any tangible way. Notice that in (5a), *ga* is within the universal quantifier's scope but is not affected by it, because it contains no free occurrence of the variable *x*. Now compare (6) with (7) and (2a) with (8):

(6) I was not reading a book (when you came in).
     "no book is such that I was reading it"
(7) A boy/Most boys did not laugh.
     "there is a boy/a majority of the boys who did not laugh"

When negation has an indefinite in its scope, as in (6), it clearly affects its interpretation in that the existence of a relevant entity can no longer be inferred. When negation is within what normally counts as the subject quantifier's scope, as in (7), negation is in no way affected by that quantifier, simply because no aspect of the interpretation of negation can ever be affected:

(2a) Every boy named a planet.

(8) Every boy named every planet/Mercury and Venus.

Likewise, while planets may vary with the boys in (2a), this is not possible in (8). Whoever named every planet or Mercury and Venus must have named the same planets; this simply follows from the meanings of these direct objects.
    Thus, we are making a distinction between (2c) and (8), for instance:

(2c) That every boy left upset a teacher.

(8) Every boy named every planet.

In neither case does *every boy* make the direct object referentially dependent. In (2c), this is so because *a teacher* is not within the scope of *every boy*. In (8), this is so because, although *every planet* is within the scope of *every boy*, its semantics precludes referential variation.[1]

1.2 *How is the scope of an operator determined?*

Scope understood as a domain is a syntactic notion; but to what extent does independently motivated syntactic structure delimit scopal options in natural language? Reinhart (1978) subsumed scope relations under the general principle (9) and proposed a very restrictive implementation, as in (10)–(11):

(9) If a rule assigns node A some kind of prominence over node B, B must be within the domain of A.

(10) **"First branching node" c-command:**
The domain of a node A consists of all and only the nodes dominated by the (non-unary) branching node α which most immediately dominates A.

(11) A logical structure in which a quantifier binding a variable x has wide scope over a quantifier binding a (distinct) variable y is a possible interpretation for a given sentence S just in case in the surface structure of S the quantified expression (QE) corresponding to y is in the domain of the QE corresponding to x.

According to (11), the surface structure of S directly determines what scope interactions are possible. If QE/1 is in the domain of QE/2 but not vice versa, QE/1 must take narrow scope. If both are in the domain of the other, the structure is potentially ambiguous. If neither QE is in the domain of the other, they must be interpreted independently. (11) is intended as a necessary but not a sufficient condition: the properties of the participating QEs may eliminate some of the predicted possibilities, as observed by Ioup (1975).

These assumptions immediately explain the starred data in (2c), (3c), and (4c): the direct object of the main clause is not within the domain of the embedded subject.

Reinhart's proposal is very attractive, because it is parsimonious (Minimalist, one might say) and establishes an extremely tight link between syntax proper and interpretive possibilities. However, as it stands it fails to account for the full range of the data, or it accounts for them using certain controversial analytical assumptions. We single out two problems.

First, the subject clearly has the direct object within its domain, but not vice versa. This predicts that both (12) and (13) have only subject wide scope readings. While these may indeed be the preferred interpretations, the so-called inverse – object wide scope – readings are also possible:

(12) Each student speaks two languages.
direct, predicted:
 "for each student, there is a potentially different pair of languages . . ."
inverse, not predicted:
 "there are two languages that each student speaks"

(13) Two students speak each language.
direct, predicted:
 "there are two students who speak each language"
inverse, not predicted:
 "for each language, there is a potentially different pair of students . . ."

Reinhart essentially denies that grammar needs to account for the unpredicted readings. As regards the type of (12), which has an indefinite in object position, she observes that the unpredicted object wide scope reading entails the predicted subject wide scope reading. It is thus difficult to tell whether there is a separate reading that requires that the pair of languages be held constant, or we are simply dealing with a special case in which the predicted reading is true. As regards the type of (13), which has a universal in object position, she points out examples that do not easily allow for inverse scope and takes these latter to be paradigmatic:

(14)   Some tourists visited all the museums.
       ?? "for each of the museums, there are potentially different tourists . . ."

Second, there are cases where the correct predictions are made but at the cost of controversial analytical assumptions involving preposing. In (15)–(16), the subject QE takes wide scope over the QE within the preposed XP:

(15)   Fond of some boy every girl is.
       "for every girl, there is some boy she is fond of"

(16)   (. . . and) break all the plates someone finally did.
       "there was someone who broke all the plates"

These data fall under the same generalization as the binding judgments in (17)–(18):

(17)   *For Ben$_i$'s car, he$_i$ is asking two grand.

(18)   For his$_i$ car, Ben$_i$ is asking two grand.

To achieve these effects, Reinhart sister-adjoins the preposed XPs to S. For example:

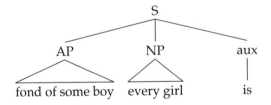

In this chapter, we are focussing on the issues related to (12)–(14); those related to (15)–(18) are taken up in Barss (this volume).

The problems we encountered raise at least the following questions:

(19)   a.   Are there solid inverse scopal readings that cannot be explained away as special cases of weaker direct readings?
       b.   Can scope options be read off of independently motivated syntactic structure, or is it necessary to create additional structure specifically for the purposes of scope interpretation?

    c. If additional structure is needed, is it constrained by similar prin-
        ciples to those that constrain "syntax proper"?

    d. What shall we make of the apparently diverse scope behavior of
        scope-bearing noun phrases?

Ever since Reinhart's pioneering proposal, the literature (some of Reinhart's
own work included) has been grappling with these questions. Not surprisingly,
each stage of theorizing attempts to answer them in its own characteristic
spirit. The survey below will bear this out.

2 Quantification in Abstract Syntax

2.1 Rules of quantification: the 1970s

Montague's classic paper, "The proper treatment of quantification in ordinary
English" (1974), presents a grammar for a small fragment of English which,
however, contains the logicosyntactic and semantic devices to handle practically any scope phenomenon. The core of his grammar is a categorial syntax
with just functional application: these days one may think of it as a Minimalist
syntax with nothing but Merge. Quantifier phrases, just like proper names,
may enter the sentence in a functional application (Merge) step. The derivation in (20) is slightly simplified, and Montague's categories t and e are relabeled
as s and np, respectively:

(20)
                      Everyone walks
                      category: s
                      translation: $\forall x[\text{person}'(x) \rightarrow \text{walk}'(x)]$

everyone   walks
category: s/(s/np)   category: s/np
translation: $\lambda P \forall x[\text{person}'(x) \rightarrow P(x)]$ translation: walk'

Syntax and interpretation proceed hand in hand. All noun phrases belong to
the category of functions s/(s/np) that take a predicate s/np as an argument
and yield a sentence s as a value; semantically, *everyone* is interpreted as the
set of properties that everyone has. Applied to the property *walk'*, this yields
the statement that everyone has the property of walking, that is, everyone walks.
A similar analysis, involving just functional application (Merge), is available
for noun phrases in non-subject position; the details, which involve some complications, are not relevant here. It is important to dispel the myth that there is
an inherent semantic necessity to impose an operator–variable structure on the
syntax of English whenever we introduce a quantifier. Once quantifiers are
assigned an appropriate interpretation (and devising such an interpretation in

terms of sets of properties is one of Montague's major achievements), merging them is perfectly well formed.

The introduction of a quantificational phrase by way of merging assigns it strictly direct scope: it will not scope over any operator (quantifier, negation, modal, etc.) that is merged later.[2] This portion of Montague's grammar makes essentially the same predictions as Reinhart's (1978) does without preposing.

Montague's grammar, however, also contains devices that create arbitrary inverse scopes. These are the rules of quantification (quantifying into nominals, verb phrases, and sentences). For illustration, we derive the inverse (object wide scope) reading of *Everyone loves someone*. Structures continue to be built bottom-up. First an open sentence, *everyone loves him$_i$*, is built with a placeholder pronoun in the object position. This placeholder is interpreted as a variable x_i. The subsequent quantification step has the following ingredients. (i) Using the quantifier phrase *someone* and the open sentence as input, a sentence is created by replacing the placeholder with the quantifier. (ii) The interpretation of the resulting sentence is built by applying the quantifier to a property that is obtained from the open sentence by abstraction. Abstraction is performed by the lambda operator; the property it forms in this case is that of being loved by everyone: $\lambda x_i[\forall y[person'(y) \rightarrow love'(x_i)(y)]]$. The result boils down to there being a person whom every person loves:

(21)   Everyone loves someone
        category: s
        translation: $\lambda P\exists x[person'(x) \wedge P(x)](\lambda x_i[\forall y[person'(y) \rightarrow love'(x_i)(y)]]) =$
        $\exists x[person'(x) \wedge \forall y[person'(y) \rightarrow love'(x)(y)]]$

someone   everyone loves him$_i$
category: s/(s/np)   category: s
translation: $\lambda P\exists x[person'(x) \wedge P(x)]$ translation: $\forall y[person'(y) \rightarrow love'(x_i)(y)]$

The narrow scope quantifier *everyone* may have been introduced either by plain Merge (as in *Everyone walks* above) or by quantifying into *he$_j$ loves him$_i$*. In this case the choice makes no semantic difference, because there is no scope interaction in the relevant portion of the sentence.

Notice that although in (21) Montague ends up with a string that corresponds to a surface English sentence, the quantification step in the derivation is a piece of abstract syntax. A structure is created that has no independent syntactic motivation and serves no other end than assigning wide scope to *everyone*.

There is a significant affinity between these ideas and May's (1977). May proposes that syntax does not end with producing the surface string. Instead, movement operations somewhat reminiscent of *wh*-movement continue to operate at an abstract level called Logical Form (LF) and append each phrase containing a quantifier to its domain. This rule is called Quantifier Raising (QR). For example, the two readings of *Everyone loves someone* have the following LF structures:

(22)

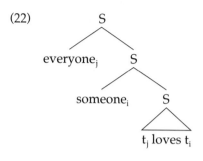

(23)

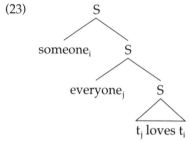

It is interesting to observe the precise match between (21) and (23). Both theories hold that on its object wide scope reading, *Everyone loves someone* is crucially associated with an abstract structure consisting of an operator comprising the material in the object noun phrase and of a sentence with a variable in the position of the direct object (a placeholder in one theory, a trace in the other). We might say that one difference between Montague's and May's syntaxes is that in Montague's, the steps straightforwardly building the surface string are interspersed with steps pertaining to its LF, while May first builds the surface structure and then rearranges it into a LF representation. Another difference is that May applies QR to all quantifier phrases without exception. An important further difference is that Montague provides an explicit compositional semantics for his syntax; we will conveniently assume that compatible syntactic proposals by others are interpreted along the same lines.

2.2 *Syntactic aspects: the 1980s*

Reinhart's approach and the Montague/May approach represent two extremes. On the former, independently motivated phrase structure imposes an absolute limitation on scope options; on the latter, there is no such absolute limitation, because structure may be built solely for the purposes of scope assignment. Nevertheless, syntactic considerations bear on scope on the latter approach as well.

First, syntactic constraints on structure building can be accommodated. For example, Rodman (1972) observed that a quantifier inside a relative clause cannot make an expression outside that relative clause referentially dependent, and modified Montague's fragment to prevent quantifying into a relative clause:

(24) Guinevere has a bone that is in every corner of the house.
      *"for every corner of the house, Guinevere has a (different) bone in that corner"

In fact, an even tighter constraint seems to be correct: a universal quantifier generally cannot affect the interpretation of expressions outside its clause.[3] Accordingly, May stipulated that QR is a clause bounded adjunction rule:

(25) A critic thinks that every book is readable.
      *"for every book, a possibly different critic thinks that it is readable"

The existence of "scope island" constraints points to the syntactic nature of the abstract structure created for the purposes of disambiguating scope. It is to be noted, however, that clause boundedness somewhat idiosyncratically constrains Quantifier Raising. The most likeminded overt operation, *wh*-movement, is not so constrained:

(26) What books does a critic think are readable?
      "what books are such that possibly different critics think they are readable"

   Second, QR interacts with pronouns, VP-ellipsis, and other phenomena in the manner of overt *wh*-movement. For example, it gives rise to crossover effects. Crossover is thought to be sensitive to either linear order or c-command, both of which are clearly syntactic in nature:

(27) a. Who does he admire?
          *"for what person x, x admires x"
      b. Who does his mother admire?
          ??"for what person x, x's mother admires x"

(28) a. He admires every man.
          *"for every man x, x admires x"
      b. His mother admires every man.
          ??"for every man x, x's mother admires x"

   Third, even though Reinhart's original assumption that no quantifier phrase takes inverse scope over another may have been too strong, an interesting subject–object asymmetry is observed in May (1985) in connection with the interaction of *wh*- and quantifier phrases:

(29) Which planet$_i$ did every boy name t$_i$?
      i.   "which planet is such that every boy named it"
      ii. "for every boy, which planet did he name"

(30) Which boy$_i$ t$_i$ named every planet?
      i.   "which boy is such that he named every planet"
      ii. *"for every planet, which boy named it"

It is convenient to think of the contrast between the (i) readings and the (ii) readings in terms of scope. Reading (i), where the *wh*-phrase has wider scope than the universal quantifier, is called the individual reading and it is generally available. Reading (ii), where the universal has wider scope than the *wh*-phrase, is called the family of questions or pair-list question reading. It is available only when the quantifier phrase c-commands the trace of *wh*-movement.

This contrast plays a central role in motivating the revisions proposed in May (1985), a work which develops a theory of scope by addressing most of the issues that were of prime concern to syntacticians in the mid-1980s.

In May (1977), QR both determines and disambiguates quantifier scope: the quantifier's c-command domain is determined by QR and the wide scope quantifier always asymmetrically c-commands the narrow scope one. In May (1985), QR determines quantifier scope, but it does not disambiguate it. In addition to assigning an absolute scope to each quantifier, the theory includes the Scope Principle that regulates their interaction:

(31) **The Scope Principle:**
      If two operators govern each other, they can be interpreted in either scopal order.

This is a feature that the new theory shares with Reinhart's.

Let us see the motivation and how the proposal works. A glance at (22) and (23) reveals that the subject wide scope reading involves a crossing dependency, while the object wide scope reading involves a nesting one. To recap:

(22) $[_S \text{ everyone}_j \ [_S \text{ someone}_i \ [_S \ t_j \text{ admires } t_i]]]$

(23) $[_S \text{ someone}_i \ [_S \text{ everyone}_j \ [_S \ t_j \text{ admires } t_i]]]$

Crossing dependencies cause ungrammaticality with two *wh*-phrases:

(32) *What does who admire?
      $[_{S'} \text{ who}_j \text{ what}_i \ [_S \ t_j \text{ admires } t_i]]$

(33) Who admires what?
      $[_{S'} \text{ what}_i \text{ who}_j \ [_S \ t_j \text{ admires } t_i]]$

The Empty Category Principle (ECP) (specifically, on Pesetsky's 1982 formulation, the Path Containment Condition) rules out (32). But then the same principle should rule out (22) as well.

If so, we have no legitimate representation for the subject wide scope reading in May's (1977) terms. May (1985) proposes that, in fact, (23) represents both readings simultaneously. This is achieved by the Scope Principle as above, in conjunction with a modified set of relevant definitions:

(34) α dominates $\beta =_{df}$ all the member nodes of α are above β.

(35) α c-commands β =_{df} every maximal projection dominating α dominates β, and α does not dominate β. Maximal projections are NP, VP, and S' (but not S).

(36) α governs β =_{df} α c-commands β, and there are no maximal projection boundaries between them.

These notions will sound familiar as they were adopted almost wholesale in *Barriers* (Chomsky 1986b). Recall that QR is Chomsky-adjunction. Under the above definitions, two phrases Chomsky-adjoined to the same projection γ will c-command each other because, in fact, the c-command domains of both extend to the next maximal projection up (they are not dominated by γ, only member nodes of it). Furthermore, since they are not separated by a maximal projection boundary, the Scope Principle says that they can be interpreted in either order. Thus, (23) with two S-adjoined quantifiers is ambiguous.

The assumption that Chomsky-adjunction extends the scope of a quantifier upwards is beneficial in connection with inverse linking. The relevant fact is that in (37), *every city* must scope over *someone* to bind *it*:

(37) Someone from every city hates it.
"for every city x, there is someone from x who hates x"

In May (1977), sentential scope could be assigned to *every city* only by S-adjunction. The assumption that *every city* extracts from the subject NP conflicts with the ungrammaticality of the corresponding *wh*-extraction (irrespective of pronoun binding):

(38) *Which city_i does [someone from t_i] hate New York?

In May (1985), *every city* only needs to adjoin to NP to have scope over the whole of S.

Let us now come back to the issue of how the theory works for *wh*-/ quantifier interaction. The ambiguous sentence in (29) has the following LF representation:

(39)

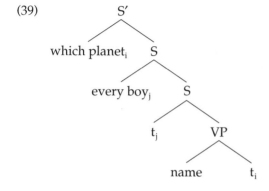

This structure contains a nested dependency and is thus approved by the ECP. Furthermore, it is ambiguous. The c-command domain of S-adjoined *every boy* extends to S′, and there is no maximal projection boundary separating it from *which planet* (S does not count as a maximal projection).

On the other hand, reversing the subject and the object in this structure gives rise to a crossing dependency and thus an ECP violation:

(40) *

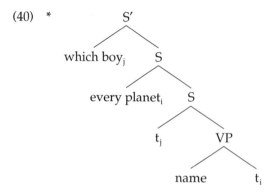

But (30), *Which boy named every planet?*, is merely unambiguous, not ungrammatical. We still need a legitimate representation for it on the correct "which boy is such that he named every planet" reading. The definitions above allow for the following, with *every planet* adjoined to VP:

(41)

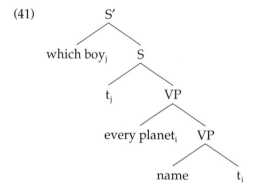

This structure does not incur an ECP-violation. On the other hand, it is not ambiguous: although VP-adjoined *every planet* c-commands *which boy*, they do not govern each other, because they are separated by a VP-boundary.

The following example shows that it is useful to distinguish mutual c-command from mutual government:

(42) [Which pilot that shot at it$_i$]$_j$ hit [every Mig that chased him$_j$]$_i$?

(42) contains two bound variable pronouns. The fact that they are legitimate indicates that *which pilot that shot at it* c-commands *him* (has *him* in its absolute

scope) and *every Mig that chased him* c-commands *it* (has *it* in its absolute scope). Nevertheless, the sentence has no family of questions interpretation because, as in (40), the *wh*-subject and the universal object do not govern each other.

VP-adjunction of a quantifier is independently motivated by coordinations like (43b):

(43)   a.   Some professor admires every student.
         i.   "there is a professor who admires every student"
         ii.   "for every student, there is a professor who admires him or her"
       b.   Some professor admires every student and hates the dean.
         i.   "there is a professor who both admires every student and hates the dean"
         ii.   *"for every student, there is a professor who both admires him or her and hates the dean"

While (43a) is ambiguous, (43b) strongly prefers the reading with a particular professor. This indicates that QR is subject to the Coordinate Structure Constraint: *every student* cannot adjoin to S by moving out of a conjunct. But then the subject wide scope reading of (43b) cannot be represented in the manner of (23). VP-adjunction of *every student* serves as a way out:

(44)   [$_S$ some professor$_j$ [$_{VP}$ every student$_i$ [$_{VP}$ t$_j$ admires t$_i$]]]

This last observation has somewhat more general significance. If subject wide scope readings can in general be represented by an unambiguous structure where the direct object adjoins to VP, then the possibility of subject wide scope does not provide much evidence for the need of ambiguous representations and the Scope Principle, contrary to what the discussion of (22) *vis-à-vis* (32) suggested. The burden of motivating the Scope Principle falls solely on the asymmetry observed in connection with *wh*-/quantifier interactions.

The Scope Principle in general and the ECP-based account of the asymmetries in *wh*-/quantifier interaction in particular have been criticized from various angles. The first extensive discussion can be found in Williams (1986, 1988), where Williams proposes to eliminate LF as a separate level of representation and to reassign its functions to other components. For further important arguments, see Liu (1990: ch. 5), Chierchia (1993), Aoun and Li (1993c), Hornstein (1995), and Beghelli (1997). As a consequence, May's specific solutions have eventually been abandoned.

3   Minimalism: The 1990s

In the early 1990s, Minimalism changed the general perspective on syntax and, accordingly, the approach to scope as laid out above became a misfit, over and beyond the specific empirical problems it might have had. A power-ful summary of the discrepancies is offered in Hornstein (1995: ch. 8). QR is an adjunction rule; no other core grammatical process involves adjunction. QR does not target a specific position; other movement rules have specific targets. QR applies in order to assign scope; other movements are feature driven.

There are two basic ways to remedy this situation. One is to eliminate QR and obtain the desired scope results as by-products of entirely independent grammatical processes. Another is to recast QR and show that it fits the Minimalist picture. The first strategy is followed by Hornstein (1995); the second is followed in some aspects of Beghelli (1993) and Beghelli and Stowell (1997).

3.1   Scope read off of A-chains

Hornstein proposes that relative scope is largely a property of A-chains. That is, the structures that determine scope are created for independent reasons and, specifically, those reasons are primarily related to case, not operator-hood. Noun phrases originate in VP-internal positions and raise to the specifiers of agreement phrases (AgrSP and AgrOP) to check case. In doing so, they leave behind copies in each link of the chain. But crucially, only one link can survive till the Conceptual–Intentional interface; all others must be deleted. Unlike in A′-chains, however, there is no preference principle forcing the dele-tion of a specific link in the chain: we are free to choose. Scope is now deter-mined by the asymmetric c-command relations of the surviving copies.[4]

To illustrate, (46) is the LF phrase marker for (45):

(45)   Someone attended every seminar.

(46)   [$_{AgrS}$ Someone [$_{TP}$ Tns [$_{AgrO}$ every seminar [$_{VP}$ someone [$_{VP}$ attended every seminar]]]]]

In both chains, one or the other member must delete. This predicts four pos-sibilities. Two of them are excluded by a version of Diesing's (1992) Mapping Hypothesis that requires that quantifiers like *every seminar* land outside VP; in the present framework, this entails that their surviving copies are always in the specifier of some AgrP.[5] The remaining structures are as follows. Parenthe-ses indicate deletion. (47) reflects the subject wide scope and (48) the object wide scope reading. (We come back to the ambiguity of *Everyone attended some seminar* later.)

(47)   [$_{AgrS}$ Someone [$_{TP}$ Tns [$_{AgrO}$ every seminar [$_{VP}$ (someone) [$_{VP}$ attended (every seminar)]]]]]

(48)   [$_{AgrS}$ (Someone) [$_{TP}$ Tns [$_{AgrO}$ every seminar [$_{VP}$ someone [$_{VP}$ attended (every seminar)]]]]]

The idea that scope ambiguities are due to the possibility of taking alternative chain links into account (put another way, to the possibility for quantifiers to reconstruct into trace positions) originates with Aoun and Li (1993c), although the chains they created and considered were A'-chains. The account extends naturally to the restrictions pronoun binding, VP-ellipsis, etc. impose on the range of possible scope interpretations.[6]

This approach has various benefits, beyond its appealing Minimalist spirit. Quantifier scope is largely clause bounded (recall (26)), a property that A-movement but not A'-movement classically has. Now this follows immediately from the fact that scope lives off of A-chains. Also, QR does not license parasitic gaps:

(49)   a.   Which paper$_i$ did you file t$_i$ without reading pg$_i$?
        b.   *You filed every paper without reading.
           [$_S$ every paper$_i$ [$_S$ you filed t$_i$ without reading pg$_i$]]

This can be explained, without explicit reference to parasitic gaps being licensed at S-structure, if the analysis of (49b) never involves A'-chains comparable to those in (49a).

3.2 *Different quantifiers, different scopes*

In at least one respect, there is a fundamental similarity between all the theories reviewed above, Hornstein's included. They hardly address the anecdotally well-known fact that different quantifier types have different scope-taking abilities. To begin with, they ignore all quantifier phrases other than those containing *every* or *some*, although those may exhibit markedly different scope behavior, and they do not even address the systematic differences between the chosen two. It turns out that scopal diversity is not only an issue for descriptive adequacy but bears on how the syntax of scope should be set up.

Reinhart (1995, 1997b), Beghelli (1993), and Beghelli and Stowell (1997) address fundamental facets of the diversity issue. Reinhart focusses on the contrast between "indefinites" and "quantifiers" with respect to islands, Beghelli and Stowell focus on the clause internal differences exhibited by a greater variety of noun phrase types.

3.2.1 *The island-free scope of indefinites*

As regards Minimalist concerns, Reinhart (1995, 1997b) assumes that QR, a covert movement operation specifically dedicated to scope assignment, is acceptable if it obeys standard constraints on movement and is forced by interface conditions, specifically the need to associate sentences with their correct truth conditions.[7] Let us assume without further argument that the behavior of universals like *every man* can indeed be accounted for along these lines. The big problem is that the scope of indefinites does not appear to obey any island constraints at all. Consider scoping out of coordinate structures, adjuncts, and relative clauses:

(50)   Everyone reported that [Max and *some lady*] disappeared.
        "there is a lady such that everyone reported that Max and this lady
        disappeared"

(51)   Most guests will be offended [if we don't invite *some philosopher*].
        "there is a philosopher such that most guests will be offended if we
        don't invite him or her"

(52)   All students believe anything [that *many teachers* say].
        "there are many teachers such that all students believe anything they
        say"

All these sentences are ambiguous. The claim that they indeed have the island-
escaping readings specified above is corroborated by the fact that *wh*-in situ
and sluicing, which Reinhart argues should be treated in a manner analogous
to indefinites, exhibit the same effects. Those cases boil down to plain matters
of grammaticality. For example:

(53)   Who reported that Max and *which lady* disappeared?

(54)   Who will be offended if we don't invite *which philosopher*?

(55)   Who believes anything that *who* says?

It turns out that the indefinite facts cannot be explained away in the manner
Reinhart (1978) had attempted to: the reading on which the indefinite takes
wide scope does not always entail the other reading. Fodor and Sag (1982) and
Ruys (1992) note the existence of examples where neither reading entails the
other. Crucially, to show that in (56), the inverse reading does not entail the
direct reading, imagine a situation with three boys. Two of them kiss Jane,
and the third kisses Jean. In this situation it is true that some girl, i.e., Jane, is
kissed by exactly two boys, but it is not true that exactly two boys kissed some
girl or other: three boys did. (To show that the direct reading does not entail
the inverse reading, imagine a situation where one boy kisses Jane, one kisses
Jean, and the third kisses no one. In this situation it is true that exactly two boys
kissed some girl or other, but not a single girl was kissed by exactly two boys.)

(56)   Exactly two boys kissed *some girl*.

But then, the island-free scope of the indefinite in (57) cannot be a matter of
entailment:

(57)   Mary dates exactly two of the men [who know *a producer I like*].
        "there is a producer I like such that Mary dates exactly two men who
        know him"

Nor can the wide scope reading be attributed to a separate, referential interpretation of the indefinite, as Fodor and Sag (1982) proposed. As they pointed out, this account predicts that indefinites cannot escape an island and take intermediate scope at the same time; Farkas (1981) showed that such readings are possible. In (58), conditions can vary with students, and triplets of arguments with conditions:

(58)   Every student has to come up with three arguments [that show that *some condition proposed by Chomsky* is wrong].
       "for every student, there should be a condition proposed by Chomsky such that the student comes up with three arguments that show that the condition is wrong"

In sum, the varying scope of indefinites is neither an illusion nor a semantic epiphenomenon: it needs to be "assigned" in some way. Suppose it is assigned by QR, and LF movement is generally immune to subjacency (as suggested in Huang 1982), while the scope of universals is confined to their clause for some other particular reason. But whether or not this solution might have worked in earlier theories, the assumption that movement before and after S-structure obeys different constraints cannot even be stated in the Minimalist theory, which does not have S-structure as a level of representation.

Given this difficulty, the varying scope of indefinites might be attributed to unselective binding. Following Lewis (1975), indefinites may be interpreted as variables, rather than existentially quantified expressions. Their existential force is then due to the fact that they are captured by an independently introduced existential quantifier. Such an existential may occur at the text level or appended to the nuclear scopes of all true quantifiers, as in Heim (1982), or appended to VP, as in Diesing (1992). In any case, the fact that unselective binding involves no movement will immediately explain why the scope of indefinites is island-free.

But there is a problem. Heim (1982) combined unselective binding with QR in the treatment of indefinites, with a good reason. Suppose an indefinite occurs inside the antecedent of a conditional and is intended to take scope over the whole conditional:

(59)   If we invite some philosopher, Max will be offended.

The interpretation that plain unselective binding produces is (60):

(60)   for some x[(if x is a philosopher and we invite x), Max will be offended]

A conditional is true if either the if-clause is false or the consequent is true. The if-clause in (60) will be false if the value of x either is not a philosopher or we do not invite it. Thus, the existence of any non-philosopher or non-invitee suffices to make (60) true. The problem stems from the fact that in (60), only the existential quantifier occurs outside the implication; the restriction *x is a philosopher* stays in its antecedent. An operation like QR, which has always been assumed to move the whole noun phrase, would not separate the existential quantifier from its restriction. Thus, syntactically ill-behaved as it might be, it appears we need QR to carry the restriction up.[8]

As a final blow, Reinhart shows that in another respect, QR would not assign the correct truth conditions. The relevant observation, made by Farkas (1981), Ruys (1992), and Kratzer (1995), pertains to the distributive interpretation of plural indefinites. Compare:

(61)   Three relatives of mine inherited a house.
    i.   "there are three relatives of mine who together inherited a house"
    ii. "there are three relatives of mine who each inherited a house"

(62)   If three relatives of mine die, I will inherit a house.
    i.   "there are three relatives of mine such that if they all die, I will inherit a house"
    ii. "there are three relatives of mine the death of each of whom will leave me with a house"

Plural indefinites can scope out of an island, but cannot distributively scope out: they cannot make another expression outside the island referentially dependent. What this indicates is that existential scope and distributivity are two separate matters: they can diverge. The traditional notion of quantifiers has distributivity built in, so to say, hence it will not make the distinction. If QR is an operation that raises quantifiers so understood, we get only the (ii) readings, which amounts to both undergeneration and overgeneration.

Thus, we need a non-QR solution to the problem of the separated restriction. There are several logically possible solutions. Reinhart chooses a variant of unselective binding, with existential quantification over choice function variables, as opposed to individual variables, as proposed in Egli and von Heusinger (1995). A choice function applies to a set and chooses an element of the set. Each choice function f may choose a different element. For example, it may be that f_1(philosopher) = Russell and f_2(philosopher) = Strawson. (59) will now be interpreted as follows. The restriction is not syntactically carried up and yet it contributes to interpretation as if it was:

(63) $\exists f[f$ is a choice function and (we invite f(philosopher) $\rightarrow$ Max will be offended)]
    "there is some choice function such that if we invite the philosopher it picks, Max will be offended" = "there is some philosopher such that if we invite him or her, Max will be offended"

If the indefinite is plural, the choice function will pick appropriate collectives from the NP-denotation; for example, *three relatives* will be interpreted as f(three relatives), which picks a collective made up of three relatives. The distributive readings of plurals are obtained with the aid of a separate distributive operator; a conclusion that is standard in the literature.

The syntactic upshot of the discussion is this. It had been assumed that QR, an operation that either is clause bounded or at least obeys Subjacency, affects phrases like *every man, some man, three men*, etc. alike. This assumption runs foul of the robust fact that the existential scope of indefinites is island-free, and the situation cannot even be remedied by making QR by default island-free. Indefinites acquire their existential scope in a manner that does not involve movement and is essentially syntactically unconstrained. The distributive interpretation of plural indefinites is due to a separate operator.

Reinhart remains undecided as to whether or not QR should be allowed, somewhat redundantly, to create island-internal distributive scopings of indefinites. In a companion paper, Winter (1997) suggests that it should not.

3.2.2   *Putting the data together*

Although Reinhart (1995, 1997b) is content with accepting QR for well-behaved quantifiers, Hornstein's (1995) objections to QR as a non-Minimalist operation seem well founded. Given that the two theories cover largely complementary items of data, one may wonder whether Reinhart's and Hornstein's insights cannot be combined.

It seems they can; moreover, such a move might solve a fatal problem in Hornstein's theory. Recall from the discussion of (45) that the ambiguity of *Someone attended every seminar* is explained as follows. Both quantifiers have two copies: in their case positions and in their VP-internal positions. By Diesing's Mapping Hypothesis, *every seminar* must have its VP-internal copy deleted, whereas *someone* can have either copy deleted. The subject wide scope reading obtains if the copy of *someone* that survives is the one in AgrS, and the object wide scope reading obtains if it is the one inside VP. But, as Hornstein points out (1995: 237–8), the ambiguity of (64) cannot be accounted for along these lines:

(64)   Everyone attended some seminar.

The reason is that by the Mapping Hypothesis, *everyone* is safely lodged in AgrS, and there is no position above it where the direct object might be located and take wider scope. Hornstein himself argues that (64) indeed only has a subject wide scope reading, and the apparent object wide scope reading is simply due to the fact that everyone may have attended the same seminar.

This line of argument is identical to Reinhart's (1978). As Reinhart (1995) points out, however, this argument, which depends on the fact that the inverse reading entails the direct reading, goes through for *every–some* but not in general – see the discussion of (56). Thus, the ambiguity of all of the following examples remains unaccounted for in Hornstein's theory, given that the definite/presuppositional subject must be interpreted VP-externally and the object wide scope reading does not entail the subject wide scope one:

(65)   Exactly half of the students attended some seminar.
       Most but not all of the students attended some seminar.
       Every second student attended some seminar.
       Two of the students attended three of the seminars.
       Neither student attended a seminar on rectangular circles.

On the other hand, if even the clause internal scope of indefinites must be obtained by existential quantification over choice functions, and the location of the existential quantifier is syntactically unconstrained, then all of (64) and (65) can be assigned an object wide scope reading simply by positing an existential quantifier somewhere – anywhere – above AgrS. Note, though, that if we must resort to assigning scope to direct object indefinites in a syntactically uncon-strained manner, the strictly A-chain based account of the behavior of subject indefinites becomes a bit of an illusion.

Interestingly, however, Hornstein's theory makes solid predictions for a kind of datum he himself never considers: sentences involving the interaction of a universal and a "modified numeral." As Liu (1990) observed, (66) is ambigu-ous but (67) is not. Modified numerals do not take island-free scope; they even resist taking inverse scope within their own clause. Similar to *more/fewer than three seminars* is the behavior of *few seminars, no seminars, exactly three seminars, more seminars than concerts*, etc.:

(66)   More/fewer than three students attended every seminar.
       i.   "more/fewer than three students are such that they attended every seminar"
       ii. "every seminar was attended by more/fewer than three students"

(67)   Every student attended more/fewer than three seminars.
       i.   "every student is such that she or he attended more/fewer than three seminars"
       ii. *"more/fewer than three seminars were attended by every student"

These judgments would be derived as follows. *Every seminar* must be inter-preted in AgrO in (66) and in AgrS in (67). In (66), *more/fewer than three students* is interpreted using either the copy in AgrS or the one in VP-internal position; the former is higher and the latter is lower than AgrO, hence the ambiguity. In (67), both positions of the modified numeral, AgrO and VP-internal, are below AgrS, whence only the subject can take wide scope.

3.2.3   A hybrid theory: A-chains plus feature driven A'-movement

To summarize, it does seem useful to assume that (i) some quantifiers, namely, modified numerals, never scope above their case position, but can be "recon-structed" into a lower link in their chains, whereas (ii) some other quantifiers, such as universals, reach a relatively high position and never "reconstruct." The question is whether the interpreted position of the latter is indeed a case position, *à la* Hornstein, and whether the impossibility to "reconstruct" them into VP is indeed prevented by pre-suppositionality, *à la* Diesing. Hornstein writes off QR because he takes it for granted that QR cannot be feature driven. It seems correct that the omnivorous rule QR that applies to all scope-bearing noun phrases in a uniform manner cannot be feature driven. Given the differential behavior of indefinites, universals, and modified numerals, such a uniform rule has no descriptive validity, to begin with. But perhaps universals and some other quantifiers are driven to their high clause internal positions by the need to check certain interpreted features, probably a different feature for each type, and the reason why they do not "reconstruct" is simply that these features are relevant for interpretation.

This is precisely the proposal in Beghelli (1993) and Beghelli and Stowell (1997).[9] Their descriptive starting point is Liu's observation that quantifiers fall into two big classes as to whether they take inverse scope (see the discussion of (66)–(67)). Beghelli and Stowell distinguish the two classes as follows:[10]

(68) a. Quantifiers that readily take inverse scope (*two men, every man,* etc.) have interpreted features that send them to relatively high designated positions, whereas

b. quantifiers that basically do not take inverse scope (*no man, more/ fewer two men,* etc.) are either sent to some relatively low interpreted position, like NegP, or do not have any feature to check beyond their case features, wherefore they are always interpreted somewhere within their A-chains.

That is to say, in this theory, only type (b) quantifiers receive the treatment that Hornstein assumes for all quantifiers.

Case (a) deserves attention because of the specific interpreted features involved. We focus on one such feature: [+distributive], to show the general plausibility of the enterprise.

Beghelli and Stowell assume (at least) the following functional projections:

(69) Ref(erential)P

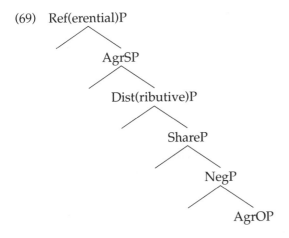

Every man and *each man*, but not *the men, a hundred men*, and *all the men* are obligatorily distributive:

(70) a.   *Every man/each man surrounded the fort.
      b.   Every man/each man lifted the table (*together).

(71) a.   The men/a hundred men/all the men surrounded the fort.
      b.   The men/a hundred men/all the men lifted the table (together).

This is accounted for by a [+dist] feature that they need to check against the distributive operator that heads DistP. Thus, specifier of DistP is the position where *every man* and *each man* land and cannot reconstruct from.

The Dist head selects as its complement a functional category (ShareP) containing the distributed share with the ability to referentially vary. The distributed share may be an existentially closed event variable, as in the correct distributive reading of (70b), or an indefinite, as in (72):

(72) Every man/each man lifted a table.

Although *the men, all the men*, or topical indefinites can also be interpreted distributively, they never occur in DistP. They are driven to the specifier of RefP, and their optional distributivity is due to an independent distributive operator, as is also argued by Reinhart. Beghelli and Stowell assimilate this latter operator to binominal *each* (Safir and Stowell 1989), which accounts for its clause bounded nature; the clause boundedness of Dist, it being a head, is straightforward.

The ambiguity of (73) and (74) is accounted for with reference to the fact that *someone* may land either in RefP or ShareP:[11]

(73) Someone attended every seminar.
      i.   [$_{RefP}$ someone [$_{DistP}$ every seminar [attended]]]
      ii. [$_{DistP}$ every seminar [$_{ShareP}$ someone [attended]]]

(74) Everyone attended some seminar.
      i.   [$_{RefP}$ some seminar [$_{DistP}$ everyone [attended]]]
      ii. [$_{DistP}$ everyone [$_{ShareP}$ some seminar [attended]]]

(75), with a modified numeral in subject position, is ambiguous, due to the fact that the subject can stay in AgrSP or reconstruct into a trace position:

(75) More than two students attended every seminar.
      i.   [$_{AgrSP}$ more than two students [$_{DistP}$ every seminar [attended]]]
      ii. [$_{DistP}$ every seminar [more than two students attended]]

On the other hand, (76) is unambiguous, because *more than two seminars* cannot get higher than AgrOP and *every student* cannot reconstruct:

(76) Everyone attended more than two seminars.
  i. [$_{DistP}$ everyone [$_{AgrOP}$ more than two seminars [attended]]]
  ii. *"there are more than two seminars that everyone attended"

To summarize, on Beghelli and Stowell's approach, too, scope is a by-product of feature checking. They argue for the existence of at least three new functional projections into which phrases are driven to check interpreted features: RefP, DistP, and ShareP. Movement into the specifiers of these positions is what takes the place of QR in their version of a Minimalist approach to scope. Reconstruction from these positions is barred by the interpretive relevance of the features checked. Hierarchy predicts that an indefinite in RefP scopes above, and an indefinite in ShareP scopes below, a universal in DistP. Modified numerals typically do not move to any of these three positions; they scope in their AgrPs or in a lower link of their chains. The assumption that AgrSP is above DistP ensures that a modified numeral subject can always potentially scope above a universal direct object.[12]

3.2.4 Crosslinguistic evidence

It is interesting to confront these theories with languages that disambiguate scope relations at Spell-Out. How do they do it? We briefly consider Hungarian and Chinese.

The surface syntactic data of Hungarian, a language that has come to be known to "wear its LF on its sleeve" (see e.g. É. Kiss 1991), provide direct support for many details of the feature driven A'-movement hypothesis. Hungarian largely disambiguates scope by the linear order of quantifiers at Spell-Out. Two important negative facts are that (i) this linear order is not obtained by simply lining up quantifiers in the desired scope order, contrary to what a Montague/May style theory would predict, and (ii) this linear order is not determined by case or grammatical functions, as a Hornstein style theory would predict. Instead, as research since the late 1970s has firmly established, each type of quantifier occurs in its specific position, easily recognizable from surface clues like the position of adverbs, the finite verb, etc.:

(77) Öt orvos   minden betegnek kevés új tablettát írt fel.
    five doctor every patient-Dat few new pill-Acc wrote up
    "there are five doctors x such that for every patient y, x prescribed few new pills to y"

Scope falls out from the hierarchy so obtained: (77) is unambiguous. Moreover, while grammatical function does not determine linear order, the order of the DP types cannot be changed at will. For example:

(78) *Öt orvos   kevés betegnek minden új tablettát írt fel.
    five doctor few patient-Dat every new pill-Acc wrote up

Thus, the Hungarian data straightforwardly support Beghelli and Stowell's general assumption that each quantifier type moves to its own characteristic position to check some feature whose existence is independent of scope interaction. But, more specifically, Szabolcsi (1997b) argues that the order and nature of these positions correspond rather closely to Beghelli and Stowell's: in the grammatical (77), the position of *öt orvos* "five doctors" is RefP and that of *minden beteg* "every patient" is DistP. The position of *kevés új tabletta* "few new pills," dubbed Predicate Operator, is in many respects analogous to AgrP/VP.

The claim that there is a position specifically related to distributivity receives particularly strong confirmation from Hungarian. Certain quantifiers, *több, mint öt NP* "more than five NP" among them, can potentially occur in more than one linear position, and their interpretations vary accordingly. In the Predicate Operator position (which is adjacent to the finite verb stem), they can support either a distributive or a collective interpretation of the sentence:

(79) Több, mint öt fiú   emelte fel az asztalt.
      more than five boys lifted up the table-Acc
      "The number of boys who lifted the table (individually or collectively) is greater than five."

When, however, they occur in the same DistP position as distributive universals canonically occupy (note the particle–verb order), they are obligatorily distributive:

(80) a. Minden fiú fel-emelte az asztalt.
          every boy up-lifted the table-Acc
          "Every boy lifted up the table (*collectively)."
      b. Több, mint öt fiú   fel-emelte az asztalt.
          more than five boy up-lifted   the table-Acc
          "More than five boys lifted up the table (*collectively)."

Let us now turn to Chinese, a language that has been argued to highlight the significance of A-chains. Aoun and Li (1993c) observe that scope in Chinese is, in some cases, disambiguated by case positions. Specifically, active sentences only have subject wide scope (81), whereas passive sentences are ambiguous (82):

(81) Yaoshi liangge nuren du guo   meiben shu . . .
      if   two women   read Asp every book
       i. "if there are two women who read every book . . ."
      ii. *"if for every book, there are two women who read it . . ."

(82) Yaoshi liangge xiansuo bei meigeren zhaodao . . .
      if   two clues   by everyone found
       i. "if there are two clues that are found by everyone . . ."
      ii. "if for everyone, there are two clues she or he finds . . ."

Hornstein takes these data to indicate that the universal is always interpreted in its case position, and the possibility for ambiguity hinges on whether the indefinite can reconstruct below it, into VP. As regards reconstructibility, he follows Aoun and Li (1993c) in attributing the contrast between actives and passives to the assumption that Chinese has no VP-internal subjects. Hence in (81), *liangge nuren* has nowhere to reconstruct. In (82), *liangge xiansuo* comes from a VP-internal complement position, into which it can reconstruct. Thus, the account of the unambiguity of actives relies as much on the assumption of no VP-internal subjects as it does on A-chains. How strong is the evidence that the datum provides for the A-chains theory of scope depends on how natural it is to assume that languages differ as to whether they have VP-internal subjects. The underlying judgment also seems to be a matter of debate: according to Liu (1990, 1997), semantically reliable quantifiers do not exhibit inverse scope in either active or passive sentences.

Further research will determine the best way to account for the spectrum of Hungarian–English–Chinese within a unified theory.

3.3 Overt or covert movement?

Beghelli and Stowell assimilate [+dist] to [+neg] as we standardly know it in that both are interpreted features that are checked covertly, at least in English. Is the assumption of covert movement necessary? Kayne (1998) argues that it is not, for either case. In what follows I briefly review Kayne's proposal for negatives. The argument for universals, *only*-phrases, etc. runs essentially parallel.

The basic idea is that a phrase like *no one* moves to check its [+neg] feature in NegP overtly, but the change in linear order that this movement brings about is covered up by subsequent remnant movement. Remnant movement affects a VP that has all material except for the verb removed from it:

(83) You married no one.
　　　... [$_{VP}$ married no one]　　　　　⇒ negative preposing
　　　... [no one/i [$_{VP}$ married t/i]]　　　⇒ VP-preposing
　　　... [(married t/i)/j [no one/i [$_{VP}$ t/j]]]

As Klima (1964) noted, (84) exhibits an ambiguity as to whether *no one* scopes in the matrix or in the complement:

(84) I will force you to marry no one.
　　i.　"there is no one that I will force you to marry"
　　ii.　"I will force that there be no one that you marry"

The narrow (complement) scope of *no one* in (84ii) is derived as above. Wide (matrix) scope in (84i) requires that *no one* check its [+neg] in the matrix NegP:

(85)   ... [$_{VP}$ force you to [$_{VP}$ marry no one]] $\Rightarrow$ negative
                                                                    preposing
       ... [no one/i [$_{VP}$ force you to [$_{VP}$ marry t/i]]] $\Rightarrow$ VP-preposing
       ... [(force you to marry t/i)/j [no one t/i [$_{VP}$ t/j]]]

If this somewhat programmatic suggestion proves to be viable, it might take
the bite of abstractness out of syntax, the syntax of scope included.

4   Conclusion

One challenge for the theory of quantifier scope in natural language is to
develop the tools, logical as well as syntactic, that are necessary to account for
the whole range of existing readings. In this chapter, we reviewed Montague's
and May's seminal proposals for one core case, asymmetrical scope. (For
cumulative, branching, and collective readings, and the role of events, see, for
example, Schein 1993.) Another challenge is to draw the proper empirical
distinction between readings that are actually available and those that are not.
We have seen that both the phrase structure position of the quantifier and its
particular semantics play a role in determining its scope taking abilities, and it
is likely that different quantifier types take scope using different mechanisms.
We reviewed May's, Hornstein's, Reinhart's, and Beghelli and Stowell's proposals in some detail. In doing so, we highlighted how each theory addresses
the dominant theoretical syntactic concerns of the era. Finally, the question
arises whether "Spell-Out syntax" is sufficient for the above two purposes.
Contrary to the mainstream assumption of LF, Reinhart, Williams, Hendriks,
and Kayne have suggested, albeit in very different ways, that it is. This issue
calls for significant further research.

NOTES

1   Beghelli et al. (1997) argue that this
    setup has empirical benefits: it can
    be used to predict what subject–
    object quantifier pairs exhibit a so-
    called branching reading in English.
    For example, *Two boys saw three films*
    and *Two boys saw every film* have a
    reading that can be paraphrased as
    "There is a set containing two boys
    and there is a set containing three/
    every film(s) such that each of the
    boys saw all of the films," but *Two*
    boys saw more than three films has
    no reading on which it can be
    paraphrased as "There is a set
    containing two boys and there is a
    set containing more than three films
    such that each of the boys saw all
    of the films."

2   Strictly speaking, this is only
    true under Montague's simple
    assumptions about logical types.
    Recent, more sophisticated versions
    of categorial grammar, e.g. Hendriks

(1993), can derive any scopal order using only functional application.

3   For potential counter-examples, see Moltmann and Szabolcsi (1994) and Farkas and Giannakidou (1996).

4   Both Hornstein (1995) and Beghelli and Stowell (1997) assume that Case is assigned in AgrP. Chomsky (1995) favors a theory with multiple specifiers. The issue does not seem settled yet; see Ura and Belletti (both this volume).

5   Operators have a restriction and a nuclear scope. Diesing's Mapping Hypothesis says that material from VP is mapped into the Nuclear Scope and is captured by Existential Closure, while material from IP is mapped into a Restrictive Clause.

6   For arguments against syntactic reconstruction, see Bittner (1994).

7   The idea that QR applies only when it makes a difference for truth conditions is explored in Fox (1995, to appear).

8   Given the semantics of conditionals, the improved formula, *for some x[x is a philosopher and (if we invite x, Max will be offended)]*, is still true if there is any philosopher that we do not invite.

9   This theory was developed simultaneously with, rather than in response to, Hornstein's and Reinhart's, but we will not elaborate on the aspects that it shares with the others.

10   According to Szabolcsi (1997b), the distinction between the two classes has a natural correlate in Discourse Representation Theory. DPs that readily take inverse scope are associated with discourse referents, while DPs that scope in situ are interpreted via "box splitting." Besides scope, this has consequences for anaphora. Szabolcsi argues for two semantic modifications of Kamp and Reyle's (1993) DRT. (i) Universals are associated with set referents, not box splitting. (ii) All referents are interpreted as variables ranging over witness sets of the generalized quantifier denoted by the DP. (For example, a witness of *two men* is any set containing two men and no non-men.) This takes care of the same problem for the sake of which Reinhart (1997b) invokes choice functions. Given these assumptions, Beghelli and Stowell's (1997) syntax can be viewed as a discourse representation structure construction algorithm.

11   This chapter does not address the issue of island-free scope.

12   For a strictly Minimalist presentation of these ideas, see Stabler (1997).

20 Deconstructing Binding

ERIC REULAND
AND MARTIN EVERAERT

0 Introduction

Among the major results of the principles and parameters (P&P) framework developed in Chomsky (1981) is the conception of Binding Theory. In
this framework, Binding Theory is one of the six subsystems of core grammar.
Binding Theory is concerned with the relations of nominal expressions with
possible antecedents.[1] An element *bound* by an antecedent depends on the
latter for its interpretation. An element that is not bound is *free*. With respect
to binding, it is assumed that nominal expressions fall into the following
categories: (i) anaphors, (ii) pronominals, and (iii) R-expressions. Anaphors
are expressions that have no capacity for inherent reference. Pronominals are
characterized by the fact that their grammatical features are drawn solely
from the set of phi-features (gender, number, and person). When overt, they
have also Case. R-expressions have some other grammatical features as well.[2]
Chomsky develops a theory of their anaphoric relations taken as syntactic
dependencies, which has since set the standard. A preliminary formulation is
given in (1):

(1) a. An anaphor is bound in a local domain.
     b. A pronominal is free in a local domain.
     c. An R-expression is free.

These conditions are referred to as "binding conditions A, B and C." In section 1 the Binding Theory will be presented in more technical detail and briefly
reviewed. Subsequently, section 2 discusses the empirical problems that have
arisen within the standard Binding Theory, and some of the ways to deal with
them. For a proper understanding of some of the core issues of debate, it
is necessary to discuss the difference between "coreference" and "bound variable interpretation," as is done in section 3. In section 4 the issue of long distance anaphora and logophoricity is discussed. In section 5 we address more

fully the typology of anaphoric expressions. Finally in section 6 the Reflexivity framework is discussed, which introduces some basic new features to the standard conception of Binding Theory.

1   Outline of the Standard Binding Theory

1.1   *Indexing and c-command*

Within the conception of Binding Theory under review the reference of an element is determined by its index. This index can be regarded as, perhaps, the sole aspect of a lexical item that is visible for whatever mental faculty assigns reference. Whereas the reference of R-expressions is inherent through an independently assigned index, a coindexed antecedent determines the reference of anaphors. Pronominals can be interpreted either by a coindexed antecedent, or by an independently assigned index. Binding Theory can then be implemented in the form of conditions on indexing; coindexed elements must match in features. This condition can be formulated as in (2):

(2)   In order to be coindexed, *a* and *b* must be non-distinct in features for person, number, and gender.

For pronominal binding this is illustrated in (3):

(3)   Bill$_i$ said he$_i$/*she$_i$ thought Mary liked him$_i$/*her$_i$

Note that the ungrammaticality indicated by the star is relative to the indexing: if *she* and *Bill* are not coindexed, (3) is grammatical.
    An illustration for anaphor binding is given in (4):

(4)   Bill$_i$ hated himself$_i$/*herself$_i$

Here, the ungrammaticality is not just relative to the indexing: if *herself* is not coindexed with *Bill*, the sentence is still out, since *herself* requires an antecedent. In English the reflexive anaphor is specified for gender, number, and person, but many languages have a 3rd person anaphor lacking a specification for gender and number. Icelandic *(sjalfan) sig* or Dutch *zich(zelf)* (cf. (5)) illustrate this option, which shows that non-distinctness rather than identity in feature composition is required for coindexing:

(5)   Wim$_i$/Marie$_i$/de katten$_i$ houdt/houden van zichzelf$_i$
      "Wim/Marie/the cats loves/love himself/herself/themselves"

In addition to matching features, binding is subject to the structural condition of *c-command*. The basic configuration is given in (6): in order for some element *b* to be able to depend for its interpretation on some element *a*, *b* must be a sister to some constituent containing *b*:

(6)　*a* [. . . *b* . . .]

More formally, c-command is defined as in (7a), and binding is, then, defined as in (7b):[3]

(7)　a.　*a* c-commands *b* iff *a* does not contain *b* and the first branching node dominating *a* also dominates *b*.
　　b.　*a* binds *b* iff *a* and *b* are coindexed and *a* c-commands *b*.

Given that anaphors must be bound, the effect is illustrated in (8):

(8)　a.　*John$_i$'s plans failed himself$_i$
　　b.　[Mary's father]$_i$ hated himself$_i$ vs. *Mary$_i$'s father hated herself$_i$

In (8a) the sentence does contain a feature compatible antecedent for *himself*, namely *John*. Yet the structure is ill formed. Since *John* does not bind *himself*, c-command failing, the latter is thus not properly interpreted. The pair in (8b) illustrates the same point in a different manner: *Mary's father* correctly binds *himself*, but *Mary* cannot bind *herself*.[4]

Note, that the intuition that binding relations reflect an inherent asymmetry between an element that depends and an element that is depended on is not captured by a coindexing notation. An alternative that immediately captures this asymmetry is the *linking* notation introduced by Higginbotham (1983). In this notation the antecedency relation is directly expressed by headed arrows, as in (3'):

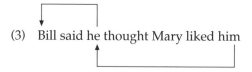

(3)　Bill said he thought Mary liked him

For reasons of space we will refrain from presenting a more extensive discussion here, but refer to Higginbotham's original article.

1.2　*The binding conditions*

The effect of binding is sensitive to locality requirements. The rough generalization is that anaphors must be bound by an antecedent that not only c-commands, but is also sufficiently "local." Pronominals can be bound, but only if the antecedent is sufficiently "non-local." Most of the work on binding has been devoted to obtaining both a precise characterization of and, ultimately, an explanation of these requirements. (9) exemplifies some basic patterns:

(9) a. *John$_i$ hates him$_i$
     b. John$_i$ thinks that Mary hates him$_i$
     c. John$_i$ hates himself$_i$
     d. *John$_i$ thinks that Mary hates himself$_i$

In (9a) the antecedent of the pronominal *him* is too local, but in (9b) it is far enough away. The reverse holds for the anaphor *himself* in (9c, d). In the standard Binding Theory "distance" is measured in terms of the notion of *governing category*:

(10) β is a governing category for α if and only if β is the minimal category containing α, a governor of α, and a SUBJECT (accessible to α).

The notion SUBJECT in (10) is defined in (11):

(11) The SUBJECT of a category is its most prominent nominal element (including the agreement features on the verb in finite clauses).

This leads to the following statement of the binding conditions (Chomsky 1981: 188):

(12) a. An anaphor is bound in its governing category.
     b. A pronominal is free in its governing category.
     c. An R-expression is free.

First we will review a couple of cases without reference to the part of the condition (10) that is in parentheses. We will then complete our overview of the standard Binding Theory with an example involving that condition.
    Consider first the contrast in (13):

(13) a. *John$_i$ expected [$_\alpha$ Mary to hate himself$_i$]
     b. [$_\beta$ John$_i$ expected [$_\alpha$ himself$_i$ to be able to hate Mary]]

In (13a) *himself* is bound by *John*, but it is easily seen that *John* is outside *himself*'s governing category α, α = IP. α is the minimal category containing the governor of *himself* (*hate*), and a SUBJECT (*Mary*). The governing category does not contain a suitable antecedent, hence condition A is violated. In (13b) *himself* receives Case from the exceptional case marker *expect*. Hence, its governing category is not α but the matrix clause β since it is the minimal category containing the governor of *himself*, *expect*, and a SUBJECT, *John*.
    Comparing (13) and (14) illustrates an important feature of the standard Binding Theory: the complementarity between anaphor binding and pronominal binding:

(14) a. John$_i$ expected [$_\alpha$ Mary to hate him$_i$]
     b. *[$_\beta$ John$_i$ expected [$_\alpha$ him$_i$ to be able to hate Mary]]

In (14a) *him* can be bound by *John* without violating any binding condition: *him* is free in its governing category α, $\alpha = \text{IP}$. In (14b) *John* is too nearby since β, and not α, is the governing category of *him*. β is the minimal category because it contains the governor of *him*, the verb *expect*; hence its governing category is the matrix clause, and the binding relation violates condition B.

(15) illustrates the opacity of finite clauses. The embedded subjects, *himself* in (15a) and *he* in (15b), are governed by INFL, the locus of the agreement features of the verb. This means that the minimal category containing *himself/he*, their governor INFL, and a subject is α, $\alpha = \text{IP}$. But α does not contain a c-commanding antecedent, hence both are free in their governing categories, which is OK for *him*, but not for *himself*:

(15)   a.   *John$_i$ expected that [$_\alpha$ himself$_i$ would be able to hate Mary]
      b.   John$_i$ expected that [$_\alpha$ he$_i$ would be able to hate Mary]

(16)–(18) illustrate the way in which the binding conditions work in NPs:

(16)   a.   John$_i$ hated [$_\alpha$ pictures of himself$_i$]
      b.   (*) John$_i$ hated [$_\alpha$ Mary's pictures of himself$_i$]

Crucially, in NPs a subject is not obligatory. The definition of governing category leads us to expect that a NP does or does not qualify as a governing category for a pronominal or anaphor it contains depending on whether it has a subject. In (16a) α, $\alpha = \text{NP}$, contains the governor of *himself*, *of*, but lacks a subject and will thus not count as a governing category. The matrix clause has a SUBJECT (*John*), thus qualifying to be the governing category for the anaphor embedded in the NP. In (16b) the NP has a subject (*Mary*), hence the NP counts as a governing category for *himself*. Therefore, condition A is violated under the intended coindexation.

(16b) is one of the type of datum that will in the end motivate a different view of binding. Although there is little discussion of this in the earlier literature, sentences of this type may be considerably better than the theory might lead us to expect, depending on the specific environment in which they are used. For that reason we have put the ungrammaticality marking in parentheses. Such cases will be discussed more in section 5. In any case, as soon as the antecedent is contained in the NP, as in (17), the judgment is again precisely as the theory leads us to expect:

(17)   John hated [$_\alpha$ Mary$_i$'s pictures of herself$_i$]

Replacing the anaphor in (17) by a pronominal, as in (18), gives the pattern to be expected by now: in (18a) *John* is outside the governing category α, $\alpha = \text{NP}$, of *him*, hence it may bind the latter. In (18b), *Mary* is inside the governing category of *her*, hence *her* may not be bound by *Mary*:

(18) a. John$_i$ hated [$_\alpha$ Mary's pictures of him$_i$]
      b. *John hated [$_\alpha$ Mary$_i$'s pictures of her$_i$]

The examples in (19) illustrate the role of the part of the condition (10) that is in parentheses:

(19) a. *[The boys]$_i$ were afraid that themselves$_i$ would be sold as slaves
      b. [The boys]$_i$ were afraid that pictures of themselves$_i$ would be on sale

The point is that there is a contrast between anaphors as subjects and anaphors properly contained in a subject. As the ungrammaticality of (19a) shows, the former always lead to a violation of condition A. This would follow if the governing category were the complement clause. It is easily seen that this is in accordance with (10), without the part in parentheses. Applying this version of (10) to (19b) also yields the complement clause as the governing category. But since *the boys* is in fact a proper antecedent for *themselves* in (19b), a modification is in order. Given the definition of accessibility in (20), the definition in (10), which would include the part of the condition in parentheses, has the required result:

(20) a. α is accessible to β iff β is in the c-command domain of α, and assignment to β of the index of α would not violate (20b).
      b. **i-within-i condition**
          *[$_\tau$ ... δ ...], where τ and δ bear the same index

In the complement clause of (19b) there would be two potential SUBJECTs, namely the phrase *pictures of themselves* and the *Agr* of the finite verb. Obviously, given (20), *pictures of themselves* is not accessible to *themselves*. However, Agr is not either, since, due to subject–verb agreement, it would share its index with the full subject *pictures of themselves*. So, a putative coindexing between *themselves* and Agr gives, by transitivity of coindexing, coindexing between *themselves* and *pictures of themselves*, in violation of (20). The effect of this is that the complement clause fails to contain a subject accessible to *themselves*, hence does not qualify as a governing category for the latter. It is easily seen that the matrix clause does qualify, hence the matrix subject is sufficiently nearby to satisfy condition A.

1.3 LF-movement

In Lebeaux (1983) it is observed that reflexives and reciprocals seem to behave differently in the (nominative) subject position of tensed sentences such as (21):

(21) a. ?[John and Mary]$_i$ didn't think that each other$_i$ would leave early
      b. *[John and Mary]$_i$ didn't think that themselves$_i$ would leave early

The fact that (21a) is grammatical is unexpected because, as we have just explained, the embedded sentence is a governing category if we follow the definition in (10). Partially on the basis of these facts, the definition of governing category is changed in Chomsky (1986a) in such a way that the matrix sentence in cases like (21) is the domain in which the anaphors must be bound. This means that both (21a) and (21b) are predicted to be grammatical. The ungrammaticality of (21b) should follow from some other principle of grammar. More specifically, Chomsky follows Lebeaux in assuming that reflexive anaphors have to move at Logical Form (LF).

The relation between a reflexive and its antecedent partly involves agreement, and since agreement often is a strictly local phenomenon, it would mean that the reflexive should move to a position in the immediate domain of the antecedent. This requirement would trigger movement of the reflexive anaphor at LF.[5] Such a movement will leave a trace (22a) which is not properly governed, violating the Empty Category Principle (ECP) (cf. Chomsky 1981); compare (22b):

(22)   a.   *... NP_i INFL-themselves$_i$ ... [$_{CP}$ ... e_i INFL ...]

   b.   *Who$_i$ do you think that e_i left

In the LF-raising analysis of Chomsky (1986a) the effects of the condition A requirement are thus partially subsumed under the ECP. This LF-head movement analysis has been further developed to account for long distance binding, and the fact that in many languages anaphors are necessarily subject bound (cf. Pica 1987, Battistella 1989, Katada 1991, Huang and Tang 1991, Cole and Sung 1994, Cole and Wang 1996, among others).

1.4   Conclusion

It is crucial to understand that Binding Theory not only deals with the distribution of reflexives, reciprocals, and pronouns. From Chomsky's "Conditions on Transformations" (1973) onwards, the study of reciprocals, reflexives, and pronouns was always tied to the study of other grammatical phenomena such as *wh*-movement, NP-movement, or control. In Chomsky (1973) the Specified Subject Condition is introduced and it is argued that both reciprocal formation and *wh*-movement appear to be subject to the Specified Subject Condition. In Chomsky (1980) the Nominative Island Constraint (NIC) not only excludes examples such as (21b), but also instances of NP-movement, under the assumption that NP-traces are anaphors subject to condition A, and even instances of *wh*-movement, under the assumption that *wh*-traces are (A'-)anaphors (cf. (22b)). Kayne (1984) argues that the Connectedness Condition, his alternative to the

ECP and devised for *wh*-movement dependencies, might also hold for anaphor antecedent dependencies (cf. also Aoun 1986, Koster 1987).

Chomsky (1981) takes the position that Binding Theory generalizes over empty categories and lexical categories. Lexical elements are partitioned by means of two features, <±Anaphor> and <±Pronominal>, resulting in the cross-classification in (23a); (23b) presents lexical and non-lexical instantiations:

(23) a. <+A,−P>   b. reflexives, reciprocals, NP-trace
          <+A,+P>   PRO
          <−A,−P>   R-expressions, *wh*-trace
          <−A,+P>   pronouns, pro

Alongside pure pronominals ([+pronominal, −anaphoric]) and pure anaphors ([−pronominal, +anaphoric]), this classification characterizes as a third category the R-expressions [−pronominal, −anaphoric]. The existence of a fourth category *PRO* is predicted [+pronominal, +anaphoric], whose distribution is limited to those positions where no governing category can be assigned. In other words, PRO is limited to ungoverned positions such as the subject position of control infinitives, the so-called *PRO-theorem* (Chomsky 1981, 1982).

The precise relationship between *wh*-movement, NP-movement or control, and the binder–bindee relationship is, of course, more complicated than we are able to discuss here. But the crucial observation is that in the LGB (*Lectures on Government and Binding*)/P&P framework the distribution of bound anaphora is always closely tied to other syntactic phenomena. It is for that reason that binding was considered part of the computational system, to use the terminology of Chomsky (1995b).

2   Some Empirical Problems

The standard Binding Theory provides a simple and appealing picture of binding relations in natural language. It clearly describes recurrent patterns in the various languages of the world. The basic complementarity between pronouns and anaphors yields a neat typology of nominal expressions in terms of the above-mentioned features. In the remainder of this chapter we will see why it has become necessary to investigate alternative conceptions of binding, despite these successes.

The crucial assumption underlying the binding research within the P&P framework is that all interpretive dependencies can be understood in terms of structural conditions on indexing. In this section we will indicate some empirical problems that have arisen with the standard conception of the Binding Theory, some of which were noted very early on.[6] We will only give some relevant facts and references. Some of the issues will be further discussed in the sections to follow.

2.1　Absence of complementarity between pronominals and anaphors in certain PPs

Right from the start it was noted that certain PPs allowed pronouns to be locally bound, just like reflexives (Lees and Klima 1963, Lakoff 1968, Chomsky 1981, Koster 1985, Kuno 1987):

(24)　a.　$John_i$ saw a snake near him_i/?$himself_i$
　　　b.　$John_i$ glanced behind him_i/$himself_i$
　　　c.　$John_i$ pulled the blanket over him_i/$himself_i$

This is clearly in violation of the binding conditions that predict that anaphors and pronominals are always in complementary distribution. The consequences for the Binding Theory are extensively discussed in Hestvik (1991), among others.

2.2　Absence of complementarity between anaphors and pronominals in the subject position of NP

Huang (1982) argues that the generalization that anaphors/pronominals in the same position have the same governing category ought to be abandoned and that distinct domains of interpretation ought to be assigned to bound anaphors and free anaphors. This position is further developed in Chomsky (1986a) on the basis of examples such as in (25):

(25)　a.　$They_i$ saw [each $other_i's$ friends]
　　　b.　$They_i$ saw [$their_i$ friends]

To account for this non-complementarity Chomsky reformulates the notions of accessible subject and governing category. It means that the binding domain of an element depends on its status as an anaphor/pronominal and that the i-within-i condition discussed in (20) is abandoned.

2.3　Picture nouns

So-called picture nouns play an important (and sometimes crucial) role in the discussion on the definition of the interpretive domain of anaphora (cf. 26a), whether c-command plays a role in the relation between anaphor and its antecedent (cf. 26b), and the level of representation at which Binding Theory should hold (cf. 26b–d):

(26)　a.　$Bill_i$ remembered that *The Times* had printed a picture of $himself_i$ in the Sunday edition
　　　b.　[Pictures of each $other_i]_x$ annoy $them_i$ (t_x)
　　　c.　[Most pictures of $herself_i]_x$ seem to $Mary_i$ t_x to be distorted
　　　d.　$John_i$ wondered which [picture of $himself_i$/$herself_j]_x$ $Mary_j$ saw t_x

The example in (26a) illustrates that picture noun anaphors often allow non-local antecedents (cf. Pollard and Sag 1994 for discussion). In (26b) the anaphor is bound by a non-commanding NP, unless one assumes the predicate is unaccusative, which would mean that at an underlying level the anaphor would be c-commanded (cf. Pesetsky 1995 for discussion of psych predicates and further references). A similar line of argumentation – binding at non-surface level – holds for the binding relation between *Mary* and *herself* in (26d). However, the reverse – binding at surface level – holds for the binding relation between *John* and *himself* in (26d) (cf. Barss 1986 for discussion and references).

Observe that in the approaches to Binding Theory of Reinhart and Reuland (1993) and Pollard and Sag (1994) the distribution of the anaphors in (26) does not fall under Binding Theory proper. For Reinhart and Reuland such anaphors are called "logophors," and Pollard and Sag use the term "exempt anaphors" to reflect the fact that they are exempt from the core binding principles.

2.4 Non-local binding of anaphors in certain environments

As noted by Ross (1970), Cantrall (1974), Kuno (1987), Zribi-Hertz (1989), Baker (1995), and many others, a variety of contexts allows anaphors to be free in their governing category in violation of condition A. This is illustrated in (27):

(27) a. There were five tourists in the room apart from myself.
      b. Physicists like yourself are a godsend.
      c. Max boasted that the queen invited Lucie and himself for a drink.

Such examples have been used to argue for discourse theoretic concepts such as "point of view" to be the relevant notion for anaphoric binding. This has led to proposals where the empirical domain of the binding theory is relegated to the domain of discourse (cf. Kuno 1987, Levinson 1987, 1991, Huang 1994), or alternatively, to the position discussed in the previous paragraph that under specified syntactic or semantic conditions anaphors fall outside the scope of Binding Theory (Reinhart and Reuland 1993, Pollard and Sag 1994).

2.5 Crosslinguistic variation in admissibility of antecedents for anaphors

Quite early on it was noted that, crosslinguistically, there were many anaphors with antecedents essentially beyond the governing category as computed by (10), or even entirely absent (Thráinsson 1976, Reis 1976, Inoue 1976, Yang 1984, Harbert 1983). The examples in (28), Norwegian, Japanese, and Icelandic respectively, illustrate this:

(28) a. Jon$_i$ bad oss hjelpe seg$_i$
         "John asked us to help him"
     b. Bill-wa$_i$ John-ga zibun$_i$-o seme-ta to   omot-ta
         Bill   John   himself blamed that thought
         "Bill thought that John blamed him"
     c. Jón$_i$ segir að María elski sig$_i$
         "John says that Maria loves-Subj him"

Often such cases are discussed under the heading of long distance binding. In general such cases were accounted for as relaxations of the notion of governing category (for example, Manzini and Wexler 1987) or the anaphors involved were classified as exceptions, so-called long distance anaphors (cf. Anderson 1986, Koster 1987).

2.6 *Disjoint reference effects*

In a number of papers the consequences for condition B of the Binding Theory of examples such as those in (29) are discussed (Chomsky 1973, 1980, Lasnik 1989, Seely 1993, Fiengo and May 1994, Berman and Hestvik 1997):

(29) a. *We voted for me
     b. We elected me
     c. *Bill$_i$ told Mary$_j$ about them$_{\{i,j\}}$
     d. Bill$_j$ was relieved that Mary$_i$ agreed to defend them$_{\{i,j\}}$

The ill-formedness of sentences such as (29a) and (29c) indicates that in order to capture condition B-type effects more is needed than just a notion of coindexing. One option is to state Binding Theory in terms of sets of indices and impose a disjointness condition. However, the well-formedness of (29b) and (29d) indicates that this is not yet sufficient. Contrasts such as in (29a, b) indicate that condition B applies at a level of representation where the full set of relations between the relevant individuals is represented. One might then suggest that (29b) is grammatical since *elect* is interpreted collectively, contrary to *vote for* in (29a). The examples in (29c, d) indicate that condition B is also sensitive to contexts where the pronoun is "half" bound, a notion whose theoretical status is still in need of further investigation.

2.7 *Thematic restrictions*

Binding Theory as formulated in section 1 is stated in strictly configurational terms. It has been frequently questioned whether nonconfigurational notions should play a role. On the basis of such examples as (30a) it has been argued that the c-command requirement on the anaphor–antecedent relationship should be replaced by a thematic prominence requirement (cf. Jackendoff 1972, 1990b, Wilkins 1988, Dalrymple 1993, Everaert and Anagnostopoulou 1997, among others, and references there). The ungrammaticality of the (30b, c) examples could be explained since in these cases the antecedent is less prominent on the thematic hierarchy than the anaphor itself (Reinhart and Reuland 1993 argue that the *about*-phrase is not part of the predicate):

(30) a. I talked to Mary$_i$ about herself$_i$
      b. *I talked about Mary$_i$ to herself$_i$
      c. (*)John$_i$ was killed by himself$_i$

Alternatively the (un)grammaticality of such examples might be argued to follow from an obliqueness constraint, i.e., a relative order of grammatical functions (see Pollard and Sag 1994 for discussion).[7] Such examples, furthermore, raised the issue of whether argument structure is the appropriate level of formulating the binding conditions (cf. Grimshaw 1990, Clark 1992b, Jackendoff 1992).

These and other empirical problems have led to several proposals to modify the Binding Theory. Some have stayed unanswered. It would clearly be beyond the scope of this contribution to give even a representative overview of problems that have been noted and solutions that have been proposed. Instead we will focus on a selection of issues that show that the Binding Theory must be modified in a more radical manner, teasing the binding conditions apart, and explaining them as effects of principles of a far lower level of granularity.

3 "Coreference" versus "Bound Variable Anaphora"

In section 1 we discussed the distribution of sentence internal anaphora as it is captured by the binding theory. In this section we will discuss a little bit more how these phenomena relate to sentence external anaphora. In essence, the discussion is about the relation between indexing and interpretation.

The simplest case of anaphora obtains when in a text distinct NPs refer to the same object, as is illustrated by the various possibilities in (31):

(31) The **chairman** came in late. The **speaker** was visibly nervous. *Everyone* had been worrying *himself* stiff. When *he$_1$* had welcomed *him$_2$*, for a moment *he$_3$* leaned back with a slight feeling of relief/panic.

Going over the various options reveals that among the NPs in bold print, the choice of interpretation is free. Admittedly, there may be tendencies favoring certain interpretations over others, depending on one's expectations about, let us say, the capacities and feelings of chairmen or speakers. Some interpretations may turn out a bit more probable than others, but what happens can be manipulated by the choice of lexical elements, and the expectations these invoke. If *he*-1 is interpreted as the chairman, and *him*-2 as the speaker – the most plausible interpretation – *he*-3 is interpreted as the speaker if the noun *relief* is chosen. But if the noun *panic* is chosen, the most likely interpretation of he-3 is the chairman. The choices are not enforced by any property of the grammar.

If two or more NPs (e.g. *chairman* and *speaker*, *chairman* and *he*) refer to the same individual they are *coreferential*. Coreference is not always possible. For instance, *he* in (32) cannot get the value of a quantificational expression such as *everyone*. This is a robust fact. There is a fundamental difference between cases with quantification like (32a) and (32b) (see the extensive literature, e.g. Heim 1982, 1998, Reinhart 1983, to appear):

(32)   a.   *Everyone* had been worrying *himself* stiff. **He** was relieved.
       b.   *Everyone* who had been worrying *himself* stiff said that **he** was
            relieved.

In (32b) the interpretation of *he* can be dependent on the interpretation of an antecedent (*everyone, no one*), showing a relation of variable binding as in (33):

(33)   *Every x* . . . said that *x* was relieved

Such an interpretation is impossible in (32a).

There is a crucial difference between variable binding and coreferentiality. Like the cases of binding discussed in section 1, variable binding is subject to c-command. If α and β belong to different sentences, this condition can never be met. Note that definite descriptions and proper names can also serve as variable binders (Reinhart 1983). However, since they are also referential and hence can be coreferential with some pronominal, the examples showing that one type of relation, namely variable binding, can break down are somewhat more complicated. Argumentation typically involves the interaction with VP-anaphora ("VP-deletion"). Consider (34):

(34)   [Bill liked his cat] and [Charley did too].

In such cases the second conjunct is dependent for its interpretation on the first conjunct. In the first conjunct, *his* can refer to Bill, Charley, or some other person. Depending on the choice in the first conjunct, we get for the second conjunct the interpretation that Charles liked Bill's cat, that Charles liked his (= Charley's) own cat, or that he liked that same other person's cat. What is impossible is the interpretation that Bill liked Charley's cat, and that Charley liked Bill's cat. An interpretation that is possible, however, is one in which Bill liked Bill's cat, and Charley liked Charley's cat. This state of affairs can only be captured by the hypothesis that *his* is either interpreted referentially or as a variable. If *his* is interpreted referentially, it is treated as a constant, and this constant is copied into the second conjunct, enforcing an identical interpretation (a "strict reading"); if it is a bound variable that property is copied, and the locally available binder provides its value (a "sloppy reading").[8] This is represented in (35):

(35) a. Bill λx (x liked *a*'s cat) & Charles λx (x liked *a*'s cat) (strict reading)
     b. Bill λx (x liked x's cat) & Charles λx (x liked x's cat) (sloppy reading)

Since the sloppy reading crucially involves variable binding, it requires that the antecedent c-command the pronoun. This is illustrated in (36):

(36) [Most of *her* friends adore *Lucie*] and [Zelda too]
     a. Lucie's friends adore Zelda
     b. NOT: Zelda's friends adore Zelda (Zelda (λx (x's friends adore x)))

It may be concluded that there are at least two types of anaphora. In the case of bound variable anaphora the anaphoric relation involves a dependency that is reflected in the interpretive process; this means that it is linguistically encoded. In the case of coreferentiality, a dependency, in so far as it can be observed at all, is not linguistically encoded. This raises an important question with respect to the relation between binding and indexing: is coindexing between two expressions necessary in order for them to be assigned the same value in the domain of discourse? It is widely accepted that this cannot be the case. A sentence such as *the morning star is the evening star* is not a tautology, even when it is known that both expressions denote Venus. Consider also a discourse such as (37) (Evans 1980):

(37) What does John feel about the murderer of his wife? Oh, I'm sure he hates him.

(37) is perfectly acceptable in the reading where *he* and *him* refer to the same individual, i.e., in a case John has actually murdered his wife but suffers from amnesia. It is certainly not a binding theory violation, which it would be if *John, the murderer of his wife, he,* and *him* were to carry the same index. Now, in cases like these one still might attempt a story, for instance invoking a difference between intended and non-intended reference. In cases such as (38) from Reinhart (1983) even this will not work:

(38) I know what Bill and Mary have in common. Mary adores Bill and *Bill* adores *him* too.

Here, clearly *Bill* and *him* are intended to corefer, yet there is no violation of condition B. There are two conclusions to be drawn from these facts. (i) If indices are to be relevant for Binding Theory, coreference cannot imply coindexing even if the implication does hold in the other direction. Rather, whatever coindexing precisely is, it must reflect only relations that are encoded by processes internal to the grammar, and not by processes relating linguistic expressions with elements in the knowledge base. (ii) If, in interpreting pronominals, directly accessing the knowledge base can "circumvent" the binding conditions, some other principle must guarantee that under most conditions condition B effects are visible nevertheless.[9] This issue is extensively discussed in Reinhart (1983), and Grodzinsky and Reinhart (1993). They argue that the choice of how a pronominal is to be interpreted is governed by the following condition:[10]

(39)   **Rule I: Intrasentential Coreference**
NP A cannot corefer with NP B if replacing A with C, C a variable A-bound by B, yields an indistinguishable interpretation.

In the case under consideration, using coreference is allowed, since the property Mary and Bill have in common is *Bill*-adoration. This property is distinct from that of SELF-adoration, which would have been ascribed to Bill if *himself* had been used in the second conjunct. No such contrast is involved in the various cases where we have seen standard condition B effects. Rule I is like a traffic rule governing which procedure will be used if two NPs are to be assigned the same value.

4   Long Distance Anaphora and Logophoricity

There is considerable variation in the domains in which anaphors must be bound, both across languages and, for anaphors of different types, within the same language. Certain anaphors may allow their first antecedent in a position considerably beyond the governing category as computed by (10). In standard Binding Theory there is no other way of describing the fact that languages differ with respect to binding phenomena than by either assuming that the anaphors themselves have different properties, or formulating parameters such as those in (40) from Manzini and Wexler (1987):

(40)   a.   a is a governing category for b iff a is the minimal category which contains b and PARAMETER.
b.   PARAMETER-values: has (i) a subject, (ii) an INFL, (iii) a Tense, (iv) an indicative Tense, (v) a root Tense.

Another line of research focussed on the classification of anaphoric elements. Should we abandon the simple anaphor/pronominal distinction in favor of a more elaborate distinction? This immediately triggered the question of whether we have to distinguish several types of reflexivization.

There is by now an extensive literature on long distance anaphora in a wide range of languages (see Reuland and Koster 1991 for an overview and discussion).[11] However, the importance of long distance anaphora for linguistic theory was first noted when Thráinsson (1976) discussed the Icelandic anaphor *sig*. He argued that Icelandic had a non-clause bounded rule, which is sensitive to semantic factors that do not seem to play any role in the "normal" clause bounded rule. Since that time Icelandic long distance phenomena have been extensively studied. That is why in this overview we will concentrate on Icelandic. The discussion of the Icelandic data also allows to discuss most relevant issues on this point.

As outlined in Thráinsson (1976), *sig* in Icelandic may take a long distance antecedent when the clause that contains *sig* is infinitive or subjunctive (i.e., the antecedent may be beyond the nearest c-commanding subject). However, if *sig* is contained in an indicative clause, it can only refer to the local antecedent. This is exemplified in (41):[12]

(41) a.   Jón$_j$ skipaði Pétri$_i$ [að PRO$_i$ raka sig$_{i,j,*k}$ á hverjum degi]
           John ordered Peter to shave-Inf himself every day
           "John ordered Peter to shave him every day"
      b.   Jón$_j$ segir [að Pétur$_i$ raki sig$_{i,j,*k}$ á hverjum degi]
           John says that Peter shave-Subj himself every day
           "John says that Peter shaves him every day"
      c.   Jón$_j$ veit [að Pétur$_i$ rakar sig$_{i,*j,*k}$ á hverjum degi]
           John knows that Peter shaves-Ind himself every day
           "John knows that Peter shaves him every day"

Various proposals have been developed to account for the long distance use of Icelandic *sig* in sentences like (41a) and (41b). These proposals can be divided into two groups according on their approach to the long distance subjunctive case. One group of approaches assumes a unified syntactic analysis of all cases of long distance *sig*, both in subjunctives and in infinitives (for instance, Anderson 1986, Everaert 1986, Harbert 1983, Koster 1987, Wexler and Manzini 1987, Pica 1987).

The other approach to long distance anaphora in Icelandic maintains that discourse factors rather than (or at least in addition to) syntactic principles rule the long distance use of *sig* out of subjunctives. Under this approach long distance *sig* is analyzed as *logophoric*. The term "logophoric" is introduced in Hagège (1974), and further elaborated in Clements (1975). It is used to characterize a class of pronouns that refer to the *"auteur d'un discours"* (the "source of a discourse" in the terms of Clements 1975).

Hagège observes that many languages have a formally distinct series of pronouns for this type of use (for instance, Mundang, Tuburi, and Ewe from the Niger–Congo family). The discourse function of such logophoric pronouns is similar to that of what traditional grammarians called *indirect reflexives*, of which the unbound use of Icelandic *sig* to be discussed below is an example. Since these pronouns bear no formal resemblance to reflexives, Hagège considers the term "indirect reflexive" inappropriate, and coins the term "logophoric." Whereas Hagège explicitly distinguishes free anaphors (indirect reflexives) from logophoric pronouns, Clements extends the notion of logophoricity so as to include free anaphors.

Clements gives the following crosslinguistic characterization of logophoric pronouns (Clements 1975: 171–2):

(i)   logophoric pronouns are restricted to reportive contexts transmitting the words or thought of an individual or individuals other than the speaker narrator;

(ii) the antecedent does not occur in the same reportive context as the logophoric pronoun;

(iii) the antecedent designates the individual or individuals whose words or thoughts are transmitted in the reported context in which the logophoric pronoun occurs.

It is this characterization that sets the tone for much of the subsequent discussion of long distance *sig* in Icelandic.

Thráinsson (1976, 1990), Maling (1984), Rögnvaldsson (1986), Sigurðsson (1990), and Sigurjónsdóttir (1992) observe that the antecedent possibilities of long distance *sig* in subjunctives are constrained not by structural conditions such as c-command but rather by discourse factors such as perspective or point of view.[13] Also, as pointed out by Thráinsson (1976, 1990), the presence of a subjunctive complement is not enough to license long distance use of *sig*. Thus, only a certain type of subjunctive allows *sig* to take a long distance antecedent, in particular, subjunctives which imply "a report from the higher subject's 'point of view'" (Thráinsson 1976: 229). Subjunctives that state a fact about the matrix subject and do not convey the higher subject's perspective or point of view, on the other hand, do not allow *sig* to be coindexed with the matrix subject:

(42) *Hann$_i$ einsetti sér ad segja sannleikann pegar dómarinn sagdi sér$_i$ hvada refsing væri
He determined himself to tell the truth when the judge told himself what the penalties were
[He resolved to tell the truth when the judge told him what the penalties would be]

Thus, it seems as if discourse information can only be accessed if there is a subjunctive. If it can, it still has to be of the "right kind."

Long distance *sig* in subjunctives in Icelandic can sometimes take as its antecedent a non-c-commanding NP. *Jón* can serve as the antecedent for *sig* in sentences like (43) from Maling (1984), although it does not c-command the anaphor:[14]

(43) [$_{NP}$ Skoðun Jóns$_i$] er [að sig$_i$ vanti hæfileika]
Opinion John's is that himself-Acc lacks-Subj talent
"John's opinion is that he lacks talent"

If *sig* in embedded subjunctives is ruled by discourse factors, we expect that the derived subject of a passive should not be able to serve as an antecedent for *sig*. A derived subject does not usually carry the perspective or point of view of the sentence (Maling 1984, Sigurðsson 1990, Reuland and Sigurjónsdóttir 1997), as is illustrated in (44):

(44) a. Jón$_i$ sagði Pétri$_j$ [að ég elskaði sig$_{i,*j}$]
          John told Peter that I loved-Subj himself
          "John told Peter that I loved SIG"
      b. *Pétri$_j$ var sagt (af Jóni$_i$) [að ég elskaði sig$_{*i,*j}$]
          Peter was told (by John) that I loved-Subj himself
          "Peter was told (by John) that I loved him"

In (44a) *sig* takes the perspective holding subject *Jón* as its antecedent, but in the passive sentence in (44b), where neither *Jón* nor *Pétur* bears the perspective of the sentence, *sig* cannot refer to the c-commanding subject or to the object of the *by*-phrase.

In this approach, cases of long distance anaphora that do not involve subjunctive are only subject to structural conditions, and the interpretation of *sig* in such cases is neither independently constrained nor licensed by discourse factors. Thus, where the c-command requirement is not met but the sentence contains a perspective holding NP as a potential antecedent, *sig* in infinitives should not be able to refer back to this NP. As we see in (45), this prediction is borne out, i.e., *sig* in infinitives cannot take a non-c-commanding NP as an antecedent, even if it is a possible perspective holder. Thus, for *sig* in infinitival clauses, discourse factors are unable to compensate for the lack of c-command. This contrasts with the situation in subjunctives discussed earlier. If the antecedent of *sig* in infinitives is only constrained by structural conditions, we expect the derived subject of a passive should be a possible antecedent for *sig*, since the subject c-commands *sig*, even if it is not a perspective holder. This is indeed the case, as witnessed by (46):

(45) *[$_{NP}$ Skoðun Jóns$_i$]$_j$ virðist [e$_j$ vera hættuleg fyrir sig$_i$]
      Opinion John's seems be-Inf dangerous for himself-Acc
      "John's opinion seems to be dangerous for him"

(46) María$_j$ var sögð (af Jóni$_i$) [e$_j$ hafa látið [mig þvo sér$_{j,*i}$]]
      Mary was said (by John) have-Inf made me wash-Inf SIG
      "Mary was said (by John) to have made me wash her (= Mary)"

To recapitulate, Reuland and Koster (1991) argue that, on a descriptive level, phenomena could be divided into three domains: short distance binding (cf. (47a), Dutch), medium distance binding (cf. (47b), Norwegian), and long distance binding (cf. (47c), Icelandic):

(47) a. Jan$_i$ wast zich$_i$/*hem$_i$
          Jan washes himself/him

    b.   Jon$_i$ bad oss hjelpe seg$_i$/ham$_i$
         John asked us help-Inf himself/him
         (John asked us to help him)
    c.   Jón$_i$ segir að Pétur elski sig$_i$/hann$_i$
         John says that Peter loves-Subj himself
         (John says that Peter loves him)

Both short distance binding and medium distance binding are syntactically governed, for instance requiring c-commanding antecedents, but differ in that anaphors and pronominals are in complementary distribution in short distance binding, but not in medium distance binding. Long distance binding should be distinguished from short and medium distance binding in that it is governed by discourse factors and not syntactically governed. More specifically, an anaphor that is long distance bound need not be c-commanded by its antecedent.

This leads to the question of what the relation between a long distance bound anaphor like *sig* and its antecedent is. Since Reinhart's (1983) work on anaphoric relations it has been established that syntactic binding requires c-command. What, then, about non-c-commanded *sig*? Does it not have to be bound, despite being an anaphor, or could we argue that it is bound despite appearances? The following contrast indicates that the latter option would lack independent support.

As discussed in Thráinsson (1991), the strict/sloppy identity ambiguity typically associated with pronouns also shows up with *sig* in the long distance subjunctive case. This can be illustrated as follows:

(48)   Jón$_i$ telur [að prófessorinn muni fella$_{subj}$ sig$_i$ á prófinu] og Ari$_j$ telur það líka
       John believes that the professor will . . .
       "John believes that the professor will fail SIG on the test and Ari believes
       so too"
       a.   = Ari believes that the professor will fail Ari on the test.
       b.   = Ari believes that the professor will fail John on the test.

However, the sloppy (i.e., bound) reading is not felicitous in cases where subjunctive *sig* is not c-commanded by its long distance antecedent. As Thráinsson puts it, in (49), the bound reading is more difficult if not impossible to get:

(49)   Skoðun Jóns$_i$ er [að sig$_i$ vanti hæfileika] og það er skoðun Péturs$_j$ líka
       Opinion John's is that SIG lacks-Subj talents and that is opinion Peter's too
       "John's opinion is that SIG lacks talents and that is Peter's opinion too"
       a.   ≠ Peter's opinion is that Peter lacks talents.
       b.   = Peter's opinion is that John lacks talents.

This is evidence that the relation between *Jón* and *sig* in (49) must be one of coreference, rather than syntactic binding.[15]

In fact, the situation is even more problematic for the view that *sig* must be bound. There are cases where *sig* may occur, and be interpreted, without any linguistic antecedent whatsoever. This is illustrated in (50) from Sigurðsson (1990: 317):

(50) María$_i$ var alltaf svo andstyggileg. Þegar Ólafur$_j$ kæmi segði hún sér$_{i/*j}$ áreiðanlega að fara.

. . .

Mary was always so nasty. When Olaf would come-Subj, she would certainly tell himself [the person whose thoughts are being presented – not Olaf] to leave.

Taking such examples seriously forces one to abandon the idea that anaphors must be syntactically bound for reasons of interpretability (see Reuland 1996, 1998a). This leads to two questions. (i) What principle governs the interpretation of anaphors when they are not syntactically bound? (ii) Why is the option of such an interpretation not always available? The first question is answered in Ariel (1990). Central in her theory is the notion of *accessibility*, which reflects the discourse prominence of an antecedent. On the basis of an investigation of cross-sentential anaphoric relations in actual texts, Ariel establishes that the degree of lexical specification of an element is inversely related to the accessibility of its discourse antecedent. Full NPs can be used anaphorically; but only felicitously if the discourse antecedent is low on the scale of accessibility. The felicitous use of pronouns requires a discourse antecedent that is more accessible.[16] An expression that is less specified, such as the Icelandic anaphor *sig*, should require a discourse antecedent that is even higher on the scale of accessibility (cf. n. 17). This is precisely what is reflected in the conditions on the logophoric interpretation of *sig* we discussed. We found structurally equivalent environments where a felicitous use of *sig* solely depended on the status of its antecedent in the discourse (cf. (44a) vs. (44b)).[17] Thus, the logophoric use of *sig* realizes an option that Ariel's theory predicts to exist. How, then, should we interpret the fact that *sig* in other than subjunctive contexts does require a syntactic binder?

It seems we have found a situation with respect to the binding requirement on anaphors (condition A) that is similar to that found earlier with respect to condition B. As observed, pronominals can be either bound by or coreferent with a c-commanding antecedent. The former situation is subject to condition B, the latter is not, potentially allowing condition B to be circumvented. Rule I acts as a traffic rule, giving priority to binding, and determining when it can be circumvented by a coreference strategy.

Precisely such a principle is needed for anaphor binding as well. A pronoun-type interpretation of "anaphors" is possible, but in most contexts anaphoric binding takes precedence. Again some traffic rule is needed to specify which option must be taken. In Reuland (1996, 1998a), elaborating on Reinhart and Reuland (1993) (see section 6), it is argued that the crucial property of syntactic anaphors is that they can be tails or intermediate members of syntactic chains. It is possible for an antecedent–anaphor relation to be syntactically encoded by chain formation, only exploiting properties of the computational system C_{HL} in the sense of Chomsky (1995b). Whenever there is a choice, using the computational system takes precedence over any other interpretive strategy. Only where the computational system has nothing to say can the effects of pragmatic conditions on interpretation be directly observed. The relevant principle can be stated as in (51):

(51) **Rule R: Variable interpretation**
      NP A cannot be interpreted as an argument/semantic variable if there is an NP B such that there is a derivation within C_{HL} yielding a chain <B, A>.[18]

An extensive discussion of how binding relations can be captured by the computational system, and to what extent, is given in Reuland (1996, 1998a). It would carry us beyond the scope of this overview to recapitulate that discussion. Let it suffice that in that discussion subjunctive morphology on the verb is argued to do precisely this: block chain formation between the subject and an anaphor such as *sig* in its domain (see the final section for some further discussion). To conclude, note that Rule R puts a different perspective on condition A; it effectively reduces it to conditions on chain formation. We will now proceed to the next challenge to standard Binding Theory.

5   Types of Anaphoric Expression

One of the major reasons to reassess the standard Binding Theory is provided by languages that divide the domain of binding relations in a rather different way than English. Such examples among languages abound. Cases that are reasonably well described include the Scandinavian languages,[19] Malayalam, Russian, Polish, Chinese, Japanese, and quite a few others. Here, we will focus on West Germanic, which despite being a closely related group of languages exhibits a very interesting diversity in anaphoric systems.[20]

There are, roughly speaking, four standard languages in this group, namely (i) English, (ii) Dutch, (iii) Frisian, and (iv) German, and it exemplifies as many different anaphoric systems. The systems differ both in the choice of anaphoric elements and in the environments in which (cognate) elements occur.

English has essentially provided the empirical basis for the standard Binding Theory with its simple two-way distinction between pronominals (*him*, etc.) and anaphors (*himself*, etc.). Nevertheless, as was already observed in Chomsky (1981), pronominals in locative PPs may be bound in their governing category, violating condition B, as in (52):

(52) John$_i$ saw a snake near him$_i$/?himself$_i$

As already noted in section 2, a variety of contexts allows anaphors to be free in their governing category in violation of condition A. This is illustrated in (53) (= (27)):

(53) a. There were five tourists in the room apart from myself.
      b. Physicists like yourself are a godsend.
      c. Max boasted that the queen invited Lucie and himself for a drink.

From the perspective of the standard Binding Theory, then, both the context in (52) and that in (53) are puzzling.

The Dutch system poses an additional challenge. Instead of having a binary pronominal/anaphor distinction it has a three-way distinction between pronominals (*hem* "him"), complex anaphors (*zichzelf* "himself"), and simplex anaphors (*zich*). A similar typology of anaphoric expressions is found in the Scandinavian languages (cf. Hellan 1988, Vikner 1985, Sigurjónsdóttir 1992), although there are some crucial distributional differences. *Zich* lacks a direct counterpart in English, and it and similar elements will be referred to and glossed as SE(-anaphors). Complex anaphors will also be referred to as SELF-anaphors. The system is illustrated in (54)–(55). In local binding environments, the occurrence of the simplex anaphor versus the complex anaphor correlates with lexical properties of the verbs (as is shown by Everaert 1986). If the predicate is inherently reflexive, as in (54), the simplex anaphor occurs. If it is not, the complex anaphor is used, as in (55):

(54) Max$_i$ gedraagt zich$_i$/*zichzelf$_i$/*hem$_i$
      Max behaves SE/himself/*him (meaning: Max behaves)

(55) a. Max$_i$ haat zichzelf$_i$/*zich$_i$/*hem$_i$
          Max hates himself/*SE/*him
      b. Max$_i$ praat met zichzelf$_i$/*zich$_i$/*hem$_i$
          Max speaks with himself/*SE/*him

The verb *gedragen* "behave" in (54) is intrinsically reflexive. This is witnessed by the fact that it cannot take any object distinct in reference from the subject. Certain verbs, like *wassen* "wash," are doubly listed in the lexicon, both as reflexive and as transitive: they clearly allow non-reflexive usage as in *Jan wast Marie* "John is washing Mary." However, without any marking (56a) allows a reflexive interpretation, but (56b), with a different verb, does not:

(56) a. Wassen is gezond
          Washing (oneself) is healthy
      b. Haten is ongezond
          Hating (only someone else) is unhealthy

A way to capture this contrast is by assuming a lexical difference between verbs like *wassen* and verbs like *haten*. For *wassen* there is both an inherently reflexive and a transitive entry, and *haten* has only a transitive entry. It is the reflexive entry for *wassen*, which allows the SE-anaphor. Its transitive entry occurs with a SELF-anaphor, as witnessed in (57):

(57)   Max$_i$ wast zich$_i$/zichzelf$_i$/*hem$_i$
       Max washes SE/himself/*him

This class of verbs, then, allows either anaphor type, unlike the purely transitive verbs such as *haten* "hate" or *praten met* "speak with," which require a complex anaphor unconditionally.

SE-anaphors also occur in locative PPs. Here, in many varieties of Dutch, they are in free variation with bound pronominals:

(58)   Max$_i$ legt het boek achter zich$_i$/hem$_i$
       Max puts the book behind SE/him

Such a relation between lexical properties of predicates and the distribution of anaphors is entirely unexpected from the perspective of the standard Binding Theory.

The following set of facts is even more puzzling. Frisian has, like English, a two-way distinction between pronominals (*him* "him") and anaphors (*himsels* "himself"), but the distribution of the pronominal is quite different from English: bound *him* occurs wherever Dutch has the anaphor *zich* or the pronominal *hem*. This is illustrated in (59)–(62):

(59)   Max$_i$ hâld him$_i$/*himsels$_i$
       Max behaves him

(60)   a.   Max$_i$ hatet himsels$_i$/*him$_i$
            Max hates himself/*him
       b.   Max$_i$ pratet mei himsels$_i$/*him$_i$
            Max speaks with himself/*him

(61)   Max$_i$ wasket him$_i$/himsels$_i$
       Max washes him/himself

(62)   Max$_i$ leit it boek efter him$_i$
       Max puts the book behind him

This pattern calls into question the very core of condition B, since (61) suffices to demonstrate that it is impossible to define a notion of governing category such that the subject is included in that of the anaphor, and excluded from that of the pronominal. Similar facts are found in Creole languages (Muysken 1993, Déchaine and Manfredi 1994), Flemish dialects and Afrikaans (cf. Everaert 1986). Older stages of English have pronominals in many positions where Modern

English requires anaphors, and thus seem to behave as Frisian (Van Gelderen to appear).

German, finally, we will claim has, again, a ternary system: a pronominal *ihn* "him," and two anaphors, a simplex anaphor *sich* and and a complex anaphor which, at least in some environments, surfaces as *sich selbst* "himself." Whereas the locally bound pronominal is ruled out in all cases of (63) and (64), and the inherent reflexives of (63) admit *sich*, a distinction between inherent and non-inherent reflexives shows up in (64), as in Dutch and Frisian:

(63) a. Max$_i$ benimmt sich$_i$/*ihn$_i$ (gut)
          Max behaves himself (well)
      b. Max$_i$ wäscht sich$_i$/*ihn$_i$
          Max$_i$ washes himself/*him

(64) a. Peter$_i$ stellte sich$_i$/??sichselbst$_i$ die Statue vor
          Peter imagined (to-himself-Dat) the statue-Prt
      b. ?*Peter$_i$ vertraute sich$_i$ seine Tochter an
          Peter entrusted to-himself-Dat his daughter-Prt
      c. Peter$_i$ vertraute seine Tochter nur sichselbst$_i$ an
          Peter entrusted his daughter only to-himself-Dat-Prt

However, unlike in Dutch and Frisian, in other than prepositionless dative contexts this distinction is not reflected in the surface form of the anaphor. Thus, in many contexts, where Dutch requires *zichzelf*, German allows *sich*, as illustrated in (65):

(65) a. Max$_i$ hasst sich$_i$/*ihn$_i$
          Max hates himself/*him
      b. Max$_i$ spricht mit sich$_i$/*ihn$_i$
          Max speaks with himself/*him

Moreover, in locative PPs *sich* is required, and the pronominal disallowed, as illustrated in (66):

(66) Max$_i$ legt das Buch hinter sich$_i$/*ihn
      Max puts the book behind himself/*him

The question is then what might cause such variation.

All this is hard to reconcile with the original binding conditions A and B. Three major questions arise from these facts. (i) How can the exceptions to binding condition A in English be accounted for? (ii) How can the contrast between simplex and complex anaphors be captured? (iii) How can a system like Frisian be understood with its pervasive violation of the standard condition B? These questions will be taken up in the next section.

6   Reflexivity

Reinhart and Reuland (1993) propose that there are two modules regulating the distribution of anaphors/pronominals. Configurational effects are due to chain formation, while the domain of reflexivization is defined over predicates without making reference to syntactic structure. Furthermore, there is no simple distinction between anaphors and pronouns. NPs are partitioned into three classes according to the properties [SELF] and R: SELF-anaphors (+SELF, –R), e.g. English *himself*; SE-anaphors (–SELF, –R), e.g. Norwegian *seg*; and pronouns/R-expressions (–SELF, +R), e.g. Norwegian *ham*. Being marked [+SELF] means that an element is able to reflexivize the predicate. The property R reflects whether or not an anaphoric expression is fully specified for phi-features. Both what we are used to call reflexives or pronouns could be –R or +R. What counts is feature specification in relation to the paradigm it is part of. This will have consequences for its ability to form a chain with other coindexed elements, as will be explained below. In the remainder of this section we will focus on Dutch and Frisian, but the analyses will, grosso modo, hold for the other languages mentioned above.

The distribution of simplex and complex anaphors in Dutch follows from the interaction between coindexing and properties or predicates. Simplex anaphors are allowed in the following environments in Dutch: (i) as the bound argument of an inherently reflexive verb (54), here repeated; (ii) as the bound argument of a locative or directional PP (58), here repeated; and (iii) as the bound subject of an ECM construction (67).[21]

(54)   Max$_i$ gedraagt zich$_i$
       Max behaves SE (meaning: Max behaves)

(58)   Max$_i$ legt het boek achter zich$_i$
       Max puts the book behind SE

(67)   Max$_i$ voelde [zich$_i$ wegglijden]
       Max felt [SE slide away]

What environments (58) and (67) have in common is that the coindexing does not involve arguments of the same predicate. The coindexed elements in (54) are arguments of the same predicate. (55), here repeated, shows that using the coindexed anaphoric element *zich* does not always lead to a reflexive predicate. In these cases using the complex anaphor is necessary:

(55)   a.   Max$_i$ haat zichzelf$_i$/*zich$_i$
            Max hates himself/*SE
       b.   Max$_i$ praat met zichzelf$_i$/*zich$_i$
            Max speaks with himself/*SE

The predicate in (54) is reflexive anyway. So, intuitively, what (58) and (67) have in common with (54) is precisely this: the coindexing does not cause a predicate to become reflexive. In none of these cases is a complex anaphor required. Intuitively, then, what sets (55) apart from the other cases is that in (55) coindexing causes the predicate to become reflexive. To put it differently, it seems as if adding SELF to the anaphor compensates for the lack of inherent reflexivity in the verb. In some sense this puts SELF and inherent reflexivity on a par. Reflexivity, then, is a property of predicates that must be linguistically licensed, either inherently, or by marking the anaphor with SELF. We will refer to this licensing as *reflexive marking*.

In order to make this precise, we need to characterize both *predicate* and *reflexive predicate*. The full set of definitions can now be given as follows (for reasons to be made clear later, we need to distinguish the notions *syntactic predicate* and *semantic predicate*):

(68) a. The *syntactic predicate* of (a head) P is P, all its syntactic arguments, and an external argument of P (subject). The *syntactic argument* of P are the projections assigned theta-role or Case by P.

  b. The *semantic predicate* of P is P and all its arguments at the relevant semantic level.

  c. A predicate is *reflexive* iff two of its arguments are coindexed.

  d. A predicate (of P) is *reflexive-marked* iff either P is lexically reflexive or one of P's arguments is a SELF-anaphor.

We can now formulate the following conditions on reflexive predicates:

(69) a. A reflexive-marked (*syntactic*) predicate is reflexive.

  b. A reflexive (*semantic*) predicate is reflexive-marked.

As we mentioned above, not all elements that are traditionally called *reflexives* are *reflexive markers* in the sense intended here. The following table summarizes the relevant properties of the elements involved:

(70)

	SELF	SE	PRONOUN
Reflexivizing function:	+	−	−
R(eferential independence):	−	−	+

Ignoring, for the moment, the distinction between semantic and syntactic predicates as expressed in the italicized parts of (69), the reader can now easily verify that the pattern observed in Dutch follows from the conditions stated. In (54) and (57) the predicate is lexically reflexive (cf. (68d)) and thus reflexive marked, satisfying conditions A/B. In (58) and (67) the predicate(s) are not reflexive marked, so condition A does not apply. Condition B does not apply either in these cases because the predicate, *achter* "behind" in (58) and *wegglijden* "to slide away" in (67), is not reflexive, i.e., does not contain two coindexed arguments. In (55) the predicate is reflexive marked if the *zichzelf* reflexive is chosen; the *zich* and *hem-variants* in (55) are not allowed because the predicate would then be reflexive but not reflexive marked.

6.1   Locally bound pronouns

Turning now to the Frisian examples (59)–(62), here repeated, we see that bound *him* occurs wherever Dutch has the anaphor *zich* or the pronominal *hem*. Ignoring the latter (cf. (62)), the distribution of *himsels* versus *him* is essentially identical to the distribution of *zichzelf* versus *zich*, cf. (59) and (61). To put it differently, whatever may be different, the conditions on reflexive marking are precisely the same in Dutch and Frisian. Again, the odd one out requiring explicit SELF-marking are the non-reflexive predicates like *haatsje* "hate" or *prate mei* "speak with" in (60):

(59)   Max$_i$ hâld him$_i$/*himsels$_i$
  Max behaves him

(60)   a.   Max$_i$ hatet himsels$_i$/*him$_i$
   Max hates himself/*him
  b.   Max$_i$ pratet mei himsels$_i$/*him$_i$
   Max speaks with himself/*him

(61)   Max$_i$ wasket him$_i$/himsels$_i$
  Max washes him/himself

(62)   Max$_i$ leit it boek efter him$_i$
  Max puts the book behind him

So far, this leaves us with two puzzles. (i) What rules out a locally bound pronominal in Dutch (and German)? (ii) What allows a locally bound pronominal in Frisian? Note that Binding condition B as formulated in (69) does not say anything about this issue. It just says that a reflexive predicate must be licensed. Although it correctly rules out the examples in (71), it incorrectly rules in the examples in (72)–(73). In (72) the predicate is lexically reflexive and reflexive; thus the binding conditions are satisfied, and in (73) no predicate is reflexive or reflexive marked and, thus, the binding conditions are vacuously satisfied:

(71)   a.   *Max$_i$ haat hem$_i$ (= 55a)
  b.   *Max$_i$ haat zich$_i$ (= 55a)
   Max hates him/himself

(72)   *Max$_i$ gedraagt hem$_i$ (= 54)
  Max behaves him

(73) *Max$_i$ voelde [hem$_i$ wegglijden]
      Max felt him slide away

Suppose we ignore Frisian, for the moment, what principle of grammar could be involved? A crucial difference between *zich* and *hem* is that the latter is fully specified for phi-features, whereas the former is not. *Zich* lacks a specification for number and gender. Inspired by the notion of a government chain in Everaert (1990), the notion of a syntactic chain can be extended so as to include any appropriate sequence of coindexation (satisfying c-command and with no barrier between any of the links), regardless of whether its links and its foot are lexical or empty (trace), dropping the stipulation that at most the head of an A-chain is non-empty. So, an A-chain is defined as in (74):

(74) **Generalized Chain definition**
      $C = (\alpha_1, \ldots, \alpha_n)$ is a chain iff C is the maximal sequence such that
      i.   there is an index i such that for all j, $1 \le j \le n$, α_j carries that index, and
      ii. for all j, $1 \le j < n$, α_j governs α_{j+1}.

Under the definition of (74) all syntactic domains in which a moved NP can bind its trace instantiate A-chains. So, all the configurations in (54), (55), and (57) are A-chains regardless of whether the tail contains a pronominal or an anaphor. Clearly, we must characterize a smaller class of such objects as well formed. But unlike the approach of Chomsky (1981 and subsequent work), which incorporates a well-formedness requirement into the definition, in accordance with Reinhart and Reuland (1993) the well-formedness of such objects can be considered a separate issue. In order to be well formed, then, A-chains must obey the condition that their tail is underspecified for at least one phi-feature. As Bouchard (1984) hypothesized that independent reference requires a full specification for phi-features, let us now understand the property +R of pronominals as standing for the morphosyntactic property of being fully specified for phi-features. Conversely, −R stands for being underspecified for (at least) one phi-feature:[22]

(75) An NP is +R iff it carries a full specification for phi-features (gender, number, person) and structural Case.

On the basis of (75) Reinhart and Reuland (1993) formulate the following well-formedness condition on chains:

(76) **Condition on A-chains**
      A maximal A-chain $(\alpha_1, \ldots, \alpha_n)$ contains exactly one link – α_1 – which is +R.

What grammatical A-chains then have in common is that the tail (all links and the foot) consists of −R NPs. So, *Max$_i$ gedraagt zich$_i$* is well formed because the tail of the chain, *zich*, is −R. *Max_i haat hem_i*, then, violates not only condition B, but also the chain condition. *Max_i gedraagt hem_i* and *Max_i voelde [hem_i wegglijden]*, on the other hand, violate the chain condition only. Whereas this might look like an unwarranted overlap between condition B and the chain condition, in fact, sentences violating two conditions are worse than those only violating one condition, in line with what should be expected if two different conditions are involved, as discussed extensively in Reinhart and Reuland (1993).[23]

What, then, about Frisian? The logic of the approach dictates what should be the case: there should be a dimension in which Frisian pronominals are underspecified and their Dutch counterparts are not. There is independent evidence that this is in fact the case.

In order to see this, first consider the pronominal system of Frisian in some more detail. Two pronominals, namely the 3rd person singular feminine and the 3rd person plural (common gender), have two object forms: both have *har* as well as *se*.[24] Often, they are used interchangeably. This is illustrated in (77):

(77) a.   Jan hat har juster sjoen
           John has her/them yesterday seen
      b.   Jan hat se juster sjoen
           John has her/them yesterday seen

However, *se* is ungrammatical when it is locally bound:

(78) $Marie_i$ wasket $harsels_i$/har_i/*se_i
       Mary washes herself/her

The ungrammaticality of the sentences with bound *se* shows that, for *se*, the chain condition works in Frisian as it does in Dutch. Therefore, we have to explain in what respects *har* is different.

Jarich Hoekstra (1994) has shown that *har* and *se* differ in Case. He concludes that the difference between *se* and *har* is that *se* requires structural Case, whereas *har* is licensed with inherent Case.[25] In accordance with Chomsky (1992), we may assume that structural Case is Case that is assigned by the agreement system. Inherent Case is then Case that is licensed under government by a lexical projection. Suppose, then, that the feature +R should be understood as requiring a full specification for *structural Case*. If so, the Dutch–Frisian contrast has nothing to do with Binding Theory. It just reflects a contrast in the Case system, which is entirely insignificant in most respects. Only, it affects the sensitivity of certain pronominal forms to the chain condition, and thus, more or less accidentally, it enlarges their potential to be locally bound.

This is, then, characteristic of the present approach to binding. Binding, chain formation, etc. are all very general processes. So is Case assignment/checking. Only, due to interaction, variations that are insignificant by themselves may yield results that are baffling on the basis of standard Binding Theory, but which become insignificant again when put into their proper perspective.

6.2   *Non-locally bound anaphors*

So far we have focussed on standard condition B phenomena, teasing them apart into effects of the revised condition B involving a property of predicates, and the chain condition. The last major puzzle involves violations of the standard condition A in English. Reconsider the following examples discussed in section ((27) = (53)):

(27)   a.   There were five tourists in the room apart from myself.
     b.   Physicists like yourself are a godsend.
     c.   Max boasted that the queen invited Lucie and himself for a drink.

In order to understand why they escape a local binding requirement the italicized parts of the revised binding conditions (69) come into play. (68d) states that a SELF-anaphor reflexive marks the predicate it is an argument of. The revised condition A then says that a syntactic predicate with the formal property of being reflexive marked must in fact have two coindexed arguments, otherwise it is marked ill formed. However, what the anaphors *myself, yourself,* and *himself* have in common is that none of them is a syntactic argument of the predicate as defined in (68a). In (27a) *apart from myself* is an adjunct, in (27b) the subject argument of the predicate formed of *be* is *physicists like yourself,* and in (27c) the object argument is *Lucie and himself.* To elaborate on the latter, it is true that there is some sense in which both *Lucie* and *himself* are arguments of *invite,* namely a semantic sense. But the syntactic object, in the sense of the constituent receiving Case, a theta-role, the constituent possibly subject to A-movement, is just the coordinated structure as a whole.

Thus, not being an argument of the syntactic predicate gives a precise reconstruction of the notion of an *exempt anaphor* discussed in Pollard and Sag (1992). Such elements, although they have the morphosyntactic form of an anaphor, need not enter a binding relation in order to be interpreted. Rather, just like Icelandic *sig* in subjunctive contexts, their interpretation is sensitive to pragmatic factors, as illustrated by the following contrast discussed by Pollard and Sag:

(79)   a.   John$_i$ was going to get even with Mary. That picture of himself$_i$ in the paper would really annoy her, as would the other stunts he had planned.
     b.   *Mary was quite taken aback by the publicity John$_i$ was receiving. That picture of himself$_i$ in the paper had really annoyed her, and there was not much she could do about it.

Structurally both text fragments are on a par. What is different is the perspective on the sentence containing the anaphor.

Given the line taken in section 3 on the division of labor between syntax, semantics, and pragmatics, the definition of reflexive marking and the revised condition A are only first steps. What is needed is to establish a relation between reflexive marking and a specific syntactic computation that is blocked in case the SELF-anaphor is not a syntactic argument of the predicate involved. A possible candidate is covert head movement, moving SELF onto the head of the predicate. It is easily seen that such movement would indeed be blocked in the cases under consideration. However, at this point no final conclusions will be drawn.

We have now seen that condition A needs to be stated in terms of syntactic predicates. So far, we have not discussed the necessity to state condition B in terms of semantic predicates. This following asymmetry will establish this need:

(80)   a.   The queen$_i$ invited both Max and herself$_i$ to our party
       b.   *The queen$_i$ invited both Max and her$_i$ to our party

The anaphor in (80a) is in an exempt position; it is nevertheless in complementary distribution with a pronoun, as we see in (80b). So, how does condition B block anaphora in (80b)? At either S-structure or LF, the predicates in (80) are not defined as reflexive, since the coindexed NPs are not coarguments of *invite* (the anaphoric expression being embedded). However, if we look at a more abstract level of semantic interpretation, the conjunction in (80) is interpreted as something equivalent to the representation in (81):

(81)   The queen (λx (x invited Max & x invited X))

This representation does contain a reflexive predicate (*x invited x*) as one of its conjuncts. If condition B applies at the stage of mapping from LF to semantic representations, like (81), it finds that in (80a), one of the arguments of this new semantic predicate which is about to be formed is, appropriately, realized in the syntax (LF) as a SELF anaphor. But in (80b), no argument is a SELF-anaphor in the syntax, so the reflexive translation is disallowed and the derivation is filtered out.

To capture such cases, then, condition B must operate on semantic predicates (i.e., at the stage of translating syntactic predicates into semantic ones). A further illustration of the relevance of semantic predicates is given by the contrasts in (82) and (83):

(82)   a.   Max$_i$ convinced both Lucie and him$_i$ [PRO to leave early]
       b.   Max$_i$ expected [both Lucie and him$_i$ to leave early]

(83)   a.   John$_i$ looked at Sally and him$_i$ together in the mirror
       b.   *John$_i$ looked at Sally and then him$_i$ in the mirror

In both (82a) and (82b) the constituent *both Lucy and him* is a syntactic argument of the predicate formed of the matrix verb; in (82a) both for reasons of Case and theta, in (82b) only for reasons of Case. In (82a) *him* (in addition to *Lucy*) is a semantic argument of *convinced*. Hence a semantic reflexive predicate is formed, which must be licensed. It is, thus, that the sentence is unacceptable under the given indexing. In (82b) the semantic object argument of *expect* is the lower clause, not *him* or *Lucy*, which means that under the given indexing no reflexive semantic argument is formed. Condition B is not violated, and the sentence is well formed.

In (83) the presence of *together* seems to force a collective interpretation for the conjunction, and the reflexive or the pronoun is permitted, while the presence of *then* in (83b) forces a distributive interpretation of the conjuncts. In accord with the notion of a semantic predicate, there would be two such predicates in (83b), forcing Condition B to come into play, accounting for its ungrammaticality.

Note that the "disjoint reference" discussed in section 2 (cf. (29)) provides independent support for the relevance of semantic predicates for condition B.

Consider how anaphora should be ruled out in (84), comparing this to (85) and (86):

(84) a. *We$_2$ voted for me$_1$
      b. *[Felix and Lucie$_1$]$_2$ praised her$_1$

(86) was observed as grammatical by Fiengo and May (1990), and the (85) cases are better, for many speakers, than (84):

(85) a. We elected me
      b. Felix and Lucie$_1$ authorized her$_1$ to be their representative

(86) Max$_1$ and Lucie talked about him$_1$

The factor determining acceptability seems to be semantic as well. While (84a, b) prefer a distributive interpretation of the plural set, (85a, b) force a collective interpretation only. This can also be verified by comparing (86) with (87):

(87) *Both Max$_1$ and Lucie talked about him$_1$

Both, in (87), forces the distributive reading (so it entails two separate acts of talking, by Max, and by Lucie). In (86), the preferred interpretation is the collective, suggesting an act of mutual talking. So this type of anaphora is excluded only under the distributive reading, and anaphora enforces the collective reading (which, for some speakers, is possible also in (84) and (87)). The interpretations of (86) and (87) are approximated in (88a, b):

(88) a. Max and Lucie (λx (x talked about him))
      b. Max (λx (x talked about x)) & Lucie (λx (x talked about him))

Under the collective interpretation in (88a), the predicate is not distributed over the two NPs in the subject, but rather, they are taken as one set. This way, no reflexive predicate is formed. Under the distributive interpretation in (88b), one of the predicates (*x talked about x*) is reflexive. None of its arguments has been reflexive marked, so condition B blocks the derivation.

The distributive interpretation of (84a) (**We voted for me*) will also contain a reflexive predicate (*x voted for x*) whose argument is one of the members of the *we*-set (i.e., *me*) which is ruled out, since *me* is not SELF-marked.

All these results are quite unexpected under any account that does not make a distinction between semantic and syntactic predicates and they show, furthermore, that condition B applies to semantic predicates.

7   Conclusion and Beyond

With the introduction of Chomsky's *Minimalist Program* the perspective on interpretive dependencies radically changes. The computational system manipulates morphological objects (lexical items and features) by Merge and Move/Attract. Dependencies are the result of Move/Attract and checking relations triggered by properties of features. Since indices are not morphological objects, it is not clear how they can be manipulated by the computational system. According to Chomsky indices are basically the expression of a relationship and they should be replaceable without loss by a structural account of the relation they annotate (Chomsky 1995b: 217). Since much of Binding Theory does indeed take indices as theoretical entities, there lies ahead the huge task of finding ways to encode anaphoric dependencies with the mechanisms available within the computational system (C_{HL}). It means that "dependency derived by coindexation" must be replaced by "dependency derived by movement." Reuland (1996, 1998a) explores ways of doing this. In essence it is shown that independently existing dependencies such as *subject–verb agreement, assignment of structural case*, and *V–I relations* which can be represented by movement forced by checking requirements can in principle be composed by a chain linking operation in the sense of Chomsky (1995b). That is, an object anaphor is linked to a verb and the verb's inflectional system by structural Case, the verb is linked to its functional system, and the functional V-system in turn is linked to the subject. In a case such as (67) a linked chain is formed between *Max* and *zich*, mediated by these relations, as in (89):

(67) Max_i voelde [zich_i wegglijden]
       Max felt [SE slide away]

(89)   Max   I   V   zich

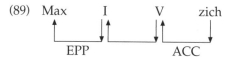

       EPP   ACC

It is argued that grammatical number on the object blocks the process of chain composition (accounting for the contrast between (67) and (73)), and that also verbal morphology such as the Icelandic subjunctive will have this effect (see the discussion at the end of section 4). Given the exploratory status of this work, for present purposes these brief remarks will have to suffice.

Not all interpretive dependencies can be brought under such a mechanism, however. For sure, also semantic and pragmatic principles must be involved that are outside C_{HL}. Some authors, in fact, explore such principles as full scale alternatives, for instance Cantrall (1974) and Kuno (1987), and, more recently, Levinson (1991) and Huang (1994), among many others. In any case, determining the division of labor between such principles is a matter for future investigation.

NOTES

1 In addition to A-binding, which is concerned with binding relations between elements in argument positions (positions to which either a theta-role or Case can be assigned), there is A'-binding, where the antecedent is not in an A-position. A standard instance of A'-binding is that of a *wh*-element binding its trace. We will not be concerned with A'-binding in this overview. Aoun (1986), among others, argues for a Binding Theory which generalizes over A- and A'-binding.

2 Taking further grammatical rather than lexical features as the defining characteristic might seem a bit surprising, but it is necessary in view of the fact that the variable bound by a *wh*-operator behaves like an R-expression. Assuming *wh* to be a grammatical, rather than a lexical feature, *wh*-words such as *who* or *what* are not distinct from the corresponding pronouns in lexical content, yet give rise to R-expressions (Chomsky 1981: 330).

3 This is the currently standard version of c-command, discussed in Reinhart (1976). It should be noted that Reinhart explicitly argued in favor of using a different definition, which in current theory could be straightforwardly stated in terms of maximal projections:

(i) *a* c-commands *b* if and only if *a* does not contain *b* and the first maximal projection dominating *a* also dominates *b*

4 See Pollard and Sag (1994) for an overview of some of the problems with the c-command requirement.

5 Under the assumption that the type of agreement involved in anaphoric binding falls under specifier–head agreement, it would mean that the anaphor has to move to the head position of which the antecedent of the anaphor occupies the specifier position, which means that the LF-movement analysis must be a case of head movement.

6 In the remainder of this chapter nothing will be said about the distribution and interpretation of reciprocals as elements subject to condition A. For recent discussion of the syntax and semantics of

reciprocals, see Heim et al. (1991) and Dalrymple et al. (1994). (cf. Nishigauchi 1992 for an interesting discussion of Japanese.)

7   É. Kiss (1987) argues, on similar grounds, for a Case hierarchy.

8   Reinhart (to appear) shows that this is somewhat of a simplification. However, for present purposes this account suffices.

9   But see Levinson (1991) for a position where all condition B effects are subsumed under discourse theoretic principles.

10 See Chien and Wexler (1990) and Avrutin (1994) for an alternative formulation of "Rule I."

11 There is an extensive literature on some East Asian languages such as Chinese (cf. Cole et al. 1990, Huang and Tang 1991, Huang 1994, and references there), Japanese (cf. Iida 1996, and references there), and Korean (Yang 1984).

12 We abstract away from the two different verb classes which have different effects on the interpretation of *sig*. With one class of verbs, like the verb *raka* "shave" exemplified in (41a), *sig* can take either a local or a long distance antecedent in the infinitive and subjunctive domain. With the other class of verbs, *sig* can only refer to the long distance antecedent. These lexical effects in Icelandic (first noted by Thráinsson) are described by Sigurjónsdóttir (1992) and Sigurjónsdóttir and Hyams (1992). Similar lexical effects have been discussed by Everaert (1986) and Reinhart and Reuland (1991) for Dutch and by Hellan (1988) for Norwegian.

13 The term logophor was introduced in Hagège (1974) in order to characterize a class of pronouns that refer to the "source of a discourse." That is, they refer to the individual cited, the speaker, as opposed to the primary speaker. Hagège observes that many languages have a formally characterized set of pronouns for this type of use, which he terms "logophors." The notion is further developed in Clements (1975).

14 Note that *sig* in Icelandic does not have a nominative form (see Everaert 1990 for a discussion of this fact). Hence, *sig* can occur in subject position only with those verbs that select a non-nominative subject, i.e., with the so-called "quirky" case verbs in Icelandic. The verb *vanta* "to lack, need" which appears in example (42a) is one of these verbs and takes an accusative subject. Quirky subjects in Icelandic have been discussed by a number of authors; see, for example, Thráinsson (1979) and Zaenen et al. (1985).

15 It should be noted, in this connection, that locally bound *sig* does not allow a strict reading. This is illustrated in (i):

(i)   Jón$_i$ rakaði sig$_i$ og Pétur$_j$ gerði pad líka.
      "John shaved SIG and Peter did so too."
      ≠ Peter shaved John

Yet in the long distance infinitive case both readings are possible:

(ii) Jón$_i$ skipaði prófessornum$_j$ [að PRO$_j$ fella$_{inf}$ sig$_i$ á prófinu] og Ari gerði pað líka.
      "John ordered the professor to fail SIG on the test and Ari did so too."
      a.   = Ari ordered the professor to fail Ari on the test.
      b.   = Ari ordered the professor to fail John on the test.

This may indicate that what forces the sloppy reading (i) is not a property of the antecedent–anaphor relation, but a property of the predicate. In (i) the copied predicate is intrinsically reflexive, whereas (ii) has no reflexive predicate (see n. 13).

16 To give an example, in a text such as (i) the repeated use of *the chairman* is odd:

> (i) The chairman came in late. When the chairman had welcomed the speaker, the chairman leaned back with a slight feeling of relief.

Replacing the second and third occurrences of the chairman by pronominals makes the text felicitous. Instead of pronominals, also epithets such as *the idiot* could be used. Since after the first mention the chairman has become a high accessibility referent, it is appropriately referred to by a linguistic element with low lexical content, such as an epithet or a pronominal. Note that using the same epithet twice is infelicitous as well. Epithets are intermediate in degree of lexical specification between full NPs and pronominals.

17 Ultimately, an understanding of these phenomena requires a more elaborated theory of discourse prominence. That is, although our results make clear that well-formedness changes with perspective, it is not at all trivial to construct an adequate theory of perspective.

18 As disussed in Reuland (1996, 1998a) cancelled derivations in the sense of Chomsky (1995b) are derivations in the sense required, in order to guarantee that mismatch in phi-features does not free an anaphor for interpretation as a semantic variable.

19 See, among others, Vikner (1985), Everaert (1986), Hellan (1988), Riad (1988), Hestvik (1990), and Sigurjónsdóttir (1992).

20 The anaphoric systems of Creole languages deserve special attention because it seems as if different anaphoric systems are lexically determined (Muysken 1993).

21 Note that it does not have to be the case that one and the same element is used in all these environments.

22 Observe that in this approach referential (in)dependence of an item finds a straightforward translation in terms of the morphological feature specification of that item. See Anagnostopoulou and Everaert (1999) for discussion.

23 This also seems to be confirmed by acquisition research (Philip and Coopmans 1996a, 1996b).

24 Note that *se* is a pronoun, not an anaphor; the plural pronoun has the form *harren* as well, but for all purposes it behaves just like *har*.

25 Hoekstra's argument is based on a number of distributional differences between *se* and *har*. For instance, locative PPs require *har* instead of *se*, as in *Ik seach it boek neist har/*se* "I saw the book next to her." The same holds true where the pronominal is licensed by an adjective, as in *It boek wier har/*se te djoer* "The book was too expensive for her." In all those cases one can argue that precisely a structural Case assigner is lacking.

21 Syntactic Reconstruction Effects

ANDREW BARSS

0 Introduction

Reconstruction is the name given to a class of intricate puzzles in the theory of anaphora, which indicate a complex interaction between the representations created by movement operations, and the core principles determining possible or impossible referential relations between NPs. To give a simple example, *which pictures of himself does Bob like best?* is as grammatical as its declarative counterpart *Bob likes this picture of himself best*. The surface representation of the interrogative seems to defy the characteristic constraints on reflexive anaphora (see below), thus motivating further analysis. The exploration of these effects has turned out to be a useful tool relevant to the understanding of movement relations, scope, and Binding Theory, as well as the general architecture of the syntactic component of the grammatical system.

The term "reconstruction" itself emanates from an enduringly popular approach to this type of problem, in which the movement operation is undone, thus "reconstructing" the pre-movement representation, allowing the binding principles to apply as if the movement had not occurred. The term is nowadays used to refer both to this one type (among several) of formal analysis, and to the empirical data itself. This blurring of terminology is somewhat unfortunate, but commonplace enough that I will follow it here.

No single review chapter can do total justice to every data paradigm and theoretical approach to reconstruction. In my remarks here I hope to provide enough of an encounter with logical shape of the problem, the major formal analysis types, and the best-understood and most widely investigated of the data paradigms that the reader may be properly prepared to take on the more advanced and controversial recent literature.

1 Setting the Scene

1.1 *Tree and dependencies*

One of the longest-standing technical results in generative grammar is the conclusion that many of the core constraints on anaphoric dependence are subject to a purely geometric relation of *c-command*. The initial discovery was made in seminal work by Lasnik (1976) and Reinhart (1976), and has remained a bedrock principle of syntactic theory ever since. C-command is generally defined over hierarchical relations in phrase markers, although argument structure based variants are occasionally proposed (see e.g. Pollard and Sag 1992, Williams 1994b). I shall take it, for purposes of the current discussion, to have the definition in (1), the definition assumed in a broad range of recent and classical work, although no particular bias is intended toward alternative definitions:

(1) A *c-commands* B iff the first branching node dominating A also dominates B, and A does not itself dominate B. (Equivalently: A c-commands B iff B is, or is contained within, a sister of A.)

The class of constraints on anaphoric dependence which critically require c-command include those subsumed under the familiar principles A, B, and C of Chomsky's (1981, 1986a) Binding Theory, briefly summed up in (2)–(4). Principle A is concerned with the regulation of the relationship between anaphors and their antecedents (where within this subtheory *anaphor* is the class of NPs containing the overt reflexive and reciprocal proforms, and NP-trace), requiring that all anaphors have an antecedent drawn from among locally c-commanding NPs. Principle B imposes a requirement of disjointness of reference between a pronominal and all locally c-commanding NPs. Principle C requires disjointness of reference between any NP which is neither an anaphor nor a pure pronominal (Chomsky's class of *R-expressions*) and any other argument NP which c-commands it. The principles are stated in (2)–(4), and standard exemplifying data are given in (5)–(7):[1]

(2) **Principle A:** If α is [+Anaphoric], α must be A-bound in the minimal CFC containing it, its governor, and a potential antecedent.[2]

(3) **Principle B:** If α is [+Pronominal], α must be A-free in the minimal CFC containing it and its governor.

(4) **Principle C:** If α is an R-expression (= [−Anaphoric], [−Pronominal]), α must be A-free (within the domain of the operator binding it).

(5) a.   Earl$_1$ knows himself$_1$.
     b.   *[Earl$_1$'s mother]$_2$ knows himself$_1$.
     c.   *Earl$_1$ said I$_2$ saw himself$_1$.
     d.   Earl$_1$ saw [$_{NP}$ several pictures of himself$_1$].
     e.   *Earl$_1$ saw [$_{NP}$ my$_2$ pictures of himself$_1$].

(6) a.   *Earl$_1$ saw him$_1$.
     b.   [Earl$_1$'s mother]$_2$ saw him$_1$.
     c.   Earl$_1$ said I$_2$ saw him$_1$.
     d.   *Earl$_1$ saw [$_{NP}$ pictures of him$_1$].
     e.   Earl$_1$ saw [$_{NP}$ my$_2$ pictures of him$_1$].

(7) a.   *He$_1$ saw Earl$_1$.
     b.   [the woman he$_1$ mentioned] said I know Earl$_1$.
     c.   *He$_1$ said I$_2$ saw Earl$_1$.
     d.   *He$_1$ saw [$_{NP}$ these pictures of Earl$_1$].
     e.   *He$_1$ saw [$_{NP}$ my$_2$ pictures of Earl$_1$].

The grammaticality contrasts between the (a) and (b) examples show the discriminating effect of c-command. Grammatical anaphora fails in (5b) because the anaphor's antecedent fails to c-command it; disjointness of reference is not forced in either (6b) or (7b), due to the lack of c-command, whereas it is enforced in (5a) and (6a), given the presence of c-command. One may think of c-command as a general, hierarchically defined, binary relation between two points in a phrase marker, rendering them "visible" to the filtering effects of the binding principles. The coindexed pairs in (5a), (6a), and (7a) are visible to the pertinent binding constraints, and the pairs in the (b) examples are not.

2   The Logical Problem of Reconstruction Introduced

The so-called "reconstruction effects" are simply a large class of apparent counter-examples to the c-command relation. The empirical data which fall into this class of problems are numerous, and I will here simply outline the basic logic of the problem with a relatively simple example, returning in later sections to more detailed and methodical consideration of more complex cases.

Consider what happens when the direct object NP in (5d) is moved leftward, either through topicalization or through *wh*-movement:

(8) [$_{NP}$ several pictures of himself$_1$]$_2$, Earl$_1$ saw e$_2$.

(9) [Which pictures of himself$_1$]$_2$ did Earl$_1$ see e$_2$?

Independent of the presence of anaphora, topicalization like that in (8) or (10) is subject to variation between speakers. Some speakers (including me) find such topicalizations perfectly acceptable; others find the construction accept-able, but only in a richer context in which an explicit set of alternatives has been established in previous discourse; and some speakers find the construc-tion unacceptable in any context:

(10) [Several pictures of Mary], Fred saw.

For speakers who accept (10), (8) is fully grammatical. And, to the best of my knowledge, all speakers of English find (9) perfect.

The problem presented by such dislocation as (8) and (9), with respect to the binding principles, should be immediately apparent: in neither case is the anaphor *himself* c-commanded by its understood antecedent *Earl*, at least not in the surface constituent structure borne by the examples. That is, at first glance, one should expect that the lack of c-command in (8) and (9) should render the examples ungrammatical, on a par with (5b). In the "visibility" metaphor of the previous section, the antecedent here is unexpectedly visible to the anaphor.

Turning to disjointness effects, we see essentially the same puzzle arise:

(11) [Pictures of $him_{2/?*1}$], $Earl_1$ saw.

(12) [Pictures of $Earl_{2/?*1}$], he_1 saw.

In (12), *he* does not c-command *Earl*, yet coreference is blocked exactly as in (7d). One might reasonably expect the failure of c-command here to render condition C irrelevant, as for (7b). But this expectation is wrong.

The example in (11), and its non-topicalized counterpart (6d), have the same status as well. Many speakers find (6d) perfect if the pronoun is com-pletely destressed, and phonologically encliticized leftward ("pictures of'im"), and marginal (with coreference) otherwise, as originally noted by Fiengo and Higginbotham (1980). Other speakers find coreference permissible regard-less of stress. For both groups, apparently topicalizing the pronoun out of the c-command domain of the antecedent has a null effect on grammaticality, indicating a null effect on the anaphoric options for the antecedent–pronoun pair. The most interesting dialect is the conservative one, since presumably the disjointness effect seen in (6d) is a (weak) condition B effect, and it is pre-served under topicalization, even though c-command does not obtain.

Wh-movement has an identical effect, as in (13) and (14):

(13) Which pictures of him did Earl see?

(14) Which pictures of Earl did he see?

So, the initial boundary of the syntactic problem is this: how can we precisely account for the lack of effect on binding relations when such extractions take place? Why should c-command be irrelevant just in case one of the elements participating in an anaphoric relation is contained within a leftward-extracted constituent? There is a descriptive facet to the problem, namely providing any precise definition of the binding principles which classifies (5d), (8), and (9) together, (6d) and (11) together, and (7d) and (12) together, and which draws a distinction between all these cases and (5b), (6b), and (7b). There is also a theoretical-conceptual facet to the problem, namely offering up a precise characterization of these data patterns which seems independently motivated, rather than simply cobbled together in a stipulative fashion to solve that exact problem. As one may imagine, there are more approaches to the reconstruction effect of the former type than the latter, and in my remark below I will try to evaluate approaches to reconstruction along both facets, including my own previous proposals on the matter.

3   Pre-LF Analyses of Reconstruction: Reconstruction Without Reconstructing

3.1   *Pre-S-structure approaches*

As a first stab, one might suppose that all the examples in (8)–(9) and (11)–(14) simply indicate that the binding principles apply to a syntactic representation prior to which overt leftward "movement" – Topicalization and *wh*-extraction, here – has not occurred. Within the derivational models of syntax typically known as the Revised Extended Standard Theory, Government Binding (GB) Theory, and Principles and Parameters (P&P) Theory, there are two technically distinct ways to achieve this result.

The first is to apply the filters of the Binding Theory to syntactic structures before any movement at all occurs, at least movement of the sort seen above (movement to non-argument positions). Two variants (at least) of this approach exist. On the first, binding principles would apply at the level D-structure, which, by definition (see Chomsky 1981, 1982) is the level of representation directly projected from the lexicon, and in which all arguments occupy theta-position. Such a view is not easily maintained in light of the fact that movement operations can feed binding principles, as shown below.

On the second variant, proposed by van Riemsdjik and Williams (1981) and extended in Williams (1986, 1994b), the overt component of the grammar (movement operations affecting pronounced word order) are divided into two sorts, A-movement and A′-movement, which are strictly ordered. A-movement derives NP-structure from D-structure, and A′-movement derives S-structure from NP-structure. The binding principles are claimed to apply at NP-structure, i.e., to the output of A-movement but prior to A′-movement:

(15) **NP-Structure Binding Theory**

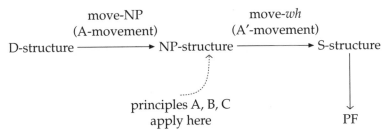

Under either such approach, the seeming c-command problem presented by (8)–(9) and (11)–(14) is just an illusion. The examples would have the following form at the point where the binding principles apply:

(8′)   Earl$_1$ saw [$_{NP}$ several pictures of himself$_1$]$_2$.

(9′)   Earl$_1$ saw [which pictures of himself$_1$]$_2$.

(11′)   Earl saw [pictures of him].

(12′)   He saw [pictures of Earl].

(13′)   Earl saw which pictures of him.

(14′)   He saw which pictures of Earl.

The problem disappears. However, both variants of the "pre-(A′-)movement" theory of binding suffer from empirical inadequacy. The problem with D-structure application of the principles is quite straightforward (see van Riemsdjik and Williams 1981, Barss 1984, 1986, for discussion): A-movement alters binding relations systematically, for all three binding principles (and hence Binding Theory cannot apply solely to the D-structure level, contrary to what the model predicts). In (16a, b) is a pair of representations related by A-movement. As inspection shows, the anaphora is regulated by the post-movement representation, not the pre-movement representation:

(16)   a.   __ seems [to himself$_1$/him$_1$] [Bill$_1$ to be handsome].
       b.   Bill$_1$ seems [to himself$_1$/*him$_1$] [e$_1$ to be handsome].

It is this sort of evidence which is taken to motivate the NP-structure model and its approach to the problem. (16) shows that the binding principles apply after NP-movement, while (8)–(9) and (10)–(14) are consistent with van Riemsdjik and Williams's view that the principles apply before, and not after, A′-movement.

However, the NP-structure model is subject to the same sort of criticism as D-structure binding is. That is, it can be easily demonstrated that the *output of* overt *wh*-movement, in some cases, forms the input to the filters of the binding theory.

Consider the contrast in (17) and (18):

(17)   The men₁ believed that the women₂ had placed (these) [portraits of [themselves/each other]₂/*₁]₃ in a scrapbook.

(18)   a.   [(these) portraits of [themselves/each other]₂/₁]₃, the men₁ believed that the women₂ had placed e₃ in a scrapbook.
       b.   I wonder [which portraits of [themselves/each other]₂/₁]₃ the men₁ believed that the women₂ had placed e₃ in a scrapbook.

(17) is unproblematic: the anaphor (*themselves* or *each other*) must be bound to the locally c-commanding NP *the women*, and cannot be bound to the distant c-commander *the men*. This follows from the locality portion of condition A.

However, (18) is ambiguous, with the anaphor possibly anteceded either by the NP which locally c-commanded it prior to extraction (*the women*), or by the intermediate NP (*the men*) which locally c-commanded it at an intermediate stage of the derivation (after the first token of A′-movement, prior to the second). The NP-structure model fails to capture the latter fact, since it strictly orders the binding principles and A′-movement, whereas factually the two seem to bear a more complex ordering relation (with either potentially occurring before the other).

So, to sum up the overview of this section: certain systematic binding paradigms indicate that the "surface" syntactic representation (the structure associated with a sentence which forms the input to the phonological system, on any theory of syntax) is not the syntactic level at which binding principles apply. Related binding paradigms indicate that it is insufficient to suppose that the binding principles apply solely prior to any extraction operations, or prior to operator movement (as in the NP-structure model). Placed together, these results indicate a most interesting, and quite complex, interplay of movement dependencies and binding relations: phrasal movement of both major types both bleeds and feeds binding relations. Even this preliminary overview indicates that the interaction of movement operations, and the c-command "meta-constraint" that determines which pairs of NPs can be inspected by the binding constraints, have implications for the overall organization of the grammatical levels of representation and the placement of specific principles within them.

In the next section I will overview a class of cases of extraction in which the generalizations observed above fail to hold. These are cases in which the material transposed to the left by movement operations is predicative in nature.

3.2   A further empirical puzzle: predicate movement and argument movement

In each of the examples of movement we have seen above (e.g. (8)–(14)), the moved material originates as an argument of a lexical predicate. As we have seen with examples (18a, b) such A′-movement of an argument expression both (i) preserves the pre-movement anaphoric options and (ii) adds additional ones.

The latter effect (ii) does not obtain when the moved material is a predicative XP, as the examples below show:

(19)   John$_1$ believes that Martin$_2$ is [$_{AP}$ very happy with himself$_{2/*1}$].

(20)   [$_{AP}$ How happy with himself$_{2/*1}$]$_3$ does John$_1$ believe that Martin$_2$ is e$_3$?

This empirical fact was first observed by Cinque (1982). Descriptively, an anaphor pied-piped in a moved predicate has exactly those anaphoric options which it has in the pre-movement representation. The implications for the overall theory of binding, and the formal analyses of reconstruction, were first investigated in detail in Barss (1986, 1987), and one analysis presented there was developed further by Huang (1993) and Takano (1995).

3.3   S-structure accounts

3.3.1   Predicate-internal subject traces

Barss (1986) presents two analyses of the critical contrast between moved arguments (which tolerate an ambiguity of antecedence) and moved predicates (which do not). On the first analysis, the strict parallelism between (19) and (20) is attributed to the presence of a theta-marked trace internal to the displaced constituent, following the (now standard) predicate internal theory of subjects developed by Manzini (1983b), Kuroda (1988), Koopman and Sportiche (1991), and McCloskey (1991). On any variant of this theory of subject theta-marking, (19) and (20) will have representations essentially of the form in (21) and (22):

(21)   John$_1$ [$_{VP}$ e$_1$ believes that Martin$_2$ is [$_{AP}$ e$_2$ very happy with himself$_{2/*1}$]].

(22)   [$_{AP}$ e$_2$ how happy with himself$_{2/*1}$]$_3$ does John$_1$ [$_{VP}$ e$_1$ believe that Martin$_2$ is e$_3$]?

Because of the presence of the trace e$_2$, the preposed material in (22) is a complete binding domain: it is a CFC, and one which contains a potential antecedent for the lexical anaphor. As a result, binding must be strictly within AP, forcing, by transitivity of indexing, *himself* to be coindexed with *John*. The same effect extends – for the same reasons – to other predicative categories, including VP and predicative NP:

(23)   [e$_4$ shave himself$_{4/*3}$], John$_4$ hopes that Martin$_3$ will.

(24)   [$_{NP}$ e$_1$ admirers of each other$_{1/*2}$], the Dukes$_2$ hoped that the Barons$_1$ became.

Thus, if this account of Cinque's asymmetry is adopted, it provides striking confirmation for the predicate internal theory of subjects, as observed in Barss (1986) and by Huang (1993).

In spite of the appeal of this analysis, there is at least one outstanding problem with it: the failure to fully generalize to condition C effects. (For this reason, Barss 1986, 1987, develops an alternative to the trace-based account, discussed briefly in sections 3.3.2 and 3.3.3.) Consider the following, all of which are ungrammatical with coreference between the pronoun and *John* (and fine with disjoint reference):

(25)   *Mary$_2$ [$_{VP}$ e$_2$ believes him$_1$ to be [$_{AP}$ e$_1$ very proud of John$_1$]].

(26)   *He$_1$ [$_{VP}$ e$_1$ believes Mary$_2$ to be [$_{AP}$ e$_2$ very proud of John$_1$]].

(27)   *[$_{AP}$ e$_1$ very proud of John$_1$] does Mary$_2$ [$_{VP}$ e$_2$ believe him$_1$ to be]?

(28)   *[$_{AP}$ e$_2$ How proud of John$_1$] does he$_1$ [$_{VP}$ e$_1$ believe Mary$_2$ to be]?

(25) and (26) are standard condition C effects: the pronoun (and the trace it binds, under the internal subjects theory) c-commands the name, and they cannot be coindexed and satisfy the binding theory. (27) follows straightforwardly under the predicate internal trace account, since the pied-piped trace still c-commands the name. The pronoun and trace must be coindexed, and the trace and the name cannot be (by condition C), and by transitivity the pronoun and name must be contra-indexed.

But (28) is not properly accounted for, since the trace internal to the moved predicate is not coindexed with the pronoun or the name: it is the trace of the lower subject *Mary*. If the only thing responsible for the ungrammaticality of (27) is the c-command of the name by e$_1$, then we should expect (28) to be fine, contrary to fact. By the same token, we should hope that any account of reconstruction sufficiently general to rule out (28) would plausibly extend also to (27).

3.3.2 A second S-structure solution

As a substitute for the predicate internal trace based analysis, Barss (1986, 1987) develops in detail an approach which is first suggested by Cinque (1982) and Hornstein (1984). On this approach, c-command is replaced by a less conservative geometric relation between anaphor and antecedent, one which combines chain theory with the path system of Kayne (1981a), May (1985), and Pesetsky (1982).

The basic idea, informally, is that a potential antecedent for an anaphor must locally c-command either it or a trace of a phrase containing it. When a phrase is iteratively moved, as in (29), there will be several potential antecedents; one which locally c-commands the anaphor itself, and others which locally c-command one of the traces:

(29) a. Mark$_5$ knows [$_{NP}$ which picture of himself$_{1/2/3/5}$]$_4$ John$_2$ [I$'_b$ [thinks [$_{CP}$ e$''_4$ [Sam$_1$ [I$'_a$ said [$_{CP}$ e$'_4$ Dan [likes e$_4$]]]]]]]].

b. chain = ([which pictures of himself]$_4$, e$'''_4$, e$''_4$, e$'_4$, e$_4$)

c. potential antecedents for *himself*:
Mark$_5$ (in virtue of local c-command of *himself*)
John$_2$ (in virtue of local c-command of e$''_4$)
Sam$_1$ (in virtue of local c-command of e$'_4$)
Dan$_3$ (in virtue of local c-command of e$_4$)

The portions of structure relevant to determination of this potential–antecedent relationship differ in each case, so that (within Barss's formalized system) each NP counts as being in distinct binding domains for the reflexive. Hence the multiple ambiguity of the example. Barss's system can be thought of as a purely "surface-level" metric for assessing possible binding relations, achieved through the abandonment of c-command in favor of a combination of c-command and chain structure. The idea is formalized within path theory, and the set of points connecting the anaphor and a potential antecedent is termed a *binding path*.

Barss captures the Cinque effect under an additional constraint on the path structure defining the potential–antecedent relation: the portions of structure connecting the anaphor and antecedent must represent whole thematic complexes (a re-encoding of Chomsky's CFC requirement on binding domains). In (30), *he* is contained within predicative AP, and the potential antecedents must be located via structure including the domain of theta-assignment of *Mary*. As a result, only *Mary* is close enough to the reflexive to count as a possible binder, blocking coindexation with the pronoun:

(30) *[$_{AP}$How proud of himself$_1$]$_3$ does [$_{IPb}$ he$_1$ [$_{I'b}$ [$_{VPb}$ believe [$_{CP}$ e$_3$ Mary$_2$ [$_{I'a}$ has [$_{VPa}$ become e$_3$]]]]]]?

Now let us return to the problematic example (28), repeated here:

(28) *[$_{AP}$How proud of John$_1$]$_3$ does [$_{IPb}$ he$_1$ [$_{I'b}$ [$_{VPb}$ believe [$_{IPa}$ Mary$_2$ [$_{I'a}$ to [$_{VPa}$ be e$_3$]]]]]]?

Recall that it was this type of example which appeared problematic for the idea that predicate internal traces underlie the Cinque effect. Within the path theoretic approach, condition C has this formulation (see Barss 1986, 1987 for original discussion, and Chierchia 1995 for extension to operator variable relations):

(31) **Condition C:** Given an R-expression R, R must connect to the root node via a binding path P such that R is not coindexed with any NP accessible to R through P.

Because *John* is contained within a predicate in (28), any well formed binding path for it must include the domain of theta-assignment of that predicate, namely the lowest clause (of which *Mary* is the subject). Since *he* is accessible to *John* through this path, coreference is blocked.

3.4   *Evaluating the second S-structure solution*

The empirical coverage of this path theoretic S-structure approach is quite large. It directly captures the increased antecedence effects induced by cyclic movement; it subsumes Cinque's asymmetry with reconstructed anaphors; and it captures the condition C effects which proved problematic for Barss's (1986) original, predicate internal trace approach to Cinque's asymmetry. Nonetheless, the path theoretic approach achieves this empirical result at some nontrivial conceptual cost. In particular, the definition of "binding path" rests on a peculiar disjunction of hierarchical domination – a geometric relation central to the subtheory of constituent structure – and chain membership, a relation belonging to one particular approach to extraction dependencies. Why should these two relations travel together? Why not domination and, say, agreement? Or Case marking? The path theoretic account, in retrospect, is a fine example of the tradeoff seen so frequently in linguistic theory between data coverage power and conceptual elegance. What it possesses in the former, it partially lacks in the latter.

In this section, we have discussed the merits and weaknesses of several representational approaches to reconstruction. As we have seen, the D-structure approach, the NP-structure approach, and the S-structure approach all suffer from non-trivial drawbacks. In the next section, I will overview the one logically remaining representational approach, under which all binding principles apply at LF (and only at LF). I will draw particularly on recent work in the Minimalist framework by Chomsky (1995b) and Reinhart (1993, 1995).

4   LF-Based Approaches: Structural Reconstruction

Consider again the basic GB grammatical model, with its three dedicated levels of syntactic representation:

(32)   DS $\rightarrow$ SS $\rightarrow$ LF

It is clear that D-structure cannot be the locus of application of the binding principles. It is equally clear that S-structure seems not to be the locus of application either, at least not if we continue to hold that c-command is a necessary ingredient in the binding principles. As we saw in section 3, there is conceptual cost associated with a precise formulation of the binding principles to hold just at S-structure. Having eliminated the alternatives, it is apparent that if the binding theory applies at any specific level of representation, that level must be LF. LF is computed from S-structure by a variety of operations, including scope assignment of quantifiers, scope assignment of interrogatives, and ellipsis resolution. Within this model, all LF-deriving operations are totally "hidden" from the phonological components, and as a result the presence or absence of a particular extraction operation in the LF-component has to be inferred from interpretive aspects of the sentence.

I will here concentrate on the LF-reconstruction theory presented by Chomsky (1993, 1995), as it is the most precisely worked out, and certainly most influential, of all purely LF-based accounts of reconstruction effects. In the next subsection I will delineate the major theoretical principles related to this theory of reconstruction, and will follow that overview with some critical comments on both the syntactic and semantic aspects of this theory.

4.1 *Movement as copying, reconstruction as selective deletion*

Within the Minimalist model presented by Chomsky in recent work (see Chomsky 1995), the derivational character of the GB model has been retained, but the notion "level of representation" has been significantly constrained. In pre-Minimalist derivational syntax, the levels D-structure, S-structure, and LF have two distinct, though related, roles to play in the architecture of the model. On the one hand, they correspond to particular points in derivations: DS constitutes the beginning, and LF the terminus, of formal syntactic operations associated with a given sentence, while S-structure corresponds to the point in the derivation immediately preceding the "branch" between LF and PF. S-structure thus has a privileged role in being the last syntactic structure which provides input to both the phonetic and semantic components. So, given a particular derivation, one can pick out the D-structure, S-structure, and LF simply by observing the flow of the derivation.

On the other hand, the levels also served an important sorting function on the various principles, filters, and constraints of the syntax. A given constraint – the Case filter, principle A, the need for INFL to agree with a Specifier, etc. – could be placed at one or another level. Indeed, the level at which a particular principle applied was in principle parameterized (see e.g. Koopman and Sportiche 1991, Lasnik and Saito 1984, 1991, for case studies in parameters of this sort). Investigation of which principles applied at which levels in which languages was a major focus of comparative syntax.

This latter function of levels of representation is almost completely given up in the Minimalist framework. No longer is it a goal of the theory to identify which level(s) a particular principle or filter applies at (in a specific language). Rather, in the more conservative terms introduced by Chomsky (1993), all level-specific syntactic principles must apply solely at LF. D-structure exists not at all, and S-structure only in the derivative sense of there being a point where the derivation branches. No principle is permitted to "name" S-structure, and thus in the latter sense of level of representation, LF is all that remains.

With this conceptually driven meta-constraint in mind, let us turn to the fate of the binding principles in Minimalist syntax. The chief components of the LF-only analysis of reconstruction include the following major ideas:

(33)   Movement is a copying operation. The immediate output representation of an instance of movement of a constituent X from point A to point B in a structure is a copy of X in position A, and another full copy in position B.

(34)   LF, the final syntactic representation, is subject to two representational economy principles:
Copy Economy: Eliminate redundancy of copies, down to recoverability.
Operator Economy: Minimize the content of operator positions.

I will illustrate these three central aspects of the theory by first considering simple reconstruction of an anaphor under Movement (for reasons of clarity, subject auxiliary inversion is ignored in the following examples). (35) is constructed by the ongoing derivation. (36) is derived from (35) by overt copying. By general rule in English-type languages, the higher copy is pronounced, the lower copies phonetically deleted, deriving the overt form *which picture of himself will John see?*:

(35)   [John will see [which picture of himself]]

(36)   [which picture of himself] [John will see [which picture of himself]]

(36) thus corresponds to what would have been called the S-structure in the pre-Minimalist model. It forms the input to LF operations.

By Copy Economy, at least one token of *which, picture, of,* and *himself,* together with the constituent structure immediately dominating them, will have to be deleted prior to LF. Several options exist, including those below:

(37)   [John will see [which picture of himself]]

(38)   [which picture of himself] [John will see ϕ][3]

(39)   [which]$_x$ John will see [ϕ_x picture of himself]

(37) is dubious, since it completely undoes the scope assignment achieved by the overt token of *wh*-movement, obliterating the relation between the *wh*-operator and its scope position (which is exactly identified with its overt landing site). (38) and (39) both satisfy Copy Economy, and in addition each retains a +*wh*-element in [Spec, CP], thus properly delimiting the scope of the interrogative.[4] The additional representational constraint Operator Economy chooses (39) over (38) as the preferred structure, since in (39) the A′-position (Spec, CP)

contains less material. (39) then seems a happy compromise between (37), which has maximal satisfaction of Operator Economy, but is likely to be semantically problematic, and (38). Almost as a side effect, the winning compromise structure (39) fully satisfies the Binding Theory, since it reconstructs the anaphor to a position c-commanded by *John*.

Similarly elegant results are achieved with condition C effects. Consider an overt derivation which constructs (40), and which subsequently derives (41) via copying:

(40) [he will see [which picture of John]]

(41) [which picture of John] [he will see [which picture of John]]

In the covert syntax, the pair of representational economy principles (34) will conspire to prefer (44) as the maximally economical (yet semantically intelligible)[5] LF representation. And, as a neat side effect, observe that the pronoun in this representation directly c-commands the name; condition C will, without any augmentation, properly block coreference between them:

(42) [he will see [which picture of John]]

(43) [which picture of John] [he will see ϕ]

(44) [which]$_x$ he will see [ϕ_x picture of John]

Under this copy and delete conception of movement, augmented with the Operator Economy principle, the basic retention of condition C effects under A'-movement is straightforwardly derived. As Chomsky (1995b: ch. 2) puts it, there is no need for any specific mechanism for Reconstruction – it all follows from independent mechanisms, at least for the rudimentary examples discussed to this point.

4.2   LF reconstruction and the moved predicate effects

In the discussion above, we observed the problems posed by example (28) for the most appealing S-structure approach to Reconstruction, the one which attributes reconstruction effects with moved predicates to the presence of a predicate internal trace. As we reviewed above, this hypothesis was criticized in Barss (1986) for its failure to straightforwardly predict the condition C effect in (28) (repeated here as (45)): since the predicate internal trace which c-commands *John* is not coindexed with the pronoun, nothing about this S-structure representation violates condition C:

(45) *[$_{AP}$ e$_2$ How proud of John$_1$]$_3$ does he$_1$ [$_{VP}$ e$_1$ believe Mary$_2$ to be e$_3$]?

In a reconsideration of these data, Takano (1995) presents an ingenious way to resurrect the essential insight of the predicate internal trace analysis in the context of Chomsky's LF-based theory of reconstruction. As Takano observes, the S-structure (45) violates Fiengo's (1977) Proper Binding Condition, stated as (46):

(46)   **Proper Binding Condition:** Traces must be bound.

Following the general spirit of Minimalism, in which all specific constraints on syntactic representation apply (solely) at LF, Takano's analysis takes the PBC to be a filter on LF. On the copy theory of movement, (45) is actually (47) at the point of Spell-Out (i.e., at S-structure):

(47) $[_{AP}$ e_2 How proud of John$_1]_3$ does he$_1$ $[_{VP}$ e_1 believe Mary$_2$ to be $[_{AP}$ e_2 how proud of John$_1]_3]$?

It is the higher copy of the trace e_2 which violates the PBC. Satisfying the PBC requires mapping (47) onto an LF like (48), by deleting the upper copy of the trace, and, presumably, the material surrounding it:

(48)   How$_4$ does he$_1$ $[_{VP}$ e_1 believe Mary$_2$ to be $[_{AP}$ e_2 e_4 proud of John$_1]_3]$?

The PBC is satisfied, in virtue of *Mary* c-commanding the preserved copy of e_2. However, as Takano argues, the lower copy of *John* is also retained (essentially parasitically on the general deletion of the upper material), and thus coindexing the pronoun and *John* violates condition C straightforwardly. Takano's analysis is similar to the original hypothesis presented in Barss (1986), that the Cinque effect – the fundamental preservation of all binding relations under predicate movement – is ultimately due to the presence of the trace. However, there is a crucial difference, as Takano's theory applies the binding principles univocally at LF. This resolves the problem Barss raised for this derivation of the Cinque effect, and remains wholly consistent with the Minimalist goal of reducing representational constraints to the LF level.

Having seen that the Cinque effect is derived without special appeal to any specific rules for Reconstruction, let us now return to the opposing data, namely the ambiguities of antecedence which arise when the anaphoric item is inside of an overtly moved argument. As discussed above, such preposing creates options for anaphora which are not present otherwise.

Within the copy theory of movement, the ambiguous example (18b) actually has something like (49) as its syntactic structure before Spell-Out, with a full copy of the *wh*-phrase in each landing site:[6]

(49)   I wonder $[_{CPa}$ [which portraits of [themselves/each other]$_{2/1}]_3$ $[_{IP}$ the men$_1$ believed $[_{CPb}$ [which portraits of [themselves/each other]$_{2/1}]_3$ that $[_{IPb}$ the women$_2$ had placed [which portraits of [themselves/each other]$_{2/1}]_3$ in a scrapbook]]]].

Since the *wh*-operator is selected by *wonder*, enough residue of the *wh*-phrase must remain at LF in the [Spec, CP$_a$] position to satisfy this selectional requirement. Chomsky (1993) proposes that the determiner *which* is retained in that position, and satisfies selection; Chomsky (1995: ch. 4) proposes that it is simply the morphosemantic feature [+*wh*] which remains in [Spec, CP$_a$]. Whichever option is taken, it is clear that the remainder of the *wh*-phrase – the non-*wh* part *portraits of each other/themselves* – need not remain in Spec, CP$_a$. Thus, on Chomsky's assumptions, both (50) and (51) are licit LF representations:

(50) I wonder [$_{CP_a}$ [which]$_3$ [$_{IP}$ the men$_1$ believed [$_{CP_b}$ [e$_3$ portraits of [themselves/each other]$_1$]$_3$ that [$_{IP_b}$ the women$_2$ had placed e$_3$ in a scrapbook]]]].

(51) I wonder [$_{CP_a}$ [which]$_3$ [$_{IP}$ the men$_1$ believed [$_{CP_b}$ that [$_{IP_b}$ the women$_2$ had placed [e$_3$ portraits of [themselves/each other]$_2$]$_3$ in a scrapbook]]]].

Crucially unlike the case with moved predicate examples (e.g. (45)), there is no requirement that the constituent reconstruct to its deepest position, and so there is an ambiguity in which copy is retained. This underlies the anaphoric ambiguity. In (50), the anaphor is sufficiently close to *the men$_1$* for that NP to grammatically antecede the anaphor. Similarly, in (51) *the women* is local to the anaphor.

Consequently, the copy theory of movement, plus the deletion theory of Economy, suffices to give a straightforward explanation of why there is a systematic anaphoric ambiguity induced by structurally displacing an anaphor as part of extracting an argument. (Very much unlike the case with the path theoretic approach reviewed in section 3, there is no complexity added to the system to take care of these effects.)

5 Reconstruction and A-Movement

The foregoing discussion has illustrated a wide range of reconstruction effects occurring under A′-movement, specifically *wh*-movement or focussing Topicalization, each of which is generally assumed to move a constituent to a non-argument position. What of A-movement? Does A-movement exhibit reconstruction effects?

We first note that the Cinque effect is essentially unobservable in A-movement. The reason for this is simply that predicates cannot undergo A-movement (which is, in the canonical case, movement of an argument NP to a Case marked position). This leaves us with the question of whether there are condition A, B, and C reconstruction effects with A-moved arguments, and the subsidiary question of whether the antecedence ambiguities of cyclic A′-movement occur as well under cyclic A-movement.

5.1   Basic anaphor reconstruction effects with A-movement

The fact that raising-to-subject constructions in general exhibit anaphor reconstruction effects is well established, and is investigated in detail by Barss (1984, 1986, 1996, 1999), Belletti and Rizzi (1988), Hoji (1985), Johnson (1985), and Williams (1994b), among many others.

In general, we will observe reconstruction effects under A-movement only in cases where there is an argument NP (the potential antecedent) which c-commands the deep position, but not the surface position, of the raised NP which contains the anaphor. Schematically this is as in (52), with α the potential antecedent argument NP and H the raising predicate:

(52) $[_{NP} \ldots \text{anaphor} \ldots]_1 [H \ldots \alpha \ldots [\ldots e_1 \ldots] \ldots \alpha \ldots]$

Thus the raising predicate (which, by definition, does not theta-mark its subject position) must have two internal arguments: one the clause from which NP_1 is raised, the other α. In the discussion below I will overview the various subtypes of raising predicate which meet this requirement.

5.1.1   Raising

Consider the English cases in (53) and (54), each of which is standardly analyzed as a raising construction:

(53)   [Old pictures of themselves$_1$]$_2$ usually strike the children$_1$ as [t$_2$ amusing].

(54)   [Each other$_1$'s houses] appear/seem to the women$_1$ [t$_2$ to be over-decorated].

There is a significant grammaticality distinction between these raising constructions and the non-movement constructions in (55) and (56), suggesting that the acceptability of (53) and (54) is a reconstruction effect induced by the NP-trace:[7]

(55)   *[Old pictures of themselves] convinced the children to pretend to be adults.

(56)   *[Each other's houses] proved to the women that they had bad taste.

This is the analog of the simplest cases of anaphor reconstruction under A'-movement like (9): binding relations are calculated as if movement had not occurred. The formal interpretation under the copy theory of movement will be just as it was for *wh*-extraction. (53), for example, will have the pre-Spell-Out representation (57), and will be mapped onto the Binding Theory-satisfying LF (58) by deletion of the higher copy:[8, 9]

(57)   [Old pictures of themselves$_1$]$_2$ usually strike the children$_1$ as [[old pictures of themselves$_1$]$_2$ amusing].

(58)   usually strike the children$_1$ as [[old pictures of themselves$_1$]$_2$ amusing]

What about cyclic A-movement – does it produce ambiguities of the type seen in cyclic A'-movement, like (59)? Apparently yes, as the acceptability of (60) on the various indexings attests:[10]

(59)   The women$_2$ asked [which pictures of themselves$_{2/3/4}$]$_1$ the men$_3$ had said that the children$_4$ had brought e$_1$ to the school fair.

(60)   The women$_2$ consider [old pictures of themselves$_{2/3/4}$]$_1$ to have struck the men$_3$ as [appearing to the children [t$_1$ be amusing]].

5.1.2   *Passive*

The cyclic A-movement example (60) shows that subject-to-subject raising can participate in an iterated sequence of A-movement dependencies, each of which preserves and expands anaphoric possibilities. This suggests that A-movement, exactly on a par with A'-movement, participates in the reconstruction effect. Since Passive is usually taken to be fundamentally the same formal operation as raising (i.e., cyclic feature driven movement to non-theta-marked A-positions), we would expect much the same pattern to hold with iterated Passive as it does in (60). The examples are difficult to construct, since we would need, effectively, a series of passivized verbs which could occur in the configuration (61), where the verb takes a (non-moved) complement NP which acts as the potential antecedent for the anaphor moved inside the Passivized constituent:

(61)   . . . [$_{NP}$ old pictures of themselves$_{i/j/k}$]$_1$ INFL V$_{pass}$ NP$_j$ [$_\alpha$ . . . t$_1$ . . .]

Unfortunately, this configuration violates Burzio's generalization (Burzio 1986), since V would have Accusative Case and fail to theta-mark its external subject. Consequently, the relevant examples are impossible to construct. However, there is one further subtype of A-movement which is relevant to the reconstruction issue, namely that seen in psych verb constructions on the analysis of Belletti and Rizzi (1988).

5.1.3   *Psych verbs*

On the influential analysis of Belletti and Rizzi (1988), one subclass of psychological predicates instantiates the schema in (52). Belletti and Rizzi argue that psych verbs of the *preoccupare/worry* class – those with experiencer subjects – are unaccusative,[11] with the surface subject raised from object position, and with the indirect object (the source argument) asymmetrically c-commanding the deep object, as in the schema (62):

(62)   NP$_1$ INFL [$_{VP}$ [$_{V'}$ V t$_1$] NP$_2$]

Belletti and Rizzi use the derived subjects analysis to resolve a long-standing puzzle in this class of verbs: an anaphor inside the surface subject can be anteceded by the apparent object:

(63)   a.   Questi pettegolezzi su di sé$_1$ preoccupano Gianni$_1$ più di ogni altra cosa.
           These gossips about himself worry John more than anything else.
        b.   *Questi pettegolezzi su di sé$_1$ descrivono Gianni$_1$ meglio di ogni biografia ufficiale.
           These gossips about himself describe John better than any official biography. (Belletti and Rizzi 1988: (57a, b))

(64)   a.   These stories about himself worry John more than anything else.
        b.   *These stories about himself describe John better than any official biography.

The non-psych verbs in the (b) examples show the typical pattern (ungrammaticality due to failure of c-command), and the (a) examples illustrate the exceptional behavior with psych verbs. This exceptional behavior is actually expected under Belletti and Rizzi's analysis, given the general participation of A-movement in reconstruction effects.

   Finally, we should expect that "psych movement" (the object-to-subject raising induced by the unaccusative psych verb), followed by subject-to-subject raising, should preserve binding relations, and this is in fact the case, as Belletti and Rizzi show in detail:

(65)   [Images of themselves]$_1$ seem [t$_1$ to have [[frightened t$_1$] [the children]]]

(66)   [Each other's accomplishments]$_1$ seem [t$_1$ to have been proven [t$_1$ to have deeply [[impressed t$_1$] [the cabinetmakers]]]].

   Taking Chomsky's copy and delete theory of movement to apply to all types of movement, the parallelism of A-movement and A'-movement under anaphor reconstruction is precisely predicted. Prior to LF-component deletion, (66), for example, will have three copies of the moved NP:

(67)   [Each other's accomplishments]$_1$ seem [[each other's accomplishments]$_1$ to have been proven [[each other's accomplishments]$_1$ to have deeply [[impressed [each other's accomplishments]$_1$] [the cabinetmakers]]]].

   By Copy Economy, three of these copies must be deleted prior to LF. Binding by *the cabinetmakers* simply reflects the option of deleting the three higher copies, retaining the lowest:

(68)   seem [to have been proven [to have deeply [[impressed [each other's accomplishments]₁] [the cabinetmakers]]]].

6   Condition C and Anti-Reconstruction Effects

In the discussion above, we focussed on anaphor reconstruction, and discussed condition C effects predominantly in the discussion of predicate extraction (section 3), noting the puzzle presented by the sharp contrast between (69) and (70):

(69)   Which picture that John₁ took at the party did he₁ decide to display in his house?

(70)   *How proud of John₁'s party did he decide he₁ should be?

We followed the initial suggestion of Cinque (1982) that this is fundamentally an asymmetry between arguments and predicates, and the analysis of Barss (1986) and Takano (1995) that the underlying cause of the more restrictive binding options in the latter case is to be attributed to a predicate internal trace of the raised subject.

There are three other major approaches to this contrast, each focussing on a more detailed examination of the apparent lack of condition C effects under *wh*-movement of arguments, as exemplified in (69). The first analysis is proposed by Friedin (1986), Lebeaux (1988), and Chomsky (1993), developing initial suggestions by van Riemsdjik and Williams (1981). The second is proposed by Heycock (1995). The third is proposed by Chierchia (1995). There is disagreement among these researchers on the nature and strength of the data, and I will present their analyses in chronological order, and note the judgments offered by the respective authors (giving my own at the end of the discussion).

To introduce useful terminology, the complete lack of condition C effects in (69) – that is, the lack of any enforced disjointness of reference between the name and pronoun, which might be expected if the extracted phrase is reconstructed – was termed "anti-reconstruction" by van Riemsdjik and Williams (1981). They note that there appears to be a contrast between (69) and (71) which they attribute to depth of embedding:

(71)   ??Which picture of John₁ did he₁ like?

In explorations of how to formally implement this suggestion, Freidin (1986) and Lebeaux (1988) propose that the contrast has fundamentally to do with whether the R-expression is embedded inside an adjunct (e.g. the relative clause in (69) and (72)) or inside an argument of the head of the extracted phrase (73):

(72)   Which report that John revised did he submit?

(73)   *Which report that John was incompetent did he submit? (Freidin 1986: (76a, b); judgments cited are his as reported in text)

In the argument-contained case, Freidin and Lebeaux suggest, there is no anti-reconstruction effect. On their judgments, disjointness of reference is forced in (73), and coreference permitted in (72).

Freidin proposes that whatever mechanism is responsible for computation of reconstruction (e.g. lowering at LF) of a phrase must reconstruct the head's subcategorized arguments, and need not reconstruct adjuncts. Thus, the postreconstruction representation for (73), but not (72), will have the name c-commanded by the pronoun, hence the condition C asymmetry.

Freidin's proposal is implemented in detail by Lebeaux (1988) and Chomsky (1993). Lebeaux suggests that adjuncts – phrases which by definition need not be present at D-structure – are inserted into syntactic representations in the course of the derivation via generalized transformations. Thus, (72) has a derivation in which the relative clause is inserted after *wh*-movement has occurred:

(74)   a.   he submit which report
       b.   [which report]$_2$ did he submit t$_2$
       c.   [which [report [that John revised]]]$_2$ did he submit t$_2$?

Since there is no derivational stage at which the relative clause (and the name it contains) is c-commanded by the pronoun, and on the assumption that reconstruction only restores material to a position it occupied at some stage of the derivation, the relative clause will not reconstruct in (74). Hence there is no condition C effect. On the elaboration of this analysis by Chomsky (1993), "reconstruction" is simply retention of material in a trace position, and deletion of the higher copy. The pre-deletion representation of (74c) will be as in (75):

(75)   [which [report [that John revised]]]$_2$ did he submit [which report]$_2$

The only copy of the relative clause is the one in [Spec, CP], hence after deletion there is no option other than to leave it in the operator position. Hence the anti-reconstruction effect with relative clauses.

Turning to the example in (73), the CP complement selected by *report* must be generated in the D-structure representation (in Lebeaux's analysis), or prior to any movement operations affecting the *wh*-phrase (on Chomsky's analysis).[12] Hence, the derivation proceeds as follows, assuming Chomsky's derivational system:

(76)   a.   he submit [which report that John was incompetent]
       b.   [which report that John was incompetent]$_2$ he submit [which report that John was incompetent]$_2$ (by movement)
       c.   [which]$_2$ he submit [report that John was incompetent]$_2$

(76c) is the LF representation. The lower copy of the CP complement is retained, the higher one deleted, by the principles in (34). Here, the pronoun c-commands the name. By Minimalist principles, condition C applies to this interface representation, precluding coreference. Hence the lack of anti-reconstruction effects with complements to heads of *wh*-phrases, and the adjunct–complement contrasts are formally derived from basic tenets of the grammatical system.

6.1 Empirical issues with anti-reconstruction

Though much of the literature on anti-reconstruction focusses on the contrastive judgments of the sort seen in (72) and (73), it is important to keep in mind that classifying (73) as a condition C effect carries a further implication, namely that it is exactly as ungrammatical, for all speakers, as (77):

(77)   *He$_1$ submitted a report that John$_1$ was incompetent.

In a re-examination of the anti-reconstruction effect (and its import for the LF position of overtly moved constituents), Chierchia (1995) notes a substantial empirical problem: some speakers simply do not find cases of the form in (73) to be strongly ungrammatical. Chierchia argues that the original proposal by van Riemsdjik and Williams – that the effect is strongly correlated with depth of embedded of the name – is correct. That is, the true asymmetry is between deep-embedding cases like (72) and (73), both classified as grammatical, and cases like (78a):

(78)   a.   ??Which pictures of John does he like best?
       b.   Which pictures of himself does John like best?

Reinhart (1983) proposes that coreference between a pronoun and a name is unacceptable (pragmatically) if there is a variant of the same structure in which a reflexive is used. Chierchia observes that the shallow-embedding[13] examples like (78a) are precisely those in which Reinhart's principle favors use of a reflexive (as the acceptability of (78b) supports). (78a) is deviant because it takes a non-optimal pathway to coreference. Crucially, this is not a purely syntactic condition C effect.

In my own investigations of this effect (reported in Barss 1994, 1996, 1999) I have polled several dozen English speakers on their judgments, and found results compatible with Chierchia's remarks. A quite small group (two) of the speakers I consulted find the robust disjointness effects inside arguments cited by Friedin and Lebeaux. The majority found the examples very mildly deviant to perfect, and, critically, the same speakers found no difference of the argument-adjunct type discussed above. By contrast, all consulted speakers found the pied-piped names inside predicates to produce total condition C-level ungrammaticality. Thus the characteristic range of judgments I have found cited by most speakers is as follows, with the judgments on (79) and (80) correlated:

(79)   Which story that Fred$_1$ found in the newspaper did he$_1$ enjoy best?
       name inside relative clause: very mildly deviant to fine

(80)   Whose story that Fred$_1$ found a mistake in the newspaper did he$_1$ enjoy best?
       name inside N-complement: very mildly deviant to fine

(81)   How proud that Fred$_1$ owns a newspaper did Mary say he$_1$ was?
       name inside moved predicate: ungrammatical

(82)   Did Mary say he$_1$ was proud that Fred$_1$ owns a newspaper?
       baseline condition C, name inside predicate: ungrammatical

(83)   He$_1$ enjoyed the financial story that Fred$_1$ found in the newspaper best.
       baseline condition C, name inside adjunct: ungrammatical

(84)   He$_1$ enjoyed my story that Fred$_1$ found a mistake in the newspaper best.
       baseline condition C, name inside N-complement: ungrammatical

What is controversial, it appears, is the status of examples like (80), and the theoretical principles that are justified by classifying them as (un)grammatical. I take the combined judgments cited by Lebeaux, Chomsky, Friedin, Chierchia, and Barss to indicate two things. First, there is inter-speaker variation of judgment on cases like (80), a fact that is by itself quite interesting and deserving of theoretical attention, as binding theoretic judgments tend to be quite stable across speakers (note, for example, the lack of variation on judgments on the other structures). Second, there is strong reason to suppose that, whatever is going on with cases like (80), it is not violation of condition C, since the same speakers who find (80) perfect (or only very mildly odd) find (84) completely ungrammatical. Chierchia's proposal, which is based on pragmatic preference strategies (which one can imagine varying in strength from speaker to speaker somewhat), seems like a promising line of attack.

7   Conclusion

This overview has shown that reconstruction is fundamentally a property of movement dependencies; and NP pied-piped inside a larger moved constituent C can, in the general case, be bound with respect to any position occupied by C at any point in the derivation. Complexities arise when the moved constituent is predicative, but this class of exceptions nonetheless follows from other basic principles of movement theory. We have seen, following Chierchia

1995, that certain cases of anti-reconstruction may require appeal to non-syntactic pragmatic preference strategies, but in the main the pattern of reconstruction effects follows what appears to be exactly what we would expect, given proper understanding of the representations derived by movement and deletion operations.

NOTES

1   The overt anaphora in (5)–(7) – where the c-commanded element is overt, and the regulated relation is between it and another NP c-commanding it – is the prototypical datum exemplifying these core constraints, and such overt anaphora will be central in the more complex examples discussed below. However, it is important to keep in mind that many versions of the Binding Theory adopt a view first formally advanced in Chomsky (1981, 1982) (and implicitly suggested in earlier work), namely that the partitioning of NPs into these subclasses extends as well to phonologically null NPs, or *empty categories*, which are taken in GB-style analyses to be present in a diverse set of environments. Within this symmetric framework, NP-trace (the EC left by movement to an argument position) is subject to condition A; PRO (the subject of control infinitivals and the like) is subject to principles A and B; and *wh*-trace is classified as an R-expression, and is thus subject to condition C. Because this typology of null categories is more controversial than the typology of overt categories, and because the technical issues which arise in this area are more complex, I leave them aside here. The reader is referred to Barss (1986: ch. 4, 1999), Lasnik and

Saito (1991), Rizzi (1990: ch. 2), and Saito (1989), for discussion.

2   Related definitions:

   i. α is A-bound by β iff α and β are coindexed, β occupies an A position, and β c-commands α.

   ii. Σ is a Complete Functional Complex (CFC) iff Σ is a subphrase marker, and for any head H contained within Σ, all thematic relations of H are assigned within Σ.

   iii. K is the least CFC containing α iff K is a CFC containing α, and there is no CFC Π which contains α and is contained by K.

3   Chomsky (1993) is unclear on the actual form, if any, of the material occupying the object position after deletion. Presumably, the position itself remains, and is syntactically of category NP. This much is needed to carry over the lexical projection of the verb's argument structure to LF. From a semantic standpoint, the position must be interpreted as a variable (over individual objects) bound to the operator, a basic result carrying over from earlier work on LF (see e.g. Higginbotham 1980, 1983, Higginbotham and May 1981, May 1985). See n. 4 for further discussion.

4   This depends, of course, on exactly what semantic analysis is provided

for such "split" *wh*-expressions, in which the *wh*-determiner is divided off from the rest of the NP. Under the theory of *wh*-operators provided by Higginbotham and May (1981), May (1985), and Higginbotham (1994), *wh*-phrases are to be interpreted strictly as restricted quantifiers. Under this view, the reconstructed LFs in, for example, (39) and (44) are uninterpretable gibberish, since the operator's restriction (its first semantic argument) is embedded inside of the second argument. For the syntax of reconstruction in this form to succeed a more liberal semantic theory for interrogatives must be adopted. One such view is developed by Reinhart (1993, 1995), in which structures like (50) and (55) are to be interpreted by taking the *wh*-determiner as binding a variable over existential choice functions, and taking the embedded material as the argument of the function variable. See Barss (1994, 1999) for discussion, and demonstration of the difficulty in extending this semantic system to the full range of reconstruction data.

5   At least insofar as each lexical item in the interrogative operator is retained in the output LF, so that there is no "deletion without recoverability." It of course remains to be shown that there is a coherent method for interpreting LFs with the syntax seen in (50) as interrogatives. Such a method is set forth by Reinhart (1993, 1995, 1997), and is discussed with respect to reconstruction by Barss (1994, 1999).

6   Within the Barriers theory of extraction, there will be additional copies of the extracted phrase adjoined to each VP separating lowest copy from the highest copy, so the representation in its full form is (i):

i.   I wonder [$_{CPa}$ [which portraits of [themselves/each other]$_{2/1}$]$_3$ [$_{IP}$ the men$_1$ [$_{VP\,CPa}$ [which portraits of [themselves/each other]$_{2/1}$]$_3$ [$_{VP}$ believed [$_{CPb}$ [which portraits of [themselves/each other]$_{2/1}$]$_3$ that [$_{IPb}$ the women$_2$ had [$_{VP\,CPa}$ [which portraits of [themselves/each other]$_{2/1}$]$_3$ [$_{VP}$ placed [which portraits of [themselves/each other]$_{2/1}$]$_3$ in a scrapbook]]]]]]]].

For reasons of expositional clarity, I suppress these VP-adjoined copies in the text example, since nothing hinges on their presence for this example (the Spec, CP copy suffices for providing a copy of the anaphor local to the higher plural NP).

7   Speakers invariably find (53) fully grammatical. I am aware of some disagreement among speakers on cases like (54), some finding it perfect, others slightly degraded (perhaps due to the linear order of the anaphor and antecedent). Even this latter group of speakers invariably judge (54) as significantly better than (55) and (56).

8   A formal question arises as to what remains, if anything, of the higher copy after deletion. This question is straightforwardly answered under Chomsky's version of Brody's (1985) theory of Case checking. Since the driving force behind the movement in the first place was to satisfy the morphological need for the NP and TNS to check their NOM case features, and such checking is achieved prior to Spell-Out, nothing requires that the raised NP remains raised after Spell-Out.

9   There are semantic subtleties which arise here that are too complex to go into detail on here. See Barss (1994, 1999) for detailed discussion. The problem is that raising predicates tend to be scopal, and shift the

interpretation of NPs over which they have scope (as originally argued by May 1977, 1985). Thus although LF reconstruction of the lower copy of the raised NP is innocuous *morphologically* (see previous note), it is not innocuous *semantically*. To give a sketch of the problem, observe that (53) does not mean what (i) means, and that this interpretive difference is not easily attributed solely to the tense difference between the two:

i.   It usually strikes the children that [old pictures of themselves are amusing]

(53) strongly prefers a semantic interpretation in which the indefinite NP containing the anaphor is associated with the quantificational adverb in the matrix clause, essentially as in (ii), while (i) prefers a separated interpretation, as in (iii):

ii. [for the usual x, x a picture of the children] it strikes the children that x is amusing
iii. [for the usual time t] it strikes the children at t [that for any x, x a picture of the children] x is amusing

The dominant interpretation for (53) is at odds with the LF-reconstruction of the raised NP into the lower clause. However, due to the complexity of the effect, I will simply refer the reader to the works cited above, particularly Barss (1999: ch. 2).

10   The judgments here are mine, and those of several speakers consulted. A reviewer notes a partial degradation of acceptability in (60) on the construal of the anaphor with the lowest NP *the children*. This is reminiscent of the effect first noted in Burzio (1986), and explored in detail by Takano (1998), of the

effects of a PP-contained NP being able to antecede, with some decrease of acceptability (for some speakers, although I find them very close to perfect), an anaphor apparently c-commanded by the PP:

i.   ?John gave some pictures of themselves$_1$ [to [the kids]$_1$] (Burzio 1986: (69b), 203)
ii. ?Some pictures of themselves$_1$ were given t [to [the kids]$_1$] (Burzio 1986: (69a), 203)

Note that the decline in acceptability of (60) noted by the reviewer is attributable to the "weak" c-command-blocking effect of the presence of the preposition, if we follow the reasoning of the text that the dependency of the anaphor on *the children* is a reconstruction effect under A-movement, a point substantiated by Burzio's example in (ii). Thus in spite of the variance in judgments, the major point discussed carries: cyclic A-movement shows reconstruction effects.

11   Specifically, the objects of these verbs consistently behave as a class with other deep objects: they cannot bind an anaphoric clitic, cannot be interpreted as *arb*, cannot be syntactically passivized, and the verb + NP cannot be embedded in the clausal causative construction.

12   In Chomsky's Minimalist derivational system, movement operations (copying) and addition of new lexical material (termed Merge) are interlaced, and apply together throughout the overt derivation. However, Chomsky (1993) imposes an Extension constraint on derivations, requiring that Merge and Move obey a cyclicity requirement which entails the result for complements described in the text. Adjuncts are exempted from

Extension, and thus Lebeaux's basic proposal is carried over into the revised derivational system.

13   Heycock (1995) reports contrastive judgments, on which examples like (78a) are judged substantially better than examples like (i):

    i.   How many stories about John is he likely to invent?

Heycock presents an interesting discussion of the semantic and pragmatic factors which might produce such differential judgments. My own judgment (and those of the speakers I have consulted) accords with that reported in Chierchia (1995), on which no significant difference is detected on (i) vs. (78a).

VI External Evaluation of Syntax

22 Syntactic Change

ANTHONY S. KROCH

0 Introduction

Over historical time languages change at every level of structure: vocabulary, phonology, morphology and syntax. How and why such change occurs are the key questions addressed by the discipline of historical linguistics. From the perspective of modern generative grammar, language change is narrowly constrained by the requirement that all languages conform to the specifications of the human language faculty; but the fact of language change, like the brute fact of the structural diversity of the world's languages, marks a limit to the biological specification of language. Just how wide a range of variation biology allows is perhaps the major open question of theoretical linguistics; but whatever that range may be, it is the field on which historical developments play themselves out. The necessity for a richly specified Universal Grammar (UG) follows from the logical problem of language acquisition, so that the synchronic linguist considers as candidate analyses only learnable ones couched in theories that specify clearly what is to be learned and what is built in. The modern study of syntactic change, the topic of this chapter,[1] is also often couched in terms of learning; but, as we will see, the study of diachrony adds complexities of its own.

Language change is by definition a failure in the transmission across time of linguistic features. Such failures, in principle, could occur within groups of adult native speakers of language, who for some reason substitute one feature for another in their usage, as happens when new words are coined and substituted for old ones; but in the case of syntactic and other grammatical features, such innovation by monolingual adults is largely unattested. Instead, failures of transmission seem to occur in the course of language acquisition; that is, they are failures of learning. Since, in an instance of syntactic change, the feature that learners fail to acquire is learnable in principle, having been part of the grammar of the language in the immediate past, the cause of the failure must lie either in some change, perhaps subtle, in the character of the evidence available to the learner, or in some difference in the learner, for example in the learner's age at acquisition, as in the case of change induced through second language acquisition by adults in situations of language contact. Our understanding of transmission failures is very limited, because our grasp of the relationship between the evidence presented to a learner and the grammar acquired is still imprecise. Studies of language acquisition generally take for granted that the evidence to which the learner is exposed is sufficient to ensure accurate learning by a competent language learner; that is, a child within the critical age period. This assumption is perfectly reasonable under normal circumstances but language change shows that there are limits to its validity. We do not know what these limits are, however, and it is not clear how to find them, given that experimentally manipulating the evidence presented to learners is neither practical nor ethical. In this context, documented cases of change have become interesting as natural experiments in language transmission. The interpretation of these experiments is, however, extremely difficult due to the limitations of the preserved evidence in quantity and sociolinguistic range and to the lack of native speaker informants. It is not surprising, therefore, that conclusive results have been hard to come by, and in what follows I will necessarily be describing as much or more the open questions and the research agenda of diachronic syntax as its established results.

1   Change and Stability

At the level of syntax, the amount of change that languages undergo over a given stretch of time varies tremendously, both from language to language and within the history of a single language. If, for example, we compare the syntax of English to that of Japanese from the medieval period to the present day, we find that English has changed enormously while Japanese has hardly changed at all. English has undergone three major word order changes: at the clause level, it has shifted from INFL-final to INFL-medial word order and from verb second to subject-verb order; and at the verb phrase level, it has changed from OV to VO order. Japanese, by contrast, has remained head final at all levels of structure. The existence of languages whose syntax has been stable over many centuries raises doubts as to the plausibility of theories of change that impute to syntax any inherent instability, and linguists differ on whether such instability exists. At the same time, syntactic change is a common phenomenon and may occur in the apparent absence of any external trigger. The English verb *do*, for example, seems to have developed spontaneously into an auxiliary from one of its main verb senses at some point in Middle English. The problem of why change occurs when and where it does is termed by Weinreich et al. (1968), in their foundational work on language change, the "actuation" problem; and it is, for all levels of structure including syntax, the biggest mystery in diachrony. The central issue here is whether languages are stable or unstable by nature; that is, leaving aside the effects of language contact and other forms of social change, should we expect languages to manifest change or stasis? We do not know the answer to this question. It is important to recognize, moreover, that the answer may be different for different levels of linguistic structure. For instance, changes in pronunciation might arise spontaneously out of the well-known phonetic variability of speech, while endogenous changes at higher levels of structure might be rare or non-existent.

Given the centrality of imperfect language acquisition to the actuation of change, we are forced, when thinking about diachrony, to go beyond the standard generative idealization of instantaneous acquisition by an ideal learner. Under the standard idealization, after all, if we have a speech community in which all of the adult members have learned grammar G for language L and this situation has been stable for at least one generation, the language can never change, for a child born into such a community must also learn G. If not, how did the child's parents learn G, given that, by hypothesis, they were exposed to L? In other words, there appears to be no room for endogenous language change, a point which has been recognized by generative theorists in recent years (Lightfoot 1991, 1999, Clark and Roberts 1993). Of course, if the conditions of linguistic transmission are altered, for example, by contact with another speech community, then change may well occur, since the linguistic experience of children of the community is likely to change. Since language change is ubiquitous, it might seem that the standard model must be overly simple in some crucial respect; and linguists have proposed various complications to allow for endogenous change. For syntax, the most obvious proposal is that change at other levels of structure, however caused, provokes grammatical reanalysis. For example, the loss of morphological case distinctions due to phonological weakening at the ends of words is generally thought to lead to rigidity of word order to compensate for the increase in ambiguity induced by the loss of case. Thus, Dutch and German differ in the rigidity of order of pre-verbal constituents in the expected way: Dutch has lost its case endings and has nearly fixed word order in the verb phrase while German, which has retained the four-case system of early Germanic, allows fairly free reordering of verb phrase constituents. Similarly, when we compare Latin to its daughter languages in the Romance family, we find that word order has in various respects become more rigid, concomitantly with the loss of case morphology.[2] There is a sense, however, in which syntactic changes induced by prior morphophonological ones are not endogenously caused. Aside from the question of what has triggered the morphophonological changes, such changes do not require that we postulate any inherent instabilities or tendencies toward change within the syntactic module of UG or the grammars of particular languages. Instead, the morphophonological changes induce syntactic change simply by altering the evidence available to the learner.

Believers in endogenous syntactic change have postulated different mechanisms that introduce instability of one form or another into the acquisition of syntax *per se*. One early generative proposal that makes room for such syntactic change is that of Andersen (1973), who suggests that child language learners faced with the linguistic data of their environment may hypothesize a grammar different from that of the speakers from whom their input comes. If the new grammar differs in its output from the original grammar only slightly, the learner may not notice the difference and so fail to correct the mistake. In other words, the child learner has direct access only to the data of language use, not to the grammar(s) that speakers use in generating that data; and the inferential process by which the child draws grammatical conclusions from the data is subject to error. There is no doubt that language transmission is sometimes imperfect, adult second language learning being the clearest such case. But the abstract possibility of imperfect transmission tells little about what changes or how much change to expect, because we do not know how accurately children learn the grammars of the speakers around them or what sorts of error they might characteristically make and not correct with maturation. Indeed, the stability of many languages over long periods of time, even with regard to small details, suggests that ordinary language acquisition cannot in general be very inaccurate. Also, even if it were, some factor or factors would have to impute a direction to its inaccuracies or to their spread in the speech community in order for observable language change to result from them. Since the time of Andersen's article, moreover, generative theory has moved in the direction of a more highly specified theory of UG, which seems to leave less room for erroneous learning, since less is learned to begin with.

Lightfoot (1991, 1999) has proposed a somewhat different approach to the relationship between learning and change. He argues forcefully against the notion of tendencies toward change inherent to syntax and against the possibility of a theory of change that would explicate such tendencies. Grammars change, in his view, when there is sufficient change in the data used by the learner to set grammatical parameters. Otherwise, they are stably transmitted. Lightfoot's view rules out endogenous change in syntax, but this leaves him with a problem in accounting for any changes not derivable from external sources like language contact or changes in phonology/morphology. One might decide that there are no such changes; certainly the case for them can be questioned. But Lightfoot leaves room for the possibility that languages may change in the absence of grammar change through drifts in the frequencies with which various sentence types are used. Eventually, this skewing of frequencies becomes so pronounced that learners are not sufficiently exposed to crucial data and thus acquire a different grammar from that of previous generations. Lightfoot's proposal does not depend on erroneous learning but it still depends on a fragile assumption; namely, on the existence of directionally consistent drifts in usage over long periods of time that are unconnected to grammar change. The evidence for such drifts is, at the least, uncertain. The best-studied cases of long-term syntactic drift are most plausibly cases of grammar competition (that is, syntactic diglossia) in which the competing forms may differ in social register, with an unreflecting vernacular variant slowly driving a conservative written one out of use (see below). Where no such process is at work, there is evidence that usage frequencies remain stable over long periods of time. Thus, one common explanation proferred for the shift from verb final to verb medial word order in the history of English is a gradual increase in the frequency of rightward extraposition of complements and adjuncts (Aitchison 1979, Stockwell 1977).[3] There is, however, no careful quantitative study of extraposition in English from a diachronic perspective that takes into account what is currently known about the syntax of the language, so the hypothesis remains a speculation. Moreover, there is a quantitative study of the required type for Yiddish, which underwent an evolution similar to that of English (Santorini 1993); and although Santorini's sample is too small to permit absolute certainty on the matter, her figures indicate that the overall frequency of extraposition, though varying considerably from text to text, neither increases nor decreases across the five centuries covered by her sample.

Another example of stability in usage where one might have expected drift is adverb placement in English. We discuss below the loss of verb to INFL (V-to-I) movement in late Middle English, for which one piece of evidence is a change in the apparent placement of pre-verbal adverbs. The canonical position of such adverbs in Modern English is between the auxiliary verb and the main verb in sentences where both are present, as in (1):

(1) Mary has always preferred lemons to limes.

In finite clauses, the adverb appears after the tensed verb when it is an auxiliary and before it when it is a main verb, as illustrated in (2):

(2) a. Lemons are always preferred to limes.
     b. Mary always prefers lemons to limes.

As is well known, Middle English manifested a different placement of the adverb in sentences like (2b). Instead of appearing before the verb, it appeared immediately postverbally:

(3) Quene Ester looked never with swich an eye. (cited in Kroch 1989b)

The difference between the order in (2b) and (3) is standardly attributed to the loss, in early Modern English, of verb movement to a functional head, INFL, which hosts tense and agreement information.[4] In Middle English, as in Modern French and many other modern European languages, verb movement, which serves to license the tense and agreement features, is visible on the surface, in the case under discussion through the change in the relative position of the main verb and adverb in (3) relative to (2b). In Modern English, by contrast, this overt movement has been replaced, for main verbs but not for auxiliaries, by a grammatically equivalent covert process. Less often discussed than the above examples is the adverb placement possibility in (4):

(4) Mary always has preferred lemons to limes.

The word order here is less common than that in (1), but it is grammatical and occurs as a regular minority pattern in both modern and Middle English texts. It is notable that the grammaticality of (4) implies that (2b) is structurally ambiguous in Modern English, but not in Middle English. Because (2b) contains only one verb and because that verb does not move in Modern English, we cannot tell whether the adverb is in the pre-INFL position or in the position between INFL and the main verb. The two possibilities can be represented as follows:

(5)   a.   [IP Mary always [I ϕ] [VP prefers lemons to limes]]
      b.   [IP Mary [I ϕ] always [VP prefers lemons to limes]]

In Middle English, the verb always moves to INFL, so that the word order in (2b) implies a pre-INFL position for the adverb; that is, the analysis in (6):

(6)   [IP Mary always [I prefers$_i$] [VP t$_i$ lemons to limes]]

Given this situation, we might have expected the following diachronic scenario in early Modern English: the gradual loss of V-to-I movement increased the frequency of examples like (2b); and since these examples were ambiguous, speakers concluded that, along with the loss of V-to-I movement for main verbs, the pre-INFL position for adverbs was becoming more frequent. This would then result in a rise in the frequency of examples like (4), where the pre-INFL position of the adverb is visible. However, no such increase occurs. On the contrary, corpus based estimates of the frequency of such examples show no change between late Middle English and today. It remains constant at about 15 per cent, with little variation from sample to sample (Kroch 1989b). Apparently, even where surface frequencies are changing, speakers are able to correctly associate such changes with their underlying grammatical cause, and they do not alter their rate of use of other structures which are string-wise but not structurally identical to those undergoing the change.

   Although they do not settle the matter, the cases we have presented cast considerable doubt on the idea that the usage frequencies of syntactic options not connected to an ongoing grammatical change ever drift in the way that Lightfoot suggests. But before we leave the issue, we should consider another case, one where Lightfoot and others have documented an undoubted long-term historical evolution which might be considered an instance of drift. The case is that of the English modals, which began as morphosyntactically normal verbs in Old English and over centuries turned into a special class of words with distinct syntactic properties, crucially the failure to occur in non-finite contexts (Lightfoot 1979, Planck 1984, Warner 1983, 1993). Here the developments are complex and involve several distinct grammatical changes. To begin with, the modals came to be unique among verbs in lacking the third person singular ending (-*s* in Modern English). This happened because they belonged to the Germanic morphological class of "preterit-present" verbs, whose present tense is historically a past form. In Old English there were several non-modal verbs of this class, but they all fell out of the language in early Middle English. A consequence of this development was that, as the second person singular *thou* with its corresponding -*st* verbal ending was replaced by *you* plus a zero inflection in early Modern English, the modals became unique among verbs in being totally uninflected. Second, the modal verbs generally resisted co-occurrence with the *to* infinitive as it spread in Middle English, while most other verbs adopted it. Thirdly, the past tense forms of the modals (*might, could, would,* and so forth) stopped signaling past tense in the course of Middle English and became instead indicators of subjunctive or conditional mood, as the morphological marking of mood on English verbs dropped out of use. Finally, the modals lost the ability to take noun phrase direct objects, the last clear signal that they were ordinary verbs. Lightfoot (1979) argues that once this last change occurred, learners no longer had sufficient evidence to catego-rize the modals as verbs and instead assigned them to a separate class, which could only occur under INFL. At this point, they became restricted to the position of the tensed auxiliary. There is no doubt that the drift described by Lightfoot is real, but its significance as a paradigm for diachronic evolution is doubtful. Warner (1983) has shown that what Lightfoot considers the signal of the reanalysis of the modals, their mid-sixteenth-century disappearance from non-finite contexts, actually occurs simultaneously with one of the changes that Lightfoot treats as a precondition for the reanalysis, the loss of direct objects, and before another putative precondition, the complete loss of verbal inflection. The loss of the second person singular occurs in the course of the seventeenth century, so the reanalysis must have taken place despite the evid-ence from this inflection. Furthermore, there are modern English auxiliaries – for example, auxiliary *do*[5] and the copula of the *is to* V construction – which have verbal inflection but cannot occur in non-finite contexts. Warner also points out that different modals appear to have lost their non-finite uses at different times, with *must* and *shall* far in advance of *can, may,* and *will*. Lightfoot (1991) accepts Warner's factual emendations but denies that they affect his conclusion that there was a reanalysis of the modals, that it occurred in the sixteenth century (though perhaps earlier for *must* and *shall*) and that it was an accumulation of exceptional properties that triggered the reanalysis. The alter-native, however, is that the modals remain verbs, just with an increasing number of exceptional features. The more general point here is that no one has given a causal account of the drift that led to the modern situation, whether it ends in grammatical reanalysis or not. We would like to know whether the history of the modals is just a series of accidents or whether some directive force is involved, but we do not. Hence, even in this well-studied case, skepticism about long-term tendencies in syntactic change remains warranted.

The single most widely cited case for long-term tendencies in syntax is that of cross-category harmony. In his wide-ranging typological studies, Greenberg established certain very general correlations among linguistic features, which linguists have ever since tried to explain. In syntax, the most important of these have been word order correlations across constituent types, which can be summarized as follows (Greenberg 1966): VO languages tend also to place adjectival and genitive modifiers after their head nouns and to be prepositional. OV languages tend to have prenominal adjectival and genitive modifiers and to be postpositional. If modifiers and complements are grouped together in opposition to heads,[6] these correlations can be seen to define two ideal word order types: head initial and head final. It has been claimed repeatedly that there is an overarching tendency in long-term linguistic evolution for languages to move in the direction of one or the other of these types because something in syntax favors cross-category harmony in directionality (Hawkins 1979, 1983). One immediate problem with this idea is that although a few languages, like Japanese or Irish, are consistently head final or head initial, most are inconsistent. For instance, English is VO and prepositional but has prenominal adjectives and genitives, while classical Latin and Farsi are OV but prepositional. Other languages, like Chinese or Yiddish, show an apparent mix of headedness at the clausal level, so that there is even controversy over whether they are VO or OV. The lack of consistency in directionality in most languages raises questions of how strong the pressure for harmony could possibly be and where in the system it could be located. Lightfoot (1979) points out that in learning a language children can have no access to any long-term tendency toward consistency. They simply learn the language to which they are exposed. Given this overwhelming fact, it is hard to see what causal force consistency could have.

Vincent (1976), relying on the work of Kuno (1974), has proposed a partial solution to finding the causal force behind cross-category harmony, based on the idea that harmony reduces perceptual complexity. As is well known, center embedded constructions are difficult to process, so much so that recursive center embedding often leads to a breakdown, as in the following standard example:

(7)   a.   The dog that the rat bit chased the cat.
       b.   *The cat that the dog that the rat bit chased died.

Kuno shows that in SOV languages like Japanese there would be many more cases of center embedding with postnominal relative clauses than there are with the actual prenominal ones, while in VSO languages the reverse holds. Within the noun phrase, there is a similar correlation. If noun phrases are head final, center embedding will be induced when a noun takes a prepositional complement/adjunct, but not when it takes a postpositional one. If noun phrases are head initial, the situation is again exactly reversed. Thus, the tendency toward harmony may be driven by a pressure to minimize center embedding. Of course, there is at least one other way of avoiding center embedding; namely, extraposition of the offending constituent. Thus, German, though an SOV language, has postnominal relatives; but these are often extraposed to the right of the verb:

(8) a. ... daß wir die Studenten [die   der Professor uns   vorgestellt
       ... that we the students   whom the professor to-us introduced
       hat] besucht haben
       has visited have
       "that we visited the students whom the professor introduced to us"
     b. ... daß wir die Studenten besucht haben [die   der Professor
       ... that we the students   visited have   whom the professor
       uns   vorgestellt hat]
       to-us introduced has

Repeated application of extraposition eliminates recursive center embedding:

(9) a. *... daß wir die Studenten [die   der Professor [der Anglistik
       ... that we the students   whom the professor who English
       lehrt]   uns vorgestellt hat] besucht haben
       teaches to-us introduced has visited   have
       "that we visited the students whom the professor who teaches Eng-
       lish introduced to us"
     b. ... daß wir die Studenten besucht haben [die   der Professor
       ... that we the students   visited have   whom the professor
       uns   vorgestellt hat] [der Anglistik lehrt]
       to-us introduced has   who English   teaches

Now, some SOV languages, Japanese among them, do not allow the sort
of extraposition found in German, but it is not clear why different languages
use different devices to mitigate the effects of center embedding. The basic
problem here is that no causal mechanism is proposed that directly relates
the processing problem posed by center embedding to language change. Until
such a mechanism has been proposed, the putative connection between processing and change cannot be evaluated (see McMahon 1994 for further
discussion).

   In recent work on the history of Germanic, Kiparsky (1996) proposes a mixed
model of the shift from OV to VO in those languages where it occurred. He
suggests that the pressure for cross-category harmony or a similar endogenous
pressure toward optimization[7] was the underlying ("effective") cause of the
shift but that there was also an enabling cause, namely the rise of verb second
(or perhaps INFL-medial) word order in subordinate clauses. Since the initial
constituent of such a verb medial subordinate clause was almost always a
subject, the surface word order in these clauses would be SVO whenever there
was no auxiliary verb. Of course, the presence of an auxiliary would lead to
S-Aux-OV order, unless the object was extraposed, which was also possible. In
any case, Kiparsky says that due to the underlying preference for harmony,
the languages shifted when the rise of verb second order in subordinate clauses
reached the point where the pressure for harmony could overcome the remaining evidence in the input. He points out that learners are ordinarily very

sensitive to the input, even to low-frequency evidence, so that, by itself, the rise of subordinate clause verb second word order would not have triggered the shift from OV to VO. In consequence, he believes that the preference for harmony was a necessary additional factor. It is difficult to tell how likely Kiparsky's scenario is to be correct. In the two cases for which we have the best evidence, English and Yiddish, there is some reason to believe that the change was triggered by language contact (Santorini 1989, Kroch and Taylor to appear); that is, by an exogenous rather than an endogenous cause. More generally, however, it is important to realize that Kiparsky does not give us an account of how a learner would evaluate the optimization pressure against the pressure to cover the input data. Just as with Vincent's proposal, we will simply not be in a position to evaluate Kiparsky's account until a more highly articulated causal model is proposed. To reach this point with respect either to Vincent's or to Kiparsky's proposal will require considerable advances in our knowledge of language processing and learning, respectively.

2   Syntactic Change and First Language Acquisition

Understanding the relationship between language acquisition and language change requires answering the question of exactly what conditions of learning lead to the acquisition of a given grammar and how much these conditions must change before a different grammar is learned. These issues are centrally addressed in the work of Lightfoot (1979, 1991, 1999), who has argued that learners do not pay attention to all of the syntactic features of the language they are acquiring. In essence, they are sensitive only to root clauses (they are "degree 0 learners" in Lightfoot's terminology)[8] and only to specific cues that provide unambiguous evidence for given parameter settings, which are triggered on exposure to those cues. Other approaches allow the learner access to properties of embedded clauses and allow the learner to entertain different parameter settings on the way to learning the correct ones (Clark 1992a). Lightfoot has argued that there is diachronic evidence in support of his model of acquisition; but while there is no doubt that diachronic developments often show the effects of changing input data on output grammars, it is less certain that such data can help us to choose among models. One case where the promise and problems of this enterprise are particularly evident is Lightfoot's (1991) analysis of the shift from OV to VO in English. His argument goes as follows: Old English was underlyingly verb final, like modern Dutch and German. Although the clearest evidence for this parameter setting is found in subordinate clause word order, child learners do not have access to this information, so they must have set the parameter on the basis of main clause evidence. The best kinds of main clause evidence were main clauses with verb final order, which were possible in Old English (unlike modern Dutch and German), and the placement of separable prefixes, which were left behind when the verb moved leftward to INFL or COMP, as it generally did in main clauses. The following examples illustrate these cases:

(10) he Gode þancode (Lightfoot 1991: (24c))
      he God   thanked
      "he thanked God"

(11) þa   *sticode* him mon   þa eagon *ut* (Lightfoot 1991: (18a))
      then stuck him someone the eyes   out
      "then his eyes were put out"

Over time these indications of the underlying position of the verb declined in frequency until, by the end of the Old English period (the twelfth century), they were no longer frequent enough for children to recognize that their language was underlyingly verb final. Instead, they reanalyzed it in accordance with the medial surface position of the verb. At the time of this reanalysis, subordinate clauses were still predominantly verb final, so that if children had had access to them as input data for acquisition, the reanalysis would not have occurred. Since main clauses had become almost entirely verb medial by the time of the reanalysis, however, we might ask what evidence there is that any such reorganization has taken place. Lightfoot's answer is that there was a catastrophic decline in the frequency of verb final word order in subordinate clauses between the end of the eleventh century and the first quarter of the twelfth, as found in the Peterborough manuscript of the Anglo-Saxon Chronicle. The relevant frequency drops from more than 50 percent verb final to less than 10 percent, apparently in striking confirmation of the hypothesis that the grammatical parameter is set on the basis of main clause word order and that subordinate clauses shift suddenly at the point of reanalysis.

However, one can raise significant linguistic and sociolinguistic objections to Lightfoot's account. Pintzuk (1991, 1993) has shown that the gradual rise of verb medial (more properly INFL-medial) word order in Old English on which Lightfoot is relying occurs in both main and subordinate clauses and, moreover, that the rate of increase is the same in the two contexts. This is an instance of the Constant Rate Effect (see below), which seems to hold in cases of grammar competition; and Pintzuk argues that Old English exhibited such competition in underlying word order; that is, that the existence of verb final main clauses, along with other features, shows that verb medial order in Old English was not a transformational variant of underlying verb final order, as it is in modern Dutch and German, but an independent parametric option. If Pintzuk is correct, the linguistic significance of the catastrophe in the Peterborough data becomes suspect; and there is, in fact, good evidence that the discontinuity is a sociolinguistic rather than a grammatical phenomenon. Up until 1122, the Peterborough manuscript was written in standard Old English and exhibited the predominantly verb final order found in other documents. In 1122, just at the apparent point of reanalysis, the handwriting changes, as does the quality of the language. It is clear from the morphology and spelling that the new scribe no longer commands literary Old English. After all, more than fifty years had now passed since the Norman Conquest, which destroyed the Old English literary culture, so that the monks trained in that culture must all have died off. The monk who took over in 1122 was certainly writing a different sort of language than the scribe before him. Instead of literary Old English, he seems to have been using something closer to his vernacular; and if so, the sharp change in frequency observed by Lightfoot reflects a dialect difference, not an internal reanalysis. The vernacular, unsurprisingly, was more innovative than the written standard; hence, the jump in frequency of the progressive INFL-medial order. It would be going too far to say that the considerations we have raised definitively refute Lightfoot's account. Rather they raise questions that have not been answered. More generally, they show how delicate the interpretation of diachronic evidence is and suggest that it is much easier to explain the past through the study of the present than vice versa.

Given a set of assumptions about UG, successful acquisition of a language's syntax clearly depends on the interaction of its structural properties with the character of the learner, so that as we learn more about the latter, we have a hope of better understanding diachrony. In addition to these matters, however, there are issues concerning the robustness of the evidence for linguistic structure being acquired that arise specifically in the context of change. Clark and Roberts (1993) make this point in discussing the loss of V2 in Middle French, an example that is worth citing at some length (see Roberts 1993 for a full discussion of the historical issues). Old French was a V2 language, like the Germanic languages; but Clark and Roberts argue that the evidence for the V2 property in Old French was relatively weak because other properties of the language obscured it in a large fraction of the sentences that a learner would hear. First of all, Old French was a partial pro-drop language so that many sentences, like (12) below, were consistent with both a V2 analysis, as in (13a), and a non-V2 analysis, as in (13b):

(12) Si firent grant joie la   nuit. (Clark and Roberts 1993: (51c))
      so made great joy the night
      "So they made great joy at night."

(13) a.   [CP si [C firent$_i$] [IP pro t$_i$ grant joie la nuit]]
      b.   [IP si [IP pro firent grant joie la nuit]]

Second, more than a third of the sentences in the Old French corpus are subject initial, as in (14):

(14) Aucassins ala   par   le forest. (Clark and Roberts 1993: (51b))
      Aucassin went through the forest
      "Aucassin walked through the forest."

Such sentences gave no evidence that the language was V2, since their word order is consistent with what would be found in a non-V2 language with underlying SVO word order; that is, a sentence like (14) is equally compatible with either of the two analyses in (15):

(15)   a.   [CP Aucassins$_i$ [C ala$_j$] [IP t$_i$ t$_j$ par le forest]]
      b.   [IP Aucassins ala par le forest]

Only sentences with overt subjects and non-subject topics, like (16) below, provided the learner of Old French, through the inversion of the subject and tensed verb, with unambiguous evidence for V2:

(16)   (Et)   lors demande Galaad   ses armes. (Clark and Roberts 1993: (51a))
      (and) then requests   Galahad his weapons.
      "And then Galahad asks for his weapons."

Sentences which give conclusive evidence for a given parameter setting are said by Clark and Roberts to "express" the parameter; and in Old French, sentences expressing the V2 parameter were frequent enough to guarantee that it was learned, despite the high frequency of sentences that did not express it.

In Middle French, certain changes occurred that reduced the frequency of sentences expressing the V2 parameter. Most clearly, the use of left dislocation began to increase at the expense of topicalization. In left dislocated sentences, illustrated in (17) below, the initial constituent binds a resumptive pronoun and is adjoined to CP, thereby generating superficial verb fourth word order:

(17)   [Les autres arts et   sciences]$_i$, Alexandre les$_i$ honoroit bien.
      the other   arts and sciences   Alexander them honored well
      "The other arts and sciences, Alexander honored (them) well."

Clearly, these sentences do not express the V2 parameter, since fronting of the direct object occurs without inversion of the subject with the tensed verb. Contrary to appearances, however, the examples are consistent with a V2 analysis. First of all, the object pronoun, being a clitic attached to the tensed verb, does not count for position, just as in all of the other V2 Romance dialects. As the following example shows, the tensed verb in a topicalized sentence inverts with the subject, as expected in a V2 language, in the presence of a pre-verbal clitic pronoun:

(18)   Toutes ces   choses te   presta Nostre Sires.
      all   these things to-you lent   our   Lord
      "All of these things our Lord lent to you."

Second, the left dislocated object is adjoined to CP and belongs to a separate intonation phrase; and in consequence, it too does not count for position. The other historical V2 languages, medieval German and Old English, for example, also exhibit this characteristic. Left dislocation is, however, infrequent in the stable V2 languages, including Old French; and as the frequency of left dislocation rises in Middle French, the evidence for V2 declines due to the concomitant drop in the frequency of sentences in which the subject and tensed verb invert.

Apparently, there was a change in the preferred prosody of French sometime during the Middle French period which favored placing a fronted constituent in a separate intonation phrase, something that is only possible with the left dislocation structure (Adams 1987). In Modern French, it is clear that sentences like (17) contain two phrase final contours and that they contrast with cases of focus movement, like (19), where there is no resumptive pronoun and the entire sentence constitutes a single intonation phrase:

(19)   Dix francs, ce truc m'a   coûté.
       ten francs this thing me-has cost.
       "Ten francs, this cost me."

It is not clear what caused the change in French prosody but it is clear what effect it had on the evidence for V2 available to learners. A further reduction in the frequency of sentences expressing the parameter may have resulted from a change in the status of subject pronouns in Middle French. It is well known that in Old French, subject pronouns, unlike object pronouns, were not clitics. By Middle French, however, they had developed into clitics; and Adams (1987) points out that the earliest apparent exceptions to V2 word order were overwhelmingly sentences with pronominal subjects, that is, with the word order XP-pro-V. If pronoun subjects by this point were clitics, these sentences would have been consistent with V2; but like the left dislocation cases, they would not express the V2 parameter. Hence, their rising frequency would have further reduced the evidence for the V2 parameter available to learners. At this point, the evidence might have become so weak that speakers abandoned the V2 hypothesis (Platzack 1995). Exactly why they should do so is, however, open to question. Clark and Roberts suggest that a combination of two factors was involved. First, sentences with the order XP-pro-V might sometimes have been taken by learners as exceptions to V2 rather than as consistent with it. This interpretation would have arisen because the clitic status of subject pronouns is less clear than that of object pronouns. Once this interpretation arose, learners would have been faced with two mutually inconsistent parameter settings for their language. In this situation, Clark and Roberts claim that learners would have opted for the grammar that assigned structurally simpler representations to sentences. The idea here is similar to the Transparency Principle of Lightfoot (1979), which states that syntactic derivations with fewer steps and whose surface outputs are closer to their underlying inputs are preferred to more complex derivations where the relationship between underlying and surface forms is more opaque.

The varying robustness of the evidence for V2 in different languages may be implicated in the different historical fate of the property across languages. Many of the medieval western European languages had the V2 property, and all of the Germanic languages except for modern English continue to obey it. English and the Romance languages, however, have lost the property. It is interesting that among the languages that retain V2, some are verb medial and some are verb final; but all of the languages that lost it are verb medial. In the case of English, the loss of V2 is subsequent to a shift from verb final to verb medial order (Kemenade 1987). This pattern raises the question of whether there are linguistic reasons why V2 might be a more stable property of verb final than of verb medial languages. Consider the following examples from German, a verb final V2 language:

(20) a. Er hat sie gesehen.
          he has her seen
      b. . . . daß er sie gesehen hat
          . . . that he her seen   has

The V2 property is generally limited to root clauses;[9] and where it does not apply, it is generally assumed that something close to the underlying order of the tensed clause will surface, as a necessary consequence of the architecture of UG; hence the verb final word order in (20b). The contrast between (20a) and (20b) gives a learner of German clear evidence that even simple subject initial sentences are V2.[10] In an underlyingly verb medial language, however, sentences equivalent to (20) provide no such evidence. This must be the point of Clark and Roberts's Old French example (14), though they do not explicitly raise the issue of the absence of a contrast with subordinate clause word order in the case of an SVO language. To see clearly what is at issue, consider the translation of the sentences in (20) into Swedish, a modern verb medial V2 language:

(21) a. Han har sett henne.
          he   has seen her
      b. . . . att han har sett henne.
          . . . that he   has seen her

Here the subordinate and main clause word orders are the same and so provide no evidence to a learner, who must rely on other sentence types, most obviously root clauses with topicalized constituents like the following, which exhibit XVS order:

(22) Boken   har jag inte köpt.
      book-the have I   not bought
      "The book, I didn't buy."

Since roughly half of the sentences in conversational speech are subject initial, a much higher proportion of the sentences heard by learners of German give evidence for V2 than for learners of Swedish. Of course, Swedish learners must hear more than enough sentences to acquire the V2 property, since all Swedish speakers acquire it; and since Swedish, like all the Scandinavian languages, has been stably V2 throughout its recorded history, the evidence must be robust. However, the diachronic syntax of English and French cast additional light on the matter of robustness. As we have seen, it is possible for changes to occur that weaken the evidence for V2 over verb medial structure for root clauses; but these changes only have their effect when they occur in a language whose underlying word order is already verb medial. In an underlyingly verb final language, surface SVO word order itself is evidence for V2. Hence, it seems that such a language could not lose the V2 property unless it first shifted from verb final to verb medial underlying order. In this way, the fact that no verb final V2 language has lost the V2 property would receive an explanation under a Clark and Roberts-type model.

It is sometimes thought that English is an example of just the path to the loss of V2 for verb final languages that this model requires, but the history and the grammar both are subject to different interpretations and the question remains very much an open one. Old English was largely verb final in subordinate clauses and verb second in root clauses; but by the beginning of Middle English (*c.*1200), the underlying order was almost entirely verb medial. At that point, the language was still verb second, but some time after 1250 verb second word order started to decline. By 1400 it was largely gone, at least in the Midlands dialects. The evidence for the verb second property was always somewhat complex in English because, in sentences with pronoun subjects, a combination of factors led to consistent verb third word order; that is, there was a systematic contrast between sentences like (23) and (24), taken from Pintzuk (1991):

(23)   &   of heom twam is eall manncynn cumen (WHom 6.52)
        and of them two   is all mankind   come

(24)   Ælc yfel he mæg don
        each evil he can   do

Since this distinction is already found in the oldest Old English documents, which date from the end of the eighth century, and V2 is stable until some time after 1250, the complexity here clearly did not interfere with the learning of the V2 property, a fact which raises questions about the relevance of the rise of subject clitics in the French case. On the other hand, it might well have been a predisposing factor, which only had its effect in combination with others, including the shift to underlying SVO word order. Another factor is that English always had certain initial adverbs that could induce verb third word order, as in the following Old English example from the Anglo-Saxon Chronicle entry for the year 892:

(25)   Her   Oswald se eadiga arcebisceop forlet   þis lif.
       in-this-year Oswald the blessed archbishop forsook this life.

Originally, only scene-setting temporal adverbs allowed this possibility, which
is also attested in medieval German; but by early Middle English the range of
adverbs that occurred with verb third word order seems to have widened, so
that, alongside cases of V2, we find, in the earliest Middle English prose (texts
in the West Midlands dialect from the first half of the thirteenth century),
examples like the following from the "Ancrene Riwle":

(26) a.   Þus Seint Iame descriueð religiun
           thus Saint James describes religion
      b.   ofte a ful haʒer smið smeðeð a ful wac   knif
           often a full skillful smith forges   a full weak knife
      c.   &   þer   god schawede him seolf to ham
           and there God showed   himself   to them

These examples might be taken as the first indications of the loss of the V2
constraint, but this interpretation is doubtful because, in the case of topicalized
arguments, V2 word order remains categorical in these texts. Nevertheless, the
widening of the class of adverbs that allow verb third order certainly reduced
the evidence available to the learner that the language was indeed V2. Again,
the importance of adverb initial, verb third sentences to the historical evolution is hard to assess. It is known that the modern verb second languages
allow verb third order with certain adverbial expressions, as in the following
German and Swedish cases:

(27)   Nichtdestotrotz, wir müssen weiter gehen.
       nevertheless   we must   further go

(28)   Utan   tvekan, hon var mycket vacker. (cited in Platzack 1995)
       without doubt   she was very   beautiful

Since these languages, crucially Swedish given the model we are exploring,
are stably V2, such sentences may not have played much of a role in the
English developments. Still, the range of adverbs that allowed verb third word
order in early Middle English seems somewhat wider than in the stable V2
languages, and this difference may have been enough to affect the behavior of
English learners.

   Although it is suggestive that V2 word order begins to decline shortly after
the definitive shift of English to verb medial order, it remains quite unclear
whether the relatively weak evidence for V2 in Middle English really did play
a role in the eventual loss of the property. At the same period (the middle of
the fourteenth century) when V2 is clearly declining in the Midlands dialects

of English, the dialect of Kent in the south preserves V2 largely without change, though the grammatical conditioning of V2 is the same in Kent as in the Midlands and though Kentish is, at that time, strictly verb medial. On the other hand, in the north the loss of V2 seems to be more advanced than in the Midlands; but in the northern dialect our best evidence says that V2 word order was equally characteristic of sentences with pronoun subjects and of those with full noun phrase subjects (Kroch and Taylor 1997, Kroch et al. 1997). In other words, the evidence for V2 was actually stronger in the dialect which lost the property first than in the dialects where the loss occurred somewhat later. As we will see below, however, there might actually be a learning based explanation for this paradoxical circumstance once we take the effects of dialect contact into account.

3   Language Contact and Syntactic Change

One actuating force for syntactic change whose existence cannot be doubted is language contact. Examples of syntactic changes due to contact abound. Perhaps the most famous is the convergence in syntactic features – for example, the absence of the infinitive – that characterizes the Balkan languages (Joseph 1983), a genetically diverse geographical *Sprachbund* in which the Romance language Romanian, various Slavic languages, Greek, and Albanian have been in contact for many centuries. Another well-known example is the contact situation in Kupwar village in Maharashtra, India, where the Dravidian language Kannada is in contact with two Indo-Aryan languages, Marathi and Urdu (Gumperz and Wilson 1971; see also Nadkarni 1975 for a similar case). Middle English may also exemplify contact effects between Scandinavian and native Anglo-Saxon due to the Viking invasions of the ninth and tenth centuries, although there is controversy about the extent of Scandinavian influence on English grammar (Jespersen 1938, Kroch et al. 1997, Thomason and Kaufman 1988). Contact can lead to the borrowing of syntactic features, as when Kupwar Kannada adopts the use of the overt copula with predicate adjectives, on the model of Indo-Aryan, where standard Kannada has a zero copula. It can also lead to the loss of features that distinguish the languages in contact, which may have happened to the case marking in Anglo-Saxon where it was in contact with Scandinavian (Jespersen 1938). Most interestingly, there is the case of substratum effects, where adult second language learners acquire their new language imperfectly and pass certain features of this "foreign dialect" on to their children, who are, however, native speakers of the foreign-influenced language. Contact-induced language change is, of course, due to imperfect learning just as in the case of the hypothesized mechanisms discussed above, but the learners involved are often adults rather than children. We do not have any precise understanding of how or why speakers adopt features from surrounding languages in preference to features of their native language or why certain features of a native language are carried over into an adult learner's second language. We do know, however, that grammatical features are not often borrowed by native speakers and, conversely, that they are likely to appear as interference effects in adult second language acquisition (Appel and Muysken 1987). Interference effects, in fact, point toward a causal account of certain kinds of contact-induced change. If a group of adults learn a second language imperfectly and if their second language usage becomes the primary linguistic data for a group of children for whom the adult learners are primary caretakers, the ordinary process of first language acquisition may lead straight-forwardly to the adoption of "foreign" or "interference" features into the native language of the children, from whom it may spread to others. In this case, unlike in the case of inaccuracies in first language acquisition, there is no mystery about the cause of imperfect transmission.

The loss of V2 in Middle English is a case of change where there is evidence that contact played a part; and given the important role that discussion of this and similar changes has played in the recent literature on diachronic syntax, the evidence is worth a brief discussion. We should note at the outset that the evidence is, as so often, not conclusive; but it is suggestive and illustrates a line of research likely to grow in importance as the availability of annotated electronic corpora makes statistical studies more practical. We summarize here the analysis presented in Kroch et al. (1997) and in Kroch and Taylor (1997), whose statistics were drawn from the Penn–Helsinki Parsed Corpus of Middle English (Kroch and Taylor 1994). Kroch and Taylor and Kroch et al. give evidence that with respect to the grammar of V2, there were two dialects in Middle English, a northern dialect in which the tensed verb moved to COMP and a southern one in which the tensed verb moved only as far as INFL. The best evidence for this dialect difference is the word order in sentences with subject pronouns. As we have mentioned, V2 in Old English exhibited a pecu-liarity not found in the other Germanic languages: Topicalized sentences with full noun phrase subjects had XVS order but those with pronoun subjects had XP-pro-V order, as illustrated in examples (23) and (24) above. This peculiarity continues into Middle English in the Midlands and the south, but there is good evidence that the northern dialect behaved differently.[11] It had inversion with pronoun subjects as well as with noun phrase subjects, just as in the other Germanic languages. The following example from the Rule of St. Benet is illustrative:

(29) þe alde sal sho calle þarto
      the old shall she call thereto

The difference between the northern and southern dialects is clear from table 22.1 of the frequency of XVS order for sentences with topicalized direct objects with full noun phrase and pronoun subjects respectively.[12]

Kroch et al. show that, although the evidence is indirect and limited, it is most probable that the dialect difference between north and Midlands/south goes back to the tenth century and may reflect Scandinavian influence on

Table 22.1 NP-V-S versus NP-S-V word order with noun phrase and
pronoun subjects

	NP subjects			Pronoun subjects		
Dialect	*Number inverted*	*Number uninverted*	*% inverted*	*Number inverted*	*Number uninverted*	*% inverted*
Midlands	50	4	93	4	84	5
North	7	0	100	58	3	95

northern Old English. As we have noted, by the fourteenth century the V2
property is clearly being lost. That loss is most advanced in northern texts
from areas in contact with the Midlands. Why should this be so? The answer
seems to lie in the nature of the contact between the dialects. At the dialect
boundary, (adult) speakers from the northern community were communicat-
ing with speakers whose usage of V2 would have seemed variable to them.
They would have analyzed topicalized sentences with full noun phrase subjects spoken by speakers with the southern grammar as exhibiting movement
of the tensed verb to COMP, since that is the analysis they would give to the
same sentences in their own dialect. But the southern speakers would have
used V3 word order with pronoun subjects, a usage that the northern speakers
would have interpreted as a violation of the V2 constraint, since they would
have had no reason to distinguish pronouns from full noun phrases in their
syntax. From these data, the northern speakers would have concluded that the
southerners were speaking a mixed language, with a V2 grammar and a non-
V2 grammar in diglossic competition (see below). If the northern speakers
accommodated to their interlocutors in the usual way, they would have produced some non-V2 sentences, but crucially with both pronoun and full noun
phrase subjects. This accommodation would have provided learners with evidence of a non-V2 grammar, which would have entered their speech community as a competitor to the V2 grammar. Speakers of the southern grammar
exposed to northern speech would not have been inclined to produce non-V2
sentences, since their northern interlocutors produced more surface V2 word
order than they themselves. If anything, the southerners would have accommodated by producing some V2 sentences with pronoun subjects and learners
might have acquired a V2 grammar with verb movement to COMP alongside
the southern V-to-INFL option. We do not know why the non-V2 grammar
won out in the north or why it eventually spread to all of Britain, but we have
some evidence that the result was not foreordained. In Chaucer, whose dialect was south-east Midlands, we find a general adherence to V2 word order
with both noun phrase and pronoun subjects. This is an instance of a south-
erner, though of unknown representativeness, picking up the northern pattern.

So it is perhaps due only to chance or the vicissitudes of social history that English today is not still V2.

4 The Diffusion of Syntactic Change

Studies of syntactic change which trace the temporal evolution of the forms in flux universally report that change is gradual. One of the most extensive studies of this type, Ellegård's study of the rise of the English auxiliary *do* (Ellegård 1953), contains a graph (figure 22.1) of the frequency of *do* + main verb against main verb alone, based on a sample of more than 10,000 tokens.

Other quantitative studies show a similar, roughly "S-shaped" curve of change. Before the rise of generative grammar, this sort of gradualness was taken for granted. Syntactic change, once actuated, was conceived primarily as a slow drift in usage frequencies, which occasionally led to the loss of some linguistic forms. New forms, whether they entered the language as innovations or borrowings, would normally affect the language only marginally at the outset and then, if adopted by the speech community, would spread and rise in frequency. With the advent of generative grammar, this way of thinking about change immediately became problematic. To begin with, generative theory, being a theory of grammatical well-formedness, is concerned with what forms are possible in natural language rather than with how often they are used. Usage frequencies might reflect stylistic preferences or psycholinguistic processing effects, but they had no place in grammatical theory. The

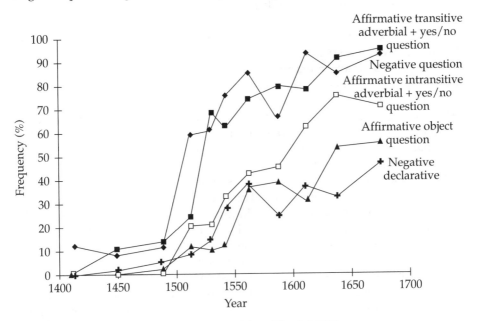

Figure 22.1 The rise of periphrastic *do* (adapted from Ellegård 1953)

gradualness of change, therefore, fell outside the domain of interest in early generative discussions. More recently, however, it has been recognized that gradualness poses something of a challenge to the theory of grammar because it characterizes not only shifts in stylistic preferences but also the diffusion of changes in syntactic parameter settings. For example, Roberts (1985) and Kroch (1989b) have argued that the rise of auxiliary *do* was a reflection of the loss of the raising of tensed main verbs to INFL, the position of tensed auxiliaries, an obligatory process which is characteristic of many European languages and which was entirely productive in Middle English. When this movement was lost, the association of tense with the verb was blocked in negative sentences, as was the movement of the verb to COMP in questions. The semantically empty auxiliary *do* was instead inserted into the INFL position, where it supported tense and, like other auxiliaries, moved to COMP when appropriate. Many analyses have been proposed for the modern English auxiliary system, but they generally share the property that auxiliary *do* is used only when V-to-I movement cannot apply. In languages where V-to-I movement is licensed for all verbs, it is obligatory and nothing like *do*-insertion occurs. Thus, it is something of a puzzle that the use of auxiliary *do* should be variable over more than 300 years of the history of English. As far as we can tell, moreover, other parametric options of syntax which undergo a change from one setting to another show the same sort of variable behavior during a more or less long period of transition. This has been shown to be true of the loss of V2 in English (Kroch 1989a), French (Fontaine 1985), and Spanish (Fontana 1993), as well as of the shift from verb final to verb medial word order in Old English, Ancient Greek, and early Yiddish (Pintzuk 1995, Taylor 1994, Santorini 1993).

Given the assumptions of generative grammar, variation in syntax which corresponds to opposed settings for basic syntactic parameters must reflect the co-presence in a speaker or speech community of mutually incompatible grammars. This is not an empirical question but a matter of the definition of the concept of parameter in the theory. In recent years, Kroch and his collaborators (see above citations) have uncovered evidence that supports this consequence of generative assumptions. They have shown, in several case studies, that the rate of change in different surface contexts reflecting a single underlying parameter change is the same. This result, known as the Constant Rate Effect, is what one expects if a single grammatical parameter is involved in a change and the mix of the two opposed settings is slowly changing over time in a given speech community. The effect is most easily illustrated in the case of the rise of auxiliary *do*. We will limit ourselves to the period from the beginning of the fifteenth century to the middle of the sixteenth in order to avoid complications introduced by the grammatical reanalyses that occur at the latter point in time (see Kroch 1989b for further discussion). When the rate of change in the use of *do* is estimated for the curves in figure 22.1,[13] the value is the same for every curve. This result is contrary to what most non-generativist students of quantitative variation have expected. The most explicit such discussion of the matter is due to Bailey (1973), who specifically claims that the rate of change should vary by context, a result that is not easily reconciled with generative assumptions. The most striking quantitative fact in the story of *do*, however, is not a fact about the use of the auxiliary itself. Ellegård also gives data about the placement of the frequency adverb *never* with respect to the tensed verb which considerably strengthens the case for a close relationship between the rate of syntactic change across contexts and the underlying grammatical nature of the change. As we noted above, in a Middle English sentence with only one verb, the canonical position for *never* was immediately postverbal. Example (3), repeated here as (30), illustrates the point:

(30)   Quene Ester looked never with swich an eye.

Since the order of verb and adverb in (30) reflects V-to-I movement, we expect the order to disappear as that movement is lost, giving way to pre-verbal placement of the adverb. This is indeed what happens, so that Modern English allows (31a), but not (31b):

(31)   a.   Jean never reads this newspaper.
      b.   *Jean reads never this newspaper.

Returning to Ellegård's quantitative data, we find that the rate at which the adverb–verb order replaces the verb–adverb order is the same as the rate of increase in the use of auxiliary *do*, thereby supporting the idea that a single parametric change underlies all of the surface contexts and that its progression is observable in the way the usage frequencies change over time.

    The Constant Rate Effect links parametric change to grammar competition, but it introduces a quantitative element into the picture that inevitably adds a non-grammatical element to the study of diachrony. Nothing in the grammatical system undergoing change accounts for the rate of the change or for the fact that the change actually goes to completion rather than stalling or even reversing.[14] Why changes spread in the way that they do is little understood, though models of the process have been proposed. Niyogi and Berwick (1997) present a dynamical systems model under which child learners do not always converge on the target grammar of the language to which they are exposed. When, as in the cases discussed above, the evidence for a given parameter setting becomes weak enough, some learners will, due to random effects, not be exposed to enough data to set the parameter correctly. The result will be a mixed population in which some speakers have the old parameter setting and some a new one. In this mixed population, the next generation of learners will, on average, have less exposure to the data needed to set the parameter in the old way. Niyogi and Berwick show how such a population evolves under a range of assumptions about the nature and distribution of the linguistic evidence. In many cases, the population will shift from the original grammar to a new one along an S-shaped trajectory.

One difficulty with the Niyogi and Berwick model, aside from its hypothetical character, however, is that it presumes that the competing parameter settings are located in different speakers, so that the quantitative element in syntactic change is located in the population, not in the individual. However, the data from the empirical studies that reveal the gradual nature of change are not consistent with Niyogi and Berwick's model in this respect. On the contrary, in all of the studies we have cited, the variation in usage that reflects different parameter settings is found within texts. Indeed, texts from the same time period generally seem more similar than different in their frequencies of the competing variants. To model this variation, it is necessary to allow for syntactic diglossia within individual authors as the normal situation during a period of change.

Again, this conclusion is a logical consequence of the general assumptions of generative theory regarding the categorical nature of grammatical parameters. Furthermore, it is necessary to allow a description of individual speakers under which they have a propensity to choose between their diglossic grammars at a characteristic average rate. This rate, moreover, seems to characterize entire speech communities, and it is what changes over time as one of the grammars slowly drives the other one out of use. This way of thinking about change is, of course, commonplace in sociolinguistics, but generativists often object to it. There is no doubt, however, that human beings, like other animals, track the frequencies of events in their environment, including the frequency of linguistic events. Confusion over this issue has arisen because sociolinguists have claimed that probabilities of use should be integrated into grammars, a proposal which is not consistent with the generative paradigm. It is not necessary, however, to make this last move in order to relate variation in usage by individuals to syntactic change. Once a community becomes diglossic with respect to a given parameter setting, every speaker will learn both settings. The choice of which criterion of well-formedness to apply in the production of a given utterance is one that falls in the domain of performance and so is not an issue for grammatical theory. How learners acquire diglossic competence is, of course, an important issue for language acquisition, but there is no doubt that they do. That members of a community should converge on roughly the same average frequency of use of a set of available variants is not surprising, nor is it surprising that this average frequency should vary over time.

The most important question raised by the fact of textual syntactic diglossia in the course of language change is why it is unstable. There is some reason to think that bilingualism in general may be linguistically unstable, since even apparently balanced bilinguals show evidence of a dominant language under experimental conditions (Cutler et al. 1992). In other words, even when children learn two languages at a young age, the one learned first or more thoroughly seems to control certain features of language processing, which may induce a tendency to prefer that language in use, all other things being equal. If this were so, then one would expect to see a shift over time in favor of the true "native" language of a community in cases of syntactic diglossia. Of course, this model depends on one of the diglossic variants being more native than the other. This would be true if, for example, it was the native variant for more speakers. It would also be true if the variants differed in social register. If one of the variants belonged to the vernacular (that is, the language learned in infancy), while the other belonged to a superposed prestige language acquired a bit later in life, then the necessary asymmetry would be established. This latter scenario seems particularly likely for the sorts of change that linguistic historians have data on. We are limited to the written language, often of societies with a low rate of literacy and sharp class distinctions in language. In these circumstances, it could easily be the case that the forms in competition in syntactic diglossia represent an opposition between an innovative vernacular and a conservative literary language. Since the former would have both a psycholinguistic advantage and the advantage of numbers, it should win out over time, even in written texts. Under this model, the gradualism found in texts might not reflect any basic mechanism of language change, but rather the psycho- and sociolinguistics of bilingualism. The actual (sudden) change in parameter setting would have occurred unobserved in the vernacular and only its competition with conservative educated usage would be accessible to study in the texts.

In some cases of change studied quantitatively, there is empirical evidence of register based diglossia behind the evolution of frequencies. The clearest such case that I know of is described in a study by Shi (1988, 1989) of the rise of the perfective aspect marker *le* in Chinese. What follows is a summary of Shi's discussion. The marker *le* did not exist in classical Chinese but it is ubiquitous in the modern language. Scholars have long known that the marker evolved out of the classical verb *liao* "to finish." Shi shows that this happened in several steps. First, *liao* started to occur with sentential subjects, but without any clear change of meaning, as in (32):

(32) [[junguan shi] liao] (Shi 1989: (7a))
       army   eat   finished
       "after the army's eating was finished . . ."

Then, it lost its main verb semantics, becoming an aspectual light verb (the so-called phase complement) in the resultative construction. At this point, it lost word stress and changed in pronunciation. This stage is observable in texts of the tenth century. Next, the new *le* became incorporated with its companion verb, so that it appeared before the direct object in a transitive sentence, as illustrated in (33):

(33) mei shi   bu ken xiawen, huai-le yi sheng (Shi 1989: (11a))
       every matter not will ask   ruin-*le* a life
       "if you don't ask questions about things, you will ruin an entire life"

At this point, the twelfth century, *le* had become an aspect marker. It was in competition with two other aspect markers *de* (from a verb meaning "to gain")

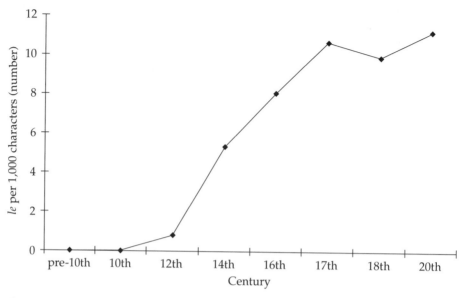

Figure 22.2   Frequency of *le* per 1,000 characters of text (Shi 1989)

and *que* (from a verb meaning "to lose"), which appeared in examples like the following:

(34)   Zixu zhuo-de Weiling (Shi 1989: (12a))
    Zixu catch-get Weiling
    "Zixu caught Weiling"

(35)   sun-que   wushi yu   ren (Shi 1989: (13a))
    damage-lose fifty   or-so man
    "they lost about fifty men"

The two markers were both perfective but were specialized to positive and negative end states of a completed action, as the examples illustrate. Aspectual *le* replaced these two markers, first *que* and then *de*, and by the fourteenth century it was the unique perfective aspect marker. At this point the grammatical change was over. Shi's quantitative data, however, show that the frequency of *le* in texts has continued to increase up to the present day. Figure 22.2, which is based on approximately 2,700 instances of *le*, is drawn from Shi (1989).

Shi raises the question of why the frequency of *le* continues to rise for 600 years after the grammatical change that introduced and spread the particle had gone to completion, and he gives the following answer. Written Chinese since the tenth century has been diglossic, using elements of both the classical language and the vernacular. The classical language lacked the aspect marker *le*, which arose in the course of the evolution of the vernacular, and it seems

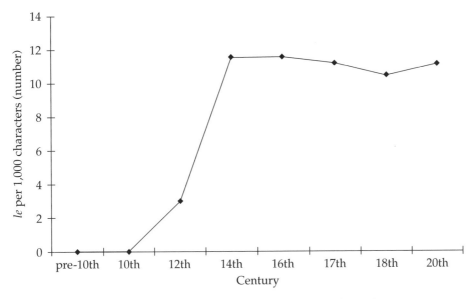

Figure 22.3 Frequency of *le* per 1,000 vernacular characters of text (Shi 1989)

that classical verbs never co-occur with *le* in mixed texts. In consequence, the rise of *le* after the fourteenth century reflects not a continuing grammatical change, but an increasing use of the vernacular language in written documents. Shi demonstrates his point by constructing an estimate of the amount of classical language in texts, using the classical interjective particle *ye* as an indicator of classical language. Over time, the frequency of *ye* declines, indexing the decline in classical usage. When the frequency of *ye* in texts is used to correct for the degree of classical admixture, the frequency evolution of *le* over time changes character dramatically, as can be seen in figure 22.3.

Figure 22.3 shows clearly that there is no change in the use of *le* in the vernacular after the fourteenth century. All of the apparent change is due to a continuing shift in the overall diglossic mix in favor of increased use of the vernacular. We do not know to what extent this Chinese case is representative of change in textual frequencies in general, but its existence warns us against assuming that changing textual frequencies have linguistic rather than sociolinguistic significance.

Given the strong possibility that textual data do not give evidence for the process of language change in a vernacular, there is a real need for the study of syntactic innovations in living languages, using sociolinguistic methods to observe unreflecting speech. Such studies do not at present exist, in part because syntactic change is relatively rare and hard to catch on the fly. In their absence, we can construct abstract models of change in the style of Niyogi and Berwick or more concrete scenarios, like the Clark and Roberts declining-evidence scenario for the loss of V2 in French or our dialect contact scenario for the loss of V2 in Middle English (see above). These are useful hypotheses, no doubt, but unless they can be further specified to make empirically testable predictions, they will remain speculative. Finding a way to derive such predictions is a major task for the future of diachronic syntax.

5   Conclusion

Weinreich et al. (1968) divide the problem of change into five related subproblems: actuation, constraints, transition, embedding, and evaluation. The actuation problem is that of why change in a particular structural feature occurs when it does in a particular language and why the change may not occur at all in other languages that share the same feature. The constraints problem is that of what changes are possible for a language in a given state. The transition problem is that of how a language moves from one state to a succeeding state. The embedding and evaluation problems are those of how a change is related to other features of the language in which it occurs and what effect it has on these other features. In the study of syntactic change within the generative tradition, these problems remain basic. They receive a somewhat different formulation than in the original work, however, because of the emphasis that generative theory places on UG and on language acquisition. This new formulation gives partial answers to some of the problems but, more importantly, it sharpens them and brings certain difficulties into focus. Consider first the actuation problem, which Weinreich et al. consider to be the heart of the matter. As we have seen, to the extent that language learning is limited to the critical period of early childhood and that children accurately learn the language of their parents, both substantive assumptions, generative theory must locate syntactic change outside the ordinary chain of grammar transmission. The constraints problem, from the generative perspective, is partly just the problem of the limits that UG places on language variation. Since children learn whatever language they are exposed to, there are no grammatical constraints, apart from those embodied in UG, on possible changes. This raises the question of why languages do not under normal circumstances undergo catastrophic reorganizations. The transition problem becomes the issue of how changes in the grammars of individuals propagate through the community. The issue of gradualness of change and how to account for it arises here, and it seems that grammatical and sociolinguistic perspectives can interact fruitfully on this problem. Finally, the embedding and evaluation problems receive a very specific answer in generative syntactic terms: to the extent that differences among the grammars of specific languages are limited to different choices of the settings of a finite number of universal syntactic parameters, the syntactic features of language subject to change are independent of one another. The issue raised here is what to make of changes that appear to be correlated with one another but are not grammatically linked, like the drift of the English modals toward specialization as auxiliaries. Although none of the problems posed by Weinreich et al. has been solved in any definitive way in consequence of work in diachronic syntax by generativists, this work has succeeded in creating a lively field with well-posed problems on its agenda and a fruitful dialectic between theoretical concerns and empirical findings.

NOTES

* Most of what I know about diachronic syntax, I have learned from years of discussion with my collaborators and colleagues in the field. Thanks for this ongoing dialog go first to my students and collaborators, especially Susan Pintzuk, Beatrice Santorini, and Ann Taylor, my collaborator on the Penn–Helsinki Parsed Corpus of Middle English. Thanks are due also to many other colleagues: Robin Clark, Antonio and Charlotte Galves, Ans van Kemenade, Paul Kiparsky, David Lightfoot, Donald Ringe, Ian Roberts, and Anthony Warner. I have mentioned a few but there are many more. Finally, I want to thank Gene Buckley, Caroline Heycock, and Beatrice Santorini for their close readings of an earlier draft of this chapter. Their suggestions have improved it, though there are undoubtedly many weaknesses left, which remain my responsibility.

1 The field of historical syntax can be divided into two parts: the study of the grammars of languages of the past and the study of changes in grammar attested in the historical record. The first subfield is best considered a branch of comparative syntax which tries to reconstruct, through textual evidence, the grammars of languages that lack living native speakers. The second subfield studies the problem of the diachronic instability of syntax and the transition between grammars. These two fields cannot be entirely separated in practice, since the study of the transition between grammars implies knowledge of the initial and end states. Nevertheless, it is the diachronic aspect of historical syntax that has the most interest for linguistics as a whole since it is in this domain that historical syntax contributes something not available from the synchronic study of extant languages. For this reason, I have chosen to focus on the diachronic aspect of historical syntax in this chapter.

2 As Kiparsky has pointed out (1996), rich case marking seems to be a necessary but not a sufficient condition for word order freedom. Icelandic, for example, has at least as rich a case marking system as German, but fairly rigid SVO word order. The one-way direction of the implication suggests that the connection between case marking and word order is indirect. The syntactic parameters ultimately responsible for the degree of word order flexibility need not make any direct reference to morphology. Instead, speakers of languages with flexible word order of certain types which lose their case marking might be expected to restrict themselves to fixed word order in their language use to avoid misunderstanding.

Learners would then not hear enough word order variation to conclude that the language allowed free word order.

3   See also Vincent (1976) for an application of this idea to the shift from SOV to SVO in the history of Romance.

4   For ease of exposition, I assume the phrase structure of *Barriers* (Chomsky 1986b) with only two functional heads at the clausal level, I(NFL) and C(OMP).

5   Auxiliary *do* certainly has the indicated property in American English. Whether it does in British English depends on the analysis of verb phrase ellipsis examples like (i):

i. He said that he'd come, and he may have done.

It is not clear whether the non-finite *do* in this example is the same morphosyntactic element as the finite auxiliary (see Pullum and Wilson 1977 for a useful discussion).

6   The decision to do so is not unproblematic. In logical form modifiers are naturally treated as functions that take their heads as arguments, mapping a phrase of a given denotation type to a larger phrase of the same type, while complements seem to be arguments of their heads, which are themselves functions. In other words, the assignment of phrases to function or argument status is reversed in the case of modifier–head and head–complement relations.

7   Kiparsky suggests that the work done by pressure for cross-category harmony could be replaced by a pressure toward simplicity of derivations (really transparency in the sense of Lightfoot 1979; see below) if one assumed the anti-symmetry theory of Kayne (1994).

The idea is that deviations from surface SVO word order would be costly because they required the postulation of leftward movement rules, which would complicate derivations and would be disfavored, all other things being equal. This variant of Kiparsky's proposal raises the same explanatory issues as the one discussed in the text.

8   More precisely, learners are sensitive to unembedded binding domains, which include the subjects of subordinate clauses under certain conditions.

9   I leave aside the West Germanic language Yiddish and the North Germanic language Icelandic, for which evidence of this limitation is largely lacking.

10 A Lightfoot-style degree 0 learner would rely on main clause evidence like the position of negation and separable prefixes to arrive at this conclusion. The contrast between the SOV and SVO verb second languages remains.

11 There are no northern prose manuscripts from before 1400 so conclusions about northern Middle English are based on indirect evidence. The best evidence comes from the Northern Prose Rule of St. Benet, an early fifteenth-century document from an isolated part of Yorkshire that seems to have preserved features from an earlier time.

12 The small number of exceptions to the pattern may be early signs of dialect contact that becomes increasingly important over time.

13 The technique used for this estimation is logistic regression, the most appropriate statistical technique for frequency data of this sort (Altmann et al. 1983, Aldrich and Nelson 1984).

14 Susan Garrett, in an unpublished study, describes a reversal in the history of Spanish negation. In the early thirteenth century the use of "any" words (*alguno*, etc.) becomes possible in negative concord contexts in place of the usual "no" words (*ninguno*, etc.). Then between 1200 and 1600 there is a modest but steady increase in their use. After 1600, this usage declines again until in the modern language it is no longer possible.

23 Setting Syntactic Parameters

JANET DEAN FODOR

1 Learnability Concerns

The study of language learnability is concerned with the "logical problem of language acquisition" (Baker and McCarthy 1981). This is the problem of how it is possible in principle to acquire a language, under various assumptions about the learning mechanism and the information provided by the environment. Some studies are very abstract (e.g. Gold 1967). Others approach more closely the properties of natural languages and human psychology, and the nature of a normal child's exposure to language (e.g. Pinker 1984). Realistic models are of the most interest, but are thin on the ground at this still early stage of the discipline.

Given that we are all living proof that natural language learning is possible, what questions could arise about learnability in principle? Chomsky (1965 and elsewhere) drew attention to "the poverty of the stimulus," the fact that the environment provides less information than the eventual adult grammar contains. This has been a key argument for the existence of innate linguistic knowledge, which must apparently substitute for the missing environmental information. The stimulus for language learning is impoverished in a number of ways. The sentences children hear (or digest) are typically simpler than those they will produce and understand as adults. Negative data, concerning what is ungrammatical in the target language, are largely absent (Marcus 1993). A child might hear *Mice often eat cheese* but no one bothers to mention that **Mice eat often cheese* is unacceptable. The language sample may include ungrammatical and incomplete sentences, idioms and exceptions, all of which could invite learners to posit overgenerating grammars. A parent's elliptical imperative *No pushing, please* should not be taken as a general model for imperative formation permitting also **Much giving me cookies, please*. Ambiguous sentences, if wrongly structured by the learner, could also lead to incorrect grammars. In English *The mouse saw the cat* means the mouse did the seeing, but a learner who mistook it to mean that the cat saw the mouse could conclude that English allows object-verb-subject word order. Learnability theory has concerned itself with each of these problems in turn.

Learning complex structures from simple input was the focus of the degree *n* research of the 1970s. The sentences of an adult language are unbounded in length and degree of embedding. Can they be projected from a subset of the language which is limited to *n* degrees of clausal embedding? Working within the Standard Theory of transformational grammar (Chomsky 1965), Hamburger, Wexler and Culicover (reported in Wexler and Culicover 1980) demonstrated degree 2 learning, given certain universal constraints of independent linguistic interest. Following this heroic work, and taking advantage of even more stringent constraints within Government Binding (GB) theory (Chomsky 1981, 1986a), Lightfoot (1989) argued that *n* can be reduced to zero "plus a little bit": the most that needs to be observed of an embedded clause is its complementizer and the subject, with all else following by general principles. (For discussion, see the commentaries following Lightfoot's paper.)

The lack of systematic negative evidence took over as the issue of main concern in the 1980s, with its moral that learning must be conservative. Changes made to the learner's developing grammar should obey the Subset Principle (SP): the language generated by the newly hypothesized grammar should be no larger than necessary to accommodate the learner's input. (This idea is evident in Gold 1967, and articulated by Angluin 1980, Berwick 1985, and others.) SP imposes a default which learners must apply, for safety reasons, when the evidence is not decisive. For example, a learner who has so far heard subjects only before verbs should assume that subjects *must* precede verbs, even though there are languages (like Italian) in which the subject may either precede or follow the verb. The standard argument for the claim that SP is necessary for successful learning is that a wrong grammar which generates a proper superset of the target language cannot be recognized as wrong without negative evidence. Examples were presented to show that the problem is real: natural languages do stand in subset/superset relations one to another (Manzini and Wexler 1987). However, it emerged that SP is too strong a remedy to match the behavior of human learners. Counter-examples to conservative learning were documented: in some domains (though by no means all) children do posit a superset of the set of well-formed adult sentences, and later retreat to the correct language (Hyams and Sigurjónsdóttir 1990).

Possible retreat mechanisms were outlined which do not require explicit negative information. A negative fact might be innately linked to a positive one and ride piggy-back on it (e.g. ungrammaticality of null subjects linked to presence of an overt expletive; Hyams 1986). The non-occurrence of a construction in an expected context might be taken as evidence of its non-existence (Chomsky 1981: ch. 1). The existence of a competing construction with the same meaning could also signal ungrammaticality, if learners rely on a preemption mechanism such as the Uniqueness Principle (Clark 1987).

SP is also too strong to allow learners to formulate valid generalizations captured by adult grammars. Under its influence, input sentences which manifest

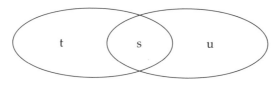

Target language

Figure 23.1   A non-subset cross-grammar ambiguity

a broad syntactic generalization would be absorbed piecemeal into the learner's grammar as a collection of individual constructional idioms. A truly conservative SP learner would be required to posit hordes of idioms and would never attain the simple generalization. (For discussion see Fodor 1994.) To avoid this misprediction, it might be assumed that learners will jettison SP in order to keep their grammars simple. But then, how is it that restricted language phenomena are transmitted from generation to generation without being overgeneralized on the way? Alternatively, it may be that learners are somehow innately equipped to know which examples they should acquire individually, and which they can and should generalize even though a more conservative grammar is possible. This would be a more elaborate variant of the traditional SP, possibly reflecting the different generalizing tendencies of different components of the grammar: morphology, lexical subcategorization, non-lexical syntax.

Many issues relating to the lack of negative data and the avoidance of (or retreat from) overgeneration have still not been fully resolved. (For instance, SP as it is usually construed is too weak as well as too strong, since two learning steps each in accord with SP can result in a superset of the target language; see Clark 1988.) But interest shifted in the 1990s to another inadequacy of learners' input: the fact that some sentence types can be generated by more than one grammar. This problem of cross-grammar ambiguity will be the focus of the remainder of this chapter, so I need not detail it here. It may be useful, though, to note how the study of cross-grammar ambiguity relates to the more familiar SP studies.

Cross-grammar ambiguity occurs when a sentence construction (setting aside here its particular lexical content) is compatible with more than one possible grammar, so that a learner cannot tell from encounter with the sentence which grammar licensed it. A subset situation is just one case of this, in fact the extreme case: *every* sentence belonging to the subset language (i.e., to both languages) of a subset/superset pair is an instance of cross-grammar ambiguity. This kind of ambiguity is dangerous. As we have noted, a superset guess, if incorrect, would never be eliminated by unambiguous evidence requiring the subset language. SP is the safe way of resolving this kind of ambiguity. By contrast, it was widely held that no harm could result from guessing freely in non-subset situations where an ambiguous sentence (*s* in figure 23.1) is shared by intersecting languages, each containing at least one sentence (*t*, *u*) not contained in the other.

If the correct grammar is guessed, all is well. If the wrong grammar is guessed, it can later be switched to the right one when an unambiguous input such as *t* is encountered. There is no simple general principle (like SP) that a wise learner could apply to resolve this kind of ambiguity, so it is just as well that no real harm can come from guessing in this situation. However, this is a case where the logical problem of language acquisition may underestimate the psychological problem of language acquisition. Though the correct grammar may be achieved eventually, the learner will have a wrong grammar (which both over- and undergenerates) in the meantime. And how long the meantime is depends on how much overlap there is between the target language and its competitors, and how often unambiguous sentences occur in the input sample. Moreover, the target is likely to overlap in a number of different respects with a number of different competing languages, so that many wrong hypotheses in need of eventual repair must be juggled at once.

The realization that non-subset grammar ambiguity is a serious practical problem has been slowly filtering into learnability studies, propelled by the insight of Clark (1992a and elsewhere) and the demonstration by Gibson and Wexler (1994). Clark has emphasized the extent of this kind of ambiguity: it is characteristic of the principles-and-parameters (P&P) theory of language that parameter values interact in complex ways in the derivations of sentences. The penalties for failing to unravel these interactions correctly may be severe. Clark showed that "harmless" temporary errors can feed further errors. This is because an incorrect grammar hypothesis may affect how subsequent inputs are structured by the learner, so that an unambiguous sentence which ought to correct the error may look like evidence for some other grammar instead. Gibson and Wexler showed that even where unambiguous evidence is available for correcting a wrong grammar guess, the learner may have gone so far astray that recovery of the correct grammar is not possible, given certain limits on how much a grammar may be changed on a single learning trial. As will be discussed below, this problem is compounded by the long-standing assumption of a simple learning mechanism which is capable of using input evidence only to disqualify wrong grammars, not as a constructive guide toward the correct grammar. If human learners were designed like this, they would have to resort to guessing a grammar even where there is enough information to make guessing unnecessary.

The agenda for learnability research must therefore include an investigation of how extensive cross-grammar ambiguity is, and how human learners manage to outsmart it. Are there effective strategies which limit the amount of misdirection due to ambiguous input? Can learners differentiate ambiguous from unambiguous input (or subset ambiguities from non-subset ambiguities) and apply strategies relevant to each? Is it inevitable that strategies which limit the randomness of guesses in ambiguous situations will render some grammars unlearnable, as in Gibson and Wexler's simulation?

These questions largely postdate the theoretical shift from rule based to principle based grammars, which created a watershed in learnability research by enabling parameter setting as the primary means for grammar acquisition. So cross-grammar ambiguity problems have mostly been formulated in terms of ambiguity of the triggers for parameter setting. Linguists and acquisition researchers have attempted to identify unambiguous triggers for all parameters postulated as part of Universal Grammar (UG). Until the seriousness of the ambiguity problem came to light, there was considerable optimism that the parametric model had left most learnability problems in the past. Previously, it had had to be supposed that children must devise rules and constraints to capture generalizations about the sentences they hear. But with the P&P theory, language learning appeared instead to be just a simple quiz. Does the target language permit or not permit phonologically null subjects? Do heads of constituents precede or follow their complements? Do interrogative phrases move (overtly) to clause initial position or remain in situ? As we will see, it matters how many such questions there are for learners to answer. It is standardly assumed that there are fewer parameters than there are possible rules in a rule based framework; otherwise, it would be less obvious that the amount of learning to be done is reduced in a parametric framework. A goal of linguistic research has been to consolidate facts and posit as few parameters as possible consistent with crosslanguage variation. It might turn out that there are 20 parameters or 30 or 100 and more. Only continued linguistic research will tell. On one recent estimate (Cinque 1999) there would be at least 32 parameters controlling the landing site for verb movement, perhaps multiplied by the number of possible verb forms (finite/infinitive/past participle, etc.). But I will make the working assumption here that there are exactly 20 binary syntactic parameters. This modest estimate is quite sufficient to raise all the questions of interest about how parameter setting could succeed in face of input ambiguity.

2   Exponential Facts of Life

2.1   *Exponential reduction*

The most welcome aspect of parameter theory for learnability research is the economy of descriptive means relative to the wealth of languages described. How many natural languages are there? Clearly a very great many, even if we set aside all differences in phonology, morphology, and the lexicon, and think only of syntactic structure. In what follows I will take a language to be an infinite set of structural descriptions of sentences, I will assume that each language in this sense is defined by a unique grammar, and I will focus on syntactic structure, using "grammar" as shorthand for "syntactic component of a grammar." If the number of languages is L, the minimum number of binary parameters there could be is n, where n is the smallest integer such that $2^n \geq L$.

For any plausible value for L, n is very much smaller than L. This is why it is important if learners can indeed distinguish which of L languages they are hearing by answering just n simple questions about it.

Because the relationship is exponential, the bigger L is, the greater the reduction the parameterization brings. If there are a thousand languages, n can be as low as 10, a reduction factor of 100. For a million languages, n need be only 20, a reduction factor of 50,000. For a billion languages, n is 30, so L is reduced by a factor greater than 30 million. In fact, the numbers are not quite this favorable unless the n-dimensional parametric space has no holes in it; that is, unless all parametric distinctions are fully orthogonal to all others, and L = exactly 2^n. But natural languages do not fully exploit the parameter space. Some parameters are inapplicable to some languages, due to incompatibility with their other parameter values or lexicon. For example, a parameter distinguishing single from multiple overt *wh*-movement is not applicable to a language whose other parameter values exclude overt *wh*-movement. A nonconfigurational language with free word order, like Warlpiri or Mohawk, will have no need of values for the standard word order parameters. For such languages there is probably no answer to the question whether the object (always *pro*, bound by the lexical phrase in adjunct position) precedes or follows the verb (see Baker 1996). Non-relevance of some parameters to some languages is of interest in learnability research, but can be largely ignored here until section 6.

It will be taken for granted here that the program of capturing natural language differences by a set of binary choices is descriptively successful and, more strongly, that it truly reflects the nature of UG. If so, then it seems that all that a child has to do to acquire any one of a million languages is to sit and listen for 20 sentences, each of which will reveal the value of one parameter. Over the first three years a child hears very approximately 2,500,000 sentences, or more than 2,000 per day, though this does not distinguish between those the child digests and those she or he merely overhears (Geoffrey Pullum, personal communication, based on statistics from Hart and Risley 1995). Since every normal child succeeds in acquiring, more or less exactly, the language to which she or he is exposed, we know that somewhere among the first five (or six or seven) million sentences a child hears there is sufficient information to determine, in conjunction with the information in UG, the correct set of parameter values for the target language. The child's only task is to extract that information from the sentences.

If there were a complaint to be raised against the parameter setting model it might be that it trivializes language acquisition. If learning is as easy as that, how could it take so long? There are some plausible answers to this. Factors such as processing limitations and the need for lexical learning would slow down an inherently efficient syntax learning device. But these need not detain us, because the real puzzle is not why real-life parameter setting is not quite as easy as this "20 questions" metaphor might suggest, but why the 20 questions mode of learning is so difficult. It is so difficult that nearly two decades after Chomsky proposed it, computational linguists and psycholinguists are still struggling to implement it in a way that is consonant with the resources of a normal child.

2.2   *Exponential re-explosion*

What all discussions overlooked, when Chomsky gave us this elegantly simple concept, was that answering a single parametric question might be as laborious (though in a different way) as hypothesizing and testing a rule was in previous learning models. It was all too easy to take it for granted that each of the small finite number of questions could be answered with a small finite amount of effort. But in fact, on perfectly plausible assumptions, reviewed below, the workload per question can be exponentially related to the number of questions there are. That is: though the exponential reduction from L languages to n parameters still holds, there is an opposite and almost equal exponential explosion from the number of parameters to the number of learning steps to set them, so that the latter is on the order of L or worse (Clark 1994). If so, the learner might just as well check out each grammar, one by one, against the input; nothing has been gained by the parameterization.

The belated recognition of this fact is what is now driving research on ways to implement parameter setting, in the hope of finding one that is relatively immune to the problems of scale that exponential complexity creates. Some ideas are discussed below. But first let us consider how compelling the evidence is that in the case of natural language, a learner cannot simply extract 20 bits of information from the language sample at a modest constant cost per item.

3   Parametric Ambiguity

3.1   *Ambiguity and workload*

To study the cost-per-parameter problem we need a measure of the learner's workload. As a rough measure that provides a common ground across otherwise different models, let us identify the workload with the number of input sentences that must be processed by the learner before learning is complete (that is, by the time the learner has settled permanently on a grammar identical, or sufficiently similar, to the target). The more sentences consumed, the slower and more laborious the acquisition process. Some learning systems may put in more work on each input sentence than others do. But if there is a practical limit on how much work a child could do per sentence before moving onto the next one in a discourse, the measure of sentences consumed is not unuseful even for such systems.

A simple argument leads to the alarming conclusion that to set one parameter could cost the learner thousands or millions of input sentences. The argument rests on the fact that the learner's language sample is a set of word strings, while syntactic parameters determine sentence *structure*. Because a string may be compatible with more than one structure, the input can be indeterminate with respect to the structural properties that the learner must have access to for parameter setting. It seems plausible that the difficulty of setting parameters is a function of how structurally indeterminate (on average) an input word string is; that is, how many distinct structural descriptions it could have. The learner's task is to identify the structural description it has in the target language. The more others it could be assigned, the greater the opportunity for errors of parameter setting; or alternatively, the greater the effort required to avoid errors.

The number of structural descriptions an input sentence could have is in the worst case a function of how many grammars there are; that is, it is bounded by L, not n. Each grammar might, in principle, assign a sentence a different derivation. So if there are 20 parameters, there could be a million or so different structural descriptions for any target language sentence, each corresponding to a different array of parameter settings. Of course this is not the least bit likely in reality. But it is important to recognize that this is the trend, the direction in which the numbers will drift in the worst case.

Consider a simple example: a sequence consisting of just a verb followed by its subject. This sequence does not have a million derivations. It is not licensed by all natural language grammars, but it is licensed by many. In some cases the parametrically relevant structure is the same. There are clusters of grammars which differ with respect to other parameters but which are alike with respect to the parameters relevant to licensing this sentence type (for example, grammars that differ only with respect to object position or the acceptability of headless relative clauses, etc.). But also, there are grammars which license a VS sentence under different parametric descriptions. For simplicity here we may bend the language facts a little and suppose there are just three relevant parameters: one that controls postposing of a subject to follow the verb, as in Italian (Burzio 1986); one that controls raising (fronting) of the verb to the Inflection position, while the subject remains in its underlying position within VP, as in Irish and Welsh (Koopman and Sportiche 1991); and one that controls raising of the verb to the Complementizer position, as in German yes/no questions, where the subject remains lower as Specifier of the Inflection phrase (Taraldsen 1986). With another stretch of the imagination we may suppose that the three parameter values which give VS order are not mutually exclusive: two or more of them may be at work in the same language (as indeed appears to be the case in Bantu languages like Shona and Swahili; see Demuth and Harford in press). In that case there would be seven ways to obtain a VS string, even if the underlying order is SV (Kayne 1994): by the parameter setting for subject postposing, by the setting for verb to I, by the setting for verb to C, by any pair of these in the same grammar, or by all three together; only the negative value for all three in the same grammar would fail to license VS order. The number of potential analyses here is not quite 2^3, but it is bounded by 2^3, not by 3. Thus, the parametric indeterminacy of any target sentence can rise *exponentially* with the number of parameters in the language domain.

Can this estimate of the degree of potential parametric ambiguity be resisted? If not, we are heading breakneck toward the conclusion that setting even one parameter can be exceedingly costly. We must re-examine the premises from which the estimate was derived. A central one is that learners' input consists only of strings, not of syntactic structures. In fact this is too severe. Let us re-consider it, along with other standard assumptions about the nature of the input for learning. These are simplistic and too extreme, but they facilitate formal work on learnability problems. They include the following:

i   Learners consult only one sentence at a time (and have no memory for prior sentences), and they do not have access to negative evidence.

ii For each language there is only one correct grammar, and the sample a learner receives is compatible only with that one grammar; that is, the input suffices to determine the target parameter settings. (Bertolo et al. 1997 and Fodor in press discuss special cases.) As part of this I will assume here, though it is unrealistic, that all sentences in the learner's sample are well formed in the target language.

iii A learner sets syntactic parameters only on the basis of sentences all of whose lexical items are known. (For discussion of problems see Stabler 1998, Fodor in press.)

iv With more bearing on the ambiguity issue, we may follow Gibson and Wexler (1994) and others in taking the input to be something more than word strings though less than full structural descriptions. It is commonly assumed that the words have been lexically categorized into nouns, verbs, determiners, etc., and that the learner knows the grammatical roles of constituents; for example, that an English learner knows that in *The cat saw the mouse, the cat* is the subject of *saw*, and *the mouse* is its object. Modifying a stronger assumption by Wexler and Culicover (1980), I will assume that a child can determine part or all of the meaning of a sentence from the verbal or non-verbal context and will not accept a syntactic analysis which contradicts that meaning.

v   Learners also use the prosodic contour to constrain the syntactic analysis of the word string (Morgan 1986). Recent work on infant perception of sentence prosody makes an excellent case for this as a practical possibility (see Nespor et al. 1996, papers in Morgan and Demuth 1996, and references there). Though prosodic phrasing does not faithfully reflect all aspects of syntactic phrasing, sensitivity to prosody implies that input strings are at least partially hierarchically structured.

On the basis of (iv) and (v) the extreme estimate of potential parametric ambiguity can be toned down. Though this will not be emphasized in the discussion below, it seems likely that semantic and prosodic information can significantly shrink the structural indeterminacy of input strings and thereby facilitate syntactic learning. (This is different, however, from the more dramatic claim implied by Mazuka 1996 and Nespor et al. 1996 that syntactic parameters may be prosodically triggered. This strikes me as less plausible, and the existing empirical evidence does not favor one hypothesis over the other.) On the other hand, the literature contains some examples of ambiguity for which neither prosody nor meaning offers significant assistance. Clark (1988) noted that an accusative subject of an infinitival complement is compatible with either Exceptional Case Marking (ECM) or structural assignment of case in infinitives. Gibson and Wexler (1994) observed that SVO word order is compatible with either the positive value of the Verb Second (V2) parameter (as in German *Die Mäuse sahen die Katze*) or the negative value (as in English *The mice saw the cat*). In both cases the meaning and prosodic contour for the competing analyses can be essentially indistinguishable. (V2 constructions permit but do not require a prosodic break before the verb.)

It seems fair to conclude, then, that the problem of parametric ambiguity does not rest solely on the simplistic assumption that learners hear only unstructured word strings. An ambiguity problem remains, even with a more inclusive concept of learners' input.

3.2   Younger learners work harder?

If a worst-case exponential relation between the number of parameters and the extent of parametric ambiguity is not assailable, the only point at which the exponential workload argument might be deflected is the postulate that parametric ambiguity *must* complicate the answering of parametric questions. That assumption also seems indisputable, but our goal must be to find a way around it if there is one. In section 4 I will argue that there is no general formula for escaping the impact of ambiguity. It depends on the particular parametric decoding procedure that a learning model employs. It also depends on how cooperative the language facts are: the structural characteristics of languages could be such as to minimize parametric ambiguity in the kinds of sentence that children typically learn from even if the rest of a language were highly ambiguous. However, first we should take a deeper look at the extent of the problem. Two points need to be made. One adds to the ambiguity load; the other can decrease it.

A plausible assumption, which will be important below, is that every syntactic parameter that contributes to the licensing of a word string does so via its effect on the structural description of the string. This is the case, for example, for the ±verb second ambiguity of SVO strings, where *The mice saw the cat* is −V2, while *Die Mäuse sahen die Katze* is +V2. On standard (though not undisputed) assumptions, the +V2 analysis has the verb in C and the subject as its Specifier, while on the −V2 analysis the verb is in some head position lower than C. In other words: parametric ambiguity is associated with structural ambiguity. We may conjecture that this is always so (see Fodor 1998a for discussion). Still, parametric ambiguity is distinct from structural ambiguity relative to a single grammar, such as in English *Flying planes can be dangerous*. A learner *qua* learner does not care about within-language ambiguity. As long as the right language has been hypothesized, that is sufficient, whether the particular analysis that was intended by the speaker was retrieved or not. Nevertheless, cross-grammar and within-grammar ambiguity can be difficult to tell apart, particularly when one is a child and does not yet know what the target grammar is. So within-language ambiguity may interfere with parameter setting. The extent of this problem is not known. Without at all underestimating its potentially damaging effects, I must set it aside here.

Second: what matters for learning is not how structurally ambiguous a string is relative to all possible grammars, but how ambiguous it is relative to grammars that the learner *has not yet excluded* as incorrect for the target language. I will call the former *gross* ambiguity and the latter *net* ambiguity. Gross ambiguity is a fact about the sentences in the learner's language sample, in relation to the domain of possible languages. (For convenience we may assume here that gross ambiguity is evenly distributed across the sentences of the sample, though in fact there is likely to be some variability; see section 6.) Net ambiguity, on the other hand, is a fact about the learner's state of knowledge as well as the language sample. It represents the uncertainty still to be eliminated before learning is complete. If learners set parameters decisively, and discard for ever the disconfirmed values, then net ambiguity will decline across the course of learning as more and more parameters are set. If the same sentence is encountered by a child at two years and again at four years, its net ambiguity will not be the same on the two occasions because the child's grammar will have advanced in the meantime. What determines learning effort is presumably net ambiguity; that is, how many structural descriptions an input sentence could have *for all the learner now knows*. If this is right, it leads to the important conclusion that a beginning learner must work harder to set a parameter than a more advanced learner would to set that same parameter.

The net ambiguity of a word string (i.e., the number of distinct structural analyses it has on the basis of grammars not yet excluded by the learner) can in principle be as high as $2^{(n-p)}$, where n is the number of parameters in the domain (all relevant to licensing the target language; see section 2.1) and p of them have so far been set (correctly) by the learner. In a domain of 20 parameters, the net ambiguity of an input could be as high as 1,048,576 (the total number of possible grammars) at the outset of learning. By the time all but one of the parameters have been set, net ambiguity would be at most 2. Thus, the first parameter setting event faces a potential net ambiguity up to half a million times higher than the potential net ambiguity for the last one (regardless of which parameters the learner happens to set first and last). The curve is the familiar exponential decline: for setting the second parameter the maximum degree of ambiguity would be half of that for setting the first; for setting the third it would be half of that; and so on. If the total number of parameters to be set is greater, the disparity between first and last is greater still. If there were 50 relevant parameters, the multiplier would be 2^{49}, which is up in the trillions. If some parameters are irrelevant to the target language, the disparity is less; for 15 relevant parameters the maximum ambiguity for setting the first is only 16,384 times higher than for setting the last. It is clear, though, that for any plausible number of parameters to be set, parameter setting difficulty is far from uniform across the course of learning if it depends on the degree of net parametric ambiguity of sentences.

The cheerful way to put this is: the task gets easier and easier as time goes on. The more parameters you set, the easier it becomes to set more of them; the more you know, the faster you learn. The disturbing side of it is: the learning task is a great deal more onerous at first than it is later on. The less you know the harder it is to learn. However small the cost of setting the last parameter may be, that cost magnified a thousand- or a million-fold for the setting of the first parameter is bound to add up to something unmanageable.

In summary: if the learner's workload is a function of parametric ambiguity, then the exponential reduction of L grammars down to n binary parameters re-explodes into estimates on the order of L for the cost of setting each parameter, at least at early stages of learning when few parameters have been set. This means that the greatest burden of learning is concentrated at a time when learners presumably have the fewest resources and are in need of the greatest assistance from the input. Once parameter setting is underway it may proceed efficiently, but early ambiguity is potentially so extreme that it is hard to see how learners ever get started. Thus, parameter setting is not a feasible means of language acquisition unless we can free it somehow from sensitivity to parametric ambiguity.

4 Parametric Decoding

Learning a language is as easy – or as difficult – as answering 20 questions. How easy that is depends on whether parametric ambiguity is the major determinant of how much work it takes to find out the answers. If parametric ambiguity is what paces parameter setting, then it is a mystery how learners manage to set their first parameter. I will consider this mystery from the psychocomputational modeler's point of view rather than the empirical study of children point of view. Later, I will consider briefly how well the two fit together.

The goal is to create a blueprint for a learning system that can extract from natural language sentences the information necessary to set 20 syntactic parameters, consuming only a reasonable number of input sentences, spread in a reasonable way over the course of learning. To do this we must find either (i) another factor which favors early learners and offsets their disadvantage with respect to ambiguity, or (ii) a method for parameter setting that is relatively insensitive to high degrees of ambiguity at any stage. I will proceed along path (ii) here. For mathematical convenience I will for the most part be treating parameters as anonymous entities with no particular linguistic content. Each is as likely to be expressed by a sentence as any other is; each is as likely to be expressed ambiguously as any other is. In fact, there can be considerable variability in these respects. To allow for this in a more interesting and realistic model entails looking at the character of natural language sentences and the relation between sentences and the grammars that license them. I take this up in section 6.

4.1   Decoding ambiguous input

Ideally, when the learning system encounters a novel kind of sentence (ambiguous or otherwise) it would know exactly which parameter values entered into the derivation by which that sentence was licensed in the grammar of its utterer. Parametric ambiguity makes this impossible, of course; the child is still trying to discern how the local adults are licensing their sentences. But at least the learner would benefit from knowing which parameter value combinations *could* have licensed that sentence. Establishing this is what I call *parametric decoding*. For example, on hearing an SVO string, the decoding device would inform the learner that it could have been derived with parameter values –V2, complement final, Specifier initial (as in English), or with +V2, complement initial, Specifier initial (as in German), or with +V2, complement final, Specifier initial (as in Swedish), or with +V2 and Specifier final, and so on. (This parameterization follows Gibson and Wexler 1994, who assumed, unlike Kayne 1994, that underlying word order differs across languages.) Encountering a parametrically unambiguous string, the decoder would report a unique parametric profile; for example, for a sequence of indirect object, finite auxiliary, subject, direct object, and thematic verb (*Den Mäusen habe ich den Käse gegeben* "I gave the cheese to the mice"), it would report the single combination: +V2, complement initial, Specifier initial (if indeed this word order is parametrically unambiguous; we may pretend that it is for now).

Once the parametric properties of an input have been decoded, the learner could follow a strategy of adopting any parameter values that are common to all analyses, in confidence that these values must be in the target grammar (since they are values without which the sentence could not have been generated). For this ideal operating system, learning would be complete as soon as each target parameter value had been unambiguously realized (*expressed*) in the learner's input. Thus, efficient parameter setting relies on efficient parametric decoding. In fact, the efficiency of decoding is seriously threatened by ambiguity.

There is a widespread view that each parameter value is associated with a "cue" which can be identified in a sentence and which then "triggers" the adoption of that parameter value. With this in mind, I examine below (section 4.2) some proposals in the literature. They divide roughly into the optimistic ones, which believe it can be done though they do not actually say how, and the pessimistic ones, which have decided that it is hopeless. The latter assume that learners do not even try to "read" parameter values accurately from sentences but operate by trial and error instead. Anyone who has read the computational literature, and been puzzled by the lack of resemblance between recent learning models and the classical picture of setting parameters by triggering, should note that this is not for lack of interest or enthusiasm for the idea of triggering. It is due largely to the difficulty of modeling the parametric decoding process that triggering presupposes. Decoding problems have had a profound effect on the directions that learnability theory has taken. In section 4.3 I describe a novel decoding method which preserves the essence of classical parameter triggering. Though somewhat unconventional, it is accurate and efficient for parametrically unambiguous input. How it can best be adapted for ambiguous input is the topic of section 5.

At best, the decoder merely presents the options, if an input sentence is parametrically ambiguous. Deciding between them is the task of the learning component. The learner might wait for a sentence which unambiguously expresses the parameter in question. But the wait may be a long one. It is even possible that *no* sentence expresses the target value unambiguously, even though it is unambiguous with respect to the language as a whole. As a simple example: in Gibson and Wexler's three-parameter domain, +V2 must be correct if some target sentences could be derived by +V2 or by −V2 with underlying SVO, and the rest could be derived by +V2 or by −V2 with underlying SOV. Thus it seems that a learner must somehow triangulate from the multiple parametric combinations for each individual sentence, to find the unique one that is common to all the sentences in the sample. This is how a linguist might go about the task. But a child is not a little linguist, and from a child's perspective there is a two-fold problem with this approach. A real-life learner cannot afford to wait to hear the whole sample before having any grammar to use for comprehension and production. And the chore of making all the cross-comparisons between large sets of parameter value combinations would be enormous. So, although this is the *logic* of the answer to parametric ambiguity, we must hope there are other ways for learners to actually go about finding the common denominator across sentences. A goal of computational psycholinguistics is to devise a way that is effective, is not too labor intensive, and is incremental, able to make progress one sentence at a time.

This is where decoding and ambiguity interact. The decoding system is the gateway through which information about sentences reaches the parameter setting system. The learner's range of options for dealing with ambiguity is limited by what the decoder can deliver. The major issue turns out to be whether or not the work of identifying a set of parameter values that can license a sentence is so effortful that it cannot reasonably be done more than once per sentence. This is important because if multiple decoding is *not* feasible, then a learner cannot know whether a sentence is parametrically ambiguous. The only way to deal with ambiguity then would be by ignoring it. The decoder would deliver just one set of parameter values for an ambiguous sentence. The learner would have no choice but to accept the information as if it were derived from an unambiguous sentence and would adopt those values, quite possibly incorrectly. If multiple decoding is feasible but only up to some limit, learners would be little better off, because incomplete decoding would still not distinguish reliably between ambiguous and unambiguous sentences. Only if it is able to check out *all* possible ways of licensing a string could the learner tell reliably (in the worst case) whether more than one way exists.

Thus, nothing short of total decoding of all ways of licensing a sentence would have to be feasible if learners are to sort ambiguous from unambiguous input accurately enough never to set a parameter on the basis of an ambiguous string. However, with ambiguity levels as high as they are in natural language (even if a million grammars per sentence is a vast exaggeration), full decoding is not a serious possibility. In order to abbreviate the discussion below, I impose here and now a blanket ban on any decoding scheme which presumes that a child analyzes (parses) and reanalyzes the same utterance more than a dozen times, or that a child conducts a single parallel parse in which more than a dozen analyses are computed simultaneously. Decoding on such a scale is not psychologically realistic. Yet as we have seen, decoding on any lesser scale provides the parameter setting device with insufficient information to do its job of triangulation accurately.

In summary: parametric ambiguity puts a tremendously heavy strain on the decoding system. If the decoding system cannot rise to the challenge, then the learner's task of finding the unique set of parameter values for the whole language, which is already substantial, is further hampered by uncertainty about the range of candidate values for individual sentences. High-precision parameter setting is then not possible.

4.2   *Decoding methods*

There was a time when we thought we knew how learners decode the parametric signatures of sentences. According to the familiar metaphor, attributed by Chomsky (1986a) to James Higginbotham, parameter setting is effected by automatic flipping of parameter switches by relevant "trigger" sentences. This neat idea holds a special place in the history of the P&P model and it is a shame to have to relinquish it, but it has been tried and found wanting – Computational linguists have turned in recent years to very different mechanisms. Figure 23.2 maps some approaches that have been devised so far. I will describe how they work, and in section 5 I will consider how they respond to heavy doses of parametric ambiguity.

Method (a) is automatic switch flipping. For it to work, each switch must be equipped with a property detector responsive to the trigger property (or properties) for that parameter; that is, the particular properties of sentences which reveal the parameter's value. Since all 20 (or 40, if parameters are not pre-set to default values) detectors check the string at once, it is reasonable to suppose that they do not process it very deeply. If they did, this model would violate the ban (section 4.1) on excessive parallel processing and would be disqualified on that ground. The trigger properties must therefore be superficial and

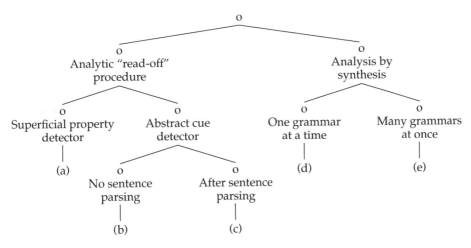

Figure 23.2 Parametric decoding methods

easily recognizable. And that is simply not true for many natural language parameters. Perhaps it is for some. Perhaps multiple overt *wh*-movement within the same clause is identifiable in a surface word string (though probably even that is not totally reliable: imagine an SOV sentence with two *wh*-arguments). However, in many cases the relevant facts are non-surface facts (e.g. the origins rather than the landing sites of movement) which are likely to be less accessible. Underlying word order is very often obscured by movement operations, and one movement operation may be masked by a later one. So even when derivational operations do not create ambiguity, there may still be no easily perceptible surface sign by which to detect the presence of a particular parameter value (Clark 1994).

Methods (b) and (c) are truer to the facts of natural language since they allow for deeper, more abstract trigger properties, as in the "cue-based theory" of Lightfoot (1997). Lightfoot's account differs from instant triggering in two ways: its cues (equivalent to trigger properties) are abstract "elements of I-language"; and the metaphor of flipping switches gives way to that of the learner "scanning sentences" for the cues. An example of what learners must watch out for is the configuration $_{SpecCP}[XP]$, which Lightfoot proposes as the cue for the positive value of the V2 parameter. Though linguistically more authentic, this approach fails procedurally in just the same way as instant triggering does. Few details are offered in the literature, but in figure 23.2 I have distinguished two possible implementations of abstract cue search. On version (b) without prior sentence parsing, the learner would have to identify the abstract cue structures from unstructured word strings. This will not work. There is no obvious way for a learner (not knowing the right grammar) to identify an XP (say, a DP) in an unstructured word string. And even if it could, it surely could not establish that this phrase is in SpecCP position, rather than in underlying subject position, or adjoined to IP by scrambling, and so forth.

With partially structured input strings as envisaged in (iv) of section 3.1, the hopelessness of this task would be diminished, but not to the point at which it would be a reliable basis for learning.

On version (c), the input is first fully parsed in order to uncover its more abstract derivational properties on the basis of which I-language cues *could* be identified. But this is quite unrealistic because it requires multiple parsings of the sentence. For instance: for purposes of recognizing the I-language cue for the +V2 parameter value, the parser must assign to the string the analysis it would have if it were licensed by the +V2 value (plus appropriate values of other parameters). Only then will the cue $_{\text{SpecCP}}[XP]$ be present for the "scanner" to find.

In other words, "scanning a sentence" for the cue for parameter value P_i (v) entails parsing the sentence with parameter value P_i (v). But a sentence cannot normally be parsed with just one parameter value, and since the learner does not yet know what the target parameter values are, it would have to parse the sentence with P_i (v) together with many combinations of values of the other parameters until it found one that succeeded for the sentence – even an unambiguous sentence. For ambiguity detection, it would (in the worst case) have to try out P_i (v) with *all* combinations of the other parameters that have not yet been set. Thus on version (c) of the cue based approach, the learner's workload explodes just as anticipated in section 3. Whether the multiple parses are conducted in parallel or sequentially, they clearly disqualify abstract cue search under the excessive processing criterion. Hence, the recognition of abstract cues is either approximate or infeasible. Reliable decoding is impossible in the absence of an effective way of spotting the cues that are present; see section 5.1 below.

The best-known representative of approach (d) is the Triggering Learning Algorithm (TLA) of Gibson and Wexler (1994). As in the second (postparsing) implementation of abstract cue search, this learner tries out grammars on input strings without knowing in advance which will work. But rather than seeking pre-defined cues for particular parameters, it takes success in parsing the sentence as the mark of whether a grammar is right for the target, or at least as a sign that it shares parameter values with the right grammar. For each input the TLA tries just one new grammar, so it satisfies the processing feasibility criterion. But given that there are a million or more grammars that could need checking, this is inevitably a slow method. In figure 23.2 this approach is filed under analysis by synthesis (ABS) methods, because the TLA does not start by observing the sentence and trying to compute the right parameter values from it; instead, it first picks a combination of parameter values and only then tries them out to see whether or not they are compatible with the sentence. It is well known that ABS methods can be very wasteful of resources if undirected. The chance of hitting on the right answer out of the blue is slim (see Fodor et al. 1974: ch. 6). To increase the efficiency of the TLA, Gibson and Wexler gave it some direction: its guesses as to which grammar to try next are influenced by feedback on the success or failure of previous guesses. Specifically, its guesses are limited to grammars which differ by no more than one parameter value from the grammar with which it most recently succeeded in parsing an input sentence. So if a grammar is successful for a while before it fails on some new input, many of its parameter values will be preserved in subsequent hypotheses. This strategy of staying in one neighborhood among the class of possible grammars, and gradually moving toward the target, is designed to save the learner from having to try out every possible grammar in the domain.

However, we have noted that parsing a sentence calls for a whole grammarful of parameter values, not just one. And this means that the TLA's positive and negative feedback, provided by success or failure in parsing input, applies to whole grammars; it cannot be attuned very closely to the correctness of individual target parameter values. Suppose, for example, that the learner has tried out a grammar, has found that it fails to parse an input sentence, and then tries parsing that sentence again after flipping parameter P7, which was previously set at the wrong value. P7 is now correctly set, so this is progress and ideally would be rewarded to encourage retention of the new value. However, it is very likely (especially early on in the course of learning) that parameters other than P7 are set wrong, and that the grammar with the correct value for P7 will fail to parse the input sentence for that reason. Hence the tentative shift to the correct value for P7 will be negatively reinforced; the learner is discouraged from making the change. (In this circumstance the TLA reverts to whatever grammar it had previously hypothesized, even though unsuccessful.)

In short: decoding is largely a hit or miss affair for the TLA due to its ABS approach, its evaluation of whole grammars, and the very ragged feedback provided by parsing success or failure. Because finding even one grammar that parses a given input is such a matter of chance, finding more than one per sentence is out of the question, so there is no possibility of ambiguity detection. The TLA therefore disregards ambiguity. It accepts any grammar it finds that works for a sentence, without checking whether others would have too. As a guessing system, it pays the price of parametric ambiguity in errors. And correcting its errors requires repeating the travails of decoding.

Method (e) in figure 23.2 represents learning systems which resemble the TLA in that they try out grammars on sentences and use parsing success as reinforcement, but which work faster by testing batches of many grammars at a time on a single input sentence. The best-known example of this is the genetic algorithm of Clark (1992a) and Clark and Roberts (1993). It records how successfully each grammar tested on a sentence can parse it, it stores the success scores of all the grammars, and it "breeds" the more successful grammars, mingling their parameter values to create a new pool of even better candidates for a next round of testing. Genetic algorithms have been a focus of recent interest for machine learning applications. But massive multiple grammar testing on each input clearly does not meet the feasibility criterion for human language processing. (Nyberg 1992 blends storage of parse success rates, as in a genetic algorithm, with TLA-like search through the grammar space.)

There is also method (f), represented by the Structural Triggers Learner (STL) of Fodor (1995, 1998a), not shown in figure 23.2 because it cuts across the tidy classification. It combines elements of the other approaches with one new twist in parametric decoding. It takes the structural cues of (b) and (c), but instead of *looking* for them in sentences, it *parses* with them as in (d) and (e), checking all parameter values simultaneously as in (a). As I will show, this can give highly efficient parameter decoding for unambiguous sentences and reliable ambiguity detection.

4.3   *The Structural Triggers decoder*

To explain the STL, let us start from cue search. This assumes that each parameter value is associated with some detectable structural property, an aspect of tree structure. I have proposed in earlier work (Fodor 1995, 1998a) that a parameter value can be *identified* with its structural cue, which I call a *treelet* or *structural trigger*, and which I take to be the deepest manifestation of the parameter value, the source of all its effects on the derivations of sentences that it contributes to. Exactly what that structural essence is may depend on the linguistic theory that is assumed. In the original P&P theory there was no very clear theory of possible parameters, and not all proposed instances took the form of a choice between tree fragments. (For discussion see Fodor 1998d.) In the Minimalist Program (Chomsky 1995b), parameter values are identified with the formal features of functional heads, which control derivational operations. For example, where the structural trigger for +V2 in Lightfoot's model is an XP in SpecCP position, in a Minimalist framework it might be a strong Specifier feature on the C head, which will attract an XP to check it. For −V2 the corresponding feature would be weak. Formal features are (very small) tree fragments, and are not themselves derivable from any deeper fact about the language. So these featural parameter values meet the needs of the STL.

The merging of the roles of parameter value and trigger (cue) into one entity (a treelet) in the STL model is of theoretical interest but is not essential to the success of the STL's parameter decoding system. All that would be lost without it is some conceptual elegance and a modicum of representational economy. More important for learnability is the fact that the decoding method works even if the structural property that defines the parameter in UG is not directly discernible in the learner's input. As long as it leaves its imprint on derivations, however non-transparently, the STL will find it.

This is how the STL works. The treelets constitute an innate (UG-supplied) lexicon of parameter values. Every natural language grammar contains some subset of these treelets, which combine with universal grammar principles and a language-specific lexicon of morphemes and words to license the sentences of the language. The learner's task is to adopt from the universal treelet lexicon the treelets that are correct for the target language. The STL adopts a treelet into its hypothesized grammar just in case it is necessary for parsing an input sentence. Encountering a sentence, the parsing component tries to parse it employing the learning component's currently hypothesized grammar. If the parse fails at some point, the parsing component is then permitted to draw on any of the innate treelets that have not yet been adopted, adding them temporarily into the learner's working grammar. At least one of the treelets in the innate parametric lexicon must be capable of unblocking the parse (unless the failure is purely lexical, which will not be considered here). If only one treelet does so, it is evidently necessary for licensing the target language and so it is added into the learner's grammar. From then on, it can be used to produce new sentences, and to parse incoming ones.

Note that a similar procedure could work if a parameter value were identified with something less concrete than a tree fragment, such as a phrase structure rule, or possibly some sort of abstract statement from which the legitimacy of such a treelet would follow; differences of this sort do not matter. The one crucial requirement is that the parsing mechanism, when it finds itself unable to continue the parse, should be able to identify efficiently any parameter value(s) capable of supplying the missing part of the parse tree so that forward parsing can proceed. We know that the parser can do this very efficiently in general, when the existing grammar suffices for the sentence. It rummages through its collection of tree-building devices to find what is needed to connect each word of the sentence into the parse tree. The STL merely extends this to include the small number of additional tree-building aids that constitute the parameter values.

The STL is representationally economical. If there are n parameters, then as few as n small tree fragments or features need to be innately represented to characterize the set of UG-defined parameter values/triggers. For 20 parameters, the innate treelet lexicon would contain 40 entries if a parameter is a choice between two treelets (e.g. a strong or a weak feature), either one of which may be adopted into the grammar of a particular natural language. There would be only 20 items in the parametric lexicon if a parameter is a choice between adopting a certain treelet (a strong feature) or not adopting it. I will not adjudicate between these two possibilities here. The STL is also procedurally economical, since it tries out all possible parameter value combinations in a single serial parse (see discussion below), using a grammar which is a perfectly normal natural language grammar such as the human sentence parser works with all the time, except only that it contains more of the UG-provided treelets than (adult) natural language grammars normally do. It is not even necessary for the learner to go through the two-step process of trying to parse an input with the currently hypothesized grammar, failing, and then parsing again using the extra treelets. The STL can just as well apply the treelet-augmented grammar right away to every sentence it encounters, as long as the treelets already adopted are given priority over others whenever there is a choice of which to employ. The extra richness of the augmented grammar may be expected to elevate the incidence of temporary ambiguity and consequent garden-pathing for the parser, but this is strictly limited to those points in sentences for which the learner's currently hypothesized grammar is inadequate and learning must occur. Elsewhere, parsing complexity remains within normal adult bounds. For example, the child is assumed to parse sentences in order to comprehend them, as adults do; and for that purpose the child's parser computes just one syntactic analysis for each sentence, as is widely assumed to be the case in adult parsing.

A serious workload explosion would result if the parser were required to compute *every* analysis of a parametrically ambiguous sentence. But this is clearly ruled out by the feasibility criterion. I assume the most the parser can be asked to do is to note when an ambiguity point arises in the course of analyzing a sentence. For example, it should flag the fact that an incoming noun might be attached into the sentence structure as either a subject or an object; or that a subject is attachable as Specifier of CP or of IP or of VP; or that a PP might be attached as daughter to VP or into an NP as a modifier of the noun. The existence of a choice point in the parse is a sign that the word string is structurally ambiguous. If the choice lies between two (or more) aspects of the learner's current grammar, it is not a parametric ambiguity. We can assume it is resolved in the usual fashion, by Minimal Attachment and/or whatever other parsing strategies are active in children; see Trueswell et al. (in press). Within-language ambiguity is excluded from further consideration here. If the choice is between the current grammar and an as yet unadopted UG treelet, it will be resolved in favor of the former, since the STL model assumes, as do all "error-driven" models, that the current grammar should not be changed as long as it continues to be compatible with the input. Or the parser's choice may be between two (or more) novel treelets, neither of which is part of the current grammar. In that case the parser may opt for one analysis rather than the other in order to assign meaning to the sentence. But the learning device – if it wants to avoid risks – must not set any parameters on the basis of the analysis the parser has chosen. In general: whenever the parser picks one route to follow and does not compute through the alternative analyses, a conservative learner will want to be notified, so that it can refrain from setting any further parameters on the basis of that sentence. No treelet utilized at or after the ambiguity point can be guaranteed correct, because the sentence may have some other structural analysis, employing other parametric treelets, that the parser does not know about.

Unlike other decoding systems that have been proposed, the STL can also reliably detect that there is no parametric ambiguity in some input sentence. Where that is so, parameter setting (adoption of a new treelet) can proceed safely. The outcome will be correct, and the learning system will know that it is correct, so that other decisions can be based on it. The new and interesting issue raised by this decoding system is what a learner should do when the parser detects that parametric ambiguity *is* (or may be) present and alerts the learning system. Should it stop learning immediately, to avoid danger of errors? That is what the earliest STL model did. It embodied the belief of many theoretical linguists that every (non-default) parameter value must have a unique trigger that is readily accessible to learners. If that is so, the wisest strategy is just patience and precision. But if the necessary unambiguous triggers do not exist, or are not guaranteed to come by frequently enough to expedite learning, then perhaps it would be more efficient overall to be less patient and less precise. Which strategy is optimal for natural languages? And which is what children do? These questions are opened for debate in sections 5.2 and 5.3.

5   Consequences of Ambiguity

We can now consider the decision strategies a learner might employ to choose which grammar to shift to when its current grammar has just failed on an input sentence. The case of interest is where the input sentence does not decide the matter because it is parametrically ambiguous – or may be, for all the learner knows. And the central question is: what effect does the degree of parametric ambiguity have on the effectiveness of different decision strategies? In particular: is there a learning model that is relatively immune to the high level of ambiguity in natural language, as children appear to be?

5.1   *Without ambiguity detection: errors*

As noted in section 4.2, learning models that meet the realistic processing load criterion are generally unable to detect parametric ambiguity, because parametric decoding other than by method (f) is such a struggle. In models other than the STL, therefore, if the decoding system can find any way to license a sentence, the learner must settle for it as if it were the only way. This is equivalent to guessing which of the possible parametric analyses of a sentence is correct. The effect of ambiguity is obvious: the greater the ambiguity, the greater the pool of candidates, so the less constrained the guess. As a result, the trajectory through the domain of possible grammars which should bring the learner's guesses closer and closer to the target is not so well directed. The feedback from parsing success is not systematically related to the learner's parametric choices. In section 4.2 we observed that a move in the right direction may fail to be positively reinforced because some other aspect of the grammar is still incorrect. Once ambiguity is added in, the opposite also occurs: the learner may be positively reinforced by parsing success when it sets a parameter to the wrong value. Hence, in an ambiguous domain, time and effort can be wasted pursuing trails that lead nowhere.

The damage done by false feedback might even be permanent. It is an open question whether an ambiguity-blind system like the TLA could be led into superset errors which are uncorrectable. This is an obvious danger in any non-deterministic model which makes errors and hopes to be able to correct them later. (I use the term *deterministic* here in the sense made familiar in parsing theory by Marcus 1980, to denote unrevisable, or "indelible," computations. In non-deterministic learning, a parameter that has been set one way could later be reset to its opposite value. See discussion by Clahsen 1990.)

Even if errors are not permanent, they can be costly. They increase the learner's total workload by requiring parameters to be reset possibly many times en route to the target grammar. This cost of making errors is beginning to be quantified (in terms of additional inputs needed before convergence on the target grammar); see Berwick and Niyogi (1996) and Sakas and Fodor (in press). Since errors are unavoidable for a non-deterministic learning procedure, the costs of error correction need to be minimized. Such a learner is therefore best paired with a highly efficient mechanism for decoding and (re)setting parameters. For this reason, the non-deterministic response to ambiguity can be evaluated most favorably if it is implemented not in the TLA framework but in combination with the treelets decoding method of the STL, which has a more constructive system for finding a candidate grammar able to parse a given sentence. A non-deterministic version of the STL is outlined in section 5.3.

For cue search systems such as Lightfoot's the consequences of ambiguity are harder to assess, because no effective method of cue recognition is specified. In a recent presentation Lightfoot (1998) adopts some aspects of the STL model, such as the identification of cues and parameter values (though, oddly, without adjusting the proposed cues to reflect the true content of the parameter values; see section 4.3 above), but he does not take advantage of the treelet parsing method for parametrically decoding the input. An input sentence receives a single parse, often incomplete, possibly incorrect; how it is assigned is unclear. "As a child understands an utterance, even partially, she has some kind of mental representation of the utterance. These are partial parses" and they are scanned for I-language cues (Lightfoot 1998: 4). This is not very informative, though it is reminiscent of other learning systems that construct parse trees by guesswork tempered by UG principles, such as Fodor (1989) and Clark (1996). In any case, it is clear from Lightfoot's description that the cue search system is not intended to be error free. In fact it is capable of errors even when correct information is available, since it does not respond to a cue until it has encountered it with some fairly substantial frequency. This is why language change occurs when the frequency of occurrence of a cue declines for any reason (e.g. loss of English verb-to-I movement by the eighteenth century, following the rise of periphrastic *do* and other changes that reduced the number of constructions in which the verb was visibly raised over another element such as the subject or negation).

Thus the cue based model makes guesses, as the TLA does. So it makes errors, at least some of which it subsequently corrects. However, the frequency sensitivity explanation for historical change suggests that, unlike the TLA, this is not a one-trial-learning device. Rather than resetting a parameter on the strength of one conflicting input sentence, this learner may be designed to collect up the weight of evidence for and against each parameter value, and to adopt a value decisively only when the evidence in favor of it exceeds some threshold. This would be similar to proposals made by Kapur (1994) and Valian (1990). To what extent such a system would make overt errors in production and perception during its period of indecisiveness concerning each parameter would depend on its strategy. It might employ on every occasion whichever value of the parameter was temporarily ahead; or it might employ both values, with probabilities in proportion to their relative standing; and so on. From the learner's point of view, the effect of increased ambiguity would be to spin out the adjudication process between the alternative values of a parameter, and postpone the time at which any values could be eliminated from consideration.

If this is what is intended by way of ambiguity management for the cue based model, it too can be implemented in a manner not unlike the non-deterministic variant of the STL to be described in section 5.3. As was observed in section 4, the concept of I-language structural cues is highly compatible with the notion of structural triggers, or treelets, on which the STL decoding system relies. So the cue based model could select any of a range of STL-type systems as its implementation, to supply the missing machinery for creating parse trees for novel input sentences. The non-deterministic STL described in section 5.3 is probably most in keeping with Lightfoot's theory.

5.2 *With ambiguity detection: delay*

The treelet-based parametric decoder of the STL model can determine that an input sentence is parametrically ambiguous though it cannot reasonably compute more than one analysis for each sentence. In fact the STL overestimates parametric ambiguity, since the parser will flag an ambiguity point when it encounters mere within-language structural ambiguities, or temporary ambiguities which are resolved later in the sentence, neither of which would in fact derail parameter setting. But though it sometimes overreacts, it never misses a parametric ambiguity. (Almost never; see discussion in Fodor 1998c.)

A learning system capable of detecting ambiguity has two choices for dealing with it. The learner can be conservative and refrain from setting parameters on the basis of any part of a sentence that is within the scope of an ambiguity. Or it can take risks by guessing which of the competing analyses is the correct one. The first strategy is suitable for a deterministic learner, and the second for a non-deterministic one, in the sense defined above. A conservative, deterministic version of the STL makes only correct decisions. As I will show, it pays the price of ambiguity in the time it must wait for unambiguous inputs to learn from (if indeed they exist). A non-deterministic version of the STL goes much faster but makes some wrong decisions; it pays for ambiguity in errors and the need for error correction, as the TLA and other guessing systems do. As noted in section 4, the earliest STL models were strictly conservative (Fodor 1995, 1998a, and the "weak STL" of Sakas and Fodor in press). But that is only possible if the input is cooperative; it may be expecting too much of the quality of input that children really receive. A version of the STL that does not always wait for perfect input might be more successful and provide a better match for human learners. We need to know, and one good way to find out is to compare the two variants to see how resilient they are to attack by parametric ambiguity.

From now on I will refer to the conservative version of the STL as the D-STL (for deterministic STL). The D-STL sets parameters (adopts new treelets) on-line, when needed to enable the parser to analyze an input sentence, but it ceases parameter setting as soon as the parser detects any ambiguity point in a sentence – a point of net ambiguity, resolved neither by the input nor by the grammar acquired so far. Parsing continues past this point for comprehension purposes, but the learning system discards the remainder of the sentence as a basis for parameter setting. It may thereby waste some reliable information, since, as noted, it sometimes perceives parametric ambiguity where none is present. But its discard policy is at least more rational than that of other models. The TLA, for example, discards many inputs – including unambiguous ones – due to decoding failures, but sets parameters on the basis of ambiguous and unambiguous inputs alike. The D-STL discards all ambiguous and some unambiguous inputs and learns from the unambiguous remainder.

The D-STL's discard rate is necessarily higher the greater the net parametric ambiguity of the target language sample. And when input is discarded, nothing is learned from it. Therefore, in a language domain which is highly ambiguous the D-STL sets parameters less frequently than when ambiguity is low; it consumes more input sentences for each parameter it sets. At the same time, the D-STL shows the progressive disambiguation effect noted in section 3.2: learning speed picks up over the course of learning as more and more parameter values are pinned down. Establishing a parameter value means that a target treelet has been adopted into the learner's grammar, where it becomes a source of certainty rather than uncertainty for the parser. On standard assumptions, to adopt one value of a parameter is to reject its other value (e.g. adopting complement initial for VP amounts to rejecting complement final for VP). So adopting a treelet has the effect of shrinking the collection of treelets waiting in the wings to be called on if the current grammar fails. And that increases the probability that the parse is rescuable by only one treelet, which would allow that treelet then to be adopted. Thus each parameter that is set makes it easier to set the next one.

Nevertheless, we have discovered from working on this model that for the D-STL, or any other conservative learning device, the delays between usable inputs can be very long indeed. The reason was touched on at the end of section 4.3: a conservative learner must discard not only parts of sentences it knows to be parametrically ambiguous (net ambiguous), but also parts of sentences which it has not fully tracked and so does not know are *not* parametrically ambiguous. This covers a lot of ground, since for a serial parsing device any part of a sentence to the right of an ambiguity is less than fully monitored. What this adds up to is that the D-STL discards input for purposes of setting one parameter, say P7, not merely if it is ambiguous with respect to P7 but also if it is ambiguous (net ambiguous) with respect to any other parameter(s). For instance, until it had determined whether the target language is +V2 or −V2, it could set no parameters controlling phenomena in the VP (e.g. indirect objects), because they would be masked by the ±V2 ambiguity to their left. Absurd as this might seem, it is a consequence of the extreme cautiousness that is necessary in a deterministic system. (Note that I assume here no meta-knowledge on the part of the learner about which parameters could or could not interact with each other in derivations.) Thus, the only usable data for parameter setting by the D-STL are sentences or parts of sentences in which, to the left of any ambiguity (within-grammar or cross-grammar ambiguity), a target treelet not yet in the learner's grammar is expressed unambiguously; that is, the sentence cannot be parsed without it.

Probabilities can be assigned to the factors relevant to speed of learning (e.g. the probability that the currently hypothesized grammar will fail on an input, the probability that the failure point at which the parse crashes precedes any ambiguity in the sentence, the probability that a unique UG treelet is able to rescue the parse), and the mathematics can be worked through to give the probability of usable data at various degrees of overall parametric ambiguity. (See Sakas and Fodor in press for mathematical considerations.) From this, the average wait between parameter setting events can be calculated. It is, unfortunately, very high indeed for anything approaching realistic degrees of ambiguity: millions of sentences, in some cases, between parameter setting events. Moreover, the average wait is less than the maximum wait, which is what counts if we are to ensure that *every* learner attains the target in a reasonable time. There are simplifying assumptions entering into these computations which are most likely too stringent for real life. Also, our calculations so far have not included the ameliorating effects of progressive disambiguation, by which the average delay between usable inputs decreases rapidly as learning proceeds. So these are by no means final estimates. But these early results stand at least as a warning that waiting for unambiguous input to learn from can be a costly strategy.

To summarize: D-STL acquisition comes close to the ideal of setting parameters accurately, once and for all, in response to unambiguous triggers supplied by the environment. But accuracy and speed do not go together. Even with its efficient treelet decoding procedure, the feasibility restriction to serial parsing entails that some unambiguous parametric information in input sentences is masked by ambiguities and is not accessible to the learning routine. Hence in the presence of parametric ambiguity, D-STL learning is accurate but very slow. It is especially slow at the beginning; ambiguity hits early learning hardest.

Is this compatible with the facts of human language learning? To the extent that children make syntactic mistakes, these would have to be attributed to faulty input, lack of lexical knowledge, semantic confusions, processing slips, etc. But this is not unrealistic. It has repeatedly been noted that children make remarkably few syntactic (as opposed to lexical or morphological) errors. This speaks in favor of conservative learning and against learning algorithms which engage in random guessing. (See, however, Bowerman 1990 on some early word order errors, e.g. *Comes feet under here.*) The slow rate of parameter setting is a legitimate concern, but is not necessarily fatal. After all, if a child has just 20 parameters to set by the age of 5, learning need go no faster than one parameter every couple of months. Even if there are 50 parameters, or 100, the time for each one is still measured in weeks, not days or minutes. This contrasts with the rate of lexical learning, which has been estimated at one word every two waking hours during the pre-school years (Pinker 1994, citing work by Nagy and Anderson).

On the other hand, the extreme effect of ambiguity on the setting of the first few parameters does seem hard to reconcile with human performance. The prediction is that – at least relative to a constant flow of information from the environment – the earliest-set parameters are set orders of magnitude more slowly than later parameters. No empirical surveys have been done to establish how many parameters children have set correctly at what ages, and whether this accelerates. Studies of particular syntactic phenomena do occasionally reveal a lag between the time at which relevant evidence appears to be available to children and the time at which they have demonstrably mastered the facts. These cases are often attributed to late maturation of some UG contribution to the construction (e.g. the maturation of A-chains, Borer and Wexler 1987; see also Wexler 1999).

Perhaps such cases should be re-examined from the perspective of conservative learning. It seems unlikely, but might these laggardly phenomena be particularly susceptible to masking by other ambiguities in the same sentence? More commonly, acquisition research reveals that children know more of the syntax of their language than they normally make use of. Constructions can be elicited which occur rarely if at all in the child's spontaneous production at that stage (e.g. a relative clause in a purpose clause at 3 years 5 months: *Jabba, please come over to point to the one that's asleep*; *wh*-extraction from a subordinate clause at 3 years 11 months: *Squeaky, what do you think that is?*; see Crain et al. 1987, Crain and Thornton 1991). And comprehension experiments with babies not yet producing any word combinations confirm that they already know some basic facts of their target language such as the surface order of subject, object, and verb (Hirsh-Pasek and Golinkoff 1991). Tentatively, then, I conclude that children exhibit no great delay in getting the early parameters set. (See also the Very Early Parameter Setting generalization of Wexler 1998.)

There is an interesting possible explanation for this which might save the D-STL. Perhaps natural languages are particularly kind to the conservative strategy for parameter setting, allowing it to be successful on sentences typical of children's early input even though for other sentences it would indeed be slow. This could reconcile the theoretical predictions of conservativism with the achievements of human learners. We know what linguistic properties would be of assistance. The beginnings of sentences are the most important: an unresolved ambiguity late in a sentence will mask less than if it were to occur at the beginning. Also, for equivalent overall amounts of ambiguity, it would be better for a sentence to have more ambiguity points with fewer treelet competitors at each, rather than fewer ambiguities with more competitors, since then the setting of one or two parameters has a good chance of eliminating an ambiguity entirely, thereby opening up later parts of sentences for further learning. Suppose these helpful properties were characteristic of relatively simple sentences such as infants comprehend and on which they presumably rely for learning, sentences such as *Where's the kitty?* or *Mommy will read you a story.* This could break the early learning bottleneck despite massive parametric ambiguity in the language as a whole. To the contrary, however, a look at natural languages makes it all too clear that early learners are faced with multiple ambiguities starting from the very first word of a sentence (see section 6). The natural language domain does not help out the D-STL; it makes deterministic early learning as difficult as it possibly could be.

5.3   *With ambiguity detection: no waiting*

The STL has a choice of strategies for responding to input ambiguity: it can exploit its ambiguity detection ability or not do so. If it does not, it is in the same boat as the TLA and other grammar guessing systems that are unable to detect ambiguity because they try out only one grammar at a time. Disregarding ambiguity is the approach of the non-deterministic variant of the STL, also known, for reasons that will be clear, as the *Parse Naturally* STL (PN-STL; Fodor 1998c).

Its parser is still a serial parser, and it does exactly what a normal (adult) human parser would normally do: it computes its favorite analysis of an input word string, based on Minimal Attachment and other innate preference principles. (Minimal Attachment says that an input word should be attached into the parse tree using the fewest possible new nodes; Fodor 1998b defends the innateness of both the parsing mechanism and its preferences.) Unlike the deterministic STL, it does not record ambiguity points. The only difference from adult sentence processing is that at a point of parse failure, the learner has access to the innate lexicon of parametric treelets. These are temporarily folded into the grammar acquired so far, as described above, so the parser's use of them is governed by Minimal Attachment and so forth, just as for other elements of the grammar. Having computed its preferred analysis, the parser reports it to the learning component without comment on ambiguity. The learner treats the parse tree as if it were correct, and adopts any new parametric treelets it contains. If the analysis *is* correct, all is well. But if a sentence is globally parametrically ambiguous, the parser's preferred analysis may differ from the target analysis, so the parameter values adopted may be incorrect. The higher the net ambiguity rate the greater the chance that this is so.

In short: the PN-STL lets the parsing strategies make decisions about how to resolve parametric ambiguities, and since these decisions cannot always be right, the PN-STL makes mistakes in setting parameters. For instance, the Minimal Chain Principle (De Vincenzi 1991) is another important parsing principle, which favors non-movement analyses over movement analyses.

This parsing preference will cause the learner to adopt −V2 rather than +V2 where there is a choice. (Gibson and Wexler 1994 also propose that learners prefer non-movement analyses, though not for parsing reasons.) This is correct for SVO strings in English but not in German. For German the V2 parameter will need resetting when a sentence is encountered for which no −V2 analysis is possible. The acquisition of +V2 in German is still not well understood, but there are some reasons for believing that the verb does not move to the C projection until Case morphology is acquired and the evidence of Accusative-initial sentences outweighs the avoidance of movement (Weissenborn 1990).

It seemed self-evident in the early days of working with the STL that its ability to more or less effortlessly detect and avoid ambiguity was a great asset not to be wasted. The PN-STL does waste this gift, but it has some good features to recommend it nonetheless. The mistakes it makes are not random or stupid ones. Its disambiguation choices are systematic, so they help to explain the uniformity of language acquisition by all normal children. They reflect the human parser's natural tendencies, which may increase the chance that the selected analysis is the one the speaker intended. The human parser is apparently a least-effort device, preferring to build structures that are as simple as possible, so even if the parser's analysis is wrong, at least the processing load is not excessive. Error correction is needed but is relatively fast given that the PN-STL does not suffer from decoding delays. Also, the PN-STL is well able to benefit from useful-but-not-quite-reliable hints about sentence structure from prosody and semantics just as adult parsing does (within bounds of modularity). These non-syntactic sources of information cannot conveniently be used by an ABS system like the TLA, which first picks a new grammar to try and only then inspects the properties of the input sentence. Nor can they be exploited by a deterministic system that cannot afford to take chances on partial cues. And a system that uses prosody to set some syntactic parameters directly could employ only a small proportion of the ubiquitous structure-sensitive prosodic patterns in natural language sentences. To extract the most benefit from prosodic and semantic cues, they should be used by a non-deterministic learner not insisting on total accuracy, where they can affect parameter setting indirectly by contributing to selection of the most likely tree structure for novel sentence constructions. Above all, the Parse Naturally system brings relief for early learners. Parametric questions are answered (albeit tentatively) as soon as they arise, so learners rapidly gain a substantial working grammar which can be used for comprehension and production until such time as the target parameter settings are stabilized.

These merits must be weighed against two disadvantages that beset all non-deterministic learning. When errors occur they can create misleading contexts for setting other parameters, thus generating even more errors (Clark 1988). This tendency is presumably exacerbated by high levels of parametric ambiguity. Also, an error-prone non-deterministic learner can never afford to dismiss the parameter values that are the competing partners of the ones it has adopted, because it may need to revert to them later. Eliminating disconfirmed values was the source of the progressive speed-up in learning rate over time discussed in section 3.2. It appears that the PN-STL sacrifices this acceleration in return for the speed it gains at the start. The effect is to flatten out the learning curve across the whole course of learning, evening up the workload – perhaps not a bad trade-off. And arguably, the PN-STL does not suffer too greatly in efficiency by its retention of unpromising-looking parameter values just in case they are needed later. The PN-STL is relatively unaffected by the number of grammars in the pool of candidates, because it considers only the most highly ranked one. Unlike other models, it selects among just those that can parse the current sentence, and attends only to the parser's preferred candidate at each choice point. Furthermore, the PN-STL can be given the capability of keeping a running tab on the success rates of all the UG treelets depending on how often they come to the rescue of a blocked parse, as suggested in section 5.1 for the cue based learner. By this means, even though it never really eliminates any treelets, the PN-STL would gain much the same advantage as if it definitively adopted some and dismissed others. Its strategy would be to give priority to the most successful treelets. The more these are used the stronger they will get, so they will streak further ahead of the others and will be, in effect, the only ones in play – except if input is subsequently encountered which offers no choice but to boost a previously low-ranked treelet. Thus, rapid narrowing of the field of likely candidates may be compatible with revision capability in case of unexpected turns in the data.

An empirical prediction of this model is that the phenomena in each language that are the hardest to learn will include those for which there exists an incorrect parametric alternative which the parsing system strongly prefers. This is not the same as claiming that all structurally complex constructions are challenging for learners. Difficulty is predicted just where the evidential support from the learner's input for the correct treelet would have to fight against the parser's disinclination on-line to assign the correct structural analysis rather than some other. Studies of adult sentence processing show that the human parsing mechanism does sometimes fail to compute a correct analysis that is highly dispreferred. To the extent that parsing preferences are innate and already active in children, we should observe slow spots in learning correlated with the known dislikes of the human parser, as in the case of the Minimal Chain preference mentioned above. More work is needed to generate exact predictions for particular languages. There is also much work to be done in establishing the error curves for PN-STL learning under various conditions of parametric ambiguity, expression rates, and so forth, to see how accuracy varies over the course of learning. For modeling the complex dynamics of error correction systems, mathematical methods are less practical, so computer simulation will be needed to evaluate the PN-STL and compare it with the performance of the deterministic STL.

5.4   Assessment

There is a family of possible STL learners, all using the innate lexicon of treelets to decode the parametric information in input sentences. Here I have utilized the general STL format to compare two different varieties incorporating some design choices proposed in other models. The purpose of the comparison is to gain insight into how the human language learning mechanism is designed, by assessing the strengths and weakness of the models, and comparing their performance with that of human learners. The D-STL emphasizes the accuracy aimed for in early switch-setting models. The PN-STL takes chances and relearns where necessary, like the TLA. They have in common their efficient decoding procedure, and the STL emphasis on sentence structure as the mediator between input word strings and grammars; parameters are concerned with aspects of that structure. The theoretical linguistic concept of a structural cue or trigger for each parameter value is preserved and is integrated into a psycholinguistic account of sentence parsing which spans adults and children, and which takes on much of the burden of the learning process.

There are more STL varieties imaginable than these two, which contrast maximally in their handling of ambiguity. A possible intermediate system would flag ambiguity points like the D-STL, but in case of ambiguity would set parameters anyway like the PN-STL. This would give the initial fast progress of the Parse Naturally approach, but the learner's confidence in a treelet could be scaled to whether it was adopted on the basis of ambiguous or unambiguous evidence. Another design that might recommend itself is the D-STL equipped with default parameter values for the child to use in language production and comprehension while waiting for decisive evidence of target values. Defaults, however, must be employed with great caution in a deterministic system, since they can engender errors (even the otherwise beneficial Subset Principle default; see Fodor 1998c). Perhaps other STL variants will emerge that are superior to these.

Formal evaluation of these models has barely begun. We know too little still about their performance characteristics for there to be a final judgment yet. The discussion so far has suggested the following rough and ready evaluation. The deterministic approach which became a practical possibility with the advent of STL decoding is the only way to achieve fully accurate parameter setting. Computationally this accuracy is essentially cost-free, but in terms of learning rate it is not, especially at early stages. The PN-STL comes closer to delivering constant rate parameter setting across the timespan of learning, despite the enormous range of uncertainty levels that children face at different stages. But the parameter setting errors of the PN-STL seem not to do justice to real children, who tend with few exceptions not to use syntactic constructions they do not know how to use correctly. Also, at present it is an open question whether the errors of the PN-STL, like those of Gibson and Wexler's TLA, may lead it into territory from which it may never retreat.

How can we advance on these approximate assessments? Computational linguistic research can continue to spell out the efficiency characteristics and convergence rates of each approach. It falls to psycholinguistics to determine which accords best with empirical data on actual parameter setting progress by children. More extensive experimental data on children's sentence processing may also be informative. One other possible source of information is the linguistic facts themselves. By comparing the properties of natural languages with how they might have been in a make-believe world better designed for learners, we may get a sharper estimate of how much of a challenge acquisition really is, and hence how robust the human learning mechanism must be. I try out this line of thought in section 6.

6 Patterns of Parametric Ambiguity in Natural Language

Is it possible to hold on to the ideal picture of rapid error free parameter setting for natural language? So far we have seen that total accuracy is probably incompatible with speed. Moreover, it appears that natural languages are designed to magnify this incompatibility. The distribution of parametric ambiguity in natural language is far more damaging for learners than it need be. It is possible, though still unclear at present, that developments in syntactic theory might ameliorate this situation. If not, deterministic learning is probably not practicable; some guesswork must be resorted to to get the job done.

6.1 String-to-structure alignment

It would have been more convenient for children if natural language parameters were all concerned with surface facts, and if every parameter value expressed by a sentence were expressed independently of the others and unambiguously. (Of course, it would be more convenient if there were no parameters at all. See Pinker and Bloom 1990 and commentaries for speculation on why human evolution did not go further and provide us with a fully formed innately specified language.) Instead, the way of natural language is to let P&P values and lexical items intermingle in a derivation so that at the surface there is no separable piece of the word string attributable to each piece of the grammar involved in the derivation. The relation between word strings and their parametric generators is thus opaque at best. And because different derivations may converge on the same word string it is also often ambiguous. A large part of the problem is that sentences have abstract structures far richer than the lexical items that realize them audibly: the non-terminal-to-terminal node ratio is high. This is particularly so for syntactic analyses since Pollock (1989), in which what were once represented as features of lexical projections now appear as functional heads with projections of their own. As Bertolo et al. (1997) have pointed out, this can create ambiguities concerning the position of a verb among the stack of inflectional heads representing tense, agreement, aspect, and so forth. A'-movement and its traces also contribute to the disproportion of inaudible to audible elements.

Neither non-terminal nodes nor empty categories would be a problem for learners if everything about them were innate. In fact, although their existence and distribution are regulated in part by innate principles, they are also to some extent parameterized. Even if the array of functional heads in the extended verbal projection is universal and totally predictable for learners with access to UG (e.g. Cinque 1999), it is still necessary for a learner to discover how that structure aligns with the words of target language sentences. For instance, in *The mouse squeaks* is *squeaks* in V or AGR_o or T or AGR_s or C? Is *the mouse* in the Specifier of V or of T or AGR_s or C? Bertolo et al. contemplate a language such that no surface facts fully determine the answers to these questions. In that case a seriously conservative learner such as the D-STL would wait forever for unambiguous input to set the verb movement parameters. The learner could never parse verbs at all for lack of knowing where they should be parked in relation to the innately prescribed non-terminal nodes in the parse tree. Even in a language where the answers are determinate, it may take quite a lot of evidence from input sentences to establish them; and a conservative learner can build no parse trees until that evidence has been encountered. Note that this is a situation in which neither prosodic nor semantic cues are of any assistance. Verb movement is a formal operation which has no effect on phonological phrasing or meaning.

The Minimalist Program suggests that morphological cues might be useful, since overt movement is driven by strong features on functional heads and there is some tendency for strong features to be overtly realized morphologically. For example, rich inflection is often cited as a predisposing factor for verb movement to I. If the correlation between overt morphological realization and strong syntactic features were exact, learners would be able to read off from the verb's morphology (once acquired) not only that the verb must have moved, but exactly which functional head it moved to within the extended verbal projection. Unfortunately it appears that this relationship is not reliable enough for learners to trust. The Minimalism based learning system of Wu (1994) treats morphological strength and syntactic strength as independent parameters (though see Pollock 1997 for a new way of relating them). The only evidence that learners can rely on, it seems, is the positional markers that linguists rely on in motivating analyses with split Infl: the adverbs which may intervene among the verbal head positions, an overtly realized negative head, and so forth. For example, Pollock (1989) used the contrast between *John often kisses Mary*/*John kisses often Mary* and **Jean souvent embrasse Marie*/*Jean embrasse souvent Marie* to argue that the finite verb moves to a higher functional head in French than in English. Adverbs and negation are audible items, and they can fix the locations of movable entities such as the verb and its arguments, within the (inaudible) extended verbal projection.

The problem with these indicators of string-to-structure alignment is that adverbs and negation are optional in sentences. So learners will receive only occasional doses of positional information. Many of the sentences children hear are not structurally disambiguated by such elements. Lack of positional markers is especially true of very simple sentences like *Mickey squeaks*, which presumably constitute the intake (the processible input) of beginning learners, who are most in need of disambiguation assistance. To make things worse, the unresolved ambiguities of verb and argument position that young children are exposed to occur often at the very beginnings of sentences (e.g. the structural position of an initial noun is multiply indeterminate). This, we have noted, is the worst possible location for an ambiguity because it will block the acquisition of any other parametric facts the sentence may contain (section 5.2). Furthermore, these ambiguities are systematic; they are not a matter of accidental overlap of word strings, which a child might be unlucky enough to encounter once but which would not recur. It is not just *Mickey squeaks* which is structurally indeterminate for learners, but *all* sentences that contain just a verb with some complements.

Thus, natural language design is extremely cruel to children: (i) natural languages have multiple positions capable of hosting the same lexical category (e.g. verb); (ii) children are not free to choose which position it should be in since there is a right and wrong answer for each language; yet (iii) UG does little to ensure that the target position is recognizable in basic sentences in which the item appears. This is especially punishing for a conservative learning strategy which demands certainty before it takes action, and for which one ambiguity can block the learning of other facts. As the extreme case of the paralysis noted by Bertolo et al. (1997), a truly conservative learner might have no grammar at all for verb placement until the verb has been observed in relation to every one of the positional landmarks that UG provides. Cinque (1999) lists 32 classes of adverb that would need to be observed, as well as multiple positions for negation.

In summary: natural languages abound in ambiguities of the worst kind for a deterministic learner: systematic ambiguities which occur early in sentences and early in a learner's career, and which are highly frequent but resolved infrequently. An artificial domain of languages in which simple sentences facilitate parameter setting can easily be created. But natural language design seems to do all it can to exacerbate the early learning problem. These observations appear to put the precision-loving deterministic STL at a disadvantage relative to the happy-go-lucky PN-STL. The former backs away from the ambiguities the primary linguistic data throw at it. The latter muddles on through until some fixed points of information finally begin to arrive; and if some never do, it has a grammar anyway.

However, the distribution of parametric ambiguity in natural languages depends not only on the language facts but also on their proper theoretical interpretation. Before we abandon forever the goal of high-precision triggering of syntactic parameters, it is appropriate to consider what difference it would make to learning if the language facts were differently analyzed.

6.2   *The problem of short sentences*

The problems circle around the properties of short sentences. Young children produce short sentences, and they show signs of comprehending short sentences better than long ones, by and large, so we assume that they learn from short sentences. Chomsky (1988: 70) wrote: "Notice that the value of the [headedness] parameter is easily learned from short simple sentences. To set the value of the parameter for Spanish, for example, it suffices to observe three-word sentences such as (3)," where (3) is *Juan habla inglés* "Juan speaks English." But this is wishful thinking. An SVO sentence does not suffice to establish head–complement order. Consider *Johann spricht Englisch*.

Though they may be easier for production and comprehension, short sentences are not necessarily simpler for acquisition than long ones are. All depends on what they leave out. A short sentence simplifies early learning by not presenting embedded questions or adverbial clauses or long distance extraction. The parameters peculiar to those constructions do not have to be set yet, and they do not create ambiguities that get in the way of setting other parameters. But a short sentence complicates learning if it leaves out the items that resolve parametric ambiguities or show the scaffolding into which the overt items fit. Ideally, the earliest sentences children attend to would be composed of items which are not themselves parameterized, and which will help to clarify the parameter settings needed for other items to come. Here, as we have seen, natural languages win no design prizes. (I am indebted to Anne Christophe and Norbert Hornstein, personal communication, for insisting on this point.)

The shortness of sentences affects different parameters to different degrees. For obvious reasons it is easier for a short sentence to reveal the positive value of the null subject parameter than the positive value of the V2 parameter. Though the particularities of different parameters cannot really be set aside, some general effects of sentence length can still be discerned. The shortness of a sentence imposes an inherent limit on how informative it can be for learners. Parametric information is carried by the overt items in a sentence: the categories of the words and the discernible relationships among them such as precedence or agreement (and also, sometimes, by what is missing). If a sentence needs more parameter values for its derivation than can be signaled by the words it contains, parametric ambiguity results. So short sentences are liable to overflow their parametric banks, so to speak, unless they are derived using only a small proportion of the full set of parameter values that generates the whole language. But this condition is hard to satisfy if a sentence consisting of just one verb has a structure with the full array of inflectional heads, all needing to be specified for weak or strong features controlling movement.

Conclusion: It could be that the best way to facilitate early learning would be to ensure that UG permits short sentences to have simple, relatively parameter-free derivations. Ambiguity overload can be kept at bay if parametric questions do not pile up unanswered, waiting until more "advanced" input is heard and absorbed.

6.3   *How much help from UG?*

We have observed that even if large chunks of language structure are innately programmed into human brains, a learner may be quite unable to tell how that structure should align with the words heard. This is parallel to the situation for syntactic categories: the categories Noun and Verb are surely innate but children still must learn which of the words they hear belong to which categories, and that is not a trivial task. The idea that innately prescribed structure is cost-free for language learners is common in linguistic research and it seems eminently plausible. It is also welcome, because it means there is no reason not to assume the innateness of many aspects of language structure. A structural configuration needed for one language can be assumed to occur, inaudibly, in other languages too, as long as there is no specific evidence to the contrary. This brings linguistic theory closer to being able to claim that all natural languages have essentially the same derivational structures – except only that not all the same parts of the universal structure are spelled out in every language.

Unfortunately, the argument that what is innate is *ipso facto* effortless for learners is not valid. It is clear now that even if the structural scaffolding of sentences is everywhere fixed and the same, any particular sentence may be highly ambiguous with respect to how its words are attached to that scaffolding. For UG to be truly helpful, it should supply innate sentence structures *and* fix their relation to surface word strings – or at least constrain that relation tightly enough that learners can rapidly fill in the rest. As long as there is substantial crosslinguistic variation with respect to how innately defined structure is overtly lexicalized, there will be ambiguities of string-to-structure alignment that may be very onerous for learners to resolve. Every bit of universal structure, even if it is not "used" in some language, can make that language harder to learn.

But UG can assist learners in two other ways. First and most obviously: whatever the facts are that adults know, a learner has a lighter time of it the more of them it knows innately. If simple sentences have rich structure, better that it should be innate than not. More interestingly: UG principles control how much invisible structure learners have to assign to word strings. Thereby they control the balance between parametric ambiguity, which is troublesome, and parametric irrelevance, which can be helpful as a way of postponing difficult questions until the input is rich enough to provide the answers. The question, then, is whether UG could permit simple sentences to have parametrically simple and unambiguous derivations. There is more than one way this could be achieved. Which if any is correct is a linguistic issue. I sketch two broad approaches here.

i   Adopt a theory of UG which matches the structural ambiguity of overt elements to their time of occurrence in learners' intake: the earliest items should be the most determinate. This would reduce the string-to-structure alignment problem by improving the balance in early language samples between the elements that need to be structurally located and the elements that can help to locate them. In earlier forms of transformational grammar before the split-Infl hypothesis, and in other linguistic frameworks such as LFG or HPSG, the verb is the fixed element in a clause, and adjuncts are positioned relative to it rather than vice versa. For target grammars of this kind, beginning learners could build correct trees for subjects and verbs right away, based on *Mickey squeaks* and other simple sentences in their conversational milieu. There would be minimal structural ambiguity to contend with at the outset, and optional elements could be added in later on.

ii Retaining the split-Infl concept, adopt a theory which entails that each sentence has only as much structure (in Infl and elsewhere) as is needed to derive its own properties (e.g. surface word order). (See, for example, Giorgi and Pianesi 1997. For an important form of argument against this idea, see Cinque 1999: ch. 6.) There would be no parametric ambiguity due to ambiguities of hidden structure (though "genuine" parametric ambiguities would still occur, such as between exceptional case marking and structural case assignment in infinitives, in the example noted by Clark 1988). Thus, a child's simplest structural hypothesis about an input sentence could be correct for that sentence even if additional parameters must be set to derive more complex sentences later.

Note that this goes beyond the suggestion that each language employs (for all its sentences) only as many functional projections as are needed to acount for the phenomena of that language (e.g. Fukui 1986, Bobaljik and Thráinsson 1998; see also discussion in Haegeman 1997 and other references there). It also differs from the proposal of Radford (1990) that functional categories are omitted from the sentence structures computed by early learners because the ability to represent them does not mature until about 2 years. It might be combined with the assumption that functional heads can be featurally underspecified, so that a learner could acknowledge that some projection must be present to provide a landing site for movement, without yet knowing what the content of the head is. This would seem promising from a learning point of view, since it allows that a child could always build just the minimal warranted structure, not committing to any more of its details than are certain.

Other proposals in a similar spirit involve defaults. Assuming that the maximal structure is present in every sentence derivation, there might be movement defaults which keep the verb and its arguments low in the structure until specific evidence of overt movement to a higher position is encountered: features controlling movement would be weak until proven strong. Or, assuming that languages differ with respect to the inventory of functional projections they employ, it would be natural for defaults to exclude any particular functional head until the input proves it necessary for reasons of morphology or movement. These alternatives may be more palatable theoretically than varying the richness of structure sentence by sentence, but they will demand some departure from full determinism of the learning procedure, since default parameter values are technically "errors" in languages which have the non-default value, so other learning decisions made on the basis of them cannot be guaranteed correct.

Whichever approach turns out to be right, it is clear that the assessment of current learning models is very much in the hands of theoretical linguistics. Linguists proposing syntactic parameters have often specified input triggers which could set those parameters. This is important. Unfortunately, as learning theory has begun to model the time course of parameter setting, we find that it has become more difficult to propose a realistic collection of triggers that will allow all parameters to be set accurately in a reasonable amount of time. For learnability theory there is therefore a great deal hanging on the outcome of current linguistic research on the richness of sentence structures, and particularly on recent reconsiderations of the linguistic evidence for and against the hypothesis that all sentences in all languages have identical hierarchies of functional projections providing potential landing sites for parameterized movement.

NOTE

* Parts of this chapter appeared in the essay "Twenty questions" written for the celebration of Noam Chomsky's 70th birthday, available at the MIT Press website (http://mitpress.mit.edu/celebration). I am grateful to Mark Baltin and Chris Collins for their ideas and advice on how to adapt it to its role in the *Handbook*. Much of its content stems from discussions with several colleagues, particularly Stefano Bertolo, Erich Groat, William Sakas, and Virginia Teller.

Bibliography

Abney, S. (1987). The English Noun Phrase in its Sentential Aspect. PhD dissertation, MIT.

Ackerman, F. (1990). The morphological blocking principle and oblique pronominal incorporation in Hungarian. In K. Dziwirek, P. Farrell, and E. Mejías-Bikandi (eds), *Grammatical Relations. A Cross-Theoretical Perspective* (pp. 1–19). Stanford: CSLI Publications.

Ackerman, F. and Webelhuth, G. (1998). *A Theory of Phrasal Predicates*. Stanford: CSLI Publications.

Ackerman, F. and Webelhuth, G. (to appear). The composition of (dis)continuous predicates. In É. Katalin Kiss (ed.), *Acta Linguistica Hungarica: Special Volume on Syntax.*

Adams, Marianne Patalino. (1987). Old French, null subjects and verb second phenomena. PhD thesis, UCLA.

Adger, D. (1996). Aspect and agreement in Scots Gaelic. In R. D. Borsley and I. Roberts (eds), *The Syntax of the Celtic Languages: A Comparative Perspective* (pp. 200–22). Cambridge: Cambridge University Press.

Åfarli, T. (1985). Norwegian verb-particle constructions as causative constructions. *Nordic Journal of Linguistics*, 8, 75–98.

Aissen, J. (1996). Pied-piping, abstract agreement, and functional projections in Tzotzil. *Natural Language and Linguistic Theory*, 14, 447–91.

Aitchison, J. (1979). The order of word order change. *Transactions of the Philological Society*, 77, 43–65.

Akmajian, A. and Wasow, T. (1975). The constituent structure of VP and AUX and the position of the verb *be*. *Linguistic Analysis*, 1, 205–45.

Akmajian, A., Steele S., and Wasow, T. (1979). The category AUX in universal grammar. *Linguistic Inquiry*, 10, 1–64.

Aldrich, J. and Nelson, F. (1984). *Linear Probability, Logit, and Probit Models*. London: Sage.

Alexiadou, A. (1997). *Adverb Placement*. Amsterdam: John Benjamins.

Alexiadou, A. and Anagnostopoulou, E. (1997). Toward a uniform account of scrambling and clitic doubling. In W. Abraham and E. van Gelderen (eds), *German: Syntactic Problems – Problematic Syntax* (pp. 143–61). Tübingen: Max Niemeyer.

Altmann, G., Buttlar, H. von, Rott, W., and Strauss, U. (1983). A law of change in language. In B. Brainerd (ed.), *Historical Linguistics* (pp. 104–15). Bochum: Studienverlag Dr N. Brockmeyer.

Anagnostopoulou, E. and Everaert, M. (1999). Towards a more complete typology of anaphoric expressions. *Linguistic Inquiry*, 30.1, 97–118.

Andersen, H. (1973). Abductive and deductive change. *Language*, 49, 765–93.

Anderson, M. (1979). Noun Phrase Structure. PhD dissertation, University of Connecticut.

Anderson, S. (1976). On the notion of subject in ergative languages. In C. Li (ed.), *Subject and Topic* (pp. 1–23). New York: Academic Press.

Anderson, S. R. (1969). West Scandinavian Vowel Systems. PhD dissertation, MIT.

Anderson, S. R. (1986). The typology of anaphoric dependencies: Icelandic (and other) reflexives. In L. Hellan and K. K. Christensen (eds), *Topics in Scandinavian Syntax* (pp. 65–88). Dordrecht: Reidel.

Anderson, S. R. (1992). *Amorphous Morphology*. Cambridge: Cambridge University Press.

Andrews, A. (1976). The VP complement analysis in Modern Icelandic. *NELS*, 6, 1–21.

Andrews, A. (1982). A note on the constituent structure of adverbials and auxiliaries. *Linguistic Inquiry*, 13, 313–17.

Andrews, A. (1990). The VP-complement analysis in Modern Icelandic. In J. Maling and A. Zaenen (eds), *Syntax and Semantics. Vol. 24: Modern Icelandic Syntax* (pp. 165–85). New York: Academic Press.

Andrews, A. D. (1982). The representation of case in modern Icelandic. In J. Bresnan (ed.), *The Mental Representation of Grammatical Relations* (pp. 427–503). Cambridge MA: MIT Press.

Andrews, A. D. (1984). Lexical insertion and the elsewhere principle in LFG. MS, Department of Linguistics, Australian National University.

Andrews, A. D. (1990). Unification and morphological blocking. *Natural Language and Linguistic Theory*, 8, 507–57.

Andrews, A. D. and Manning, C. (1993). Information spreading and levels of representation in LFG. Report no. CSLI-93-176. Stanford: CSLI.

Androutsopoulou, A. (1995a). The licensing of adjectival modification. In *Proceedings of WCCFL*. Stanford: CSLI.

Androutsopoulou, A. (1995b). The distribution of the definite determiner and the syntax of Greek DPs. MS, UCLA.

Androutsopoulou, A. (1997). On Remnant DP-Movement in Modern Greek. MA thesis, UCLA.

Angluin, D. (1980). Inductive inference of formal languages from positive data. *Information and Control*, 45, 117–35.

Anttila, A. (1997). Morphological Variation. PhD dissertation, Stanford University.

Anttila, A. (to appear). Deriving variation from grammar. In F. Hinskens, R. van Hout, and L. Wetzels (eds), *Variation, Change and Phonological Theory*. Amsterdam: John Benjamins.

Aoun, J. (1986). *Generalized Binding*. Dordrecht: Foris.

Aoun, J. and Li, Y.-H. A. (1993a). *Wh*-elements in situ: syntax or LF? *Linguistic Inquiry*, 24, 199–238.

Aoun, J. and Li, Y.-H. A. (1993b). On some differences between Chinese and Japanese *wh*-elements. *Linguistic Inquiry*, 24, 365–72.

Aoun, J. and Li, Y.-H. A. (1993c). *Syntax of Scope*. Cambridge MA: MIT Press.

Aoyagi, H. and Ishii, T. (1994). Agreement-inducing vs. non-agreement-inducing NPIs. *Proceedings of NELS*, 24, 1–15.

Appel, R. and Muysken, P. (1987). *Language Contact and Bilingualism*. London: Edward Arnold.

Ariel, M. (1990). *Accessing Noun-Phrase Antecedents*. London: Croom Helm.

Aronoff, M. (1976). *Word Formation in Generative Grammar*. Cambridge MA: MIT Press.

Ashton, E. O. (1982). *Swahili Grammar (Including Intonation)*. Harlow: Longman.

Austin, P. (in press). Word order in a free word order language: the case of Jiwarli. *Language*.

Austin, P. and Bresnan, J. (1996). Non-configurationality in Australian aboriginal languages. *Natural Language and Linguistic Theory*, 14, 215–68.

Avrutin, S. (1994). Psycholinguistic Investigations in the Theory of Reference. PhD dissertation, MIT.

Babby, L. (1987). Case, prequantifiers, and discontinuous agreement in Russian. *Natural Language and Linguistic Theory*, 5, 91–138.

Babby, L. H. (1980). *Existential Sentences and Negation in Russian*. Ann Arbor MI: Karoma.

Bach, E. (1979). Control in Montague grammar. *Linguistic Inquiry*, 10, 515–31.

Bailey, C.-J. (1973). *Variation and Linguistic Theory*. Washington DC: Center for Applied Linguistics.

Bailyn, J. (1995a). A Configurational Approach to Russian "Free" Word Order. PhD dissertation, Cornell University.

Bailyn, J. (1995b). Underlying phrase structure and "short" verb movement in Russian. *Journal of Slavic Linguistics*, 3.1, 13–58.

Bailyn, J. (1995c). Configurational case assignment in Russian syntax. *Linguistic Review*, 12, 315–60.

Bailyn, J. and Rubin, E. (1991). The unification of instrumental case assignment in Russian. In W. Harbert and A. J. Toribio (eds), *Cornell Working Papers in Linguistics*, 9 (pp. 99–126). Ithaca NY: Department of Modern Languages and Linguistics.

Baker, C. L. (1970). Notes on the description of English questions: the role of an abstract question morpheme. *Foundations of Language*, 6, 197–219.

Baker, C. L. (1995). Contrast, discourse prominence, and intensification, with special reference to locally-free reflexives in British English. *Language*, 71, 63–101.

Baker, C. L. and McCarthy, J. J. (eds), (1981). *The Logical Problem of Language Acquisition*. Cambridge MA: MIT Press.

Baker, M. (1985). The Mirror Principle and morphosyntactic explanation. *Linguistic Inquiry*, 16, 373–416.

Baker, M. (1988). *Incorporation: A Theory of Grammatical Function Changing*. Chicago: Chicago University Press.

Baker, M. (1991). On some subject/object non-asymmetries in Mohawk. *Natural Language and Linguistic Theory*, 9, 537–76.

Baker, M. (1996). *The Polysynthesis Parameter*. Oxford: Oxford University Press.

Baker, M. (1997a). On the distinction between adjectives and verbs. Unpublished paper, McGill University.

Baker, M. (1997b). Thematic roles and syntactic structure. In L. Haegeman (ed.), *Elements of Grammar* (pp. 73–137). Dordrecht: Kluwer.

Baker, M. and K. Hale (1990). Relativised minimality and pronoun incorporation. *Linguistic Inquiry*, 21, 289–97.

Baker, M., Johnson, K. and Roberts, I. (1989). Passive arguments raised. *Linguistic Inquiry*, 20, 219–51.

Baltin, M. (1987). Do antecedent-contained deletions exist? *Linguistic Inquiry*, 18, 579–96.

Baltin, M. (1989). Heads and projection. In M. Baltin and A. S. Kroch (eds), *Alternative Conceptions of Phrase Structure* (pp. 1–16). Chicago: University of Chicago Press.

Baltin, M. (1992). On the characterisation and effects of d-linking: comments on Cinque. In R. Freidin (ed.), *Current Issues in Comparative Grammar* (pp. 249–56). Dordrecht: Kluwer.

Baltin, M. (1995). Floating quantifiers, PRO, and predication. *Linguistic Inquiry*, 26, 199–248.

Baltin, M. (in preparation). Ellipsis and the representation of arguments.

Barbosa, P., Fox, D., Hagstrom, P., McGinnis, M., and Pesetsky, D. (eds), (1998). *Is the Best Good Enough? Optimality and Competition in Syntax*. Cambridge MA: MIT Press and MIT Working Papers in Linguistics.

Barker, M. A. R. (1964). *Klamath Grammar*. Berkeley: University of California Press.

Barss, A. (1984). Chain binding. Generals examination paper, MIT.

Barss, A. (1986). Chains and Anaphoric Dependence: On Reconstruction and its Implications. PhD dissertation, MIT.

Barss, A. (1987). Paths, connectivity, and featureless empty categories. In A. Cardinaletti, G. Cinque, and G. Giusti (eds), *Constituent Structure* (pp. 9–34). Dordrecht: Foris.

Barss, A. (1994). Anaphora and the timing of dependency formation. MS, University of Arizona.

Barss, A. (1996). Derivations and reconstruction. *Studies in the Linguistic Sciences*, 24.2, 19–38.

Barss, A. (1999). Derivations and dependencies. MS, University of Arizona.

Bartsch, R. (1976). *The Grammar of Adverbials*. Amsterdam: North Holland.

Battistella, E. (1989). Chinese reflexivization: a movement to Infl approach. *Linguistics*, 27, 987–1012.

Bayer, J. (1984). COMP in Bavarian. *Linguistic Review*, 3, 209–74.

Bayer, J. (1996). *Directionality and Logical Form*. Dordrecht: Kluwer.

Bayer, J. and Kornfilt, J. (1994). Against Scrambling as an instance of move-alpha. In N. Corver and H. van Riemsdijk (eds), *Studies on Scrambling. Movement and Non-Movement Approaches to Free Word-Order Phenomena* (pp. 17–60). Berlin: de Gruyter.

Beck, S. (1996). Quantified structures as barriers for LF movement. *Natural Language Semantics*, 4, 1–56.

Beckman, J., Dickey, L., and Urbanczyk, S. (eds), (1995). Papers in Optimality Theory. *University of Massachusetts Occasional Papers*, 18. Amherst: University of Massachusetts.

Beghelli, F. (1993). A Minimalist approach to quantifier scope. In A. Schafer (ed.), *Proceedings of NELS*, 23 (pp. 65–80).

Beghelli, F. (1997). The syntax of distributivity and pair-list readings. In A. Szabolcsi (ed.), *Ways of Scope Taking* (pp. 349–408). Dordrecht: Kluwer.

Beghelli, F. and Stowell, T. (1997). Distributivity and negation: the syntax of *each* and *every*. In A. Szabolcsi (ed.), *Ways of Scope Taking* (pp. 71–109). Dordrecht: Kluwer.

Beghelli, F., Ben-Shalom, D., and Szabolcsi, A. (1997). Variation, distributivity, and the illusion of branching. In A. Szabolcsi (ed.), *Ways of Scope Taking* (pp. 29–71). Dordrecht: Kluwer.

Belletti, A. (1981). Frasi ridotte assolute. *Rivista di grammatica generativa*, 6, 3–32.

Belletti, A. (1982). On the anaphoric status of the reciprocal construction in Italian. *Linguistic Review*, 2, 101–38.

Belletti, A. (1988). The case of unaccusatives. *Linguistic Inquiry*, 19, 1–34.

Belletti, A. (1990). *Generalized Verb Movement: Aspects of Verb Syntax*. Turin: Rosenberg and Sellier.

Belletti, A. (1994). Verb positions: evidence from Italian. In D. Lightfoot and N. Hornstein (eds), *Verb Movement* (pp. 19–40). Cambridge: Cambridge University Press.

Belletti, A. (forthcoming). Italian/Romance clitics: structure and derivation. In H. van Riemsdijk (ed.), *Clitics in the Languages of Europe*. Berlin: de Gruyter.

Belletti, A. (in preparation). Aspects of the clause structure and derivation of comparative clauses. MS, University of Siena.

Belletti, A. and Rizzi, L. (1981). The syntax of *ne*: some theoretical implications. *Linguistic Review*, 1, 117–54.

Belletti, A. and Rizzi, L. (1988). Psych-verbs and theta theory. *Natural Language and Linguistic Theory*, 6, 291–352.

Belletti, A. and Rizzi, L. (1996). Su alcuni casi di accordo del participio passato in francese e in italiano. In P. Benincà, G. Cinque, T. De Mauro, and N. Vincent (eds), *Italiano e dialetti nel tempo. Saggi di grammatica per Giulio Lepschy* (pp. 7–22). Rome: Bulzoni.

Belletti, A. and Shlonsky, U. (1995). The order of verbal complements: a comparative study. *Natural Language and Linguistic Theory*, 13.3, 489–526.

Benincà, P. (1994). *La variazione sintattica*. Bologna: Il Mulino.

Benincà, P. and Vanelli, L. (1982). Appunti di sintassi veneta. In M. Cortelazzo (ed.), *Guida ai dialetti veneti. Vol. 4* (pp. 7–38). Padua: CLEUP.

Bennis, H. and Haegeman, L. (1984). On the status of agreement and relative clauses in West Flemish. In W. de Geest and Y. Putseys (eds), *Sentential Complementation* (pp. 33–55). Dordrecht: Foris.

Benua, L. (1995). Identity effects in morphological truncation. In J. Beckmann, L. Dickey, and S. Urbanczyk (eds), Papers in Optimality Theory (pp. 77–136). *University of Massachusetts Occasional Papers*, 18. Amherst: University of Massachusetts.

Benveniste, E. (1966). *Problèmes de linguistique générale*. Paris: Gallimard.

Berman, J. (1996). Topicalization vs. left-dislocation of sentential arguments in German. In M. Butt and T. H. King (eds), *LFG-Workshop. Proceedings of the First LFG Conference*. Rank Xerox Research Centre, Grenoble, August 26–8. On-line, CSLI Publications: http://www-csli.stanford.edu/publications/

Berman, J. (1997). Empty categories in LFG. In M. Butt and T. H. King (eds), *Proceedings of the LFG97 Conference*, University of California, San Diego. On-line, CSLI Publications: http://www-csli.stanford.edu/publications/

Berman, J. (1998). On the syntax of correlative *es* and finite clauses in German – an LFG analysis. In *Proceedings of the ESSLLI–98 Workshop on Constraint-Based Theories of Germanic Syntax*, Saarbrücken (pp. 5–19). To be published in revised form as: On the cooccurrence of *Es* with a finite clause in German: an LFG analysis. In T. Kiss and D. Meurers (eds), *Topics in Constraint-Based Germanic Syntax*. Stanford: CSLI Publications.

Berman, S. and Hestvik, A. (1997). Split antecedents, noncoreference, and DRT. In H. Bennis, P. Pica, and J. Rooryck (eds), *Atomism and Binding* (pp. 1–29). Dordrecht: Foris.

Bernini, G. and Ramat, P. (1992). *La frase negativa nelle lingue d'Europa*. Bologna: Il Mulino.

Bernstein, J. (1991a). DPs in French and Walloon: evidence for parametric variation in nominal head movement. *Probus*, 3, 1–26.

Bernstein, J. (1991b). Nominal enclitics in Romance. *MIT Working Papers in Linguistics*, 14, 51–66.

Bernstein, J. (1992). On the syntactic status of adjectives in Romance. *CUNYForum*, 17, 105–22.

Bernstein, J. (1993a). Topics in the Syntax of Nominal Structure across Romance. PhD dissertation, CUNY.

Bernstein, J. (1993b). The syntactic role of word markers in null nominal constructions. *Probus*, 5, 5–38.

Bernstein, J. (1997). Demonstratives and reinforcers in Romance and Germanic languages. *Lingua*, 102, 87–113.

Bernstein, J. (1999). Focusing the "right" way in romance determiner phrases. MS, Syracuse University. To appear in *Probus*, 13.1.

Bernstein, J., Cowart, W. and McDaniel, D. (in press). Bare singular effects in genitive constructions. *Linguistic Inquiry*, 30.

Bertolo, S., Broihier, K., Gibson, E., and Wexler, K. (1997). Cue-based learners in parametric language systems: application of general results to a recently proposed learning algorithm based on unambiguous superparsing. Paper presented at the 19th Annual Conference of the Cognitive Science Society, August, Stanford.

Berwick, R. C. (1985). *The Acquisition of Syntactic Knowledge*. Cambridge MA: MIT Press.

Berwick, R. C. and Niyogi, P. (1996). Learning from triggers. *Linguistic Inquiry*, 27.4, 605–22.

Besten, H. den (1983). On the interaction of root transformations and lexical deletive rules. In W. Abraham (ed.), *On the Formal Syntax of the Westgermania* (pp. 47–131). Amsterdam: John Benjamins.

Bhat, D. N. S. (1994). *The Adjectival Category: Criteria for Differentiation and Identification*. Amsterdam: John Benjamins.

Bhatt, R. and Yoon, J. (1992). On the composition of COMP and parameters of V2. In D. Bates (ed.), *Proceedings of the Tenth WCCFL* (pp. 41–53). Stanford: CSLI Publications.

Bhattacharya, T. (to appear). DP-internal NP movement. *UCL Working Papers*, 10.

Bianchi, V. and Figuereido Silva, M. C. (1994). On some properties of agreement-object in Italian and in Brazilian Portuguese. In M. L. Mazzola (ed.), *Issues and Theory in Romance Linguistics: Selected Papers from the XXIV LSRL* (pp. 181–97). Washington DC: Georgetown University Press.

Bierwisch, M. (1963). *Grammatik des deutschen Verbs*. Berlin: Akademie Verlag.

Bittner, M. (1994). *Case, Scope and Binding*. Dordrecht: Kluwer.

Bittner, M. and Hale, K. (1995). Remarks on definiteness in Warlpiri. In E. Bach, A. Kratzer, E. Jelinek, and B. Partee (eds), *Quantification in Natural Languages* (pp. 81–105). Dordrecht: Kluwer.

Bittner, M. and Hale, K. (1996a). The structural determination of case and agreement. *Linguistic Inquiry*, 27, 1–68.

Bittner, M. and Hale, K. (1996b). Ergativity: toward a theory of heterogeneous class. *Linguistic Inquiry*, 27, 531–601.

Blake, B. (1994). *Case*. Cambridge: Cambridge University Press.

Blasco Ferrer, E. (1986). *La lingua sarda contemporànea: grammatica del logudorese e del campidanese*. [*The Sardinian Language Today: Grammar of Logudorese and Campidanese*]. Cagliari: Edizioni della Torre.

Blevins, J. P. (1995). Syncretism and paradigmatic opposition. *Linguistics and Philosophy*, 18, 113–52.

Bobaljik, J. (1993). On ergativity and ergative unaccusative. *MIT Working Papers in Linguistics*, 19, 45–88.

Bobaljik, J. (1995). Morphosyntax: The Syntax of Verbal Inflection. PhD dissertation, MIT.

Bobaljik, J. (1998). Adjacency and the autonomy of syntax: Holmberg's Generalization revisited. Paper presented at the 10th Conference of Nordic and General Linguistics, Reykjavík.

Bobaljik, J. and Carnie, A. (1996). A Minimalist account of Irish word order. In R. D. Borsley and I. Roberts (eds), *The Syntax of the Celtic Languages: A Comparative Perspective* (pp. 223–40). Cambridge: Cambridge University Press.

Bobaljik, J. and Jonas, D. (1996). Subject positions and the roles of TP. *Linguistic Inquiry*, 27, 195–236.

Bobaljik, J. and Thráinsson, H. (1998). Two heads aren't always better than one. *Syntax*, 1.1, 37–71.

Boersma, P. (1997). How we learn variation, optionality, and probability. On-line, Rutgers University: Rutgers Optimality Archive, ROA-221-1097, http://ruccs.rutgers.edu/roa.html

Bolinger, D. (1971). *The Phrasal Verb in English*. Cambridge MA: Harvard University Press.

Bonet, E. (1995). Feature structure of Romance clitics. *Natural Language and Linguistic Theory*, 13, 607–47.

Borer, H. (1984). *Parametric Syntax: Case Studies in Semitic and Romance Languages*. Dordrecht: Foris.

Borer, H. (1994). Deconstructing the construct. MS, University of Massachusetts, Amherst.

Borer, H. (1996). The construct in review. In J. Lecarme, J. Lowenstamm, and U. Shlonsky (eds), *Studies in Afro-Asiatic Languages* (pp. 30–61). The Hague: Holland Academic Graphics.

Borer, H. and Wexler, K. (1987). The maturation of syntax. In T. Roeper and E. Williams (eds), *Parameter Setting* (pp. 123–72). Dordrecht: Reidel.

Börjars, K. and Vincent, N. (1997). Double case and the "wimpishness" of morphology. Paper presented at the LFG97 Conference, July 9–11, University of California, San Diego.

Börjars, K., Vincent, N., and Chapman, C. (1997). Paradigms, periphrases and pronominal inflection: a feature-based account. In G. Booji and J. van Marle (eds), *Yearbook of Morphology* (pp. 1–26). Dordrecht: Kluwer.

Borsley, R. and Roberts, I. (1996). *The Syntax of the Celtic Languages*. Cambridge: Cambridge University Press.

Borsley, R. D., Rivero , M.-L., and Stephens, J. (1996). Long head movement in Breton. In R. Borsley and I. Roberts, *The Syntax of the Celtic Languages* (pp. 53–74). Cambridge: Cambridge University Press.

Bošković, Ž. (1997a). Superiority effects with multiple *wh*-fronting in Serbo-Croatian. *Lingua*, 102, 1–20.

Bošković, Ž. (1997b). *The Syntax of Nonfinite Complementation*. Cambridge MA: MIT Press.

Bošković, Ž. (1998). Multiple *wh*-fronting and economy of derivation. *Proceedings of the West Coast Conference on Formal Linguistics*, 16, 49–63.

Bošković, Ž. (to appear). Sometimes in SpecCP, sometimes in-situ. In R. Martin and J. Uriagereka (eds), *Step by Step: Papers on Minimalist Syntax in Honor of Howard Lasnik*. Cambridge MA: MIT Press.

Bouchard, D. (1984). *On the Content of Empty Categories*. Dordrecht: Foris.

Bouchard, D. (1998). The distribution and interpretation of adjectives in French: a consequence of bar phrase structure. *Probus*, 10, 139–83.

Bouton, L. F. (1970). *Antecedent Contained Pro-Forms*. Chicago: Chicago Linguistics Society.

Bowerman, M. (1990). Mapping thematic roles onto syntactic functions: are children helped by innate linking rules? *Linguistics*, 28, 1253–89.

Bowers, J. (1975). Adjectives and adverbs in English. *Foundations of Language*, 13, 529–62.

Bowers, J. (1987). Extended X-bar theory, the ECP and the Left Branch Condition. In M. Crowhurst (ed.), *Proceedings of the West Coast Conference on Formal Linguistics*, 6, 47–62. Stanford: Stanford Linguistics Association.

Bowers, J. (1991). The syntax and semantics of nominals. In S. Moore and A. Wyner (eds), *Proceedings of the First Semantics and Linguistic Theory Conference, Cornell Working Papers in Linguistics*, 10 (pp. 1–30). Ithaca NY: Department of Modern Languages and Linguistics, Cornell University.

Bowers, J. (1993a). The syntax of predication. *Linguistic Inquiry*, 24.4, 591–656.

Bowers, J. (1993b). The syntax and semantics of stage level and individual level predicates. Paper read at the Third Semantics and Linguistic Theory Conference, UC Irvine.

Bowers, J. (1997a). Case and agreement. MS, Cornell University.

Bowers, J. (1997b). A binary analysis of resultatives. In R. C. Blight and M. J. Moosally (eds), *Texas Linguistic Forum 38: The Syntax and Semantics of Predication* (pp. 43–58). Austin TX: Department of Linguistics, University of Texas at Austin.

Bowers, J. (1998). Toward a minimalist theory of grammatical and thematic relations. MS, Cornell University.

Brame, J. (1981). The general theory of binding and fusion. *Linguistic Analysis*, 7.3, 277–325.

Brame, M. (1982). The head-selector theory of lexical specifications and the nonexistence of coarse categories. *Linguistic Analysis*, 10.4, 321–5.

Brandi, L. and Cordin, P. (1989). Two Italian dialects and the null subject parameter. In O. Jaeggli and K. Safir (eds), *The Null Subject Parameter* (pp. 111–42). Dordrecht: Kluwer.

Bresnan, J. (1971a). Note on the notion "identity of sense anaphora." *Linguistic Inquiry*, 2, 589–97.

Bresnan, J. (1971b). Sentence stress and syntactic transformations. *Language*, 47, 257–81.

Bresnan, J. (1972). Theory of Complementation in English Syntax. PhD dissertation, MIT.

Bresnan, J. (1973). Syntax of the comparative clause construction in English. *Linguistic Inquiry*, 4, 275–343.

Bresnan, J. (1976). On the form and functioning of transformations. *Linguistic Inquiry*, 7.1, 3–40.

Bresnan, J. (1977). Transformations and categories in syntax. In R. E. Butts and J. Hintikka (eds), *Basic Problems in Methodology and Linguistics* (pp. 262–82). Dordrecht: Reidel.

Bresnan, J. (1978). A realistic transformational grammar. In J. M. B. Halle and G. A. Miller (eds), *Linguistic Theory and Psychological Reality* (pp. 1–59). Cambridge MA: MIT Press.

Bresnan, J. (1982a). Control and complementation. In J. Bresnan (ed.), *The Mental Representation of Grammatical Relations* (pp. 282–390). Cambridge MA: MIT Press.

Bresnan, J. (ed.), (1982b). *The Mental Representation of Grammatical Relations*. Cambridge MA: MIT Press.

Bresnan, J. (1982c). The passive in lexical theory. In J. Bresnan (ed.), *The Mental Representation of Grammatical Relations* (pp. 3–86). Cambridge MA: MIT Press.

Bresnan, J. (1998a). Morphology competes with syntax: explaining typological variation in weak crossover effects. In P. Barbosa, D. Fox, P. Hagstrom, M. McGinnis, and D. Pesetsky (eds), *Is the Best Good Enough? Optimality and Competition in Syntax* (pp. 59–92). Cambridge MA: MIT Press and MIT Working Papers in Linguistics.

Bresnan, J. (1998b). Markedness and morphosyntactic variation in pronominal systems. Paper presented at the workshop Is Syntax Different? Common Cognitive Structures for Syntax and Phonology in Optimality Theory, December 12–13, CSLI, Stanford University.

Bresnan, J. (1998c). Pidgin genesis in Optimality Theory. In M. Butt and T. H. King (eds), *Proceedings of the LFG98 Conference*, University of Queensland, Brisbane. On-line, CSLI Publications: http://www-csli.stanford.edu/publications/

Bresnan, J. (forthcoming a). *Lexical-Functional Syntax*. Oxford: Blackwell.

Bresnan, J. (forthcoming b). The lexicon in Optimality Theory. Paper presented at Annual CUNY Conference on Human Sentence Processing, Special Session on the Lexical Basis of Syntactic Processing: Formal and Computational Issues, March 20, Rutgers University.

Bresnan, J. (forthcoming c). The emergence of the unmarked pronoun. In G. Legendre, J. Grimshaw, and S. Vikner (eds), *Optimality Theoretic Syntax*. Cambridge MA: MIT Press.

Bresnan, J. (in press a). Optimal syntax. In J. Dekkers, F. van der Leeuw, and J. van de Weijer (eds), *Optimality Theory: Phonology, Syntax, and Acquisition*. Oxford: Oxford University Press.

Bresnan, J. (in press b). The emergence of the unmarked pronoun: Chicheŵa pronominals in Optimality Theory. *BLS–23*.

Bresnan, J. and Kanerva, J. (1989). Locative inversion in Chicheŵa: a case study of factorization in grammar. *Linguistic Inquiry*, 20, 1–50.

Bresnan, J. and Mchombo, S. A. (1987). Topic, pronoun, and agreement in Chicheŵa. *Language*, 63, 741–82.

Bresnan, J. and Mchombo, S. A. (1995). The lexical integrity principle: evidence from Bantu. *Natural Language and Linguistic Theory*, 13, 18–252.

Bresnan, J. and Zaenen, A. (1990). Deep unaccusativity in LFG. In K. Dziwirek, P. Farrell, and E. Mejías-Bikandi (eds), *Grammatical Relations: A Cross-Theoretical Perspective* (pp. 45–57). Stanford: CSLI Publications.

Brockett, C. (1994). *Mo*: quantificational evidence for a non-quantificational anaylsis. In M. Koizumi and H. Ura (eds), Formal Approaches to Japanese Linguistics 1, *MIT Working Papers in Linguistics*, 24 (pp. 45–59).

Brodie, B. L. (1985). English Adverb Placement in Generalized Phrase Structure Grammar. *Ohio State University Working Papers in Linguistics*, 1–63.

Brody, M. (1985). On the complementary distribution of empty categories. *Linguistic Inquiry*, 16.4, 505–46.

Brody, M. (1995). *Lexico-Logical Form*. Cambridge MA: MIT Press.

Brown, K. (1991). Double modals in Hawick Scots. In P. Trudgill and J. K. Chambers (eds), *Dialects of English. Studies in Grammatical Variation* (pp. 74–103). London: Longman.

Browning, M. (1987). Null Operator Constructions. PhD dissertation, MIT. Published (1991) New York: Garland.

Browning, M. and Karimi, E. (1994). Scrambling to object position in Persian. In N. Corver and H. van Riemsdijk (eds), *Studies on Scrambling: Movement and Non-Movement Approaches to Free Word-Order Phenomena* (pp. 61–100). Berlin: de Gruyter.

Brugè, L. (1996). Demonstrative movement in Spanish: a comparative approach. *University of Venice Working Papers in Linguistics*, 6.1.

Burton, S. and Grimshaw, J. (1992). Coordination and VP-internal subjects. *Linguistic Inquiry*, 23, 305–13.

Burzio, L. (1981). Intransitive Verbs and Italian Auxiliaries. PhD dissertation, MIT.

Burzio, L. (1986). *Italian Syntax*. Dordrecht: Reidel.

Burzio, L. (1991). The morphological basis of anaphora. *Journal of Linguistics*, 27, 81–105.

Butt, M. and King, T. H. (eds), (1996). *LFG-Workshop. Proceedings of the First LFG Conference*. Rank Xerox Research Centre, Grenoble, August 26–8. On-line, CSLI Publications: http://www-csli.stanford.edu/publications/

Butt, M. and King, T. H. (eds), (1997). *Proceedings of the LFG97 Conference*, University of California, San Diego. On-line, CSLI Publications: http://www-csli.stanford.edu/publications/

Butt, M. and King, T. H. (eds), (1998). *Proceedings of the LFG98 Conference*, University of Queensland, Brisbane. On-line, CSLI Publications: http://www-csli.stanford.edu/publications/

Butt, M., Dalrymple, M., and Frank, A. (1997). An architecture for linking theory in LFG. In M. Butt and T. H. King (eds), *Proceedings of the LFG97 Conference*, University of California, San Diego. On-line, CSLI Publications: http://www-csli.stanford.edu/publications/

Campos, H. and Kempchinsky, P. (eds), (1995). *Evolution and Revolution in Linguistic Theory: Essays in Honor of Carlos Otero*. Washington DC: Georgetown University Press.

Cantrall, W. (1974). *View Point, Reflexives and the Nature of Noun Phrases*. The Hague: Mouton.

Cardinaletti, A. and Guasti, M. T. (eds), (1995). *Syntax and Semiotics. Vol. 28: Small Clauses*. New York: Academic Press.

Cardinaletti, A. and Roberts, I. (1991). Clause structure and X-second. MS, University of Venice and University of Geneva.

Carlson, G. N. (1977). A unified analysis of the English bare plural. *Linguistics and Philosophy*, 1, 413–56.

Carnie, A. (1995). Non-Verbal Predication and Head Movement. PhD dissertation, MIT.

Carnie, A., Pyatt, E., and Harley, H. (1996). VSO order as raising out of IP? Some evidence from Old Irish. MS. To appear in *Studies in the Linguistic Sciences*, 24.

Carrier, J. and Randall, J. (1992). The argument structure and syntactic structure of resultatives. *Linguistic Inquiry*, 23, 173–234.

Carstens, V. (1991). The Morphology and Syntax of Determiner Phrases in Kiswahili. PhD dissertation, UCLA.

Carstens, V. (1998). Features and movement in DPs. MS, Cornell University.

Carter, R. (1976). Some linking regularities in English. MS, University of Paris.

Carter, R. (1988). Some linking regularities. In B. Levin and C. Tenny (eds), *On Linking: Papers by Richard Carter* (pp. 1–92). Cambridge MA: Center for Cognitive Science, MIT.

Casalegno, P. (1987). Sulla logica dei plurali. *Teoria*, 2, 125–43.

Cattell, R. (1976). Constraints on movement rules. *Language*, 52, 18–50.

Chamorro, A. (1992). On Free Word Order in Mohawk. MA thesis, McGill University.

Chao, W. (1987). On Ellipsis. PhD dissertation, University of Massachusetts, Amherst.

Cheng, L. and Sybesma, R. (to appear). Bare and not-so-bare nouns and the structure of NP. *Linguistic Inquiry*.

Cheng, L. L.-S. (1991). On the Typology of *Wh*-Questions. PhD dissertation, MIT.

Cheng, L. L.-S. (1995). On dou-quantification. *Journal of East Asian Linguistics*, 4, 197–234.

Cheng, L. L.-S. and Huang, C.-T. (1996). Two types of donkey sentences. *Natural Language Semantics*, 4, 121–63.

Cheng, L. L.-S., Huang, C.-T. J., and Tang, C.-C. J. (1997). Negative particle questions: a dialectal comparison. In J. Black and V. Motapanyane (eds), *Micro-Parametric Syntax: Dialectal Variation in Syntax* (pp. 41–74). Philadelphia: John Benjamins.

Cheshire, J., Edwards, V., and Whittle, P. (1993). Non-standard English and dialect levelling. In J. Milroy and L. Milroy (eds), *Real English. The Grammar of English Dialects in the British Isles* (pp. 53–96). London: Longman.

Chien, Y.-C. and Wexler, K. (1990). Children's knowledge of locality conditions in binding as evidence for the modularity of syntax and pragmatics. *Language Acquisition*, 1, 225–95.

Chierchia, G. (1984). Topics in the Syntax and Semantics of Infinitives and Gerunds. PhD dissertation, University of Massachusetts, Amherst.

Chierchia, G. (1985). Formal semantics and the grammar of predication. *Linguistic Inquiry*, 16, 417–43.

Chierchia, G. (1989). A semantics for unaccusatives and its syntactic consequences. MS, Cornell University.

Chierchia, G. (1993). Questions with quantifiers. *Natural Language Semantics*, 1, 181–234.

Chierchia, G. (1995). *Dynamics of Meaning*. Chicago: Chicago University Press.

Chierchia, G. and Turner, R. (1988). Semantics and property theory. *Linguistics and Philosophy*, 11, 261–302.

Choe, H. S. (1995). Focus and topic movement in Korean and licensing. In K. É. Kiss (ed.), *Discourse Configurational Languages* (pp. 269–334). Oxford: Oxford University Press.

Choe, J. W. (1987). LF movement and pied-piping. *Linguistic Inquiry*, 18, 348–53.

Choi, H.-W. (1996). Optimizing Structure in Context: Scrambling and Information Structure. PhD dissertation, Stanford University. On-line, Rutgers University: Rutgers Optimality Archive, http://ruccs.rutgers.edu/roa.html

Choi, H.-W. (forthcoming). Focus scrambling and reconstruction in binding. In G. Legendre, J. Grimshaw, and S. Vikner (eds), *Optimality Theoretic Syntax*. Cambridge MA: MIT Press.

Chomsky, N. (1955). The logical structure of linguistic theory. MS, Harvard University and MIT. Revised (1956) version published in part (1975) New York: Plenum and (1985) Chicago: University of Chicago Press.

Chomsky, N. (1957). *Syntactic Structures*. The Hague: Mouton.

Chomsky, N. (1959). On certain formal properties of grammars. *Information and Control*, 2, 137–67. Reprinted in R. D. Luce, R. Bush, and E. Galanter (eds), (1965). *Readings in Mathematical Psychology II*. New York: Wiley.

Chomsky, N. (1962). The logical basis of linguistic theory. In *Proceedings of the Ninth International Congress of Linguists*.

Chomsky, N. (1964). *Current Issues in Linguistic Theory*. The Hague: Mouton.

Chomsky, N. (1965). *Aspects of the Theory of Syntax*. Cambridge MA: MIT Press.

Chomsky, N. (1970). Remarks on nominalization. In R. Jacobs and P. Rosenbaum (eds), *Readings in English Transformational Grammar* (pp. 184–221). Waltham MA: Ginn.

Chomsky, N. (1973). Conditions on transformation. In S. Anderson and P. Kiparsky (eds), *A Festschrift for Morris Halle* (pp. 232–86). New York: Holt, Rinehart, and Winston.

Chomsky, N. (1975). *Reflections on Language*. New York: Pantheon.

Chomsky, N. (1976). Conditions on rules of grammar. *Linguistic Analysis*, 2, 303–51. Reprinted in (1977) *Essays on Form and Interpretation*. New York: North Holland.

Chomsky, N. (1977). On *wh*-movement. In P. Culicover, T. Wasow, and A. Akmajian (eds), *Formal Syntax* (pp. 71–132). New York: Academic Press.

Chomsky, N. (1980). On binding. *Linguistic Inquiry*, 11, 1–46.

Chomsky, N. (1981). *Lectures on Government and Binding*. Dordrecht: Foris.

Chomsky, N. (1982). *Some Concepts and Consequences of the Theory of Government and Binding*. Cambridge MA: MIT Press.

Chomsky, N. (1986a). *Knowledge of Language: Its Nature, Origin, and Use*. New York: Praeger.

Chomsky, N. (1986b). *Barriers*. Cambridge MA: MIT Press.

Chomsky, N. (1988). *Language and Problems of Knowledge: The Managua Lectures*. Cambridge MA: MIT Press.

Chomsky, N. (1989). Some notes on economy of derivation and representation. *MIT Working Papers in Linguistics*, 10, 43–74. Also in R. Freidin (ed.), *Principles and Parameters in Comparative Grammar* (pp. 417–54). Cambridge MA: MIT Press.

Chomsky, N. (1991). Some notes on economy of derivation and representation. In R. Freidin (ed.), *Principles and Parameters in Comparative Grammar* (pp. 417–54). Cambridge MA: MIT Press.

Chomsky, N. (1992). A Minimalist Program for linguistic theory. *MIT Occasional Papers in Linguistics*, 1.

Chomsky, N. (1993). A Minimalist Program for linguistic theory. In K. Hale and S. J. Keyser (eds), *The View from Building 20: Essays in Linguistics in Honor of Sylvain Bromberger* (pp. 1–52). Cambridge MA: MIT Press.

Chomsky, N. (1994). Bare phrase structure. *MIT Occasional Papers in Linguistics*, 5. Also in G. Webelhuth (ed.), (1995). *Government and Binding Theory and the Minimalist Program*. Oxford: Blackwell.

Chomsky, N. (1995a). Categories and transformations. In *The Minimalist Program* (pp. 219–394). Cambridge MA: MIT Press.

Chomsky, N. (1995b). *The Minimalist Program*. Cambridge MA: MIT Press.

Chomsky, N. (1998a). Minimalist inquiries: the framework. *MIT Working Papers In Linguistics*.

Chomsky, N. (1998b). Some observations on economy in generative grammar. In P. Barbosa, D. Fox, P. Hagstrom, M. McGinnis, and D. Pesestsky (eds), *Is the Best Good Enough? Optimality and Competition in Syntax* (pp. 115–27). Cambridge MA: MIT Press.

Chomsky, N. (1999). Derivation by phase. MS, MIT.

Chomsky, N. and Lasnik, H. (1977). Filters and control. *Linguistic Inquiry*, 8, 425–504.

Chomsky, N. and Lasnik, H. (1993). The theory of principles and parameters. In J. Jacobs, A. von Stechow, W. Sternefeld, and T. Vennemann (eds), *Syntax: An International Handbook of Contemporary Research. Vol. 1* (pp. 506–69). Berlin: de Gruyter.

Christensen, K. (1986). Norwegian *ingen*: a case of post-syntactic lexicalization. In Ö. Dahl and A. Holmberg (eds), *Scandinavian Syntax* (pp. 21–35). Stockholm: Department of Linguistics, University of Stockholm.

Chung, S. (1970). Negative Verbs in Polynesian. Senior honors thesis, Harvard University.

Chung, S. (1973). The syntax of nominalizations in Polynesian. *Oceanic Linguistics*, 12, 641–86.

Chung, S. and McCloskey, J. (1987). Government, barriers and small clauses in Modern Irish. *Linguistic Inquiry*, 18, 173–237.

Chung, S., Ladusaw, W. A., and McCloskey, J. (1995). Sluicing and logical form. *Natural Language Semantics*, 3, 239–82.

Churchward, C. M. (1953). *Tongan Grammar*. London: Oxford University Press.

Cinque, G. (1980). On extraction from NP in Italian. *Journal of Italian Linguistics*, 5, 47–99.

Cinque, G. (1982) Constructions with left peripheral phrases, "connectedness," move-α, and ECP. MS, University of Venice.

Cinque, G. (1990a). Ergative adjectives and the lexicalist hypothesis. *Natural Language and Linguistic Theory*, 8, 1–39.

Cinque, G. (1990b). *Types of A'-Dependencies*. Cambridge MA: MIT Press.

Cinque, G. (1994a). On the evidence for partial N-movement in the Romance DP. In G. Cinque, J. Koster, J.-Y. Pollock, L. Rizzi, and R. Zanuttini (eds), *Paths toward Universal Grammar: Studies in Honor of Richard S. Kayne* (pp. 85–110). Washington DC: Georgetown University Press.

Cinque, G. (1994b). Sull'ordine relativo di alcune classi di avverbi in italiano e in francese. In G. Borgato (ed.), *Teoria del linguaggio e analisi linguistica – XX Incontro di Grammatica Generativa* (pp. 163–77). Padua: Unipress.

Cinque, G. (1995). *Italian Syntax and Universal Grammar*. Cambridge: Cambridge University Press.

Cinque, G. (1997). Adverbs and the universal hierarchy of functional projections. MS, University of Venice.

Cinque, G. (1999). *Adverbs and Functional Heads*. Oxford: Oxford University Press.

Clahsen, H. (1990). Constraints on parameter setting: a grammatical analysis of some acquisition stages in German child language. *Language Acquisition*, 1, 361–91.

Clark, E. (1987). The principle of contrast: a constraint on language acquisition. In B. MacWhinney (ed.), *Mechanisms of Language Acquisition*. Hillsdale NJ: Lawrence Erlbaum.

Clark, R. (1988). On the relationship between the input data and parameter setting. *Proceedings of the NELS*, 19, 48–62.

Clark, R. (1992a). The selection of syntactic knowledge. *Language Acquisition*, 2.2, 83–149.

Clark, R. (1992b). Towards a modular theory of coreference. In C.-T. Huang and R. May (eds), *Logical Structure and Linguistic Structure* (pp. 49–78). Dordrecht: Kluwer.

Clark, R. (1994). Finitude, boundedness and complexity. In B. Lust, G. Hermon, and J. Kornfilt (eds), *Syntactic Theory and First Language Acquisition: Cross-Linguistic Perspectives. Vol. 2: Binding, Dependencies, and Learnability* (pp. 473–89). Hillsdale NJ: Lawrence Erlbaum.

Clark, R. (1996). Complexity and the induction of tree adjoining grammars. *IRCS Report*, 96–14. Philadelphia: Institute for Research in Cognitive Science, University of Pennsylvania.

Clark, R. and Roberts, I. (1993). A computational model of language learnability and language change. *Linguistic Inquiry*, 24.2, 299–345.

Clements, G. N. (1975). The logophoric pronoun in Ewe: its role in discourse. *Journal of West African Languages*, 10, 141–77.

Cole, P. and Hermon, G. (1994). Is there LF *wh*-movement? *Linguistic Inquiry*, 25, 239–62.

Cole, P. and Sung, L.-M. (1994). Head movement and long-distance reflexives. *Linguistic Inquiry*, 25, 355–406.

Cole, P. and Wang, C. (1996). Antecedents and blockers of long-distance reflexives. *Linguistic Inquiry*, 27, 357–90.

Cole, P., Hermon, G., and Sung, L.-M. (1990). Principles and parameters of long-distance reflexives. *Linguistic Inquiry*, 21, 1–22.

Collins, C. (1994a). Economy of derivation and the generalized Proper Binding Condition. *Linguistic Inquiry*, 25, 45–61.

Collins, C. (1994b). Serial verb constructions and the theory of multiple feature checking. MS, Cornell University.

Collins, C. (1995). Towards a theory of optimal derivations. In Papers on Minimalist Syntax, *MIT Working Papers in Linguistics*, 27, 65–103.

Collins, C. (1997). *Local Economy*. Cambridge MA: MIT Press.

Collins, C. (1999). Eliminating labels. MS, Cornell University.

Collins, C. and Thráinsson, H. (1993). Object shift in double object constructions and the theory of Case. *MIT Working Papers in Linguistics*, 19, 131–74.

Collins, C. and Thráinsson H. (1996). VP-internal structure and object shift in Icelandic. *Linguistic Inquiry*, 27.3, 391–444.

Comorovski, I. (1989). Discourse-linking and the *wh*-island constraint. *Proceedings of NELS*, 19.

Comrie, B. (1979). Degrees of ergativity: some Chukchee evidence. In F. Plank (ed.), *Ergativity: Toward a Theory of Grammatical Relations* (pp. 219–40). New York: Academic Press.

Comrie, B. (1989). *Language Universals and Linguistic Typology* (2nd edn). Chicago: University of Chicago Press.

Contreras, H. (1986). Spanish bare NPs and the ECP. In I. Bordelois, H. Contreras, and K. Zagona (eds), *Generative Studies in Spanish Syntax* (pp. 25–49). Dordrecht: Foris.

Cornilescu, A. (1992). Remarks on the determiner system of Rumanian: the demonstratives *al* and *cel*. *Probus*, 4, 189–260.

Corver, N. (1990). The Syntax of Left Branch Extractions. PhD dissertation, University of Tilburg.

Corver, N. (1991). Evidence for DegP. *Proceedings of NELS*, 21.

Corver, N. (1997). The internal structure of the Dutch extended adjectival projection. *Natural Language and Linguistic Theory*, 15.2, 289–368.

Corver, N. and van Riemsdijk, H. (eds), (1994a). *Studies on Scrambling: Movement and Non-Movement Approaches to Free Word-Order Phenomena*. Berlin: de Gruyter.

Corver, N. and van Riemsdijk, H. (1994b). Introduction: approaches to and properties of Scrambling. In N. Corver and H. van Riemsdijk (eds), *Studies on Scrambling: Movement and Non-Movement Approaches to Free Word-Order Phenomena* (pp. 1–15). Berlin: de Gruyter.

Costa, J. (1996). Scrambling in European Portuguese. *Proceedings of SCIL VIII*, MIT Working Papers in Linguistics.

Crain, S. and Thornton, R. (1991). Recharting the course of language acquisition: studies in elicited production. In N. Krasnegor, D. Rumbaugh, M. Studdert-Kennedy, and R. Schiefelbusch (eds), *Biological and Behavioural Aspects of Language Acquisition* (pp. 321–39). Hillsdale NJ: Lawrence Erlbaum.

Crain, S., Nakayama, M., and Murasugi, K. (1987). Structure dependence in grammar formation. *Language*, 63, 522–43.

Crisma, P. (1990). Functional Categories inside the Noun Phrase: A Study of the Distribution of Nominal Modifiers. Thesis, University of Venice.

Crisma, P. (1993). On adjective placement in Romance and Germanic event nominals. *Rivista di Grammatica Generativa*, 18, 61–100.

Crisma, P. (1996). On the configurational nature of adjectival modification. In K. Zagona (ed.), *Grammatical Theory and Romance Languages – Current Issues in Linguistic Theory* 133 (pp. 59–71). Amsterdam: John Benjamins.

Crisma, P. (1997). L'articolo nella prosa inglese antica e la teoria degli articoli nulli [The Article in Old English Prose and the Theory of Null Articles]. PhD dissertation, University of Padua.

Curme, G. O. (1931). *Syntax*. Boston/New York: D.C. Heath.

Cutler, A., Mehler, J., Norris, D., and Segui, J. (1992). The monolingual nature of speech segmentation by bilinguals. *Cognitive Psychology*, 24, 381–410.

Czepluch, H. (1990). Word order variation in a configurational language: against a uniform Scrambling account in German. In W. Abraham, W. Kosmeijer, and E. Reuland (eds), *Issues in Germanic Syntax* (pp. 163–95). Berlin: de Gruyter.

Dahl, Ö. (1979). Typology of sentence negation. *Linguistics*, 17.1/2, 79–106.

Dalrymple, M. (1993). The syntax of anaphoric binding. *CSLI Lecture Notes*, 36.

Dalrymple, M. and Kaplan, R. M. (1997). A set-based approach to feature resolution. In M. Butt and T. H. King (eds), *Proceedings of the LFG97 Conference*, University of California, San Diego. On-line, CSLI Publications: http://www-csli.stanford.edu/publications/

Dalrymple, M., Kaplan, R. M., Maxwell, J. M., and Zaenen, A. (eds), (1995). *Formal Issues in Lexical-Functional Grammar*. Stanford: CSLI Publications.

Dalrymple, M., Mchombo, S. A., and Peters, S. (1994). Semantic similarities and syntactic contrasts between Chichewa and English reciprocals. *Linguistic Inquiry*, 25, 145–63.

Dalrymple, M., Sheiber, S. M., and Pereira, F. C. N. (1991). Ellipsis and higher-order unification. *Linguistics and Philosophy*, 14, 399–452.

Dayal, V. (1994). Scope marking as indirect *wh*-dependency. *Natural Language Semantics*, 2, 137–70.

Dayal, V. (1996). *Locality in Wh-Quantification*. Dordrecht: Kluwer.

Dayal, V. (in preparation). *Wh*-in-situ inside complex noun phrases: a semantics without reconstruction. MS, Rutgers University.

Dayley, J. (1985). *A Tzutujil Grammar*. Berkeley and Los Angeles: University of California Press.

de Hoop, H. (1992). Case Configuration and Noun Phrase Interpretation. PhD dissertation, University of Groningen.

De Vincenzi, M. (1991). *Syntactic Parsing Strategies in Italian*. Dordrecht: Kluwer.

Déchaine, R.-M. and Manfredi, V. (1994). Binding domains in Haitian. *Natural Language and Linguistic Theory*, 12, 203–57.

Déchaine, R.-M. and Manfredi, V. (1998). SVO ergativity and abstract ergativity. *Recherches Linguistiques de Vincennes*, 27, 71–94.

Dekkers, J., van der Leeuw, F., and van de Weijer, J. (eds), (in press). *Optimality Theory: Phonology, Syntax, and Acquisition*. Oxford: Oxford University Press.

Del Gobbo, F. (1999). Chinese nominal phrases: current studies. MS, UCIrvine.

DeLancey, S. (1981). An interpretation of split ergativity and related patterns. *Language*, 57, 626–57.

Delfitto, D. (1993). A propos du statut lexical de l'article partitif en français: quelques hypothèses sur l'interaction entre mophologie et forme logique. In A. Hulk et al. (eds), *Du lexique à la morphologie: du côté de chez Zwaan*. Amsterdam: Rodopi.

Delfitto, D. (to appear). Bare plurals. In H. van Rjemsdijk and M. Everaert (eds), *Encyclopedia of Syntactic Case Studies*. Wassenaar: NIAS.

Delfitto, D. and Schroten, J. (1992). Bare plurals and the number affix in DP. *Probus*, 3, 155–85.

Delsing, L.-O. (1988). The Scandinavian noun phrase. *Working Papers in Scandinavian Syntax*, 42, 57–79.

Delsing, L.-O. (1993). The Internal Structure of Noun Phrases in the Scandinavian Languages. PhD dissertation, University of Lund.

Demuth, K. and Gruber, J. S. (1995). Constraining XP sequences. In V. Manfredi and K. Reynolds (eds), *Niger-Congo Syntax and Semantics* 6 (pp. 1–30). Boston MA: Boston University African Studies Center.

Demuth, K. and Harford, C. (in press). Verb raising and subject inversion in comparative Bantu. *Journal of African Languages and Linguistics*.

den Besten, H. (1975). A note on designating lexical delenda. MS, University of Amsterdam.

den Besten, H. (1983). On the interaction of root transformations and lexical deletive rules. In W. Abraham (ed.), *On the Formal Syntax of the Westgermania* (pp. 47–132). Amsterdam: John Benjamins.

den Besten, H. and Edmonson, J. (1983). The verbal complex in Continental West Germanic. In W. Abraham (ed.), *On the Formal Syntax of the Westgermania* (pp. 155–216). Amsterdam: John Benjamins.

den Besten, H. and Webelhuth, G. (1989). Stranding. In G. Grewendorf and W. Sternefeld (eds), *Scrambling and Barriers* (pp. 77–92). Amsterdam/Philadelphia: John Benjamins.

den Dikken, M. (1995). *Particles: On the Syntax of Verb–Particle, Triadic and Causative Constructions*. Oxford: Oxford University Press.

den Dikken, M. (1996). The minimal links of verb (projection) raising. In W. Abraham, S. D. Epstein, H. Thráinsson, and C. J.-W. Zwart (eds), *Minimal Ideas. Syntactic Studies in the Minimalist Framework* (pp. 67–96). Amsterdam: John Benjamins.

Déprez, V. (1989). On the Typology of Syntactic Positions and the Nature of Chains. PhD dissertation, MIT.

Déprez, V. (1994). Parameters of object movement. In N. Corver and H. van Riemsdijk (eds), *Studies on Scrambling. Movement and Non-Movement Approaches to Free Word-Order Phenomena* (pp. 101–52). Berlin: de Gruyter.

Diesing, M. (1992). *Indefinites*. Cambridge MA: MIT Press.

Diesing, M. (1996). Semantic variables and object shift. In H. Thráinsson, S. D. Epstein, and S. Peter (eds), *Studies in Comparative Germanic Syntax* II (pp. 66–84). Dordrecht: Kluwer.

Diesing, M. (1997). Yiddish VP order and the typology of object movement in Germanic. *Natural Language and Linguistic Theory*, 15, 369–427.

Diesing, M. and Jelinek, E. (1993). The syntax and semantics of object shift. *Working Papers in Scandinavian Syntax*, 51.

Diesing, M. and Jelinek, E. (1995). Distributing arguments. *Natural Language Semantics*, 3, 123–76.

Dixon, R. M. W. (1972). *The Dyirbal Language of North Queensland*. Cambridge: Cambridge University Press.

Dixon, R. M. W. (1979). Ergativity. *Language*, 55, 59–138.

Dixon, R. M. W. (1982a). Semantic neutralisation for phonological reasons. In *Where Have All the Adjectives Gone? And Other Essays in Semantics and Syntax* (pp. 235–8). Berlin: Mouton.

Dixon, R. M. W. (1982b). *Where Have All the Adjectives Gone? And Other Essays in Semantics and Syntax*. Berlin: Mouton.

Dixon, R. M. W. (1994). *Ergativity*. Cambridge: Cambridge University Press.

Dobrovie-Sorin, C. (1987). A propos de la structure du groupe nominal en Roumain. *Rivista di Grammatica Generativa*, 12, 123–52.

Dobrovie-Sorin, C. (to appear). Spec, DP and (in)definiteness spread: from Rumanian genitives to construct state nominals. In V. Motapanyane (ed.), *Comparative Studies in Romance Syntax*. The Hague: Holland Academic Graphics.

Dobrovie-Sorin, C. and Laca, B. (1996). Generic bare NPs. MS, University of Paris VII and University of Strasbourg.

Dokulil, M. (1994). On morphological oppositions. In P. A. Luelsdorff, J. Panevová, and P. Sgall (eds), *Praguiana. 1945–1990* (pp. 113–30). Amsterdam: John Benjamins. Original work (1958).

Donati, C. (1996). Elementi di sintassi della comparazione. PhD dissertation, University of Florence.

Dowty, D. (1979). *Word Meaning and Montague Grammar: The Semantics of Verbs and Times in Generative Semantics and in Montague's PTQ*. Dordrecht/Boston: Reidel.

Dowty, D. (1982). Grammatical relations and Montague Grammar. In P. P. Jacobson and G. K. Dordrecht (eds), *The Nature of Syntactic Representation* (pp. 79–130). Dordrecht: Reidel.

Dowty, D. (1991). Thematic protoroles and argument selection. *Language*, 67, 547–619.

Dryer, M. (1989). Universals of negative position. In E. Moravscsik, J. Wirth, and M. Hammond (eds), *Studies in Syntactic Typology* (pp. 93–124). Amsterdam: John Benjamins.

Dryer, M. (1992). The Greenbergian word order correlations. *Language*, 68, 81–138.

Duffield, N. (1991). The construct state in Irish and Hebrew: Part 1. MS, Heinrich Heine University, Düsseldorf.

Duffield, N. (1996). On structural invariance and lexical diversity in VSO languages: arguments from Irish noun phrases. In R. Borsley and I. Roberts (eds), *The Syntax of the Celtic Languages* (pp. 314–40). Cambridge: Cambridge University Press.

É. Kiss, K. (1987). *Configurationality in Hungarian*. Dordrecht: Reidel.

É. Kiss, K. (1991). Logical structure in linguistic structure. In H.-May (ed.), *Logical Structure and Linguistic Structure* (pp. 387–426). Dordrecht: Kluwer.

É. Kiss, K. (1994). Scrambling as the base generation of random complement order. In N. Corver and H. van Riemsdijk (eds), *Studies on Scrambling: Movement and Non-Movement Approaches to Free Word Order Phenomena* (pp. 221–56). Berlin: de Gruyter.

Ebert, K. (1970). Referenz. Sprechsituation und die bestimmten Artikel in einem Nordfriesischen Dialekt. PhD dissertation, University of Kiel.

Egli, U. and von Heusinger, K. (1995). The epsilon operator and e-type pronouns. In U. Egli, P. E. Pause, C. Schwarze, A. von Stechow, and G. Wienold (eds), *Lexical Knowledge in the Organization of Language* (pp. 121–41). Amsterdam: John Benjamins.

Eide, K. and Afarli T. (1997). A predication operator: evidence and effects. MS, Department of Linguistics, NTNU (Trondheim).

Ellegård, A. (1953). *The Auxiliary Do: The Establishment and Regulation of its Use in English*. Stockholm: Almqvist and Wiksell.

Elman, J., Bates, E. A., Johnson, M. H., Karmiloff-Smith, A., Parisi, D., and Plunkett, K. (1995). *Rethinking Innateness: A Connectionist Perspective on Development*. Cambridge MA: MIT Press.

Emonds, J. (1976). *A Transformational Approach to English Syntax: Root, Structure-Preserving, and Local Transformations*. New York: Academic Press.

Emonds, J. (1978). The verbal complex V'–V in French. *Linguistic Inquiry*, 9, 151–75.

Emonds, J. (1980). Word order in generative grammar. *Journal of Linguistic Research*, 1, 33–54.

Emonds, J. (1994). Two principles of economy. In J. K. Cinque, J.-Y. Pollock, L. Rizzi, and R. Zanuttini (eds), *Paths Toward Universal Grammar: Studies in Honor of Richard S. Kayner* (pp. 155–72). Washington DC: Georgetown University Press.

Engdahl, E. (1986). *Constituent Questions*. Dordrecht: Reidel.

Engdahl, E. (1983). Parasitic gaps. *Linguistics and Philosophy*, 6, 5–34.

Epstein, S. D. (1992). Derivational constraints on A'-chain formation. *Linguistic Inquiry*, 23, 235–59.

Epstein, S. D. (in press). Un-principled syntax and the derivation of syntactic relations. In S. D. Epstein and N. Hornstein (eds), *Working Minimalism*. Cambridge MA: MIT Press.

Epstein, S. D., Thráinsson, H., and Zwart, C. J.-W. (1996). Introduction. In W. Abraham, S. D. Epstein, H. Thráinsson, and C. J.-W. Zwart (eds), *Minimal Ideas. Syntactic Studies in the Minimalist Framework* (pp. 1–66). Amsterdam: John Benjamins.

Espinal, M. T. (1992). Expletive negation and logical absorption. *Linguistic Review*, 9, 333–58.

Evans, G. (1980). Pronouns. *Linguistic Inquiry*, 11.2, 337–62.

Everaert, M. (1986). *The Syntax of Reflexivization*. Dordrecht: Foris.

Everaert, M. (1990). Nominative anaphors in Icelandic: morphology or syntax? In W. Abraham, W. Kosmeijer, and E. J. Reuland (eds), *Issues in Germanic Syntax* (pp. 277–305). Berlin: de Gruyter.

Everaert, M. (1991). Contextual determination of the anaphor/pronominal distinction. In J. Koster and E. J. Reuland (eds), *Long-distance Anaphora* (pp. 49–76). Cambridge: Cambridge University Press.

Everaert, M. and Anagnostopoulou, E. (1997). Thematic hierarchies and binding theory: evidences from Greek. In F. Corblin, D. Godard, and J.-M. Marandin (eds), *Empirical Issues in Formal Syntax and Semantics* (pp. 433–60). Bern: Peter Lang.

Evers, A. (1975). *The Transformational Cycle in Dutch and German*. Bloomington IN: Indiana University Linguistics Club.

Eyer, J. A. and Leonard, L. (1995). Functional categories and specific language impairment: a case study. *Linguistic Acquisition*, 4, 177–203.

Faarlund, J.-T. (1977). Transformational syntax in dialectology: Scandinavian word order varieties. In T. Fretheim and L. Hellan (eds), *Papers from the Trondheim Syntax Symposium*. Department of Linguistics, University of Trondheim.

Faarlund, J.-T. (1990). *Syntactic Change: Toward a Theory of Historical Syntax*. Berlin: de Gruyter.

Falk, C. (1990). On double object constructions. *Working Papers in Scandinavian Syntax*, 46, 53–100.

Faltz, L. M. (1977). Reflexivization: A Study in Universal Syntax. PhD dissertation, University of California at Berkeley. Distributed by University Microfilm International, Ann Arbor ML and London.

Fanselow, G. (1990). Scrambling as NP-movement. In G. Grewendorf and W. Sternefeld (eds), *Scrambling and Barriers* (pp. 113–40). Amsterdam: John Benjamins.

Farkas, D. (1981). Quantifier scope and syntactic islands. In R. Hendrik, C. S. Masek, and M. F. Miller (eds), *Papers from CLS*, 17 (pp. 59–66).

Farkas, D. and Giannakidou, A. (1996). How clause-bounded is the scope of universals? In T. Galloway and J. Spence (eds), *Proceedings from Semantics and Linguistic Theory*, VI (pp. 35–53). Ithaca NY: Cornell University.

Farmer, A. (1984). *Modularity in Syntax*. Cambridge MA: MIT Press.

Farmer, A., Hale, K., and Tsujimura, N. (1986). A note on weak crossover in Japanese. *Natural Language and Linguistic Theory*, 4, 33–42.

Fassi Fehri, A. (1980). Some complement phenomena in Arabic, lexical grammar, the complementizer phrase hypothesis and the non-accessibility condition. MS, University of Rabat.

Fassi Fehri, A. (1989). Generalized IP structure, case and VS word order. *MIT Working Papers in Linguistics*, 10, 75–113.

Fassi Fehri, A. (1993). *Issues in the Structure of Arabic Clauses and Words*. Dordrecht: Kluwer.

Fassi Fehri, A. (1997). Arabic antisymmetrical adjectives. *Linguistic Research*, 2.2, 1–51.

Ferguson, K. Scott. (1996). Shortest move and object case checking. In W. Abraham, S. D. Epstein, H. Thráinsson, and C. J.-W. Zwart (eds), *Minimal Ideas. Syntactic Studies in the Minimalist Framework* (pp. 97–111). Amsterdam: John Benjamins.

Fiengo, R. (1974). Semantic Conditions on Surface Structure. PhD dissertation, MIT.

Fiengo, R. (1977). On trace theory. *Linguistic Inquiry*, 8, 35–61.

Fiengo, R. and Higginbotham, J. (1980). Opacity in NP. *Linguistic Analysis*, 7, 395–421.

Fiengo, R. and May, R. (1990). Anaphora and ellipsis. MS, CUNY and University of California at Irvine.

Fiengo, R. and May, R. (1994). *Indices and Identity*. Cambridge MA: MIT Press.

Fillmore, C. (1965). *Indirect Object Constructions in English and the Ordering of Transformations*. The Hague: Mouton.

Fillmore, C. (1968). The case for Case. In E. Bach and R. T. Harms (eds), *Universals in Linguistic Theory* (pp. 1–88). London: Holt, Rinehart, and Winston.

Finer, D. L. (1994). On the nature of two A'-positions in Selayarese. In N. Corver and H. van Riemsdijk (eds), *Studies on Scrambling. Movement and Non-Movement Approaches to Free Word-Order Phenomena* (pp. 153–84). Berlin: de Gruyter.

Fodor, J. A., Bever, T. G., and Garrett, M. F. (1974). *The Psychology of Language*. New York: McGraw-Hill.

Fodor, J. D. (1989). Principle-based learning. *CUNYForum*, 14, 59–67.

Fodor, J. D. (1994). How to obey the subset principle: binding and locality. In B. Lust, G. Hermon, and J. Kornfilt (eds), *Syntactic Theory and First Language Acquisition: Cross-Linguistic Perspectives. Vol. 2: Binding, Dependencies and Learnability* (pp. 429–51). Hillsdale NJ: Lawrence Erlbaum.

Fodor, J. D. (1995). Fewer but better triggers. *CUNYForum*, 19, 39–64.

Fodor, J. D. (1998a). Unambiguous triggers. *Linguistic Inquiry*, 29.1, 1–36.

Fodor, J. D. (1998b). Learning to parse? *Journal of Psycholinguistic Research*, 27.2, 285–318.

Fodor, J. D. (1998c). Parsing to learn. *Journal of Psycholinguistic Research*, 27.3, 339–74.

Fodor, J. D. (1998d). What is a parameter? Address to Linguistic Society of America, January, MS, Graduate Center, City University of New York.

Fodor, J. D. (in press). Learnability theory: decoding trigger sentences. In R. C. Schwartz (ed.), *Linguistics, Cognitive Science, and Childhood Language Disorders*. Hillsdale NJ: Lawrence Erlbaum.

Fodor, J. D. and Sag, I. (1982). Referential and quantificational indefinites. *Linguistics and Philosophy*, 3, 419–72.

Foley, W. (1991). *The Yimas Language of New Guinea*. Stanford: Stanford University Press.

Foley, W. and Van Valin, R. D. (1984). *Functional Syntax and Universal Grammar*. Cambridge: Cambridge University Press.

Fontaine, C. (1985). Application de methodes quantitatives en diachronie: l'inversion du sujet en français. Master's thesis, University of Quebec, Montreal.

Fontana, J. M. (1993). Phrase Structure and the Syntax of Clitics in the History of Spanish. PhD thesis, University of Pennsylvania.

Fox, D. (1993). Chain and binding – a modification of Reinhart and Reuland's "reflexivity." MS, MIT.

Fox, D. (1995). Economy and scope. *Natural Language Semantics*, 3, 283–341.

Fox, D. (forthcoming). *Economy and Semantic Interpretation*. Cambridge MA: MIT Press.

Frampton, J. (1991). Relativized Minimality: a review. *Linguistic Review*, 8, 1–46.

Frampton, J. (1997). Expletive insertion. In C. Wilder, H.-M. Gartner, and M. Bierwisch (eds), *The Role of Economy Principles in Linguistic Theory* (pp. 36–57). Berlin: Academia Verlag.

Frank, A., King, T. H., Kuhn, J., and Maxwell, J. M. (1998). Optimality Theory style constraint ranking in large scale LFG grammars. In M. Butt and T. H. King (eds), *Proceedings of the LFG98 Conference*, University of Queensland, Brisbane. On-line, CSLI Publications: http://www-csli.stanford.edu/publications/

Fraser, B. (1976). *Verb–Particle Combinations in English*. New York: Academic Press.

Freidin, R. (1978). Cyclicity and the theory of grammar. *Linguistic Inquiry*, 9, 519–49.

Freidin, R. (1986). Fundamental issues in the theory of binding. In B. Lust (ed.), *Studies in the Acquisition of Anaphora. Vol. 1* (pp. 151–90). Dordrecht: Reidel.

Friedeman, M. A. (1992). The underlying position of external arguments in French. *GenGenP*, 1–2, 123–44.

Friedeman, M. A. and Siloni, T. (1997). Agr_{obj} is not $Agr_{participle}$. *Linguistic Review*, 14, 69–96.

Fu, J., Roeper, T., and Borer, H. (1996). The VP within nominalizations. MS, University of Massachusetts, Amherst.

Fukui, N. (1986). A Theory of Category Projection and its Applications. PhD dissertation, MIT. Revised version (1995) as *Theory of Projection in Syntax*. Stanford: CSLI Publications and Cambridge University Press.

Fukui, N. (1988). Deriving the differences between English and Japanese: a case study in parametric syntax. *English Linguistics*, 5, 249–70.

Fukui, N. (1991). Strong and weak barriers: remarks on the proper characterization of barriers. In H. Nakajima (ed.), *Current English Linguistics in Japan* (pp. 78–93). Berlin: de Gruyter.

Fukui, N. (1993). Parameters and optionality. *Linguistic Inquiry*, 24, 399–420.

Fukui, N. (1995). The principles-and-parameters approach: a comparative syntax of English and Japanese. In M. Shibatani and T. Bynon (eds), *Approaches to Language Typology* (pp. 327–72). Oxford: Oxford University Press.

Fukui, N. (1997). Attract and the A-over-A principle. In L. C.-S. Liu and K. Takeda (eds), *UCI Working Papers in Linguistics*, 3, 51–67.

Fukui, N. and Saito, M. (1992). Spec–head agreement, X′-compatibility, and optionality. Paper presented at MIT Colloquium, Cambridge MA.

Fukui, N. and Speas, M. (1986). Specifiers and projection. *MIT Working Papers in Linguistics*, 8, 128–72.

Fukui, N. and Takano, Y. (1998). Symmetry in syntax: merge and demerge. *Journal of East Asian Linguistics*, 7, 27–86.

Gambarotto, M. (1995). La questione dei determinanti in russo. Tesi di laurea, University of Venice.

Gazdar, G., Pullum, G., and Sag, I. (1982). Auxiliaries and related phenomena in a restrictive theory of grammar. *Language*, 58, 591–638.

Gazdar, G., Klein, E., Pullum, G. K., and Sag, I. (1985). *Generalized Phrase Structure Grammar*. Cambridge MA: Harvard University Press.

Geach, P. (1962). *Reference and Generality*. Ithaca NY: Cornell University Press.

Genabith, J. van and Crouch, R. (1996). F-structures, QLFs and UDRSs. In M. Butt and T. H. King (eds), *LFG-Workshop. Proceedings of the First LFG Conference*. Rank Xerox Research Centre, Grenoble, August 26–8. On-line, CSLI Publications: http://www-csli.stanford.edu/publications/

Gibson, E. and Wexler, K. (1994). Triggers. *Linguistic Inquiry*, 25, 407–54.

Gil, D. (1987). Definiteness, NP configurationality and the count–mass distinction. In E. Reuland and A. ter Meulen (eds), *The Representation of (In)definiteness* (pp. 254–69). Cambridge MA: MIT Press.

Giorgi, A. and Longobardi, G. (1991). *The Syntax of Noun Phrases: Configuration, Parameters and Empty Categories*. Cambridge: Cambridge University Press.

Giorgi, A. and Pianesi, F. (1997). *Tense and Aspect: From Semantics to Morphosyntax*. New York: Oxford University Press.

Giusti, G. (1991). The categorial status of quantified nominals. *Linguistische Berichte*, 136, 438–52.

Giusti, G. (1993a). *La sintassi dei determinanti* [*The Syntax of Determiners*]. Padua: Unipress.

Giusti, G. (1993b). Enclitic articles and double definiteness: a comparative analysis of nominal structure in Romance and Germanic. *University of Venice Working Papers in Linguistics*, 3, 83–94. Reprinted in *Linguistic Review*, 11, 231–55.

Giusti, G. (1997). The categorial status of determiners. In L. Haegeman (ed.), *The New Comparative Syntax* (pp. 95–123). London: Longman.

Givón, T. (1997). Grammatical relations: an introduction. In T. Givón (ed.), *Grammatical Relations: A Functionalist Perspective* (pp. 1–84). Amsterdam: John Benjamins.

Gold, E. M. (1967). Language identification in the limit. *Information and Control*, 10, 447–74.

Goldberg, A. (1996). Words by default: optimizing constraints and the Persian complex predicate. *BLS*, 22, 132–46.

Gosu, A. (1988). On the distribution of genitive phrases in Rumanian. *Linguistics*, 26, 931–49.

Greenberg, J. (1966). Some universals of grammar with particular reference to the order of meaningful elements. In J. H. Greenberg (ed.), *Universals of Language* (pp. 73–113). Cambridge MA: MIT Press.

Greenberg, J. (1996). *Language Universals: With Special Reference to Feature Hierarchies*. The Hague: Mouton.

Grewendorf, G. (1988). *Aspekte der deutschen Syntax: Eine Rektions-Bindungs-Analyse.* Tübingen: Gunter Narr Verlag.

Grewendorf, G. and Sabel, J. (1994). Long Scrambling and incorporation. *Linguistic Inquiry*, 25, 263–308.

Grewendorf, G. and Sternefeld, W. (1990a). Scrambling theories. In G. Grewendorf and W. Sternefeld (eds), *Scrambling and Barriers* (pp. 3–37). Amsterdam: John Benjamins.

Grewendorf, G. and Sternefeld, W. (eds), (1990b). *Scrambling and Barriers.* Amsterdam: John Benjamins.

Grimshaw, J. (1990). *Argument Structure.* Cambridge MA: MIT Press.

Grimshaw, J. (1991). Extended projection. MS, Brandeis University.

Grimshaw, J. (1997). Projection, heads, and optimality. *Linguistic Inquiry*, 28, 373–422.

Grimshaw, J. and Samek-Lodovici, V. (1998). Optimal subjects and subject universals. In P. Barbosa, D. Fox, P. Hagstrom, M. McGinnis, and D. Pesetsky (eds), *Is the Best Good Enough? Optimality and Competition in Syntax* (pp. 193–219). Cambridge MA: MIT Press and MIT Working Papers in Linguistics.

Grinder, J. and Postal, P. (1971). Missing antecedents. *Linguistic Inquiry*, 2, 269–312.

Grodzinsky, Y. and Reinhart, T. (1993). The innateness of binding and coreference. *Linguistic Inquiry*, 24, 69–101.

Grosu, A. (1988). On the distribution of genitive phrases in Rumanian. *Linguistics*, 26, 931–49.

Gruber, J. S. (1965). Studies in Lexical Relations. PhD dissertation, MIT. Published as *MIT Working Papers in Linguistics*, GRUB01. Also in *Lexical Structures in Syntax and Semantics* 1. Amsterdam: North Holland.

Gruber, J. S. (1973). Hóã kinship terms. *Linguistic Inquiry*, 4, 427–49.

Gruber, J. S. (1994). Principles of a configurational theta-theory. In Y.-S. Kim, B.-C. Lee, K.-J. Lee, H.-K. Yang, and J.-Y. Yoon (eds), *A Festschrift for Dong-Whee Yang: Explorations in Generative Grammar* (pp. 69–111). Seoul: Hankuk.

Gruber, J. S. (1996). Configurational accounts of thematic linking regularities: the possessional–spatial asymmetry. In A.-M. Di Sciullo (ed.), *Configurations.* Ithaca NY: Cornell Cascadilla Press.

Gruber, J. S. (1997). Modularity in a configurational theta-theory. In A.-M. Di Sciullo (ed.), *Projections and Interfaces: Essays on Modularity* (pp. 155–200). Oxford: Oxford University Press.

Gruber, J. S. and Collins, C. (1997). Argument projection, thematic configurationality and Case theory. In A.-M. Di Sciullo (ed.), *Projections and Interfaces: Essays on Modularity* (pp. 130–54). Oxford: Oxford University Press.

Guasti, M. T. (1992). Verb syntax in Italian child grammar. *GenGenP*, 1–2, 145–62.

Guilfoyle, E. (1988). Parameters and functional projection. *Proceedings of NELS*, 18, 193–207.

Guilfoyle, E. (1993). Functional Categories and Phrase Structure Parameters. PhD dissertation, McGill University, Montreal.

Gumperz, J. and Wilson, R. (1971). Convergence and creolization. a case from the Indo-Aryan/Dravidian border in India. In D. Hymes (ed.), *Pidginization and Creolization of Languages* (pp. 151–67). Cambridge: Cambridge University Press.

Gupta, A. (1980). *The Logic of Common Nouns.* New Haven: Yale University Press.

Haegeman, L. (1992). *Theory and Description in Generative Syntax: A Case Study in West Flemish.* Cambridge: Cambridge University Press.

Haegeman, L. (1993a). Object clitics in West Flemish. *GenGenP*, 1, 1–30.

Haegeman, L. (1993b). Some speculations on argument shift, clitics and crossing in West Flemish. In W. Abraham and J. Bayer (eds), *Dialektsyntax* (pp. 131–60). Opladen: Westdeutscher Verlag.

Haegeman, L. (1994). Root infinitives, tense and truncated structure. *GenGenP*, 1, 12–41.

Haegeman, L. (1997). Elements of grammar. In L. Haegeman (ed.), *Elements of Grammar: Handbook in Generative Syntax* (pp. 1–71). Dordrecht: Kluwer.

Haegeman, L. (1998). Inversion, non-adjacent inversion, and adjuncts in CP. MS, University of Geneva.

Hagège, C. (1974). Les pronoms logophoriques. *Bulletin de la Société de Linguistique de Paris*, 69, 287–310.

Haider, H. (1988). Tracking systems. In L. Maracz and P. Muysken (eds), *Configurationality* (pp. 185–206). Dordrecht: Foris.

Haider, H. (1997). Typological implications of a directionality constraint on projections. In A. Alexiadou and T. A. Hall (eds), *Studies on Universal Grammar and Typological Variation* (pp. 17–33). Amsterdam: John Benjamins.

Haider, H. and Prinzhorn, M. (eds) (1986). *Verb Second Phenomena in Germanic Languages*. Dordrecht: Foris.

Haider, H., Olsen, S., and Vikner, S. (1995). Introduction. In H. Haider, S. Olsen, and S. Vikner (eds), *Studies in Comparative Germanic Syntax* (pp. 1–45). Dordrecht: Kluwer.

Haïk, I. (1987). Bound VPs that need to be. *Linguistics and Philosophy*, 10, 503–30.

Hale, K. (1978). The structure of English sentences. Class notes. MIT.

Hale, K. (1983). Warlpiri and the grammar of nonconfigurational languages. *Natural Language and Linguistic Theory*, 1, 5–49.

Hale, K. (1992). Basic word order in two "free word order" languages. In D. Payne (ed.), *Pragmatics of Word Order Flexibility* (pp. 63–82). Amsterdam: John Benjamins.

Hale, K. (1994). Core structures and adjunction in Warlpiri syntax. In N. Corver and H. van Riemsdijk (eds), *Studies on Scrambling: Movement and Non-Movement Approaches to Free Word-Order Phenomena* (pp. 185–220). Berlin: de Gruyter.

Hale, K. and Keyser, J. (1991). On the syntax of argument structure. *Lexical Project Working Papers*, 34.

Hale, K. and Keyser, J. (1993). On argument structure and lexical expression of syntactic relations. In K. Hale and J. Keyser (eds), *The View from Building 20: Essays in Linguistics in Honor of Sylvain Bromberge* (pp. 53–109). Cambridge MA: MIT Press.

Hale, K. and Keyser, J. (1997). On the double object construction. MS, Department of Linguistics and Philosophy, MIT.

Hale, M. and Reiss, C. (1997). Formal and empirical arguments concerning phonological acquisition. On-line, Rutgers University: Rutgers Optimality Archive, ROA–170–0197, http://ruccs.rutgers.edu/roa.html

Halle, M. and Marantz, A. (1993). Distributed morphology and the pieces of inflection. In K. Hale and S. J. Keyser (eds), *The View from Building 20: Essays in Linguistics in Honor of Sylvain Bromberger* (pp. 111–76). Cambridge MA: MIT Press.

Hamblin, C. L. (1973). Questions in Montague English. *Foundations of Language*, 10, 41–53.

Hankamer, J. and Sag, I. (1976). Deep and surface anaphora. *Linguistic Inquiry*, 7, 391–428.

Harada, S.-I. (1976). Honorifics. In M. Shibatani (ed.), *Syntax and Semantics. Vol. 5: Japanese Generative Grammar* (pp. 499–561). New York: Academic Press.

Harbert, W. (1983). On the definition of binding domains. In *Proceedings of the West Coast Conference of Formal Linguistics*, 2, 102–13.

Hardt, D. (1992). VP ellipsis and semantic identity. In S. Berman and A. Hestvik (eds), *Proceedings of the Stuttgart Ellipsis Workshop*. Stuttgart.

Hardt, D. (1993). Verb Phrase Ellipsis: Form, Meaning and Processing. PhD dissertation, University of Pennsylvania.

Hardt, D. (1997). Dynamic interpretation of verb phrase ellipsis. *Linguistics and Philosophy*, 22, 185–219.

Harley, H. (1995). Subjects, Events and Licensing. PhD dissertation, MIT.

Harris, J. (1991). The exponence of gender in Spanish. *Linguistic Inquiry*, 22, 27–62.

Harris, Z. (1946). From morpheme to utterance. *Language*, 22, 161–83.

Harris, Z. (1951). *Methods in Structural Linguistics*. Chicago: University of Chicago Press.

Hart, B. and Risley, T. R. (1995). *Meaningful Differences in the Everyday Experience of Young Children*. Baltimore MD: Paul H. Brookes.

Hasegawa, N. (1991). Affirmative polarity items and negation in Japanese. In C. Georgopoulos and R. Ishihara (eds), *Interdisciplinary Approaches to Language: Essays in Honor of S.-Y. Kuroda* (pp. 271–84). Dordrecht: Kluwer.

Haspelmath, M. (1997). *Indefinite Pronouns*. Oxford: Oxford University Press.

Hawkins, J. A. (1979). Implicational universals as predictors of word order change. *Language*, 55, 618–48.

Hawkins, J. A. (1983). *Word Order Universals*. New York: Academic Press.

Hayes, B. (in press). Gradient well-formedness in Optimality Theory. In J. Dekkers, F. van der Leeuw, and J. van de Weijer (eds), *Optimality Theory: Phonology, Syntax, and Acquisition*. Oxford: Oxford University Press.

Hazout, I. (1991). Verbal Nouns: Theta-Theoretic Studies in Hebrew and Arabic. PhD dissertation, University of Massachusetts, Amherst.

Heath, J. (1986). Syntactic and lexical aspects of nonconfigurationality in Nunggubuyu (Australia). *Natural Language and Linguistic Theory*, 4, 375–408.

Heim, I. (1982). The Semantics of Definite and Indefinite Noun Phrases. PhD dissertation, University of Massachusetts.

Heim, I. (1997). Predicates or formulas? Evidence from ellipsis. In A. Lawson and E. Cho (eds), *Proceedings of SALT VII*. Cornell University: CLC Publications.

Heim, I. (1998). Anaphora and semantic interpretation: a reinterpretation of Reinhart's approach. In U. Sauerland and O. Percus (eds), The Interpretative Tract, *MIT Working Papers in Linguistics*, 25.

Heim, I., Lasnik, H., and May, R. (1991). Reciprocity and plurality. *Linguistic Inquiry*, 22, 63–101.

Helke, M. (1971). The Grammar of English Reflexives. PhD dissertation, MIT.

Hellan, L. (1988). *Anaphora in Norwegian and the Theory of Grammar*. Dordrecht: Foris.

Hellan, L. and Platzack, C. (1995). Pronouns in Scandinavian: an overview. *Working Papers in Scandinavian Syntax*, 56, 47–69.

Hendrick, R. (1988). *Anaphora in Celtic and Universal Grammar*. Dordrecht: Kluwer.

Hendriks, H. (1993). Studied Flexibility, Categories and Types in Syntax and Semantics. PhD dissertation, University of Amsterdam.

Hestvik, A. (1990). LF-movement of Pronouns and the Computation of Binding Domains. PhD dissertation, Brandeis University.

Hestvik, A. (1991). Subjectless binding domains. *Natural Language and Linguistic Theory*, 9.3, 455–96.

Hestvik, A. (1992a). LF-movement of pronouns and antisubject orientation. *Linguistic Inquiry*, 23.4, 557–94.

Hestvik, A. (1992b). Subordination and strict identity of interpretation of reflexives. In S. Berman and A. Hestvik (eds), *Proceedings of the Stuttgart Ellipsis Workshop*. Stuttgart.

Hewitt, M. S. and Crowhurst, M. J. (to appear). Conjunctive constraints and templates in Optimality Theory. *NELS*, 26.

Heycock, C. (1995). Asymmetries in reconstruction. *Linguistic Inquiry*, 26.4, 547–70.

Higginbotham, J. (1980). Pronouns and bound variables. *Linguistic Inquiry*, 11, 679–708.

Higginbotham, J. (1983). Logical form, binding and nominals. *Linguistic Inquiry*, 14, 395–420.

Higginbotham, J. (1985). On semantics. *Linguistic Inquiry*, 16, 547–94.

Higginbotham, J. (1987). Indefiniteness and predication. In E. J. Reuland and A. G. B. ter Meulen (eds), *The Representation of (In)definiteness* (pp. 43–70). Cambridge MA: MIT Press.

Higginbotham, J. (1994). Interrogatives. In K. Hale and S. J. Keyser (eds), *The View from Building 20: Essays in Linguistics in Honor of Sylvain Bromberge* (pp. 195–227). Cambridge MA: MIT Press.

Higginbotham, J. and May, R. (1981). Questions, quantifiers, and crossing. *Linguistic Review*, 1, 41–79.

Higgins, F. R. (1989). The history of control and raising in Modern English. Paper presented at the MIT Workshop on Control, May.

Hirschbühler, P. (1982). VP deletion and across-the-board quantifier scope. In J. Pustejovsky and P. Sells (eds), *Proceedings of NELS*, 12 (pp. 132–9).

Hirsh-Pasek, K. and Golinkoff, R. (1991). Language comprehension: a new look at some old themes. In N. Krasnegor, D. Rumbaugh, M. Studdert-Kennedy, and R. Schiefelbusch (eds), *Biological and Behavioural Aspects of Language Acquisition* (pp. 310–20). Hillsdale NJ: Lawrence Erlbaum.

Hjelmslev, L. (1953). *Prolegomena to a Theory of Language*. Madison: University of Wisconsin Press. Original work (1943).

Hoekstra, J. (1994). Pronouns and Case: on the distribution of Frisian *harren* and *se* (them). *Leuvense bijdragen*, 83, 47–65.

Hoji, H. (1985). Logical Form Constraints and Configurational Structures in Japanese. PhD dissertation, University of Washington.

Hoji, H. (1986). Scope interpretation in Japanese and its theoretical implications. *Proceedings of WCCFL*, 5, 87–101.

Holmberg, A. (1986). Word Order and Syntactic Features in Scandinavian Languages and English. PhD dissertation, University of Stockholm.

Holmberg, A. (1991a). The distribution of Scandinavian weak pronouns. In H. van Riemsdijk and L. Rizzi (eds), *Clitics and their Hosts: Eurotyp Working Papers*, 1 (pp. 155–74). Tilburg.

Holmberg, A. (1991b). On the Scandinavian double object construction. *Papers from the Twelfth Scandinavian Conference of Linguistics* (pp. 141–55). Institute of Linguistics, University of Iceland.

Holmberg, A. (ed.), (1992). *Papers from the Workshop on the Scandinavian Noun Phrase*. Report 32, Dept of General Linguistics, University of Umeå.

Holmberg, A. (1997). The true nature of Holmberg's Generalization. *NELS*, 27, 203–17.

Holmberg, A. and Platzack, C. (1988). On the role of inflection in Scandinavian syntax. *Working Papers in Scandinavian Syntax*, 42, 25–42.

Holmberg, A. and Platzack, C. (1991). On the role of inflection in Scandinavian syntax. In W. Abraham, W. Kosmeijer, and E. Reuland (eds), *Issues in Germanic Syntax* (pp. 93–118). Berlin: de Gruyter.

Holmberg, A. and Platzack, C. (1995). *The Role of Inflection in Scandinavian Syntax.* Oxford: Oxford University Press.

Hopper, P. and Thompson, S. (1984). The discourse basis for lexical categories in universal grammar. *Language*, 60, 703–52.

Hornstein, N. (1977). S and X' convention. *Linguistic Analysis*, 3, 137–76.

Hornstein, N. (1984). *Logic as Grammar.* Cambridge MA: MIT Press.

Hornstein, N. (1994). An argument for minimalism: the case of antecedent-contained deletion. *Linguistic Inquiry*, 25, 455–80.

Hornstein, N. (1995). *Logical Form.* Oxford: Blackwell.

Horvath, J. (1997). The status of "*wh*-expletives" and the partial *wh*-movement construction in Hungarian. *Natural Language and Linguistic Theory*, 15, 509–72.

Huang, C.-T. J. (1981/2). Move *wh* in a language without *wh*-movement. *Linguistic Review*, 1, 369–416.

Huang, C.-T. J. (1982). Logical Relations in Chinese and the Theory of Grammar. PhD dissertation, MIT.

Huang, C.-T. J. (1984). On the distribution and reference of empty pronouns. *Linguistic Inquiry*, 15, 531–74.

Huang, C.-T. J. (1993). Reconstruction and the structure of VP: some theoretical consequences. *Linguistic Inquiry*, 24, 103–38.

Huang, C.-T. J. (1995). Logical form. In G. Webelhuth (ed.), *Government and Binding Theory and the Minimalist Program* (pp. 125–75). Oxford: Blackwell.

Huang, C.-T. J. and Tang, C.-C. J. (1991). The local nature of the long-distance reflexive in Chinese. In J. Koster and E. J. Reuland (eds), *Long-Distance Anaphora* (pp. 263–82). Cambridge: Cambridge University Press.

Huang, Y. (1994). *The Syntax and Pragmatics of Anaphora.* Cambridge: Cambridge University Press.

Huddleston, R. (1978). The constituent structure of VP and Aux. *Linguistic Analysis*, 4, 31–59.

Hudson, R. (1977). The power of morphological rules. *Lingua*, 42, 73–89.

Hudson, R. (1997). I aren't and multiple inheritance. MS, Department of Phonetics and Linguistics, University College London.

Hughes, G. A. and Trudgill, P. (1979). *English Accents and Dialects: An Introduction to Social and Regional Varieties of English.* London: Edward Arnold.

Hyams, N. (1986). *Language Acquisition and the Theory of Parameters.* Dordrecht: Reidel.

Hyams, N. (1996). The underspecification of functional categories in early grammar. In H. Clashen (ed.), *Generative Perspectives on Language Acquisition* (pp. 91–127). Amsterdam: John Benjamins.

Hyams, N. and Sigurjónsdóttir, S. (1990). The development of long distance anaphora: cross-linguistic comparison with special reference to Icelandic. *Language Acquisition*, 1, 57–93.

Ihalainen, O. (1991). On grammatical diffusion in Somerset folk speech. In P. Trudgill and J. K. Chambers (eds), *Dialects of English. Studies in Grammatical Variation* (pp. 104–19). London: Longman.

Iida, M. (1996). *Context and Binding in Japanese.* Stanford: CSLI Publications.

Ingria, R. J. P. (1990). The limits of unification. *Proceedings of the 28th Annual Meeting of the Association for Computational Linguistics*, 194–204.

Inoue, K. (1976). Reflexivization: an interpretive approach. In M. Shibatabi (ed.), *Syntax and Semantics. Vol. 5: Japanese Generative Grammar* (pp. 117–91). New York: Academic Press.

Ioup, G. (1975). *The Treatment of Quantifier Scope in a Transformational Grammar.* PhD dissertation, CUNY.

Ishi, Y. (1991). *Operators and Empty Categories in Japanese.* PhD dissertation, University of Connecticut.

Ishii, T. (1977). *An Asymmetry in the Composition of Phrase Structure and its Consequences.* PhD dissertation, UCIrvine.

Iwakura, K. (1977). The auxiliary system in English. *Linguistic Analysis,* 3, 101–36.

Jackendoff, R. (1969). An interpretive theory of negation. *Foundations of Language,* 5, 218–41.

Jackendoff, R. (1972). *Semantic Interpretation in Generative Grammar.* Cambridge MA: MIT Press.

Jackendoff, R. (1976). Toward an explanatory semantic representation. *Linguistic Inquiry,* 7, 89–150.

Jackendoff, R. (1977). *X′ Syntax: A Study of Phrase Structure.* Cambridge Mass: MIT Press.

Jackendoff, R. (1987). The status of thematic relations in linguistic theory. *Linguistic Inquiry,* 18, 369–411.

Jackendoff, R. (1990a). On Larson's treatment of the double object construction. *Linguistic Inquiry,* 21, 427–56.

Jackendoff, R. (1990b). *Semantic Structures.* Cambridge MA: MIT Press.

Jackendoff, R. (1992). Mme Tussaud meets the binding theory. *Natural Language and Linguistic Theory,* 10, 1–33.

Jackobson, R. (1984). Structure of the Russian verb. In L. R. Waugh and M. Halle (eds), *Roman Jakobson: Russian and Slavic Grammar. Studies 1931–81* (pp. 1–14). Berlin: Mouton. Original work (1932).

Jacobson, P. (1990). Raising as function composition. *Linguistics and Philosophy: An International Journal,* 13.4, 423–75.

Jacobson, P. (1992). Antecedent contained deletion in a variable-free semantics. In C. Barker and D. Dowty (eds), *SALT,* 2 (pp. 193–213).

Jaeggli, O. (1980). Remarks on *to* contraction. *Linguistic Inquiry,* 11, 239–45.

Jaeggli, O. (1986). Passive. *Linguistic Inquiry,* 17, 587–633.

Jaeggli, O. and Safir, K. (eds), (1989a). *The Null Subject Parameter.* Dordrecht: Kluwer.

Jaeggli, O. and Safir, K. (1989b). The null subject parameter and parametric theory. In O. Jaeggli and K. Safir (eds), *The Null Subject Parameter* (pp. 1–44). Dordrecht: Kluwer.

Jang, Y. (1997). On the so-called adjunct predicates in Korean. In R. C. Blight and M. J. Moosally (eds), *Texas Linguistic Forum. Vol. 38: The Syntax and Semantics of Predication* (pp. 149–59). Austin TX: Department of Linguistics, University of Texas at Austin.

Jayaseelan, K. A. (1990). Incomplete VP deletion and gapping. *Linguistic Analysis,* 20, 64–81.

Jayaseelan, K. A. (1995). Anaphors as pronouns. *Studia Linguistica,* 51.2, 186–234.

Jelinek, E. (1984). Empty categories, case, and configurationality. *Natural Language and Linguistic Theory,* 2, 39–76.

Jelinek, E. (1988). The case split and pronominal arguments in Choctaw. In L. Marácz and P. Muysken (eds), *Configurationality: The Typology of Asymmetries.* Dordrecht: Foris.

Jelinek, E. and Demers, R. (1994). Predicates and pronominal arguments in Straits Salish. MS, University of Arizona.

Jespersen, O. (1946). *The Growth and Structure of the English Language*. Garden City NY: Doubleday.

Johnson, K. (1985). A Case for Movement. PhD dissertation, MIT.

Johnson, K. (1988). Verb raising and *have*. McGill Working Papers in Linguistics: Special Issue on Comparative German Syntax (pp. 156–67).

Johnson, K. (1991). Object positions. *Natural Language and Linguistic Theory*, 9, 577–636.

Johnson, M. (forthcoming). Comments on the paper by Bresnan. Paper presented at Annual CUNY Conference on Human Sentence Processing, Special Session on the Lexical Basis of Syntactic Processing: Formal and Computational Issues, March 20, Rutgers University.

Johnson, M. and Bayer, S. (1995). Features and agreement in lambek categorial grammar. In G. V. Morrill and R. T. Oehrle (eds), *Formal Grammar: Proceedings of the Conference of European Summer School in Logic, Language and Information, Barcelona, 1995* (pp. 123–37).

Jonas, D. (1994). The TP-parameter in Scandinavian syntax. In C. Hedlund and A. Holmberg (eds), Papers from the Workshop on Scandinavian Syntax (pp. 33–60). *Gothenburgh Working Papers in Syntax*, University of Gothenburgh, Gothenburgh.

Jonas, D. (1996a). Clause structure, expletives and verb movement. In W. Abraham, S. D. Epstein, H. Thráinsson, and C. J.-W. Zwart (eds), *Minimal Ideas. Syntactic Studies in the Minimalist Framework* (pp. 167–88). Amsterdam: John Benjamins.

Jonas, D. (1996b). Clause Structure and Verb Syntax in Scandinavian and English. PhD dissertation, Harvard University.

Jonas, D. and Bobaljik, J. (1993). Specs for subjects: the role of TP in Icelandic. *MIT Working Papers in Linguistics*, 18, 59–98.

Jónsson, J. G. (1996). Clausal Architecture and Case in Icelandic. PhD dissertation, University of Massachusetts, Amherst.

Josefsson, G. (1992). Object shift and weak pronominals in Swedish. *Working Papers in Scandinavian Syntax*, 49, 59–94.

Josefsson, G. (1993). Scandinavian pronouns and object shift. *Working Papers in Scandinavian Syntax*, 52, 1–28.

Joseph, B. (1976). Raising in Modern Greek: a copying process? *Harvard Studies in Syntax and Semantics*, II, 241–78.

Joseph, B. D. (1983). *The Synchrony and Diachrony of the Balkan Infinitive: A Study in Areal, General, and Historical Linguistics*. Cambridge: Cambridge University Press.

Kadmon, N. and Landman, F. (1993). Any. *Linguistics and Philosophy*, 16, 353–422.

Kahrel, P. and van den Berg, R. (1994). *Typological Studies in Negation*. Amsterdam/ Philadelphia: John Benjamins.

Kallulli, D. (1996). Bare singulars and bare plurals: mapping syntax and semantics. *Proceedings of Console 5*. University of Leiden Press.

Kamp, H. and Reyle, U. (1993). *From Discourse to Logic*. Dordrecht: Kluwer.

Kang, E. (1997). On Korean small clauses. MS, Cornell University.

Kaplan, R. and Bresnan, J. (1982). Lexical-Functional Grammar: a formal system for grammatical representation. In J. Bresnan (ed.), *The Mental Representation of Grammatical Relations* (pp. 282–390). Cambridge MA: MIT Press.

Kapur, S. (1994). Some applications of formal learning theory results to natural language acquisition. In B. Lust, G. Hermon, and J. Kornfilt (eds), *Syntactic Theory and*

First Language Acquisition: Cross-Linguistic Perspectives. Vol. 2: Binding Dependencies and Learnability (pp. 491–508). Hillsdale NJ: Lawrence Erlbaum.

Karttunen, L. (1977). The syntax and semantics of questions. *Linguistics and Philosophy*, 1, 3–44.

Karttunen, L. (1984). Features and values. *Proceedings of Coling 84*, 28–33.

Katada, F. (1991). The LF representation of anaphors. *Linguistic Inquiry*, 22, 287–313.

Kawashima, R. (1994). The Structure of Noun Phrases and the Interpretation of Quantificational NPs in Japanese. PhD dissertation, Cornell University.

Kayne, R. (1981a). Unambiguous paths. In R. May and J. Koster (eds), *Levels of Syntactic Representation* (pp. 143–83). Dordrecht: Foris.

Kayne, R. (1981b). On certain differences between French and English. *Linguistic Inquiry*, 12.3, 349–71.

Kayne, R. (1981c). ECP extensions. *Linguistic Inquiry*, 12, 93–133.

Kayne, R. (1984). *Connectedness and Binary Branching*. Dordrecht: Foris.

Kayne, R. (1985). Principles of particle constructions. In J. Guéron, H.-G. Obenauer, and J.-Y. Pollock (eds), *Grammatical Representation*. Dordrecht: Foris.

Kayne, R. (1989a). Facets of Romance past participle agreement. In P. Benincà (ed.), *Dialect Variation and the Theory of Grammar* (pp. 85–103). Dordrecht: Foris.

Kayne, R. (1989b). Notes on English agreement. *CIEFL Bulletin*, 1, 40–67.

Kayne, R. (1991). Romance clitics, verb movement and PRO. *Linguistic Inquiry*, 22, 647–86.

Kayne, R. (1994). *The Antisymmetry of Syntax*. Cambridge MA: MIT Press.

Kayne, R. (1998). Overt vs. convert movement. *Syntax*, 1, 128–91.

Kayne, R. and Pollock, J.-Y. (1978). Stylistic inversion, successive cyclicity, and move NP in French. *Linguistic Inquiry*, 9, 595–621.

Keenan, E. (1980). Passive is phrasal not (sentential or lexical). In H. v. d. H. T. Hoekstra and M. Moortgat (eds), *Lexical Grammar*. Dordrecht: Foris.

Keenan, E. (1987). *Universal Grammar: 15 Essays*. London: Croom Helm.

Keenan, E. (1988). On semantics and the binding theory. In J. Hawkins (ed.), *Explaining Language Universals* (pp. 104–55). Oxford: Blackwell.

Kemenade, A. van. (1987). *Syntactic Case and Morphological Case in the History of English*. Dordrecht: Foris.

Kennedy, C. (1994). Argument contained ellipsis. *Report LRC-94-03*. Santa Cruz: Linguistics Research Center.

Kennedy, C. (1997). Antecedent contained deletion and the syntax of quantification. *Linguistic Inquiry*, 28, 662–88.

Kennedy, C. (to appear). VP deletion and "nonparasitic" gaps. *Linguistic Inquiry*.

Kennedy, C. and Merchant, J. (1997). Attributive comparatives and bound ellipsis. MS, University of California, Santa Cruz.

Kester, E.-P. (1993). The inflectional properties of Scandinavian adjectives. *Studia Linguistica*, 47, 139–53.

Kester, E.-P. (1996). The Nature of Adjectival Inflection. PhD dissertation, Utrecht University.

Kikuchi, A. (1987). Comparative deletion in Japanese. MS, Yamagata University.

Kim, J.-B. and Sag, I. (1996). French and English negation: a lexicalist alternative to head movement. MS, Department of Linguistics, Stanford University.

Kim, S. (1991). Chain Scope and Quantification Structure. PhD dissertation, Brandeis University.

Kim, S. and Lyle, J. (1996). Parasitic gaps, multiple questions, and VP ellipsis. *Proceedings of the West Coast Conference on Formal Linguistics* (pp. 287–301).

Kim, S. and Maling, J. (1997). A crosslinguistic perspective on resultative formation. In R. C. Blight and M. J. Moosally (eds), *Texas Linguistic Forum 38: The Syntax and Semantics of Predication* (pp. 189–204). Austin TX: Department of Linguistics, University of Texas at Austin.

Kim, S.-Y. (1996). Dependencies: A Study of Anaphoricity and Scrambling. PhD dissertation, Harvard University.

King, T. H. (1995). *Configuring Topic and Focus in Russian*. Stanford: CSLI Publications.

Kiparsky, P. (1973). Elsewhere in phonology. In S. Anderson and P. Kiparsky (eds), *A Festschrift for Morris Halle* (pp. 93–106). New York: Holt, Rinehart, and Winston.

Kiparsky, P. (1996). The shift to head-initial VP in Germanic. In S. Epstein, H. Thráinsson, and S. Peters (eds), *Studies in Comparative Germanic Syntax*, 2 (pp. 140–79). Dordrecht: Kluwer.

Kishimoto, H. (1992). LF pied-piping: evidence from Sinhala. *Gengo Kenkyuu [Language Study]*, 102, 46–87.

Kitagawa, Y. (1986). Subjects in Japanese and English. PhD dissertation, University of Massachusetts, Amherst.

Kitahara, H. (1994). Target A: A Unified Theory of Movement and Structure-Building. PhD dissertation, University of Harvard.

Kitahara, H. (1995). Target A: deducing strict cyclicity from derivational economy. *Linguistic Inquiry*, 26, 47–77.

Kitahara, H. (1996). Raising quantifiers without quantifier raising. In W. Abraham, S. D. Epstein, H. Thráinsson, and C. J.-W. Zwart (eds), *Minimal Ideas* (pp. 189–98). Amsterdam: John Benjamins.

Kitahara, H. (1997). *Elementary Operations and Optimal Derivations*. Cambridge MA: MIT Press.

Klima, E. (1964). Negation in English. In J. A. Fodor and J. J. Katz (eds), *The Structure of Language* (pp. 246–323). Readings in the Philosophy of Language. Englewood Cliffs NJ: Prentice-Hall.

Koizumi, M. (1993). Object Agreement Phrases and the Split VP Hypothesis. *MIT Working Papers in Linguistics* 18: 99–148.

Koizumi, M. (1995). Phrase Structure in Minimalist Syntax. PhD dissertation, MIT.

Koopman, H. (1983). *The Syntax of Verbs*. Dordrecht: Foris.

Koopman, H. (1984). *Verb Movement and Universal Grammar*. Dordrecht: Foris.

Koopman, H. and Sportiche, D. (1985). Theta theory and extraction. *GLOW Newsletter*, 14, 57–8.

Koopman, H. and Sportiche, D. (1986). A note on long extraction in Vata and the ECP. *Natural Language and Linguistic Theory*, 4, 357–74.

Koopman, H. and Sportiche, D. (1991). The position of subjects. *Lingua*, 85, 211–58.

Kornfilt, J. (1984). Case Marking, Agreement, and Empty Categories in Turkish. PhD dissertation, Harvard University.

Kornfilt, J. (1990). Naked partitive phrases in Turkish. MS, Syracuse University.

Koster, J. (1978). *Locality Principles in Syntax*. Dordrecht: Foris.

Koster, J. (1985). Reflexives in Dutch. In J. Gueron, H. Obenauer, and J.-Y. Pollock (eds), *Grammatical Representation* (pp. 141–68). Dordrecht: Foris.

Koster, J. (1987). *Domains and Dynasties*. Dordrecht: Foris.

Koster, J. and Reuland, E. J. (eds) (1991). *Long Distance Anaphora*. Cambridge: Cambridge University Press.

Kratzer, A. (1993). On external arguments. *University of Massachusetts Occasional Papers*, 17. Amherst: University of Massachusetts.

Kratzer, A. (1995). Scope or pseudo-scope? Are there wide scope indefinites? In S. Rothstein (ed.), *Events and Grammar*. Dordrecht: Kluwer.

Kravmskyv, J. (1972). *The Article and the Concept of Definiteness in Language*. The Hague: Mouton.

Kroch, A. (1989a). The loss of the verb-second constraint in Middle English and Middle French. Paper presented at the 9th Annual Meeting of the Association quebecoise de linguistique, Montreal, Quebec.

Kroch, A. (1989b). Reflexes of grammar in patterns of language change. *Language Variation and Change*, 1, 199–244.

Kroch, A. and Taylor, A. (eds) (1994). Penn–Helsinki Parsed Corpus of Middle English. Philadelphia: Department of Linguistics, University of Pennsylvania. Available by anonymous ftp from babel.ling.upenn.edu

Kroch, A. and Taylor, A. (1997). Verb movement in Old and Middle English: dialect variation and language contact. In A. van Kemenade and N. Vincent (eds), *Parameters of Morphosyntactic Change* (pp. 297–325). Cambridge: Cambridge University Press.

Kroch, A. and Taylor, A. (to appear). Dialect differences in the grammar of the XV/VX alternation in Middle English. Proceedings of the 5th Diachronic Generative Syntax Conference, York.

Kroch, A., Taylor, A., and Ringe, D. (1997). The Middle English verb-second constraint: a case study in language contact and language change. In S. Herring, P. van Reenen, and L. Schoesler (eds), *Textual Parameters in Older Language*. Philadelphia: John Benjamins.

Kroeger, P. (1993). *Phrase Structure and Grammatical Relations in Tagalog*. Stanford: CSLI Publications.

Kuno, S. (1973). *The Structure of the Japanese Language*. Cambridge MA: MIT Press.

Kuno, S. (1974). The position of relative clauses and conjunctions. *Linguistic Inquiry*, 5, 117–36.

Kuno, S. (1981). The syntax of comparative clauses. In R. Hendrick, C. Masek, and M. M. Frances (eds), *Chicago Linguistics Society* (pp. 136–55). Chicago: University of Chicago Press.

Kuno, S. (1987). *Functional Syntax: Anaphora, Discourse and Empathy*. Chicago: University of Chicago Press.

Kuno, S. and Takami, K. (1997). Remarks on negative islands. *Linguistic Inquiry*, 28, 553–76.

Kuroda, S.-Y. (1965). Generative Grammatical Studies in the Japanese Language. PhD dissertation, MIT.

Kuroda, S.-Y. (1988). Whether we agree or not: a comparative syntax of English and Japanese. In W. J. Poser (ed.), *Papers from the Second International Workshop on Japanese Syntax* (pp. 103–43). Stanford: CSLI. Also in *Linguisticae Investigationes*, 12, 1–47.

Ladusaw, W. A. (1992). Expressing negation. In C. Barker and D. Dowty (eds), *Proceedings of the Conference on Semantics and Linguistic Theory*, 2 (pp. 237–59). Columbus: Ohio State University.

Ladusaw, W. and Dowty, D. (1988). Toward a nongrammatical account of thematic roles. In W. Wilkins (ed.), *Syntax and Semantics. Vol. 21: Thematic Relations* (pp. 72–7). New York: Academic Press.

Laenzlinger, C. (1996). Comparative Studies in Word Order Variations: Adverbs, Pronouns and Clause Structure in Romance and Germanic. PhD thesis, University of Geneva.

Laka, I. (1990). Negation in Syntax: On the Nature of Functional Categories and Projections. PhD thesis, MIT.

Lakoff, G. (1968). Pronouns and reference. Indiana Linguistics Club. Reprinted in J. D. McCawley (ed.), *Syntax and Semantics. Vol. 7: Notes from the Linguistic Underground* (pp. 275–336). New York: Academic Press.

Lamarche, J. (1991). Problems for No-movement to NumP. *Probus*, 3, 215–36.

Lambek, J. (1958). The mathematics of sentence structure. *American Mathematical Monthly*, 65, 154–70. Reprinted in W. Buszkowski, W. Marciszewski, and J. van Benthem (eds), *Categorial Grammar*. Amsterdam: John Benjamins.

Langendoen, D. T. (1970). *Essentials of English Grammar*. New York: Holt, Rinehart, and Winston.

Lappin, S. and McCord, M. (1990). Anaphora resolution in slot grammar. *Computational Linguistics*, 16, 197–212.

Larson, R. (1988). On the double object construction. *Linguistic Inquiry*, 19, 335–91.

Larson, R. (1990). Double objects revisited: reply to Jackendoff. *Linguistic Inquiry*, 21, 589–632.

Larson, R. (1991). Promise and the theory of control. *Linguistic Inquiry*, 22, 103–39.

Larson, R. and Segal, G. (1995). *Knowledge of Meaning: An Introduction to Semantic Theory*. Cambridge MA: MIT Press.

Lasnik, H. (1972). Analyses of Negation in English. PhD dissertation, MIT.

Lasnik, H. (1976). Remarks on coreference. *Linguistic Analysis*, 2, 1–22. Reprinted in (1989) *Essays on Anaphora*. Dordrecht: Kluwer.

Lasnik, H. (1989). *Essays on Anaphora*. Dordrecht: Kluwer.

Lasnik, H. (1992). Case and expletives: notes toward a parametric account. *Linguistic Inquiry*, 23, 381–405.

Lasnik, H. (1993). Lectures on minimalist syntax. *Uconn Occasional Papers* 1. Cambridge MA: MIT Working Papers in Linguistics.

Lasnik, H. (1995a). Verbal morphology: *Syntactic Structures* meets the Minimalist Program. In H. Campos and P. Kempchinsky (eds), *Evolution and Revolution in Linguistic Theory* (pp. 251–75). Georgetown: Georgetown University Press.

Lasnik, H. (1995b). Case and expletives revisited: on greed and other human failings. *Linguistic Inquiry*, 26, 615–33.

Lasnik, H. (1995c). Last resort and Attract-F. In L. Gabriele, D. Hardison, and R. Westmoreland (eds), *Proceedings of the Sixth Annual Meeting of the Formal Linguistics Society of Mid-America* (pp. 62–81). Bloomington IN: Indiana University.

Lasnik, H. (1995d). Last resort. In S. Haraguchi and M. Funaki (eds), *Minimalism and Linguistic Theory* (pp. 1–32). Tokyo: Hituzi Syobo. Reprinted, with minor corrections, in (1999), *Minimalist Analysis*. Oxford: Blackwell.

Lasnik, H. (1995e). Last resort. In *Proceedings of the First Numazu Conference on Formal Linguistics*.

Lasnik, H. (1995f). A note on pseudogapping. In Papers on Minimalist Syntax, *MIT Working Papers in Linguistics*, 27, 143–63. Reprinted, with minor corrections, in (1999), *Minimalist Analysis*. Oxford: Blackwell.

Lasnik, H. (1999). On feature strength: three minimalist approaches to overt movement. *Linguistic Inquiry*, 30, 197–217.

Lasnik, H. and Saito, M. (1984). On the nature of proper government. *Linguistic Inquiry*, 15, 235–89. Reprinted in (1990) *Essays on Restrictiveness and Learnability*. Dordrecht: Kluwer.

Lasnik, H. and Saito, M. (1991). *On the Subject of Infinitives*. In L. Dobrin et al. (eds), *Papers from the 27th Regional Meeting, Chicago Linguistics Society* (pp. 324–43).

Lasnik, H. and Saito, M. (1992). *Move α*. Cambridge MA: MIT Press.

Lasnik, H. and Stowell, T. (1991). Weakest crossover. *Linguistic Inquiry*, 22, 687–720.

Lazzeroni, R. (1997). La baritonesi come segno dell'individuazione: il caso del vocativo indoeuropeo. MS, University of Pisa.

Lebeaux, D. (1983). A distributional difference between reciprocals and reflexives. *Linguistic Inquiry*, 14, 723–30.

Lebeaux, D. (1988). Language Acquisition and the Form of the Grammar. PhD dissertation, University of Massachusetts, Amherst.

Lebeaux, D. (1990). The grammatical nature of the acquisition sequence: adjoin-α and the formation of relative clauses. In J. de Villiers and L. Frazier (eds), *Language Processing and Language Acquisition* (pp. 13–82). Dordrecht: Kluwer.

Lebeaux, D. (1991). Relative clauses, licensing, and the nature of the derivation. In S. Rothstein (ed.), *Perspectives on Phrase Structure: Heads and Licensing* (pp. 209–39). San Diego: Academic Press.

Lecarme, J. (1989). Genitive constructions in Somali: the notion of internal complements for nominals. Paper presented at the 20th International Conference on African Linguistics, University of Illinois.

Lecarme, J. (1994). Construct state and genitive assignment in Somali. MS, CNRS, Sophia Antipolis.

Lee, H. (1998). Discourse competing with syntax: prominence and "misplaced" *que* in child French. Paper presented at the workshop Is Syntax Different? Common Cognitive Structures for Syntax and Phonology in Optimality Theory, December 12–13 CSLI, Stanford University.

Lee, R. K. (1994). Economy of Representation. PhD dissertation, MIT.

Lee, Y.-S. and Santorini, B. (1994). Towards resolving Webelhuth's Paradox: evidence from German and Korean. In N. Corver and H. van Riemsdijk (eds), *Studies on Scrambling: Movement and Non-Movement Approaches to Free Word-Order Phenomena* (pp. 257–300). Berlin: de Gruyter.

Lees, R. and Klima, E. (1963). Rules for English pronominalization. *Language*, 39, 17–28.

Lees, R. B. (1960). *The Grammar of English Nominalization*. The Hague: Mouton.

Lefebvre, C. and Muysken, P. (1988). *Mixed Categories: Nominalizations in Quechua*. Dordrecht: Kluwer.

Legendre, G. (1997). Secondary predication and functional projections in French. *Natural Language and Linguistic Theory*, 15, 43–87.

Legendre, G., Grimshaw, J., and Vikner, S. (eds) (forthcoming). *Optimality Theoretic Syntax*. Cambridge MA: MIT Press.

Legendre, G., Smolensky, P., and Wilson, C. (1998). When is less more? Faithfulness and minimal links in *wh*-chains. In P. Barbosa, D. Fox, P. Hagstrom, M. McGinnis, and D. Pesetsky (eds), *Is the Best Good Enough? Optimality and Competition in Syntax* (pp. 249–89). Cambridge MA: MIT Press and MIT Working Papers in Linguistics.

Lema, J. and Rivero, M.-L. (1990). Long head movement: ECP vs. HMC. *Proceedings of NELS*, 20, 333–47.

Lema, J. and Rivero, M.-L. (1991). Types of verbal movement in Old Spanish: modals, futures and perfects. *Probus*, 3, 237–78.

Lema, J. and Rivero, M.-L. (1992). Inverted conjugations and V-second effects in Romance. In C. Lauefer and T. Morgan (eds), *Theoretical Analyses in Contemporary Romance Linguistics* (pp. 311–28). Amsterdam: John Benjamins.

Levin, B. (1993). *English Verb Classes and Alternations: A Preliminary Investigation*. Chicago: University of Chicago Press.

Levin, B. and Rappaport, M. (1986a). The formation of adjectival passives. *Linguistic Inquiry*, 17.4, 623–61.

Levin, B. and Rappaport, M. (1986b). What to do with theta-roles. In W. Wilkins (ed.), *Syntax and Semantics. Vol. 21: Thematic Relations* (pp. 7–36). New York: Academic Press.

Levin, B. and Rappaport Hovav, M. (1995). *Unaccusativity: At the Synyax–Semantics Lexical Interface*. Cambridge MA: MIT Press.

Levin, N. (1978). Some identity-of-sense deletions puzzle me. Do they you? *Proceedings of the Fourteenth Annual Meeting of the Chicago Linguistic Society*, 229–40.

Levin, N. (1986). *Main-Verb Ellipsis in Spoken English*. New York: Garland.

Levinson, S. (1987). Pragmatics and the grammar of anaphora. *Journal of Linguistics*, 23, 379–434.

Levinson, S. (1991). Pragmatic reduction of the Binding Conditions revisited. *Journal of Linguistics*, 25, 445–72.

Lewis, D. (1975). Adverbs of quantification. In E. L. Keenan (ed.), *Formal Semantics of Natural Language* (pp. 3–15). Cambridge: Cambridge University Press.

Li, Y.-H. A. (1992). Indefinite *wh* in Mandarin Chinese. *Journal of East Asian Linguistics*, 1, 125–56.

Li, Y.-H. A. (1997). Structures and interpretations of nominal expressions. MS, UCLA.

Lidz, J. (1995). Morphological reflexive marking: evidence from Kannada. *Linguistic Inquiry*, 26.4, 705–10.

Lidz, J. (1996). Dimensions of Reflexivity. PhD dissertation, University of Delaware.

Lightfoot, D. (1979). *Principles of Diachronic Syntax*. Cambridge: Cambridge University Press.

Lightfoot, D. (1989). The child's trigger experience: Degree–0 learnability. *Behavioural and Brain Sciences*, 12, 321–75.

Lightfoot, D. (1991). *How to Set Parameters: Arguments from Language Change*. Cambridge MA: MIT Press.

Lightfoot, D. (1997). Catastrophic change and learning theory. *Lingua*, 100, 171–92.

Lightfoot, D. (1998). The development of grammars. *Glot International*, 3.1, 3–8.

Lightfoot, D. (1999). *The Development of Language: Acquisition, Change, and Evolution*. Malden MA: Blackwell.

Lin, J.-W. (1992). The syntax of *zenmeyang* "how" and *weishenme* "why" in Mandarin Chinese. *Journal of East Asian Linguistics*, 1, 293–331.

Liu, F.-H. (1990). Scope and Dependency in English and Chinese. PhD dissertation, UCLA.

Liu, F.-H. (1997). *Linguistik Aktuell. Vol. 16: Scope and Specificity*. Amsterdam: John Benjamins.

Lobeck, A. (1987a). Syntactic Constraints on Ellipsis. PhD dissertation, University of Washington.

Lobeck, A. (1987b). VP ellipsis in infinitives: Infl as a proper governor. In J. McDonough and B. Plunkett (eds), *Proceedings of NELS* (pp. 425–41). Amherst: GLSA.

Lobeck, A. (1992). Licensing and identification of ellipted categories in Englis. In S. Berman and A. Hestvik (eds), *Proceedings of the Stuttgart Ellipsis Workshop*. Stuttgart.

Lobeck, A. (1995). *Ellipsis: Functional Heads, Licensing and Identification*. New York: Oxford University Press.

Lois, X. (1986). Les groupes nominaux sans déterminant en espagnol. MS, University of Paris VIII.

Longobardi, G. (1994). Reference and proper names: a theory of N-movement in syntax and logical form. *Linguistic Inquiry*, 25, 609–65.

Longobardi, G. (1995). Construct state across languages: a minimalist interpretation. MS, University of Venice.

Longobardi, G. (1996). The syntax of N-raising: a minimalist theory. *OTS Working Papers*. Research Institute for Language and Speech, University of Utrecht.

Longobardi, G. (1998). Comparative semantics and syntactic parameters. MS, University of Trieste.

López, L. (1994). The syntactic licensing of VP-ellipsis: a comparative study of Spanish and English. In M. L. Mazzola (ed.), *Issues and Theory in Romance Linguistics: Selected Papers from the Linguistic Symposium on Romance Languages XXIII* (pp. 333–54). Washington DC: Georgetown University Press.

Lumsden, J. S. (1992). Underspecification in grammatical and natural gender. *Linguistic Inquiry*, 23, 469–86.

Lutz, U. and Müller, G. (eds), (1995). *Studies on Wh-Scope Marking*. Arbeitspapiere des SFB 340, University of Stuttgart and University of Tübingen.

Lyons, J. (1968). *Introduction to Theoretical Linguistics*. Cambridge: Cambridge University Press.

Mahajan, A. K. (1990). The A/A-Bar Distinction and Movement Theory. PhD dissertation, MIT.

Mahajan, A. K. (1994a). Against the relevance of subjacency at LF: the case of Hindi *wh*. *Linguistic Inquiry*, 25, 171–8.

Mahajan, A. K. (1994b). Toward a unified theory of Scrambling. In N. Corver and H. van Riemsdijk (eds), *Studies on Scrambling: Movement and Non-Movement Approaches to Free Word Order Phenomena* (pp. 301–30). Berlin: de Gruyter.

Maki, H. (1995). The Syntax of Particles. PhD dissertation, University of Connecticut.

Maling, J. (1976). Notes on quantifier postposing. *Linguistic Inquiry*, 7, 708–18.

Maling, J. (1984). Non-clause-bounded reflexives in Modern Icelandic. *Linguistics and Philosophy*, 7, 211–41.

Maling, J. (1986). Clause-bounded reflexives in Modern Icelandic. In L. Hellan and K. K. Christensen (eds), *Topics in Scandinavian Syntax* (pp. 53–63). Dordrecht: Reidel.

Maling, J. and Zaenen, A. (1978). The non-universality of a surface filter. *Linguistic Inquiry*, 9, 475–97. Also in J. Maling and A. Zaenen (eds), *Syntax and Semantics. Vol. 24: Modern Icelandic Syntax*. San Diego: Academic Press.

Mandelbaum, D. (1994). Syntactic Conditions on Saturation. PhD dissertation, CUNY.

Manzini, M. R. (1983a). On control and control theory. *Linguistic Inquiry*, 14.3, 421–46.

Manzini, M. R. (1983b). Restructuring and Reanalysis. PhD dissertation, MIT.

Manzini, R. (1992). *Locality*. Cambridge MA: MIT Press.

Manzini, R. and Wexler, K. (1987). Parameters, binding theory, and learnability. *Linguistic Inquiry*, 18, 413–44.

Marácz, L. (1988). Locality and correspondence effects in Hungarian. In A. Cardinaletti, G. Cinque, and G. Guisti (eds), *Constituent Structure* (pp. 203–35). Dordrecht: Foris.

Marantz, A. (1984). *On the Nature of Grammatical Relations*. Cambridge MA: MIT Press.

Marantz, A. (1991). Case and licensing. *Proceedings of ESCOL '91*, 234–53.

Marantz, A. (1995). The minimalist program. In G. Webelhuth (ed.), *Government and Binding Theory and the Minimalist Program* (pp. 349–82). Oxford: Blackwell.

Marcus, G. F. (1993). Negative evidence in language acquisition. *Cognition*, 46, 53–85.

Marcus, M. P. (1980). *A Theory of Syntactic Recognition for Natural Language*. Cambridge MA: MIT Press.

Martí, N. (1995). *De* in Catalan elliptical nominals: a partitive case marker. *Catalan Working Papers in Linguistics*, 4, 243–65.

Martin, J. (1995). On the Syntactic Structure of Spanish Noun Phrases. PhD thesis, University of Southern California.

Martin, R. (1992). On the distribution and case features of PRO. MS, University of Connecticut.

Martin, R. (1996). A Minimalist Theory of PRO and Control. PhD dissertation, University of Connecticut.

Matthews, P. H. (1972). *Inflectional Morphology*. Cambridge: Cambridge University Press.

Maxwell, J. T. and Kaplan, R. M. (1995). A method for disjunctive constraint satisfaction. In M. Dalrymple, R. M. Kaplan, J. M. Maxwell, and A. Zaenen (eds), *Formal Issues in Lexical-Functional Grammar* (pp. 381–401). Stanford: CSLI Publications.

May, R. (1977). The Grammar of Quantification. PhD dissertation, MIT.

May, R. (1981). Movement and binding. *Linguistic Inquiry*, 12, 215–43.

May, R. (1985). *Logical Form: Its Structure and Derivation*. Cambridge MA: MIT Press.

Mazuka, R. (1996). Can a grammatical parameter be set before the first word? Prosodic contributions to early setting of a grammatical parameter. In J. L. Morgan and K. Demuth (eds), *Signal to Syntax: Bootstrapping from Speech to Grammar in Early Acquisition* (pp. 313–30). Mahwah NJ: Lawrence Erlbaum.

McCarthy, J. J. and Prince, A. S. (1995). Generalized alignment. In J. Beckman, L. Dickey, and S. Urbanczyk (eds), Papers in Optimality Theory (pp. 249–384), *University of Massachusetts Occasional Papers*, 18. Amherst: University of Massachusetts.

McCawley, J. (1968). Concerning the base component of a transformational grammar. *Foundations of Language*, 4, 243–69.

McCawley, J. D. (1988). *The Syntactic Phenomena of English*. Chicago: University of Chicago Press.

McCloskey, J. (1984). Raising, subcategorization and selection in Modern Irish. *Natural Language and Linguistic Theory*, 1.4, 441–85.

McCloskey, J. (1991). Clause structure, ellipsis and proper government in Irish. *Lingua*, 85, 259–302.

McCloskey, J. (1993). The scope of verb-movement in Irish. *Natural Language and Linguistic Theory*.

McCloskey, J. (1996). Subjects and subject positions in Irish. In R. Borsley and I. Roberts (eds), *The Syntax of the Celtic Languages* (pp. 241–83). Cambridge: Cambridge University Press.

McCloskey, J. (1997). Subjecthood and subject positions. In L. Haegeman (ed.), *Elements of Grammar: Handbook in Generative Syntax* (pp. 197–236). Dordrecht: Kluwer.

McCloskey, J. and Hale, K. (1984). On the syntax of person–number inflection in Modern Irish. *Natural Language and Linguistic Theory*, 1, 487–533.

McConnell-Ginet, S. (1982). Adverbs and logical form. *Language*, 58, 144–84.

McDaniel, D. (1989). Partial and multiple *wh*-movement. *Natural Language and Linguistic Theory*, 7, 565–604.

McDaniel, D., Chiu, B., and Maxfield, T. (1995). Parameters for *wh*-movement types: evidence from child English. *Natural Language and Linguistic Theory*, 13, 709–53.

Mchombo, S. and Ngunga, A. (1994). The syntax and semantics of the reciprocal construction in Ciyao. *Linguistic Analysis*, 24, 3–31.

McMahon, A. (1994). *Understanding Language Change*. Cambridge: Cambridge University Press.

Merchant, J. (1996). Object Scrambling and quantifier float in German. *NELS*, 26, 179–93.

Miceli, G. and Caramazza, A. (1988). Dissociation of inflectional and derivational morphology: evidence from aphasia. *Brain and Language*, 35, 24–65.

Miller, J. (1993). The grammar of Scottish English. In J. Milroy and L. Milroy (eds), *Real English. The Grammar of English Dialects in the British Isles* (pp. 99–138). London: Longman.

Milner, J. C. (1987). *De la syntaxe à l'interpretation*. Paris: Seuil.

Milroy, J. and Milroy, L. (eds), (1993). *Real English. The Grammar of English Dialects in the British Isles*. London: Longman.

Milsark, G. (1974). Existential Sentences in English. PhD dissertation, MIT.

Milsark, G. (1977). Toward an explanation of certain peculiarities of the existential construction in English. *Linguistic Analysis*, 3, 1–29.

Mithun, M. (1987). Is basic word order universal? In R. Tomlin (ed.), *Coherence and Grounding in Discourse* (pp. 281–328). Amsterdam: John Benjamins.

Mohammad, M. (1988). The Sentential Structure of Arabic. PhD Dissertation, University of Southern California.

Mohanan, K. P. (1980). Grammatical relations and anaphora in Malayalam. MS, MIT.

Mohanan, K. P. (1982). Grammatical relations and clause structure in Malayalam. In J. Bresnan (ed.), *The Mental Representation of Grammatical Relations* (pp. 504–89). Cambridge MA: MIT Press.

Mohanan, K. P. (1983). Move NP or lexical rules? Evidence from Malayalam causativization. In L. Levin, M. Rappaport, and A. Zaenen (eds), *Papers in Lexical-Functional Grammar* (pp. 47–111). Bloomington IN: Indiana University Linguistics Club.

Moltmann, F. (1989). Adjectives and argument structure in German. MS, MIT.

Moltmann, F. and Szabolcsi, A. (1994). Scope interactions with pair-list quantifiers. In M. González (ed.), *Proceedings of NELS, 24* (pp. 381–95).

Montague, R. (1974). The proper treatment of quantification in ordinary English. In R. H. Thomason (ed.), *Formal Philosophy: Selected Papers of Richard Montague* (pp. 247–71). New Haven and London: Yale University Press.

Moore, J. (1998). Turkish copy-raising and A-chain locality. *Natural Language and Linguistic Theory*, 16, 149–89.

Morgan, J. L. (1986). *From Simple Input to Complex Grammar*. Cambridge MA: MIT Press.

Morgan, J. L. and Demuth, K. (eds), (1996). *Signal to Syntax: Bootstrapping from Speech to Grammar in Early Acquisition*. Mahwah NJ: Lawrence Erlbaum.

Morimoto, Y. (1998). Dative objects in Japanese *-sa* nominalization. In M. Butt and T. H. King (eds), *Proceedings of the LFG98 Conference*, University of Queensland, Brisbane. On-line, CSLI Publications: http://www-csli.stanford.edu/publications/

Morin, Y.-C. (1986). A morphological convergence between liaison and schwa deletion in the Picard and Walloon dialects of French. In H. Anderson (ed.), *Sandhi Phenomena in the Languages of Europe* (pp. 211–22). Berlin: de Gruyter.

Müller, G. (1997). *Incomplete Category Fronting: A Derivational Approach to Remnant Movement in German*. Dordrecht: Kluwer.

Müller, G. and Sternefeld, W. (1996). Ā-chain formation and economy of derivation. *Linguistic Inquiry*, 27, 480–511.

Müller, G. and Sternefeld, W. (1994). Scrambling as A-bar Movement. In N. Corver and H. van Riemsdijk (eds), *Studies on Scrambling. Movement and Non-Movement Approaches to Free Word-Order Phenomena* (pp. 331–85). Berlin: de Gruyter.

Murasugi, K. (1992). Crossing and Nested Paths: NP Movements in Accusative and Ergative Languages. PhD dissertation, MIT.

Mustanoja, T. (1973). *Ælmighty* in Early English: a study in positional syntax. *Wiener Beiträge zur Englischen Philologie*, 75, 204–12.

Muysken, P. (1982). Parametrizing the notion "head." *Journal of Linguistic Research*, 2.3, 57–75.

Muysken, P. (1993). Reflexives of Ibero-Romance reflexive clitic+verb combinations in Papiamentu: thematic grids and grammatical relations. In F. Byrne and D. Winford (eds), *Focus and Grammatical Relations in Creole Languages* (pp. 285–301). Amsterdam: John Benjamins.

Muysken, P. and Smith, N. (1994). Reflexives in the Creole languages: an interim report. In D. Adone and I. Plasg (eds), *Creolization and Language Change* (pp. 45–64). Tübingen: Max Niemeyer Verlag.

Nadkarni, M. V. (1975). Bilingualism and syntactic change in Konkani. *Language*, 51, 672–83.

Nakamura, M. (1994). An economy account of *wh*-extraction in Tagalog. *Proceedings of the Twelfth West Coast Conference on Formal Linguistics*, 405–20.

Nakamura, M. (1997). Object extraction in Bantu applicatives: some implications from Minimalism. *Linguistic Inquiry*, 28, 252–80.

Napoli, D. (1979). Reflexivization across clause boundaries in Italian. *Journal of Linguistics*, 15, 1–28.

Napoli, D. J. (1985). Verb phrase deletion in English: a base-generated analysis. *Journal of Linguistics*, 21, 281–319.

Neeleman, A. (1994). Scrambling as a D-structure phenomenon. In N. Corver and H. van Riemsdijk (eds), *Studies on Scrambling. Movement and Non-Movement Approaches to Free Word-Order Phenomena* (pp. 387–429). Berlin: de Gruyter.

Nespor, M., Guasti, M., and Christophe, A. (1996). Selecting word order: the rhythmic activation principle. In U. Kleinhenz (ed.), *Interfaces in Phonolgy* (pp. 1–26). Berlin: Akademie Verlag.

Nichols, J. (1986). Head-marking and dependent-marking grammar. *Language*, 62, 56–119.

Nichols, J. (1992). *Linguistic Diversity in Space and Time*. Chicago: University of Chicago Press.

Nielsen, Ø. (1997). Adverbs and A-shift. *Working Papers in Scandinavian Syntax*, 59, 1–31.

Nishigauchi, T. (1990). *Quantification in the Theory of Grammar*. Dordrecht: Kluwer.

Nishigauchi, T. (1992). Syntax of reciprocals in Japanese. *Journal of East Asian Linguistics*, 1.2, 157–96.

Nishiyama, K. (1998). The Morphosyntax and Morphophonogy of Japanese Predicates. PhD dissertation, Cornell University.

Niyogi, P. and Berwick, R. (1997). Evolutionary consequences of language learning. *Linguistics and Philosophy*, 20, 697–719.

Nordlinger, R. (1998). *Constructive Case: Evidence from Australian Languages*. Stanford: CSLI Publications.

Nyberg, E. (1992). A Non-Deterministic Success-Driven Model of Parameter Setting in Language Acquisition. PhD dissertation, Carnegie Mellon University.

Obenauer, H. (1983). On the identification of empty categories. *Linguistic Review*, 4, 153–202.

Obenauer, H. (1994). Aspects de la syntaxe A-barre. Thèse de doctorat d'état, University of Paris VIII.

Ochi, M. (1997). Move or Attract?: Attract F and the pied-piping chain. Open Linguistics Forum, Ottawa.

Ochi, M. (1999). Some consequences of Attrac-F. *Lingua*, 109, 81–107.

Ogwueleka, O. S. (1987). Thematic Roles and Syntactic Processes in Igbo. PhD dissertation, Obafemi Owolowo University, Ille-Ife, Nigeria.

Oka, T. (1993). Minimalism in Syntactic Derivation. PhD dissertation, MIT.

Orton, H. and Dieth, E. (eds), (1962–). *Survey of English Dialects*. Leeds: E. J. Arnold for the University of Leeds.

Ottósson, K. G. (1991). Icelandic double objects as small clauses. *Working Papers in Scandinavian Syntax*, 48, 77–97.

Ottósson, K. G. (1993). Double-object small clauses and reanalysis in Icelandic passives. *Proceedings of the Eleventh WestCoast Conference on Formal Linguistics*, 371–87.

Ouhalla, J. (1988). The Syntax of Head Movement: A Study of Berber. PhD dissertation, University College, London.

Ouhalla, J. (1990). Sentential negation, Relativized Minimality and the aspectual status of auxiliaries. *Linguistic Review*, 7, 183–231.

Ouhalla, J. (1991). *Functional Categories and Parametric Variation*. London: Routledge.

Ouhalla, J. (1996a). Remarks on the binding properties of *wh*-pronouns. *Linguistic Inquiry*, 27, 676–707.

Ouhalla, J. (1996b). The construct state in Berber. In J. Lecarme, J. Lowenstamm, and U. Shlonsky (eds), *Studies in Afro-Asiatic Languages* (pp. 278–301). The Hague: Holland Academic Graphics.

Palmer, F. R. (1994). *Grammatical Roles and Relations*. Cambridge: Cambridge University Press.

Palmer, H. E. and Blandford, F. G. (1969). *A Grammar of Spoken English* (3rd edition, revised and rewritten by Roger Kingdon). Cambridge: W. Heffer and Sons.

Parry, M. M. (1996). La negazione italo-romanza: variazione tipologica e variazione strutturale. In P. Benincà, G. Cinque, T. de Mauro, and N. Vincent (eds), *Italiano e dialetti nel tempo. Saggi di grammatica per Giulio C. Lepschy* (pp. 225–57). Rome: Bulzoni.

Parry, M. M. (1997). Negation. In M. Miaden and M. M. Parry (eds), *The Dialects of Italy*. London: Routledge.

Partee, B. H. (1965). Subject and Object in Modern English. PhD dissertation, MIT.

Partee, B. and Bach, E. (1984). Quantification, pronouns, and VP anaphora. In J. Groenendijk, T. Janssen, and M. Stokhof (eds), *Truth, Interpretation and Information*. Dordrecht: Foris.

Payne, J. R. (1985). Negation. In T. Shopen (ed.), *Language Typology and Syntactic Description. Vol. I: Clause Structure* (pp. 197–242). Cambridge: Cambridge University Press.

Pearce, E. (1997). Genitive case in the Maori DP. *Welllington Working Papers in Linguistics*, 9, 31–55.

Pearce, E. (to appear). The syntax of genitives in the Maori DP. *Canadian Journal of Linguistics/Revue Canadienne de Linguistique*.

Pensalfini, R. (1997). Nonconfigurationality as restrictions on encyclopedic information. MS, MIT.

Perlmutter, D. (1971). *Deep and Surface Structure Constraints in Syntax*. New York: Holt, Rinehart, and Winston.

Perlmutter, D. (1978). Impersonal passives and the unaccusative hypothesis. *Proceedings of Fourth Annual Meeting of the Berkeley Linguistics Society* (pp. 157–89).

Perlmutter, D. (1982). Syntactic representation, syntactic levels, and the notion of subject. In P. Jacobson and G. Pullum (eds), *The Nature of Syntactic Representation* (pp. 283–304). Dordrecht: Reidel.

Perlmutter, D. (1984). Working 1s and inversion in Italian, Japanese, and Quechua. In D. Perlmutter and C. Rosen (eds), *Studies in Relational Grammar*, 2 (pp. 292–330). Chicago: University of Chicago Press.

Perlmutter, D. and Postal, P. (1977). Toward a Universal Characterization of Passivization. *Proceedings of the 3rd Annual Meeting of the Berkeley Linguistics Society*.

Perlmutter, D. and Postal, P. (1984). The 1-advancement exclusiveness law. In D. Perlmutter and C. Rosen (eds), *Studies in Relational Grammar*, 2 (pp. 81–125). Chicago: University of Chicago Press.

Perlmutter, D. and Postal, P. (1983). Some proposed laws of basic clause structure. In D. M. Perlmutter (ed.), *Relational Grammar* I. Chicago: University of Chicago Press.

Pesetsky, D. (1982). Paths and Categories. PhD dissertation, MIT.

Pesetsky, D. (1987). *Wh*-in-situ: movement and unselective binding. In E. Reuland and A. ter Meulen (eds), *The Representation of (In)definiteness* (pp. 98–129). Cambridge MA: MIT Press.

Pesetsky, D. (1989). Language-particular processes and the earliness principle. MS, MIT.

Pesetsky, D. (1995). *Zero Syntax*. Cambridge MA: MIT Press.

Pesetsky, D. (1997). Optimality theory and syntax: movement and pronunciation. In D. Archangeli and D. T. Langendoen (eds), *Optimality Theory* (pp. 134–70). Oxford: Blackwell.

Petersen, H. P., J. í L. Jacobsen, Z. S. Hansen, and H. Thráinsson (1998). Faroese: An Overview for Students and Researchers. MS, Reykjavik and Tórshavn.

Philip, W. and Coopmans, P. (1996a). The role of referentiality in the acquisition of pronominal anaphora. In K. Kusumoto (ed.), *Proceedings of NELS*, 26 (pp. 241–55).

Philip, W. and Coopmans, P. (1996b). The role of feature specification in the acquisition of pronominal anaphora in Dutch. In W. Philip and F. Wijnen (eds), *Connecting Children's Language and Linguistic Theory* (pp. 73–106). Amsterdam Series in Child Language Development 5.

Pica, P. (1985). Subject, tense and truth: towards a modular approach to binding. In J. Guéron, H. G. Obenauer, and J.-Y. Pollock (eds), *Grammatical Representation* (pp. 259–91). Dordrecht: Foris.

Pica, P. (1987). On the nature of the reflexivization cycle. *NELS*, 17, 483–99.

Pica, P. and Synder, W. (1995). Weak crossover, scope, and agreement in a minimalist program. *Proceedings of WCCFL*, 13, 334–49.

Picallo, M. C. (1991). Nominals and nominalization in Catalan. *Probus*, 3, 279–316.

Picallo, M. C. (1994). Catalan possessive pronouns: the avoid pronoun principle revisited. *Natural Language and Linguistic Theory*, 12, 259–99.

Pierce, A. (1989). On the Emergence of Syntax: A Cross-Linguistic Study. PhD dissertation, MIT.

Pinker, S. (1984). *Language Learnability and Language Development*. Cambridge MA: Harvard University Press.

Pinker, S. (1989). *Learnability and Cognition: The Acquisition of Argument Structure*. Cambridge MA: MIT Press.

Pinker, S. (1994). *The Language Instinct: How the Mind Creates Language*. New York: W. Morrow.

Pinker, S. and Bloom, P. (1990). Natural language and natural selection. *Behavioural and Brain Sciences*, 13, 707–84, with commentaries.

Pintzuk, S. (1991). Phrase Structures in Competition: Variation and Change in Old English Word Order. PhD thesis, University of Pennsylvania.

Pintzuk, S. (1993). Verb seconding in Old English: verb movement to Infl. *Linguistic Review*, 10, 5–35.

Pintzuk, S. (1995). Phrase structure variation in Old English. *Language Variation and Chang*, 7, 152–67.

Planck, F. (1984). The modals story retold. *Studies in Language*, 8, 305–64.

Platzack, C. (1987). The Scandinavian languages and the null subject parameter. *Natural Language and Linguistic Theory*, 5, 377–401.

Platzack, C. (1992). Functional categories and early Swedish. In J. Meisel (ed.), *The Acquisition of Verb Placement: Functional Categories and V2 Phenomena in Language Development* (pp. 63–82). Dordrecht: Kluwer.

Platzack, C. (1995). The loss of verb second in English and French. In A. Battye and I. Roberts (eds), *Language Change and Verbal Systems* (pp. 200–26). Oxford: Oxford University Press.

Platzack, C. and Holmberg, A. (1989). The role of AGR and finiteness. *Working Papers in Scandinavian Syntax*, 43, 51–76.

Poletto, C. (1991). The aspect projection: an analysis of the "passé surcomposé." MS, University of Padua.

Poletto, C. (1993a). *La sintassi del soggetto nei dialetti italiani settentrionali*. Vol. 12 of *Monografie*. Padua: Unipress.

Poletto, C. (1993b). Subject clitic–verb inversion in north eastern Italian dialects. In A. Belletti (ed.), *Syntactic Theory and the Dialects of Italy* (pp. 204–51). Turin: Rosenberg and Sellier.

Pollard, C. and Sag, I. (1987). *Information-Based Syntax and Semantics. Vol. I: Fundamentals*. Stanford: CSLI Publications.

Pollard, C. and Sag, I. (1992). Anaphors in English and the scope of the binding theory. *Linguistic Inquiry*, 23, 261–305.

Pollard, C. and Sag, I. (1994). *Head-Driven Phrase Structure Grammar*. Stanford and Chicago: CSLI and University of Chicago Press.

Pollock, J.-Y. (1989). Verb movement, universal grammar and the structure of IP. *Linguistic Inquiry*, 20, 365–424.

Pollock, J.-Y. (1997). Notes on clause structure. In L. Haegeman (ed.), *Elements of Grammar* (pp. 237–79). Dordrecht: Kluwer.

Poole, G. (1995). Constraints on local economy. In P. Barbosa, D. Fox, P. Hagstrom, M. McGinnis, and D. Pesetsky (eds), *Is the Best Good Enough? Optimality and Competition in Syntax* (pp. 385–98). Cambridge MA: MIT Press.

Porterfield, L. and Srivastav, V. (1998). (In)definiteness in the absence of articles: evidence from Hindi and Indonesian. *Proceedings of WCCFL*, 7, 265–76.

Poser, W. J. (1992). Blocking of phrasal constructions by lexical items. In I. A. Sag and A. Szabolcsi (eds), *Lexical Matters* (pp. 111–30). Stanford: CSLI Publications.

Postal, P. (1969). On so-called "pronouns" in English. In D. Reibel and S. Schane (eds), *Modern Studies in English* (pp. 201–24). Englewood Cliffs NJ: Prentice-Hall.

Postal, P. (1971). *Cross-Over Phenomena*. New York: Holt, Rinehart, and Winston.

Postal, P. (1972). Some further limitations of interpretive theories of anaphora. *Linguistic Inquiry*, 3, 349–71.

Postal, P. (1974). *On Raising*. Cambridge MA: MIT Press.

Postal, P. (1990). Some unexpected English restrictions. In K. Dziwirek et al. (eds), *Grammatical Relations: A Cross-theoretical Perspective* (pp. 365–85). Stanford: CSLI.

Postal, P. (1994). Parasitic and pseudoparasitic gaps. *Linguistic Inquiry*, 25.1, 63–117.

Postal, P. and Pullum, G. (1988). Expletive noun phrases in subcategorized positions. *Linguistic Inquiry*, 19, 635–70.

Potsdam, E. (1996a). English verbal morphology and VP ellipsis. In K. Kusumoto (ed.), *Proceedings of NELS* (pp. 353–68).

Potsdam, E. (1996b). Syntactic Issues in the English Imperative. PhD dissertation, University of Santa Cruz.

Potsdam, E. (1997). NegP and subjunctive complements in English. *Linguistic Inquiry*, 28, 533–41.

Prince, A. and Smolensky, P. (1993). *Optimality Theory: Constraint Interaction in Generative Grammar*. RuCCS Technical Report 2. Piscateway NJ: Rutgers University Center for Cognitive Science.

Pullum, G. and Wilson, D. (1977). Autonomous syntax and the analysis of auxiliaries. *Language*, 53, 741–88.

Pullum, G. K. and Zwicky, A. M. (1997). Licensing of prosodic features by syntactic rules: the key to auxiliary reduction. Paper presented at the 1997 Linguistic Society of America meeting, Chicago.

Pustejovsky, J. (1987). Paper presented at the MIT Workshop on Sentential Complementation.

Radford, A. (1990). *Syntactic Theory and the Acquisition of English Syntax*. Oxford: Blackwell.

Rapoport, T. (1991). Adjunct-predicate licensing and D-structure. In *Perspectives on Phrase Structure* (pp. 159–87). San Diego: Academic Press.

Raposo, E. (1987). Case theory and Infl-to-Comp: the inflected infinitive in European Portuguese. *Linguistic Inquiry*, 18, 85–109.

Reinhart, T. (1976). The Syntactic Domain of Anaphora. PhD dissertation, MIT.

Reinhart, T. (1977). Quantifier scope: how labor is divided between QR and choice functions. *Linguistics and Philosophy*, 20, 335–97.

Reinhart, T. (1978). Syntactic domains for semantic rules. In F. Günthner and S. J. Schmidt (eds), *Formal Semantics and Pragmatics for Natural Languages* (pp. 107–30). Dordrecht: Reidel.

Reinhart, T. (1983). *Anaphora and Semantic Interpretation*. London: Croom Helm.

Reinhart, T. (1993). Interpreting *wh*-in-situ. MS, Tel-Aviv University.

Reinhart, T. (1995). Interface strategies. *OTS Working Papers* TL–94–003. Revised version to appear with MIT Press.

Reinhart, T. (1997a). *Wh*-in-situ in the framework of the Minimalist Program. *Natural Language Semantics*, 6.1, 29–56.

Reinhart, T. (1997b). Quantifier scope: how labor is divided between QR and choice functions. *Linguistics and Philosophy*, 20, 335–97.

Reinhart, T. (1998). *Wh*-in-situ in the framework of the Minimalist Program. *Natural Language Semantics*, 6, 29–56.

Reinhart, T. (1999). Syntactic effects of lexical operations: reflexives and unaccusatives. *OTS Working Paper*. Utrecht Institute of Linguistics.

Reinhart, T. (to appear). Strategies of anaphora resolution. In H. Bennis, M. Everaert, and E. Reuland (eds), *Interface Strategies*. Amsterdam: Royal Netherlands Academy of Arts and Sciences.

Reinhart, T. and Reuland, E. J. (1991). Anaphors and logophors: an argument structure perspective. In J. Koster and E. J. Reuland (eds), *Long Distance Anaphora* (pp. 283–321). Cambridge: Cambridge University Press.

Reinhart, T. and Reuland, E. J. (1993). Reflexivity. *Linguistic Inquiry*, 24, 657–720.

Reinholtz, C. and Russell, K. (1994). Quantified NPs in pronominal argument languages: evidence from Swampy Cree. In J. Beckman (ed.), *NELS 25* (pp. 389–403). Amherst: GLSA.

Reis, M. (1976). Reflexivierung in deutsche A.c.I.-konstruktionen: ein transformations-grammatisches Dilemma. *Papiere zur Linguistik,* 9, 5–82.

Remacle, L. (1952). *Syntaxe du parler wallon de La Gleize* 1 [*The Syntax of La Gleize Walloon* 1]. Paris: Belles Lettres.

Reuland, E. J. (1996). Pronouns and features. In K. Kusumoto (ed.), *Proceedings of NELS,* 26 (pp. 319–33). Amherst: GSLA.

Reuland, E. J. (1997). Logophoricity as orientation. In J. Don and T. Sanders (eds), *UiL OTS Yearbook* (pp. 71–83). Utrecht: Utrecht Institute of Linguistics OTS.

Reuland, E. J. (1998a). Primitives of binding. *Working Paper, Utrecht Institute of Linguistics OTS.* Utrecht University.

Reuland, E. J. (1998b). Structural conditions on chains and binding. In P.N. Tamanji and K. Kosumoto (eds), *Proceedings of NELS,* 28, (pp. 341–56). Amherst: GSLA.

Reuland, E. J. and Koster, J. (1991). Long-distance anaphora: an overview. In J. Koster and E. J. Reuland (eds), *Long-Distance Anaphora* (pp. 1–25). Cambridge: Cambridge University Press.

Reuland, E. J. and Reinhart, T. (1992). Binding conditions and chains. In D. Bates (ed.), *The Proceedings of the Tenth West Coast Conference on Formal Linguistics.* Stanford: Stanford Linguistics Association, CSLI, Leland Stanford Junior University.

Reuland, E. J. and T. Reinhart (1995). Pronouns, anaphors and Case. In H. Haider, S. Olsen, and S. Vikner (eds), *Studies in Comparative Germanic Syntax* (pp. 241–69). Dordrecht: Kluwer.

Reuland, E. J. and Sigurjónsdóttir, S. (1997). Long distance binding in Icelandic: syntax or discourse? In H. Bennis, P. Pica, and J. Rooryck (eds), *Atomism in Binding* (pp. 323–34). Dordrecht: Foris.

Riad, T. (1988). Reflexivity and predication. *Working Papers in Scandinavian Syntax,* 36.

Richards, N. (1997). What Moves Where When in Which Language? PhD dissertation, MIT.

Richards, N. (1998). The principle of minimal compliance. *Linguistic Inquiry,* 29, 599–629.

Riemsdijk, H. van. (1982). *A Case Study in Syntactic Markedness.* Dordrecht: Foris.

Riemsdjik, H. van and Williams, E. (1981). NP-structure. *Linguistic Review,* 1, 171–217.

Riemsdijk, H. van and Williams, E. (1986). *Introduction to the Theory of Grammar.* Cambridge MA: MIT Press.

Ritter, E. (1986). NSO noun phrase in a VSO language. MS, MIT.

Ritter, E. (1988). A head-movement approach to construct-state noun phrases. *Linguistics,* 26, 909–29.

Ritter, E. (1991). Two functional categories in noun phrases: evidence from Modern Hebrew. In S. Rothstein (ed.), *Syntax and Semantics* 26 (pp. 37–62). San Diego: Academic Press.

Ritter, E. (1993). Where's gender? *Linguistic Inquiry,* 24, 795–803.

Rivero, M.-L. (1991). Patterns of V-raising in long head movement, and negation: Serbo-Croatian vs. Slovak. *Linguistic Review,* 8, 319–51.

Rivero, M.-L. (1994). The structure of the clause and V-movement in the languages of the Balkans. *Natural Language and Linguistic Theory,* 12, 63–120.

Rizzi, L. (1982). *Issues in Italian Syntax.* Dordrecht: Foris.

Rizzi, L. (1986a). Null objects in Italian and the theory of PRO. *Linguistic Inquiry,* 17, 501–57.

Rizzi, L. (1986b). On chain formation. In H. Borer (ed.), *Syntax and Semantics. Vol. 19: The Syntax of Pronominal Clitics* (pp. 65–95). New York: Academic Press.

Rizzi, L. (1987). Three issues in Romance dialectology. *GLOW Paper*. Venice.

Rizzi, L. (1990). *Relativized Minimality*. Cambridge MA: MIT Press.

Rizzi, L. (1992a). Argument/adjunct (a)symmetries. *Proceedings of NELS*, 22, 365–81.

Rizzi, L. (1992b). Direct perception, government and thematic sharing. *GenGenP*, 0, 39–52.

Rizzi, L. (1993). On the status of referential indices. In A. Kasher (ed.), *The Chomskyan Turn* (pp. 273–99). Cambridge MA: Blackwell.

Rizzi, L. (1994). Some notes on linguistic theory and language development: the case of root infinitives. *Language Acquisition*, 3, 371–93.

Rizzi, L. (1996). Residual verb second and the *wh*-criterion. In A. Belletti and L. Rizzi (eds), *Parameters and Functional Heads* (pp. 63–90). Oxford: Oxford University Press.

Rizzi, L. (1997). The fine structure of the left periphery. In L. Haegeman (ed.), *Elements of Grammar* (pp. 281–337). Dordrecht: Kluwer.

Rizzi, L. and Roberts, I. (1989). Complex inversion in French. *Probus*, 1, 1–39.

Roberts, I. (1985). Agreement parameters and the development of the English modal auxiliaries. *Natural Language and Linguistic Theory*, 3, 21–58.

Roberts, I. (1987). *The Representation of Implicit and Dethematized Subjects*. Dordrecht: Foris.

Roberts, I. (1988). Predicative APs. *Linguistic Inquiry*, 19, 703–10.

Roberts, I. (1991). Excorporation and minimality. *Linguistic Inquiry*, 22, 209–18.

Roberts, I. (1993a). The nature of subject clitics in Franco-Provençal Valdotain. In A. Belletti (ed.), *Syntactic Theory and the Dialects of Italy* (pp. 319–53). Turin: Rosenberg and Sellier.

Roberts, I. (1993b). *Verbs and Diachronic Syntax. A Comparative History of English and French*. Dordrecht: Kluwer.

Roberts, I. (1994). Two types of head-movement in Romance. In N. Hornstein and D. Lightfoot (eds), *Verb Movement* (pp. 207–42). Cambridge: Cambridge University Press.

Roberts, I. (1995). Object movement and verb movement in Early Modern English. In H. Haider, S. Olsen, and S. Vikner (eds), *Studies in Comparative Germanic Syntax* (pp. 269–84). Dordrecht: Kluwer.

Roberts, I. (1997). Directionality and word order change in the history of English. In A. van Kemenade and N. Vincent (eds), *Parameters of Morphosyntactic Change* (pp. 397–426). Cambridge: Cambridge University Press.

Roberts, I. (1998). *Have/be*-raising, Move-F and Procrastinate. *Linguistic Inquiry*, 29, 113–25.

Roberts, I. and Roussou, A. (1997). Interface interpretation. MS, University of Stuttgart and University of Cyprus.

Roberts, I. and Roussou, A. (1998). The EPP as a condition on the tense dependency. MS, University of Stuttgart and University of Cyprus. To appear in P. Svenonius (ed.), *Subjects, Expletives and the EPP*.

Roca, F. (1996). La determinación y la modificación nominal en español [Nominal Determination and Modification in Spanish]. PhD dissertation, Universitat Autonomà de Barcelona.

Rodman, R. (1972). The proper treatment of relative clauses in Montague grammar. In R. Rodman and B. H. Partee (eds), Papers in Montague Grammar (pp. 80–94), *UCLA Occasional Papers in Linguistics*.

Roeper, T. (1987). Implicit arguments and the head–complement relation. *Linguistic Inquiry*, 18, 267–310.

Rögnvaldsson, E. (1986). Some comments on reflexivization in Icelandic. In L. Hellan and K. K. Christensen (eds), *Topics in Scandinavian Syntax* (pp. 89–102). Dordrecht: Reidel.

Rögnvaldsson, E. (1982). *Um orðaröð og færslur í nútímaíslensku.* Master's thesis, University of Iceland. Published (1990) Reykjavik: Institute of Linguistics, University of Iceland.

Rögnvaldsson, E. (1987). OV word order in Icelandic. In R. D. S. Allen and M. P. Barnes (eds), *Proceedings of the Seventh Biennial Conference of Teachers of Scandinavian Languages in Great Britain and Northern Ireland* (pp. 33–49). University College, London.

Rögnvaldsson, E. (1992). Word order changes in the VP in Icelandic. Paper given at the Second Diachronic Generative Syntax Conference, November, University of Pennsylvania, Philadelphia.

Rögnvaldsson, E. (1995). Old Icelandic: a non-configurational language? *NOWELE, 26,* 3–29.

Rooth, M. (1992a). Ellipsis redundancy and reduction redundancy. In S. Berman and A. Hestvik (eds), *Proceedings of the Stuttgart Ellipsis Workshop.* Stuttgart.

Rooth, M. (1992b). A theory of focus interpretation. *Natural Language Semantics, 1,* 117–21.

Ross, J. R. (1967a). Constraints on Variables in Syntax. PhD dissertation, MIT. Published (1986) as *Infinite Syntax!.* Norwood NJ: Ablex.

Ross, J. R. (1967b). On the cyclic nature of English pronominalization. In *To Honor Roman Jakobson* (pp. 1699–82). The Hague: Mouton. Reprinted in D. Reiber and S. Schane (eds), *Modern Studies in English* (pp. 187–200). Englewood Cliffs NJ: Prentice-Hall.

Ross, J. R. (1969). Guess who? In R. I. Binnick, A. Davison, G. M. Green, and J. L. Morgan (eds), *Papers from the Fifth Regional Meeting of the Chicago Linguistic Society* (pp. 252–86). Chicago: Chicago Linguistic Society, University of Chicago.

Ross, J. R. (1970). On declarative sentences. In R. Jacobs and P. Rosenbaum (eds), *Readings in English Transformational Grammar* (pp. 222–72). Waltham MA: Ginn.

Ross, J. R. (1972). Act. In D. Davidson and G. Harmman (eds), *Semantics of Natural Language* (pp. 70–125). Dordrecht: Reidel.

Ross, J. R. (1983). Inner Islands. MS, MIT.

Rothstein, S. (1983). The Syntactic Form of Predication. PhD dissertation, MIT.

Rothstein, S. (1995). Pleonastics and the interpretation of pronouns. *Linguistic Inquiry,* 26, 499–529.

Rothstein, S. (1997). Predicational "be." In R. C. Blight and M. J. Moosally (eds), *Texas Linguistic Forum 38: The Syntax and Semantics of Predication* (pp. 281–93). Austin TX: Department of Linguistics, University of Texas at Austin.

Rouveret, A. (1994). *Syntaxe du gallois: principes généraux et typologie.* Paris: CNRS.

Rouveret, A. (1989). Cliticisation et temps en portugais européen. *Revue des Langues Romanes,* 2, 337–71.

Rouveret, A. (1995). *Principes généraux et variation typologique: une syntaxe du gallois.* Paris: CNRS.

Rouveret, A. and Vergnaud, J.-R. (1980). Specifying reference to the subject: French causatives and conditions on representations. *Linguistic Inquiry,* 11, 97–202.

Rubin, E. (1990). Italian psych verbs in a theory of predication. In Y. No and M. Libucha (eds), *Proceedings of the Seventh Eastern States Conference on Linguistics* (pp. 227–39). Ohio State University.

Rudin, C. (1982). Who what to whom said: an argument from Bulgarian against successive cyclicity. *Papers from the Seventeenth Regional Meeting of the Chicago Linguistic Society*, 353–60.

Rudin, C. (1988). On multiple questions and multiple *wh*-fronting. *Natural Language and Linguistic Theory*, 6, 445–501.

Runner, J. T. (1995). Noun Phrase Licensing and Interpretation. PhD dissertation, University of Massachusetts, Amherst.

Rutten, J. (1991) Infinitival Complements and Auxiliaries. PhD dissertation, University of Amsterdam.

Ruys, E. (1992). The Scope of Indefinites. PhD dissertation, University of Utrecht, OTS.

Sadler, L. (1997). Clitics and the structure-function mapping. In M. Butt and T. H. King (eds), *Proceedings of the LFG97 Conference*, University of California, San Diego. Online, CSLI Publications: http://www-csli.stanford.edu/publications/

Safir, K. (1985). *Syntactic Chains*. Cambridge and New York: Cambridge University Press.

Safir, K. (1996). Semantic atoms of anaphora. *Natural Language and Linguistic Theory*, 14, 545–89.

Safir, K. and Stowell, T. (1989). Binominal *each*. In *Proceedings of NELS*, 18, 426–50.

Sag, I. (1976). Deletion and Logical Form. PhD dissertation, MIT.

Saito, M. (1985). Some Asymmetries in Japanese and their Theoretical Implications. PhD dissertation, MIT.

Saito, M. (1989). Scrambling as semantically vacuous A′ movement. In M. Baltin and A. Kroch (eds), *Alternative Conceptions of Phrase Structure* (pp. 182–200). Chicago: Chicago University Press.

Saito, M. (1992). Long distance scrambling in Japanese. *Journal of East Asian Linguistics*, 1, 69–118.

Saito, M. (1994a). Additional *wh*-effects and the adjunction site theory. *Journal of East Asian Linguistics*, 3, 195–240.

Saito, M. (1994b). Scrambling and the functional interpretation of *wh*-phrases. In Y.-S. Kim et al. (eds), *Explorations in Generative Grammar: A Festschrift for Dong-Whee Yang* (pp. 571–88). Seoul: Hankuk.

Saito, M. (1997). Quantifier interpretation in Japanese and English: differences and non-differences. Paper presented at the Workshop on Japanese Syntax in a Comparative Context, LSA Linguistic Institute, Cornell University, Ithaca NY.

Saito, M. and Fukui, N. (1998). Order in phrase structure and movement. *Linguistic Inquiry*, 29.3.

Saito, M. and Murasugi, K. (1998). Subject predication with IP and DP. In K. Johnson and I. Roberts (eds), *Beyond Principles and Parameters: Essays in Memory of Osvaldo Jaeggli* (pp. 159–82). Dordrecht: Kluwer.

Sakas, W. G. and Fodor, J. D. (in press). The structural triggers learner. In S. Bertolo (ed.), *Parametric Linguistics and Learnability: A Self-Contained Tutorial for Linguistics*. Cambridge: Cambridge University Press.

Sánchez, L. (1995a). Aspectual adjectives and the structure of DP and VP. *Probus*, 7, 167–80.

Sánchez, L. (1995b). Syntactic Structures in Nominals: A Comparative Study of Spanish and Southern Quechua. PhD dissertation, USC.

Sánchez, L. (1996). Word order, predication and agreement in DPs in Spanish, Southern Quechua and Southern Andean bilingual Spanish. In K. Zagona (ed.), *Grammatical Theory and Romance Languages – Current Issues in Linguistic Theory* 133 (pp. 209–18). Amsterdam/Philadelphia: John Benjamins.

Santelmann, L. (1993). The distribution of double determiners in Swedish: *Den* support in *Do*. *Studia Linguistica*, 47, 154–76.

Santorini, B. (1989). *The Generalization of the Verb-Second Constraint in the History of Yiddish*. PhD thesis, University of Pennsylvania.

Santorini, B. (1993). The rate of phrase structure change in the history of Yiddish. *Language Variation and Change*, 5, 257–83.

Schachter, P. (1977a). Constraints on coordination. *Language*, 53, 86–103.

Schachter, P. (1977b). Does she or doesn't she? *Linguistic Inquiry*, 8, 763–6.

Schein, B. (1993). *Plurals and Events*. Cambridge MA: MIT Press.

Schladt, M. (to appear). The typology and grammaticalization of reflexives. In Z. Frajzyngier and T. Curl (eds), *Reflexives: Forms and Functions*. Amsterdam: John Benjamins.

Schlyter, S. (1974). Une hiérarchie d'adverbes et leur distribution – par quelle transformation? In C. Rohrer and N. Ruwet (eds), *Actes du Colloque Franco-Allemand de Grammaire Transformationnelle. Vol. II* (pp. 76–84).

Schmitt, C. (1996). *Aspect and the Syntax of Noun Phrases*. PhD dissertation, University of Maryland, College Park.

Schneider-Zioga, P. (1987). Syntax screening. MS, USC, Los Angeles.

Schutze, C. (1997). *Infl in Child and Adult Language: Agreement, Case and Licencing*. PhD dissertation, MIT.

Schwartz, L. (1993). On the syntactic alignment of attributive and identificational constructions. In R. Van Valin (ed.), *Advances in Role and Reference Grammar* (pp. 433–64). Amsterdam/Philadelphia: John Benjamins.

Seely, T. Daniel. (1993). Binding plural pronominals. *CLS*, 29, 305–17.

Selkirk, E. (1977). Some remarks on noun phrase structure. In P. Culicover, T. Wasow, and A. Akmajian (eds), *Formal Syntax* (pp. 285–316). New York: Academic Press.

Selkirk, E. (1982). *The Syntax of Words*. Cambridge MA: MIT Press.

Sells, P. (1987). Aspects of logophoricity. *Linguistic Inquiry*, 18, 445–79.

Sells, P. (1996). Case, categories, and projection in Korean and Japanese. In H.-D. Ahn, M.-Y. Kang, Y.-S. Kim, and S. Lee (eds), *Morphosyntax in Generative Grammar (Proceedings of 1996 Seoul International Conference on Generative Grammar)* (pp. 47–62). Seoul: Korean Generative Grammar Circle, Hankuk.

Sells, P. (1997a). Optimality and economy of expression in Japanese and Korean. In *Proceedings of the 7th Japanese/Korean Conference*. Stanford: CSLI Publications.

Sells, P. (1997b). Positional constraints and faithfulness in morphology. In S. Kuno et al. (eds), *Harvard Studies in Korean Linguistics 7*. Cambridge MA: Harvard University Press.

Sells, P. (1998a). Scandinavian clause structure and object shift. In M. Butt and T. H. King (eds), *Proceedings of the LFG98 Conference*, University of Queensland, Brisbane. On-line, CSLI Publications: http://www-csli.stanford.edu/publications/

Sells, P. (1998b). Syntactic positioning as alignment: object shift in Swedish. Paper presented at the workshop Is Syntax Different? Common Cognitive Structures for Syntax and Phonology in Optimality Theory, December 12–13, CSLI, Stanford University.

Senegupta. (1990). *Scrambling in Bangla*. PhD dissertation, University of Massachusetts, Amherst.

Shi, Z.-Q. (1988). *The Present and the Past of the Particle le in Mandarin Chinese*. PhD thesis, University of Pennsylvania.

Shi, Z.-Q. (1989). The grammaticalization of the particle *le* in Mandarin Chinese. *Language Variation and Change*, 1, 99–114.

Shieber, S. M. (1986). *An Introduction to Unification-Based Approaches to Grammar*. Stanford: CSLI Publications.

Shlonsky, U. (1987). Null and Displaced Subjects. PhD dissertation, MIT.

Shlonsky, U. (1989). The hierarchical structure of agreement. MS, Haifa University.

Shlonsky, U. (1991a). Hebrew construct state nominals, Arabic verb-initial clauses and the head movement constraint. MS, University of Quebec at Montreal.

Shlonsky, U. (1991b). Quantifiers as functional heads: a study of quantifier float in Hebrew. *Lingua*, 84, 159–80.

Shlonsky, U. (1992). Resumptive pronouns as a last resort. *Linguistic Inquiry*, 23, 443–68.

Shlonsky, U. (1994a). Agreement in Comp. *Linguistic Review*, 11, 351–75.

Shlonsky, U. (1994b). Semitic clitics. *GenGenP*, 2, 1–11.

Siegel, D. (1973). Nonsources of unpassives. In J. P. Kimball (ed.), *Syntax and Semantics. Vol. 2* (pp. 301–17). New York and London: Seminar Press.

Siegel, D. (1974). Topics in English Morphology. PhD dissertation, MIT.

Sigurðsson, H. Á. (1986). Verb post-second in a V2 language. In Ö. Dahl and A. Holmberg (eds), *Scandinavian Syntax* (pp. 138–49). Institute of Linguistics, University of Stockholm.

Sigurðsson, H. Á. (1989). Verbal Syntax and Case in Icelandic in a Comparative GB Approach. PhD dissertation, University of Lund. Reprinted (1992) Málvísindastofnun Háskóla Íslands.

Sigurðsson, H. Á. (1990). Long distance reflexives and moods in Icelandic. In J. Maling and A. Zaenen (eds), *Modern Icelandic Syntax* (pp. 309–46). New York: Academic Press.

Sigurjónsdóttir, S. (1992). Binding in Icelandic: Evidence from Language Acquisition. PhD dissertation, UCLA. Published (1993) as *UCLA Working Papers in Psycholinguistics*, 2.1.

Sigurjónsdóttir, S. and Hyams, N. (1992). Reflexivization and logophoricity: evidence from the acquisition of Icelandic. *Language Acquisition*, 2, 359–413.

Siloni, T. (1990). Hebrew noun phrases: generalized noun raising. MS, University of Geneva.

Siloni, T. (1991). Noun raising and the structure of noun phrases. *MIT Working Papers in Linguistics*, 14, 255–70.

Siloni, T. (1994). Noun Phrases and Nominalizations. PhD dissertation, University of Geneva.

Siloni, T. (1997). *Noun Phrases and Nominalizations*. Dordrecht: Kluwer.

Simpson, J. (1983). Aspects of Warlpiri Morphology and Syntax. PhD dissertation, MIT.

Simpson, J. (1991). *Warlpiri Morpho-Syntax: A Lexicalist Approach*. Dordrecht: Kluwer.

Simpson, J. and Bresnan, J. (1983). Control and obviation in Warlpiri. *Natural Language and Linguistic Theory*, 1, 49–64.

Singh, M. (1992). Determining the definiteness of noun phrases. *MIT Working Papers in Linguistics*, 16, 191–205.

Sleeman, P. (1996). Licensing Empty Nouns in French. PhD dissertation, University of Amsterdam.

Smith, H. (1994). Dative sickness in Germanic. *Natural Language and Linguistic Theory*, 12, 677–736.

Smith, J. (1997). Noun faithfulness: on the privileged behaviour of nouns in phonology. On-line, Rutgers University: Rutgers Optimality Archive, http:-//ruccs.rutgers.edu/roa.html

Smolensky, P. (1996a). The initial state and "richness of the base" in Optimality Theory. Technical Report JHU-CogSci-96-4, Department of Cognitive Science, Johns Hopkins University.

Smolensky, P. (1996b). Generalizing optimization in OT: a competence theory of grammar "use." Paper presented at the Workshop on Optimality Theory and Cognition, December 6, CSLI, Stanford University.

Speas, M. (1986). Adjunctions and Projections in Syntax. PhD dissertation, MIT.

Speas, M. (1990). *Phrase Structure in Natural Language.* Dordrecht: Foris.

Spencer, A. and Zwicky, A. (eds), (1998). *The Handbook of Morphology.* Oxford: Blackwell.

Sportiche, D. (1983). Structural Invariance and Symmetry. PhD dissertation, Cambridge MA: MIT.

Sportiche, D. (1988). A theory of floating quantifiers and its corollaries for constituent structure. *Linguistic Inquiry,* 19, 425–49.

Sportiche, D. (1995). French predicate clitics and clause structure. In A. Cardinaletti and M. T. Guasti (eds), *Syntax and Semantics Vol. 28: Small Clauses* (pp. 287–324). New York: Academic Press.

Sportiche, D. (1996). Clitic constructions. In J. Rooryck and L. Zaring (eds), *Phrase Structure and the Lexicon* (pp. 213–76). Dordrecht: Kluwer.

Sportiche, D. (to appear). Subject clitics in French and Romance: complex inversion and clitic doubling. In K. Johnson and I. Roberts (eds), *Studies in Comparative Romance Syntax.* Dordrecht: Kluwer.

Sproat, R. (1985). Welsh syntax and VSO structure. *Natural Language and Linguistic Theory,* 3, 173–216.

Sproat, R. and Shih, C. (1988). Prenominal adjectival ordering in English and Mandarin. *NELS,* 18, 465–89.

Sproat, R. and Shih, C. (1991). The cross-linguistic distribution of adjective ordering restrictions. In C. Georgopoulos and R. Ishihara (eds), *Interdisciplinary Approaches to Language. Essays in Honor of S.-Y. Kuroda* (pp. 565–93). Dordrecht: Kluwer.

Srivastav-Dayal, V. (1993). Binding facts in Hindi and the scrambling phenomenon. In M. Butt, T. King and G. Ramchand (eds), *Word Order in South Asian Languages.* Stanford: CSLI.

Stabler, E. (1997). Computing quantifier scope. In A. Szabolcsi (ed.), *Ways of Scope Taking* (pp. 155–183). Dordrecht: Kluwer.

Stabler, E. (1998). Acquiring languages with movement. *Syntax,* 1.1, 72–97.

Starke, J. (1997). LOC: A Sketch with Special Reference to Anaphora. MS, University of Geneva.

Starke, M. (1995). On the format of small clauses. In A. Cardinaletti and M. T. Guasti (eds), *Syntax and Semantics Vol 28: Small Clauses* (pp. 237–69). New York: Academic Press.

Steriade, D. (1995). Underspecification and markedness. In J. Goldsmith (ed.), *Handbook of Phonological Theory* (pp. 114–74). Oxford: Blackwell.

Stockwell, R. P. (1977). Motivations for exbraciation in Old English. In N. C. Li (ed.), *Mechanisms of Syntactic Change* (pp. 291–314). Austin TX: University of Texas Press.

Stockwell, R. P., Schachter, P., and Partee, B. H. (1973). *The Major Syntactic Structures of English.* New York: Holt, Rinehart and Winston.

Stowell, T. (1981). Origins of Phrase Structure. PhD dissertation, MIT.

Stowell, T. (1982). The tense of infinitives. *Linguistic Inquiry*, 13, 561–70.

Stowell, T. (1983). Subjects across categories. *Linguistic Review*, 2, 285–312.

Stowell, T. (1989a). Raising in Irish and the projection principle. *Natural Language and Linguistic Theory*, 7.3, 317–59.

Stowell, T. (1989b). Subjects, specifiers and X-bar theory. In M. Baltin and A. Kroch (eds), *Alternative Conceptions of Phrase Structure* (pp. 232–62). Chicago: University of Chicago Press.

Stowell, T. (1991). Determiners in NP and DP. In K. Leffel and D. Bouchard (eds), *Views on Phrase Structure* (pp. 37–56). Dordrecht: Kluwer.

Stowell, T. (1998). Perfect tense. MS, UCLA.

Sumangala, L. (1992). Long Distance Dependencies in Sinhala: The Syntax of Focus and *Wh* Questions. PhD dissertation, Cornell University.

Suñer, M. (1998). Object-shift: comparing a Romance language to Germanic. MS, Cornell University.

Svenonius, P. (1996). The optionality of particle shift. *Working Papers in Scandinavian Syntax*, 57, 47–75.

Szabolcsi, A. (1981). The possessive construction in Hungarian: a configurational category in a non-configurational language. *Acta Linguistica Academiae Scientiarum Hungaricae*, 31, 261–89.

Szabolcsi, A. (1983). The possessor that ran away from home. *Linguistic Review*, 3, 89–102.

Szabolcsi, A. (1987). Functional categories in the noun phrase. In I. Kenesei (ed.), *Approaches to Hungarian* 2 (pp. 167–89). Szeged: JATE.

Szabolcsi, A. (1989). Noun phrases and clauses: is DP analogous to IP or CP? In J. Payne (ed.), *Proceedings of the Colloquium on Noun Phrase Structure*, Manchester.

Szabolcsi, A. (1992). Subordination: articles and complementizers. In I. Kenesei and C. Pléh (eds), *Approaches to Hungarian*, 4 (pp. 123–37). Szeged: JATE.

Szabolcsi, A. (1994). The noun phrase. In F. Kiefer and K. É. Kiss (eds), *Syntax and Semantics Vol. 27: The Syntactic Structure of Hungarian* (pp. 179–274). San Diego: Academic Press.

Szabolcsi, A. (1997a). Quantifiers in pair-list readings. In A. Szabolcsi (ed.), *Ways of Scope Taking* (pp. 311–47). Dordrecht: Kluwer.

Szabolcsi, A. (1997b). Strategies for scope taking. In A. Szabolcsi (ed.), *Ways of Scope Taking* (pp. 109–55). Dordrecht: Kluwer.

Szabolcsi, A. and Zwarts, F. (1997). Weak islands and an algebraic semantics for scope taking. In A. Szabolcsi (ed.), *Ways of Taking Scope* (pp. 217–62). Dordrecht: Kluwer.

Takahashi, D. (1993). Movement of *wh*-phrase in Japanese. *Natural Language and Linguistic Theory*, 11, 655–78.

Takahashi, D. (1994a). Minimality of Movement. PhD dissertation, University of Connecticut.

Takahashi, D. (1994b). Sluicing in Japanese. *Journal of East Asian Linguistics*, 3, 265–300.

Takahashi, D. (1997). Move F and null operator movement. *Linguistic Review*, 14, 181–96.

Takano, Y. (1995). Predicate fronting and internal subjects. *Linguistic Inquiry*, 26, 327–40.

Takano, Y. (1998). Object shift and scrambling. *Natural Language and Linguistic Theory*, 16.4, 817–89.

Tallerman, M. (1996). Fronting constructions in Welsh. In R. Borsley and I. Roberts (eds), *The Syntax of the Celtic Languages* (pp. 97–124). Cambridge: Cambridge University Press.

Talmy, L. (1978). Figure and ground in complex sentences. In J. Greenberg (ed.), *Universals of Human Language: Syntax. Vol. 4* (pp. 625–49). Stanford: Stanford University Press.

Talmy, L. (1985). Lexicalization patterns: semantic structure in lexical forms. In T. Shopen (ed.), *Language Typology and Syntactic Description* (pp. 57–149). Cambridge: Cambridge University Press.

Tancredi, C. (1992). Deletion, Deaccenting and Presupposition. PhD dissertation, MIT.

Tang, C.-C. J. (1990). Chinese Phrase Structure and the Extended X'-theory. PhD dissertation, Cornell University.

Tang, J. (1989) Chinese Reflexives. *Natural Language and Linguistic Theory*, 7, 93–121.

Taraldsen, T. (1986). On verb second and the functional content of syntactic categories. In H. Haider and M. Prinzhorn (eds), *Verb-Second Phenomena in Germanic Languages*. Dordrecht: Foris.

Taraldsen, T. (1990). D-projections and N-projections in Norwegian. In M. Nespor and J. Mascaró (eds), *Grammar in Progress* (pp. 419–31). Dordrecht: Foris.

Taraldsen, T. (1995). On agreement and nominative objects in Icelandic. In H. Heider, S. Olsen, and S. Vikner (eds), *Studies in Comparative Germanic Syntax* (pp. 307–27). Dordrecht: Kluwer.

Taylor, A. (1994). The change from SOV to SVO in Ancient Greek. *Language Variation and Change*, 6, 1–37.

Tellier, C. (1988). Universal Licensing: Implications for Parasitic Gap Constructions. PhD dissertation, McGill University, Montreal.

Tenny, C. (1989). The aspectual interface hypothesis. *Lexicon Project Working Papers*, 31. Cambridge MA: Center for Cognitive Sciences, MIT.

Tenny, C. (1994). *Aspectual Roles and the Syntax–Semantics Interface*. Dordrecht: Kluwer.

Terzi, A. (1997). PRO and null Case in finite clauses. *Linguistic Review*, 14, 335–60.

Tesar, B. and Smolensky, P. (1996). The learnability of Optimality Theory: an algorithm and some basic complexity results. Technical Report, Cognitive Science Department, Johns Hopkins University, and Rutgers Center for Cognitive Science, Rutgers University.

Thomason, S. G. and Kaufman, T. (1988). *Language Contact, Creolization and Genetic Linguistics*. Berkeley: University of California Press.

Thornton, R. J. (1990). Adventures in Long-Distance Moving: The Acquisition of Complex *Wh*-Questions. PhD dissertation, University of Connecticut.

Thráinsson, H. (1976). Reflexives and subjunctives in Icelandic. *NELS*, 6, 225–39.

Thráinsson, H. (1979). *On Complementation in Icelandic*. New York: Garland.

Thráinsson, H. (1986). V1, V2, V3 in Icelandic. In H. Haider and M. Prinzhorn (eds), *Verb-Second Phenomena in the Germanic Languages* (pp. 169–94). Dordrecht: Foris.

Thráinsson, H. (1990). A semantic reflexive in Icelandic. In J. Maling and A. Zaenen (eds), *Modern Icelandic Syntax* (pp. 289–307). New York: Academic Press.

Thráinsson, H. (1991). Long-distance reflexives and the typology of NPs. In J. Koster and E. J. Reuland (eds), *Long-Distance Anaphora* (pp. 49–75). Cambridge: Cambridge University Press.

Thráinsson, H. (1996). On the (non-)universality of functional categories. In W. Abraham, S. D. Epstein, H. Thráinsson, and C. J.-W. Zwart (eds), *Minimal Ideas. Syntactic Studies in the Minimalist Framework* (pp. 253–81). Amsterdam: John Benjamins.

Thráinsson, H. (1997). The chapters by Kiparsky, Roberts and Weerman: an epilogue. In A. van Kemenade and N. Vincent (eds), *Parameters of Morphosyntactic Change* (pp. 495–508). Cambridge: Cambridge University Press.

Thráinsson, H. (1999). Review of Holmberg and Platzack 1995: *The Role of Inflection in Scandinavian Syntax. Journal of Linguistics.*

Thráinsson, H., Epstein, S. D., and Peter, S. (1996). Introduction. In H. Thráinsson, S. D. Epstein, and S. Peter (eds), *Studies in Comparative Germanic Syntax* II (pp. vii–xxxix). Dordrecht: Kluwer.

Toman, J. (1982). Aspects of multiple *wh*-movement in Polish and Czech. In R. May and J. Koster (eds), *Levels of Syntactic Representation* (pp. 293–302). Dordrecht: Foris.

Tomaselli, A. (1989). La sintassi del verbo finito nelle lingue germaniche. PhD Dissertation, University of Pavia.

Tomioka, S. (1997). Focussing Effects in VP Ellipsis and NP Interpretation. PhD dissertation, University of Massachusetts.

Toribio, J. (1990). Specifier–head agreement in Japanese. *Proceedings of WCCFL*, 9, 535–48.

Torrego, E. (1987). Empty categories in nominals. MS, University of Massachusetts, Boston.

Travis, L. (1984). Parameters and Effects of Word Order Variation. PhD dissertation.

Travis, L. (1988). The syntax of adverbs. In *McGill Working Papers in Linguistics: Special Issue on Comparative Germantic Syntax* (pp. 280–310). Montreal: Department of Linguistics, McGill University.

Treviño, E. (1991). Clitic movement, minimality and negation in Spanish. MS, University of Ottawa.

Trudgill, P. and Chambers, J. K. (eds), (1991). *Dialects of English. Studies in Grammatical Variation*. London: Longman.

Trueswell, J. C., Sekerina, I., Hill, N. M., and Logrip, M. L. (in press). The kindergarten-path effect: studying on-line sentence processing in young children. *Cognition.*

Tsai, W.-T. D. (1994a). On Economizing the Theory of A-Bar Dependencies. PhD dissertation, MIT.

Tsai, W.-T. D. (1994b). On nominal islands and LF extraction in Chinese. *Natural Language and Linguistic Theory*, 12, 121–75.

Ueyama, A. (1994). Against the A/A'-movement dichotomy. In N. Corver and H. van Riemsdijk (eds), *Studies on Scrambling. Movement and Non-Movement Approaches to Free Word-Order Phenomena* (pp. 459–86). Berlin: de Gruyter.

Underhill, R. (1976). *Turkish Grammar*. Cambridge MA: MIT Press.

Unseth, P. (1994). Verbal negation in Majang. Paper presented at the 25th Annual Conference on African Linguistics, Rutgers University.

Ura, H. (1993). On feature-checking for *wh*-traces. *MIT Working Papers in Linguistics*, 18, 243–80.

Ura, H. (1994). Varieties of raising and the feature-based bare phrase structure theory. *MIT Occasional Papers in Linguistics*, 7. Cambridge MA: MIT Working Papers in Linguistics.

Ura, H. (1995). Towards a theory of "strictly derivational" economy condition. *MIT Working Papers in Linguistics*, 27, 243–67.

Ura, H. (1996). Multiple Feature Checking: A Theory of Grammatical Function Splitting. PhD dissertation, MIT.

Ura, H. (forthcoming). *Checking Theory and Grammatical Functions in Universal Grammar*. Oxford: Oxford University Press.

Ura, H. (in press). A theory of grammatical functions in the minimalist program. In G. Alexandrova et al. (eds), *The Minimalist Parameter: Papers Deriving from the Open Linguistics Forum "Challenges of Minimalism"* (pp. 31–48). Amsterdam: John Benjamins.

Urbanczyk, L. (1995). Double reduplications in parallel. In J. Beckman, L. Dickey, and S. Urbanczyk (eds), Papers in Optimality Theory (pp. 499–531). *University of Massachusetts Occasional Papers*, 18. Amherst: University of Massachusetts.

Uriagereka, J. (1995). Aspects of the syntax of clitic placement in Western Romance. *Linguistic Inquiry*, 26, 79–123.

Uriagereka, J. (in press). Multiple spell-out. In S. D. Epstein and N. Hornstein (eds), *Working Minimalism*. Cambridge MA: MIT Press.

Valian, V. (1990). Null subjects: a problem for parameter setting models of language acquisition. *Cognition*, 35, 105–22.

Valois, D. (1991). The Internal Syntax of DP. PhD dissertation, UCLA.

Van Gelderen, E. (to appear). Bound pronouns and non-local anaphors: the case of earlier English. In Z. Frajzyngier and T. Curl (eds), *Reflexives: Forms and Functions*. Amsterdam: John Benjamins.

Van Valin, R. (1981). Grammatical relations in ergative languages. *Studies in Language*, 5, 361–94.

Van Valin, R. (1985). Case marking and the structure of the Lakhota clause. In J. Nichols and A. Woodbury (eds), *Grammar Inside and Outside the Clause*. Cambridge: Cambridge University Press.

Van Valin, R. (1990). Semantic parameters of split intransitivity. *Language*, 66.2, 221–60.

Van Valin, R. (1993). *Advances in Role and Reference Grammar*. Amsterdam/Philadelphia: John Benjamins.

Van Valin, R. and LaPolla, R. (1997). *Syntax: Structure, Meaning and Function*. Cambridge: Cambridge University Press.

Vangsnes, Ø. A. (1995). Referentiality and argument positions in Icelandic. *WPSS*, 55, 89–109.

Vangsnes, Ø. A. (1996a). A configurational approach to noun phrase interpretation. In J. Costa, R. Goedemans, and R. van de Vijver (eds), *Proceedings of ConSOLE* 4.

Vangsnes. Ø. A. (1996b). The role of gender in (mainland) Scandinavian possessive constructions. *Working Papers in Scandinavian Syntax*, 58, 1–28.

Vendler, Z. (1967). *Linguistics in Philosophy*. Ithaca NY: Cornell University Press.

Vergnaud, J.-R. (1974). French Relative Clauses. PhD dissertation, MIT.

Vergnaud, J.-R. (1985). *Dépendances et Niveaux de Représentation en Syntaxe*. Amsterdam: John Benjamins.

Vergnaud, J.-R. and Zubizarreta, M. L. (1992). The definite determiner and the inalienable constructions in French and English. *Linguistic Inquiry*, 23.4, 595–652.

Vijay-Shanker, K. and Joshi, A. K. (1990). Unification based tree adjoining grammars. In J. Wedekind (ed.), *Unification-Based Grammars*. Cambridge MA: MIT Press.

Vikner, S. (1985). Parameters of Binder and Binding Category in Danish. *Working Papers in Scandinavian Syntax*, 23.

Vikner, S. (1989). Object shift and double objects in Danish. *Working Papers in Scandinavian Syntax*, 44, 141–55.

Vikner, S. (1991). Verb Movement and the Licensing of NP-Positions in the Germanic Languages. PhD dissertation, University of Geneva. Second version, University of Stuttgart, September.

Vikner, S. (1994a). *Verb Movement and Expletive Subjects in the Germanic Languages*. Oxford/New York: Oxford University Press.

Vikner, S. (1994b). Scandinavian object shift and West Germanic Scrambling. In N. Corver and H. van Riemsdijk (eds), *Studies on Scrambling. Movement and Non-Movement Approaches to Free Word-Order Phenomena* (pp. 487–517). Berlin: de Gruyter.

Vikner, S. (1995). *Verb Movement and Expletive Subjects in the Germanic Languages*. New York/Oxford: Oxford University Press.

Vikner, S. (1997a). V-to-I movement and inflection for person in all tenses. In L. Haegeman (ed.), *The New Comparative Syntax* (pp. 189–213). London: Longman.

Vikner, S. (1997b). The interpretation of object shift, Optimality Theory and Minimalism. *Working Papers in Scandinavian Syntax*, 60, 1–24.

Vincent, N. (1976). Perceptual factors in word order change in Latin. In M. Harris (ed.), *Romance Syntax* (pp. 54–68). Salford: University of Salford.

Vincent, N. (1998a). Competition and correspondence in syntactic change: null arguments in Latin and Romance. Paper delivered at the 5th Diachronic Generative Syntax Conference (DIGS5), May 30–June 1, University of York.

Vincent, N. (1998b). The development of the Romance auxiliary split: an OT approach. Paper presented at the workshop Is Syntax Different? Common Cognitive Structures for Syntax and Phonology in Optimality Theory, December 12–13, CSLI, Stanford University.

Vincent, N. and Börjars, K. (1996). Suppletion and syntactic theory. In M. Butt and T. H. King (eds), *LFG-Workshop. Proceedings of the First LFG Conference*. Rank Xerox Research Centre, Grenoble, August 26–8. On-line, CSLI Publications: http://www-csli.stanford.edu/publications/

von Stechow, A. (1996). Against LF pied-piping. *Natural Language Semantics*, 4, 57–110.

Wahba, W. A.-F. B. (1991). LF movement in Iraqi Arabic. In C.-T. J. Huang and R. May (eds), *Logical Structure and Linguistic Structure* (pp. 253–76). Dordrecht: Kluwer.

Warner, A. (1983). Review of D. Lightfoot, *Principles of Diachronic Syntax*. *Journal of Linguistics*, 19, 187–209.

Warner, A. (1993). *English Auxiliaries: Structure and History*. Cambridge: Cambridge University Press.

Wasow, T. (1972). Anaphoric Relations in English. PhD dissertation, MIT.

Wasow, T. (1977). Transformations and the lexicon. In P. Culicover, T. Wasow, and A. Akmajian (eds), *Formal Syntax* (pp. 327–60). New York: Academic Press.

Wasow, T. (1980). Major and minor rules in lexical grammar. In H. v. d. H. T. Hoekstra and M. Moortgat (eds), *Lexical Grammar*. Dordrecht: Foris.

Watanabe, A. (1992a). *Wh*-in-situ, subjacency, and chain formation. *MIT Occasional Papers in Linguistics*, 2.

Watanabe, A. (1992b). Subjacency and S-structure movement of *wh*-in-situ. *Journal of East Asian Linguistics*, 1, 255–91.

Watanabe, A. (1993). Agr-based Case Theory and its Interaction with the A-bar System. PhD dissertation, MIT.

Watanabe, A. (1995). The conceptual basis of strict cyclicity. In Papers on Minimalist Syntax, *MIT Working Papers in Linguistics*, 27, 269–91.

Watanabe, A. (1996). *Case Absorption and Wh-Agreement*. Dordrecht: Kluwer.

Watanabe, A. (1997). Movement of [+interpretable] features. Paper presented at the Workshop on Japanese Syntax in a Comparative Context, LSA Linguistic Institute, Cornell University.

Webber, B. (1978). A Formal Approach to Discourse Anaphora. PhD dissertation, Harvard University.

Webelhuth, G. (1984–5). German is Configurational. *Linguistic Review*, 4, 203–46.

Webelhuth, G. (1989). Syntactic Saturation Phenomena and the Germanic Languages. PhD dissertation, University of Massachusetts, Amherst.

Webelhuth, G. (1992). *Principles and Parameters of Syntactic Saturation*. New York: Oxford University Press.

Webelhuth, G. (ed.), (1995a). *Government and Binding Theory and the Minimalist Program*. Oxford: Blackwell.

Webelhuth, G. (1995b). X-bar theory and Case theory. In G. Webelhuth (ed.), *Government and Binding Theory and the Minimalist Program* (pp. 15–95). Oxford: Blackwell.

Weber, D. (1989). *A Grammar of Huallaga (Huanuco) Quechua*. Berkeley: University of California Press.

Weerman, F. (1989). *The V2 Conspiracy. A Synchronic and a Diachronic Analysis*. Dordrecht: Foris.

Weerman, F. (1997). On the relations between morphological and syntactic case. In A. van Kemenade and N. Vincent (eds), *Parameters of Morphosyntactic Change* (pp. 427–59). Cambridge: Cambridge University Press.

Weinreich, U., Labov, W., and Herzog, M. I. (1968). Empirical foundations for a theory of language change. In W. P. Lehmann and Y. Malkiel (eds), *Directions for Historical Linguistics: A Symposium* (pp. 95–195). Austin TX: University of Texas Press.

Weissenborn, J. (1990). Functional categories and verb movement in early German: the acquisition of German syntax reconsidered. In M. Rothweiler (ed.), *Spracherwerb und Grammatik: Linguistische Untersuchungen zum Erwerb von Syntax und Morphologie* (pp. 190–224). *Linguistische Berichte*, special issue 3/1990.

Wells, R. S. (1947). Immediate constituents. *Language*, 23, 81–117.

Wexler, K. (1994). Optional infinitives, head movement and the economy of derivation. In D. Lightfoot and N. Hornstein (eds), *Verb Movement* (pp. 305–50). Cambridge: Cambridge University Press.

Wexler, K. (1998). Very early parameter setting and the Unique Checking Constraint: a new explanation of the optional infinitive stage. *Lingua*, 106, 23–79.

Wexler, K. (1999). Maturation and growth of grammar. In W. C. Ritchie and T. K. Bhatia (eds), *Handbook of Child Language Acquisition*. San Diego: Academic Press.

Wexler, K. and Culicover, P. (1980). *Formal Principles of Language Acquisition*. Cambridge MA: MIT Press.

Wexler, K. and Manzini, R. (1987). Parameters and learnability in binding theory. In T. Roeper and E. Williams (eds), *Parameter Setting* (pp. 41–76). Dordrecht: Reidel.

White, L. and Prevost, P. (1997). Truncation and missing inflection in second language acquisition. MS, McGill University.

Wilkins, W. (1988). Thematic structure and reflexivization. In W. Wilkins (ed.), *Syntax and Semantics Vol. 21: Thematic Relations* (pp. 190–213). New York: Academic Press.

Williams, E. (1974). Rule Ordering in Syntax. PhD dissertation, MIT.

Williams, E. (1975). Small clauses in English. In J. Kimball (ed.), *Syntax and Semantics. Vol. 4*. New York: Academic Press.

Williams, E. (1977). Discourse and logical form. *Linguistic Inquiry*, 8, 101–39.

Williams, E. (1980). Predication. *Linguistic Inquiry*, 11, 203–38.

Williams, E. (1983a). Against small clauses. *Linguistic Inquiry*, 14, 203–38.

Williams, E. (1983b). Syntactic versus semantic categories. *Linguistics and Philosophy*, 6, 423–46.

Williams, E. (1984). Grammatical relations. *Linguistic Inquiry*, 15, 639–73.

Williams, E. (1986). A reassignment of the functions of LF. *Linguistic Inquiry*, 17, 265–99.

Williams, E. (1988). Is LF distinct from S-structure? A reply to May. *Linguistic Inquiry*, 19, 135–47.

Williams, E. (1994a). A reinterpretation of the evidence for verb movement in French. In D. Lightfoot and N. Hornstein (eds), *Verb Movement* (pp. 189–206). Cambridge: Cambridge University Press.

Williams, E. (1994b). *Thematic Structure in Syntax*. Cambridge MA: MIT Press.

Williams, E. S. (1980). Passive. MS, University of Massachusetts.

Williamson, J. (1984). Studies in Lakhota Grammar. PhD dissertation, UCSD.

Williamson, J. (1987). An indefiniteness restriction for relative clauses in Lakhota. In E. Reuland and A. ter Meulen (eds), *The Representation of (In)definiteness* (pp. 168–90). Cambridge MA: MIT Press.

Winter, Y. (1997). Choice functions and the scopal semantics of indefinites. *Linguistics and Philosophy*, 20, 399–466.

Wood, M. M. (1993). *Categorial Grammars*. London and New York: Routledge.

Wu, A. (1994). The Spellout Parameters: A Minimalist Approach to Syntax. PhD dissertation, UCLA.

Wyngærd, G. (1989). Object shift as an A-movement rule. *MIT Working Papers in Linguistics*, 11, 256–71.

Wyngærd, G. and Zwart, J.-W. (1991). Reconstruction and vehicle change. In F. Drijkoningen and A. v. Kemenade (eds), *Linguistics in the Netherlands*.

Yang, C. D. (1997). Minimal computation: derivation of syntactic structures. MS, MIT.

Yang, D.-W. (1984). The extended binding theory of anaphors. *Theoretical Linguistic Research*, 1, 195–218.

Yip, M., Maling, J., and Jackendoff, R. S. (1987). Case in tiers. *Language*, 63, 217–50.

Zaenen, A., Maling, J., and Thráinsson, H. (1985). Case and grammatical functions: the Icelandic passive. *Natural Language and Linguistic Theory*, 3, 441–83. Also in J. Maling and A. Zaenen (eds), *Modern Icelandic Syntax* (pp. 95–136). San Diego: Academic Press.

Zagona, K. (1988a). Proper government of antecedentless VPs in English and Spanish. *Natural Language and Linguistic Theory*, 6, 95–128.

Zagona, K. (1988b). *Verb Phrase Syntax: A Parametric Study of English and Spanish*. Dordrecht: Kluwer.

Zamparelli, R. (1993). Pre-nominal modifiers, degree phrases and the structure of AP. *University of Venice Working Papers in Linguistics*, 3, 138–63.

Zamparelli, R. (1994). Aspects of a ADJP = DP = CP hypothesis. MS, University of Rochester.

Zamparelli, R. (1995). Layers in the Determiner Phrase. PhD dissertation, University of Rochester.

Zanuttini, R. (1991). Syntactic Properties of Sentential Negation: A Comparative Study of Romance Languages. PhD thesis, University of Pennsylvania.

Zanuttini, R. (1997). *Negation and Clausal Structure*. Oxford: Oxford University Press.

Zidani-Eroglu, L. (1997). Exceptionally case-marked NPs as matrix objects. *Linguistic Inquiry*, 28.2, 219–30.

Zribi-Hertz, A. (1989). A-type binding and narrative point of view. *Language*, 65, 695–727.

Zwart, C. J.-W. (1993a). Dutch Syntax: A Minimalist Approach. PhD dissertation, University of Groningen.

Zwart, C. J.-W. (1993b). Verb movement and complementizer agreement. In J. Bobaljik and C. Phillips (eds), Papers on Case and Agreement. *MIT Working Papers in Linguistics*, 18, 297–341.

Zwart, C. J.-W. (1996). "Shortest move" vs. "fewest steps." In W. Abraham, S. D. Epstein, H. Thráinsson, and C. J.-W. Zwart (eds), *Minimal Ideas. Syntactic Studies in the Minimalist Framework* (pp. 239–61). Amsterdam: John Benjamins.

Zwart, C. J.-W. (1997). *The Morphosyntax of Verb Movement: A Minimalist Approach to the Syntax of Dutch*. Dordrecht: Kluwer.

Zwicky, A. (1981). Stranded *to* and phonological phrasing. *Linguistics*, 20, 3–58.

Zwicky, A. M. and Pullum, G. K. (1983). Cliticization vs. inflection: English *n't*. *Language*, 59, 502–13.

Index